Argentina

Sandra Bao

Gregor Clark, Bridget Gleeson,
Andy Symington, Lucas Vidgen

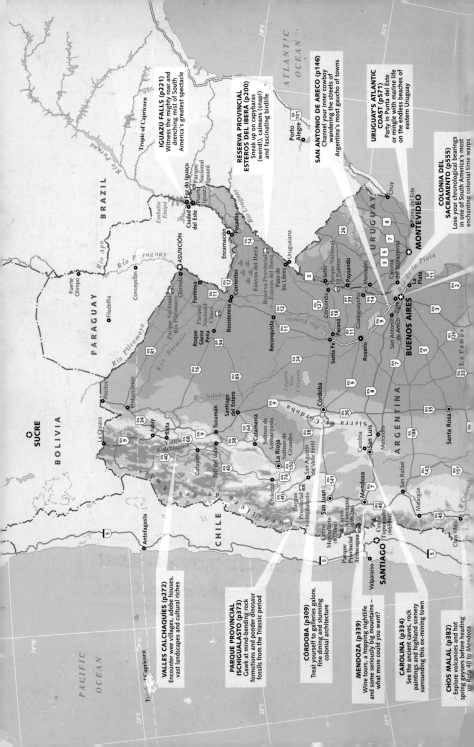

IGUAZÚ FALLS (p221)
Witness the mighty roar and drenching mist of South America's greatest spectacle

RESERVA PROVINCIAL ESTEROS DEL IBERÁ (p200)
Sneak up on capybaras (weird!), caimans (snap!) and fascinating birdlife

SAN ANTONIO DE ARECO (p146)
Channel your inner cowboy wandering the streets of Argentina's most gaucho of towns

URUGUAY'S ATLANTIC COAST (p571)
Party in Punta del Este or mingle with marine life on the endless beaches of eastern Uruguay

COLONIA DEL SACRAMENTO (p555)
Lose your chronological bearings in one of South America's most enchanting colonial time warps

VALLES CALCHAQUÍES (p272)
Encounter wee villages, adobe houses, vast landscapes and cultural riches

PARQUE PROVINCIAL ISCHIGUALASTO (p373)
Gawk at mind-bending rock formations and ponder dinosaur fossils from the Triassic period

CÓRDOBA (p309)
Treat yourself to galleries galore, fine dining and stunning colonial architecture

MENDOZA (p339)
Wine tours, a hopping nightlife and some seriously big mountains – what more could you want?

CAROLINA (p334)
See the ancient caves, rock paintings and highland scenery surrounding this ex-mining town

CHOS MALAL (p382)
Explore volcanoes and hot spring geysers before heading up Ruta 40 to Mendoza

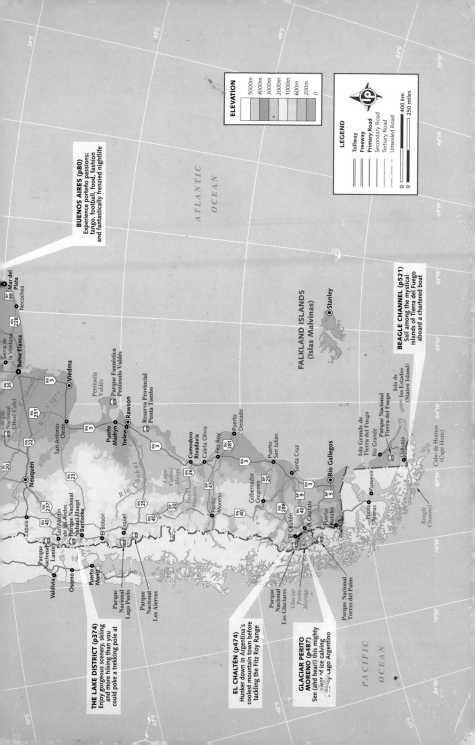

ELEVATION

5000m
4000m
3000m
2000m
1000m
600m
200m
0

LEGEND

Tollway
Freeway
Primary Road
Secondary Road
Tertiary Road
Unsealed Road

0 — 400 km
0 — 250 miles

ATLANTIC
OCEAN

PACIFIC
OCEAN

FALKLAND ISLANDS
(Islas Malvinas)

● Stanley

BUENOS AIRES (p80)
Experience porteño passions:
tango, football, food, fashion
and fantastically frenzied nightlife

THE LAKE DISTRICT (p374)
Enjoy gorgeous scenery, skiing
and more hiking than you
could poke a trekking pole at

EL CHALTÉN (p474)
Hunker down in Argentina's
coolest mountain town before
tackling the Fitz Roy Range

**GLACIAR PERITO
MORENO (p487)**
See (and hear!) this mighty
river of ice calving
along Lago Argentino

BEAGLE CHANNEL (p521)
Sail among the mystical
islands of Tierra del Fuego
aboard a chartered boat

Mar del Plata
Necochea
Viedma
Bahía Blanca
Sierra de la Ventana
Neuquén
Zapala
San Antonio Oeste
Peninsula Valdés
Parque Faunística Peninsula Valdés
Reserva Provincial Punta Tombo
Rawson
Puerto Madryn
Trelew
Comodoro Rivadavia
Caleta Olivia
Puerto Deseado
Fitz Roy
Puerto San Julián
Santa Cruz
Gobernador Gregores
Perito Moreno
Río Gallegos
El Chaltén
El Calafate
Puerto Natales
Parque Nacional Torres del Paine
Parque Nacional Los Glaciares
Glaciar Perito Moreno
Punta Arenas
Porvenir
Isla Grande de Tierra del Fuego
Río Grande
Parque Nacional Tierra del Fuego
Ushuaia
Isla de los Estados (Staten Island)
Cabo de Hornos (Cape Horn)
Beagle Channel
San Martín de los Andes
Parque Nacional Nahuel Huapi
Bariloche
El Bolsón
Esquel
Parque Nacional Lago Puelo
Parque Nacional Los Alerces
Puerto Montt
Osorno
Valdivia
Parque Nacional Lanín
Parque Nacional Lihué Calel
Río Negro
Río Chubut
Lago Colhué Huapi
Lago Musters

On the Road

SANDRA BAO
Coordinating Author
Researching is hard work, stomping from one hotel to another. This time I took a break – tossed aside my notes, got on a horse and looked at the Argentine countryside from a gaucho's perspective. It wasn't easy imagining a romantic, isolated pampas with 10 other tourists riding alongside, but the ride was great nonetheless.

BRIDGET GLEESON
The snow started falling harder as we boarded a boat in Parque Nacional Los Glaciares, South (p487). We couldn't see anything – it was white all around, and tourists were slipping on the deck and bumping each other with umbrellas. Then the clouds parted. We fell silent as the massive crystal-blue Glaciar Perito Moreno suddenly loomed before us.

GREGOR CLARK
OK, I admit it: I love baby farm animals. And Uruguay in springtime is kind of a rural paradise. If you want to feed a baby cow or sheep, just ask at one of the country's *estancias turísticas*, and they'll likely turn you loose with your very own bottle.

LUCAS VIDGEN
One of the only true bonuses about researching in Argentina during winter was that the ski resorts were still open. Here I am, hard at work in Los Penitentes (p355), outside of Mendoza at the end of the season. Snow conditions? Sheet ice. Views? Absolutely unbelievable.

ANDY SYMINGTON
From the northwestern town of Chilecito (p305) you can explore the region's industrial heritage with a steep, bumpy 4WD ascent to the abandoned mine at La Mejicana, high up in the mountains at nearly 5km of altitude. The landscape is rugged, bleak and utterly spectacular.

For full author biographies see p640

BEST OF ARGENTINA

Round up the best of Argentina – the wine, the fishing, the tango, the mountaineering, the skiing, the literature, the beef, the architecture, the clubbing – and you have the building blocks for one of the most exciting journeys you'll ever take. No joke. While *so many* things in Argentina are exciting, some things are better defined as 'mind blowing.' We've cobbled together a collection of the latter. Put as many on your To Do list as possible.

MICHAEL TAYLOR

Classic Argentina

Whether it's as simple as *dulce de leche* (that delicious milk caramel Argentines spread on just about everything) or as complex as the tango, some things are quintessentially Argentine. Stereotypical? Perhaps, but they're lots of fun too, and prime makings for great experiences and fond memories.

Author Tip
First-class overnight buses often provide wine with dinner. It's a welcome perk, but it's usually a cheap swill. So bring your own bottle (and a corkscrew). Not only will it make dinner that much tastier, it'll make the ride that much more relaxing. Sleep well!

① The Andes
Stretching nearly the whole length of Argentina's western edge, this amazing mountain range offers high deserts (p270), scenic lakes (p374), great hiking (p478) and the continent's highest peak, Cerro Aconcagua (p356).

② Football (Soccer)
Take a deep breath and get ready for the most concentrated 90 minutes of emotional rollercoastering you've ever experienced. And pray for goals (p130)!

③ Gauchos
The gaucho is as much a state of mind as a cultural icon. You can experience both by heading into the pampas, to towns such as San Antonio de Areco (p146) where tradition trumps all.

④ Tango
Go on, give it a try. So what if it's one of the world's most sophisticated dances (p50). It's so sexy, you'll soon be fired up enough to make it through that long Buenos Aires night.

⑤ Estancias
There's something definitively Argentine about *estancias* – those don't-fence-me-in ranches with endless views, peace and quiet and plenty of home-cooked food. Opportunities for livin' the county life are ample, too (p598).

⑥ Penguins
There are several places in the country to see these critters close-up – including Punta Tombo (p441), Cabo Dos Bahías (p442), Parque Nacional Monte León (p453) and Ushuaia (p524). The mother lode of penguins, though, is in Antarctica (p523).

⑦ The Jesuit Missions
Journey to northeast Argentina – and even into Paraguay for the day – to wander among the astonishing ruins of the Jesuit missions (p217), built by indigenous laborers in the 17th century.

⑧ Argentines
Ultrafriendly, fun-loving, engaging and warm, Argentines are, without a doubt, one of the highlights of any trip to Argentina. Just asking someone for directions can lead to loads of fun...

Natural Wonders

With its head in the tropics and its toes in Antarctica, it's hardly surprising Argentina kicks out such a barrage of natural wonders. Few places in the world offer so many opportunities for jaw-dropping, speech-stopping encounters with planet Earth. Although the journeys are long, access is usually easy. The rewards? Unforgettable.

❶ Glaciar Perito Moreno
What Iguazú Falls is to water, the Perito Moreno (p487) is to ice. The glacier calves with such force into the steel-blue waters of Lago Argentino you'll forever remember the sounds with glazed-over eyes.

❷ Tierra del Fuego
Maybe it's the austral light or just knowing that the next step south is Antarctica. Whatever it is, this trove of mystical islands (p511), cut off from the northern world by the Strait of Magellan, is indescribably magical.

❸ Reserva Faunística Península Valdés
Never mind the Galápagos, this superb coastal reserve (p430) is a wildlife lover's dream, with sea lions, elephant seals, guanacos, rheas, Magellanic penguins, seabirds and – most famously – endangered southern right whales.

❹ Quebrada de Humahuaca
Etched into the Andes near the Bolivian border, this spectacular valley (p252) is home to traditional villages, epic views, unique food and plenty of proof that erosion can be nature's greatest artist. No wonder it made Unesco's World Heritage list!

❺ Iguazú Falls
There are waterfalls and there are waterfalls. And then there's Iguazú (p221). Nothing can prepare you for the sight and sound of so much water falling so hard from so many jungle-clad cliffs.

❻ Reserva Provincial Esteros del Iberá
Vast wetlands, shimmering lagoons, fiery red sunsets, gauchos, capybaras, caimans, birds – this enormous reserve (p200) is the stuff of dreams, where you can experience traditional Argentine life and some of the continent's most visible wildlife all in one go.

❼ Valles Calchaquíes
From Parque Nacional Los Cardones, where fawn-colored guanacos dart among giant cacti, to the traditional adobe villages of Cachi and Molinos, this vast network of valleys (p272) cradles some of Argentina's most scenic treasures.

❽ Valle de Calingasta
You might look a little funny pulling off the road, getting out of your vehicle, throwing your arms into the sky and spinning around in deranged, oblivious bliss – but you probably wouldn't be the first. This stretch of the Andes (p367) is *that* beautiful.

The Taste of Argentina

Argentines take barbecuing and beef to heights you cannot imagine. They make fabulous red, white and sparkling *vino* (wine). Their pizzas vie with those of New York, Naples and Chicago. The pasta? Superb. The coffee? Excellent. And despite recent inflation, you can *still* eat big while spending less than you would in New York, Chicago, Naples…

Author Tip

Foreigners often have difficulty stomaching the stuff that Argentines love to grill, including intestines, blood sausage, kidneys, chewy short ribs and even chewier cuts such as *vacio* (similar to flank steak). If that's the case with you, be sure to order the prime cuts (see p62).

❶ Wine

Exploring Argentina by the glass will take you – and your palate – from the malbecs and cabernets of Mendoza (p351) to the crisp torrontés of Cafayate (p277) and to the succulent syrahs of San Juan (p364). A bottle a day – make that your motto.

❷ Ice Cream

Argentine ice cream, from Buenos Aires to Patagonia, gives the French and Italian versions a run for their money. The capital's *heladerías* (ice-creameries; p120) are a great place to start lickin'.

❸ Mate

Although most first-time *mate* drinkers can barely choke the stuff down, this strong green tea, sipped communally from a gourd with a filtering metal straw, is a cultural delight (p65).

❹ Beef

Whether you're dining on prime cuts in a swanky Buenos Aires *parrilla* (steak house) or digging into a sizzling tabletop grill of chewy, flavorful, close-to-the-bone cuts in a family-style eatery, you're bound to get your fill of Argentina's most famous food (p62).

❺ Cafes

Nothing beats the feeling of sipping an espresso drink in an old-time cafe, especially in Buenos Aires (p121). Cafe culture has always been a key element in Argentine life. Imbibe!

City Life

Buenos Aires might reign supreme in this category, but Argentina's other cities offer urban fun on an altogether different level. Despite being the country's next biggest cities, they exude a small-town feel, and friendliness seems to permeate most facets of life, from the nightclub floor to the local *parrilla* (steak house).

❶ Buenos Aires

The Argentine capital (p80) is one of the world's most exhilarating cities, with astounding art, fascinating neighborhoods, fabulous food and a passionate population blazingly devoted to having fun *all…night…long.*

❷ Córdoba

Argentina's second city (p309) boasts the country's finest colonial center, with a gorgeous central plaza and exquisite Jesuit architecture. And the people? They're some of the friendliest you'll find anywhere.

❸ Mendoza

Grab your corkscrew and venture to the heart of wine country. Basking in the sun beneath the Andes' highest peaks, Mendoza (p339) is a stunning city of shade trees and *vino*.

❹ Salta

Only one thing beats an evening stroll around Salta's historic central plaza – drinking an ice-cold beer at one of its outdoor cafes. On a hot summer's evening, beneath the old buildings, it's pretty close to perfect (p260).

Contents

Regional Map Contents

THE ANDEAN NORTHWEST p244

NORTHEAST ARGENTINA p178

CÓRDOBA & THE CENTRAL SIERRAS p308

MENDOZA & THE CENTRAL ANDES p338

URUGUAY p534

BUENOS AIRES pp82–3

THE PAMPAS & THE ATLANTIC COAST p141

THE LAKE DISTRICT p375

PATAGONIA p419

TIERRA DEL FUEGO p512

Destination Argentina

Get a few people free associating on the word 'Argentina,' and it's quickly apparent why the country has long held travelers in awe: tango, Patagonia, beef, football, Tierra del Fuego, passion, the Andes. The classics alone make a formidable wanderlust cocktail.

Just wait till you get here. Arriving in Buenos Aires is like jumping aboard a moving train. Outside the taxi window, a blurred mosaic of drab apartment blocks and haphazard architecture whizzes by as you shoot along the freeway toward the center of the city. The driver – probably driving *way* too fast while chain-smoking and talking incessantly about government corruption – finally merges off the freeway. Then the people appear, the cafes, the purple jacaranda flowers draped over the sidewalks, *porteños* (residents of Buenos Aires) in stylish clothing walking purposefully past the newspaper stands and candy kiosks and handsome early-20th-century stone facades.

Despite the enormity of the capital city – which is home to a whopping 30% of the country's population – visitors seem to find its groove with surprising ease. The real shocker, after experiencing the art, music, cafes, shopping and all-night revelry of Buenos Aires, comes when you leave it. Aside from a handful of cities such as Rosario, Córdoba, Mendoza and La Plata, Argentina is pretty darn empty. Population centers are small, and even provincial capitals can have the feel of a friendly town. While these places can be worthy destinations in themselves, their real purpose is usually to springboard people into Argentina's greatest attraction: the natural world.

From the mighty Iguazú Falls in the subtropical north, to the thunderous, crackling advance of the Perito Moreno Glacier in the south, Argentina is a vast natural wonderland. The country beholds some of the Andes' highest peaks, several of which top 6000m near Mendoza and San Juan. It's home to wetlands that rival Brazil's famous Pantanal, massive ice fields in Patagonia, mountains painted in rustic colors, deserts dotted with cacti, cool lichen-clad Valdivian forests, glacial lakes, Andean salt flats, a spectacular Lake District, penguins, flamingos, caimans, capybaras and more.

But Argentina's cosmopolitan and natural marvels are only part of a very complex equation. Visitors will also experience a country at odds with itself – a potential economic powerhouse not fully in control of its destiny. Argentina dips into an economic crisis every dozen years, frustrating its citizens to no end. This has manifested in the recent low approval ratings of Cristina Kirchner, the country's first elected female president, who took office in 2007 (following in the footsteps of her husband, Nestor Kirchner). This country, like most of the rest of the world, is currently down – but not out. Argentines do have an overly healthy dose of skepticism, but it's tempered by a hope their country will one day pick itself up and leave its erratic reputation behind.

Travelers who dig beneath the tourist-office version of Argentina will find a country full of passion and beauty. They'll find amicable, seductive and engaging people fascinated with strangers who visit their land, many from countries they want Argentina to aspire to emulate. You can be one of those lucky enough to know the Argentine people, their land and their culture. This is a place people dream about visiting, and many fall in love with it once they arrive.

FAST FACTS

Area: 2.8 million sq km

Population: 40,150,000

Capital: Buenos Aires

Primary language: Spanish

Secondary languages: Quechua, Aymara, Toba (Qom) & others

Time: GMT minus 3hr (depending on daylight savings time)

GDP per capita: US$8235

Inflation: 15%, highly variable

Unemployment rate: 9-10%

Beef consumption per capita: 70kg per year

Getting Started

Forget everything you've heard about the challenges of travel in South America. Argentina is different. It's easy. Comfortable buses run on set schedules, petty theft is relatively rare (except perhaps in Buenos Aires), overnight buses are luxurious and the streets are safe. But the country does have its quirks, and knowing a few particulars before you go will make your journey all the more enjoyable.

This section will help you know when to visit (wait, August is ski season?), how much you might spend (prices have skyrocketed) and where to go for more information. Argentina is still a remarkable deal, and you can do it on a budget or live it luxuriously. It all depends on what you want out of your trip.

WHEN TO GO

Argentina's seasons are the reverse of those of the northern hemisphere. The best time to visit Buenos Aires is in spring (September through November), when the jacarandas are in bloom and temperatures are blissfully cool, and in fall (March through May). Summer (December through February) in the capital is hot and humid. Mendoza, Córdoba and the Lakes District are all spectacular during fall: the leaves put on an epic display, temperatures are comfortable and the crowds are thin.

See Climate Charts (p600) for more information.

Summer is the best time to hit Patagonia, when the weather's milder and more services are available. In other seasons, public transportation becomes trickier as services thin out. Northern Argentina can be brutally hot in summer and is best visited in spring. Winter (June through August) and fall in this region are also pleasant.

Ski season runs mid-June through mid-October, and the resorts are most expensive and most crowded in July and August when every *porteño* (person from Buenos Aires) seems to be on the slopes.

The most expensive times to travel are the Argentine vacation months of January, February and July.

COSTS & MONEY

After the economic collapse of 2001/02 Argentina devalued the peso and the country became instantly affordable. Travel was cheap. In the following years the economy stabilized, inflation reared its head and the world became hip to the Argentine bargain. Prices rose. Although Argentina has become pricier, it's still good value, especially if you're traveling on the euro or the UK pound.

DON'T LEAVE HOME WITHOUT...

- Checking the visa situation (see p611)
- Tampons – tough to find in smaller towns
- Ziplock bags – to waterproof your gizmos
- Duct tape – make a mini-roll around a pencil stub or lighter
- Handy wipes – great for overnight bus rides
- Swiss Army knife – must contain a corkscrew!
- Ear plugs
- Universal sink plug – a must for hand-washing clothes

RATES ON THE RISE

Lonely Planet aims to give its readers as precise an idea as possible of what things cost. Rather than slapping hotels or restaurants into vague budget categories (which can still leave you guessing), we publish the actual rates and prices that businesses quote to us during research. The problem is that prices change, especially somewhere such as Argentina, where inflation runs rampant. But we've found that readers prefer to have real numbers in their hands so they can make the calculations once they're on the road and then apply them across the board. This is still more precise than price ranges.

Argentina is no longer the rock-bottom bargain it was before 2005, but it remains good value. Where else can you enjoy a steak dinner with a good bottle of wine for under US$20? Or an amazing scoop of ice cream for under US$3? Certainly not in Europe or the USA. Although we anticipate prices will continue to rise, we've still opted to provide the prices given to us at the time of research. Our advice: call or check a few hotel or tour-operator websites before budgeting your trip, just to make sure you're savvy about going rates.

If you're on a budget, you can get by on AR$80 to AR$100 per day (outside Patagonia) by sleeping in hostel dorm beds or cheap hotels and eating at the cheapest nontouristy restaurants. Things get pricier when you add tours, entertainment and travel. Outside the capital and Patagonia, midrange travelers can get by comfortably on AR$180 to AR$200 per person per day if traveling with a companion, staying in a comfy hotel and eating at decent restaurants.

Buenos Aires and especially Patagonia are more expensive than the rest of Argentina. In the capital, good hotel rooms start at around AR$200 per double. In the provinces you can land a good hotel for AR$160 per double, while an extra AR$50 will get you something very comfortable.

Except in Patagonia, a pasta dinner can be as cheap as AR$15 per person at a no-frills family joint, while a full gourmet meal at a top-end restaurant can cost around AR$100 per person. In Patagonia a cheap restaurant meal starts at around AR$25.

HOW MUCH?

Midrange hotel AR$180-250

Five-hour bus ride AR$75

Slice of pizza AR$4

Sirloin steak AR$30

Average in-city cab ride AR$20

TRAVELING RESPONSIBLY

Since our inception in 1973, Lonely Planet has encouraged our readers to tread lightly, travel responsibly and enjoy the magic that independent travel affords. International travel is growing at a massive rate, and we still firmly believe in the benefits it can bring – but, as always, we encourage you to consider the impact your visit will have on both the global environment and the local economies, cultures and ecosystems.

Whenever you can, patronize the businesses listed in the Lonely Planet GreenDex (p666), which have proven that they're dedicated to sustainable travel. In all situations, try to support local businesses rather than large and international chains – it keeps profits and employment local. Whenever hiking, climbing, flying or otherwise enjoying the great outdoors, do your best to adhere as strictly as possible to the ethics of **Leave No Trace** (www.lnt .org), principles created by outdoor enthusiasts to minimize impact on the environment.

Although Argentina lacks a large indigenous population (unlike the Andean nations to the north), it does have its share of indigenous communities, primarily in the Chaco (p241) and in the Lakes District (p374). Whenever visiting or traveling through these communities, be sensitive to local beliefs and customs and avoid playing the gawker.

And don't forget the obvious: learn the language! Even if you blow it, you're attempt will be appreciated.

For more on sustainable travel, see p72.

TOP PICKS

Chile **Buenos Aires** ARGENTINA

NATIONAL PARKS

Argentina is a nature-lover's dream, and its parks are truly one of the best reasons to be here. For a complete list, see p76, but don't miss the following:

- Parque Nacional Los Glaciares (p478)
- Parque Nacional Iguazú (p221)
- Reserva Provincial Esteros del Iberá (p200)
- Reserva Faunística Península Valdés (p430)
- Parque Provincial Ischigualasto (p373)

WEIRD & WACKY PLACES

After all, everywhere has its oddities. The following offbeat places will get you thinking just how *interesting* Argentina can be. ¡Que raro!

- Museo Rocsen (p330) Possibly the most eclectic museum you'll ever visit
- Difunta Correa Shrine (p367) Honoring the mother of all mothers
- Tierra Santa (p102) Religious theme park without holy roller coasters
- Gaucho Antonio Gil shrines (p200) Nods to Argentina's Robin Hood – with a gaucho twist
- Parque El Desafío, Gaiman (p440) Recycling for art – or just a bunch of junk

MOVIES

Argentina has both inspired and produced countless outstanding movies. Here are our noninclusive, totally biased choices.

- *El bonaerense* (2002), directed by Pablo Trapero (see p47)
- *The Motorcycle Diaries* (2004), directed by Walter Salles
- *Histórias mínimas* (2002), directed by Carlos Sorin
- *La ciénaga* (2001), directed by Lucrecia Martel (see p47)
- *Nueve reinas* (2000), directed by Fabián Bielinsky
- *El secreto de sus ojos* (2009), directed by Juan José Campanella
- *Pizza, birra, faso* (1998), directed by Adrián Caetano and Bruno Stagnaro

CLASSIC LITERATURE

Be they works by Argentine authors or by foreigners writing about Argentina, the following are perfect for those long bus rides across the Argentine pampas.

- *Kiss of the Spider Woman* (1976), by Manuel Puig
- *Hopscotch* (1963), by Julio Cortázar
- *Labyrinths: Selected Stories & Other Writings* (1962), by Jorge Luis Borges
- *The Tunnel* (1948), by Ernesto Sábato
- *In Patagonia* (1977), by Bruce Chatwin
- *The Honorary Consul* (1973), by Graham Greene

TRAVEL LITERATURE

After years out of print, Lucas Bridges' classic, *Uttermost Part of the Earth* (1947), was republished in 2008. Bridges brilliantly describes his life among the indigenous peoples of Tierra del Fuego – a must-read for anyone heading south.

Another newly released account of an old journey is Ernesto 'Che' Guevara's offbeat *The Motorcycle Diaries* (2003), in which the young medical student recounts his eye-opening journey by motorcycle in 1951 and 1952 through Argentina, Chile, Brazil, Venezuela, Peru and Colombia.

In *Bad Times in Buenos Aires* (1999), Miranda France covers everything from Argentine condoms to psychoanalysis in a wry (and sometimes overbearingly negative) account of her stay in the capital in the 1990s.

If you're going to be wandering down to Patagonia (and even if you're not), pick up Bruce Chatwin's *In Patagonia* (1977), one of the most informed syntheses of life and landscape for any part of South America. For a glimpse into some gripping Patagonian mountaineering, read Gregory Crouch's *Enduring Patagonia* (2001), in which the author details his ascents of Cerro Torre's brutal west face and several other wild climbs.

Nick Reding's *The Last Cowboys at the End of the World: The Story of the Gauchos of Patagonia* (2001) takes place mostly in Chile, but is equally pertinent to the conditions and changes in neighboring Argentine Patagonia.

Frequently reprinted, William Henry Hudson's *Idle Days in Patagonia* (1893) is a romantic account of the 19th-century naturalist's adventures in search of migratory birds. Also check out his *The Purple Land* (1885) and *Far Away and Long Ago* (1918).

INTERNET RESOURCES

For websites about specific topics (such as hostels, relocating to Argentina, or gay and lesbian resources), see the appropriate section in the Directory (p596). For websites about Buenos Aires, see p93.

The following should get you started (all are in English or have an English link):

Argentimes (www.theargentimes.com) Expat-run newspaper out of Buenos Aires, with wide-ranging, at times in-depth, articles on Argentina.

Argentine Post (www.argentinepost.com) Good interesting articles on Buenos Aires and Argentina.

Argentina's Travel Guide (www.argentinastravel.com) Lots of information and fun articles on the country.

Argentina Turística (www.argentinaturistica.com) Packed with information on Argentina and its cities, and much more.

Bloggers in Argentina (www.bloggersinargentina.blogspot.com) A collection of Argentine bloggers; a good personal way to get a taste of the country.

Buenos Aires Herald (www.buenosairesherald.com) An international view of the country and world from the website of Buenos Aires' excellent, main English-language newspaper.

Latin American Network Information Center (www.lanic.utexas.edu/la/argentina/) Has a long list of Argentine websites. It's hardly complete, but you're bound to find something useful.

Lonely Planet (www.lonelyplanet.com) Succinct summaries on traveling to most places on earth; postcards from other travelers; and the Thorn Tree bulletin board, where you can ask questions before you go or dispense advice when you get back.

Events Calendar

Although Argentina is less prone to wild festivals than other South American countries, there are several fiestas that might be worth planning your trip around. Aside from the ones listed here, nearly every town in Argentina has its own fiesta, many of which are covered in the destination chapters. For a list of national public holidays, see p603.

JANUARY

FESTIVAL NACIONAL DEL FOLKLORE
late Jan

Near the city of Córdoba, the town of Cosquín hosts the National Festival of Folk Music (p320; www.aquicosquin.org, in Spanish) during the last week of January. It's the country's largest and best known *folklórico* (folk music) festival.

FEBRUARY–MARCH

CARNAVAL
late Feb–early Mar

Though not as rockin' in Argentina as it is in Brazil, this celebration is rowdy in the northeast, especially in Gualeguaychú (p204) and Corrientes (p196). In the northwest (particularly Quebrada de Humahuaca) there's more emphasis on traditional music and dancing. Montevideo, the capital of Uruguay, also has a good Carnaval (see p547).

FIESTA NACIONAL DE LA VENDIMIA
late Feb–early Mar

Mendoza city's National Wine Harvest Festival (p345) kicks off with parades, folkloric events and a royal coronation – all in honor of Mendoza's intoxicating beverage. For more information, see www.vendimia.mendoza.gov.ar, in Spanish.

MAY

DÍA DE VIRGEN DE LUJÁN
May 8

Thousands of devout believers make a 65km pilgrimage to the pampas town of Luján (p144) in honor of the Virgin Mary; other large pilgrimages to Luján take place in early October, early August, late September and on December 8.

JULY–AUGUST

EXPOSICIÓN RURAL
late Jul–early Aug

Get a glimpse of Argentina's obsession with its cattle and other livestock – horses, sheep, chickens etc. Gauchos do their thing, farm machinery is on display and there are plenty of meaty things to eat.

FESTIVAL Y MUNDIAL DE TANGO
mid–late Aug

Buenos Aires' best tango dancers perform at venues throughout the city during the two-week Tango Festival (p108). There's also a world-class competition and plenty of classes and workshops.

SEPTEMBER

SOUTH AMERICAN MUSIC CONFERENCE
exact date varies

This is Buenos Aires' biggest electronic music party (p108). It features the who's who of the electronic world, with networking conferences held during the day and 50,000 party-goers at night.

OCTOBER

FIESTA NACIONAL DE LA CERVEZA/OKTOBERFEST
early Oct

Join the swillers and oompah bands at Argentina's National Beer Festival, Villa General Belgrano's Oktoberfest (p326) in the Central Sierras. For more details, check out http://elsitiodelavilla.com /oktoberfest.

EISTEDDFOD
late Oct

This lively Welsh festival, featuring plentiful grub and choral singing, takes place in the Patagonian towns of Trelew (p437) and Trevelin (p465). It's a great one for inducing those 'wait-am-I-really-in-South-America?' moments.

NOVEMBER

DÍA DE LA TRADICIÓN
early–mid-Nov

The Day of Traditional Culture festival kicks off with a salute to the gaucho and is especially significant in San Antonio de Areco (p147), the most classically gaucho of towns. However, it is also important – and decidedly less touristy – in the mountain town of San José de Jáchal (p371), in San Juan.

MARCHA DEL ORGULLO GAY
mid-Nov

Buenos Aires' Gay Pride Parade (p108) draws thousands of gay, lesbian and transgendered citizens, as well as their supporters, who march (with the music up loud!) from Plaza de Mayo to the Congreso.

Itineraries
CLASSIC ROUTES

NORTHERN LOOP

Two to Four Weeks / Buenos Aires to Parque Nacional Iguazú

From lively **Buenos Aires** (p80), head to **Mendoza** (p339), smack in the heart of wine country. Take a day trip to **Puente del Inca** (p355) and the **Cristo Redentor** (p357) monument. Then, take an overnight bus to **Córdoba** (p309) to explore Argentina's finest colonial center.

Journey to **Tucumán** (p280) for some eclectic architecture and one of Argentina's liveliest street scenes. Head northwest to mellow lakeside **Tafí del Valle** (p286) for a day, then on to beautiful **Cafayate** (p276) to knock back some local torrontés wine. Sober up and journey through the epic **Quebrada de Cafayate** (p279) to **Salta** (p260), whose central plaza is one of Argentina's finest. From there, journey into the otherworldly **Valles Calchaquíes** (p272) to the adobe villages of **Cachi** (p272) and **Molinos** (p274). Next up, take in the beauty of the magnificently eroded Andean valley, **Quebrada de Humahuaca** (p252), where you can bed down overnight in lively little **Tilcara** (p254).

Return to Salta. From there, bus across the Chaco or fly via Buenos Aires for the grand finale: two days at **Parque Nacional Iguazú** (p223).

Covering more than 4000km, the Northern Loop takes you to four of Argentina's finest cities, through the forgotten Valles Calchaquíes to villages plucked from centuries past, and to one of South America's greatest natural spectacles, Iguazú Falls.

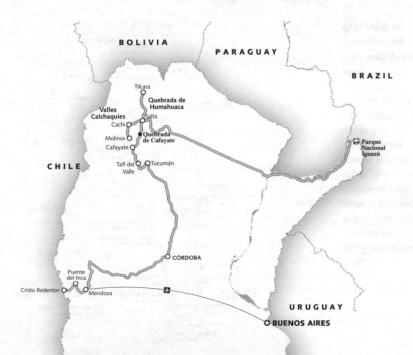

GRAND LOOP
Six to 12 Weeks / Buenos Aires to Buenos Aires

From **Buenos Aires** (p80), head south for whale watching at **Reserva Faunística Península Valdés** (p430). Take the long bus ride south to **Ushuaia** (p518) in Tierra del Fuego and on the way, stop for penguin watching at **Reserva Provincial Punta Tombo** (p441), dolphin spotting at **Reserva Natural Ría Deseado** (p450) and coastal bird-watching at **Parque Nacional Monte León** (p453).

After reaching Ushuaia allow for several days of exploration. Then, follow the two-week Patagonian Passage itinerary (p27) before winding your way up to the **Lake District** (p374), with a chocolate stop in **Bariloche** (p401). Bump down the lake-studded **Ruta de los Siete Lagos** (Seven Lakes Route; p392) to the leafy resort of **San Martín de los Andes** (p391) before exploring the Valdivian forests of **Parque Nacional Lanín** (p389).

From San Martín, head to **Aluminé** (p385) for rafting or fly-fishing and then on to gorgeous little **Villa Pehuenia** (p386) for a day or two of hiking and relaxation. Next, explore the breathtaking volcanic landscapes around **Malargüe** (p360) and continue north to **Mendoza** (p339) for wine tasting and more mind-blowing Andean scenery. From Mendoza, journey via **San Juan** (p364) to **Parque Provincial Ischigualasto** (p373), and then head east to explore the colonial center of **Córdoba** (p309).

From Córdoba, cut north to **Tucumán** (p280), then through the wildly eroded canyon of **Quebrada de Cafayate** (p279) to **Salta** (p260). From there head in to **Quebrada de Humahuaca** (p252) for a few days. Travel across the rugged Chaco, to visit **Reserva Provincial Esteros del Iberá** (p200). Continue northeast to the **Jesuit missions** (p217) near Posadas and finish beneath the massive falls of **Parque Nacional Iguazú** (p223). Fly back to Buenos Aires and party till your plane leaves.

The Grand Loop traverses more than 8800km, from Tierra del Fuego and Los Glaciares in the south, through the beautiful Lake District, to the traditional villages and Andean scenery of northwest Argentina. Throwing a couple of flights into this itinerary makes it manageable in less time.

ROADS LESS TRAVELED

RUTA NACIONAL 40   Four to Eight Weeks / Abra Pampa to Torres del Paine

Argentina's quintessential road trip, RN 40 travels the length of the Argentine Andes through some of the country's remotest regions. Much of it remains unpaved, and requires perseverance, time and self reliance. As you travel, you'll see an Argentina that most people – even most Argentines – never do. Much of the route is doable by bus, but some stretches require your own vehicle.

RN 40 starts south of **Abra Pampa** (p259) in the northwest, but the steep stretches before **Cachi** (p272), in the wildly scenic **Valles Calchaquíes** (p272), are impossible without a 4WD. Alternatively, start at Cachi. Further south, you'll hit lovely **Cafayate** (p276) before passing tiny **Huaco** (p372) and traditional **San José de Jáchal** (p371). Take a breather in **Mendoza** (p339) – you've been going *at least* a week now – and then explore the volcanic landscapes around **Malargüe** (p360). To avoid road closures, travel south of Malargüe in summer.

Continue south via tranquil **Buta Ranquil** and explore the lagoons and hot springs around **Chos Malal** (p382). Detour to the national parks of **Lanín** (p389) and **Nahuel Huapi** (p410) for epic hiking before hitting **Bariloche** (p401). Drive **El Calafate** (p482), where you can see the mind-altering Perito Moreno Glacier. Take a side trip to **El Chaltén** (p474) for superb hiking in the Fitz Roy Range before continuing back down along RN 40 to **Puerto Natales** (p500), Chile. From there, explore **Parque Nacional Torres del Paine** (p505) before doglegging west to **Río Gallegos** (p453) to fly back to Buenos Aires (unless you continue south a bit to Ushuaia, on RN3; it's as far south as any highway in the world goes).

RN 40 travels nearly the entire length of Argentina, more than 5000km, from just south of the Bolivian border in the north, nearly to Tierra del Fuego in the south. Some stretches require a private vehicle, others a 4WD (or, sans the 4WD, good walking shoes, plenty of food and water, and a need for adventure).

FORGOTTEN ANDES & NATIONAL PARKS   Two to Three Weeks / San Luis to Corrientes

This journey off the beaten track will turn up tiny villages, empty roads and rarely visited provincial parks. Begin in the small provincial capital of **San Luis** (p331), from where you can visit **Parque Nacional Sierra de las Quijadas** (p334), whose wildly eroded lunar landscape is similar to San Juan's Parque Provincial Ischigualasto – sans the people. Bus over to **San Juan** (p364), rent a car and head for the hills: drive up to **Barreal** (p368) in the breathtaking Valle de Calingasta for hiking, rafting, climbing and land sailing beneath the country's highest peaks. Head up RP 412 to the traditional towns of **Rodeo** (p371), **San José de Jáchal** (p371) and **Huaco** (p372), but stop en route for a dip in the thermal baths of **Pismanta** (p372). Take RN 40 back to San Juan and bus out to the fascinating **Difunta Correa Shrine** (p367) – and don't forget to leave a bottle of water as an offering to this patron saint of truck drivers (especially if you hitchhike!).

From San Juan, take an overnight bus to **Córdoba** (p309), a colonial city that foreigners often skip. After a day or two exploring the city and the Jesuit *estancias* (ranches) of the **Central Sierras** (p318), grab an overnighter to **Resistencia** (p233), an odd city of sculptures and the nearest hub to diverse **Parque Nacional Chaco** (p237). From **Corrientes** (p194), catch some live *chamamé* (folk music of northeast Argentina) and head to **Reserva Provincial Esteros del Iberá** (p200), a wetlands preserve and wildlife sanctuary comparable to Brazil's Pantanal.

By now you'll be aching for human contact: either join the crowds at **Iguazú Falls** (p223), a full day's travel away, or head back to Buenos Aires, flying from Corrientes or journeying overland.

Just because the crowds head elsewhere doesn't mean this 2850km trip lacks sights. In fact, the forgotten back roads and little-visited villages and parks make this a very special trip through an Argentina that most foreigners never see.

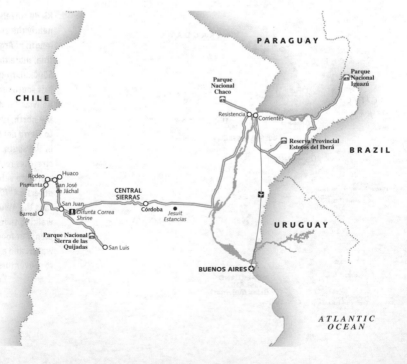

TAILORED TRIPS

PATAGONIAN PASSAGE   Patagonia, Tierra del Fuego & the Lake District

Though the sadistic manage this national-parks circuit in 10 days, two weeks is really the minimum. It's the end of the world, after all, so don't sell yourself short. Begin in **Ushuaia** (p518), in Tierra del Fuego, and visit nearby **Parque Nacional Tierra del Fuego** (p528). Take a hopper flight to **El Calafate** (p482) and visit spectacular Perito Moreno Glacier in **Parque Nacional Los Glaciares** (p487). Bus down to **Puerto Natales** (p500) and hike the famous **Parque Nacional Torres del Paine** (p505). Head north again to **El Chaltén** (p474) for mind-altering hikes in the **Fitz Roy area** (p478). Then back to El Calafate for your return flight to Buenos Aires. *Chau!*

With an extra two weeks, begin the trip by heading south (by bus or plane) from Buenos Aires and stop in **Puerto Madryn** (p424) on your way down for whale watching at **Reserva Faunística Península Valdés** (p430). After exploring the national parks mentioned above, fly from El Calafate up to **Bariloche** (p401). From here, hike yourself silly in the Lake District national parks of **Nahuel Huapi** (p410) and **Lanín** (p389). Before your flight back to Buenos Aires, you may even be able to squeeze in trips to nearby **Parque Nacional Lago Puelo** (p417) and **Parque Nacional Los Alerces** (p465).

ADVENTURES IN WINE   Mendoza, San Juan & the Andean Northwest

Prime your palate for this trip through Argentina's world-class wine countries. Following the oenologist's trail will not only give you a serious sampling of the country's finest libation, you'll be introduced to many of its most interesting regions. Uncork your trip in beautiful **Mendoza** (p339), Argentina's Andes-flanked wine capital. Be certain to stop at **Bodega La Rural** (p352), home of South America's largest (and best) wine museum. Squeeze in a day trip up RN 7 to **Puente del Inca** (p355) thermal baths and the lung-busting heights of the **Cristo Redentor** (p357), on the Chilean border.

Take a crack-of-dawn bus to **San Rafael** (p358), rent a bike and ride out to the city's wineries, making **Bianchi Champañera** (p358) your last stop for a bit of bubbly. The next day, head to **San Juan** (p364) to try the excellent syrah and regional whites produced near this leafy provincial capital. Pause between sips and squeeze in a day trip to **Parque Provincial Ischigualasto** (p373) or up RN 40 to **San José de Jáchal** (p371) if you have the time. From San Juan take an overnight bus to **Tucumán** (p280), and head the next day to lovely little **Cafayate** (p276) to hit a few wineries and dazzle your taste buds with the regional torrontés white wine. Return to Tucumán for your flight to Buenos Aires.

History

Like all Latin American countries, Argentina has a tumultuous history, one tainted by periods of despotic rule, corruption and hard times. But it's also an illustrious history, a story of a country that was once one of the world's economic powerhouses, a country that gave birth to the tango, to international icons such as Evita Perón and Che Guevara, and to some of the world's most important inventions (the public bus, the coronary bypass and the ballpoint pen come to mind). Understanding Argentina's past is paramount to understanding its present and, most importantly, to understanding Argentines themselves.

NATIVE PEOPLES

Human migration to the Americas began nearly 30,000 years ago, when the ancestors of Amerindians, taking advantage of lowered sea levels during the Pleistocene epoch, walked from Siberia to Alaska via a land bridge across the Bering Strait. They eventually reached what's now Argentina around 10,000 BC. One of Argentina's oldest and impressive archaeological sites is Cueva de las Manos (Cave of the Hands; p472) in Patagonia, where mysterious cave paintings, mostly of left hands, date from 7370 BC.

By the time the Spanish arrived, much of present-day Argentina was inhabited by highly mobile peoples who hunted the guanaco (a wild relative of the llama) and the rhea (a large bird resembling an emu) with bow and arrow or *boleadoras* – heavily weighted thongs that could be thrown up to 90m to ensnare the hunted animal. (Today, replica *boleadoras* are sold at artisan shops throughout the country – pick up a set and give them a hurl at a stationary object for an idea of the skill required to take down a guanaco!)

The Argentine pampas was inhabited by the Querandí, who were hunters and gatherers legendary for their spirited resistance to the Spanish. The Guaraní, indigenous to the area from northern Entre Ríos through Corrientes and into Paraguay and Brazil, were semisedentary agriculturalists, raising sweet potatoes, maize, manioc and beans, and fishing the Río Paraná.

Of all of Argentina, the northwest was the most developed. Several indigenous groups, most notably the Diaguita, practiced irrigated agriculture in the valleys of the eastern Andean foothills. The region's inhabitants were influenced heavily by the Tiahanaco empire of Bolivia and by the great Inca empire, which expanded south from Peru into Argentina from the early 1480s. In Salta province the ruined stone city of Quilmes (p289) is one of the best-preserved pre-Incan indigenous sites, where some 5000 Quilmes, part of the Diaguita civilization, lived and withstood the Inca invasion. Further north in Tilcara (p254) you can see a completely restored *pucará* (walled city), about which little is known.

Journey back in time to the epoch of Patagonia's first human inhabitants and see how their world changed in the centuries that followed in *Patagonia: Natural History, Prehistory and Ethnography at the Uttermost End of the Earth* (1997), by Colin McEwen et al.

TIMELINE

10,000 BC	7370 BC	4000 BC
Humans, having crossed the Bering Strait approximately 20,000 years earlier, finally reach the area of modern-day Argentina. The close of one of the world's greatest human migrations nears.	Toldense culture makes its first paintings of hands inside Patagonia's famous Cueva de las Manos. The paintings prove humans inhabited the region this far back – and had a preference for painting the left appendage.	The indigenous Yaghan, later referred to as Fuegians by the English-speaking world, begin populating the southernmost islands of Tierra del Fuego. Humans could migrate no further south.

In the Lake District and Patagonia, the Pehuenches and Puelches were hunter-gatherers, and the pine nuts of the araucaria, or pehuén tree, formed a staple of their diet. The names Pehuenches and Puelches were given to them by the Mapuche, who entered the region from the west as the Spanish pushed south. Today there are many Mapuche reservations, especially in the area around Junín de los Andes (p387).

Until they were wiped out by Europeans, there were indigenous inhabitants as far south as Tierra del Fuego, where the Selk'nam, Haush, Yaghan and Alacaluf peoples lived as mobile hunters and gatherers. Despite frequently inclement weather they wore little or no clothing, but constant fires (even in their bark canoes) kept them warm and gave the region its Spanish name, Tierra del Fuego (Land of Fire).

ENTER THE SPANISH

Just over a decade after Christopher Columbus (Cristóbal Colón in Spanish) accidentally encountered the Americas, other Spanish explorers began probing the Río de la Plata estuary. (Columbus was actually Italian, but he undertook his expedition sailing under the Spanish flag.) Most early explorations of the area were motivated by rumors of vast quantities of silver. Spaniard Sebastian Cabot optimistically named the river the Río de la Plata (River of Silver), and to drive the rumors home, part of the new territory was even given the Latin name for silver (*argentum*). But the mineral riches that the Spanish found in the Inca empire of Peru never panned out in this misnamed land.

The first real attempt at establishing a permanent settlement on the estuary was made by Spanish aristocrat Pedro de Mendoza in 1536. He landed at present-day Buenos Aires and, not one to mince words, named the outpost Puerto Nuestra Señora Santa María del Buen Aire (Port Our Lady St Mary of the Good Wind). After the colonists tried pilfering food from the indigenous Querandí, the natives turned on them violently. Within four years Mendoza fled back to Spain without a lick of silver, and the detachment of troops he left behind beat it upriver to the gentler environs of Asunción, present-day capital of Paraguay.

NORTHWEST SUPREMACY

Although Spanish forces reestablished Buenos Aires by 1580, it remained a backwater in comparison to Andean settlements founded by a separate and more successful Spanish contingency moving south from Alto Perú (now Bolivia). With ties to the colonial stronghold of Lima, capital of the viceroyalty of Peru, and financed by the bonanza silver mine at Potosí, the Spanish founded some two dozen cities as far south as Mendoza (1561) during the latter half of the 16th century. Santiago del Estero, founded in 1553, is the country's oldest permanent settlement. The main force in this northward

Argentina's national beer, Quilmes, is named after the now decimated indigenous group of northwest Argentina.

The most comprehensive, though not necessarily most readable, book on Argentine history is David Rock's *Argentina 1516-1987: From Spanish Colonization to Alfonsín* (1987). It's worth the grunt.

AD 1480s	1536	1553
The Inca empire expands into present-day Argentina's Andean northwest. At the time, the region was inhabited by Argentina's most advanced indigenous cultures, including the Diaguita and Tafí.	Pedro de Mendoza establishes Puerto Nuestra Señora Santa María del Buen Aire on the Río de la Plata. But the Spaniards anger the indigenous Querandí, who soon drive the settlers out.	Francisco de Aguirre establishes Santiago del Estero, furthering Spain's expansion into present-day Argentina from Alto Perú. Today the city is the country's oldest permanent settlement.

orientation was the protectionist King of Spain, whose mercantile policy decreed that commerce between Spain and the colonies had to be routed through Lima.

The two most important population centers at the time were Tucumán (founded in 1565) and Córdoba (1573). Tucumán lay in the heart of a rich agricultural region and supplied Alto Perú with grains, cotton and livestock. Córdoba became an important educational center, and Jesuit missionaries established *estancias* (ranches) in the surrounding sierras to supply Alto Perú with mules, foodstuffs and wine. Córdoba's Manzana Jesuítica (Jesuit Block; p312) is now the finest preserved group of colonial buildings in the country, and several Jesuit *estancias* in the Central Sierras (p318) are also exquisitely preserved. These sites, along with the central plazas of Salta (founded in 1582) and Tucumán, boast the country's finest colonial architecture.

THE JESUITS

Northeast Argentina, along the upper regions of the Río Uruguay and Río Paraná, was colonized later with the help of Jesuit missionaries, who concentrated the indigenous Guaraní in settlements. Starting around 1609, the Jesuits established 30 missions, including the marvelously preserved San Ignacio Miní (p218), which should be on every architecture-lover's hit list.

Perhaps as many as 100,000 indigenous people lived in the Jesuit settlements, which resembled other Spanish municipalities but operated with a political and economic autonomy that did not apply to other Iberian settlers. Wary of the Jesuits' accumulating wealth and power, the Spanish crown expelled them in 1767, and the mission communities disintegrated rapidly, almost fading into the wilderness.

South America's oldest university is Córdoba's Universidad Nacional de Córdoba, founded in 1613 and elevated to university status in 1622.

BUENOS AIRES: BOOTLEGGER TO BOOMTOWN

As the northwest prospered, Buenos Aires suffered the Crown's harsh restrictions on trade for nearly two centuries. But because the port was ideal for trade, frustrated merchants turned to smuggling, and contraband trade with Portuguese Brazil and nonpeninsular European powers flourished. The increasing amount of wealth passing through the city fueled much of its initial growth.

With the decline of silver mining at Potosí in the late 18th century, the Spanish Crown was forced to recognize Buenos Aires' importance for direct transatlantic trade. Relaxing its restrictions, Spain made Buenos Aires the capital of the new viceroyalty of the Río de la Plata – which included Paraguay, Uruguay and the mines at Potosí – in 1776.

Although the new viceroyalty had internal squabbles over trade and control issues, when the British raided the city in 1806 and again in 1807, the response was unified. Locals rallied against the invaders without Spanish help and chased them out of town.

The Mission (1986), starring Robert De Niro and Jeremy Irons, is an epic film about the Jesuit missions and missionaries in 18th-century South America. It's the perfect kickoff for a trip to northern Argentina's missions.

1561	1565	1573
The city of Mendoza is founded by Spaniards traveling east from Santiago, Chile, during their push to establish access to the Río de la Plata, where Spanish ships could deliver more troops and supplies.	Diego de Villarroel founds the city of San Miguel de Tucumán (referred to today simply as Tucumán), Argentina's third-oldest. The city was relocated further east 120 years later.	The city of Córdoba is founded by Tucumán Governor Jerónimo Luis de Cabrera, establishing an important link on the trade routes between Chile and Alto Perú.

AN ABBREVIATED HISTORICAL WHO'S WHO

■ **José de San Martín** (1778–1850) Argentina's national hero, who led the country and southern South America to independence from Spain. Best quote: 'I only want lions in my regiment.'

■ **Domingo Faustino Sarmiento** (1811–88) Argentine author, educator and president of Argentina (1868–74). Famous words: 'It would be fun to make an offer to England, just to see how much muslin and cotton it would give to own these plains of Buenos Aires.'

■ **General Julio Argentino Roca** (1843–1914) Minister of War (1877–79); President of Argentina (1843–1914). Famous for: wiping out much of Patagonia's indigenous population in the 1879 Conquest of the Desert.

■ **Raúl Alfonsín** (1927–2009) First democratically elected president (1983–89) following the Dirty War. Famous quote: 'The house is in order.'

■ **Ernesto Guevara de la Serna** (1928–67) Born in Rosario, Argentina, and known as Che Guevara, the most legendary of revolutionaries. Famous quote: 'I don't care if I fall as long as someone else picks up my gun and keeps on shooting.'

■ **Juan Domingo Perón** (1895–1974) President of Argentina (1946–55); husband of Evita. Famous quote: 'The people are my only descendants.'

■ **María Eva Duarte de Perón** (1919–52) Known to the world as 'Evita'; championed social rights as First Lady to President Perón. Famous quote: 'If I fall, look out for the crash. There won't be anyone left standing.'

■ **Jorge Rafael Videla** (1925–) Former military general and leader of military coup that unseated Isabel Perón in 1976; de facto president until 1981.

■ **Carlos Menem** (1930–) President of Argentina (1989–99). Famous for: curbing inflation after the Dirty War, selling off state enterprises, corruption.

■ **Domingo Cavallo** (1946–) Argentine Minister of Economy under Carlos Menem. Famous for: pegging the peso to the US dollar in 1991 and instituting *el corralito* (a freeze on withdrawals) in 2001.

■ **Fernando de la Rúa** (1937–) President of Argentina (1999–2001); resigned amid economic crisis that rocked Argentina. Best campaign ad: 'They say that I'm boring.'

■ **Eduardo Duhalde** (1941–) Interim president (2002–03) following resignation of Fernando de la Rúa. Famous for: devaluing the peso in 2002.

■ **Roberto Lavagna** (1942–) Minister of Economy (2002–05) under interim President Eduardo Duhalde. Credited with: handling the economic crisis and arranging Argentina's debt swap with the IMF.

■ **Nestor Kirchner** (1950–) President of Argentina (2003–07). Nicknames: 'K' and 'El Pingüino' ('the penguin;' he hails from Patagonia).

■ **Cristina Fernández de Kirchner** (1953–) Current president of Argentina; former First Lady to Nestor Kirchner.

1580	**1609**	**1767**
Buenos Aires is reestablished by Spanish forces, but the city remains a backwater for years, in comparison with the growing strongholds of Mendoza, Tucumán and Santiago del Estero in central and northwestern Argentina.	Jesuits begin building missions in northeast Argentina, including San Ignacio Miní (1610), Loreto (1632) and Santa Ana (1633), concentrating the indigenous Guaraní into settlements known as *reducciones*.	The Spanish Crown expels the Jesuits from all of New Spain, and the mission communities decline rapidly.

The late 18th century also saw the emergence of the legendary gauchos of the pampas (see the boxed text, p148). The South American counterpart to North America's cowboys, they hunted wild cattle and broke in wild horses that had multiplied after being left behind by previous expeditions on the Río de la Plata.

INDEPENDENCE & INFIGHTING

Toward the end of the 18th century, criollos (Argentine-born colonists) became increasingly dissatisfied and impatient with Spanish authority. The expulsion of British troops from Buenos Aires gave the people of the Río de la Plata new confidence in their ability to stand alone. After Napoleon invaded Spain in 1808, Buenos Aires finally declared its independence on May 25, 1810. To commemorate the occasion, the city's main square was renamed Plaza de Mayo.

For an interpretation of the gaucho's role in Argentine history, check out Richard W Slatta's book *Gauchos and the Vanishing Frontier* (1983).

Independence movements throughout South America soon united to expel Spain from the continent by the 1820s. Under the leadership of General José de San Martín and others, the United Provinces of the Río de la Plata (the direct forerunner of the Argentine Republic) declared formal independence at Tucumán on July 9, 1816.

Despite achieving independence, the provinces were united in name only. With a lack of any effective central authority, regional disparities within Argentina – formerly obscured by Spanish rule – became more obvious. This resulted in the rise of the caudillos (local strongmen), who resisted Buenos Aires as strongly as Buenos Aires had resisted Spain.

Argentine politics was thus divided between the Federalists of the interior, who advocated provincial autonomy, and the Unitarists of Buenos Aires, who upheld the city's central authority. For nearly two decades bloody and vindictive conflicts between the two factions left the country nearly exhausted.

THE REIGN OF ROSAS

In the first half of the 19th century Juan Manuel de Rosas came to prominence as a caudillo in Buenos Aires province, representing the interests of rural elites and landowners. He became governor of the province in 1829 and, while he championed the Federalist cause, he also helped centralize political power in Buenos Aires and proclaimed that all international trade be funneled through the capital. His reign lasted more than 20 years (to 1852), and he set ominous precedents in Argentine political life, creating the infamous *mazorca* (his ruthless political police force) and institutionalizing torture.

One of the best-known contemporary accounts of postindependence Argentina is Domingo Faustino Sarmiento's *Life in the Argentine Republic in the Days of the Tyrants* (1868). Also superb is his seminal classic, *Facundo, Or Civilization & Barbarism* (1845).

Under Rosas, Buenos Aires continued to dominate the new country, but his extremism turned many against him, including some of his strongest allies. Finally, in 1852, a rival caudillo named Justo José de Urquiza (once a staunch supporter of Rosas) organized a powerful army and forced Rosas from power. Urquiza's first task was to draw up a constitution, which was

1776	1806–07	1810
Spain names Buenos Aires the capital of the new viceroyalty of the Río de la Plata. The territory includes the areas of present-day Paraguay, Uruguay and the mines at Potosí (Bolivia).	Attempting to seize control of Spanish colonies during the Napoleonic Wars, British forces raid Buenos Aires in 1806 and in 1807. Buenos Aires militias defeat British troops without Spain's help, which kindles ideas of independence.	Buenos Aires declares its independence from Spain on May 25, although actual independence is still several years off. The city names the Plaza de Mayo in honor of the event.

formalized by a convention in Santa Fe on May 1, 1853. The Constitution (still in force today despite its frequent suspension) pointed to the triumph of Unitarism, and subsequent economic developments confirmed Buenos Aires' power in the coming decades.

THE FLEETING GOLDEN AGE

Elected the Republic of Argentina's first official president in 1862, Bartolomé Mitre was concerned with building the nation and establishing infrastructure. His goals, however, were subsumed by the War of the Triple Alliance (or Paraguayan War), which lasted from 1865 to 1870. Not until Domingo Faustino Sarmiento, an educator and journalist from San Juan, became president did progress in Argentina really kick in. Sarmiento is still revered for his promotion of education, and his childhood home in San Juan is now a museum (p364). In Buenos Aires there's also a museum honoring him (p103).

Buenos Aires' economy boomed and immigrants poured in from Spain, Italy, Germany and Eastern Europe. The city's population grew more than sevenfold from 1869 to 1895. The new residents worked in the port area, lived tightly in the tenement buildings and developed Buenos Aires' famous dance – the tango – in the brothels and smoky nightclubs of the port (see the boxed text, p124). Basque and Irish refugees became the first shepherds, as both sheep numbers and wool exports increased nearly tenfold between 1850 and 1880.

Still, much of the southern pampas and Patagonia were inaccessible for settlers because of fierce resistance from indigenous Mapuche and Tehuelche. Nicolás Avellaneda, elected Argentina's president in 1874, took care of that. In 1879 Avellaneda's Minister of War, General Julio Argentino Roca, carried out a ruthless campaign of extermination against the indigenous people in what is known as the Conquista del Desierto (Conquest of the Desert). The campaign doubled the area under state control and opened up Patagonia to settlement and sheep. The Vía Cristi memorial (p388) in Junín de los Andes is likely the region's most impressive and moving tribute to the Mapuche lives lost in this 'war.'

By the turn of the 20th century Argentina had a highly developed rail network (financed largely by British capital), fanning out from Buenos Aires in all directions. Still, the dark cloud of a vulnerable economy loomed. Because of inequities in land distribution, the prosperity of the late 19th century was far from broad. Industry could not absorb all the immigration. Labor unrest grew. As imports surpassed exports, the economy showed signs of stress. Finally, with the onset of the world-wide Great Depression, the military took power under conditions of considerable social unrest. An obscure but oddly visionary colonel, Juan Domingo Perón, was the first leader to try to come to grips with the country's economic crisis.

Take a more personalized look into Argentina's past with Monica Szurmuk's *Women in Argentina* (2001), a collection of travel narratives by women – both Argentine and foreign – who traveled here between 1850 and 1930.

July 9 1816	1829	1852
After successful independence movements throughout South America, the United Provinces of the Río de la Plata (Argentina's forerunner) declares formal independence from Spain at Tucumán.	Federalist caudillo Juan Manuel de Rosas becomes governor of Buenos Aires province and de facto ruler of the Argentine Confederation. He rules the confederation with an iron fist for more than 20 years.	Federalist and former Rosas ally Justo José de Urquiza defeats Rosas at the Battle of Caseros and, in 1853, draws up Argentina's first constitution, making him the leader of a divided republic.

THE PERÓN DECADE

A fascinating, fictional-
ized version of the life of
ex-president Juan Perón,
culminating in his return
to Buenos Aires in 1973,
is Tomás Eloy Martínez'
The Perón Novel (1998).

Juan Perón emerged in the 1940s to become Argentina's most revered, as well as most despised, political figure. He first came to national prominence as head of the National Department of Labor, after a 1943 military coup toppled civilian rule. In this post he organized relief efforts after a major earthquake in San Juan, which earned praise throughout the country. In the process he also met Eva (Evita) Duarte, the radio actor who would become his second wife and make her own major contribution to Argentine history (see the boxed text, opposite). With the help of Evita, Perón ran for and won the presidency in 1946.

During previous sojourns in fascist Italy and Nazi Germany, Perón had grasped the importance of spectacle in public life and also developed his own brand of watered-down Mussolini-style fascism. He held massive rallies from the balcony of the Casa Rosada, with the equally charismatic Evita at his side. Although they ruled by decree rather than consent, the Peróns legitimized the trade-union movement, extended political rights to working-class people, secured voting rights for women and made university education available to any capable individual.

Argentine writer Uki
Goñi's The Real Odessa
(2002) is the best
and probably most
meticulously researched
book about Argentina's
harboring of Nazi war
criminals during the
Perón administration.

Economic difficulties and rising inflation undermined Juan Perón's second presidency in 1952, and Evita's death the same year dealt a blow to both the country and the president's popularity. In late 1955 a military coup sent him into exile in Spain and initiated nearly three decades of catastrophic military rule.

PERÓN'S EXILE & RETURN

During their exile, Perón and his associates constantly plotted their return to Argentina. In the late 1960s increasing economic problems, strikes, political kidnappings and guerrilla warfare marked Argentine political life. In the midst of these events, Perón's opportunity to return finally arrived in 1973, when the beleaguered military relaxed their objections to Perón's Justicialist party (popularly known as the Peronistas) and loyal Peronista Hector Cámpora was elected president. Cámpora resigned upon Perón's return, paving the way for new elections easily won by Perón.

For a glimpse into the life
of Argentina's beloved
Eva Perón, check out Julie
M Taylor's Eva Perón:
The Myths of a Woman
(1979).

After an 18-year exile, Perón once again symbolized Argentine unity, but there was no substance to his rule. Chronically ill, Perón died in mid-1974, leaving a fragmented country to his ill-qualified third wife – and vice president – Isabel.

THE DIRTY WAR & THE DISAPPEARED

In the late 1960s and early '70s, antigovernment feeling was rife, and street protests often exploded into all-out riots. Armed guerrilla organizations such as the Ejército Revolucionario del Pueblo (ERP; People's Revolutionary Army) and the Montoneros emerged as radical opponents of the military,

1862	1865	1865–70
Bartolomé Mitre is elected president of the newly titled Republic of Argentina and strives to modernize the country by expanding the railway network, creating a national army and postal system, and more.	Over 150 Welsh immigrants, traveling aboard the clipper *Mimosa*, land in Patagonia and establish Argentina's first Welsh colony in the province of Chubut.	The War of the Triple Alliance is fought between Paraguay and the allied countries of Argentina, Brazil and Uruguay. Paraguay loses and Argentina gains control of territory along the Río de la Plata and upper Río Paraná.

EVITA, LADY OF HOPE

'I will come again, and I will be millions.'

Eva Perón, 1952

From her humble origins in the pampas, to her rise to power beside President Juan Perón, María Eva Duarte de Perón is one of the most revered political figures on the planet. Known affectionately to all as Evita, she is Argentina's beloved First Lady, in some ways even eclipsing the legacy of her husband, who governed Argentina from 1946 to 1955.

At the age of 15 Eva Duarte left her hometown of Junín for Buenos Aires, looking for work as an actor. After stints in theater and film she landed a job in radio. In 1944 Duarte attended a benefit at Buenos Aires' Luna Park for victims of an earthquake in San Juan. Here she met Colonel Juan Perón, head of the National Department of Labor, who was entranced by her intensity and vision. They were married by 1945.

Shortly after Perón won the presidency in 1946, Evita went to work in the office of the Department of Labor and Welfare. During Perón's two terms, Evita empowered her husband both through her charisma and by reaching out to the nation's poor, who came to love her dearly. She created the Fundación Eva Perón, through which she built housing for the poor, created programs for children, and extended subsidies and distributed clothing and food items directly to needy families. She fervently campaigned for the aged, urging her husband to add elderly rights to the constitution and successfully pushing through a law granting pensions to elderly people in need. The foundation created medical trains and buses that traveled the country, offering health services directly to the poor. Evita created the Partido Peronista Femenino (Peronista Feminist Party), and in 1947 successfully advocated for a law extending suffrage to women.

When Perón ran for his second term in 1952, thousands gathered in the streets of Buenos Aires demanding Evita be his running mate. She accepted publicly, but declined in a radio announcement the following day, due to opposition within the military government. The same year, at age 33, Evita died of cancer on July 26.

Although remembered for extending social justice to those she called the country's *descamisados* (shirtless ones), Evita's rule with Perón was not free from controversy. Together they ruled with an iron fist, jailing opposition leaders and closing opposition newspapers. When *Time* magazine referred to her as an 'illegitimate child' she banned the publication, and when she traveled to Europe in 1947 she was refused entrance to Buckingham Palace. However, there is no denying the extent to which she empowered women at all levels of Argentine society and helped the country's poor.

When Evita said she'd return to 'be millions' in a speech shortly before her death, she probably had no idea of her words' prophetic truth. Today she enjoys near-saint status (many have petitioned the Vatican unsuccessfully) and has practically become a pop icon after the release of the Hollywood musical *Evita*, starring Madonna (a serious bone of contention in Argentina). She is loved throughout the world. In Argentina she was, for many, 'our Lady of Hope.'

To get a little closer to Evita, stop by the Museo Evita (p102) or visit her tomb in the Recoleta cemetery (p101).

Eva speaks for herself, to some degree, in her ghostwritten autobiography *La razón de mi vida* (My Mission in Life; 1951), well worth a read for Evitaphiles.

1868	1869–95	1872–79
Domingo Faustino Sarmiento, an educator and journalist from San Juan, is elected president. He encourages immigration to Argentina, ramps up public education and pushes to Europeanize the country.	The Argentine economy booms, immigration skyrockets as Italian and Spanish immigrants flood in, and Buenos Aires' population grows from 90,000 to 670,000. The tango emerges in Buenos Aires .	José Hernández publishes his epic poem, 'El Gaucho Martín Fierro,' in two parts: 'El Gaucho Martín Fierro' (1872) and 'La Vuelta de Martín Fierro' (1879). General Julio Roca slaughters thousands of indigenous people.

Hectór Olivera's 1983 film *Funny Dirty Little War,* available on DVD, is an unsettling but excellent black comedy set in a fictitious town just before the 1976 military coup.

the oligarchies and US influence in Latin America. Perón's bumbling widow, Isabel, along with her adviser, José López Rega, created the Triple A (Alianza Argentina Anticomunista), a death squad to take on the revolutionary groups. With increasing official corruption exacerbating Isabel's incompetence, Argentina found itself plunged into chaos.

On March 24, 1976, a bloodless military coup led by army general Jorge Rafael Videla took control of the Argentine state apparatus and ushered in a period of terror and brutality. Videla's sworn aim was to crush the guerrilla movements and restore social order, and much of the Argentine press and public gave their support. During what the regime euphemistically labeled the Process of National Reorganization (known as El Proceso), security forces went about the country arresting, torturing, raping and killing anyone on their hit list of suspected leftists.

During the period between 1976 and 1983, often referred to as the Guerra Sucia or Dirty War, human-rights groups estimate that some 30,000 people 'disappeared.' To disappear meant to be abducted, detained, tortured and probably killed, with no hope of legal process. Ironically, the Dirty War ended only when the Argentine military attempted a real military operation: liberating the Falkland Islands (Islas Malvinas) from British rule.

Jacobo Timerman, an Argentine publisher and journalist who was outwardly critical of the 1976–83 military regime, was arrested and tortured by the military. He details the experience in his esteemed memoir *Prisoner Without a Name, Cell Without a Number* (1981).

THE FALKLANDS/MALVINAS WAR

Under military rule, Argentina's economy continued to decline and eventually collapsed in chaos. El Proceso was coming undone.

In late 1981 General Leopoldo Galtieri assumed the role of president. To stay in power amid a faltering economy and mass social unrest, Galtieri played the nationalist card and launched an invasion in April 1982 to dislodge the British from the Falkland Islands, which had been claimed by Argentina as its own Islas Malvinas for nearly a century and a half.

Overnight, the move unleashed a wave of nationalist euphoria that then subsided almost as fast. Galtieri underestimated the determined response of British Prime Minister Margaret Thatcher, and after only 74 days Argentina's ill-trained, poorly motivated and mostly teenaged forces surrendered ignominiously. The military regime collapsed, and in 1983 Argentines elected civilian Raúl Alfonsín to the presidency.

AFTERMATH OF THE DIRTY WAR

In his successful 1983 presidential campaign, Alfonsín pledged to prosecute military officers responsible for human-rights violations during the Dirty War. He convicted high-ranking junta officials (such as ex-presidents Galtieri, Videla and Roberto Viola, and ex-Admiral Emilio Massera) for kidnapping, torture and homicide, but when the government attempted to also try junior officers, these officers responded with uprisings in several different parts of the country. The timid administration succumbed to military demands and

1926	1946	1952
Novelist and poet Ricardo Güiraldes publishes *Don Segundo Sombra,* a classic work of gaucho literature evoking the spirit of the gaucho and its impact on Argentine society.	With Eva at his side, Juan Perón is elected president and makes sweeping changes to the Argentine political structure. Evita soon embarks on her social-assistance programs to help lower-class women and children.	Eva Perón dies of cancer on July 26 at age 33, one year into her husband's second term as president. Her death would severely weaken the political might of her husband.

LAS MADRES DE LA PLAZA DE MAYO

In 1977, after a year of brutal human-rights violations under the leadership of General Jorge Rafael Videla, 14 mothers marched into the Plaza de Mayo in Buenos Aires. They did this despite the military government's ban on public gatherings and despite its reputation for torturing and killing anyone it considered dissident. The mothers, wearing their now-iconic white head scarves, demanded information about their missing children, who had 'disappeared' as part of the government's efforts to quash political opposition.

The group, which took on the name Las Madres de la Plaza de Mayo (The Mothers of Plaza de Mayo), developed into a powerful social movement and was the only political organization that overtly challenged the military government. Las Madres were particularly effective as they carried out their struggle under the banner of motherhood, which made them relatively unassailable in Argentine culture. Their movement showed the power of women – at least in a traditional role – in Argentine culture, and they are generally credited with helping to kick start the reestablishment of the country's civil society.

After Argentina's return to civilian rule in 1983, thousands of Argentines were still unaccounted for, and Las Madres continued their marches and their demands for information and retribution. In 1986 Las Madres split into two factions. One group, known as the Founding Line, dedicated itself to recovering the remains of the disappeared and to bringing military perpetrators to justice. The other, known as the **Asociación Madres de Plaza de Mayo** (www.madres.org) held its last yearly protest in January 2006, saying it no longer had an enemy in the presidential seat. Both groups, however, still hold silent vigils every Thursday afternoon in remembrance of the disappeared – and to protest other social causes.

For more information see also www.abuelas.org.ar.

produced the Ley de la Obediencia Debida (Law of Due Obedience), allowing lower-ranking officers to use the defense that they were following orders, as well as the Ley de Punto Final, declaring dates beyond which no criminal or civil prosecutions could take place. At the time, these measures eliminated prosecutions of notorious individuals such as Navy Captain Alfredo Astiz, who was implicated in the disappearance of a Swedish-Argentine teenager and the highly publicized deaths of two French nuns. (In 2003, however, the Ley de la Obediencia Debida and Ley de Punto Final were repealed – and in 2005 declared unconstitutional. Thus, Dirty War crime cases have been reopened – including that of Astiz.)

During the 1995 presidential campaign, Dirty War issues resurfaced spectacularly when journalist Horacio Verbitsky wrote *The Flight: Confessions of an Argentine Dirty Warrior* (1996), a book based on interviews with former Navy Captain Adolfo Scilingo, in which Scilingo acknowledges throwing political prisoners, alive but drugged, into the Atlantic. In 2005 Scilingo was found guilty of numerous counts of human-rights abuses, becoming the first Dirty War official to be tried abroad (in Spain).

Nunca Más (Never Again; 1984), the official report of the National Commission on the Disappeared, systematically details military abuses from 1976 to 1983, during Argentina's Dirty War.

1955	**1976–83**	**1982**
After the economy slides into recession President Perón loses further political clout and is finally thrown from the presidency and exiled to Spain after another military coup.	Under the leadership of General Jorge Videla, a military junta takes control of Argentina, launching the country into the Dirty War. In eight years an estimated 30,000 people 'disappear.'	With the economy on the brink of collapse once again, General Leopoldo Galtieri, now in control, invades the Falkland Islands/Islas Malvinas, unleashing a wave of nationalism and distracting the country from its current state.

In recent years, several other officers have been convicted for Dirty War crimes. In December 2007 Héctor Febres, who worked at Buenos Aires' Naval Mechanics School (the country's most notorious detention center; now a memorial space) was found dead from cyanide poisoning in his prison cell just days before he was to be sentenced for human-rights violations. In 2008 Luciano Benjamin Menendez, a former general, was given a life sentence for the murders of four activists; seven other officers were also convicted. And in August 2009 Santiago Omar Riveros (another general) was found guilty for his involvement in the torture and murder of a 15-year-old youth. His former intelligence chief, Fernando Verplaetsen, was also sentenced, as were four other officers.

Yet despite these arrests, most of the criminals of El Proceso still walk the streets, either in Argentina or abroad. As frightening and as recent as this chapter in Argentine history is, most Argentines feel an atrocity such as the Dirty War could never happen again.

THE MENEM YEARS

Set in the 1970s during Argentina's Dirty War, Lawrence Thornton's *Imagining Argentina* (1991) is an enthralling novel about a Buenos Aires playwright who acquires the ability to see *desaparecidos,* people who 'disappeared' at the hands of the military.

Carlos Menem, whose Syrian ethnicity earned him the nickname 'El Turco' (The Turk), was elected president in 1989. Menem quickly embarked on a period of radical free-market reform. In pegging the peso to the US dollar, he effectively created a period of false economic stability, one that would create a great deal of upward mobility among Argentina's middle class. Despite the sense of stability, his policies are widely blamed for Argentina's economic collapse in 2002, when the overvalued peso was considerably devalued.

According to the BBC, Menem's presidency was characterized by rampant government corruption and the privatization of state-owned companies. He sold off YPF (the national oil company), the national telephone company, the postal service and Aerolíneas Argentinas, all to foreign companies, and much of the profit was never accounted for. He also changed the constitution to allow himself to run for a second term (which he won in 1995), and unsuccessfully tried again so he could run for a third term in 1999. Amid accusations of corruption, Menem finally stepped down.

Adding to his scandals, Menem married Chilean Cecilia Bolocco, a former Miss Universe 35 years his junior. In 2001 he was charged with illegally dealing arms to Croatia and Ecuador and placed under house arrest. After five months of judicial investigation, the charges were dropped; the following day he announced he would run again for president. In 2003 he did, only to withdraw after the first round. A failed 2007 bid for governor of his home province of La Rioja has pretty much written him off politics.

'LA CRISIS'

At the end of Menem's second term in 1999, the country faced economic crisis. Fernando de la Rua succeeded Menem in the 1999 elections, inheriting an unstable economy and US$114 billion in foreign debt. With the Argentine

1983	1989–99	1999–2000
After the failure of the Falklands War and with an economy on the skids, Raúl Alfonsín is elected the first civilian leader of the country since 1976.	Carlos Menem serves as president. During his presidency, he pegs the Argentine peso to the US dollar, sells off state-owned companies and paves the way for the 2002 economic crisis.	Fernando de la Rua succeeds Menem as president, inheriting a failing economy. Agricultural exports slump and strikes begin occurring throughout the country. The IMF grants Argentina US$40 million in aid.

peso pegged to the US dollar, Argentina was unable to compete on the international market and exports slumped. A further decline in international prices of agricultural products pummeled the Argentine economy, which depended heavily on farm-product exports.

By 2001 the Argentine economy teetered on the brink of collapse, and the administration, with Minister of Economy Domingo Cavallo at the wheel, took measures to end deficit spending and slash state spending, including employee salaries and pensions. After attempted debt swaps and talk of devaluing the peso, middle-class Argentines began emptying their bank accounts. Cavallo responded to the run on the banks by placing a cap of US$250 per week on withdrawals, a measure that would become known as 'el corralito' (meaning small enclosure or playpen). It was the beginning of the end.

By mid-December unemployment hit 18.3% and unions began a nationwide strike. Things came to a head on December 20 when middle-class Argentines took to the streets banging pots and pans, in what became known as the *cacerolazo* (from the word *cacerola,* meaning pan), in protest of De la Rua's handling of the economic situation. Rioting spread throughout the country, leaving more than 25 dead, and President de la Rua resigned. Three interim presidents had resigned by the time Eduardo Duhalde took office in January 2002, becoming the fifth president in two weeks. Duhalde devalued the peso in January 2002 and announced that Argentina would default on US$140 billion in foreign debt, the biggest default in world history. For Argentina it was 'la crisis,' an economic collapse that sent poverty skyrocketing and foreign investors running.

> Placing the blame squarely on neoliberalism and the IMF, Marcela López-Levy's *We are Millions* (2003) is one of the only books published that tackles Argentina's economic crisis of 2000–02.

THE KIRCHNER YEARS

Duhalde's Minister of Economy, Roberto Lavagna, negotiated a take-it-or-leave-it deal with the IMF in which Argentina would pay only the interest on its debts. Simultaneously, devaluation of the peso meant that Argentina's products were suddenly affordable on the world market, and by 2003 exports were booming. The surge was great for the country's GNP (its growth rate of nearly 9% was Latin America's largest), but prices at home skyrocketed, plunging more of Argentina's already shaken middle class into poverty – and those already in poverty into dire economic straits.

A presidential election was finally held in April 2003, and Santa Cruz Governor Nestor Kirchner emerged victoriously (by default) after his opponent, former president Carlos Menem, bowed out of the election. Although Menem emerged from the first round of voting with more percentage points than Kirchner, it quickly became clear that Menem would lose horrendously.

By the end of his term in 2007, Kirchner had become one of Argentina's most popular presidents. Risking backlash from the military, Kirchner immediately reversed amnesty laws that protected members of the 1976–83 junta against being charged for atrocities committed during the Dirty War,

2001	2002	2003
The Argentine economy goes into tailspin; President de la Rua places caps on bank withdrawals – known as 'el corralito' – and later resigns amid violent protests throughout the country.	Interim president Eduardo Duhalde devalues the peso, and Argentina defaults on its US$140 billion international debt (including US$800 million owed to the World Bank), the largest default in world history.	Nestor Kirchner is elected president of Argentina after Carlos Menem bows out of the presidential race, despite winning more votes in the first round of elections.

and by 2008 several major players had been arrested, charged and tried in both Argentina and Spain. He took a heavy stance against government corruption, impeaching two supreme-court justices and forcing the resignation of another. He steered the economy away from strict alignment with the US and realigned it with that of Argentina's South American neighbors. And in 2005 he paid off Argentina's entire debt to the IMF in a single payment. By the end of Kirchner's presidency in 2007, unemployment had fallen to just under 9% – from a high of nearly 25% in 2002.

Despite Kirchner's successes and the recovery of the economy – not to mention the great rise in optimism nationwide – poverty and inflation remain serious issues. Many from Argentina's middle classes have regained their footholds, but many others, particularly those who were already living at or below the poverty line, have found their economic shackles impossible to break.

Gargantuan in size and vast in scope, *The Argentina Reader* (2002), edited by Gabriella Nouzeilles and Graciela Montaldo, is a thorough compilation of some of the most important essays, excerpts and stories from Argentine history and culture.

When the presidential seat went up for grabs in 2007, Argentines expressed their satisfaction with Kirchner's policies by electing his wife, well-known Senator Cristina Fernández de Kirchner, as president. Cristina won the presidency with a whopping 22% margin over her nearest challenger and became Argentina's first elected female president.

ARGENTINA TODAY

When Cristina became 'la Presidenta', she faced two major challenges: tackling poverty and curbing inflation (unofficially estimated at 15% or more). Unlike her husband Nestor's successful tenure, however, hers has been rocky: racked with scandals, tax bungles and plummeting approval ratings.

During her first days as president, a Venezuelan-American entering Argentina from Venezuela was found with almost US$800,000 cash in his suitcase, and lied about its origins. *Time* magazine wrote that US attorneys claimed this was Hugo Chavez' way of aiding Kirchner's election campaign, an allegation the Venezuelan president denied.

In March 2008 Kirchner significantly raised the export tax on soybeans, infuriating farmers who soon went on strike and blockaded highways; the tax was later rescinded. Then in June 2009, her power base was shattered when her ruling party lost its majority in both houses of Congress in the mid-term elections. Soon after, she enacted an unpopular law set to break apart Clarín, a media conglomerate that often shone unfavorably on her presidency (see p45).

The latest bad news for Cristina? In early 2010 she controversial dismissed Martin Redrado, the Central Bank's governor, for refusing to hand over US$6.5 billion in reserves to ostensibly help pay Argentina's international debt.

What's next for the Kirchners and Argentina? While the government remains optimistic on economic growth, it's more likely the country's slowdown will continue. Argentina will also need to regain the confidence of international markets and pay back debts to private investors. Best of luck to whoever wins the next presidential race.

2005	2007	2009
The Argentine Supreme Court declares an amnesty law unconstitutional which, until now, protected former military officers accused of human-rights abuses during the 1973–86 military dictatorship.	Former First Lady Cristina Fernández de Kirchner is elected president. Isabel Perón, former president and wife of Juan Perón, is arrested in Spain in connection with military crimes committed during the Dirty War.	Raul Alfonsín dies; Cristina Kirchner's popularity ratings dive-bomb, along with the country's economy; small-use marijuana is decriminalized; Argentina claims first legal same-sex marriage in Latin America.

The Culture

Whether it's for the country's world-famous tango or its renowned rock and roll, the paintings of Antonio Berni, or the prose of Jorge Luis Borges, Argentina is no less than a cultural goldmine.

THE NATIONAL PSYCHE

Throughout Latin America, Argentines endure a reputation for being a bit cocky. 'How does an Argentine commit suicide?' goes the old joke. 'By jumping off his ego.'

Traveling to Argentina, you'll find that the Argentine stereotype has a nugget of truth to it. But anyone who spends some time here finds the stereotype immediately challenged by warmth, friendliness and the gregarious social nature that more accurately defines the Argentine psyche. There's simply no denying the fact that Argentines are some of the most welcoming, sociable, endearing folks on the planet.

Opinionated, brash and passionate, Argentines are quick to engage in conversation and will talk after dinner or over coffee until the wee hours of the morning. Argentina's most visible customs are entirely social in nature. Look no further than the ritual of drinking *mate* (p65) and the famous *asado* (barbecue; p62).

While Argentines are friendly and passionate they also have a subtle broodiness to their nature, especially *porteños* (residents of Buenos Aires). This stems from a pessimism Argentines have acquired watching their country, one of the world's economic powerhouses during the late 19th and early 20th centuries, descend into a morass of immense international debt. They've endured military coups, severe government repression, and year after year they've seen their beloved Argentina, rich in resources, people and beauty, plundered by corrupt politicians.

But the broodiness is just a part of the picture. Add everything together and you get a people who are fun, fiery, opinionated and proud. And you'll come to love them for it.

The first usable ballpoint pens were designed and created in Argentina by the Hungarian László Bíró. Hence the name biro (in Britain) and *birome* (in Argentina) for ballpoint pen.

LIFESTYLE

Although Buenos Aires holds more than one-third of the country's population, it's surprisingly unlike the rest of Argentina or, for that matter, much of Latin America. The city's core neighborhoods, especially the Microcentro, are more akin to New York than Caracas. As throughout the country, one's lifestyle in the capital depends mostly on money. A modern flat rented by a young advertising creative in Buenos Aires' Las Cañitas neighborhood differs greatly from a family home in one of the city's impoverished *villas* (poor neighborhoods), where electricity and clean water are luxuries and street crime is a daily occurrence.

Geography and ethnicity also play important roles. Both of these Buenos Aires homes have little in common with that of an indigenous family living in an adobe house in a desolate valley of the Andean northwest, where life is eked out through subsistence agriculture and earth goddess Pachamama outshines Evita as a cultural icon. In regions such as the pampas, Mendoza province and Patagonia, a provincial friendliness surrounds a robust, outdoor lifestyle.

By Latin American standards, Argentina has a large middle class, though it shrank significantly after the economic crisis that began in 1999. Quiet, tree-lined, middle-class neighborhoods are still common throughout the country,

Like in Australia or Turkey, voting is obligatory in Argentina – though an exception is made if you're over 70.

SOCIAL DOS & DON'TS

When it comes to social etiquette in Argentina, there aren't many wildly obscure dos or don'ts, but knowing a few social intricacies will keep you on the right track.

Dos

- Greet people you encounter with *buenos días* (good morning), *buenas tardes* (good afternoon) or *buenas noches* (good evening).
- Use *usted* (the formal term for 'you') when addressing elders and in formal situations.
- Dress for the occasion.
- Accept and give *besos* (kisses) on the cheek.
- Tip the luggage handlers and bathroom caretakers.
- In small villages, greet people on the street and when walking into a shop.
- Be seen eating ice cream at all times, especially in northern Argentina.

Don'ts

- Don't refer to the Islas Malvinas as the Falkland Islands (if you're British, don't refer to them at all).
- Don't cheer for the wrong *fútbol* (soccer) team in the wrong place.
- Don't hand someone the salt when they ask you to pass it to them at the table; place the shaker on the table in front of them. (It's a superstition.)
- Don't suggest Italian or US pizza might taste better than Argentine pizza.

---

but large sectors of the population have yet to experience the economy's revival. On the other side of the spectrum, wealthy city dwellers are moving into *'countries'* (gated communities) in surprising numbers. The question that remains is how this shift away from the city – from its cafes and other pillars of Argentine social life – will affect the cultural landscape.

One thing that all Argentines have in common is their devotion to family. The Buenos Aires advertising exec joins her family for weekend dinners, and the cafe owner in San Juan meets cousins and friends out at the family *estancia* (ranch) for a Sunday *asado*. Children commonly live with their parents until they're married, especially within the country's poorer households.

> Argentines almost always exchange a kiss on the cheek in greeting – even among men. In formal and business situations, though, it is better to go with a handshake.

Argentine culture has long been known for its machismo and an accompanying dose of misogyny, but things are changing. Women are breaking out of their traditional roles – especially among the country's youth – and men are becoming more accepting of that fact. Argentina's workforce is more than 40% female, and women currently occupy a third of Argentina's congressional seats. In 2007 Argentina elected its first female president, Cristina Fernández de Kirchner.

ECONOMY

Since colonial times the Argentine economy has relied on agricultural exports (hides, wool, beef and grains) gleaned from the fertile pampas. Until the late 19th century the economy resembled that of most Latin American countries, with much of the land and profits in the hands of relatively few. The economy boomed after Argentina began reaping the benefits of exportation in the 1870s, but with the onset of WWI, foreign investment in Argentina ceased and exports plummeted. After the Great Depression of 1929 delivered the final punch, Argentina's economy crumbled.

Juan Perón (p34) helped revive the Argentine economy by encouraging the development of a state-supported industrial base. Before long, however, many state enterprises became havens for corruption, including the proliferation of 'ñoquis,' or ghost employees, which contributed to inflation rates often exceeding 50% per month.

Inflationary chaos was finally broken by Carlos Menem (1989–99; see p38), who reduced public-sector employment, sold off state enterprises, restricted labor-union activities and, most importantly, pegged the peso to the US dollar. His approach eliminated short-term budget deficits, but finally collapsed by the end of his second term. After the peso was devalued in 2002, the country was once again able to compete in the world market, and later even went through an economic boom for several years.

Like most other countries, Argentina was hit by the recent global economic crisis. Commodity prices dropped, hurting exports, and the worst drought in 50 years deeply affected beef production. Tax revenues have fallen, while inflation and unemployment continue to be problematic. The tourism industry took a big hit, and many local businesses – from entertainment venues to restaurants – have seen fewer consumers due to the swine flu epidemic. At least Argentines are quite used to their economy being a bumpy roller-coaster ride.

POPULATION

The majority of Argentines live in cities. Of the country's population of more than 40 million people, 13 million live in greater Buenos Aires alone. The country's second-biggest city is Córdoba (1,531,500), followed by Rosario (1,161,000), Mendoza (929,000, with the inclusion of greater Mendoza), Tucumán and La Plata. What's left is a country with *lots* of open space (which you'll have to cross any time you want to go somewhere).

Compared to countries such as Bolivia, Peru and Ecuador, Argentina has a small indigenous population. Historically, native populations were relatively thin along the coast and in the pampas, and those who did not die from hard labor and disease were eradicated during the Conquista del Desierto (Conquest of the Desert; see p33). Unlike other Latin American countries, Argentina was built more on the backs of imported European labor – primarily Italian and Spanish – than indigenous or African slavery. The most visible indigenous cultures in Argentina today are found in the Lake District, the Andean northwest, and in and around the Chaco.

Three Argentines have won the Nobel Prize for Science, while two have won the Nobel Prize for Peace: Carlos Saavedra Lamas (1936) and Adolfo Perez Esquivel (1980).

SPORTS

Fútbol (soccer) is Argentina's passion and is by far the most popular sport in the country. The national team has been to the World Cup final four times and has triumphed twice, in 1978 and 1986. The Argentine team also won Olympic gold twice, at the 2004 and 2008 games. Argentines devote a great deal of time following the Boca Juniors, River Plate and other club teams, and the fanatical behavior of the country's *hinchas* or *barra brava* (hooligans) rivals that of their European counterparts. For a foreigner's view of Argentine *fútbol* (via the team Argentinos Juniors), check out www.handofdan.com.

Rugby's popularity has increased in Argentina ever since Los Pumas, their national team, beat France in the first game of the 2007 Rugby World Cup and *again* in the semi finals. As an indicator of just how popular the sport has become, the Superclásico (the famed soccer match between Boca and River Plate) was rescheduled so it wouldn't conflict with Los Pumas' quarter final match.

Horse racing, polo and boxing are also popular, followed by tennis, golf, basketball and car racing. The Dakar Rally took place mostly in Argentina in both 2009 and 2010. The country also has some of the best polo horses and players in the world.

Jimmy Burns' *The Hand of God* (1997) is the definitive English-language book about soccer legend Diego Maradona and makes for a great read even if you're not a soccer fanatic.

FÚTBOL & DIEGO MARADONA *Andy Symington*

You don't have to travel long in Argentina to realize that *fútbol* (soccer) is the number one thing here; there are impromptu games everywhere, and paraphernalia of Boca Juniors, River Plate or one of the other big sides (mostly based in Buenos Aires) is ubiquitous. The country is an assembly line of thoroughbred talent, the best of which quickly moves to Europe, where the salaries are many times higher; this weakens the local leagues but doesn't dim the passion of the supporters.

Argentine football traditionally combines a South American flair in attack with a rugged Italianate defense, a very effective synthesis that has won the national team two World Cups. Defensive rocks such as Daniel Passarella, Oscar Ruggeri and Roberto Ayala have been complemented by midfielders and attackers such as twinkletoed Osvaldo Ardiles, lethal Gabriel Batistuta or, more recently, unpredictable genius Juan Román Riquelme, muscular Carlos Tévez and, perhaps destined to be the best of all, mercurial Lionel Messi.

Best of all bar one, that is. Debate rages over who is the sport's greatest-ever player. Many say Brazil's Pelé takes the garland, but just as many would award it to Diego Armando Maradona, whose life has been equal parts controversy and brilliance. Born in 1960 in abject poverty in a Buenos Aires shantytown, Maradona played his first professional game for Argentinos Juniors before his 16th birthday. Transferring to his beloved Boca Juniors, he continued to prosper and, after a good showing at the 1982 World Cup, moved first to Barcelona in Spain, and then to Naples in Italy. This was the start of a phenomenal few years. His genius inspired unfashionable Napoli to two league titles, and in 1986 he single-handedly won a very average Argentina side the World Cup. In the quarterfinal against England, he scored the first with his hand – later saying the goal was scored partly by the hand of God – and the second with his feet, after a mesmerizing run through the flummoxed English defense that led to it being named the goal of the century by FIFA.

But the big time also ruined Diego. Earning huge sums of money, Maradona became addicted to cocaine and the high life and, as his body began to feel the strain over the years, a succession of drug bans, lawsuits and weight issues meant that by his eventual retirement in 1997 he had been a shadow of his former self for some years.

After retiring from football, he was rarely out of the news: overdoses, heart attacks, detox, his own TV program, offbeat friendships and enmities – all par for the course in the Maradona circus. And then he was back in football, as manager of the national side. It was an unlikely appointment and one that was heavily criticized as Argentina flirted with failure to qualify for the 2010 World Cup. Once they achieved qualification, Maradona suggested in a press conference that his critics could pleasure him orally. Cue controversy and a two-month ban from FIFA. Yet, however many colorful chapters he writes, those numerous moments of magic in the number 10 shirt have sealed immortality.

Among the best-known national sports figures are soccer legends Diego Maradona, Gabriel Batistuta and Lionel Messi (voted FIFA World Player of the Year in 2009); the late boxers Oscar Bonavena and Carlos Monzón; ex–Formula One racers Juan Manuel Fangio (see p172) and Carlos Reutemann; and basketball phenomenon Emanuel Ginóbili, who holds a championship ring with the NBA's San Antonio Spurs.

> Although Gabriel Batistuta will forever live in Diego Maradona's shadow, he scored a record 56 goals for the Argentine national soccer team, while Maradona scored 34.

Tennis stars include Guillermo Vilas, Gabriela Sabatini and David Nalbandian. In 2009 Juan Martín del Potro defeated Roger Federer to win the US Open tennis championship. In golfing news, Argentine golfer Ángel Cabrera won the US Open in 2007, and in 2009 followed up by taking top spot at the Masters Tournament.

Pato is Argentina's traditional sport, played on horseback and mixing elements from both polo and basketball. It was originally played with a duck (a 'pato') but now, thankfully, uses a ball encased in leather handles. Despite its long history, relatively few people follow it.

MULTICULTURALISM

More than 95% of the Argentine population claims to be of European descent (mainly Spanish and Italian). However, on closer inspection, Argentina is a country that has been influenced by numerous cultures – cultures whose distinctive traits, although Argentinized, are still apparent today.

In the mid-19th century, Italians, Basques, English, Ukrainians and other European immigrants began flooding into Argentina. As a result, you'll still find Welsh-Argentines in Chubut province, German surnames and physical traits in Misiones province, Bulgarians and Yugoslavs in Roque Sáenz Peña, and Ukrainians in La Pampa province. Argentina also has a substantial Jewish population of about 300,000 (see p211). Middle Eastern immigrants, though fewer in number, have attained great political influence – the most high-profile being former president Carlos Menem, who was of Syrian ancestry.

Immigrants from Asia are a visible presence in Buenos Aires and are becoming increasingly so in the interior. The first Japanese Argentines arrived during the late-19th-century immigration boom, and became the most integrated Asian population in Argentina. There are around 30,000 people of Japanese descent in the country. Koreans, who number around 20,000, are a more recent immigrant group. The Chinese-Argentine population is the largest; numbering around 65,000, and there's a miniature Chinatown in Buenos Aires' Belgrano neighborhood.

According to Argentina's census bureau, Argentina is home to some 600,000 self-recognized indigenous people. Of the more than 30 recognized *pueblos indígenas* (indigenous groups), the largest is the northern Patagonia's Mapuche, with some 200,000 members. In northwest Argentina there are more than 50,000 Kolla and nearly as many Toba. The country's other significant groups include the Wichí in Chaco, the Mocoví in Santa Fe, the Guaraní in northeastern Argentina, the Huarpe of central Argentina and the Tehuelche of northern Patagonia.

For more on the indigenous cultures of the Gran Chaco, see p241. For more on the Mapuche of northern Patagonia, see p397.

> Buenos Aires' Jewish community of a third of a million people is the largest of its kind in Latin America.

> Argentines tend not to shy away from assigning stereotypes. Fair-complexioned people are called *Rusos* (Russians), Asians are called *Chinos* (Chinese) and if anyone is overweight, they may be labeled a *gordo* (fatty).

MEDIA

Since the end of the military dictatorship in 1983, Argentina has enjoyed a free press. Argentina today boasts over 100 daily newspapers, hundreds of radio stations and more than 40 TV stations. Nearly all are privately owned, and many engage in a fair amount of political analysis and criticism. A few large conglomerates dominate print and TV, but smaller print publications bring a variety of opinions to the table. That said, there's a fair amount of self-censorship among the largest TV stations and newspapers, which is where most folks get their news.

KIRCHNER VS CLARÍN

In the June 2009 midterm elections, Cristina Kirchner lost her party's backing – most importantly in Buenos Aires province, where much of her power base had been. Blaming the Clarín Group (who runs Argentina's most widely read newspaper) for negative press, before she lost her majority in Congress, Kirchner rushed through the 'Ley de Medios K' – an anti-monopoly media law critics claimed was specifically targeted at Clarín. The conglomerate, after all, owns several newspapers, magazines and TV, cable and radio stations. While many support de-monopolizing large news corporations, others fear that the subsequent regulatory agency created would give government too much media control – and denounce this new law as a bully tactic created when things don't go the way of *la presidenta*.

RELIGION

Roman Catholicism is the official state religion, though only a relatively small percentage of Argentines attend mass regularly. Even so, the church still holds much sway over the culture; up until recently, the president of Argentina had to be Catholic. As in the rest of Latin America, the religion sometimes morphs into a fascinating blend of indigenous tradition or local belief and official church doctrine. Shrines adorned with water bottles and car parts and devoted to the female saint Difunta Correa (see p370) add color to roads throughout the country. You are also likely to see shrines decorated with red flags honoring the saintlike 'Gauchito' Antonio Gil (p200), a sort of gaucho Robin Hood worshipped by many.

Argentina has one of the world's largest Jewish populations, and Buenos Aires has a large and active Jewish community. Other religious communities include Evangelical Protestants, Jehovah's Witnesses, Hare Krishnas and Mormons.

Visitors to Recoleta and Chacarita cemeteries in Buenos Aires will see pilgrims going to the resting places of Juan and Eva Perón, psychic Madre María and tango singer Carlos Gardel. Followers come to communicate, leave offerings and ask for favors by praying at the tombs.

WOMEN IN ARGENTINA

As throughout Latin America, Catholicism has, until recently, played a major role in defining the place of women in society. Over the past few decades, Argentine women have made huge strides in their struggle for social and economic independence and equality. Although Argentina's famous machismo is still alive and well, men have been forced to take women seriously in the workplace, and women are increasingly excelling in jobs across the entire economic spectrum. That said, the glass ceiling still exists in some professions, and the core of many businesses remains a boys' club.

In the political realm, women have made a huge impact. One only need consider Eva Perón (Evita), the country's most enduring political icon. Women such as those involved with Las Madres de la Plaza de Mayo (p37) exerted a unique power through their roles as mothers. In 2007 Cristina Fernández de Kirchner became the country's first elected female president.

For information on what to expect as a woman traveling to Argentina, see p612.

ARTS

Artistically, Argentina is one of Latin America's most compelling countries, with a rich literary heritage and vibrant, evolving scenes in cinema, theater and music. And, of course, few places in the world attract so many people who simply want to learn to dance like the locals.

Literature

Journalist, poet and politician José Hernández (1831–86) gave rise to the 'gauchesco' literary tradition with his epic poem *Martín Fierro*, which acknowledged the role of the gauchos in Argentina's development. Argentine writing only reached an international audience during the 1960s and 1970s, when the stories of Jorge Luis Borges, Julio Cortázar, Ernesto Sábato, Adolfo Bioy Casares and Silvina Ocampo, among many others, were widely translated for the first time.

As a half-Jewish, half-English Argentine who was educated in Europe, Jorge Luis Borges (1899–1986) was influenced by everything from Jewish cabalists to HG Wells, Cervantes and Kafka. His tight, precise, paradoxical *ficciones* (fictions) are part essay and part story, blurring the line between

Under the old Argentine constitution, Carlos Menem had to convert from Islam to Catholicism to become president.

Argentines are pretty well-read – their literacy rate is around 97.2%.

myth and truth, underscoring the idea that reality is a matter of perception and that an infinite number of realities can exist simultaneously. His early stories such as 'Death and the Compass' and 'Streetcorner Man' offer a metaphysical twist on Argentine themes, and his later works, including 'The Lottery in Babylon,' 'The Circular Ruins' and 'Garden of the Forking Paths,' are works of fantasy.

Despite being discovered and influenced by Borges in the 1940s, the writing of Julio Cortázar (1914–84) was considerably different. His short stories and novels are more anthropological and concern people living seemingly normal lives in a world where the surreal becomes commonplace. Cortázar's most famous book is *Hopscotch,* which requires the reader to first read the book straight through, then read it a second time, 'hopscotching' through the chapters in a prescribed but nonlinear pattern.

The contemporary, postboom generation of Argentine writers is more reality-based, often reflecting the influence of popular culture and directly confronting the political realities of the authoritarian Argentina of the 1970s. One of the most famous postboom Argentine writers is Manuel Puig (author of *Kiss of the Spider Woman*). In the Argentine tradition, Puig did much of his writing in exile, fleeing Argentina during the Perón years and ultimately settling in Mexico.

Osvaldo Soriano (1943–97), perhaps Argentina's most popular contemporary novelist, wrote *A Funny Dirty Little War* (1986) and *Winter Quarters* (1989). Juan José Saer (1937–2005) penned short stories and complex crime novels, while Rodrigo Fresán (1963–), the youngest of the postboom generation, wrote the international bestseller *The History of Argentina.*

Other notable contemporary writers include Federico Andahazi, Ricardo Piglia and Tomás Eloy Martínez.

Jorge Luis Borges' short-story collections in English include *Labyrinths, The Aleph, A Universal History of Iniquity* and – if you want it all in one big, not-so-backpackable tome – *Collected Fictions.*

Victoria Ocampo (1890–1979) was a famous writer, publisher and intellectual who founded *Sur,* a renowned cultural magazine of the 1930s. For more on her, see the boxed text, p168. You can also visit her old mansion near Buenos Aires (p137).

Cinema

Since the end of the military dictatorship, film has emerged as one of Argentina's most vibrant and creative art forms. Argentine cinema has achieved international stature, and many Argentine films are available abroad.

One of the best places to start is Luis Puenzo's *The Official Story* (1985), which deals with the controversial theme of the Dirty War and won an Oscar for best foreign-language film. Perhaps the best internationally known film to deal with Argentina is Héctor Babenco's Oscar-winning *Kiss of the Spider Woman* (1985), based on Manuel Puig's novel.

Today's cutting-edge Argentine cinema includes director Lucrecia Martel's *La ciénaga* (The Swamp; 2001), which tells the story of the crises within two families in Salta. In 2004 she released the acclaimed *La niña santa* (The Holy Girl). Pablo Trapero's gritty yet applauded *El bonaerense* (2002) tells of a young rural locksmith forced to leave his family to join the notoriously corrupt Buenos Aires provincial police force. Also check out Juan José Campanella's *El hijo de la novia* (The Son of the Bride), which was nominated for an Oscar for best foreign-language film in 2002.

Mariano Llinás is another popular director. His documentary film *Balnearios* (2002) shows how the influx of outsiders shapes and changes people's existence in little tourist towns. Two films by director Carlos Sorín capture the quiet spirit and vast emptiness of Patagonia: *Historias mínimas* (Intimate Stories; 2002) and *El perro* (Bonbón: El Perro; 2004).

Tristán Bauer's powerful, award-winning *Illuminados por el fuego* (Blessed by Fire; 2005) tells the story of the 1982 Falklands War through the eyes of a young soldier. And in 2005 Juan Diego Solanas won top prize at the Stockholm Film Festival for his well-executed *Nordeste* (Northeast), which tackles difficult social issues such as child trafficking.

Want to learn more about the history and beginnings of Argentine cinema? Check out www.surdelsur.com/cine/cinein/indexingles.html.

Other recent Argentine films include Damián Szifron's *Tiempo de valientes* (2005), Daniel Burman's *Derecho de familia* (2006), Adrián Caetano's *Crónica de una fuga* (2006) and Lucía Puenzo's *XXY* (2007). Campanella's *El secreto de sus ojos* (2009) was Argentina's highest-grossing movie the year it was released. For more top films, see p20.

Argentina's biggest film event is the Buenos Aires International Festival of Independent Film (Bafici), held in April. Check out www.bafici.gov.ar for more information.

Music & Dance

Music and dance are unavoidable in Argentina, and none is more famous than the tango. But tango is a Buenos Aires thing. The rest of the country (and much of Buenos Aires, for that matter) grooves to different sounds, be it *chamamé* in Corrientes, *cuarteto* in Córdoba or *cumbia villera* in the poor neighborhoods of Buenos Aires.

TANGO

There's no better place to dive into tango than through the music of the genre's most legendary performer, singer Carlos Gardel (1887–1935). Violinist Juan D'Arienzo's *orquesta* (orchestra) reigned over tango throughout the 1930s and into the 1940s. Osvaldo Pugliese and Héctor Varela are important bandleaders from the 1940s, but the real giant of the era was *bandoneón* (small type of accordion) player Aníbal Troilo.

Modern tango is largely dominated by the work of *bandoneón* maestro Astor Piazzolla who moved the genre from the dance halls into the concert halls – *tango nuevo*, as it was called, was now for the ear. Piazzolla paved the way for the tango fusion which emerged in the 1970s and continues to this day with *tango electrónica* groups such as Gotan Project and Bajofondo Tango Club.

While in Buenos Aires, keep an eye out for Orquesta Típica Fernández Fierro (www.fernandezfierro.com), who put a new twist on traditional tango songs; but also perform their own new creations. Another young orchestra to watch out for is Orquesta Típica Imperial (www.orquestaimperial.com), who regularly play at *milongas* (tango dance halls) around Buenos Aires.

Influential contemporary tango singers include Susana Rinaldi, Daniel Melingo and Adriana Varela.

FOLK MUSIC

Traditional music is generally known as *folklore* or *folklórico*. It's sort of an umbrella genre that captures numerous styles and there are many contemporary branches (*chamamé, chacarera, carnavalito* and *copla*) that are popular throughout the countryside, claiming fans of all ages. Los Chalchaleros are a northern *folklórico* institution who have turned out more than 40 albums over a 50-plus year career. One of Argentina's greatest contemporary *folklórico* musicians is accordionist Chango Spasiuk, a virtuoso of Corrientes' *chamamé* music. Peteco Carabajal (master of the *chacarera*), León Gieco (Argentina's Bob Dylan) and *charango* player Jaime Torres are other big names in *folklórico*. Horacio Guarany is a contemporary *folklórico* singer whose 2004 album *Cantor de Cantores* was nominated for a Latin Grammy in the Best Folk Album category.

Atahualpa Yupanqui (1908–92), however, is by far Argentina's most important *folklórico* musician of the 20th century. Yupanqui's music emerged alongside the *nueva canción* (literally 'new song') movement that swept Latin America during the 1960s. *Nueva canción* was deeply rooted in folk music and its lyrics often dealt with social and political themes of the era. The genre's grande dame was Argentina's Mercedes Sosa (1935–2009), one of the best-known Argentine folk singers outside South America and winner of several Latin Grammy awards.

ROCK & POP

Argentina is famous throughout the Spanish-speaking world for its *rock en español* (Spanish-language rock). Musicians such as Charly García (formerly a member of the pioneering groups Sui Generis and Serú Girán), Fito Páez and Luis Alberto Spinetta are national icons. Soda Stereo, Sumo, Los Fabulosos Cadillacs and Los Pericos rocked Argentina throughout the 1980s and maintain wild popularity. Bersuit Vergarabat, who put out its first album in 1992, endures as one of Argentina's best rock bands with a musical complexity that is arguably without peer. R&B-influenced Ratones Paranóicos opened for the Rolling Stones in 1995, while La Portuaria – who fuse Latin beats with jazz and R&B – collaborated with David Byrne in 2006.

Other popular national groups include the offbeat Babasónicos; punk rockers Ataque 77; rockers Los Piojos, Los Redonditos de Ricota, Dividos, Catupecu Machu and Gazpacho; and metal-meets-hip-hop Illya Kuryaki and the Valderramas. Also, don't miss contemporary and eclectic Kevin Johansen, an American-Argentine who sings in both English and Spanish.

Born in Córdoba in the early 1940s, *cuarteto* is Argentina's original pop music: despised by the middle and upper classes for its arresting rhythm and offbeat musical pattern (called the '*tunga-tunga*'), as well as its working-class lyrics, it is definitely music from the margins. Although definitively *cordobés* (from Córdoba), it's played in working-class bars, dance halls and stadiums throughout the country. The most famous *cuarteto* group is La Barra.

Cumbia villera is a relatively recent musical phenomenon: a fusion of *cumbia* (originally a Colombian dance music) and gangsta posturing with a punk edge and reggae overtones. This spawn of Buenos Aires shantytowns has aggressive lyrics that deal with marginalization, poverty, drugs, sex and the Argentine economic crisis. Gauchin, Los Pibes Chorros, Yerba Brava and Damas Gratis are Argentina's best known *cumbia villera* groups.

Finally, *murga* is a form of athletic musical theater composed of actors and percussionists. Primarily performed in Uruguay, *murga* in Argentina is more heavily focused on dancing than singing. You'll mostly see this exciting musical art form at Carnaval celebrations (see p547).

ELECTRÓNICA

Electrónica, or dance music, exploded in Argentina in the 1990s and has taken on various forms in popular music. Hybrid *bandas electrónicas* (electronic bands) are led by the likes of Intima, Mujik and Adicta. DJ-based club and dance music is increasingly popular. Argentina's heavyweights include Hernán Cattáneo, Ricky Ryan, Bad Boy Orange (the reigning king of Argentine drum 'n' bass), Diego Ro-K (who has been around since the mid-1980s, and is known as the Maradona of Argentine DJs), Fabian Dellamonica and Zucker.

CLASSICAL MUSIC & BALLET

Buenos Aires' Teatro Colón (see p98) is one of the world's premier opera houses and hosts top world talent. Unfortunately, tickets are hard to come by, as many of the theater's 3500 seats are held by season ticketholders. In May 2010 the Colón should be finished with its remodel, so check the current situation.

One person who never had problems getting into Teatro Colón is Argentine Julio Bocca, one of the most important ballet dancers of the 20th century. At age 19 he was invited to join the American Ballet Theatre by Mikhail Baryshnikov, and in 1990 started his own troupe, Ballet Argentino, which has been wildly popular at home. Bocca danced a farewell performance in 2006 and retired in 2007.

Charly García's version of the Argentine national anthem does what Jimi Hendrix did for 'The Star-Spangled Banner,' but it earned García a court appearance for 'lacking respect for national symbols.'

Julio Bocca, Argentina's famous ballet star, once posed nude with his long-time dance partner (Eleonora Cassano) for Argentine *Playboy*.

THE TANGO

The air hangs heavy, smoky and dark. Streams of diffused light illuminate a large, open space. A lone woman, dressed in slit skirt and high heels, sits with legs crossed at one of the small tables surrounding a wooden dance floor. She casually looks here and there, in search of the subtle signal. Her gaze sweeps over several tables and suddenly locks onto a stranger's eyes, and there it is: the *cabezazo*, a quick tilt of his head. She briefly considers the offer, then nods with a slight smile. The man approaches her and she rises to meet him, and the new pair head out toward the dance floor.

The tango hasn't always been quite so mysterious, but it does have a long and somewhat complex history. Though the exact origins can't be pinpointed, the dance is thought to have started in Buenos Aires in the 1880s. Legions of European immigrants, mostly lower-class men, arrived in the great village of Buenos Aires to seek their fortunes. Missing their motherlands and the women they left behind, they sought out cafes and bordellos to ease the loneliness. Here the men mingled and danced with waitresses and prostitutes. It was a strong blend of machismo, passion and longing, with an almost fighting edge to it.

Small musical ensembles were soon brought in to accompany early tangos, playing tunes influenced by pampas *milonga* verse, Spanish and Italian melodies and African *candombe* drums. (The *bandoneón*, a small accordion, was brought into these sessions and has since become an inextricable part of the tango orchestra.) Here the tango song was also born. It summarized the new urban experience for the immigrants and was permeated with nostalgia for a disappearing way of life. Themes ranged from profound feelings about changing neighborhoods to the figure of the mother, male friendship and betrayal by women. Sometimes, raunchy lyrics were added.

The perceived vulgarity of the dance was deeply frowned upon by the reigning elites, but it did manage to influence some brash young members of the upper classes, who took the novelty to Paris and created a craze – a dance that became an acceptable outlet for human desires, expressed on the dance floors of elegant cabarets. The trend spread around Europe and even to the USA, and 1913 was considered by some 'the year of the tango.' When the evolved dance returned to Buenos Aires, now refined and famous, the tango finally earned the respectability it deserved. The golden years of tango were just beginning.

Gardel & the Tango

In June 1935 a Cuban woman committed suicide in Havana; meanwhile, in New York and in Puerto Rico two other women tried to poison themselves. And it was all over the same man – a man none of them had ever met. The man was tango singer Carlos Gardel, El Zorzal Criollo, the songbird of Buenos Aires, and he had just died in a plane crash in Colombia.

Though born in France, Gardel was the epitome of the immigrant *porteño*. When he was three his destitute single mother brought him to Buenos Aires. In his youth he worked at a variety of menial jobs, but he also managed to entertain his neighbors with his rapturous singing. A performing career began after he befriended Uruguayan-born José Razzano, and the two of them sang together in a popular duo until Razzano lost his voice. From 1917 onward, Gardel performed solo. Carlos Gardel played an enormous role in creating the tango *canción* (song). Almost single-handedly, he took the style out of Buenos Aires' tenements and brought it to Paris and New York. His crooning voice, suaveness and overall charisma made him an immediate

Architecture

Argentina lacks the great pre-Columbian architecture of Andean South America, though a few significant archaeological sites exist in the Andean northwest. This region has notable, if not abundant, Spanish colonial architecture in cities such as Salta and Tucumán, and in villages in isolated areas such as the Quebrada de Humahuaca. Some of the country's most splendid colonial architecture is in Córdoba (p309), whose historic center is arguably Argentina's finest. Carmen de Patagones is also home to some outstanding colonial architecture. Buenos Aires itself has scattered colonial examples, but success in Latin American countries. His star rose in tango's golden years of the 1920s and 1930s and Gardel became a recording star. Unfortunately, his later film career was tragically cut short by that fatal plane crash.

Every day a steady procession of pilgrims visits Carlos Gardel's sarcophagus in the Cementerio de la Chacarita in Buenos Aires, where a lit cigarette often smolders between the metal fingers of his life-size statue. The large, devoted community of his followers, known as *gardelianos,* cannot pass a day without listening to his songs or watching his films. Another measure of his ongoing influence is the common saying that 'Gardel sings better every day.' Elvis should be so lucky.

Tango at a Milonga Today

Despite a long evolution from its origins, tango is still sensual and erotic. The upper bodies are held upright and close, with faces almost touching. The man's hand is pressed against the woman's back, guiding her, with their other hands held together and out. The lower body does most of the work. The woman's hips swivel, her legs alternating in short or wide sweeps and quick kicks, sometimes between the man's legs. The man guides, a complicated job since he must flow with the music, direct the woman, meld with her steps and avoid other dancers. It's a serious business, and while dancing the pair wear hard expressions. Smiling and chatting are reserved for between songs. At an established *milonga* (tango dance hall), choosing an adequate partner involves many levels of hidden codes, rules and signals that dancers must follow. After all, no serious dancer wants to be caught with someone stepping on her toes – and expensive tango heels. In fact, some men will only ask an unknown woman to dance after the second song, so as not to be stuck for the four tango songs that make a session. It's also considered polite to dance at least two songs with any partner; if you are given a curt *'gracias'* after just one, consider yourself excused.

Your position in the area surrounding the dance floor can be critical. At some of the older *milongas,* the more-established dancers have reserved tables. Ideally, you should sit where you have easy access to the floor and to other dancers' line of sight. You may notice couples sitting further back, while singles sit right at the front. And if a man comes into the room with a woman at his side, she is considered 'his' for the night. For couples to dance with others, they either enter the room separately, or the man may signal his intent by asking another woman to the floor. Then 'his' woman becomes open for asking.

The *cabezazo* – the quick tilt of the head, eye contact and uplifted eyebrows – can happen from way across the room. The woman to whom the *cabezazo* is directed either nods yes and smiles, or pretends not to have noticed. If she says yes, the man gets up and escorts her to the floor. If you're at a *milonga* and don't want to dance with anyone, don't look around too much – you could be breaking some hearts.

So what is the appeal of the tango? Experienced dancers will say that the adrenaline rush you get from an excellent performance is like a successful conquest: it can lift you to exhilarating heights. But the dance can also become addictive – once you have fallen for the passion and beauty of the tango's movements you may spend your life trying to attain a physical perfection that can never be fully realized. The true *tanguero* attempts to make the journey as graceful and passionate as possible.

is essentially a turn-of-the-20th-century city, with architectural influences that are predominantly French.

Catholicism has provided Argentina with some of its finest monuments, from the lonely, picturesque churches of the Andean northwest to the colonial cathedral in Córdoba and the neo-Gothic basilicas of Luján and La Plata, to the Jesuit ruins of Misiones province. Recent architecture tends to the large and impersonal, with modernistic glass buildings dominating downtown areas, most notably the new high-rise developments of Buenos Aires' Puerto Madero.

Visual Arts

Although the visual arts have waxed and waned over the years, they've always been a fundamental part of Argentine expression. Lino Spilimbergo (1896–1964) and Antonio Berni (1905–81) are two of Argentina's greatest painters; check out the ceiling murals in Buenos Aires' Galerías Pacífico (see p95) for a taste of their work.

Benito Quinquela Martín (1890–1977) put the working-class *barrio* of La Boca on the artistic map by painting brightly colored oils of life on Buenos Aires' waterfront. Beyond classification, Xul Solar (1887–1963; see p101) was a multitalented phenomenon who painted colorful Kandinsky- and Klee-inspired dreamscapes. Other Argentine virtuosos include Tucumán-born Víctor Hugo Quiroga and *porteño* painter Guillermo Kuitca. Meanwhile, some contemporary artists to watch for are multimedia queens Graciela Sacco and Liliana Porter, conceptual artists Roberto Jacoby and photographers Arturo Aguiar and Sebastián Friedman.

To appreciate one of Buenos Aires' most prolific forms of contemporary painting, you never have to step inside – just watch for the ubiquitous street stencils (www.bsasstencil.org) or graffiti (www.bagraff.com).

Buenos Aires' streets are home to graffiti and stencil art, which can be just as inspirational as anything found indoors. A more traditional form of popular painting in Buenos Aires' is *filete*, the ornamental line painting that once graced the capital's horse carts, trucks and buses.

Given its French origins, official public sculpture tends toward the pompously monumental – think equestrian statues of military figures. A welcome exception is the work of the late Rogelio Yrurtia, some of whose works deal sympathetically with the struggles of working people (such as his *Canto al Trabajo* in Plazoleta Olazábal in San Telmo). An even more extreme exception is pop artist Marta Minujín, known for making huge prominent sculptures in the capital – some out of food. Meanwhile, León Ferrari's artworks deal with antireligious and political themes that always stir up controversies.

Famous Argentine illustrator Florencio Molina Campos (1891–1959) drew cartoonish gaucho scenes with a comical twist. To get to know his art, check out the Centro Cultural Usina Vieja (see p147) in San Antonio de Areco.

Other influential Argentine sculptors are Lucio Fontana, Enio Iommi, Alberto Heredia, Juan Carlos Distéfano and Yoël Novoa. Well-known women include Norma D'Ippolito, Lucia Pacenza and Claudia Aranovich.

In Buenos Aires, keep an eye out for the giant metal flower *Floralis Genérica* in Recoleta's Plaza de las Naciones Unidas (p101); it was created by architect Eduardo Catalano. Outside the capital, the city of Resistencia (p233) is famous for its outdoor sculptures.

Theater

Theater is important in Argentina, and not only in cosmopolitan Buenos Aires. The country's legendary performers include Lola Membrives, Luis Sandrini and Federico Luppi, while its most famous contemporary playwrights and directors include Juan Carlos Gené, Ciro Zorzoli, Lorena Vega, Ricardo Bartis, José Muscari and Daniel Veronese.

Buenos Aires has a vibrant independent theater scene that's well worth tapping (see p128). The official theater season is June to August, but there are always performances on Buenos Aires' Av Corrientes, and at smaller theater companies in the city. In summer some of the best shows are seen in the provincial beach resort of Mar del Plata (see p171).

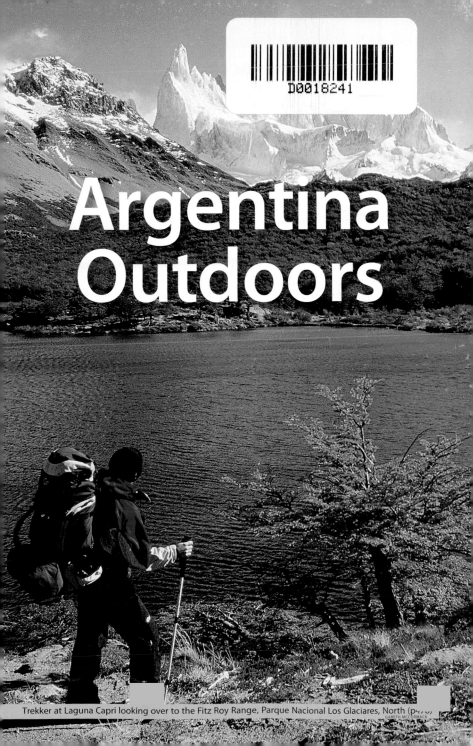

Argentina
Outdoors

Trekker at Laguna Capri looking over to the Fitz Roy Range, Parque Nacional Los Glaciares, North (p470)

GARETH MCCORMACK

Whether to the rugged wilderness of Patagonia or the massive peaks of the Andes, Argentina has long allured the world's most adventurous souls. For anyone with a little grit and a love of the great outdoors, it's more than just a magnet. It's a mecca. Mountaineering, hiking and fishing have long been Argentina's classic outdoor pursuits, but these days locals and visitors alike are doing much more. They're kite surfing in the Andes, snowboarding near Bariloche, paragliding in the Central Sierras and sneaking up on caimans in Esteros del Iberá. And they're always, always having fun.

HIKING & TREKKING

Argentina is home to some seriously superb stomping. The Lake District is probably the country's most popular hiking destination, with outstanding day and multiday hikes in several national parks, including Nahuel Huapi (p410) and Lanín (p389). Bariloche is the best base for exploring the former, San Martín de los Andes the latter.

Patagonia, needless to say, has out-of-this-world hiking. South of Bariloche, El Bolsón (p412) is an excellent base for hiking both in the forests outside of town and in nearby Parque Nacional Lago Puelo (p417). Parque Nacional Los Glaciares offers wonderful hiking in and around the Fitz Roy Range; base yourself in El Chaltén (p474) and wait out the storms (in the brewery, of course).

If you've come this far south, you might as well head to Parque Nacional Torres del Paine (p505), in Chile, for some of the continent's most epic hiking. Tierra del Fuego also has great hiking, most conveniently in Parque Nacional Tierra del Fuego (p528).

Hiking in Parque Nacional Los Glaciares (p478)
GARETH MCCORMACK

Then there are the high Andean peaks west of Mendoza (p343). Although these areas are more popular for mountaineering, there's some great trekking here as well. The northern Andes around Quebrada de Humahuaca (p252) are also good.

Most sizable towns in the Lake District and Patagonia have a hiking and mountaineering club called Club Andino. These can be good places to get information, maps and current conditions. We've listed the clubs in Information sections throughout this book (Bariloche, Junín de los Andes, El Bolsón and Ushuaia all have one).

Lonely Planet's *Trekking in the Patagonian Andes* is a great resource to have if you're planning some serious trekking.

MOUNTAINEERING

The Andes are a mountaineer's dream, especially in San Juan and Mendoza provinces,

Mountains, lakes and lush countryside in Parque Nacional Nahuel Huapi (p410)

ANDREW BAIN

where some of the highest peaks in the Western hemisphere are found. While the most famous climb is Aconcagua (p356), the highest peak in the Americas, there are plenty of others in the Andes – many of them more interesting and far more technical. Near Barreal (p368), the Cordón de la Rameda boasts five peaks over 6000m, including the mammoth Cerro Mercedario, which tops out at 6770m. The region is less congested than Aconcagua, offers more technical climbs and is preferred by many climbers. Also near here is the majestic Cordillera de Ansilta (p368), with seven peaks scraping the sky at between 5130m and 5885m.

The magnificent and challenging Fitz Roy Range (p478), in southern Patagonia, is one of the world's top mountaineering destinations, while the mountains of Parque Nacional Nahuel Huapi (p410) offer fun for all levels.

Rock Climbing

Patagonia's Parque Nacional Los Glaciares (p478), home to Cerro Torre and Cerro Fitz Roy, is one of the most important rock-climbing destinations in the world. Cerro Torre is considered one of the five toughest climbs on the planet. The nearby town of El Chaltén is a climber's haven, and several shops offer lessons and rent equipment. If you don't have the time or talent for climbs of the Cerro Torre magnitude, there are plenty of other options.

Los Gigantes (p320), in the Central Sierras, is fast becoming the country's de facto sport-climbing capital, with lots of high-quality granite. Operators in Córdoba (p313) offer lessons and transportation. There's also climbing around Carolina (p334).

In Mendoza province, Los Molles (p362) is a small, friendly hub for rock climbing, and there's more nearby at Chigüido (near Malargüe). Around Mendoza city are the draws of Los Arenales and El Salto.

Cerro Otto, in Parque Nacional Nahuel Huapi (p410), has popular climbing routes. Finally, in the pampas, there's some climbing in Tandil (p150) and Mar del Plata (p165).

FISHING
Where to Fish

Together, Patagonia and the Lake District constitute one of the world's premier fly-fishing destinations, where introduced trout species (brown, brook, lake and rainbow) and landlocked Atlantic salmon reach massive sizes in cold rivers surrounded by spectacular scenery. It's an angler's paradise.

In the Lake District, Junín de los Andes (p387) is the self-proclaimed trout capital of Argentina, and lining up a guide to take you to Parque Nacional Lanín's superb trout streams is easy. Nearby Aluminé (p385) sits on the banks of Río Aluminé, one of the country's most highly regarded trout streams. Bariloche (p404) is another excellent base.

Casting a rod, Tierra del Fuego (p511)
MICHAEL TAYLOR

Further south, Parque Nacional Los Alerces (p465) has outstanding lakes and rivers, and you can take day trips to El Chaltén's Lago del Desierto or Laguna Larga (p481). The Río Grande, on Tierra del Fuego's Isla Grande (p514), is famous for holding some of the largest sea-running brown trout in the world. Other important mainland Patagonian rivers include Río Negro, Río Gallegos and Río Santa Cruz. There's also an *estancia* (ranch) in this area, dedicated to anglers (p456), and deep-sea fishing is a possibility in Camarones (p442).

In subtropical northeast Argentina, the wide Río Paraná (p179) attracts fly-fishers, spin fishers and trollers from around the world, who pull in massive river species such as surubí (a massive catfish) and dorado (a troutlike freshwater game fish). The dorado, not to be confused with the salt-water mahi mahi, is an extremely powerful swimmer and is said to be one of the most exciting fish to catch on a fly.

There's also great fishing in Mendoza (p345), Uspallata (p353) and Barreal (p368).

Guides & Services

A fly rod makes a great addition to any backpack. If you're traveling around Patagonia, especially the Lake District, you can easily throw a pack rod into your bag and fish wherever you feel like (provided you're licensed, of course). But if you really want to fish, nothing can take the place of having a good guide. In smaller towns such as Junín de los Andes, you can usually go to the local tourist office and request a list of local fishing guides. Better yet, most tourist offices can set you up with a list of established fishing operators. Another good option for independent anglers heading to the Lake District is the **Asociación de Guías Profesionales de Pesca del Parque Nacional Nahuel Huapi y Patagonia Norte** (www.guiaspatagonicos.com.ar), which maintains a list and contact details of licensed guides for northern Patagonia and the Lake District.

In northern Argentina, which doesn't have a tourist infrastructure as accommodating as the Lake District's, it's virtually impossible to fish without a guide – and usually a boat.

For more info about fly-fishing, contact **Asociación Argentina de Pesca con Mosca** (☎ in Buenos Aires 011-4773-0821; www.aapm.org.ar). For more about fishing in Tierra del Fuego, see p516.

Rules & Regulations

In the Lake District and Patagonia, the season runs November to between mid- and late April. In the northeast the season runs February to October. Certain lakes and streams on private land may stay open longer.

Trout fishing is almost always mandatory catch and release. Throughout Patagonia (including the Lake District), native species should *always* be thrown back. These are usually smaller than trout and include perca (perch), puyen (common galaxias, a narrow fish native to the southern hemisphere), Patagonian pejerrey and the rare peladilla.

Fishing licenses are required everywhere and are available at tackle shops, the local *club de caza y pesca* (hunting and fishing club), and sometimes at tourist offices and YPF gas stations. For most of the country, prices are AR$75 per day, AR$250 per week and AR$350 for the season. Trolling fees cost extra. In Tierra del Fuego, prices are higher. There may also be additional fees for preferential zones.

> ### MUSH!
>
> You can't say you've done it all until you've tried dog sledding. Argentina's a great place to start. Operators near Caviahue (p382) offer dog sledding, as do operators in San Martín de los Andes (p391). And how about dog sledding at the end of the world, in Ushuaia (p522)? Obviously, this activity is possible only when there's snow, during the winter months of June to October (though in Ushuaia the season might be longer).

SKIING & SNOWBOARDING

Although still not as internationally known as the slopes in neighboring Chile, Argentina's mountains can be outstanding. Most locations offer superb powder, good cover and plenty of sunny days. Many resorts have large ski schools with instructors from all over the world, so language is not a problem. At some of the older resorts equipment can be a little antiquated, but in general the quality of skiing more than compensates.

There are three main snow-sport areas: Mendoza, the Lake District and Ushuaia. Mendoza is home to Argentina's premier resort, Las Leñas (p362), which has the best snow and the longest runs. The Lake District is home to several low-key resorts, including Cerro Catedral (p411), near Bariloche, and Cerro Chapelco (p396), near San Martín de los Andes. Although the snow doesn't get as powdery here, the views are far superior to Las Leñas. And Esquel, further south in Patagonia, *does* have great powder at its La Hoya resort.

The world's most southerly commercial skiing is near Ushuaia (see p522). The ski season everywhere generally runs mid-June to mid-October.

Skiing with superb views and incredibly dry powder snow, Las Leñas (p362)

CHRISTIAN ÅSLUND

CYCLING

Cycling is a popular activity among Argentines, and spandex-clad cyclists are a common site along the road, despite the fact that you'll never see a bicycle lane. There are some outstanding paved routes for cyclists, especially in the Lake District and, to a lesser extent, in the Andean northwest.

In the Lake District's Parque Nacional Nahuel Huapi (p410), there are several excellent loops (including the Circuito Chico) that skirt gorgeous lakes and take in some of Patagonia's most epic scenery. Cyclists often take their bikes on the Cruce de Lagos (p409), a famous two-day boat/bus journey across the Andes to Chile. Instead of bussing the road stretches, they ride.

In the northwest, there are several excellent road routes, including the highway from Tucumán to Tafí del Valle; the direct

Cycling around Mendoza's wineries (p344)
ANDREW PEACOCK

road from Salta to Jujuy; and – arguably most spectacular of all – Quebrada de Cafayate (p279). The Central Sierras (p318) are also great candidates for cycling, and the mostly paved network of roads rolls past a countryside that is, at times, reminiscent of Scotland. Mendoza boasts some epic routes through the Andes, but most are doable only for the seasoned cyclist – those lacking thighs of glory can entertain themselves pedaling between wineries in Maipú (p352).

For more info on the logistics of getting around Argentina on two wheels, see p617.

Mountain Biking

The opportunities for mountain biking are endless. However, the sport is fairly undeveloped here, and you'll find few places that have true single tracks for mountain bikers. Even if you leave your bike at home, you'll find ample opportunity to ride. At most outdoor hubs (such as Bariloche) you can rent a mountain bike for a day of independent pedaling or for guided mountain-bike rides, a fantastic way to see parts of an area you otherwise wouldn't. Places with mountain-bike rentals and guides include Córdoba (p318), Alta Gracia (p326), La Cumbrecita (p327), La Cumbre (p322) and Villa General Belgrano (p327) in Córdoba province; Villa la Angostura (p399), Bariloche (p401), El Bolsón (p414), Esquel (p457) and Junín de los Andes (p387) in the Lake District; Mendoza (p339), San Rafael (p358) and Uspallata (p353) in Mendoza province; Barreal (p368) in San Juan province; and Cafayate (p276), Catamarca

---

SAILING: NO WATER NECESSARY

In San Juan province's Parque Nacional El Leoncito (p371), the Pampa El Leoncito has become the epicenter of *carrovelismo* (land sailing). Here, people zip across the dry lake bed beneath Andean peaks in so-called sail cars. If you're interested, head straight to Barreal (p370).

(p293), Humahuaca (p256) and also Tilcara (p254) in the Andean northwest. Puerto Madryn (p424), on the Atlantic Coast, and Rosario (p179), in Northeast Argentina, also have bike rentals.

WHITE-WATER RAFTING & KAYAKING

Although its rivers can't compare to neighboring Chile's when it comes to white-water action, Argentina does have some excellent river running. Currently, Río Mendoza and Río Diamante, in Mendoza province (see p344), are the reigning white-water destinations, while Río Juramento near Salta (p265) and Río Atuel (see p360) have exciting possibilities, too.

If you want great scenery, however, it's all about Patagonia. The Río Hua Hum and Río Meliquina, near San Martín de los Andes (see p392), and Río Limay and Río Manso, near Bariloche (see p404) are both spectacular. So is Río Aluminé, near wee Aluminé (p385). From the Patagonian town of Esquel (p457) you can join a rafting trip on the incredibly scenic, glacial-fed Río Corcovado. A relatively unknown rafting destination is Barreal (p369), but it's more about the epic Andean scenery than the rapids. Scenic class II to III floats are possible on most of these rivers, while class IV runs are possible on the Ríos Mendoza, Diamante, Meliquina, Hua Hum and Corcovado. Experience is generally unnecessary for guided runs.

Kayaking is possible on many of the rivers mentioned, and also around Ushuaia (round Cape Horn! see p522), El Chaltén (p481), Viedma (p422), Puerto Madryn (p426), Paraná (p193), Gualeguaychú (p204), Rosario (p183) and Salta (p265).

PARAGLIDING & SKYDIVING

Paragliding is popular in Argentina and it's a great place to take tandem flights or classes. Why? Because it's so affordable and there are some outstanding places to do it. Many agencies in Bariloche (p405) offer paragliding, and views are superb. Tucumán (p282) and Salta (p265) have options in the Andean Northwest. Perhaps the best place of all, however, is La Cumbre (p322), in Córdoba's Central Sierras.

Both La Cumbre and Alta Gracia (p326) are the places to go for skydiving in Córdoba province, while on the coast, Mar del Plata (p169) offers aerial thrills, too.

SLOPE OF THE WIND

From around the world, windsurfing and kite-surfing fanatics drag an insane amount of gear to an isolated spot in the central Andes: Dique Cuesta del Viento, literally 'slope of the wind reservoir' (p371). The reservoir, near the wee village of Rodeo, in San Juan province, is one of the best windsurfing and kite-surfing destinations on the planet. Its consistent and extremely powerful wind blows every afternoon – without fail – from October to early May. We checked it out, and it blew us away!

Paragliding at Cerro Otto (p410)
CHRISTIAN KAPTEYN / ALAMY

Getting up close to Iguazú Falls' Garganta del Diablo by boat (p223) is awe inspiring (and a bit damp)
MARGIE POLITZER

Food & Drink

Argentines love eating. A great deal of their social and political life involves a table, be it for a leisurely coffee, an informal meal or an elegant banquet. The food must meet two criteria: abundance and a good price-to-quality relationship. Sophistication is not a national feature, and beef and pasta are the two pillars upon which the national menu is based. That's not to say sophistication doesn't exist. On the contrary. In Buenos Aires and other Argentine cities, you'll find plenty of slick international restaurants – Japanese, Middle Eastern, Mexican, Southeast Asian, Brazilian, you name it – that serve intricately prepared dishes. But traditional Argentine food, which is rooted in Italian and Spanish cooking, is generally more modest.

As for libations, Argentina is fast becoming synonymous with wine – *good* wine. The number of wineries and vineyards is skyrocketing, not just in Mendoza province (the heart of Argentine wine country) but in northwest Argentina and even northern Patagonia. And despite rising inflation and economic instability, sampling fine wine in this country remains an affordable luxury.

For details on Uruguayan food and drink, see p537.

Argentines eat a lot of beef. Per capita, they down nearly 70kg of the stuff per year. Compare that to 43kg in the US and 37kg in Australia.

STAPLES & SPECIALTIES

Most visitors (unless they're vegetarian, heaven forbid) follow the same splurge-and-purge pattern when they get to Argentina: they arrive, gorge themselves on the country's famous beef and then, by day four, start moaning for something different – *anything* but more beef! Rest assured, beef is only part of the story.

Beef

But first things first. When it comes to national cuisine, beef is the operative word. Argentina produces what is arguably the world's best, and it consumes more per capita than any other country. The most important thing to keep in mind when partaking in the experience is the difference between prime cuts (such as sirloin, tenderloin, ribeye and others) versus some of the more unusual cuts that Argentines often grill. The former are usually tender and juicy and offer foreigners the exquisite grilled-beef experience they expect. The latter include everything from short ribs and T-bone to small intestines, all of it with plenty of fat and grilled to a state of well-doneness resulting in lots of flavor and *lots* of chewing. It may not be your idea of tastiness. If not, stick with the prime cuts. For the complete lowdown on beef, see the boxed text, p62.

Mollejas (sweetbreads; the thymus or pancreas) are a delicacy and an acquired taste. They look fatty at first, so concentrate instead on their tenderness and sublime flavor.

Italian

Thanks to Argentina's Italian heritage, the national cuisine oozes with influences carried across the Atlantic by the wave of Italian immigrants who entered the country during the late 19th century. Along with an animated set of speaking gestures, they brought their love of (and recipes for) pasta, pizza, gelato, olive oil and more.

Many restaurants make their own pasta – look for *pasta casera* (handmade pasta) – and those that don't almost invariably buy it fresh. *Ravioles* (ravioli), *sorrentinos* (large, round, filled pasta parcels similar to ravioli), *ñoquis* (gnocchi), *fideos* (spaghetti) and *tallerines* (fettuccine) are just some of the varieties of pasta you'll encounter. Standard sauces include *tuco* (tomato sauce), *estofado* (beef stew, popular with ravioli) and *salsa blanca*

Italian food is everywhere in Argentina, thanks to its rich Italian heritage, and the strongest influence is Genoese, since so many hail from Genoa.

THE BEEF ON BEEF

You walk into a traditional *parrilla* (steak house), breezing past the stuffed bull and sizzling *asado* (barbecue grill) at the entrance, and sit down hungry, knife and fork in hand. You don't know a word of Spanish, you've never had to choose between more than two or three cuts of steak in your life and the menu has at least 10 different choices. What do you do? Don't fret. We'll give you a better idea of what will show up on your plate.

But first, you should have an idea of where Argentina's famous beef comes from. When the first Spaniards came over to Argentina from Europe, with the intention of colonizing the area, they brought some cows. Because stubborn locals were unwilling to let themselves be dominated, the Spaniards' first efforts at a colony proved unfruitful. They ended up abandoning their herds in the pampas and moving away. The cattle, on the other hand, found the bovine equivalent of heaven: plenty of lush, fertile grasses on which to feed, with few natural predators to limit their numbers. Things were great until the Europeans decided to start recolonizing the pampas and capturing the cattle for their own use. (The gauchos, however, had been taking advantage of these free-roaming meals-on-the-hoof all along.)

Today, intermixing with other European bovine breeds has produced a pretty tasty beef. Why is it so good? Any Argentine will say it's because free-range Argentine cows eat nutritious pampas grass, lacking in the massive quantities of corn, antibiotics and growth hormones that American or European stocks are given in feedlots. This makes for a leaner, more natural-tasting meat, though these days things are changing somewhat: inoculations against disease do occur, and the feedlot system is gaining a serious foothold – see p157.

The average intake of beef is around 70kg per person per year, though in the past Argentines ate even more. Most of this consuming takes place at the family *asado,* often held on Sunday in the backyards of houses all over the country (if you are lucky enough to be invited to one, make sure you attend). Here the art of grilling beef has been perfected. This usually involves cooking

(béchamel). Perhaps as an Argentine touch (and to the chagrin of budget travelers), sauce is sometimes *not* included in the price of the pasta – you pay for it separately.

Then, of course, there's pizza. Big, piping-hot extra-cheesy *porciones* (slices) or whole pizzas are sold at *pizzerías* throughout the country, but pizza is especially popular (and arguably at its artery-clogging best) in Buenos Aires. The traditional way to polish off a couple of slices is by topping each with a slice of *fainá* (a sort of chickpea patty sliced to match) and washed down with a glass of *moscato* (muscatel). Most *pizzerías* also sell empanadas.

Spanish

Spanish cooking is less popular than Italian, but forms another bedrock of Argentine food. In the country's Spanish restaurants you'll find paella, as well as other typically Spanish seafood preparations. (Beware that Argentine seafood is usually mediocre, at best.) Most of the country's *guisos* and *pucheros* (types of stew) are almost all descendants of Spain.

Although Italians might argue that empanadas – small, stuffed pastries ubiquitous throughout Argentina – are the country's take on the calzone, they're actually Spanish in origin. Empanadas are prepared differently throughout Argentina (for example, you'll find spicy ground-beef empanadas in the Andean northwest and ham-and-cheese empanadas in Buenos Aires) and make for a tasty quick meal.

Regional Dishes

Although it's the national food, beef is really a regional dish. It's a pampas thing. Cows don't stay tender roaming the barren Andean northwest, or the scrub forests of the Chaco, or the steppes of windswept Patagonia. When you're

Shirley Lomax Brooks' *Argentina Cooks! Treasured Recipes from the Nine Regions of Argentina* does a great job remaining true to its title.

with coals and using only salt to prepare the meat. On the grill itself, which is often waist high and made of bricks, slanted runners funnel the excess fat to the sides to avoid flare-ups, and an adjustable height system directs the perfect amount of heat to the meat.

Emerging from this family tradition, the commercial steak house offers a little bit of everything. The *parrillada* (mixed grill) might have an assortment of *chorizo* (beef or pork sausage), *pollo* (chicken), *costillas* (ribs) and *carne* (beef). It can also come with more exotic items such as *chinchulines* (small intestines), *tripa gorda* (large intestine), *molleja* (thymus gland or sweetbreads), *ubre* (udder), *riñones* (kidneys) and *morcilla* (blood sausage). You can order a *parrillada* for as many people as you want; the steak house adjusts its servings according to the party's size.

You could skip the mixed grill and dive right into the prime beef cuts. Here's a guide:

- **bife de chorizo** – sirloin; a thick, juicy and popular cut
- **bife de costilla** – T-bone; a cut close to the bone; also called *chuleta*
- **bife de lomo** – tenderloin; a thinly cut, more tender piece
- **cuadril** – rump steak; often a thin cut
- **ojo de bife** – ribeye; a choice smaller morsel
- **tira de asado** – shortribs; thin strips of ribs and meat sliced crosswise
- **vacío** – flank steak; textured and chewy, but very tasty

If you don't specify, your steak will be cooked *a punto* (medium). To get it pink on the inside ask for *jugoso* (medium rare). *Vuelta y vuelta* or *poco hecho* means rare, and well done is *bien hecho*. Be sure not to miss *chimichurri*, a tasty sauce often made of olive oil, garlic and parsley. Also try *salsa criolla*, a condiment made of diced tomato, onion and parsley – it's harder to find.

outside the provinces of Buenos Aires, Santa Fe, Córdoba and La Pampa – Argentina's cattle-producing region – it's best to try something different.

Although the term *comida típica* can refer to any of Argentina's regional dishes, it often refers to food from the Andean northwest. Food from this region, which has roots in pre-Columbian times, has more in common with the cuisines of Bolivia and Peru than with the Europeanized food of the rest of Argentina. It's frequently spicy (thanks to the liberal use of chilies) and is hard to find elsewhere (most Argentines are suspicious of anything spicier than a pinch of black pepper). Typical dishes can include everything from *locro* (a hearty and often outstanding corn or mixed-grain stew with sausage or other meat), to tamales, *humitas* (sweet tamales) and fried empanadas.

In Patagonia, lamb almost wipes beef off the map. Along the coast, seafood is a popular choice and includes fish, oysters and king crab. In the Lake District, game meats such as venison, wild boar and trout are popular. In the west, the provinces of Mendoza, San Juan and La Rioja pride themselves on *chivito* (young goat). River fish, such as the dorado, pacú (a relative of the piranha) and surubí (a type of catfish), are staples in the northeast.

Torta galesa (Welsh cake) is a delicious fruitcake unknown in Wales. Welsh settlers in Argentina created it to tide them over during the harsh Patagonian winters, when food was scarce.

Meals

Argentines are not great breakfast eaters, and bacon-and-eggs people may find themselves fighting hunger pangs by midmorning. A typical breakfast consists of *café con leche y medialunas* (coffee with milk, and croissants), although hotels catering to tourists offer American-style breakfasts. The croissants come *dulce* (sweet) or *salada* (plain). *Tostadas* (toast), with *manteca* (butter) and/or *mermelada* (jam), is an alternative. *Facturas* (sweet pastries), which can be found at any *confitería* (cafe serving light meals) and most bars, are a common snack.

Argentines make up for breakfast at lunch and dinner, although the three-course lunch is now far less common. While most places begin service around noon, the popular time to lunch is between 1pm and 1:30pm. Dinner can begin at 8pm, but an Argentine will seldom eat before 9pm (10pm is far more common), and meals can draw out long after midnight on weekends.

Sandwiches & Snacks

In big cities it's easy to snack at any time on almost anything you desire. *Kioscos* (kiosks) are all over town and provide sweets, cookies, ice cream and packaged sandwiches. On many streets you'll find *pancho* (hot dog) and *garapiñadas* (sugar-roasted peanuts) sellers preparing and selling treats from their carts. A more substantial snack is the aforementioned empanada, which is cheap and filling, and comes either *al horno* (baked) or *frito* (fried).

Sandwiches de miga (thin, crustless sandwiches, usually with cheese and ham) are very popular teatime snacks, usually available at bakeries. *Pebetes* are heartier sandwiches made on oblong bread rolls. *Lomitos* (steak sandwiches) are by far the pinnacle of Argentine sandwiches, and few things can beat a really good, cholesterol-packed *super lomito* (a *lomito* served with a slice of ham and fried egg on top of the meat). The one thing that can: the *choripán*, a classic sandwich made with two ingredients: *chorizo* (beef or pork sausage) and *pan* (bread). Top it with *chimichurri* sauce, and you're set!

> *Chimichurri* is a classic Argentine steak and sausage condiment. An old joke attributes the name to a Spanish-language corruption of 'Che, mi curry!' – 'hey, my curry!' which is what the British soldiers yelled in restaurants in the 19th century.

Desserts & Sweets

Argentina is one of the world's highest per capita consumers of sweets. From the multitude of candy bars that pour from streetside kiosks to the national addiction to *dulce de leche* (milk caramel), there's no shortage of sweetness in Argentina.

Two of Argentina's most definitive treats are *dulce de leche* and *alfajores* (round, cookie-type sandwiches stuffed with anything from apple preserves to *dulce de leche*). Each region of Argentina has its own version of the *alfajor*, and many argue that those from Santa Fe are the best.

> With its Central European heritage, Bariloche (p401) is Argentina's reigning capital of chocolate. Can't make it? Try a bar of Águila from any supermarket.

Helado (ice cream) is outstanding in Argentina, especially in Buenos Aires. Based on the Italian tradition, there are three basic types: the large-scale brands, such as Frigor (Nestlé); the semi-artisanal, produced by chains such as Freddo; and the artisanal, made by small *heladerías* (ice-creameries). *Helados* are eaten all year long and flavors are extremely varied. Helados Jauja in Bariloche (p407) is often credited with making the country's best ice cream, but parlors such as Una Altra Volta and Persicco in Buenos Aires (p120) are arguably on par.

> Ice cream is one of Argentina's greatest treats, more akin to Italian gelato than its creamy counterparts in France and the US.

In restaurants, fruit salad and ice cream are almost always on the menu. *Flan* is a baked custard that comes with a choice of either cream or *dulce de leche* topping. *Queso y dulce* consists of slices of fresh cheese with candied *membrillo* (quince) or *batata* (sweet potato). The former is typical of northern Argentina and can be outstanding.

DRINKS
Alcoholic Drinks

Over the last decade Argentina has exploded onto the international wine map, and its reputation for producing fine wines continues to grow. Argentine wines scale the entire price range from very cheap to very expensive. Mendoza is Argentina's premier wine region, but the provinces of San Juan, La Rioja and Salta (primarily around Cafayate) also produce excellent wines. Mendoza is known for its malbec, while San Juan is famous for its syrah and Cafayate for its torrontés, a crisp, dry white wine.

MATE & ITS RITUAL

Nothing captures the essence of *argentinidad* (Argentinity) as well as the preparation and consumption of *mate* (pronounced *mah*-tay), perhaps the only cultural practice that truly transcends the barriers of ethnicity, class and occupation in Argentina. More than a simple drink, *mate* is an elaborate ritual, shared among family, friends and coworkers. In many ways, sharing is the whole point.

Yerba mate is the dried, chopped leaf of *Ilex paraguayensis*, a relative of the common holly. Also known as Paraguayan tea, it became commercially important during the colonial era on the Jesuit missions' plantations in the upper Río Paraná. Europeans quickly took to the beverage, crediting it with many admirable qualities. The Austrian Jesuit Martin Dobrizhoffer wrote that *mate* 'provokes a gentle perspiration, improves the appetite, speedily counteracts the languor arising from the burning climate and assuages both hunger and thirst.' Production declined after the Jesuits' expulsion in 1767, but since the early 20th century it has increased dramatically.

Argentina is the world's largest producer and consumer of *yerba mate*. Argentines consume an average of 5kg per person per year, more than four times their average intake of coffee. It's also popular in parts of Chile, southern Brazil, Paraguay and, in particular, Uruguay, which consumes twice as much per capita as Argentina.

Preparing *mate* is a ritual in itself. In the past, upper-class families even maintained a slave or servant whose sole responsibility was preparing and serving it. Nowadays, one person, the *cebador* (server), fills the *mate* gourd almost to the top with *yerba*, heating but not boiling the water in a *pava* (kettle) and pouring it into the vessel. Drinkers then sip the liquid through a *bombilla*, a silver straw with a bulbous filter at its lower end that prevents the *yerba* leaves from entering the tube. Gourds can range from simple calabashes to carved wooden vessels to the ornate silver museum pieces of the 19th century. *Bombillas* also differ considerably, ranging in materials from inexpensive aluminum to silver and gold with intricate markings, and in design from long straight tubes to short, curved models.

There is an informal etiquette for drinking *mate*. The *cebador* pours water slowly as he or she fills the gourd. The gourd then passes clockwise, and this order, once established, continues. A good *cebador* will keep the *mate* going without changing the *yerba* for some time. Each participant drinks the gourd dry each time. A simple *'gracias'* will tell the server to pass you by. Don't hold the *mate* too long before passing it on, or someone might tell you *'no es un microfono'* ('it's not a microphone!').

An invitation to partake in *mate* is a cultural treat and not to be missed, although the drink is an acquired taste and novices may find it bitter and very hot at first. Because drinking *mate* is a fairly complex process, it is rarely served in restaurants or cafes, except in teabag form. For a foreigner, it is therefore easy to spend an entire holiday in Argentina without ever experiencing it. The simple solution is to do what traveling Argentines do: buy a thermos (stores rarely lack a thermos shelf), a *mate* gourd, a *bombilla* and a bag of herb.

Before drinking from your gourd, you must first cure it by filling it with hot water and *yerba* and letting it soak for 24 hours. When it's ready, you have to fill your thermos; nearly all restaurants, cafes and hotels are used to filling thermoses, sometimes charging a small amount. Simply whip out your thermos and ask: *'¿Podía calentar agua para mate?'* ('Would you mind heating water for *mate*?'). Even gas stations are equipped with giant tanks of precisely heated water for drinkers on the road. Once you have your water, you're off to the park to join the rest of the locals drinking *mate* in the shade.

If you'd like to find out more about *mate*, visit a *mate* museum – there's one in Tigre (p138) and another in Posadas (p214).

The wine list is called *la carta de vinos* and most fine restaurants have one. Sommeliers are scarce. For more on Argentine wine, see p351.

If Argentina has a national beer, it's Quilmes. Following close behind are Isenbeck, Warsteiner, Andes and the Brazilian Brahma. Order a *porrón* and you'll get a half-liter bottle, or a *chopp* and you'll get a frosty mug of draft.

Unless you order it with a meal, beer is usually served with a free snack, such as peanuts or potato chips.

At the harder end of the spectrum, it's all about Fernet Branca, a bitter, herbed Italian digestif (45% alcohol), originally intended as medicine, but now gulped down as a Coca Cola cocktail by Argentines everywhere. *Fernet con Coke* is by far Argentina's favorite cocktail, and despite many claims that it won't give you hangover, it will (trust us).

Another popular beverage (and one that won't knock you on your ass) is Gancia, a locally produced aperitif of Italian origin. It hurts by itself, but when whipped up with soda and lemon, it makes a delicious summertime drink called *Gancia batido.* Unusual beverages, more popular in the country than in cities, are *caña,* distilled from sugarcane, and a local gin *(ginebra)* made by Bols y Llave.

Nonalcoholic Drinks

Argentines are great coffee drinkers, and they like it strong. They drink coffee with milk in the morning and innumerable cups of *café solo* (basically espresso, but weaker) during the day (a stronger espresso is called *ristretto*). An espresso with a drop of milk is a *café cortado,* while a *lágrima* is mostly milk with a drop or two of coffee. *Cafe de filtro* is regular, drip-filter coffee, but it's rarely served in cafes.

Black and herbal teas are also available, in varieties such as *manzanilla* (chamomile) and *peperina* (an Argentine mint). Of course, there are *mates* (see p65). In the cooler seasons, try a *submarino:* a bar of chocolate placed in a glass of very hot milk and allowed to melt slowly.

Although fresh fruit is plentiful in the markets, fruit juices in bars and *confiterías* are usually limited to *exprimido de naranja* (freshly squeezed orange juice) and *pomelo* (grapefruit). A *licuado* is fruit liquefied in a blender with milk or water.

Gaseosas (soft drinks) are big business in Argentina, from Coke to *amargos Serrano* (a herbal infusion) and flavored mineral waters.

Even in big cities such as Buenos Aires, the *agua de canilla* (tap water) is drinkable. In restaurants, however, most people order bottled mineral water – ask for *agua con gas* (with bubbles) or *agua sin gas* (without). In older, more traditional restaurants, carbonated water in a spritzer bottle *(un sifón de soda)* is great for drinking, though Argentines often mix it with cheap wine.

CELEBRATIONS

Food during the holidays in Argentina is similar to that in Europe and the US. At Christmas, stores begin to fill up with many of the items typical in the northern hemisphere, although here in the south it's hot, hot, hot this time of year. During Semana Santa (Holy Week), fish and seafood hold sway, but whatever the occasion, the *asado* (barbeque) almost always reigns supreme. You may need to make restaurant reservations during holiday periods.

WHERE TO EAT & DRINK

Argentines love to dine out, and there is no lack of places to find a bite to eat. Bars or pubs (the latter which often have a pseudo-British touch) often have a limited range of snacks and meals available.

Confiterías are open all day and much of the night, and usually offer a long list of drink choices and appetizers, along with typical Argentine standbys such as pasta, pizza and meats. Cafe life is typical of Buenos Aires, and much financial, romantic, social and political business is conducted in these institutions. For the best meats, however, you'll need to head to a

---

If you love Argentine wine but don't want to lug those heavy bottles home, check out www.anuvawines.com. You can also book a wine tasting in Buenos Aires, then have a few vintages affordably shipped to your home outside Argentina.

With all the boutique wineries and newly planted varietals in Argentina, it's important to remember the past: Vasco Viejo is the country's classic table wine. At about AR$8 per bottle, it's rough but cheap!

When you order a beer at many restaurants, you often have to settle for a huge bottle, what's known as a *tres-quartos* (three-quarters), which is 0.75L. Smaller bottles are often unavailable. Ah shucks!

parrilla (steak restaurant) where your carnal choices can be dizzying (see the boxed text, p62).

Typical restaurants tend to be open only at meal times (1pm to 3:30pm or 4pm for lunch and 9pm to 1am or 2am for dinner). In Buenos Aires (especially in the Palermo Viejo neighborhood) you can choose from a wide variety of cuisines, such as Chinese, Japanese, Middle Eastern, Indian, Brazilian and Mexican. Outside the capital you're often stuck with the standard pasta, pizza and meat choices.

A *tenedor libre* (literally, 'free fork') is an all-you-can-eat restaurant. If you're hungry, these are great value and offer a wide range of foods, nearly always including a salad bar and *asado*. Quality is usually decent, and drinks cost extra.

Restaurant reservations are taken but are really only necessary on weekends at better restaurants, especially during peak times in hotspots like Mar del Plata or Bariloche. If in doubt, call ahead. Expect to linger over your meal and chat over coffee or drinks afterward. Your bill will rarely be presented until you ask for it, by saying, *'la cuenta, por favor'* ('the bill, please'). A waiter is a *mozo* and a waitress *señorita* (or *moza*).

Menus come in two types: a regular à la carte menu and *menú fijo* or *menú del día*, which refer to fixed-price meals, sometimes including a drink. Many menus are 'translated' into English, with results ranging from useful to hilarious to incomprehensible.

At fancier restaurants, your final bill may arrive with a *cubierto* (small cover charge for bread and use of utensils). This is not a tip, which is usually around 10% and a different charge from the *cubierto*. In 2007 smoking was banned from restaurants throughout Argentina, and most establishments enforce the ban.

VEGETARIANS & VEGANS

Recently, health foods and organic products have become more accessible in Argentine cities, but outside Buenos Aires vegetarian restaurants are scarce. Most menus do include a few vegetarian choices, and pastas are a nearly ubiquitous (and usually excellent) option, provided you don't order a meat sauce, of course. At *parrillas*, salads, baked potatoes, *provoleta* (a thick slice of grilled provolone cheese) and, occasionally, roasted vegetables, all make good alternatives to meat. Outside the *parrilla*, you'll find plenty of vegetarian options, including *pizzerías* and *empanaderías* (empanada shops). At the latter, look for empanadas made with *acelga* (Swiss chard) and *choclo* (corn), both generally free of meat.

Sin carne means 'without meat,' and the words *soy vegetariano/a* ('I'm a vegetarian') will come in handy when explaining to an Argentine why you don't eat their nation's renowned steaks.

Vegans will have a much harder time than vegetarians in Argentina. Pasta, often homemade, can include eggs, and fried vegetables can be fried in lard. There isn't a word for 'vegan' in Argentina. You'll need to be creative to survive here. Some tips: *fugazza* is a cheeseless pizza often served at *pizzerías*; and Indian restaurants do exist in Buenos Aires. Good luck.

For tips on where to eat *sin carne* in Buenos Aires, see p116.

EATING WITH KIDS

Argentines adore children, and eating out with the kids is common. A number of restaurants incorporate special menus for the junior brigade, but all (save perhaps the five-star outfits) will cater to your reasonable demands – from serving half portions to preparing something special in the kitchen.

Some early Jesuit priests tried to ban the Guaraní from drinking *mate* during church services, arguing that all that liquid intake gave rise to the need to urinate – distracting them from the sermon.

Especially in Buenos Aires, look out for *panettone* (a large, muffin-shaped sweet bread originally from Italy) around Christmas time – some of the loaves are as beautiful as they are delicious.

At many finer Argentine restaurants, you'll be charged a per-person *cubierto*; this is a small 'fee' for bread and the use of utensils. It's not the tip, which should be paid separately.

EAT YOUR WORDS

Want to make sure you don't order cow brains or testicles by mistake? Get behind the cuisine scene by getting to know the language. For pronunciation guidelines, see p629. For useful phrases at a restaurant, see p632.

Food Glossary

MEAT

achuras	a-*choo*-ras	organ meats
bife	*bee*-fe	general name for steak (*bife de chorizo* is thick and boneless, similar to New York strip)
cabrito	ka-*bree*-to	goat (kid)
carbonada	kar-bo-*na*-da	typical beef, corn, pumpkin and vegetable stew, with peaches in season
centolla	sen-*to*-zha	southern king crab
cerdo	*ser*-do	pork
chinchulines	cheen-choo-*lee*-nes	small intestine
chivito	chee-*vee*-to	young goat (kid)
choripán	cho-ree-*pan*	Argentina's answer to the hot dog, made with spicy *chorizo*
chorizo	cho-*ree*-so	sausage (also *salchicha* and *morcilla*)
churrasco	choo-*ras*-ko	grilled beef
ciervo	*syer*-vo	venison
cordero patagónico	kor-*de*-ro pa-ta-*go*-nee-ko	Patagonian lamb, celebrated for its lean, herb-flavored meat
criadillas	kree-a-*dee*-zhas	testicles
empanada	em-pa-*na*-da	pastry similar to a turnover, usually filled with beef and fried or baked
hígado	*ee*-ga-do	liver
jamón	kha-*mon*	ham
langostino	lan-gos-*tee*-no	shrimp or prawn
lechón	le-*chon*	suckling pig
lengua	*len*-gwa	tongue
matambre	ma-*tam*-bre	flank or skirt steak, usually stuffed, rolled up and eaten cold
mollejas	mo-*zhe*-khas	sweetbreads; either the thymus or pancreas, a popular part of an *asado*
morcilla	mor-*see*-zha	black pudding (blood sausage)
panceta	pan-*se*-ta	bacon
pavo	*pa*-vo	turkey
pejerrey	pe-khe-*ray*	a very fine river fish
pollo	*po*-zho	chicken
salpicón	sal-pi-*kon*	a vegetable and meat (usually chicken, tuna or beef) salad eaten cold
sesos	*se*-sos	brains
surubí	soo-roo-*bee*	large, delicate river fish
ternera	ter-*ne*-ra	veal
ubre	*oo*-bre	udder

OTHER FOOD

alfajor	al-fa-*khor*	a sandwich biscuit (cookie) usually filled with *dulce de leche*
arroz	a-*ros*	rice
budín de choclo	boo-*deen* de *chok*-lo	a corn souffle
chimichurri	chee-mee-*choo*-ri	an Argentine herb marinade, also used as a dressing

dulce de batata	*dool*·se de ba·*ta*·ta	sweet potato (yam) preserve, frequently eaten with cheese
dulce de leche	*dool*·se de *le*·che	caramelized milk, Argentina's most popular sweet
dulce de membrillo	*dool*·se de mem·*bree*·zho	quince preserve, frequently eaten with cheese
escabeche	es·ka·*be*·che	an oil, vinegar and herb marinade
helado	e·*la*·do	ice cream
mantecol	man·te·*kol*	sweet made with ground peanuts and sugar
medialuna	me·dya·*loo*·na	croissant
morron	mo·*ron*	red pepper
palta	*pal*·ta	avocado
pan dulce	pan *dool*·se	a sweet bread containing dried fruit, nuts and some brandy, similar to *panettone*
puchero	poo·*che*·ro	local version of a French *pot au feu* or the Spanish *cocido*
torta galesa	*tor*·ta ga·*le*·sa	a rich fruit cake, created by the Welsh colony in Patagonia

Environment

Argentina. For anyone raised on *National Geographic* and adventure stories, the name is loaded with images: the Magellanic penguins of the Patagonian coast, the windswept mysteries of Tierra del Fuego, the vast emptiness of the pampas, the towering Andes, and the raging Iguazú Falls. Spanning from the subtropics to the edge of Antarctica, the country is simply unmatched in natural wonders.

THE LAND

Argentina is big – *really* big. With a total land area of about 2.8 million sq km, excluding the South Atlantic islands and the Antarctic quadrant claimed as national territory, Argentina is the world's eighth-largest country, only slightly smaller than India. It stretches from La Quiaca on the Bolivian border, where summers can be brutally hot, to Ushuaia in Tierra del Fuego, where winters are experienced only by seasoned locals and the nuttiest of travelers. It's a distance of nearly 3500km, an expanse that encompasses a vast array of environments and terrain. The Andean chain runs the length of Argentina, from the Bolivian border in the north to the South Atlantic, where it disappears into the islands of Tierra del Fuego.

The Central & Northern Andes

In the extreme north, the Andes are basically the southern extension of the Bolivian *altiplano*, a thinly populated high plain between 3000m and 4000m in altitude, punctuated by even higher volcanic peaks. Although days can be surprisingly hot (sunburn is a serious hazard at high altitude), frosts occur almost nightly. The Andean northwest (p243) is also known as the *puna*.

Further south, in the arid provinces of San Juan and Mendoza (p337), the Andes climb to their highest altitudes, with 6962m Cerro Aconcagua (p356) topping out as the highest point in the western hemisphere. Here, their highest peaks lie covered in snow through the winter. Although rainfall on the eastern slopes is inadequate for crops, perennial streams descend from the Andes and provide irrigation water, which has brought prosperity to the wine-producing Cuyo region (the provinces of Mendoza, San Juan and San Luis). Winter in San Juan province is the season of the *zonda*, a hot, dry wind descending from the Andes that causes dramatic temperature increases (see p364).

> At its mouth, the Río de la Plata is an amazing 200km wide, making it the widest river in the world – though some consider it more like a river estuary.

The Chaco

East of the Andes and the Andean foothills, much of northern Argentina consists of subtropical lowlands. This arid area, known as the Argentine Chaco, is part of the much larger Gran Chaco (p233), an extremely rugged, largely uninhabited region that extends into Bolivia, Paraguay and Brazil. The Argentine Chaco encompasses the provinces of Chaco, Formosa and Santiago del Estero, the western reaches of Jujuy, Catamarca and Salta provinces, and the northernmost parts of Santa Fe and Córdoba.

The Chaco has a well-defined winter dry season, and summer everywhere in the Chaco is brutally hot. Rainfall decreases as you move east to west. The wet Chaco, which encompasses the eastern parts of Chaco and Formosa provinces and northeast Santa Fe, receives more rain than the dry Chaco, which covers central and western Chaco and Formosa provinces, most of Santiago del Estero and parts of Salta.

Mesopotamia

Also referred to as the Litoral (as in littoral), Mesopotamia is the name for the region of northeast Argentina (p177) between the Río Paraná and Río Uruguay. It's a region defined, as its names suggest, by its rivers, both a dominant part of the landscape. Here, the climate is mild, and rainfall is heavy in the provinces of Entre Ríos and Corrientes, which make up most of Mesopotamia. Hot and humid Misiones province, a politically important province surrounded on three sides by Brazil and Paraguay, contains part of Iguazú Falls, which descend from southern Brazil's Paraná Plateau. Shallow summer flooding is common throughout Mesopotamia and into the eastern Chaco, but only the immediate river floodplains become inundated in the west. Mesopotamia's rainfall is evenly distributed throughout the year.

Iguazú Falls consists of more than 275 individual falls that tumble from heights as much as 80m. They stretch for nearly 3km and are arguably the most amazing waterfalls on earth.

The Pampas & Atlantic Coast

Bordered by the Atlantic Ocean and Patagonia and stretching nearly to Córdoba and the Central Sierras, the pampas (p140) are Argentina's agricultural heartland. Geographically, this region covers the provinces of Buenos Aires and La Pampa, as well as southern chunks of Santa Fe and Córdoba.

This area can be subdivided into the humid pampas, along the Litoral, and the arid pampas of the western interior and the south. More than a third of the country's population lives in and around Buenos Aires, where the humid climate resembles Sydney's or New York City's in the spring, summer and autumn. Annual rainfall exceeds 900mm, but several hundred kilometers westward it's less than half that. Buenos Aires' winters are relatively mild.

The pampas are an almost completely level plain of wind-borne loess (a fine-grained silt or clay) and river-deposited sediments. The absence of nearly any rises in the land to speak of makes the area vulnerable to flooding from the relatively few, small rivers that cross it. Only the granitic Sierra de Tandil (484m; p150) and the Sierra de la Ventana (1273m; p154), in southwestern Buenos Aires province, and the Sierra de Lihué Calel (p158) disrupt the otherwise monotonous terrain.

The largest dinosaur ever discovered was the Argentinosaurus huinculensis, uncovered in Neuquén province; the herbivore measured a massive 40m long and 18m high.

Moving south along the Atlantic coast from the Argentine capital, the province of Buenos Aires features the sandy, often dune-backed beaches that attracted the development of seaside resorts such as Mar del Plata and Necochea. Inland it's mostly the grasslands of the pampas. South of Viedma, cliffs begin to appear but the landscape remains otherwise desolate for its entire stretch south through Patagonia.

Patagonia & the Lake District

Ever-alluring Patagonia is the region of Argentina south of the Río Colorado, which flows southeast from the Andes and passes just north of the city of Neuquén. The Lake District is a subregion of Patagonia. Province-wise, Patagonia consists of Neuquén, Río Negro, Chubut and Santa Cruz. It's separated from Chilean Patagonia by the Andes.

The Andean cordillera is high enough that Pacific storms drop most of their rain and snow on the Chilean side. In the extreme southern reaches of Patagonia, however, enough snow and ice still accumulate to form the largest southern hemisphere glaciers outside of Antarctica.

East of the Andean foothills, the cool, arid Patagonian steppes support huge flocks of sheep, whose wool is almost all exported to Europe. For such a southerly location, temperatures are relatively mild, even in winter, when more uniform atmospheric pressure moderates the strong gales that blow most of the year.

Except for urban centers such as Comodoro Rivadavia (the center of coastal Patagonia's petroleum industry) and Río Gallegos (the hub for wool and meatpacking), Patagonia is thinly populated. Tidal ranges along the

GREEN ARGENTINA *Sarah Gilbert*

If you're in Argentina long enough, you're sure to hear a local say, in tones of either exaspera-
tion or resignation, that the root of the country's troubles is this: *'No hay control de nada!'* In
other words, nothing is organized, and nothing is under control. One look at the filth floating
in Buenos Aires' Río Riachuelo or the rampant urban development gobbling up the country's
coastline confirms this theory.

The unfortunate irony is that while Argentina has one of the best environmental protection
programs in South America, the rules are very poorly enforced. Conservationists say this is the
single biggest problem facing Argentina's natural environment.

Argentina is a developing country where around 10 million people live in poverty – one-third
of those in extreme poverty. It is also a country with vast natural resources and large tracts of
wilderness. This combination creates a dilemma faced by many countries in a similar position –
how to improve the day-to-day lives of their populations using what resources are available
without too much negative environmental impact. So while it's understandable that Argentina
wants to develop economically to lift its citizens' standard of living, this often comes at the
expense of the environment. At the same time, cleaning up the rivers or protecting the forests
can all too often seem less urgent than the many other critical problems that take up the lion's
share of government and social-sector resources. And as with most countries, the costs of failing
to properly protect its natural resources is not factored into Argentina's economic formula.

Of course, it's not just domestic policy and development that are having an impact. Global
climate change is affecting Argentina, too, with Patagonia's melting glaciers grabbing frequent
headlines here. Argentina is already South America's second-highest carbon emitter, and increased
development is creating ever more energy consumption. At the same time, according to Greenpeace,
a football field's worth of the country's native forest is cut down each hour.

Conservation in Argentina

Super-rich in biodiversity, Argentina boasts 18 distinct ecological regions with 20,000 plants, 700 fish,
150 amphibian, 250 reptile, 350 mammal and 1000 bird species. Argentines are justifiably proud of this
immense natural wealth and of the network of national parks and reserves that help protect it.

On the whole, though, Argentina's resources have been overexploited and imperiled over the
300-odd years since Europeans arrived. At the beginning of the 20th century there were 1.05
million sq km of native forest and jungle. There are now 320,000 sq km left, and what is left has
been compromised. Forests, fish stocks, water and soil have all been overexploited and continue
to be so, and environmental awareness remains fairly low.

On the bright side, however, Argentina has lost very few of its native species since colonization, and compared to most countries, it is still full of wild, untouched places. Meanwhile,
important and creative conservation work is being done. Argentina's foremost environmental
organization, **Fundación Vida Silvestre** (www.vidasilvestre.org.ar), has its own network of reserves,
occasionally passing areas on to national parks for protection. Vida Silvestre works closely with
private landowners to create *refugios* (protected areas managed by joint agreement) that help
preserve wildlife and indigenous plant species throughout the country.

Sustainable Travel

Tourism has grown exponentially since the 2001 currency crisis made Argentina affordable to a
greater number of travelers. This is a plus for the economy, of course, but in many ways it's a plus
for the environment, too. Argentina's extraordinary natural beauty is its main attraction, and the
increase in tourism revenue proves that the country's wild places are worth preserving for economic
as well as environmental reasons. Nonetheless, with the increase in visits to all national parks, it's
important to note that the tourism boom places a strain on Argentina's fragile ecosystems.

Sustainable travel and ecotourism are still fairly novel concepts in Argentina, and are often misun-
derstood. If you see the 'eco' tag attached to a tour group or lodge, it's as likely as not that it simply
means 'something to do with nature.' As yet, there's no official certification program for the travel
industry, and anyone can hang a tour-guide sign on their door. Until a proper scheme is in place, it's up
to travelers to support those businesses that are helping develop a sustainable tourism industry.

While true ecolodges may be scarce, there are plenty of travel options in Argentina that contribute to the wealth and wellbeing of Argentina's people, cultural heritage and natural environment, whether it's a stay at a historic *estancia* (ranch) or buying organic wine from an Argentine-owned winery.

Sustainable travel also involves energy-saving and carbon-reducing practices. Where possible, rent a bike or a horse rather than a car. While popular, activities such as quad biking and jet-skiing can have a negative impact on wildlife and create unnecessary noise pollution. Even if locals don't always seem to get it, respectful travelers can easily take care with their garbage. In hotel rooms try using the fan instead of the air-conditioner, and re-use your towels.

The harsh truth for travelers who want to reduce their carbon footprint is that flying is the single worst thing you can do. Unfortunately, in a country as large as Argentina, it's hard for most of us to avoid planes, and the absence of a fast and reliable railway system doesn't help. Carbon offsetting schemes are one way to mitigate the negative effects of your flights (see p615).

Sustainable Gems

The popularity of rural tourism, the resilience of indigenous communities and the creativity and enterprise of Argentina's people all mean that you can find plenty of ways to contribute to the country's sustainable development while traveling here. For starters, see this book's GreenDex (p666).

Argentina has a rich agricultural history, and throughout the country you'll find historic *estancias*, which often conserve large green spaces and forested areas, while helping to preserve part of the country's rural and architectural heritage. A few use alternative energy and nearly all of them are Argentine-owned, employing locals and buying produce from local farmers.

You'll find *estancias* listed throughout this guide, including standouts such as **Estancia y Bodega Colomé** (see p275), where alternative energy and Argentina's oldest vines help produce excellent organic wine; and the Unesco World Heritage–listed **Estancia Santa Catalina** (p324), whose owners blend tourism with heritage preservation and happily inform guests of the area's rich history.

Argentina's indigenous tribes may be less visible than their counterparts in neighboring countries such as Peru and Bolivia, but they have held on to their traditions in many regions, particularly in the north. You can help support economic development in communities by buying handicrafts directly from indigenous artisans, some of whom run their own cooperatives, or by visiting enterprises such as the Mapuche-operated **Batea Mahuida ski park** (p386). Also, **Anda Responsible Travel** (see p94) runs tours that benefit local communities around Argentina.

Argentina's national parks (see p76) offer an impressive array of spectacular landscapes to explore, while provincial and municipal parks protect green spaces and unique ecosystems. According to the Fundación Vida Silvestre, tourism is a threat to nearly all of Argentina's parks. Too often success is measured in terms of the volume of visitors, without considering their effects on the wildlife and fauna. The worst example of this is Iguazú, which welcomes over a million visitors per year without measuring their impact. One park that's doing better at managing human intervention is **Reserva Provincial Esteros del Iberá** (p200), where boat trips through the marshes are controlled.

Interpretive material can be scant in many parks. Eco-conscious tour companies offer an opportunity to learn more about the environment you're in. Worth recommending is **Seriema Nature Tours** (www.seriemanaturetours.com), which works closely with the Ornithological Association of Argentina and runs tours throughout the country for bird-watchers, botanists and nature photographers.

Environmental & Social Organizations

Greenpeace (www.greenpeace.org.ar, in Spanish) and Argentine environmental NGO **Fundación Vida Silvestre** (www.vidasilvestre.org.ar, in Spanish) operate nationally in Argentina. Greenpeace does its usual crucial mix of public awareness and lobbying, while Vida Silvestre is on the ground, working with landowners and nature lovers to preserve important ecosystems throughout the country.

NGOs in the social sector are also participating. **Responde** (www.responde.org.ar, in Spanish) helps small villages to build healthy local economies, often in the form of sustainable tourism, thus preserving regional culture and stemming uncontrolled urban sprawl in the big cities, while the many NGOs in Buenos Aires' slums are campaigning to improve the quality of the urban environment.

For information on volunteering opportunities with NGOs for travelers, see p611.

Atlantic coast are too great for major port facilities. In the valley of the Río Negro and at the outlet of the Río Chubut (near the town of Trelew), people farm and cultivate fruit orchards.

Tierra del Fuego

The world's southernmost permanently inhabited territory, Tierra del Fuego (aka Land of Fire) consists of one large island (Isla Grande), unequally divided between Chile and Argentina, and many smaller ones, some of which have been the source of longtime contention between the two countries. When Europeans first passed through the Strait of Magellan (which separates Isla Grande from the Patagonian mainland), the fires stemmed from the activities of the now endangered Yaghan people; nowadays, the fires result from the flaring of natural gas in the region's oil fields.

The northern half of Isla Grande, resembling the Patagonian steppes, is devoted to sheep grazing, while its southern half is mountainous and partly covered by forests and glaciers. As in Patagonia, winter conditions are rarely extreme, although hiking and outdoor camping are not advisable except for experienced mountaineers. For most visitors, though, the brief daylight hours during this season may be a greater deterrent than the weather.

The *carpincho*, or capybara, is the world's largest rodent, weighing up to 65kg. Its skin makes a beautiful spotted leather and its meat tastes like pork. Despite overhunting in some places, they're not endangered; it's a good thing they breed like rodents!

WILDLIFE

With such variances in terrain and such great distances, it's no wonder Argentina supports a wide range of flora and fauna. Subtropical rainforests, palm savannas, high-altitude deserts and steppes, humid-temperate grasslands, alpine and sub-Antarctic forests and rich coastal areas all support their own special life forms. The most exciting part is that visitors – especially those from the northern hemisphere – will find many of Argentina's plants and animals unfamiliar. Take the capybara, for instance, the world's largest rodent, or the araucaria (pehuén), a conifer appropriately deemed the monkey puzzle tree in English. To protect these environments, Argentina has created an extensive system of national and provincial parks (p76), which are often the best places to experience the country's unique wildlife.

Animals

Northeast Argentina boasts the country's most diverse animal life. One of the best areas on the continent to enjoy wildlife is the swampy Esteros del Iberá (p200), in Corrientes province, where animals such as swamp deer, capybara and caiman, along with many large migratory birds, are common. It's comparable – arguably even better – than Brazil's more famous Pantanal.

Peninsula Valdés (p430) is one of only two places on earth where killer whales (orcas) have been known to hunt sea lions by beaching themselves. You'd be *very* lucky to witness this phenomenon, however.

CAPYBARAS Andy Symington

Treading, with its webbed feet, a very fine line between cute and ugly, the capybara is a sizable semiaquatic beast that you're bound to encounter in the Iberá area. Weighing in at up to 75kg, the carpincho, as it's known in Spanish, is the world's largest rodent.

Very much at home both on land and in the water, the gentle and vaguely comical creature eats aquatic plants and grasses in great quantity. They form small herds, with a dominant male living it up with four to six females. The male can be recognized by a protrusion on its forehead that emits a territory-marking scent. The lovably roly-poly babies are born in spring.

Though protected in the Iberá area, the capybara is farmed and hunted elsewhere for its skin, which makes a soft, flexible leather. The meat is also considered a delicacy in traditional communities.

In the drier northwest the most conspicuous animal is the domestic llama, but its wild cousins, the guanaco and vicuña, can also be seen. Your odds of seeing them are excellent if you travel by road through Parque Nacional Los Cardones (p272) to Salta. Their yellow fur is often an extraordinary puff of color against the cactus-studded backdrop. Many migratory birds, including flamingos, inhabit the high saline lakes of the Andean northwest.

In less densely settled areas, including the arid pampas of La Pampa province, guanacos and foxes are not unusual sights. Many bodies of water, both permanent and seasonal, provide migratory bird habitats.

Most notable in Patagonia and Tierra del Fuego is the wealth of coastal wildlife, ranging from Magellanic penguins, cormorants and gulls to sea lions, fur seals, elephant seals, orcas and whales. Several coastal reserves, from Río Negro province south to Tierra del Fuego, are home to enormous concentrations of wildlife that are one of the region's greatest visitor attractions. Inland on the Patagonian steppe, as in the northwest, the guanaco is the most conspicuous mammal, but the flightless rhea, resembling the Old World ostrich, runs in flocks across the plains.

For more on Patagonia's marine wildlife, see the boxed text, p434.

Plants

When it comes to plant life, the country's most diverse regions are in northeast Argentina, the Lake District, the Patagonian Andes and the subtropical forests of northwest Argentina.

The high northern Andes are dry and often barren, and vegetation is limited to ichu (sparse bunch grasses) and low, widely spaced shrubs, known collectively as tola. In Jujuy and La Rioja provinces, however, huge, vertically branched cardón cacti add a rugged beauty to an otherwise empty landscape. In the Andean precordillera, between the Chaco and the Andes proper, lies a strip of dense, subtropical montane cloud forest known as the Yungas. Spanning parts of Salta, Jujuy and Tucumán provinces, the Yungas are kept lush by heavy summertime rains, and are one of the most biologically diverse regions in the country. The Yungas are home to three national parks: Parque Nacional Calilegua (p250), Parque Nacional Baritú (p252) and Parque Nacional El Rey (p251).

The wet Chaco is home to grasslands and gallery forests with numerous tree species, including the quebracho colorado and caranday palm. The dry Chaco, although extremely parched, is still thick with vegetation. Its taller trees include the quebracho colorado, quebracho blanco, algarrobo, palo santo, and a dense understory of low-growing spiny trees and shrubs. Both quebracho and algarrobo trees produce highly valued hard woods that have lead to widespread deforestation throughout both regions of the Chaco.

In Mesopotamia rainfall is sufficient to support swampy lowland forests as well as upland savanna. Misiones' native vegetation is mostly dense subtropical forest, though its upper elevations are studded with araucaria pines.

The once lush native grasses of the Argentine pampas have suffered under grazing pressure and the proliferation of grain farms that produce cash crops such as soy beans. Today very little native vegetation remains, except along watercourses like the Río Paraná.

Most of Patagonia lies in the rain shadow of the Chilean Andes, so the vast steppes of southeastern Argentina resemble the sparse grasslands of the arid Andean highlands. Closer to the border there are pockets of dense *Nothofagus* (southern beech) and coniferous woodlands that owe their existence to the winter storms that sneak over the cordillera. Northern Tierra del Fuego is a grassy extension of the Patagonian steppe, but the heavy rainfall of the mountainous southern half supports verdant southern beech forests.

The funny-looking *araucaria araucana*, or monkey puzzle tree, grows in the Chilean and Argentine Lake Districts (p389). It has long scaly branches and produces edible pine nuts.

Conservación Patagónica (www.patagonialand trust.org) has purchased 460,000 acres in Patagonia and Esteros del Iberá in order to preserve them.

NATIONAL PARKS & PROTECTED AREAS

Park	Features	Activities	Best Time to Visit
Monumento Natural Laguna de los Pozuelos (p260)	High-altitude lake; abundant bird life, including three species of flamingos	bird-watching, walking, wildlife watching	Nov-Mar
Parque Nacional Baritú (p252)	Nearly virgin subtropical montane forest	walking, wildlife watching, visiting traditional communities	Jun-Sep
Parque Nacional Calilegua (p250)	Transitional lowland forest, subtropical montane forest and subalpine grassland	walking, wildlife watching, bird-watching	May-Nov
Parque Nacional Los Cardones (p272)	Montane desert park with striking cardón cacti and wandering guanacos	walking, photography, geology	Sep-May
Parque Nacional El Rey (p251)	Lush subtropical forest and coniferous Andean forest	walking, wildlife watching, bird-watching	May-Nov
Parque Nacional Río Pilcomayo (p242)	Subtropical marshlands and palm savannas; colorful birds, caimans and nocturnal mammals	swimming with piranhas, boat trips, bird-watching	Jun-Sep
Parque Nacional Chaco (p237)	Dense, subtropical thorn forests, marshes, palm savannas and colorful birds; very accessible but rarely visited	walking, 4WD trips, tree admiration	Apr-Oct
Parque Nacional Iguazú (p223)	Home of the awesome Iguazú Falls; also subtropical rainforest and abundant birds, mammals and reptiles	walking, boat trips, gawking	Oct-Mar
Parque Nacional Mburucuyá (p199)	Quebracho and palm forests, estuaries and islands; capybaras, foxes, gazunchos, river wolves and swamp deer (swamp deer?!)	walking, wildlife watching, bird-watching	year-round
Reserva Provincial Esteros del Iberá (p200)	Tranquil wetland reserve; arguably a better wildlife site than Brazil's Pantanal	boat trips, wildlife, bird-watching, horseback riding	Mar-Dec famous
Parque Nacional El Palmar (p208)	On the Río Uruguay; home to the last extensive stands of yatay-palm savanna	walking, horseback riding, cycling, tree admiration	year-round
Parque Nacional Talampaya (p305)	Rich desert scenery and extraordinary geological, paleontological and archaeological resources	geology, cycling, 4WD trips, walking	Sep-Nov & Mar-May
Parque Nacional Copo (p293)	Dense dry Chaco forest, mostly flat, home to the last of the region's threatened wildlife	walking, wildlife and bird-watching	Apr-Oct
Parque Provincial Ischigualasto (p373)	Known as Valley of the Moon; surreally scenic paleontological preserve with wild rock formations	hiking, bike tours, full-moon tours	Apr-Sep
Parque Nacional El Leoncito (p371)	760 sq km of barren Andean precordillera; home to guanacos, foxes and peregrine falcons	hiking, landsailing, astronomy	year-round
Parque Nacional Quebrada del Condorito (p328)	Stunning rocky grasslands across the Pampa de Achala in the Sierras Grande; condors, condors, condors	hiking, condor watching	Apr-Sep
Parque Nacional Sierra de las Quijadas (p334)	Polychrome desert canyons and the site of major dinosaur discoveries; wonderfully quiet	photography, paleontology, hiking	Apr-Sep
Parque Provincial Aconcagua (p356)	Home of the western hemisphere's highest peak, 6960m Aconcagua	hiking, mountain climbing	Dec-Mar
Parque Provincial Volcán Tupungato (p357)	Centerpiece: 6650m summit of Tupungato, a more challenging climb than nearby Aconcagua	hiking, mountain climbing	Dec-Mar

Park	Features	Activities	Best Time to Visit
Parque Nacional Lihué Calel (p158)	Pinkish peaks, isolated valleys, petroglyphs and a surprising range of fauna and flora	hiking, archeological interest, wildlife spotting	Sep-Oct, Mar-Apr
Parque Provincial Payunia (p362)	Boasts a higher concentration of volcanic cones (over 800 of them) than anywhere else in the world	hiking, photography, bird-watching	year-round
Parque Nacional Laguna Blanca (p380)	Desolate lake, lots of nothingness; ancient volcanoes and lava flows, nesting colonies of black-necked swans, Andean flamingos	hiking, photography, bird-watching	Sep-Dec
Parque Nacional Lanín (p389)	Extensive forests of monkey puzzle trees (araucaria) and southern beech capped by the perfect cone of Volcán Lanín	hiking, photography, visiting Mapuche communities	Dec-Mar
Parque Nacional Nahuel Huapi (p410)	An area of 7580 sq km around the exquisite Lago Nahuel Huapi; lakes, views, trees, fun – and lots of people	hiking, snow sports, fishing	Dec-Mar
Parque Nacional Los Arrayanes (p399)	Tiny park inside Parque Nacional Nahuel Huapi; protects stands of the unique arrayán tree	hiking, photography, boat cruises	Dec-Mar
Parque Nacional Lago Puelo (p417)	Lago Puelo, an aquamarine, low-altitude lake set among high Andean peaks	fishing, boating, hiking	Dec-Mar
Parque Nacional Los Alerces (p465)	Unique Valdivian forest, which includes impressive specimens of the redwood-like alerce tree	hiking, boating, fishing	Nov-Apr
Reserva Faunística Península Valdés (p430)	Wildlife enthusiast's dream; whales, sea lions, Magellanic penguins	wildlife watching, diving, boat tours	Jun-Dec
Reserva Provincial Punta Tombo (p441)	Known for its enormous nesting colony of burrowing Magellanic penguins	wildlife watching, walking	Sep-Mar
Parque Nacional Perito Moreno (p473)	Awesome glacial lakes, alpine peaks, Andean-Patagonian forest and guanacos; way off the beaten track	hiking, wildlife watching, horseback riding	Nov-Mar
Monumento Natural Bosques Petrificados (p450)	Isolated park featuring immense specimens of petrified *Proaraucaria* trees	hiking, fossil-finding	year-round
Parque Nacional Monte León (p453)	Argentina's first coastal national park outside Tierra del Fuego,	hiking, wildlife watching, bird-watching	year-round
Parque Nacional Los Glaciares (p478 & p487)	Home to Argentina's must-sees: the famous Glaciar Perito Merino and the awesome pinnacles of the Fitz Roy Range	hiking, glaciers, backpacking, climbing	Nov-Mar
Parque Nacional Tierra del Fuego (p528)	Argentina's first shoreline national park: alpine glaciers and peaks, marine mammals, seabirds, shorebirds and extensive southern beech forests	hiking, kayaking	Nov-Mar

* Parks are listed generally north to south, west to east.

NATIONAL & PROVINCIAL PARKS

Argentina's national parks lure visitors from around the world. One of Latin America's first national-park systems, Argentina's dates from the turn of the 20th century, when explorer and surveyor Francisco P Moreno donated 75 sq km near Bariloche to the state in return for a guarantee that the parcel would be preserved for the enjoyment of all Argentines. This area is now part of Parque Nacional Nahuel Huapi (p410) in the Andean Lake District.

Since then the country has established many other parks and reserves, mostly but not exclusively in the Andean region. There are also important provincial parks and reserves, such as the Reserva Faunística Península Valdés (p430), which do not fall within the national-park system but deserve attention. In general, the national parks are more visitor-oriented than the provincial parks, but there are exceptions: Parque Nacional Perito Moreno has few visitor services, for example, while Península Valdés has many.

Before seeing the parks, visitors to Buenos Aires should stop in at the **Administración de Parques Nacionales** (National Parks Administration; ☎ 4311-6633; www .parquesnacionales.gov.ar; Santa Fe 690) for maps and brochures, which are often in short supply in the parks. Most national parks are free, but some charge an entry fee of around AR$25. The premier parks, however, cost the most: Parque Nacional (PN) Iguazú and PN Tierra del Fuego, for example, both charge AR$50, and PN Los Glaciares charges AR$75. (Argentines and children pay less.)

Admission to provincial parks varies in cost from free to AR$40, but official fees can be deceiving. At some parks you'd have to set off flares just to find someone to pay; at others (such as Parque Provincial Ischigualasto in San Juan), you may be required to hire a guide, which can increase the price by anywhere from AR$20 to AR$220 per person. At Parque Provincial Aconcagua, hiking permits cost AR$150 to AR$300 and climbing permits AR$500 to AR$1500. See p76 for a list of parks.

ENVIRONMENTAL ISSUES

Although Argentina boasts one of South America's largest systems of parks and reserves, much of those areas – not to mention the extremely sensitive regions around and between them – face serious threat. Deforestation is a major issue in the Chaco, where cultivation of genetically modified soy, sunflower crops and lumber are impacting on the health of the forests. It's equally troubling in the Yungas and the subtropical rainforests of Misiones province, where tea plantations and timber companies continue to destroy some of Argentina's most biologically diverse areas. The result is that many of the country's protected areas, especially those in the Gran Chaco and the Mesopotamia, are virtual islands in a sea of environmental degradation.

With Argentina's economic collapse and the country's subsequent ability to compete on the international market, production of soy has skyrocketed and become Argentina's single most important cash crop. Farmers throughout the pampas now plant monocrops of genetically modified, herbicide-resistant soy, which is rapidly depleting the ground of its minerals, accelerating deforestation and contributing to high levels of herbicide in soils throughout the region.

The good news is that 2007 saw the passing of the Ley de Bosques (National Forest Law), which levied a one-year nationwide moratorium on the clearing of native forests until proper management regulations could be established. The law, largely a project of Greenpeace Argentina and Fundación Vida Silvestre (see the boxed text, p72), was a major victory for environmentalists. However, Cristina Kirchner delayed putting the law into effect for over a

---

Fundación Vida Silvestre (www.vidasilvestre.org. ar, in Spanish) is one of Argentina's top environmental organizations and has partnered with the WWF since 1988.

US environmentalist Doug Tompkins, founder of The North Face and Esprit clothing companies, owns about 8000 sq km of land in Argentine and Chilean Patagonia, as well as in northeastern Argentina. Most of his land is set aside for conservation.

Most of Patagonia's glaciers are shrinking at an alarming rate, but the active Perito Moreno Glacier (p487) is considered 'stable' – it's advancing at roughly the same pace as it calves ice.

UNESCO WORLD HERITAGE SITES

The UN Educational, Scientific and Cultural Organization (Unesco) has designated the following sites in Argentina World Heritage sites. The first was Parque Nacional Los Glaciares (1981) and the most recent was the magnificent Quebrada de Humahuaca (2003).

- Cueva de las Manos (p472)
- Jesuit *estancias* (ranches) of Córdoba province: (p324, p325 and p324)
- Jesuit Missions of the Guaraní: San Ignacio Miní (p218), Santa Ana (p217) and Loreto (p217)
- Manzana Jesuítica (Jesuit Block), Córdoba (p312)
- Parque Nacional Iguazú (p223)
- Parque Nacional Los Glaciares (p478 and p487)
- Parque Nacional Talampaya (p305)
- Parque Provincial Ischigualasto (p373)
- Quebrada de Humahuaca (p252)
- Reserva Faunística Península Valdés (p430)

year but in February 2009 was finally spurred on to implement it by activists who demanded action.

Another high-profile issue is global warming, which, according to scientists, is taking a major toll on the Southern Patagonian Ice Field, which is melting far faster today than it was before the 1990s. Ironically, global warming and glacial retreat have become such big news these days that more people than ever are booking tours to see Argentina's glaciers and Antarctica before they're…gone forever?

As international headlines point south, national headlines point north – to the Botnia paper mill that opened in 2007 across the Río Uruguay from the Argentine town of Gualeguaychú (p203). Owned by Finnish company Botnia, the Uruguayan mill has sparked widespread protest from Argentina, which views it as an environmental catastrophe. For more, see p536.

The Canadian company Barrick Gold currently operates a massive goldmine in San Juan province that has taken a dramatic toll on both the landscape and the people. Locals and environmentalists in and around the town of San José de Jáchal (p371), as well as winemakers and other groups from the province, have fervently protested Barrick's use of highly toxic cyanide, which is contaminating both soil and groundwater. In late 2009 the company began construction of its highly controversial Pascua Lama gold-and-silver mining project on the Argentina-Chile border, with the goal to begin production in 2012. The project received intense criticism after reports surfaced that Barrick planned to 'relocate' three Andean glaciers (by some estimates, that meant removal of 20 hectares of ice) in order to mine. Chile approved the mine but forbade the transfer of glaciers, and Barrick has stated that no ice will be moved.

Argentina is the world's third-highest producer of soybeans, after the USA and Brazil, but interestingly, Argentines don't really eat soy. More than 90% of the country's soybeans are exported.

Buenos Aires

Mix together a beautiful European-like city with attractive residents (call them *porteños*), gourmet cuisine, awesome shopping, a frenzied nightlife and top-drawer activities, and you get Buenos Aires, a cosmopolitan metropolis with both slick neighborhoods and equally downtrodden areas – but that's part of the appeal. It's an elegant, seductive place with a ragged edge, laced with old-world languor and yet full of contemporary attitude. BA is somehow strangely familiar, but unlike any other city in the world.

In between cutting-edge designer boutiques, ritzy neighborhoods and grand parks are unkempt streets full of spewing buses and bustling fervor. Seek out the classic BA: the old-world cafes, colonial architecture, fun outdoor markets and diverse communities. Rub shoulders with the formerly rich and famous in Recoleta's cemetery, making sure to sidestep the ubiquitous dog piles on the sidewalks. Fill your belly at a *parrilla* (steak restaurant), then spend the night partying away in Palermo Viejo's trendiest dance club. Hunt for that antique gem in a dusty San Telmo shop, or visit on Sunday for the *barrio's* spectacularly popular fair. Learn to sweep your leg dancing the sultry tango, and then attend a super-passionate *fútbol* match between River and Boca. These unforgettable adventures (and many more) are just waiting for you to go out and experience them.

Everyone knows someone who has been here and raved about it. You've put it off long enough. Come to Buenos Aires and you'll understand why so many people have fallen in love with this amazing city, and even decided to stay. There's a good chance you'll be one of them.

HIGHLIGHTS

- Commune with BA's rich and famous dead at the **Recoleta cemetery** (p101)
- Marvel at those amazingly high leg kicks at a tango show in **San Telmo** (p124)
- Shop the fun and stylish designer boutiques in **Palermo Viejo** (p129)
- Feast on tasty steaks or more exotic cuisine in Palermo's **Las Cañitas** (p119)
- Party all night long in BA's chic and super-happening nightclubs in **Palermo** (p126)

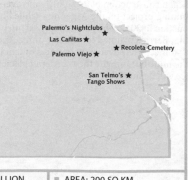

Palermo's Nightclubs ★
Las Cañitas ★
Palermo Viejo ★
★ Recoleta Cemetery
San Telmo's ★
Tango Shows

| ■ TELEPHONE CODE: 011 | ■ POPULATION: 3 MILLION | ■ AREA: 200 SQ KM |

HISTORY

Buenos Aires was settled in 1536 by Pedro de Mendoza, an adventurous and aristocratic Spaniard who financed his own expedition to South America. Food shortages and attacks by indigenous groups prompted Mendoza's hasty departure in 1537; to add insult to injury, he died at sea on the way home. Meanwhile, other expedition members left the settlement, sailed 1600km upriver and founded Asunción (now capital of Paraguay).

By 1541 the original settlement was completely abandoned. In 1580 a new group of settlers moved downriver from Asunción under Juan de Garay's command and repopulated Mendoza's abandoned outpost.

For the next 196 years Buenos Aires was a backwater and a smuggler's paradise, due to trade restrictions imposed by mother Spain. All the same, its population had grown to around 20,000 by 1776, the year Spain decreed the city capital of the enormous new viceroyalty of Río de la Plata. Suddenly Buenos Aires was a very important place, and many *porteños* have had a notoriously high opinion of themselves and their city ever since.

After repelling British invasions in 1806 and 1807, *porteños* reckoned they could handle themselves without Spain's help (or interference). Napoleon's 1808 conquest of Spain led to BA's *cabildo* (town council) cutting ties with the mother country in May 1810. Decades of power struggles between BA and the other former viceregal provinces ensued, escalating more than once into civil war.

Finally in 1880 the city was declared the federal territory of Buenos Aires, a separate entity from the surrounding province of the same name, and the nation's capital forevermore.

Buenos Aires' population by then was nearly half a million, and waves of immigrants (chiefly Spanish and Italian) continued to roll in. Many of them settled on the southern edge of town, to work in the booming port and the meat-processing industry. The 1871 yellow-fever epidemic had already driven the wealthy northward, and now the middle class abandoned La Boca and San Telmo to the newcomers.

The nation's agricultural exports soared from 1880 to 1914, which resulted in great wealth accumulating in BA. Well-heeled *porteños* built opulent French-style mansions, and the government spent lavishly on public works, including parks, ornate offices and a subway. Much of the unique look BA sports today dates from this period, although Av 9 de Julio's transformation into a block-wide megaboulevard didn't occur until the late 1930s.

But the boom times didn't last forever. Immigration burgeoned, export prices began to drop and workers became frustrated and militant. The Wall Street crash of 1929 dealt the final blow to the country's markets, and soon the first of many military coups took over. It was the end of Argentina's Golden Age.

Immigration to Buenos Aires kept climbing, but now it was mostly mestizos (people of mixed Indian and Spanish descent) from the rest of Argentina. Shantytowns popped up and social problems grew as the city failed to absorb its increasing population. The capital was the center of the country's economy, but as its prosperity waned there were no other centers of commercialism to help.

Pollution, poverty, unemployment and decaying infrastructure were constant problems in the 19th century, and even today greater Buenos Aires holds an astounding one-third of Argentina's population. Extreme governments and a roller-coaster economy have been constant plagues, but at least the 20th century saw a turn-around in the country's direction, though the recent global financial crisis has had an impact. For more on Argentina's roller-coaster history, see p28.

ORIENTATION

Buenos Aires is a huge city, but most places of interest to travelers are concentrated in just a few easily accessible neighborhoods.

At the heart of the city is the Microcentro, the downtown business center; it's small enough that you can walk around it fairly easily. Further south is San Telmo, known for its tango and its Sunday antiques market. South of here is La Boca, famous for its colorful houses clad in corrugated metal.

West of the Microcentro is Congreso, BA's seat of politics. To the north is Retiro (with the city's main train and bus station) and northwest, Recoleta, upscale areas of museums and fancy stores. Further north are Palermo and Belgrano, upper-middle-class suburbs with spacious parks and plenty of shopping.

BA's Ezeiza airport is about 35km south of the center; see p135 for details. Aeroparque Jorge Newbery airport is northwest of downtown BA.

(Continued on page 92)

BUENOS AIRES

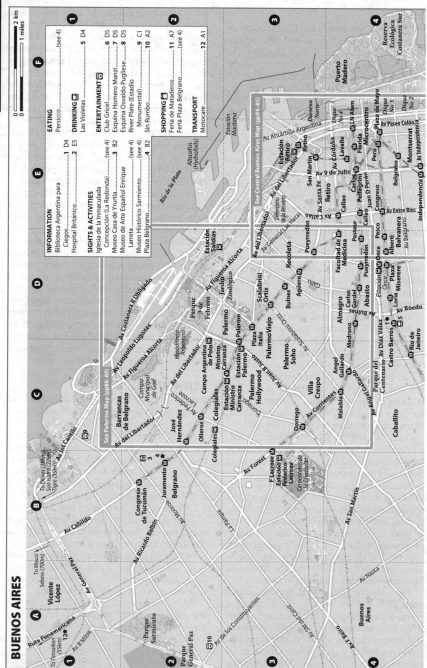

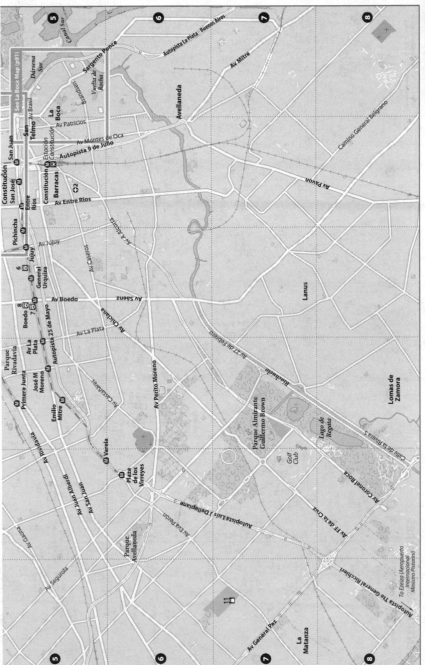

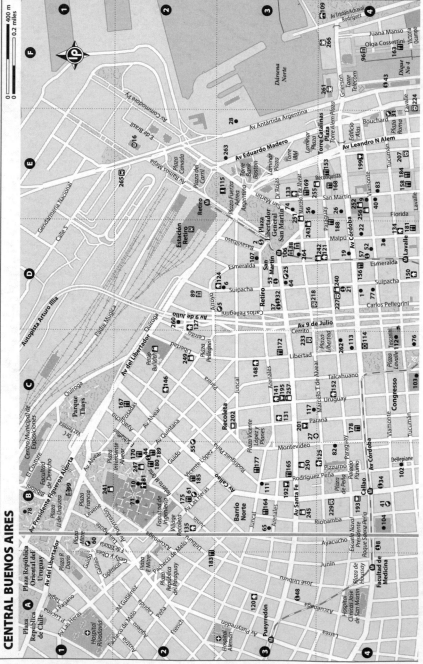

CENTRAL BUENOS AIRES

BUENOS AIRES

CENTRAL BUENOS AIRES (pp84–5)

BUENOS AIRES

CENTRAL BUENOS AIRES (pp84–5)

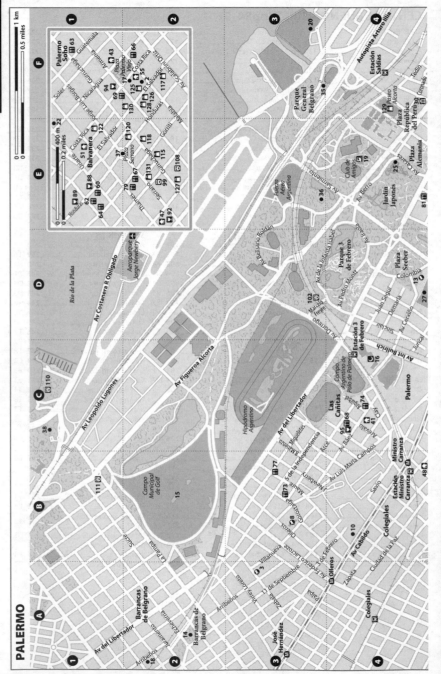

PALERMO

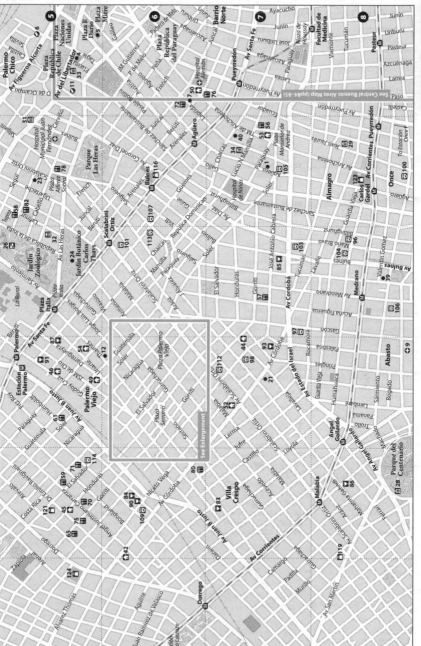

BUENOS AIRES

PALERMO (pp88–9)

LA BOCA

0 ————— 400 m
0 ————— 0.2 miles

See Central Buenos Aires Map (pp84–85)

Areas considered unsafe for tourists

Areas considered unsafe for tourists

SIGHTS & ACTIVITIES		
Boca Juniors	1	B3
Fundación Proa	2	C4
La Bombonera Stadium	(see 1)	
Museo de Bellas Artes de La Boca Benito Quinquela Martín	3	C4
Museo de la Pasión Boquense	4	B3
Museo Histórico de Cera	5	C4
Museo Histórico Nacional	6	A2

SLEEPING		
Casa Bolívar	7	A2
Sandanzas	8	A1

EATING		
El Samovar de Rasputín	9	C4
Il Matterello	10	C3
Parrilla 1880	11	A2

ENTERTAINMENT		
Centro Cultural Torquato Tasso	12	A2
El Samovar de Rasputín	13	C4

SHOPPING		
Moebius	14	A1

(Continued from page 81)

INFORMATION

Bookstores

El Ateneo (Map pp84-5; ☎ 4325-6801; Florida 340; ⏲ 9am-10pm Mon-Fri, to 5pm Sat) Modern bookstore with several branches; see also p132.

Walrus Books (Map pp84-5; ☎ 4300-7135; Estados Unidos 617; ⏲ noon-8pm Tue-Sun) The best English-language bookstore for quality new and used literature and nonfiction.

Concierge Services

BA Cultural Concierge (☎ 011-15-5457-2035; www .baculturalconcierge.com) Madi Lang's concierge service will help you plan itineraries, arrange airport transport, get a cell phone, run errands, reserve theater tickets, send a care package, scout out a potential apartment and do a thousand other things for your trip to run smoothly.

Cultural Centers

Centro Cultural Borges (Map pp84-5; ☎ 5555-5359; www.ccborges.org.ar; cnr Viamonte & San Martín) One of BA's best, offering cheap art exhibits, music and workshops.

Ciudad Cultural Konex (Map pp88-9; ☎ 4864-3200; www.ciudadculturalkonex.org; Sarmiento 3125) Apart from workshops and exhibitions, it stages theatrical performances and percussion shows; see p129.

Centro Cultural Recoleta (Map pp84-5; ☎ 4807-6340; www.centroculturalrecoleta.org; Junín 1930) Features art exhibits, a cinema, a kids' science museum and outdoor films in summer.

Centro Cultural Ricardo Rojas (Map pp84-5; ☎ 4954-5523; www.rojas.uba.ar; Corrientes 2038)

Exceptionally good, offering a very wide range of quality offerings, including inexpensive classes.

Centro Cultural San Martín (Map pp84-5; ☎ 4374-1251; www.ccgsm.gov.ar; Sarmiento 1551) An excellent cultural resource, offering many free or inexpensive offerings.

There are also several foreign cultural centers, all offering libraries, cultural events and classes:

Alianza Francesa (Map pp84-5; ☎ 4322-0068; www .alianzafrancesa.org.ar; Av Córdoba 946)

British Arts Centre (Map pp84-5; ☎ 4393-2004; www.britishartscentre.org.ar; Suipacha 1333)

Instituto Goethe (Map pp84-5; ☎ 4318-5600; www .goethe.de/buenosaires; Av Corrientes 319)

Emergency

Ambulance (☎ 107)

Police (☎ 911)

Tourist police (Comisaría del Turista; Map pp84-5; ☎ 4346-5748, 0800-999-5000; Av Corrientes 436; ⏲ 24hr) Provides interpreters and helps victims of robberies and rip-offs.

Immigration

Immigration office (Map pp84-5; ☎ 4317-0200; Antártida Argentina 1355; ⏲ 7:30am-1:30pm Mon-Fri) Offers 90-day visa extensions for AR$300.

Internet Access

Internet cafes and *locutorios* (private telephone offices) with internet access are very common everywhere in the center; you can often find

---

BUENOS AIRES IN...

Two Days

Start with a stroll in **San Telmo** (p98) and duck into some antiques stores. Walk north to **Plaza de Mayo** (p96) for a historical perspective, then wander the **Microcentro** (p95), perhaps veering east to **Puerto Madero** (p97) – a great spot for a break.

Keep heading northward into **Retiro** (p100) and **Recoleta** (p101), stopping off at the **Museo Nacional de Bellas Artes** (p101) to admire some impressionism. Be sure to visit the **Cementerio de la Recoleta** (p101) to commune with BA's bygone elite. For dinner and nightlife, **Palermo Viejo** (p102) is hard to beat.

On day two take in the **Congreso** neighborhood (p98) or head to **La Boca** (p99). Shop on **Av Santa Fe** (p129) or **Palermo Viejo** (p129), and at night catch a **tango show** (p124) or a performance at the **Teatro Colón** (p126).

Four Days

Follow the two-day itinerary, then on your third day add a trip to **Tigre** (p137) or **Colonia** (p555) in Uruguay. On the fourth day think about seeing some museums, taking a **tango lesson** (see boxed text, p125), going to the **Mataderos fair** (see boxed text, p133) if it's a weekend, or checking out **Palermo's parks** (p101). Be sure to find yourself a good steak restaurant for your last meal.

one by just walking a couple of blocks in any direction. Rates are cheap and connections are quick. Many cafes and restaurants have free wi-fi.

Internet Resources

The following websites are devoted to Buenos Aires; all are in English or have an English link. For general websites on Argentina, see p21.

Argentine Post (www.argentinepost.com) Useful wide-ranging articles on BA and Argentina.

Budgetba (www.budgetba.blogspot.com) Sporadic entries, but you could save a peso or two.

Bue (www.bue.gov.ar) The city's official website; click 'agenda' for a calendar of happenings.

Buenos Aires Expatriates Group (www.baexpats.org) Popular expat website.

Craigslist (www.buenosaires.en.craigslist.org) Find everything from an apartment to a job to a lover.

Expatargentina (www.expatargentina.wordpress.com) One expat's eclectic musings on living in BA.

Good Morning BA (www.goodmorningba.com) All-around guide to Buenos Aires.

Goodairs (www.goodairs.com) Interesting compilation of articles by a renowned local writer.

Landing Pad BA (www.landingpadBA.com) Good alternative articles on Buenos Aires.

Salt Shaker (www.saltshaker.net) Best for its detailed restaurant reviews.

What's up Buenos Aires (www.whatsupbuenosaires .com) Hip stuff to do today.

Libraries

Biblioteca Lincoln (Map pp84–5; ☎ 5382-1536; www .bcl.edu.ar; Maipú 672) Located inside the Instituto Cultural Argentino-Norteamericano (ICANA); good for English newspapers, magazines and books.

Biblioteca Nacional (Map pp88–9; ☎ 4806-9764; Agüero 2502) BA's main library and downright ugly; occasionally hosts author talks.

The Alianza Francesa, British Arts Centre and Instituto Goethe also have foreign libraries (see opposite).

Media

BA's most popular newspapers are the entertaining, tabloid-like *Clarín* and the more moderate and upper-class *La Nación*. *Página 12* provides a leftist perspective and often breaks important stories. *Ámbito Financiero* is the voice of the business sector, but it also provides good cultural coverage.

The English-language daily *Buenos Aires Herald* covers Argentina and the world from

---

NEED AN OFFICE – FOR AN HOUR OR A DAY?

The brainchild of one of BA's many expat entrepeneurs, **Areatres** (Map pp88–9; ☎ 4120-3333; www.areatresworkplace.com; Malabia 1720) is a secure working office where you can rent a desk, cubicle, office or meeting room. There are fax and copy services, complete internet and wi-fi connections, networking social events, a business lounge, a large presentation room and even a zenlike patio in back for the stress-prone. Facilities are cutting-edge – it's like you never left Silicon Valley.

---

an international perspective, while the livelier *Argentimes* (also in English) has fewer but more in-depth articles. German speakers have *Argentinisches Tageblatt*. These newspapers are available on the internet. International newspapers such as the *New York Times*, the *Guardian* and *Le Monde* are available at many newspaper kiosks, as are magazines such as *Time*, *Newsweek* and the *Economist*.

Cable TV lives a healthy life in Buenos Aires; international channels include CNN, BBC and ESPN. There are also plenty of reality shows, bimbo-led dance parties and *telenovelas* (soap operas).

Dozens of FM stations serve BA: FM 92.7 has tango, 95.1 has entertainment news and dance and 98.3 has Argentine rock.

Medical Services

Dental Argentina (☎ 4828-0821; www.dental-argen tina.com.ar; Uruguay 292, 9B) Dental services with English-speaking professionals. Also at Laprida 1621, 2B.

Hospital Británico (Map pp82–3; ☎ 4304-1081; www .hospitalbritanico.org.ar; Perdriel 74) Also has a clinic at Marcelo T de Alvear 1573 (Map pp84–5).

Hospital Italiano (Map pp88–9; ☎ 4959-0200; www .hospitalitaliano.org.ar; Gascón 450) Highly regarded hospital.

Medicalls (☎ 4823-5999, 011-15-5156-8384; www .medicalls.com.ar) Tourist-oriented medical attention with English-speaking doctors and dentists; both house calls and clinical services available.

Money

Banks and *cambios* (money-exchange offices) are common in the city center; banks have longer lines and more-limited opening hours but may offer better rates. Avoid the shady figures on Av Florida, offering 'cambio, cambio, cambio' to passing pedestrians. Using these unofficial street changers is not recommended; there are quite a few fake bills floating about.

ATMs are the best way to get pesos in Argentina – they're everywhere. There may be limits per withdrawal, but you can withdraw several times per day; some systems let you take nearly AR$1000 out at one time. A fee of AR$11.46 may be charged on ATM transactions by the *local* bank (not including charges by your home bank). Beware: this is a *per transaction* fee.

Even in Buenos Aires it's hard to change traveler's checks. Only a few fancy hotels and banks will take them, and you won't get a favorable rate. One exception is American Express (see following), but you'll have to line up.

The following local representatives can help you replace lost or stolen cards:

American Express (Map pp84–5; ☎ 0810-555-2639; Arenales 707) Also changes traveler's checks 10am to 3pm Monday to Friday.

MasterCard (Map pp84–5; ☎ 4340-5700; Perú 151)

Visa (Map pp84–5; ☎ 4379-3400; Corrientes 1437, basement fl)

Post

The post office has branches located all over the city.

Correo Internacional (Map pp84–5; ☎ 4316-1777; Av Antártida Argentina; ☼ 10am-5pm Mon-Fri) Only for shipping international parcels over 2kg.

DHL Internacional (Map pp84–5; ☎ 4314-2996; www .dhl.com.ar; Av Córdoba 783)

Federal Express (Map pp84–5; ☎ 0810-333-3339; www.fedex.com; Maipú 753)

OCA (Map pp84–5; ☎ 4311-5305; www.oca.com.ar; Viamonte 526) For domestic packages.

Telephone

The easiest way to make a phone call in BA is at a *locutorio* (small telephone office). Street phones require coins or *tarjetas telefónicas* (magnetic phone cards available at many kiosks). Faxes are cheap and widely available at most *locutorios* and internet cafes. For more on telephone services, including cell phones, see p608.

Tourist Information

There are several small government tourist offices or kiosks in BA; hours vary throughout the year. The official tourism site of Buenos Aires is www.bue.gov.ar and the government site is www.buenosaires.gov.ar. Many regions also have tourist offices in BA; see p609.

Florida tourist kiosk (Map pp84–5; Diagonal Norte & Perú)

Puerto Madero tourist kiosk (Map pp84–5; ☎ 4315-4265; Dique 4)

Recoleta tourist kiosk (Map pp84–5; Quintana 596)

Retiro tourist office (Map pp84–5; ☎ 4313-0187; ☼ 7:30am-2:30pm Mon-Fri) In Retiro bus terminal.

Secretaría de Turismo de la Nación (Map pp84–5; ☎ 4312-5550; www.turismo.gov.ar; Av Santa Fe 883; ☼ 9am-5pm Mon-Fri) Dispenses information on Buenos Aires, but focuses on Argentina as a whole.

South American Explorers (Map pp84–5; ☎ 5275-0137; www.saexplorers.org; Roque Saénz Peña 1142, 7A; ☼ 10am-5pm Mon-Fri, 10am-1pm Sat) A plethora of information and services for the independent traveler, but requires annual membership.

Travel Agencies

The following agencies all arrange tours in BA and Argentina, and staff speak English. For more on city tours, see p107.

Anda Responsible Travel (Map pp88–9; ☎ 3221-0833; www.andatravel.com.ar; Agüero 1131, 1st fl) Organizes tours around BA and Argentina with a 'sustainable' focus in mind, by introducing travelers to local communities, fair-trade organizations and social projects.

HI Travel (Map pp84–5; ☎ 4511-8723; www.hihostels.com; Florida 835, ground fl) Hostelling International's travel office.

Say Hueque (Map pp84–5; ☎ 5199-2517; www .sayhueque.com; Viamonte 749, 6th fl) Friendly company that offers 'independent' packages around BA and Argentina. Also at Guatemala 4845, 1st floor in Palermo (Map pp88–9).

Tangol (Map pp84–5; ☎ 4312-7276; www.tangol .com; Florida 971, Suite 31) Offers city tours, tango shows, guides to *fútbol* games, air tickets and countrywide packages – plus much more.

Wow Argentina (Map pp84–5; ☎ 5239-3019; www .wowargentina.com.ar; Av Santa Fe 882, 12F) Small agency catering to a middle- and upper-class clientele.

DANGERS & ANNOYANCES

Buenos Aires has been getting a bad rap these past few years. Crime does exist (as it does in any big city) and you'll notice that *porteños* are very security conscious, but in general BA is fairly safe. In many places you can comfortably walk around at all hours of the night, even as a lone woman. People stay out very late, and there's almost always somebody else walking down any street at any time. However, you should be careful at night in some neighborhoods, including Constitución (around the train station), the eastern border of San Telmo, and La Boca (where, outside tourist streets, you should be careful even during the day).

Crime against tourists is almost always of the petty sort, such as pickpocketing in crowded markets or buses, or bag snatches when you're not looking – things smart travelers can certainly guard themselves against. Be wary of the old 'mustard trick' – someone pointing out whatever 'goo' on your clothing, placed there by an accomplice, and offering to clean it up (along with your valuables).

Minor nuisances include the lack of respect shown by vehicles toward pedestrians, lax pollution controls and high noise levels. For dealing with taxis, see p136.

If you've been robbed in some way, contact the tourist police (see Emergency, p92) to file a claim. There's also **Defensoría del Turista** (Map pp84-5; ☎ 4302-7816, 011-15-4046-9682; Defensa 1250; ☯ 11am-6pm Tue-Fri), a sort of ombudsman that helps tourists who have been ripped off or 'abused.'

Remember to use your head wherever you are: don't flash any wealth, don't stagger around drunk, always be aware of your surroundings and look like you know exactly where you're going (even if you don't). And realize that if you're reasonably careful, the closest thing to annoyance you'll experience is being shortchanged, tripping on loose sidewalk tiles, stepping on the ubiquitous dog pile or getting flattened by a crazy bus driver. Watch your step.

SIGHTS
Microcentro
BA's Microcentro is where the big city hustles: here you'll see endless crowds of business suits and power skirts yelling into cell phones as they hasten about the narrow streets in the shadows of skyscrapers and old European buildings.

Florida, a long pedestrian street, is in some ways the main artery of this neighborhood. It's always jammed during the day with businesspeople, shoppers and tourists seeking vehicle-free access from north to south without the ubiquitous bus fumes and honking taxis. Buskers, beggars and street vendors thrive here as well, adding color and noise. Renovated old buildings, such as beautiful Galerías Pacífico (near Florida and Av Córdoba) add elegance to the area.

Further south is BA's busy financial district, where there are several museums to investigate. After that comes Plaza de Mayo, often filled with people resting on benches or taking photos of the surrounding historic sites.

GALERÍAS PACÍFICO
Covering an entire city block, this beautiful French-style **shopping center** (Map pp84-5; ☎ 5555-5110; ☯ 10am-9pm Mon-Sat, noon-9pm Sun) dates from 1889 and boasts vaulted ceilings with paintings done in 1954 by muralists Antonio Berni, Juan Carlos Castagnino, Manuel Colmeiro, Lino Spilimbergo and Demetrio Urruchúa. All were adherents of the *nuevo realismo* (new realism) school of Argentine art. For many years the building was semiabandoned, but a joint Argentine-Mexican team repaired and restored the murals in 1992.

The beautiful structure, which is dotted with fairy lights at night, is now a central meeting place sporting upscale stores and a large food court. Tourist-oriented tango shows take place in front on pedestrian Florida, and the excellent Centro Cultural Borges takes up the top floor.

MUSEO MITRE
Bartolomé Mitre, who became Argentina's president in 1862, resided at this colonial house, now a **museum** (Map pp84-5; ☎ 4394-8240; San Martín 336; admission AR$5; ☯ 2-7:30pm Mon, Tue, Thu & Fri). After leaving office, he founded the influential daily *La Nación*, still a *porteño* institution. The museum provides a good reflection of 19th-century upper-class life. It's full of Mitre's personal effects, such as home decorations and furniture.

MUSEO DE LA POLICÍA FEDERAL
In the heart of the financial district, this **museum** (Map pp84-5; ☎ 4394-6857; San Martín 353, 7th fl; admission free; ☯ 2-6pm Tue-Thu) proudly displays a whole slew of uniforms, medals, guns, drug paraphernalia and gambling exhibits. Avoid taking your kids into the room way in back – grisly forensic photos, along with dummies of murder victims, are barf-bag specials.

MUSEO HISTÓRICO DR ARTURO JÁURETCHE
This **museum** (Map pp84-5; ☎ 4331-1775; Sarmiento 364; admission free; ☯ 10am-6pm Mon-Fri) makes some sense of Argentina's chaotic economic history. Well-lit displays about paper money and

counterfeiting are no doubt scrutinized by BA's current money forgers. The million-peso bill from 1981 gives an idea of the hyperinflation *porteños* had to deal with.

CORREO CENTRAL BUILDING
This massive beaux arts building (Map pp84–5), filling an entire city block, used to house BA's main post office. It took 20 years to complete and was originally modeled on New York City's main post office. In late 2009 the structure was being remodeled into offices and exhibition spaces for Argentina's bicentennial; it may be worth checking out during your tenure to see what's going on.

PLAZA DE MAYO
Planted between the Casa Rosada, the Cabildo and the city's main cathedral is grassy Plaza de Mayo (Map pp84–5), BA's ground zero for the city's most vehement protests. In the plaza's center is the **Pirámide de Mayo**, a small obelisk built to mark the first anniversary of BA's independence from Spain. Looming on the plaza's north side is the impressive **Banco de la Nación** (1939), the work of famed architect Alejandro Bustillo.

Today the plaza attracts camera-toting tourists, the occasional camera thief, and activists. And if you happen to be here on Thursdays at 3:30pm, you'll see the Madres de la Plaza de Mayo; these 'mothers of the disappeared' continue to march as a memorial to their lost children (see p34).

CABILDO
The mid-18th-century town council, now a **museum** (Map pp84–5; ☎ 4342-6729; Bolívar 65; admission AR$1; ⏰ 10:30am-5pm Tue-Fri, 11:30am-6pm Sun & holidays) is not the size it once was, due to the building of surrounding avenues, but still has a section of the *recova* (colonnade) that once spanned Plaza de Mayo. The museum inside offers scanty exhibits, but a lively crafts market sets up in the patio on Thursday and Friday – and the cafe is a great place to relax.

CASA ROSADA
Taking up the whole east side of the Plaza de Mayo is the unmistakable pink facade of the Casa Rosada (Pink House; Map pp84–5). Though the offices of 'La Presidenta' Cristina Kirchner are here, the presidential residence is in the calm suburb of Olivos, north of the center.

The side of the palace facing Plaza de Mayo is actually the back of the building. It's from these balconies, however, that Juan and Eva Perón, General Leopoldo Galtieri, Raúl Alfonsín and other politicians have preached to throngs of impassioned Argentines. Pop celebrity Madonna also crooned from here for her movie *Evita*.

The salmon-pink color of the Casa Rosada, which positively glows at sunset, could have come from President Sarmiento's attempt to make peace during his 1868–74 term (blending the red of the Federalists with the white of the Unitarists). Another theory is that the color comes from painting the palace with bovine blood, which was a common practice in the late 19th century.

There are free 20-minute **tours** (☎ 4344-3600) in Spanish available on Saturday and Sunday from 10am to 6pm; just walk in and join the next group waiting for a tour. The **Museo de la Casa Rosada**, off to the southern side, was being renovated at research time but might be open during your tenure.

CATEDRAL METROPOLITANA
BA's baroque **cathedral** (Map pp84–5; ☎ 4331-2845; www.catedralbuenosaires.org.ar; cnr Av Rivadavia & San Martín; ⏰ 8am-7pm Mon-Fri, 9am-7:30pm Sat & Sun) is a significant religious and architectural landmark, but more importantly it contains the tomb of General José de San Martín – Argentina's most revered hero. Outside the cathedral you'll see a flame keeping his spirit alive.

Tours of the church and crypt are given at 3:30pm Monday to Saturday; tours of just the crypt are at 11:30am Monday to Friday. All tours are in Spanish. Occasional free choir concerts are also on offer (check the website).

MANZANA DE LAS LUCES
The Manzana de las Luces (Block of Enlightenment) includes the city's oldest colonial church, the Jesuit **Iglesia San Ignacio**. During colonial times this was BA's center of learning, and it still symbolizes high culture in the capital. The first to occupy this block were the Jesuits, and two of the five original buildings of the Jesuit Procuraduría still remain. Dating from 1730, these buildings include defensive tunnels discovered in 1912. The Universidad de Buenos Aires has occupied the site since independence in 1810. **Tours** (Map

pp84-5; ☎ 4331-9534; Perú 272; AR$7) in Spanish are available; drop by for a schedule.

MUSEO DE LA CIUDAD

Wander among the permanent and temporary exhibitions on *porteño* life and history at this **city museum** (Map pp84-5; ☎ 4343-2123; Defensa 219; admission AR$1, Wed free; ☾ 11am-7pm). Salvaged doors and ancient hardware have found a home next door at the museum's annex. Nearby, at the corner of Defensa, is the **Farmacia de la Estrella**, a functioning homeopathic pharmacy with gorgeous woodwork and elaborate late-19th-century ceiling murals.

MUSEO ETNOGRÁFICO JUAN B AMBROSETTI

This small but attractive **anthropological museum** (Map pp84-5; ☎ 4345-8196; Moreno 350; admission AR$3; ☾ 1-7pm Tue-Fri, 3-7pm Sat & Sun) displays collections from the Andean northwest, Patagonia and elsewhere in South America. Beautiful indigenous artifacts, including intricate jewelry and Mapuche ponchos, are presented, while an African and Asian room showcases priceless items. Tours are available in English and Spanish (call for hours).

BASÍLICA DE SANTO DOMINGO

Further south, this 18th-century **Dominican basilica** (cnr Defensa & Av Belgrano) has a colorful history. On its left tower are the replicated scars of shrapnel from fire against British troops who holed up here during the 1806 invasion. The **museum** (Map pp84-5; ☎ 4331-1668; admission by donation; ☾ by appointment) displays the flags that were captured from the British.

Puerto Madero

The newest and least conventional of the capital's 48 official barrios is Puerto Madero, located east of the Microcentro. Once an old waterfront, it's now a wonderful place to stroll, boasting cobbled paths and a long line of attractive brick warehouses that have been converted into ritzy new lofts, business offices and upscale restaurants. Today Puerto Madero holds BA's most expensive real estate, though it also has a bumpy history.

In the mid-19th century competing commercial interests began to fight over the location of a modernized port for Argentina's burgeoning international commerce. Puerto Madero was finally chosen, and the city's mudflats were transformed into a series of modern basins and harbors consistent with the aspirations and ambitions of a cosmopolitan elite. It was completed in 1898, but Puerto Madero had exceeded its budget and was tarnished by scandal – suspicions arose from the sale of surrounding lands likely to increase in value. The practical side of the scheme didn't go so well either: by 1910 the amount of cargo was already too great for the new port, and poor access to the rail terminus at Plaza Once made things even worse. Only the 1926 completion of Retiro's Puerto Nuevo solved these problems.

MUSEO FORTABAT

Rivaling Palermo's MALBA museum for cutting-edge looks is this fancy **art museum** (Map pp84-5; ☎ 4310-6600; www.coleccionfortabat.org.ar; Olga Cossettini 141; admission AR$15; ☾ noon-9pm Tue-Fri, 10am-9pm Sat & Sun). It shows off the collection of multi-millionairess Amalia Lacroze de Fortabat, Argentina's wealthiest woman. The museum's airy salons exhibit works by famous Argentine and international artists – look for Warhol's take on Fortabat herself. Movable aluminum panels above the roof open and close, keeping sun off the glassy ceiling. Call ahead for tours in English.

FRAGATA SARMIENTO

Over 23,000 Argentine naval cadets and officers have trained aboard this 85m **ship** (Map pp84-5; ☎ 4334-9386; Dique No 3; admission AR$2; ☾ 10am-7pm), which sailed around the world 40 times between 1899 and 1938 but never participated in combat. On board are the records of its voyages, nautical items and even the stuffed remains of Lampazo (the ship's pet dog).

RESERVA ECOLÓGICA COSTANERA SUR

The beautifully marshy land of this **nature preserve** (Map pp84-5; ☎ 4893-1588; Av Tristán Achával Rodríguez 1550; ☾ 8am-7pm Tue-Sun) makes it a popular site for weekend outings, when hundreds of picnickers, cyclists and families come for fresh air and natural views. If you're lucky you may spot a river turtle or a coypu; bird-watchers will adore the 200-plus bird species that pause to rest here (for private flora and fauna tours see Seriema Nature Tours, p108). You can rent bikes just outside the park entrance on the weekends (daily in summer).

Congreso

Congreso is an interesting mix of old-time cinemas and theaters, bustling commerce and hard-core politics. The buildings still hold that European aura, but there's more grittiness here than in the Microcentro: it has a more local city feel, with an atmosphere of faded elegance and fewer fancy crowds.

Separating Congreso from the Microcentro is Av 9 de Julio, 'the widest street in the world!,' as proud *porteños* love to boast. While this may be true – it's 16 lanes at its widest – the nearby side streets Cerrito and Carlos Pellegrini make it look even broader. At Avs 9 de Julio and Corrientes lies the city's famous **Obelisco**, 67m high and built in 1936 in only a month; it's the destination of *porteño* sports fans when they have a big win to celebrate.

Plaza Lavalle is surrounded by the austere neoclassical **Escuela Presidente Roca** (1902), the French-style **Palacio de Justicia** (1904) and the landmark **Teatro Colón**. Nearby is the **Templo de la Congregación Israelita**, Argentina's largest synagogue. About 10 blocks south of Plaza Lavalle is the **Palacio del Congreso**, together with its plaza and obligatory monument.

TEATRO COLÓN

Started in 1880 and finished in 1908, the **Teatro Colón** (Map pp84-5; ☎ 4378-7344; www.teatrocolon.org.ar; Cerrito 618) is a major landmark and gorgeous world-class facility for opera, ballet and classical music. It was the southern hemisphere's largest theater until the Sydney Opera House was built in 1973. Opening night featured Verdi's *Aïda*, and visitors have been wowed ever since. Even at times of economic hardship, the elaborate Colón remains a high national priority.

Renovations halted the excellent tours (offered in several languages), but work should have been finished by May 2010 for Argentina's bicentennial celebrations.

PALACIO DEL CONGRESO

Colossal and topped with a green dome, the **Palacio del Congreso** (Map pp84-5; ☎ 4010-3000, ext 2410; Hipólito Yrigoyen 1849) cost more than twice its projected budget and set a precedent for contemporary Argentine public-works projects. It was modeled on the Capitol Building in Washington, DC, and was completed in 1906. Across the way, the **Monumento a los Dos Congresos** honors the congresses of 1810 in BA and 1816 in Tucumán, both of which led to Argentine independence.

Inside the Congreso, free guided tours are given of the **Senado** at 11am and 4pm every weekday except Wednesday; go to the entrance on Hipólito Yrigoyen and be sure to bring photo ID.

PALACIO DE LAS AGUAS CORRIENTES

About six blocks west of Plaza Lavalle, this gorgeous and eclectic Swedish-designed waterworks building (1894) is topped by French-style mansard roofs and covered in 170,000 glazed tiles and 130,000 enameled bricks. If you like quirky museums, check out the small **Museo del Patrimonio** (Map pp84-5; ☎ 6319-1104; cnr Córdoba & Riobamba; admission free; 🕑 9am-1pm Mon-Fri) on the 2nd floor; it's full of pipe fittings, tiles and odd toilets. Guided visits offer a backstage glimpse of the building's inner workings (call for schedules). Bring photo ID and enter via Riobamba.

San Telmo

Full of charm and personality, San Telmo is one of BA's most attractive and historically rich barrios. Narrow cobbled streets and low-story colonial housing retain an old-time feel, though the tourist dollar continues to bring about changes.

Historically, San Telmo is famous for the violent street fighting that took place when British troops, at war with Spain, invaded the city in 1806. British forces advanced up narrow Defensa, but an impromptu militia drove the British back to their ships. The victory gave *porteños* confidence in their ability to stand apart from Spain, even though the city's independence had to wait another three years.

After this San Telmo became a fashionable, classy neighborhood, until in the late 19th century a yellow-fever epidemic hit, driving the rich north into present-day Recoleta. Many older mansions were subdivided and became *conventillos* (tenements) to house poor families. A few years ago these *conventillos* attracted artists and bohemians looking for cheap rent, but these days they're likelier to be filled with fancy shops, new hostels, gay couples or rich expats.

The heart of San Telmo is **Plaza Dorrego**, which hosts a famous Sunday antiques market (see the boxed text, p133). Nearby, the baroque, neocolonial **Iglesia Nuestra Señora de Belén** (Map pp84-5; Humberto Primo 340) was a Jesuit school until 1767, when the Bethlemite order took it over. Also worth a peek is **Mercado San Telmo**, an old fruit and vegetable market that still functions today; it's located in the center of the block bordered by Estados Unidos, Bolívar, Carlos Calvo and Defensa.

EL ZANJÓN DE GRANADOS

One of the more unique places in Buenos Aires is this amazing **architectural site** (Map pp84-5; ☎ 4361-3002; Defensa 755; 30min/1hr tour AR$25/40; ☺ tours on the hour from 11am-3pm Mon-Fri, every half hour 1-6pm Sun). Below the remains of a mansion, a series of old tunnels, sewers and water wells going back to 1730 were discovered. They have been meticulously reconstructed brick by brick, and very attractively lit, and this 'museum' offers a fascinating glimpse into the city's architectural past. Choose between hour-long tours during the week or half-hour tours on Sundays. It's best to call and reserve, especially if you need English-speaking guides.

MUSEO HISTÓRICO NACIONAL

This **national historical museum** (Map p91; ☎ 4307-1182; Defensa 1600; admission free; ☺ 11am-6pm) is located at the supposed site of Pedro de Mendoza's original founding of the city in 1536. Major figures of Argentine historical periods, such as San Martín, Rosas and Sarmiento, are represented, along with a few artifacts and paintings. Exhibits are a bit sparse, but the security is great – be prepared to hand over your bag while you look around.

MUSEO PENITENCIARIO

Just off the plaza, this **prison museum** (Map pp84-5; ☎ 4361-0917; Humberto Primo 378; admission AR$2; ☺ 2:30-5:30pm Wed-Fri, 1-7pm Sun) occupies a building that was first a convent, then a women's prison. Don't miss the tear-gas canisters used for riot control, the tennis balls used to hide drugs and the effeminate mannequins sporting past prison fashions. Cool old jail cells, too.

MUSEO DE ARTE MODERNO

Housed in a former tobacco warehouse, this roomy **museum** (Map pp84-5; Av San Juan 350) exhibited the works of contemporary Argentine artists, as well as temporary exhibitions. In 2009 it was closed for major remodeling, with plans to integrate the old cinema museum next door.

MUSEO DEL TRAJE

This small **clothing museum** (Map pp84-5; ☎ 4343-8427; Chile 832; admission free; ☺ 3-7pm Tue-Sun) is always changing its wardrobe. You can hit upon roaring '60s garb, Victorian dresses, vintage hippie wear or matador outfits. Come by and see what hot fashions the dummies are donning when you're in town.

La Boca

Blue collar and raffish to the core, La Boca is very much a locals' neighborhood. In the mid-19th century, La Boca became home to Spanish and Italian immigrants who settled along the Riachuelo, the sinuous river that divides the city from the surrounding province of Buenos Aires. Many came during the booming 1880s and ended up working in the many meat-packing plants and warehouses here, processing and shipping out much of Argentina's vital beef exports. After sprucing up the shipping barges, the port dwellers splashed leftover paint on the corrugated-metal sidings of their own houses – unwittingly giving La Boca what would become one of its claims to fame. Unfortunately, some of the neighborhood's color also comes from the rainbow slick of industrial wastes on the river.

Caminito, near the southern edge of La Boca, is the barrio's most famous street, and on weekends busloads of camera-laden tourists come here for photographs and to browse the small crafts fair while watching tango dancers perform for spare change. A riverside pedestrian walkway offers a close-up sniff of the Riachuelo, while a few museums provide mental stimulation. Four blocks inland is **La Bombonera stadium** (Brandsen), home of the Boca Juniors football team – the former club of disgraced superstar Diego Armando Maradona.

> **BOCA WARNING**
>
> La Boca is not the kind of neighborhood for casual strolls – it can be downright rough in spots. Don't stray far from the riverside walk, El Caminito or La Bombonera stadium, especially while toting expensive cameras. And certainly don't cross the bridge over the Riachuelo. There's nothing you'd really want to see outside the touristy areas, anyway.

FUNDACIÓN PROA

This elegant **art foundation** (Map p91; ☎ 4104-1000; www.proa.org; Av Don Pedro de Mendoza 1929; admission AR$10; ☾ 11am-7pm Tue-Sun) exhibits works by only the most cutting-edge national and international contemporary artists in both traditional and more unusual mediums. Visit the rooftop terrace – the views are excellent and you can grab a meal or drink in the fancy restaurant.

MUSEO DE BELLAS ARTES DE LA BOCA BENITO QUINQUELA MARTÍN

On display at this modern **museum** (Map p91; ☎ 4301-1080; Av Don Pedro de Mendoza 1835; suggested donation AR$5; ☾ 10am-6pm Tue-Fri, 11am-7pm Sat & Sun) are the works of Benito Quinquela Martín, which center on La Boca's port history. There are also paintings by more contemporary Argentine artists, along with a small but excellent collection of painted wood bowsprits (carved statues decorating the front of ships).

OTHER MUSEUMS

High-tech and spiffy, the **Museo de la Pasión Boquense** (Map p91; ☎ 4362-1100; www.museoboquense.com; Brandsen 805; admission AR$20; ☾ 10am-7pm) chronicles La Bombonera stadium, some soccer idols' histories, past highlights (on many videos), the championships, the trophies and, of course, the gooooals. It's located right under the stadium; peek at the pitch for a few extra pesos.

Wax reconstructions of historical figure-heads (literally just their heads!) and dioramas of scenes in Argentine history are the specialty of the small and very tacky **Museo Histórico de Cera** (Map p91; ☎ 4301-1497; www.museodecera.com.ar; Del Valle Iberlucea 1261; admission AR$10; ☾ 10am-6pm Mon-Fri, 11am-8pm Sat & Sun). There are also stuffed snakes and creepy wax limbs depicting bite wounds – barely worth the price of admission.

Retiro

Well-located Retiro is one of the ritziest neighborhoods in BA – but it hasn't always been this way. The area was the site of a monastery during the 17th century, and later became the *retiro* (country retreat) of Agustín de Robles, a Spanish governor. Since then, Retiro's current **Plaza Libertador General San Martín** – which sits on a bluff – has played host to a slave market, a military fort and even a bullring. Things are more quiet and exclusive these days.

French landscape architect Carlos (Charles) Thays designed the leafy Plaza San Martín, whose prominent monument is the obligatory equestrian statue of José de San Martín. Surrounding the plaza are several landmark public buildings, such as the **Palacio San Martín**, an art nouveau mansion originally built for the elite Anchorena family and sometimes open to the public; the huge and beautiful **Palacio Paz**; and the 120m-high **Edificio Kavanagh** (1935), once South America's tallest building.

The 76m **Torre de los Ingleses**, across Av del Libertador from Plaza San Martín, was a donation by the city's British community in 1916. Opposite the plaza is the impressive and busy **Retiro train station** (Estación Retiro), built in 1915 when the British controlled the country's railroads. Don't wander behind the station – it's a shantytown.

PALACIO PAZ

This gorgeous **palace** (Map pp84-5; ☎ 4311-1071, ext 147; Santa Fe 750; tours in Spanish AR$18; ☾ tours 11am & 3pm Tue-Fri, 11am Sat), also called the Círculo Militar, was once the private residence of José C Paz, founder of the still-running newspaper *La Prensa*. Inside are ornate rooms, salons and halls with wood-tiled floors, marble walls and gilded details. Nearly everything was ordered from Europe and assembled here. Tours in English (AR$34) are at 3:30pm Wednesday and Thursday.

MUSEO DE ARMAS

If you're big on weaponry, don't miss this extravagant **museum** (Map pp84-5; ☎ 4311-1071; Santa Fe 702; admission AR$6; ☾ 1-7pm Mon-Fri) showcasing over 2000 bazookas, grenade launchers, machine guns, muskets, pistols, lances and swords – even the gas mask for a combat horse is on display. Don't miss the Japanese suits of armor.

MUSEO DE ARTE HISPANOAMERICANO ISAAC FERNÁNDEZ BLANCO

This neocolonial-era mansion turned **museum** (Map pp84-5; ☎ 4327-0228; Suipacha 1422; admission AR$1, free Thu; ☾ 2-7pm Tue-Fri, 11am-7pm Sat & Sun) holds some gorgeous pieces of silverwork, religious paintings, Jesuit statuary and antiques. There's been no effort to place items in any historical context, but everything is in great condition, and an attractive garden provides a peaceful sanctuary. Call ahead for tours in English, German or French.

TEATRO NACIONAL CERVANTES & MUSEO NACIONAL DEL TEATRO

Six blocks west of Plaza San Martín, you can't help but notice the lavishly ornamented **Teatro Cervantes** (Map pp84-5; ☎ 4815-8883; www.teatrocervantes.gov.ar; Av Córdoba 1155). The landmark building dates from 1921 and holds a historical theater with a grand tiled lobby and plush red-velvet chairs. Enjoy the elegance – however faded – with a tour (call for current schedule).

Exhibits at the tiny, low-key **Museo Nacional del Teatro** (Map pp84-5; ☎ 4815-8883, ext 156; cnr Córdoba & Libertad; admission free; ☼ 10am-6pm Mon-Fri) trace the history of Argentine theater from its colonial beginnings. Check out the gaucho suit worn by Carlos Gardel and the *bandoneón* that once belonged to Paquita Bernardo, Argentina's first musician to play this accordion-like instrument.

Recoleta & Barrio Norte

BA's wealthiest citizens live and breathe in Recoleta, the city's most exclusive and fashionable neighborhood. In the 1870s many upper-class *porteños* relocated here from San Telmo during a yellow-fever epidemic. Today you can best see the wealth of this sumptuous quarter on **Av Alvear**, where many of the old mansions (and newer international boutiques) are located.

Full of lush parks, classy museums and French architecture, Recoleta is best known for its **Cementerio de la Recoleta**. Next door to the cemetery, the 1732 **Iglesia Nuestra Señora del Pilar** is a baroque colonial church with a small **museum** (donation AR$4; ☼ 10:30am-6:15pm Mon-Sat, 2:30-6:15pm Sun) to the left and upstairs, while just in front the **Plaza Intendente Alvear** hosts the city's most popular *feria artesanal* (crafts fair; see the boxed text, p133). A little further north is the sinuous sculptural flower **Floralis Genérica**, whose giant metal petals close up at night – if all the gears are working, that is.

CEMENTERIO DE LA RECOLETA

Wander for hours in this amazing **cemetery** (Map pp84-5; ☎ 4803-1594; cnr Junín & Guido; admission free; ☼ 7am-6pm) where 'streets' are lined with impressive statues and marble sarcophagi. Crypts hold the remains of the city's elite: past presidents, military heroes, influential politicians and the rich and famous. Hunt down Evita's grave, and bring your camera – there are some great photo ops here. Tours in English are available at 11am on Tuesday and Thursday (call to confirm). For a great map and information, order Robert Wright's PDF map at www.recoletacemetery.com.

MUSEO NACIONAL DE BELLAS ARTES

Arguably Argentina's top **fine-arts museum** (Map pp84-5; ☎ 5288-9900; www.mnba.org.ar; Av del Libertador 1473; admission free; ☼ 12:30-8:30pm Tue-Fri, 9:30am-8:30pm Sat & Sun) is a must-see for art lovers. It showcases works by Renoir, Monet, Gauguin, Cézanne and Picasso, along with many classic Argentine artists such as Xul Solar and Edwardo Sívori. There are also temporary exhibits, a small gift shop and a cinema.

MUSEO XUL SOLAR

Xul Solar was a painter, inventor and poet, and this **museum** (Map pp88-9; ☎ 4824-3302; www.xulsolar.org.ar; Laprida 1212; admission AR$10; ☼ noon-8pm Tue-Fri, to 7pm Sat, closed Jan) highlights over 80 of his bizarre, surreal and even cartoonish paintings; the guy was in a class by himself.

Palermo

Palermo is heaven on earth for BA's middle class. Its large, grassy parks – regally punctuated with grand monuments – are popular destinations on weekends, when families fill the shady lanes, cycle the bike paths and paddle on the peaceful lakes. Many important museums and elegant embassies are also located here, and certain subneighborhoods of Palermo have become some of the city's hottest destinations for shopping and nightlife.

Palermo's green spaces haven't always been for the masses. The area around **Parque 3 de Febrero** (Map pp88-9) was originally the 19th-century dictator Juan Manuel de Rosas' private retreat and became public parkland after his fall from power. Within these green spaces you'll find the **Jardín Japonés** (Map pp88-9; ☎ 4804-4922; www.jardinjapones.org.ar; cnr Avs Casares & Berro; admission Mon-Fri AR$5, Sat & Sun AR$8; ☼ 10am-6pm, to 7pm Sat & Sun), a peaceful paradise with koi ponds, teahouse and cultural offerings; the surprisingly decent **Jardín Zoológico** (see p102), BA's main zoo; and the nearby **Jardín Botánico Carlos Thays**, which will appeal to both botanists and cat lovers (it's full of feral felines). There's also the **Planetario Galileo Galilei** (Map pp88-9; ☎ 4771-9393; www.planetario.gov.ar; cnr Avs Sarmiento & Belisario Roldán), a planetarium with shows throughout the week and summer telescope viewings. Just south of the zoo is the landmark of **Plaza Italia**, Palermo's main transport hub.

BUENOS AIRES

PALERMO VIEJO

Roughly bounded by Av Santa Fe, Scalabrini Ortiz, Av Córdoba and Dorrego is trendsetting **Palermo Viejo** (Map pp88-9). It's further divided into Palermo Hollywood (north of the train tracks) and Palermo Soho (south of the tracks), both full of beautiful old buildings, leafy sidewalks and cobbled streets. Dozens of ethnic, ultramodern restaurants cater to anyone yearning for Japanese, Vietnamese, Greek or even Norwegian food, though modern international cuisine tops the list (see p119). There are also great guesthouses, bars and clubs; hanging out in **Plaza Serrano** on any weekend night is a blast. And the shopping! Buenos Aires' most cutting-edge designers have opened up dozens of boutiques here, and there are also many fancy housewares stores and other fun themed shops. You can wander around for hours and even days in this exciting area.

One of the capital's most trendsetting areas is **Palermo Viejo** (see the boxed text, above), with fine shopping, dining and nightlife. Another popular but much smaller Palermo neighborhood, **Las Cañitas**, is further north. Many restaurants and other nightspots here attract hordes of hip folk at night, when Av Báez clogs with traffic. Southeast of Las Cañitas is the landmark **Centro Islámico Rey Fahd** (☎ 4899-0201; www.ccislamicoreyfahd.org.ar; Av Int Bullrich 55), built by Saudis on land donated by former president Carlos Menem. Tours in Spanish are offered on Tuesday and Thursday at noon (call to confirm, and dress conservatively).

Even if you're devoutly Catholic, you'll find **Tierra Santa** (Map pp88-9; ☎ 4784-9551; www.tierrasanta-bsas.com.ar; Av Costanera R Obligado 5790; admission AR$25; ☒ call for hours) a very tacky place. The 'world's first religious theme park' boasts animatronic dioramas including of Adam and Eve and the Last Supper, but its pièce de résistance is a giant Jesus rising from a fake mountain – aka, the resurrection (every half hour).

MUSEO DE ARTE LATINOAMERICANO DE BUENOS AIRES (MALBA)

Sparkling inside its glass walls, this airy **modern arts museum** (Map pp88-9; ☎ 4808-6511; www.malba.org.ar; Av Figueroa Alcorta 3415; admission AR$15, Wed AR$5; ☒ noon-8pm Thu-Mon, to 9pm Wed) is BA's fanciest. Art patron Eduardo Costantini displays his limited but fine collection, which includes work by Argentines Xul Solar and Antonio Berni, plus some pieces by Mexicans Diego Rivera and Frida Kahlo. A cinema screens art-house films, and there's an excellent cafe for watching the beautiful people.

JARDÍN ZOOLÓGICO

Artificial lakes, pleasant walking paths and over 350 species of animals entertain the crowds at this relatively good **zoo** (Map pp88-9; ☎ 4011-9900; www.zoobuenosaires.com.ar; cnr Avs Las Heras & Sarmiento; admission AR$12-22; ☒ 10am-6pm Tue-Sun Oct-Mar, to 5pm Apr-Sep). Most of the enclosures offer decent spaces, and some buildings are impressive in themselves – check out the elephant house. An aquarium, a monkey island, a petting zoo and a large aviary are other highlights.

MUSEO NACIONAL DE ARTE DECORATIVO

Located in the stunning beaux-arts mansion called Palacio Errázuriz (1911), this **museum** (Map pp88-9; ☎ 4802-6606; www.mnad.org; Av del Libertador 1902; admission from AR$5; ☒ 2-7pm Tue-Sun) displays the posh belongings of Chilean aristocrat Matías Errázuriz. Everything from Renaissance religious paintings and porcelain dishes to Italian sculptures and artwork by El Greco and Rodin can be admired. The outside cafe in front is a fine place to refresh yourself on a sunny day. Admission prices vary according to the exhibition on show.

MUSEO EVITA

Everybody who is anybody in Argentina has their own museum, and Eva Perón is no exception. You can see her immortalized in **Museo Evita** (Map pp88-9; ☎ 4807-9433; Lafinur 2988; local/foreigner AR$4/14; ☒ 11am-7pm Tue-Sun) through videos, historical photos, books, old posters and newspaper headlines – even her fingerprints are recorded. The prize memorabilia, however, would have to be her wardrobe: dresses, shoes, handbags, hats and blouses stand proudly behind shining glass, forever pressed and pristine.

MUSEO DE ARTE POPULAR JOSÉ HERNÁNDEZ

This modest-sized **museum** (Map pp88-9; ☎ 4803-2384; Av del Libertador 2373; admission AR$3, Wed & Sat AR$1, Sun free; ☒ 1-7pm Wed-Fri, 10am-8pm Sat & Sun) has permanent exhibitions on Mapuche crafts, such as exquisite ponchos and (at the opposite end of the spectrum) gaudy Carnaval costumes. Diverse changing exhibitions range from folk crafts to modern toys.

Belgrano

Bustling Av Cabildo, the racing heartbeat of Belgrano, is an overwhelming jumble of noise and neon; it's a two-way street of clothing, shoe and housewares shops that does its part to support the mass consumerism of *porteños*. For a bit more peace and quiet step away from the avenue, where Belgrano becomes a leafy barrio of museums, parks and good eateries.

Only a block east of Av Cabildo, **Plaza Belgrano** (Map pp82–3) is the site of a modest but fun weekend market (see the boxed text, p133). Near the plaza stands the Italianate **Iglesia de la Inmaculada Concepción**, a church popularly known as 'La Redonda' because of its impressive dome.

Just across the plaza is the **Museo de Arte Español Enrique Larreta** (Map pp82-3; ☎ 4784-4040; Juramento 2291; admission AR$1; ◷ 2-8pm Mon -Fri, 10am-8pm Sat & Sun), which displays the well-known novelist's gorgeous art collection. Also close by is the **Museo Histórico Sarmiento** (Map pp82-3; ☎ 4782-2354; Juramento 2180; admission AR$5, Thu free; ◷ 1-6pm Mon-Fri, 2-6pm Sat & Sun), which displays the memorabilia of Domingo F Sarmiento, one of Argentina's most famous, forward-thinking presidents.

About five blocks north, the **Museo Casa de Yrurtia** (Map pp82-3; ☎ 4781-0385; O'Higgins 2390; admission AR$5; ◷ 3-7pm Tue-Fri, 1-7pm Sun) honors the well-known Argentine sculptor Rogelio Yrurtia. His old house and garden is full of his large sculptures and other artists' works; look for Picasso's *Rue Cortot, Paris.*

Four blocks northeast of Plaza Belgrano, French landscape architect Carlos Thays took advantage of the contours of **Barrancas de Belgrano** (Map pp88–9) to create an attractive, wooded public space on one of the few natural hillocks in the city. On Sunday evenings the bandstand is host to a *milonga* (tango dance school; see boxed text, p125).

Across Juramento (and the train tracks) from the Barrancas, Belgrano's small **Chinatown** (Map pp88–9) takes up a few blocks, offering decent Chinese restaurants (mostly closed on Monday) and cheap goods.

Once & Around

BA's most ethnically colorful neighborhood is Once, with sizable groups of Jews, Peruvians and Koreans. The cheap market around Once train station (Map pp82–3) always bustles, with vendors selling their goods on sidewalks and crowds everywhere, making it a fun spot to wander around. The nearby **Museo Casa Carlos Gardel** (Map pp88-9; ☎ 4964-2071; Jean Jaurés 735; admission AR$1; ◷ 11am-6pm Mon & Wed-Fri, 10am-7pm Sat & Sun) offers tango fans some insight into the dance's most famous singer.

For high-class shopping, wander through **Mercado de Abasto** shopping mall (see p133); it has especially good kids' entertainment. West of Once is Caballito, a calm residential neighborhood. Here you'll find the **Museo Argentino de Ciencias Naturales** (Map pp88-9; ☎ 4982-6595; Ángel Gallardo 490; admission AR$3; ◷ 2-7pm), a good natural-science museum that's definitely worth a peek for its musty taxidermy and cool skeleton room.

ACTIVITIES

The extensive greenery in Palermo provides good areas for recreation, especially on weekends when the ring road around the rose garden is closed to motor vehicles. Recoleta has grassy parks also, if you can avoid the dog piles. Best of all is the Reserva Ecológica Costanera Sur (p97), an ecological paradise just east of Puerto Madero; it's excellent for walks, runs, bike rides and even a bit of wildlife viewing.

Cycling

Bike paths interlace Palermo's Parque 3 de Febrero (Map pp88–9), where rental bikes are available in good weather; look for them on Av de la Infanta Isabel on weekends in winter and daily in summer. The Reserva Ecológica Costanera Sur (see p97) also has bike rentals with a similar schedule.

For safe family cycling, head to Nuevo Circuito KDT in Palermo's **Parque General Belgrano** (Map pp88-9; ☎ 4807-7700; Salguero 3450; admission AR$3). Here, **Sprint Haupt** (☎ 4807-6141; Salguero 3450; ◷ Tue-Sun) rents bicycles for use around a plain 1200m concrete bike path (RSVP and bring your passport). Nearby there's a rather run-down, banked velodrome, but you'll have to bring your own specialized bicycle. They're both under the overpass and over the pedestrian bridge.

For information on bike tours, see p107.

Horseback Riding

If you want to get out of town for a few hours and hop on a horse, forget those touristy *estancias* (ranches) and check out **Caballos a la Par** (☎ 011-15-5248-3592; www.caballos-alapar.com). Guided rides are given in a provincial park about an hour's drive from Buenos Aires. Services are professional and equipment of high quality; moonlight rides available.

Swimming

Some upscale hotels have decent-sized pools, but they charge hefty prices for nonguests to swim and use their facilities – if they allow them. It's better to find a health club with an indoor pool (see right). Otherwise there's Palermo's **Club de Amigos** (Map pp88-9; ☎ 4801-1213; www.clubdeamigos.org.ar; Figueroa Alcorta 3885; admission AR$20, pool extra), which has a pool open December to February. Call for public swimming times.

Golf & Tennis

Benos Aires' most convenient golf course is the 18-hole **Campo Municipal de Golf** (Map pp88-9; ☎ 4772-7261; Av Tornquist 1426; ☒ Tue-Sun, sometimes open Mon). Practice your long shots at the **Costa Salguero Driving Range** (Map pp88-9; ☎ 4805-4732; cnr Avs Costanera & Salguero), which also has a golf store, a cafe and a 9-hole, family-friendly course.

There are eight clay tennis courts available for casual hire at **Parque General Belgrano** (Map pp88-9; ☎ 4807-7879; Salguero 3450; admission AR$3); rates are AR$20 to AR$25 per hour. Try to reserve 48 hours in advance; bring your own equipment. **Club de Amigos** (Map pp88-9; ☎ 4801-1213; www.clubdeamigos.org.ar; Figueroa Alcorta 3885; admission AR$20, court hire AR$66-76) also has tennis courts.

THE SPA LIFE

Scrub that dead skin off – you've earned it. Other than the places listed here, several hotels also have spa services, including the **Four Seasons** (p113), the **Palacio Duhau – Park Hyatt** (p113) and **Home Hotel** (p115).

Aqua Vita Spa (Map pp84-5; ☎ 4812-5989; www.aquavitamedicalspa.com; Arenales 1965)

Espacio Oxivital (Map pp88-9; ☎ 4775-0010; www.espaciooxivital.com.ar; Nicaragua 4959)

Evian Spa (Map pp88-9; ☎ 4807-4688; www .aguaclubspa.com; Cerviño 3626)

Health Clubs

Some gyms may require a medical checkup before using their services.

The king of BA's gyms is **Megatlon** (Map pp84-5; ☎ 4322-7884; www.megatlon.com; Reconquista 335; day/week/month AR$82.50/180/330), with about 15 branches throughout the city. Expect decent gym services, including many classes; some have an indoor pool. Hours vary depending on the branch. Other gyms include **Le Parc** (Map pp84-5; ☎ 4311-9191; www.leparc.com; San Martín 645; day-use fee AR$80), **Sport Club Cecchina** (Map pp84-5; ☎ 5199-1212; www.sportclub.com.ar; Bartolomé Mitre 1625; day-use fee AR$40) and **YMCA** (Map pp84-5; ☎ 4311-4785; www .ymca.org.ar; Reconquista 439; day-use fee AR$35).

Yoga & Pilates

Most gyms and some cultural centers schedule yoga and Pilates classes. Even some health-oriented restaurants, such as Arte Sano (see p116) or Natural Deli (p119) offer yoga, tai chi and/or meditation. There are significant discounts for weekly or monthly class packages.

YOGA IN THE PARK?

And now for something completely different – **Eco Yoga Park** (☎ 4901-0744; 011-15-6507-0577; http://ecoyogapark.blogspot.com), located about 1½ hours west of Buenos Aires, near Luján.

Run by friendly Hare Krishnas, this pretty countryside retreat comes complete with grassy lawns, ecologically built *cabañas* (some made of cob), organic vegetable garden, yoga studio, art shop and meditation hall shaped like a giant beehive. The tiny restaurant serves vegetarian meals, much of it from the garden, and easy yoga classes are offered daily. **Accommodations** (incl meals AR$110, with 4 hours of volunteering AR$60) are all in rustic but comfortable hostel-type bunks with shared facilities. Other than doing perhaps some volunteer work and taking part in the yoga and meditation activities, there's not much to do except relax.

All religious denominations are welcome. There are just a few rules: no alcoholic drinks, drugs, smoking or meat-eating allowed on premises.

Buena Onda Yoga (☎ 011-15-5423-7103; www
.buenaondayoga.com; per class AR$40) Taught by several
American women expats at several locations around BA.
Private classes are available.

Centro Valletierra (Map pp88-9; ☎ 4833-6724; www
.valletierra.com; Costa Rica 4562; per class AR$50) This
slick Palermo Viejo studio has Hatha, Iyengar and Ashtanga
yoga classes plus meditation.

Tamara Di Tella Pilates (Map pp84-5; ☎ 4813-1216;
www.tamaraditella.com; cnr Juncal & R Peña) The
'Pilates Queen' has over a dozen branches with modern
facilities.

Vida Natural (Map pp88-9; ☎ 4826-1695; www
.vidanatural.com.ar; Charcas 2852; per class AR$40) This
natural-therapy center in Palermo offers Ashtanga, Hatha
and Iyengar yoga. Therapeutic massage and harmonizing
Tibetan bowls also available.

WALKING TOUR

Start at leafy **Plaza San Martín** (**1**; p100), designed by French landscape architect Carlos
Thays. If you like guns, swords and can-
nons, stop in at the **Museo de Armas** (**2**; p100).
Otherwise, head down pedestrian Florida to
the elegant **Galerías Pacífico** (**3**; p95), one of the
capital's most beautiful malls. Take a peek

inside at the ceiling murals, or watch one of
the pass-the-hat tango shows that are often
just outside.

From here head west on Córdoba, cross-
ing the impressive **Av 9 de Julio** (**4**). Soon you'll
come to the lovely **Teatro Cervantes** (**5**; p101)
and the notable **Templo de la Congregación
Israelita** (**6**). Walk south along Libertad to the
Teatro Colón (**7**; p98), one of BA's most impressive buildings; take a tour if you've got time.
Then keep going south and turn left at Av
Corrientes. You'll soon bisect Av 9 de Julio
again, but under the shadow of BA's famous
67m **Obelisco** (**8**). Just after you cross, turn left
at Carlos Pellegrini and then right at pedestrian Lavalle; keep going until the junction
at Florida.

WALK FACTS

Start: Plaza San Martín
End: Heladería Cadore
Distance: 5km
Duration: about four hours, depending on
breaks

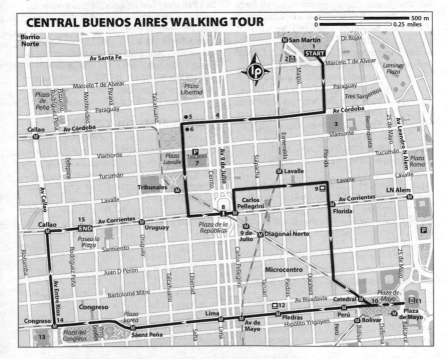

CENTRAL BUENOS AIRES WALKING TOUR

If you need a break, stop at the classic cafe **Richmond** (9; p122) – the old atmosphere can't be beat. After your *café con leche* (coffee with milk), keep buzzing south on Florida and then down Diagonal Roque Sáenz Peña to **Plaza de Mayo** (10; p96). Tour the **Casa Rosada** (11; p96), then head west on Av de Mayo past **Café Tortoni** (12; p124), the city's most famous and touristy cafe, to the **Palacio del Congreso** (13; p98). Note the rococo **Confitería del Molino** (14), a now-defunct cafe that presently molders in BA's air. For a special treat, walk north four blocks and one block west to **Heladería Cadore** (15; p120) for a delicious ice-cream cone.

COURSES

Visitors have many opportunities to study almost anything in BA, from Spanish to cooking to tango (see the boxed text, p125). Most cultural centers (p92) offer a wide variety of classes at affordable rates.

Language

BA is a major destination for students of Spanish, and good institutes are opening up all the time. Nearly all organize social activities and home-stay programs, and all have private classes. Below are just a few institutes; it's always best to ask around for current recommendations.

For something different, contact **Español Andando** (☎ 5278-9886; www.espanol-andando.com). You'll walk around town with a guide, learning Spanish by interacting with *porteños* on the street. Or try **Spanglish** (www.spanglishexchange .com), set up like speed dating; you'll speak five minutes in English and five in Spanish, then switch partners.

DWS (Map pp88-9; ☎ 4777-6515; www.daniela wasser.com.ar; Av Córdoba 4382) Friendly and has free internet computers.

Expanish (Map pp84-5; ☎ 4322-0011; www.expan ish.com; Viamonte 927, 1st fl, suites A & B) Housed in a lovely building; offers good services.

IBL (Map pp84-5; ☎ 4331-4250; www.ibl.com.ar; Florida 165, 3rd fl) Very central and offers eight levels of Spanish instruction.

One on One (Map pp84-5; ☎ 3528-4452; www.one ononeargentina.com.ar; Rodríguez Peña 617, 4th fl) Small school with tailor-made courses; several languages taught.

University of Buenos Aires (UBA; Map pp84-5; ☎ 4343-5981; www.idiomas.filo.uba.ar; 25 de Mayo 221) Regular and intensive, long-term classes (one to four months). Italian, German, French, Portuguese and Japanese also taught. Cheap, but classrooms are run-down.

Verbum (Map pp88-9; ☎ 4861-7571; www.verbum .biz; Salguero 553) Also offers trainee and internship programs for those who want to remain in Argentina.

VOS (Map pp84-5; ☎ 4812-1140; www.vosbuenos aires.com; Marcelo T de Alvear 1459) Very welcoming institute located just outside Recoleta.

Cooking

Those proficient in Spanish and seeking long-term cooking classes can try the highly regarded **Instituto Argentino de Gastronomía** (IAG; Map pp84-5; ☎ 5032-1414; www.iag.com.ar; Montevideo 968) or **Mausi Sebess** (☎ 4791-4355; www.mausisebess .com; Av Maipú 594, Vicente López).

Taking cooking classes in a small group or privately are probably the best options for short-term visitors who don't speak Spanish. There are several options in BA, a few with expat chefs who have their own 'closed door' restaurant (see p117).

A Little Saigon (☎ 011-15-6056-8823; www.alittlesai gon.com) Chef Thuy Lam will instruct you on how to make authentic Vietnamese cuisine from old family recipes.

Cooking with Teresita (☎ 011-15-4293-5992; www .try2cook.com) Learn to cook cuisine from Argentina and other South American countries.

Dan Perlman (www.saltshaker.net/class-schedule) Ex-New Yorker Dan Perlman teaches Italian, Mediterranean, Asian and vegetarian classes.

Norma Soued (☎ 011-15-4470-2267; www.argentine cooking.blogspot.com) Will teach you to make typical Argentine cuisine such as empanadas and traditional stews.

Samuel Warde (☎ 011-15-5740-9267; www.wynnwo ods.com/classes) Customized cooking classes by a feisty ex-Texan. All kinds of cuisine, including vegan and raw food.

BUENOS AIRES FOR CHILDREN

Those with kids have it good in BA. On weekends Palermo's parks bustle with families taking walks or picnicking. Shopping malls fill with strollers, while zoos, museums and theme parks also make good child-friendly destinations.

Good green spots in the city include Palermo's **Parque 3 de Febrero** (Map pp88-9), where on weekends traffic isn't allowed on the ring road around the rose garden (and you can rent bikes, boats and in-line skates nearby). Other good stops here include a planetarium (p101), a zoo (p102) and a Japanese garden (p101). If you're downtown and need a nature break, think about the Reserva Ecológica Costanera Sur (p97), a large nature preserve with good bird-watching, pleasant gravel paths and no vehicular traffic.

Shopping malls make safe destinations for families (especially if it's raining), and most come with a playground, a video arcade, a multiplex and toy shops. **Paseo Alcorta** (Map pp88-9; ☎ 5777-6500; Salguero 3172) is particularly good, while the Abasto (p133) boasts a full-blown children's museum (actually a fancy playground) and a mini-amusement park.

In San Telmo, check out the puppet museum, **Museo Argentino del Títere** (Map pp84-5; ☎ 4304-4376; Piedras 905; admission free; ☷ 3-6pm Tue-Sun), which has inexpensive weekend shows (call for schedule) that will amuse the little urchins.

In Recoleta visit the **Museo Participativo de Ciencias** (Map pp84-5; ☎ 4806-3456; www.mpc.org .ar; Junín 1930; admission AR$15; ☷ 3:30-7:30pm), in the Centro Cultural Recoleta (p92). This hands-on science museum has interactive displays that focus on fun learning. Hours vary widely depending on the season; check during your tenure. A bit outside the center, in Caballito, is the good Museo Argentino de Ciencias Naturales (natural science museum; p103).

Heading to Tigre (p137), north of the city, makes a great day excursion. Get there via the Tren de la Costa; it ends right at Parque de la Costa, a typical amusement park with fun rides and activities. Take a boat trip on the delta or wander the market for fruit and housewares.

Outside the city is the exceptional zoo, **Parque Temaikén** (☎ 03488-436-900; www.temaiken .com.ar; RP 25, Km 1, Escobar; adult/child 3-10 AR$48/35; ☷ 10am-7pm Tue-Sun Dec–mid-Mar, to 6pm mid-Mar–Dec). Only the most charming animal species are on display (think meerkats, pygmy hippos and white tigers), roaming freely around natural enclosures. An excellent aquarium comes with touch pools, and plenty of interactive areas provide mental stimulation. Taxis from the center cost around AR$120 and take 40 minutes, or grab bus 60 marked 'Escobar' from Plaza Italia.

To help calm down temper tantrums, visit one of BA's dozens of ice-cream shops; see the boxed text, p120, for suggestions.

For more particulars on traveling with children in Argentina, see p599.

TOURS

There are plenty of organized tours, from the large tourist-bus variety to more intimate car trips to guided bike rides to straight-up walks. Other than the following listings, there are also travel agencies (p94), most of which broker tours or offer their own.

The City of Buenos Aires organizes **free monthly tours** (☎ 4114-5791; www.bue.gov.ar) from August to December, with themes ranging from art to historic bars to particular neighborhoods. Stop by any government tourist office (p94) for a schedule.

If you have an MP3 player and are self-sufficient, check out www.mptours.com. You can download unique self-guided tours and maps of BA neighborhoods for US$12.50 each, walking, stopping and listening at your leisure. The city also has audio tours (www .bue.gov.ar/audioguia) and they're free by calling a number on your cell phone.

All companies listed below offer tours in English and possibly other languages; some companies listed under 'Group Tours' also do private tours.

Group Tours

Anda Responsible Travel (☎ 3221-0833; www .andatravel.com.ar; Agüero 1131, 1st floor; per person from AR$40) Most notable for its La Boca tour, which gets travelers involved with local organizations working towards improving the lives of its citizens.

BA Free Tour (☎ 011-15-6395-3000; www.bafreetour .com) Free (well, donation) morning and afternoon walking tours given by enthusiastic young guides who love their city. Even if you can't give anything you're welcome to join.

BA Walking Tours (☎ 5773-1001; www.ba-walking -tours.com; per person AR$100) Various kinds of city walking tours with historical, cultural, political and architectural perspectives.

Buenos Aires Bus (☎ 5239-5160; www.buenosaires bus.com; ticket AR$50) Hop-on, hop-off topless bus with a dozen stops. Runs every 30 minutes at designated stops (see website).

Cultour (☎ 011-15-6575-4593; www.cultour.com.ar; per person from AR$55) Good tours run by teachers and students from UBA (University of Buenos Aires). Prepare to learn the historical and cultural facets of Buenos Aires.

Eternautas (☎ 5031-9916; www.eternautas.com; tour prices vary) An interesting range of tours given by historians. Some have economic, religious or cultural themes. Walking tours (in Spanish) are from AR$10 per person.

Graffitimundo (☎ 011-15-3683-3219; www.graffiti mundo.com; per person AR$75) Expat-run tours of some of BA's best graffiti, by those in the know. Learn artists' history and the local culture of graffiti (and stencil art too).

La Bicicleta Naranja (Map pp84-5; ☎ 4362-1104; www.labicicletanaranja.com.ar; Pasaje Giuffra 308; tours AR$105, bike rental per hr AR$10) Offers various bike tours around the city; tour price includes helmet, lock and guide.

Urban Biking (☎ 4568-4321; www.urbanbiking.com) Offers similar services to La Bicicleta Naranja.

Private Tours

BA Local (☎ 011-15-4870-5506; www.balocal.com; tours from AR$450) Christina Wiseman, an ex–New Yorker, specializes in personal shopping tours and off-the-beaten-path (or regular city) tours.

Bitch Tours (☎ 011-15-6157-3248; www.bitchtours .blogspot.com; tours from AR$380) Agustina Menendey is actually not a bitch, and she will give off-beat custom tours for the right (cool) people.

Bob Frassinetti (☎ 011-15-6965-1955; admin@fras sinetti.com) Bohemian Bob can take you to art galleries, studios, secondhand shops and markets – plus hunting for arts and antiques around Argentina.

Buenos Tours (☎ 011-15-3221-1048; www.buenos tours.com; tours from AR$380) Arranges well-run city tours guided by friendly, knowledgeable and responsible local expats.

Seriema Nature Tours (☎ 4312-6345; www.seriema tours.com) It does nature tours to all South America, but around BA the most popular outings are to Costanera Sur and Reserva Natural Otamendi. It also has a two-day 'Birding of the Pampas' tour.

Sylvia Zapiola (☎ 4822-1187, 011-15-3555-3639; tours from AR$300) Feisty Argentine and professional guide who has lived abroad; does general city orientation tours and special services such as airport pickup.

FESTIVALS & EVENTS

There are festivals happening in BA all the time, and they celebrate nearly everything imaginable – including tango, horses, gauchos, cinema, art, wine, fashion and books. Spring is when the lion's share of these events occur. Check with tourist offices for exact dates as they vary from year to year. Palermo's **La Rural** (aka Predio Ferial; Map pp88-9; Av Santa Fe) is the venue for many of the city's bigger events.

January & February

Carnaval (late February) Get sprayed with foam while enjoying Afro-Latin *murga* (musical theater) rhythms on Av de Mayo. BA's Carnaval is relatively tame, but there's still a chance for water-balloon fights.

Chinese New Year (date depends on the lunar calendar) Head to Belgrano's tiny Chinatown for food, firecrackers and festivities.

April

Feria del Libro (www.el-libro.org.ar; La Rural) The largest book festival in Latin America, attracting over a million book lovers for three weeks (April to May).

Festival International de Cine Independiente (www.bafici.gov.ar) Highlights national and international independent films at venues all around town.

June & July

arteBA (www.arteba.com; La Rural) Popular event highlighting contemporary art, introducing exciting new young artists, and showing off top gallery works.

Exposición Rural (www.exposicionrural.com.ar; La Rural) The mother of all livestock fairs, with lots of bull(s). Late July to early August.

August

Fashion BA (www.bafweek.com) Spots the city's latest designer threads and hottest models. A fall collection shows in February or March; both events are at La Rural.

Festival y Mundial de Tango (www.mundialdetango .gov.ar; various venues) Masterful tango performances, tango movies, classes, workshops, conferences and competitions in venues all over the city.

September

Vinos y Bodegas (www.expovinosybodegas.com.ar; La Rural) A can't-miss event for wine aficionados, offering vintages from over 100 Argentine *bodegas* (wineries).

Casa Foa (www.casafoa.com) The city's top-notch architecture, design and decoration fair, located at a different renovated (and usually historical) building each year. Runs September to October.

South American Music Conference (www.samc.net) BA's biggest electronic music party, featuring networking conferences during the day and 50,000 party-goers at night.

November

Marcha del Orgullo Gay (www.marchadelorgullo.org .ar) Thousands of BA's gay, lesbian and transgender citizens proudly march from Plaza de Mayo to the Congreso.

Gran Premio Nacional The country's biggest horse race and a fine family event, held in Palermo's opulent and French-styled *hipódromo*.

Día de la Tradición Held in San Antonio de Areco (see p146), but a worthwhile day trip if you like gauchos.

December

Campeonato Abierto de Pato (www.fedpato.com.ar) Showcases Argentina's quirky traditional sport involving horseback riders wrestling over a handled ball.

Campeonato Abierto de Polo (☎ 4343-0972; www .aapolo.com) Watch the world's best polo players thunder up and down Palermo's polo fields.

Creamfields (www.creamfieldsba.com) BA's answer to the UK's outdoor, all-night, cutting-edge electronic-music and dance party, with over 100 international DJs and bands.

Festival Buenos Aires Danza Contemporánea (www.buenosairesdanza.com.ar) A major contemporary dance party that occurs every two years. Performances, seminars and workshops happen in various cultural centers and theaters.

SLEEPING

Over the last few years Buenos Aires has seen its accommodation options increase exponentially. Boutique hotels and guesthouses, especially, have mushroomed in neighborhoods such as San Telmo and Palermo, and hostels are a dime a dozen. You shouldn't have trouble finding the type of place you're looking for, but it's still a good idea to make a reservation beforehand – especially during any holidays or the busy summer months of November through January.

Many places will help you with transportation to and from the airport if you reserve ahead of time. The most expensive hotels will take credit cards, but cheaper places might not (or may include a surcharge for credit-card payment). Some kind of breakfast, whether it be continental or buffet, is included nearly everywhere; the same goes for internet access, wi-fi and air-con.

At Hostelling International (HI) hostels, buying a membership card (AR$60) gives a discount off listed prices. Another hostel club is www.minihostels.com. For top-end hotels, we've listed rack rates; look at their websites for significantly reduced rates.

Prices below are for high season (roughly November to February). Rates can skyrocket during peak seasons (Christmas and Easter) or drop during slow seasons.

For a list of apartment-rental websites, see below.

Microcentro

As well as being very central, the Microcentro has the best range and the largest number of accommodations in the city. Toward the north you'll be close to the popular pedestrian streets of Florida and Lavalle, as well as the neighborhoods of upmarket Retiro and Recoleta. The Plaza de Mayo area contains the bustling banking district and many historical buildings, and is within walking distance of San Telmo. During the day the whole area is very busy, but nights are much calmer as businesspeople flee the center after work. Don't expect creative cuisine in this area – for that you'll have to head to Palermo.

BUDGET

our pick **Portal del Sur** (Map pp84-5; ☎ 4342-8788; www .portaldelsurba.com.ar; Hipólito Yrigoyen 855; dm AR$40-50, s/d AR$160/180; ✷ ▣ ☞) Located in a charming

---

SHORT- & LONG-TERM RENTALS

Any hotel, hostel or guesthouse should significantly discount a long-term stay, so negotiate a deal in advance. There are also many guesthouses that specialize in weekly or monthly stays, and these offer a more intimate experience. If you're interested in spending time with a host family, check out www.coret.com.ar. To rent a room in a house, check out www.sparerooms.com.ar.

Traditionally you need a local's lien to help you cover rent for an apartment, but so many long-term foreigners have poured into BA that a plethora of rental agencies and websites have popped up to help them find housing without this requirement. Expect to pay a much higher monthly rate for this service, however; locals usually commit to at least one year when obtaining a lease for unfurnished apartments, and consequently pay less. Sites to check:

www.adelsur.com
www.alojargentina.com.ar
www.apartmentsba.com
www.barts.com.ar
www.buenosaireshabitat.com
www.friendlyapartments.com (gay oriented)
www.oasisba.com
www.roomargentina.com
www.stayinbuenosaires.com
www.tucasargentina.com
www.yourhomeinargentina.com.ar

If you'd like someone to check out an apartment before you rent it, Madi Lang at www.bacul turalconcierge.com can make sure the place isn't on a busy street, outlying neighborhood or near a construction site.

old building, this is one of the city's best hostels. Beautiful dorms and sumptuous, hotel-quality private rooms surround a central open area, which features a kitchen and dining area. The highlight is the lovely rooftop deck with views and attached airy, common lounge. Has free tango lessons, Spanish lessons and walking tour.

HI Obelisco Suites (Map pp84-5; ☎ 4328-4040; www .hihostels.com; Av Corrientes 830; dm AR$45; s/d AR$100/140; 🕸 🖳 ⊚) This apartment-like HI hostel features large dorms (four to eight beds) and pleasant private rooms; every three rooms share a bathroom and a kitchenette. Common areas include a trendy bar-lounge with a pool table, and separate small rooms for Spanish classes and watching TV. Lots of activities are on offer as are occasional free dinners.

Milhouse Youth Hostel (Map pp84-5; ☎ 4345-9604; www.milhousehostel.com; Hipólito Yrigoyen 959; dm/d AR$48/210; 🕸 🖳 ⊚) Best known as BA's premiere party hostel, this popular HI spot offers a plethora of activities and services. Dorms and private rooms are tiny but fairly well kept, and most surround a pleasant open patio. Common spaces are large and boisterous, and include a bar in the basement, a TV lounge on the mezzanine and a rooftop terrace above. There's a gorgeous annex building nearby.

Hotel Alcázar (Map pp84-5; ☎ 4345-0926; Av de Mayo 935; s AR$120-150, d AR$150-170; 🖳 ⊚) One of BA's best budget deals, the old Alcázar now has simple remodeled rooms (get one with an outside window) that are mostly small, but clean and good value. It's centrally located and just steps away from the famous Tortoni Cafe, which is handy since breakfast isn't included. There are also some nice interior tiled patios. Reserve ahead.

MIDRANGE & TOP END

Suipacha Inn (Map pp84-5; ☎ 4322-0099; www.ho telsuipacha.com.ar; Suipacha 515; s AR$180, d AR$200-240; 🕸) This well-located hotel is a good deal in the Microcentro – it's only a couple of blocks from the Obelisco. It could use a facelift, but you do get small, basic and tidy rooms, most with a fridge, a microwave, a sink and a safe box. Treat yourself and upgrade to a more spacious 'special' room, as they don't cost too much more.

Hotel Frossard (Map pp84-5; ☎ 4322-1811; www .hotelfrossard.com.ar; Tucumán 686; s/d AR$200/230; 🕸 🖳 ⊚) This intimate hotel is a little gem, boasting 24 high-ceilinged rooms of different sizes in a charming older building. Singles are tiny and doubles are small, but triples have more breathing room. The location is excellent; the pedestrian streets of Florida and Lavalle are just a block away.

Moreno Hotel (Map pp84-5; ☎ 4334-3638; www .morenobuenosaires.com; Moreno 376; r AR$750; 🕸 🖳 ⊚) Located in an atmospheric historical building is this otherwise modern, minimalist hotel. The rooms are beautiful – some are huge and come with a loft. The best part is the 6th-floor rooftop terrace; there's also a contemporary restaurant. You can opt to make your stay carbon-neutral by 'donating' AR$12 per night (don't worry – it gets paid even if you don't).

Tryp Hotel (Sol Meliá; Map pp84-5; ☎ 5222-9600; www .solmelia.com; San Martín 474; d AR$830; 🕸 🖳 ⊚) A good modern and upscale choice in the center, the Tryp (aka Sol Meliá) is a large hotel on the cutting edge of hip. On offer are large, contemporary rooms in cool earthy colors, featuring flat-panel TVs, glass desks and large elegant headboards framing comfortable beds. Business travelers should note the meeting room with attached rooftop deck.

NH City & Tower (Map pp84-5; ☎ 4121-6464; www .nh-hotels.com; Bolívar 160; d AR$950; 🕸 🖳 ⊚ 🕸) The NH chain's signature style is hip minimalism, with muted earth tones and natural design accents. Expect classy, tasteful rooms and excellent services – this particular hotel has a small but beautiful rooftop swimming pool with city views. Prices can vary at the several other NH branches in town.

Congreso

Congreso and Tribunales contain many of the city's older theaters, cinemas and cultural centers. Lively Av Corrientes has many modest shops, services and bookstores. The Plaza de Congreso area is always moving, sometimes with mostly peaceful public demonstrations. Generally, this area is not quite as packed as the Microcentro and has a less business and touristy flavor, but still bustles day and night.

BUDGET

Sabatico Hostel (Map pp84-5; ☎ 4381-1138; www .sabaticohostel.com.ar; Mexico 1410; dm AR$40-45; r AR$120-170; 🕸 🖳 ⊚) Located off the tourist-beaten path in an atmospheric neighborhood is this exceptional, well-maintained hostel. Rooms are small but pleasant and the great common areas include a nice kitchen, airy patio hall and wonderful rooftop terrace with soaking pool. There's occasional live music on weekends.

Kilca Hostel (Map pp84–5; ☎ 4381-1966; www.kilcabackpacker.com; Mexico 1545; dm AR$46, s/d AR$115/145; 🖳 🛜) The slightly artsy Kilca is in the Montserrat neighborhood, which is cool – fewer tourists and more local activity. It has a laid-back atmosphere and is located in an early 1900s house with rooms that feature exposed brick and high ceilings with beams. There's a funky kitchen and small leafy courtyards that are good for relaxing.

Hotel Sportsman (Map pp84–5; ☎ 4381-8021; www.hotelsportsman.com.ar; Av Rivadavia 1425; s/d from AR$50/80) For a taste of how backpacker lodgings in BA used to be, check into this oldie but goodie. It's a classic, ancient hotel with creaky wood staircase, an old iron elevator and mazelike hallways leading to basic but decent rooms with either shared or private bathrooms. Character abounds, and there's a kitchen – but only for heating up water. No breakfast, but it's still an awesome deal.

El Jardín del Tango (☎ 4952-9829; http://sites.google.com/site/jardindeltango; s/d from AR$135/170) Tango aficionado and expat Rachel Stevenson runs three guesthouses in Buenos Aires' colorful and very local Once neighborhood, just west of Congreso. All have just one or two rooms or apartments available and are homey and comfortable. Rachel's own place, Casa Rosa, comes with her two cats. Reservations essential.

Hotel Reina (Map pp84–5; ☎ 4381-2496; www.reinahotel.com; Av de Mayo 1120; s AR$120-150, d AR$150-200; 🖳) This charming old building still has a subdued elegance that's apparent in the grand halls, the classic elevator and the original light fixtures. Some rooms are simple, while others are lovely – with high ceilings, wood floors and balconies (try for the 2nd floor). Tango classes can be given in the airy salon; breakfast is good.

MIDRANGE & TOP END

Yira Yira Guesthouse (Map pp84–5; ☎ 4812-4077; www.yirayira.com.ar; Uruguay 911 1B; s/d/tr AR$133/190/228; 🖳 🛜) Run by the helpful Paz, who lives onsite, is this intimate apartment with four large rooms facing the central living area. It's a good place to meet other travelers and very well located, smack in the center of the downtown neighborhoods. Two-night minimum stay and RSVP required.

Fiamingo Apart Hotel (Map pp84–5; ☎ 4374-4400; www.fiamingoapart.com.ar; Talcahuano 120; s/d AR$205/245; 🖳 🛜) Great for families, the Fiamingo features huge suites that lean more toward comfortable and convenient than fancy. All come with attached kitchenettes (there are no stoves – just microwaves and sinks). Staff are friendly, and windows are double-paned for peace and quiet. It's a great deal for the price; reserve ahead of time.

Hotel Bonito (Map pp84–5; ☎ 4381-2162; www.bonitobuenosaires.com; Chile 1507, 3rd fl; r AR$266-418; 🖳 🛜) Lovely boutique hotel with just five artsy, gorgeous rooms mixing the traditional and contemporary. Some have a loft, cupola sitting area or Jacuzzi; floors can be wood or acid-finished concrete. Warm atmosphere, with small bar area and good breakfast.

Design Suites (Map pp84–5; ☎ 4814-8700; www.designsuites.com; MT de Alvear 1683; r AR$684-990; 🖳 🛜) Futuristically elegant, with that minimalist style so popular in trendy BA hotels these days, Design Suites offers a great location and exclusive atmosphere. All suites have flat-panel TVs, gorgeous decor and small kitchenettes (no stoves, just microwaves). The downstairs lounge is elegant; too bad you can't dip into the pool.

San Telmo & Around

South of the Microcentro, San Telmo has some of the most traditional atmosphere in Buenos Aires. Buildings are more charming and historical than those in the center, and tend to be only a few stories high. Many restaurants and fancy boutique stores have opened here in recent years, and there are some good bars, tango venues and other nightspots for entertainment. Most accommodation options here are hostels, humble hotels or upscale guesthouses rather than five-star hotels.

BUDGET

Garden House (Map pp84–5; ☎ 4305-0517; www.gardenhouseba.com.ar; San Juan 1271; dm AR$36-40, s & d AR$125-170; 🖳 🛜) A bit off the beaten tourist path is this friendly hostel with two dorms (four and eight beds) and six doubles (a couple with pretty patios) and some casual but cozy common spaces. Most rooms share bathrooms. It's far from the center, but the good vibes are worth the trek. Cheap but excellent Thursday-night *asados* (barbecues) take place on the terrace.

Art Factory (Map pp84–5; ☎ 4343-1463; www.art factoryba.com.ar; Piedras 545; dm AR$38, s AR$105-125, d AR$120-170; ✖ 🖳 🛜) Friendly and uniquely art-themed, this fine hostel offers more private rooms than most – and all feature huge murals, painted and decorated by different artists from around the world. Even the hallways and water tanks have colorful cartoonish themes, and the 1850s mansion adds an elegant old touch to the atmosphere. Large rooftop terrace and bar-lounge area.

Sandanzas Hostel (Map p91; ☎ 4300-7375; www .sandanzas.com.ar; Balcarce 1351; dm AR$40-45, d AR$140-180; 🖳) This friendly hostel has just 28 beds and is enthusiastically run by its five young owners, all artists or social workers. It's a colorful place with good-sized dorms, six doubles (three with bathroom) and occasional cultural events. The location is in a gritty blue-collar neighborhood near Plaza Lezama. Free tango classes and bike rentals.

Brisas del Mar (Map pp84–5; ☎ 4300-0040; Humberto Primo 826; s AR$60-70, d AR$70-80) Long-running old cheapie hotel with no luxuries – except for cable TV. Has basic but decent budget rooms, some even musty, and downstairs ones share outside bathrooms. Upstairs rooms are brighter; all face tiled hallways lined with plants.

MIDRANGE & TOP END

Lugar Gay (Map pp84–5; ☎ 4300-4747; www.lugargay .com.ar; Defensa 1120; dm AR$95-133, s AR$152-228, d AR$190-304; ✖ 🖳 🛜) This intimate guesthouse is for gay men only, offering eight small but elegant rooms – half with shared bathrooms and most featuring stunning views of the pretty church in back. It's a maze of catwalks, spiral staircases and sunny terraces (nude sunbathing welcome), plus a tango salon, a tiny cafe and a closet kitchenette. Two Jacuzzis – one indoor, one outside – translate into fun nights.

Casa Bolivar (Map p91; ☎ 4300-3619; www.casa bolivar.com; Bolívar 1701; r AR$373-612; ✖ 🖳 🛜) Fourteen spacious studios and loft apartments have been lovingly renovated into attractive and modern spaces at this amazing mansion, some with incredible original details such as carved doorways or painted ceilings. Separate entrances join with common hallways connecting through the complex, and there are lovely garden patios in which to relax.

Mansion Dandi Royal (Map pp84–5; ☎ 4307-7623; www.hotelmansiondandiroyal.com; Piedras 922; s AR$368, d AR$506-620; ✖ 🖳 🛜 🖻) Catering mainly to tango fanatics, this 1903 family mansion has been renovated into a luxurious themed hotel complete with murals, glass chandeliers and a curved wooden staircase. The 29 rooms are gorgeous; most come with antique furniture, claw-foot tubs and high ceilings. There's a small but lovely rooftop pool and a sunny patio, while tango classes, *milongas* and shows take place in the wonderful wood-floored basement studios or next-door salon.

Axel Hotel (Map pp84–5; ☎ 4136-9393; www.axelho tels.com; Venezuela 649; r AR$1135-1965; ✖ 🖳 🖻) BA's first five-star gay hotel is certainly a showpiece from the bottom up – the lobby boasts a multistory wall fountain and a peek at the top-floor swimming pool. Stairways are also glassy and rooms are fabulously contemporary, with acid-concrete floors. There's a large back garden with another (outdoor) pool, two bar-lounges, a restaurant, saunas, Jacuzzis and a gym. Sunday pool parties in summer; DJ parties on Fridays. Make sure to check its website – prices vary.

Retiro

Retiro is a great, central place to be, *if* you can afford it – many of BA's most expensive hotels, along with some of its richest inhabitants, are settled here. Close by are leafy Plaza San Martín, the Retiro bus station and many upscale stores and business services. Recoleta and the Microcentro are just a short stroll away.

MIDRANGE & TOP END

Hotel Central Córdoba (Map pp84–5; ☎ 4311-1175; www .hotelcentralcordoba.com.ar; San Martín 1021; s AR$150, d AR$170-200; ✖ 🛜) Possibly Retiro's most affordable hotel is the Central Córdoba. Rooms are neat and feature desk areas and tiled floors, but don't leave much space to move around. Ask for an inside room if you want quiet. The location is spot on – some key bars are within easy staggering distance – and it's very popular, so book well ahead.

Dazzler Suites Arroyo (Map pp84–5; ☎ 5276-7700; www.dazzlersuitesarroyo.com; Suipacha 1359; d from AR$340; ✖ 🖳 🛜 🖻) Contemporary in a minimalist way, this hotel sits in a good location close to Recoleta. There's a snazzy lobby area with patio beyond and to the side. Rooms are comfortably modern and all come with kitchenette; some have two bedrooms. Perks include an open-air swimming pool, gym and international restaurant; the breakfast is good.

Aspen Suites (Map pp84-5; ☎ 4313-9011; www.aspensuites.com.ar; Esmeralda 933; d from AR$425; ✂ 🖵 🛜) This six-story building is hardly luxurious – the halls could use a lick of paint and views out the window vary – but the modern, spacious suites all have fully equipped kitchenettes and dining areas. Bigger 'deluxe' suites and one-bedroom apartments are also available; good for families.

Hotel Bel Air (Map pp84-5; ☎ 4816-0016; www.hotelbelair.com.ar; Arenales 1462; r from AR$460; ✂ 🖵 🛜) The lobby bar here is downright sensuous, and the nearby lounge has upscale travelers and business folks sitting pretty. Upstairs, rooms are nicely designed in warm colors and have modern furnishings, though they're not super luxurious. Great location between the Retiro and Recoleta.

Four Seasons (Map pp84-5; ☎ 4321-1200; www.fourseasons.com/buenosaires; Posadas 1086; d from AR$2415; ✂ 🖵 🛜 🏊) No surprise here – the Four Seasons offers all the perks that define a five-star hotel, such as great service and white terry-cloth robes. Rooms are large and beautiful, with contemporary furnishings and decorations, and the finest suites (AR$4600 to AR$36,800!) are located in an old luxurious mansion next door. There's also a gorgeous spa and an outdoor heated swimming pool.

Recoleta & Barrio Norte

Most of the accommodations in Recoleta (Barrio Norte is more of a subneighborhood) are expensive, and what cheap hotels there are tend to be full much of the time. Buildings here are grand and beautiful, befitting the city's richest barrio, and you'll be close to Recoleta's famous cemetery, along with its lovely parks, museums and boutiques.

BUDGET & MIDRANGE

Southernhouse Hostel (Map pp88-9; ☎ 4961-6933; www.southernhouseba.com; TM de Anchorena 1117; dm AR$40, s AR$100, d AR$140-160; ✂ 🖵 🛜) This maze-like hostel is rather ho-hum, with small dorms (though each has its own bathroom). There are a dozen private rooms and a tiled outside patio, but the highlight here is its location, between Palermo, Recoleta and Once.

Recoleta Hostel (Map pp84-5; ☎ 4812-4419; www.hirecoleta.com.ar; Libertad 12116; dm AR$40-48, r AR$138-165; ✂ 🖵 🛜) Long-running hostel in an awesome location. Hardly intimate, though, and a bit rough around the edges despite it being an HI hostel. Segregated dorms (four to 10

beds), seven private rooms, tiny kitchen and sunny rooftop terrace. Lots of stairs, so be in shape. Strangely, Friday and Saturday rates can be higher.

Hotel Lion D'or (Map pp84-5; ☎ 4803-8992; www.hotel-liondor.com.ar; Pacheco de Melo 2019; s AR$150-180, d AR$190-250; ✂ 🛜) These digs have their charm (it's an old embassy), but rooms vary widely – some are small, basic and dark, while others are absolutely grand and may include a (non-working) fireplace. All are clean and good value, and while a few are a bit rough around the edges, most have been modernized for comfort. There's a great old marble staircase, and the elevator is just fabulous. No breakfast; some rooms share bathrooms.

TOP END

Art Hotel (Map pp84-5; ☎ 4821-4744; www.arthotel.com.ar; Azcuénaga 1268; s AR$285, d AR$360-740; ✂ 🖵 🛜) Stunningly beautiful, this boutique hotel features a small covered patio with an interesting wall of mirrors and a wonderful rooftop terrace with a Jacuzzi and a wood deck. Rooms (some small) boast a contemporary mix of decor – think concrete floors, plasma TVs and ironwork details – along with romantic canopied beds and original high doors.

Onze Trendy Hotel (Map pp88-9; ☎ 4821-2873; www.onzehotelboutique.com; Ecuador 1644; d AR$380-570; ✂ 🖵 🛜) With a name like this, how can you resist? Gorgeous from the get-go, this boutique hotel offers 11 rooms with unique touches such as dressing rooms and traditional *mantas* (hand-woven blankets) for decoration. Try for upstairs rooms; they're more interesting, and some rooms have balconies. It's a lovely place with great service and an exclusive feel.

Marseille des Anges (Map pp84-5; ☎ 5219-2526; www.marseilledesanges.com; Arenales 1392; s/d AR$395/482; ✂ 🖵 🛜) A great choice and well-located in snazzy Recoleta. Rooms are large and comfortable, and the best come with balcony or front-facing window. All have great bathrooms with cutting-edge multispray showers. The overall feel here is friendly and intimate, and the atmosphere traditional with modern comforts.

Palacio Duhau – Park Hyatt (Map pp84-5; ☎ 5171-1234; www.buenosaires.park.hyatt.com; Av Alvear 1661; d from AR$3015; ✂ 🖵 🛜 🏊) One of the loveliest five-star hotels in BA, the Park Hyatt consists of two wings – a newer building on Av Posadas and the renovated Palacio Duhau.

In between is a gorgeously terraced grassy garden with fountains and patios, overlooked by the palace's large restaurant balcony. Rooms are luxuriously wonderful, and swanky amenities include a fine spa, an indoor pool, a wine and cheese bar, an art gallery and even a teahouse.

Palermo

Despite being about a 10-minute taxi ride from the center, Palermo is the top choice for many travelers. Not only is it full of extensive parklands – which are great for weekend jaunts and sporting activities – but you'll have heaps of cutting-edge restaurants, designer boutiques and hip dance clubs at your fingertips. Many of these places are located in the extensive subneighborhood of Palermo Viejo (p102). All are connected to the center by bus or Subte.

BUDGET
Palermo House Hostel (Map pp88–9; ☎ 4832-1815; www.palermohouse.com.ar; Thames 1754; dm AR$38-50, d AR$133-152; ❄ ☐ ☎) It's a bit of an odd layout, with reception on the 3rd floor – but this is where everyone hangs out anyway. It's one big room, with a whole bank of windows making it bright and welcoming – and the metal deck makes a very welcome addition. Good dorms and private rooms with high ceilings are down one floor.

Hostel Suites Palermo (Map pp88–9; ☎ 4773-0806; www.hostelsuites.com; Charcas 4752; dm/d AR$49/195; ❄ ☐ ☎) One of the more pleasant large cheapies in town is this HI hostel in a fine old mansion and former geriatric home. Maybe this explains why it's not a party place, but a rather peaceful spot with good, large dorms and 11 small, private rooms. There's a rooftop terrace for hanging out, and lots of events on offer.

Kapaké Hostel (Map pp88–9; ☎ 4773-1150; www.kapake.com.ar; Paraguay 5570; dm AR$57-76, s/d AR$170/266; ❄ ☐ ☎) Wonderful, slightly upscale hostel on the edge of Palermo Hollywood and just 1½ blocks from a Subte stop. Common spaces have a great feel and modern amenities (think flat-screen TV), with nice patio and roof terrace areas for *asados*. Reserve private rooms in advance; there are only two. Intimate and secure.

ourpick Zentrum Hostel Boutique (Map pp88–9; ☎ 4833-9518; www.zentrumhostel.com.ar; Costa Rica 4520; dm AR$57, r AR$266-323; ❄ ☎) The Zentrum is

more like a small boutique hotel – there are only three private rooms, plus one that has bunks for six people. There's no kitchen, but the wood deck upstairs is awesome, and the location right on Plaza Palermo Viejo can't be beat.

MIDRANGE
Gorriti 4290 (Map pp88–9; ☎ 4862-8300; www.gorriti4290.com.ar; Gorriti 4290; d AR$190-304; ❄ ☐ ☎) For an intimate stay, seek out this small, friendly spot. There are only four rooms (three with shared bathrooms) and all are simple yet comfortable, with quality beds and linens. The common area is interesting – there's a catwalk above the dining room, and sunny rooftop patio. The owners live on-site; good breakfast.

Kala Petit Hotel (Map pp88–9; ☎ 4773-1331; www.kalapetithotel.com; Thames 1263; d from AR$228; ❄ ☐ ☎ ☎) Family-run, it's a great midrange deal in Palermo, especially because there's a small garden with pool and *asado* area in back – plus a nice kitchen available for guests. Rooms are simple but pleasant, and most share bathroom. In an old house, with good breakfast.

Palermo Viejo B&B (Map pp88–9; ☎ 4629-4773; www.palermoviejobb.com; Niceto Vega 4629; s AR$285, d AR$323-437; ❄ ☐ ☎) Small B&B in a remodeled *casa chorizo* – a long, narrow house. The six rooms all front an outdoor hallway and are simple but quite comfortable; two have lofts. All come with fridge and good breakfast.

TOP END
Craft Hotel (Map pp88–9; ☎ 4833-0060; www.crafthotel.com; Nicaragua 4583; r AR$506-690; ❄ ☐ ☎) Contemporary hotel with clean lines and artsy recycled touches; the stairs are made from old colorful wood panels. Rooms have Scandinavian aesthetics and come with flat-screen TVs, MP3 docks, cement floors, showers (yes – often *in* the room!) and sometimes balconies. This hotel's best feature, however, has to be the rooftop lounge area. Free bike rental.

ourpick Miravida Soho (Map pp88–9; ☎ 4774-6433; www.miravidasoho.com; Darregueyra 2050; r from AR$508; ❄ ☐ ☎) Run by a helpful Canadian, this lovely guesthouse comes with six beautifully remodeled, elegant rooms. All are very comfortable, and one has a private terrace and chandelier over the bathtub. There's a wine cellar, table-and-bar area for the evening wine tastings, small relaxing patio and it even has an elevator. It serves an American-style breakfast.

248 Finisterra (Map pp88-9; ☎ 4773-0901; www .248finisterra.com; Av Báez 248; r from AR$574; ⌘ ▯ ☜) Smack in the middle of Las Cañitas' nightlife lies this elegant, Zenlike boutique hotel. There are four classes of minimalist rooms, with most being good sized and all beautifully contemporary. Best of all is the rooftop terrace, with wood lounges and a Jacuzzi. Service is attentive, and security good.

Home Hotel (Map pp88-9; ☎ 4778-1008; www .homebuenosaires.com; Honduras 5860; r from AR$598; ⌘ ▯ ☜ ⌘) Sleek with Scandinavian designs, Home is a friendly, intimate little paradise of a hotel. Rooms come beautifully decorated with simple, modern lines and vintage wallpaper accents. The highlight is in the back, however; here you'll find an excellent bar and a grassy garden with a glorious pool. The basement spa is icing on the cake.

Vain Boutique Hotel (Map pp88-9; ☎ 4774-8246; www.vainuniverse.com; Thames 2226; r from AR$637; ⌘ ▯ ☜) Located in a lovely renovated building, the Vain typifies the new Palermo Viejo style of boutique minimalism. The 15 rooms here have been tastefully done up along contemporary lines – black headboards, white bedspreads and simple furnishings. All have high ceilings and wood floors, and you get a welcome drink on arrival.

EATING

Eating out in Buenos Aires makes for a gastronomical highlight. Not only are the typical *parrillas* (steak houses) a dime a dozen, but the city's Palermo Viejo neighborhood boasts the most varied ethnic cuisine in the country. You can find Armenian, Brazilian, Mexican, Indian, Japanese, Southeast Asian and Middle Eastern cuisines – and even fusions of several. Most are acceptable and some are exceptional.

Microcentro eateries tend to cater to the business crowd, while nearby Puerto Madero is full of elegant and pricey restaurants. Congreso is pretty traditional, cuisine-wise, except for its 'little Spain' neighborhood. Recoleta is another expensive neighborhood with touristy dining options on Roberto M Ortiz (near the cemetery). San Telmo keeps attracting more and more worthwhile restaurants.

Reservations are usually unnecessary except at the most popular restaurants – or if it's the weekend. The most thorough online guide to BA restaurants is www.guiaoleo .com, in Spanish; for English there's www .saltshaker.net.

Microcentro

Parrilla al Carbón (Map pp84-5; ☎ 4328-0824; Lavalle 663; mains AR$11-32; ⌚ lunch & dinner) Cheap *parrilla* doesn't come easier than this. Go for a quick *choripan* (sausage sandwich; AR$6) at the counter in front of the grill. For more comfort and a better view of the TV, snag one of the few crowded tables and order a half-portion of the *vacío* (a chewy but tasty flank cut).

California Burrito Company (CBC; Map pp84-5; ☎ 4328-3057; Lavalle 441; mains AR$22-36; ⌚ 8:30am-11pm Mon-Fri) At this modern Mexican joint, flour tortillas are loaded up with your choice of meat, rice, beans and salsa, and rolled into large San Francisco–style burritos the likes of which BA has never before seen. Tacos and salads are lighter options, and the house margaritas are a nice touch. It's also in Palermo at Godoy Cruz 1781 (Map pp88–9).

Broccolino (Map pp84-5; ☎ 4322-7754; Esmeralda 776; mains AR$24-45; ⌚ lunch & dinner) Pick from over 25 sauces (including squid ink!) for your pasta, with a choice of rigatoni, fusilli, pappardelle and all sorts of stuffed varieties. If you can't decide on your topper, try the delicious Sicilian sauce (spicy red peppers, tomato and garlic) or the pesto with mushrooms and garlic. Portions are large and the bread homemade.

Granix (Map pp84-5; ☎ 4343-4020; Florida 165, 1st fl; all-you-can-eat AR$35; ⌚ lunch Mon-Fri) Stepping into this large, modern lacto-ovo-vegetarian eatery will make you wonder if *porteños* have had enough steak already. Pick from the many hot appetizers and mains; there's also a great salad bar and plenty of desserts. It's only open for weekday lunches, and located in a shopping mall. Takeout is available.

Puerto Madero

Fresh Market (Map pp84-5; ☎ 5775-0335; cnr Villaflor & Olga Cossettini; mains AR$45-52; ⌚ breakfast, lunch & dinner) It's not on the water, but a sidewalk table does just fine at this upscale cafe-restaurant. Choose from stir-fried veggies, grilled salmon or broccoli ravioli with garlic sauce, and sit pretty with Puerto Madero's wealthy residents. There's a luscious dessert case inside, so be sure to take a peek.

MEATLESS IN BUENOS AIRES

Argentine cuisine is internationally famous for its succulent grilled meats, but this doesn't mean vegetarians – or even vegans – are completely out of luck.

Most restaurants, including *parrillas*, serve a few items acceptable to most vegetarians, such as green salads, omelettes, pizza and pasta. Key words to beware of include *carne* (beef), *pollo* (chicken), *cerdo* (pork) and *cordero* (lamb). *Sin carne* means 'without meat,' and the phrase *soy vegetariano/a* (I'm a vegetarian) will come in handy when explaining to an Argentine why in the world you don't want to tuck into a prime *bife de chorizo* (sirloin).

Luckily for nonmeat-eaters, vegetarian restaurants have become somewhat trendy in Buenos Aires recently. For cafeteria-style places close to the Microcentro there's **Granix** (p115), **Lotos** (Map pp84-5; ☎ 4814-4552; Córdoba 1577; mains AR$10-17; ☑ 11:30am-6pm Mon-Fri, 11:30am-4pm Sat) and **Arte Sano** (Map pp88-9; ☎ 4963-1513; Lucio Mansilla 2740; mains AR$15-21; ☑ 8am-10pm Mon-Fri, 9am-8pm Sat). **Pura Vida** (p118) has nutritious juice combinations plus a few veggie snacks.

The Palermo Viejo area has more upscale options, including **Bio** (p120), **Meraviglia** (p119) and **Artemesia** (Map pp88-9; ☎ 4863-4242; José Antonio Cabrera 3877; mains AR$25-40; ☑ dinner Tue-Sat). **Krishna** (p119) is a long-running hippie-Indian spot with good options.

There are many more vegetarian places in BA, plus many Indian restaurants. For a list, check out www.happycow.net – but be aware their BA section includes some places that have closed.

Siga la Vaca (Map pp84-5; ☎ 4315-6801; Av Alicia Moreau de Justo 1714; lunch AR$49-61, dinner AR$61-62; ☑ lunch & dinner) Only the truly hungry should set foot in this excellent all-you-can-stuff *parrilla*. Work your way from the appetizer salad bar to the grill, where the meat hangs out. Eat slowly and pace yourself, and you'll only need to eat once that day. One drink and a dessert are included in the price, which varies depending on the meal and day.

Rodizio (Map pp84-5; ☎ 4334-3638; Av Alicia Moreau de Justo 838; all-you-can-eat AR$130; ☑ lunch & dinner) Pure heaven for meat lovers is this Brazilian-style *churrasquería* (all-you-can-eat restaurant). You don't even have to queue up – just sit pretty at your table and knife-wielding waiters come by to slice chunks of meat off long spits, right onto your plate. The cuts vary, so be choosy and pace yourself. An extensive appetizer-salad buffet, along with one dessert and a coffee, are included in the price.

Congreso

Pizzería Güerrín (Map pp84-5; ☎ 4371-8141; Av Corrientes 1368; slices AR$3-4.50; ☑ 11am-2am) Just point at a prebaked slice behind the glass counter and eat standing up with the rest of the guys. To be more civilized, sit down and order your pizza freshly baked – this way you'll also get to choose from a greater variety of toppings. Empanadas and plenty of desserts are also available.

Cervantes II (Map pp84-5; ☎ 4372-5227; Juan D Perón 1883; mains AR$19-38; ☑ lunch & dinner) It's a

modern and unpretentious spot with a touch of old-world atmosphere. Locals order an *agua de sifón* (soda water) to go along with the *bife de chorizo* (sirloin) or *ravioles con tuco* (ravioli with sauce). Short orders such as *milanesas* (breaded steaks) and omelettes are also available. Portions are large and the service is efficient.

our pick **Chan Chan** (Map pp84-5; ☎ 4382-8492; Hipólito Yrigoyen 1390; mains AR$22-33; ☑ lunch & dinner Tue-Sun) A welcome newcomer to Congreso's dining scene is this very popular and artsy Peruvian joint. Dishes range from duck to rabbit to lamb (don't worry – no guinea pig), plus of course their delicious mixed ceviches and plenty of seafood choices. Try the *chicha morron* – a tasty corn-based fruity drink. Reasonable prices and good service mean there's often a wait.

Chiquilín (Map pp84-5; ☎ 4373-5163; Sarmiento 1599; mains AR$28-45; ☑ lunch & dinner) Going strong for over 80 years, Chiquilín is a large and comfortable restaurant with a classic atmosphere that adds a bit of personality (think ham legs hanging from the ceiling). The best food here is the *parrilla* and the pasta, though there is also seafood, omelettes and specialty salads, along with plenty of desserts.

San Telmo & Constitución

Bar El Federal (Map pp84-5; ☎ 4300-4313; cnr Perú & Carlos Calvo; snacks AR$15-30; ☑ 8am-2am) This historic bar with classic atmosphere dates from 1864; check out the amazing counter area. The specialties here are sandwiches (especially turkey breast) and *picadas* (shared appetizer plates), but there are also pastas, salads and desserts. Sidewalk tables are the perfect perch for you to watch San Telmo go by.

Bar Plaza Dorrego (Map pp84-5; ☎ 4361-0141; Defensa 1098; mains AR$20-39; ❧ 8am-2am Sun-Thu, to 3am Fri & Sat) You can't beat the atmosphere at this traditional joint; sip your *cortado* (coffee with milk) by a picture window and watch the world pass by. Meanwhile, traditionally suited waiters, tango music and scribbled graffiti on the counters take you back in time – at least until your hamburger lands on the table. Sitting at a sidewalk table is another experience in itself.

Parrilla 1880 (Map p91; ☎ 4307-2746; Defensa 1665; mains AR$20-45; ❧ lunch & dinner Tue-Sun) A good, solid *parrilla* away from the more touristy sections of San Telmo. The atmosphere is thick with history and locals come here to enjoy juicy cuts of meat from the open grill in front. The half portion of *bife de chorizo* is plenty big for one person. Lots of other dishes such as pastas, omelettes and salads are also available.

Gran Parrilla del Plata (Map pp84-5; ☎ 4300-8858; Chile 594; mains AR$21-36; ❧ lunch & dinner) There's nothing too fancy at this traditional *parrilla* – just old-time atmosphere and generous portions of good grilled meats at decent prices. There are also pastas for that vegetarian who gets dragged along. The cowhide-covered chairs are a great touch; this place a local favorite.

Mash (Map pp84-5; ☎ 011-15-5507-0572; Mexico 518; mains AR$25-37; ❧ dinner Tue-Sat) Run by a rather eccentric gay Brit and his Argentine partner (who both ran eateries across Europe) is this cozy restaurant-bar in San Telmo. The menu is small, but the dishes exotic and tasty; they range from Tandoori chicken to fajitas to Thai green curry to lamb rogan josh.

Café San Juan (Map pp84-5; ☎ 4300-1112; Av San Juan 450; mains AR$35-50; ❧ lunch & dinner Tue-Sun) Some of San Telmo's best international cuisine can be found at this family-run restaurant. The pork *bandiola* is deliciously tender, and the crushed-almond shrimp is a real treat – but everything is good. This is a great spot to try seafood; it's brought in daily from Patagonia.

Casal de Catalunya (Map pp84-5; ☎ 4361-0191; Chacabuco 863; mains AR$45-70; ❧ lunch Tue-Sat, dinner daily) Unsurprisingly big on seafood, this excellent Catalan restaurant offers garlic shrimp, mussels and clams in tomato sauce and fish of the day with *aioli* (garlic mayonnaise). Other typical Spanish dishes include *jamón serrano* (*prosciutto*-like ham), seafood paella and suckling pig. Don't miss the luscious *crema Catalana* for dessert.

La Boca

El Samovar de Rasputín (Map p91; ☎ 4302-3190; De Valle Iberlucea 1251; mains AR$15-22; ❧ 10am-8pm Tue-Sun) On warm summer days choose the street seating at this atmospheric old joint, with great tourist-watching opportunities. The food is nothing new – basic pasta, sandwiches, *milanesas*

THE SECRET'S OUT

A Buenos Aires culinary offshoot that has been getting a bit of press lately is the so-called 'closed-door restaurant' scene, or *puertas cerradas*. These restaurants are only open a few days per week, are pricey prix fixe and you have to ring a bell to enter. Most won't even tell you the address until you make reservations (mandatory, of course). But if you want that spine-tingling feeling brought on by discovering something off the beaten path – or just like being part of an exclusive group – these places are for you.

We'll let you in on the secret with a few starting points. At **Casa Saltshaker** (www.casasaltshaker .com) you'll be dining in chef and sommelier Dan Perlman's actual apartment in Barrio Norte. Vegetarians shouldn't miss **Casa Felix** (www.diegofelix.com), which serves a fish-based menu but does vegetarian or vegan dishes on request. Wine lovers will love **Casa Coupage** (www.casacoupage .com.ar), run by two friendly Argentine sommeliers in their beautiful home. And for something exotic there's **Cocina Sunae** (http://cocinasunae.blogspot.com), which serves up very tasty (and at times spicy) pan-Asian food.

All are great for meeting fellow diners, since tables are usually communal and the atmosphere intimate. And there are many more not listed here; do a little search and enjoy discovering BA's 'underground' dining scene!

and *parrilla* – but there's good live rock and blues at 10pm (see p127).

Il Matterello (Map p91; ☎ 4307-0529; Martín Rodríguez 517; mains AR$25-40; ☯ lunch Tue-Sun, dinner Tue-Sat) The food is exceptional at this Genovese trattoria. Try the *lasagne bolognese* or the *tagliatelle alla rucola* (tagliatelle with arugula). For a special treat, the house *tortelli verde* (small pasta pillows stuffed with cheese and garlic) is hard to beat.

Retiro

Filo (Map pp84-5; ☎ 4311-0312; San Martín 975; mains AR$25-46; ☯ lunch & dinner) Your choice is likely to be excellent at this artsy restaurant, as it does a great job cooking up the 20 varieties of pizza and 15 kinds of salads (try the smoked salmon). Other tasty choices include *panini*, pasta and meats, along with a whirlwind of desserts.

Al Carbón (Map pp84-5; ☎ 4312-5604; Reconquista 875; mains AR$32-44; ☯ lunch & dinner Mon-Sat) This attractive, modern and upscale *parrilla* restaurant is on a pedestrianized street downtown. Plenty of good beef is slapped on the grill, and there are also lamb, pork and fish dishes available – mostly well presented. Homemade pastas and plenty of dessert options round out the menu.

Gran Bar Danzón (Map pp84-5; ☎ 4811-1108; Libertad 1161; mains AR$34-65; ☯ dinner) It's hard to be hipper than this popular lounge bar–restaurant. A cool-looking conservation system makes it possible for many wines to be offered by the glass, one of which should go well with the duck *confit* with *taleggio* cheese, rabbit ravioli or risotto with king crab.

Empire Bar (Map pp84-5; ☎ 4312-5706; Tres Sargentos 427; mains AR$36-61; ☯ lunch & dinner Mon-Fri, dinner Sat) This trendy place is good for its tasty Thai cuisine, though the spice factor is toned down for Argentine taste buds. The kitchen puts out crispy wrapped prawns, *paneng* pork in red curry and *tom ka gai* (chicken-and-coconut-milk soup). There are also nearly 80 kinds of vodkas.

Sipan (Map pp84-5; ☎ 4315-0763; Paraguay 624; mains AR$40-70; ☯ lunch & dinner Mon-Sat) Either come very hungry or with a friend, 'cause the plates at this attractive Japanese-Peruvian restaurant are meant to be shared. Both traditional ('criollo') and Asian-influenced creative dishes ('*chifa*') are available; try the 'Sipan roll' (with shrimp, crab, avocado and cream cheese) or well-spiced ceviches.

Recoleta & Barrio Norte

Pura Vida (Map pp84-5; ☎ 4806-0017; Uriburu 1489; juices AR$10-17, snacks AR$16-21; ☯ 9:30am-10pm Mon-Sat) Step into this healthy juice bar for fruit blends and smoothies. The Green Monster (celery, cucumber and apple) is especially refreshing, and you can add wheatgrass, yogurt, spirulina or bee pollen to your selection. Sandwiches, wraps and salads are available. A second branch (Map pp84-5) has opened in central BA at Reconquista 516.

El Sanjuanino (Map pp84-5; ☎ 4805-2683; Posadas 1515; mains AR$16-25; ☯ lunch & dinner) The cheapest food in Recoleta, attracting both penny-pinching locals and thrifty tourists. Sit on the main floor or in the basement and order spicy empanadas, tamales or *locro* (a spicy stew), or take your food to go – Recoleta's lovely parks are just a couple of blocks away.

Cumaná (Map pp84-5; ☎ 4813-9207; Rodriguez Peña 1149; mains AR$18-27; ☯ lunch & dinner) Cumaná specializes in deliciously homey, stick-to-your-ribs pot stews, which are filled and baked with squash, corn, potatoes and/or meats, among other tidbits. Also popular are the pizzas, empanadas, pastas and calzones. Come early if you want a table.

Rodi Bar (Map pp84-5; ☎ 4801-5230; Vicente López 1900; mains AR$20-36; ☯ breakfast, lunch & dinner Mon-Sat) A great option for well-priced, unpretentious food in upscale Recoleta. This traditional restaurant with fine old-world atmosphere and extensive menu offers something for everyone, from inexpensive combo plates to relatively unusual dishes such as liver stuffed with nuts. Opens very early in the morning.

Grant's (Map pp84-5; ☎ 4801-9099; General Las Heras 1925; lunch AR$22-30, dinner AR$30-33; ☯ lunch & dinner) This *tenedor libre* (all-you-can-eat) offers a fantastic assortment of foods too numerous to mention. There are also plenty of *parrilla* and dessert selections. The price depends on the meal and on the day of the week; drinks are mandatory and cost extra.

Como en Casa (Map pp84-5; ☎ 4816-5507; www .tortascomoencasa.com; Riobamba 1239; mains AR$22-32; ☯ breakfast, lunch & dinner Tue-Sat, breakfast & lunch Sun & Mon) Gorgeous cafe-restaurant in Barrio Norte, with an elegant atmosphere. Best for its shady patio, complete with large fountain and surrounded by grand buildings – a must on a warm day. This location has a few dinner options; their other branches (see website) have mostly fancy pastries and sandwiches, salads or crepes.

Natural Deli (Map pp88-9; ☎ 4822-1228; Laprida 1672; mains AR$24-30; ☺ 8am-9:30pm Mon-Sat, 9am-8:30pm Sun) Modern, organic deli offering delicious natural foods. Choose from creative gourmet sandwiches and wraps, fresh salads or vegetarian tarts. You can add echinacea and ginseng to their healthy juices and *licuados*, and there's even a small health food store for take-home treats. Also at Gorostiaga 1776 (Map pp88–9), which has a yoga studio.

La Olla de Felix (Map pp84-5; ☎ 4811-2873; Juncal 1693; mains AR$30-42; ☺ lunch & dinner Mon-Fri, dinner Sat) This wonderful French bistro comes full of personality and cozy atmosphere – there's a different soup tureen on every table (as decoration) and animated Felix Rueda, the chef, is often on the dining floor greeting return patrons. There are only five items on the menu, which changes daily, but all are well-prepared, tasty choices – and the service is attentive.

Munich Recoleta (Map pp84-5; ☎ 4804-3981; RM Ortiz 1871; mains AR$36-60; ☺ lunch & dinner Wed-Mon) This traditional old place hasn't changed much since Borges was a regular and enjoying its great food; try the *brochettes* (shish kebabs), grilled salmon or nine kinds of ravioli. Just make sure you can stomach the trophy animal heads looking down at you from the wall.

our pick **Oviedo** (Map pp88-9; ☎ 4821-3741; Beruti 2602; mains AR$45-70; ☺ lunch & dinner) Chef Martin Rabaudino oversees one of the best kitchens in the city. This is a truly elegant place, with professional service and a classy atmosphere. Fish and meat dishes are the specialty; choose from tempting and nonpretentious dishes such as quail with mushrooms, shrimp risotto and seafood paella. The wine list is excellent.

Palermo
BUDGET
La Fábrica del Taco (Map pp88-9; ☎ 4833-3534; Gorriti 5062; tacos AR$7-13; ☺ lunch & dinner Tue-Sun) You might just feel like you're back in a Mexican beach town at this very casual, colorful taco joint. Authentic Mexican cooks hover at the front grill, slapping together those tasty and familiar tacos (al pastor, carne asada, pollo con queso, vegetariano). There are even *aguas frescas de tamarindo* and jamaica. *Chimichurri* (sauce made of olive oil, garlic and parsley) on the menu, however, brings you back to BA.

Meraviglia (Map pp88-9; ☎ 4775-7949; cnr Gorriti & Angel J Carranza; mains AR$16-20; ☺ 9am-8pm Mon-Sat) Wonderful new airy and bright vegetarian cafe with small but high-quality menu.

Choose granola and yogurt for breakfast, and well-prepared salads, tarts and sandwiches for lunch or late afternoon snack. Everything is freshly made with mostly organic ingredients, and a few healthy products are available for purchase.

El 22 Parrilla (Map pp88-9; ☎ 4833-7876; Gorriti 5299; mains AR$17-40; ☺ lunch & dinner) A cheap unpretentious *parrilla* isn't that easy to find in upscale Palermo Viejo. This casual family-style joint is an exception, serving up huge portions for great prices. The lunch specials are an even better deal, especially if you score a sidewalk table. Several branches around Palermo.

Krishna (Map pp88-9; ☎ 4833-4618; Malabia 1833; mains AR$18-27; ☺ lunch & dinner Tue-Sun) With colorful decor and low tables, Krishna offers a vegetarian Indian food experience with a multireligious theme – look for Ganesh mixing it up with Jesus, the star of David and even Jimi Hendrix. Order the *thali*, *koftas* (balls of ground vegetables) or stuffed soya *milanesa*, and there's chai, lassis and alcohol-free beer to help wash it all down.

Las Cholas (Map pp88-9; ☎ 4899-0094; Arce 306; mains AR$18-30; ☺ lunch & dinner) Las Cholas found the golden rule of many successful restaurants: quality food, trendy design and bargain prices. Traditional Argentine foods such as *locro* and *cazuelas* (meat and veggie stews) are worth a shot, but the *parrilla* is also excellent. Expect a wait and so-so service.

MIDRANGE
Il Ballo del Mattone (Map pp88-9; ☎ 4776-4247; Gorriti 5934; mains AR$20-45; ☺ lunch daily, dinner Tue-Sat) The homemade pastas here can be hit or miss, but the atmosphere – full of funky, artsy touches – is priceless. Not surprisingly, the owner is an artist and the little patio in back has a graffiti mural. Friday nights can be packed – a DJ often spins. Its cafe, a few doors down, is a more peaceful proposition.

our pick **Sarkis** (Map pp88-9; ☎ 4772-4911; Thames 1101; mains AR$22-38; ☺ lunch & dinner) There's a reason this long-standing, Middle Eastern restaurant is still around – the food is awesome. For appetizers, don't miss the *boquerones* (marinated sardines) or *hojas de repollo rellenas* (stuffed grape leaves). Follow up with lamb in yogurt sauce. At night a fortune teller reads diners' coffee grounds.

Don Julio (Map pp88-9; ☎ 4832-6058; Guatemala 4699; mains AR$22-45; ☺ lunch & dinner) A p*arrilla* highly recommended for its exceptional meat dishes –

LICKING YOUR WAY THROUGH BA

Because of Argentina's Italian heritage, Argentine *helado* is comparable to the best ice cream in the world. Amble into an *heladería* (ice-cream shop), order up a cone (pay first) and the creamy concoction will be artistically swept up into a mountainous peak. Important: *granizado* means with chocolate flakes.

Here are some of the tastiest *heladerías* in town:

Dylan (Map pp84-5; ☎ 0810-3333-9526; Perú 1086, San Telmo)

Freddo (Map pp84-5; ☎ 0810-3337-3336; cnr Quintana & RM Ortiz, Retiro) Many branches; check www.freddo .com.ar, in Spanish.

Heladería Cadore (Map pp84-5; ☎ 4374-3688, Av Corrientes 1695, Congreso)

Persicco (☎ 0810-333-7377) Belgrano (Map pp82-3; Vuelta de Obligado 2092); Las Cañitas (Map pp88-9; Migueletes 886); Palermo (Map pp88-9; Salguero 2591)

Una Altra Volta (Map pp88-9; ☎ 4805-1818; Av del Libertador 3060, Palermo) Also at the corner of Quintana and Ayacucho, Recoleta (Map pp84–5).

Vía Flaminia (Map pp84-5; ☎ 4342-7737;l Av Florida 121, Microcentro)

it's as good as its fancier neighbors, but with much more traditional feel. Nice corner location with sidewalk tables, and the wine list is also better than average.

Bio (Map pp88-9; ☎ 4774-3880; Humboldt 2199; mains AR$23-36; ☿ lunch daily, dinner Tue-Sun) The health-conscious should make a beeline to this casual corner joint, which specializes in healthy, organic and vegetarian fare. Feed your body and soul quinoa risotto, seitan curry, mushroom stir-fries and mustard tofu with yamani rice.

Bar Uriarte (Map pp88-9; ☎ 4834-6004; Uriarte 1572; mains AR$25-48; ☿ lunch & dinner) One of Palermo's trendiest and best restaurants, and beautiful to boot. Sample the marinated pork with ginger and salvia, cooked in their adobe oven (where their gourmet pizza is baked). Other delicious dishes include the lamb carpaccio or *noquis* de ricotta.

Mama Racha (Map pp88-9; ☎ 4833-4950; Costa Rica 4602; mains AR$26-33; ☿ breakfast, lunch & dinner) Sitting on the rooftop terrace on a hot day, looking over Plaza Palermo Viejo, you might feel life can't get any better than this. Then your salmon and arugula salad with lemonade arrives, and you'll know it can. The wood-block menu also has good creative salads, sandwiches and breakfast choices, but service can be slow.

Novecento (Map pp88-9; ☎ 4778-1900; Av Báez 199; mains AR$30-49; ☿ breakfast, lunch & dinner) Full breakfasts (a rarity in BA) are served at this elegant corner restaurant; go for the French toast, eggs benedict or waffles with fig syrup. There's brunch on weekends, when dishes are brought to you (all-you-can-eat; AR$90 for two). Dinner means things like beef carpaccio and salmon farfalle.

Voulezbar (Map pp88-9; ☎ 4802-4817; Cerviño 3802; mains AR$33-49; ☿ breakfast, lunch & dinner Mon-Sat) It's worth the trek out to Palermo Chico to sit at this popular corner cafe. Fresh, creative cuisine includes Patagonian trout and shrimp risotto. For lighter, less expensive fare, come for lunch – the baby calamari, grilled squash and lox salads are awe-inspiring, or try a burger or even the tasty *ceviche*.

TOP END

Miranda (Map pp88-9; ☎ 4771-4255; Costa Rica 5602; mains AR$37-52; ☿ lunch & dinner) Popular for its reasonably priced steaks, Miranda is a fashionable, modern *parrilla* with concrete walls, high ceilings and rustic wood furniture, but the food is the main attraction here. The meat is good quality and grilled to perfection, and if you score a sidewalk table on a warm day, life for a carnivore just doesn't get much better.

Olsen (Map pp88-9; ☎ 4776-7677; Gorriti 5870; mains AR$37-54; ☿ lunch & dinner Tue-Sat, 10:30am-8pm Sun) Olsen is famous for its Sunday brunch, but dinner isn't bad either; order manchego cheese ravioli or slow-cooked lamb with krein cabbage. Lunches are prix fixe and the best deal, plus you can see the peaceful garden better. The popular bar serves more than 50 kinds of vodka, assiduously kept at -18°C.

Astrid & Gastón (Map pp88-9; ☎ 4802-2991; Lafinur 3222; mains AR$40-70; ☿ lunch & dinner Mon-Sat) Likely BA's fanciest Peruvian restaurant, dishes include cream of shrimp soup, crab with avocado and cherry tomatoes, duck in dark beer sauce and – of course – several kinds of delicious *ceviche*. Excellent pisco sours (if a bit pricey), exquisite desserts and very attentive service.

Azema (Map pp88-9; ☎ 4774-4191; AJ Carranza 1875; mains AR$42-58; ⏲ dinner Mon-Sat) Run by eccentric chef Paul Jean Azema (who has cooked for Kurt Cobain, among others) is this restaurant that serves up 'French colony cuisine' – an interesting array of Asian, French and Argentine fusions. Dishes run the gamut from Vietnamese spring rolls to Tandoori chicken salad to rabbit in Dijon mustard and Chardonnay. Seafood dishes are great and the kitchen isn't afraid of using its spices.

DRINKING
Cafes
Cafes are an integral part of *porteño* life, and you shouldn't miss popping into one of these beloved hangouts to sip dainty cups of coffee and nibble biscuits with the locals. There are plenty of cafes in the city, and while you're walking around seeing the sights you're bound to run across one and find an excuse for a break. Some cafes are old classics and guaranteed to take you back in time.

Most cafes serve all meals and everything in between: breakfast, brunch, lunch, afternoon tea, dinner and late-night snacks. For a background on these enduring legacies of Argentine social history, see the boxed text (below).

Café de los Angelitos (Map pp84-5; ☎ 4952-2320; Rivadavia 2100) Originally called Bar Rivadavia, this spot was once the haunt of poets, musicians…even criminals. Recently restored to its former glory, this historic cafe is now an elegant hangout, modernized by offering tango shows to tourists. Come during the day, order a cup of tea and enjoy a slice of the shady past.

Clásica y Moderna (Map pp84-5; ☎ 4812-8707; Av Callao 892) Catering to the literary masses since 1938, this cozy and intimate bookstore-cafe continues to ooze history from its atmospheric brick walls. It's nicely lit, offers plenty of reading material and serves upscale meals. There are also regular live performances of folk music, jazz, bossa nova and tango.

El Gato Negro (Map pp84-5; ☎ 4374-1730; Av Corrientes 1669) Tea-lined wooden cabinets and a spicy aroma welcome you to this pleasant little sipping paradise. Enjoy cups of imported coffee or tea along with breakfast and dainty *sandwiches de miga* (thinly sliced white-bread sandwiches). Tea is sold by weight, and exotic herbs and spices are also on offer.

La Biela (Map pp84-5; ☎ 4804-0449; Av Quintana 600) A Recoleta institution, this classic landmark has been serving the *porteño* elite since the 1950s, when racing-car champions used to come here for their java jolts. The outdoor front terrace is unbeatable on a sunny afternoon, especially when the nearby weekend *feria* (street market) is in full swing – but it'll cost you 20% more.

La Puerto Rico (Map pp84-5; ☎ 4331-2215; Adolfo Alsina 416) One of the city's historic cafes, going strong since 1887. Located a block south of Plaza de Mayo, it serves great coffee and pastries, the latter baked on the premises. Old photos on the walls hint at a rich past and the Spanish movies that have been filmed here. A good place to come that's not too touristy.

our pick **Las Violetas** (Map pp82-3; ☎ 4958-7387; Rivadavia 3899) Dating back to 1884, this historic coffeehouse was renovated in 2001. Lovely awnings and stained-glass windows, high ceilings, cream-colored Ionic columns and gilded

---

BUENOS AIRES' CAFES

Thanks to its European heritage, Buenos Aires has a serious cafe culture. *Porteños* will spend hours dawdling over a single *café cortado* (coffee with milk) and a couple of *medialunas* (croissants), discussing the economy, politics or that latest football game.

Some of the capital's cafes have been around for over a hundred years, and many still retain much of their original atmosphere. They've always been the haunts of Argentina's politicians, anarchists, intellectuals, artists and literary greats. **London City** (p122) boasts that Julio Cortázar wrote his masterpiece *The Prizes* at one of its tables, while the **Richmond** (p122) says Jorge Luis Borges drank hot chocolate there. The most famous is **Café Tortoni** (p124), which is beautiful but way too touristy.

Most cafes offer a surprisingly wide range of food and drinks; you can order a steak as easily as a *cortado*. Some double as bookstores or host live music, tango shows and other cultural events. Hanging out at one of these atmospheric cafes is part of the Buenos Aires experience – and also makes a welcome break from all that walking you'll be doing.

details make this cafe the most beautiful in BA. Breakfast, lunch and dinner service is available, along with a luxurious afternoon tea. Located in Almagro.

London City (Map pp84-5; ☎ 4343-0328; Av de Mayo 599) This swank and classy cafe has been serving java addicts for over 50 years, and claims to have been the spot where Julio Cortázar wrote his first novel. Your hardest work here, however, will most likely be choosing which luscious pastry to consume with your freshly brewed coffee.

Nucha (Map pp84-5; ☎ 4813-9507; Paraná 1343) There *must* be something in the tempting pastry counter – perhaps cheesecake, *medialunas* (croissants) or lightly layered afternoon cake – to go with your imported tea, iced coffee or *mate* (tea-like beverage) at this cute cafe. Crowds flood in for afternoon tea and tasty lunch sandwiches, but breakfast is also served.

Richmond (Map pp84-5; ☎ 4322-1341; Florida 468) Feel like challenging the local male population to a billiards game or a chess match? Then head to the basement at this very traditional cafe. Better yet, go to the main room and sink into a leather chair to admire the Dutch chandeliers and English-style surroundings while sipping hot chocolate – just like Jorge Luis Borges did.

Bars

In a city that never sleeps, finding a good drink (or cup of tea) is as easy as walking down the street. Whether you're into trendy lounges, Irish pubs, traditional cafes or sports bars, you'll find them all within the borders of Buenos Aires.

Argentines aren't huge drinkers and you'll be lucky to see one rip-roaring drunk. One thing they *do* do, however, is stay up late.

pMost bars and cafes are open until two or three in the morning, and often until 5am on weekends – or until the last customer stumbles out the door.

And if you like to party with the young international crowd, check out **Buenos Aires Pub Crawl** (☎ 011-15-5464-1886; www.pubcrawlba.com; per person AR$60). Transport to several bars and a nightclub is included, as are free pizza and some beer or wine.

CENTRAL BUENOS AIRES

Casa Bar (Map pp84-5; ☎ 4816-2712; Rodríguez Peña 1150) Run by an American ex-pilot, who spent years rebuilding an old house into this atmospheric bar. Attractions include 50 beers to choose from, US football on TV, pancakes on weekends and BA's best spicy chicken wings. Has a tiny patio in back for smokers.

Debar (Map pp84-5; ☎ 4381-6876; Av Rivadavia 1132) A popular bar in an area not known for its nightlife, Debar has some of BA's greatest rock and hip-hop beats. Businesspeople come for an after-work *trago* (drink), while travelers and expats hit it later in the evening. With a happy hour that runs until midnight every night, everyone is happy. Also does lunch on weekdays.

El Alamo (Map pp84-5; ☎ 4813-7324; Uruguay 1175) El Alamo draws US students and expats with US football, baseball and basketball on TV (not to mention beer pong games on Tuesday). The music's rock, there's pub food for the hungry and they've got a great way of attracting women – every day from noon to midnight, the ladies drink beer for free. Happy hour indeed.

Gibraltar (Map pp84-5; ☎ 4362-5310; Perú 895) One of BA's classic expat pubs, with a cozy atmosphere and an excellent bar counter for those traveling alone. Great exotic food too – try the

---

WINE TASTING 101

Big on wine? There are a few ways to taste what Argentina's best grapes have to offer. Try a wine tasting!

Casa Coupage (Map pp88-9; ☎ 4833-6354; www.casacoupage.com.ar; Güemes 4382) Run by a friendly Argentine couple, both sommeliers, in their beautiful Palermo Soho apartment. Includes light tables for the wine and a food pairing meal.

Anuva Wines (☎ 4777-4661; www.anuvawines.com) US native Daniel Karlin organizes wine tastings – try five boutique vintages with food pairings. Best of all, he'll send your wines to the USA (arguably BA's most affordable wine-shipping service) and can deliver within the city.

Nigel Tollerman (☎ 4966-2500; www.0800-vino.com) Private wine tastings run by enthusiastic Brit Nigel Tollerman, in his atmospheric basement cellar. He'll also deliver fine-quality Argentine wines to your hotel, and has a premium-wine storage service.

generous Thai, Indian or English dishes, or the sushi on Sunday. For a little friendly competition head to the pool table in back, grabbing a well-priced pint of beer along the way.

Le Cigale (Map pp84-5; ☎ 4312-8275; 25 de Mayo 722) Sultry and moody downtown lounge very popular with both foreigners and *porteños*. There's different music every night, with live bands on Thursday and DJs on Saturday. But it's most popular on 'French Tuesday,' when electronica and French drinks draw the heavy crowds in.

Milión (Map pp84-5; ☎ 4815-9925; Paraná 1048) This elegant and sexy bar is in a renovated mansion. The garden out back is a leafy paradise, overlooked by a solid balcony that holds the best seats in the house. There are elegant tapas to accompany the wide range of cocktails (pay first, then catch the bartender's eye!), while downstairs a restaurant serves international dishes.

Puerta Roja (Map pp84-5; ☎ 4362-5649; Chacabuco 733) There's no sign and you have to ring the bell, but once inside there's hot music and cool vibes, with low lounge furniture in the main room and a pool table tucked behind. Come early for a good seat and to munch on the excellent and cheap food options – there's little space to eat later. Adventurous? Try their 'chili bomb' cocktail.

PALERMO

Many hotels and restaurants in Palermo have great bars; try Home Hotel (p115), **Casa Cruz** (Map pp88-9; ☎ 4833-1112; Uriarte 1658) or **Bangalore** (Map pp88-9; ☎ 4779-2621; Humboldt 1416). For the hippest scene in town, head to Plaza Serrano (in Palermo Viejo) and settle in at one of the many trendy bars surrounding the plaza.

878 (Map pp88-9; ☎ 4773-1098; Thames 878) Enter into a wonderland of elegant, low lounge furniture and red brick walls; if you're a whiskey lover, there are over 100 kinds to try. Tasty classic and original cocktails also lubricate the crowds, happy to revel in the jazz, bossa nova and good old rock music playing on the speakers.

Congo (Map pp88-9; ☎ 4833-5857; Honduras 5329) The highlight at this beautiful and trendy bar is the back patio – *the* place to be seen on hot summer nights. The music is tops too, with DJs spinning almost every night, and inside are elegant low lounges in creative spaces. Full food menu available, along with some tasty, stiff cocktails.

El Carnal (Map pp88-9; ☎ 4772-7582; Niceto Vega 5511) The open-air roof terrace, with its bamboo lounges and billowy curtains, can't be beat for a cool chill-out on a warm summer night. Thursday means pre-Niceto Club drinks, on Friday reggae rocks, and Saturday is dominated by pop and '80s beats.

Kim y Novak (Map pp88-9; ☎ 4777-9081; Güemes 4900) Popular with the gay and expat crowds, this intimate corner bar has great *onda* (vibes). Come before 2am if you want to chat, because it really gets packed in the early hours – especially later in the week when the basement dance floor opens. Try their house drink, the JoJo – made of vodka, ginger, lime and sugar.

Mundo Bizarro (Map pp88-9; ☎ 4773-1967; Serrano 1222) This futuristically retro and stylishly slick lounge bar is open all night on weekends, when everything from old-time American music to hip DJs and jazz stir up the airwaves. Thursday night is ladies' night; if you feel lucky hop on the pole and grab some attention. For the hungry there are hamburgers, or sushi on Monday.

Sugar (Map pp88-9; ☎ 011-15-6894-2002; Costa Rica 4619; ⏳ Tue-Sun) Palermo Soho bar that's super popular for its happy hour, which runs from 8pm to midnight – pints, glasses of wine or mixed drinks are AR$5 each. Attracts foreign students and expats (it's partially expat-run); all servers speak some English. Great eclectic mix of music, from James Brown to the Killers. Come early to avoid lines; weekends have a drink minimum.

Van Koning (Map pp88-9; ☎ 4772-9909; Av Báez 325) Great rustic spaces make this intimate Las Cañitas pub feel like the inside of a boat; after all, it's a 17th-century-style seafaring theme complete with dark-wood beams, flickering candles and blocky furniture. Filled with Dutch expats on the first Wednesday of the month.

ENTERTAINMENT

Nonstop Buenos Aires offers endless possibilities for entertainment. Dozens of venues offer first-rate theatrical productions, independent or contemporary movies, sultry tango shows, raging dance parties and exciting sports matches.

Most newspapers publish entertainment supplements on Friday; the *Buenos Aires Herald* does one in English called *Get Out*. Also check www.whatsupbuenosaires.com.

Major entertainment venues often require booking through **Ticketek** (☎ 5237-7200; www .ticketek.com.ar). The service charge is about 10% of the ticket price. At *carteleras* (discount ticket offices), you can buy tickets at 20% to 50% off for many entertainment events. Here are three:

Cartelera Baires (Map pp84–5; ☎ 4372-5058; www .carterabaires.com; Av Corrientes 1382) In Cine Lorange.

Cartelera Espectáculos (Map pp84–5; ☎ 4322-1559; www.123info.com.ar; Lavalle 742) Right on pedestrian Lavalle.

Cartelera Vea Más (Map pp84–5; ☎ 6320-5319; www .veamasdigital.com.ar; Corrientes 1660, local 2)

Tango

Sensationalized tango shows aimed at tourists are common, and 'purists' don't consider them authentic – though this doesn't necessarily make them bad. Modest shows are more intimate and cost far less, but you won't get the theatrics, the costume changes or the overall visual punch. For discount tickets to some shows, check the *carteleras* (see earlier). Still young, but with some potential, is this tango show review website www.tangotix .com.

For free (that is, donation) tango, head to Galerías Pacíficos, where there are daily performances in front on the pedestrian street. On Sunday in San Telmo, dancers do their thing in Plaza Dorrego (and it's *crowded* – watch your bag). Another good bet is weekends on Caminito in La Boca. All of these dancers are pretty good, so remember to toss some change into their hats.

For tango tours, check www.tangofocus .com. The following is a list of tango shows; for classes and *milongas*, see the boxed text, opposite.

Bar Sur (Map pp84–5; ☎ 4362-6086; cnr Estados Unidos & Balcarce; show & dinner AR$220, show only AR$150) Best for its intimate, traditional atmosphere – there are only a dozen or so tables so everyone gets a good look at the dancers. The schedule is also very flexible – nightly shows run continuously from 8:30pm to 2am, so just show up anytime (though you might need to reserve a table).

Café Tortoni (Map pp84–5; ☎ 4342-4328; www .cafetortoni.com.ar; Av de Mayo 829; show AR$60–70) Buenos Aires' landmark cafe has become overrun with tourists, but the tango shows are relatively good and still affordable. There are up to four shows nightly, but reserve ahead because they do fill up.

Centro Cultural Torquato Tasso (Map p91; ☎ 4307-6506; www.torquatotasso.com.ar; Defensa 1575; shows AR$50–120) One of BA's best live-music venues, with top-name tango *music* performances. Attracts bands that mix genres together, such as fusing tango or *folklórico* with rock; keep an eye out for La Chicana, Sexteto Mayor or Fernández Fierro.

El Balcón (Map pp84–5; ☎ 4362-2354; Humberto Primo 461, 1st fl) Located above Plaza Dorrego, this restaurant puts on free shows – but you have to order some food to see them. Shows run at 10pm Saturday and from 1pm to midnight on Sunday.

El Querandí (Map pp84–5; ☎ 5199-1770; www .querandi.com.ar; Perú 302; show & dinner AR$330, show only AR$190) This large corner tango venue is also an elegant restaurant with an upscale atmosphere. The excellent show is one of the better ones in town, taking you through the evolution of tango over the years. One plus is a high stage, which makes viewing easier.

Esquina Homero Manzi (Map pp82–3; ☎ 4957-8488; www.esquinahomeromanzi.com.ar; Av San Juan 3601; show & dinner AR$270-310) An impressively refurbished old cafe, Homero Manzi was named after one of Argentina's most famous tango lyricists. Today you can take tango lessons here, then sit back and watch the show.

Esquina Osvaldo Pugliese (Map pp82–3; ☎ 4931-2142; Boedo 909; show AR$25-28) Also called Recuerdo Café, this casual venue has a small stage in more modest surroundings, with just a few performers doing the fancy footwork. It's at a fraction of the price of Homero Manzi's much fancier tango show, just a block away. Shows Friday and Saturday.

Los 36 Billares (Map pp84–5; ☎ 4381-5696; www .los36billares.com.ar; Av de Mayo 1265) A combination restaurant-cafe-bar–billiards hall, this atmospheric old place has been around for nearly 100 years. It boasts pool tables in back and billiards tables in the basement. Free tango shows Monday through Thursday, minimum AR$20 Friday and Sunday, AR$20 shows (with AR$20 minimum consumption) on Saturday. The food is not great, however.

Piazzolla Tango (Map pp84–5; ☎ 4344-8201; www .piazzollatango.com; Florida 165; show & dinner AR$320, show only AR$210) This beautiful art nouveau theater used to be a red-light cabaret venue. The show put on here now is a combination of old and new; it's based on tradition, but some moves are so athletic they seem more like circus acts.

MILONGAS & TANGO CLASSES

Tango has experienced a renaissance, both at the amateur and professional levels and among all ages. Classes are available just about everywhere, from youth hostels and cultural centers to all the *milongas* (social dance events); and many are now taught in English. Group classes cost anywhere from AR$15 to AR$40, depending on the teacher; private classes cost much more.

Milongas start either in the afternoon or the evening. They're affordable, usually costing AR$10 to AR$30. Don't be surprised to see different *milongas* put on at a single venue, depending on the time or day. Each *milonga* is run by a different promoter, so each will have its own vibe, style, music and table arrangement, as well as age levels and experiences. For a long list of *milongas* and instructors, snag the free *Caserón Porteño Tango Map Guide* or magazines such as *El Tangauta* (www.eltangauta.com) or *BA Tango* (www.londontango.wordpress.com); they're often available from tango shoe stores, tango venues and tourist offices. Or check www.buenosairesmilongas.com.

For a unique outdoor experience, head to the bandstand at the Barrancas de Belgrano park, where the casual *milonga* 'La Glorieta' takes place on Sunday evenings at around 8pm (free tango lessons given earlier).

Club Gricel (Map pp82-3; ☎ 4957-7157; www.clubgriceltango.com.ar; La Rioja 1180) This old classic (far from the center, take a taxi) attracts an older, well-dressed crowd. Wonderful aging wood dance floor and occasional live orchestras.

Confitería Ideal (Map pp84-5; ☎ 5265-8069; www.confiteriaideal.com; Suipacha 384, 1st fl) The mother of all historic tango halls, with many classes and *milongas* offered pretty much continuously. Live orchestras often accompany dancers; shows almost nightly. Good for beginners.

El Beso (Map pp84-5; ☎ 4953-2794; Riobamba 416) Another traditional and popular place that attracts some very good dancers. Located upstairs, with an intimate feel and a convenient bar as you enter.

La Catedral (Map pp88-9; ☎ 011-15-5325-1630; Sarmiento 4006, 1st fl) If tango can be trendy and hip, this is where you'll find it. The grungy warehouse space is very casual, with funky art on the walls and jeans on the dancers. A great place to come to learn tango, especially if you're young.

La Marshall (Map pp84-5; ☎ 4912-9043; www.lamarshall.com.ar; Maipú 444, 1st fl) Held in Plaza Bohemia on Wednesday and everyone's welcome, but La Marshall is best known for being a gay *milonga*. Come at 10pm for a class, then at 11:30pm the *milonga* starts.

La Viruta (Map pp88-9; ☎ 4774-6357; www.lavirutatango.com; Armenia 1366) Located in the basement of the Asociación Cultural Armenia building. *Milongas* take place Wednesday through Sunday evenings. Best for 'nuevo tango' – mixed dance styles, with rock, salsa and folk music thrown in.

Niño Bien (Map pp84-5; ☎ 4147-8687; Humberto Primo 1462, 1st fl) Takes place on Thursday in Centro Región Leonesa and attracts a wide range of aficionados. It has a beautiful atmosphere, a large ballroom and a great dance floor, but it still gets very crowded (come early and dress well). It's far from the center – it's best to take a taxi.

Salon Canning (Map pp88-9; ☎ 4832-6753; Av Scalabrini Ortiz 1331) Some of BA's finest dancers grace this traditional venue, with a great dance floor and live orchestras. Well-known tango company **Parakultural** (www.parakultural.com.ar) often stages good events here.

Sin Rumbo (Map pp82-3; ☎ 4571-9577; Tamborini 6157) One of the oldest, most traditional tango joints in BA, Sin Rumbo has given rise to a few famous tango dancers. It's a local neighborhood place that attracts older professionals. Best on Friday. Far from the center in Villa Urquiza; take a taxi.

There are many more popular venues, such as Porteño Bailarín, Villa Malcolm, Sunderland and Nuevo Salón Argentina (with its El Arranque *milongas*).

Taconeando (Map pp84-5; ☎ 4307-6696; www.taconeando.com; Balcarce 725; dinner show AR$180, show only AR$140) One of the smaller and more reasonably priced upscale shows. There's tango dancing after the professionals are done. Shows Thursday to Sunday only

Nightclubs

BA's *boliches* (discos) are the throbbing heart of its world-famous nightlife. To be cool, don't arrive before 2am (or even 3am) and dress as stylishly as you can. Taking a nap before dinner helps keep you up all night. Admission sometimes includes a drink; women often pay less than men. Payment for admission and drinks is nearly always in cash only. Some clubs offer dinners and shows before the dancing starts.

Check out the website www.whatsupbue nosaires.com for current happenings. There are many last-minute parties happening in BA at any one time, so ask around. Massively popular annual event-parties include the South American Music Conference (see p108) and Creamfields (see p108).

For one of BA's biggest and most unique parties, check out **La Bomba de Tiempo** (www .labombadetiempo.com); it's at 7pm every Monday at Ciudad Cultural Konex (p129).

Bahrein (Map pp84-5; ☎ 4314-8886; www.bahre inba.com; Lavalle 345; ☼ Tue-Sat) Bahrein is hugely popular for its Tuesday night drum 'n' bass parties – highlighted with fast, aggressive electronic rhythms by resident DJ Bad Boy Orange. Trance, house and popular tunes round out the music menu, while an elegant upstairs restaurant provides much-needed energy. The club used to be a bank; check out the basement 'vault.'

Club Aráoz (Map pp88-9; ☎ 4832-9751; www.clu baraoz.com.ar; Aráoz 2424; ☼ Thu-Sat) Also known as 'Lost,' this small club's finest hour is on Thursday, when hip-hop rules the roost and the regulars start break dancing around 2am. It's popular with young Americans, and there's no dress code – a good thing, since it gets hot and sweaty. A great casual place to hang with friends, and drinks are well-priced as well.

Crobar (Map pp88-9; ☎ 4778-1500; cnr Paseo de la Infanta Isabel & Freyre; ☼ Fri & Sat) The current darling of the BA club world. Friday nights always feature international DJs mashing up the latest electronic selections, while Saturday has more commercial beats and a younger crowd. There's also a back room for those who prefer classic rock, '80s remixes and occasional live bands, while the main levels are strewn with mezzanines and walkways for those perfect viewpoints.

Maluco Beleza (Map pp84-5; ☎ 4372-1737; www .malucobeleza.com.ar; Sarmiento 1728; ☼ Wed & Fri-Sun) Located in an old mansion is this popular Brazilian *boliche*. It gets really packed with crowds happily grinding to samba fusion music and watching lithe, half-naked dancers squirming on the stage; it's lots of fun. Upstairs it's darker and more laid-back. If you're craving Brazilian cuisine, get here at 10pm on Wednesday for the dinner.

Museum (Map pp84-5; ☎ 4771-9628; www.museum club.com.ar; Perú 535; ☼ Wed, Fri & Sat) This cavernous disco is best known for its Wednesday night 'after-office' party (read: meat market), which starts at 8pm. It's a huge space with multiple balconies and a great sound system. Saturday nights feature incredible light shows and techno/house music. Note the amazing building, an old factory designed by Eiffel (who also did that Parisian landmark).

Niceto Club (Map pp88-9; ☎ 4779-9396; www.nic etoclub.com; Niceto Vega 5510; ☼ Thu-Sat) One of the city's biggest and long-running crowd-pullers, Club 69 is back in the saddle after a few years off. Expect everything from half-naked break-dancers to large humping drag queens in elaborate costumes; very popular with the gay crowd. Buenos Aires' biggest DJs entertain, with edgy international acts an occasional treat. Get buzzed beforehand at El Carnal (p123), just across the street.

Pachá (Map pp88-9; ☎ 4788-4280; www.pachabue nosaires.com; near cnr Av Costanera Norte & La Pampa; ☼ Fri & Sat) Famous international DJs spin tunes for the youthful, spruced-up and snobby crowds at this huge electronica club (slightly past its peak but still fun). Laser lightshows and a great sound system keep the blissed-out masses entranced. Saturday nights are best, but don't come until after 4am – giving you time to party watching the sunrise on the terrace (bring your shades).

Rumi (Map pp88-9; ☎ 4782-1307; www.rumiba.com; Av Figuero Alcorta 6442; ☼ Tue-Sat) If you're looking for glamour, fashion and possible celebrity sightings, then ultracool and highbrow Rumi is your mecca. Dress well to satisfy the picky bouncers, then enter into a wonderland of electronica, hip-hop and house beats. Famous DJs spin on Wednesday nights, but weekends are equally popular; if you're gay, come on Thursday.

Classical Music

Teatro Colón (Map pp84-5; ☎ 4378-7344; www.teatro colon.org.ar; Libertad 621) BA's premier venue for the arts, Teatro Colón has hosted prominent figures such as Placido Domingo and Luciano Pavarotti. There's also ballet, opera and occasional free concerts. See also p98.

La Scala de San Telmo (Map pp84-5; ☎ 4362-1187; www.lascala.org.ar; Pasaje Giuffra 371) This small San Telmo venue puts on classical and contemporary concerts featuring piano, tango, musical comedy and musical-related workshops.

Teatro Avenida (Map pp84–5; ☎ 4384-0519; www
.balirica.org.ar; Av de Mayo 1222) This beautiful 1906
venue highlights mostly classical music, ballet and flamenco – but its biggest strength
is opera.

Teatro San Martín (Map pp84–5; ☎ 0800-333-5254;
www.teatrosanmartin.com.ar; Av Corrientes 1530) Along
with art exhibitions, ballet, photography, cinema and theater, this large complex also hosts
classical ensembles.

Teatro Coliseo (Map pp84–5; ☎ 4816-3789; www
.fundacioncoliseo.com.ar; MT de Alvear 1125) Classical
arts entertain here, with occasional surprises
such as Argentine-American rock star Kevin
Johansen.

Live Music
ROCK & BLUES
The following are smaller venues that showcase mostly local groups; international stars
tend to play at large venues such as soccer
stadiums or Luna Park (see below). Blues isn't
as popular as rock, but still has its own loyal
following.

El Samovar de Rasputín (Map p91; ☎ 4302-3190;
Del Valle Iberlucea 1232; ☾ Sat) Located across
from its original location (where there are
photos of Napo, the hippie-ish owner, with
Keith Richards, Eric Clapton and Pavarotti).
Argentine bands entertain with rock and blues
most of the time. Bus 29 gets you here from
the city center.

La Trastienda (Map pp84–5; ☎ 4342-7650; www
.latrastienda.com; Balcarce 460; ☾ nightly) The large
theater in the back of the restaurant here can
entertain over 700 people, and showcases all
sorts of live groups (mostly rock and reggae). Look for headers such as Charlie Garcia,
Los Divididos, Marilyn Manson and the
Wailers.

Luna Park (Map pp84–5; ☎ 5279-5279; www.lunapark
.com.ar; cnr Bouchard & Corrientes) Originally a boxing
stadium, this huge stadium has a capacity of
15,000 and is the fateful location where Juan
Perón met Eva Duarte (aka Evita), and where
Maradona got married.

Mitos Argentinos (Map pp84–5; ☎ 4362-7810; Humberto
Primo 489; ☾ Fri & Sat) This cozy old brick house in
San Telmo has lots of tables, a perfectly sized
stage and a small balcony above. Known for
its tributes to *rock nacional* (Argentine rock)
bands; good for scouting out upcoming new
talent. Limited dinner options.

ND/Ateneo (Map pp84–5; ☎ 4328-2888; www.ndate
neo.com.ar; Paraguay 918; ☾ nightly) Theater with

good acoustics and quality concerts, especially rock, jazz and folk. Also puts on films,
theater and other artsy shows, and in 2008
hosted the Buenos Aires International Jazz
Festival.

JAZZ
Clásica y Moderna cafe (p121) occasionally
hosts jazz groups.

Notorious (Map pp84–5; ☎ 4815-8473; www.notori
ous.com.ar; Av Callao 966; ☾ nightly) Slick and intimate, this is one of BA's premier jazz venues.
Up front is a CD store; in back, the restaurant-
cafe (overlooking a verdant garden) hosts live
jazz shows every night.

Thelonious Bar (Map pp88–9; ☎ 4829-1562; www
.theloniousclub.com.ar; Salguero 1884; ☾ nightly) Cozily
ensconced on the 1st floor of an old mansion,
this intimate, dimly lit and artsy jazz bar has
high brick ceilings and a good sound system.
There's great jazz lineups, with DJs entertaining into the early morning hours. Come early
for dinner and good seats.

FLAMENCO & FOLK
With so many *porteños* boasting Spanish ancestry, it's not surprising that there are a few
flamenco venues in town. Most are located in
Congreso's Spanish neighborhood, near the
intersection of Salta and Av de Mayo.

Música folklórica also has its place in BA.
There are several *peñas* (folk-music clubs) in
the city, but other venues occasionally host
folk music – keep your eyes peeled.

Ávila Bar (Map pp84–5; ☎ 4383-6974; Av de Mayo 1384;
dinner-shows AR$90; ☾ Wed-Sat) Long-running and cozy
Spanish restaurant with pricey shows,
but tasty meals are thrown in (drinks extra).
Reserve on weekends.

Cantares (Map pp84–5; ☎ 4381-6965; www.cantares
tablao.com.ar; Av Rivadavia 1180; shows AR$80; ☾ Wed-Sat)
This intimate flamenco venue once hosted the
Spanish poet Federico García Lorca. Dances
are highly authentic. Lessons also available.

Guayana (Map pp84–5; ☎ 4381-4350; Lima 27;
☾ daily, shows Fri & Sat) For great local working-
class flavor, try this nondescript *confitería*
(cafe offering light meals) with cheap food and
surprisingly good music. Live tango and folk
tunes play from 10pm on Friday and Saturday
night. Reserve a table on Saturday night.

La Peña del Colorado (Map pp88–9; ☎ 4822-1038;
Güemes 3657; ☾ nightly) Nightly folkloric shows are
awesome at this rustic, brick-and-stucco restaurant-bar, and afterwards audience members

GAY & LESBIAN BA

There is a live and kicking gay scene in BA, and it's become even livelier since December 2002, when Buenos Aires became Latin America's first city to legalize same-sex unions (then in December 2009, two Argentine men became Latin America's first legally married gay couple). This is likely one reason Buenos Aires has outstripped Rio as South America's number one gay destination. And while BA's November **Marcha del Orgullo Gay** (gay pride parade; www.marchadelorgullo.org.ar) is pretty limited for now, other gay-oriented events – such as an annual **film festival** (www.diversa.com.ar) and even a **tango festival** (www.festivaltangoqueer.com.ar) – have popped up. Let's not forget either that the 2007 gay World Cup took place here.

For general information, there's **Lugar Gay** (p112) in San Telmo. It's a casual B&B but also acts as an information center and organizes activities for guests and nonguests alike. City tours are given by **Comunidad Homosexual Argentina** (CHA; ☎ 4361-6382; www.cha.org.ar). Other resources include **Grupo Nexo** (☎ 4374-4484; www.nexo.org), while gay websites in English include www.thegayguide.com.ar and www.buenosaires.queercity.info.

There are quite a few choices for gay-owned accommodations, such as the **Axel Hotel** (p112), **Lugar Gay** (p112) and **Bayres B & B** (Map pp88-9; www.bayresbnb.com). For information on gay-tolerant apartments, check the two gay websites above or www.friendlyapartments.com; also see p109.

There's lots of gay-oriented literature; keep an eye out for La Otra Guía (www.laotraguiaweb.com.ar), Gay Maps (www.gaymaps.org) and The Ronda (www.theronda.com.ar), available at many businesses. Heftier magazines such as Imperio can be bought at some newsstands.

There is plenty of nightlife to keep you out all night long. Gay-friendly restaurants include fancy **Chueca** (Map pp84-5; ☎ 4115-7214; Olga Cossetini 1545), **Empire Bar** (p118) and **Rave** (Map pp88-9; ☎ 4833-7832; Gorriti 5092).

Popular gay bars include the glitzy **Bulnes Class** (Map pp88-9; ☎ 4861-7492; Bulnes 1250), loud **Sitges** (Map pp88-9; ☎ 4861-3763; Av Córdoba 4119) and casual **Flux** (Map pp84-5; ☎ 5252-0258; MT de Alvear 980). **Pride Café** (Map pp84-5; ☎ 4300-6435; Balcarce 869) and **Kim y Novak** (p123) attract mixed crowds, while **Casa Brandon** (Map pp88-9; ☎ 4858-0610; www.brandongayday.com.ar; LM Drago 236; ☽ Wed-Sun) is a restaurant-bar–art gallery–cultural center. For a fun night of 'guided' drinking, check out **Out & About Pub Crawl** (www.outandaboutpubcrawl.com).

For dancing, rough-and-tumble **Amerika** (Map pp88-9; ☎ 4865-4416; Gascón 1040; ☽ Thu-Sun) and sexy **Glam** (Map pp88-9; ☎ 4963-2521; José Antonio Cabrera 3046; ☽ Thu-Sat) are some of the best traditional nightclubs. On Friday nights **Crobar** (see pp88–9) is popular with gays, while **Axel Hotel** (see pp84–5) has summer pool parties on Sunday, and Friday night DJ parties year-long. Ask around for the most current hot gay cruising spots or parties such as Friday night's **Fiesta Plop** (www.facebook.com/fiestaplop).

Lesbians don't have nearly as much choice as gay men. There's the long-running, intimate **Bach Bar** (Map pp88-9; JA Cabrera 4390) and, for dancing, trendy **Verona** (Map pp84-5; ☎ 011-15-5427-2962; Hipólito Yrigoyen 968; ☽ Fri & Sat) – best visited on Saturday, when it's lesbians-only allowed in. For more information on the lesbian scene, check out **La Fulana** (www.lafulana.org.ar), a sort of lesbian cultural center.

Finally, gay classes and milongas are given at **La Marshall** (www.lamarshall.com.ar), **Tango Queer** (Map pp88-9 and Map pp84-5; www.tangoqueer.com) and **Lugar Gay** (p112).

pick up guitars to make their own entertainment. Try the tasty northern Argentine food, and wash it down with mate.

Tiempo de Gitanos (Map pp88-9; ☎ 4776-6143; www.tiempodegitanos.com.ar; El Salvador 5575; dinner-shows AR$70-90; ☽ Wed-Sun) This Palermo Hollywood venue offers good flamenco shows in an intimate restaurant setting, but – unlike the dancing – the tapas and seafood paella might be less than authentic. Reserve in advance.

Theater

Av Corrientes, between Avs 9 de Julio and Callao, has traditionally been the capital's center for theater, but there are now dozens of venues throughout the city. The following venues include both the traditional and the alternative. See also Teatro Colón (p98 and p126) and Teatro San Martín (p127).

Abasto Social Club (Map pp88-9; ☎ 4862-7205; www.abastosocialclub.com.ar; Humahuaca 3649) A small venue with weekend performances and concerts, along with a cafe-bar. Various classes and workshops.

Ciudad Cultural Konex (Map pp88-9; ☎ 4864-3200; www.ciudadcultural.org; Sarmiento 3131) Has multidisciplinary performances that often fuse art, culture and technology. It hosts an amazing Monday-night percussion show called La Bomba de Tiempo.

El Camarín de las Musas (Map pp88-9; ☎ 4862-0655; www.elcamarindelasmusas.com.ar; Mario Bravo 960) Trendy venue offering contemporary dance, plays and theatrical workshops. There's a good cafe-restaurant in front.

Espacio Callejón (Map pp88-9; ☎ 4862-1167; www.callejonteatro.com.ar; Humahuaca 3759) A small independent venue showcasing new theater, music and dance, and offers a few classes.

Teatro Nacional Cervantes (Map pp84-5; ☎ 4816-4224; www.teatrocervantes.gov.ar; Libertad 815) Architecturally gorgeous theater featuring three halls, a grand lobby and red-velvet chairs – but could use a facelift. Has good productions at affordable prices. See also p101.

Teatro Gran Rex (Map pp84-5; ☎ 4322-8000; Av Corrientes 857) A huge theater seating 3500, this place hosts a myriad of musical productions, from Cyndi Lauper to Kenny G.

Teatro Presidente Alvear (Map pp84-5; ☎ 4374-6076; www.teatrosanmartin.com.ar; Av Corrientes 1659) Inaugurated in 1942 and named after an Argentine president whose wife sang opera, this theater holds over 700 and shows many musical productions, including tango.

Cinemas

BA is full of cinemas, both historical neon classics and slick modern multiplexes. The traditional cinema districts are along pedestrian Lavalle (west of Florida) and on Av Corrientes, but newer cineplexes are spread throughout the city; most large shopping malls have one. Tickets cost AR$15 to AR$20; matinees and midweek shows are cheapest.

Check out the *Buenos Aires Herald* for original titles of English-language films. Except for kids' films, most movies remain in their original language (with Spanish subtitles).

Sports

Fútbol is a national obsession and witnessing a live game part of the BA experience; see the boxed text, p130. For specifics on Argentine *fútbol*, check out www.afa.org.ar and www.futbolargentino.com.ar (both in Spanish).

The most popular clubs are **Boca Juniors** (Map p91; ☎ 4362-2260; www.bocajuniors.com.ar; Brandsen 805) and **River Plate** (Map pp82-3; ☎ 4789-1200; www.cariverplate.com.ar; Presidente Figueroa Alcorta 7597), but Buenos Aires has two dozen professional football teams – the most of any city in the world.

Other popular spectator sports include rugby, basketball, polo and field hockey. *Pato* (like rugby on horseback) deserves an honorable mention for being the most 'traditional.'

SHOPPING

Despite a major drop in the purchasing power of the Argentine peso over the last few years, Buenos Aires' citizens continue to shop as if there's no tomorrow. Just a peek into the nearest mall on a weekend will have you wondering how people who seem to be making so little can spend so much. As the saying goes, 'An Argentine will make one peso and spend two.'

In the Microcentro, Florida is a multipurpose pedestrian strip that buzzes with shoppers, while Av Santa Fe is a bit less pedestrian-friendly but equally prominent as the city's main shopping artery. San Telmo is ground zero for antiques, and Av Pueyrredón near Once train station is *the* place for cheap (and low-quality) clothing. Jewelry shops are found on Libertad south of Corrientes. Leather jackets and bags are cheapest on Calle Murillo (600 block), in Villa Crespo.

For the most unique and avant garde fashions, Palermo Viejo is the place to be. Here the city's youthful and up-and-coming designers have set up shop alongside trendy boutiques (not to mention dozens of fashionable restaurants). Not only are the fashions creative and beautiful, but compared with the US and Europe they're bargains.

As in other Western countries, bargaining is not acceptable in most stores. High-price items such as jewelry and leather jackets can be exceptions, especially if you buy several. At street markets you can try negotiating for better prices – just keep in mind you may be talking to the artists themselves, who generally don't make much money. San Telmo's antiques fair is an exception; prices here are often inflated for tourists.

One thing to be aware of is whether you're quoted in pesos or dollars. Most sellers quote in pesos, but a few unscrupulous ones switch to dollars after striking a deal. Make sure of your position if you have any doubts.

BUENOS AIRES

GOING TO A FÚTBOL GAME David Labi

In the land where Maradona is God, going to see a *fútbol* (soccer) match is a religious experience. The *superclásico* match between the two classic *porteño* teams Boca Juniors and River Plate has been called the number one sporting event to do before you die; but even the less-celebrated games will give you insight into a national passion.

Barring summer (January and February) and winter (July and August) breaks, two leagues and two international cup competitions provide plenty of opportunities for viewing silky ball-skills and learning some colorful vocabulary you won't find in any phrasebook.

If you want to see a *clásico* – a match between two of the major teams – it is inadvisable to go to the stadium to buy tickets. People will have been waiting there all night, and the atmosphere is not exactly friendly. Plus Boca doesn't even put tickets for its key matches on sale – all tickets go to *socios* (members). Instead, you're better off going with an agency such as Tangol (see p94) or www.vamosalacancha.com. Expect to pay around AR$250 for a *clásico*, and AR$400 for a *superclásico*. Not cheap, but it's much easier (and safer) getting a ticket this way.

For lesser games, it's perfectly easy to get your own ticket. Keep an eye on the clubs' websites, which inform when and where tickets will be sold. Boca sell tickets on match day mornings, while River tends to sell three days in advance. Some tickets can be nabbed online, at www.ticketek.com.ar.

The official price for *popular* (terraces/bleachers) tickets is AR$30 to AR$35, while *platea* (seated stands) can vary from AR$60 to AR$200 – and even higher for serious VIP territory.

Dress down, and try to look inconspicuous when you go. Take only minimum cash and keep your camera close. You probably won't get in with water bottles, and food and drink in the stadium is meager and expensive. Arrive no later than an hour before kick off, and even two or three hours for the big matches (just enjoy the insane build-up to the game). And most importantly – don't wear the opposing team's colors. Perhaps gray is the safest bet?

Bearing all this in mind, you're ready to have some fun! The *superclásico* is justly the most famous game. You can feel the Boca stadium, dubbed La Bombonera (chocolate box) because of its shape, shake as the crowd jumps. And you might even glimpse God himself swinging his shirt above his head, in his lifetime seat above an enormous portrait. That's Maradona, just to make it clear.

For more on *fútbol* and Maradona, see p44.

Antiques & Art

Appetite (Map pp84-5; ☎ 4331-5405; Chacabuco 551; ⏱ 2-7pm Mon-Sat) To see what's happening in the contemporary erotic art world, take a peek into this grungy space and expect fantasy, sexual and sometimes violent themes.

En Buen Orden (Map pp84-5; ☎ 011-15-5936-2820; Defensa 894; ⏱ 11am-6:30pm) If you like sorting through endless shelves full of knickknacks such as old jewelry, little medals, old lace, musty shoes and antique figurines, then this place is for you.

Galería Ruth Benzacar (Map pp84-5; ☎ 4313-8480; Florida 1000; ⏱ 11:30am-8pm Mon-Fri) The first contemporary art gallery in BA, this underground space shows off internationally known Argentine artists such as Leandro Erlich, Jorge Macchi, Flavia Darin and Nicola Costantino. You're welcome to show up and have a look around.

Gil Antiguedades (Map pp84-5; ☎ 4361-5019; Humberto Primo 412; ⏱ 11am-1pm & 3-7pm Tue-Sun) Find antiques galore here, including baby dolls, china plates, old lamps, feather fans, Jesus figures and huge glass bottles. Best of all is the basement – it's stuffed with some amazing vintage clothing and accessories, some of which is in their annex.

Imhotep (Map pp84-5; ☎ 4862-9298; Defensa 916; ⏱ 11am-6pm Sun-Fri) Come find the funkiest old knickknacks at this eccentric shop. Small oddities such as Indian statuettes, ceramic skulls, Chinese snuff boxes, precious stone figurines and gargoyles make up some of the bizarre trinkets here. Larger prize finds may include a boar's head or a slot machine.

Mercado de las Pulgas (Map pp88-9; cnr Álvarez Thomas & Dorrego; ⏱ 10am-6pm Tue-Sun) This dusty and dim covered flea market sells antiques such as old furniture, glass soda bottles, ceramic vases, paintings, bird cages, elegant mirrors and metal garden furniture. Prices aren't cheap, so bargain.

Camping Equipment

Camping Center (Map pp84-5; ☎ 4314-0305; Esmeralda 945; ☺ 10am-7pm Mon-Fri, to 5pm Sat) This modern store carries new, high-quality camping and mountaineering equipment, rock-climbing gear and general backpacking products. There's also plenty of expensive, outdoor name-brand clothing imported from the USA.

Montagne (Map pp84-5; ☎ 4312-9041; Florida 719; ☺ 10am-8:30pm Mon-Sat, noon-8pm Sun) This shop sells outdoor clothing that is stylish, good quality and made in Argentina. Choose from a small selection of tents, backpacks and camping gear upstairs. There are several other Montagne branches.

Wildlife (Map pp84-5; ☎ 4381-1040; Hipólito Yrigoyen 1133; ☺ 10am-8pm Mon-Fri, 10am-1pm Sat) Crampons, knives, tents, backpacks, climbing ropes, foul-weather clothing and military gear can be found at this somewhat musty-smelling place. Sell your stuff here, too.

Children

Owoko (Map pp88-9; ☎ 4502-9905; El Salvador 4694; ☺ 11am-8pm Mon-Sat, 3-7pm Sun) Every purchase at this small kids' clothes store comes with a free story booklet about Planet Owoko and its colorful characters, who are (conveniently) immortalized on cute T-shirts, pants and accessories.

Recursos Infantiles (Map pp88-9; ☎ 4834-6177; JL Borges 1766; ☺ 3-8pm Mon, 8am-8pm Tue-Sun) Small but fun, this kids' store offers some pretty unique toys – and all are made in Argentina. Books in Spanish and a small rack of cute clothes keep mom busy, and a tiny cafe on the premises caters to hungry little bellies.

TAXES & REFUNDS

Taxes are included in quoted or marked prices: what you see is what you pay. Some places, however, might add a *recargo* (surcharge) to credit-card purchases – ask before you buy.

If you buy more than AR$70 in merchandise from a store that displays a 'Tax-Free Shopping' sticker, you're entitled to a tax refund. Just ask the merchant to make out an invoice for you (you'll need ID); upon leaving the country show the paperwork to a customs official, who'll stamp it and tell you where to obtain your refund.

Clothing & Accessories

Bolivia (Map pp88-9; ☎ 4832-6284; Gurruchaga 1581; ☺ 11am-8pm Mon-Sat, 3-8pm Sun) There's almost nothing here that your young, hip and possibly gay brother wouldn't love, from the striped cut-off cowboy shirts to the floral Puma sneakers to the Mexican-bag-fabric plastic belts. Metrosexual to the hilt, and paradise for the man who isn't afraid of patterns, plaid or pastels. There are branches in town.

Gabriella Capucci (Map pp84-5; ☎ 4815-3636; Av Alvear 1477; ☺ 10:30am-8pm Mon-Sat) All-original sequined T-shirts, wispy scarves, vintage tops, velvet pillows and eclectic accessories fill this ever-changing, girly boutique. Crocheted flowers decorate camouflage, satin and animal prints, and the costume jewelry is wild.

Hermanos Estebecorena (Map pp88-9; ☎ 4772-2145; El Salvador 5960; ☺ 11am-8pm Mon-Sat) The Estebecorena brothers apply their highly creative skills toward original, highly stylish, very functional men's clothing that makes the artsy types swoon. Selection is limited, but what's there really counts.

Moebius (Map p91; ☎ 4361-2893; Defensa 1356; ☺ 10:30am-1:30pm & 3-8:30pm Tue-Sat, noon-8:30pm Sun) Highly original bags, retro knickknacks, handmade jewelry and ingeniously designed women's clothes are highlights here, but you'll never know exactly what you'll find. The recycled-material items are always the most fun.

Nadine Zlotogora (Map pp88-9; ☎ 4831-4203; El Salvador 4683; ☺ 11am-8pm Mon-Sat) Nadine's gorgeous dresses and tops combine feminine styles with nearly magical fabrics, creating fantastically romantic wearables. Thick and billowy base textiles are layered with lacy tulle and silky edging – a feast for the eyes as well as the skin.

Objeto (Map pp88-9; ☎ 4771-4934; Gurruchaga 1335; ☺ 11am-8pm Mon-Sat) The designers here display some of the wackiest, most outrageously fun clothes in town. Outfits are less frilly and more substantial than most of their *porteño* designer colleagues – think of dresses with multiple patterns accented with cartoons or silhouetted figures. Great gear for parties.

Rapsodia (Map pp88-9; ☎ 4833-5814; El Salvador 4757; ☺ 10am-9pm) With fabrics from linen to leather, street casual to sequins, this larger boutique shop is a must for fashion mavens. There are cutting-edge jeans, wild bikinis and even a small kids' section, plus sofas for the guys to sit on as they wait. Several branches in town.

Crafts & Souvenirs

Arte y Esperanza (Map pp84-5; ☎ 4343-1455; Balcarce 234; ✆ 10am-6pm Mon-Fri) This store sells fair-trade, handmade products that include many from Argentina's indigenous craftspeople. Items are well-made and include jewelry, pottery, textiles, *mate* gourds, baskets, woven bags and animal masks (along with other wood-carved items). Also in Retiro at Suipacha 892 (Map pp84-5).

Atípica (Map pp88-9; ☎ 4833-3344; El Salvador 4510; ✆ 2-8pm Mon-Fri, 11am-7pm Sat) This tiny shop stocks crafts from Argentine artists who use indigenous techniques for their works. All are handmade and unique, and include picture frames, wall hangings, mask replicas, gourd bowls, small boxes, textiles and jewelry. Quality is high and prices fair.

Kelly's Regionales (Map pp84-5; ☎ 4311-5712; Paraguay 547; ✆ 10am-8pm Mon-Fri, to 3pm Sat) Cowhides, Mapuche ponchos, animal masks, alpaca knives and *mate* gourds are all good ethnic buys at this large souvenir shop, but plenty of cheap souvenir knickknacks also line the shelves.

Housewares

Calma Chicha (Map pp88-9; ☎ 4831-1818; Honduras 4909; ✆ 10am-8pm Mon-Fri, 11am-8pm Sat, noon-8pm Sun) Big on leather, this fun household spot has a variety of butterfly chair styles and brightly colored cowhide rugs. Penguin pitchers, flowery plastic tablecloths and thick sheepskins are other must-haves.

Cualquier Verdura (Map pp84-5; ☎ 4300-2474; Humberto Primo 517; ✆ noon-8pm Thu-Sun) Located in a lovely, refurbished old house, this very fun store sells eclectic items from vintage clothing to entertaining soaps to recycled floppy-disc lamps to novelty toys. Note the *mate*-drinking Buddha above the fountain in the patio.

Music

El Ateneo (Map pp84-5; ☎ 4325-6801; Florida 340; ✆ 9am-10pm Mon-Fri, to 5pm Sat) Buenos Aires' landmark bookseller stocks a limited number of books in English and also has a decent selection of music CDs. There are several branches within the city, including a gorgeous branch in the Gran Splendid, an old renovated cinema (Map pp84-5; Av Santa Fe 1860). Hours vary by store.

Zival's (Map pp84-5; ☎ 5128-7500; www.tangostore .com; Av Callao 395; ✆ 9:30am-10pm Mon-Sat) One of the better music stores in town, especially when it comes to tango, jazz and classical music. Listening stations and a big sale rack are pluses, and it'll ship CDs, DVDs and sheet music abroad too (check the website). Also in Palermo Viejo at Serrano 1445 (see Map pp88-9).

Shoes & Leather Goods

28 Sport (Map pp88-9; ☎ 4833-4287; Gurruchaga 1481; ✆ 11am-8pm Mon-Sat) Focusing on only one product and one style – men's 1950s sport-style shoes – the cobblers here can concentrate on quality and craftsmanship. Inspiration comes from football, boxing and bowling shoes, and only 12 pairs of each design are produced.

Casa López (Map pp84-5; ☎ 4311-3044; MT de Alvear 640/658; ✆ 9am-8pm Mon-Fri, 9:30am-7pm Sat, 10am-6pm Sun) Start up the limousine and make sure there's enough room for some of BA's finest selection of quality leather jackets, luggage, bags and accessories. A downside: service is almost too attentive. Another branch is at Galerías Pacífico (p95).

Mishka (Map pp88-9; ☎ 4833-6566; El Salvador 4673; ✆ 11am-8pm Mon-Sat) Well-regarded designer Chelo Cantón was an architect in a previous incarnation, but now creates glittery, low-heeled shoes with a retro-hip, feminine and slightly conservative vibe. There are purses and bags also and another branch in Paseo Alcorta shopping mall (see p107).

Rossi y Carusso (Map pp84-5; ☎ 4814-4774; Av Santa Fe 1377; ✆ 9:30am-8pm Mon-Fri, 10am-7pm Sat) Fine leather goods line the shelves at this upscale shop. Choose from fancy boots, belts, bags, saddles, gaucho knives and the occasional silver *mate* vessel. All are made from Argentine materials, and most are exclusive designs.

Shopping Malls

Alto Palermo (Map pp88-9; ☎ 5777-8000; Av Coronel Díaz 2098; ✆ 10am-10pm) This popular, shiny mall offers dozens of clothing shops, bookstores, jewelry boutiques, and electronics and houseware stores. Look for Timberland, Lacoste, Hilfiger and Levis (plus many Argentine brand names, too). Services include a food court, cinema complex and a good kids' area on the 3rd floor.

Buenos Aires Design (Map pp84-5; ☎ 5777-6000; Av Pueyrredón 2501; ✆ 10am-9pm Mon-Sat, noon-9pm Sun) The trendiest and finest home furnishings are all under one roof here. This is the ideal place to look for that snazzy light fixture,

BUENOS AIRES STREET MARKETS

Some of BA's best crafts and souvenirs are sold at its many street markets, often by the artists themselves. You may have to sort through some tacky kitsch, but you'll also find creative and original art. A plus is the 'free' (donation) entertainment from buskers and mimes.

Feria Artesanal (Map pp84-5; Plaza Intendente Alvear; ☼ 10am-7pm) Recoleta's hugely popular fair, with hundreds of booths and a range of creative goods. Hippies, mimes and tourists mingle; nearby restaurants provide refreshment. Biggest on weekends; located just outside the cemetery.

Feria de Mataderos (Map pp82-3; ☎ Mon-Fri 4342-9629, Sun 4687-5602; www.feriademataderos.com.ar; cnr Avs Lisandro de la Torre & de los Corrales; ☼ 11am-8pm Sun & holidays Apr-Dec, 6pm-midnight Sat Jan-Mar) This unique market is far off in the barrio of Mataderos. There are shows of horsemanship, folk dancing and cheap authentic treats to be had. From downtown, take bus 155, 180 or 126 (one hour); taxis cost at least AR$50. Confirm hours beforehand; it could be closed in January.

Feria de San Telmo (Map pp84-5; Plaza Dorrego; ☼ 10am-5pm Sun) Locals and tourists alike come to this wonderful *feria;* you'll find antique seltzer bottles, jewelry, artwork, vintage clothing, collectibles and donation tango shows. Lots of fun, but keep an eye on your wallet. Some vendors hang around on Saturdays also.

Feria Plaza Belgrano (Map pp82-3; cnr Juramento & Cuba; ☼ 10am-8pm Sat & Sun) Belgrano's pleasant market is great on a sunny weekend. You'll find high-quality imaginative crafts, as well as some kitschy junk. Good for families as it's calmer and less touristy than the more central *ferias*.

Feria Plaza Serrano (Map pp88-9; Plaza Serrano; ☼ noon-7pm Fri-Sun) Costume jewelry, hand-knit tops, funky clothes, hippie bags and leather accessories fill the crafts booths at this small but lively fair on fashionable Plaza Serrano in Palermo Viejo.

streamlined toilet or reproduction Asian chair. Also good for everyday appliances and housewares, along with cute decor and a few knickknacks.

Galerías Pacífico (Map pp84-5; ☎ 5555-5110; cnr Florida & Av Córdoba; ☼ 10am-9pm Mon-Sat, noon-9pm Sun) Centrally located right on pedestrian Florida, this gorgeous mall with murals on the ceiling is always full of shoppers and tourists. Donation tango shows often play outside. For more information, see p95.

Galería Bond (Map pp84-5; Av Santa Fe 1670; ☼ 10am-9pm Mon-Sat) For the edgiest tattoos and piercings in town, you can't beat this grungy shopping center. Buenos Aires' skateboarder-wanna-bes and punk rockers come here to shop for the latest styles and sounds. Expect everything from Hello Kitty to heavy metal.

Mercado de Abasto (Map pp88-9; ☎ 4959-3400; cnr Corrientes & Anchorena; ☼ 10am-10pm) One of the most beautiful malls in BA, this remodeled old market holds more than 200 shops, a large cinema, a covered plaza, a kosher McDonald's, a good children's museum and even a small amusement park.

Wine

See also p122 for wine-tasting options and wine delivery services.

Lo de Joaquin Alberdi (Map pp88-9; ☎ 4832-5329; www.lodejoaquinalberdi.com.ar; JL Borges 1772; ☼ 11am-

9:30pm) Excellent wine shop in Palermo Soho that carries only Argentine brands. Wine tastings with food pairings happen on Thursday.

GETTING THERE & AWAY
Air

Buenos Aires is Argentina's international gateway and easily accessible from North America, Europe and Australasia, as well as other capital cities in South America.

Almost all international flights arrive at BA's Ezeiza airport, about 35km south of the center. Ezeiza is a modern airport with good services such as ATMs, restaurants and duty-free shops. There's also an overpriced internet cafe and iffy wi-fi. For more on arriving in Ezeiza, see the boxed text, p135.

Most domestic flights use Aeroparque Jorge Newbery airport, a short distance north of downtown BA. Flight information for both airports, in English and Spanish, is available at ☎ 5480-6111 or www.aa2000.com.ar.

Boat

BA has a regular ferry service to and from Colonia (see p555) and Montevideo (see p539), both in Uruguay. Ferries leave from the **Buquebus terminal** (Map pp84-5; cnr Avs Antártida Argentina & Córdoba). There are many more launches in the busy summer season.

BUENOS AIRES

Bus

If you're heading out of town you'll probably have to visit BA's modern **Retiro bus terminal** (Map pp84-5; Av Antártida Argentina). It's 400m long, three floors high and has slots for 75 buses. The bottom floor is for cargo shipments and luggage storage, the top for purchasing tickets and the middle for everything else. There's an **information booth** (☎ 4310-0700; ☺ 24hr) that will help you find the right long-distance bus company to your destination; it's located near the escalators at the southern end of the terminal. Other services include a **tourist office** (☎ 4313-0187; ☺ 7:30am-2:30pm Mon-Fri) near Puente 3, on the main floor under bus counter 105; telephone offices (some with coin-accessed internet), cafes and many small stores.

You can buy a ticket to practically anywhere in Argentina and departures are fairly frequent to the most popular destinations. Reservations are not necessary except during peak summer and winter holiday seasons (January, February and July). And remember to keep an eye on your bags!

Here are some sample destinations; be aware that ticket prices vary widely according to bus company, class, season and inflation.

Destination	Cost (AR$)	Duration (hr)
Bariloche	245	20
Comodoro Rivadavia	308	24
Córdoba	150	10
Foz do Iguaçu (Brazil)	200	19
Mar del Plata	90	6
Mendoza	250	13
Montevideo (Uruguay)	140	9
Puerto Iguazú	280	19
Puerto Madryn	270	20
Punta del Este (Uruguay)	159	12
Rosario	50	4
Santiago (Chile)	260	22

Retiro bus terminal is connected to the local bus system, but it's a giant snarl and hard to figure out. There's a nearby Subte station and Retiro train station. Street taxis are numerous, though *remises* (call taxis) are generally more secure – there are two small *remise* booths near bus slots 8 and 9 that are open 24 hours.

Train

Privately run trains mostly connect Buenos Aires' center to its suburbs and nearby provinces. The three main central stations are served by Subte, see p136. Here are some destinations outside BA:

Destination(s)	Station	Contact
Bahía Blanca/Carmen de Patagones*	Constitución (Map pp82–3)	(☎ 4304-0028; www.ferrobaires.gba.gov.ar)
Concordia/Posadas	Federico Lacroze** (Map pp82–3)	(www.trenesdellitoral.com.ar)
La Plata***	Constitución (Map pp82–3)	(☎ 0800-1-2235-8736)
Luján***	Once (Map pp82–3)	(☎ 0800-333-3822; www.tbanet.com.ar)
Mar del Plata or Tandil or Pinamar	Constitución (Map pp82–3)	(☎ 4304-0028; www.ferrobaires.gba.gov.ar)
San Isidro/Tigre/ Rosario/Córdoba or Tucumán	Retiro (Map pp84–5)	(☎ 0800-333-3822; www.tbanet.com.ar, www.ferrocentralsa.com.ar)
San Isidro/Tigre	Olivos**** (off Map pp82–3)	www.trendelacosta.com.ar

* The weekly Bahía Blanca–Carmen de Patagones leg is very slow and services are canceled periodically.
** Federico Lacroze station is reached by Subte line B.
*** La Plata is reached via the suburban Roca line; Luján by the Sarmiento line.
**** Olivos station is reached by taking the suburban Mitre line from Retiro.

GETTING AROUND
To/From the Airport

If you're traveling solo, the best way to and from Ezeiza is to take a shuttle with transfer companies such as **Manuel Tienda León** (MTL; Map pp84-5; ☎ 4315-5115; www.tiendaleon.com; cnr Av Eduardo Madero & San Martín). You'll see its stand immediately as you exit airport customs. Shuttles cost AR$40 to AR$45 one way, run every half hour from 6am to midnight and take about 40 minutes, depending on traffic (for two people the price is AR$70). It'll deposit you either at its office (from where you can take a taxi) or at some central hotels. Avoid its taxi service at the airport, which is overpriced at AR$146; if you want to take a taxi just go past the transport 'lobby' area, through the doors to the reception area and – avoiding *all* touts – find the freestanding city taxi stand (blue sign that says 'Taxi Ezeiza'), which charges AR$98 to the center (or save AR$3 and head outside the airport doors to another taxi stand called GCBA, with a yellow sign). For tips on how to avoid getting ripped off in a taxi, see p136.

EZEIZA ARRIVAL & DEPARTURE TIPS

As of January 2010, citizens from several countries have to pay a 'reciprocity fee' *(tasa de reciprocidad)* when they land in Ezeiza. This is equal to what Argentines are charged for visas to visit those countries. These fees include US$131 for US citizens, US$70 for Canadians and US$100 for Australians. The fee is payable in cash, credit card or traveler's check and is usually good for 10 years (per entry for Canadians though – sucks, eh?).

To change money at Ezeiza, don't go to any *cambio* (exchange house). Their rates are bad; for better rates, pass the rows of transport booths, go outside the doors into the reception hall and veer sharply to the right to find Banco de la Nación's small office; it's open 24 hours and has an ATM (there's another ATM nearby, next to Farmacity, and yet another way beyond, at the airline counters).

For shuttles and taxis from Ezeiza to the center, see opposite. There's a helpful **tourist information booth** (24hr) just beyond the city's taxi stand.

When leaving Ezeiza on an international flight, passengers had to pay a departure tax. Tickets bought after March 2009, however, should have this tax included in the ticket price.

If you're heading straight to Aeroparque (the domestic airport), taxis from Ezeiza cost about AR$115; MTL's shuttles are AR$45.

Real shoestringers can take public bus 8, which costs AR$2 and can take up to two hours to reach the Plaza de Mayo area. Catch it outside the Aerolíneas Argentinas terminal, a short walk (150m) from the international terminal. You'll need change for the bus; there's a Banco de la Nación just outside customs.

If you're living it big, however, contact US expat Fred at **Silver Star Transport** (in the USA 214-502-1605, in Argentina 011-15-6826-8876; www.silverstarcar.com). He'll pick you up at Ezeiza in his Lincoln town car and deliver you to your hotel for AR$295. Fred also does city tours.

There are also car-rental agencies at Ezeiza, but we generally don't recommend driving in Buenos Aires.

To get from Aeroparque to the city center, take public bus 33 or 45 (don't cross the street; take them going south). MTL has shuttles to the center for AR$15; taxis cost around AR$25.

Bicycle

BA is not a great city for cycling. Traffic is dangerous and hardly respectful toward bicycles; the biggest vehicle wins the right of way, and bikes are low on the totem pole. Still, some spots call out for two-wheeled exploration, such as Palermo's parks and the Reserva Ecológica Costanera Sur; on weekends and some weekdays you can rent bikes at these places. You can also join city bike tours (see p107); these companies sometimes rent bikes.

Bus

BA has a huge and complex bus system. If you want to get to know it better, you'll have to buy a *Guia T* (bus guide); they're sold at any newsstand, but try to find the handy pocket version (AR$8). Just look at the grids to find out where you are and where you're going, and find a matching bus number. If you are familiar with BA, check www.xcolectivo.com.ar. Most routes (but not all) run 24 hours.

Save your change like it's gold; local buses do not take bills. Bus ticket machines on board will, however, give you small change from your coins. Most rides around town cost AR$1.25. Offer your seat to the elderly, pregnant and women with young children.

Route	Bus no
Microcentro to Palermo Viejo	111
Microcentro to Plaza Italia (Palermo)	29, 59, 64
Retiro to Plaza de Mayo/San Telmo	22
Recoleta to Congreso/San Telmo/La Boca	39
Plaza Italia to Microcentro/San Telmo	29
Plaza Italia to Once/Plaza de Mayo/La Boca	64
Plaza Italia to Retiro/Plaza de Mayo/La Boca	152, 29
Plaza Italia to Recoleta/Microcentro/Constitución	59

Car

Anyone considering driving in BA should know that most local drivers are reckless, aggressive and even willfully dangerous. They'll ignore speed limits, road signs, lines and traffic signals. They'll tailgate mercilessly and honk even before signals turn green. Buses are a nightmare to reckon with, potholes are everywhere, traffic is a pain and parking can be a bitch. Pedestrians seem to beg to be run over at times.

On the other hand, public transport is great and taxis are cheap and plentiful.

If, after all these tips, you still insist on renting a car, expect to pay around AR$190 per day. You'll need to be at least 21 years of age and have a valid driver's license; having an international driver's license isn't crucial. You'll need to present a credit card and your passport, though.

Avis (Map pp84-5; ☎ 4326-5542; www.avis.com.ar; Cerrito 1527)

Hertz (Map pp84-5; ☎ 4816-8001; www.hertzargen tina.com.ar; Paraguay 1138)

New Way (Map pp84-5; ☎ 4515-0331; www.new wayrentacar.com; Marcelo T de Alvear 773)

Victory (Map pp84-5; ☎ 4381-4731; victory_renta car@hotmail.com; Lima 509)

Motorcycle

For motorcycle rentals, be at least 25 years of age and head to **Motocare** (Map pp82-3; ☎ 4782-1500; www.motocare.com.ar; Esteban Echeverria 738, Vicente Lopez). Honda Transalps 650 and 700 cost about AR$420 per day with a five-day minimum (it's cheaper by the month). Bring your own helmet and riding gear. Crossing into Chile, Uruguay, Paraguay and Brazil is allowed (permissions required for the latter three countries). If you buy a motorcycle here you can negotiate to sell it back, possibly saving money in the long term. Staff are English-speaking.

Car-rental company Victory rents scooters, too.

Subte (Underground) & Train

BA's **Subte** (☎ 4555-1616; www.subte.com.ar) opened in 1913 and is the quickest way to get around the city, though it can get mighty hot and crowded during rush hour. It consists of Líneas (Lines) A, B, C, D, E and H. Four parallel lines run from downtown to the capital's western and northern outskirts, while Línea C runs north–south and connects the two major train stations of Retiro and Constitución. Línea H runs from Once south to Av Caseros, with future expansion plans.

One-ride magnetic cards for the Subte cost AR$1.10. To save time and hassle buy several rides, since queues can get backed up. If you're planning on staying in BA for a while, the **Monedero card** (www.monedero.com.ar) is a convenient, rechargeable card that you can use to enter the Subte, plus buy some products at the stations and get certain discounts.

At some stations platforms are on opposite sides, so make sure of your direction *before* passing through the turnstiles.

Subte trains operate from 5am to (around) 10:30pm Monday to Saturday and 8am to (around) 10pm on Sunday and holidays. Service is frequent on weekdays; on weekends you'll wait longer.

By contrast, the suburban train system is of little use to travelers:

Belgrano line (www.ferrovias.com.ar) Retiro station to the northern suburbs.

Mitre line (www.tbanet.com.ar) Retiro to Belgrano, San Isidro, Tigre and beyond.

Roca line Constitución station to the southern suburbs and La Plata.

San Martín line Retiro to the northern suburbs.

Sarmiento line (www.tbanet.com.ar) Once station to the southwestern suburbs and Luján.

Taxi & Remise

Buenos Aires' very numerous (about 38,000) and cheap taxis are conspicuous by their black-and-yellow paint jobs. The meter should always be used and the fare ticks upwards about every two blocks when the vehicle is moving (you'll pay for waiting in stuck traffic, too). It's customary to let drivers keep small change. Taxis looking for passengers will have a red light lit on the upper right corner of their windshield.

Almost all taxi drivers are honest workers making a living, but there are a few bad apples in the bunch. Do not to give the driver large bills; not only will they usually not have change, but there have been cases where the driver quickly and deftly replaces a larger bill with a smaller (or fake) one. One solution is to state how much you are giving them and ask if they have change ('¿*Tiene usted cambio de un veinte?*' – Do you have any change for a 20?).

Be especially wary of receiving counterfeit bills; at night have the driver *prender la luz* (turn on the light) so you can carefully count and check your change (look for a watermark on bills).

Pretend to have an idea of where you're going; a few taxis offer the 'scenic' route (though also be aware there are many one-way streets in BA). A good way to do this is to give the taxi driver an intersection rather than a specific address. Also, if you are obviously a tourist going to or from a touristy spot, don't ask how much the fare is beforehand; this makes quoting an upped price, rather than using the meter, tempting.

Finally, make an attempt to snag an 'official' taxi. These are usually marked by a roof light and license number printed on the doors. Official drivers must display their license on the back of their seat or dashboard; you can write down the taxi's details in case of problems or forgotten items.

Most *porteños* recommend you call a *remise* instead of hailing street cabs. *Remises* look like regular cars and don't have meters. They cost a bit more than street taxis but are more secure, since an established company sends them out. Most hotels and restaurants will call a *remise* for you.

AROUND BUENOS AIRES

So you've spent days tramping on noisy and busy streets, visiting all the sights and smells of BA. You're ready to get away from the capital and experience something different and more peaceful. So where do you go?

Luckily, there are several trips that can be done in a day, but a few are better if you have more time to spare. Luján (p144) is a religious mecca, while San Antonio de Areco (p146) features peace and the occasional gaucho theme. La Plata (p142) is a mini-version of Buenos Aires, with an amazing cathedral.

For something different, head across the Río de la Plata into neighboring Uruguay; Montevideo (p539) is a laid-back capital city with a much slower pace, while Colonia (p555) offers some cobbled streets and old-time atmosphere. The ritzy resort of Punta del Este (p576) provides sun, sand and stars – celebrities, that is.

Some options much closer to BA are presented following.

SAN ISIDRO

About 22km north of Buenos Aires is peaceful and residential San Isidro, a charming suburb of cobblestone streets lined with graceful buildings. The historic center is at Plaza Mitre and its beautiful neo-Gothic cathedral; on weekends the area buzzes with a crafts fair. There's a **tourist office** (☎ 4512-3209; Libertador 16362; ☼ 8am-5pm Mon-Fri, 10am-6pm Sat & Sun) at the plaza.

A stroll through the rambling neighborhood streets behind the cathedral will turn up some luxurious mansions (as well as more-modest houses) and the occasional view toward the coast. Close by is also the Tren de la Costa's San Isidro station, with a fashionable outdoor shopping mall to explore.

Once owned by Argentine icon, General Pueyrredón, the **Museo Histórico Municipal General Pueyrredón** (☎ 4512-3131; Rivera Indarte 48; admission free; ☼ 10am-6pm Tue & Thu, 2-6pm Sat & Sun) is an old colonial villa set on spacious grounds with faraway views of the Río de la Plata. Don't miss the algarrobo tree under which Pueyrredón and San Martín planned strategies against the Spanish. To get here from the cathedral, follow Av Libertador five blocks, turn left on Peña and after two blocks turn right onto Rivera Indarte.

Even more glamorous is the Unesco site **Villa Ocampo** (☎ 4732-4988; Elortondo 1837; admission Thu & Fri ARS6, Sat & Sun ARS15; ☼ 12:30-6pm Thu-Sun), a wonderfully restored mansion and reminder of a bygone era. Victoria Ocampo was a writer, publisher and intellectual who dallied with the literary likes of Borges, Cortázar, Sabato and Camus. The gardens are lovely here; tours and a cafe are also available.

Getting There & Away

The best way to reach San Isidro is via the **Tren de la Costa** (www.trendelacosta.com.ar), whose BA terminal (Maipú) is in the suburb of Olivos. Get to Maipú station in BA on bus 59 or 152; some 60s buses also go (ask the bus driver). The Mitre train line from Retiro train station (downtown) also reaches Maipú (at Mitre station). You can also go directly to San Isidro with buses 60 and 168.

TIGRE & THE DELTA

The city of Tigre (35km north of BA) and the surrounding delta region is one of the most popular weekend getaways for weary *porteños*. The city itself has a few pleasant attractions, but it's really the delta just beyond Tigre that everyone's after. Latte-colored waters – rich with iron from the jungle streams flowing from inland South America – will hardly remind you of a blue paradise, but there are hidden gems in this marshy region. Boat rides into the delta offer peeks at local stilt houses and colonial mansions, and you can explore along some peaceful trails. Many lodgings are located throughout the region, making getaways complete. All along the shorelines are signs of water-related activity, from kayaking to wakeboarding, canoeing to sculling.

Information

Tourist Office (☎ 4512-4497; www.tigre.gov.ar; ☯ 8am-6pm) Located behind McDonald's; will help you sort out the complex delta region. There's a smaller booth (☎ 4512-4547) at the train station.

Sights & Activities

Tigre itself is very walkable and holds some attractions. Be sure to check out the **Puerto de Frutos** (Sarmiento 160; ☯ 10am-6:30pm), where vendors sell mostly housewares, wicker baskets and dried flowers, along with a modest selection of fruits. Weekends are best, when a large crafts fair sets up. Nearby is Tigre's amusement park, **Parque de la Costa** (☎ 4002-6000; www.parquedelacosta.com.ar; admission AR$38-49). Call for current hours.

The **Museo Naval** (Naval Museum; ☎ 4749-0608; Paseo Victorica 602; admission AR$3; ☯ 8:30am-5:30pm Mon-Fri, 10:30am-6:30pm Sat & Sun) traces the history of the Argentine navy with an eclectic mix of historical photos, model boats and airplanes, artillery displays and pickled sea critters. For something special, visit the **Museo del Mate** (☎ 4506-9594; www.elmuseodelmate.com; Lavalle 289; admission AR$10; ☯ 10am-6pm Tue-Sun), which has over 2000 items dedicated to the national drink. There's a *mate* cafe as well (of course).

Tigre's fanciest museum is the **Museo de Arte Tigre** (☎ 4512-4093; Paseo Victorica 972; admission AR$5; ☯ 9am-7pm Wed-Fri, noon-7pm Sat & Sun). Located in an old (1912) social club, this beautiful art museum showcases famous Argentine artists from the 19th and 20th centuries. The building itself is worth a visit.

The waterways of the delta offer a glimpse into how locals live along the peaceful canals, with boats as their only transportation. Frequent commuter launches depart from Estación Fluvial (located behind the tourist office) for various destinations in the delta (AR$17 to AR$31 round trip). A popular destination is the **Tres Bocas neighborhood**, a half-hour boat ride from Tigre, where you can take residential walks on thin paths connected by bridges over narrow channels. There are several restaurants and accommodations here. The **Rama Negra** area has a quieter and more natural setting with fewer services, but is an hour's boat ride away.

Several companies offer inexpensive boat tours (AR$30 to AR$45, 1½ hours), but commuter launches give you flexibility if you want to go for a stroll or stop for lunch at one of the delta's restaurants.

Tours

Bonanza Deltaventura (☎ 4728-1674; www.delta ventura.com) Offers adventures that include walks, canoe trips, bike rides, horseback rides and *asados*.

El Dorado Kayak (☎ 011-15-6503-6961; www .eldoradokayak.com) Does kayaking tours deep inside the delta; all equipment and lunch included.

Floating Tours (☎ 4572-5078; www.tigredeltatours .wordpress.com) Door-to-door service from BA to Tigre; boat trips with small groups and English-speaking guides.

Sleeping & Eating

The huge delta is dotted with dozens of accommodation possibilities, from camping to B&Bs to *cabañas* to beach resorts to activity-oriented places. The further out you are, the more peace and quiet you'll experience (but bring mosquito repellent). Since places are relatively hard to reach – you generally arrive by boat – the majority also provide meals.

The Tigre tourist office has photos of and information on all accommodation places, and many are listed on its website (www .vivitigre.com.ar). The following places are in Tigre itself. Prices listed are for Saturday night, when you should always book ahead; on weekdays, rates can plummet up to 30%.

Tigre Hostel (☎ 4749-4034; www.tigrehostel.com.ar; dm AR$60, s AR$120-180, d AR$240-300; ☐ ☏) Located in an old mansion, this hostel offers large dorms and nice bunks, but the kitchen is ordinary. Private rooms are spacious and some share bathrooms. A large garden and back decks are great hangout areas, and an annex nearby has more rooms.

Casona La Ruchi (☎ 4749-2499; www.casonalaruchi .com.ar; Lavalle 557; s/d AR$160/210; ☐ ☏ ☒) This family-run B&B is in a beautiful mansion (built in 1893) that's showing its age. Most of the five romantic bedrooms have balconies; all have shared bathrooms with original tiled floors. There's a pool and large garden out back.

Hotel Villa Victoria (☎ 4731-2281; www.hotel villavictoria.com; Liniers 566; AR$350-535; ☒ ☐ ☒) Run by an Argentine-Swedish family, this boutique hotel is more like a fancy guesthouse. Only six simple yet elegant rooms are available, and there's a clay tennis court and pool out back. Swedish, French and English are spoken.

La Soñada (☎ 4731-4004; www.bybtigre.com.ar; Anastasio El Pollo 1786; r AR$380-590; ☒ ☐ ☒) For a homey feel, there's this casual, family-run place. The five rooms are comfortable but not luxurious, and there's a large grassy garden with pool and covered dining area.

As far as food goes, Tigre's cuisine is not cutting-edge, but dining can be atmospheric. Stroll Paseo Victorica, the city's pleasant riverside avenue. For an upscale meal, try **Maria Luján** (☎ 4731-9613; mains AR$36-55; ☺ breakfast, lunch & dinner), which also has a great patio boasting river views.

Getting There & Away

There are four main ways to get to Tigre. From Retiro train station (downtown BA) take a train straight to Tigre (one hour). You can also take bus 60 (marked 'Panam') straight to Tigre (1½ hours).

The nicest way to reach Tigre, however, is via the **Tren de la Costa** (www.trendelacosta.com.ar; local/foreigner AR$7/12; trains every half hour) – a pleasant electric train with attractive stations and some water views. This train line starts in the suburb of Olivos; to get there, take a train from Retiro station (Mitre Line) and get off at the Mitre station – then cross the bridge to the Tren de la Costa. Buses 59, 60 and 152 also go to the Tren de la Costa.

You can also take the commuter boat **Sturla** (Map pp84-5; ☎ 4731-1300; www.sturlaviajes.com .ar; cnr Grierson & Juana Manso) straight to Tigre from Puerto Madero. However, there's only one per day, at 6:30pm from Monday to Friday (AR$15, one hour).

The Pampas & the Atlantic Coast

Evita's shirtless masses, the lawless and romantic gaucho, the wealthy landowner with his palatial country estate and the defiant Indian – all these classic Argentine characters have their origins in the pampas. In fact, in its early days, Argentina *was* the pampas – the fight for independence was born on the Río de la Plata, and Argentina's immigrant identity was forged by the Europeans who filled the pampean towns.

The seemingly endless fertile grasslands that make up this region financed Argentina's golden years, its natural grasses and easily cleared land yielding huge returns. Buenos Aires province is still the nation's economic and political powerhouse: this is where all that juicy beef comes from, and it's also home to around 40% of Argentina's voters.

While the pampas is often overlooked by travelers, it does hold some hidden gems, many of which make worthwhile side trips from Buenos Aires. A visit to lovely San Antonio de Areco offers a taste of living gaucho culture, while the hills around Tandil and Sierra de la Ventana are a picturesque mix of the wild and the pastoral, with plenty of opportunities for hiking and climbing. And although the beaches can't compare with Brazil's, they make a good escape from the city's summer heat.

One of the best ways to get to know the pampas is to spend a day or so at one of the region's many historic *estancias*, where the huge sky and luscious green plains, the gauchos' horsemanship and the faded elegance of Argentina's belle epoque can all be experienced first-hand.

HIGHLIGHTS

- Peek through a natural rock 'window' atop the mountain **Cerro de la Ventana** (p156)
- Soak up the sun and crowds in the Atlantic Coast's largest city, **Mar del Plata** (p165)
- Sample some country life – and deli meats and cheese – in pleasant **Tandil** (p150)
- Go gaucho in **San Antonio de Areco** (p146), the prettiest town in the pampas
- Check out the lagoon, spot flamingos and hike the dunes at **Mar Chiquita** (p164)

- POPULATION: 15.4 MILLION
- AREA: 451,011 SQ KM

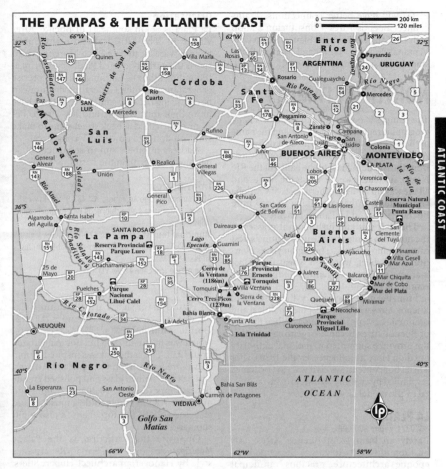

Climate

Temperatures on the pampas fluctuate wildly through the year, from lows of -6°C up to highs of 38°C, although such extremes are rare and the temperature is generally comfortable. The region is divided into two main climatic zones: the wet (or humid) pampas along the coast, where much of the rain falls, and the dry pampas to its west. There can be as much as 1000mm of rainfall per year (thanks to occasional heavy rainfalls rather than an extended rainy period), although drought is the largest single problem for farmers in the region.

National & Provincial Parks

The pampas and coast are home to a small but excellent selection of protected areas. The Parque Provincial Ernesto Tornquist (p156) is a hikers' paradise, where you can scale the peaks of Cerro de la Ventana (1186m) or check out the stunning Garganta del Diablo (Devil's Throat) gorge. Parque Nacional Lihué Calel (p158) is set in a near-desert landscape with surreal granite rock formations and is home to a wealth of animal species. More modest Parque Provincial Miguel Lillo (p173) is a leafy haven right by downtown Necochea.

Getting There & Away

There are flights from Buenos Aires to Santa Rosa, Bahía Blanca and Mar del Plata. Buses from nearly every town run to most destinations in the country, although, of course, larger cities (such as Santa Rosa, La Plata and Mar del

Plata) will have better connections. Trains connect Buenos Aires' Constitución station with La Plata, Luján Bahía Blanca, Sierra de la Ventana, Pinamar, Tandil and Mar del Plata, stopping at smaller towns along those routes.

NORTHERN PAMPAS

The pampas is both a general term for a large geographic region of fertile plains and the name of the province that lies to the west of Buenos Aires. The pampas grasslands roll southwards from the Río de la Plata to the banks of the Río Negro, stretching west towards the Andes and all the way up to the southern parts of Córdoba and Sante Fe provinces, taking in the entire Buenos Aires and La Pampa provinces.

The rich soil and lush natural grasses of the northern pampas make it Argentina's best cattle-raising country. The region yields plentiful hides, beef, wool and wheat for global markets, stamping Argentina on the world's economic map.

From the mid-19th century, the province of Buenos Aires was the undisputed political and economic center of the country. When the city of Buenos Aires became Argentina's capital, the province submitted to national authority but didn't lose its influence. By the 1880s, after a brief but contentious civil war, the province responded by creating its own provincial capital in the model city of La Plata.

LA PLATA

☎ 0221 / pop 800,000

Barely an hour from Buenos Aires, this bustling university town has the same belle epoque architecture, gracious municipal buildings, leafy parks and nightlife, all on a smaller scale. The big tourist draws are its natural history museum, one of Argentina's best, and the imposing neo-Gothic cathedral.

When Buenos Aires became Argentina's new capital, Governor Dardo Rocha founded La Plata in 1882 to give the province of Buenos Aires its own top city. Rocha chose engineer Pedro Benoit's elaborate city plan, based upon balance and logic, with diagonal avenues crossing the regular 5km-square grid pattern to connect the major plazas, creating a distinctive star design. Elegant on paper, this blueprint creates confusion at many intersections, with up to eight streets going off in all directions. However, it probably made La Plata South America's first completely planned city.

Orientation

La Plata is 56km southeast of Buenos Aires via RP 14. The cathedral and many public buildings are located on Plaza Moreno, which sports the graffiti-covered Piedra Fundacional (Founding Stone) – marking the city's precise geographical center. General navigation can be confusing because some intersections have more than four corners and it's easy to become disoriented. Check street signs to make sure you don't go down the wrong street.

Address numbers run in sequences of 50 per block rather than the customary 100.

Information

ACA (Automóvil Club Argentina; ☎ 482-9040; cnr Av 51 & Calle 9) Argentina's auto club; good for provincial road maps.

Municipal tourist office (☎ 427-1535; www.laplata .gov.ar; ☼ 9am-6pm Mon-Fri, 9am-4pm Sat & Sun) Just off Plaza San Martín.

Post office (cnr Calle 4 & Av 51)

Sights

La Plata's main sights are all within walking distance. Near Plaza Moreno is the neo-Gothic **cathedral** (☎ 423-3931; ☼ 10am-7pm), which was begun in 1885 but not inaugurated until 1932. The cathedral was inspired by medieval predecessors in Cologne and Amiens, and has fine stained glass and polished granite floors; tours (daily at 10:30am, 2:30pm and 4pm) are AR$10 and include a museum and elevator ride to the top. There's also a gift shop and cafe.

Opposite the cathedral is the **Palacio Municipal**, designed in German Renaissance style by Hanoverian architect Hubert Stiers. On the west side of the plaza, the **Museo y Archivo Dardo Rocha** (☎ 427-5591; Calle 50, No 933; admission free; ☼ 9am-5pm Mon-Fri, 3-6pm Sat & Sun) was the vacation house of the city's creator and contains period furniture and many of his personal knickknacks.

Two blocks northeast, the **Teatro Argentino** (☎ 0800-666-5151; www.teatroargentino.ic.gba.gov.ar; Av 51, btwn Calle 9 & Calle 10) is a fantastically ugly concrete monolith, but boasts great acoustics and quality ballet, symphony and opera performances. Two blocks further northeast, in front of Plaza San Martín is the ornate **Palacio de la Legislatura**, also in German Renaissance style. Nearby, catch the French Classic **Pasaje Dardo Rocha**, once La Plata's main railroad station and now the city's major cultural center,

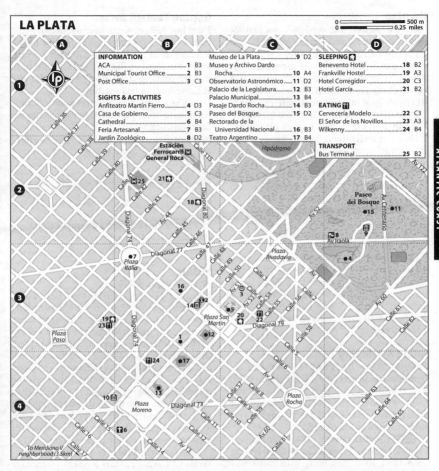

LA PLATA

INFORMATION		
ACA	**1**	B3
Municipal Tourist Office	**2**	B3
Post Office	**3**	C3

SIGHTS & ACTIVITIES		
Anfiteatro Martín Fierro	**4**	D3
Casa de Gobierno	**5**	C3
Cathedral	**6**	B4
Feria Artesanal	**7**	B3
Jardín Zoológico	**8**	D2
Museo de La Plata	**9**	D2
Museo y Archivo Dardo Rocha	**10**	A4
Observatorio Astronómico	**11**	D2
Palacio de la Legislatura	**12**	B3
Palacio Municipal	**13**	B4
Pasaje Dardo Rocha	**14**	B3
Paseo del Bosque	**15**	D2
Rectorado de la Universidad Nacional	**16**	B3
Teatro Argentino	**17**	B4

SLEEPING		
Benevento Hotel	**18**	B2
Frankville Hostel	**19**	A3
Hotel Corregidor	**20**	C3
Hotel García	**21**	B2

EATING		
Cervecería Modelo	**22**	C3
El Señor de los Novillos	**23**	A3
Wilkenny	**24**	B4

TRANSPORT		
Bus Terminal	**25**	B2

containing two museums. Also close by is the Flemish Renaissance **Casa de Gobierno**, housing the provincial governor and his retinue. A few blocks to the northwest are the original buildings of the **Rectorado de la Universidad Nacional** (1905), which was once a bank but is now the university administrative offices. On Sundays, check out the lively **feria artesanal** (crafts fair) on Plaza Italia.

Plantations of eucalyptus, gingko, palm and subtropical hardwoods cover **Paseo del Bosque**, parkland expropriated from an *estancia* (ranch) at the time of the city's founding. It attracts a collection of strolling families, smooching lovers and sweaty joggers. Various interesting sights are strewn within, such as the open-air **Anfiteatro Martín Fierro** (marked

Teatro de Aire Libre), that hosts music and drama performances; the **Observatorio Astronómico** (☎ 423-6593; call for schedule); the modest **Jardín Zoológico** (☎ 427-3925; admission AR$5; ☼ 10am-6pm, closed Mon); and the **Museo de La Plata** (☎ 425-7744; admission AR$6; ☼ 10am-6pm, closed Monday). Popular with school groups, this notable museum has paleontological, zoological, archaeological and anthropological collections of famous Patagonian explorer Francisco P Moreno. Countless display rooms offer something for everyone: Egyptian tomb relics, Jesuit art, amusing taxidermy, amazing skeletons, mummies, ancient pottery, scary insects and reconstructed dinosaurs. There's also a cafe. Arrange English tours in advance.

THE PAMPAS & THE ATLANTIC COAST

Sleeping

Frankville Hostel (☎ 482-3100; www.frankville .com.ar; Calle 46, No 781; dm AR$40-45, d AR$110; 🖳 🛜) Currently La Plata's only hostel – and luckily it's a decent one. Rooms are small with shared baths outside, but they're clean and have lockers. Nice back patio for socializing. HI (Hostelling International) card discount.

Hotel García (Calle 2, No 525; s AR$50-65, d AR$85) Friendly and clean, this budget place near the bus terminal offers 20 small, basic rooms. Showers are open – so everything in the bathroom gets wet – but the cable TV makes up for it.

Benevento Hotel (☎ 423-7721; www.hotelbenevento .com.ar; Calle 2, No 645; s AR$161-203, d AR$242; 🔌 🖳 🛜) This charmingly renovated hotel offers beautiful rooms with high ceilings and cable TV. Most have wood floors, plus balconies overlooking the busy street.

Hotel Corregidor (☎ 425-6800; www.hotelcorregi dor.com.ar; Calle 6, No 1026; s/d AR$303/340; 🔌 🖳 🛜) No surprises here – carpeted, modern rooms are pleasant and comfortable, catering to business people. Some have patios, and there's a small gym. Reserve from March to mid-December.

Eating & Drinking

Wilkenny (☎ 483-1772; cnr Calle 11 & 50; mains AR$21-39; 🕑 breakfast Mon-Fri, lunch & dinner daily) Popular place with traditional Irish pub feel and a decent range of food such as salads, sandwiches and pastas. On Friday and Saturday nights you might catch some live music.

our pick Cervecería Modelo (☎ 421-1321; cnr Calles 5 & 54; mains AR$25-35; 🕑 breakfast, lunch & dinner) Dating from 1894, its ceiling hung with hams and peanut shells strewn on the floor, this classic place serves ice-cold ales to a happy crowd. There are great sidewalk tables, and it's not too old to boast a big-screen TV and wi-fi.

El Señor de los Novillos (☎ 422-5553; Calle 46, btwn Calles 10 & 11; mains AR$25-36; 🕑 lunch Thu-Sun, dinner Tue-Sun) A modern, classy *parrilla* with a good atmosphere, decent prices and no pretensions.

A 10-minute taxi ride from the center, in the bohemian neighborhood Meridiano V, you'll find **Bar Imperio** (Calle 17, btwn Calles 70 & 71), **Mirapampa** (cnr Calles 17 & 71) and **Ciudád Vieja** (cnr Calles 17 & 71), all offering live music from Thursday through Sunday nights. The area is popular with students, and on Sundays there are market stalls showcasing the creations of local fashion designers.

Getting There & Away

Plaza bus 129 connects Buenos Aires with La Plata every 20 minutes (AR$8.50, one hour). It leaves from the side street Martín Zuvería, located in front of Buenos Aires' Retiro train station, making stops along Ave 9 Julio and at Constitución train station.

La Plata's bus terminal has plenty of connections to other parts of Argentina, including the following:

Destination	Cost (AR$)	Duration (hr)
Bahía Blanca	132-143	8-10
Bariloche	230	23
Córdoba	120	12
Mar del Plata	86-95	5
Mendoza	190	18

La Plata is also served by Buenos Aires' Roca suburban train line, with regular services from the Constitución station.

LUJÁN

☎ 02323 / pop 80,000

Luján is a pleasant riverside town that several times per year overflows with pilgrims making their way to Argentina's most important shrine. It's also busy on weekends (but worth visiting anytime), boasting a huge Spanish-style plaza with imposing neo-Gothic cathedral, as well as a couple of interesting museums. The riverside area is lined with restaurants and barbecue stands selling *choripan* (a spicy pork sausage in a crunchy roll); you can rent boats for a paddle on the river and on festive days there are games and rides. A chairlift carryies sightseers over the grubby river – an oddly charming touch.

On the first Saturday in October thousands of Catholics start a 65km pilgrimage walk from Buenos Aires to Luján (see boxed text, opposite). Other large gatherings occur on May 8 (**Virgin's day**), the first weekend in August (the colorful **Peregrinación Boliviana**), the last weekend in September (the 'gaucho' pilgrimage – watch for horses) and December 8 (**Immaculate Conception Day**).

Orientation & Information

Most places of interest are within three blocks of the basilica, though Plaza Colón – five blocks southeast via Calle San Martín – is another center of activity.

Post office (Mitre 575)

Tourist office (☎ 427082; 🕑 8am-5pm Mon-Fri, 10am-6pm Sat & Sun) Near the river at the west end of Lavalle, in the domed, yellow building.

OUR LADY OF LUJÁN

Argentina's patron saint is a ubiquitous presence – you can spot her poster on butcher shop walls, her statue in churches throughout the country and her image on the dashboards of many a Buenos Aires taxi. She can be recognized by her stiff, triangular dress, the half-moon at her feet and the streams of glory radiating from her crowned head.

Her legend begins in 1630, when a Portuguese settler in Tucumán asked a friend in Brazil to send him an image of the Virgin for his new chapel. Unsure what style of Virgin was required, the friend sent two – including one of the Immaculate Conception, her hands clasped before her in prayer. After setting out from the port of Buenos Aires, the cart bearing the statues got bogged near the river of Luján and only moved when the Immaculate Conception was taken off. Its owner took it as a sign, and left the statue in Luján so that a shrine could be built there. The other statue continued its journey to the northwest.

Since then the Virgin of Luján has been credited with a number of miracles – from curing tumors and sending a fog to hide early settlers from warring Indians, to protecting the province from a cholera epidemic. She was rewarded for her trouble in 1886 when Pope Leo XIII crowned her with a golden coronet set with almost 500 pearls and gems.

The massive pilgrimage to her basilica, where the original statue is still venerated, starts on the first Saturday in October. Throngs of the faithful walk the 65km from the Buenos Aires neighborhood of Liniers to Luján – a journey of up to 18 hours. If you arrive on the first Sunday in October (for Día de Virgen de Luján), you'll spot families of exhausted pilgrims snoozing in the square, enjoying barbecues by the river and filling plastic bottles with holy water from the fountain.

Sights

BASÍLICA NUESTRA SEÑORA DE LUJÁN

Every year over five million pilgrims from throughout Argentina visit Luján to honor the Virgin for her intercession in affairs of peace, health, forgiveness and consolation. The terminus of their journey is this imposing **basilica**, built from 1887 to 1935. The neo-Gothic church is made from a lovely rose-colored stone that glows in the setting sun. The statue of the Virgin, which dates from 1630, sits in the high chamber behind the main altar. Under the basilica you can tour a **crypt** (☎ 420058; admission AR$3; Ⓨ frequent between 10am-5pm) that's inhabited by Virgin statues from all over the world. Masses take place in the basilica several times a day.

COMPLEJO MUSEOGRÁFICO ENRIQUE UDAONDO

This gorgeous colonial-era **museum complex** (☎ 420245; admission AR$1; Ⓨ 2:30-5:30pm Wed-Fri, 10:30am-5:30pm Sat, Sun & holidays) rambles with several display rooms, pretty patios and gardens. The Sala General José de San Martín showcases Argentina's battles for independence, while the Sala de Gaucho contains some beautiful *mate* ware, horse gear and other gaucho paraphernalia. Near the entrance is a room portraying an old prison chamber, as the *cabildo* (town hall) used to be a lockup.

The nearby **Museo de Transporte** (☎ 420245; admission AR$1; Ⓨ 1:30-5:30pm Wed, 12:30-5:30pm Thu & Fri, 10:30am-5:30pm Sat, Sun & holidays) has a remarkable collection of horse-drawn carriages from the late 1800s. Also on display is the first steam locomotive to serve the city from Buenos Aires and a monster of a hydroplane that crossed the Atlantic in 1926. The most offbeat exhibits, however, are the stuffed and scruffy remains of Gato and Mancha, the hardy Argentine criollo horses ridden by adventurer AF Tschiffely from Buenos Aires to New York. This trip took 2½ years, from 1925 to 1928.

Buy tickets in the office at the intersection between the two museums.

Sleeping

Luján can easily be done on a day trip from Buenos Aires. If you decide to overnight on a weekend, however, be sure to reserve ahead. Rates drop on weekdays.

Hostel Estación Luján (☎ 429101; www.estacion lujanhostel.com.ar; 9 de Julio 978; dm AR$60, r AR$150-170; Ⓧ 🖳 🛜) Run by a friendly family, this small, modern hostel is just steps from the basilica. There are just four clean rooms, some with balcony, plus kitchen use and a large common area.

Hotel Hoxón (☎ 429970; www.hotelhoxon.com.ar; 9 de Julio 760; s AR$128-145, d AR$218-230; Ⓧ 🖳 🛜 🛒)

The best and biggest in town, with modern, clean and comfortable rooms. Superiors are carpeted and come with fridge and air-con. The swimming pool comes with raised sun deck.

Hotel del Virrey (☎ 420797; www.hoteldelvirreylujan .com.ar; San Martín 129; r AR$200; ☒ ☜) Right near the basilica is this modern hotel offering small but good rooms.

Eating

Pilgrims won't go hungry in Luján – the central parts of San Martín, 9 de Julio and the riverfront are all lined with restaurants.

Cervecería Berlín (☎ 426767; San Martín 151; mains AR$10-20; ☾ lunch & dinner) With tables on its small front deck, this is a good choice on a warm day. Food isn't fancy – burgers, sandwiches and waffles – but there are plenty of drinks.

Café La Basílica (☎ 428376; San Martín 101; mains AR$21-45; ☾ 8am-7pm Mon-Thu, 8am-midnight Fri & Sat, 8am-7pm Sun) This classic corner bar offers satisfying meals of homemade pastas and grilled meats. There's English translation on the menu.

L'Eau Vive (☎ 421774; Constitución 2112; 3-course menu AR$45; ☾ lunch & dinner Tue-Sat, lunch only Sun) Just 2km from the town center you'll find this friendly French restaurant run by Carmelite nuns from around the world. Taxis here cost less than AR$10, or take bus 501 from the center.

Getting There & Away

Lujan's **bus terminal** (Av de Nuestra Señora de Luján & Almirante Brown) is just three blocks north of the basilica. From Buenos Aires, take Transportes Atlántida's bus 57 from outside the Plaza Italia or Once train stations, which leaves every half-hour (AR$10, two hours). There are also daily train departures from Estación Once in Buenos Aires, but you need to change trains in Moreno.

SAN ANTONIO DE ARECO
☎ 02326 / pop 23,000

Nestled among lush farmlands, San Antonio de Areco is probably the prettiest town in the pampas. An easy drive from the capital, it welcomes many day-tripping *porteños* (residents of Buenos Aires) who come for the peaceful atmosphere and picturesque colonial streets. The town dates from the early 18th century and preserves a great deal of criollo and gau-

cho traditions, especially among its artisans, who produce very fine silverwork and saddlery. Gauchos from all over the pampas show up for November's Día de la Tradición, where you can catch them and their horses strutting the cobbled streets in all their finery.

San Antonio de Areco's compact town center and quiet streets are very walkable. Around the Plaza Ruiz de Arellano, named in honor of the town's founding *estanciero* (*estancia* owner), are several historic buildings, including the *iglesia parroquial* (parish church).

The *puente viejo* (old bridge; 1857), across the Río Areco, follows the original cart road to northern Argentina. Once a toll crossing, it's now a pedestrian bridge leading to San Antonio de Areco's main attraction, the Museo Gauchesco Ricardo Güiraldes. **Kayaking** is possible on the river.

Orientation

San Antonio de Areco is 113km west of Buenos Aires via RN 8. The main drag is V Alsina, though the town's numerous sites of interest and shops are scattered throughout the surrounding streets.

Information

There are a few banks with ATMs around the Plaza Ruiz de Arellano.

Cyber Play (Ruiz de Arellano 285) Internet access.

Post office (cnr Alvear & Av Del Valle)

Tourist office (☎ 453165; cnr E Zerboni & Ruiz de Arellano; ☾ 8am-7pm Mon-Fri, 8am-8pm Sat & Sun)

Sights
MUSEO GAUCHESCO RICARDO GÜIRALDES

Inaugurated by the provincial government in 1938, a decade after the death of Ricardo Güiraldes, author of the gaucho novel *Don Segundo Sombra* (see the boxed text, p148), this **museum** (☎ 455839; cnr R Güiraldes & Sosa; admission AR$8; ☾ 11am-5pm Wed-Mon) in Parque Criollo is a sort of gaucholand of restored or fabricated buildings, including an old flour mill, a re-created *pulpería* (tavern) and a colonial-style chapel. The main deal is a 20th-century reproduction of an 18th-century *casco* (ranch house), which holds a wooden bed belonging to Juan Manuel de Rosas (a famous Argentine *caudillo*, or warlord), lots of gorgeous horse gear and various works of gauchesco art. Two rooms are dedicated to Güiraldes himself.

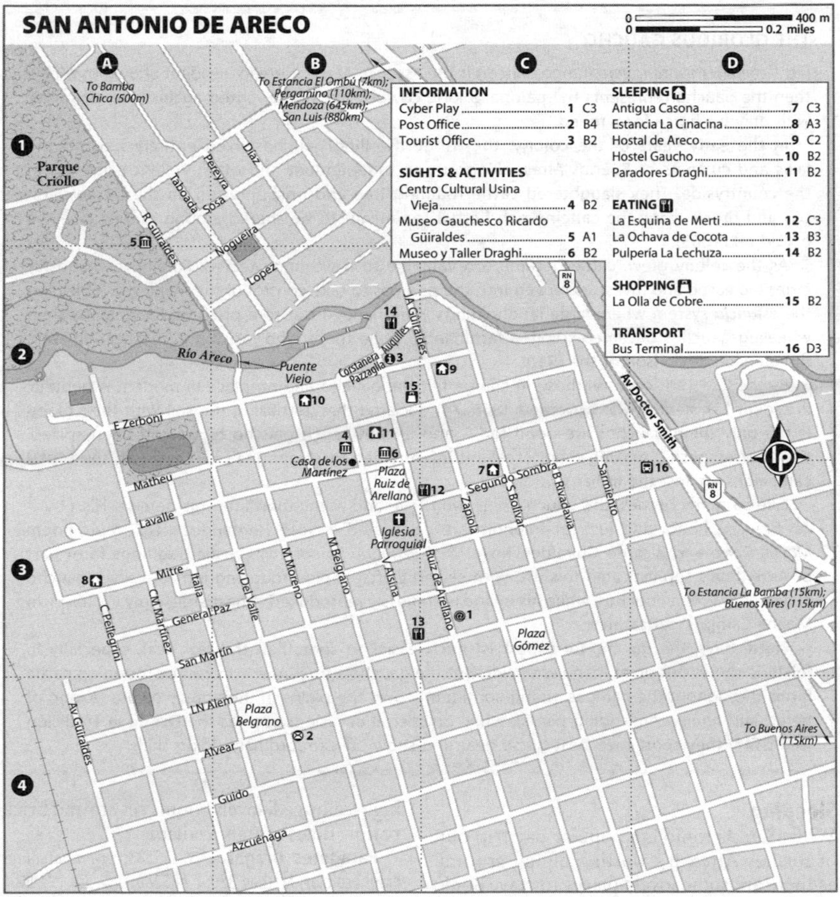
SAN ANTONIO DE ARECO
0 400 m
0 0.2 miles
INFORMATION
Cyber Play 1 C3
Post Office 2 B4
Tourist Office 3 B2
SIGHTS & ACTIVITIES
Centro Cultural Usina Vieja 4 B2
Museo Gauchesco Ricardo Güiraldes 5 A1
Museo y Taller Draghi 6 B2
SLEEPING
Antigua Casona 7 C3
Estancia La Cinacina 8 A3
Hostal de Areco 9 C2
Hostel Gaucho 10 B2
Paradores Draghi 11 B2
EATING
La Esquina de Merti 12 C3
La Ochava de Cocota 13 B3
Pulpería La Lechuza 14 B2
SHOPPING
La Olla de Cobre 15 B2
TRANSPORT
Bus Terminal 16 D3
To Bamba Chica (500m)
To Estancia El Ombú (7km); Pergamino (110km); Mendoza (645km); San Luis (880km)
Parque Criollo
Río Areco
Puente Viejo
Casa de los Martínez
Plaza Ruiz de Arellano
Iglesia Parroquial
Plaza Gómez
Plaza Belgrano
To Estancia La Bamba (15km); Buenos Aires (115km)
To Buenos Aires (115km)
Av Doctor Smith
Segundo Sombra
RN 8

MUSEO Y TALLER DRAGHI

This small **museum and workshop** (☎ 454219; Lavalle 387; admission AR$10; ⏲ 10:30am-12:30pm & 1-4pm Mon-Sat, 10:30am-12:30pm Sun) highlights an exceptional collection of silver *facónes* (gaucho knives), beautiful horse gear and intricate *mate* paraphernalia. There's also some jewelry and leather bags; everything is for sale.

CENTRO CULTURAL USINA VIEJA

Set in an old power plant dating from 1901, the **Centro Cultural Usina Vieja** (☎ 456202; V Alsina 660; admission AR$1.50; ⏲ 11am-5pm Tue-Sun) is an eclectic museum with a funky collection of ancient radios, typewriters, sewing machines and record players. Farm equipment, sculptures, an old-time grocery store and even a small airplane are also on display, as are rotating exhibits of local artists' work and some of Florencio Molina Campos' amusing caricatures of gaucho life.

Festivals & Events

San Antonio de Areco is the symbolic center of Argentina's vestigial cowboy culture, and puts on the country's biggest gaucho celebration on **Día de la Tradición** (in early to mid-November; call the tourist office for exact dates). If you're in the area, don't miss it; attractions include a horseback procession through the town, displays of horsemanship, folk dancing, craft exhibitions and guided tours of historic sites. Main events take place at Parque Criollo.

THE PAMPAS & THE
ATLANTIC COAST

THE GLORIOUS GAUCHO

If the melancholy *tanguero* (tango dancer) is the essence of the *porteño* (resident of Buenos Aires), then the gaucho represents the pampa: a lone cowboy-like figure, pitted against the elements, with only his horse for a friend.

In the early years of the colony, the fringe-dwelling gauchos lived entirely beyond the laws and customs of Buenos Aires, eking out an independent and often violent existence in the countryside. They slaughtered cattle roaming free and unsupervised on the fertile pampas and drank *mate,* the caffeine-rich herbal tea meant to be shared among friends (see the boxed text, p65).

As the colony grew, cattle became too valuable to leave unprotected. Foreign demand for hides increased and investors moved into the pampas to take control of the market, establishing the *estancia* system where large landholdings were handed out to a privileged few. Many freewheeling gauchos became exploited farmhands, while those who resisted domestication were threatened with prison or the draft.

By the late 19th century, those in charge felt the gaucho had no place in modern Argentina. President Sarmiento (who governed 1868–74) declared that 'fertilizing the soil with their blood is the only thing gauchos are good for' – and already much gaucho blood had been spilled, their horsemanship making them excellent infantrymen for Argentina's civil war and the brutal campaigns against the Indians.

Like so many heroes, the gaucho only won love and admiration after his demise. His physical bravery, honor and lust for freedom are celebrated in José Hernández's 1872 epic poem *Martin Fierro* and Ricardo Güiraldes' novel *Don Segundo Sombra*. His rustic traditions form part of Argentina's sophisticated folk art, with skilled craftspeople producing intricate silver gaucho knives and woven ponchos, while his image is endlessly reproduced – most amusingly in Florencio Molina Campos' caricatures.

These days, the gaucho-for-export is much easier to spot than the real deal, especially in folkloric shows put on at many *estancias*. But the gaucho's true inheritors can be found on cattle farms throughout the pampas, riding confidently over the plains in their dusty *boinas* (a kind of beret) and *bombachas* (riding pants), while on special occasions such as the Día de la Tradición (see p147) they sport their best horse gear and show off extraordinary riding skills.

Sleeping

While San Antonio is a popular day trip out of Buenos Aires, it's worth hanging around as there are some lovely places to stay. Book on weekends.

Hostel Gaucho (☎ 453625; www.hostelgaucho.com.ar; Zerboni 308; dm/r AR$50/120; 🖳 🛜) This is Areco's only hostel, and it's a good one. Dorms and rooms are small but fine, and there's a grassy garden (with *parrilla*) in back. Bike rentals and tours available. Private rooms cost AR$150 on Saturday night.

Hostal de Areco (☎ 456118; www.hostaldeareco.com .ar; Zapiola 25; s/d AR$100/140) Clustered with two other hotels, which aren't as personable but do have pools, this place has a pleasant salon and nice large grassy garden in back. Room rates rise to AR$160 on weekends for both singles and doubles.

our pick **Antigua Casona** (☎ 456600; www.antiguaca sona.com; Segundo Sombra 495; s AR$150-180, d AR$200-250; 😵) This restored traditional home offers five high-ceilinged, lovely rooms set around brick patios. Bikes rentals available.

Paradores Draghi (☎ 455583; www.paradores draghi.com.ar; Matheu 380; r AR$280; 😵 🖳 🛜 🐾) Five large, gorgeous rooms (two with kitchenette) are available at this tranquil place. There's a grassy garden with beautiful pool, greenhouse breakfast room and two patios in which to relax.

ESTANCIAS

Estancia La Cinacina (☎ 452045; www.lacinacina.com .ar; B Mitre 9; día de campo AR$120, r AR$304-380; 🕙 Tue & Fri-Sun; 😵 🐾) On the edge of town, this *estancia* offers comfortable lodgings in a pretty park setting.

Bamba Chica (☎ 15-5893-7412, 15-5893-7413; www .bambachica.com.ar; Ruta 8, Km 116; día de campo AR$160, s/d AR$550/650; 😵 🐾) Located 500m from the Museo Gauchesco in Areco. For something fancier, try its sister *estancia* (www.la-bamba .com.ar).

El Ombú (☎ 02326-492080, in Buenos Aires 011-4737-0436; www.estanciaelombu.com; RP 31, cuartel VI, Villa Lía; día de campo AR$265, s/d AR$760/1216; 🏊 🍴) At this historical *estancia*, on 300 hectares about 20km from Areco, stays include all meals, drinks and most activities such as horseback riding and golf or tennis at a nearby country club.

For more *estancias* in the province, see the boxed text, p152.

Eating

San Antonio de Areco has a considerable assortment of character-filled cafes and restaurants to choose from. Some host *peñas* (folk-music clubs) on weekends – ask the locals or the people at the tourist office.

Pulpería La Lechuza (☎ 454542; Costanera Aquiles Pazzaglia, btwn Ruiz de Arellano & E Zerboni; mains AR$18-35; 🕐 lunch & dinner Fri & Sat only) Enjoy a huge lunch of empanadas and barbecued beef under the trees or grab a *choripan* to go and enjoy it by the riverbank. There's folk dancing at night (AR$12 cover charge).

La Ochava de Cocota (☎ 452176; cnr V Alsina & LN Alem; mains AR$18-36; 🕐 breakfast, lunch & dinner Wed-Sat & Mon, dinner only Sun) A cafe serving homemade cakes and quiches by day, and cocktail bar serving cheese plates and pizzas by night, with a welcoming, woody aroma and a laid-back feel.

La Esquina de Merti (☎ 456705; Ruiz de Arellano 147; snacks AR$5-15; 🕐 breakfast, lunch & dinner) Areco's only restaurant that doesn't close in the afternoon – luckily it has great old atmosphere. Typical *parrilla* at mealtimes, with mostly sandwiches and empanadas for teatime.

Shopping

San Antonio de Areco's artisans are known throughout the country. *Mate* paraphernalia, *rastras* (silver-studded belts) and *facónes*, produced by skilled silversmiths, are the most typical items. The tourist office has an extensive list of artists and their trades.

If you're looking for a gift of artisanal chocolates or *alfajores* (cookie-type sandwiches), try **La Olla de Cobre** (☎ 453105; Matheu; 🕐 10am-1pm & 3:30-8:30pm Mon & Wed-Fri, 10am-1pm & 2:30-8:30pm Sat & Sun, closed Tue) You can sit down for a coffee or drinking chocolate as well.

Getting There & Away

General Belgrano and Chevallier run frequent buses from Buenos Aires to Areco (AR$27, two hours). A few long-distance services are available.

SOUTHERN PAMPAS

Spreading out from the capital, the pampas region extends south beyond the borders of Buenos Aires province and west into the province of La Pampa.

In the southern part of Buenos Aires province, the endlessly flat plain is punctuated by sierras, or hills. The Sierras de Tandil are ancient mountain ranges, worn to soft, low summits with heights that barely reach 500m. A little to the west, Sierra de la Ventana's jagged peaks rise to 1300m, attracting hikers and climbers.

Further west again, in the province of La Pampa, are the modest granite boulders of Parque Nacional Lihué Calel.

The hillside towns of Tandil and Sierra de la Ventana offer lots of outdoor activities and a relaxing country atmosphere – both make good side trips from Buenos Aires. La Pampa's provincial capital of Santa Rosa doesn't offer much in its own right, but is a decent resting point for overland travelers on their way west or south.

CHASCOMÚS

☎ 02241 / pop 47,000

This pretty town sits on the shores of Laguna Chascomús, a popular fishing spot. Its broad jacaranda-lined main street, Av Lastra, leads from RN 2, on the way to Mar del Plata, directly to the lagoon. Horses and bikes can be rented along the shore, and there's a paved road all the way around the lagoon (which is 34km in circumference). The **tourist information office** (☎ 430405; 🕐 8am-7pm Mon-Fri, 9am-7pm Sat & Sun), located at the fishing pier close to town, provides maps and information on lodgings and activities. There's another **tourist office** (☎ 426300; 🕐 1-5pm Fri, 9am-2pm Sat & Sun) at the bus terminal.

Sights include the excellent **Museo Pampeano** (☎ 430982; Av Lastri & Muñiz; admission free; 🕐 9am-3pm Tue-Fri, 10:30am-4:30pm Sat & Sun), filled with artifacts from the area's various former inhabitants – indigenous people, the gauchos and the wealthy landowners. Note the interesting chair made from animal bones. Also worth a look are the historical buildings of the city's center, including the **Capilla de los Negros** (Av Costanera & Presidente Perón). Here's a little-known fact: Buenos Aires province and the capital were once home to a significant African population that vanished in the

THE PAMPAS & THE ATLANTIC COAST

19th century – some say because they were conscripted into the war against Paraguay. In Chascomús, black people were refused entry to the main cathedral, so they built this chapel where you can still note their fusion of Catholicism with African beliefs.

There are several camp grounds near the lake, the pick of which is **Camping 6 de Septiembre** (☎ in Buenos Aires 011-15-5182-3836; www.seisdeseptiembre.com.ar; per person AR$20 plus per tent AR$20; 🔊), which also offers cabins that sleep up to four (AR$250). It's 8km from the bus terminal.

Several hotels lie along the lakeshore, including **La Posada** (☎ 423503; laposadachascomus@ hotmail.com; Av Costanera España 18; r AR$220-270; 🔊 🛜), with four large and comfortable rooms with kitchenette and front patio. Or splurge and head 12km around the lake to **Estancia La Alameda** (☎ in Buenos Aires 011-15-5228-2817; www .estancialaalameda.com; día de campo AR$100, s/d AR$495/660; 🔊 🛜), a country estate with all the usual *estancia* activities (*asado* lunch, *folklore* show, horseback rides).

Chascomús' bus terminal is 3km from town (taxis AR$6). Several buses run from Buenos Aires (AR$27, two hours).

TANDIL
☎ 02293 / pop 140,000
Pretty Tandil sits at the northern edge of the Sierras de Tandil, a 2.5-million-year-old mountain range worn down to gentle, grassy peaks and rocky outcroppings – perfect for rock climbing and mountain biking. It exudes a rare combination of laid-back country charm and the energy of a thriving regional city. The town center is leafy and relaxed, with many places observing the afternoon siesta. Later in the evening, however, locals crowd the squares and streets, shopping and partaking in the city's cultural offerings. On a side note, Tandil is known for nurturing a disproportionate number of Argentina's tennis stars – the latest of which is Juan Martín del Potro.

The town arose from Fuerte Independencia, a military outpost established in 1823 by Martín Rodríguez. In the early 1870s, it was the scene of one of the province's most remarkable battles, when renegade gauchos, followers of the eccentric healer Gerónimo de Solané (popularly known as Tata Dios), gathered in the hills before going on a murderous rampage against landowners and recent

immigrants. The immigrants prevailed, and the culinary skills they brought from Europe have made the area an important producer of specialty foods. Today, Tandil is famous for its cheeses and cured meats, which can be sampled in eateries and stores throughout town.

Orientation
Tandil is 384km south of Buenos Aires via RN 3 and RN 226, and 170km northwest of Mar del Plata via RN 226. The main commercial streets are Gral Rodríguez and 9 de Julio, while the center of social activity is Plaza de Independencia, a two-block area bounded by Gral Rodríguez, Belgrano, Chacabuco and Gral Pinto.

Information
ACA (Automóvil Club Argentina; ☎ 425463; Gral Rodríguez 399) Auto club; good for provincial road maps.
Hospital (Hospital Municipal Ramón Santamarina; ☎ 422210; Gral Paz 1406)
Post office (Gral Pinto 621)
Tourist kiosk (Plaza Independencia, cnr Grals Pinto & Rodríguez; 🕒 10am-6pm Mon, 9am-8pm Tue-Sat, 9am-12:30pm & 3:30-6pm Sun) Might move in the future.
Tourist office (☎ 432225; www.tandil.gov.ar; Av Com Espora 1120; 🕒 9am-8pm Mon-Fri, 9am-6pm Sat, 9am-3pm Sun)

There's another **tourist office** (☎ 432092) at the bus terminal.

Sights
Tandil's museums include the historical **Museo Tradicionalista Fuerte Independencia** (☎ 435573; 4 de Abril 845; admission AR$5; 🕒 2-6pm Mar-Nov, 4-8pm Dec-Feb), which exhibits a large and varied collection on the town's history. Photographs (captioned in Spanish) commemorate major events, and the place is filled with relics – from carriages to ladies' gloves – donated by local families. The **Museo de Bellas Artes** (☎ 432067; Chacabuco 353; admission by donation; 🕒 8:30am-12:30pm & 5-9pm Tue-Fri, 5-9pm Sat & Sun) has temporary exhibits of Argentine and international artists.

The walk to **Parque Independencia** from the southwestern edge of downtown offers good views of the city, particularly at night, while the central **Plaza de Independencia**, surrounded by the typical municipal buildings and a church, is where the townspeople stroll in the evenings, often to the sounds of music from the bandstand.

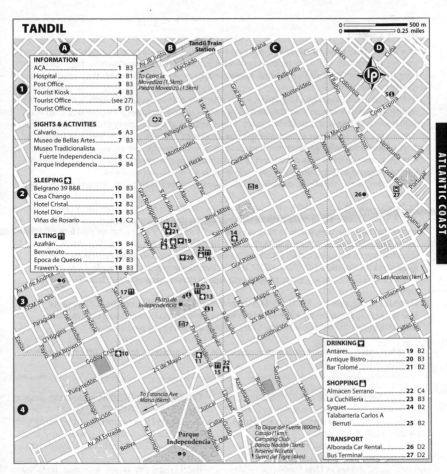

TANDIL

0　　　　　　　　　500 m
0　　　　　　　0.25 miles

INFORMATION
ACA.. **1** B3
Hospital.................................. **2** B1
Post Office........................... **3** B3
Tourist Kiosk....................... **4** B3
Tourist Office................. (see 27)
Tourist Office..................... **5** D1

SIGHTS & ACTIVITIES
Calvario.................................. **6** A3
Museo de Bellas Artes....... **7** B3
Museo Tradicionalista
　Fuerte Independencia....... **8** C2
Parque Independencia........ **9** B4

SLEEPING
Belgrano 39 B&B................ **10** B3
Casa Chango........................ **11** B4
Hotel Cristal........................ **12** B2
Hotel Dior............................ **13** B3
Viñas de Rosario................. **14** C2

EATING
Azafrán................................. **15** B4
Benvenuto............................ **16** B3
Epoca de Quesos................ **17** B3
Frawen's............................... **18** B3

DRINKING
Antares.................................. **19** B2
Antique Bistro..................... **20** B3
Bar Tolomé.......................... **21** B2

SHOPPING
Almacen Serrano................ **22** C4
La Cuchillería...................... **23** B3
Syquet.................................. **24** B3
Talabartería Carlos A
　Berruti.............................. **25** B2

TRANSPORT
Alborada Car Rental........... **26** D2
Bus Terminal....................... **27** D2

At the north edge of town, where Tata Dios gathered his supporters over a century ago, the Piedra Movediza (a 300-ton 'rocking stone') teetered precariously atop **Cerro La Movediza** for many years, before finally falling in 1912. A 'replica' nonmoving stone was built in 2007. Take bus 503 (blue).

Calvario, a hill ostensibly resembling the site of Christ's crucifixion, attracts masses of visitors at Easter, when a passion play is held.

The **Reserva Natural Sierra del Tigre** (admission AR$6; ☼ 9am-7:30pm in summer, till 6pm in winter, closed Wed & rainy days) is just south of town, at the end of Calle Suiz, off Av Don Bosco. The rocky hills are fun to climb, and in spring the reserve is filled with fragrant wild flowers. The peaks offer views of the town to one side

and the patchwork pampean farms stretching out from the other. A somewhat incongruous collection of animals – llamas and donkeys among them – have free run of the park, while their natural predator, the puma, is sadly caged.

Activities
The **Dique del Fuerte**, only 12 blocks south of Plaza Independencia, is a huge reservoir that you can easily walk around in a couple of hours. In summer, the Balneario Municipal runs several **swimming pools** and you can rent **canoes** and **kayaks**. There are also a few restaurants nestled along its shoreline.

To go horseback riding in the Reserva Natural Sierra del Tigre or other surrounding

THE PAMPAS & THE ATLANTIC COAST

DÍA DE CAMPO

One of the best ways to enjoy the wide open spaces of the pampas is to visit an *estancia* (ranch). Argentina's late-19th-century belle epoque saw wealthy landowning families adorn their ranches with lavish, often fanciful homes and designer gardens, which they used as their country retreats.

Those glorious days being long gone, a rich selection of these establishments is now open to tourists. The *día de campo* – or 'day in the country' – usually includes a huge *asado* (barbecue grill) lunch with drinks, a tour of the historic home and use of the property's horses, bicycles and swimming pool. Some places also offer a *show gauchesco*, featuring folk dances and traditional feats of horsemanship, while others host polo matches. *Estancias* are an excellent sustainable tourism option, helping to preserve part of the country's past while also providing an impressive guest-to-tree ratio. Overnight stays generally include all meals and activities.

Here are some stand-out options in the pampas (rates include all meals and are per person):

La Candelaria (☎ 02227-424404; www.estanciacandelaria.com; RN 205, Km 114.5, Lobos; día de campo AR$200, r from AR$400; ☢) The original family went bust building their French-style castle, whose grounds were designed by Charles Thays, responsible for many of Buenos Aires' public parks. Polo matches are often held.

Santa Rita (☎ 02227-495026; www.santa-rita.com.ar; RN 205, Lobos; día de campo AR$160, r AR$305; ☢) A somewhat eccentric restoration rescued this colonial-era home, whose chapel is one of the oldest in the province.

Bella Vista de Guerrero (☎ 02245-481234; www.bellavistadeguerrero.com; RN 2, Castelli; día de campo AR$300, s/d AR$1525/2180; ☢) Boasts a magnificently restored mansion, gourmet cuisine, luxurious rooms and a day spa.

El Roble (☎ in Buenos Aires 011-4807-3450; www.insidethepampas.com; NR 47, near Luján; día de campo AR$270, r AR$380) Run by a young British-Argentine couple, experience an authentic working cattle farm in the lovely pampas. Area activities include horseback rides, herding cattle and visiting gaucho festivals.

For a few more options in the province, see under San Antonio de Areco (p148) or check www .estanciasargentinas.com.

---

areas, call **Gabriel Barletta** (☎ 427725, 02293-15-509609; cabalgatasbarletta@yahoo.com.ar; half-day tours per person AR$100). For bike rentals, contact **Sergio** (☎ 452454, 02293-15-647234).

Several tour agencies offer a range of activities around the town and the sierras. The highly trained guides at **Chao Tandil** (☎ 432542; www.chaotandil.com.ar) offer trekking, canoeing, rappelling, mountain biking and rock climbing.

Sleeping

Reservations are a must during summer, Easter week and holiday weekends. If you have your own transport, the many cabañas along Av Don Bosco are a good option – the tourist office provides lists of fully equipped cabins, many of which have pools.

Camping Club Banco Nacion (☎ 423125; www .campingcbntandil.com.ar; Av Don Bosco & Yugoslavia; per person AR$20; ☢) Out of town, towards the *reserva*, this campground also offers dorm-style lodgings, as well as *parrillas* and outdoor activities.

Casa Chango (☎ 422260; www.casa-chango.com.ar; 25 de Mayo 451; dm/s/d AR$50/80/130; ☐ ☎) A decent hostel located in a rambling old building with great old tiles, a nice back garden and crumbling patios. Choose between huge dorms or tiny private rooms.

Hotel Cristal (☎ 443970; hotelcristal_tandil@yahoo .com.ar; Gral Rodríguez 871; s/d AR$100/148; ☐) A basic but comfortable hotel, with a sunny garden where guests can enjoy breakfast.

Belgrano 39 B&B (☎ 426989, 02293-15-607076; Belgrano 39; r AR$280 & 400; ☢) There's just two rooms here – one comfortable double and one huge loft room that sleeps four or five – plus huge, lovely gardens and pool. Run by a one-of-a-kind British woman; phone ahead.

Las Acacias (☎ 423373; www.posadalasacacias.com .ar; Brasil 642; s/d AR$270/340; ☐ ☎ ☢) Located in an old dairy, this wonderful place has nine elegant rooms set around the gardens. Rustic atmosphere and tasteful decor; prices drop outside summer.

Hotel Dior (☎ 431901; www.hoteldior.com; Gral Rodríguez 475; r AR$320; ☒ ☐ ☎) This three-star place's comfortable rooms feature bouncy beds and good-sized bathrooms. Try for a room with balcony offering views of the square and the hills beyond town.

Viñas del Rosario (☎ 444776; www.vinasdelrosario .com; Gral Paz 625; d/tr AR$350/470; ✖ 🖳 🛜) Fine old building with three simple but beautiful rooms and a small grassy garden with Jacuzzi. Central location.

Estancia Ave Maria (☎ 422843; www.avemariatandil .com.ar; s/d from AR$610/850; 🖳 🛜 🔊) This historical and beautiful *estancia* offers home-cooked meals and elegant, comfortable rooms, some with views of the hills. Prices include half-board, plus activities such as horseback rides. Take Juan B Justo 6km west of town.

Eating

Frawen's (☎ 426339; Gral Rodríguez 499; mains AR$15-26; ✓ breakfast, lunch & dinner) Breakfast on the plaza? Frawen's is your spot: light and sunny, with heaps of sidewalk seating, this place is a great start to your day.

Carajo (☎ 436669; cnr Saavedra Lamas & García; mains AR$17-36; ✓ lunch & dinner Tue-Sat, dinner only Sun, closed Mon) With a great outdoor terrace overlooking the Dique del Fuerte, this place is unbeatable on a warm sunny day. The meat is pretty good as well.

Benevento (☎ 447001; cnr San Martín & L N Alem; pasta AR$20-24; ✓ lunch & dinner Tue-Sun) These guys do only pasta, and they do it very well – it's all homemade and deliciously fresh. Try the *tallarines* with smoked ham, asparagus and vodka cream. Big takeout counter.

our pick **Epoca de Quesos** (☎ 448750; cnr San Martín & 14 de Julio; mains AR$21-34; ✓ 9am-10pm) Stuffed with tourists on a busy weekend, Epoca de Quesos sells over 130 local cheeses and dozens of cured meats. Taste at the counter or snag a table in the pleasant garden out back, and order a sampler plate with specialty beer.

Azafrán (☎ 436800; cnr Fte Independencia & Constitución; mains AR$26-34; ✓ lunch & dinner Wed-Mon) This small and smartly decorated restaurant does fine gourmet dishes like tagliatelle with mushrooms, or trout in lime and aromatic rice. Reservations are a good idea.

Drinking

For a small town, Tandil has several good bars.

Antares (☎ 446636; 9 de Julio 758; ✓ 6:30pm-late) One of Antares many branches, it sports the typical Antares look – an attractive, modern restaurant-pub with just-for-looks copper tap cylinders behind the bar. Live music on weekends.

Bar Tolomé (☎ 422951; cnr Gral Rodríguez & Bmé Mitre; ✓ 7:30pm-late) Dead midweek and lively on weekends (when there's loud, live music), this relaxed bar serves pizzas and sandwiches when a beer's not enough.

Antique Bistro (☎ 449339; Gral Rodríguez 687; ✓ 7pm-late) A sophisticated mood prevails at this tiny old-fashioned piano bar, where live folk and tango bands perform from 11:30pm Thursday to Saturday nights.

Shopping

Cold cuts and cheese are what Tandil is famous for, but there are also plenty of finely crafted gaucho knives that will come in handy when slicing the salami.

La Cuchillería (☎ 444937; San Martín 780; ✓ 9am-1pm & 5-9pm Mon-Sat) From 8cm whittlers to 36cm *facónes*, this high-end knife shop sells a wide array of quality handmade blades.

Talabartería Carlos A Berruti (☎ 425652; Gral Rodríguez 787; ✓ 9:15am-1pm & 4:30-8:30pm Mon-Sat) Especially good for leather, this store also stocks an assortment of *mates*, knives, silverwork and ponchos.

Almacen Serrano (☎ 448102; cnr Av Avellaneda & Gral Rodríguez; ✓ 9am-1pm & 4:30-9pm Mon-Thu, 9am-9pm Fri & Sat, 10am-9pm Sun) Sells cheese, salamis and hams from the region, as well as locally made beers and sweets.

Syquet (☎ 422122; cnr Bmé Mitre & Gral Rodríguez; ✓ 9am-1pm & 5-9pm Tue-Thu, 9am-9pm Fri-Mon) More cheeses, meats and beers, plus *dulce de leche* (milk caramel), jams and liqueurs made from chocolate and honey.

Getting There & Away

Tandil's bus terminal is within walking distance of its town center, if you don't mind walking 12 blocks. Otherwise taxis will cost about AR$7.

Popular long-distance destinations:

Destination	Cost (AR$)	Duration (hr)
Buenos Aires	74	5¼
Córdoba	174	16
Mar del Plata	32	3
Mendoza	250	16
Necochea	25	3
Rosario	125	11

Trains from Buenos Aires' Constitución station go to Tandil.

THE PAMPAS & THE ATLANTIC COAST

Getting Around

Tandil's excellent public transportation system reaches every important sight. Bus 500 (yellow) goes to Dique del Fuerte, bus 501 (red) goes to the bus terminal, and bus 503 (blue) goes to Cerro La Movediza, the university and the bus terminal.

For car rental, try **Alborada** (☎ 441950; cnr Gral Pinto & Saavedra).

SIERRA DE LA VENTANA

☎ 0291 / pop 5000

The Río Sauce winding gently through it, this leafy town fills up on weekends, with families from around the province flocking to its pretty bathing spots and picturesque hills.

Sierra de la Ventana's main attraction is the wealth of outdoor activity it offers: hiking up the nearby peaks, trout fishing and bathing in the streams and pools, riding on horse or bicycle through the hills, and climbing or rappelling among the rocks.

To reach the town from Bahía Blanca (125km to its south), take RN 33 to Tornquist, then RP 76. Sierra de la Ventana is divided into two sectors by Río Sauce Grande: Villa Tivoli has all of the businesses and services, while Villa Arcadia is a more residential area.

Information

Banco Provincia (San Martín 260) The town's only bank; it has an ATM.

Cyber Intersierra (Av San Martín 403) Internet access; look for the striped awning.

Post office (cnr Av Roca & Alberdi)

Tourist office (☎ 491-5303; Av del Golf; ☷ 8am-8pm) Across the tracks from the train station.

Activities

Lots of outdoor pursuits are on offer in this region, and you can tackle most on your own. For hiking guides try **Luan & Ventur** (☎ 491-5005; luan_ventur@hotmail.com; Av San Martín 140), which goes to Garganta del Diablo (see p156), the only way to explore that gorge. It also offers hikes to Cerro Tres Picos (see opposite), as well as activities such as rappelling and horseback riding.

Based in Villa Ventana, **Eco Ventania** (☎ 491-0245; www.ecoventania.com.ar; Siete Colores, btwn Pillahuinco & Cruz del Sur, Villa Ventana) offers similar activities, as well as jeep tours and photographic safaris, while **Campo Equino** (☎ 0291-15-643-1582; campoequino@celt.com.ar; RP 76, Km 230) specializes in horseback riding.

Sergio Rodriguez (☎ 491-5355; sergiorodriguez turismo@infovia.com.ar; cnr Av San Martín & Iguazú), also known as GeoTur, does tours to a nearby winery, an *estancia* or area highlights.

For bike rentals head to **El Tornillo** (☎ 0291-15-431-1812; Roca 142; ☷ 10am-7pm, closed in afternoons during hot weather).

Sleeping

Book ahead in summer and during long weekends.

Camping El Paraíso (☎ 0291-15-407-4530; camping_elparaiso@yahoo.com.ar; Los Tilos 150; campsites per person AR$15, s/d/tr/q cabañas AR$45/70/85/95) This decent campground is pretty central, with shady sites and various services. Small cabañas have bunks and outside baths are available.

Hostería Maiten (☎ 491-5073; Iguazú 93; s/d AR$60/120) Sixteen very basic but clean rooms cluster around a leafy garden patio at this central, friendly and family-run place.

Aihuen Parque Hotel (☎ 491-5074; www.com-tur .com.ar/aihuen; Tornquist; s/d AR$75/150; ☷) About four blocks from the main drag, where Tornquist meets the river, is this charmingly old-style hotel on grassy grounds. It's hardly luxurious, with creaky wood floors and simple furnishings, but there's certainly some atmosphere.

Hotel Atero (☎ 491-5002; cnr Av San Martín & Güemes; s/d AR$120/180; ☷ ☷ ☷) Comfortable and homey rooms, some with balconies overlooking the street, make this a good midrange choice. It's right in the middle of town, and has a restaurant.

Hotel Provincial (☎ 491-5024; hotelprovincialsierrad elaventana@yahoo.com.ar; Drago 130) A grand old place with a major remodel planned. Call ahead of time to see where it's at.

Estancia El Retiro (☎ 491-5034; www.golfyestancias .com.ar; per person AR$380; ☷) Splash out at this 70-hectare *estancia* complete with Anglo-Norman castle and sweeping views of the sierras. Activities include trout fishing and bird-watching. Take RP 72, about 3km south of town.

Eating

Some restaurants close one day per week outside the December to March summer months.

Parrilla Rali-Hué (☎ 491-5220; San Martín 307; mains AR$18-25; ☷ lunch & dinner) It's beef only at this plastic-tablecloth joint, where locals flock to dine on the *parrillada* (mixed grill) for two – great value at AR$46.

Sol y Luna (☎ 491-5316; Av San Martín 393; mains AR$18-35; ☺ lunch & dinner) An attractive place serving everything from homemade pastas and pizzas to *parrilla* and fresh trout. Vegetarians will welcome the soy burgers and other nonmeat specials.

La Rueda (☎ 491-5359; Av San Martín 256; mains AR$20-37; ☺ breakfast, lunch & dinner Wed-Mon) A friendly restaurant serving your typical meats and pastas, along with creative dishes such as pork chops with apple purée. Great rustic furniture and sidewalk tables.

Getting There & Around

Condor Estrella (☎ 491-5091) buses to Buenos Aires (AR$105, eight hours, six times weekly) and Bahía Blanca (AR$25, two hours, once or twice daily) leave from a small office on Av San Martín, a block from the YPF gas station. There are more services to Bahía Blanca with local *combi* (long-distance bus) companies such as **Ventana Bus** (☎ 0291-15-468-5101).

There are several trains per week from Buenos Aires (AR$34 to AR$55); some arrive at Tornquist, 48km away.

Transporte Silver (☎ 491-5533; Av San Martín 156) runs a door-to-door service between Sierra de la Ventana and Tornquist (AR$13, one hour), stopping at Villa Ventana (AR$9, 25 minutes) and Parque Provincial Ernesto Tornquist (AR$11, 40 minutes). The minibuses run two or three times daily (more in summer, December to March).

AROUND SIERRA DE LA VENTANA
☎ 0291

The hills around Sierra de la Ventana constitute Argentina's oldest mountain range, and are the site of much hiking, horseback riding, picnicking and general pleasure seeking during the warmer months. Hiking trails can get very crowded during school holidays and weekends, and accommodations fill up fast in the high season.

Villa Ventana

Just 17km northwest of Sierra de la Ventana, fast-growing Villa Ventana offers a quieter base from which to explore the area's delights. Its dirt roads are shaded by tall trees and birdsong fills the air, but on long weekends and holidays the serenity factor drops dramatically.

There's a **tourist office** (☎ 491-0795; ☺ 8am-2pm & 3:30-6pm Mon-Thu, to 7pm Fri-Sun) at the entrance to town.

SLEEPING & EATING

There are campgrounds in town, but campers are better off heading to Campamento Base, just outside the park (see p156).

Hosteria La Peninsula (☎ 491-0012; cnr Golondrina & Cruz del Sur; s/d AR$50/100; ☒) Right next to the tourist office, Villa Ventana's oldest hotel is pretty basic, but its rooms are comfortable enough. The pool (when it's operating) is a welcome addition.

Cabañas La Ponderosa (☎ 491-5491; www.villa laponderosa.com.ar; Cruz del Sur; cabañas from AR$200) This central spot on the plaza offers good-sized, homey and very comfortable wood cabañas, some with loft and all with kitchenette. They sleep from two to five people.

our pick **Posada Agua Pampas** (☎ 491-0210; www .aguapampas.com.ar; cnr Calle Las Piedras & Canario; r from AR$260; ☒ ☐ ☎ ☒) The town's best stay, this place is built from local stone and recycled wood, right down to the hollow-log bathtubs. It also boasts a gray-water system to irrigate its extensive lawns. This doesn't mean luxury takes a back seat – rooms are gorgeous, each with its own deck, and there are wonderful indoor and outdoor pools plus spa services and a restaurant.

Rancho Villa (☎ 491-0235; cnr Cruz del Sur & Zorzal; mains AR$10-25; ☺ breakfast, lunch & dinner) This little teahouse, one of several in town, has outdoor tables where you can snack on locally made *alfajores* and quick meals such as steak sandwiches.

Da Roberto (☎ 0291-15-468-1459; cnr Cruz del Sur & Carpintero; mains AR$32-48; ☺ lunch Fri-Tue, dinner Thu-Tue) Run by an Italian chef influenced by the slow food movement, this restaurant cooks up great pastas and pizzas. It's intimate, with good rustic atmosphere.

GETTING THERE & AWAY

Transportes Silver minibuses (AR$7.50, 20 minutes) connect Sierra de la Ventana with Villa Ventana two to three times a day. A *remise* (taxi) will cost around AR$35. From Bahía Blanca (AR$23, two hours), take the buses that leave for Sierra de la Ventana and ask to be dropped off at Cerro de la Ventana, which is on the way.

Cerro Tres Picos

The 1239m Cerro Tres Picos, southwest of Villa Ventana but accessed from RP 76, is a worthwhile excursion. Since this is the private property of Estancia Funke, there is a charge – AR$15 to spend the day walking, cooking a barbecue lunch and enjoying the swimming spots (if there's been enough rain), or AR$25 to make the 10-hour climb to the top of Cerro Tres Picos, where you can pitch your tent in a natural cave. There is also basic accommodation with kitchen access available (AR$35 with your sleeping bag, AR$45 without). Contact **Monica Silva** (☎ 494-0058; www.funketurismo.com) to arrange visits. Some food is sold here, but it's best to bring your own.

Parque Provincial Ernesto Tornquist

This 67-sq-km **park** (☎ 491-0039; admission AR$10; ☉ 8am-5pm Dec-Mar, 9am-5pm Apr-Nov), 25km from Sierra de la Ventana, draws visitors from throughout the province. There are two entrances. The first is 5km west of Villa Ventana and home to the **Centro de Visitantes**, which has a small display on local ecology. The main hike here is **Cerro Bahía Blanca** (three hours roundtrip), offering great views. If you have a car, you can hire a guide in town (ask at the tourist office) and drive to the **Reserva Integral** (four to five hours round-trip) to see some cave paintings.

The park's highlight, however, is at its other entrance, 4km further west. The five-hour (roundtrip) hike to 1186m **Cerro de la Ventana** leads to a window-shaped rock formation near its peak. The climb offers dramatic views of surrounding hills and the distant pampas. Register with rangers before 11am at the trailhead, and take plenty of water and sun protection.

If you don't have the energy, there are shorter destinations such as **Piletones** (three hours round-trip) and **Garganta Olvidada** (one hour round-trip). To visit the gorge at **Garganta del Diablo** (six hours round-trip), you must go with a tour company (see p154).

Transportes Silver minibuses from Sierra de la Ventana (AR$11, 40 minutes) and Villa Ventana (AR$6, 15 minutes) head to the park two or three times daily (more in summer).

SLEEPING

Campamento Base (☎ 0291-491-0999; RP 76, Km 224; campsites per person AR$22) This campground at Cerro de la Ventana has shaded campsites and basic dorms (AR$30) with kitchens.

Hotel El Mirador (☎ 0291-494-1338; www.complejoelmirador.com.ar; RP 76, Km 226; s/d from AR$225/270, cabins from AR$540; ☒ ☒ ☎) A short distance from Cerro de la Ventana, pleasant A-frame cabins

(sleeping up to eight) and an ample hotel offer all the amenities, including an all-day restaurant serving meats and pastas.

SANTA ROSA
☎ 02954 / pop 110,000

About 600km from Buenos Aires – and a long way from pretty much anywhere else – Santa Rosa is unlikely to be of interest unless you find yourself traveling overland, in which case it's a convenient stopping point and transport hub. It's a pleasant enough place, however, with a small-town feel, friendly people and one ugly cathedral. You can also explore Parque Nacional Lihué Calel, 220km southwest of Santa Rosa, an isolated but pretty park that's home to a surprising assortment of vegetation and wildlife.

The city was founded in 1892 by French, Spanish and Italian immigrants who arrived with the expansion of the railroads. But one measure of Santa Rosa's continuing isolation and insignificance is that until 1951 the surrounding area remained a territory rather than a province.

Santa Rosa is also a university town, with the University of La Pampa attracting students from around the region.

Orientation

North of Av España, the city consists of a standard grid centered on the spotless but nearly shadeless Plaza San Martín. Most businesses are on the plaza and its surrounding streets, while the modern Centro Cívico, seven blocks east on Av Pedro Luro, is another center of activity.

Information

You'll find several ATMs in the city center.
ACA (☎ 422435; Av San Martín 102) Argentina's auto club; good for provincial road maps. At the plaza.
Municipal tourist office (☎ 436555; Luro 365; ☉ 8am-7pm Mon-Fri, 10am-2pm & 5-7pm Sat & Sun) In the bus terminal; don't confuse it with the nearby (and more visible) 24-hour information office at the terminal.
Post office (Hilario Lagos 258)
Provincial tourist office (☎ 424404; www.turismolapampa.gov.ar; cnr Luro & San Martín; ☉ 7am-9pm Mon-Fri, 9:30am-9pm Sat & Sun) Across from the bus terminal.

Sights & Activities

The **Museo Provincial de Historia Natural** (☎ 422693; Quintana 116; admission free; ☉ 8am-noon Mon-Fri, 7-10pm Sun) has a taxidermy collection featuring

THE PAMPAS & THE
ATLANTIC COAST

HOME, HOME ON THE...FEEDLOT?

They've always been one of Argentina's biggest tourist attractions – those juicy, grass-fed steaks full of seriously beefy taste. But these days, it's in danger of disappearing. Stuffing cattle into pens and feeding them grain is becoming a standard way of finishing them off. Today, around 40% of Argentina's cows slaughtered each year – around 15 million head – experience their last few months in a feedlot.

Carnivorism was not always mass produced in Argentina. The country's agriculturally rich and vast pampas plains were ideal grounds for raising beef. Up until 2001, around 90% of cattle ate only their natural food: grass. But several recent developments have changed this. The price of agricultural crops such as soybeans, of which Argentina is one of the world's top producers, has skyrocketed, making it more lucrative grow the legume than dedicate space to cattle. Also, a severe drought in recent years dealt another blow to the beef industry, causing a big decline in cattle birth rates.

But perhaps the biggest factor detrimental to the grass-fed cattle has been government subsidies for feedlot development, with the intention of producing beef more quickly than before. It's less profitable to raise a fully grass-fed cow – which takes much longer to reach maturity – than a grain-fed one. And the Argentine government also passed legislation keeping beef prices artificially low within its borders, while at the same time using taxes to discourage cattle ranchers from making profits by exporting beef. (At a consumption rate of over 70kg per capita – one of the highest in the world – Argentines eat the majority of their country's beef anyway.) So even more ranchers have turned pastureland into soy or corn rows to stay alive.

Despite a relatively recent drop in agricultural prices and delay in subsidy payments, the feedlot system is here to stay – and it's even more likely to grow. Some estimate that by 2015, 75% of Argentine cattle will live out their last few months in dirt-floor corrals, limiting their movements and eating an un-cow-like diet of grains. They'll be shot full of immunizations and antibiotics, which are crucial to treating ailments brought on by these unnatural conditions. Their beef will be slightly less tasteful and nutritious, yet more tender – due to the lower percentage of muscle, plus higher fat. And the modern world of commercial beef production will finally have caught up to Argentina, wiping away a part of its history, reputation...and that famous Argentine pride.

birds of the pampas. There are also some live snakes and a bit about local dinosaur fossil discoveries.

The **Museo Provincial de Artes** (☎ 427332; cnr 9 de Julio & Villegas; admission free; ☇ 8am-8pm Mon-Fri, 6-9:30pm Sat & Sun) features local and national artists, with several rooms showcasing temporary exhibitions. **Teatro Español** (☎ 455325; Hilario Lagos 54) is Santa Rosa's major performing-arts venue and dates from 1927.

Laguna Don Tomás, 1km west of the city center, is the place for locals to sail, swim, play sports or just stroll.

Sleeping & Eating

Camping Municipal Don Tomás (☎ 434568; Av Uruguay; campsites per person AR$3) Basic but OK camping facilities include picnic tables. From the bus terminal, take the local 'circular' bus (taxis AR$15). It's at the west end of Av Uruguay.

Residencial Atuel (☎ 422597; www.atuel.aehglp.org .ar; Luro 356; s/d AR$100/120; ☒) Just steps from the bus terminal, this friendly place has worn but

tidy rooms with cable TV. It's certainly good enough for one night.

Hotel San Martín (☎ 414814; www.hsanmartin .com.ar; cnr Alsina & Pelligrini; s/d AR$120/190; ☒ ☐ ☎) Opposite the defunct train station, the San Martín offers clean and quiet rooms in a reasonably central location.

Hotel Calfucurá (☎ 433303; www.hotelcalfucura .com; San Martín 695; s/d AR$175/235; ☒ ☎ ☒) Santa Rosa's best hotel, with modern atmosphere, handy location near the bus terminal and very comfortable carpeted rooms.

La Recova (☎ 424444; cnr Yrigoyen & Avellaneda; meals AR$12-32; ☇ breakfast, lunch & dinner) Good for breakfast, this modern place right on Plaza San Martín does the whole *confitería* (cafe) thing to perfection.

Arándalo (☎ 560200; Yrigoyen 731; set menu AR$58; ☇ lunch & dinner Mon-Sat) A block from the bus terminal, this upscale and beautiful restaurant has no surprises on its menu. Your set meal includes an appetizer, main, dessert and drink.

Getting There & Away

Aerolíneas (☎ 433076) flies to Buenos Aires once a week. The airport is 3km from town (taxis AR$20).

The **bus terminal** (Luro 365) is seven blocks from the plaza. Long-distance buses include Bahía Blanca (AR$62, five hours), Neuquén (AR$120, seven hours), Buenos Aires (AR$150, eight hours), Puerto Madryn (AR$120 to AR$150, 10 hours), Mendoza (AR$180, 12 hours) and Bariloche (AR$170, 12 hours).

For car rentals there's **Rent Auto** (☎ 450040; cnr Avs Luro & Harris).

RESERVA PROVINCIAL PARQUE LURO
☎ 02954

Home to a mix of introduced and native species, as well as over 150 species of birds, this 75-sq-km **reserve** (☎ 499000; www.parqueluro.gov.ar; admission AR$4; ☼ 9am-7pm) is a delightful spot to while away some easy hours. It's more peaceful on weekdays: the picnicking masses from Santa Rosa descend en masse at the weekends.

The park's curious history explains its unusual assortment of beasts. At the turn of the 20th century, a wealthy local and keen hunter, Doctor Pedro Luro, created Argentina's first hunting preserve in these woods, importing exotic game species such as Carpathian deer and European boar. He also built an enormous French-style mansion (now a museum) to accommodate his European guests. As sport hunting fell out of vogue and the European aristocracy suffered the upheavals of WWI and the Great Depression, Luro went broke. The reserve was sold, then neglected, its animals escaping through the fence or falling victim to poachers.

Since its acquisition by the province in 1965, Parque Luro has served as a refuge for native species such puma and wild fox, along with exotic migratory birds, including flamingo. You reach the **Centro de Interpretación** by following the path from the entrance. There you'll find good material on local ecology and early forest exploitation, as well maps of the various hiking trails throughout the park.

Tours of the **Castillo Luro** (per person AR$8), as the museum is known, offer insight into the luxurious eccentricities that Argentine landowners could afford to indulge in the first half of the 20th century. Note, for instance, the walnut fireplace – an obsession that Luro was able to satisfy only by purchasing an entire Parisian restaurant.

Besides the museum, there are picnic areas, a restaurant and the **Sala de Caruajes**, a collection of turn-of-the-century carriages. **Camping** (☎ 02954-15-590606; campsites per person AR$10) is possible; it's best to take food, though there's a small store. There are also nice **cabañas** (☎ 02954-15-590330; AR$180) available that sleep up to four.

Parque Luro is about 35km south of Santa Rosa, and is tricky to get to without a car. From the bus terminal, you'll need to catch the Dumascat bus to General Acha (AR$16) and ask to be dropped off at the park entrance. Find out when the bus returns to Santa Rosa. Taxis cost AR$70 each way (negotiate your return time), or you can rent a car in Santa Rosa; try **Rent Auto** (☎ 450040; cnr Avs Luro & Harris).

PARQUE NACIONAL LIHUÉ CALEL
☎ 02952

In the local indigenous language of Pehuenche, Lihué Calel means Sierra de la Vida (Range of Life), and describes the series of small, isolated mountain ranges and valleys that mark this nearly featureless pampean landscape.

This desert-like **park** (☎ 436595; www.lihuecalel .com.ar; admission free) is a haven for native cats such as puma and yagouaroundi. You can easily spot armadillo, guanaco, mara (Patagonian hare) and vizcacha, while birdlife includes the rhea-like ñandú and many birds of prey such as the carancho (crested caracara). Though you're unlikely to encounter them unless you overturn rocks, be aware of the highly poisonous pit vipers commonly known as yarará.

Though Lihué Calel receives only about 400mm of rainfall per year, water is an important factor in the landscape. Sudden storms can create brief but impressive waterfalls over granite boulders near the visitors center. Even when the sky is cloudless, the subterranean streams in the valleys nourish the *monte* (a scrub forest with a surprising variety of plant species). Within the park's 10 sq km exist 345 species of plants, nearly half the total found in the entire province.

Until General Roca's Conquest of the Desert (see p33), Araucanian Indians successfully defended the area against European invasion. Archaeological evidence, including petroglyphs, recalls their presence and that of their ancestors. Lihué Calel was the last refuge of the Araucanian leader Namuncurá, who eluded Argentine forces for several years before finally surrendering.

Located 220km southwest of Santa Rosa, the salmon-colored granite peaks do not exceed 600m, but still offer enjoyable hiking, and a variety of subtle environments that change with the seasons.

More information is available at the **visitors center**, where there's a small museum.

Sights & Activities

From the park campground, a signed nature trail follows an intermittent stream through a dense thorn forest of caldén and other typical trees. The trail leads to a petroglyph site, unfortunately vandalized. The friendly and knowledgeable rangers accompany visitors if their schedule permits.

A trail marks the gradual climb to the 589m peak, which bears the charming name **Cerro de la Sociedad Científica Argentina**. Watch for flowering cacti such as *Trichocereus candicans* between the boulders, and remember that the granite is very slippery when wet. From the summit, there are outstanding views of the entire sierra and its surrounding marshes and salt lakes, such as Laguna Urre Lauquen to the southwest.

About 8km from the visitors center is **Viejo Casco**, the ruins of the old house of former Estancia Santa María, whose land the provincial government expropriated before transferring it to the national park system. It's possible to make a circuit via the **Valle de las Pinturas**, where there are some undamaged petroglyphs. Ask rangers for directions.

Sleeping

Near the visitors center is a comfortable and free campground with shade trees, firepits (bring wood), picnic tables, toilets and showers. Stock up on food before arriving; the nearest decent supplies are at the town of Puelches, 35km south.

Your best option for accommodation is at a *hospedaje* (family home) in Puelches. The provincial tourist office, opposite the bus terminal in Santa Rosa, can arrange a stay and transport to the park; contact it for more details.

Getting There & Away

Getting to Parque Nacional Lihué Calel isn't easy. There's a daily minibus that heads to Puelches at 6pm (AR$30, three hours) and can drop you off at the park if you're camping. Check with the tourist office for possible new public transport options during your trip.

Driving is the best way to visit the park. In Santa Rosa, try **Rent Auto** (☎ 450040; cnr Avs Luro & Harris).

ATLANTIC COAST

Argentines can justly claim Latin America's highest peak (Cerro Aconcagua), its widest avenue (Buenos Aires' 9 de Julio) and perhaps its prettiest capital, but its beaches aren't tropical paradises strewn with palm trees. There's no white sand here, the winds can be fierce and the water is cloudy rather than turquoise. Despite all this Argentina's beaches are hardly unpleasant places in summer, and each January and February they reliably attract tens of thousands of well-heeled *porteños* escaping the capital's unrelenting heat. In fact, so many people flock to the shore that at times you might have a hard time finding a free spot to spread your towel.

So if you don't mind the lively summer crowds, the Atlantic Coast offers a wonderful escape. Mar del Plata is a bustling metropolis in its own right, with a rich cultural life and a great annual film festival. Pinamar attracts a hip crowd, while tiny Mar Chiquita boasts a worthwhile bird-watching reserve. And if you want to avoid the heaps of *porteños* seeking sand and surf in the high season, try visiting in the shoulder months of December and March, when the weather is still warm enough to enjoy the beaches and their activities. In the dead of winter, however, coastal towns here take on an abandoned feel and the foul weather can become downright depressing. Mar de Plata is an exception – the coast's largest city offers something to do all year round.

Accommodation prices vary widely along the coast, depending on the season. They rise sharply from mid-December through February, when reservations are crucial (and a few places require minimum-nights stays). Prices then start declining in March but rise again during Easter, after which most places close down until November. In the places that do stay open, bargains can be found during these cooler months.

Prices and opening hours noted in this chapter are for the January–February high season. In other months, opening hours (especially at tourist offices and restaurants) are much shorter.

SAN CLEMENTE DEL TUYÚ

☎ 02252 / pop 13,000

With absolutely none of the glitz or glamour of the resorts down the coast, family-oriented San Clemente is a favorite for low-key beachgoers. While eating and sleeping options are more limited than its bigger neighbors, they're good enough to keep you happy if you're on a short break from Buenos Aires.

Calle 1 is the main drag, just a block from the beach. The **tourist information office** (☎ 423-249; cnr Av Costanera & 63; ◷ 9am-9pm) is across from the beach.

Sights & Activities

A few kilometers north of San Clemente del Tuyú are several protected areas, including **Reserva Natural Municipal Punta Rasa**, managed by the environmental NGO **Fundación Vida Silvestre** (☎ in Buenos Aires 011-4331-3631). At the tip of Cabo San Antonio, where the Río de la Plata meets the Atlantic, the park is essentially a beach with a wet pampas grassland beyond it. A path leads through the park, which is visited by more than 100,000 migratory birds each year – some from as far off as Alaska. This reserve and its neighboring parks area are some of the last protected areas of pampas grassland in the province. There's no public transport to the park, which is 10km from the center of town, and no visitors center. A *remise* will cost around AR$26. **Seriema Nature Tours** (☎ in Buenos Aires 011-4312-6345; www.seriema naturetours.com) offers two-day bird-watching tours of the area.

Parque Nacional Campos del Tuyú, 26km west of San Clemente del Tuyu, was declared a national park in late 2007, and is the only national park in Buenos Aires province. At the time of research, it was not yet open to visitors, though there are plans to make it accessible. Call **National Parks** (☎ in Buenos Aires 011-4311-0303; ◷ 9am-5pm Mon-Fri) to check.

Mundo Marino (☎ 430300; www.mundomarino .com.ar; admission AR$66; ◷ 10am-8pm), 3km northwest of the center of San Clemente, is South America's largest marine park and home to a selection of marine and terrestrial mammals. It offers entertainment such as seal and dolphin shows.

The popular recreation center **Termas Marinas** (☎ 423000; www.termasmarinas.com.ar; admission AR$43; ◷ 10am-7pm) is just north of town and features mineral-rich thermal baths set in a leafy park. There's also a cafe and a beauty spa.

Sleeping

Hotel 5 Avenue (☎ 421035; Calle 5, No 1561; s/d AR$55/100) Just a block and a half from the beach, and a safe distance from the noise of downtown's bars and nightspots, this friendly place offers worn budget rooms with tiny bathrooms.

Hotel Top (☎ 522005; www.hoteltopsanclemente.com .ar; Av Costanera 1657; s/d AR$65/130) Almost too good of a deal, with 24 small but tidy rooms with cable TV, and right on the beach. Call to make sure prices haven't gone up.

Campamento ACA (☎ 421124; www.acasanclemente .com.ar; Av 2; campsites for 2 with tent AR$67) A big camping spot near the beach, just a few blocks from the town's center, there's a store, restaurant, kid's play area and plenty of sites – each with barbeque pit and table. In January only ACA members can stay.

Brisas Marinas (☎ 522219; www.brisas-marinas.com .ar; Calle 13, No 50; r AR$180-200; 🖥 🛜) A reasonably attractive choice just steps from the beach, with simple, nice and clean rooms. Some rooms have balconies in front, and there's afternoon tea service.

Gran Hotel Fontainebleau (☎ 421187; www .fontainebleau.com.ar; Calle 3, No 2290; s/d AR$310/350; ❄ 🖥 🛜 🛒) The pick of the beachfront high-rises, the Fontainebleau has fine (though not luxurious) rooms, many with balconies overlooking the sea.

Eating

Balneario Eden (☎ 526342; cnr Av 11 & the beach; mains AR$14-30; ◷ breakfast, lunch & dinner) With a patio overlooking the sand, this place offers burgers and snacks all day, with plenty of well-priced seafood and *parrilla* options.

Confiteria La Marca (☎ 521125; Calle 1, No 2385; mains AR$20-30; ◷ breakfast, lunch & dinner) Modern, attractive *confitería* with good coffee, tempting homemade pastries and the usual selection of main dishes (pizzas, meats). Sports on the TV.

La Parrillita (☎ 526300; Calle 1, No 2178; mains AR$28-44; ◷ lunch & dinner) One of San Clemente's best *parrillas*, right on the main drag, it also serves homemade pastas. It's only open Friday to Sunday outside summer months (December to March).

El Vaskito (☎ 421268; cnr Av Costanera & Calle 19; mains AR$30-50; ◷ lunch & dinner) A recommended place for grilled fish and other fresh seafood, it also serves pastas and meats. Try one of the seafood stews.

Getting There & Away

The **bus terminal** (cr Avs Talas and Naval) is about 25 blocks from the town center. There are local buses and taxis (AR$15) to the center. Frequent buses connect San Clemente to Buenos Aires (AR$80, 4½ hours), Pinamar (AR$16, 2½ hours) and also Mar del Plata (AR$39, 4½ hours).

PINAMAR

☎ 02254 / pop 40,000

Located about 120km northeast of Mar del Plata, Pinamar is a very popular beach destination for middle-class *porteños*, boasting pleasantly warm waters. Its large main drags are Av Libertador, which runs parallel to the beach, and Av Bunge, which runs perpendicular. It's a busy place in summer, so if you're seeking a bit of tranquility, head to its southern and more residential neighborhoods of Ostende and Valeria, which are less conveniently located but offer more affordable sleeping options. Even further south is woodsy Cariló, Argentina's most exclusive resort and home to expensive mansions, chic boutiques and fashionable restaurants.

Pinamar was founded and designed in 1944 by architect Jorge Bunge, who figured out how to stabilize the shifting dunes by planting pines, acacias and pampas grass. It was the refuge for the country's upper echelons, but is now somewhat less exclusive, with the best-heeled beachgoers heading for Uruguay's Punta del Este (see p576), leaving Pinamar to a more laid-back crowd.

Pinamar's film festival, **Pantalla Pinamar** (www.pantallapinamar.com), takes place in March and there are concerts and parties on the beach around New Year.

Information

ACA (☎ 482744; Del Cazón 1365) Good for provincial road maps.
Municipal hospital (☎ 491770; Shaw 250)
Municipal tourist office (☎ 491680; cnr Av Bunge & Shaw; ◷ 8am-9pm)
Post office (Jasón 524)

Activities

The main activity in Pinamar is simply relaxing and socializing on the *balneario*-lined beach, which stretches all the way from north of the town down to Cariló. But the area also offers a wealth of outdoor activities, from windsurfing and waterskiing to horseback riding and fishing. You can also ride bicycles in the wooded areas near the golf course, or through the leafy streets of nearby Cariló.

For bike rentals, try **Leo** (☎ 488855; Av Bunge 1111; per hr/day AR$10/30; ◷ 9am-8pm). If you want to learn how to kite surf, go to Sport Beach, the last *balneario* located about 5km north of Av Bunge. To try sand boarding, contact **Aventura Pinamar** (☎ 493531; www.aventurapinamar.com.ar); it also has jeep tours and off-road vehicles. There are many more options for activities – ask at the tourist office.

Sleeping

Pinamar lacks real budget accommodations – it's worth heading to Ostende and Valeria, a few kilometers away, where you'll find low-key lodgings close to the beach, but away from the action and bustle of Av Bunge. Reservations are a must in January, when some places have a week minimum stay. Prices following are for summer, but off-season rates are up to 40% lower.

Albergue Bruno Valente (☎ 482908; cnr Mitre & Nuestras Malvinas, Ostende; dm AR$50) In Ostende, about 10 blocks south of Pinamar's center, is this seriously ugly hostel in a decaying old building – but it's just steps from the beach. Cheap and institutional; don't expect great service.

Camping Saint Tropez (☎ 482498; www.sainttropezpinamar.com.ar; cnr Quintana & Nuestras Malvinas, Ostende; campsite for 2 persons with tent AR$52; ◷ Oct-Apr) Due to its choice beachfront location, this small site fills up quickly in summer. Apartments also available (from AR$200).

Hospedaje Acacia (☎ 485175; Del Cangrejo 1358; d AR$180) Good basic cheapie a few blocks from Pinamar's tourist office and about a 15-minute walk to the beach. There's a little garden patio in back.

Hosteria Candela (☎ 486788; Nicolas Jorge 434, Valeria; r AR$200) Just two blocks from the beach at Valeria, with good-sized rooms and a nice grassy garden in back, this place is a good option.

Hotel Trinidad (☎ 48983; hoteltrinidad@telpin.com.ar; Del Cangrejo 1370; r AR$230; ◌) Right near Hospedaje Acacia and a good budget option in Pinamar, it offers decent, darkish rooms with small bathrooms and cable TV. Prices drop to AR$180 in February.

Hotel Mojomar (☎ 407300; www.hotelmojomar.com.ar; Burriquetas 247; d from AR$340) A minimalist new hotel nicely located three blocks off Av Bunge, but a block from the beach. Beautiful lobby and small, comfortable rooms; go for a suite if you need more space.

Hotel Las Calas (☎ 405999; www.lascalashotel.com.ar; Av Bunge 560; r AR$460; ✿ 🖳) This boutique-style hotel has lovely tasteful rooms with king-size beds – the bigger ones with a loft. There's also a small but great wood sundeck, games room and gym. It's right on the main drag, in the middle of the bustle.

Next door to Hosteria Candela are **Posada Amarela** (☎ 487428; www.posadaamarela.com.ar) and **Hosteria la Sirena** (☎ 486714), both offering similar deals.

Eating

The beach is lined with restaurants serving fresh, inexpensive meals like fried calamari and burgers.

Acqua & Farina (☎ 570278; cnr Cerezo & Boyero, Cariló; mains AR$20-35; ✆ lunch & dinner) Head to Cariló for the best thin-crust pizza around, as well as fresh salads and homemade pastas.

Cantina Tulumei (☎ 488696; Bunge 64; mains AR$20-38; ✆ lunch & dinner) A good place for reasonably priced, quality seafood. Fish is prepared in at least nine different sauces, or go for the shrimp soup and octopus salad. Homemade pastas also available.

Halles Bistro (☎ 407300; Burriquetas 247; mains AR$20-50; ✆ lunch & dinner) Located right under the Hotel Mojomar is this unpretentious restaurant run by chef Fernando Lo Coco, who uses fresh, local ingredients to make whip up creative dishes like squash raviolis with almond cream sauce. Great pastries available, too.

Tante (☎ 494949; De las Artes 35; mains AR$26-46; ✆ breakfast, lunch & dinner) This classy restaurant, bar and tea room was the home of a well-known soprano who wowed the crowds at Teatro Colón in the '50s. Now specializes in gourmet meat dishes and European specialties like fondue.

Getting There & Away

Pinamar's bus terminal is about eight blocks north of the town center, just off Av Bunge. Destinations include Buenos Aires (AR$80, five hours), Mar del Plata (AR$24, 2½ hours) and San Clemente del Tuyú (AR$16, 2½ hours). There are frequent buses to nearby Villa Gesell (AR$5, 30 minutes).

Trains run from Buenos Aires Constitución train station to Pinamar's Estación Divisadero, about 2km north of town.

VILLA GESELL

☎ 02255 / pop 30,000

Smaller and less flashy than its neighbors Pinamar and Mar del Plata, laid-back Villa Gesell is still a hit with the younger crowd. Uniquely for the coastal towns, it offers a wood-planked beach boardwalk, making walks along the sands much easier. It's also known for summer choral performances and rock and folk concerts, and there are plenty of outdoor activities to enjoy. The town is compact, with most services located on its main drag, Av 3, three blocks from the beach.

In the 1930s, merchant, inventor and nature lover Carlos Gesell designed this resort of zig-zag streets, planting acacias, poplars, oaks and pines to stabilize the shifting dunes. Though he envisioned a town merging with the forest he had created, it wasn't long before high-rise vacation shares began their malignant growth and the trees started to disappear.

Information

ACA (☎ 462273; Av 3, btwn Paseos 112 & 113) Argentina's auto club; for provincial road maps.

Hospital Municipal Arturo Illía (☎ 462618; cnr Paseo 123 & Av 8)

Post office (cnr Av 3 & Paseo 108)

Tourist office (☎ 478042; Av 3, No 820; ✆ 8am-midnight) Conveniently located in the center. Less convenient is its main branch (Av Buenos Aires at Camino de los Pioneros), near the entrance to town.

Sights & Activities

The **Muelle de Pesca** (Playa & Paseo 129), Gesell's 15m fishing pier, offers year-round fishing for mackerel, rays, shark and other marine species.

You can rent surf gear from **Windy** (☎ 474626; www.windyplayabar.com.ar; Paseo 104), down on the beachfront. For bicycle rentals try **Casa Macca** (☎ 468013; cnr Av 3 & Paseo 126). Horseback riding is another popular activity.

Aventura Faro Querandí (☎ 468989; cnr Av 3 & Paseo 132) runs four-hour tours in 4WD jeeps to a local lighthouse.

For a totally different atmosphere visit **Mar de las Pampas**, an exclusive woodsy neighborhood that's a 15-minute bus ride south from Villa Gesell's bus terminal. It has sandy streets, expensive lodging (rented only by the week in summer) and upscale services – all dropped into a pine forest. The beach here is less crowded, too. Beyond Mar de las Pampas is **Mar Azul**, another (less exclusive) beach town.

Sleeping

Campgrounds here charge around AR$30 to AR$35 per person per night. Most close at the end of March, but three at the southern end of town on Av 3 (at the beach) are open all year: **Camping Casablanca** (☎ 470771; www.autocampingcasablanca.com), **Camping Mar Dorado** (☎ 470963; www.mardorado.com.ar) and **Camping Monte Bubi** (☎ 470732; www.montebubi.com.ar). All have lots of services and cabaña-style accommodations. The Mar Azul bus from the terminal goes right by.

La Deseada Hostel (☎ 473276; www.ladeseadahostel.com.ar; cnr Av 6 & Paseo 119; dm AR$75; ▯) One of the best-looking hostels on the coast; tucked away six blocks from the beach and a 15-minute walk from the center. Dorms have eight beds; prices outside January drop to AR$50 to AR$60.

Hospedaje Villa Gesell (☎ 466368; www.hospedajevillagesell.8k.com; Av 3, No 812; d/tr AR$100/150) You can't get more cheap or central than this simple spot with 10 budget rooms. The scruffy little patio area saves it from total mediocrity.

Los Médanos (☎ 463205; Av 5, No 549; d AR$130) Downstairs rooms here are more modern, and the best ones are near the back garden, so try to score one of these. There's also a 13-bed dorm room (the converted garage) for women only (AR$45). Limited kitchen use.

Hotel Tamanacos (☎ 468753; tamanacos@gesell.com.ar; cnr Paseo 103 & Av 1; s/d AR$160/270; ⬙) Not far from the beach, this cute hotel has some great common areas, particularly the front patio. The small rooms have tiny baths, but with beach umbrellas provided you won't be in them most of the time.

Residencial Viya (☎ 462757; www.gesell.com.ar/viya; Av 5, No 582, btwn Paseos 105 & 106; d AR$170) Rooms are simple, with open-shower bathrooms, but they're comfortable enough at this family-run *residencial* on a quiet street. The best rooms open to the central leafy garden.

Costa Bonita (☎ 462457; www.gesellcostabonita.com.ar; Av 4, No 648; r AR$210; ▯ ⬙) Fourteen tastefully-decorated rooms with high ceilings are available at this small guesthouse in a residential neighborhood near the center. Upstairs rooms have more light. There's also a tiny garden patio area to hang out in.

Hotel Merimar (☎ 462243; www.gesell.com.ar/hotelmerimar; cnr Paseo 107 & Playa; r AR$320; ⬙) Rooms here have old carpets and outdated furniture, but if you score a beachfront room with balcony (reserve ahead!), the views are worth it. If you can't get a view, at least the breakfast salon has them, and you're still near the beach.

Belle Maison (☎ 462335; www.bellemaison.com.ar; Calle 4, btwn Paseos 106 & 107; r from AR$350; ▯ ⬙) Just five lovely rooms are available at this boutique hotel, actually a large house in a residential neighborhood near the center. Common spaces include a small garden, and there's even a bar counter inside.

Eating

La Pachamama (☎ 468727; Av 2, No 411; empanadas AR$3, pizzas AR$17-25; ⬙ lunch & dinner) This casual eatery bakes up delicious Salta-style empanadas and fresh pizzas – perfect for a quick budget meal. Great outdoor booths in front.

Sutton 212 (☎ 460674; cnr Paseo 105 & Ave 2; mains AR$18-35; ⬙ 9:30am-late) This lively restaurant serves well-made classics like burgers and wok-fried noodles. There's live bossa nova and jazz at dinner, then a DJ later in the evening, when the place becomes a happening bar.

La Delfina (☎ 465863; cnr Paseo 104 & Av 2; mains AR$20-31; ⬙ lunch & dinner) A huge menu means there's something for everyone at this popular *parrilla*. If you need some extra protein, try the 'El Supremo' *bife de chorizo* – a steak that comes with two eggs and bacon. There's also a low-calorie section and everything in-between.

ourpick Las Margaritas (☎ 456377; Av 2, No 484, btwn Paseos 104 & 105; mains AR$30-49; ⬙ dinner) Charmingly cozy and quiet, this place serves excellent homemade pasta, including a shrimp and squid ink ravioli. The tiramisú is to die for. Reservations essential in summer.

Entertainment

Villa Gesell comes alive with music in the summer months, when venues book everything from rock to choral music.

Cine Teatro Atlas (☎ 462969; Paseo 108, btwn Avs 3 & 4) Such rock-and-roll greats as Charly García and Los Pericos have played this small theater, which doubles as a cinema (www.cinesdelacosta.com) during off-season months.

Anfiteatro del Pinar (☎ 467123; cnr Av 10 & Paseo 102) There are musical performances in January, February and Semana Santa. Gesell's Encuentros Corales, an annual gathering of the country's best choirs, takes place annually in this lovely amphitheater.

Pueblo Límite (☎ 452845; www.pueblolimite.com; Av Buenos Aires 2600; admission AR$12-30) A sort of small town megadisco, this complex has three dance clubs, a restaurant, two bars and cheap food booths in the front.

THE PAMPAS & THE ATLANTIC COAST

Shopping

Feria Artesanal, Regional y Artística (FARA; Av, 3 btwn Paseos 112 & 113; ☻ nightly mid-Dec–mid-Mar) This is an excellent arts and crafts fair, with lots of handmade jewelry and decorative objects in carved wood and glass, as well as paintings and the usual range of souvenirs.

Getting There & Away

The **bus terminal** (cnr Av 3 & Paseo 140) is 30 blocks south of the town center; a local bus ride to the center takes 20 minutes.

Destinations include Buenos Aires (AR$88, six hours), Mar del Plata (AR$19, two hours) and Pinamar (AR$5, 30 minutes). You can buy bus tickets in the town center at **Central de Pasajes** (cnr Av 3 & Paseo 107), saving you a trip to the terminal.

MAR CHIQUITA

☎ 0223 / pop 400

Despite being so very *chiquita* (petite), this spot merits special mention as one of the best destinations for nature lovers within an easy distance of Buenos Aires. It's a humble little gem of a place, with no high-rises, no *balnearios* and no stress. People come to fish and windsurf, but what really makes Mar Chiquita special is its lagoon – it's a rare ecosystem that's home to a wealth of bird and fish species.

This windy town is 34km from Mar del Plata, about 2km towards the beach from the highway. Most of the town's houses are vacation homes owned by residents from Mar del Plata, meaning that on summer weekends the population here can go up dramatically. The **visitors center** (☎ 469-1158; cnr Belgrano & Rivera del Sol; ☻ erratic) overlooks the lake; if it's not open, call nearby Santa Clara's **tourist office** (☎ 460-2433). Bring money – there are no banks or ATMs here.

Sights & Activities

Most visitors come here to explore the **Reserva Mar Chiquita**, a Unesco World Biosphere Reserve. It takes in several types of landscapes and ecosystems, including pampean grasslands and the coastal dunes to the north. The star attraction, however, is the **Albúfera Mar Chiquita**, a 35km-long lagoon that is the only one of its kind in Argentina – and one of only a few in the world.

Sheltered by a chain of sand dunes and fed by creeks from the Sierras de Tandil, the lagoon alternately drains into the ocean or absorbs seawater, depending on the tides. This has created a unique ecosystem boasting a huge biodiversity, and is a paradise for birdwatchers. Over 220 species, 86 of which are migratory, have been recorded. Chilean flamingos are common, along with various species of swans, plovers and sandpipers. There are also over 55 fish species in the lagoon, making it a popular fishing spot.

Land tours of the area (AR$35 per person) depart from the visitors center at 9am daily, and run depending on conditions (reserve ahead). You can also go on a boat tour with **Marcelo Gustavo Pons** (☎ 687-9084), depending on the tides and weather.

The lagoon is also a great spot for windsurfing and kite surfing; for rentals and lessons, contact Hostería Bariloche (see below). And if you want to go horseback riding, contact **Pedro** (☎ 0223-15-455-4985) at Estancia Nahuel Rucá.

Just 6km south of Mar Chiquita, **Mar de Cobo** offers another tranquil coastal experience. Backed by dunes and featuring smooth rocks that make excellent beach furniture, the place has yet to be invaded by summer crowds. There are a few comfortable *hosterías;* (lodging houses) try **Posada del Solar** (☎ 469-1252; www .posadadelsolar.com; Av M Cobo & la costa; d AR$150; ⚐).

Sleeping & Eating

Campgrounds include **Camping Santa Rosa** (☎ 469-1300; cnr River del Sol & Lugones; campsites per person AR$20).

Hostería Bariloche (☎ 469-1254; mchpao@hotmail .com; cnr Beltran & Echeverría; s/d from AR$80/120; ⚐) This friendly, family-run place offers 10 homey rooms and apartments, along with a sea-view lounge and spacious *parrilla* area. Meals can be provided in the low season, and Paula is a great source of information on the area.

Hotel Mar Chiquita (☎ 469-1046; www.hotel -marchiquita.com.ar; Echeverria; r AR$320; ⚐) A largeish hotel with basic rooms that don't offer great value, though the balconies overlooking the beach have nice views. Restaurant and pool on premises.

Mar Chiquita has only a few restaurants, all facing the lagoon along Rivera del Sol. All are open only on weekends outside summer.

Lo de Pedro (Rivera del Sol 1400; mains AR$20-45; ☻ lunch & dinner) Good restaurant for homemade pastas, fish and seafood.

Getting There & Away

Rápido del Sud runs frequently up and down the coast, and can let you off at the highway 2km outside Mar Chiquita (but does not enter town). Local bus 221 (AR$5, 1½ hours) enters the town, but runs only every two hours in summer to/from Mar del Plata. Double-check with the driver if you're heading out, as some 221 buses stop short of Mar del Plata.

MAR DEL PLATA
☎ 0223 / pop 700,000

It's worth going to Mar del Plata ('Mardel') on a summer weekend if only so you'll never again be tempted to say, 'Gee, this beach is crowded.' There's a couple of places where you could get a few swimming strokes in without taking somebody's eye out, but mostly it's shoulder-to-shoulder sun-frazzled *porteños*. During the week, and especially outside of summer, the crowds disperse, hotel prices drop and the place takes on a much more relaxed feel.

First impressions of the extremes to which this resort town has taken itself can be abhorrent. But, after spending a few days on its comically packed beaches, watching street performers on the beachside Plaza Colón or exploring the wonders of the port, it's hard not to give in to the adoration the country feels for the place. If summer crowds aren't your bottle of lotion, visit in spring or autumn, when prices are lower and the area's natural attractions are easier to enjoy.

History

Europeans were slow to occupy this stretch of the coast, so Mardel was a late bloomer. Not until 1747 did Jesuit missionaries try to evangelize the southern pampas indigenous people; the only reminder of their efforts is the body of water known as Laguna de los Padres.

More than a century later, Portuguese investors established El Puerto de Laguna de los Padres. Beset by economic problems in the 1860s, they sold out to Patricio Peralta Ramos, who founded Mar del Plata proper in 1874. Peralta Ramos helped develop the area as a commercial and industrial center, and later as a beach resort. By the turn of the century, many upper-class *porteño* families owned summer houses, some of which still grace Barrio Los Troncos.

Since the 1960s the 'Pearl of the Atlantic' has lost some of its exclusivity as the Argentine elite sought refuge in resorts such as nearby

Pinamar or Punta del Este (Uruguay). Still, Mar del Plata remains the most thriving Argentine beach town.

Orientation

Mar del Plata, 400km south of Buenos Aires via RN 2, sprawls along 8km of beaches, though most points of interest are in the downtown area. On street signs, the coastal road is called Av Peralta Ramos, but most people refer to it as Blvd Marítimo; it turns into Av Martínez de Hoz further south.

Peatonal San Martín is the downtown pedestrian mall, and Rivadavia is pedestrianized through the summer. To the town center's south lies the leafy upscale neighborhood of Los Troncos, where along Av LN Alem you'll find another small commercial center.

Information

CULTURAL CENTERS

Alianza Francesa (☎ 494-0120; La Rioja 2065; ☒ 1:30-8:30pm Mon, Wed & Fri, 9:30am-8:30pm Tue & Thu, 9:30am-12:30pm Sat) Culture for Francophiles.
Asociación Argentina de Cultura Inglesa (☎ 495-6513; San Luis 2498) Has a library with newspapers, magazines and books in English, as well as occasional films and lectures.
Centro Cultural Osvaldo Soriano (☎ 499-7877; cnr Catamarca & 25 de Mayo) Offers a variety of affordable activities ranging from film screenings and theater to popular music, jazz, *folklore* and tango.

MEDICAL SERVICES

Hospital (☎ 477-0960; JB Justo 6700, btwn Tres Arroyos & Calle 164)

MONEY

There are several money exchanges along San Martín and Rivadavia.
Jonestur (San Martín 2574)
La Moneta (Rivadavia 2623)

POST

Post office (Av Luro 2460 & Santiago del Estero)

TOURIST INFORMATION

ACA (☎ 491-2096; Av Colón 2450) Auto club; good for provincial road maps.
Municipal tourist office (☎ 495-1777; www .turismomardelplata.gov.ar; Blvd Marítimo, edificio Casino local 51; ☒ 8am-10pm) Exceptionally helpful. A smaller office is at San Luis 1949.
Provincial tourist office (☎ 495-5340; www .turismo.gba.gov.ar; Blvd Marítimo, edificio Casino local 48; ☒ 8am-9pm) Basic information on Buenos Aires province.

THE PAMPAS & THE ATLANTIC COAST

MAR DEL PLATA

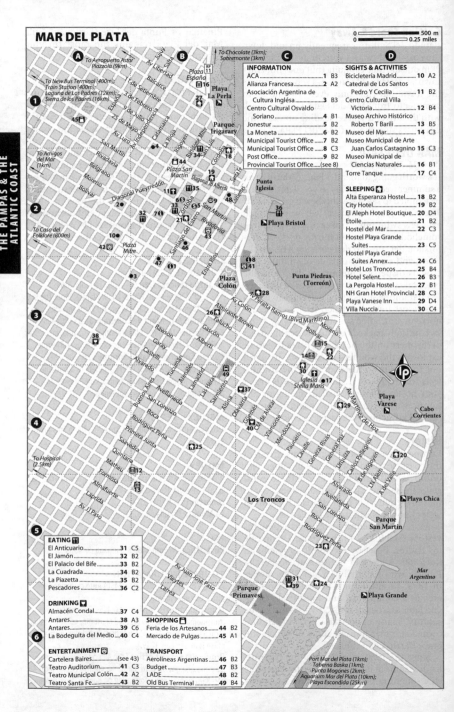

0 ──────── 500 m
0 ──────── 0.25 miles

INFORMATION

ACA	**1** B3
Alianza Francesa	**2** A2
Asociación Argentina de Cultura Inglésa	**3** B3
Centro Cultural Osvaldo Soriano	**4** B1
Jonestur	**5** B2
La Moneta	**6** B2
Municipal Tourist Office	**7** B2
Municipal Tourist Office	**8** C3
Post Office	**9** B2
Provincial Tourist Office	(see 8)

SIGHTS & ACTIVITIES

Bicicletería Madrid	**10** A2
Catedral de Los Santos Pedro Y Cecilia	**11** B2
Centro Cultural Villa Victoria	**12** B4
Museo Archivo Histórico Roberto T Barili	**13** B5
Museo del Mar	**14** C3
Museo Municipal de Arte Juan Carlos Castagnino	**15** C3
Museo Municipal de Ciencias Naturales	**16** B1
Torre Tanque	**17** C4

SLEEPING

Alta Esperanza Hostel	**18** B2
City Hotel	**19** B2
El Aleph Hotel Boutique	**20** B2
Etoile	**21** B2
Hostel del Mar	**22** C3
Hostel Playa Grande Suites	**23** C5
Hostel Playa Grande Suites Annex	**24** C6
Hotel Los Troncos	**25** B4
Hotel Selent	**26** B3
La Pergola Hostel	**27** B1
NH Gran Hotel Provincial	**28** C3
Playa Vanese Inn	**29** D4
Villa Nuccia	**30** C4

EATING

El Anticuario	**31** C5
El Jamón	**32** B2
El Palacio del Bife	**33** B2
La Cuadrada	**34** B2
La Piazetta	**35** B2
Pescadores	**36** C2

DRINKING

Almacén Condal	**37** C4
Antares	**38** A3
Antares	**39** C6
La Bodeguita del Medio	**40** C4

ENTERTAINMENT

Cartelera Baires	(see 43)
Teatro Auditorium	**41** C3
Teatro Municipal Colón	**42** A2
Teatro Santa Fe	**43** B2

SHOPPING

Feria de los Artesanos	**44** B2
Mercado de Pulgas	**45** A1

TRANSPORT

Aerolíneas Argentinas	**46** B2
Budget	**47** B3
LADE	**48** B2
Old Bus Terminal	**49** B4

Sights
BEACHES
Mar del Plata's beaches are safe and swimmable, if impossibly crowded in the summer. Downtown fronts onto the most central beach, **Playa Bristol**, with its wharf and fishermen's club bearing the huge neon Quilmes sign; the boardwalk here, next to the casino area, is always packed with activity. The next beach to the north is **Playa La Perla**, favored by a younger crowd and filled with *balnearios*. To the south of Playa Torreón are **Playa Varese** and **Cabo Corrientes**, a pair of small waveless beaches that are protected by small rocky headlands.

South of these beaches, at the more fashionable end of town, lies **Playa Grande**, also crowded with *balnearios*. Just past the port you'll find the huge **Punta Mogotes** complex – slightly more chilled and favored by families, who fill the *balnearios* to overflowing in January.

Beyond the lighthouse and the limits of Mar del Plata proper, along the road called **Costanera Sur** is a less urbanized area. Though the beaches are still filled with yet more *balnearios* in the summer, they're a quieter option if you're here outside of the peak season.

For the adventurous, there's **Playa Escondida** (www.playaescondida.com.ar), some 25km south of Mardel and possibly Argentina's only legal nude beach. Bus 221 gets you there.

CATEDRAL DE LOS SANTOS PEDRO Y CECILIA
Facing the leafy Plaza San Martín at San Luis, this neo-Gothic building features gorgeous stained glass, an impressive central chandelier from France, English tiled floors and a ceiling of tiles from other European countries.

CENTRO CULTURAL VILLA VICTORIA
Victoria Ocampo (see the boxed text, p168), founder of the literary journal *Sur*, hosted literary salons with prominent intellectuals from around the world at this, her summer chalet. It's now a **cultural center** (☎ 492-0569; Matheu 1851; admission AR$3-10; ☼ 5-9:30pm) that features changing art and cultural exhibitions.

TORRE TANQUE
This interesting, medieval water storage **tower** (☎ 451-4681; cnr Falucho & Mendoza; admission free; ☼ 8am-2:45pm Mon-Fri), atop Stella Maris hill, was finished in 1943 and offers great views over Mar del Plata. There's a tiny museum inside; after checking it out, climb the spiral stairs or take the elevator.

AQUARIUM MAR DEL PLATA
Located 10km south of the center, near the lighthouse, is Mar del Plata's **aquarium** (☎ 467-0100; www.aquariummardelplata.com; Av Martínez de Hoz 5600; adult/child 3-10yr AR$65/45; ☼ 10am-8pm). Animals on display include penguins, flamingoes, crocodiles and lots of fish. There are sealion, dolphin and water-skiing shows, along with a cinema. You can also swim with sharks (among other watery creatures) and sit on the beach. Get here on bus 221 or 511.

MUSEUMS
Built in 1909 as the summer residence of a prominent Argentine family, the Villa Ortiz Basualdo is now the **Museo Municipal de Arte Juan Carlos Castagnino** (☎ 486-1636; Av Colón 1189; admission AR$4, Wed free; ☼ 5-10pm). Resembling a Loire Valley castle, its Belgian interior exhibits paintings, photographs and sculptures by Argentine artists.

In the Villa Emilio Mitre (1930), another former summer residence of the Argentine oligarchy, the **Museo Archivo Histórico Municipal Roberto T Barili** (☎ 495-1200; Lamadrid 3870; admission AR$4; ☼ 8am-5pm Mon-Fri, 2-6pm Sat & Sun) houses a superb collection of late-19th-century photographs, along with other exhibits recalling Mar del Plata's colorful past.

Housing the most extensive seashell collection you're ever likely to see, the **Museo del Mar** (☎ 451-3553; Av Colón 1114; admission AR$18; ☼ 10am-10pm, shorter hrs Apr-Dec) exhibits more than 30,000 shells, representing 6000 species from around the world. The museum also contains a small tide pool, an aquarium and a cafe.

Kids and science fans might enjoy the **Museo Municipal de Ciencias Naturales** (☎ 473-8791; Av Libertad 3099; admission AR$4, Wed free; ☼ 9am-4:30pm Mon & Wed-Fri, 3-6:30pm Sat & Sun), a small science museum with a small aquarium, scary spiders, lots of butterflies and dinosaur bones.

PORT MAR DEL PLATA
Mar del Plata is one of the country's most important fishing ports and seafood-processing centers. At **Baquina de Pescadores** – the picturesque wharf about 5km south of the Mardel's center – fisherfolk and stevedores follow their routine on and around orange wooden boats.

LITERARY LADY OF LA PLATA

She was 'the most beautiful cow in the pampas' according to French novelist Pierre Drieu, and Jorge Luis Borges called her 'the most Argentine of women'. In the 1920s and 1930s, Victoria Ocampo gathered writers and intellectuals from around the globe to her home in Mar del Plata each summer, creating a formidable literary and artistic salon.

Victoria (1890–1979) was born to one of those upper-class Argentine families whose habit it was to escape the oppressive heat of Buenos Aires during summer and head for the coast. In keeping with the Europhilia of the time, the Ocampos' *veraneo*, or summer home, Villa Victoria (see p167), was imported piece by piece from Scandinavia. Over the years, the house hosted such luminaries as Borges, Gabriela Mistral, Igor Stravinsky, Le Corbusier and Rabindranath Tagore.

She never went to university (her parents' social class regarded women's education as superfluous), but Victoria's voracious appetite for knowledge and love of literature led her to become Argentina's leading lady of letters. She founded the literary magazine *Sur*, which introduced writers like Virginia Woolf and TS Eliot to Argentine readers. She was an indefatigable traveler and a pioneering feminist among incurable *machistas*.

Having no regard for convention, Ocampo was loathed as much as she was loved, scandalizing society by driving her own automobile when such a thing was unheard of among society women. A ferocious opponent of Peronism, chiefly because of Perón's interference with intellectual freedom, Victoria was arrested at Villa Victoria at the age of 63. She entertained her fellow inmates by reading aloud and acting out scenes from novels and cinema.

If Victoria is remembered as a lively essayist and great patroness of writers, her younger sister, Silvina, was the literary talent, writing both short stories and poetry. She won several literary prizes for her works, and in 1940 married Adolfo Bioy Casares, a famous Argentine writer and friend of Jorge Luis Borges.

As for the tradition of the *veraneo*, it's still going strong. Many wealthy families still have mansions in leafy Los Troncos, where Villa Victoria stands, but Argentines of all social classes save vacation time and cash to squeeze themselves onto a patch of sand, whether in humble San Clemente del Tuyú or upper-crust Cariló, and spend the summer running into everyone they know.

They're monitored by sea lions who have established a large colony – all male – down the *escollera sur* (southern jetty), about a 10-minute walk from the fishing boats in an ugly industrialized section. There are often sea lions lazing around the boat staging area, if you don't want to walk so far.

In the early morning, unfazed by the chilly sea breeze, the fishermen load their nets and crates before spending the day at sea, escorted by the sea lions. At about 5pm, the pier gets noisy and hectic as the returning fishermen sort and box the fish, bargain for the best price and tidy up their boats and tools. The sea lions return to seek or fight over a resting spot at their colony. Braving their horrendous stench affords excellent opportunities for photography: separated by a chain-link fence, you can approach very closely.

Just past the colony is the port's fantastic graveyard of **ruined ships**, half-sunken and rusting in the sun. Here the *escollera sur* begins its long stretch over 2km out to sea, with panoramic views of the city from its tip. Climb the yellow ladders and walk on top of the sea wall for the best views. You can walk back to the **Centro Comercial del Puerto** and close the day in one of its great restaurants.

Local buses 221, 511, 522, 551, 562 and 593 go to the wharf from downtown. A taxi costs AR$20.

LAGUNA DE LOS PADRES

A popular weekend destination for *marplatenses*, this lake offers a bucolic setting and a range of activities, including bird-watching, fishing, water sports, biking, hiking and rock climbing. The area was first settled in 1746 as a Jesuit Mission aimed at rounding up the nomadic tribes of the area – there's a replica of the original chapel by the lake's shore. You can camp by the lake, and there are good places to eat in the pleasant nearby town of Sierra de los Padres.

The lake is just 12km out of Mardel along RN 226; the town is 4km further. Bus 717 (from Av Luro in Mardel) goes to **Sierra de los Padres**, but it doesn't take the side road to the lake – you'll have to get off at the highway and walk a kilometer just to reach the shore, or double back from Sierra de los Padres in a *remise*.

Activities

Mar del Plata and its surrounds offer plenty of opportunity to enjoy outdoor activities and adventure sports.

Biking is a good, green way to get around town. The streets of Los Troncos are relatively calm and pleasant for cycling. Bicycles can be rented from **Bicicletería Madrid** (☎ 494-1932; Yrigoyen 2249, Plaza Mitre; per hr/day AR$10/40; ☺ 9:30am-1pm & 3:30-7:30pm Mon-Fri, 9:30am-8pm Sat, 10am-8pm Sun).

The **Escuela Argentina de Surfistas Profesionales** (☎ 0223-15-400-2072) offers surfing classes and rents boards at Playa Grande during the summer. Find it at the beach, near the Yacht Club.

You can go horseback riding in the picturesque hills of Sierra de los Padres; contact **Estancia Ituzaingó** (☎ 460-0797, 0223-15-527-6317; www.estanciaituzaingo.com.ar; Ruta 226, Km 10).

As the sea lions attest, Mar del Plata is one of the best spots for fishing in Argentina. The rocky outcrop at **Cabo Corrientes**, just north of Playa Grande, is a good spot to try, as are the two breakwaters – **Escollera Norte** and **Escollera Sur** – at the port. Freshwater fishing is popular at Laguna de los Padres (see opposite), while **Mako Team** (☎ 493-5338; www.makoteam.com.ar) offers ocean fishing excursions. You can rent gear from **Complejo Recreativo Islas Malvinas** (☎ 0223-15-562-5430), right near the lake.

The rocky cliffs by the sea and the hills of Sierra de los Padres make for excellent climbing and rappelling. **Acción Directa** (☎ 474-4520; www.acciondirecta.com.ar) runs a school – it also offers mountain biking, canoeing and overnight active camping trips.

For those really looking to get the heart racing, there's a skydiving outfit just outside of town that offers daily jumps, weather permitting. Contact **Aeroclub Mar del Plata** (☎ 464-2151; RP 88, Km 96).

Tours

Crucero Anamora (☎ 489-0310; www.an amoracrucero.com.ar) This 30m boat offers one-hour harbor tours (AR$39) several times daily in summer and twice daily on weekends in winter from Dársena B at the port.
Municipal Tourist Office (Blvd Marítimo) Emtur conducts free organized tours (called 'Paseos Para Gente Inquieta') of various city sights.

Festivals & Events

Mar del Plata's elaborate tourist infrastructure guarantees a wide variety of special events throughout the year. It's worth being in town for the city's **International Film Festival** (www.mardelplatafilmfest.com), which takes place in November. Launched in 1950, though interrupted for decades by Argentina's political and economic woes, it is South America's most important film festival, attracting participants from all over the world.

In January Mar del Plata also celebrates **Fiesta Nacional de los Pescadores** (Fisherman's Festival), which sees locals cooking up seafood feasts and a traditional procession where a statue of Our Lady, Star of the Sea – patron saint of fishermen – is carried through the streets.

Another large celebration is February's **Fiesta Nacional del Mar** (National Sea Festival), which includes the election and coronation of a 'Sea Queen' and her princesses, along with plenty of music.

Sleeping

It's worth reiterating that prices start climbing in November and December, are highest in January and February, then drop off in March. In the off season many of Mar del Plata's hotels and *residenciales* close their doors.

BUDGET

Rates at Mar del Plata's crowded campgrounds, mostly south of town, are around AR$17 per person; the tourist office prints out information about their facilities.

Hostel del Mar (☎ 486-3112; www.hosteldelmar .ar; Av Colón 1051; dm AR$50-60; s/d AR$80/160; 🖳 🛜) A very casual, small hostel just 1½ blocks from the beach. Nice grassy back garden, and it offers bike and surfboard rentals (along with surfing lessons). The two tiny private rooms have bunks.

Alta Esperanza Hostel (☎ 495-8650; www.altaesper anzahostelfrentealmar.blogspot.com; Av Peralta Ramos 1361; dm AR$60-70; 🖳 🛜) Proud to be Mardel's first waterfront hostel, in an interesting, Tudor-like building. Offers six- to 10-bed dorms only, and best for nonparty types – this is a place to relax. Occasional art shows or cultural events will be hosted here.

La Pergola Hostel (☎ 493-3695; www.lapergolahostel .com.ar; Yrigoyen 1093; dm AR$50-60; 🖳 🛜) A decent hostel in an amazing old Tudor-like building, it has nice wood-floor dorms, some with balcony and partial sea views, and there's a great terrace with pergola. The dining/communal/games area is in the 'cold' basement, though. Private rooms are available during slow times.

Hostel Playa Grande Suites (☎ 451-2396; www.hostelplayagrande.com.ar; Quintana 168; dm AR$65, r AR$200; 🖳 🛜) Near an upscale strip of shops, restaurants and bars is this slightly fancy hostel with nice hang-out areas. It's big on surfing, offering gear and lessons. Staff will also set up activities like horseback riding, paragliding, scuba diving and rock climbing. Rooms are mostly privates; its annex, two blocks away, has mostly dorms.

MIDRANGE & TOP END

Playa Vanese Inn (☎ 451-1813; www.playavareseinn.com.ar; Gascón 715; s/d AR$130/270; 🖳 🛜) Fifteen simple, comfortable and good-sized rooms with concrete floors are on offer at this nice little *hostería*. It's just 1½ blocks from the beach and has cable TV; reserve ahead, as its popular.

City Hotel (☎ 495-3018; www.cityhotelmardelplata.com; Diagonal JB Alberdi 2561; d AR$250-310) This worker-owned cooperative has an old-school feel and a delightful back garden. It's worth paying a bit extra for the 'superior' rooms – they're larger, have balconies and the bathrooms come with bathtubs.

Hotel Selent (☎ 494-0878; www.hotelselent.com.ar; Arenales 2347; d AR$280; 🖳 🛜) Well located not far from the beach action, this friendly, family-run hotel is nicely set back from the street. The tiled rooms are simple and clean, and the atmosphere is fairly peaceful.

Etoile (☎ 493-4968; Santiago del Estero 1869; d AR$280; 🛜) Its central location, plus spacious rooms (each has its own long 'entry' space with sofa), make this place good value. Get a quieter room in back – they're still bright.

Hotel Los Troncos (☎ 451-8882; www.hotellostroncos.com.ar; Rodríguez Peña 1561; d AR$290; 🖳 🛜) This small hotel, which actually looks more like a guesthouse, is located in a leafy residential neighborhood. It's far from the beach, but has a large and pleasant grassy garden with lounges. Rooms are very nice and comfortable.

our pick **El Aleph Hotel Boutique** (☎ 451-4380; www.elalephmdq.com.ar; LN Alem 2542; r AR$330-400; 🖳 🖳 🛜) Six lovely rooms and suites are set around covered wood walkways and a grassy garden, offering an upscale paradise. The feel is exclusive but relaxed, with afternoon tea and wine tastings available. Reservations are crucial; no children under 16 and cash payment only.

Villa Nuccia (☎ 451-6593; www.villanucia.com.ar; Almirante Brown 1134; d AR$350-420; 🖳 🖳 🛜) A beautiful boutique hotel in an old renovated house, rooms are simple but elegant and spacious, and a couple have balconies. There's a large green lawn out back with a swimming pool and Jacuzzi; afternoon tea service is offered. Run by a young, traveling Argentine couple.

NH Gran Hotel Provincial (☎ 499-5900; www.nhgrandhotelprovincial.com; Blvd Marítimo 2502; r from AR$620; 🖳 🖳 🛜 🖳) One of Mardel's best stays, and typical NH style – elegant and minimalist. Rooms are beautiful, of course, most offering beach and sea views, and all the expected services are here, including outdoor pool, indoor pool (coming) and even a casino.

Eating

Mar del Plata's numerous restaurants, pizzerias and snack bars often struggle to keep up with impatient crowds between December and March, and there are always long lines. For fresh seafood head south of town to the port, which has several restaurants cooking up the catch of the day.

El Jamón (☎ 493-7447; cnr Bolívar & Bartolomé Mitre; mains AR$20-26; 🕑 lunch & dinner Mon-Sat) There's little atmosphere at this neighborhood favorite, with plastic plants swinging from the beams. It's still full of locals, however, all enjoying the lamb roast, Spanish-style octopus or beef pasta (menu choices change daily).

Piedra Buena (☎ 480-1632; Centro Comercial Puerto, Port Mar del Plata; mains AR$20-32; 🕑 dinner daily Jan, lunch & dinner Wed-Sun Feb-Dec) One of the best seafood restaurants down at the port, and the most atmospheric, there's a huge menu – the seafood bisque comes highly recommended. Across the way is Santa Rita, a much more casual joint but still good.

La Cuadrada (☎ 494-6949; 9 de Julio 2737; mains AR$20-45; 🕑 dinner) A wonderfully eclectic place with a personality disorder – it's a tea house, cultural center, restaurant and theater. There's a wide range of teas, along with pastries, for your afternoon enjoyment, and the restaurant has good, well-priced food. It also does dinner shows with *folklore*, tango and murga music (among many other kinds).

Pescadores (☎ 493-1713; Blvd Marítimo & Av Luro; AR$24-38; 🕑 lunch & dinner) Located out on the fishing pier (under the giant 'Quilmes' sign), this seafood restaurant offers great water views – especially from its 2nd floor. The menu runs through typical Mardel offerings of meat, pasta and seafood, but you're here for the views.

La Piazetta (☎ 494-5113; San Luis 1652; mains AR$24-39; ☻ lunch & dinner) Popular with the locals, this Italian restaurant offers fine homemade pastas, along with meat and fish dishes and a great assortment of salads. The AR$38 lunch special is a good deal.

El Palacio del Bife (☎ 494-7727; Córdoba 1857; mains AR$25-39; ☻ lunch & dinner) A highly recommended, classy *parrilla* with a massive menu. Come hungry and come wanting meat, although the homemade pastas are also worth a try. Takeout food is discounted by 20%.

Taberna Baska (☎ 480-0209; 12 de Octubre 3301; mains AR$30-52; ☻ lunch & dinner) Just a few blocks inland from the port is this renowned Basque restaurant. It has old-school atmosphere, and serves up delicious dishes like garlic shrimp, mixed seafood stews, fish in seven kinds of sauce, and baby squid in ink and saffron.

Amigos del Mar (☎ 491-6054; Guido 2056; mains AR$45-60; ☻ dinner, closed Mon Easter-Nov) Apart from the hearty *buenas noches* greeting on arrival, this Japanese restaurant is the real deal. It has bamboo screens, jangly background music and a sushi sashimi platter that's worth the trek 1.5km west (or AR$15 taxi ride) on its own.

El Anticuario (☎ 451-6309; Bernardo de Irigoyen 3819; AR$50-80; ☻ dinner) Proponents of the slow food philosophy, upscale Anticuario serves very good Mediterranean and seafood dishes like black halibut in oyster sauce, seafood paella or king crab in garlic.

Drinking

At the Playa Grande end of town, the areas along Bernardo de Irigoyen and LN Alem, between Almafuerte and Rodríguez Peña, are popular nightlife magnets.

Antares (☎ 492-4455; Córdoba 3025; ☻ 8pm-late) The eight homebrews on tap at Mar del Plata's only microbrewery include imperial stout, pale ale and barley wine – excellent cures for the Quilmes blues. Food is available and there is live music most weekends. There's another branch at Irigoyen 3851.

La Bodeguita del Medio (☎ 486-3096; Castelli 1252; ☻ 7pm-late) Named after one of Hemingway's favorite haunts, the mojitos at this atmospheric joint do him proud and are two-for-

one between 7pm and 9pm. The Cuban dishes and bar snacks all go down well, and there's occasional live music.

Almacén Condal (☎ 451-3460; cnr Alsina & Garay; ☻ 9am-late) For traditional old atmosphere, you can't beat this funky corner bar. Talk to the locals at the long bar while munching the pub grub – it's sure to take you back in time.

Entertainment

NIGHTCLUBS

After tanning on the beach all day, Argentines take their hot, bronzed bodies to the nightclubs and dance until the morning hours. The most popular clubs are along Av Constitución, about 3km from downtown, and don't really get started until after 1am. Bus 551 from downtown runs along the entire avenue. Keep your eyes peeled during the day for discount flyers handed out along San Martín and Rivadavia.

Sobremonte (☎ 479-2600; Av Constitución 6690; ☻ midnight-dawn nightly Dec-Mar, midnight-dawn Thu-Sat Apr-Nov) Ground zero for the city's most fashionable summertime clubbers, Sobremonte has three throbbing discos, a Mexican restaurant and a lounge all under one roof.

Chocolate (☎ 479-4848; Av Constitución 4451; ☻ midnight-dawn Dec-Mar, midnight-dawn Thu-Sat Apr-Nov) This is another long-time favorite, with two floors, a patio and a standard soundtrack covering everything from techno to *rock nacional* (Argentine rock).

LIVE MUSIC

The tourist information office has information on current performances.

Casa del Folklore (☎ 472-3955; San Juan 2543; ☻ 9pm-late, Fri & Sat only winter) Music usually gets underway after 11pm at this lively *peña* (folk music club) northwest of downtown, where there's plenty of food, drink and dancing.

THEATER

When Buenos Aires shuts down in January, hundreds of shows come from the capital to Mar del Plata. *Carteleras* (discount ticket offices) offer half-price tickets to movies and theater presentations; try **Cartelera Baires** (Santa Fe 1844, Local 33).

Teatro Auditorium (☎ 493-6001; Blvd Marítimo 2280) Part of the casino complex, this place offers quality musical theater.

Other venues include **Teatro Municipal Colón** (☎ 499-6555; Yrigoyen 1665) and **Teatro Santa Fe** (☎ 492-0856; Santa Fe 1854).

Shopping

Mar del Plata is famous for sweaters and jackets. Shops along Av JB Justo, nicknamed 'Avenida del Pullover', have competitive, near-wholesale prices. For an upscale experience, stroll along Calle Güemes.

Feria de los Artesanos (Plaza San Martín) Vendors set up their stalls every summer afternoon on Plaza San Martín to sell everything from *mate* gourds and knives to sweaters and silverwork.

Mercado de Pulgas (Plaza Rocha; ☉ 11am-6pm Thu-Sun) This relaxed flea market, selling everything including the kitchen sink, is at 20 de Septiembre between San Martín and Av Luro, seven blocks northwest of Plaza San Martín.

Getting There & Away

AIR

Aerolíneas Argentinas (☎ 496-0101; Moreno 2442) has several daily flights to Buenos Aires (from AR$285). **LADE** (☎ 491-1484; Corrientes 1537) is cheaper but flies much less frequently.

BUS

Mar del Plata's bus terminal is planning on moving to near the train station, some 2km northwest of the beach. There will likely be local bus services to the town center (plus of course taxis). There will be plenty of connections to destinations all over Argentina, including the following:

Destination	Cost (AR$)	Duration (hr)
Bahía Blanca	90	7
Bariloche	300	18-20
Buenos Aires	100	5½
Comodoro Rivadavia	280	24
Córdoba	210	16-18
Mendoza	295	20
Necochea	25	2¼
Pinamar	24	2½
Puerto Madryn	220	16½
Tandil	32	3
Villa Gesell	19	2

TRAIN

The **train station** (☎ 475-6076; Av Luro 4700 at Italia; ☉ 6am-midnight) is about 2km from the beach.

El Marplatense chugs on Friday from Buenos Aires to Mar del Plata; it returns to BA on Sunday (AR$90). The regular train does the Buenos Aires–Mardel route twice daily (AR$52 to AR$69, seven hours). Reserve tickets well ahead in summer.

Getting Around

Aeropuerto Astor Piazzola (☎ 478-3990; RN 2, Km 396) is 10km north of the city. To get there by bus, take bus 542 from the corner of Blvd Marítimo and Belgrano. A taxi or *remise* costs about AR$25.

Despite Mar del Plata's sprawl, frequent buses reach just about every place in town. However, most buses take magnetic cards that must be bought ahead of time at *kioskos* and charged up. Popular bus 221 is an exception: it takes either coins or bills. The tourist office is a great resource for more transport details.

Car rentals are available at **Budget** (☎ 495-2935; Córdoba 2270); the cheapest model goes for AR$200 per day including 200km.

BALCARCE

Named for Argentina's most famous racing driver, the **Museo del Automovilismo Juan Manuel Fangio** (☎ 02266-425540; www.museofangio.com; cnr Dardo Rocha & Mitre, Balcarce; adult/child 6-18yr AR$20/12; ☉ 10am-7pm), one of the country's finest, preserves a multimillion-dollar collection of classic and racing cars in Fangio's birthplace of Balcarce, 70km northwest of Mar del Plata. The museum stresses the worldwide exploits of Fangio and his contemporaries, but also makes an effort to put automotive history into a global context.

El Rápido runs frequent buses from Mar del Plata (AR$12, 1½ hours).

NECOCHEA

☎ 02262 / pop 89,000

Totally pumping in summer and near dead in winter, Necochea's beach-town feel is undisturbed by the high-rises that keep springing up. With 70km of beachfront, it's fairly certain that you'll be able to find a spot to lay your towel. Windy Necochea also has the best waves on the coast, attracting surfers throughout the year. The foresty Parque Provincial Miguel Lillo is a great bonus here, as are the walking and horseback riding opportunities out to the west of town. Another plus is that Necochea offers some of the best-value lodging on the coast.

Most of Necochea's services, such as the post office, banks and bus terminal, are inland about 3km from the beach.

Information

ACA (☎ 422106; Av 59, No 2073) Argentina's auto club; good for provincial road maps.

Municipal hospital (☎ 422405; Av 59, btwn Calles 100 & 104)
Municipal tourist office (☎ 438333; cnr Avs 2 & 79; ⊗ 8am-9pm) On the beach.
Post office (Calle 6, No 4065)

Sights & Activities
The dense pine woods of **Parque Provincial Miguel Lillo**, a large greenbelt along the beach, are widely used for cycling, horseback riding, walking and picnicking. Horses and bikes can both be rented inside the park.

The Río Quequén Grande, rich in rainbow trout and mackerel, also allows for easy rafting, particularly around the falls at **Saltos del Quequén**. At the village of **Quequén** at the river's mouth, several stranded shipwrecks offer good opportunities for exploration and photography below sculpted cliffs. The **faro** (lighthouse) is another local attraction.

With some of the best waves along the Atlantic coast, Necochea is a hit with surfers. There's a surf school at the **Monte Pasuvio camping ground** (☎ 451482, 02262-15-530975; Calle 502, No 1160), across the river in Quequén, where you can arrange classes and rent boards year-round.

Sleeping
Note that some accommodations are open from December to Easter only; call ahead. The following are all within four blocks of the beach.

Jamming Hostel (☎ 450753; www.jamminghostel .com.ar; Calle 502, No 1685; dm/r AR$50/150) This interesting adobe-style hostel is near the beach in Quequén, 1km beyond the river that separates the two towns and 6km from the bus terminal (a taxi costs around AR$12). Some rooms have water views. It's big on skateboarding and surfing culture (a surf school is nearby).

Hospedaje La Casona (☎ 423345; lacasonahlc@yahoo .com.ar; Calle 6, No 4356; d AR$100) This welcoming place offers guests basic rooms, a spacious garden with a *parrilla*, as well as a games room and small library. There are also apartments with kitchenette (AR$160).

Hotel Mirasol (☎ 525158; www.mirasolhotel.com.ar; Calle 4, No 4133; d AR$160) With an excellent location right on the square, this place has comfortable budget rooms, some with refrigerator and TV. Open all year.

Hotel Flamingo (☎ 420049; flamingoneco@hotmail .com; Calle 83, No 333; d AR$180; 🛜) Choose from three kinds of rooms here, from basic, dark and musty to big, bright and modern (the latter are upstairs).

Hotel España (☎ 422896; www.hotel-espana.com .ar; Calle 89, No 215; d AR$250-275; 🛜) This small hotel sits a half block from the beach, offering comfortable, carpeted rooms (some with balcony). Room sizes vary, so ask to look at a couple.

Hostería del Bosque (☎ 420002; www.hosteria-del bosque.com.ar; Calle 89, No 350; d AR$280-390; ⊠ 🖵 🛜) This *hostería* is by far the most atmospheric place to stay in town. Rooms are large and comfortable, and some have views of Parque Lillo across the street. Nice grassy garden in back.

Eating & Drinking
There are plenty of dining options around Plaza San Martín. Many of the *balnearios* have eateries where you can grab a bite beachside. In low season many restaurants are only open on weekends.

Chimichurri Asador (☎ 420642; Calle 83, No 345; mains AR$16-30; ⊗ lunch & dinner) Only carnivores are welcome at this *parrilla*, favored by locals for its delicious meats.

Sotavento (☎ 02262-15-406442; Pinolandia; mains AR$20-38; ⊗ lunch & dinner) A modern restaurant right on the beach offering good service, well-prepared gourmet dishes and sea views. It's about 1km south of Calle 89.

Taberna Española (☎ 525126; Calle 89, No 360; mains AR$25-55; ⊗ lunch & dinner) For the Spanish take on the whole seafood thing, there's this well-regarded restaurant. The 'special' menu includes a starter, main dish and dessert (AR$37). Reservations essential.

Antares (☎ 421976; Calle 4, No 4266; AR$20-45; ⊗ dinner Tue-Sun) Yet another branch of the beautiful bar-restaurant chain. There's a decent selection of pub-style food, along with several craft-style beers (actually brewed in Mar del Plata).

If you need a drink, check out the bars on Calle 87 between Calles 4 and 6.

Getting There & Away
The **bus terminal** (Av 58, btw Calle 47 & Av 45) is 3.5km from the beach (taxis cost AR$8, or take local bus 513). Destinations include Buenos Aires (AR$111, seven hours), Mar del Plata (AR$25, 2¼ hours), Tandil (AR$25, three hours) and Bahía Blanca (AR$45, five hours).

THE PAMPAS & THE
ATLANTIC COAST

BAHÍA BLANCA

☎ 0291 / pop 325,000

Grandiose buildings, an attractive plaza and boulevards lined with shade trees and palms lend oft-overlooked Bahía Blanca the feel of a cosmopolitan city in miniature. While its chief advantage is as a resting point during overland trips from Buenos Aires to Patagonia, there are a few things to see in town, and plenty of good eating and entertainment options.

The hordes of sailors who dock here, at what is now South America's largest naval base, attest to Bahía Blanca's militaristic beginnings. In an early effort to establish military control on the periphery of the pampas, Colonel Ramón Estomba situated the pompously named Fortaleza Protectora Argentina at the natural harbor of Bahía Blanca in 1828.

Orientation

Bahía Blanca is 654km southwest of Buenos Aires via RN 3, and 278km north of Viedma via RN 3. Bahia Blanca's streets change their names at Av San Martín/Zelarrayán and at Av Colón/Hipólito Irigoyen.

Information

ACA (☎ 455-0076; Chiclana 305) Argentina's auto club; good for provincial road maps.

Hospital Privado del Sur (☎ 455-0270; Las Heras 164)

Post office (Moreno 34)

Pullman Tour (☎ 455-3344; San Martín 171) Change money and traveler's checks here.

Tourist office (☎ 456-2668; Alsina 370; ☽ 8am-3pm Mon-Fri) The bus terminal also has a tourist office (open 7am to 1pm), and there's a kiosk planned at Drago just north of O'Higgins.

Sights & Activities

On the outskirts of town – in a former customs building that's hardly noticeable among the massive grain elevators and fortress-like power plant of Puerto Ingeniero White – the **Museo del Puerto** (☎ 457-3006; Guillermo Torres 4131; admission by donation; ☽ 8am-1:30pm Mon-Fri, 5-9pm Sat & Sun) is an iconoclastic tribute to immigrants and their heritage, and includes an archive with documents, photographs and recorded oral histories. The best time to visit is for a weekend afternoon tea, when local groups prepare regional delicacies, each week representing a different immigrant group.

Live music often accompanies the refreshments. Bus 500 from the plaza goes to the museum.

The neoclassical **Teatro Municipal** (cnr Alsina & Zapiola Dorrego) is the main performing-arts center in the city. In the same building is **Museo Histórico** (☎ 456-3117; admission free; ☽ 4-8pm Tue-Sun). Displays include indigenous artifacts and collections that represent important episodes in the life of the region, such as its founding as a military base and the arrival of the railways. Also worth checking out is **Museo de Arte Contemporáneo** (☎ 459-4006; Sarmiento 454; admission free; ☽ 2-8pm Tue-Fri, 4-8pm Sat & Sun), showcasing local and national artists.

From Thursday to Sunday, an afternoon **artisans market** takes over Plaza Rivadavia, opposite the Municipalidad.

Sleeping

Catering mainly to the business set, accommodations in Bahía Blanca are generally more expensive than in other Argentine towns its size; however, good deals can be found.

Bahía Blanca Hostel (☎ 452-6802; www.bahiablanca hostel.com; Soler 701; dm AR$38, s AR$45-60, d AR$75-85; 🖳 ☜) Located in old hotel, this hostel isn't exactly cozy – but it's friendly and cheap. There are lots of basic private rooms, most set around an old patio, and the cheapest share bathrooms.

Firenze Hotel (☎ 455-7746; www.firenzehotel.com.ar; Rondeau 39; s/d AR$80/130; ☜) A great deal for what you get, this small hotel has 17 simple, pretty rooms in a remodeled old building.

Hotel Victoria (☎ 452-0522; General Paz 84; s/d AR$110/150; ☜) This well-kept old building has good, comfortable rooms around a central courtyard.

Hotel Muñiz (☎ 456-0060; www.hotelmuniz.com.ar; O'Higgins 23; s AR$125-190, d AR$185-250; 🕮 🖳 ☜) Set in a beautiful old building in a very central location, the Muñiz offers three levels of decent rooms – along with great old atmosphere.

Rio Oja Apart Hotel (☎ 481-9922; www.aparthotelrio -oja.com.ar; Estados Unidos 65; s/d AR$165/200; 🕮 ☜) If you're just passing through town, this modern hotel is a good choice – it's right at the bus terminal. Rooms are efficient and come with a tiny closet kitchenette.

Hotel Argos (☎ 455-0404; www.hotelargos.com; España 149; s/d AR$250/300; 🕮 🖳 ☜) Bahía Blanca's best, with large, quiet and carpeted rooms. Breakfast is filling, the gym modern and the service good.

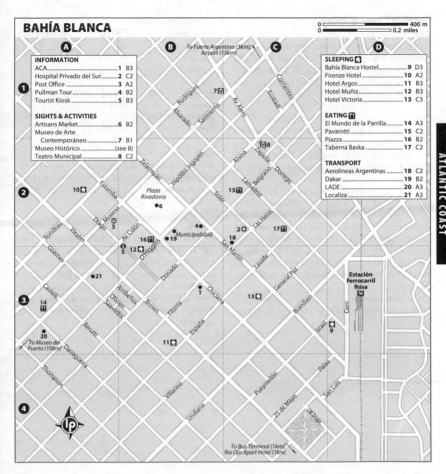

BAHÍA BLANCA

INFORMATION	
ACA	**1** B3
Hospital Privado del Sur	**2** C2
Post Office	**3** A2
Pullman Tour	**4** B2
Tourist Kiosk	**5** B3

SIGHTS & ACTIVITIES	
Artisans Market	**6** B2
Museo de Arte Contemporáneo	**7** B1
Museo Histórico	(see 8)
Teatro Municipal	**8** C2

SLEEPING	
Bahía Blanca Hostel	**9** D3
Firenze Hotel	**10** A2
Hotel Argos	**11** B3
Hotel Muñiz	**12** B3
Hotel Victoria	**13** C3

EATING	
El Mundo de la Parrilla	**14** A3
Pavarotti	**15** C2
Piazza	**16** B2
Taberna Baska	**17** C2

TRANSPORT	
Aerolíneas Argentinas	**18** C2
Dakar	**19** B2
LADE	**20** A3
Localiza	**21** A3

THE PAMPAS & THE ATLANTIC COAST

Eating

Piazza (☎ 452-2707; cnr O'Higgins & Chiclana; mains AR$18-35; ⏲ breakfast, lunch & dinner) A popular cafe on the plaza, with an imaginative menu (including pizza and salads) and a fully stocked bar. Don't miss the chocolate mousse (AR$11).

Taberna Baska (☎ 450-2500; Lavalle 284; mains AR$25-48; ⏲ lunch & dinner Mon-Sat) Seafood dishes and classics like Spanish tortilla (potato omelet) are very well done at this relaxed place, part of the Basque social club.

Pavarotti (☎ 450-0077; Belgrano 272; mains AR$28-47; ⏲ lunch & dinner) Sophisticated dishes such as seafood stew, along with gourmet pastas, large meat and cheese plates and the ensalada '9 de Julio' (mixed lettuces with cheese, nuts, olives and croutons), make this place special.

El Mundo de la Parrilla (☎ 454-6446; Av Colón 379; à la carte AR$35-42; ⏲ lunch & dinner Sun-Fri, dinner only Sat) Reservations are a must at this buzzing *parrilla*, which locals agree is the best in town. The *tenedor libre* (AR$45 for women, AR$48 for men!) sees an endless procession of succulent grilled meats brought to your table, along with salad and drinks.

Drinking

For a night out on the town in Bahía Blanca, head to Fuerte Argentino, about nine blocks northeast from Plaza Rivadavia, where *boliches* (nightclubs) and bars are clustered in a convenient cul-de-sac. There is a pleasant sculpture garden nearby where you can catch your breath.

Getting There & Away

AIR

Bahía Blanca's airport is 15km east of town. **Aerolineas Argentinas** (☎ 456-0561; San Martín 298) hops to Buenos Aires (AR$435). **LADE** (☎ 452-1063; Darragueira 21) does the same trip for about AR$300, but only every 15 days.

BUS

Bahía Blanca's **bus terminal** (Brown 1700) is about 2km southeast of Plaza Rivadavia. Taxis to the city enter cost AR$12 to AR$15; there are local buses also, but you'll have to buy a magnetic card at a *kiosco* to use them.

There are several businesses – including *locutorios* (private telephone offices) and the travel agent **Dakar** (Chidana 102) – right at the south end of Plaza Rivadavia that sell bus tickets, saving you a trip to the bus terminal for information. These different businesses sell different bus company's tickets, so ask around if you want a particular schedule, company or price.

Condor Estrella and Expreso Cabildo each offer two or three daily services to Sierra de la Ventana.

Some long-distance destinations:

Destination	Cost (AR$)	Duration (hr)
Bariloche	143	12-14
Buenos Aires	125-160	9
Córdoba	160-192	13-15
Mar del Plata	85	7
Mendoza	210-265	16
Neuquén	70-95	7½
Sierra de la Ventana	23	2
Trelew	122-135	10-12

CAR

If you're using Bahía Blanca as a base to explore the nearby sierras and the coast, hiring a car could be the best way. Try **Localiza** (☎ 456-2526; Av Colón 194).

TRAIN

Trains leave from the **Estación Ferrocarril Roca** (☎ 452-9196; www.ferrobaires.gba.gov.ar; Av Cerri 750) for Buenos Aires daily Monday to Saturday at around 7pm (AR$40 to AR$66, 12 to 15 hours). Once a week there's also a very slow service south to Carmen de Patagones, though it tends to get cancelled from time to time.

Northeast Argentina

Northeast Argentina is defined by its water. Muscular rivers roll through flat green pastureland that they flood at will, the crashing roar of spectacular waterfalls reverberates through the surrounding jungle, and fragile wetlands support myriad birdlife, snapping caimans and cuddly capybaras. The peaceful Río Iguazú, meandering through the tropical forest between Brazil and Argentina, dissolves in fury and power in the world's most awe-inspiring cataracts.

The river then merges gently into the Río Paraná, one of the world's mightiest watercourses, which surges southward, eventually forming the Río de la Plata near Buenos Aires. Along its path are some of the country's most interesting cities: elegant Corrientes, colonial Santa Fe and booming Rosario, as well as Posadas, gateway to the ruined splendor of the Jesuit missions, whose dreams of social utopia in the jungle quickly foundered. The Paraná is joined by the Río Paraguay, west of which stretches the dry scrubland of the Chaco – whose more remote parts are named 'El Impenetrable' – and, eventually, the Río Uruguay, whose course down the Uruguayan border is interrupted by the unusual and spectacular Saltos del Moconá falls. Along its length are also several relaxed waterside towns: attractive Colón, and Gualeguaychú, whose exuberant Carnaval goes on for weeks.

Dotted throughout the region are excellent reserves and national parks, representative of the biological diversity of this tract of country. The shallow freshwater lakes of the Esteros del Iberá harbor a stunning richness of wildlife that's easily seen among the aquatic plants.

NORTHEAST ARGENTINA

HIGHLIGHTS

- Drop your jaw in stunned amazement at the beauty and power of the **Iguazú Falls** (p221)
- Get personal with the mighty Paraná in livable, lovable **Rosario** (p179)
- Coo at the cute capybaras of the **Reserva Provincial Esteros del Iberá** (p200)
- Munch delicious freshwater fish by the Río Uruguay in pretty **Colón** (p207)
- Ponder a unique experiment in humanity at the ruined **Jesuit missions** (p214)

★ Iguazú Falls

★ Jesuit Missions

★ Reserva Provincial Esteros del Iberá

★ Colón

★ Rosario

- POPULATION: 7.52 MILLION
- AREA: 501,487 SQ KM

NORTHEAST ARGENTINA

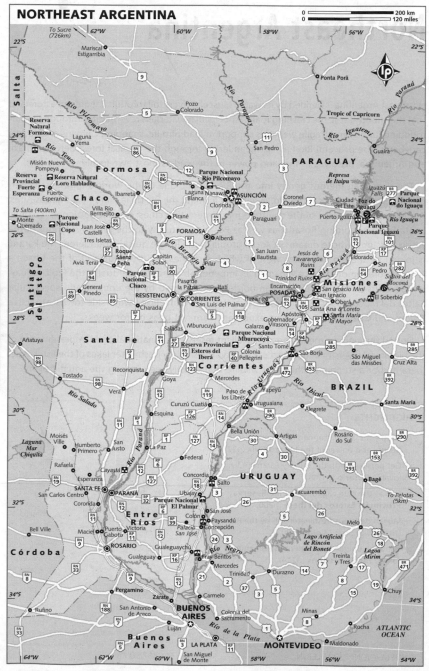

Climate

Over such a large area, temperatures vary widely, getting more tropical as you head north. The riverside cities north of Rosario all tend to be humid, but the Chaco is particularly dry. Winter in the southern part of the region can be fairly cold, with occasional subzero temperatures.

National Parks & Reserves

There are some excellent national parks within the region, varying from the dry savannas of the Chaco to the rainforests of Misiones. In the far northeast, Parque Nacional do Iguaçu (p224) and Parque Nacional Iguazú (p223) are the access points for viewing the incredible Iguazú Falls, and also provide a habitat for orchids, big cats, birdlife and other flora and fauna.

Nowhere will you see as much wildlife as in the wetlands of Reserva Provincial Esteros del Iberá (p200) and its nearby counterpart Parque Nacional Mburucuyá (p199), while it's the haunting elegance of yatay palm trees that makes Parque Nacional El Palmar (p208) special.

Deforestation has denuded much of the Chaco area, so the scrub forests and marshes of Parque Nacional Chaco (p237) and Parque Nacional Río Pilcomayo (p242) are especially valuable, as are the natural reserves further west in the region (see the boxed text, p239).

Getting There & Away

There are flights from Buenos Aires to Rosario, Santa Fe, Paraná, Posadas, Puerto Iguazú, Resistencia, Corrientes and Formosa. Bus connections are available from most towns to destinations all over the country and there is limited train service from Buenos Aires to Rosario and to Posadas.

ALONG THE RÍO PARANÁ

The mighty Río Paraná, the continent's second-longest river at 4000km, dominates the geography of Northeast Argentina. Several of the nation's more interesting cities lie along it, and interact with it on a daily basis. All have their town centers a sensible distance above the shorelines of this flood-prone monster, but have a costanera (riverbank) that's the focus of much social life. The river is still important for trade, and large oceangoing vessels ply it as far

as Rosario, a city whose wonderfully friendly inhabitants and optimistic outlook make it a great destination.

Santa Fe and Paraná have a relaxing sleepy feel – who can blame them with the humidity the Paraná generates? – and attractive traditional architecture, while beautiful Corrientes is the home of chamamé music (a local musical style derived from polka) and launch pad for the wonderful Esteros del Iberá wetlands.

The Paraná is the demesne of enormous river fish – surubí, dorado and pacú among others – that attract sportfishers from around the world. Their distinctive flavor enlivens the menu of the region's restaurants; make sure you try them.

ROSARIO

☎ 0341 / pop 1.2 million

The boom times are back for Rosario, birthplace of both the Argentine flag and 'Che' Guevara, and an important riverport. The derelict buildings of the long costanera have been converted into galleries, restaurants and skate parks, and the river beaches and islands buzz with life in summer. The center – a curious mishmash of stunning early-20th-century buildings overshadowed by ugly apartments – has a comfortable, lived-in feel, and the down-to-earth rosarinos (people from Rosario) are a delight. All are very proud of the city's current claim to fame: Lionel Messi, a golden boy of world soccer, is Rosario born and bred.

History

Rosario's first European inhabitants settled here informally around 1720 without sanction from the Spanish crown. After independence Rosario quickly superseded Santa Fe as the province's economic powerhouse, though, to the irritation of rosarinos, the provincial capital retained political primacy.

The Central Argentine Land Company, an adjunct of the railroad, was responsible for bringing in agricultural colonists from Europe, for whom Rosario was a port of entry. From 1869 to 1914 Rosario's population grew nearly tenfold to 223,000, easily overtaking the capital in numbers. The city's role in agricultural exports and its economic ties to the beef market of the Chicago Mercantile Exchange earned it the nickname 'Chicago Argentino'.

Though the decline of economic and shipping activity during the 1960s led to a drop in Rosario's population and power, its importance

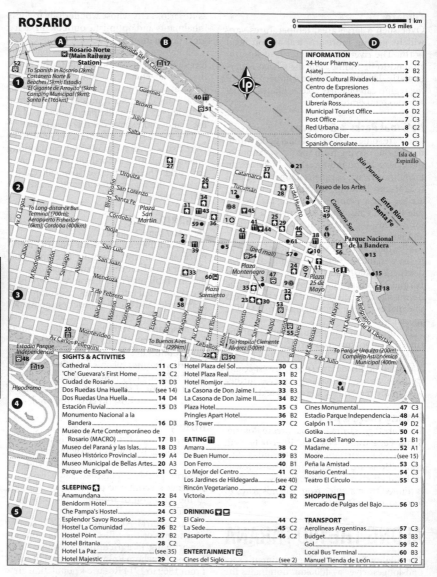

ROSARIO

0 — 1 km
0 — 0.5 miles

as a port was rivaled only by Buenos Aires. Its title as Argentina's second city, however, was later usurped by Córdoba – a status still hotly contested by *rosarinos*.

Nationalistic Argentines cherish Rosario, which is home to a monument to the nation's flag, as Cuna de la Bandera (Cradle of the Flag).

Orientation

Rosario displays a very regular grid pattern, except where the curvature of the bluffs above the river channel dictates otherwise. The traditional focus of urban activities is Plaza 25 de Mayo, but the *peatonales* (pedestrian streets) of San Martín and Córdoba mark the commercial center. There are some 70 square blocks of open space in Parque Independencia, southwest of downtown.

Information

BOOKSTORES

Librería Ross (☎ 448-5378; www.libreriaross.com.ar; Córdoba 1347) Has a small selection of classics in English.

CULTURAL CENTERS

Centro Cultural Rivadavia (☎ 480-2401; San Martín 1080) On Plaza Montenegro, this is a good place to find out what's happening in town. Its galleries provide a showcase for the local arts community.

Centro de Expresiones Contemporáneas (☎ 480-2243; www.cecrosario.org.ar; cnr Av del Huerto & Paseo de los Artes) Recycled historical buildings now providing space for special exhibitions.

INTERNET ACCESS

There are numerous places to get online, and plenty of spots offer free wi-fi, including the plane-shaded Plaza 25 de Mayo (network: mr_gratuita).

Red Urbana (Av Corrientes 563; per hr AR$2.50; ⏰ 24hr)
Sicómoro Ciber (Laprida 966; per hr AR$2.50; ⏰ 8am-late, from 2pm Sun)

MEDICAL SERVICES

There are several 24-hour pharmacies in the center of town, including one at the corner of San Lorenzo and Entre Ríos.

Hospital Clemente Alvarez (☎ 480-8111; Rueda 1110) Southwest of the city center.

MONEY

Banks and ATMs are all over, with a cluster along Santa Fe near Plaza 25 de Mayo. Exchanges along San Martín and Córdoba change traveler's checks (with commission) and cash. Street changers may pass false notes.

POST & TELEPHONE

There are many *locutorios* (private telephone offices) around the center.

Post office (Córdoba 721)

TOURIST INFORMATION

Municipal tourist office (☎ 480-2230; www.rosarioturismo.com; Av del Huerto; ⏰ 9am-7pm Mon-Sat, 9am-6pm Sun) Near the waterfront. There's another office at the long-distance bus terminal.

TRAVEL AGENCIES

Asatej (☎ 425-6002; www.asatej.com; Shopping del Siglo, 2nd fl, Roca 848) Nonprofit student travel agency.

Sights & Activities

MUSEO DEL PARANÁ Y LAS ISLAS

Thanks to the romantic, engaging murals of local painter Raúl Domínguez, this **museum** (☎ 439-8679; Estación Fluvial; admission free; ⏰ 1-7pm Sat-Sun), on the 1st floor of the waterfront Estación Fluvial, is worthwhile. Life on the islands of the Paraná so enchanted Domínguez that he created this small museum, filling it with photographs, artifacts, historical documents and his own paintings.

PLAZA 25 DE MAYO

Rosario's **cathedral** (⏰ 7:40am-12:30pm & 4:30-8:30pm Mon-Sat, 8am-1pm & 5-9:30pm Sun) is a slender construction with a high single nave and dome decorated with stained-glass panels depicting the life of the Virgin. It's one of several attractive buildings around this square, which is effectively the center of old Rosario.

Nearby, Manuel Belgrano, who designed the Argentine flag, rests in a crypt beneath the colossal 78m-high **Monumento Nacional a La Bandera** (☎ 480-2238; Santa Fe 581; admission AR$2; ⏰ 9am-6pm Tue-Sun, 2-6pm Mon Apr-Sep, to 7pm daily Oct-Mar), a chillingly nationalistic construction in pitiless stone. The monument's redeeming attributes are its location near the Paraná waterfront, with stirring views of the river and its islands from the tower, accessed by elevator (no disabled access).

MUSEO HISTÓRICO PROVINCIAL

The well-presented collection of this **museum** (☎ 472-1457; Parque Independencia; admission AR$1; ⏰ 9am-5pm Tue-Fri, 2-6pm Sat & Sun) features plenty of postindependence exhibits plus excellent displays on indigenous cultures from all over Latin America. Particularly interesting is the collection of Baroque religious art from the southern Andes. Information is presented in Spanish only.

MUSEO MUNICIPAL DE BELLAS ARTES

This **museum** (☎ 480-2542; cnr Av Carlos Pellegrini & Blvd Oroño; admission AR$4; ⏰ 2-8pm Mon & Wed-Fri, 1-7pm Sat & Sun) is worth a visit for its brilliantly inventive juxtapositions of fine art – and there are a couple of exceptional European paintings here – with contemporary artworks from the MACRO (see p182) collection. A *St Andrew* by Ribera, for example, is beautifully matched with a haunting photo portrait by Pierre Gonnord.

MUSEO DE ARTE CONTEMPORÁNEO DE ROSARIO (MACRO)

Housed in a brightly painted grain silo on the waterfront, this **gallery** (☎ 480-4981; www.mac romuseo.org.ar; Av de la Costa at Blvd Oroño; donation AR$3; ⏱ 2-8pm Thu-Tue) is part of Rosario's impressive riverbank renewal. It features temporary exhibitions, mostly by young local artists, of varying quality, housed in small galleries spread over eight floors. There's a good view of the river islands from the *mirador* (viewpoint) at the top and an attractive cafe-bar, Davis, by the river.

LA COSTANERA

One of Rosario's most attractive features is its waterfront, where what was once home to derelict warehouses and train tracks is rapidly being reclaimed for the fun of the people. It stretches some 15km from its southern end at Parque Urquiza to the Embarcadero Costa Alta, near the city's northern edge, just short of the suspension bridge that crosses into Entre Ríos province. It's an appealing place to wander and watch what's going on, from the plentiful birdlife and impromptu football games to massive cargo ships surging past on the river.

The grassy **Costanera Sur**, just below downtown, includes plenty of space for jogging and courting, as well as La Fluvial (Estación Fluvial) building. This offers boats across to the islands as well as several upmarket eating and drinking options, and the Museo Del Paraná y las Islas (p181).

Heading further north, you pass various cultural venues before reaching the **Parque de España** and its mausoleum-like edifice. Beyond here is a zone of bars and restaurants that gets lively at weekends, and then the Museo de Arte Contemporáneo de Rosario (MACRO; above).

In summer, however, it's the **Costanera Norte**, about 5km north of downtown, that attracts the crowds, as this stretch, along with the islands, offers the best places to swim. The stretch along the busy Av Carrasco, north of Av Puccio, has the most to offer, including the **Rambla Cataluña**, a tree-lined riverfront with small sandy beaches, shoreline cafes, bars, volleyball nets and tanning sunbathers.

The widest beach is further north at **Balneario La Florida** (admission AR$2; ⏱ Oct-Apr), with services including umbrellas, showers, clothing check and outdoor bars. The sidewalk stops at La Florida and picks up again at its northern edge at **Costa Alta**, where there are more beaches and a pier with boats to the islands.

To get to Rambla Cataluña take bus 153 from the center of town 6km north to Av Puccio (here the bus turns inland).

RIVER ISLANDS

Rosario sits on the banks of the Río Paraná upper delta, an area characterized by largely uninhabited, subtropical islands and winding *riachos* (streams). **Isla Invernada** and **Isla del Espinillo**, the two main islands visible from Rosario's shore, are accessible by boat in summer. Out of season, you'll have to take a tour by kayak with a tour operator (see Tours, opposite).

Boats from Costa Alta leave every 20 minutes (AR$3 roundtrip), from 9am to 8pm in summer, for the various *balnearios* (swimming beaches) along the western shore of Isla Invernada. They are all pretty similar, with sandy beaches, gregarious summer crowds, cafes, ice-cream stands, umbrella rentals, music, billboards and boats from the mainland. Bring plenty of sunblock.

From **Estación Fluvial** (Ferry station; ☎ 447-3838; www.lafluvialrosario.com.ar) there are hourly boats at weekends, and daily in summer (AR$15 roundtrip) to the southern *balnearios* of Costa Esperanza (which offers everything from quad bikes to boat trips), Vladimir and Oasis. There are also cruises and charters on yachts available from this ticket office in summer.

Nearby, the **Ciudad de Rosario** (☎ 449-8688; www.barcocr1.com) offers two-hour cruises on the Paraná for AR$19; it leaves on weekends and holidays at 2:30pm and 5pm, or 5pm and 7:30pm in summer.

COMPLEJO ASTRONÓMICO MUNICIPAL

Those interested in more distant environments can visit the planetarium at the **municipal observatory** (☎ 480-2554; Parque Urquiza; admission free), which has shows (AR$5) at 5pm and 6pm Saturday and Sunday from May to September. At 8pm Wednesday through to Friday (clouds permitting), visitors can view the astral skies through its 2250mm refractor telescope and 4500mm reflecting telescope. On Thursdays and Fridays from noon to 2pm there's a sunwatching session.

'CHE' GUEVARA'S FIRST HOME

This apartment building at Entre Ríos 480, designed by Alejandro Bustillo, was where Ernesto Guevara Lynch and Celia de la Serna lived in 1928 after the birth of their son, Ernesto Guevara de la Serna, popularly known as 'Che'. According to biographer Jon Anderson, young Ernesto's birth certificate was falsified (he was born more than a month before the official date of June 14), but this was certainly Che's first home, although briefly. It's now a private flat, so you can't go inside, but fans of this revolutionary figure still enjoy such trivia, and may want to also check out the Guevara family home in Córdoba (see p326).

Tours

Dos Ruedas Una Huella (☎ 0341-15-571-3812; www .bikerosario.com.ar; Zeballos 327) is a friendly, professional set-up offering recommended bike tours of the city (AR$75, 3½ hours) and kayak trips on the Río Paraná (AR$115, 3½ hours) in several languages. You can combine the two on a full-day trip (AR$165, six hours) or head off on a two-day kayak trip, with camping and *asado* (barbecue grill) included.

Courses

Rosario's a great place to hang out for a while, and **Spanish in Rosario** (☎ 437-2860; www.spanishinro sario.com; Carrasco 1260) offers enjoyable language programs to help you put that time to good use. It can arrange family stays and volunteer work placements.

Festivals & Events

Every June Rosario celebrates **Semana de la Bandera** (Flag Week), climaxing in ceremonies on June 20, the anniversary of the death of Manuel Belgrano, the flag's designer. From mid-October to early November, the **Festival de Jazz** takes place in various venues around town. Pick up a copy of the *AC* (Agenda Cultural) magazine from the tourist office for event listings. Also in November, the national **Encuentro de Colectividades**, a tribute to the country's immigrants, is celebrated with fancy dress, music and food stalls.

Sleeping

Booming Rosario has a huge number of places to stay. There are over 30 hostels (ask the tourist office for a list) and an ever-increasing herd of midrange hotels.

BUDGET

Camping Municipal (☎ 471-2806; cnr Lisandro de la Torre & Costanera; campsites per person AR$9; 🅿) At Granadero Baigorria, 9km north of the center, this has a pleasant riverfront location and is popular with young Argentines. Take bus 35 from the center (Plaza Sarmiento is one option). In summer you can also camp at a couple of sites on the river islands, but don't rely on this, as members get priority.

Hostel La Comunidad (☎ 424-5302; www.lacomunidad hostel.com; Roca 453; dm/d AR$35/110; 🖳 🛜) Occupying a gorgeous old Rosario building, this spot has lofty ceilings and a light, airy feel. The dorms have handsome wooden bunks and floorboards; a cute private room is also available. There's a bar, lounge area and peaceful vibe.

La Casona de Don Jaime (www.youthhostelrosario.com .ar; 🖳 🛜) | (☎ 527-9964; Roca 1051; dm/d without bathroom AR$38/110); || (☎ 530-2020; San Lorenzo 1530; dm/d AR$42/140) There's plenty of punch for your peso at this friendly pair of hostels. The original, on Roca, is for the party crowd, with dark dorms off a pretty central patio noisy with reggae from the Roots bar-restaurant out the front. The second is quieter and cleaner, with a tango theme to its high-ceilinged dorms and rooms with attached bathrooms. Discounts midweek and for HI (Hostelling International) members.

Che Pampa's Hostel (☎ 424-5202; www.chepampas .com; Rioja 812; dm/d AR$40/125; 🆓 🖳 🛜) Designed with verve and panache, this is one of the best-looking hostels we've ever seen. Plush colors and stylish touches characterize the comfortable dorms, which have a bit of road noise. There are also private rooms available, as well as almost any facility (DVDs, excellent kitchen, barbecue area, patio) you care to mention. The enthusiastic staff caps off an excellent place to stay.

Hostel Point (☎ 440-9337; www.hostelpoint.com.ar; Catamarca 1837; dm AR$40-45, tw AR$100; 🖳 🛜) Handy for the riverbank action, this newish hostel features very friendly owners and a rooftop terrace for *parrillas* (mixed grills). The dorms are simple but comfortable; it's worth paying the extra five pesos to upgrade to the quieter, roomier five-bed ones.

Anamundana (☎ 424-3077; www.anamundanahostel .com; Montevideo 1248; dm/d AR$45/120; 🆓 🖳 🛜) A block from the Pellegrini eat-street strip, this wins points for comfortable mattresses, warm personal service and an appealing private double. Breakfast is above average, and it's cheaper midweek.

Hotel Britania (☎ 440-6036; San Martín 364; s/d AR$80/100) Handy for the river and tourist office, this likable old place features welcoming owners and a variety of rooms (some windowless) with TV and OK bathrooms. It's kept clean, but noise echoes, especially at weekends from nearby bars.

Hotel Romijor (☎ 421-7276; Laprida 1050; s/d AR$90/120; 🔁) Spacious darkish rooms and warm personal service are the features of this old-fashioned and handily central hotel. There are a couple of cheaper rooms without TV and heating.

Hotel La Paz (☎ 421-0905; www.hotellapazrosario.com.ar; Barón de Maua 36; s/d AR$110/140; 🔁 ▢ 🛜) Well positioned on Plaza Montenegro, and still looking good after 60 years in operation, this welcoming hotel has resisted the price hikes in recent years and consequently offers excellent value for money. Family rooms at the front have balconies overlooking Plaza Montenegro.

MIDRANGE & TOP END

Pringles Apart Hotel (☎ 447-4050; www.pringlesapart.com.ar; Santa Fe 1470; s/d AR$210/230; 🔁 🛜 🖳) Put thoughts of potato snacks aside and book ahead for this top-value spot. The spacious apartments sleep up to three people and have a decent kitchen, comfy beds and a small balcony.

Plaza Hotel (☎ 421-6446; www.hotelesplaza.com; Barón de Maua 26; s/d AR$258/269; 🔁 ▢ 🛜) There's some serious '70s action going on in the lobby here, and if floral print means 'seethe' rather than 'soothe' for you, avoid the rooms, but otherwise it's a comfortable place with an excellent location on Plaza Montenegro. Service is helpful.

Hotel Plaza del Sol (☎ 421-9899; www.hotelesplaza.com; San Juan 1055; r AR$316; 🔁 ▢ 🛜 🖳) The balconied rooms of this fine hotel are uninspired, but spacious and well equipped, and are shaded by the public areas, complete with strategically placed sculptures. There's a fabulous pool and sundeck area on the 11th floor. Service is good and the breakfast buffet is huge.

our pick Esplendor Savoy Rosario (☎ 429-6000; www.esplendorsavoyrosario.com; San Lorenzo 1022; r AR$600; 🔁 ▢ 🛜 🖳) Even among Rosario's many elegant early-20th century buildings, this art nouveau gem is a standout and has recently reopened after a complete renovation. Rooms feature modern conveniences that seem to blend well with the centenarian features. An indoor pool, elegant cafe-bar and roof garden are among the other attractions. The rates listed are rack rates; you'll find much better prices online or as a walk-up.

Also recommended:

Benidorm Hotel (☎ 421-9368; www.hotelbenidorm.com.ar; San Juan 1049; s/d AR$80/130; 🛜) A decent no-frills option behind Plaza Montenegro.

Hotel Majestic (☎ 440-5872; www.hotelmajestic.com.ar; San Lorenzo 980; s/d/ste AR$220/260/302; 🔁 ▢ 🛜) Stylish rooms in a stately old central building. The suites are much more spacious.

Hotel Plaza Real (☎ 440-8800; www.plazareal hotel.com; Santa Fe 1632; r standard/superior/luxury AR$360/425/550; 🔁 ▢ 🛜 🖳) Luxurious rooms, apartments and suites in a modern building with rooftop pool. Fine facilities, a cracking breakfast and polite friendly service.

Ros Tower (☎ 529-9000; www.rostower.com.ar; Mitre 295; r AR$600; 🔁 ▢ 🛜 🖳) Great service and facilities in this new and sleek business-spa hotel with top river views from many rooms.

Eating

Central Rosario seems empty come suppertime. That's because half the city is out on Av Carlos Pellegrini. Between Buenos Aires and Moreno there's a vast number of family-friendly eateries, including several barn-like *parrillas* (steak restaurants), dozens of pizza places, several all-you-can-eat buffet joints and ice creameries. It's unsubtle but it's where everyone goes. Just stroll along and take your pick. Most places have terraces on the street.

De Buen Humor (☎ 449-0999; Rioja 1560; ice cream from AR$6; ⏱ 10am-8pm) Ice cream here comes from happy cows, they say. We can't vouch for that, but anyone with a sweet tooth will be mooing contentedly at the optimism-filled decor, patio seating, and tasty cones, concoctions and fruit salads.

Victoria (☎ 425-7665; cnr San Lorenzo & Roca; light meals AR$10-28; ⏱ 7:30am-late Mon-Sat, 8pm-late Sun) This busy and atmospheric cafe-cum-bar in an old brick building offers a AR$22 lunch special and delicious salads. Also, it's a great place for a beer and has wi-fi.

Rincón Vegetariano (☎ 411-0833; Mitre 720; all you can eat AR$13; ⏱ lunch & dinner Mon-Sat) With over 50 meat-free hot and cold dishes to eat in or take out, this is a real haven if barbecued meat ain't your thing. There are deals for two people.

Los Jardines de Hildegarda (☎ 426-1168; riverbank near España; dishes AR$11-21; ♡ noon-late Tue-Sun) Right by the river, this offbeat spot serves a short menu of pasta, mussels, pizza and potato dishes, as well as tasty *licuados* and plenty of relaxation. The setting is delightful – some may say better than the food. Take the lift down from next to Don Ferro restaurant.

our pick **Lo Mejor del Centro** (☎ 421-9983; Santa Fe 1171; mains AR$16-32; ♡ lunch & dinner) When this *parrilla* went bust, the staff were left high and dry, but the local government let them reopen it as a cooperative, and what a great job they've done. The meat's as good as you'll taste in Rosario, but there's also homemade pasta, creative salads and a warm, convivial buzz at the tightly packed tables.

Don Ferro (☎ 421-1927; riverbank near España; mains AR$17-56; ♡ lunch & dinner) A very good-looking *parrilla* in what was once Rosario's train station, with a delightful terrace on the platform, excellent service and seriously delicious meat.

Amarra (☎ 447-7550; cnr Buenos Aires & Av Belgrano; mains AR$25-40; ♡ lunch & dinner Mon-Sat) Smart but relaxed, this restaurant opposite the tourist office has a stylish split-level interior and serves up some very imaginative dishes, beautifully presented and prepared. Its specialty is fish, but the meat is also delicious. A huge paella for two people costs AR$60, and the weekday lunch is great value.

Drinking

Rosario has a great number of *restobares*, which function as hybrid cafes and bars, and generally serve a fairly standard selection of snacks and plates. Many are good for either a morning coffee or an evening glass of wine – or anything in between.

La Sede (☎ 425-4071; Entre Ríos 599) In a striking modernist building, this is a very Argentine cafe with a literary feel. Come here to read a book, enjoy the cakes and quiches or, at weekends, catch an offbeat live performance of something or other.

El Cairo (☎ 449-0714; cnr Sarmiento & Santa Fe; ♡ 7am-1am Mon-Thu, 7am-3am Fri & Sat, 4pm-1am Sun) High ceilinged and elegant, with huge panes of glass for people-watching (and vice versa), this classic Rosario cafe is good at any time of day, but especially in the evening, when it mixes a decent cocktail and puts on good Argentine pub grub.

Pasaporte (☎ 448-4097; cnr Maipú & Urquiza; ♡ 8am-late Mon-Sat) A sublimely cozy spot with a pretty terrace and timeworn wooden furniture, including little window booths, the Pasaporte is a favorite for morning coffee with workers from the customs department opposite. But it also has a great evening atmosphere, particularly when the rain's pouring down outside.

Entertainment
CINEMA & THEATER

Cines del Siglo (☎ 425-0761; www.holidaycines.com.ar; Roca 848; tickets AR$10-12) In the Shopping del Siglo center.

Cines Monumental (☎ 530-7070; www.cinesmonumental.com.ar; San Martín 997; tickets AR$12-14) Multiscreen complex in the *peatonal* in San Martín. You can smell the popcorn a block away. Half price on Tuesdays.

Teatro El Círculo (☎ 448-3784; www.teatro-elcirculo.com.ar; Laprida 1235) The city's main performing arts venue is in a lovely building dating from 1904.

LIVE MUSIC

Galpón 11 (☎ 480-2946; riverbank at Cabral) This is a big bare rock venue in an old riverside warehouse.

La Casa del Tango (☎ 480-2415; riverbank at España) This new tango center has info on performances around town, fun Friday evening lessons for only AR$7 and stages various events, including a tango show on Saturdays at 9pm (AR$13). There's also a good cafe and restaurant where the waiters dance tango at dinnertime Wednesday to Saturday.

Peña la Amistad (☎ 411-0339; Maipú 1111; ♡ 10pm-late Fri & Sat) For a different night out, head down to this folksy spot, where a harp and guitar duo bang out traditional music accompanied by the smell of roasting meat, stamping feet and corks being popped.

NIGHTCLUBS

Clubs open their doors shortly after midnight, but remain deserted until after 2am, when lines begin to form. There are several clubs northwest of downtown along Rivadavia and around the Costanera Norte.

Gotika (www.gotikacityclub.com.ar; Mitre 1539; admission AR$10-20; ♡ Fri-Sun) Set behind the imposing facade of a former church, this place kicks off at weekends with a variety of music from drum'n'bass to house.

Moore (Estación Fluvial; admission AR$10; ☺ Fri-Sat Mar-Nov) One of the few central nightclubs, this is atmospherically located in the Estación Fluvial building with an outdoor deck and packed upstairs dance floor.

Madame (cnr Brown & Francia; admission AR$15; ☺ 11pm-5:30am Fri-Sat) One of South America's bigger clubs, this draws people from Buenos Aires at weekends. Fridays have an age minimum of 25.

SPORTS

Rosario has two rival soccer teams with several league titles between them. **Newell's Old Boys** (☎ 421-1180; www.nob.com.ar) plays in red and black at Estadio Parque Independencia, where the club is based, and has a long, proud history of producing great Argentine footballers. **Rosario Central** (☎ 421-0000; www .rosariocentral.com; Mitre 857) plays in blue and yellow stripes at **Estadio 'El Gigante de Arroyito'** (☎ 438-9595; cnr Blvd Avellaneda & Génova). Buy tickets from the stadiums or Rosario Central's club office.

Shopping

Mercado de Pulgas del Bajo (Av Belgrano; ☺ from 4pm Sat & Sun) A small flea market by the tourist office, where dealers sell everything from silverwork to leather goods.

Getting There & Away

AIR

Aerolíneas Argentinas (☎ 420-8138; Córdoba 852) no longer services Rosario's airport. **Sol** (☎ 0810-444-4765; www.sol.com.ar) flies daily to Buenos Aires (AR$360) and also services Mendoza, Córdoba and Tucumán. **Gol** (☎ 530-1150; www .voegol.com; Santa Fe 1515) serves Porto Alegre and Brasilia in Brazil.

BUS

The **long-distance bus terminal** (☎ 437-3030; www .terminalrosario.com.ar, in Spanish; Cafferata & Santa Fe) is 25 blocks west of the city center. From downtown, any bus along Santa Fe will do the trick.

Rosario is a major transport hub and there are direct daily services to nearly all major destinations, including international services to Paraguay, Brazil, Chile and Uruguay. **Manuel Tienda de León** (☎ 0810-888-5366; www .tiendaleon.com.ar; San Lorenzo 935) offers a direct service to or from Buenos Aires' international airport for AR$140. It does pickups from hotel.

Some sample destinations:

Destination	Cost (AR$)	Duration (hr)
Buenos Aires	58	4
Córdoba	71	7
Corrientes	118	12
Mar del Plata	95	7½
Mendoza	140	11
Paraná	32	2
Posadas	160	16
Resistencia	114	10
Salta	150	16
Santa Fe	28	2
Santiago del Estero	109	10
Tucumán	132	12

TRAIN

From **Rosario Norte train station** (Av del Valle 2700; www.tbanet.com.ar), unreliable services to Buenos Aires (AR$40, seven hours) leave at 4:45am Monday to Friday, returning at 6:43pm. There are four other weekly trains, run by **Ferrocentral** (www.ferrocentralsa.com.ar) that stop here en route between Buenos Aires and Córdoba, and Buenos Aires and Tucumán (see p286), a more interesting trip.

Take bus 138 from San Juan and Mitre to the station.

Getting Around

To get to **Aeropuerto Fisherton** (Fisherton Airport; ☎ 451-1226), 8km west of town, take a *remise* (taxi), which costs AR$30 to AR$35. A reliable *remise* operator is **Primera Clase** (☎ 454-5454).

From the local bus terminal on Plaza Sarmiento, bus services run virtually everywhere (see www.rosariobus.com.ar). Have the AR$1.75 fare in exact change; otherwise buy a *tarjeta magnética* (magnetic bus card) from any kiosk (AR$3.20/9.30 for two/six trips). To get to the city center from the long-distance terminal, take a bus marked 'Centro' or 'Plaza Sarmiento'. It's about AR$10 in a taxi.

To rent a car, try **Budget** (☎ 449-4500; www .budget.com.ar; Mendoza 1547) or one of the several car-rental agencies at the airport.

To rent a bike, head to **Dos Ruedas Una Huella** (☎ 0341-15-571-3812; www.bikerosario.com.ar; Zeballos 327; per half-day/day/week AR$40/50/150), which has well-equipped town bikes. You'll need your passport and an AR$150 deposit.

SANTA FE

☎ 0342 / pop 454,238

There's quite a contrast between Santa Fe's relaxed center, where colonial buildings age gracefully in the humid heat and nobody

SANTA FE

0 — 400 m
0 — 0.2 miles

INFORMATION
Lavadero Junin	1	C2
Municipal Tourist Office	(see 34)	
Post Office	2	B2
Provincial Tourist Office	3	B4
Telepública	4	C2

SIGHTS & ACTIVITIES
Casa de Gobierno	5	B4
Catedral	6	B4
Convento y Museo de San Francisco	7	B4
Iglesia de la Compañía	8	B4
Museo Etnográfico y Colonial Provincial	9	B4
Museo Histórico Provincial	10	B4

SLEEPING
Conquistador Hotel	11	C2
Hostal Santa Fe de la Veracruz	12	C2
Hostel Santa Fe	13	C1
Hotel Constituyentes	14	C2
Hotel Emperatriz	15	C2
Hotel España	16	C2
Hotel Galeón	17	C2
Hotel Royal	18	C2
Hotel Zavaleta	19	C2

EATING
Bodegas del Castelar	20	B4
Círculo Italiano	21	C2
Club Social Sirio Libanés	22	C2
El Brigadier	23	B4
La Victoria	24	C1
Las Delicias	25	C2
Merengo	26	B3
Merengo	(see 20)	
Restaurante España	(see 16)	

DRINKING
El Sheik	27	C1
Morrison Bar	28	C1
Suite	29	C1

ENTERTAINMENT
Passage	30	C1
Teatro Municipal Primero de Mayo	31	B3

TRANSPORT
Aerolíneas Argentinas	32	B3
Avis	33	B3
Bus Terminal	34	C2

NORTHEAST ARGENTINA

seems to get beyond an amble, and a Friday night in the Recoleta district where university students in dozens of bars show the night no mercy. Capital of its province, but with a small-town feel, Santa Fe is an excellent place to visit for a day or two.

Santa Fe de la Veracruz (it's full title), was moved here in 1651 from its original location at Cayastá, 75km to the north. The first Santa Fe was founded in 1573 by Juan de Garay, but by the mid-17th century the location proved intolerable for the original Spanish settlers. Wearied by constant raids by indigenous people, floods and isolation, they packed up the place and moved it to its current location on a tributary of the Río Paraná. Several picturesque colonial buildings remain.

In 1853 Argentina's first constitution was ratified by an assembly that met here, which is a source of great pride to the city. Santa Fe hit the headlines again in 2003, when a sudden flood caused havoc. About 100,000 people had to be evacuated, and 24 people perished.

Orientation

Santa Fe's remaining colonial buildings are within a short walk of Plaza 25 de Mayo, the town's functional center. Av San Martín, north of the plaza, is the major commercial street and part of it forms an attractive *peatonal* with palm trees and terraces.

To the east, a bridge crosses the river, then a tunnel beneath the Paraná connects Santa Fe with its twin city of Paraná in Entre Ríos.

Information

Long-distance telephone services are in the bus terminal and at *locutorios* downtown. Several banks with ATMs can be found along the *peatonal*.

Hospital Provincial José María Cullen (☎ 457-3340; Av Freyre 2150)

Lavadero Junín (☎ 452-1096; Av Rivadavia 2834; ♥ Mon-Sat) Laundry.

Municipal tourist office (☎ 457-4124; www .santafeciudad.gov.ar; Belgrano 2910; ♥ 7am-8pm) In the bus terminal.

Provincial tourist office (☎ 458-9476; www.turismo -santafe.org.ar; cnr Amenábar & Av San Martín; ♥ 7am-6pm Mon & Wed-Thu, 7am-1pm Tue & Fri) Helpful office for provincial exploration.

Telepública (Rivadavia 2871) Call shop and internet.

Sights

CONVENTO Y MUSEO DE SAN FRANCISCO

The principal historical landmark is this Franciscan monastery and **museum** (☎ 459-3303; Amenábar 2257; admission by donation; ♥ 8am-noon & 4-7pm summer, 3:30-6:30pm winter, closed Sun except for church), built in 1680. The walls, which are more than 1m thick, support a roof made from Paraguayan cedar and hardwood beams held together by fittings and wooden spikes, rather than by nails. While the museum section is mediocre, the church is beautiful, with an exquisite wooden ceiling and a fine polychrome Christ by the grumpy Spanish master Alonso Cano – it was sent as a sympathy gift to Santa Fe by the Queen of Spain when the town moved. Note also the tomb of Padre Magallanes, a priest who was killed by a jaguar that took refuge in the church when it was driven from the shores of the Paraná during the floods of 1825. The cloister has a carved wooden balustrade and is redolent with the perfume of flowers. The monastery is still home to one monk, who is helped out by a trio of priests.

MUSEO HISTÓRICO PROVINCIAL

In a lovable 17th-century building, this **museum** (☎ 457-3529; Av San Martín 1490; admission AR$1; ♥ 8:30am-7pm Tue-Fri, 3-6pm Sat & Sun Apr-Sep; 8:30am-noon & 3-7:30pm Tue-Fri, 4:30-7:30pm Sat & Sun Oct-Dec, 8:30am-noon & 4:30-8:30pm Tue-Fri, 5:30-8:30pm Sat & Sun Jan-Mar) has a variety of possessions and mementos of various provincial governors and caudillos (provincial strongmen), as well as some religious art and fine period furnishings, including a sedan chair once used to carry around the Viceroy of Río de la Plata.

MUSEO ETNOGRÁFICO Y COLONIAL PROVINCIAL

Run with heartwarming enthusiasm, this **museum** (☎ 457-3550; 25 de Mayo 1470; admission AR$1; ♥ 8:30am-noon & 3:30-8:30pm Tue-Fri, 5:30-8:30pm Sat & Sun mid-Dec–Feb, 8:30am-noon & 2-7pm Tue-Fri, 4-7pm Sat & Sun Mar–mid-Dec) has a chronological display of stone tools, Guaraní ceramics, jewelry, carved bricks and colonial objects. Highlights include a set of *tablas* – a colonial game similar to backgammon – and a scale model of the original Santa Fe.

PLAZA 25 DE MAYO

The center of colonial Santa Fe is a peaceful square framed by many fine buildings. The vast **Casa de Gobierno** (Government House) was built in 1909 and replaced the demolished colonial *cabildo* (town council), seat of the 1852 constitutional assembly. On the square's east side, the exterior simplicity of the Jesuit **Iglesia de la Compañía** masks an ornate interior. Dating from 1696, it's the province's best-preserved colonial church. On the square's north side the city's **catedral** is a little underwhelming by comparison, and dates from the mid-18th century.

GRANJA LA ESMERALDA

Nobody likes to see wild animals locked in confined spaces, but this **experimental zoo** (☎ 457-9202; Av Aristóbulo del Valle 8700; admission AR$5; ♥ 8am-7:30pm Mon-Fri, 10am-7:30pm Sat & Sun) has a wild and woodsy feel to it that makes it stand apart from most other zoos in the country. Provincial native fauna is mainly represented, including toucans, pumas, jaguars and a giant anteater. Many of the animals have been rescued after experiencing problems in the wild. Bus 10 bis, from Av Rivadavia, goes to the farm.

Sleeping

The vaguely seedy area around the bus terminal is the budget hotel zone. It's not dangerous – just the central location for various vice-fuelled transactions. Many hotels offer a discount for cash payment.

Hostel Santa Fe (☎ 455-4000; www.santafe-hostel .com; Blvd Gálvez 2173; dm/d AR$40/120; ▣ ▨) Tucked behind a tour agency called Latitud Sur, this new hostel has two airless but not-too-crowded dorms with lockers, and a private double. There's also a small pool and it's very handy for the Recoleta nightlife.

Hotel Constituyentes (☎ 452-1586; www.hotelcon stituyentes.com.ar; San Luis 2862; s/d with bathroom AR$100/120, without bathroom AR$60/80; ✕ ▣ � 🖵 🛜) Plenty of value is to be had at this relaxed place near the bus terminal. The rooms are spacious with cable TV and blasting hot showers. Rooms at the front suffer from street noise. Breakfast is a few pesos extra.

Hotel Emperatriz (☎ 453-0061; emperatrizhotel@arnet. com.ar; Irigoyen Freyre 2440; s/d AR$102/145; ✕ 🛜) Sipping *mate* (a tea-like drink) and chatting with the courteous old gentleman on the front desk, it's easy to fall in love with this other-era place. It's not luxury, but it's a slice of an Argentina that won't be around in a few years' time.

Hostal Santa Fe de la Veracruz (☎ 455-1740; www .hostalsf.com; Av San Martín 2954; s/d standard AR$169/270, s/d superior AR$235/290; ✕ 🖵 🛜) Decorated with indigenous motifs, this hotel offers spacious superior rooms and decent standards at a fair price. It'll soon be time for redecorating though – those dozen shades of beige are looking a little dated. Siesta fans will love the 6pm checkout.

Hotel Galeón (☎ 454-1788; www.hotelgaleon.com .ar; Belgrano 2759; s/d AR$176/232; ✕ 🖵 🛜) Bright, unusual, and all curved surfaces and weird angles, this cheery place is a breath of fresh air. There's a variety of room types, none of which is a conventional shape; the beds are seriously comfortable and the bathrooms pleasant. It's handy for the bus, too.

Conquistador Hotel (☎ 400-1195; www.lin eaverdedehoteles.com.ar; 25 de Mayo 2676; s/d AR$270/318; ✕ 🖵 🛜 ▣) The Conquistador lays on the charm, with sauna, hydromassage, fluffy bathrobes, gymnasium and a huge buffet breakfast. The beds in the twins and singles are happily queen-sized. The pool is outdoor, so only open in summer. Slightly cheaper rooms at the Hotel España across the road give you access to the same facilities.

Also recommended:

Hotel Royal (☎ 452-7359; Irigoyen Freyre 2256; r without bathroom AR$60) Basic, with gloomy rooms, but it's cheap and near the bus terminal…it'll do for a night.

Hotel Zavaleta (☎ 455-1841; www.zavaletahotel .com.ar; Hipólito Yrigoyen 2349; s/d standard AR$135/180, s/d superior AR$180/216; ✕ 🖵 🛜) Welcoming plazaside hotel near the bus terminal.

Eating

On Belgrano, across from the bus terminal, several very good, inexpensive places serve Argentine staples, such as empanadas, pizza and *parrillada* (mixed grill including steak).

Merengo (☎ 459-3458; Av General López 2634; alfajores from AR$1.50; ⏰ 9am-6pm) Since 1851 little Merengo has been making some of the town's best *alfajores santafesinos* (Santa Fe's sugar-crusted version of the country's favorite snack). There's another branch on Av San Martín.

Las Delicias (☎ 453-2126; Av San Martín 2882; cakes & pastries from AR$2, snacks AR$10-19; ⏰ 8am-midnight) Delightfully old-fashioned and elegant, with a great shady terrace, this bakery offers some of the most sinful pastries and cakes imaginable; it also does breakfast, afternoon tea and sandwiches. Service is traditional and correct.

La Victoria (cnr 25 de Mayo & Santiago del Estero; pizza AR$10-20, all-you-can-eat pizza AR$16.90; ⏰ lunch & 8pm-late) Right in the middle of La Recoleta nightlife district and still pumping at 3am, the Victoria is the place to come before, after or in between bars to have a few drinks and load up on good pizza and snacks.

Club Social Sirio Libanés (25 de Mayo 2740; meals AR$15-30; ⏰ lunch & dinner Tue-Sun) In a rather aristocratic dining room, attentive waiters serve well-prepared Middle Eastern–style dishes; it's a pleasingly unusual place to eat. You enter down the end of a passageway.

Restaurante España (Av San Martín 2644; mains AR$15-46) This hotel restaurant has a huge menu that covers the range of fish (both locally caught and from the sea), steaks, pasta, chicken and crepes, with a few Spanish dishes thrown in to justify the name. The wine list is a winner, too.

Círculo Italiano (☎ 456-3555; Hipólito Yrigoyen 2457; meals AR$20-35; ⏰ lunch & dinner) Part of the Italian social club, Círculo Italiano prepares good, moderately priced lunch specials (AR$25 to AR$30 Monday to Friday) and tasty pasta. Come for the ritzy atmosphere, the waiters in linen jackets, the complimentary pâté or the extensive wine list. Stay for the classic rock on the sound system.

El Brigadier (☎ 458-3367; San Martín 1670; mains AR$20-35; ⏰ lunch & dinner) Half a block from Plaza 25 de Mayo, this refurbished restaurant offers an elegant interior and tasty cuts of meat and river fish that win out, despite a few strange quirks in the service department.

Bodegas del Castelar (☎ 452-2229; Av San Martín 1601; mains AR$25-45; ⏰ lunch & dinner) Run by the upmarket hotel of the same name, this spot appeals for its terrace on the stately Plaza 25 de Mayo – a fine spot for a sunset drink – as well as for its service and pricy but high-quality dishes, which include a couple of fondues (AR$50 to AR$70 for two people) and a copious platter of cheeses and meats (AR$52). Cheaper snacks are also available and there's plenty of wine to try.

El Quincho de Chiquito (☎ 460-2608; cnr Brown & Obispo Vieytes; set menu AR$35; ☒ lunch & dinner) This legendary place is a local institution, and *the* place to go to eat river fish. It's on the *costanera* some 6km north of downtown. There are few frills to the service, and no choice about the menu: four or five courses of delicious surubí, sábalo or pacú are brought out to you. You won't leave hungry. Drinks are extra but cheap. Think AR$10 each way in a taxi (staff will call you one to take you back) or catch bus 16 from any point on the waterfront road.

Drinking & Entertainment

Santa Fe's nightlife centers on the intersection of 25 de Mayo and Santiago del Estero, the heart of the area known as La Recoleta, which goes wild on weekend nights – a crazy contrast to the sedate pace of life downtown. Places change name and popularity rapidly, so just head to the zone and take a look around the dozens of bars and clubs. Many have a cover charge redeemable for a drink. A few are listed here to get you started.

Morrison Bar (25 de Mayo 3426; ☒ from 8pm Wed-Sat) An attractive bar with a popular attached nightclub.

El Sheik (25 de Mayo 3452) Laid-back without being tranquil, this place attracts a young crowd with its cheap drinks and good music.

Passage (☎ 453-3435; Av San Martín 3243; admission AR$5) This venue has been dishing out rock, electronica and Latin grooves for years, and it is still a good place to cut loose.

Suite (25 de Mayo 3249) Trendy lighting design and a roof terrace are the attractions at this handsome preclub venue.

THEATER

Teatro Municipal Primero de Mayo (☎ 459-7777; Av San Martín 2020) Designed in the French neo-renaissance style so common in Argentina at the turn of the 20th century, this theater presents both drama and dance performances.

SPORT

The city's best football team, **Colón** (☎ 459-8025; www.clubcolon.com.ar), is in the top division. It

plays at the **Brigadier Estanislao López stadium** (cnr Dr Zavalla & Pietranera), where you can also pick up tickets.

Getting There & Away

AIR

Aerolíneas Argentinas (☎ 452-5959; 25 de Mayo 2287) has five weekly flights to Buenos Aires (AR$373). **Sol** (☎ 0810-444-4765; www.sol.com.ar) flies the same route Monday to Saturday (AR$290).

BUS

From the **bus terminal** (☎ 457-2490; www.terminalsantafe.com; Belgrano 2940) there are services throughout the country. Following are some sample fares:

Destination	Cost (AR$)	Duration (hr)
Buenos Aires	77	6
Córdoba	63	5
Corrientes	92	9
Mendoza	165	13
Paraná	4	40min
Paso de los Libres	60	9
Posadas	156	14
Resistencia	94	9
Rosario	28	2
Salta	188	16
Tucumán	134	11

Getting Around

Aeropuerto Sauce Viejo (☎ 457-0642) is 7km south of town on RN 11. A *remise* will cost about AR$30. To rent a car, try **Avis** (☎ 458-3123; www.avis.com.ar; 9 de Julio 2003).

CAYASTÁ

A fascinating day trip from Santa Fe takes you to that city's original location, the **Cayastá ruins** (Santa Fe la Vieja; admission AR$1; ☒ 9am-1pm & 2-6pm Tue-Fri, noon-6pm Sat & Sun Apr-Sep, 9am-1pm & 3-7pm Tue-Fri, 10am-1pm & 4-7pm Sat & Sun Oct-Mar), picturesquely set beside the Río San Javier, which has actually eroded away a good portion of them.

There's ongoing archaeological excavation and conservation here (and a campaign for Unesco status underway), but the most fascinating find by far has been the Iglesia de San Francisco. The Spanish and mestizo inhabitants of old Santa Fe were buried directly beneath the earth-floored church, and nearly 100 graves have been excavated, including those of Hernando Arias de Saavedra (known as 'Hernandarias'), the first locally born governor of Río de la Plata province,

EXPLORING SANTA FE PROVINCE

With perhaps a brief stop in Rosario or Santa Fe itself, most travelers bang straight on through this fascinating region, their compass set for attractions further north. If you have more time, however, there are many things worth discovering, all within easy reach by bus or car from Santa Fe.

Some 43km south of the city, **Coronda** is famous for its strawberries *(frutillas)*. There are several places to try and buy, and also a couple of fine river beaches. Further south, at **Puerto Gaboto**, you can see the reasonably conserved remains of the country's oldest Spanish fort, Sancti Spíritu, dating from 1527. It's a few kilometers east of the main road – turn or jump off the bus at Maciel.

Forty kilometers northwest of Santa Fe, the town of **Esperanza** has an interesting history. It was the first of the many planned agricultural colonies that were established in Argentina in the mid-19th century and peopled by immigrants from Central Europe. There's an interesting museum with the story of the settlement. Nearby, **San Carlos Centro** is worth a visit for its bell factory. The bells (mostly for churches) are carefully handcrafted in an intriguing process. Glassware and sweets are also produced in this hardworking community.

West of Esperanza, turn north at the booming town of Rafaela to explore the cheese-making village of **Humberto Primero**, and the Jewish traditions of **Moisés Ville** (see the boxed text, p211). There are hotels in Esperanza and farmstay accommodations available in the area. For details, get in touch with the **provincial tourist office** (☎ 458-9476; www.turismo-santafe.org.ar; cnr Amenábar & Av San Martín; ☀ 7am-6pm Mon & Wed-Thu, 7am-1pm Tue & Fri) in Santa Fe.

and his wife, Gerónima de Contrera, daughter of Juan de Garay, who founded Santa Fe and Buenos Aires.

You can also see the remains of two other churches and the *cabildo*, as well as a reconstructed period house. Near the entrance to the site is an attractive and excellent museum housing the finds from the site, including some fine indigenous pottery with parrot and human motifs.

Last entry is strictly one hour before closing.

There's a mediocre restaurant at the site and a couple of decent *parrillas* in town. Several spots offer simple lodgings and boat trips on the river. **Cabañas Cayastá** (☎ 03405-493300; www .cayasta.com; cabin for 2/4 people AR$200/300; ⊠ ⚎) is a riverside resort offering cabin accommodation and a spa.

Cayastá is 76km northeast of Santa Fe on RP 1. Paraná Medio bus company departs regularly from Santa Fe's bus terminal (AR$14, 1½ hours). Ask the driver to drop you at 'las ruinas', 1km short of Cayastá itself.

PARANÁ

☎ 0343 / pop 247,310

Comfortably down-at-heel and unpretentious, likable Paraná seems surprised at its own status as capital of Entre Ríos province. Perched on the hilly banks of its eponymous

river, it's a sleepy, slow-paced city. The nicest part of town is the riverside where a pretty park slopes down to the *costanera*, where there are beaches, bars, boat trips and hundreds of strollers and joggers. After the defeat of Rosas at the battle of Caseros, Paraná was the capital of the Argentine Confederation (which didn't include Buenos Aires) from 1853 to 1861.

Orientation

Paraná sits on a high bluff on the east bank of the Río Paraná, 500km north of Buenos Aires. A tunnel beneath the main channel of the Paraná connects the city to Santa Fe.

The city plan is more irregular than most Argentine cities, with diagonals and curving boulevards. Plaza 1 de Mayo is the town center and is crossed by the *peatonal* José de San Martín. Street names change on all sides of the plaza. At the northern end of San Martín, more than 1km of riverfront and the bluffs above it have been transformed into the lovely Parque Urquiza.

Information

There are several banks with ATMs within a couple of blocks of Plaza 1 de Mayo.

Hospital San Martín (☎ 423-4545; www.hospitalsan martin.org.ar; Presidente Perón 450)

Lavadero Belgrano (Av Belgrano 306) Laundry.

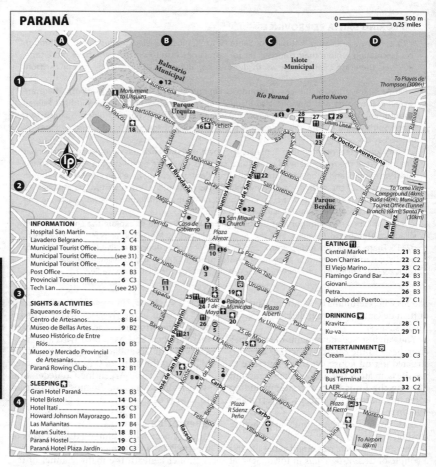

Municipal tourist office (www.turismoenparana.gov
.ar; 8am-8pm) Main office (423-0183; Buenos Aires
132); River branch (420-1837; cnr Av Doctor Laurencena
& José de San Martín); Bus station branch (420-1862; Av
Ramírez 2300) Good brochures and helpful attitude.

Provincial tourist office (422-2100; www.turismo
.entrerios.gov.ar; Laprida 5; 8am-8pm) Don't rely on it
being open. There's another branch by the Santa Fe tunnel.

Tech Lan (Av Urquiza 1071; per hr AR$2.50) One of dozens
offering internet access and phone calls.

Sights & Activities

MUSEO HISTÓRICO DE ENTRE RÍOS

Flaunting local pride, this modern **museum**
(420-7869; Buenos Aires 286; admission AR$2; 8am-
12:30pm & 3-8pm Tue-Fri, 9am-noon & 5-7pm Sat, 9am-noon
Sun) on Plaza Alvear contains information on

the short-lived Republic of Entre Ríos and the
battle of Monte Camperos, as well as *mate*
paraphernalia and numerous solid wooden
desks and portraits of Urquiza. Much of it
was the collection of a local poet.

A small permanent collection of oils, illustrations and sculptures by provincial artists is
complemented by temporary exhibitions at
the **Museo de Bellas Artes** (420-7868; Buenos Aires
355; admission variable; 8am-noon & 4-8pm Tue-Fri, 10am-
noon & 4-7pm Sat, 10am-noon Sun) on Plaza Alvear.

MUSEO Y MERCADO PROVINCIAL DE ARTESANÍAS

Promoting handicrafts from throughout
the province, the **Museo y Mercado Provincial de
Artesanías** (420-8891; Av Urquiza 1239; admission free;

8am-1pm & 4-7pm Mon-Fri, 8am-1pm Sat, 9am-noon Sun) is a likable little place. Ask the curator to explain things to you; you'll be amazed at the intricacy of some of the work, like the hats made from tightly woven palm fibers. In December there are folk music performances in the garden.

Similar traditional *artesanías* (handicrafts) are on display and sale at the **Centro de Artesanos** (☎ 422-4493; cnr Av 9 de Julio & Carbó; 5-9pm in summer, 9am-noon & 4-8pm rest of year).

RIVER ACTIVITIES

From the northern edge of downtown, Parque Urquiza slopes steeply downward to the banks of the Río Paraná. During the summer months the waterfront fills with people strolling, fishing and swimming. Beware of *jejenes* (biting insects) in summer.

There's a stretch of beach west of the **Paraná Rowing Club** (☎ 431-2048) at which, for AR$40 per day, you can access facilities, including a private beach, swimming pool and showers (AR$5 for beach only). There's also a cafe-restaurant on the water.

A better beach, **Playas de Thompson**, is 1km further east, beyond the port.

Various operators offer boat trips, but the best is **Baqueanos del Río** (☎ 423-4893, 0343-15-611-2170), which offers excursions in wooden boats and knows a hell of a lot about the river and its ecosystem. Ring or email to book a trip (AR$20 per hour). Boats leave from the eastern end of the *costanera*, by the tourist office. **Paraná en Kayak** (☎ 422-7143; www.paranaenkayak .ar) offers easy kayak trips on the river.

Festivals & Events

Every February Paraná hosts the **Fiesta Nacional de Música y Artesanía Entrerriana**, featuring regional folk music and crafts.

Sleeping

Paraná Hostel (☎ 422-8233; www.paranahostel.com .ar; Pazos 159; dm/d/q AR$39/90/160;) The mix of centrality and tranquility (when the disco nearby isn't pumping) is great at this relocated hostel, which offers a tree-shaded back patio and garden as well as smart furnishings, good facilities and comfy dorms. The rate includes breakfast, kitchen, *mate* and internet.

Hotel Itatí (☎ 423-1500; hoteles_itati@hotmail .com; Belgrano 135; s/d AR$55/85;) Welcoming management make up for the worn carpets and ageing sheets at this curiously designed budget hotel. Heating costs a little extra, as does internet use. The dark rooms are fine for the price, with tiny bathrooms.

our pick **Las Mañanitas** (☎ 421-8324; www.lasma nianitas.com.ar; Carbó 62; s/d AR$100/130;) There's a summer-house feel about this delightfully relaxed little place, which has nine rooms alongside a courtyard and garden with pool. The rooms are unremarkable but well priced, but it's the light style and grace of the whole ensemble that makes this a winner.

Gran Hotel Paraná (☎ 422-3900; www.hotelesparana .com.ar; Av Urquiza 976; s AR$150-280, d AR$200-350;) Fine service is a major plus at this large hotel on the main square. Bypass the unremarkable standards for a 'plus' room or the newly refurbished superior rooms, which are much bigger. If you don't mind a bit of traffic noise, try for a room with a balcony on the square. There's a health spa and a high-quality restaurant. The breakfast buffet is rocking.

Paraná Hotel Plaza Jardín (☎ 423-1700; www .hotelesparana.com.ar; Av 9 de Julio 60; r standard/superior AR$175/225;) Set in a lovely old colonial building, this hotel has a peaceful patio that's great for a break from the midday heat. The superior rooms are much more spacious and stylish, and worth the upgrade. It's significantly cheaper outside of summer.

Maran Suites (☎ 423-5444; www.maran.com.ar; cnr Av Rivadavia & Blvd Bartolomé Mitre; s AR$295, d AR$395-440;) Towering over the western end of Parque Urquiza, this sleek modern hotel has a rare combination of style and warmhearted personal service. Try to get a room as high as possible for city or river views. All the rooms are very spacious and decorated with flair; the 'presidential' suites (AR$978) are big enough to get lost in and boast a Jacuzzi with memorable vistas over the water.

Also recommended:

Toma Vieja Campground (☎ 433-1721; Av Blas Parera; campsites AR$10) Scenic site of the old waterworks overlooking the river. Take bus 5 from the bus terminal or bus 1 from the plaza.

Hotel Bristol (☎ 431-3961; bristolpna@yahoo.com .ar; Alsina 221; s/d with bathroom AR$65/105, without bathroom AR$45/65;) Right by the bus terminal. Well kept and quiet.

Howard Johnson Mayorazgo (☎ 420-6800; www .hjmayorazgo.com.ar; Etchevehere s/n; r AR$360-400;) The long curved facade of this remodeled five-star dominates the waterfront from above. Great views from large windows and a casino.

Eating

The **central market** (cnr Carlos Pellegrini & Bavio) is good to buy food in the morning.

Flamingo Grand Bar (☎ 431-1711; cnr Urquiza & José de San Martín; light meals AR$10-20; ◷ 8am-10pm) Smart seats and a plaza-side location make this a favorite throughout the day, from morning croissants and juices through to *lomitos* (steak sandwiches) and lunch specials to decent à la carte plates and *picadas* (shared appetizer plate).

El Viejo Marino (☎ 432-9767; Av Doctor Laurencena 341; mains AR$15-25; ◷ lunch & dinner Wed-Mon) There's an uncomplicated, brightly lit and cheery atmosphere under the thatched roof at this restaurant near the river. It offers *milanesas* (breaded fish cutlets) and the like, river fish both filleted and whole, and a *parrillada* for AR$26 that'll feed two.

Giovani (☎ 423-0527; Av Urquiza 1045; pasta AR$9-20, mains AR$19-40; ◷ lunch & dinner) With as-it-should-be service and thoughtful touches like free coffee, this stylish restaurant in the center of town serves excellent meats from the *parrilla* and delectable pasta. Fish isn't such a strong point.

Quincho del Puerto (☎ 423-2045; Av Doctor Laurencena 350, fish AR$20-33; ◷ lunch & dinner Tue-Sun) This is a popular spot for river fish just back from the *costanera*. There are various options, including the tasty (but bony) pacú and surubí.

Petra (☎ 423-0608; 25 de Mayo 32; lunch/dinner AR$23/24; ◷ lunch & dinner) With a huge range of mostly Chinese food on offer, this redoubtable all-you-can-eat joint sits on the square. The standard is quite a lot better than you might expect – it's rather a bargain. Drinks not included.

Don Charras (☎ 425-5972; cnr José de San Martín & San Lorenzo; mains AR$25-39; ◷ lunch & dinner Tue-Sun) Thatched and atmospheric, this *parrilla* is a popular Paraná choice. Fridays and Saturdays see fire-roasted lamb, goat and beef, but you can enjoy the usual char-grilled selection and solicitous service otherwise.

Drinking & Entertainment

Paraná is very quiet midweek, but things get busier on Friday and Saturday nights. Most of the action is at the eastern end of the riverfront, by the port. Here, **Kravitz** (www.kravitz dance.com.ar; Figueroa s/n; ◷ 11pm-late Fri & Sat) plays the usual mix of mainstream *marcha*, house and salsa. Nearby, **Ku-va** (cnr Güemes & Liniers Lineal; ◷ 8pm-late Tue-Sun) offers plenty of atmosphere in an attractive old post office building. At **Cream** (www.creamparana.com.ar; Uruguay 190; ◷ Thu-Sat), you'll feel ancient if you're over 30.

Getting There & Around

AIR

The airport is 6km south of town, accessible only by *remise* (AR$25). **LAER** (☎ 0810-777-5237; www.laersa.com.ar; José de San Martín 918) flies to Buenos Aires on weekdays.

BUS

The **bus terminal** (☎ 422-1282; Av Ramírez) is opposite Plaza Martín Fierro. Buses 1, 4, 5 and 9 run between the terminal and the town center for AR$1.75. Paraná is a hub for provincial bus services, but Santa Fe is more convenient for long-distance trips. Buses leave every 30 minutes for Santa Fe (AR$4, 40 minutes).

Destinations include the following:

Destination	Cost (AR$)	Duration (hr)
Buenos Aires	77	6½
Colón	39	4-5
Concordia	42	4-5
Córdoba	66	6
Corrientes	96	10
Gualeguaychú	39	4-5
Paso de los Libres	60	6
Rosario	32	3

CORRIENTES

☎ 03783 / pop 316,782

Stately Corrientes sits below the confluence of the Paraná and Paraguay rivers just across the water from its twin city, Resistencia. One of the nation's most venerable cities, dignified Corrientes has elegant balconied buildings dating from the turn of the 20th century that lend a timeworn appeal to its colorful streets. Like many such cities, the *costanera* is everybody's destination of choice for strolling, licking ice creams or sipping *mate* with friends.

The city is famous for both its Carnaval, which attracts big crowds to its colorful parades, and for being the setting of Graham Greene's novel *The Honorary Consul*.

Corrientes is a magnet for regional indigenous crafts, which artisans sell in the evening on Plaza JB Cabral and in the Museo de Artesanías. Guaraní culture has a strong presence.

Corrientes was originally called Vera de los Siete Corrientes, after its founder Juan Torres de Vera y Aragón and the shifting *corrientes* (currents) of the Paraná. During colonial times Corrientes suffered repeated indigenous uprisings before establishing itself as the first Spanish settlement in the region.

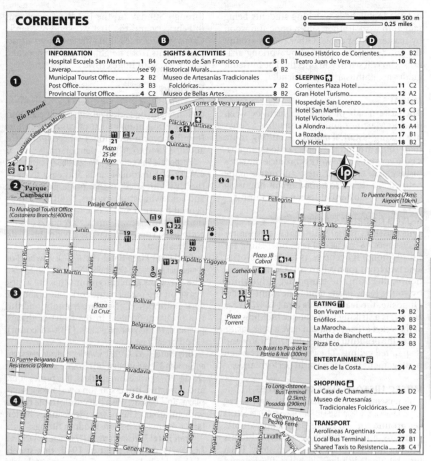

CORRIENTES

INFORMATION	
Hospital Escuela San Martín......	**1** B4
Laverap...................................(see 9)	
Municipal Tourist Office	**2** B2
Post Office.................................	**3** B3
Provincial Tourist Office............	**4** C2

SIGHTS & ACTIVITIES	
Convento de San Francisco	**5** B1
Historical Murals........................	**6** B2
Museo de Artesanías Tradicionales	
Folclóricas............................	**7** B2
Museo de Bellas Artes................	**8** B2

Museo Histórico de Corrientes................	**9** B2
Teatro Juan de Vera............................	**10** B2

SLEEPING	
Corrientes Plaza Hotel	**11** C2
Gran Hotel Turismo	**12** A2
Hospedaje San Lorenzo	**13** C3
Hotel San Martín	**14** C3
Hotel Victoria.....................................	**15** C3
La Alondra	**16** A4
La Rozada	**17** B1
Orly Hotel...	**18** B2

EATING	
Bon Vivant	**19** B2
Enófilos	**20** B3
La Marocha	**21** B2
Martha de Bianchetti	**22** B2
Pizza Eco	**23** B3

ENTERTAINMENT	
Cines de la Costa	**24** A2

SHOPPING	
La Casa de Chamamé..................	**25** D2
Museo de Artesanías	
Tradicionales Folclóricas........(see 7)	

TRANSPORT	
Aerolíneas Argentinas	**26** B2
Local Bus Terminal	**27** B1
Shared Taxis to Resistencia......	**28** C4

NORTHEAST ARGENTINA

Orientation

Corrientes has a regular grid, but the center is more spread out than in most Argentine cities. Plaza 25 de Mayo, near the river and its lively *costanera*, is one of the two main squares; the other is Plaza JB Cabral, from which the *peatonal* along Junín, the main shopping street, heads westwards for six blocks. On the west side of town, Puente Belgrano crosses the Río Paraná to Resistencia.

Information

Locutorios and internet places are easy to find. There are many banks with ATMs on 9 de Julio between La Rioja and Córdoba.

Hospital Escuela San Martín (☎ 420697; Av 3 de Abril 1251)

Laverap (Pasaje González 1071) Laundry.

Municipal tourist office (☎ 474733; www.ciudad decorrientes.gov.ar; bus terminal; ☻ 7am-10pm) Other branches at the corner of Junín and San Juan, and on the Costanera at the end of Junín.

Provincial tourist office (☎ 427200; www.corrientes turistica.gov.ar; 25 de Mayo 1330; ☻ 7am-9pm Mon-Fri, 8am-8pm Sat & Sun)

Sights

MUSEO DE ARTESANÍAS TRADICIONALES FOLCLÓRICAS

This intriguing **museum** (Quintana 905; admission free; ☻ 8am-9pm Mon-Sat) is set in a converted colonial house with an interior courtyard. There are two small displays of fine traditional *artesanía* as well as a good shop selling craft products, but the highlight is watching students being taught to work leather, silver, bone and wood by master craftspeople. Other rooms around the courtyard are occupied by working artisans who will sell to you directly. The museum guides are enthusiastic and friendly.

MURALS

The eastern side of Calle San Juan, between Plácido Martínez and Quintana, has a series of striking **historical murals**, extending more than 100m around the corner onto Quintana. These very attractive works chronicle the city's history since colonial times – full marks to the council. There's also a monument honoring Corrientes' substantial Italian community.

MUSEO DE BELLAS ARTES

This **museum** (☎ 436722; San Juan 634; admission free; ✆ 9am-noon & 6-9pm Tue-Sat) is as interesting for the old house it occupies as for the artworks. The two front rooms have an eclectic permanent collection; the temporary exhibitions by young local artists tend to be avant-garde. Opposite, the **Teatro Juan de Vera** (☎ 427743; San Juan 637) is a striking belle epoque building; ask at the ticket office if you can have a peek inside to see the beautiful treble-galleried theater and its painted ceiling. The cupola retracts when management fancies a starlit performance.

MUSEO HISTÓRICO DE CORRIENTES

This **museum** (☎ 475916; 9 de Julio 1044; admission free; ✆ 8am-noon & 4-8pm Tue-Fri, 9am-noon & 4-7pm Sat) is set around an attractive patio and exhibits weapons, antique furniture, coins and items dealing with religious and civil history. It's a little bit higgledy-piggledy, but staff are proud of the exhibition and keen to chat. The room on the War of the Triple Alliance is the most interesting.

CONVENTO DE SAN FRANCISCO

This colonial **monastery** (Mendoza 450) dates from the city's founding, and was beautifully restored in 1939. The small colonnade is modelled on Bernini's at St Peter's in Rome, and the monastery has its own museum, the **Museo Francisco** (☎ 422936; admission free; ✆ 8am-noon & 5-9pm Mon-Fri), with religious art and artefacts.

Festivals & Events

Corrientes' traditionally riotous **Carnaval Correntino** competes with Gualeguaychú's for the title of the country's best. Celebrated Friday through Sunday on the last three weekends in February and the first weekend of March, Carnaval's parades along the *costanera* attract participants from neighboring provinces and countries, with huge crowds.

Sleeping

Corrientes has comparatively few accommodations. During Carnaval, the provincial tourist office maintains a list of *casas de familia* (family accommodations) where lodging is about AR$40 to AR$50 per person.

Hospedaje San Lorenzo (☎ 421740; San Lorenzo 1136; d AR$90; ✖) Inconspicuous and easy to miss, the tiny entrance to this place guards bare and somewhat stuffy rooms, but it's in a good central location and is one of few budget options. It's not sleazy, but it's a rendezvous for couples so rooms all have saggy double beds. No breakfast.

Corrientes Plaza Hotel (☎ 466500; www.hotel-corrientes.com.ar; Junín 1549; s/d AR$170/250; ✖ ▢ 🛜 ▧) The Plaza has generous rooms that are a little heavy on the pastel paintwork, but otherwise very commodious. Staff are friendly, and this is a pretty good deal in the heart of things, particularly if you pay cash (10% discount). Good breakfast.

Orly Hotel (☎ 420280; www.hotelorlycorrientes.com.ar; San Juan 867; s/d standard AR$172/222, r superior AR$352; ✖ ▢ 🛜) Spruce and spotless, this professional and attractive three-star job overlooks a small plaza, and has smallish but comfortable rooms with minibar. The new wing features better, larger rooms with more modern fittings.

Gran Hotel Turismo (☎ 433174; Entre Ríos 650; s/d AR$180/210; ✖ ▧) Built in 1948, this stately old hotel is in low-slung Californian style and has an attractive restaurant, a large pool, a bar and an excellent riverside location. The rooms are slightly worn, but it's a charming old place and a lot more atmospheric than most other hotels in town.

Hotel San Martín (☎ 421061; hsanmartin@impsat1.com.ar; Santa Fe 955; s/d AR$185/230; ✖ ▢ 🛜) Right on Plaza JB Cabral, this place has reasonable rooms with excellent showers. Though no rooms face over the plaza, each floor has a shared balcony where you can sit and watch things going on down below. The hotel lets itself down with small meannesses: breakfast costs extra, and you virtually need a retina scan to get the remote for the TV from reception.

La Alondra (☎ 430555; www.laalondra.com.ar; Av 3 de Abril 827; tw/ste AR$544/726; ✖ 🛜 ▧) Sumptuously furnished with dark-wood antiques, this wonderfully renovated house is an oasis of relaxation from the unappealing main road. Most of the seven rooms that surround a small finger-shaped pool are suites boasting plush king-sized beds and characterful bathrooms fitted with claw-foot tubs. Wonderfully handsome public areas and classy service add up to a most impressive package. There are often deals below the above prices.

Also recommended:

Hotel Victoria (☎ 435547; hotelvictoria1@hotmail .com; Av España 1050; s/d AR$115/130; ✂ ▯ ☞) One of two decent adjacent budget choices near Plaza JB Cabral.

La Rozada (☎ 433001; www.larozada.com; Plácido Martínez 1223; r AR$385; ✂ ▯ ☞) Handsome, artistic rooms and duplex apartments make this an intriguing new option in a battleship-gray historical building near the riverfront.

Eating

Look out for *mbaipú*, a traditional *correntino* dish of fried beef and onions topped with toasted flour and cheese.

Martha de Bianchetti (☎ 423008; cnr 9 de Julio & Mendoza; pastries from AR$3; ✇ 8am-1pm & 4-11pm Mon-Sat) An old-fashioned, Italian-style bakery and cafe, this serves mind-altering pastries and excellent coffee; each cup comes with *chipacitos* (small cheese pastries). All the yummy treats are warm when the doors open.

Pizza Eco (☎ 425900; Hipólito Yrigoyen 1108; pizza AR$12-26; ✇ 7am-1pm & 5pm-3am) Both the atmosphere and the pizza rate well at this friendly spot, tucked in an attractive corner building. The tasty empanadas are also worthy of praise.

Bon Vivant (☎ 467902; Junín 918; mains AR$13-32; ✇ lunch & dinner) After the fierce heat of the *cor-*

rentino day, it's great to be able to eat outside once the sun goes down. With a terrace in the middle of the *peatonal*, good steaks, pizza, warm service and more-than-fair prices, this place does the trick. It's also popular with young locals for a beer.

La Marocha (☎ 438699; cnr Salta & Quintana; meals AR$15-30; ✇ lunch & dinner) This cute little restaurant-bar right on Plaza 25 de Mayo has a wider-than-normal selection of salads, meat dishes and some excellent daily specials. Also a good range of wines and cocktails.

ourpick Enófilos (☎ 439271; Junín 1260; mains AR$25-45; ✇ lunch & dinner Mon-Sat) An *enófilo* is a wine-lover, so the cellar gets plenty of attention at this attentive upstairs restaurant on the *peatonal*. The wine 'list' is displayed in a small temple at the room's center; traditional *correntino* ingredients like succulent surubí river fish are given creative flair, and fine cuts of meat are showcased to great advantage with exquisite sauces and fresh vegetables. It's a great place to get off the pizza, pasta and *parrilla* treadmill. There's a set menu available on weekdays for AR$50.

Drinking & Entertainment

The area near the intersection of Junín and Buenos Aires has several bars and clubs pumping along at weekends. The *costanera* also sees some action, with several bars and *boliches* (nightclubs) in the new Costanera Sur zone south of the bridge to Resistencia.

Puente Pexoa (☎ 451687; RN 12 at Virgen de Itatí roundabout; ✇ from 8:30pm Fri & Sat) Corrientes is the heartland of the lively music and dance known as *chamamé* (see the boxed text, below), and seeing a live performance is memorable. This relaxed restaurant features *chamamé* dances

---

CHAMAMÉ

Tango? What's that? Up here they dance the *chamamé*, one of the country's most intoxicating musical forms. Rooted in the polka, which was introduced by European immigrants, it is also heavily influenced by the music and language of the indigenous Guaraní. Its definitive sound is the accordion, which is traditionally accompanied by the guitar, the *guitarrón* (an oversized guitar used for playing bass lines), the larger *bandoneón* (accordion) and the *contrabajo* (double bass). Of course, a *conjunto* (band) is hardly complete without a singer or two.

Chamamé is as much a dance as it is a musical genre, and it's a lively one. It is a dance for a couple, except when the man takes his solo *zapateo* (folkloric tap dance). Corrientes province is the heart of *chamamé* and is therefore the easiest place to find a live performance. Sitting in on an evening of music and dancing – or taking to the floor if you're brave – is one of the joys unique to the province.

Check out the Spanish-only website www.corrienteschamame.com for details of performances, and online tunes to introduce you to the genre.

every weekend and it can be outrageous fun when the dancing starts. Men and women show up in full gaucho regalia, and up to four *conjuntos* (bands) may play each night, usually starting around 11pm. A taxi costs around AR$25 or grab bus 102.

Cines de la Costa (☎ 460360; cnr 25 de Mayo & Av Costanera General San Martín) A cinema in the casino complex on the *costanera*, it shows both Hollywood hits and alternative choices.

Shopping

Museo de Artesanías Tradicionales Folclóricas (Quintana 905; ⌚ 8am-noon & 4-9pm Mon-Sat) The shop attached to this museum sells a wide range of traditional handicrafts.

La Casa de Chamamé (Pellegrini 1790) This CD shop specializes in Corrientes' roots music, plus you can listen before you buy.

Getting There & Away

AIR

Aerolíneas Argentinas (☎ 428678; Junín 1301) flies to Buenos Aires daily (AR$577), and three times weekly to Asunción (AR$1179), Paraguay. It also flies to both destinations from nearby Resistencia.

BUS & TRAIN

The **long-distance bus terminal** (Av Maipú, btwn Manatiales & Nicaragua) is 3km east of the center. Nearby Resistencia has better long-distance bus connections to the west and northwest (see p237). Buses to Resistencia (AR$2.50, 40 minutes) leave frequently from the **local bus terminal** (cnr Av Costanera General San Martín & La Rioja). Faster are the shared taxis that zip you into Resistencia for AR$3. They leave from the same intersection, and also from the corner of Av 3 de Abril and Santa Fe. Minibuses to Paso de la Patria (AR$6) and Itatí (AR$12) leave from behind the market at the corner of Belgrano and Roca. Sample destinations and fares:

Destination	Cost (AR$)	Duration (hr)
Buenos Aires	165	12
Concordia	89	7
Córdoba	140	14
Mercedes	30	3½
Paraná	98	10
Paso de los Libres	44	6
Posadas	55	4
Puerto Iguazú	100	9
Rosario	118	12
Salta	130	14
Santa Fe	98	9

Getting Around

Local bus 105 (AR$1.75) goes to the **airport** (☎ 458684), about 10km east of town on RN 12. Bus 6 runs between the local bus terminal and the long-distance bus terminal on Av Maipú. Bus 103 connects the long-distance bus terminal with downtown; a taxi will cost AR$12 to AR$15.

AROUND CORRIENTES
Paso de la Patria
☎ 09783 / pop 3498

This humid but appealingly laid-back town stretches along the Río Paraná 38km northeast of Corrientes. A popular summer and weekend destination, the town's raison d'être is fishing: the annual **Fiesta Internacional del Dorado**, in mid-August, centers on a two-day competition for the carnivorous dorado, known as the 'tiger of the Paraná' for its fighting nature.

The **tourist office** (☎ 494400; www.pasodelapa triaturismoypesca.com; 25 de Mayo 425; ⌚ 7am-9pm) can arrange river trips and accommodation. A whole day fishing with everything included costs around AR$250 to AR$350 for two people; an hour's boat trip leaving the finned tribes unmolested costs about AR$25. The best accommodation choice is one of the many houses available for rent (by the day or week). Prices start at AR$100 per day for a small house. There are several well-equipped campgrounds and hotels, often booked out by large fishing parties.

Buses run every two hours to and from Corrientes (AR$4, one hour). Two operators, **Silvitur** (☎ 494260; Espana 926) and **Mir** (☎ 494654; Rioja & 12 Octubre) run hourly minibuses (AR$6, 40 minutes), which will pick you up and drop you off where you please. It's worth booking ahead. In Corrientes, these leave from the corner of Belgrano and Roca. A taxi from Corrientes to Paso is AR$55.

Itatí

One of Argentina's most revered figures, the **Virgin of Itatí**, resides 68km from Corrientes, beyond Paso de la Patria. Tradition has it that the figure was found by a group of Guaraní in 1615 atop a pillar of stone, accompanied by otherworldly light and music; a mission was built on the spot. Others say the wooden figure was sculpted by Guaraní at the mission. However she came to be, she's now visited by up to two million people a year and has her home in a massive **basilica**, completed in 1950. It's quite a surreal sight in this remote riverside spot. There are numerous pilgrimages by different groups throughout the year. It's worth being here on July 9, when pilgrims arrive in horses and carts from San Luis del Palmar. Regular minibuses (AR$12, one hour) run to Itatí from the corner of Belgrano and Roca in Corrientes.

PARQUE NACIONAL MBURUCUYÁ
☎ 03782

Well off the beaten track, this **national park** (☎ 498907; informesmburucuya@apn.gov.ar) lies about 180km southeast of Corrientes. It belongs to the same ecoregion as the Esteros del Iberá, and although visitor services are nowhere near as advanced, it offers greater biodiversity.

The park holds three natural regions: the Chaco, characterized by palm, carob and quebracho forests, pastures and riverine estuaries; the Paraná Forest, with magote islands, pindó palms and tacuarazú cane; and the Spinal Zone, with its xerófilo forests, yatay palms and grasslands. There is an abundance of fauna: 150 species of birds have been spotted, as well as capybaras, caimans, foxes, swamp deer and the near-extinct maned wolf.

At present there are only two walking trails within the park. The **Sendero Yatay** passes through 2.5km of forests and grassland dotted with yatay palms to a lookout point on the Estero Santa Lucía. The **Sendero Aguará Popé** has explanatory signs along its 1.2km length as it winds through a variety of environments and crosses a small creek where caimans are often spotted.

The **visitor center** (🕑 9am-5pm) is 9km into the park. Both trails leave from near here.

Sleeping & Eating
Camping is the only option within the park itself. There's a small, rustic **campground** (campsites free) with toilets and drinking water next to the visitor center. In Mburucuyá, 12km west of the park, there are simple places to stay and eat, as well as a small supermarket and a *chamamé* museum.

Getting There & Away
There are four daily buses from Corrientes to the town of Mburucuyá (AR$20, three hours). There, *remises* congregate on the plaza. The half-hour trip to the visitor center will cost

around AR$50, or a little more if you want the driver to wait while you walk the trails. Take note that the access road to the park is unpaved, sandy and often impassable after heavy rains, even in a 4WD. Call the visitor center first to check on conditions.

MERCEDES
☎ 03773 / pop 30,961

The main access point for the spectacular Esteros del Iberá wetlands, Mercedes is a handsome gaucho town with a mighty easy pace to life. Its claim to fame is the nearby – and utterly surreal – roadside shrine to the gaucho Antonio Gil, an enormously popular religious phenomenon (see the boxed text, p200), 9km west of town.

There's an irregularly attended tourist information office at the bus terminal. The town's HI hostel also runs a helpful **information booth** (🕑 9-11am & 3:30-7pm) there. If it's closed, head to the hostel itself.

There are several telephone and internet places near the plaza, and various banks with ATMs.

Sleeping & Eating
Delicias del Iberá (☎ 423167; www.deliciasdelibera .com; Rivas 688; dm/s/d AR$43/80/120; 🖫) Two blocks north of the plaza, this warmly welcoming hostel is a valuable fount of information about the reserve, whether or not you are staying here. The comfortable and quiet dorms and rooms face a central patio, and there's a grassy garden out the back, past the kitchen. The hostel will pay your taxi from the bus terminal, where it also maintains an information office. There's 20% off for HI members.

Hotel Itá Pucú (☎ 421015; Batalla de Salta 647; r per person AR$50; 🖫) Two blocks east of the plaza, this friendly low-roofed hotel has a sort of spaghetti-western feel, and OK rooms that open onto a grassy garden. Breakfast is extra.

Hotel Sol (☎ 420283; San Martín 519; s/d AR$80/120; 🖫 🖀) Round the corner from the Itá Pucú, this welcoming spot has good rooms for the price, but the highlight is the stunning patio: a riot of plants, birdsong and gleaming chessboard tiles.

Mercedes Gran Hotel (☎ 421820; mercedesgra nhotel@fibertel.com.ar; Guazú 750; s/d AR$100/190; 🖫) This once-appealing place on the north side of town has gone to the dogs recently. Nonetheless, it's still technically Mercedes' best. Smallish rooms are redeemed by big

---

'GAUCHITO' GIL

Spend time on the road anywhere in Argentina and you're bound to see at least one roadside shrine surrounded by red flags and votive offerings. These shrines pay homage to Antonio Gil, a Robin Hood–like figure whose shrine and burial place just out of Mercedes attracts tens of thousands of pilgrims every year.

Little is known for sure about 'El Gauchito,' as he is affectionately known, but many romantic tales have sprung up to fill the gaps. What is known is that he was born in 1847 and joined the army – some versions say to escape the wrath of a local policeman whose fiancée had fallen in love with him – to fight in the War of the Triple Alliance.

Once the war ended, Gil was called up to join the Federalist Army, but went on the run with a couple of other deserters. The trio roamed the countryside, stealing cattle from rich landowners and sharing it with poor villagers, who in turn gave them shelter and protection. The law finally caught up with the gang, and Gil was hung by the feet from the espinillo tree that still stands near his grave, and beheaded.

So how did this freeloading, cattle-rustling deserter attain saintlike status? Moments before his death, Gil informed his executioner that the executioner's son was gravely ill. He told the soldier that if he were buried – not the custom with deserters – the man's son would recover.

After lopping off Gil's head, the executioner carried it back to the town of Goya where a judicial pardon awaited Gil. On finding that his son was indeed seriously ill, the soldier returned to the site and buried the body. His son recovered quickly, word spread and a legend was born.

'Gauchito' Gil's last resting place is now the site of numerous chapels and storehouses holding thousands of votive offerings – including T-shirts, bicycles, pistols, knives, license plates, photographs, cigarettes, hair clippings and entire racks of wedding gowns – brought by those who believe in the gaucho's miracles. January 8, the date of Gil's death, attracts the most pilgrims. If you are driving past, the story goes that you must sound your horn or suffer long delays on the road – or, more ominously, never arrive at all.

---

balconies and leafy, quiet grounds. Apparently the pool was too much trouble to maintain and is out of use.

Sabor Único (☎ 420314; San Martín 1240; mains AR$12-28; ☀ lunch & dinner) Just about the town's best eating option, this offers several usual favorites as well as a couple of more typical *correntino* dishes.

Getting There & Away

The **bus terminal** (☎ 420165; cnr San Martín & Perreyra) is six blocks west of the plaza. Buses run regularly both ways. Destinations include Buenos Aires (AR$135, nine hours), Paso de los Libres (AR$12 to AR$20, three hours), Resistencia (AR$32, four hours) and Corrientes (AR$30, 3½ hours).

For information about transport to Colonia Pellegrini and the Esteros del Iberá, see p203.

RESERVA PROVINCIAL ESTEROS DEL IBERÁ

This stunning wetland reserve is home to an abundance of bird and animal life, and is one of the finest places to see wildlife in South America. Although tourism has been increasing substantially in recent years, Esteros del Iberá remains comparatively unspoiled. The main base for visiting the park is the sleepy village of **Colonia Pellegrini**, 120km northeast of Mercedes; it offers a variety of excellent accommodations and trips to the reserve. Rural *estancias* (ranches) in the larger area also make excellent bases.

The lakes and *esteros* (estuary) are shallow, fed only by rainwater, and thick with vegetation. Water plants and other vegetation accumulate to form *embalsados* (dense floating islands), and this fertile habitat is home to a stunning array of life. Sinister black caimans bask in the sun while busy capybaras (see the boxed text, p74) feed around them. Other mammals include the beautiful orange-colored marsh deer, howler monkeys (officially the world's noisiest animal), the rare maned wolf, coypu, otters and several species of bat.

There are some 350 species of bird present in the reserve, including colorful kingfishers, delicate hummingbirds, parrots, spoonbills, kites, vultures, several species of egret and heron (including the magnificent rufescent tiger-heron), cormorants, ducks, cardinals and the enormous southern screamer, which would really light up Big Uncle Bob's eyes at a Christmas roast. *Ibera: Vida y Color* (AR$20), on sale at La Cabaña, among other places, has beautiful photos of most of the birds, plants and animals you may see.

Information

The enthusiastic **municipal tourist office** (🕑 7:30am-7:30pm) is at the entrance to the village, after crossing the causeway en route from Mercedes, and it's the best source of general information. The reserve's **visitors center** (🕑 7:30am-noon & 2-6pm), on the Mercedes side of the causeway, has an exhibition, audiovisual presentation and short paths.

Note that as yet there is no bank or ATM in Colonia Pellegrini, so take plenty of cash. Internet access is currently limited to the more expensive lodgings.

Activities & Tours

The best way to appreciate the area is by boat. The classic trip is a two- to 2½-hour excursion in a *lancha* (small passenger motorboat; AR$60 to AR$80), which takes you around the Laguna Iberá and its *embalsados*. You'll see myriad bird and animal life, elegant lilies, water hyacinths and other aquatic plants. There are abundant caimans and capybaras, and you also may see deer, otters, coypu and howler monkeys. Birdlife includes cormorants, grebes, herons, egret, rails, kingfishers and ducks. The guide will punt you remarkably close to the creatures. You can also take a night trip; go prepared with plenty of insect repellent!

The short path opposite the visitors center gives you a sporting chance of seeing howler monkeys up close, and their other paths introduce you to the different plants and habitats of the area. Longer, guided walks are available, as are horseback rides (AR$40), although these are more for the ride's sake than for wildlife spotting. Several of the lodges offer a *día del campo* – a day's excursion to a ranch that incorporates horseback riding, an *asado* and other gaucho pursuits.

The Laguna Iberá is only a small part of the 13,000-sq-km area of the Esteros. Some 80km north, at Galarza, is the Laguna Galarza and the larger Laguna de Luna, which also can be explored by boat.

Many of the lodges can organize these activities; if you are staying at one they are usually included in the price. If not, there are many other options. Organize boat trips at the campsite (from where most trips leave). There are several local, independent guides in town; the tourist office has a list. Note that few guides speak English; if you want an English-speaking guide, it's best to go through one of the lodges.

NORTHEAST ARGENTINA

ECOLOGICAL ISSUES IN THE IBERÁ

With increasingly unpredictable weather systems assailing Argentina's pasturelands, it will come as no surprise to learn that the wildlife-rich wetlands of the Esteros del Iberá are under threat from a variety of sources. At times in Argentina, water is at a premium, but illegal pumping to irrigate farmland may be the least of the area's problems.

The Esteros have a delicate ecosystem, and environmentalists are understandably anxious that it not be harmed. To this end, US entrepreneur Doug Tompkins has been buying up large tracts of land around the reserve and proposes to donate them to the Argentine government if it guarantees national park status for the area.

But many locals, as well as feeling shorn of traditional access and irrigation rights by Tompkins' purchases, feel that foreign interest has a more sinister purpose. For under this part of northern Argentina – and extending into Brazil, Uruguay and Paraguay – is the Guaraní Aquifer, an immense body of underground fresh water that, with drinking water likely to become an increasingly valuable global resource, is becoming an issue of major political importance. Nationalistic Argentines (and there are plenty of those) feel that this aquifer may eventually help put the nation back in a significant position on the global stage and (understandably, given South America's deplorable history of outside exploitation) view with suspicion the meddling of other nations. It's hard to feel optimistic for the future of the capybaras and caimans once interests such as this are involved.

Check out www.theconservationlandtrust.org for Tompkins' position and www.salvemosalibera. org, in Spanish, for current water-theft issues.

Sleeping

COLONIA PELLEGRINI

Colonia Pellegrini's accommodations are mushrooming, with more than 20 at last count. They are divided between *hospedajes*, usually simple rooms behind a family home, and posadas (inns) or *hosterías*, comfortable lodges that offer full-board rates, always including three meals a day plus afternoon tea. Most offer two free excursions daily, and provide bikes, canoes or kayaks for guests' use. All can book a transfer from Mercedes or Posadas for you.

Camping Iberá (☎ 03773-15-629656; www.coloniapel legrini.gov.ar; Mbiguá s/n; per person 1st/subsequent days AR$25/15) This municipal campground right by the lake is where to go for wildlife-spotting boat trips. It's worth booking campsites ahead, as there aren't so many, but nearly all have their own *quincho* (thatched roof building) with tables and chairs around the barbecue.

Hospedaje San Cayetano (☎ 03773-15-400929; www.iberasancayetano.com.ar; cnr Yacaré & Aguapé; r per person AR$30-40, d AR$120; ☎) This friendly budget choice with lawn, plunge pool, simple kitchen and *parrilla* offers a variety of rooms, from simple flop-downs with shared bathroom to pretty twins, doubles and family rooms with good beds and showers. Rooms can be private or shared, and prices are somewhat negotiable. The boss runs good boat trips and does transfers.

Hospedaje Los Amigos (☎ 03773-15-493753; hospedaje losamigos@gmail.com; cnr Guasú Virá & Aguapé; s/d AR$40/80) An excellent budget choice, with a kindly owner, this offers spotless rooms with big beds and decent bathrooms for a pittance. You can also eat simply but well here.

Hostería Ñandé Retá (☎ 03773-499411; www.nan dereta.com; s/d AR$160/254, 3 days & 2 nights incl full board s/d AR$990/1500; ☎ ☎) This place has been around longer than any, and is still one of the most pleasing. Surrounded by pines and eucalypts, it's got a peaceful, hidden-away feel that is highly seductive. It's very family friendly, the rooms are colorful, service excellent and the pool is a decent size.

Posada Aguapé (☎ 03773-499412; www.iberaesteros .com.ar; Yacaré s/n; s in small/large r AR$188/269, incl full board AR$464/576, d AR$221/322, incl full board AR$804/1040; ☎ ☎) This luxurious colonial-style posada is in a beautiful setting above the lake. It has more amenities than any other place in town, including a wide variety of excursions. Service is multilingual and excellent.

Irupé Lodge (☎ 03752-438312; www.irupelodge .com.ar; Yacaré s/n; s/d standard AR$237/288, s/d superior AR$368/448; ☎ ☎) On the lake near the causeway, this rustic lodge makes you feel very welcome. While the rooms are satisfactory, artistic wooden furniture, a pool and views across the water are the highlights. Superior cabins have private verandas and are more sizable.

Posada Ypa Sapukai (☎ 03773-420155; www.ibera turismo.com.ar; Mburucuyá s/n; s/d incl boat trip AR$256/320, s/d incl full board AR$832/1040; ☎ ☎) Secluded and rustic, this has grounds (with hammocks and chairs for lounging) that stretch down to the lake and small rooms that are pretty good value. It wins points for the name, which means 'The Cry of the Lake'.

Posada de La Laguna (☎ 03773-499413; www.posada delalaguna.com; Guasú Virá s/n; s/d US$136/178, incl full board US$225/300; ☎ ☎ ☎) Simple and elegant, in wide grounds by the lake at the end of town, rooms have paintings by the owner. The emphasis is on rural style and relaxation (ie no TV), and the staff pull it off, with friendly service and great guided trips. Meals are excellent.

Also recommended:

Corazón del Iberá (☎ 03773-431526; www.cora zondelibera.com.ar; cnr Ñangapiry & Yaguareté; s/d AR$70/120) Neat clean rooms and a little veranda. Runs good horseback-riding trips.

Hospedaje Jabirú (☎ 03773-15-413750; Yaguareté s/n; s/d AR$70/120) Spotless rooms sleeping up to five in a pretty adobe bungalow run by the friendly folk of Yacarú Porá restaurant next door.

FURTHER AFIELD

Estancia Rincón del Socorro (☎ 03782-497073; www .rincondelsocorro.com; r per person incl full board & excursions US$220; ☎ ☎) Off the Mercedes road, 31km south of Pellegrini, this ranch, owned by ecocampaigner Doug Tompkins, is a place to come to terms with the big sky and abundant wildlife around here. It's substantial country comfort rather than luxury; the pretty rooms interconnect, making them great for family stays, while freestanding cabins sleep two. Around the complex, vast lawns blend into pastureland and contemplation. If this isn't remote enough, head over to San Alonso, its sister *estancia*, only reachable by plane.

Estancia San Lorenzo (☎ 03756-481292; www.es tanciasanlorenzo.com; d per person incl full board & excursions AR$837) This divine little four-room *estancia* in Galarza is run by its exceptionally friendly owners who cook, talk, guide you on horseback and buzz you around the nearby lagoons to spy on caimans and capybaras. The food, all of it homemade, is superb (and seemingly endless). It can be tough to get there without a 4WD, but they'll pick you up (AR$500 return) from Gobernador Virasoro (80km away), which is easily reached by bus or car from Posadas.

Hotel Puerto Valle (☎ 03786-425700; www.hotel puertovalle.com; RN 12, Km 1282; d incl full board US$327-375; ☒ ☜ ☒) This luxurious option is on the bank of the Paraná near the northeastern tip of the Esteros. It boasts five impeccable rooms in spacious grounds that include a caiman farm. Meals are excellent.

Eating

All of the midrange and top-end accommodations options put meals on for their guests. If you ask nicely in advance, and they have space, most of them will let nonguests eat. There are other simple options in town.

La Cabaña (cnr Yaguareté & Curupí; lomitos AR$6-10) This tiny *artesanía* shop also does tasty *lomitos* (steak sandwiches) and coldish beer.

Yacarú Porá (☎ 03773-15-413750; cnr Caraguatá & Yaguareté; mains AR$12-22; ☯ 10am-midnight) Run with charm and enthusiasm, this attractive tin-roofed bungalow guarantees a warm welcome. The food is prepared to order and features generous portions of meat with tasty sauces, chicken dishes, empanadas, omelets and *milanesas* (breaded cutlets).

Getting There & Away

The road from Mercedes to Colonia Pellegrini (120km) is unsealed, and departures are limited. Bus services are unreliable and painfully slow, but theoretically leave Mercedes at 12:30pm Mondays to Saturday for Colonia Pellegrini (AR$40, four to five hours); check at the bus terminal information office.

A faster and more reliable way to get there is by combi or 4WD transport. This costs AR$300 for as many people as you can fit in the vehicle. Arrange this through the hostel in Mercedes, or contact **Beto** (☎ 03773-15-515862), who lives opposite Hostería Ñandé Retá in Colonia Pellegrini. There may already be a trip arranged that you can join.

The Mercedes road isn't as bad as everyone says it is, and is drivable in a normal car except after heavy rain. The road from Posadas is worse (take the turning between Gobernador Virasoro and Santo Tomé if you're in a normal car). Drivers charge AR$600 for a charter to

Posadas, or AR$450 to Gobernador Virasoro, from where frequent buses head the 80km on to Posadas.

There's no gas station in Pellegrini; the closest are in Mercedes and at the main road junction near Santo Tomé. Fill up before you head in. A couple of places in Pellegrini can sell you petrol and diesel if you're in a fix.

ALONG THE RÍO URUGUAY

The second of the two great rivers that converge above Buenos Aires to form the Río de la Plata, the Río Uruguay divides the country of the same name from Argentina, and also forms part of the border with Brazil. Bridges provide easy access to these neighbors, whose influences have blended with those of indigenous and immigrant groups in the area. The riverside towns on the Argentine side offer plenty and are very popular summertime destinations for *porteños* (people from Buenos Aires).

GUALEGUAYCHÚ
☎ 03446 / pop 75,516
A mellow little riverside place, Gualeguaychú is very quiet out of season and you won't find much to do apart from stroll by the river or in the lush Parque Unzué – which makes it very appealing if you've just come from Buenos Aires, for example. Argentine holidaymakers begin to arrive in December, and in January and February the place really kicks off, with the country's longest and flashiest Carnaval.

Orientation

Some 220km north of Buenos Aires, Gualeguaychú sits on the east bank of its namesake river, a tributary of the Uruguay. Plaza San Martín, occupying four square blocks, is the center of its grid pattern; each block covers 50, rather than 100, street numbers. Nearby the General Libertador San Martín toll bridge leads to the Uruguayan city of Fray Bentos – when it's not blocked, that is (see the boxed text, p536).

Information

There are several banks, most with ATMs, along Av 25 de Mayo.
Laverap (Bolívar 702) Laundry.
Telecentro (25 de Mayo 570; per hr AR$2.50; ☯ 7:30am-11pm) Calls and internet.

NORTHEAST ARGENTINA

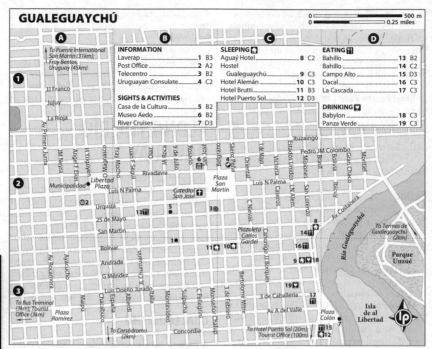

GUALEGUAYCHÚ

0 — 500 m
0 — 0.25 miles

INFORMATION
Laverap 1 B3
Post Office 2 A2
Telecentro 3 B2
Uruguayan Consulate.........4 C2

SIGHTS & ACTIVITIES
Casa de la Cultura 5 B2
Museo Aedo 6 B2
River Cruises 7 D3

SLEEPING
Aguaý Hotel 8 C2
Hostel
   Gualeguaychú..................9 C3
Hotel Alemán 10 C3
Hotel Brutti...........................11 B3
Hotel Puerto Sol..................12 D3

EATING
Bahilio 13 B2
Bahilio 14 C2
Campo Alto 15 D3
Dacal 16 C3
La Cascada 17 C3

DRINKING
Babylon 18 C3
Panza Verde 19 C3

Tourist office (☎ 423668; www.gualeguaychuturism
o.com; Plazoleta de los Artesanos s/n; ☼ 8am-10pm summer, 8am-8pm winter) Thatched hut by the Av Costanera,
south of Plaza Colón. A branch at the bus terminal keeps
the same hours.

Sights & Activities

A handful of colonial buildings remain in
Gualeguaychú, in addition to more recent
ones important in Argentine political and
literary history. The **Museo Aedo** (San José 105;
admission AR$2; ☼ 9-11:45am & 4-7pm Wed-Sat, 9-11:45am
Sun), just off Plaza San Martín, is the municipal
museum, occupying the oldest house in town
(c 1800). It features mostly antique furniture
and weaponry. A free guided tour in rapid-fire
Spanish is available.

Dating from the early 20th century, the
unusual **Casa de la Cultura** (☎ 427989; 25 de Mayo)
has occasional public exhibitions, and is the
place to contact for entrance to other historic houses around town and the museum, if
there's nobody there during opening hours.

Southwest of the center, the **Corsódromo** (Blvd
Irazusta) is the main site for Gualeguaychú's
lively Carnaval.

Gualeguaychú's highlight is **Parque Unzué**, a
sizable and elegant riverside park across the
bridge from the center. It's great for swimming, picnicking, camping, fishing and relaxing. Near the park is **Termas de Gualeguaychú**
(☎ 499167; www.gualeguaychutermal.com.ar; RP 42, Km
2.5; admission AR$20; ☼ 8am-midnight), a popular
complex of shallow thermal pools at various
temperatures.

A stroll along Av Costanera yields views
across the river to the park and various inlets and landscapes. There are various river-
cruise options lasting from one to six hours.
One of the several operators, **Litoral Aventura**
(☎ 1563-2266; www.litoralaventura.com.ar) also offers
kayaking.

Festivals & Events

Gualeguaychú's summer **Carnaval** is big and
brassy, so make a stop here any weekend from
mid-January to late February. Admission to
the Corsódromo costs AR$25, plus another
AR$10 to AR$20 to guarantee a seat.

Every October, on the Día de la Raza
weekend, high-school students build and parade floats through the city during the **Fiesta**

Provincial de Carrozas Estudiantiles. Other local celebrations include numerous *jineteadas* (rodeos) throughout the year.

Sleeping

There's a string of decent budget hotels along Bolívar between Bartolomé Mitre and Monseñor Chalup, and three hostels in town. All prices are significantly lower out of season. On the eastern bank of the river by Parque Unzué are several clusters of cabins and bungalows. The simplest charge around AR$120 for two to four people. The tourist office will give you a list of them. Several campgrounds both in Parque Unzué and along the riverside north of the bridge open in summer and charge from AR$15 to AR$20 per person. Pack mosquito repellent.

Hostel Gualeguaychú (☎ 424371; www.hostelguale guaychu.com.ar; G Méndez 290; dm incl breakfast AR$40; 🞐) A relaxed place near the water with an emphasis on Argentine *folklore*: there are musical instruments to use, and the owners run an impressive shop of artisanal *mate* paraphernalia next door. There's a kitchen for guest use and you're close to the summer nightlife.

Hotel Brutti (☎ 426048; Bolívar 591; s/d AR$70/120; 🛜) A favorite of 50-something traveling salesmen, this is one of the cheaper and more reliable choices in town. The rooms facing the front are lighter, but there's a bit of morning noise from the market opposite.

Hotel Alemán (☎ 426153; Bolívar 535; s/d AR$140/200; 🞐 🛜) This welcoming spot is a home-like place, with a faux-Alpine exterior and a bright central courtyard complete with a replica renaissance fountain. Rooms are well kept, with decent bathrooms.

Hotel Puerto Sol (☎ 434017; www.hotelpuertosol .com.ar; San Lorenzo 477; d AR$210; 🞐 🖵 🛜 🞈) Cordial and bright, this spot near the water has an appealing summer-camp feel about it with its pastel paint job, outdoor sitting area, board games and small pool on a river island that staff take you to by boat. Prices are a fair bit cheaper outside the height of summer, and single rates (AR$162) are available.

Aguaý Hotel (☎ 422099; www.hotelaguay.com.ar; Av Costanera 130; s/d AR$240/350; 🞐 🖵 🛜 🞈) All rooms in this stylish modern hotel are spacious and have balconies (most with great views over the river) and excellent bathrooms. There's a small gym, a rooftop pool and spa. It's at least 50 pesos cheaper outside the summer months.

Eating & Drinking

Bahillo (ice-cream cones from AR$3.50-7; 🕒 10am-9pm) Head to one of its two branches (corner of Av Costanera and San Lorenzo, and corner of Díaz and 25 de Mayo) for quality ice cream.

La Cascada (☎ 432451; Av Costanera near Av A del Valle; mains AR$11-28; 🕒 lunch & dinner) Spacious, cheerful and simple, this place does the Entre Ríos basics well. Cheap *parrillada*, all the classic river fish (check out the photos of some of the monster surubí in the menu) and a range of salads – it's all here.

Campo Alto (☎ 429593; cnr San Lorenzo & Concordia; mains AR$15-32, all you can eat AR$26; 🕒 lunch & dinner) Thatched-roof bungalows, occasional live music and shady outdoor seating make this *asador libre* (all-you-can-eat barbecue) one of the most enjoyable eating options in town.

Dacal (☎ 427602; cnr San Lorenzo & Andrade; mains AR$15-40; 🕒 lunch & dinner) One of the better places to eat in town, with a long menu and a no-nonsense outdoor and indoor dining areas, Dacal looks right across the *costanera* to the river, and serves good fish, pasta and meat.

Panza Verde (cnr LN Alem & Luis Doello Jurado; 🕒 from 6pm Thu-Sun) A happening little neighborhood bar that also does *parrilla* and serves *picadas* (snacks). On a clear, balmy night, the rooftop terrace is the place to be.

Babylon (G Méndez 276; 🕒 nightly Dec-Feb) Near the waterfront, this is one of the livelier summer disco-bars, with a roof terrace.

Getting There & Around

The **bus terminal** (☎ 440688; Jurado & Artigas) is 3km southwest of the plaza. For AR$2, infrequent buses – routes 2 and 3 – stop on Artigas across from the bus terminal and take circuitous routes to the town center. For AR$6 to AR$7 a taxi will drop you anywhere downtown.

Buses to Fray Bentos (Uruguay) were suspended at the time of research because of the blockade of the road, due to the Botnia papermill (see the boxed text, p536).

Destinations include the following:

Destination	Cost (AR$)	Duration (hr)
Buenos Aires	47	3½
Colón	15	2
Concepción	11	1¼
Concordia	26	4
Paraná	39	4-5
Paso de los Libres	49	7
Rosario	61	7½
Santa Fe	41	5½

NORTHEAST ARGENTINA

CONCEPCIÓN

☎ 03442 / pop 65,954

Set around a stately plaza, Concepción del Uruguay (its full name) is a typical riverside town, wondering what to do with itself now that trade on the Río Uruguay has died off. It makes a decent stopover on the way north, has a couple of excellent places to stay and boasts the sumptuous Palacio San José outside town.

Orientation & Information

The parallel streets Rocamora, Galarza and 9 de Julio run east through the center of town to the river. On the way, Rocamora becomes pedestrianized and passes one block north of the central Plaza General Francisco Ramírez; Galarza runs along he northern edge of the plaza; and 9 de Julio hits the middle of the plaza, continuing on the other side.

There is an ATM at the bus terminal and the Shell gas station opposite has 24-hour internet access.

Municipal tourist office (☎ 425820; www.concep cionturismo.gov.ar; 9 de Julio 844; ⏰ 7am-8pm Mon-Fri, 7am-10pm Sat & Sun) Well prepared and helpful, but not clearly marked, it's two blocks west of the plaza.

Telecentro Uruguay (3 de Febrero 63; per hr AR$3) Internet and phone calls just off the plaza.

Sights

The principal sights are around the noble main plaza, where the earthy-pink colored **basilica** (⏰ 8am-noon & 5-8pm) holds court. To the left of the altar, a sunken crypt (modeled on that of Napoleon in the Invalides in Paris) holds the remains of Justo José de Urquiza, first president of Argentina. Not far away, the **Museo Casa de Delio Panizza** (cnr Entrerriano & Galarza; admission AR$2; ⏰ 9am-noon & 4-7pm) dates from the late 18th century and holds a collection of 19th-century bric-a-brac.

Concepción has a long riverfront, but it doesn't offer much, though development is in the pipeline. The beaches are better to the northeast of town.

The region's primary attraction, however, is **Palácio San José**, 33km west of town (see opposite).

Sleeping

Residencial Centro (☎ 427429; www.nuevorescentro .com.ar; Moreno 130; twd AR$70/80; ✗ 🛜) The best budget deal in town has a variety of rooms around a courtyard. They vary slightly in price according to size and if they have air-con; there's more light in the ones upstairs.

Antigua Fonda (☎ 433734; www.antiguafonda.com .ar; España 172; s/d AR$80/120; ✗ 🛜) Likable owners have created this new option from part of what was once an historic Concepción hotel (though you wouldn't know). Pleasing rooms in cream colors surround a small grassy garden, with artistic touches and a relaxing vibe. Improvements are ongoing – there was no breakfast at the time of research, but guests could use a kitchen. It's a block west and three south of the plaza.

Grand Hotel Casino (☎ 425586; www.grandpala ciotexier.com.ar; cnr Eva Perón & Rocamora; s/d AR$160/250; ✗ 💻 🛜) This stately old place at the end of the pedestrian precinct has a charm from bygone years that plucks at the heartstrings. It's well priced, even though the rooms can be a little cramped. Try to picture the adjoining casino as it once would have been, without the ugly slot machines that disgrace it today.

ourpick Antigua Posta del Torreón (☎ 432618; www.postadeltorreon.com.ar; Almafuerte 799; s/d AR$170/240; ✗ 💻 🛜) This intimate and classy hotel a block west and four south of the plaza offers a real haven for a relaxing stay. It's an elegantly refurbished 19th-century mansion, with rooms surrounding a postcard-pretty courtyard replete with fountain and small swimming pool.

Eating

Café de la Plaza (☎ 433292; cnr Urquiza & Galarza; light meals AR$6-18; ⏰ 8am-2pm & 4pm-late) On the northwest corner of the plaza, this offbeat place has a bit of everything, with a terrace, chessboard tiles, tasty coffee, wooden bench-booths, food and regular live music (AR$10 admission). The decor blends traditional and industrial, and pulls it off. Applause.

El Conventillo de Baco (☎ 433809; España 193; dishes AR$15-45; ⏰ lunch & dinner) Near the Antigua Posta del Torreón hotel, this new restaurant has both indoor and outdoor dining in an attractive patio space and specializes in well-prepared river fish and seafood, with dishes like calamari stew and glazed pork as specialties.

Getting There & Around

The **bus terminal** (☎ 422352; cnr Galarza & Chiloteguy) is 10 blocks west of the plaza. Bus 1 (AR$1.50) runs between them, a *remise* costs AR$4 to AR$5.

Destinations include the following:

Destination	Cost (AR$)	Duration (hr)
Buenos Aires	51	4½
Colón	6	¾
Concordia	22	3
Gualeguaychú	11	1¼
Paraná	41	5
Paso de los Libres	40	6-7
Paysandú (Uruguay)	13	1½

PALACIO SAN JOSÉ
☎ 03442

Topped by twin towers and surrounded by elegant gardens, Justo José de Urquiza's ostentatious pink **palace** (☎ 432620; RP 39, Km 30; adult/child AR$5/1; ☼ 8am-7pm Mon-Fri, 9am-6pm Sat & Sun) is 33km west of Concepción via RP 39. Set around an elegant arched patio, with a walled garden out the back, it was built partly to show up Urquiza's arch rival in Buenos Aires, Juan Manuel de Rosas, and partly to show the power and wealth of Entre Ríos province. Local *caudillo* (provincial strongman) Urquiza, commanding an army of provincial loyalists, Unitarists, Brazilians and Uruguayans, was largely responsible for Rosas' downfall in 1852 and the eventual adoption of Argentina's modern constitution; he was effectively Argentina's first president.

Sometime allies like Domingo Sarmiento and Bartolomé Mitre supped at Urquiza's 8.5m dining-room table and slept in the palatial bedrooms. The bedroom where Urquiza was murdered by a mob sent by Ricardo López Jordán is a permanent shrine, created by Urquiza's wife.

If you don't mind walking the final 3km to the palace, you can get a Caseros-bound bus from Concepción and get the driver to drop you at the turnoff, but an easier option is to take a *remise* direct from Concepción. **Sarbimas** (☎ 427777) will take up to four people there and back, including a two-hour wait, for AR$65. There's a mediocre restaurant at the palace and picturesque grounds for picnicking.

COLÓN
☎ 03447 / pop 19,288

The most appealing destination for riverside relaxation in Entre Ríos, Colón is a very popular summer getaway for Argentine holidaymakers. Its population almost doubles in January, but the pretty town takes it all in its stride. With numerous places to stay, a thriving handicrafts scene and worthwhile, out-of-the-ordinary restaurants, it's a great place to be. It's also the best base for visiting the Parque Nacional El Palmar (p208).

One of three main Entre Ríos border crossings, Colón is connected to the Uruguayan city of Paysandú by the Puente Internacional General Artigas. The center of the action is Plaza San Martín, a block back from the river, and the street 12 de Abril running up to it.

Information
Ciber Barnet (Lavalle 32; per hr AR$2.50) Internet half a block from the main drag.
Tourist office (☎ 421969; www.colon.gov.ar; cnr Gouchón & Av Costanera; ☼ 6am-8pm Mon-Fri, 8am-8pm Sat & Sun) Occupies the former customs building, built by Urquiza. There is also an office in the bus terminal open holidays only.

Sights & Activities
Strolling around the riverbank and quiet leafy streets is the highlight here. Check out beautiful Calle Alejo Peyret, a street back from the river: it's dotted with well-preserved 19th-century buildings, with traditional green roofs and shutters. Old-style streetlamps give it a romantic cast at night. On the southern edge of town, **Parque Quirós** is handsome and tranquil.

The **Termas de Colón** (☎ 424717; www.termasdeentrerios.gov.ar; cnr Lavalle & Sabatier; admission AR$10; ☼ 9am-8pm), at the northern edge of town, is a thermal spa with 10 indoor and outdoor pools, ranging from 33°C to 40°C. The source is a 1500m-deep well drilled to tap the region's abundant geothermal aquifers.

In February the city hosts the **Fiesta Nacional de la Artesanía**, a crafts fair held in Parque Quirós that features high-standard live folkloric entertainment.

ENTERING URUGUAY

There are three main crossings linking Argentina with its eastern neighbor Uruguay (see p533). From south to north these are Gualeguaychú–Fray Bentos, Colón–Paysandú and Concordia–Salto. All three are theoretically open 24 hours, but at the time of research the Gualeguaychú crossing was still blocked due to ongoing protests about the Botnia papermill (see the boxed text, p536). See Visas, p593, for Uruguayan entry requirements.

There are numerous *artesanía* shops selling everything from *mate* gourds to pickled coypu. **La Casona** (☎ 425097; www.artesanoslacasona .com; 12 de Abril 106; ⏰ 9am-noon & 5-8pm), on the corner of the plaza, is a cooperative selling a wide range of handmade goods.

There are various boat trips available to explore the river and the Islas Vírgenes. Expect to pay AR$25 to AR$35 for a one- to two-hour excursion.

It's also worth visiting the nearby village of **San José**, 8km northwest, where in 1857 European pioneers established the country's second agricultural colony. An interesting regional **museum** (☎ 470088; Urquiza 1127; admission AR$2; ⏰ 9am-noon & 3-6pm Tue-Sun) displays period tools and memorabilia.

Sleeping

There are numerous summer campgrounds (think AR$30 for a two-person tent), cabins, bungalows and apartments available for rental. The tourist office can supply you with a list.

Hotel Futuro (☎ 423712; Urquiza 168; s/d AR$80/130; ✶) Despite the name, don't expect a glimpse forward in time, unless various shades of lime green come back into fashion in a big way. It's family run and comfortable enough, with a good location near the plaza. Some rooms are much better than others, with spacious bathrooms.

ourpick **Hostería 'Restaurant del Puerto'** (☎ 422698; www.hosteriadecolon.com.ar; Alejo Peyret 158; d AR$220; ✶ ▢ ⌨ ✷) In what has a strong claim to be Colón's loveliest house (on its prettiest street), it has cracking characterful rooms decorated faithfully in keeping with the 1880 building, with enormous windows, plenty of wood and noble rustic furniture. The family duplexes (AR$320) are a good deal, as are the regular half-price midweek discounts. All rooms surround a patio dominated by a fragrant Paraguay jasmine; there's also a heated pool and Jacuzzi. It's not a restaurant, though.

Hotel Plaza (☎ 421043; www.hotel-plaza.com.ar; cnr 12 de Abril & Belgrano; d standard/superior AR$250/460; ✶ ▢ ⌨ ✷) This Colón staple has been around for a while, but it certainly never looked like this before. A sleek refit has left it looking modern and glistening. The rooms aren't quite as posh; the superiors are the new ones, with quality bathrooms. But the combination of plaza-side location (some rooms in each category have balconies) and decent-sized heated pool out the back make it a winner.

Eating & Drinking

There are numerous places to eat. Hit Urquiza for traditional Argentine options, or Alejo Peyret for more unusual choices.

Juanes (☎ 421942; cnr 12 de Abril & Paso; meals AR$12-45; ⏰ 10am-late) With outdoor seating wrapping round a corner of the plaza, this offers classy *licuados*, salads and *lomitos* to keep the snackers in business, and more substantial meals with decent wine selections. Good *tragos* until quite late make it a solid all-round favorite.

El Sótano de los Quesos (☎ 427163; cnr Chacabuco & Av Costanera; mixed plates for 1/2 persons AR$20/38; ⏰ 3:30-9pm Tue-Fri, 10:30am-9pm Sat & Sun) Near the tourist office, this intriguing spot serves a wide variety of artisanal cheeses and other delicacies at pretty thatched tables on a lawn looking over the port. There's also locally made wine and beer on hand, and a cellar shop whose aromas will almost compel you to buy.

La Cosquilla del Ángel (☎ 423711; Alejo Peyret 180; mains AR$25-50; ⏰ lunch & dinner) Colón's best restaurant combines comfortably elegant decor, a big welcome and top service with a whimsical and unpretentious approach, particularly in the curiously named dishes, and the intriguing restaurant name, which translates to 'The Angel's Tickle.' Many of the dishes combine sweet and savory flavors; try the *mollejitas* (or *mollejas*; sweetbreads) if you're a fan. The pasta is also highly recommended and the wine list is well above average.

Getting There & Around

Colón's **bus terminal** (☎ 421716; cnr Rocamora & 9 de Julio) is seven blocks inland (roughly west) of the river and eight blocks north of the main shopping and entertainment street, 12 de Abril. A *remise* into the center costs AR$5 to AR$6.

Destinations include Buenos Aires (AR$55, five hours), Gualeguaychú (AR$15, two hours) via Concepción (AR$6, 40 minutes), Concordia (AR$17, 2½ hours) via Ubajay (AR$8, 1½ hours) and Paysandú, Uruguay (AR$10, 45 minutes).

For details about crossing into Uruguay, see the boxed text, p207.

PARQUE NACIONAL EL PALMAR
☎ 03447

On the west bank of the Río Uruguay, midway between Colón and Concordia, 8500-sq-km **Parque Nacional El Palmar** (☎ 493049; www .elpalmarapn.com.ar; RN 14, Km 199; Argentine/foreigner/car

AR$8/25/4) preserves the last extensive stands of yatay palm on the Argentine littoral. In the 19th century the native yatay covered large parts of Entre Ríos, Uruguay and southern Brazil, but the intensification of agriculture, ranching and forestry throughout the region destroyed much of the palm savanna.

Most of the remaining palms in El Palmar are relics, some more than two centuries old, but under protection from grazing and fire they have once again begun to reproduce. Reaching a maximum height of about 18m, with a trunk diameter of 40cm, the larger specimens clustered throughout the park accentuate a striking and soothing subtropical landscape that lends itself to photography. The grasslands and the gallery forests along the river and creeks shelter much wildlife, including birds, mammals and reptiles.

Park admission (valid for 48 hours) is collected at the entrance on RN 14 from 7am to 7pm, but the gate is open 24 hours.

Sights & Activities

All the park's main facilities are 12km down a good dirt road leading from the entrance. Here, the **visitors center** (8am-7pm) has displays on natural history. You can organize canoeing, cycling and horseback-riding trips around the park. These cost AR$30 to AR$60, depending on route and duration. Decent dirt roads lead off the main access road to three viewpoints. **Arroyo Los Loros**, a short distance north of the campground by gravel road, is a good place to observe wildlife. South of the visitor center is Arroyo El Palmar, a pleasant stream accessed at two viewpoints, **La Glorieta** and **El Palmar**. These have short marked trails, and the latter has a hide for bird-watching. There are three other short trails near the visitors center, and another bird-watching hide near the Río Uruguay. Guided walks are available by prior arrangement.

Early morning and just before sunset are the best times to view wildlife. The most conspicuous bird is the rhea, but there are also numerous parakeets, cormorants, egrets, herons, storks, caracaras, woodpeckers and kingfishers. Among the mammals, the capybara and vizcacha are common sights, but there are also foxes, raccoons and wild boar. The latter, an introduced species, damage the palms and are being reduced.

Vizcachas inhabit the campground; their nocturnal squeaks and reflective eyes sometimes disturb campers, but they are harmless (as are the enormous toads that invade the showers and toilets at night). The same is not true of the yarará, a deadly pit viper that inhabits the savannas. Bites are rare, but watch your step and wear high boots and long trousers when hiking. Staff recommends you keep to the marked trails.

There is excellent access to the river for swimming and boating from the campground.

Sleeping & Eating

In Ubajay there are basic rooms in the bus terminal complex as well as other cheap lodgings.

Camping El Palmar (☎ 423378; campsites per person/tent AR$12/10) This sociable campground across the parking lot from the visitors center is the only place to stay that's in the park. It has shady, level campsites, hot showers and electricity. The shop here sells snacks and food, including massive slabs of beef for the barbecues; opposite, there's a restaurant next to the visitors center, serving tasty full meals.

La Aurora del Palmar (☎ 421549; www.auroradelpalmar.com.ar; RN 14, Km 202; campsites AR$6 plus AR$12 per adult; d without shower AR$140, d/q AR$200/250; ✕ ☑) Between Ubajay and the park entrance, this property, as well as being a cattle ranch and citrus farm, has a protected palm forest at least as spectacular as those in the national park itself. It's an original, well-run place with shady campsites, family duplex rooms in a pretty bungalow, and rustic wooden rooms in renovated railway carriages. There's a good swimming pool and a restaurant. Canoeing, horseback riding, and palm safaris are available (AR$40/100 for each/all three). Various packages are offered. too, and it's cheaper midweek.

Getting There & Away

El Palmar is on RN 14, a major national highway, so there are frequent north–south bus services. Any bus running north towards Concordia will drop you at the park entrance, 12km from the visitors center. You could walk or hitchhike from here or else stay on the bus a further 6km to Ubajay, from where a *remise* will cost you AR$40 to AR$50 to the visitor center. Ask the Telecentro alongside the bus terminal to call you one. There's also a school bus that heads into the park on weekdays at noon and in the afternoon from Ubajay that will take you for free if it has space.

Several agencies in Colón offer half-day trips to the park, which include a guided walk. **LHL** (☎ 422222; lhlcolon@arnet.com.ar; 12 de Abril 119) near the plaza is one: the trip costs AR$40 to AR$55 depending on numbers, plus the park entry fee.

CONCORDIA
☎ 0345 / pop 138,099
This pleasant agricultural service town on the Río Uruguay won't keep you spellbound for weeks at a time, but makes a convenient stop for a night. It's a working rather than a tourist town, and has a fine central plaza, interesting cathedral, and riverside beaches and fishing. It also offers a border crossing, via the Represa Salto Grande hydroelectric project, to the Uruguayan city of Salto.

The mainstay of the local economy is citrus fruit, and you can smell the tang in the air at times.

Information
There are several banks with ATMs in the vicinity of Plaza 25 de Mayo.
Lavasped (☎ 422-4375; Urquiza 502) Laundry.
Municipal tourist office (☎ 421-2137; turismo@ concordia.gov.ar; Urquiza 636; 🕑 8am-9pm) Next to the cathedral. The information desk at the bus terminal also has tourist info.
Telecentro (Pellegrini at Plaza 25 de Mayo; per hr AR$2.50) For phone calls and internet access.

Sights & Activities
On the west side of Plaza 25 de Mayo, the 19th-century **Catedral San Antonio de Padua** is the city's signature landmark. It's one of the region's more interesting cathedrals, with an ornate *retablo* (altarpiece) and stained-glass windows with scenes from the life of Christ.

Facing Plaza Urquiza, at the corner of Entre Ríos and Ramírez, the **Palacio Arruabarrena** (1919) is a fabulous building, blending French neo-renaissance architecture with art nouveau touches. It contains the **Museo Regional de Concordia** (☎ 421-1883; admission free; 🕑 8am-1pm & 2-8pm Mon-Fri, 9am-6pm Sat & Sun). The display is mostly about Italian immigration to the region, but there's also some fine furniture, including a mirror that belonged to Urquiza. The interior is badly in need of restoration, but Concordia – hit hard by the economic crisis – has nowt in the bank.

The **Museo Judío de Entre Ríos** (☎ 421-4088; www.museojudioer.org.ar; Entre Ríos 476; admission AR$10; 🕑 8:30am-12:30pm Sun-Fri) has three rooms detailing the arrival and struggles of the Jewish gauchos (see the boxed text, opposite), their way of life and the Holocaust seen through the eyes of one who experienced it. There's also a room for temporary exhibitions.

In the riverside Parque Rivadavia, at the northeastern edge of town, are the ruins of **Castillo San Carlos** (1888), built by a French industrialist who mysteriously abandoned the property years later. French writer Antoine de Saint-Exupéry briefly lived in the building; there's a monument to *The Little Prince* nearby. There's no charge for wandering around the ruins, but watch the kids.

CONCORDIA

0   200 m
0   0.1 miles

INFORMATION
Lavasped..**1** A4
Municipal Tourist Office...............**2** A3
Post Office.....................................**3** B3
Telecentro......................................**4** B3

SIGHTS & ACTIVITIES
Catedral San Antonio de Padua....**5** A3
Museo Judío de Entre Ríos.............**6** A4
Museo Regional de Concordia.....(see 7)
Palacio Arruabarrena.....................**7** A1

SLEEPING
Hotel Concordia.............................**8** B4
Hotel El Palmar.............................**9** A4
Hotel Pellegrini............................**10** B4
Hotel Salto Grande......................**11** A3

EATING
Cristóbal Café...............................**12** B3
El Reloj...**13** B3
Malaika..**14** B3

To Uruguayan Consulate (50m)
To Bus Terminal (1.5km); Castillo San Carlos (5km); Parque San Carlos (5km); San Carlos Inn (5km); Complejo Termal Concordia (8km); Represa Salto Grande (18km)
To Launches to Salto (Uruguay) (1.2km)

THE GAUCHO JUDÍO

The gaucho is one of Argentina's archetypal images, but it's a little-known fact that many a gaucho was of Jewish origin. The first recorded instance of mass Jewish immigration to Argentina was in the late 19th century, when 800 Russian Jews arrived in Buenos Aires, fleeing persecution from Czar Alexander III.

The Jewish Colonization Association, funded by a wealthy German philanthropist, began to distribute 100-hectare parcels of land to immigrant families in the provinces of Entre Ríos, Santa Fe, Santiago del Estero, La Pampa and Buenos Aires.

The first major colony was in Moisés Ville in Santa Fe province, which became known at the time as Jerusalem Argentina. Today there are only about 300 Jewish residents left in town (15% of the population), but many Jewish traditions prevail: the tiny town boasts four synagogues, the bakery sells Sabbath bread, and kids in the street use Yiddish slang like 'schlep' and 'schlock.'

These rural Jews readily assimilated into Argentine society, mixing their own traditions with those of their adopted country, so that it was not unusual to see a figure on horseback in baggy pants, canvas shoes and skullcap on his way to throw a lump of cow on the *asado* (barbecue). Many of their descendants have since left the land in search of education and opportunities in the cities. Argentina's Jews number about 300,000, making them Latin America's largest Jewish community.

To learn more about the *gauchos judíos*, visit the museum at Concordia (opposite).

Concordia has a good thermal spa, the **Complejo Termal Concordia** (☎ 425-1963; www.ter masconcordia.com.ar; admission AR$35; ☼ 9am-10pm) to the north of town. Bus 7 runs there every half-hour from San Lorenzo, four blocks west of the bus terminal.

Festivals & Events

The city holds its **Fiesta Nacional de Citricultura** (National Citrus Festival) the first week in December. Concordia's **Carnaval** celebrations (around February or March) are also lively. Carnaval Tuesday, the main day, is 47 days before Easter Sunday.

Sleeping

Hotel Pellegrini (☎ 422-7137; Pellegrini 443; s/d AR$65/120) By far the best budget choice, this friendly family-run spot offers spotless rooms with TV and bathroom three blocks south of the plaza. Book ahead, as it's popular.

Hotel Concordia (☎ 421-6869; La Rioja 518; s/d AR$80/110; ☒) Cheap and cheerful choice occupying a cavernous building. Rooms vary in light, size and mattress quality. Bathrooms, some accessed via in-room stairs, are decent.

Hotel El Palmar (☎ 421-6050; www.palmarhotel .com.ar; Urquiza 517; s/d standard AR$154/180, s/d superior AR$230/280; ☒ ☐ ☞) A couple of blocks south of the plaza, the Palmar offers cramped rooms with balconies that feel a little overpriced. They're gradually being done up – the su-

perior rooms offer plenty more space and modern convenience, but the standard rooms have that unmissable feel of gentle decline that characterizes so many Argentine hotels.

Hotel Salto Grande (☎ 421-0034; www.ho telsaltogrande.net; Urquiza 581; s/d AR$171/203; ☒ ☐ ☞ ☒) Just south of the main plaza, this polished, modern hotel offers excellent service and, at time of research at least, prices that hadn't risen in quite some time, making it excellent value. Deluxe rooms have better views and minibar, but aren't a great deal better than the standards.

San Carlos Inn (☎ 431-0725; www.hotelsancarlosinn .com.ar; Parque San Carlos; r standard/superior AR$275/315; ☒ ☐ ☞ ☒) Set in the lush grounds of the Parque Rivadavia, the resort-style San Carlos Inn is a quiet spot to rest up. The superior rooms have balconies, river views, better beds and decent TVs, and they don't cost much more.

Eating

Cristóbal Café (☎ 421-5736; cnr Pellegrini & 1 de Mayo; meals AR$10-30; ☼ breakfast, lunch & dinner) The terrace, complete with director's chairs and palm trees, is the best thing about this attractive, popular spot on the plaza. There's an interesting – if overpriced – menu, but the interior suffers from too much music and TV, and tables so closely packed you'll learn all about your neighbor's kidney complaints.

NORTHEAST ARGENTINA

El Reloj (☎ 422-2822; Pellegrini 580; pizza AR$15-25; ☽ lunch & dinner) This spacious brick-walled pizzeria has good ambience and a staggering selection of options. A haven for the indecisive as the staff doesn't grumble about doing half and halves. It also does *parrilla*.

Malaika (☎ 422-4867; 1 de Mayo 59; dishes AR$18-42; ☽ 8am-2am) Trendy eating has arrived in Concordia in the form of this relaxed and handsome cafe-bar on the plaza. It serves a variety of tasty meals, with salads, pizza, tapas, snacks and more elaborate fare, including plenty of vegetarian options and daily specials. Decent wines, caring service and a romantic mood seal the deal. Also lunches for AR$22.

Getting There & Away
The **bus terminal** (☎ 421-7235; cnr Justo & Hipólito Yrigoyen) is 13 blocks north of Plaza 25 de Mayo. Four daily buses (none on Sunday) go to Salto, Uruguay (AR$15, 1¼ hours).

Destinations include the following:

Destination	Cost (AR$)	Duration (hr)
Buenos Aires	75	5½
Colón	17	2½
Concepción	20	3
Corrientes	89	7
Gualeguaychú	26	4
Paraná	42	4½
Paso de los Libres	32	4
Posadas	100	8

From the port beyond the east end of Carriego, launches cross the river to Salto (AR$10, 15 minutes) four times between 9am and 6pm Monday to Saturday.

The Buenos Aires–Posadas train line runs through Concordia. For details about crossing into Uruguay, see the boxed text, p207.

Getting Around
Bus 2 (AR$1.75) takes Yrigoyen south from the bus terminal to the center. On its northward run catch it on Pellegrini in front of Banco de la Nación. A taxi to the bus terminal from the center should cost about AR$6.

PASO DE LOS LIBRES
☎ 03772 / pop 40,494
The name (meaning 'Crossing of the Free') is the most romantic thing about this border town on the banks of the Río Uruguay. It faces the much larger Brazilian city of Uruguaiana on the opposite bank, and is connected to it by a well-used bridge. There's little to detain the traveler, but the town has a picturesque central plaza and a couple of reasonable places to stay if you want to stop for the night.

Orientation & Information
Situated on the west bank of the Uruguay, Paso de los Libres has a standard rectangular grid, centered on Plaza Independencia. The principal commercial street is Av Colón, one block west. It's good for shopping, catering to the flourishing cross-border traffic. The international bridge to Uruguaiana, Brazil, is about 10 blocks southwest.

There's no tourist office, but try the ACA (Automóvil Club Argentino) office near the border complex before the bridge or the Intendencia (Town Hall) on the plaza. There are maps of town all over the center. You'll find a bank with an ATM on the plaza.

Libres Cambio (Av Colón 901) Changes money.
Telecentro (Madariaga 660; per hr AR$2.50) Internet and phones half a block from the plaza.

Sleeping & Eating
Hotel Las Vegas (☎ 423490; Sarmiento 554; s/d AR$90/140; ☒ ☎) Despite the burgundy carpets and '70s feel, this is a newish place in the center of town. The rooms are dark but comfortable and have bathrooms with good showers. The rooms up the back have more light and space.

Hotel Alejandro Primero (☎ 424100; Coronel López 502; s/d AR$165/280; ☒ ☐ ☎ ☒) A surprisingly good hotel, this has a swish lobby and restaurant area and slightly less impressive but very spacious rooms. Ask for one with views over the river and Uruguaiana in Brazil on the other side.

El Nuevo Mesón (☎ 03772-15-468117; Colón 587; mains AR$15-30; ☽ lunch & dinner) It's nothing out of the ordinary to look at, but this offers really well-prepared dishes and caring service. There's pizza, *parrilla* and more elaborate creations, but it's all low priced and very tasty indeed. Grab a table outside if the weather's fine.

Getting There & Away
The **bus terminal** (☎ 425600) is at the corner of Av San Martín and Santiago del Estero. Several buses daily head to Buenos Aires (AR$98, 9½ hours) and Posadas (AR$56, six hours). Some go via Concordia, Colón, Concepción and Gualeguaychú. More buses bypass the town,

but can drop you off at the Esso gas station on RN 14, where you can get a taxi to take you the last 16km to downtown.

Tata/El Rápido serves Corrientes (AR$44, six hours) via Mercedes (AR$12 to AR$20, three hours), from where you can visit the Esteros del Iberá.

Buses to Uruguaiana, Brazil (AR$2), leave frequently from 7am onwards, stopping on Av San Martín at Av Colón and across from the bus terminal (by the castle-like building).

For information about visa requirements for crossing into Brazil, see the boxed text, p225. The frontier is open 24 hours.

Getting Around

The area between the bus terminal and downtown is a little dodgy at night. Minibuses (AR$1.50) run from the corner below the bus terminal into town. A taxi to the town center is AR$10.

YAPEYÚ

☎ 03772 / pop 1650

It would be untruthful to call this delightfully peaceful place a one-horse town: there are many horses, and the sound of their hooves thumping the reddish earth in the evening is one of the nicest things about it. Yapeyú was founded in 1626 as the southernmost of the Jesuit missions, and at its height had a population of more than 8000 Guaraní tending as many as 80,000 head of cattle. After the order was expelled in 1767, the mission started to decline, and was finally destroyed by Brazilian raiders in the early 19th century. Many houses in the area are built of red sandstone blocks salvaged from mission buildings. Another historical note: José de San Martín, Argentina's greatest national hero and known as 'the Liberator', was born here in 1778. Yapeyú is a great spot to relax; the sort of place where locals will greet you on the street.

Sights & Activities

Everything in town is within easy walking distance of the central Plaza San Martín. On its south side is the **Museo de la Cultura Jesuítica** (admission free; ☯ 8am-noon & 3-6pm Tue-Sun), set among the ruins of what was once the mission's church and cloister. If you read Spanish, it's an excellent museum, with a comprehensive overview of the missions in Argentina, Brazil and Paraguay and detailed information on all aspects of those fascinating communities. The

photographic displays are also good, and the museum would make a useful first stop on a tour of the Jesuit zone.

It's a measure of the esteem that Argentines hold for the Liberator that they have built **Casa de San Martín** (admission free; ☯ 8am-noon & 2:30-6pm), an ornate building to protect the ruins of the house where he was born in 1778 and lived his first three years. The house actually dates from the early 17th century and was one of the Jesuit buildings. San Martín's parents' remains are here, and a campaign is underway to bring the man himself (he currently rests in the cathedral of Buenos Aires). No chance. Near the house, the incomplete arch is a Falklands/Malvinas War memorial and represents Argentina without the Malvinas.

On the southern edge of town, four blocks south of the plaza, the army barracks house another museum, the **Museo Sanmartiniano** (admission free; ☯ 8am-10pm). As well as various San Martín paraphernalia, it also has some objects from the Jesuit period, including a wooden Christ found in mud by the river. Charmingly, and typically for provincial museums in Argentina, there are also a couple of objects that aren't really on the program: an unusually twisted eucalyptus branch, for example.

On the west side of the plaza, the Gothic-spired parish **church** dates from 1899, but contains some important images from the Jesuit period.

Sleeping & Eating

Hotel San Martín (☎ 493120; Sargento Cabral 712; s/d AR$70/110; ✿) Handily located right on the plaza and next to the Jesuit ruins and San Martín's house, this is Yapeyú's only hotel. Rooms have TVs and face an echoey inner courtyard; there's not much natural light if you want privacy. The hotel also has a basic restaurant.

El Paraíso Yapeyú (☎ 493056; www.termasdeyapeyu .com.ar; cnr Paso de los Patos & San Martín; bungalow for 1/2/6 people AR$110/165/350; ✿ ⬛) This complex of comfortable modern bungalows (sleeping up to six) offers excellent value in a waterfront location – the Uruguay is mighty impressive right here. There's a pool and *parrilla* restaurant by the river.

Comedor del Paraíso (☎ 03772-15-433983; Gregoria Matorras s/n; mains AR$10-17; ☯ 7am-midnight) This simple and friendly spot is just down from the Casa de San Martín on a street named after the Liberator's mother. There's no menu as such, just a limited choice from what's available. Portions are small but very cheap. If you ask a few hours beforehand, staff can organize other dishes for you. There are river views and out the front is a large, 300-year-old palo borracho tree, in which, they say, a young San Martín used to play.

Getting There & Away

The small bus terminal is two blocks west of the plaza. There are four to five daily buses (AR$5 to AR$12, one hour) to Paso de los Libres, with some continuing to Concordia and beyond. In the other direction, there are daily services to Posadas (AR$48, five hours). More buses stop on the highway at the edge of the town.

POSADAS & THE JESUIT MISSIONS

The narrow northeastern province of Misiones juts out like an Argentine finger between Brazilian and Paraguayan territory and is named for the Jesuit missions (see the boxed text, p220) that were established in the region and whose ruins are a major attraction. Today San Ignacio Miní is the best restored; it and other ruins (including those across the border in Paraguay; see the boxed text, p218) are easily accessed from the provincial capital, Posadas. Buses churn through Misiones en route to the Iguazú Falls in the north of the province, but a detour will take you to another stunning cascade – the Saltos del Moconá on the Río Uruguay (see the boxed text, p222).

The landscape here is an attraction. Approaching Misiones from the south you will see a change to gently rolling low hills, stands of bamboo, and papaya and manioc plantations. The highway passes tea and *mate* plantations growing from the region's trademark red soil – the province is the main producer of *mate*, Argentina's staple drink.

POSADAS

☎ 03752 / pop 279,961

Capital of Misiones, and a base for visiting the ruins of the Jesuit missions after which the province is named, Posadas is a modern city that gazes across the wide Río Paraná to Encarnación in Paraguay. Brightly colored street signs vie for attention on the bustling, humid streets, and shady trees stand guard

in the several parks and plazas. Posadas is a stopover for travelers on their way north to Paraguay or Iguazú, but has plenty of charm of its own, if little in the way of sights.

Posadas was the gateway to the pioneering agricultural communities of interior Misiones and in 1912 was linked with Buenos Aires by the Urquiza railway. The city lost some of its low-lying areas to flooding from the Yacyretá dam, a major hydroelectric project completed in 1997 that forced the relocation of 40,000 people.

Orientation

Posadas is on the south bank of the upper Río Paraná, 300km south of Puerto Iguazú. A handsome bridge links Posadas with the Paraguayan city of Encarnación.

Plaza 9 de Julio is the center of Posadas' standard grid; the impressive 19th-century facade of the Casa de Gobierno (Government House) stretches along almost its entire east side. Av Bartolomé Mitre is the southern boundary of the center and leads east to the international bridge.

Information

There are several ATMs around the plaza, and call centers and internet places nearby.

ACA (Automóvil Club Argentina; ☎ 436955; cnr Córdoba & Colón) Maps and route information.

Cambios Mazza (Bolívar) Changes traveler's checks.

Guayrá (☎ 433415; www.guayra.com.ar; San Lorenzo 2208) Very helpful tour agency, one of many offering half-day tours to the Jesuit missions (AR$150 to AR$200 for up to four missions), the Paraguayan missions, Saltos del Moconá and more.

Hospital General R Madariaga (☎ 447775; Av López Torres 1177) About 1km south of downtown.

Provincial tourist office (☎ 447539; www.turismo .misiones.gov.ar; Colón 1985; ☺ 7am-8pm) Has well-informed staff. There's another office at the bus terminal, open the same hours.

Su Lavandería (☎ 03752-15-353479; La Rioja 1778; per load AR$20; ☺ 8am-8pm) Fast laundry.

Sights

Guayrá (see above) organises tours to the nearby missions (see p217).

The mighty Paraná itself is the main sight of Posadas, apart from a couple of desultory museums. Better than these is the **Palacio del Mate** (☎ 449974; Rivadavia 1846; ☺ 9am-8pm), a newly reopened art gallery with temporary exhibitions and some displays on the *mate*-growing process.

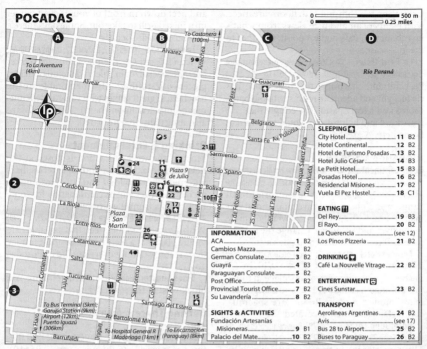

POSADAS

SLEEPING		
City Hotel	11	B2
Hotel Continental	12	B2
Hotel de Turismo Posadas	13	B2
Hotel Julio César	14	B3
Le Petit Hotel	15	B3
Posadas Hotel	16	B2
Residencial Misiones	17	B2
Vuela El Pez Hostel	18	C1

EATING		
Del Rey	19	B3
El Rayo	20	B2
La Querencia	(see 12)	
Los Pinos Pizzeria	21	B2

DRINKING		
Café La Nouvelle Vitrage	22	B2

ENTERTAINMENT		
Cines Sunstar	23	B2

TRANSPORT		
Aerolíneas Argentinas	24	B2
Avis	(see 17)	
Bus 28 to Airport	25	B2
Buses to Paraguay	26	B2

INFORMATION		
ACA	1	B2
Cambios Mazza	2	B2
German Consulate	3	B2
Guayrá	4	B3
Paraguayan Consulate	5	B2
Post Office	6	B2
Provincial Tourist Office	7	B2
Su Lavandería	8	B2

SIGHTS & ACTIVITIES		
Fundación Artesanías		
Misioneras	9	B1
Palacio del Mate	10	B2

Guaraní culture is strong in this part of Argentina, and you'll see Guaraní artists selling their wares throughout the center. Particularly fine pieces are displayed and sold at **Fundación Artesanías Misioneras** (☎ 441229; funda cionartesaniasmisioneras@gmail.com; cnr Alvarez & Arrechea; ☽ 9am-12:30pm & 5-8pm Mon-Sat).

Festivals & Events
Posadas celebrates **Carnaval** (in February or March, depending on the year) with great gusto, and seems to try to outdo other northern cities in the skimpiness of dancers' costumes.

Sleeping
Look out for the reopening of **Hotel de Turismo** (Bolívar 2176), closed for major renovation and modernization at the time of research.

BUDGET
Vuela El Pez Hostel (☎ 438706; www.vuelaelpez.com .ar; 25 de Mayo 1216; dm/tw AR$30/95, d without bathroom AR$75; ☒ ⌨ 🖳 🕮) Atop a bluff near the cos-tanera, this unsigned building contains a very laid-back hostel indeed. Decent dorms and

dark but good-value private rooms surround a small pool. Other features include a kitchen, DVD player and a liberal atmosphere.

La Aventura (☎ 465555; www.complejolaaventura .com; cnr Avs Urquiza & Zapiola; dm AR$35, cabins from AR$170; ☒ ⌨ 🖳) This is a sort of HI-affiliated holi-day camp, 4km from the center (bus 3 or 13 from Ayacucho, or a AR$7 taxi ride). Cabins sleep up to four; there are also dorm beds and hotel rooms. In the large, leafy grounds are a river beach, a good restaurant, a pool, tennis court, minigolf and more.

Residencial Misiones (☎ 430133; Av Azara 1960; s/d AR$50/60) Offering seriously cheap rooms in a characterful central building, this is a budget option for those who aren't hygiene freaks. The mattresses are in reverse gear already, and nei-ther the near-useless kitchen nor the bathrooms are up to much, but it gains points for the low prices and the staff's caring attitude. Rooms vary in quality, so have a look at a few.

City Hotel (☎ 439401; www.misionescityhotel.com .ar; Colón 1754; s/d AR$102/170; ☒ 🖳 🕮) Bang on the plaza, the City has just about the biggest sign in a big-sign town. Rooms vary; some are rather uninspiring with lino floors, but others, right up on the 10th and 11th floors, are nicer, with plenty of air and nice views from what's just about the city's highest point. Cheaper in the low-season.

Le Petit Hotel (☎ 436031; www.hotellepetit.com .ar; Santiago del Estero 1630; s/d AR$120/170; ✖ ☎) Peaceful and charming, this little place has clean, light and adequate rooms with big bathrooms and a leafy patio. The couple that run it are kind and helpful, and you'll feel right at home here. A great spot.

MIDRANGE & TOP END

Hotel Continental (☎ 440990; www.hoteleramisiones .com.ar; Bolívar 1879; s/d standard AR$193/237, s/d superior AR$249/309; ✖ ☐ ☎) A mite overpriced but bang on the plaza, this cavernous hotel has many rooms with superb views over the square to the river and Paraguay. Change the carpets please. Ten percent off if you pay cash.

Posadas Hotel (☎ 440888; www.hotelposadas.com.ar; Bolívar 1949; s/d AR$200/245; ✖ ☐ ☎) With by far the best-looking interior of any place in town, the Posadas has that gravitas missing from many modern hotels. Rooms are spacious, comfortable and well decorated.

Hotel Julio César (☎ 427930; www.juliocesarhotel .com.ar; Entre Ríos 1951; s/d AR$250/300; ✖ ☐ ☎ ☎) This four-star job in the city center has light, spacious, summery rooms with fridge and pleasing bathrooms, and better service than it used to. The slightly pricier superior rooms are identical but on higher floors.

Eating

Casual eateries near the intersection of Bolívar and San Lorenzo are popular meeting spots for a light meal outdoors or an ice cream. The *costanera* also has several options.

El Rayo (☎ 439901; Bolívar 2089; light meals AR$6-15; ☽ lunch & dinner) No-frills and effective, this joint is thronged at lunchtime for its delicious empanadas, *lomitos* and good-value pizza. Service comes with a smile, too. Thumbs up.

Los Pinos Pizzeria (☎ 423713; cnr Buenos Aires & Sarmiento; pizza AR$12-27; ☽ 4pm-late) The place to go for pizza, draft beer or empanadas. There's a well-stocked bar and classical music on the sound system during the week; weekends things get a bit livelier. The lovely old building began as a pharmacy.

Del Rey (☎ 436798; cnr Tucumán & Ayacucho; mains AR$15-25; ☽ lunch & dinner) Value is high at this sociable neighborhood *parrilla*, which will toss impressive quantities of barbecued chicken and beef down in front of you or even parcel up a mixed grill to take-out. Some days there's all-you-can-eat specials.

La Querencia (☎ 437117; Bolívar 322; mains AR$18-40; ☽ lunch & dinner) On the plaza, this upmarket *parrilla* specializes in *galeto* (delicious chicken pieces with stuffing). Also memorable are the brochettes (giant spikes with various delicious meats impaled upon them). The salads are also unusually well prepared.

Drinking & Entertainment

Most of the weekend action is down at the new *costanera*, where a knot of eateries, bars and nightclubs go loud and late. Head north up Buenos Aires and its continuation for some nine blocks from the city center.

Café La Nouvelle Vitrage (☎ 429619; Bolívar 1899) With a vaguely French feel, this amiable cafe on the plaza has a comfy interior and a terrace perfect for watching everyday life in Posadas go by.

Cines Sunstar (Bolívar 1981) This cinema is a block west of the plaza.

Getting There & Away
AIR

Aerolíneas Argentinas (☎ 422036; Ayacucho 1728) flies five times weekly to Buenos Aires (AR$610).

BUS

Buses to Encarnación, Paraguay (AR$3.50), leave every 20 minutes from the corner of San Lorenzo and Entre Ríos. With border formalities, the trip can take more than an hour, but is usually quicker.

Everyone gets out to clear Argentine emigration. The bus may leave without you; hang onto your ticket to catch the next one. The same happens on the Paraguayan side. There's a handy tourist office right by Paraguayan immigration, and official moneychangers hanging around. Make sure you get small denominations: a 100,000 guaraní note is hell to change. At the time of writing there were 4630 guaraní to US$1 or 1200 guaraní to AR$1.

Launches (AR$3) across the Río Paraná to Encarnación had been suspended at time of research.

For transport from Posadas to the Esteros del Iberá, see p203.

Posadas' **bus terminal** (☎ 425800; RN 12 & Av Santa Catalina) can be reached from downtown by buses 8, 15, 21 or 24 (AR$1.40). Think AR$16 in a taxi.

All of the following destinations are served at least daily, most are served several times a day. Travel times are approximate.

Destination	Cost (AR$)	Duration (hr)
Buenos Aires	165	14
Corrientes	55	4
Paso de los Libres	56	6
Puerto Iguazú	45	5
Resistencia	60	5
Rosario	160	16
Santa Fe	156	14
Tucumán	210	18
Yapeyú	48	5

Bus services to San Ignacio (AR$8, one hour) begin at 5:15am and depart half-hourly.

TRAIN
From **Garupá train station** (☎ 491101; www.trenes dellitoral.com.ar), 10km from Posadas, the battered old Gran Capitán runs to Buenos Aires' Federico Lacroze train station at 6pm on Sunday, leaving from Buenos Aires at 10pm on Friday. It theoretically takes 27 hours, but usually takes many more. The cheapest class costs AR$65, while a sleeping berth costs AR$225.

Getting Around
Bus 28 (AR$1.40) goes to the airport from San Lorenzo (between La Rioja and Entre Ríos). A *remise* costs about AR$30. **Avis** (☎ 430050; www .avis.com.ar; Azará 1908) is a recommended car-rental agency.

AROUND POSADAS
Santa Ana & Loreto
Atmospherically decaying in the humid forest, these two Jesuit missions are both off RN 12 between Posadas and San Ignacio, the site of another (better restored) mission.

At **Santa Ana** (☯ 7am-6pm), which was founded in 1633 but moved here in 1660, dense forest has been partially removed to reveal a settlement that had over 7000 Guaraní inhabitants at its peak. The enormous plaza, 140m square, attests to the importance of the settlement.

The muscular church's thick walls have been propped up with interior scaffolding; a few photogenic strangler figs grow atop them, lending a dramatic effect to what must have been a magnificent building, though none of its decorative embellishments remain. The church was designed by the Italian architect Brasanelli, who also worked on the San Ignacio church.

To the right side of the church is the cemetery, which was used by villagers into the latter half of the 20th century but is now neglected. Crypts with doors agape reveal coffins fallen from their shelves and burst open; if this place doesn't give you the willies, you haven't watched enough horror movies.

Behind the church, a channel and reservoir remain from what was a sophisticated irrigation system.

Loreto (☯ 7am-6:30pm), founded in 1632, has even fewer visible remains than Santa Ana, and may not be worth the effort to visit via public transport. The old adobe latrine and a chapel are partially restored, but the jungle is king here again, and it's difficult to interpret the tumbled mossy stones among the trees. It's undeniably atmospheric, though. It was one of the more important missions, and a printing press was built here – the first in the southern part of the continent.

Admission for both Loreto and Santa Ana is via a **joint ticket** (Argentines/other Latin Americans/other nationalities AR$15/20/25) that includes San Ignacio Miní and Santa María la Mayor. Both Santa Ana and Loreto are staffed by knowledgeable students, who give recommended tours, included in the admission price. The missions have small museums and kiosks at their entrances.

GETTING THERE & AWAY
Buses heading north from Posadas stop at the turnoffs on RN 12 for both sites. Santa Ana's is at Km 43, from where it's a 1km walk to the ruins. Loreto's is at Km 48, with a 3km walk. It can be intensely hot, so take plenty of water. You may be able to hitch a lift on the school bus on your way back; ask at Loreto mission. You can get a *remise* from San Ignacio to take you to both, including waiting time, for about AR$70. If you can't see one around the center, call **Andi** (☎ 03752-15-273747), who knows plenty about the area.

Santa María la Mayor
Further afield, this is the fourth mission on the joint admission ticket for San Ignacio, Santa Ana and Loreto. A sizable plaza is the main feature, with the church very ruinous. The settlement was a large one, with printing press and prison; the chapel is a 20th-century addition. It's a relaxing place surrounded by jungle that's great for bird-watching, with toucans and trogons easily spotted. The visitor center has a good bird identification pamphlet.

VISITING THE PARAGUAYAN MISSIONS

From Posadas there's a tempting and very rewarding day trip to two of the Jesuit missions in Paraguay. The ruined but majestic churches at Trinidad and Jesús de Tavarangüe have been carefully restored and preserve some fabulous stonework.

From Posadas, cross by bus to Encarnación (see p216) and get off at the bus terminal. From here, there are buses (most marked Ciudad del Este) every half-hour or so to Trinidad (G5000, 40 minutes). Get the driver to let you off at the turnoff to the ruins; it's then a 700m walk.

The **Trinidad ruins** (admission G5000; ☽ 7am-7pm, to 5:30pm in winter) are spectacular, with the red-brown stone of the church contrasting strongly with the flower-studded green grass and surrounding hillscapes. Unlike at the Argentine missions, there is much decoration preserved here: the scalloped niches still hold timeworn sculptures, and the font and elaborate baroque pulpit are impressive. The doorways are capped with fine, carved decoration. You can climb to the top of one of the walls, but careful with the kids – there's no guardrail up there. An earlier church and bell tower have also been restored here. There's a hotel and restaurant by the ruins.

For **Jesús de Tavarangüe**, walk back to the main road and turn right. At the gas station 100m away is the turnoff to Jesús, 12km away. Shared taxis (G5000) wait here to fill, and buses (G4000) pass every two hours. You can get a taxi to take you to Jesús de Tavarangüe, wait for you and bring you back to the turnoff for about G20,000.

The restored **church** (admission G5000; ☽ 7am-7pm, to 5:30pm in winter) at Jesús de Tavarangüe was never finished. The spectacular trefoil arches (a nod to Spain's Moorish past) and carved motifs of crossed swords and keys make it perhaps the most picturesque of all the Jesuit ruins. The treble-naved church, with green grass underfoot, is on a similarly monumental scale as Trinidad. You can climb the tower for views of the surrounding countryside.

Head back to the main road by bus or taxi; buses back to Encarnación stop by the gas station. Last stop is at or by the bus terminal; buses back to Posadas leave from the bus stop outside the bus terminal, opposite the school.

Note: you may need a visa to enter Paraguay. Currently, Americans, Canadians, Australians and New Zealanders do; Israelis, Brits and other EU citizens don't. A single-entry visa costs US$45 from the Paraguayan consulate in Posadas and can be ready in about an hour. You'll need passport photos, a copy of your passport, proof of an onward ticket and possibly proof of sufficient funds (a credit card may do). You can risk going through without getting your passport stamped, but the fine is US$75 if you get caught, which is possible on your way back through.

The ruins are right on the RP 2 road between Concepción de la Sierra and San Javier, 110km southeast of Posadas. To get there, take a bus from Posadas to Concepción de la Sierra. There, change to a San Javier–bound service and ask the driver to let you off at the ruins, which are some 25km down the road. You can get a San Javier–bound bus direct from Posadas, but make sure it runs via the ruins – some go a different way.

SAN IGNACIO
☎ 03752 / pop 6312

The best preserved of the Argentine missions, San Ignacio Miní is the central attraction of this small town north of Posadas. You could visit from Posadas or on your way to Iguazú, but a better idea is to stay the night; the hotels are comfortable, and you'll have a chance to check out the sound-and-light show at the

ruins as well as Quiroga's house; both are worthwhile.

San Ignacio is 56km northeast of Posadas via RN 12. From the highway junction, the broad Av Sarmiento leads about 1km to the center, where Rivadavia leads six blocks north to the ruins. At the highway junction is a helpful **tourist office** (☽ 7am-9pm).

Sights
SAN IGNACIO MINÍ

These **mission ruins** (☎ 470186; www.misiones-jesuiticas.com.ar; entrance Calle Alberdi s/n; Argentines/Latin Americans/other nationalities AR$15/20/25; ☽ 7am-7pm) are the most complete of those in Argentina and impress for the quantity of carved ornamentation still visible and for the amount of restoration done. No roofs remain, but many of the living quarters and workshops have been re-erected.

First founded in 1610 in Brazil, but abandoned after repeated attacks by slavers, San Ignacio was established at its present site in 1696 and functioned until the Jesuits finally gave in to the order of expulsion in 1768. The ruins, rediscovered in 1897 and restored between 1940 and 1948, are a great example of 'Guaraní baroque.' At its peak, the *reducción* had a Guaraní population of nearly 4000.

The entrance is on the north side on Calle Alberdi, where the first stop is the **interpretation center**. It's an impressive display with plenty of unbiased information (in Spanish and English) about the missions from both the Jesuit and Guaraní perspectives. You can listen to Guaraní music, including some religious pieces composed at the missions, and inspect a virtual model of San Ignacio as it would have been.

The ruins themselves feature interactive panels that provide multilingual information, or you can join an informative free tour if you wish; guides speak English and some speak French and German, too. You first pass between rows of Guaraní houses before arriving at the plaza, on one side of which is the enormous red sandstone church. Impressive in its dimensions, it is the focal point of the settlement. While the red-brown stone is very picturesque, the buildings were originally white. Before lime was widely available, it was obtained by burning snail shells.

By the church, the cloisters preserve some ornately carved balustrades and the original flooring of some of the rooms off it. Just before the exit is another museum containing some excellent carved paving stones.

In summer it's worth trying to avoid visiting between 10am and 1pm, as the site gets particularly busy with tour groups at these times.

In theory, there is a *Luz y Sonido* (Sound-and-Light show) at the ruins every night from mid-September to March, and sporadically at other times. It's included in the price of the ticket and the time varies slightly between 7pm and 8pm.

The admission ticket is valid for 15 days, and includes entry to the nearby ruins at Santa Ana and Loreto (p217), and also to Santa María la Mayor (p217), a little further afield.

CASA DE HORACIO QUIROGA

The Uruguayan novelist and poet Horacio Quiroga was a get-back-to-nature type who found his muse in the rough-and-ready Misiones backwoods lifestyle. His **house** (☎ 470124; Av Quiroga s/n; admission AR$7; ◷ 8am-6:45pm) at the southern end of town (a 20- to 30-minute walk) is a simple affair, which he built himself out of stone.

To reach it, you walk a trail through the sugarcane, where panels (in English, too) detail the events of a deeply tragic life so full of shotgun accidents and doses of cyanide it's almost funny.

Grand views of the Paraná (which you'll have to crane to see if the vegetation is high) inspired Quiroga to write his regionally based stories that transcend time and place without abandoning their setting. Some of his short fiction is available in English translation in *The Exiles and Other Stories*.

Next to the stone house is a replica of his initial wooden house, built for the 1996 biographical film *Historias de Amor, de Locura y de Muerte* (Stories of Love, Madness and Death).

Sleeping & Eating

Adventure Hostel (☎ 470955; www.sihostel.com; Independencia 469; dm/d AR$34/140; ⚅ ▢ ⊚ ▣) Next to the plaza two blocks south of the church, this new hostel has darkish and slightly institutional (whitewashed brick) but comfortable dorms and private rooms, and excellent facilities. There's everything from ping-pong and DVDs to seesaws in the spacious grounds, and staff can order food in for you, too.

Hotel San Ignacio (☎ 470047; hotelsanignacio@arnet.com.ar; cnr Sarmiento & San Martín; s/d AR$70/100, 5-person cabana AR$150; ⚅ ▢) Located in the town center near where the bus stops, this is an excellent choice for its clean, quiet, comfortable rooms, great bathrooms, benevolent owners, and an attached bar and internet cafe. The A-frame cabins out the back are great value for groups. The bar does simple tasty food. You may never find it easier to be the best pool player in town, but the table football is a different story.

Hotel Portal del Sol (☎ 470005; www.portaldelsol hotel.com; Rivadavia 1115; s/d AR$90/115; ⚅ ▢ ⊚ ▣) Between the town center and the ruins, this place is a fair bit better than it looks. The restaurant is mediocre, but the rooms are rather attractive, with a contrast between the light linen and the dark wooden furniture. Guests can use the pool at the nearby Carpa Azul tent restaurant.

NORTHEAST ARGENTINA

A TRIUMPH OF HUMANITY

For a century and a half from 1609, one of the world's great social experiments was carried out in the jungles of South America by the Society of Jesus (the Jesuits). Locating themselves in incredibly remote areas, priests set up *reducciones* (missions), where they established communities of Guaraní whom they evangelized and educated, while at the same time protecting them from slavery and the evil influences of colonial society. It was a utopian ideal that flourished and led Voltaire to describe it as 'a triumph of humanity which seems to expiate the cruelties of the first conquerors.'

For the Guaraní who were invited to begin a new life in the missions, there were many tangible benefits, including security, nourishment and prosperity. Mortality declined immediately, and the mission populations grew rapidly. At their peak, the 30 Jesuit *reducciones* spread across what's now Argentina, Brazil and Paraguay were populated by more than 100,000 Guaraní. Each mission had a minimum of Europeans: two priests was the norm, and the Guaraní governed themselves under the Jesuits' spiritual authority. The Jesuits made no attempt to force the Guaraní to speak Spanish and only sought to change those aspects of Guaraní culture – polygamy and occasional cannibalism – that clashed with Catholic teaching. Each Guaraní family was given a house and children were schooled.

The typical *reducción* consisted of a large central plaza, dominated by the church and *colegio*, which housed the priests and also contained art workshops and storerooms. The houses of the Guaraní occupied the rest of the settlement in neat rows; other buildings might include a hospital, a *cotiguazú* (big house) that housed widows and abandoned wives, and a *cabildo* where the Guaraní's chosen leader lived.

The settlements were self-sufficient; the Guaraní were taught agriculture, and food was distributed equally. As time went on and the missions grew, the original wooden buildings were replaced by stone ones, and the churches, designed by master architects with grandiose utopian dreams, were stunning edifices with intricate baroque stonework and sculpture comparable with the finest churches being built in Europe at the time.

Indeed, the missions' most enduring achievement was perhaps artistic. The Guaraní embraced the art and music they were introduced to and, interweaving European styles with their own, produced beautiful music, sculpture, dance and painting in the so-called 'Guaraní baroque' style. It was perhaps the Jesuits' religious music that most attracted the Guaraní to Catholicism.

However, mission life necessarily had a martial side. Raiding parties of *bandeirantes* from Brazil regularly sought slaves for sugar plantations, and the Jesuits were resented by both Spanish and Portuguese colonial authorities. There were regular skirmishes and battles until a notable victory over an army of 3000 slavers at Mbororó in 1641 ushered in a period of comparative security.

The mission period came to an abrupt end. Various factors, including envy from colonial authority and settlers, and a feeling that the Jesuits were more loyal to their own ideas than those of the crown, prompted Carlos III of Spain to ban them from his dominions in 1767, following the lead of Portugal and France. With the priests gone, the communities were vulnerable, and the Guaraní gradually dispersed. The decaying missions were then ruined in the wars of the early 19th century.

The 1986 film *The Mission* is about the last days of the Jesuit missions. Most intriguing is the casting of a Colombian tribe, the Waunana (who had had almost no contact with white people) as the Guaraní.

Almost nothing remains of several of Argentina's 15 missions, but those well worth visiting include San Ignacio Miní (p218), Loreto and Santa Ana (p217), Yapeyú (p213) and Santa María la Mayor (p217). The fabulous Paraguayan missions at Jesús de Tavarangüe and Trinidad can be easily visited on a day trip from Posadas (see the boxed text, p218). There are others to visit not too far away in southern Brazil.

La Aldea (Los Jesuitas s/n; dishes AR$12-25; ⊗ 8am-midnight) Near the *artesanía* stalls at the ruins exit, this barn of a place has tables out the front, inside and on the rear deck. It serves excellent pizza and *minutas* (snacks), and is one of the only eating options open late at night.

Don Valentín (☎ 03752-15-647961; Alberdi 444; mains AR$14-30; ⊗ 8am-5:30pm) Across from the entrance to the ruins, Don Valentín is a step up from the production-line operations serving tour groups along here. It has a shady terrace and cordial service, but doesn't stay open for dinner.

Getting There & Away

Fast buses on RN 12 stop at the arch on the main road, at the entrance to town, but plenty enter San Ignacio, stopping on Av Sarmiento in the center of town, by the church. Services between Posadas (AR$8, one hour) and Puerto Iguazú (AR$40, four to five hours) are frequent.

If you're not staying, the friendly kiosk next to the church, right where buses stop, will look after baggage for a couple of pesos.

IGUAZÚ FALLS

One of the planet's most awe-inspiring sights, the Iguazú Falls are simply astounding. A visit is a jaw-dropping, visceral experience, and the power and noise of the cascades live forever in the memory. An added benefit is the setting: the falls lie split between Brazil and Argentina in a large expanse of national park, much of it rainforest teeming with unique flora and fauna. There are thousands of species of insects, hundreds of species of birds and many mammals and reptiles.

The falls are easily reached from either side of the Argentine–Brazilian border, as well as from nearby Paraguay. Most visitors choose either to stay in Foz do Iguaçu, on the Brazilian side, or in Argentina's Puerto Iguazú. Both have a wide range of accommodation choices.

History & Environment

Álvar Núñez Cabeza de Vaca and his expedition in 1542 were the first Europeans to view the falls. According to Guaraní tradition the falls originated when an Indian warrior named Caroba incurred the wrath of a forest god by escaping downriver in a canoe with a young girl, Naipur, with whom the god was infatuated. Enraged, the god caused the riverbed to collapse in front of the lovers, producing a line of precipitous falls over which Naipur fell and, at their base, turned into a rock. Caroba survived as a tree overlooking it.

Geologists have a more prosaic explanation. The Río Iguaçú's course takes it over a basaltic plateau that ends abruptly just short of the confluence with the Paraná. Where the lava flow stopped, thousands of cubic meters of water per second now plunge down as much as 80m into sedimentary terrain below.

Before reaching the falls, the river divides into many channels with hidden reefs, rocks and islands separating the many visually distinctive cascades that together form the famous *cataratas* (waterfalls). In total, the falls stretch around for more than 2km.

Seeing the Falls

The Brazilian and Argentine sides offer different views and experiences of the falls. Go to both (perhaps to the Brazilian first) and hope for sun. The difference between a clear and an overcast day at the falls is vast, only in part because of the rainbows and butterflies that emerge when the sun is shining. Ideally you should allow for a multiple-day stay to have a better shot at optimal conditions.

While the Argentine side – with its variety of trails and boat rides – offers many more opportunities to see individual falls close up, the Brazilian side yields the more panoramic views. You can easily make day trips to both sides of the falls, no matter which side of the border you choose to base yourself.

National Parks

The Brazilian and Argentine sides of the falls are both designated national parks: Parque Nacional do Iguaçu and Parque Nacional Iguazú, respectively. High temperatures, humidity and rainfall encourage a diverse habitat, and the parks' rainforest contains more than 2000 identified plant species, countless insects, 400 species of birds and many mammals and reptiles.

THE OTHER FALLS

Iguazú's aren't the only spectacular falls in Misiones province: the remote and unusual **Saltos del Moconá** also live long in the memory. A geological fault in the bed of the Río Uruguay divides the river lengthwise, and water spills over the shelf between the two sections, creating a waterfall some 3km long and up to 15m high, depending on the water level.

The falls are at the eastern edge of Misiones province roughly equidistant from Posadas and Puerto Iguazú. From Posadas, several daily buses leave for El Soberbio (four hours); from here it's 75km to the falls, mostly paved. From the end of the road, if the river is low, you can pick your way along to the falls, but you'll see them much better by taking a boat trip.

Lodges organize trips to the falls and the various parks and reserves that protect the zone, as does friendly **Yabotí Jungle** (☎ 03755-495266, 03755-15-652853; mocona4x4@yahoo.com.ar; Av Corrientes 481, El Soberbio), which charges AR$130 for a four-hour trip to the falls (AR$390 minimum); the speedboat trip, with Brazilian and Argentine jungle reserves on each side, is an attraction in itself. Operators in Posadas and Puerto Iguazú also arrange trips. The same operators also run trips to remote Guaraní *aldeas* (villages) for AR$80.

Most important: the falls aren't always visible; if the river is high, then you're out of luck. Ring ahead to find out. December to March is normally the best time.

El Soberbio itself is an interesting place, a service center for a lush agricultural area growing tobacco, citronella and manioc. There's a ferry crossing to Brazil, and blond heads are everywhere, a legacy of German and Eastern European immigrants joining the native Guaraní population.

There are several places to stay, including **Hostal Del Centro** (☎ 03755-495133; cnr Rivadavia & San Martín; r per person AR$50), right in the center of town but built around a grassy courtyard; rooms are good for this price and there's a kitchen you can use.

Hilltop **Hostería Puesta del Sol** (☎ 03755-495161; www.h-puestadelsol.com.ar; Suipacha s/n; s/d AR$95/180; 🅿 🛜 🖦) offers decent rooms in a relaxing complex with spectacular views and a huge (summertime) pool. Half-board rates are available for an extra AR$25 each, and there are bungalows for groups.

Several jungly lodges are closer to the falls. Accommodation in these places is generally in elegant rustic cabins with great views. Rates (except for Aldea Yaboty) include meals.

Aldea Yaboty (☎ 03755-15-553069; www.aldeayaboty.com; r/cabin AR$200/300)
Don Enrique Lodge (☎ 011-4743-2070; www.donenriquelodge.com.ar; s/d US$180/260)
Posada la Bonita (☎ 03755-15-680380; www.posadalabonita.com.ar; s/d AR$342/532)
Posada La Misión (☎ 011-5199-0185; www.lodgelamision.com.ar; d AR$530)

Resembling the tropical Amazonian rainforest to the north, the forests of the falls region consist of multiple levels, the highest a closed 30m canopy. Beneath the canopy are several additional levels of trees, plus a dense ground-level growth of shrubs and herbaceous plants. One of the most interesting is the guapoy (strangler fig), an epiphyte that uses a large tree for support until it finally asphyxiates its host.

Mammals and other wildlife are present but not easily seen in the parks, because many are either nocturnal or avoid humans – which is not difficult in the dense undergrowth. This is the case, for instance, with large cats such as the puma and jaguar. The largest mammal is the tapir, which is a distant relative of the horse, but most common is the coati, a relative of the raccoon. It is not unusual to see iguanas, and watch out for snakes.

Tropical bird species add a dash of color, with toucans and various species of parrot easily seen. The best time to see them is early morning along the forest trails.

Despite regular official denials, the heavy impact of so many visitors to the area has clearly driven much of the wildlife further into the parks, so the more you explore responsibly, the more you'll see.

Dangers & Annoyances

The Río Iguaçu's currents are strong and swift; tourists have been swept downriver and drowned in the area of Isla San Martín. Of course, don't get too close to the falls proper.

The heat and humidity are often intense around the falls, and there's plenty of hungry insect life.

While you're very unlikely to see a jaguar, be aware that they are 'respect' beasts. Official jaguar tactics are: don't run, make yourself look big and speak loudly.

On both sides, you're almost certain to encounter coatis. Don't feed them; though these clownish omnivores seem tame, they become aggressive around food, and will bite and scratch. Both parks have a medical point in case of coati attack.

You are likely to get soaked, or at least very damp, from the spray at the falls, so keep your documents and camera protected in plastic bags.

PARQUE NACIONAL IGUAZÚ
☎ 03757

On the Argentine side, this **park** (☎ 491469; www.iguazuargentina.com; adult/child 6-12yr AR$60/30, Mercosur nationals AR$30, Argentines AR$20; ☺ 8am-6pm Apr-Sep, 7:30am-6:30pm Oct-Mar) has plenty to offer, and involves a fair amount of walking. The spread-out complex at the entrance has various amenities, including lockers, an ATM and a restaurant. There's also an exhibition, **Ybyrá-retá**, with a display on the park and Guaraní life essentially aimed at school groups. The complex ends at a train station, where a train runs every half-hour to the Cataratas train station, where the waterfall walks begin, and to the Garganta del Diablo. You may prefer to walk: it's only 650m along the 'Sendero Verde' path to the Cataratas station, and a further 2.3km to the Garganta and you may well see capuchin monkeys along the way.

There's more than enough here to detain you for a couple of days, and admission is reduced by 50% if you visit the park again the following day. You need to get your ticket stamped when leaving on the first day to get the discount.

Sights

Walking around is the best way to see the **falls**, with sets of paths offering different perspectives over the cascades. It really is worth getting here by 9am: the gangways are narrow and getting stuck in a conga line of tour groups in searing heat and humidity takes the edge off the experience.

Two circuits, the **Paseo Superior** (650m) and **Paseo Inferior** (1400m), provide most of the viewing opportunities via a series of trails, bridges and *pasarelas* (catwalks). The Paseo Superior is entirely level and gives good views of the tops of several cascades and across to more. The Paseo Inferior descends to the river (no wheelchair access), passing delightfully close to more falls on the way. At the bottom of the path, a free launch makes the short crossing to **Isla San Martín**, an island with a trail of its own that gives the closest look at several falls, including **Salto San Martín**, a huge, furious cauldron of water. It's possible to picnic and swim on the lee side of the island, but don't venture too far off the beach.

From Cataratas train station, train it or walk the 2300m to the Garganta del Diablo stop, where an 1100m walkway across the placid Río Iguazú leads to one of the planet's most spectacular sights, the **Garganta del Diablo** (Devil's Throat). The lookout platform is perched right over this amazingly powerful and concentrated torrent of water, a deafening cascade plunging to murky destination; the vapors soaking the viewer blur the base of the falls and rise in a smoke-like plume that can often be seen several kilometers away. It's a place of majesty and awe, and should be left until the end of your visit. The last train to the Garganta leaves at 5pm, and we recommend taking it, as it'll be a far less crowded experience. If you walk, you'll see quite a lot of wildlife around this time of day, too.

THE RIDE OF A LIFETIME

If you think that the walkways give you a close-up view of Iguazú Falls, think again – you have actually been denied a once-in-a-lifetime photo opportunity.

In the early days of Iguazú's popularity as a tourist attraction, you could hire a local with a rowboat who would take you right out to the edge of the falls and keep the boat there by rowing madly against the current while you and your friends took photos, spat and did all that other stuff you do at the edge of a waterfall.

But the inevitable has a way of happening, and so it was that one day in 1938 the rower found himself overpowered by the current, and the boat – with seven German tourists on board – went sliding over the edge. There were no survivors and these boat trips were immediately prohibited.

And so ends the history of a foolish but exhilarating sightseeing option.

NORTHEAST ARGENTINA

Activities

Relatively few visitors venture beyond the immediate area of the falls to appreciate the park's forest scenery and wildlife, but it's well worth doing. On the falls trails you'll see large lizards, coatis and several species of birds, but you'll see much more on one of the few trails through the dense forest.

Along the road past the visitor center (you can also access it via a path from the Estación Central trailhead) is the entrance to the **Sendero Macuco** nature trail, which leads through dense forest to a nearly hidden waterfall, **Salto Arrechea**. The first 3km of the trail to the top of the waterfall is almost completely level, but there is a steep lateral drop to the base of the falls and beyond to the Río Iguaçu, about 650m in all. This part of the trail is muddy and slippery – watch your step and figure about 1¼ hours each way from the trailhead. Early morning is best, with better opportunities to see wildlife, including toucans and bands of caí monkeys. Take insect repellent.

Iguazú Jungle Explorer (☎ 421696; www.iguazujunglexplorer.com) is a well-run set-up that offers the following three excursions: a speedboat ride to the bottom of several of the waterfalls, including an exhilarating drenching under the San Martín torrent (AR$75, 15 minutes); a quiet dinghy ride down the upper Iguazú (AR$35, 30 minutes); and a one-hour trip combining a descent to the river in flatbed trucks along the Sendero Yacaratiá, and then a trip upriver through rapids to the falls (AR$150, one hour). Discounts are offered for combining any of these tours.

For five consecutive nights per month, **full moon walks** (☎ 491469; www.iguazuargentina.com; AR$130) visit the Garganta del Diablo. There are three departures nightly; the first one, at 8pm, offers the spectacle of the inflated rising moon; the last, at 9:30pm, sees the falls better illuminated. Don't expect to see wildlife. The price includes admission, and a cocktail and dinner afterwards. Extra bus departures from Puerto Iguazú cater for moonwalkers.

Sleeping & Eating

There's one hotel within the park. The numerous snack bars offer predictably overpriced snacks and drinks. The food is awful; bring a picnic or eat at one of the two restaurants, La Selva or Fortín.

Sheraton International Iguazú (☎ 491800; www.sheraton.com/iguazu; r with forest/falls view AR$1100/1330; ⊠ ⎚ ⎙ ⊗ ⊗) With a privileged position in the park itself and looking right up the river to the most spectacular section of the falls, the Sheraton backs it up with professional service and spacious rooms with balconies, though it looks a little tired in parts. You're paying for the view here, so you might as well upgrade to see the falls. Rooms are usually substantially cheaper if booking online. Readers have been disappointed with the restaurant.

Fortín (☎ 491040; all-you-can-eat AR$50; ⊠ 10am-5pm) Well located near the old hotel (now the park medical center), this offers a decent buffet spread with fairly mediocre *parrilla* choices. It's the closest acceptable lunch spot to the falls walkways. It doesn't appear on park maps.

La Selva (☎ 491459; tenedor libre AR$55; ⊠ 11am-3:30pm) During your visit, this restaurant will get talked up so much you'll fear the worst, but it's actually quite OK, with a decent buffet of hot and cold dishes, and all-you-can-eat *parrillada*. The information kiosks dotted around the complex sometimes give out vouchers offering a substantial discount.

Getting There & Away

The park is 20km southeast of Puerto Iguazú. From Puerto Iguazú's bus terminal, buses leave half-hourly for the park (AR$5, 40 minutes) between 6:40am and 7:40pm, with return trips between 7:20am and 8:20pm. The buses make flag stops at points along the highway. A taxi from town to the park entrance is AR$50.

PARQUE NACIONAL DO IGUAÇU (BRAZIL)

On the Brazilian side, this **park** (☎ 3521-4400; www.cataratasdoiguacu.com.br; 7yr & older R$21.15, Mercosur nationals R$18.15, Brazilians R$13.65; ⊠ 9am-6pm summer, 9am-5pm winter) is entered via an enormous visitor center, which has a snack bar, an ATM and big lockers (R$3), among other amenities. Parking here costs R$12, but it's free at the Parque das Aves opposite.

Tickets can be purchased using Brazilian, Argentine, Paraguayan and US currency, and last admission is one hour before closing. After buying tickets, you pass through to an exhibition giving information (in Portuguese, English and Spanish) about the geology, history and biodiversity of the falls region. Behind the building, double-decker buses await to take you into the park proper. Keep your eyes peeled for animals.

ENTERING BRAZIL

If you're on a day trip, formalities are minimal. Argentine officials will stamp your passport as you leave the country, but Brazil usually unofficially tolerates day entry (even if you need a visa) without stamping you in.

If you are staying a while, or heading on into Brazil, you will need to get stamped in. Get off the bus at Brazilian immigration (then catch the next one on). Citizens of the USA, Australia, Canada and Japan, among others, will need a visa to officially enter Brazil. You can arrange one at the **Brazilian consulate** (☎ 03757-421348; Córdoba 264) in Puerto Iguazú, or before you leave home. If you do stay a while in Brazil, note that you may face a tax on your return to Argentina; for details, see the boxed text, p614.

The first stop is the **Trilha do Poço Preto** (☎ 3529-9627; www.macucoecoaventura.com.br; per person R$100), a 9km guided hike through the jungle on foot or by bike. The trail ends at Taquara Island, where you can kayak or take a boat cruise to Porto Canoas. You can also return via the Bananeiras Trail.

The second stop is for the two-hour **Macuco Safari** (☎ 3574-4244; www.macucosafari.com.br; per person R$140), which includes a 3km trailer ride through the jungle, a 600m walk to a small waterfall and then a boat ride up towards the falls. Don't confuse it with the Macuco trail on the Argentine side. Alight here, too, for the **Bananeiras Trail** (☎ 3529-9627; www.macucoecoaventura.com.br; per person R$80), a 2km walk passing lagoons and observing aquatic wildlife, which ends at a jetty where you can take boat rides or silent 'floating' excursions in kayaks down to Porto Canoas. If you plan to do any of these, chat with one of the agents touting them around the park visitor center; they can get you a discount. There are full-day packages offered for around R$228, including lunch, that should be reserved the day before.

The third, and principal, stop is at the Hotel Tropical das Cataratas (see right). This is where the main waterfall observation trail starts. At the beginning of the trail is also **Cânion Iguaçu** (☎ 3529-6040; www.campodedesafios.com.br), an activity center offering rafting (R$70), abseiling (R$50), rock climbing (R$40) and a canopy tour (R$50).

From here you walk 1.5km down a paved **trail** with brilliant views of the falls on the Argentine side, the jungle and the river below. Every twist of the path reveals a more splendid view until the trail ends right under the majestic Salto Floriano, which will give you a healthy sprinkling of water via the wind it generates. A catwalk leads out to a platform with majestic vistas, with the Garganta del

Diablo close at hand, and a perspective down the river in the other direction. If the water's high, it's unforgettable; a rainbow is visible in the spray on clear afternoons.

An elevator heads up to a viewing platform at the top of the falls at Porto Canoas, the last stop of the double-decker buses. Porto Canoas has a gift shop, a couple of snack bars (burgers R$4 to R$7) and an excellent buffet restaurant (see p226).

The park and restaurant are open for evening visits once a month on the night of the full moon.

Activities

Just opposite the park entrance, **Helisul** (☎ 3529-7474; www.helisul.com) runs 10-minute chopper jaunts at 450m over the Brazilian side of the falls. The environmental impact is debatable (the Argentines suspended their service for this reason), but it's undeniably exhilarating. There are open panels in the windows for photography. The ride costs R$190 per person; it's best done after you've visited the falls themselves. You can also charter the helicopter for a 35-minute trip that takes in the Itaipú dam and triple frontier.

Opposite Helisul, the **Parque das Aves** (☎ 3529-8282; www.parquedasaves.com.br; admission R$25; ☒ 8:30am-5:30pm) is a large bosky bird park. It has a huge assortment of our feathered friends, mostly Brazilian, with good information in English and Spanish. The highlight is the walk-through aviaries, where you can get up-close and personal with toucans, macaws and hummingbirds.

Sleeping & Eating

Hotel das Cataratas (☎ 2102-7000; www.hoteldascataratas.com; r standard/superior/deluxe R$921/1017/1181; ☒ ☐ ☒) This elegant pinkish hotel, which is not as old as it looks, is right in the park and near the falls. It appeals enormously for its location, but the rooms are elegant and not much more; only a handful have views of the falls. The staff and facilities are, however, commendable. Major renovations, due to last until 2011, are giving the still-open hotel a major facelift. Don't miss climbing the belvedere for the view.

Porto Canoas (☎ 3521-4400; buffet R$35; ☘ 11:30am-4pm Tue-Sun) After the falls, you (and your camera trigger finger) deserve a break. This spot is surprisingly good, with a long pleasant terrace overlooking the river just before it descends into maelstrom – a great spot for a beer – and a worthwhile buffet lunch with plenty of salads and tasty hot dishes.

Getting There & Around

'Parque Nacional' buses run from Foz do Iguaçu's urban bus terminal (you pay the fare entering the terminal) to the park entrance (R$2.20, 45 minutes) every 22 minutes between 6am and 7pm, and then every hour until midnight, making stops along Av Juscelino Kubitschek and Av das Cataratas.

A taxi from Foz to the park entrance costs around R$35.

To access the Brazilian park from Puerto Iguazú, take the bus to Foz do Iguaçu but get off a couple of stops after crossing the international bridge (the driver will announce it). Here, cross the road, and wait for the Parque Nacional bus at the bus stop opposite. Repeat the process at the same stop on the way back. If you're only planning to spend a day visiting the park, border formalities are minimal (see the boxed text, p225).

PUERTO IGUAZÚ

☎ 03757 / pop 31,515

Little Puerto Iguazú sits at the confluence of the Ríos Paraná and Iguazú and looks across to Brazil and Paraguay. It doesn't really feel like Argentina any more. There's no center and little feeling of community – everyone is here to see the falls or to make a buck out of them. Still, it's quiet, safe and has good transport connections and many excellent places to stay and eat.

Orientation

Some 300km northeast of Posadas via RN 12, Puerto Iguazú has an irregular city plan, but is small enough that you will find your way around easily. The main drag is the diagonal

Av Victoria Aguirre, but most services are just north of this in a criss-cross of streets meeting at odd angles.

Information

Argecam (☎ 423085; Av Victoria Aguirre 1164) Changes money.

Banco de la Nación (Av Victoria Aguirre s/n) Has an ATM.

Hospital (☎ 420288; cnr Av Victoria Aguirre & Ushuaia) **Internet** (Bompland 127; per hr AR$4) Equipped with headsets.

Lavandería Central (P Moreno 215) Laundry.

Macro (cnr Av Misiones & Bompland) ATMs.

Tourist office (☎ 420800; www.iguazuargentina .com; Av Victoria Aguirre 396; ☘ 7am-1pm & 2-9pm Mon-Fri, 8am-noon & 4-8pm Sat & Sun) There's another office at the airport.

Sights

There's little to see in the town itself, but a kilometer west of the town center along Av Tres Fronteras is the **Hito Argentino**, a small obelisk at the impressive confluence of the Ríos Paraná and Iguazú. From here you can see Brazil and Paraguay, with similar markers on their sides. A fairly desultory *artesanía* market is also here.

Five kilometers out of town on the way to the national park, **GüiráOga** (☎ 03757-15-465011; www.guiraoga.fundacionazara.org.ar; admission AR$30; ☘ 8:30am-6pm, last entry 4:30pm) is an animal hospital and center for rehabilitation of injured wildlife. It also carries out valuable research into the Iguazú forest environment, and has a breeding program for endangered species. You get driven around the park by one of the biologists and get to meet the creatures in a natural state. The visit takes about 80 minutes and is recommended.

Tours

Numerous local operators offer day tours to the Brazilian side of the falls (AR$50 to AR$110 depending on what's included), some taking in the Itaipú dam as well. **Venteveo Turismo** (☎ 424062; www.venteveoturismo .com.ar) is one of many that have offices at the bus terminal, and has been recommended by readers.

Sleeping

There are many sleeping options for all budgets, including a string of resort-type hotels between town and the national park.

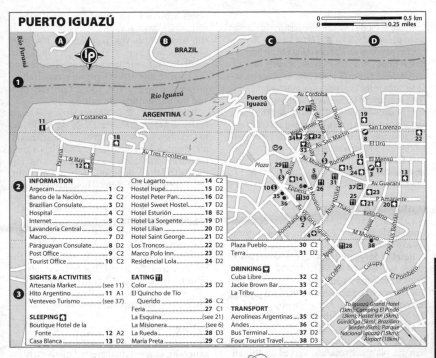

PUERTO IGUAZÚ

0		0.5 km
0		0.25 miles

BRAZIL

Río Paraná

Río Iguazú

ARGENTINA

Av Costanera

Puerto
Iguazú

Av Córdoba

San Lorenzo

El Urú

Av San Martín

Plaza

Av Misiones

El Mensú

Bonpland

Av Guaraní

Av Tres Fronteras

T de Mayo

Corrientes

Paraná

Eppens

Av Victoria Aguirre

Bonpland

Av Núñez

Alvar Núñez

Thays

P Amarante

Belgrano

M Moreno

Fray Luis Beltrán

Curupy

El Pombero

Las Cedros

Tareferos

INFORMATION
Argecam	1	C2
Banco de la Nación	2	C2
Brazilian Consulate	3	D2
Hospital	4	C2
Internet	5	C2
Lavandería Central	6	C2
Macro	7	D2
Paraguayan Consulate	8	D2
Post Office	9	C2
Tourist Office	10	C2

SIGHTS & ACTIVITIES
Artesanía Market	(see 11)	
Hito Argentino	11	A1
Venteveo Turismo	(see 37)	

SLEEPING
Boutique Hotel de la Fonte	12	A2
Casa Blanca	13	D2
Che Lagarto	14	C2
Hostel Irupé	15	D2
Hostel Peter Pan	16	D2
Hostel Sweet Hostel	17	D2
Hotel Esturión	18	B2
Hotel La Sorgente	19	D1
Hotel Lilian	20	D2
Hotel Saint George	21	D2
Los Troncos	22	D2
Marco Polo Inn	23	D2
Residencial Lola	24	D2

EATING
Color	25	D2
El Quincho de Tío Querido	26	C2
Feria	27	C1
La Esquina	(see 21)	
La Misionera	(see 6)	
La Rueda	28	D3
María Preta	29	C2
Plaza Pueblo	30	C2
Terra	31	D2

DRINKING
Cuba Libre	32	C2
Jackie Brown Bar	33	C2
La Tribu	34	C2

TRANSPORT
Aerolíneas Argentinas	35	C2
Andes	36	C2
Bus Terminal	37	D2
Four Tourist Travel	38	D3

To Iguazú Grand Hotel
(3km); Camping El Pindó
(3km); Hostel Inn (5km);
GüiráOga (5km); Brazilian
Border (6km); Parque
Nacional Iguazú (15km);
Airport (18km)

NORTHEAST ARGENTINA

BUDGET

Hostel Sweet Hostel (☎ 424336; www.hostelsweethos
tel.com.ar; El Mensú 38; dm/d AR$30/100; ✆ ❑ ❒ ❄) Everything's casual at this likable place, with a decent backyard pool and chill-out area with pool table. Dorms and rooms are funny shapes, but comfortable with bathrooms; TV costs a little extra. Casual also extends to the reservations department, so that booking you made might not be set in stone. Good breakfast.

Hostel Peter Pan (☎ 423616; www.peterpanhostel
.com; Av Córdoba 267; dm/d AR$35/140; ✆ ❑ ❄ ❒) Handy for the bus terminal, this hostel features comfortable (if a little stuffy) dorms with lockers, and good private rooms. The highlight is the centerpiece – a sizable swimming pool in a hammock-filled patio.

Marco Polo Inn (☎ 425559; www.marcopoloinniguazu
.com; Av Córdoba 158; dm/d AR$40/140; ✆ ❑ ❄ ❒) Built motel style with plenty of space, this friendly hostel is right opposite the bus terminal. The dorms are darkish but come with lockers and bathroom, and there's a host of other facilities like ping-pong and a pool. It's popular, so book. Substantial HI discount.

Hostel Inn (☎ 421823; www.hostel-inn.com; RN 12, Km 5; dm/r AR$45/170; ✆ ❑ ❄ ❒) This is more resort than hostel, and you get a lot for your pesos, as the spotless place is set in expansive grounds and has a big pool and all the backpacker-friendly facilities you can imagine. The dorms are commodious and air-conditioned. Most readers love it to bits, though some complain about CHS (cool hostel syndrome): you'll know whether it's for you or not. It's 5km into town, but the falls buses (AR$1 to the town center) will stop right outside. HI discount applies.

Residencial Lola (☎ 423954; Av Córdoba 255; s/d AR$50/80; ❑) Plenty of price gouging goes on in Puerto Iguazú, but it stops at Lola's front door. This cheap, cheerily run spot is very close to the bus terminal and features compact, clean rooms with bathroom for a pittance.

Hotel Lilian (☎ 420968; hotellilian@yahoo.com
.ar; Fray Luis Beltrán 183; s/d AR$115/155; ✆ ❑) Run by a hospitable family, this friendly place of-fers plenty of value, with bright and cheerful rooms around a patio. The superior rooms only cost around AR$15 more, but have a balcony and heaps of natural light. All the bathrooms are spacious and spotless.

Also recommended:

Camping El Pindó (☎ 421795; elpindo@yahoo.com.ar; per tent/person AR$15/10; 🐾) At Km 3.5 of RN 12 on the southern edge of town, it's easily reached on the bus.

Hostel Irupé (☎ 03757-15-453606; Misiones 80; dm/s/d AR$30/70/80; 🖳) Good value for private rooms. Go for rooms at the back, which have more light.

Che Lagarto (☎ 422206; www.chelagarto.com; Av Brasil 24; dm/d AR$40/140; 🐾 🖳 🛜 🐾) The new Iguazú version of this popular hostel chain was still being built at the time of research, but we liked the central location, big deck and relaxation space.

Casa Blanca (☎ 421320; www.casablancaiguazu.com .ar; Av Guaraní 121; s/d AR$150/160; 🐾 🖳 🛜 🐾) A little somber but spotless and welcoming.

MIDRANGE & TOP END

For a luxury option inside the Parque Nacional Iguazú there's the Sheraton International Iguazú (p224).

Hotel La Sorgente (☎ 424252; www.lasorgenteho tel.com; Av Córdoba 454; s/d AR$264/310; 🐾 🖳 🛜 🐾) Book ahead for a real treat at this stylish but homey posada. Set around a verdant garden, life couldn't be easier here – if you can't face the long walk around the pool, take the bridge across it. Twin rooms have queen-sized beds; cozy upstairs doubles overlook the pool and banana plants. Breakfast, served in the authentic Italian restaurant, gets the seal of approval, too.

our pick Los Troncos (☎ 424337; www.hotellostron cosiguazu.com; San Lorenzo 154; d AR$305; 🐾 🖳 🛜 🐾) Original and peaceful, these 10 two-level apartments climb a hill like a forest staircase and are all equipped with their own balcony gazing out over plentiful greenery. Artful use of wood is the signature here; you'll likely fall in love with the bar and deck area. Prepare to stay longer than you planned.

Hotel Saint George (☎ 420633; www.hotelsaintgeorge .com; Av Córdoba 148; s/d standard AR$327/408, s/d superior AR$425/488; 🐾 🖳 🛜 🐾) The Saint George has been around for years and is reliable for comfort, service and organization. It's right across from the bus terminal (some bus noise) and offers excellent facilities, including a garden and new spa complex. Superior rooms are significantly larger, with two big double beds. Fifty pesos more gets you a buffet dinner.

Boutique Hotel de la Fonte (☎ 420625; www .bhfboutiquehotel.com; cnr Corrientes & 1 de Mayo; r AR$380-600; 🐾 🖳 🛜 🐾) This unusual new place features characterful individual rooms and suites around a tree-filled courtyard garden romantically lit at night. It's enthusiastically run by a couple who'll make you feel most welcome and part of the family. Numerous small decorative touches make this more than the sum of its parts. There's a classy Italian-influenced restaurant, and a saltwater pool and hot tub among the palms.

Hotel Esturión (☎ 420100; www.hotelesturion.com; Av Tres Fronteras 650; r/apt AR$600/1200; 🐾 🖳 🛜 🐾) Set in spacious landscaped grounds near the triple-frontier lookout, the Esturión has a great pool area, public areas and tennis courts. The rooms feel tired, but some are better than others. Service is top class. There are 10 highly elegant *cabaña* apartments in the lodge annex across the road (www.esturionlodges.com).

Iguazú Grand Hotel (☎ 498050; www.casinoiguazu .com; RN 12, Km 1640; r from AR$1532; 🐾 🖳 🛜 🐾) Don't let the tacky ads for the attached casino put you off this classy place, just short of the bridge across to Brazil. It's comfortably the most upmarket hotel on either side of the falls, with excellent service, pretty grounds and the town's best restaurant.

Eating

Restaurants in Puerto Iguazú are pricey but generally of good quality, and open early for dinner to cater for tourists.

A really nice place to eat is the *feria* in the north of town. This market is full of stalls selling Argentine wines, sausages, olives and cheese to visiting Brazilians, and several of them put out mixed deli platters, other simple regional dishes and cold beer for very few pesos. Readers have recommended Ramona's *barraca*, but there are plenty of good ones to choose from.

La Misionera (☎ 424580; P Moreno 207; empanadas AR$2; ⏰ 10am-midnight) Excellent empanadas with a variety of fillings, and decent pizza from this well-regarded central bakery.

Plaza Pueblo (☎ 424000; Av Victoria Aguirre s/n; snacks AR$12-25; ⏰ 10am-10pm) This courtyard terrace is bang in the heart of town but set back from the road, so feels peaceful. It serves beer, pizza and excellent burgers and *lomitos*, all with a smile.

Color (☎ 420206; Av Córdoba 135; mains AR$20-48; ⏰ lunch & dinner) This remodeled pizza'n'*parrilla* packs them in to its tightly spaced tables, so don't discuss state secrets. But the prices are fair for this strip, and the meat comes out redolent of wood smoke; try the *picaña*, a tender rump cut. *Parrillada* for four comes to AR$90; a mixed grill of river fish is AR$70.

Terra (Av Misiones 125; mains AR$24-32; ☺ dinner Mon-Sat) Chalked signatures of myriad satisfied customers mark the walls of this chilled bar-restaurant that specializes in well-prepared wok dishes, with pasta and salads as other options. The streetside terrace fills fast.

María Preta (☎ 420441; Av Brasil 39; mains AR$25-50; ☺ lunch & dinner) The indoor-outdoor eating area and evening guitarist make this a popular dinner choice, whether it's for steaks that are actually cooked the way you want them, for a wide range of typical Argentine-Spanish dishes, or for something a little snappier: caiman fillet. Sometimes a pun's just got to be.

El Quincho de Tío Querido (☎ 420151; Bompland 110; mains AR$30-55; ☺ dinner) Lively with the buzz of both tourists and locals, this popular *parrilla* has the usual grill favorites (*parrillada* for two is AR$67) as well as giant 'baby beef' steaks and a range of interesting specials with occasionally comic translations (we enjoyed 'loin with blow, camp bacon'). There's live music and limited outdoor seating. The wine list is pricey.

La Esquina (☎ 420633; cnr Av Córdoba & P Amarante; mains AR$36-52, buffet AR$55; ☺ lunch & dinner) With a balmy, softly lit terrace and solicitous service, La Esquina is a romantic dinner option that backs up the atmosphere with cracking food. There are some unusual combinations of flavors here with excellent results. Try the papaya, carrot, orange and palm-heart salad to kick things off.

La Rueda (☎ 422531; Av Córdoba 28; mains AR$34-67; ☺ lunch & dinner) A mainstay of upmarket eating in Puerto Iguazú, this culinary heavyweight still packs a punch. The salads are imaginative and delicious, as are the river fish (dorado, pacú and surubí) creations. The homemade pasta is cheaper but doesn't disappoint. Service is good but slow. The only card it accepts is Amex.

Drinking & Entertainment

Thanks to ever-increasing tourism and Brazilians from Foz looking for a cheap night out on the weakened peso, Puerto Iguazú's nightlife is lively. The action centers on Avenida Brasil, where at **La Tribu** (Av Brasil 149) the drinks are expensive but the terrace appealing. Opposite, Jackie Brown Bar pulls in the weekend punters, while the unsubtle

Cuba Libre around the corner gets the cross-border Brazilian crowd living it up on the dance floor.

Getting There & Away

Aerolíneas Argentinas (☎ 420168; Av Victoria Aguirre 295) flies from Iguazú five times daily to Buenos Aires (AR$687). **LAN** (☎ 424296) flies the route (AR$663) three times daily and somewhat more reliably. **Andes** (☎ 425566; www.andesonline .com; Av Victoria Aguirre 279) flies Monday to Friday to and from both Salta and Córdoba.

The **bus terminal** (☎ 420854; cnr Avs Córdoba & Misiones) has departures for all over the country. The following is a sample of fares available; competition keeps them low on the popular routes.

Destination	Cost (AR$)	Duration (hr)
Buenos Aires	215	19
Córdoba	296	23
Corrientes	100	9
Paraná	212	15
Posadas	45	5
Resistencia	100	10
San Ignacio	40	4
Santa Fe	180	13

There are international services, as well as Brazilian domestic services, across the border in Foz do Iguaçu (p232). Some buses to Brazilian destinations like Curitiba or São Paulo leave from the Puerto Iguazú bus terminal, too.

Getting Around

Four Tourist Travel (☎ 422962; M Moreno 58) runs an airport shuttle for AR$15 per person; it needs to be booked in advance. A *remise* costs AR$60.

Frequent buses cross to Foz do Iguaçu, Brazil (AR$5/R$3, 35 minutes), and to Ciudad del Este, Paraguay (AR$5/R$3/G6000, one hour), from the local side of the bus terminal. All will stop near the roundabout at the edge of town.

Groups wanting to see both sides of the falls (and the Itaipú dam) may find a taxi or *remise* a good idea; figure on it costing up to AR$250 for a full day of sightseeing. The tourist office may be able to arrange such trips for less. A taxi to Foz do Iguaçu costs around AR$50; to the Brazilian falls (with waiting time) it's AR$120.

For information on entering Brazil, see the boxed text, p225.

NORTHEAST ARGENTINA

FOZ DO IGUAÇU (BRAZIL)

☎ 045 / pop 308,900

Hilly Foz is the main base for the Brazilian side of the falls, and also gives you a good chance to get a feel for a Brazilian town. It's much bigger and more cosmopolitan than Puerto Iguazú, and has a keep-it-real feel that its Argentine counterpart lacks. On the downside, it's noisier, more chaotic and has more crime. It's not a pretty place, but there's something appealing about it nonetheless.

In the '70s the Itaipú hydroelectric project led to the city's population exploding (from 34,000) and commercial opportunities across the river in Ciudad del Este attracted many new ethnic communities. Today Foz is home to several thousand Lebanese people and smaller communities of Japanese and Koreans.

Orientation

Foz do Iguaçu is at the confluence of Río Iguaçu and Río Paraná; the Ponte Tancredo Neves links the city to Puerto Iguazú, Argentina, across the Río Iguaçu, while the Ponte da Amizade connects it to Ciudad del Este, Paraguay, across the Paraná. Fifteen kilometers upstream is Itaipú, the world's largest operating hydroelectric project.

The city's compact, hilly center has a fairly regular grid. Av das Cataratas leads 20km to the falls, passing the turnoff for the Argentine border on the way. BR 277 leads west to Ciudad del Este and northeast to Curitiba and beyond. The main downtown thoroughfare is Av Juscelino Kubitschek, often referred to simply as 'JK' (zho-ta-*ka*). Parallel to it is more pleasant Av Brasil, the main commercial street.

Information

Hotels and restaurants in town accept dollars, Paraguayan guaraníes and Argentine pesos, but it's always cheaper to pay in Brazilian reais. There are useful foreign-card ATMs in the Muffato supermarket (p232) near the local bus terminal.

Guia Mara Lavanderia (☎ 3523-9641; Rua Tarobá 834) Laundry.

HSBC (Av Brasil 1131) One of several banks with an ATM around this area.

Municipal tourist office (☎ 3521-1455; www .iguassu.tur.br; Praça Getúlio Vargas; ☷ 7am-10pm); local bus terminal (☷ 7am-6pm); long-distance bus terminal (☎ 3522-2590; ☷ 7am-6pm) Helpful and gives out a useful map and info sheet. Also a booth at the airport, which opens until the last flight.

Paraguayan Consulate (☎ 3523-2898; Rua Marechal Deodoro da Fonseca 901; ☷ 8:30am-12:30pm & 1:30-3:30pm Mon-Fri)

Phoenix Cyber (Rua Barão do Rio Branco 616; per hr R$2) One of many internet places.

Post office (cnr Juscelino Kubitschek & Rua Barão do Rio Branco)

Safira Turismo (☎ 3523-9966; Av Brasil 567) Changes traveler's checks (6% commission) and cash.

Teletur (☎ 0800-451516; ☷ 7am-11pm) Maintains a toll-free information service with English-speaking operators.

Dangers & Annoyances

Don't make your way down to the Río Paraná; it's a sketchy neighborhood around the *favela* (shanty town) down there. Muggings of tourists are not unknown in Foz, so travel by taxi late at night.

Sights

With a capacity of 14 million kilowatts, the binational **Itaipú Dam** (Usina Hidrelétrica Itaipú) is still, for now, the largest hydroelectric project in the world. A controversial project, it plunged Brazil way into debt and necessitated large-scale destruction of rainforest and the displacement of 10,000 people. But it cleanly supplies nearly all of Paraguay's energy needs, and 20% of Brazil's.

The structure is highly impressive; at some 8km long and 200m high, it is a memorable sight, especially when the river is high and a vast torrent of overflow water cascades down the spillway. The **Centro de Recepção de Visitantes** (☎ 0800-645-4645; www.itaipu.gov.br; Tancredo Neves 6702; ☷ 8am-6pm Sun-Thu, 8am-9pm Fri-Sat) is 10km north of Foz. From here, regular tours (*visita panorâmica*; R$19) run daily at 8am, 9am, 10am, 2pm, 3pm and 3:30pm; more detailed ones (*circuito especial*; R$36), which take you into the power plant itself, leave daily at 8:30am, 9am, 10:30am, 11am, 2pm, 2:30pm, 4pm and 4:30pm. There are extra visits at weekends (when there are also floodlit night viewings available), as well as a variety of other attractions within the complex, including a museum, wildlife park and river beaches.

Across Av Juscelino Kubitschek from Foz's downtown local bus terminal, Conjunto C Norte buses (R$2.20) run north every 10 minutes from 5:30am until 11pm. It's better to catch the bus on the street rather than from inside the terminal, as the bus makes a long circuit of the city after leaving the terminal before passing by it again.

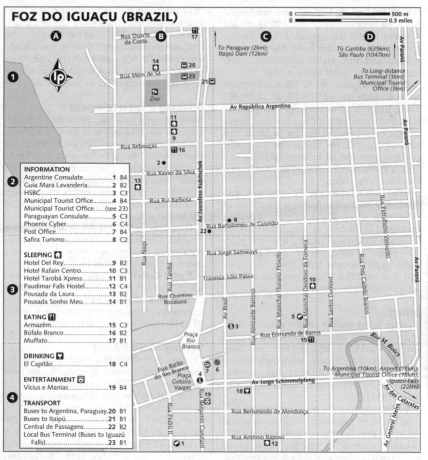

FOZ DO IGUAÇU (BRAZIL)

To Paraguay (2km);
Itaipú Dam (12km)

To Curitiba (635km);
São Paulo (1047km)

To Long-distance
Bus Terminal (3km);
Municipal Tourist
Office (3km)

Av República Argentina

Zoo

Rua Duarte
da Costa

Rua Mem de Sá

Rua Reboução

Rua Xavier da Silva

Rua Rui Barbosa

Rua Bartolomeu de Gusmão

Rua Jorge Samways

Travessa Julio Passa

Rua Quintino
Bocaiuva

Praça
Rio
Branco

Rua Edmundo de Barros

Rio M. Boicy

To Argentina (10km); Airport (18km);
Municipal Tourist Office (18km);
Iguazú Falls
(22km)

Rua Barão
do Rio Branco

Praça
Getúlio
Vargas

Av Jorge Schimmelpfeng

Rua Berlamindo de Mendonça

Rua Antônio Raposo

INFORMATION
Argentine Consulate..............1 B4
Guia Mara Lavanderia...........2 B2
HSBC...................................3 C3
Municipal Tourist Office.........4 B4
Municipal Tourist Office.....(see 23)
Paraguayan Consulate...........5 C3
Phoenix Cyber.......................6 C4
Post Office............................7 B4
Safira Turismo.......................8 C2

SLEEPING
Hotel Del Rey........................9 B2
Hotel Rafain Centro..............10 C3
Hotel Tarobá Xpress..............11 B1
Paudimar Falls Hostel............12 C4
Pousada da Laura..................13 B2
Pousada Sonho Meu..............14 B1

EATING
Armazém..............................15 C3
Búfalo Branco.......................16 B2
Muffato................................17 B1

DRINKING
El Capitão.............................18 C4

ENTERTAINMENT
Vícius e Manias......................19 B4

TRANSPORT
Buses to Argentina, Paraguay.20 B1
Buses to Itaipú......................21 B1
Central de Passagens.............22 B2
Local Bus Terminal (Buses to Iguazú
      Falls)............................23 B1

NORTHEAST ARGENTINA

Tours

There are numerous travel agencies in Foz, and most hotels also have a tour desk. All can book you trips to either side of the falls, visits to Itaipú dam, walks and boat rides.

Sleeping

Hotels and posadas in Foz will substantially lower their prices from those listed if they're not full. Ask!

Paudimar Falls Hostel (☎ 3028-5503; www.paudimarfalls.com.br; Rua Antônio Raposo 820; dm R$23-25, r R$75; ⚒ ▯ 🛜 ▧) It's an excellent HI hostel at the south end of town with bags of facilities, helpful staff and a lively atmosphere. You can also camp here. There's another branch in big grounds off the road to the falls, 13km from town.

Pousada da Laura (☎ 3523-0101; www.pousadalaura .com; Rua Naipi 671; dm/d R$30/80; ▯) This budget stalwart couldn't be more relaxed or welcoming. There's no luxury, but the clean, quiet, bright rooms with bathroom, tasty breakfast and delightful people give it an appeal far beyond what you expect at first glance.

ourpick Pousada Sonho Meu (☎ 3573-5764; www .sonhomeufoz.com.br; Rua Mem de Sá 262; s/d R$80/120; ⚒ ▯ 🛜 ▧) What from the outside looks like an administrative building becomes a delightful little oasis barely 50m from the local bus terminal. Guests have use of a kitchen and pool table, and are made to feel exceedingly welcome. Rooms are artistically decorated with bamboo. Rates almost halve in the low season.

NORTHEAST ARGENTINA

Hotel Del Rey (☎ 3523-2027; www.hoteldelreyfoz .com.br; Rua Tarobá 1020; s/d R$120/165; ❄ 🖳 � 🖳) A recent facelift has upgraded this friendly, spotless and convenient hotel. The rooms are spacious and comfortable, facilities are excellent and the breakfast buffet is huge.

Hotel Tarobá Xpress (☎ 2102-7700; www.hoteltaroba .com.br; Rua Tarobá 1048; s/d R$120/170; ❄ 🖳 ⓐ 🖳) You'll likely need to book for this popular place that's handy for the bus terminal. Value is high here considering the facilities and professional staff; the tiled rooms are bright and spacious and all have minifridges and cable TV. There's also a sauna and small gym. Breakfast is excellent.

Hotel Rafain Centro (☎ 3521-3500; www.rafain centro.com.br; Rua Marechal Deodoro da Fonseca 984; s/d R$179/225; ❄ 🖳 ⓐ 🖳) Much more appealing than some of the hulking megahotels around town, the Rafain is a cracking four-star place with plenty of style, artistic detail and top-notch staff. Rooms have large balconies and fine facilities. Prices can come down substantially.

Eating

It's easy to eat cheaply. Many places will do you a soft drink and *salgado* (baked or fried snack) for as little as R$2, and there are cheap local places where a buffet lunch costs around R$7 to R$12. Thanks to the Lebanese community, there are dozens of shawarma (kebab) places (R$5).

Muffato (☎ 2102-1800; Av Juscelino Kubitschek 1565; per kg R$14.90; ☉ 8:30am-10pm) Want to eat where the locals eat? Trust us on this one. Inside a hideous hypermarket near the bus terminal is a place with little atmosphere but one that serves a very typical, very tasty and cheap Brazilian pay-by-weight (the food, not you) buffet.

Armazém (☎ 3572-0007; www.armazemtrapiche.com .br; Rua Edmundo de Barros 446; mains R$18-45; ☉ dinner daily, lunch Sat & Sun) A block off Schimmelpfeng, this well-frequented restaurant serves top-shelf Brazilian food. As well as various chicken and beef dishes (all huge and just about enough for two) with a variety of tasty sauces, it offers more offbeat dishes such as wild boar, ostrich and caiman. There's a terrace outside and weekend live music.

Búfalo Branco (☎ 3523-9744; Rua Rebouças 530; tenedor libre R$47; ☉ noon-11:30pm) This spacious Foz classic continues to draw locals and tourists alike for its classy *rodízio*, which features delicious roast meats, including excellent beef, as well as more unusual choices like chicken hearts and turkey balls. The salad bar is truly excellent, and includes tasty Lebanese morsels and sushi rolls. There's a good if overpriced choice of Brazilian wines. Look diffident outside the door and you might get a cheaper deal.

Drinking & Entertainment

Make sure you have the classic Brazil experience: an ice-cold bottle of Skol in a plastic insulator served in a no-frills local bar with red plastic seats. Unbeatable. For a healthier tipple, the many juice bars give you the chance to try exotic fruits such as *acerola*, *açaí* or *cupuaçu*.

Nightlife in the city centers on Av Jorge Schimmelpfeng, a couple of blocks east of the tourist office.

El Capitão (☎ 3572-1512; Av Jorge Schimmelpfeng s/n; pizza R$25) This buzzy and friendly staple has a big terrace, well-poured *chopp* (beer), and a menu of pizza and other food.

Vícius e Manias (☎ 523-9161; Rua Benjamin Constant 107; ☉ 10pm-5am Thu-Sun) Popular central *discoteca* with reasonably priced drinks. There's an admission or minimum consumption of R$5 to R$15, but it's often free for women.

Getting There & Away

There are daily flights to Rio de Janeiro, Curitiba and São Paulo, Brazil, operated by **Gol** (www .voegol.com.br) and **TAM** (www.tam.com.br).

Long-distance bus destinations served daily from Foz include Curitiba (R$90, 10 hours), São Paulo (R$140, 16 hours) and Rio de Janeiro (R$193, 22 hours). You can buy tickets with a small surcharge at many central travel agencies, including **Central de Passagens** (☎ 3523-4700; www.centraldepassagens.com; Av Juscelino Kubitschek 526).

Getting Around

For the airport or falls, catch the 'Aeropuerto/ Parque Nacional' bus from the local bus terminal or one of the stops along Av Juscelino Kubitschek; the trip takes 30 minutes and costs R$2.20, paid as you enter the terminal. A taxi costs about R$35.

The **long-distance bus terminal** (rodoviária; ☎ 3522-3336; Costa e Silva) is 5km northeast of downtown. To get downtown, taxi it for R$12 or walk downhill to the bus stop and catch any 'Centro' bus (R$2.20).

Buses to Puerto Iguazú (R$3) run along Rua Mem de Sá alongside the local bus terminal half-hourly from 8am until 8pm; they stop along Juscelino Kubitschek. Buses for Ciudad del Este, Paraguay (R$3), run every 15 minutes (half-hourly on Sundays); catch them on JK opposite the local bus terminal. The bridge can back up badly due to Paraguayan customs checks.

THE GRAN CHACO

The Gran Chaco is a vast alluvial lowland, stretching north from the northern edges of Santa Fe and Córdoba provinces, across the entire provinces of Chaco and Formosa, and into western Paraguay, eastern Bolivia and along the southwestern edge of Brazil. It reaches west through most of Santiago del Estero province, drying up as it goes, and skirts the southeastern edge of Salta province. The western side, known as the Chaco Seco (Dry Chaco), has been deemed the Impenetrable, due to its severe lack of water across an endless plain of nearly impassable thorn scrub.

In the Chaco Húmedo (Wet Chaco) to the east, the gallery forests, marshes and palm savannas of Parque Nacional Chaco, as well as the subtropical marshlands of Parque Nacional Río Pilcomayo, offer excellent birding opportunities. These areas are best visited in the cooler, drier months of April through November.

Resistencia, with a unique commitment to sculpture, is the most interesting city out here and is a good place to start learning about the region's indigenous cultures like the Toba.

Crossing the Gran Chaco from Formosa to Salta along the northern RN 81 is brutal and can take nearly two days; RN 16 from Resistencia is much faster.

History

In colonial times, Europeans avoided the hot, desolate Chaco, whose few hunter-gatherer peoples resisted colonization and were not numerous enough to justify their pacification for *encomiendas* (the colonial labor system). Today, about 85,000 Guaycurú (Toba and Mocoví) and Mataco peoples remain in the region.

Early Spanish settlements were soon abandoned after indigenous resistance. Later, Jesuit missionaries had some success, but the order's expulsion in 1767 again delayed European settlement.

In the mid-19th century, woodcutters from Corrientes entered the region's forests to exploit the valuable hardwood quebracho, whose name literally means 'axe breaker.' This eventually opened the region to agricultural expansion, which has primarily taken the form of cotton and cattle production. Many new settlers came from Central Europe from the 1930s.

Deforestation continues apace in the Chaco, with vast areas being cleared to plant soya, of which Argentina is now one of the world's major producers. This has impacted heavily on Toba tribes, whose traditional environment is being destroyed.

RESISTENCIA

☎ 03722 / pop 359,590

Chaco's provincial capital is perched on the edge of the barely populated wilderness of the Chaco. It isn't the most likely candidate for the garland of artistic center of northern Argentina, yet baking-hot Resistencia has strong claims to that title – its streets are studded with sculpture (half a thousand and more) and there's a strong boho-cultural streak that represents a complete contrast to the tough cattle-and-dust solitudes that characterize the province.

First settled in 1750, Resistencia grew rapidly with the development of the tannin industry and subsequent agricultural progress. It acquired its name after successful resistance against numerous indigenous attacks throughout the 19th century.

Resistencia's museums and cultural centers are particularly worthwhile if you are interested in the Toba indigenous culture (see the boxed text, p241)

Orientation

Enormous Plaza 25 de Mayo is the focus of the city center. It has fountains and numerous sculptures, and is planted with quebracho, ceibo, lapacho and other native trees.

Street names change at the plaza. Av Sarmiento is the main access route from RN 16, which leads east to Corrientes, and west to Roque Sáenz Peña and beyond. Av 25 de Mayo leads northwest from the plaza to RN 11, which goes north to Formosa and the Paraguayan border.

NORTHEAST ARGENTINA

RESISTENCIA

0 — 500 m
0 — 0.25 miles

INFORMATION

Centro Cultural Leopoldo Marechal	1	C2
C-Net Cyber	2	B2
Hospital Perrando	3	D3
Municipal Tourist Office	4	C2
Post Office	5	C1

SIGHTS & ACTIVITIES

El Fogón de los Arrieros	6	C2
Museo del Hombre Chaqueño	7	C2
Statue of Fernando	8	C1

SLEEPING

Gran Hotel Royal	9	C2
Hotel Alfil	10	B2
Hotel Amerian	11	B1
Hotel Colón	12	B2
Hotel Covadonga	13	C2
Hotel Luxor	14	B1
Hotel Marconi	15	B1
Residencial Bariloche	16	C2

EATING

Kebon	17	C1
La Bianca	18	C2
Parrillada Don Abel	19	B1
Pizzería Los Campeones	20	B1

DRINKING

El Fogón de los Arrieros	(see 6)	
El Viejo Café	21	C2
Zingara	22	C1

ENTERTAINMENT

Peña Nativa Martín Fierro	23	D2

SHOPPING

Artesanía Stalls	24	C2
Chac Cueros	25	C1
Fundación Chaco Artesanal	26	C1

TRANSPORT

Aerochaco	27	D1
Aerolíneas Argentinas	28	C2
Buses to Airport	29	C1
Buses to Bus Terminal	30	B2
Buses to Corrientes	31	C1
Shared taxis to Corrientes	32	C2

Information

There are several ATMs around Plaza 25 de Mayo.

Centro Cultural Leopoldo Marechal (☎ 452738; Pellegrini 272; ⊗ 9am-noon & 4-8pm Mon-Sat) The place to go to learn about indigenous issues and visiting Toba communities.

C-Net Cyber (cnr Perón & Necochea; per hr ARS2) Fastish internet and phone calls.

Hospital Perrando (☎ 452583; Av 9 de Julio 1099)

Municipal tourist office (☎ 458289; www.mr.gov.ar; Plaza 25 de Mayo; ⊗ 7am-1pm & 2-8pm Mon-Fri, 8am-noon & 3-7pm Sat, 6-9pm Sun) In a kiosk on the southern side of the plaza, there's helpful and knowledgeable staff, with good bilingual city information.

Provincial tourist office (☎ 423547; www.chaco.gov.ar/turismo; Sarmiento 1675; ⊗ 7am-8:30pm Mon-Fri, 8am-1pm & 2-7pm Sat & Sun) Good info about the Chaco and visiting the Impenetrable.

Sights
SCULPTURES

At last count, there were over 500 sculptures around the city, a number that is set to increase with every Bienal (see opposite). The streets are packed with them, especially around the plaza and north up Av Sarmiento. Calle Perón/Arturo Illia, a block south of the plaza, is also well endowed. Every Bienal, a brochure is printed with a sculpture walking tour around the city. The most likely place to get hold of the latest one is at the **MusEUM** (☎ 415020; www.bienaldelchaco.com; admission free; ⊗ 8am-noon & 3-8pm Mon-Sat), an open-air workshop on the north side of Parque 2 de Febrero. Several of the most impressive pieces are on display here, and this is where (during the Bienal and quite frequently at other times) you can catch sculptors at work.

EL FOGÓN DE LOS ARRIEROS

Founded in 1942, this is a cultural center, art gallery and bar that for decades has been the driving force behind Resistencia's artistic commitment and progressive displays of public art. Still the keystone of the region's art community, it is now famous for its eclectic collection of art objects from around the Chaco and Argentina. The **museum** (☎ 426418; Brown 350; admission AR$5; ☺ 8am-noon Mon-Sat) also features the wood carvings of local artist and cultural activist Juan de Dios Mena. Check out the irreverent epitaphs to dead patrons in the memorial garden; it's called 'Colonia Sálsipuedes' (Get out if you can).

MUSEO DEL HOMBRE CHAQUEÑO

This small but excellent **museum** (Museum of Chaco Man; ☎ 453005; JB Justo 280; admission free; ☺ 8am-noon & 4-8pm Mon-Sat) is run by enthusiastic staff (some English spoken) who will talk you through the displays covering the three main pillars of Chaco population: the indigenous inhabitants (there are some excellent ceramics and Toba musical instruments here), the *criollos* who resulted from interbreeding between the European arrivals and the local populations, and the 'gringos' – the wave of mostly European immigration that arrived from the late 19th century onwards. Best of all is the mythology room upstairs, where you'll get to meet various quirky characters from *chaqueño* popular religion.

Festivals & Events

During the third week of July in even years, the **Bienal de Escultura** (www.bienaldelchaco.com) brings 10 renowned Argentine and international sculptors to Resistencia. Arranging themselves around the fountain at the open-air museum in Parque 2 de Febrero, they have seven days to complete a sculpture under the public gaze. The medium changes every time, and there's a parallel competition for students.

Sleeping

Camping Parque 2 de Febrero (☎ 458366; Av Avalos 1100; campsites AR$10) This well-staffed campground has good facilities, including shade, but can get crowded and noisy in high season – not least because of the dance clubs across the road. Bus 9 will get you there from the north side of the plaza.

Hotel Luxor (☎ 447252; camorsluxor@hotmail.com; Remedios de Escalada 19; s/d AR$46/68; ☒) The town's cheapest option is a central and decent enough place that caters for traveling salespeople, the odd backpacker and local couples looking for a few hours away from disapproving parents' eyes. Breakfast, TV and air-con all cost extra.

Hotel Alfil (☎ 420882; Santa María de Oro 495; s/d AR$60/90; ☒) A few blocks south of the plaza, the Alfil is a reasonable budget choice. The interior rooms are dark but worthwhile if the significant street noise in the exterior rooms (with their strangely inaccessible balconies) will bother you. Air-con is AR$10 extra, but it's a decent deal despite the lack of breakfast.

Hotel Colón (☎ 422861; hotelcolon@gigared.com. ar; Santa María de Oro 143; s/d AR$105/155, apt AR$190; ☒ 🖳 ☜) Art deco fans mustn't miss this

---

A TOWN'S BEST FRIEND

Stray dogs wandering the streets of South American towns sometimes inspire fear, even outright panic. Not in Resistencia – in the late 1950s and early '60s, a stray dog inspired the love of the entire town, and Víctor Marchese's statue on Calle Mitre, in front of the Casa de Gobierno, immortalizes him.

His name was Fernando. As the story goes, he wandered the streets and slept in doorways and finally befriended a bank manager, who allowed Fernando to join him for breakfast every morning in his office. Before long, Fernando was the delight of downtown, inspiring people's daydreams with his daily, carefree adventures in the Plaza 25 de Mayo. In a town devoted to the arts, Fernando was bohemianism in fur, and was a welcome regular at El Fogón de los Arrieros (see above). When Fernando died in 1963, the municipal band played a funeral march and people across town shut their shades in respect. He is buried at El Fogón de los Arrieros, where another sculpture by Marchese marks his grave.

1920s classic, a few steps south of the plaza. It's an amazingly large and characterful building with some enticingly curious period features. Rooms show their age, but the refurbished apartments are very spick-and-span.

Hotel Covadonga (☎ 444444; www.hotelcovadonga .com.ar; Güemes 200; s/d ARS215/255; ❄ ❑ ⧉ ⧳) With an excellent location close to the plaza and restaurants, this upmarket hotel has fine facilities, including a pool, sauna and Jacuzzi, and personable staff. The public areas are slickly furnished, and the recently renovated rooms feature streetside balconies and attractive wooden floors.

Hotel Amerian (☎ 452400; www.hotelcasinogala .com.ar; Perón 330; s/d ARS385/424, ste ARS626-1980; ❄ ❑ ⧉ ⧳) This swish casino-hotel is the city's smartest choice, with various grades of room and slick service. As well as the slot machines, there's also a sauna, gym and a self-contained spa complex.

Other recommendations:

Residencial Bariloche (☎ 421412; Obligado 239; s/d ARS70/90; ❄) This simple place has quite reasonable rooms for a low price within easy striking distance of the plaza.

Gran Hotel Royal (☎ 439694; www.granhotelroyal .com.ar; Obligado 211; s/d ARS115/159; ❄ ⧉) It has spotless and comfortable rooms, albeit somewhat uninspired.

Hotel Marconi (☎ 421978; Perón 352; s/d ARS100/130; ❄ ⧉) Simple, clean and central.

Eating

La Bianca (☎ 449230; Colón 102; dishes ARS12-25; ❨ lunch & dinner Wed-Mon) Busy and bustling, this long-time local split-level favorite keeps 'em coming for its well-priced pasta, pizza and soufflés. There's also meat and salad dishes in generous quantities. A cheap and cheerful banker.

Parrillada Don Abel (☎ 449252; Perón 698; meals ARS15-33; ❨ lunch & dinner, closed dinner Sun) This *parrilla* is inside a homey *quincho* (thatched-roof building) and serves substantial portions of pasta and grilled surubí, in addition to the usual grilled beef. It has a convivial family buzz to it at the weekend.

Kebon (☎ 422385; Don Bosco 102; mains ARS17-48; ❨ lunch & dinner Mon-Sat) Popular and not lacking in quality, this corner restaurant has a wide choice of fish and meat dishes, with a series of elaborate sauces to choose from. Service is attentive and the portions gener-

ous, but the place somehow lacks a little bit of atmosphere. The take-out *rotisería* next door is a bargain.

Pizzería Los Campeones (☎ 443864; Perón 300; pizza ARS18-32; ❨ lunch & 6pm-2am) This down-home pizzeria, with sidewalk seating on a very busy street, also serves unbeatable slices at ARS3 to ARS4 a pop.

Drinking & Entertainment

El Fogón de los Arrieros (☎ 426418; Brown 350; ❨ 9:30pm-1am) Stopping into El Fogón's friendly bar – a local institution for decades – is almost mandatory. The attached cultural center presents occasional live music and small-scale theatrical events, including Thursday night tango.

El Viejo Café (☎ 459399; Pellegrini 109; ❨ 7am-late Sun-Thu, 1pm-late Fri & Sat) In an elegant old edifice, with an eclectically decorated interior, this is a fine choice at any time of day. Its terrace is a sweet spot for a sundowner, and it gets lively later on weekends.

Zingara (☎ 452059; Güemes 282; ❨ 6pm-3am) Central and buzzy, this upbeat bar has a lively terrace, good people running it and a wide selection of music. They mix a decent drink, too. A fine choice.

Peña Nativa Martín Fierro (☎ 423167; Av 9 de Julio 695) Try this traditional place on Friday night from 9pm for live folk music and *parrillada*.

Shopping

There's a selection of *artesanía* stalls on the southern side of the plaza.

Chac Cueros (☎ 433604; Güemes 186) Chac Cueros specializes in high-quality goods made from the hide of capybaras, which is valued for the suede produced from their tan, naturally dimpled skin.

Fundación Chaco Artesanal (☎ 448427; Av Sarmiento 234) Selection of indigenous crafts as well as CDs from the Toba choir (see the boxed text, p241).

Getting There & Away

AIR

Aerolíneas Argentinas (☎ 446802; JB Justo 184) flies to Buenos Aires' Aeroparque (ARS582, six times weekly). Weekday flights go to Asunción, Paraguay (ARS1187, one hour). **Aerochaco** (☎ 0810-345-2422; www.aerochaco.net; Av Sarmiento 715) services Buenos Aires, Córdoba, Salta, Puerto Iguazú and other destinations from Resistencia.

BUS

Resistencia's **bus terminal** (☎ 461098; cnr MacLean & Islas Malvinas) serves destinations in all directions. Buses make the rounds between Corrientes and Resistencia (AR$2.50, 40 minutes) at frequent intervals throughout the day. You can also catch a bus to Corrientes from the city center, on Av Alberdi just south of the plaza. Better are the shared taxis (AR$3, 20 minutes) that congregate on Frondizi near Plaza 25 de Mayo.

There are frequent daily services to the destinations listed following:

Destination	Cost (AR$)	Duration (hr)
Asunción (Paraguay)	32	5
Buenos Aires	138	13
Córdoba	144	12
Formosa	25	2
Mendoza	240	24
Mercedes	32	4
Posadas	60	5
Puerto Iguazú	100	10
Roque Sáenz Peña	27	2
Rosario	114	10
Salta	126	10
Santa Fe	94	9
Santiago del Estero	121	7½
Tucumán	138	12

Getting Around

Aeropuerto San Martín is 6km south of town on RN 11; take bus 2 from the northwest corner of the plaza. The bus terminal is a AR$10 taxi ride from the city center, or you can take bus 3 or 10 from opposite the Hotel Colón. City buses cost AR$1.75.

PARQUE NACIONAL CHACO

Preserving several diverse ecosystems that reflect subtle differences in relief, soils and rainfall, this very accessible **park** (☎ 03725-499161; admission free; ☒ visitor center 9am-7pm) protects 150 sq km of the humid eastern Chaco. It is 115km northwest of Resistencia via RN 16 and RP 9.

Ecologically, it falls within the 'estuarine and gallery forest' subregion of the Gran Chaco, but the park encompasses marshes, grasslands, palm savannas, scrub forest and denser gallery forests. The most widespread ecosystem is the *monte fuerte*, where mature specimens of quebracho, algarrobo and lapacho reach above 20m, while lower strata of immature trees and shrubs provide a variety of habitats at distinct elevations. The hard-wooded quebracho colorado tree used to be widespread across northern Argentina, but overlogging almost led to its complete disappearance.

Scrub forests form a transitional environment to seasonally inundated grasslands, punctuated by caranday and pindó palms. Marshes and gallery forests cover the smallest areas, but they are biologically the most productive. The meandering Río Negro has left several shallow oxbow lakes where dense aquatic vegetation flourishes.

Mammals are few and rarely seen, but birds are abundant, including the rhea, jabirú, roseate spoonbill, cormorant, common caracara and other less conspicuous species. The most abundant insect species is the mosquito, so visit during the cooler, drier winter and bring repellent.

Activities

Hiking and bird-watching are the principal activities here, best done in the early morning or around sunset. Some areas are accessible only while cycling or horseback riding; find out about the rental of bicycles or horses and hiring of guides in Capitán Solari, 6km east of the park; ask at the *municipalidad* (town hall).

Sleeping & Eating

The *municipalidad* in Capitán Solari provides information on locals who rent rooms to travelers at a fair price. One such is **Señora Nilda Ocampo** (☎ 03725-15-458977) who charges AR$25 per person. Camping is the only option in the park. There are shaded campsites with cold-water showers, toilets and fire pits with wood – and it's free.

Weekends can be crowded with visitors, but at other times you may have the park to yourself. On busy weekends a vendor from Resistencia sells meals, but it's better to bring everything you'll need.

Getting There & Away

Capitán Solari is 2½ hours from Resistencia by bus. La Estrella runs five buses daily each way (AR$15.50).

From Capitán Solari, the park information may be able to organize you transport; otherwise you can walk, hitch or take a *remise* (AR$15) the 5km to the park. The road may be impassable for motor vehicles in wet weather.

ROQUE SÁENZ PEÑA

☎ 03732 / pop 76,794

Something of a frontier town, Presidencia Roque Sáenz Peña (its full cumbersome name) is well out in the Chaco, and is the gateway to the 'Impenetrable' beyond. It's known for its thermal baths, fortuitously discovered by drillers seeking potable water in 1937, and makes an appealing stop, with a rugged, friendly feel to the place.

Roque is primarily a service center for cotton and sunflower growers and, as the Chaco province grows nearly two-thirds of the country's cotton crop, in May it hosts the **Fiesta Nacional del Algodón** (National Cotton Festival).

Orientation & Information

The town straddles RN 16, which connects Resistencia with Salta. Its regular grid plan centers on willow-shaded Plaza San Martín; Av San Martín is the principal commercial street.

Av San Martín has several banks with ATMs and numerous places to make phone calls or use the internet.

Post office (Belgrano 602, at Mitre)

Tourist office (Brown 541; ☢ 6:30-11:30am & 2:30-8pm) In the thermal baths complex.

Sights

Roque's **Complejo Termal Municipal** (Thermal Baths Complex; ☎ 430030; www.elchacotermal.com.ar; Brown 545; ☢ 6:30-11:30am & 2:30-8pm) draws its saline water from 150m below ground. The center, around since the 1930s, is now a top-class facility, offering thermal baths (AR$7), saunas and Turkish baths (AR$8) that are a little cheaper in the morning session. Treatments on offer include kinesiology, massage and aromatherapy.

At the junction of RN 16 and RN 95, 4km east of downtown, the town's spacious and nationally renowned **Parque Zoológico** (☎ 424284; adult/child AR$4/1; ☢ 9am-6pm Mon-Fri, 8am-6pm Sat & Sun) and botanical garden emphasizes birds and mammals found in the Chaco region, alongside a few lions, tigers and bears. Featured species are tapir and jaguar, but there are also crocodiles, llamas, monkeys, a bafflingly large chicken pen, snakes, condors and vultures.

The zoo has two large artificial lakes frequented by migratory waterfowl. A small snack bar operates, but the aroma from nearby enclosures is a bit of an appetite killer. Bus 2 goes from Calle Moreno to the zoo (AR$1) and a *remise* will cost AR$15; it's also within reasonable walking distance, if it's not too hot.

Sleeping

Orel Hotel (☎ 429645; cnr Saavedra & San Martín; s/d AR$80/120; ☢ ☐) The rooms are simple, clean and colorful, and have cable TV. Some have windows looking out on to the street (noisy), others face the hallway (and lack privacy). Still, it's not a bad deal.

Hotel Familiar (☎ 429906; Moreno 486; s/d AR$80/120; ☢) A welcoming little place a block from the main drag. The rooms are clean and quiet, if dark, and the people take an interest in their guests.

Hotel Presidente (☎ 424498; San Martín 771; s/d AR$120/170; ☢ ☐ ☢) With plush red carpet and mirrors everywhere, including on the doors of the rooms, this looks like a cross between a Colombian narco-trafficker's mansion and a top-of-the-market '70s brothel. It's a very pleasing place in the heart of town, with friendly staff and, for this price, excellent rooms with minibar and big comfortable beds.

Hotel Gualok (☎ 420715; San Martín 1198) Right next to the spa complex, the faded town centerpiece was being transformed into five-star luxury at the time of research and should be open by the time you read this.

Eating

Ama Nalec (☎ 420348; Moreno 601; ice creams from AR$3; ☢ 10am-1pm & 5pm-late) This busy corner place does tempting little pastries and very tasty ice cream, a godsend in Roque's paralyzing heat. It has some unusual flavors – figs in cognac is worth a lick.

Saravá (cnr San Martín & 25 de Mayo; dishes AR$8-18; ☢ 8am-midnight) A popular spot serving the regular range of steak, chicken, burgers and sandwiches, as well as icy fruit licuados, Saravá has a full bar and is on a busy corner in the heart of town, so get an outdoor table.

Bien, José! (☎ 431725; 25 de Mayo 531; mains AR$8-20; ☢ dinner) Warm personal service melds with delicious meat empanadas and decent *parrilla* choices at this good-value restaurant. Every generation is called José here, so ask one of them what the daily special is and enjoy. Twenty meters up the road, Rovetti does enormous *milanesas* for AR$20.

Giuseppe (☎ 425467; Moreno 680; small pizza AR$9-20, mains AR$9-23; ☢ lunch & dinner) This place has slightly staid decor but is very popular in the evening for its tasty pizza and interesting pasta combinations. Try not to sit down the side – the kitchen belts out so much heat you expect brimstone and horned waiters.

PENETRATING THE IMPENETRABLE

If you have a yen to get off the beaten track, the more remote areas of the Chaco are for you. The key access point for the Impenetrable is the town of **Juan José Castelli**, 115km north of Roque Sáenz Peña, and served by two daily buses from Resistencia (AR$20, five hours) via Roque. From Juan José Castelli, you can head west along *ripio* (gravel) roads to remote Fuerte Esperanza (shared *remises* run this route), which has two nature reserves in its vicinity – **Reserva Provincial Fuerte Esperanza** and **Reserva Natural Loro Hablador**. Both conserve typical dry Chaco environments, with algarrobo and quebracho trees, armadillos, peccaries and many bird species. **Loro Hablador**, 40km from Fuerte Esperanza, has a good campground and short walking trails with ranger guides. Fuerte Esperanza has two simple *hospedajes* (family homes). Further north, **Misión Nueva Pompeya** was founded in 1899 by Franciscans who established a mission station for Matacos in tough conditions. The main building, with its square-towered church, is a surprising sight in such a remote location.

Various operators offer excursions and packages, which include visits to the reserves, Misión Nueva Pompeya and indigenous communities in the area. **Carlos Aníbal Schumann** (☎ 03732-471473; www.ecoturchaco.com.ar; Av San Marín 500, Juan José Castelli) comes recommended and also runs a campground and lodge in Villa Río Bermejito, a riverside settlement 67km northeast of Juan José Castelli. **Tantanacuy** (☎ 03722-15-640705; http://chacoagreste.com.ar) is a *hostería* (lodging house) between Castelli and Fuerte Esperanza that offers packages including accommodation, transfers and excursions.

Heading west from Roque Sáenz Peña, RN 16 heads past the access to the Parque Nacional Copo (p293), which is part of the same ecoregion.

Getting There & Away

The **bus terminal** (☎ 420280; Petris, btwn Avellaneda & López) is seven blocks east of downtown; take bus 1 from Mitre. There are regular buses to Resistencia (AR$27, two hours), and services running west to Tucumán, Santiago del Estero and Salta also stop here. There are also services to JJ Castelli.

FORMOSA
☎ 03717 / pop 198,074

Travelers heading to Formosa might get a mystified 'Why?' from residents of other Argentine cities, but it's quite a sweet little city and provincial capital set on a horseshoe bend of the Río Paraguay. It makes a decent place to stop (far better than Clorinda) en route to Paraguay or Parque Nacional Río Pilcomayo. It's blazingly hot in summer, with high humidity levels, but as the sun goes down, its riverside area makes a great place to stroll. You can even duck across the river for a taste of Paraguay if you wish.

Orientation

Formosa is 169km north of Resistencia and 113km south of Clorinda (on the border with Paraguay) via RN 11. The center of town is Plaza San Martín, a four-block public park beyond which Av 25 de Mayo, the heart of the city, continues to the shores of the Río Paraguay.

Information

There are banks with ATMs along Av 25 de Mayo between the plaza and the river.
Post office (Plaza San Martín at 9 de Julio)
Provincial tourist office (☎ 425192; turismo@ formosa.gov.ar; Uriburu 820; ☾ 7am-8pm Mon-Fri) On the plaza. A foreign visitor makes the staff's week. There's a tourist info booth in the bus terminal, too.
Telecom (Av 25 de Mayo 245; per hr AR$2.50) Internet and phone calls.

Sights & Activities

In Casa Fotheringham, a pioneer residence that was the province's first government house, the **Museo Histórico** (cnr Belgrano & Av 25 de Mayo; admission free; ☾ 8am-noon Mon, 8am-noon & 3-7pm Tue-Fri, 9am-noon & 6-8pm Sat & Sun) focuses on the foundation and development of Formosa. The museum is small and well organized. The province was part of the Paraguayan Chaco until the 19th-century War of the Triple Alliance, and the museum also houses uniforms, weapons and relics from the period. There are a few old indigenous weavings on display as well.

Six kilometers south of town, **Laguna Oca** is a wetland area that has a popular beach, with food kiosks and canoe hire; once you wander away from the weekend crowds, there's a great deal of birdlife to be spotted.

Festivals & Events

Formosa's annual **Fiesta del Río**, lasting a week in mid-November, features an impressive nocturnal religious procession in which 150 boats from Corrientes sail up the Río Paraguay.

In April, the **Encuentro de Pueblos Originarios de América** brings together delegations from various indigenous groups from Argentina, Paraguay, Bolivia and further afield, with associated cultural spectacles.

Sleeping & Eating

Hotel San Martín (☎ 426769; Av 25 de Mayo 380; s/d AR$90/120; ✦) OK for the price, but otherwise uninteresting, the San Martín is surprisingly quiet for its central location. Some rooms are definitely better than others, so have a look around if you can.

Hotel Plaza (☎ 426767; www.hotelplazaformosa.com.ar; Uriburu 920; s/d AR$120/140; ✦ ▢ 🛜 ✦) The name don't lie: it's right on the plaza, and has a welcoming feel to it. The rooms are nothing special, but there's a small swimming pool and a good restaurant.

Hotel Internacional de Turismo (☎ 437333; hotel deturismo@hotmail.com; cnr Av 25 de Mayo & San Martín; s/d AR$200/230; ✦ ▢ 🛜 ✦) Overlooking the river and the pretty, disused station, this large and somewhat impersonal hotel offers rooms with views across to Paraguay and decent facilities. Big balconies and an excellent swimming pool and sundeck are also on offer.

Raíces (☎ 427058; Av 25 de Mayo 65; mains AR$15-42; ✦ lunch & dinner) Despite the garish sign, this is a refined and classy place, with a fine selection of surubí dishes, among many other well-prepared offerings, and a good wine list.

El Tano Marino (☎ 420628; Av 25 de Mayo 55; mains AR$13-36; ✦ lunch & dinner, closed dinner Sun) Next door to Raíces, this similarly reliable restaurant has an Italian touch, but also features many of the usual Argentine favorites, river fish dishes and correct service. It also has a decent wine list.

Shopping

Casa de las Artesanías (San Martín 82; ✦ 8am-1pm & 4-8pm Mon-Sat) In an historic building near the river, this artisans' cooperative sells wood carvings, weavings and other items that range from shoddy to beautiful. Proceeds go to the indigenous communities – the Mataco, Toba and Pilaga – who make the crafts.

Getting There & Away

AIR

Aerolíneas Argentinas (☎ 429314; Av 25 de Mayo 601) flies five times weekly to Buenos Aires (AR$601).

BOAT

Boats leave from the riverport for the rapid crossing to Alberdi, basically a typically shambolic Paraguayan cheap-goods market. It costs AR$5 to go and AR$4 to come back.

BUS

Formosa's **bus terminal** (☎ 451766; cnr Gutñiski & Antártida Argentina) is 15 blocks west of the plaza. Destinations include the following:

Destination	Cost (AR$)	Duration (hr)
Asunción (Paraguay)	24	2
Buenos Aires	150	16
Clorinda	19	1¾
Laguna Blanca	19	3
Resistencia	25	2

Getting Around

The airport is 4km south of town along RN 11, so taxi are inexpensive. The bus marked Tejón passes by the bus terminal on its way to the airport. A taxi between the terminal and center costs AR$6 to AR$8.

CLORINDA

☎ 03718 / pop 47,004

Bustling Clorinda has a Paraguayan feel already with its street markets and intense heat, and most visitors are indeed here to cross the border to Asunción via the San Ignacio de Loyola bridge. While the town's energy can be briefly infectious, there's nothing much to do or see. Two footbridges take you across to the similar Paraguayan town of Nanawa on the other side of the river.

There's inexpensive lodging at the **Hotel San Martín** (☎ 421211; 12 de Octubre 1150; s/d AR$60/80; ✦), which, with its exposed brick walls and understated decor, scrapes together a bit of style. **La Pupuruchi** (☎ 425291; San Martín 548; mains AR$8-16; ✦ lunch & dinner) is a hugely popular lunch spot on the main street with an excellent salad bar.

There are several bus terminals in Clorinda; the most useful is the Godoy company's one at San Martín and Paraguay. They have regular cross-border departures to Asunción, as well as services south to Formosa (AR$19, 1¾ hours), Resistencia (AR$42, 3¾ hours) and Buenos Aires (AR$165, 18 hours).

INDIGENOUS GROUPS OF THE GRAN CHACO Danny Palmerlee and Andy Symington

With some 50,000 members, the **Toba** of the Gran Chaco are one of Argentina's largest indigenous groups, but invisibility nonetheless seems to stalk them. Toba protests in 2009 highlighted the stark reality that many communities suffer from abandoned government facilities and, in some, people actually die of starvation. Few Argentines had any idea about the struggles of this *pueblo olvidado* (forgotten people).

As a traveler, it's easy to zip through the sun-scorched Chaco without ever noticing the presence of *indígenas* (indigenous people), except, perhaps, for the crafts sold at government-sponsored stores or along the roadside. In Resistencia, the Toba live in *barrios* (neighborhoods) that are separated from the rest of the city. And those who don't live in the city either live in towns that travelers rarely visit (such as Juan José Castelli or Quitilipi) or deep within the Argentine Impenetrable, in settlements reached only by dirt roads that are impossible to navigate if you don't know the way. If you do know the way (or you go with someone who does), you'll find Toba *asentamientos* (settlements) that are unlike anything else in Argentina. People live in extreme poverty (although there's always a church) and, except for the occasional government-built health center, nearly all buildings are made of adobe, with dirt floors and thatched roofs.

The Toba refer to themselves as Komlek (or Qom-lik) and speak a dialect of the Guaycurú linguistic group, known locally as Qom. They have a rich musical tradition (the Coro Toba Chelaalapi, a Toba choir founded in 1962, has Unesco World Heritage designation). Along with basket weaving and ceramics, the Toba are known for their version of the fiddle, which they make out of a gas can.

The region's most numerous indigenous group is the **Wichí**, with a population of over 60,000. Because the Wichí remain extremely isolated (they live nearly 700km from Resistencia, in the far northwest of Chaco province and in Formosa and Salta provinces) they are the most traditional of its groups. They still obtain much of their food through hunting, gathering and fishing. The Wichí are known for their wild honey and for their beautiful *yica* bags, which they weave with fibers from the chaguar plant, a bromeliad native to the arid regions of the Chaco. Like the Toba, most Wichí live in simple adobe huts.

The **Mocoví** are the Gran Chaco's third-largest indigenous group, with a population of 17,000, concentrated primarily in southern Chaco province and Santa Fe province. Like the Toba, the Mocoví speak a dialect of the Guaycurú linguistic group. Until the arrival of Europeans, the Mocoví sustained themselves primarily through hunting and gathering, but today they rely mostly on farming and seasonal work. They are famous for their burnished pottery, which is the most developed of the Chaco's indigenous pottery.

For more information on the Toba, Wichí or Mocoví, stop by Resistencia's Centro Cultural Leopoldo Marechal (see p234), which has crafts exhibits sponsored by the Fundación Chaco Artesanal and helpful staff, and the Museo del Hombre Chaqueño (p235). To journey into the Argentine Impenetrable to visit the Toba or Wichí, see the boxed text, p239.

NORTHEAST ARGENTINA

LAGUNA BLANCA

☎ 03718 / pop 6508

The handiest base for visiting the Parque Nacional Río Pilcomayo (see p242), Laguna Blanca is a spread-out settlement where people move slowly, mostly on scooters and bicycles. Cattle, horses, bananas and citrus keep people in business here, and the town is renowned for its grapefruit, celebrated during **Fiesta del Pomelo** in mid-July. To the south of town is a large reserve owned by the Toba.

Laguna Blanca is 55km west of Clorinda and 126km northwest of Formosa. Most services are around the plaza. On its northeastern side are a bank with ATM, and Maxi Compras Plaza, a shop where *remises* congregate.

Sleeping & Eating

Residencial Guaraní (☎ 470024; cnr San Martín & Sargento Cabral; s/d AR$40/55; ☒) One of two places to stay, this is a great little spot with comfortable rooms (AR$10 extra for air-con) with sizable bathrooms set around a beautiful patio with a well and shaded by mango trees. It also has the best restaurant (dishes AR$8 to AR$22) in town, which far exceeds expectations; it's open for lunch and dinner.

El Monumental (25 de Mayo btwn RN 86 & San Martín; meals AR$9-16; ☯ lunch & dinner) A friendly local with a simple dynamic: good cheap food, cold beer, plastic tables outside and the local radio station belting out classic '80s rock.

Getting There & Away

Godoy and Tres Destinos run to Laguna Blanca from Formosa five times daily (AR$19); the trip takes three hours, a little less via Riacho rather than Clorinda (AR$7, 1½ hours). Shared taxis (AR$12) shuttle between Clorinda and Laguna Blanca, leaving from Av San Martín in Clorinda, a block west of the footbridge, and the plaza in Laguna Blanca.

PARQUE NACIONAL RÍO PILCOMAYO

East of Laguna Blanca is the wildlife-rich marshland of 600-sq-km Parque Nacional Río Pilcomayo. Its outstanding feature is shallow, shimmering **Laguna Blanca** (not to be confused with the town) where, at sunset, caimans lurk on the lake's surface. Other animals are likelier to be heard than seen; species such as tapirs, anteaters and the maned wolf are present. Birds are abundant, with rheas, parrots, cormorants, jabirú and raptors easily spotted. The park has grasslands studded with caranday palms, and thicker riverine vegetation.

There are two distinct parts of the park that you can access. The visitors center at **Estero Poí** is 11km from the center of Laguna Blanca, 3km east along the highway and 8km north along a dirt road. From the visitors center, a roughish 14km vehicle track runs down to the Río Pilcomayo; it's along here that you've got most chance of seeing wildlife.

The visitors center at Laguna Blanca is 3km north of the main road from the turnoff 2km west of Laguna Naick-Neck, and 9km east of Laguna Blanca town. Here, there's a small nature display (from roadkill) and a boardwalk leading to the lake itself, where there's a rickety wooden observation tower, platforms out on the water and boats that the rangers can take you out in. The water is shallow, and the caimans not a concern, but a sign advises swimming with footwear because of the piranhas… It's especially tranquil and appealing here late in the day, after picnickers and daytrippers have left, but take repellent.

Sleeping & Eating

Both the Estero Poí and Laguna Blanca centers have shady free campsites, with basic bathrooms and barbecues with wood. The shower water is saline and most people prefer the lake. A shop sells simple food and cold drinks just outside the Laguna Blanca park entrance, but you're better off bringing supplies from Laguna Blanca town or Clorinda.

Getting There & Away

Buses between Clorinda and Laguna Blanca will drop you off at either of the national park turnoffs, but you'd have to walk or hitch from there. A *remise* from Laguna Blanca town to either park visitors center will charge from AR$30; more if it waits for you. Ask at Maxi Compras Plaza in Laguna Blanca.

The Andean Northwest

In stark contrast with the low, flat, humid northeast, Argentina's northwest sits lofty, dry and tough beneath the mighty Andes. Nature works its magic here with stone: weird, wonderful and tortured rockscapes are visible throughout, from the imposing formations of the Parque Nacional Talampaya in the far south to the twisted strata of the Quebrada de Cafayate; from the jagged ruggedness of the Valles Calchaquíes to the palette of colors of the Quebrada de Humahuaca. And always to the west is the brooding presence of magnificent peaks.

The area has an Andean feel with its traditional handicrafts, Quechua-speaking pockets, coca leaves, llamas, the indigenous heritage of the inhabitants, Inca ruins, and the high, arid puna (Andean highlands) stretching west to Chile and north to Bolivia. The region's cities were Argentina's first colonial settlements and have a special appeal. The quiet gentility of Santiago del Estero recalls bygone centuries, Salta's beauty makes it a favorite stop for travelers, while resolutely urban Tucumán, a sugarcane capital, seems to look firmly to the future.

Several popular routes await. From Salta you can take in the cactus sentinels of Parque Nacional Los Cardones on your way to gorgeous Cachi, and then head down through the traditional weaving communities of the Valles Calchaquíes to Cafayate, home of some of Argentina's best wines. Another route from Salta soars into the mountains to the puna mining settlement of San Antonio de los Cobres, heads north to the spectacular salt plains of the Salinas Grandes, and then down to the visually wondrous and history-filled Quebrada de Humahuaca.

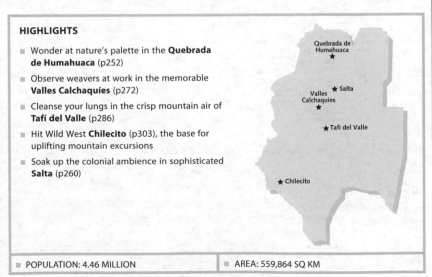

HIGHLIGHTS

- Wonder at nature's palette in the **Quebrada de Humahuaca** (p252)
- Observe weavers at work in the memorable **Valles Calchaquíes** (p272)
- Cleanse your lungs in the crisp mountain air of **Tafí del Valle** (p286)
- Hit Wild West **Chilecito** (p303), the base for uplifting mountain excursions
- Soak up the colonial ambience in sophisticated **Salta** (p260)

Quebrada de Humahuaca ★

★ Salta
Valles Calchaquíes ★

★ Tafí del Valle

★ Chilecito

- POPULATION: 4.46 MILLION
- AREA: 559,864 SQ KM

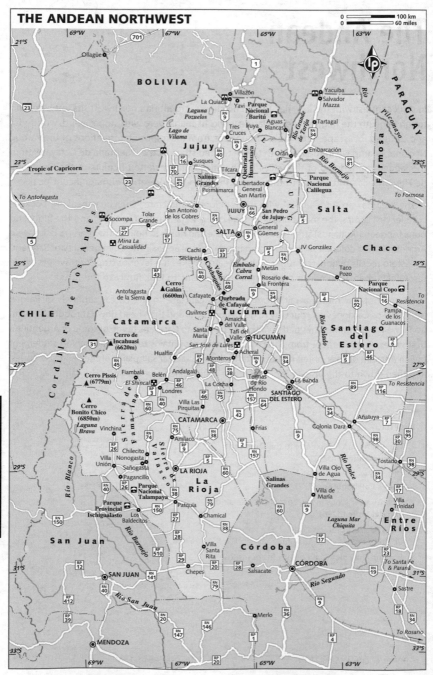

THE ANDEAN NORTHWEST

Climate

Dryness and cold characterize the extreme northwest's weather. Drought is often a problem and many zones are virtual desert. Although the zone's crossed by the Tropic of Capricorn, the altitudes here keep things chilly. To the south and east, however, temperatures are much warmer, and you'll sweat it out in the steamy cloud forest of Parque Nacional Calilegua or the scorching summer of La Rioja.

National Parks

This region holds some important national parks, mostly in Jujuy and Salta provinces. Parque Nacional Calilegua (p250) preserves subtropical cloud forest and is home to an array of birdlife, as well as pumas and jaguars. The less accessible Parque Nacional El Rey (p251) is the most biologically diverse park in the country and teems with birdlife, including toucans. Far-flung Parque Nacional Baritú (p252) contains subtropical montane forest and is home to monkeys, big cats, otters and forest squirrels. Between Salta and Cachi, Parque Nacional Los Cardones (p272) is full of cactus-studded photo opportunities. Much further south, Parque Nacional Talampaya (p305) has aboriginal petroglyphs, photogenic rock formations and unique flora and fauna, while in the far east of the region, Parque Nacional Copo (p293) harbors anteaters, parrots and the fabulous quebracho colorado tree.

Getting There & Away

There are flights from Buenos Aires to Jujuy, Salta, Tucumán, Santiago del Estero, Catamarca and La Rioja, and flights from Salta to Córdoba and Iguazú. Salta has the most flights. Bus connections are generally available for destinations all over the country, particularly from the large cities of Tucumán and Salta. Slow trains from Buenos Aires make it to Tucumán.

JUJUY & SALTA PROVINCES

Intertwined like yin and yang, Argentina's two northwestern provinces harbor an inspiring wealth of natural beauty and traditional culture, of archaeological sites and appealing urban spaces, of national parks and wineries. Bounded by Bolivia to the north and Chile to the west, the zone climbs from the sweaty cloud forests of Las Yungas westward to the puna highlands and some of the most majestic peaks of the Cordillera de los Andes.

The two capitals – comfortable Jujuy and colonial, beloved-of-travelers Salta – are launch pads for exploration of the jagged chromatic ravines of the Quebrada de Cafayate and Quebrada de Humahuaca; for the villages of the Valles Calchaquíes, rich in artisanal handicrafts; for the stark puna scenery; for nosing of the aromatic Cafayate torrontés whites; or for rough exploration in the remote national parks of El Rey or Baritú.

JUJUY

☎ 0388 / pop 278,336 / elev 1201m

Of the trinity of northwestern cities, Jujuy lacks the colonial sophistication of Salta or urban vibe of Tucumán, but nevertheless shines for its livable feel, enticing restaurants and gregarious, good-looking locals. It's got the most indigenous feel of any of Argentina's cities. The climate is perpetually springlike; the city is the highest provincial capital in the country.

San Salvador de Jujuy (commonly called simply Jujuy) was founded in 1593 as the most northerly Spanish colonial city in present-day Argentina. It was the third attempt to found a city in this valley, after the previous two incarnations had been razed by miffed indigenous groups who hadn't given planning permission.

On August 23, 1812, during the wars of independence, General Belgrano ordered the evacuation of Jujuy. Its citizens complied in what is famously known as the *éxodo jujeño*. All possessions that could not be loaded on the mules were burned, along with the houses, in a scorched-earth retreat. Belgrano reported that most citizens were willing. They were able to return to what was left of their city in February 1813. The province of Jujuy bore the brunt of conflict during these wars, with Spain launching repeated invasions down the Quebrada de Humahuaca from Bolivia.

The city's name is roughly pronounced *hu-hui;* if it sounds like an arch exclamation of surprise, you're doing well.

Orientation

Jujuy sits above the Río Grande floodplain where the smaller Río Xibi Xibi meets it. It consists of two parts: the old city, with a

THE ANDEAN NORTHWEST

JUJUY & SALTA PROVINCES

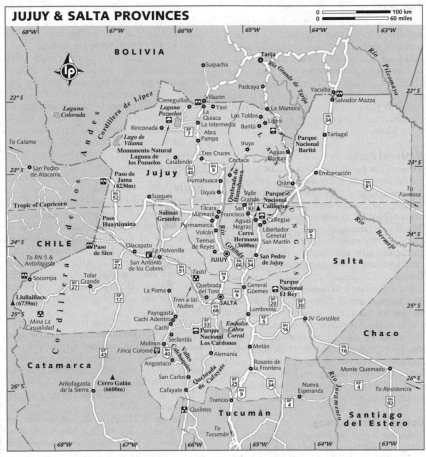

fairly regular grid pattern between the Ríos Grande and Xibi Xibi, and a newer area south of the Xibi Xibi that sprawls up the slopes of the nearby hills. All of interest is within walking distance of the main square, Plaza Belgrano.

Information

There are many central banks with ATMs. Call centers and internet places abound.

ACA (Automóvil Club Argentino; ☎ 422-2568; cnr Av Senador Pérez & Alvear) Maps and route information.

Hospital Pablo Soria (☎ 422-1228; cnr Patricias Argentinas & Av Córdoba)

La Zona (☎ 422-5233; Lavalle 340; per hr ARS2) Good cybercafe with extra facilities available.

Laverap (Belgrano 1214) Laundry.

Municipal tourist office (☎ 402-0254; Av Urquiza 354; ☽ 7am-10pm) Simple, friendly office in the old train station. There's another at the bus terminal.

Provincial tourist office (☎ 422-1343; www.turismo .jujuy.gov.ar; Gorriti 295; ☽ 7am-10pm Mon-Fri, 8am-10pm Sat & Sun) Excellent office with good brochures and staff.

Sights

CATEDRAL

Jujuy's 1763 **catedral** (cathedral; Plaza Belgrano; ☽ 8am-12:30pm & 5pm-8:30pm) replaced a 17th-century predecessor destroyed by the Diaguita. The outstanding feature, salvaged from the original church, is the gold-laminated baroque pulpit, probably built by local artisans trained by a European master.

MUSEO ARQUEOLÓGICO PROVINCIAL

The **Museo Arqueológico Provincial** (☎ 422-1315; Lavalle 434; admission AR$2; 🕑 8am-8pm Mon-Fri, 9am-1pm & 3-7pm Sat & Sun) is definitely worth a visit. The standout exhibit is a vivid 3000-year-old fertility goddess figure, depicted with snakes for hair and in the act of giving birth. She's a product of the advanced San Francisco culture, which existed in Las Yungas from about 1400 BC to 800 BC. There's also a selection of skulls with cranial deformities (practiced for cosmetic reasons) and mummified bodies displayed with what might have been their typical possessions. Staff hand out a booklet that has information in English.

CABILDO & MUSEO POLICIAL

On the plaza, the attractively colonnaded **cabildo** (colonial town hall) houses the **Museo Policial** (☎ 423-7715; admission free; 🕑 8am-1pm & 4-9pm Mon-Fri, 9am-noon & 6-8pm Sat & Sun). Police museums in Argentina are funny things, with grisly crime photos, indiscriminate homage to authority and the odd quirky gem, in this case the discovery that in 1876 you could expect a five peso fine if you wanted carnal knowledge of a llama.

MUSEO HISTÓRICO PROVINCIAL

During Argentina's civil wars, a bullet pierced the imposing wooden door of this colonial house, killing General Juan Lavalle, a hero of the wars of independence. The story of Lavalle unfolds in **Museo Histórico Provincial** (☎ 422-1355; Lavalle 256; admission AR$2; 🕑 8am-8pm Mon-Fri, 9am-1pm & 4-8pm Sat & Sun). There is also religious and colonial art, as well as exhibits on the independence era, the evacuation of Jujuy and 19th-century fashion. There are some English labels, and guides on hand to answer questions.

IGLESIA Y CONVENTO SAN FRANCISCO

While the Franciscan order has been in Jujuy since 1599, **Iglesia y Convento San Francisco** (cnr Belgrano & Lavalle) dates only from 1912. Nevertheless, its **Museo Histórico Franciscano** (☎ 423-3434; admission AR$2; 🕑 9am-3pm & 5-9pm Mon-Fri), alongside on Belgrano, retains a strong selection of colonial art from the Cuzco school, which came about when monks taught indigenous Peruvians the style of the great Spanish and Flemish masters; this school gradually developed a high-quality style of its own that still exists today.

CULTURARTE

An attractive modern space, the **Culturarte** (☎ 424-9539; cnr San Martín & Sarmiento; admission free; 🕑 8:30am-midnight Mon-Fri, 8:30am-1pm & 4:30pm-midnight Sat & Sun) showcases exhibitions by well-established Argentine contemporary artists. There's also a cafe-bar with a great little balcony elevated over the street.

MERCADO DEL SUR

Jujuy's lively market, opposite the bus terminal, is a genuine trading post where indigenous Argentines swig *mazamorra* (a cold maize soup) and peddle coca leaves (see boxed text, p249). Simple eateries around here serve hearty regional specialties; try *chicharrón con mote* (stir-fried pork with boiled maize) or spicy *sopa de maní* (peanut soup).

Tours

Several Jujuy operators offer trips to the Quebrada de Humahuaca, Salinas Grandes, Parque Nacional Calilegua and other provincial destinations. See the Provincial Tourist Office (opposite) for a full listing.

Noroeste (☎ 423-7565; www.paisajesdelnoroeste.tur.ar; San Martín 136) Based at Club Hostel (below), it hits the Quebrada de Humahuaca area, Salinas Grandes and more.

Festivals & Events

In August, Jujuy's biggest event, the weeklong **Semana de Jujuy**, commemorates Belgrano's evacuation of the city during the wars of independence. The next-largest gathering is the religious pilgrimage known as the **Peregrinaje a la Virgen del Río Blanco** on October 7.

Sleeping

BUDGET

There are lots of cheap *residenciales* in the chaotic streets around the bus terminal.

Club Hostel (☎ 423-7565; www.noroestevirtual.com.ar; San Martín 134; dm/s/d AR$35/70/120; 🖥 🛜 🛄) In a new location across the road, this busy hostel has good dark dorms that have lockers, bathrooms and only four berths per room. The private rooms with bathrooms are also decent, and there's a kitchen and tiny Jacuzzi out the back. HI (Hotel International) discount applies. Friendly staff also operate a tour agency.

Hostal Casa de Barro (☎ 422-9578; www.casadebarro.com.ar; Otero 294; s/d without bathroom AR$40/75) Light-hearted and genuinely welcoming, this original and enjoyable place has rooms that are bright and chirpy, and shared bathrooms

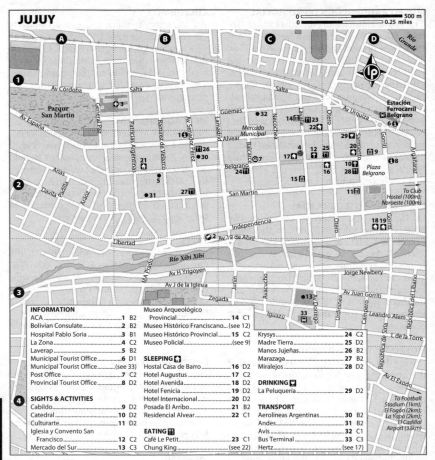

INFORMATION
ACA	1 B2
Bolivian Consulate	2 B2
Hospital Pablo Soria	3 B1
La Zona	4 C2
Laverap	5 B2
Municipal Tourist Office	6 D1
Municipal Tourist Office	(see 33)
Post Office	7 C2
Provincial Tourist Office	8 D2

SIGHTS & ACTIVITIES
Cabildo	9 D2
Catedral	10 D2
Culturarte	11 D2
Iglesia y Convento San Francisco	12 C2
Mercado del Sur	13 C3
Museo Arqueológico Provincial	14 C1
Museo Histórico Franciscano	(see 12)
Museo Histórico Provincial	15 C2
Museo Policial	(see 9)

SLEEPING
Hostal Casa de Barro	16 D2
Hotel Augustus	17 C2
Hotel Avenida	18 D2
Hotel Fenicia	19 D2
Hotel Internacional	20 D2
Posada El Arribo	21 B2
Residencial Alvear	22 C1

EATING
Café Le Petit	23 C1
Chung King	(see 22)
Krysys	24 C2
Madre Tierra	25 D2
Manos Jujeñas	26 B2
Marazaga	27 B2
Miralejos	28 D2

DRINKING
La Peluqueria	29 D2

TRANSPORT
Aerolineas Argentinas	30 B2
Andes	31 B2
Avis	32 C1
Bus Terminal	33 C3
Hertz	(see 17)

that are very clean. The place is decorated throughout with rock-art motifs. There's a comfy lounge and a kitchen, and breakfast is included.

Residencial Alvear (☎ 422-2982; restaurantechunking@arnetbiz.com.ar; Alvear 627; s/d with bathroom AR$78/95, without bathroom AR$38/76) A variety of rooms is tucked away behind the Chung King restaurant (see opposite). They're OK for the price, but select carefully (upstairs) as some of those with shared bathroom are a little poky. The further back, the quieter it gets.

MIDRANGE
Hotel Avenida (☎ 423-6136; www.quintar.com.ar; Av 19 de Abril 469; s/d AR$80/140) There's a curious cast of characters at the aged Avenida, but they all mean well. Once quite upmarket, it's seen better days but is still a reasonable choice by the river. Rooms at the front have huge windows looking across to greenery, but suffer from street noise. Bag a discount.

Hotel Fenicia (☎ 423-1800; www.quintar.com.ar; Av 19 de Abril 427; s/d standard AR$132/216, s/d superior AR$180/264; 🅿 🖳 🛜) This hotel overlooks the Xibi Xibi; its rooms are a bit run-down, but worth the price for the views from their great balconies. Modernized superior rooms are better value, while the penthouse (AR$780) has the best views of all.

Hotel Internacional (☎ 423-1599; www.hinternacionaljujuy.com.ar; Belgrano 501; s/d AR$150/190; 🅿 🖳 🛜) Perched on a corner of the plaza, this high-rise has smallish but bright cream-colored rooms with good-looking clean bathrooms. Some have spectacular views out over the plaza, and nice touches include a morning paper put under your door. Good value.

Hotel Augustus (☎ 423-0203; www.hotelaugustus .com.ar; Belgrano 715; s/d AR$182/230; ✂ 💻 ☎) Smack on the pedestrian street (er, block), this offers personable service and value for money. The mattresses feel newish, and are draped with fleur-de-lis bedspreads. Half the rooms have pleasant balconies. You can use the pool at a hotel just a 15-minute cab ride away.

Posada El Arribo (☎ 422-2539; www.elarribo.com; Belgrano 1263; s/d AR$210/255; ✂ 💻 ☎ 🐾) An oasis in the heart of Jujuy, this highly impressive family-run place is a real visual feast. The renovated 19th-century mansion is wonderful, with high ceilings and wooden floors; there's patio space galore and a huge garden. The modern annex behind doesn't lose much by comparison, but go for an older room if you can.

Eating

Café Le Petit (Lavalle 415; cakes AR$5-8; ☺ 9am-8pm) A stately and well-loved salon with classic, refined decor, where you can take your well-deserved break for coffee and rather tasty cake.

Manos Jujeñas (☎ 424-3270; Av Senador Pérez 381; mains AR$14-26; ☺ lunch & dinner) One of Jujuy's best addresses for no-frills traditional slow-food cooking, this fills up with a contented buzz on weekend evenings. There are several classic northeastern dishes to choose from, but it's the *picante* – chicken, tongue or mixed – that's the pride of the house.

COCA CHEWING

Once you get seriously north, you see signs outside shops advertising *coca* and *bica*. The former refers to the leaves, mainly grown in Peru and Bolivia, which are used to produce cocaine. *Bica* refers to bicarbonate of soda, an alkaline that, when chewed along with the leaves (as is customary among Andean peoples), releases their mild stimulant effect and combats fatigue and hunger. Chewing coca and possessing small amounts for personal use is legal, but only in the northern provinces of Salta and Jujuy. Taking them into other provinces or into Chile is illegal, and there are plenty of searches.

Chung King (☎ 422-2982; Alvear 627; mains AR$14-34; ☺ lunch & dinner) This is a popular, worthwhile restaurant with an extensive Argentine menu including good-value daily specials (AR$18 to AR$24); it has an even more popular attached pizzeria. In fact, despite the name, about the only chow you can't get here is Chinese.

Miralejos (☎ 422-4911; Sarmiento 368; meals AR$15-32; ☺ 8am-midnight) This is plaza-side dining at its finest. Miralejos offers the full gamut of steak and pasta (with a wide choice of interesting sauces), with a few local trout dishes thrown in. The outside tables are a great place for breakfast and the eclectic music selection is interesting, to say the least.

Krysys (☎ 423-1126; Balcarce 272; mains AR$15-40; ☺ lunch & dinner Mon-Sat) The best *parrilla* (steak restaurant) option is this central, upscale place offering all your barbecued favorites in a relaxed atmosphere. But there's plenty more on the menu, with a range of tasty sauces to go with your choice of chicken, pork or beef, and various appetizing avocado starters. Prices are fair, and you'll get the meat the way you want it cooked.

Marazaga (☎ 424-3427; Av Senador Pérez 222; mains AR$32-45; ☺ dinner) This place offers traditional Andean plates alongside trendy new creations. The vegetarian crepe starter is filling and tasty; but the pork with honey-mustard sauce could do with a more dignified bed than crinkle-cut chips. But, as in Russian roulette, there are more positive than negative outcomes.

our pick Madre Tierra (☎ 422-9578; Belgrano 619; 4-course lunch AR$35; ☺ 7am-6pm Mon-Sat) This place is a standout. The vegetarian food – there's a daily set menu – is excellent and the salads, crepes and soups can be washed down with fresh juice. It's an earthy place where the simple, home-cooked food makes a welcome change. The bakery out the front does a range of wholesome breads.

Drinking & Entertainment

Jujuy's folkloric *peñas* (folk music clubs) tend to be a cab ride away and open weekend nights only. One of the best is **El Fogón** (☎ 0388-15-588-2040; RN9; ☺ 8pm-late Sat) on the southeastern edge of town; another is **La Yapa** (☎ 402-0637; Mejías 426, Barrio Malvinas; ☺ 8pm-late Fri & Sat). The big *boliches* (nightclubs) are also out on RN9 south of town, while **La Peluquería** (Alvear 526; ☺ 8pm-late Thu-Sun) isn't a hairdresser but a big, popular central pub with an elevated stage for live music.

THE ANDEAN NORTHWEST

Getting There & Away

AIR

Andes (☎ 431-0279; www.andesonline.com.ar; San Martín 1283) flies six times weekly to Buenos Aires (AR$712) via Salta (AR$68), with connections to Puerto Madryn and Iguazú. **Aerolíneas Argentinas** (☎ 422-7198; Av Senador Pérez 355) services Buenos Aires' Aeroparque Jorge Newbery (AR$827) once daily.

BUS

The old-school **bus terminal** (☎ 422-1375; cnr Av Dorrego & Iguazú) has provincial and long-distance services, but Salta has more alternatives.

Buses coming from Salta run to San Pedro de Atacama (AR$160) around 8:30am on Monday, Wednesday and Friday; book it in advance with Andesmar or Pullman. Geminis do the same run on Tuesday, Thursday and Sunday.

There are frequent services south to Salta and north to the Quebrada de Humahuaca and the Bolivian border at La Quiaca. Sample destinations and fares:

Destination	Cost (AR$)	Duration (hr)
Buenos Aires	210	23
Catamarca	96	10
Córdoba	166	14
General Libertador San Martín	19	2
Humahuaca	13	3
La Quiaca	35	4-5
Mendoza	210-250	20
Purmamarca	9	1¼
Salta	23	2
Salvador Mazza	69	6-7
Susques	26	4-5
Tilcara	10	1¾
Tucumán	62	5

Getting Around

Jujuy's El Cadillal airport is 33km east of the center. A shuttle service leaves from the Hotel Internacional at 12.30pm to coincide with flights (AR$20). Otherwise it's AR$65 in a *remise* (radio taxi).

If you're after a rental car, **Avis** (☎ 424-4938; www.avis.com; Güemes 864) or **Hertz** (☎ 422-9582; www.hertz.com.ar; Belgrano 715), in Hotel Augustus, are central choices; there are also branches at the airport.

AROUND JUJUY

Situated in a deep green valley above a mostly dry riverbed, the hot springs of **Termas de Reyes** are just 19km from Jujuy; the mineral-rich water emerges at a natural temperature of 50ºC. They are so named (Kings' Springs) because indigenous chiefs used to bathe in them for their magical properties.

There's a public **pool** (admission AR$15; 9am-8:30pm), and free campsite here, as well as the upmarket **Hotel Termas de Reyes** (☎ 0388-492-2522; www.termasdereyes.com; s/d AR$210/360;), with a central-European feel, very comfortable rooms (views cost more) and spa treatments. It doesn't accept under-16s as guests.

Bus 1C runs hourly (AR$1.75, 45 minutes) from Calle Gorriti near the Jujuy tourist office.

PARQUE NACIONAL CALILEGUA
☎ 03886

Jujuy province's eastern portion is Las Yungas, a humid and fertile subtropical zone mostly devoted to the sugarcane industry. Here, arid, treeless altiplano gives way to the dense cloud forest of the Serranía de Calilegua, whose preservation is the goal of this accessible 760-sq-km park. At the park's highest elevations, about 3600m, verdant Cerro Hermoso reaches above the forest for boundless views of Chaco to the east. Birdlife is abundant and colorful, but the tracks of rare mammals, such as pumas, tapirs and jaguars, are easier to see than the animals themselves.

Information

The park's **headquarters** (☎ 422046; calilegua@apn.gov.ar; 7am-2pm Mon-Fri) is in Calilegua village, 5km north of the town of Libertador General San Martín. It has general park information, but the ranger at the **park entrance** (admission free; 9am-6pm) in Aguas Negras has more information about trails and conditions. There's another ranger station at Mesada de las Colmenas, 13km past Aguas Negras and 600m higher. The trails are well marked.

Receiving 1000mm to 1800mm of precipitation a year, but with a defined winter dry season, Calilegua comprises a variety of ecosystems. The transitional *selva* (jungle), from 350m to 500m above sea level, consists of tree species common in the Gran Chaco, such as deciduous lapacho and palo amarillo. Between 550m and 1600m, the cloud forest forms a dense canopy of trees more than 30m tall, punctuated by ferns, epiphytes and lianas, often mist covered. Above 1200m, the montane forest is composed of conifers, aliso and queñoa. Above 2600m this grades into moist grasslands, which become drier as one proceeds west toward the Quebrada de Humahuaca.

The 230 bird species at home in the park include condors, brown eagles, torrent ducks and colorful toucans. Important mammals include tapirs, pumas, jaguars, collared peccaries and otters. The presence of the road through the middle of the park, the nearby hydro-station and regular gravel harvesting in the riverbed mean that, on the trails near Aguas Negras, there's little chance of spotting reclusive species.

Activities

The best places for bird and mammal watching are near the stream courses in the early morning or late afternoon. From the ranger station at Mesada de las Colmenas, follow the steep, rugged trail down to a beautiful creek marked with numerous animal tracks, including those of large cats. The descent takes an hour, the ascent twice that.

There are seven marked trails in the park, from 20-minute strolls to tough four-hour hikes. From the campground, a short **Guaraní cultural trail**, dotted with weird signboards, introduces you to the lower tropical forest. For waterbirds, head to **La Lagunita**, about 1½ hours' walk from Aguas Negras. The **La Junta trail** starts 3km up the road from Aguas Negras, and is a four-hour return walk with steepish climbs rewarded by great views over the park.

Vehicles with clearance can get right through the 23km of park, if there's no rain. The road offers outstanding views of Cerro Hermoso and the nearly impenetrable forests of its steep ravines.

From Valle Grande, beyond the park boundaries to the west, it's possible to hike in a week to Humahuaca along the Sierra de Zenta, or to Tilcara.

Sleeping & Eating

Camping is the only option in the park itself. The developed **campground** (Aguas Negras) is some 300m from the ranger station at the entrance. It is free and has bathrooms and shower, but no shop. There are simple homestay accommodations at San Francisco, 39km from Aguas Negras, beyond the western end of the park.

Nearby Libertador General San Martín is a sizable town devoted to processing sug-

arcane, whose sickly sweet smell pervades all corners. Places to stay include **Hotel Los Lapachos** (☎ 423790; Entre Ríos 400; s/d AR$80/100; ⊠), which tries hard with its scalloped handbasins and wine-red carpets, a block from the plaza. Eating, except at the upmarket Posada del Sol hotel outside town, is dire. **Parador 34** (cnr Belgrano & RN 34; mains AR$9-22; ⊠ 6am-midnight), on the highway in the center, is esteemed hereabouts, but offers little besides bright lights, internet, a huge TV, and overcooked steak, chicken and rabbit.

Little Calilegua, 5km north, is a much more appealing place to stay, with a tumbledown tropical feel and a deafening chorus of cicadas. Near the park office, **Jardín Colonial** (☎ 430334; San Lorenzo s/n; s/d without bathroom AR$25/50) is a lovely bungalow with rooms, a shady porch and a verdant, sculpture-filled garden.

Getting There & Away

Numerous buses between Jujuy/Salta and the Bolivian border at Salvador Mazza stop at Libertador General San Martín and Calilegua, and some will let you off on the highway at the junction for the park, 3km north of Libertador and 2km south of Calilegua. It's 8km from here to the ranger station at Aguas Negras; there's enough traffic to hitchhike.

A daily bus (at 8:30am) goes from Libertador General San Martín to Valle Grande (two hours) through the park. It passes the Aguas Negras ranger station at 9am. The return bus passes around 6pm; perfect for day trips to the park. It's also easy to get a taxi from either Libertador or Calilegua to Aguas Negras (AR$20 to AR$30).

PARQUE NACIONAL EL REY

East of Salta, **Parque Nacional El Rey** (elrey@apn.gov.ar) is at the southern end of the Las Yungas subtropical corridor and protects a habitat that is the most biologically diverse in the country. The park takes its name from the *estancia* (ranch) that formerly occupied the area and whose expropriation led to the park's creation.

The park's emblem is the giant toucan, which is appropriate because of the abundant birdlife, but the mosquito might be just as appropriate (also check yourself for ticks, although they don't carry disease). Most of the same mammals found in Calilegua and Baritú are also here.

BOLIVIA VIA SALVADOR MAZZA

RN 34 continues past Calilegua to Argentina's northernmost settlement, Salvador Mazza (also known as Pocitos, the name of the defunct station), one of the country's two major frontiers with Bolivia. Here you cross the **frontier** (✆ 24hr), and take a shared taxi 5km to the larger Bolivian settlement of Yacuiba, which has weekly flights to La Paz, and buses to Tarija (US$14, 12 hours) and Santa Cruz (US$11, 15 hours). There's no Bolivian consulate, so get your visa in Jujuy or Salta if you need one. At the time of research, US nationals needed a visa, but citizens of the EU, UK, Canada, Australia, New Zealand and South Africa did not. Salvador Mazza is served by numerous buses from Jujuy, Salta and other northern cities. Bolivia is one hour behind Argentina.

At the time of writing the exchange rate for bolivianos was AR$1 to B$1.80 and US$1 to B$6.90.

There are various well-marked trails, some accessible by vehicle. **Laguna Los Patitos**, 2km from park headquarters, offers opportunities to observe waterbirds. Longer trails lead to moss-covered **Pozo Verde**, a three- to four-hour climb to an area teeming with birdlife. Two other trails are of similar day-trip length; rangers recommend a three-day stay to really get to know the park. Trails involve multiple river crossings, so bring waterproof shoes or get your feet wet.

Entry is free and the best time to visit is between April and October.

There is free camping at the park's headquarters, with toilets, drinkable water, cold showers and power from 7pm to 10pm. There is no shop. Contact the **National Parks Administration** (APN; ✆ 0387-431-2683; www.parquesnacionales.gov.ar; España 366; ✆ 8am-3pm Mon-Fri) in Salta for up-to-date info or check the rangers' blog (http://pnelrey.blogspot.com).

It's tough to get here. The last 46km are on rough *ripio* (gravel) road that's almost impassable if it's been raining. Last fuel is at General Güemes, 160km from the park, so consider taking extra gas. If you aren't hiring a 4WD, the easiest way to get here is via guided tour from Salta (p265). Public transportation gets as far as Lumbreras, 91km short of the park.

PARQUE NACIONAL BARITÚ

Hugging the Bolivian border, Baritú is the northernmost of the three Las Yungas parks conserving subtropical montane forest. Like Calilegua and El Rey, it harbors a large number of threatened mammals, including black howler and capuchin monkeys, southern river otters, Geoffroy's cats, jaguars and tapirs. The park's emblem is the forest squirrel, which inhabits the moist forest above 1300m.

Admission is free and information can be obtained at **park headquarters** (✆ 03878-450101; baritu@apn.gov.ar) or **National Parks Administration** (APN; ✆ 0387-431-2683; www.parquesnacionales.gov.ar; España 366; ✆ 8am-3pm Mon-Fri) in Salta.

Here, Che Guevara's psychopathic disciple Masetti tried to start the Argentine revolution by infiltrating from Bolivia in 1963. The only road access is through Bolivia. From RN 34, 90km beyond Calilegua, head for Orán then Aguas Blancas. Crossing into Bolivia, you hug the north bank of Río Bermejo, heading westward 113km, before crossing back into Argentina at La Mamora. A further 17km gets you to Los Toldos, and another 26km brings you to Lipeo, a hamlet at the northwest corner of the park. It has a ranger station but no other services. Los Toldos has accommodations, telephone and a supermarket. The drive to the park usually requires a 4WD.

From Lipeo, there are various trails, including to the hot springs of **Cayotal**, two hours away, and to the remote hamlet of **Baritú**, a four-hour walk each way through impressive cedar forest. You can rent horses in Lipeo for this ride. Locals in Lipeo and Baritú can offer accommodation in their homes.

QUEBRADA DE HUMAHUACA

North of Jujuy, the memorable Quebrada de Humahuaca snakes its way upward toward Bolivia. It's a harsh but vivid landscape, a dry but river-scoured canyon overlooked by mountainsides whose sedimentary strata have been eroded into spectacular scalloped formations that reveal a spectrum of colors in undulating waves. The palette of this Unesco World Heritage–listed valley changes constantly, from shades of creamy white to rich, deep reds; the rock formations in places recall a necklace of sharks' teeth, in others the knobbly backbone of some unspeakable beast. The canyon's southern stretches are overlooked by cardón cactus sentinels, but these peter out beyond Humahuaca as the road rises.

Dotting the valley are dusty, picturesque, indigenous towns that have a fine variety of places to stay, plus pretty, historic adobe churches, and homey restaurants serving warming *locro* (a stew of maize, beans, beef, pork and sausage) and llama fillets. The region has experienced a tourism boom in recent years and gets very full in summer, when accommodation prices soar.

There are many interesting stops along this colonial post route between Potosí (Bolivia) and Buenos Aires; buses along the road run every 40 minutes or so, so it's quite easy to jump off and on as required. The only spot to hire a car hereabouts is in Jujuy, or further south in Salta. The Quebrada de Humahuaca itself shows its best side early in the morning, when the colors are more vivid and the wind hasn't got up.

Purmamarca

☎ 0388 / pop 510 / elev 2192m

Little Purmamarca, 3km west of the highway, sits under the celebrated Cerro de los Siete Colores (Hill of Seven Colors), a spectacular and jagged formation resembling the marzipan fantasy of a megalomaniac pastry chef. The village is postcard pretty, with ochre adobe houses and ancient algarrobo trees by the bijou 17th-century church. This, and its proximity to Jujuy, has made it perhaps the northwest's most over-touristed spot; if you're looking for an authentic Andean village, move on. Nevertheless, Purmamarca is an excellent place to shop for woven goods; a flourishing poncho market sets up on the plaza every day.

There's an ATM on the plaza, as well as an **information office** (☒ 8am-1pm & 2-7pm), with maps that include the easy but spectacular 3km walk around the *cerro* (hill), whose striking colors are best appreciated in the morning or evening sunlight.

SLEEPING & EATING

Hostería Bebo Vilte (☎ 490-8038; Salta s/n; camping per person AR$20, dm/d without bathroom AR$40/100, with bathroom AR$150/220) Behind the church, this is a popular place offering good motel-style rooms with bathroom, simpler interior rooms and dorms with shared bathroom and a camping area with barbecues. Prices are much more realistic outside of high summer.

El Pequeño Inti (☎ 490-8089; elintidepurmamarca@hotmail.com; Florida s/n; s/d AR$90/110) Small and enticing, this is a fine little choice just off the plaza. Offering value (for two), it has unadorned rooms with comfortable beds and marine-schemed bathrooms.

CHILE VIA SUSQUES

The paved road climbs doggedly from Purmamarca through spectacular bleak highland scenery to a 4150m pass, then crosses a plateau partly occupied by the Salinas Grandes. You hit civilization at **Susques**, 130km from Purmamarca, which has gas and an ATM.

Susques is well worth a stop for its terrific village **church** (admission by donation; ☒ 8am-6pm). Dating from 1598, it has a thatched roof, cactus-wood ceiling and beaten-earth floor, as well as charismatic, naïve paintings of saints on the whitewashed adobe walls. There's a tourist office on the main road, and basic places to stay, including, opposite the bank, friendly **La Vicuñita** (☎ 03887-490207; atamabel@imagine.com.ar; San Martín 121; s/d with bathroom AR$30/60, r per person without bathroom AR$20), which serves up tasty meals, too.

AndesBus runs Tuesday, Thursday, Saturday and Sunday from Jujuy to Susques (AR$26, four to five hours) via Purmamarca.

Beyond Susques, the road continues a further 154km (fuel up in Susques) to the Paso de Jama (4230m), a spectacular journey. This is the Chilean border, although Argentine **emigration** (☒ 8am-10pm) is some way before it. No fruit, vegetables or coca leaves are allowed into Chile – they check. The paved road continues toward San Pedro de Atacama, Calama and Antofagasta in Chile. Buses from Salta and Jujuy travel this route. Nationals of the USA, Canada, Australia, South Africa, New Zealand and the EU do not need a visa to enter Chile. However, a fee is payable for US (US$131), Canadian (US$132) and Australian (US$61) citizens – that's what Chileans pay to apply for a visa for those nations.

Huaira Huasi (☎ 490-8070; www.huairahuasi.com.ar; Ruta 52, Km 5; d/apt AR$260/500; ❌ 🖳 🛜) One of a handful of characterful hotels on the main road above town, this stands out for its valley views and handsome terracotta-colored adobe buildings. There are two apartments that sleep five and are just beautifully decorated with local fabrics and cardón wood; rooms are obviously smaller but still lovely. Good value.

Los Colorados (☎ 490-8182; www.loscoloradosjujuy .com.ar; Chapacal s/n; apt for 2/4 people AR$320/460; 🖳) Looking straight out of a science-fiction movie, these strange but inviting apartments are tucked right into the *cerro*, and blend in with it. They are stylish and cozy; fine places to hole up for a while.

Los Morteros (☎ 490-8002; Salta s/n; mains AR$30-45; ☽ lunch & dinner) Warmly lit and stylish, this is the town's best restaurant, serving dishes such as local trout, or lamb stew with quinoa.

El Rincón de Claudia Vilte (Libertad s/n; admission AR$10, mains AR$12-30; ☽ lunch & dinner) Minstrels serenade diners in nearly every eating establishment, but if you want the whole local music deal over your meal, this is the best *folklore* (folk music) option, though the food is mediocre.

GETTING THERE & AWAY
Buses to Jujuy (AR$9, 1¼ hours) run every one to two hours; others go to Tilcara (AR$3, 30 minutes) and Humahuaca (1¼ hours, AR$8). There's at least one bus every day (bar Monday) to Susques (AR$20, three to four hours) via Salinas Grandes.

Purmamarca has no gas station; the closest can be found 25km north, at Tilcara, or south, at Volcán. Westward, the next gas station is in Susques, a 130km steep climb away.

Tilcara
☎ 0388 / pop 4358 / elev 2461m

Picturesque Tilcara, 23km further up the valley from the Purmamarca turnoff, is many people's choice as their Quebrada de Humahuaca base and offers a wide accommodations choice – from luxury boutique retreats to hostels. The mixture of local farmers getting on with a centuries-old way of life and arty urban refugees looking for a quieter existence has created an interesting balance on the town's dusty streets.

Tilcara is connected by a bridge to RN 9. The main street, Belgrano, runs from the access road to the square, Plaza Prado, and on another block to the church.

INFORMATION
There are several central internet places and call centers as well as a bank with ATM just off the plaza on Lavalle.

Tourist office (☎ 495-5135; mun_tilcara@cootepal .com.ar; Belgrano 366; ☽ 8am-9pm Mon-Fri, 8am-1pm & 2-9pm Sat, 8am-noon Sun) Good information on walks and has a list of accommodation prices.

SIGHTS
Pucará
The reconstructed pre-Columbian fortification, the **pucará** (walled city; ☎ 495-5073; admission incl Museo Arqueológico AR$10, Mon free; ☽ 8am-6pm), is 1km south of the center across an iron bridge. Its situation is undeniably strategic, commanding the river valley both ways and, though the site was undoubtedly used before, the ruins date from the 11th to 15th centuries. The 1950s reconstruction has taken liberties; worse yet is the earlier, ridiculous monument to pioneering archaeologists bang where the plaza would have been. Nevertheless, you can get a feel of what would have been a sizable fortified community. Most interesting is the 'church,' a building with a short paved walkway to an altar; note the niche in the wall alongside. The site itself has great views and, seemingly, a cardón for every soul that lived and died here. For further succulent stimulation, there's a cactus garden by the entrance.

Museo Arqueológico
The Universidad de Buenos Aires runs the well-presented **Museo Arqueológico** (☎ 495-5006; Belgrano 445; admission incl pucará AR$10, Mon free; ☽ 9am-6pm) of regional artifacts. There are some artifacts from the *pucará*, and exhibits give an insight into the life of people living around that time. The room dedicated to ceremonial masks is particularly impressive. The museum is in a striking colonial house on Plaza Prado.

ACTIVITIES
Of several interesting walks around Tilcara, the most popular is the two-hour hike to **Garganta del Diablo**, a pretty canyon and waterfall. Head toward the *pucará*, but turn left along the river before crossing the bridge. The path to the Garganta leaves this road to the left just after a sign that says *'Cuide la flora y fauna.'* Swimming is best in the morning, when the sun is on the pool.

Tilcara Mountain Bike (☎ 0388-15-500-8570; tilcarabikes@hotmail.com; Belgrano s/n; ☺ 8am-7pm) is a friendly setup just past the bus terminal that hires out well-maintained mountain bikes (AR$8/40 per hour/day) and provides a helpful map of trips in the area.

There are several places for horseback riding with or without a guide. You'll see phone numbers for *cabalgatas* (horseback rides) everywhere, and most accommodations can arrange it for you.

TOURS

Based in the Posada de Luz, **Caravana de Llamas** (☎ 495-5326; www.caravanadellamas.com) is a recommended llama-trekking operator running half-day excursions (AR$140) around Tilcara, day trips in the Salinas Grandes (AR$180) and multiday excursions, including a five-day marathon from Las Yungas lowlands to Tilcara (AR$1750 to AR$2600). The guide is personable and well informed about the area. Llamas are pack animals: you walk, they carry the bags.

FESTIVALS & EVENTS

Tilcara celebrates several festivals during the year, the most notable of which is January's **Enero Tilcareño**, with sports, music and cultural activities. February's **Carnaval** is equally important as in other Quebrada de Humahuaca villages, as is April's **Semana Santa** (Holy Week). August's indigenous **Pachamama** (Mother Earth) festival is also worthwhile.

SLEEPING

There are heaps of simple hostels; another budget option is a *casa de familia* (room in a private home with shared bathroom). They are invariably spotless, and you get a room to yourself for around AR$20 to AR$30 per person. One is **Genara de Vargas** (☎ 495-5399; Lavalle 439), whose well-kept house is opposite the hospital.

Casa los Molles (☎ 495-5410; www.casalosmolles .com.ar; Belgrano 155; dm/d without bathroom AR$38/90; ▣ ☎) Run with laissez-faire friendliness by a young couple, this hostel three blocks uphill from the square has a rustic feel, views and a garden to lounge around in. There's plenty of kitchen space and a good social scene.

Hostel Malka (☎ 495-5197; www.malkahostel.com .ar; San Martín s/n, Barrio Malka; dm/s/d AR$50/150/220, d

without bathroom AR$180; ☎) This rustic complex up a path three blocks west of the church is a special place, both hotel and hostel. The welcoming owners, secluded, shady situation, thoughtfully different dorms, and new stone-clad rooms with hammocks and deckchairs out front make it the sort of place you end up staying longer than you expected. There's a good breakfast included and HI discount.

Hotel de Turismo (☎ 495-5720; www.hoteldeturismo.8k .com; Belgrano 590; s/d AR$150/195; ▨ ▣ ☎ ▩) These ACA hotels always lack character, but the facilities are good for the price. The rooms aren't huge but some have little balconies. The central location, mountain views and pool (summer only) make it a safe bet. It's much cheaper off-season.

Cerro Chico (☎ 495-5744; www.cerrochico.com; d/q AR$220/280; ☎ ▩) Two kilometers from town down a dirt road, this attractive complex of cabins climbs a hill with gorgeous Quebrada views and a remote, relaxing feel. The standard cabins are compact but handsome, and the pool area is a great little spot. Turn left straight after crossing the bridge into Tilcara and follow the signs.

Posada de Luz (☎ 495-5017; www.posadadeluz .com.ar; Ambrosetti 661; r AR$240-320; ▩ ☎) With a nouveau-rustic charm, this little place is a fantastic spot to unwind for a few days. More expensive rooms have sitting areas, but all feature pot-bellied stoves and individual terraces with deckchairs and views out over the valley. There are just six rooms, so book ahead.

our pick Rincón de Fuego (☎ 495-5130; www.rin condefuego.com; Ambrosetti 445; s AR$270-365; d AR$305-415; ▨ ▣ ☎) Romantic and welcoming, this posada (inn) is tucked away at the top of town; it's a fine spot to retreat to with someone you love. Effective, artistic use of bare stone and adobe lends much atmosphere; the rooms are darkish but seductive, with woodstoves. The common areas are exquisitely cozy, and breakfast features bread baked in the patio's clay oven.

EATING

Peña de Carlitos (☎ 495-5331; Lavalle 397; dishes AR$11-18; ☺ lunch & dinner) Hit the corner of the square for this cheery longstanding local restaurant, which offers live folkloric music with no cover charge every night, more of a mix of locals and visitors than in most places, and low-priced regional dishes.

El Patio (☎ 495-5044; Lavalle 352; mains AR$15-36; ⊙ lunch & dinner) Tucked away between the plaza and the church, this has a lovely shaded patio and garden seating. It offers a wide range of tasty salads, inventive llama dishes and a far-from-the-madding-crowd atmosphere.

Los Puestos (☎ 495-5100; cnr Belgrano & Padilla; meals AR$16-40; ⊙ lunch & dinner) Though a little touristy – we can't guarantee you won't be treated to a rendition of 'Sounds of Silence' on the pan-pipes at lunchtime – this makes up ground with its decor of local stone and chunky wood. Tasty regional specialties feature heavily – bar-becued llama (AR$24) is one – but it's small touches, such as tiny bread rolls straight from the clay oven, that win friends.

Escuela Gastronómica del Norte Argentino (☎ 495-5264; Bolívar 651; mains AR$25-29; ⊙ lunch Thu-Sun, dinner Wed-Sat) This hospitality school restaurant offers earnest service and a short but inventive menu of mostly local ingredients like corn lasagne and local trout.

GETTING THERE & AWAY
The bus terminal is about 500m south of the town center. There are services roughly every 45 minutes to Jujuy (AR$10, 1¾ hours), and north to Humahuaca (AR$3, 45 minutes) and La Quiaca (AR$20, 3½ hours). There are several services daily to Purmamarca (AR$3, 30 minutes) and six to Salta (AR$31, four hours).

Around Tilcara
The town of **Maimará**, 8km south, is a typical adobe valley settlement set beneath the spectacular and aptly named Paleta del Pintor (Painter's Palette) hill. Just off the main road, its hillside cemetery is a surprising and different sight with a picturesque backdrop. Take photos respectfully; bear in mind that locals bury their loved ones here. The town also has a worthwhile anthropological and historical museum and places to stay if you fancy overnighting.

Part of a chain that ran from Lima to Buenos Aires during viceregal times, **La Posta de Hornillos** (admission AR$3; ⊙ 8am-6pm) is a beautifully restored staging post 11km south of Tilcara. Founded in 1772, it was the scene of several important battles during the wars of independence, and remained an important stop on the road to Bolivia until 1908, when the La Quiaca railway opened. The interesting exhibits include leather suitcases, some impressively fierce swords and a fine 19th-century carriage.

Some 15km north of Tilcara, the road crosses the **Tropic of Capricorn**, marked by a large sundial, *artesanía* (handcraft) offerings and a pair of photo-hungry alpacas.

Any of the frequent buses running north–south along the Quebrada will drop you off or pick you up at these spots.

Uquía
☎ 03887 / pop 525 / elev 2818m
It's not often that you imagine the heavenly hosts armed with muzzle-loading weapons, but in this roadside village's fabulous 17th-century **church** (admission by donation; ⊙ 10am-noon & 2-4pm) that's just what you see. A restored collection of Cuzco school paintings – the *ángeles arcabuceros* (arquebus-wielding angels) – features Gabriel, Uriel et al putting their trust in God but keeping their powder dry. There's also a gilt *retablo* (retable) with fine painted panels. By the church, **Hostal de Uquía** (☎ 490508; elportillo@cootepal.com.ar; s/tw/d AR$110/165/175; ⊠) is a neat place with decent rooms and restaurant.

Humahuaca
☎ 03887 / pop 7985 / elev 2989m
The Quebrada's largest settlement is also its most handsome, with atmospheric cobblestoned streets, adobe houses and quaint plazas. You can feel the nearby puna here, with chilly nights, sparse air and a quiet Quechua population. Humahuaca feels less affected by tourism than the towns further south, and is the better for it. There are good handicrafts shops around town, and folk musicians strum and sing in the more popular restaurants.

ORIENTATION & INFORMATION
Straddling the Río Grande east of RN 9, Humahuaca is very compact. The town center is between the highway and the river. The disused railway runs through the middle of town. The main square, Plaza Gómez, has the church and *cabildo*; another plaza, San Martín, is near the bus terminal.

There are two places on Corrientes a block from the plaza that have internet access and open until midnight. The **tourist office** (Plaza Gómez s/n; ⊙ 10am-9pm Mon-Fri) is in the *cabildo*; there's also an ATM on this plaza. The tourist office on the highway is usually shut, but young rascals outside sell pamphlets that the other office gives out free.

SIGHTS & ACTIVITIES

Built in 1641, Humahuaca's **Iglesia de la Candelaria** (Buenos Aires) faces Plaza Gómez. Nearby, the lovably knobbly **cabildo** is famous for its clock tower, where a life-size figure of San Francisco Solano emerges at noon to deliver a benediction. From the plaza, a staircase climbs to the **Monumento a la Independencia**, a vulgarity produced by local sculptor Ernesto Soto Avendaño. The sculpture exemplifies *indigenismo*, a widespread tendency in Latin American art that romantically but patronizingly extols the virtues of native cultures overwhelmed by colonialism.

The organization of mountain guides, **Hasta las Manos** (☎ 421075; www.hlmexpeditions.com.ar; Av Ejército del Norte s/n), is recommended for exciting multiday treks with mules to the Calilegua or Baritú national parks, with a stunning change in terrain as you descend into the subtropical forest systems. They also offer sandboarding at Abra Pampa (AR$160 for the day) and high-mountain excursions.

Ser Andino (☎ 421659; Jujuy 221) rents out bikes.

FESTIVALS & EVENTS

Besides **Carnaval**, which is celebrated throughout the Quebrada de Humahuaca in February, Humahuaca observes February 2 as the day of its patron, the **Virgen de Candelaria**.

SLEEPING

The boutique hotel boom hasn't yet hit Humahuaca, which keeps it real with cheap family-run accommodations and a couple of midrange hotels. Prices given are for summer high season; they rise for Carnaval and drop for the rest of the year.

Posada El Sol (☎ 421466; www.posadaelsol.com.ar; Barrio Milagrosa s/n; dm AR$41, d with/without bathroom AR$180/116; 🖳) In a peaceful location, signposted

800m across the river bridge, this curious, appealing adobe hostel has a variety of quirky dorm rooms with lockers, and pretty doubles under traditional cane ceilings. Some dorms are cramped, but this place is more than the sum of its parts. Kitchen use, breakfast and taxi from the bus terminal are included, and there's HI discounts.

Posada La Churita (☎ 421055; lachurita@argentina .com; Buenos Aires 456; r per person AR$45) Run by warm-hearted and motherly Olga, this is one of a few unheated cheapies on this street. In theory, the rooms are dorms, but you may well get one to yourself. The shared bathrooms are clean and hot water reliable. Guests have use of the kitchen and a common area with tables.

Inti Sayana (☎ 421917; www.intisayanahostal.com .ar; La Rioja 83; s/d AR$90/110) Spacious rooms with decent beds – good for families and groups – surround a little courtyard at this pleasing *hostal*. The guitar-playing owner is helpful and friendly, and can offer advice on what to do around town.

Naty Hostería (☎ 421022; www.hosterianaty.com.ar; Buenos Aires 488; s/d AR$90/120) Right in the heart of town, this has a friendly boss, photos of nearby places you want to go to, and rooms of varying shapes and sizes at a fair price. Breakfast is included.

Hostal La Soñada (☎ 421228; www.hostallasoniada .com.ar; San Martín s/n; s/d AR$90/130; 🛜) Just across the tracks from the center, this is run by a kindly local couple and features spotless rooms with colorful bedspreads and good bathrooms. Breakfast is served in the attractive common area, and guests feel very welcome.

EATING & DRINKING

Casa Vieja (cnr Buenos Aires & Salta; mains AR$14-30; 😋 lunch & dinner) This warm and attractive corner restaurant is hung with basketry and

---

TOREO DE LA VINCHA

You won't see bullfighting in Argentina – it was banned in the 19th century – but the unusual fiestas of **Casabindo** feature a *toro* (bull) as the central participant. This tiny and remote adobe puna village celebrates the Assumption on August 15 in style, and thousands make the journey to see the main event – man against beast in a duel of agility and wits.

The bull's horns are garlanded with a red sweatband that contains three silver coins. *Promesantes* (young men from the village) armed with only a red cloth then try to distract the animal's attention and rob it of its crown. The successful torero then offers the coins to the Virgin. The bull is unharmed. The festival has its origins in similar Spanish fiestas.

Casabindo is west of the Quebrada, accessible via a rough road beyond Purmamarca. Tour operators in Jujuy (p247) and Tilcara (p255) run trips to the festival.

THE ANDEAN NORTHWEST

large dreamcatchers. It serves simple llama dishes, and also a tasty bean and quinoa stew. Portions are generous. There's live music nightly from 9pm.

El Portillo (☎ 424-9000; cnr Tucumán & Corrientes; mains AR$14-30; ✆ 8am-midnight) Attractively decorated with cactus-wood furniture and booth tables, this popular restaurant has poor service and a simple menu, which mostly consists of llama in a variety of rather similar creamy sauces. There's live music every night from 8pm.

Aisito (Arías s/n; ✆ 10pm-late) Head across the railway tracks from the bus terminal and turn right at the river to reach this unsigned bar. Locals gather in the attractive interior to bash out local music until rather late. A real find.

SHOPPING
The handicrafts market, near the train station, has woolen goods, souvenirs and atmosphere. Near the plaza, **Manos Andinas** (Buenos Aires 401) sells fair-trade *artesanía*.

GETTING THERE & AWAY
The **bus terminal** (cnr Belgrano & Entre Ríos) is three blocks south of the plaza. There are regular buses to Salta (AR$36, 4½ hours) and Jujuy (AR$13, 2¼ hours), and to La Quiaca (AR$15, three hours). There are three daily buses to Iruya (AR$14, three hours).

Iruya
☎ 03887 / pop 1070 / elev 2780m

There's something magical about Iruya, a remote village just 50km from the main road but a world away in other respects. It makes a great destination to relax for a few days, and also allows proper appreciation of the Quebrada de Humahuaca region away from the busy barreling highway.

The journey is worth the trip in itself. Turning off RN 9, 26km north of Humahuaca, the *ripio* road ascends to a spectacular 4000m pass that marks the Jujuy–Salta provincial boundary. Here, there's a massive *apacheta* (a cairn that accumulates stone by stone, left by travelers for luck). The plastic bottles are from liquid offerings to Pachamama.

The road then winds down into another valley, where smallholders farm potatoes, onions and beans, and reaches Iruya, with its pretty yellow-and-blue church, steep streets, adobe houses and spectacular mountainscapes (with soaring condors). It's an indigenous community with fairly traditional values, so respect is called for. Chatting with the friendly locals is the highlight of most travelers' experiences here. You can also hike in the surrounding hills – ask for a local guide – or visit other communities in the valley. **Pablo Harvey** (☎ 0387-15-458-8417; pharvey_ar@yahoo.com.ar) runs unusual and recommended night walks with stargazing, music and Andean legends for AR$15 per person.

Iruya has a **tourist office** (Calle San Martín), but opening hours are irregular. There's a bank but no ATM in town.

SLEEPING & EATING
There are many cheap places to stay in locals' homes. We won't recommend any – spreading the wealth is best here – but can confirm that they are spotless and offer value for money (AR$20 to AR$30 per person in a private room).

Federico III (☎ 03887-15-629152; www.complejofederico.com.ar; cnr San Martín & Salta; r per person AR$100) A more upmarket option, just above the plaza at the bottom of town; pretty whitewashed rooms surround a little courtyard. Some rooms have views.

Hostería Iruya (☎ 482002; www.hosteriadeiruya.com.ar; s/d AR$195/235, with view AR$240/275) At the top of the town, this place has light white rooms with wide beds, a spacious common area and a picturesque stone terrace with memorable views. It's worth the extra cash for the big-windowed rooms with valley vistas. There's a decent restaurant here (mains AR$20 AR$30). Note that credit cards are not accepted.

Several simple *comedores* (basic cafeterias) serve local cuisine. At **Comedor Iruya** (cnr Lavalle & San Martín; dishes AR$5-15; ✆ 10am-9pm), genial Juan and Tina serve delicious home-style meat and salad dishes in a cozy tin-roofed atmosphere.

GETTING THERE & AWAY
Buses from Humahuaca (AR$14, three hours) leave three times daily; there are also two daily direct buses from Tilcara (AR$19, four hours).

There is 50km of *ripio* road to negotiate off RN 9. In summer it often becomes impassable due to rain. You'll often see villagers hitchhiking – it's a good way to meet locals. A parking fee (AR$2) is sometimes charged entering Iruya.

THE ANDEAN NORTHWEST

LA QUIACA

☎ 03885 / pop 13,761 / elev 3442m

Truly the end of the line, La Quiaca is 5171km north of Ushuaia, and a major crossing point to Bolivia. It's a cold, windy place that has decent places to stay and eat, but little to detain you. Once a bustling railroad terminus, La Quiaca's main sign of life these days is weary Bolivians trudging between the border and the bus terminal toting heavy bags. Nevertheless, it's not seedy, and noble stone buildings recall more optimistic times.

The road to La Quiaca is intriguing. After leaving the Quebrada de Humahuaca, paved RN 9 passes through **Abra Pampa**, a forlornly windy town 90km north of Humahuaca, and climbs through picturesque and typical altiplano landscapes. Nightly frosts make agriculture precarious, so people focus subsistence efforts on livestock (llamas, sheep, goats) that can survive on the sparse ichu grass. Look for the endangered vicuña off main routes.

La Quiaca is divided by its defunct train tracks; most services are west of them. North of town, a bridge across the river links La Quiaca with Villazón, Bolivia.

Information

Change money on the Bolivian side of the border or at the bus terminal. Call centers and internet places abound in town.

ACA (Automóvil Club Argentino; cnr Internacional & Bustamante) Maps and motorist services.

Banco Macro (Árabe Siria 445) Has an ATM.

Information kiosk (☺ 9:30am-1:30pm & 4-7pm) Run by a hostel, this offers decent information opposite the bus terminal.

Tourist office (☎ 422644; turismo@laquiaca.com.ar; ☺ 7am-7pm) Branches at the border, and at the southern entrance to town.

Sleeping & Eating

Hospedaje Frontera (☎ 422269; cnr Belgrano & Árabe Siria; s/d without bathroom AR$30/50) Nights can get a little chilly here, but the darkish, motel-style rooms are clean and proper behind a popular local restaurant. Bathrooms (shared) have hot water, and management is welcoming.

Copacabana Hostel (☎ 423875; www.hostelco pacabana.com.ar; Pellegrini 141; r per person without bathroom AR$30; ▣) Across the tracks from the center, and a block up the street with the Banco de la Nación on the corner, this place offers small, rather sweet heated pink rooms with shared bathroom and amiable staff.

Hotel de Turismo (☎ 422243; hotelmun@laquiaca.com .ar; cnr Árabe Siria & San Martín; s/d AR$95/140; ▣ ◌ ▣) A very good deal, this friendly hotel offers handsome heated rooms with parquet floors and fine bathrooms. It's the best option in town.

Hostería Munay (☎ 423924; www.munayhotel.jujuy .com; Belgrano 51; s/d AR$100/135) Set back from the pedestrian street (but you can still drive in and park), this is a reassuring option with cheery rooms decorated with *artesanía* and featuring small bathrooms, big beds and heating. It's cheaper for walk-ins.

If coming from Bolivia, things get better eating-wise a few hours down the road. The Hotel de Turismo is the best bet; *bife de chorizo* (sirloin steak) with the works is AR$25, the set lunch AR$20. The down-home **Frontera** (mains AR$11-21) has meat plates, Spanish omelet and decent *tallarines al pesto* (noodles with pesto), plus a set lunch for AR$14.

BOLIVIA VIA VILLAZÓN

Crossing from La Quiaca to Villazón, Bolivia, walk, get a taxi or local bus to the bridge, and then walk across, clearing **immigration** (☺ 24hr). At the time of research, US nationals needed a visa, but citizens of the EU, UK, Canada, Australia, New Zealand and South Africa did not. Bolivia is much nicer than Villazón promises, so head past the cut-price stalls and straight to the bus terminal or train station. A couple of cheap but reliable accommodation options are by the bus terminal and the plaza if you need them. Buses head to Tupiza (B$10, 2¼ hours), La Paz (B$80 to B$120, 20 hours) via Potosí (B$40, 10 hours), Oruro and Tarija (B$40, eight hours). The train station is 1.5km north of the border crossing – a taxi costs B$3 per person. There are four weekly train services to Tupiza (B$13 to B$51, three hours), Uyuni (B$36 to B$152, six hours) and Oruro (B$65 to B$230, 13 hours). Check www.fca.com.bo for schedules. Bolivia is one hour behind northern Argentina.

At the time of writing the exchange rate for bolivianos was AR$1 to B$1.80 and US$1 to B$6.90.

Getting There & Away

The chaotic **bus terminal** (cnr Belgrano & España) has frequent connections to Jujuy (AR$35, four to five hours), Salta (AR$65, eight hours), Buenos Aires (AR$190, 27 hours) and intermediate points. There is no transportation to Bolivia, but a few Argentine buses leave directly from Villazón's bus station.

YAVI

☎ 03887 / pop 207 / elev 3440m

Picturesque, atmospheric, indigenous Yavi, 16km east of La Quiaca via paved RP 5, more than justifies a detour, and is a great little lazy hideaway. Apart from the tumbledown romanticism of its adobe streets, the village preserves two fascinating colonial-era buildings.

Yavi's **church** (admission by donation; ☺ 9am-noon & 3-6pm Tue-Fri, 9am-noon Sat & Sun, 3-6pm Mon) is perhaps the most fascinating in northern Argentina. Built by the local marquis in the late 17th century, it preserves stunning altarpieces in sober baroque style, covered in gold leaf and adorned with excellent paintings and sculptures, mostly from the Cuzco school, but including one fine Flemish original. The translucent onyx windows also stand out.

Opposite, the **Casa del Marqués Campero** was the house of the marquis himself, a Spanish noble whose family dominated the regional economy in the 18th century. Now a **museum** (admission AR$3; ☺ 9am-1pm & 2-6pm Mon-Fri, 9am-6pm Sat & Sun), it displays beautifully restored furniture, exhibits on more recent puna life and a lovable library.

Near Yavi are several short walks in the Cerros Colorados – to rock paintings and petroglyphs at **Las Cuevas** or to springs at **Agua de Castilla**. Ask for directions at the museum or accommodations.

As well as a good free campground by the river, there are several places to stay. **Hostal de Yavi** (☎ 421659; www.hostaldejavi.blogspot.com; Güemes 222; dm/d AR$25/120) offers simple, comfortable rooms and an informal atmosphere with decent meals (AR$30 a dish). **Hostería Pachamá** (☎ 03885-423235; www.pachamahosteria.net; cnr Pérez & Ruta 5; s/d AR$60/100) has rather charming rooms set around an adobe courtyard, and a pretty eating area, while likeable **La Casona** (☎ 03885-422316; mccalizaya@hotmail.com; cnr Pérez & San Martín; cm AR$20, d with/without bathroom AR$80/50) has gnarled wooden floors and rustic rooms with stoves for winter nights.

Shared taxis and pickups (AR$5, 20 minutes) run to Yavi from La Quiaca's Mercado Municipal on Hipólito Yrigoyen; departures are frequent between 6am and 8am but slower after that. Otherwise, it's AR$25 or so in a taxi.

MONUMENTO NATURAL LAGUNA DE LOS POZUELOS

Coots, geese, ducks, three species of flamingo and many other birds breed along the barren shores of this 160-sq-km lake, an important wetland habitat at an altitude of nearly 4000m. There's also a large vicuña population hereabouts.

A car is the best transportation option, but fuel up: there is no gasoline available beyond Abra Pampa, midway between Humahuaca and La Quiaca. Make sure you also take plenty of drinking water. Be aware that heavy summer rains can make the unpaved routes off the main highway impassable.

There's a ranger station at Río Cincel, south of the lake. From near here, a 7km road heads north to a parking lot near the lakeshore. Or not; you may have to walk up to 3km depending on the water levels, which are highest in April and lowest in November. Take binoculars in any event, as you'll likely find yourself a long way from the flamingoes.

From Abra Pampa there are midmorning buses daily to Rinconada, west of the lake, where there are simple accommodations. On request, the bus will drop you off at the ranger station, but you'll have to walk from there to the lake. Camping is possible on exposed sites, with basic infrastructure, at the ranger station.

There are three main access routes to the lake: from just north of Abra Pampa; from La Quiaca west via Cieneguillas; and from La Intermedia, halfway between Abra Pampa and La Quiaca, where a road makes its way west over the hills to Pozuelos village.

SALTA

☎ 0387 / pop 468,583 / elev 1187m

Sophisticated Salta is a favorite of many travelers, smoothing ruffled psyches with its profusion of services, engaging active minds with its outstanding museums, and lighting romantic candles with its plaza-side cafes and the live *música folklórica* of its popular *peñas*. It offers the facilities of a large town, retains the comfortable vibe of a smaller place and preserves more colonial architecture than most places in Argentina.

It's the most touristed spot in northwest Argentina, and has numerous accommodation options. The center bristles with travel and tour agents: this is the place to get things organized for onward travel. Nevertheless, there's a poorer Salta readily visible if you venture toward the city's outskirts, with a large population of indigenous farmfolk from the province and Bolivia searching, often in vain, for a better life in the big city.

History

Founded in 1582, Salta lies in a basin surrounded by verdant peaks. This valley's perpetual spring attracted the Spaniards, who could pasture their animals in the surrounding countryside and produce crops that it was not possible to grow in the frigid Bolivian highlands, where the mining industry created enormous demand for hides, mules and food. When the extension of the Belgrano railroad made it feasible to market sugar to the immigrant cities of the pampas, the city recovered slightly from its 19th-century decline. In recent years, growth has been rapid as numerous families have settled here in search of work, fleeing the economic conditions in rural areas.

Orientation

Although Salta has sprawled considerably, most points of interest are within a few blocks of central Plaza 9 de Julio. North–south streets change their names on either side of the plaza, but the names of east–west streets are continuous. East of the center, Cerro 20 de Febrero and Cerro San Bernardo overlook the town.

Information

BOOKSTORES

Feria del Libro (☎ 421-0359; Buenos Aires 83) Large selection.
Librería San Francisco (☎ 431-8456; Caseros 362) Decent selection of English books, mostly classics.

IMMIGRATION

Migraciones (☎ 422-0438; Maipú 35; ☽ 7am-2pm Mon-Fri) Twelve blocks west of the plaza, near Caseros.

INTERNET ACCESS & TELEPHONE

There are dozens of internet cafes and call centers dotted throughout the town center. One central option for both is **Telecentro** (Alvarado 766; per hr AR$3; ☽ 10am-11pm).

LAUNDRY

Laverap (Santiago del Estero 363; service wash AR$15) One of many. Most accommodations also have a (dearer) service.

MEDICAL SERVICES

Hospital San Bernardo (☎ 432-0445; Tobías 69)

MONEY

Cambio Dinar (B Mitre 101) Changes traveler's checks (high commission) and cash.
Citibank (cnr España & Balcarce) Changes euros and US dollars, and has a high ATM withdrawal limit.

POST

Post office (Deán Funes 140)

TOURIST INFORMATION

ACA (Automóvil Club Argentino; ☎ 431-0551; cnr Rivadavia & B Mitre) Road maps and route advice.
Municipal tourist office (☎ 437-3340; www .saltalalinda.gov.ar; Caseros 711; ☽ 9am-9pm) Efficient multilingual staff.
National Parks Administration (APN; ☎ 431-2683; www.parquesnacionales.gov.ar; España 366; ☽ 8am-3pm Mon-Fri) On the 3rd floor of the Aduana building, it offers excellent information and advice on the region's national parks. Contact this place before going to the more remote parks such as El Rey or Baritú.
Provincial tourist office (☎ 431-0950; www.turismo salta.gov.ar; Buenos Aires 93; ☽ 8am-9pm Mon-Fri, 9am-8pm Sat & Sun) Top marks – friendly, efficient and multilingual. Ask staff about the condition of the roads if heading out in a rental car.

TRAVEL AGENCIES

There are numerous agencies along Buenos Aires, between Caseros and Alvarado, and all around the town center that can book airfares and bus tickets. See p265 for tour operators.

Sights

MUSEO DE ARQUEOLOGÍA DE ALTA MONTAÑA (MAAM)

Perhaps the premier museum in northern Argentina, **MAAM** (☎ 437-0499; www.maam.org .ar; B Mitre 77; Argentines/foreigners AR$10/30, ☽ 11am-7.30pm Tue-Sun) has a serious and informative exhibition focusing on Inca culture and, in particular, the child sacrifices the Inca left on some of the Andes' most imposing peaks (see boxed text, p264).

The centerpiece of the display is the mummified body of one of the three children (rotated every six months) discovered at the peak

SALTA

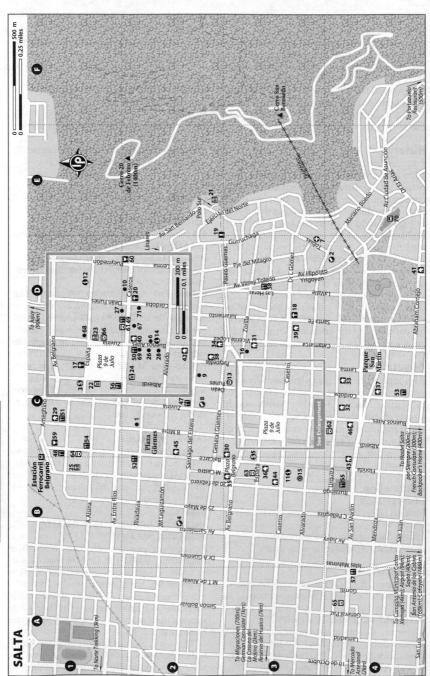

of Llullaillaco during the 1999 expedition. It was a controversial decision to display the bodies (visitors may choose to view or not) and it is a powerful experience to come face-to-face with them. The intricately plaited hair and clothes are perfectly preserved, and their faces reflect – who knows? – a distant past or a typical 21st-century Salta face; a peaceful passing or a tortured death. You decide.

The grave goods that accompanied the children impress by their immediacy, with colors as fresh as the day they were produced. The *illas* (small votive figurines of animals and humans) are of silver, gold, shell and onyx, and many are clothed in textiles. It's difficult to imagine that a more privileged look at pre-Columbian South American culture will ever be offered us. Also exhibited is the 'Reina del Cerro,' a mummy robbed from an Inca tomb in the 1920s that finally ended up here after a turbulent history. Some good videos give background information about the mummies and the expedition. Most of the museum's information panels are reproduced on laminated sheets in various languages. Take a jacket: comfortable mummy temperature can be pretty chilly for the rest of us. There's a library as well as a good cafe-bar with terrace and wi-fi.

PAJCHA – MUSEO DE ARTE ÉTNICO AMERICANO

This eye-opening private **museum** (☎ 422-9417; www.museodearteetnico.com.ar; 20 de Febrero 838; admission AR$10; ☑ 10am-1pm & 4-8pm Mon-Sat) is a must-see if you're interested in indigenous art and culture. Six exquisitely presented rooms present contemporary and recent artisanal work from all over Latin America. The quality of the pieces (which include amazing macaw-feather creations, religious sculpture from the Cuzco school, tools of the trade of Bolivian *kallawaya* healers and finely crafted Mapuche silver jewelry) is extraordinarily high, testament to decades of study and collection by the anthropologist founder. It's an exquisite dose of color and beauty, and run with great enthusiasm by the English-speaking management, who will give you a worthwhile guided tour for an extra AR$15.

MUSEO HISTÓRICO DEL NORTE

Set on the plaza in the *cabildo*, the **Museo Histórico del Norte** (☎ 421-5340; Caseros 549; admission AR$3, free Sun; ☑ 9am-6pm Tue-Fri, 9am-1:30pm Sat & Sun) has a collection that ranges from pre-Columbian ceramics through to colonial-era religious painting and sculpture (admire the

THE ANDEAN NORTHWEST

THE CHILDREN GIVEN TO THE MOUNTAIN

The phrase 'human sacrifice' is sensationalist, but it is a fact that the Inca culture from time to time offered the lives of high-born children to please or appease their gods. The Inca saw this as an offering to ensure the continued fertility of their people and the land. The high peaks of the Cordillera de los Andes were always considered sacred, and were chosen as sites for the sacrifices. The Inca felt that the children didn't die as such, but were reunited with their forefathers, who watched over the communities from the highest peaks.

The children, carefully selected for the role, were taken to the ceremonial capital of Cuzco, where they were the centerpieces of a large celebration – the *capacocha*. Ceremonial marriages between them helped to cement diplomatic links between tribes across the Inca empire. At the end of the fiesta, they were paraded twice around the plaza, and then had to return home in a straight line – an arduous journey that could take months. Once home, they were feted and welcomed, and then taken into the mountains. They were fed, and given quantities of *chicha* (an alcoholic drink made from fermented maize) to drink. When they passed out, they were taken up to the peak of the mountain and entombed in their drunken sleep, presumably never to awaken.

Three such children were found in 1999 near the peak of **Llullaillaco**, a 6739m volcano some 480km west of Salta, on the Chilean border. It's the highest known archaeological site in the world. The cold, low pressure and lack of oxygen and bacteria helped to preserve the bodies almost perfectly. The Doncella (Maiden) was about 15 at the time of death, and was perhaps an *aclla* (a 'virgin of the sun'), a prestigious role in Inca society. The other two, a boy and girl both aged six to seven (the girl damaged by a lightning strike), had cranial deformations that indicated they came from high-ranking families. They were accompanied each by an *ajuar* (a selection of grave goods), which included textiles and small figurines of humanoids and camelids.

The mummies' transfer to Salta was controversial. Many felt they should have been left where they were discovered, but this, once the location was known, would have been impossible. Whatever your feelings on them, and the role of archaeology, they offer an undeniably fascinating glimpse of Inca religion and culture.

---

fine pulpit from Salta's Jesuit church), and displays on Salta in the 19th and 20th centuries. The endless series of portraits of Salta's governors wouldn't be out of place in a beard-and-moustache museum, while the transportation collection includes a somber hearse used for children's funerals and an enormous 1911 Renault that puts any Hummer to shame. The building itself, with cobbled patio and gallery overlooking the plaza, is lovely.

MUSEO DE ARTE CONTEMPORÁNEO

The **Museo de Arte Contemporáneo** (MAC; ☎ 437-0498; Zuviría 90; admission AR$2; ☉ 9am-8pm Tue-Sat, 4-8pm Sun) has on display the work of contemporary artists from Salta, as well as other parts of Argentina and the wider world. The space itself is well lit and expertly curated. Exhibitions change regularly and are usually of high quality.

CATEDRAL

Salta's pink **catedral** (cnr España & B Mitre; ☉ 7am-noon & 4:30-8pm) was consecrated in 1878 and harbors the ashes of (among other notables) General Martín Miguel de Güemes, a *salteño* (resi-

dent of Salta) and independence hero; even today, the gauchos of Salta province proudly flaunt their red-striped *ponchos de güemes* (traditional Salta ponchos). The high baroque altarpiece is the other central feature.

IGLESIA SAN FRANCISCO

Two blocks east of the plaza, the magenta-and-yellow **Iglesia San Francisco** (cnr Caseros & Córdoba; ☉ 7:30am-noon & 5-9pm) is Salta's most striking landmark. The exuberant facade is topped by a slender tower; inside, the single nave is ornately painted to resemble stucco-work. There are several much-venerated images here, including the Niño Jesús de Aracoeli, a rather spooky crowned figure. There's a lovely garden cloister, accessed via guided tour (which run on demand in Spanish; donation appropriate) that takes in a mediocre museum of religious art and treasures.

CONVENTO DE SAN BERNARDO

Only Carmelite nuns may enter 16th-century **Convento de San Bernardo** (cnr Caseros & Santa Fe), but visitors can approach the blindingly whitewashed adobe building (consider sunglasses) to admire the carved, 18th-century algarrobo door. The church, too, is open for visits before Mass early weekday mornings, Saturday evenings and Sunday mornings.

CERRO SAN BERNARDO

For outstanding views of Salta and its surroundings, take the **teleférico** (cable car; ☎ 431-0641; one way/roundtrip AR$10/20; ☻ 10am-7pm) from Parque San Martín to the top of Cerro San Bernardo. A trail that takes you up the hill begins at the Güemes monument at the top of Paseo Güemes. Atop is a *confitería* (cafe offering light meals), whose terrace has the best views, a watercourse and *artesanía* shops.

Just above the Güemes monument, on the lower slopes of Cerro San Bernardo, is the friendly **Museo Antropológico** (☎ 422-2960; www.antropologico.com.ar; cnr Ejército del Norte & Polo Sur; admission AR$3; ☻ 9am-7pm Mon-Fri, 10am-6pm Sat). It has good representations of local ceramics, especially from the Tastil ruins (Argentina's largest pre-Inca town), and some well-designed displays in its attractive, purpose-built spaces.

RESERVA DEL HUAICO

This 60-hectare **cloud forest reserve** (☎ 0387-15-489-0118; www.reservadelhuaico.com.ar; Mariano Moreno s/n, San Lorenzo; 4hr guided tour AR$60; ☻ 8am-noon & 2-6pm) is in San Lorenzo, 8km west of Salta, and run by a not-for-profit nature foundation. Entry is by appointment only and includes a four-hour guided walk along the reserve's 15km of trails. Despite Salta's proximity, the bird-watching is extraordinarily good: more than 205 species have been recorded, with 100 of those – including guans, tanagers, parrots, hummingbirds and woodpeckers – all common. A taxi from Salta costs AR$20, or you can get any San Lorenzo–bound bus (AR$1.25). Get off at the *municipalidad* (city hall) and it's a 1km walk along Mariano Moreno to the reserve.

Courses

Salta appeals as a spot for a Spanish course. **Bien Argentino** (☎ 0387-15-475-8679; www.bien-argentino.com.ar; Pje Zorrilla 239) is one operator.

Tours

Salta is the base for a range of innovative tours, offered by many companies. For city tours (AR$60) and excursions in the Salta area, try any of the travel agencies on Buenos Aires, between Caseros and Alvarado. Other popular trips head to Cafayate (AR$120), Cachi (AR$140), San Antonio de los Cobres (the *Tren a las Nubes* route; AR$190), Salinas Grandes (AR$290) and Humahuaca (AR$150). Several operators offer horseback riding, rafting and kayaking; paragliding, abseiling, climbing and hiking are also available.

Some operators:

Clark Expediciones (☎ 497-1024; www.clarkexpediciones.com) Professional agency offering trips with highly competent English-speaking guides to the region's national parks and remote uplands. They're serious about bird-watching; trips include a half/full day in the Reserva Huaico (US$70/140), two days to Parque Nacional El Rey (US$340) and multiday tailored itineraries. Book well ahead.

Norte Trekking (☎ 436-1844; www.nortetrekking.com; Libertador 1151, Barrio Grand Bourg) One of four agencies specifically approved for trips to Parque Nacional El Rey, it runs various multiday hikes, with some guaranteed departure dates listed on its website.

Salta Rafting (☎ 421-4114; www.saltarafting.com; Buenos Aires 88) Runs two-hour white-water rafting trips on the Class III Río Juramento, 100km from Salta (AR$150 including a barbecue lunch; transportation to/from Salta AR$60 extra). At the same location are spectacular 400m ziplines across a canyon (four-/nine-line trip AR$120/180). Also runs mountain-biking excursions.

Sayta (☎ 0387-15-683-6565; www.sayta.com.ar; Chicona) This *estancia* 40km from Salta runs excellent horseback-riding days, with optional *asado* (barbecue grill). It's also a place you can stay to experience a taste of Argentine gaucho life. A half-day with/without lunch costs AR$170/125, and full-board accommodation for a night is AR$230 (with a day's riding AR$345). Prices include transfers from Salta.

Tastil (☎ 431-1223; www.turismotastil.com.ar; Caseros 468) One of the operators with a variety of day trips and multiday excursions. Some use a characterful but pricey open truck (MoviTrack) while cheaper ones go in a minibus.

Turismo la Posada (☎ 421-6544; www.turismolaposada.com.ar; Buenos Aires 94) This multilingual company has a good variety of trips, and offers horseback riding, hiking and rafting.

Sleeping
BUDGET

Camping Municipal Carlos Xamena (☎ 423-1341; Av Libano; campsites per person/tent AR$3.20/4.80; ☻) One of Argentina's best campgrounds, this has 500 tent sites and a huge pool (it takes a week to fill). It's typically loud in summer. Take bus 3B from Ituzaingó between San Martín and Mendoza. There's a supermarket near the campground.

Inti Huasi (☎ 431-0167; www.intihuasihostel.com.ar; Abraham Cornejo 120; dm/d AR$30/90; 🖳 🛜) A short stroll from the bus terminal, this hostel has a really appealing atmosphere, with plenty of socializing in the good kitchen and grassy patio area. Dorms are spacious and comfortable, and you feel like you're crashing at a mate's place.

Correcaminos (☎ 422-0731; www.saltahostel.com; Vicente López 353; dm/d without bathroom AR$33/90; 🖳 🛜) 'Roadrunner' is a cheap-and-cheerful hostel that boasts a well-used bar and pool table. Dorms are spacious if a little stuffy in summer, but the location and laid-back vibe are appealing. It runs another hostel opposite, with a more modern kitchen and fewer beds in the dorms, but without the courtyard space.

Residencial Balcarce (☎ 431-8135; www.residencialbalcarce.com.ar; Balcarce 460; s/d without bathroom AR$35/60, with bathroom AR$60/100) Just south of Plaza Güemes, a small entrance disguises a large interior at this value-packed place. In many ways, it's a standard *residencial*, with unadorned rooms with decent bathrooms, but the friendly service, grapevine-shaded patio and high hygiene levels make it a sound choice.

Hostel Terra Oculta (☎ 421-8769; www.terraoculta.com; Córdoba 361; dm/d AR$35/80; 🖳 🛜) Handily located between the bus terminal and town center, this laid-back, labyrinthine spot is an upbeat hostel that sensibly has its light, comfortable dorms well separated from the excellent rooftop bar, where the action can go loud and late.

Hostel Salta por Siempre (☎ 423-3230; www.saltaporsiempre.com.ar; Tucumán 464; dm/d AR$40/120; 🖳 🛜) It's eight blocks south of the plaza, but worth the trudge to this super-friendly hostel. The quiet and handsome building has glisteningly clean colorful rooms with bathroom – some dorms have beds, others bunks – a proper kitchen and attractive shared spaces. Breakfast is included.

Backpacker's Home (☎ 423-5910; www.backpackerssalta.com; Buenos Aires 930; dm/d AR$52/170; 🖳 🛜 🖳) Souvenir shops have given way to panelbeaters by the time you've walked the kilometer or so from the center, but this instant-social-life hostel appeals for the great backyard bar and pool area. Rates include breakfast and dinner. HI discounts apply.

Residencial Elena (☎ 421-1529; Buenos Aires 256; s/d AR$80/130; 🛜) Set in a neocolonial building with a charming interior patio, this has a choice location not far south of the plaza. Though it's on a busy central street, it's very quiet, and the longtime Spanish owners keep it shipshape.

Hostal El Alcázar (☎ 422-3800; www.hostalelalcazar.com; Balcarce 81; s/d AR$90/125; 🖳 🛜) Reliable and central, this offers clean private rooms with bathroom but also has hostel-like facilities (eg a good kitchen) and a laid-back traveler-friendly attitude. It's a decent deal at Salta prices.

Munay Hotel (☎ 422-4936; www.munayhotel.jujuy.com; Av San Martín 656; s/d AR$100/135; 🛜) With everything you could want in a budget hotel – a handy location, staff who are pleased to see you, well-furnished and clean bedrooms, shower curtains and breakfast – this is one to book ahead.

MIDRANGE

Provincial Plaza (☎ 432-2000; www.provincialplaza.com.ar; Caseros 786; s/d/tw AR$160/185/250; 🗶 🖳 🛜 🖳) Rooms are serviceable rather than spectacular at this central four-star option, but the price is more than fair for the quality. Twin rooms are more expensive than doubles, but a lot more spacious; superior and executive rooms are higher up the building with views. The pool is outdoors, on the roof.

Aldaba Hotel (☎ 421-9455; www.aldabahotel.com; B Mitre 910; s/d AR$170/260; 🗶 🖳 🛜) A block away from the *peña* action of Calle Balcarce, this six-room place is nevertheless superbly quiet and tranquil. Run with a personal touch, it's decorated with restrained modern elegance, and boasts super-comfortable beds and friendly service. Rooms vary widely in size (but not price); there are plans to add a few new ones on the ground floor.

our pick Bloomers B&B (☎ 422-7449; www.bloomers-salta.com.ar; Vicente López 129; s AR$200, d AR$240-270; 🗶 🖳 🛜) Break any or all of the Ten Commandments if need be, but make sure you get one of the five rooms at this exquisitely stylish yet relaxed and comfortable guesthouse. The second B here stands for brunch, served until noon and replete with good things. The color-themed rooms are all different and all delightful. The good company and laissez-faire environment makes you feel like a guest in a friend's home, but few of our friends have a place this pretty.

Hotel Candela (☎ 422-4473; www.hotellacandela.com.ar; Pueyrredón 346; d AR$215-330; 🗶 🖳 🛜 🖳) Decked out like a country villa with an L-shaped pool and grassy garden, this is nevertheless central and features excellent staff, good facilities and comfortable rooms, including a duplex apartment out the back. Different grades of room differ chiefly by size. The decor is one of easy elegance, with an eclectic range of art on the walls.

Hotel del Antiguo Convento (☎ 422-7267; www.hoteldelconvento.com.ar; Caseros 113; r AR$230; 🍽 🖵 📶 🏊) There really is nothing *antiguo* (old) or conventlike about this place: rooms are modern and sunny and there's a great little pool area out the back. A duplex apartment next to it sleeps four and goes for AR$340.

Also recommended:

Bonarda Boutique Hotel (☎ 421-5786; www.hotelbonarda.com; Urquiza 427; s/d AR$170/225; 🍽 📶) Some parts of this not-quite-convincing 'boutique' hotel are attractive; others feel like they've been done on the cheap. Rooms open inward onto a spacious interior courtyard; some are airier than others.

Marilian Hotel (☎ 421-6700; www.hotelmarilian.com.ar; Buenos Aires 176; s/d AR$200/250; 🍽 🖵 📶) Nestled among the tour agencies, this hotel offers bright and pretty white-tiled rooms with hanging headrests and small but new bathrooms.

TOP END

Carpe Diem (☎ 421-8736; www.carpediemsalta.com.ar; Urquiza 329; s/d AR$240/300; 🖵) There's a real home-from-home feel about this B&B that's full of thoughtful touches, like home-baked bread at breakfast, enticing places to sit about with a book and a computer with internet connection in the attractive rooms. A single with shared bathroom in the garden is small but a good deal at AR$120.

Hotel Salta (☎ 426-7500; www.hotelsalta.com; Buenos Aires 1; s/d standard AR$248/350, s/d superior AR$339/430; 🍽 🖵 📶 🏊) You pay extra for location here (but what a location) on a corner of the postcard-pretty central plaza, in a stately, traditional hotel. Facilities are good and service excellent, but the rooms are a tad disappointing. Try to grab one with a view of the church and Cerro San Bernardo. Superior rooms are bigger than the compact standards, and have bathtubs.

Alejandro I (☎ 400-0000; www.alejandro1hotel.com.ar; Balcarce 252; r standard/superior/executive AR$415/478/550; 🍽 🖵 📶 🏊) Astronauts, cosmonauts or Google Earth aficionados might know whether Salta's most upmarket hotel is visible from orbit – it certainly is, for better or worse, from the whole city. The rooms are slick and modern, and get pricier and larger as you move higher up the building. The restaurant is reader-recommended, and service is swift and efficient.

Design Suites (☎ 01-15-199-7465; www.designsuites.com; Belgrano 770; r/ste AR$648/733; 🍽 🖵 📶 🏊) We're not 100% sure whether the look of this place – all exposed concrete and urban-trendy design – works in a colonial city such as Salta, but it's an undeniably attractive space. The excellent, quiet rooms have floor-to-ceiling windows, and the rooftop pool and Jacuzzi space offers memorable nighttime views of town. Service is willing.

Eating

It's a toss-up between Salta and Tucumán for Argentina's best empanadas, but they're wickedly toothsome in both places. Locals debate the merits of fried (in an iron skillet – juicier) or baked (in a clay oven – tastier). Numerous places specialize in them, including the *peñas*. The taxi drivers' favorite is **Patio de la Empanada** (cnr San Martín & Islas Malvinas; 🕐 10am-midnight), where various stalls surround an indoor-outdoor eating area; a dozen will set you back AR$15.

Mercado Central (cnr Florida & Av San Martín) This large, lively market is very interesting, as well as one of the cheapest places to eat in town. You can supplement inexpensive pizza, empanadas and *humitas* (stuffed corn dough) with fresh fruit and vegetables.

Bio's Diet (☎ 421-5771; Santiago del Estero 496; dishes AR$8-16; 🕐 lunch & dinner Mon-Sat) This mostly vegetarian little restaurant mostly functions as a take-out, but has a few simple wooden tables. Daily dishes are displayed at the glass counter.

New Time Café (☎ 431-6461; Caseros 602; snacks AR$8-19; 🕐 8am-late) In the race for the accolade of Salta's best plaza cafe, this two-level corner spot wins by several lengths. It offers shady (in the afternoon) tables, great views of the *cabildo*, Cerro San Bernardo and cathedral, and wi-fi. It also serves coffee and food, though it isn't the cheapest. Live music some nights.

Jovi II (☎ 432-9438; Balcarce 601; mains AR$15-30; 🕐 lunch & dinner) A long terrace overlooking the palms of Plaza Güemes is just one reason to like this popular local restaurant that does a huge range of dishes well, without frills and in generous portions. Several rabbit dishes, tasty fish and a succulent plate of the day are backed up by excellent service.

La Céfira (☎ 421-4922; Córdoba 481; pasta AR$16-29; 🕐 lunch Fri-Sun, dinner Tue-Sat) This handsomely styled dining room a few blocks south of the center is a cut far above the usual gnocchi-with-four-cheese-sauce joints. Delicious homemade pasta includes such temptations as squid-ink ravioli with crab, or spinach fettuccini with salmon and caper sauce. Tasty salads seal the deal.

Entre Indyas (☎ 474-3879; Buenos Aires 44; dishes AR$18-25; ⏰ 10am-3pm & 8-11pm) This intimate little spot transcends its shopping-arcade location with tasty vegetarian cuisine, blending Indian and Peruvian traditions. There's no menu as such, just three or four daily specials, which might include shitake ceviche, stirfried vegetable chapatis, or quinoa and corn salads.

El Solar del Convento (☎ 421-5124; Caseros 444; mains AR$18-40; ⏰ lunch & dinner) Warmly decorated and popular, this reliable touristy choice offers solicitous service – the free apéritif wins points – and a varied menu. It specializes in *lomo* (sirloin) with tasty sauces, and also has fish dishes and *parrillada* (mixed grill including steak) options. The wine list offers lots of (priced-up) provincial choices.

Viejo Jack (☎ 422-3911; Av Virrey Toledo 145; mains for 2 AR$22-36; ⏰ lunch & dinner) Far enough out of the tourist zone to be authentic, but not so far it's a pain in the backside to get to, this is a down-to-earth spot very popular with locals for its *parrillada* and pasta. The serves are huge – designed for two – but you'll get a single portion (still a big slab of meat) for 70% of the price.

La Leñita (☎ 421-4865; cnr Balcarce & A Alsina; mains AR$28-42; ⏰ lunch & dinner) This popular *parrilla* hits meaty heights on what is a hit-and-miss dining street. There's fine *carne* (meat), with a wide range of cuts, and solicitous service whether you're in a suit or singlet. The versatile staff serenade diners with Salta *folklore* halfway through dinner.

José Balcarce (☎ 421-1628; www.cocinadealtura.com .ar; cnr Mitre & Necochea; mains AR$30-50; ⏰ dinner Mon-Sat) Exposed stone walls, ambient music and solicitous service set the scene for a satisfying gourmet dining experience here. Starters like llama carpaccio could be followed by sea bass with passionfruit and ginger, or other highland-type dishes involving lamb or trout. The wine list sees each grape variety described in human terms – merlot is a sensitive listener, with gay tendencies. Close to Salta's best.

Café del Tiempo (☎ 432-0771; Balcarce 901; dishes AR$33-45; ⏰ 7pm-late) Decked out to resemble a Buenos Aires cafe, this has prices to match but offers a stylish terrace in the heart of the Balcarce zone; a top spot for a drink. There's

some sort of performance or live music every night. Most of the dishes – including international offerings such as chop suey, sushi and ceviche – are designed to share, and the *picadas* (shared appetizer plates) are great for a group.

Drinking & Entertainment

See the boxed text (opposite) for info on *peñas* – the classic Salta night-time experience. The two blocks of Balcarce north of Alsina, and the surrounding streets, are the main nightlife zone. Bars and clubs around here follow the typical boom-bust-reopen-with-new-name pattern, so just follow your nose.

Macondo (☎ 431-7191; Balcarce 980; ⏰ 8pm-late) After all the *folklórica* music on this street, the indie '90s–'00s mix in this trendy bar might come as a relief. Popular with locals and tourists, it keeps it lively until late.

Plaza de Almas (☎ 422-8933; Pueyrredón 6; ⏰ 9am-late Mon-Sat) Offering an eclectic mix of *artesanía* shops, a bar, lounge, cafe and restaurant, this Tucumán classic has seamlessly moved into Salta. The most atmospheric place for a drink near the plaza.

Casa de Cultura (☎ 421-6042; Caseros 460) This cultural center near the plaza has regular live events. It runs the whole gamut here: you're as likely to catch a Houdini-style magician as a classical ballet performance.

Cine Ópera (☎ 421-3520; Urquiza 560; tickets AR$10) This is the most central of Salta's several cinemas, showing Hollywood standards and more offbeat fare in original version.

Teatro Provincial (☎ 422-4515; Zuviria 70) Great new theater in a '40s building on the plaza.

Shopping

An artisan's market sets up every Sunday along Balcarce, stretching a couple of blocks south from the bus terminal.

Mercado Artesanal (☎ 439-2808; Av San Martín 2555; ⏰ 8am-8:30pm) For souvenirs, this provincially sponsored market is the most noteworthy place. Articles include native handicrafts, such as hammocks, string bags, ceramics, basketry, leather work and the region's distinctive ponchos. To get here, take bus 2, 3 or 7 from downtown.

Getting There & Away

AIR

Salta's **airport** (SLA; ☎ 424-3115) is 9.5km southwest of town on RP 51. **Andes** (☎ 437-3514; www. andesonline.com; España 478) flies six times weekly to Buenos Aires (AR$660), and also services

PEÑAS OF SALTA

Salta is famous Argentina-wide for its *folklore* (folk music), which is far more national in scope than tango. A *peña* is a bar or social club where people eat, drink and gather to play and listen to *folklore*, which often traditionally took the form of an impromptu jam session.

These days, the Salta *peña* is quite a touristy experience, with scheduled performances, CD sales, tour groups and high prices, and it's difficult to find an authentic spot. There are a couple (ask around) where folk musicians hang out in their spare time, and you may catch a spontaneous performance. Nevertheless, the standard Salta *peña* is a great deal of fun. Traditional fare is empanadas and red wine – delicious, but most of the places offer a wider menu including *parrillada* (mixed grill including steak) and 'Andean cuisine', with llama meat and quinoa featuring.

Peña heartland is Calle Balcarce, between Alsina and the train station. There are several here, along with other restaurants, bars and *boliches* (nightclubs) – it's Salta's main nightlife zone. Things typically get moving at 9.30pm, but go on till late, especially at weekends.

Some *peñas* to get you started:

La Vieja Estación (☎ 421-7727; www.viejaestacion-salta.com.ar; Balcarce 885; show AR$12-15, mains AR$18-45; ⓧ 8pm-3am Tue-Sun) The best established of the Balcarce *peñas*, with a stage, wooden tables and three live shows per night. Tasty empanadas and *locro* (a stew of maize, beans, beef, prok and sausage), and a wide range of other choices.

La Casona del Molino (☎ 434-2835; Luis Burela 1; mains AR$18-35; ⓧ lunch & 9pm-5am Tue-Sun) This former mansion, about 20 blocks west of Plaza 9 de Julio, is a Salta classic that goes sinfully late at weekends. It has several spacious rooms, each with different performers who work around the tables rather than on a stage.

Peña Boliche Balderrama (☎ 421-1542; www.boliche-balderrama.com.ar; Av San Martín 1126; show AR$20; ⓧ 9pm-1.30am) With cheap but unremarkable food, this is Salta's most touristy *peña*. It can be a lot of fun, but feels contrived these days.

La Casa de Güemes (☎ 422-8978; España 730, mains AR$13-28; ⓧ lunch & 9pm-late) This central historic house was once occupied by Güemes, a *salteño* (resident of Salta) independence hero who looms large in gaucho and *folklore* culture hereabouts. Decent, fairly priced food – with some worthwhile lunch specials – and good local music.

Córdoba (AR$402), Puerto Iguazú (AR$602) and Jujuy (AR$68). Through Buenos Aires you can connect to its other destination, Puerto Madryn. **Aerolíneas Argentinas** (☎ 431-1331; Caseros 475) flies three times daily to Buenos Aires' Aeroparque Jorge Newbery (AR$813). **LAN** (☎ 421-7330; www.lan.com; Buenos Aires 88) flies the same route twice daily.

Aerosur (☎ 432-0149; www.aerosur.com; Buenos Aires 88) flies three times weekly to Santa Cruz, Bolivia (AR$537).

Flights are heavily oversubscribed, so try to book well ahead.

BUS

Salta's **bus terminal** (☎ 401-1248; Av Hipólito Yrigoyen), southeast of downtown, has frequent services to all parts of the country. The information desk is in the middle of the concourse.

Two companies, Andesmar and Pullman, do the run to San Pedro de Atacama, Chile, at around 7am on Monday, Wednesday and Friday. Geminis, an inferior service, does it on Tuesday, Thursday and Sunday. It goes via Jujuy and the Paso de Jama, takes 10 to 11 hours and costs AR$180. It's worth reserving

a few days before. The buses go on to service Calama, Antofagasta, Iquique and Arica.

Ale Hermanos (☎ 427-1127) goes daily to San Antonio de los Cobres (AR$25, 5½ hours), while **Marcos Rueda** (☎ 421-4447) serves Cachi (AR$37, 4½ hours), departing daily at 7am and also at 1.30pm Tuesday and Saturday, at 3.30pm Thursday and at 5pm Sunday.

Sample fares to other destinations:

Destination	Cost (AR$)	Duration (hr)
Buenos Aires	210	22
Cafayate	35	4
Catamarca	91	8
Córdoba	160	14
Jujuy	23	2
La Quiaca	50	8
La Rioja	117	10
Mendoza	230	18
Puerto Iguazú	235	21
Resistencia	126	10
Río Gallegos	530	48
Salvador Mazza	72	6
San Juan	201	16
Santiago (Chile)	305	25
Santiago del Estero	68	6
Tucumán	55	4½

THE ANDEAN NORTHWEST

CAR

Many travelers choose to rent a car for a few days in Salta in order to see the surrounding highlands and valleys. There are many agencies; cruise around getting quotes, as there are often special offers available. Most will do airport or city pick-ups. Typically, companies charge AR$170 to AR$220 per day for a week's hire, or triple that for a 4WD. The stretches between San Antonio de los Cobres and La Poma (en route to Cachi), and north of Salinas Grandes toward Abra Pampa are usually 4WD only, but the *ripio* road between San Antonio and Salinas Grandes is normally passable in a standard car. Always check with the provincial tourist office for current conditions.

You can't take rental cars into Bolivia, but it is possible to take them into Chile. Companies require a few days' notice of this to process the paperwork, which will cost you an extra AR$300 or so.

Some companies:

AndarSalta (☎ 431-0720; www.andarsalta.com.ar; Buenos Aires 88) Decent prices; cheaper if you pay cash.

Asís (☎ 431-1704; www.asisrentacar.com.ar; Buenos Aires 68) Straight talking and fairly priced.

Europcar (☎ 421-8848; Córdoba 20; www.europcar .com.ar) Good weekly deals.

Noa (☎ 431-7080; www.noarentacar.com; Buenos Aires 1) In the Hotel Salta.

TRAIN

Salta no longer has train services, except the *Tren a las Nubes* (see below).

Getting Around

Bus 6 from San Martín near Buenos Aires runs to the airport (AR$1.25), otherwise it's a AR$17 *remise* (taxi ride). There are also bookable shuttle buses that do hotel pickups (AR$15).

Local bus 5 (AR$1.25) connects the train station and downtown with the bus terminal.

TREN A LAS NUBES

Argentina's most famous train ride is up and running again, after an uncertain start to the century. From Salta, the *Tren a las Nubes* (Train to the Clouds) leaves the Lerma Valley to ascend the multicolored Quebrada del Toro, continuing past Tastil ruins and San Antonio de los Cobres, before continuing a little further to the trip's highlight – a stunning viaduct 64m high and 224m long. It spans an enormous desert canyon at **La Polvorilla**,

4220m above sea level, and is a magnificent engineering achievement unjustifiable on any reasonable economic grounds. Though it seems underwhelming at first glimpse, it's very impressive once you get up close. This is the train's last stop, but the track actually continues to the high Paso de Socompa on the Chilean border, 571km west of Salta.

The trip is a touristy one, with *folklore* performances, karaoke and multilingual commentary. It's a long day – leaving Salta at 7am, and not getting back until 11pm. Some people choose to get off in San Antonio, spend the night there and make their own way back. The train runs only on Saturday, and the return trip costs US$120, which includes breakfast and snacks, but not lunch or dinner; you can eat in the dining car or take a picnic.

There's an **office** (☎ 422-3033; www.trenalasnubes .com.ar; ⏰ 8am-10pm Mon-Fri, from 6am Sat) at Salta station where you can book tickets; most travel agents along Calle Buenos Aires can also do this for you.

Many tour operators in Salta (see p265) run trips along the road that parallels the train's route, which is also a spectacular ascent; they include the viaduct and cost around AR$190.

SAN ANTONIO DE LOS COBRES

☎ 0387 / pop 4274 / elev 3775m

This dusty little mining town is on the puna 168km west of Salta, and over 2600m above it. It's suffered greatly since the deterioration of the region's mining and associated railway, and relies heavily on tourism and the *Tren a las Nubes* for income. It's a very typical highland settlement, with adobe houses, almost deserted streets and a serious drop in temperature as soon as the sun goes down. It's not the place for cutting-edge nightlife or street art, but is worth stopping in to get the feel of this facet of Argentine and South American life. You can head north from here to the Quebrada de Humahuaca via the Salinas Grandes and Purmamarca, and, some of the year, south to Cachi (see p274).

In colonial times, transportation from northwestern Argentina depended on pack trains; one route passed through here, crossing the rugged elevations of the Puna de Atacama to the Pacific and then on to Lima. It was a rugged journey, taking 20 days to cover the 800km.

There's a tourist office near the bridge in the center of town, and a little kiosk at the

THE ANDEAN NORTHWEST

eastern entrance to town. In theory they are open 8am to 8pm, but it's a fiction; try your luck.

Sights
There's little to see in town – though the sunsets are spectacular – but 16km to the west is the viaduct at La Polvorilla, the last stop of the *Tren a las Nubes* (opposite). From the parking lot, which has a couple of *artesanía* shops, you can climb up a zigzag path to the top of the viaduct and walk across it. *Remises* in San Antonio charge about AR$30 for the return journey.

Sleeping & Eating
Hostal del Cielo (☎ 490-9912; www.vivirenloscobres.org.ar; Belgrano s/n; dm AR$35) This basic but very friendly hostel is on the edge of town, heading toward the viaduct. Buses from Salta will drop you here if you ask, otherwise it's about 1km from the center. There are two spotless, comfortable dorms; bathrooms are also mighty clean; HI members get breakfast included. There's a small anthropological museum next door.

El Palenque (☎ 490-9019; hostalelpalenque@hotmail.com; Belgrano s/n; d without bathroom AR$60, tr/q with bathroom AR$90/120) Welcoming and tidy, this is a fine choice a few blocks from the center, past the church. It looks closed from outside, but it's not. The rooms are insulated and (comparatively) warm, there's hot water and sound family ownership.

Hostería de las Nubes (☎ 490-9059; www.maresur.com; Caseros 441; s/d AR$160/200; 🛜) The best place to stay and eat in town, this has attractively simple decoration in its comfortable rooms, which boast doubleglazing and heating.

Book ahead. The restaurant (mains AR$15 to AR$25; open noon to 2pm and 7pm to 9.30pm) serves a short menu of local dishes; all are well prepared and nourishing.

Simple restaurants are dotted along Belgrano; these are good bets for empanadas, *milanesas* (breaded cutlets) and local staples.

Getting There & Away
There are daily buses from Salta (AR$25, 5½ hours) with Ale Hermanos. See also the *Tren a las Nubes* (opposite). There's precious little transportation running over the Paso de Sico to Chile these days; if you are trying to hitchhike, ask around town for trucks due to leave. From San Antonio, a good *ripio* road runs 97km north, skirting the Salinas Grandes to intersect with the paved RP52.

SALINAS GRANDES
Bring sunglasses for this spectacular **salt plain** in a remote part of the puna, at some 3350m above sea level. Once a lake dried up in the Holocene this is now a 525-sq-km crust of salt up to half a meter thick. On a clear day, the blinding contrast between the bright blue sky and the cracked and crusty expanse of white is spellbinding.

The *salinas* (salt plains) are in Salta province, but are most easily reached by heading west along the paved RP 52 from Purmamarca in Jujuy province. About 5km west of the intersection of RP52 and RN40 (the good *ripio* road that heads north 97km from San Antonio de los Cobres), there's a saltmining building; opposite, you can drive onto the salt pan to check out the rectangular basins from which the salt is periodically dug out. A few

---

WESTERN SALTA PROVINCE

If you thought San Antonio de los Cobres was remote, think again. Hundreds of kilometers of Salta province stretch west of here, and include two passes to Chile: the barren **Paso de Sico** and the remote rail and road crossing at **Socompa**. Sixty kilometers west of San Antonio, **Olacapato** is Argentina's highest village, at 4090m above sea level. All the area's settlements are mining camps or grew up around the railway that serviced the mines; many are abandoned now.

From Olacapato you can continue west to the Paso de Sico, or head southwest across *salares* (salt flats) to **Tolar Grande**, where there are accommodations in private homes. Beyond here it's 139km to the Paso de Socompa, or 131km southward to the abandoned mine of **La Casualidad**, the end of the road and one of Argentina's most remote spots. Needless to say, it's a trip only possible in summer, and an arduous one. Take all your fuel needs from San Antonio, where you can buy 200L drums, and inform police of your plans. Don't wander off-road around Mina La Casualidad, as some landmines from a 1970s dispute with Chile are still around.

artisans sell decent stone carvings and llamas made from salt here. A couple of places to buy drinks and food are on the road nearby.

The inevitable 'salt hotel' hasn't appeared yet. The closest places to stay are San Antonio and Susques. The only way of reaching the *salinas* by public transportation is to jump off a Susques-bound bus from Jujuy or Purmamarca. Check the timetables carefully before doing this; on some days it's possible to catch a bus back to Purmamarca a couple of hours later, but on other days it's not. This road has enough traffic to hitchhike.

Otherwise, hire a car, grab a *remise* from Purmamarca, or take a tour from Jujuy or Salta. From the latter, it's a hellishly long day, unless you opt to overnight in Purmamarca.

The *salinas* are spectacular, but the otherworldly *salares* (salt flats) in southwestern Bolivia are even more so; if you're heading that way (or have already been), you might want to prioritize other attractions.

VALLES CALCHAQUÍES

The Valles Calchaquíes is one of Argentina's most seductive off-the-beaten-track zones: a winning combination of rugged landscapes, traditional workshops, strikingly attractive adobe villages and some of Argentina's best wines. Small but sophisticated Cafayate, with its wineries and paved highway, presents quite a contrast to more remote settlements such as Angastaco or Molinos, while Cachi, accessible from Salta via a spectacular road that crosses the Parque Nacional Los Cardones, is another peaceful and popular base. The vernacular architecture in these valleys merits special attention – even modest adobe houses might have neoclassical columns or Moorish arches.

In these valleys, indigenous Diaguita (Calchaquí) put up some of the stiffest resistance to Spanish rule. In the 17th century, plagued by labor shortages, the Spaniards twice tried to impose forced labor obligations on the Diaguita, but found themselves having to maintain armed forces to prevent the Diaguita from sowing their own crops and attacking pack trains.

Military domination did not solve Spanish labor problems, since their only solution was to relocate the Diaguita as far away as Buenos Aires, whose suburb of Quilmes bears the name of one group of these displaced people. The last descendants of the 270 families transported to the viceregal capital had died or had

dispersed by the time of Argentine independence. The productive land that had sustained the Diaguita for centuries was formed by the Spaniards into large rural estates, the haciendas of the Andes.

Parque Nacional Los Cardones

Occupying some 650 sq km on both sides of the winding RP 33 from Salta to Cachi across the Cuesta del Obispo, Parque Nacional Los Cardones takes its name from the candelabra cactus known as the cardón, the park's most striking plant species.

In the treeless Andean foothills and puna, the cardón has long been an important source of timber for rafters, doors, window frames and similar uses. You see it often in vernacular buildings and the region's colonial churches. According to Argentine writer Federico Kirbus, clusters of cardónes can be indicators of archaeological sites: the indigenous people of the puna ate its sweet black seed, which, after passing through the intestinal tract, readily sprouted around their latrines. Certainly, many a *pucará* in the region bristles with these otherworldly sentinels.

Los Cardones is free to enter and still has no services – though a visitor center on the main road is gradually being renovated – but there is a **ranger office** (☎ 03868-496005; San Martín s/n) in Payogasta, 11km north of Cachi. Take plenty of water and protection from the sun. Buses between Salta and Cachi will stop for you, but verify times. Most people disembark at Valle Encantada, which is the most accessible, picturesque part of the park.

Cachi

☎ 03868 / pop 2189 / elev 2280m

The biggest place by some distance hereabouts, enchanting Cachi is nevertheless little more than a village, albeit one surrounded by stunning scenery. Overlooked by noble mountains, it boasts fresh highland air, sunny days and crisp nights. The cobblestones, adobe houses, tranquil plaza and opportunities to explore the surrounds mean that it's the sort of place that eats extra days out of your carefully planned itinerary.

On the west side of the plaza, the **Mercado Artesanal** (☎ 491902; oficinadeturismo.cachi@gmail.com; Güemes s/n; ⏰ 8am-8pm) is both a handicraft shop and the tourist office.

Opposite, the simple but attractive **Iglesia San José** (1796) has graceful arches and a barrel-vaulted ceiling of cardón wood. The confessional and other features are also made of cardón, while the holy water lives in a large *tinaja* (a big clay vessel for storing oil).

Next door, Cachi's **Museo Arqueológico** (☎ 491080; admission by AR$5 or AR$10 donation; 🕑 10am-7pm Mon-Sat, 10am-1pm Sun) is a well-presented and professionally arranged account of the surrounding area's cultural evolution, with good background information on archaeological methods, all in Spanish. Don't miss the wall in the secondary patio, composed of stones with petroglyphs.

Two kilometers southwest of the center, on the edge of town, **Todo lo Nuestro** (☎ 0387-15-458-5668; jorgeafpark@hotmail.com; admission AR$10; 🕑 9am-7pm) is a labor of love that features replica buildings from several phases of the valley's history. It's a fascinating project; in some of the buildings it really feels as if the occupants have just stepped out for a minute. There's a rustically styled restaurant here, too.

ACTIVITIES

A short walk from Cachi's plaza brings you to a **viewpoint** and then its picturesque hilltop **cemetery**; nearby is a rather unlikely airstrip. A longer walk (an hour and a bit) takes you to **Cachi Adentro**, a tiny village where there's not a great deal to do save swing on the seats in the demi-plaza or sip a soda from the only store. It's a particularly lovely walk in summer, when the streams and cascades are alive with water. From here, you could return a longer way (about 26km roundtrip): bear left past the church and then take a left down the road labelled Camino de las Carreras. This road winds around the valley and eventually crosses the river; shortly afterwards, turn left when you hit a bigger road (or right for 2km to the lovely Algarrobal campground); and this will lead you back to Cachi via the hamlet of La Aguada.

There's a handful of rather unremarkable **archaeological sites** dotted around the valley; these are signposted and also appear on the tourist office map of the area, and make destinations for picturesque hikes or drives.

For more strenuous hiking and mountaineering, **Santiago Casimiro** (☎ 03868-15-638545; santiagocasimiro@hotmail.com; Barrio Cooperativa Casa 17) is a local guide. Many locals hire out **horses**; look for signs or ask in the tourist office. After all that endeavor, you can always cool off in the municipal **pool**.

SLEEPING

Camping Municipal (☎ 491902; cachi@salnet.com.ar; campsites AR$15-20; 🖭) On a hill southwest of the plaza, this offers shaded campsites with individual barbecues surrounded by hedges; the municipal pool is here. There's also a hostel with basic dorms (with/without bathroom AR$20/12) and a couple of cabins (AR$125); reservations must be made at the tourist office.

Hotel Nevado de Cachi (☎ 491912; s/d with bathroom AR$60/80, s without bathroom AR$30) Just off the plaza and right by the bus stop, this is a decent budget choice with rooms around a patio. Beds are comfortable, and bathrooms – both shared and private – work well enough. Prices are a bit negotiable and vary slightly by room; try for the upstairs double round the back.

ACA Hostería Cachi (☎ 491105; www.soldelvalle.com.ar; Av ACA s/n; s/d AR$203/302; 🖭 🖳 🖭 🖭) With its hilltop position, this family-friendly hotel has the best views in town, and there are worse ways to spend your day than relaxing poolside checking them out. Rooms are comfortable and unexciting but picturesquely surround a patio; there's even a little zoo.

El Cortijo (☎ 491034; www.elcortijohotel.com; Av ACA s/n; s/d from AR$250/295; 🖭 🖭) Opposite the ACA Hostería Cachi entrance, this stylish small hotel offers rooms that aren't large but are decorated with finesse, and some – particularly 'Los Padres', with its own private terrace with loungers (doubles AR$380) – have fabulous views of the sierra. There's an original-looking restaurant and various further improvements in the works.

La Merced del Alto (☎ 490020; www.lamerceddelalto.com; s/d AR$599/701; 🖳 🖭 🖭 🖭) Built of traditional whitewashed adobe with ceramic floors and cane ceilings, this hotel across the river from town is designed to look like an historic monastery. It offers excellent facilities and great peace and quiet, with cool, restrained rooms looking over either the hills beyond (slightly more expensive) or the interior patio. Public areas include a most inviting lounge, a good restaurant, and a rustic spa area offering massage treatments, a pool and Jacuzzi with sierra views. Service is multilingual and top-notch.

El Molino de Cachi (☎ 491094; www.bodegaelmolino.com.ar; d AR$610; 🖭) With just six rooms, this converted mill makes a highly relaxing rural base for exploring the area. Four kilometers from the center of Cachi, it's also a winery. It doesn't take walk-ins, so book ahead. No children or credit cards.

Other options:

La Mamama (☎ 491305; Suárez 590; dm/r without bathroom AR$20/40) A welcoming spot on the bus stop street, with simple rooms with saggy mattresses and a Cachi-casual feel.

Hostal del Inkañan (☎ 491135; luisreicolque@hot mail.com; Güemes s/n; dm/d without bathroom AR$30/80) Decent rooms around a grassy patio uphill from the plaza.

EATING

For local dishes such as *locro* and *humitas*, best are the various no-frills *confiterías* and *comedores* around the plaza and across from the Hotel Nevado de Cachi.

Platos y Diseño (☎ 0387-15-513-3861; Güemes s/n; dishes AR$10-25; ⏱ lunch & dinner) Uphill from the plaza, this has a relaxing dining area with local art and photos on the walls, slow but amiable service and decent for-the-tourists traditional dishes.

Ashpamanta (☎ 0387-15-451-4267; Bustamante s/n; dishes AR$15-35; ⏱ lunch & dinner) Compact and snug, this likable little place has a short but tasty menu of pasta, salads and a couple of more elaborate mains – quinoa risotto or pan-fried fillets with vegetables – that are prepared in an open kitchen behind the bar.

Oliver (☎ 491903; Ruíz de los Llanos 160; mains AR$15-40; ⏱ 8am-midnight) On the plaza, this homey, multilevel, wooden-tabled restaurant is a reliable choice for tasty pizza, bruschetta and a couple of creative meaty mains. The terrace on the plaza is also a fine place for a sundowner. Wine prices are mostly over the odds.

GETTING THERE & AWAY

Marcos Rueda (☎ 491063) buses run between Salta and Cachi. It's a spectacular ride, winding up to the Cuesta del Obispo pass, then traveling through the cactus-studded Parque Nacional Los Cardones. Buses to Salta (AR$37, 4½ hours) leave at 9.05am Monday to Saturday. There's a 3pm service on Monday, Thursday and Friday, and a 3.30pm service on Sunday. Seclantás is serviced daily and Molinos five times weekly, while three buses Monday through Saturday run to Cachi Adentro (AR$2.20, 30 minutes).

There are four weekly buses north to La Poma (AR$17, 1¼ hours), an old hacienda town that, as far as public transport goes, is the end of the line. The road beyond, to San Antonio de los Cobres, is an arduous, spectacular ascent that criss-crosses a river and travels by lonely goat farms to a 4895m pass.

It's only passable in a non-4WD vehicle at certain times of year (normally September to December); phone the **police** (☎ 0387-490-9051) for advice. Otherwise, you'll have to approach San Antonio the long way round.

Seclantás

☎ 03868 / pop 306 / elev 2100m

Charming Seclantás is a quiet little place that's the spiritual home of the Salta poncho. There are many weavers' workshops in town, and north of here, along the road to Cachi, artisans' homes are marked with a sign indicating that you can drop in and peruse their wares; the stretch of road has been dubbed the **Route of the Artisans**. One of them, Señor Tero, is well known hereabouts for having woven a poncho worn by Pope John Paul II.

Seclantás' **church**, pretty in yellow, dates from 1835; the evocative **cemetery** is at the top of town.

Places to stay in Seclantás are clustered around the plaza. Among them, **Hostería La Rueda** (☎ 498041; cnr Cornejo & Ferreyra; s/d with bathroom AR$70/90, without bathroom AR$50/70) is hospitable and spotless, and features comfortable, pretty, common areas and decent rooms. The campground is just behind the church, and has a pool that's open to the public.

There's a daily bus from Cachi to Seclantás (AR$12, 1¼ hours, two on Saturday); it continues to Molinos some days.

Molinos

☎ 03868 / pop 927 / elev 2020m

If you thought Cachi was laid-back, wait until you see Molinos, a lovely little backwater with a collection of striking adobe buildings in gentle decline; a stroll through the streets will reveal some real gems. Its picturesque appeal is augmented by shady streets and good accommodations. There's an ATM on the plaza.

Molinos takes its name from the still-operational flour mill on the Río Calchaquí. The town's restored 18th-century **Iglesia de San Pedro de Nolasco**, in the Cuzco style, features twin bell towers and a traditional tiled roof. Like Angastaco, Molinos was a waystation on the trans-Andean route to Chile and Peru. Well into the 20th century, pack trains passed here with skins, wool and wood for sale in Salta and subsequent shipment to Buenos Aires.

About 1.5km west is the **Criadero Coquera** (☎ 0387-15-407-1259) where the government's agricultural research arm raises vicuñas and manages to shear them without damaging their health; alongside is the **Casa de Entre Ríos**, part of the former Estancia Luracatao, where there's a fine artisans' market with spectacular *ponchos de güemes* for sale. There are two simple rooms (AR$30 per person) here.

The *hospedajes* (family homes) scattered around town are more like homestays than anything. **Los Cardones de Molinos** (☎ 494061; cardonesmolinos@hotmail.com; cnr Sarmiento & San Martín; r per person with/without bathroom AR$50/40) is an excellent choice, with comfortable rooms with cactus furniture. You're treated as one of the family and can use the kitchen; the exceptionally welcoming and accommodating owner is a good source of local advice. Breakfast is included.

Across from the church, adobe **Hacienda de Molinos** (☎ 494094; www.haciendademolinos.com.ar; Cornejo s/n; s/d standard AR$300/380, r superior AR$450-510; 🖳 🛜 🛒) is also known as the Casa de Isasmendi, after Salta's last colonial governor, who was born, lived and died in this sprawling residence in a town that was a stronghold of royalist resistance. It's been picturesquely restored, with sober, handsome rooms with inviting beds, antique furniture, cane ceilings and great bathrooms, set around lovely patio spaces. It's on the edge of the village and utterly peaceful. There's a good restaurant.

There's a daily bus to Molinos from Cachi (AR$17, two hours) on Monday, Wednesday, Friday, Saturday and Sunday. It returns from Molinos at 7am Monday, Tuesday, Thursday and Saturday, and 2pm on Sunday.

Angastaco
☎ 03868 / pop 881 / elev 1955m

Tiny Angastaco sits among some of the most dramatically tortuous rockscapes of the valley route. Forty kilometers south of Molinos and 54km north of San Carlos, it resembles other oasis settlements placed at regular intervals in the Valles Calchaquíes, with vineyards, fields of anise and cumin, and the ruins of an ancient *pucará*.

Angastaco has a gas station but no bank. There is a tourist office on the square, as well as an **archaeological museum** in the municipal building. Both are open irregular hours, but ask around in the *municipalidad* or police station and someone will help. **Horseback riding** is easily arranged via the Hostería Angastaco.

Angastaco's major fiesta is on December 8, the day of the **Virgin of the Valley**, the village's patron. On February 17 and 18, the **grape vintage** and making of foot-trodden *vino patero* is celebrated with a festival.

FINCA COLOMÉ

Some of Argentina's finest wines are produced at this ecological **bodega** (☎ 03868-494044; www .bodegacolome.com; tasting AR$30-50; 🕙 10:30am-6pm), which is set (as they say hereabouts) 'where the devil lost his poncho,' some 20km down a spectacular gravel road west from Molinos. The vineyards (including some ancient pre-phylloxera European vines) and hotel enjoy a stunning natural setting, surrounded by hills and mountains that seem to change color hourly. Forward thinking on environmental, social and cultural fronts is also in evidence: the complex is electrically self-sufficient, has funded substantial infrastructural improvements in the local community and now boasts a stunning **museum** (admission free; 🕙 2-6pm) designed by artist James Turrell, with a permanent exhibition of nine of his works. These are utterly memorable installations involving light and the strange frontiers of our own perception; it's a remarkable place. Both bodega and museum visits should be booked ahead by phone or email (museo@colomeargentina.com). The bodega also serves salads and baguettes (AR$27 to AR$29) for a light lunch.

The **hotel** (www.estanciacolome.com; d AR$1486; 🗶 🖳 🛜 🛒) features chic and relaxing rooms accompanied by excellent multilingual service and a raft of facilities, including a picturesque pool surrounded by the grapevines and beds of lavender. Apart from lolling about reading novels and enjoying the wine, you could also head off on some of the impressive criollo horses – really trained by whispering rather than the lash – to explore the surrounding hillscapes. The restaurant (book ahead) is open to visitors, with a short changing menu of just two mains (AR$45 to AR$60), one of which is vegetarian.

Not far from Colomé, Bodega El Humanao is also worth a visit for its beautifully balanced cabernet-malbec blend, among others.

Hospedaje El Cardón (☎ 0387-15-459-0021; r per person with/without bathroom AR$30/20) is a decent budget choice. It's 50m to your right (the one with the fancy porch) if you're standing facing the church. **Hostería Angastaco** (☎ 491123; s/d AR$40/70; ☲) feels a bit abandoned but offers excellent value for its rooms with artisanal throws on the beds and cardón chests. There's a restaurant and summer-only pool.

At research time, the only public transportation was one bus that headed south to San Carlos and Cafayate at 6am Monday to Friday and 4pm Sunday (no Saturday service). Transport options to Molinos, 40km north, are limited. **Moisés López** (☎ 0387-15-410-2130) and **Miguel Pastrana** (☎ 0387-15-4819-0146) will run the route in a car or truck for AR$120 total. There's also a transport that takes kids from the boarding school in Molinos home to Angastaco at around 5pm on Friday, and returns them to Molinos at around 6am on Monday; they'll take tourists for free if there's room. Otherwise, it's a hitchhike or long walk. Hitchhiking is very slow hereabouts; take water.

San Carlos
☎ 03868 / pop 1887

A sizable traditional village, San Carlos, 22km north of Cafayate, is connected to it by paved road, a pleasant shock if you're arriving from the north. Most visitors push on through to Cafayate or Angastaco, but there's a special place to stay here in **La Casa de los Vientos** (☎ 495073; Barrio Cemitigre; r AR$120), which is signposted off the main road at the Cachi end of town. Built in the traditional manner of adobe, with terracotta tiles and cane ceilings, it incorporates some ingenious environmental innovations. The owners are potters, and the rooms (all different) are decorated with rustic flair and beauty.

CAFAYATE
☎ 03868 / pop 10,714 / elev 1683m

Argentina's second center for quality wine production, Cafayate is a popular tourist destination but still has a tranquil small-town feel. It's easily reached from Salta via the spectacular Quebrada de Cafayate, and is also the southern terminus of the Valles Calchaquíes route. With a selection of excellent accommodations for every budget, and several wineries to visit in and around town, Cafayate invites laying up for a while to explore the surrounding area. It also has many young artists and craftspeople, so check out the *artesanía*.

Cafayate is famous for its torrontés, a grape producing aromatic dry white wine, but the bodegas hereabouts also produce some fine reds from cabernet sauvignon, malbec and tannat.

Orientation
Cafayate sits at the foot of the Valles Calchaquíes, near the junction between RN 40, which goes northwest to Molinos and Cachi, and RN 68, which goes to Salta through the Quebrada de Cafayate. Through town, RN 40 is Av General Güemes.

Information
Banco de la Nación (Plaza San Martín) ATM on the plaza; also changes money.
La Red (Toscano 79; per hr AR$3) Internet access on the plaza.
Locutorio (Av General Güemes & Belgrano)
Tourist information kiosk (☎ 422442; Plaza San Martín; ☷ 8am-9pm) On the northeast corner of the plaza.

Sights & Activities
MUSEUMS
The private **Museo Arqueológico** (☎ 421054; cnr Colón & Calchaquí; admission by donation; ☷ 11:30am-9pm Mon-Fri, 11:30am-3pm Sat) is the collection left by enthusiastic archaeologist Rodolfo Bravo and well worth a visit. Sourced mostly from grave sites in a 30km radius from Cafayate, the collection consists of an excellent array of ceramics, from the black and gray wares of the Candelaria and Aguada cultures to late Diaguita and Inca pottery, all well displayed across two rooms. While there's not much explanation, the material speaks for itself.

The **Museo de Vitivinicultura** (Av General Güemes; admission AR$2; ☷ 8am-8pm) details the history of local wine production and displays a range of antiquated winemaking equipment. It's pretty dry, but ambitious plans for new, interactive wings might just have transformed it by the time you visit.

RÍO COLORADO
A 6km walk southwest of town leads you to the Río Colorado. Follow the river upstream for about 1½ hours to get to a 10m **waterfall**, where you can swim. There's a second waterfall further up. Look out for hidden **rock paintings** on the way (for about AR$10, local

THE ANDEAN NORTHWEST

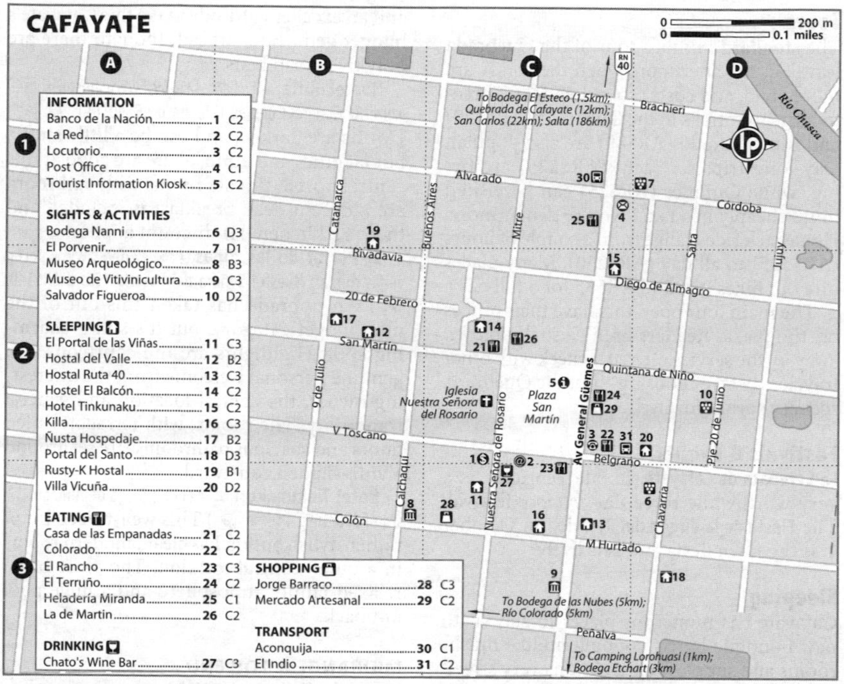
CAFAYATE
0 200 m
0 0.1 miles
A
B
C
D
1
2
3
INFORMATION
Banco de la Nación 1 C2
La Red 2 C2
Locutorio 3 C2
Post Office 4 C1
Tourist Information Kiosk 5 C2
SIGHTS & ACTIVITIES
Bodega Nanni 6 D3
El Porvenir 7 D1
Museo Arqueológico 8 B3
Museo de Vitivinicultura 9 C3
Salvador Figueroa 10 D2
SLEEPING
El Portal de las Viñas 11 C3
Hostal del Valle 12 B2
Hostal Ruta 40 13 C3
Hostel El Balcón 14 C2
Hotel Tinkunaku 15 C2
Killa 16 C3
Ñusta Hospedaje 17 B2
Portal del Santo 18 D3
Rusty-K Hostal 19 B1
Villa Vicuña 20 D2
EATING
Casa de las Empanadas 21 C2
Colorado 22 C2
El Rancho 23 C3
El Terruño 24 C2
Heladería Miranda 25 C1
La de Martin 26 C2
DRINKING
Chato's Wine Bar 27 C3
SHOPPING
Jorge Barraco 28 C3
Mercado Artesanal 29 C2
TRANSPORT
Aconquija 30 C1
El Indio 31 C2
RN 40
To Bodega El Esteco (1.5km); Quebrada de Cafayate (12km); San Carlos (22km); Salta (186km)
Brachieri
Río Chusca
Alvarado
Córdoba
Catamarca
Buenos Aires
Mitre
Salta
Jujuy
Rivadavia
Diego de Almagro
20 de Febrero
San Martín
Quintana de Niño
9 de Julio
Iglesia Nuestra Señora del Rosario
Plaza San Martín
Av General Güemes
Pje 20 de Junio
V Toscano
Belgrano
Calchaquí
Nuestra Señora del Rosario
Chavarría
Colón
M Hurtado
To Bodega de las Nubes (5km); Río Colorado (5km)
Peñalva
To Camping Lorohuasi (1km); Bodega Etchart (3km)

children will guide you). If you want to ride out to the trailhead, you can leave your bike at the nearby house for a few pesos. You could combine this walk with a visit to Bodega de las Nubes (right). Note: if the river is high after rains in January and February, the route to the waterfall becomes strenuous and dangerous.

WINERIES

Several wineries offer tours and tastings in and around the town. Some are small, easy-going and friendly, while others are larger, with a cooler welcome.

The tour and tastings are short and bright at **Bodega Nanni** (☎ 421527; www.bodegananni.com; Chavarría 151; tours with tasting AR$5; ⏱ 9:30am-1pm & 2:30-6:30pm Mon-Sat, 11am-1pm & 3-6pm Sun), a small, central winery with a lovely grass patio. Its wines are organic, uncomplicated and drinkable.

Tiny **Salvador Figueroa** (☎ 421289; Pje 20 de Junio 25; tasting AR$5; ⏱ 9:30am-12:30pm & 3-7pm) is a friendly family winery in town that produce sonly 5000 bottles of torrontés and malbec per year with small hand-operated equipment. Nearby, **El Porvenir** (☎ 422007; www.bodegasel-porvenir.com; Córdoba 32) focuses on quality wine production. The tour is free, but tastings cost AR$30, AR$60 or AR$90 depending on which wines you want to try.

Diageo-owned **Bodega El Esteco** (☎ 421283; www.elesteco.com.ar; tours AR$20; ⏱ tours 10am, 11am, noon, 2:30pm, 3:30pm, 4.30pm & 5:30pm Mon-Fri, 10am, 11am & noon Sat), on the northern edge of town, is a smart and attractive winery producing some of the region's best wines and offering upmarket accommodations.

Three kilometers south of town, **Bodega Etchart** (☎ 421310; www.pernodricard.com.ar; RN 40; ⏱ 9am-noon & 1-5pm Mon-Sat) offers a cheerful free tour including tasting. It produces some six million bottles of quality torrontés, cabernet and malbec per year.

Five kilometers west of town along the road to Río Colorado (it's signposted 'Mounier'), small, organic and friendly **Bodega de las Nubes** (☎ 422129; ⏱ 9:30am-5:30pm Mon-Sat) has a fabulous position at the foot of the jagged hills. The short tour and tasting nominally costs AR$15, but if you buy wine it's not charged. It also does tasty picadas here. Ring ahead to check it is open and if you want to eat. Grape-picking day in March is lots of fun, with volunteers welcomed.

Tours

The standard minibus tour of the Quebrada leaves in the afternoon, when the colors are more vivid, and costs around AR$60. Three-to four-hour treks in the Quebrada (AR$120) and Río Colorado (AR$80) are also popular. Day-long trips to Cachi (AR$225) are tiring, while Quilmes (AR$75) can be visited more cheaply in a taxi if you're two or more. Horseback rides range from a couple of hours (AR$125) to all day (AR$250). Many places hire out bikes (around AR$35 for a full day).

The main tour operators have their offices on the plaza. Readers aren't usually blown away by the service offered – check with other travelers before choosing – but the Quebrada scenery speaks for itself.

Festivals & Events

La Serenata de Cafayate, in late February, is a very worthwhile three-day *folklore* festival. The **Fiesta de la Virgen del Rosario**, on October 4, is the town fiesta and gets lively.

Sleeping

Cafayate has numerous places to stay, with new boutique hotels popping up like mushrooms and simple *hospedajes* on every street.

BUDGET

Camping Lorohuasi (☎ 422292; campsites per person/tent AR$5/6; ☒) This municipal campground 10 minutes' walk from the center along Av General Güemes can get dusty when the wind blows. Facilities are OK, and there's a small grocery store.

Ñusta Hospedaje (☎ 421852; nusta.hospedaje@arnet.com.ar; Catamarca 15; r per person AR$35; ☞) Excellent value is to be had at this warm-hearted family guesthouse with a variety of simple, comfortable rooms and a generous spirit. There's an annex with more rooms a block further down the road.

Hostel El Balcón (☎ 421739; www.elbalconhostel.com.ar; 20 de Febrero 110; dm AR$30-40, d/tw AR$180/200; ☒) Travelers either love or hate this place. The rooftop bar's a great spot, but the spacious dorms suffer from noise at weekends and there's a mercenary feel to the setup – staff sell its tours hard.

Rusty-K Hostal (☎ 422031; rustykhostal@gmail.com; Rivadavia 281; dm AR$40, d with/without bathroom AR$120/100; ☒ ☞) The peace of the vine-filled patio garden here is broken only by the occasional pock-pock of table tennis. Cute doubles and an excellent attitude make this Cafayate's budget gem. Book ahead, though: there are only five dorm beds.

Hostel Ruta 40 (☎ 421689; www.hostel-ruta40.com; Av General Güemes 178; dm/d AR$40/140; ☒ ☞) Dorms are darkish and can be a little stuffy, but facilities and atmosphere are good at this central hostel. Private rooms with bathroom are a decent deal, breakfast is included and there's a kitchen. HI discount applies.

El Portal de las Viñas (☎ 421098; www.portalvinas.com.ar; Nuestra Señora del Rosario 155; d AR$140; ☒) An upgrade has taken this out of the ultrabudget category, but it's still a charming spot. Highlights are the courteous and genuine personal welcome from the interesting owner, the central location and general tranquility. The rooms, with terracotta-tiled floors and spacious bathrooms, are set around a vine-shaded courtyard.

Hotel Tinkunaku (☎ 421148; Diego de Almagro 12; s/d AR$90/169; ☒ ☞ ☒) This well-priced if not rather stylish option has clean, modern rooms in a quiet, central location. The place has a relaxed family atmosphere and a huge pool out back.

MIDRANGE & TOP END

Hostal del Valle (☎ 421039; www.welcomeargentina.com/hostaldelvalle; San Martín 243; s/d AR$124/186; ☒ ☞) This enticing place offers myriad flowering pot plants, and pretty rooms with large, inviting beds and excellent bathrooms. There are a couple of smaller, darker rooms that are a little cheaper but still worthwhile. Breakfast is served in a rooftop conservatory with privileged views.

Villa Vicuña (☎ 422145; www.villavicuna.com.ar; Belgrano 76; s/d AR$200/300; ☒ ☒ ☞) Peacefully set around twin patios, this offers an intimate retreat with beautiful, spotless rooms with big beds and reproduction antique furniture. Service and breakfast are good, and you can lose hours deciphering the offbeat mural sculpture in the courtyard.

Portal del Santo (☎ 422400; www.portaldelsanto.com.ar; Chavarría 250; s/d AR$220/280; ☒ ☞) Cool white elegance is the stock in trade of this hospitable hotel that resembles a colonial palace with its arched arcades. The lower rooms open onto the front porch and also the inviting back garden and pool area; the rooms on the top floor (double/suite AR$320/500) have mountain views and a little more space. The suites sleep four.

ourpick Killa (☎ 422254; www.killacafayate.com.ar; Colón 47; s/d/ste AR$303/355/396; ✗ 🖥 📶 🐾) Classy, comfortable and well run, this handsome and recommendable hotel has colonial style given warmth by its creative use of natural wood, stone and local *artesanía*. The gorgeous rooms – not a TV in sight – have great bathrooms, and the upstairs suites – worth the small extra investment – have cracking views and private balcony spaces. There's a pretty pool area and impeccable hospitality.

Eating

Heladería Miranda (Av General Güeme; ice cream from AR$4; ⏱ 10am-10pm) A frequent dilemma in Argentina is whether to go for a rich red cabernet or a dry white torrontés, but it doesn't usually occur in ice-cream parlors. It does here: the Miranda's wine ice creams are Cafayate's pride and joy.

Casa de las Empanadas (☎ 454111; Mitre 24; dishes AR$2-24; ⏱ lunch & dinner) No-frills and pretty tasty local dishes are the reason to come to this friendly spot off the plaza. There are empanadas beyond the usual chicken or meat range, as well as *humitas*, *locro* and *tamales*.

El Rancho (☎ 421256; www.elranchocafayate.com.ar; V Toscano 4; mains AR$13-25; ⏱ lunch & dinner) A cut above the string of hit-and-miss places around the plaza, this has a short, simple menu, including *locro* and some good chicken dishes. It's owned by a bodega, so competition wines are overpriced. It appeals on winter nights, with a crackling fire, and the nights when a blind guitarist plays unobtrusive *folklórica*.

La de Martín (☎ 03868-15-455836; Mitre 25; mains AR$15-30; ⏱ lunch & dinner) Goat stew, local dishes and the odd llama special sit alongside reliable *parrillada* at this not-too-touristy place, with helpful waiters and fair prices.

Colorado (☎ 421280; Belgrano 26; mains AR$24-42; ⏱ lunch & dinner) Microbrewed beers, Mexican dishes, spinach and blue cheese salad, and a Thai red curry are among the things that make this welcoming bar-restaurant a break from the norm in these parts.

El Terruño (☎ 422460; Av General Güemes 30; mains AR$30-45; ⏱ lunch & dinner) Plaza-side seating and polite service are backed up by the food at this restaurant, which curiously has two menus, one of which is less traditional, with dishes like salmon and avocado salad, and boned lamb fillets.

Drinking

Chato's Wine Bar (Nuestra Señora del Rosario 132; ⏱ 7pm-midnight) Run by a cordial English-speaking boss, this unpretentious place is Cafayate's only true wine bar and a great place to try fairly priced local drops by the glass and have a chat.

Shopping

There are numerous *artesanía* shops on and around the central plaza. The **Mercado Artesanal** (Av General Güemes; ⏱ 9am-10pm) cooperative features many locals' work. For fine silver, check out the workshop of **Jorge Barraco** (☎ 421244; Colón 157).

Getting There & Away

El Indio (Belgrano s/n) has three to four buses daily to Salta (AR$35, four hours). There are also three to four daily services to San Carlos (AR$5, 40 minutes), and a bus to Angastaco (AR$14, two hours) leaving at 11am Monday through Friday and 6.30pm on Sunday (no Saturday service). **Aconquija** (cnr Av General Güemes & Alvarado) leaves three to four times daily for Tucumán (AR$44, five to 6½ hours) via Amaicha del Valle and Tafí del Valle (AR$24.50, four hours); three buses go to Santa María (AR$13, two hours).

Getting Around

Taxis congregate around the plaza and can be useful for reaching out-of-town bodegas. If there's none around, call ☎ 422128.

QUEBRADA DE CAFAYATE

North of Cafayate, the Salta road heads through the barren and spectacular Quebrada de Cafayate, a wild landscape of richly colored sandstone and unearthly rock formations. Carved out by the Río de las Conchas, the canyon's twisted sedimentary strata exhibit a stunning array of tones, from rich red ochre to ethereal green. While you get a visual feast from the road itself – it's one of the country's more memorable drives or rides – it's worth taking the time to explore parts of the canyon. The best time to appreciate the canyon is in the late afternoon, when the low sun brings out the most vivid colors.

A short way north of Cafayate, Los Médanos is an extensive dune field that gives way to the canyon proper, where a series of distinctive landforms are named and signposted from the road. Some, such as El Sapo (the

THE ANDEAN NORTHWEST

Toad) are fairly underwhelming, but around the Km 49 mark, the adjacent Garganta del Diablo (Devil's Throat) and Anfiteatro (Amphitheatre) are much more impressive. Gashes in the rock wall let you enter and appreciate the tortured stone, whose clearly visible layers have been twisted by tectonic upheavals into extraordinary configurations.

These landmarks are heavily visited, and you may be followed by locals hoping for some pesos for a bit of 'guiding.' *Artesanía* sellers and musicians hover around these landmarks, but there's no reliable place to buy food or water.

Getting There & Away

There are several ways to see and explore the canyon. Tours from Salta are brief and regimented; it's much better to take a tour from closer Cafayate (p278). Renting a car is possible in Salta but not Cafayate,where bikes are easily hired instead; you could also combine the bus, hitchhiking and walking.

Here's the lowdown for those without a private vehicle: disembark from any El Indio bus (with your rental bike or by foot), tour around for a while and then flag another bus later on. Be aware of the schedules between Salta and Cafayate, and carry food and plenty of water in this hot, dry environment. A good place to start your exploration is the Garganta del Diablo; several other attractions are within easy walking distance of here.

TUCUMÁN & AROUND

Though it's the country's second-smallest province, Tucumán has played a significant role in Argentina's story. It was here that independence was first declared, and the massive sugar industry is of great economic importance. While this monoculture has enabled the province to develop secondary industry, it has also created tremendous inequities in wealth and land distribution, as well as ecological problems.

The city of Tucumán is full of heat and energy, in complete contrast to the lung-cleansing air of Tafí del Valle, up in the hills to the west. Beyond, Argentina's most important pre-Columbian site is Quilmes, on the Cafayate road. South of Tucumán, Santiago del Estero province is a backwater with an enjoyably sleepy feel.

TUCUMÁN

☎ 0381 / pop 738,479 / elev 420m

With nigh on all three-quarters of a million souls in its greater urban area, Tucumán, the cradle of Argentine independence, is the nation's fifth-largest city and feels like it, with a metropolitan bustle that can come as quite a shock after the more genteel provincial capitals elsewhere in the northwest. You may not like it at first, but don't be put off. This isn't the usual patter: Tucumán really rewards time spent getting to know it. You may find you prefer it at night, when the fumes and heat of the day have lulled, and the cafes and bars come to life.

Tucumán (San Miguel de Tucumán is its full name) is baking hot, energetic and brash, with a blue-collar feel and a down-to-earth quality. It also has a lively cultural scene, and its stylish cafe-bars, great bookstores, art exhibitions and traditional *peñas* make its serene neighbors seem a bit provincial. Less advanced is the courtship behavior of the average *tucumano* (inhabitant of Tucumán) – women can expect higher-than-usual numbers of *piropos* (flirtatious remarks) here.

History

Founded in 1565, Tucumán only distinguished itself from the rest of the region in the culmination of the early-19th-century ferment, when it hosted the congress that declared Argentine independence in 1816. Dominated by Unitarist merchants, lawyers, soldiers and clergy, the congress accomplished little else; despite a virtual boycott by Federalist factions, it failed to agree on a constitution that would have institutionalized a constitutional monarchy in hopes of attracting European support.

Unlike other colonial cities of the northwest, Tucumán successfully reoriented its economy after independence. Modern Tucumán dates from the late 19th century and owes its importance to location; at the southern end of the frost-free zone of sugarcane production, it was close enough to Buenos Aires to take advantage of the capital's growing market. By 1874 the railway reached the city, permitting easy transportation of sugar, and local and British capital contributed to the industry's growth. Economic crises in the 1960s and the early years of the 21st century hit Tucumán hard, but sugarcane's growing use as a fuel source means there's plenty of optimism about the future.

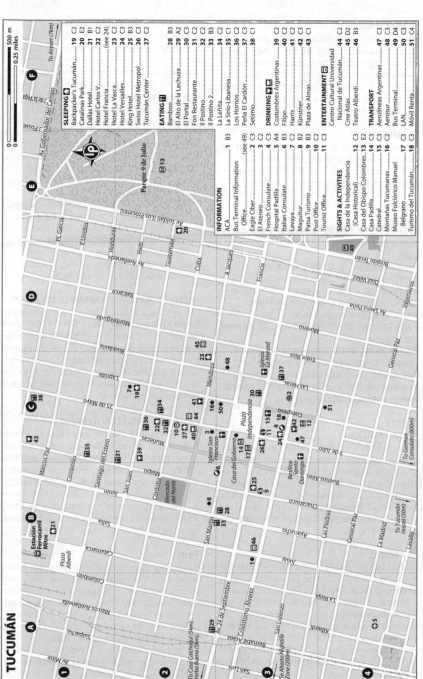

TUCUMÁN

INFORMATION
ACA.......................................1 B3
Bus Terminal Information
  Office..............................(see 49)
Eagle Ciber............................2 C3
El Ateneo..............................3 C2
French Consulate.......................4 C1
Hospital Padilla.......................5 A4
Italian Consulate......................6 C2
Lavaya.................................7 C2
Maguitur...............................8 B3
Patsa Turismo..........................9 B3
Post Office...........................10 C3
Tourist Office........................11 C3

SIGHTS & ACTIVITIES
Casa de la Independencia
  (Casa Histórica)....................12 C3
Casa del Obispo Colombres.13 E2
Casa Padilla..........................14 C3
Catedral..............................15 C3
Montañas Tucumanas...16 C3
Museo Folclórico Manuel
  Belgrano............................17 C3
Turismo del Tucumán...18 C3

SLEEPING
Backpacker's Tucumán........19 C2
Catalinas Park........................20 E2
Dallas Hotel..........................21 B1
Hotel Carlos V........................22 C2
Hotel Francia.....................(see 24)
Hotel La Vasca........................23 C2
Hotel Versailles......................24 C3
King Hotel............................25 B3
Swiss Hotel Metropol..........26 C3
Tucumán Center.......................27 C2

EATING
Bamboo................................28 B3
El Alto de la Lechuza...........29 A2
El Portal.............................30 C3
Fon Restaurante.......................31 C2
Il Postino............................32 B3
Il Postino 2..........................33 B3
La Leñita.............................34 C3
La Sirio-Libanesa....................35 C1
Los Hornos............................36 C3
Peña El Cardón........................37 C3
Setimio...............................38 C1

DRINKING
Costumbres Argentinas........39 C2
Filipo................................40 C3
Harris................................41 C2
Künstner..............................42 C3
Plaza de Almas........................43 C1

ENTERTAINMENT
Centro Cultural Universidad
  Nacional de Tucumán............44 C2
Cine Atlas............................45 D2
Teatro Alberdi........................46 B3

TRANSPORT
Aerolíneas Argentinas.........47 C3
Aerosur...............................48 C3
Bus Terminal..........................49 D4
LAN...................................50 C3
Móvil Renta...........................51 C4

THE ANDEAN NORTHWEST

Orientation

Tucumán's geographical focus is the rectangular Plaza Independencia, site of major public buildings such as the cathedral and Casa de Gobierno, which are spectacularly floodlit at night. Street names change north and south of Av 24 de Septiembre, west of Av Alem/Mitre and east of Av Avellaneda/Av Sáenz Peña.

Information

Tucumán is bristling with internet cafes and call centers. Many downtown banks have ATMs.

ACA (Automóvil Club Argentino; ☎ 431-1522; Crisóstomo Álvarez 901) Argentina's auto club; good source for provincial road maps.

Eagle Ciber (Crisóstomo Álvarez 381; per hr AR$2) Cybercafe.

El Ateneo (25 de Mayo 182) Excellent bookshop. Also maps, a small selection of airport novels in English, and a cafe.

Hospital Padilla (☎ 429-0969; Alberdi 550)

Lavaya (☎ 431-2366; Laprida 460) Laundry.

Maguitur (☎ 431-0032; San Martín 765; ◷ 8:30am-2pm & 4-6:30pm Mon-Fri, 10am-noon Sat) Cashes traveler's checks and changes money.

Patsa Turismo (☎ 421-6806; Chacabuco 38) The Amex representative.

Tourist office (☎ 430-3644; www.tucumanturismo .gov.ar; 24 de Septiembre 484; ◷ 8am-10pm Mon-Fri, 9am-9pm Sat & Sun) On the plaza, staff are helpful and knowledgeable. There's another office at the bus terminal, opposite platform 12, open the same hours.

Sights

CASA PADILLA

Alongside the Casa de Gobierno, this partly restored mid-19th-century house first belonged to provincial governor José Frías (1792–1874), then to his mayor son-in-law Ángel Padilla. A display of European art, Chinese porcelain and period furniture make up the collection housed by the **museum** (25 de Mayo 36; admission free; ◷ 9am-1pm Tue-Sun).

CATEDRAL

Tucumán's neoclassical **cathedral** (◷ 8:30am-1pm & 4:30-10pm) is a handsome presence on Plaza Independencia, and has a Doric facade with a pediment depicting the Exodus. Curiously, Moses is receiving bunches of grapes in the desert; a reference to the fertility of Tucumán's surrounding area. The interior has a petite wooden choir, cheerily alive ceiling paintings, and a canvas of the Annunciation behind the altar.

CASA DE LA INDEPENDENCIA (CASA HISTORICAL)

Unitarist lawyers and clerics (Federalists boycotted the meeting) declared Argentina's independence from Spain on July 9, 1816, in the dazzlingly whitewashed late-colonial **Casa de la Independencia** (☎ 431-0826; Congreso 151; admission AR$5; ◷ 10am-6pm). Portraits of the signatories line the walls of the room where the declaration was signed, the only actual original part of the structure – the rest has been rebuilt. There's plenty of information in Spanish on the lead-up to these seismic events, but you can also get a guided tour (free) in English.

There's a sound-and-light show nightly except Thursday at around 8:30pm; entry is AR$10/5 per adult/child. The ticket office opens 15 minutes before the show.

Next to the building is an open area with various *artesanía* stalls and stands selling traditional foods like *locro* and *humitas*.

MUSEO FOLCLÓRICO MANUEL BELGRANO

Occupying a colonial house, pleasant **Museo Folclórico Manuel Belgrano** (☎ 421-8250; Av 24 de Septiembre 565; admission free; ◷ 9am-1pm & 3-8pm Tue-Sun) features a good collection of traditional gaucho gear, indigenous musical instruments (check out the *charangos* made from an armadillo shell) and weavings, as well as some indigenous pottery.

CASA DEL OBISPO COLOMBRES

In the center of Parque 9 de Julio (formerly Bishop Colombres' El Bajo plantation), handsome 18th-century **Casa del Obispo Colombres** (☎ 452-2332; admission free; ◷ 8am-1pm & 3-8pm) is a museum dedicated to the sugar industry, which the active cleric (an important figure in the independence movement) effectively set up. The information panels are translated into English.

Tours

Tucumán province is hitching its horse firmly to the tourism wagon, and any number of tour operators offer excursions from sedate city strolls to canoeing, challenging hikes and paragliding; the city has hosted the Paragliding World Cup. The tourist office can supply a fuller list. One worthwhile hikes is the beautiful, accessible, four-day hike from Tucumán to Tafí del Valle.

Some companies offering tours:

Canoas y Aventuras (☎ 485-0814; canoasyaventuras@ yahoo.com.ar) Offers canoeing excursions and a long day-hike through subtropical forest to some pretty waterfalls (AR$90 per person).

Montañas Tucumanas (☎ 0381-15-609-3336; www .montanastucumanas.com; Laprida 196) A cordial and professional setup, this offers hiking, climbing, canyoning, rappelling and more, both in locations near Tucumán and further afield.

Tucumán Parapente (☎ 0381-15-444-7508; www .tucumanparapente.com.ar) Excellent tandem paragliding flights over the Yungas forests, as well as instruction.

Turismo del Tucumán (☎ 422-7636; tucumantur@ sinectis.com.ar; Crisóstomo Álvarez 435) Guided trips to spots of interest around the province, including Tafí del Valle and Quilmes (AR$210), or a circuit in Las Yungas (AR$100).

Walter 'Paco' Castro (pacoflight@hotmail.com) Reader-recommended hang-gliding instructor who offers tandem flights (AR$250 per person).

Festivals & Events

Celebrations of the **Día de la Independencia** (Argentina's Independence Day) on July 9 are vigorous in Tucumán, the cradle of the country's independence. *Tucumanos* also celebrate the **Batalla de Tucumán** (Battle of Tucumán) on September 24.

Sleeping

Most of Tucumán's hotels are overpriced, but you can negotiate substantial discounts, particularly if paying cash.

BUDGET

Tucumán Hostel (☎ 420-1584; www.tucumanhostel.com .ar; Buenos Aires 669; dm AR$35, d with/without bathroom AR$95/85; 🖳 🛜 🐛) It's easy to like this breezy hostel seven blocks south of the plaza; with solid dorm beds and enthusiastic staff, it makes a fine base. The bathrooms are very clean, as is the kitchen, and there's also a bar. If lounging around the pool at the back, be careful not to get brained by falling fruit from the avocado tree.

Backpacker's Tucumán (☎ 430-2716; www.back packerstucuman.com; Laprida 456; dm AR$45, s with/without bathroom AR$100/110, d with/without bathroom AR$120/130; 🖳) This reliable hostel is a short walk away from the lively 25 de Mayo eating scene, and has a relaxed, airy charm allied to plenty of facilities. The dorms are spacious, with fans and high ceilings, the rooms tight but comfortable and the cool patio spaces make attractive common areas. HI discount applies.

Casa Calchaquí (☎ 425-6974; www.casacalchaqui .com; Lola Mora 92, Yerba Buena; dm/s/d AR$45/100/140; 🐛 🖳 🛜 🐛) Six kilometers west of the center in the upmarket barrio of Yerba Buena, this is a welcome retreat from the sweaty city. Hammocks, a wide green lawn, bar service and a minipool make it a top spot to relax. Add to that comfortable bunks and doubles, a kitchen and *parrilla*, and friendly multilingual hosts. Yerba Buena also has many good restaurants and nightlife choices. Grab a taxi (AR$15) or bus 102 or 118 from opposite the bus terminal. Casa Calchaquí also hires out bikes.

Hotel La Vasca (☎ 421-1828; www.redcarlosv.com .ar; Mendoza 289; s with/without bathroom AR$76/63, d with/without bathroom AR$100/83; 🐛 🛜) Everyone deserves to have 3m-high doors to their room, and you can in this central budget choice. Rooms are around two courtyards – go for an upstairs room at the back if you can – and decorated with original oils by the owner. Staff are welcoming.

King Hotel (☎ 431-0211; Chacabuco 18; s/d AR$85/100; 🐛) Traveling salespeople keep returning to this hotel because it's comfortable, clean and in the heart of things. Prices are very fair by Tucumán standards. It often fills up by midafternoon, so you might want to book ahead.

MIDRANGE & TOP END

Dallas Hotel (☎ 421-8500; www.dallashotel.com.ar; Corrientes 985; s/d AR$180/235; 🐛 🛜) Run with a smile, this likable place has padded doors that give way softly to reveal sizable rooms with decent beds. There are plenty of popular bar-restaurants nearby; make sure you also check out the beautiful train station around the corner. It's 10% off if you pay cash.

Hotel Francia (☎ 431-0781; www.franciahotel.com; Cristósomo Álvarez 467; s/d AR$190/239; 🐛 🖳 🛜) A block from the plaza, this features decent modern-ish rooms with French prints on the walls and good bathrooms. It will usually lower the above rate for walk-ins.

Hotel Versailles (☎ 422-9760; www.hotelversaill estuc.com.ar; Crisóstomo Álvarez 481; s/d AR$209/256; 🐛) There is indeed a certain French elegance to this understated, old-fashioned hotel. The rooms are compact and look a little tired for the price, but the public areas have a worn stately appeal. It often will heavily discount prices if you ask; it's not worth the cash otherwise.

Hotel Carlos V (☎ 431-1666; www.redcarlosv.com; 25 de Mayo 330; s/d AR$215/265; 🍴 💻 🛜) There's something rather charming about the rooms here – it must be the parchment-colored walls and bright bedspreads, for they certainly aren't huge. Offering a fine central location and fairly classic ambience, as well as a busy cafe-restaurant, this is a decent Tucumán address.

Swiss Hotel Metropol (☎ 431-1180; www.swisshotelmetropol.com.ar; 24 de Septiembre 524; s/d AR$346/438; 🍴 💻 🛜 🏊) The modern rooms and spacious bathrooms on offer here are perhaps slightly offset by the tiny balconies (standing room only). The fantastic rooftop pool makes up for a lot though, as does the very central location.

Tucumán Center (☎ 452-5555; www.tucumancenterhotel.com.ar; 25 de Mayo 230; s/d AR$396/449, ste for 4 AR$1040; 🍴 💻 🛜 🏊) It's hard to fault this upmarket, business-class hotel bang in the center of town. Service and facilities – including a small gym and outdoor pool – are first-rate, and the huge beds are mighty comfortable. Suites come with space to spare and a bathtub with bubbles. It offers big discounts in summer; check the website for specials.

Catalinas Park (☎ 450-2250; www.catalinaspark.com; Av Soldati 380; s/d standard AR$420/480, s/d superior AR$492/548; 🍴 💻 🛜 🏊) Several Tucumán hotels charge this sort of price for what is barely three-star comfort. Not so at this spot by the large Parque 9 de Julio. Offering commodious (if not huge) rooms with great views, and a range of comforts that include a pleasant outdoor pool, babysitting service, sauna and anticipatory staff, this is as it should be. There's even a chopper should you fancy an aerial excursion.

Eating

Tucumán is very famous for its excellent eggy empanadas, which you'll find everywhere. Calle 25 de Mayo is eat street, studded with modern cafe-bars offering a variety of traditional and international cuisines. If you want to blend in here, you'd better have an ice cream in your hand at all times; there are several ice-creameries around the plaza that can sort you out.

`our pick` **El Portal** (☎ 422-6024; Av 24 de Septiembre 351; dishes AR$2.50-26; 🕙 10am-11pm) Half a block east of Plaza Independencia, this rustic indoor/outdoor eatery has a tiny but perfectly formed menu, based around empanadas, *locro* and the like. Delicious and authentic.

Il Postino (☎ 421-0440; cnr 25 de Mayo & Córdoba; pizza & pasta AR$10-25; 🕙 7am-2am) Pizza and pasta are served with panache in this atmospheric brick warehouse eatery. It's popular with all, and you often have to wait for a table. It's worth it: the standard (of the pizza especially) is sky-high. It also serves various tapas-sized portions. There's another branch nearby in Junín 86.

Peña El Cardón (☎ 497-8235; Las Heras 50; dishes AR$10-24; 🕙 lunch Tue-Sun, dinner Tue-Sat) This historical and traditional *peña* gives a good idea of what these places were like before they started putting on touristy shows. There are regular cultural events, a pretty patio and delicious empanadas. Live *folklore* music on Fridays and Saturdays starts about 10pm, goes very late and gets rowdy.

El Alto de la Lechuza (☎ 0381-15-477-9527; Av 24 de Septiembre 1199; dishes AR$12-26; 🕙 8pm-late Thu-Sat) Founded in 1939 and billing itself as Argentina's oldest *peña*, this place offers standard *parrilla* and pasta fare, plus a few regional specialties. The real reason to come here, though, is the music: the venue has hosted many Argentine luminaries.

Fon Restaurante (☎ 421-8715; Maipú 435; all-you-can-eat AR$15; 🕙 lunch Mon-Sat) The lunchtime buffet at this vegetarian restaurant has mostly Chinese dishes, with a few local favorites such as *ensalada rusa* (Russian salad) and empanadas thrown in. It's not gourmet, but it does the job.

La Sirio-Libanesa (Maipú 575; set menus AR$19-28; 🕙 lunch daily, dinner Mon-Sat) The restaurant at the Syrian-Lebanese society offers tasty Levantine cuisine that makes a welcome change of scene. Mashed eggplant, tasty *kipe naye* (marinated raw mincemeat) and tabouleh salad all feature; the set lunch is AR$19 and there are several other set menus, as well as à la carte.

La Leñita (☎ 422-9196; 25 de Mayo 377; mains AR$28-39; 🕙 lunch & dinner) One of the best *parrilla* restaurants around in this part of the world, this wins few points for interior design (who thought the sports bar look was a good idea?), but stands out for service and the sheer quality of the meat. Try *picanha* (rump steak) or the delicious *mollejitas* (sweetbreads). Sit strategically to avoid the air-con's arctic wind.

Setimio (☎ 431-2792; Santa Fe 512; dishes AR$28-45; 🕙 7:30pm-1:30am Mon-Sat) Wall-to-wall wine bottles decorate this smart wine shop and restaurant, whose short menu features a pair of posh salads, chicken stirfry, crusted salmon and other toothsome delights. Several wines are available by the glass, and you can pick any of the several hundred bottles from the shelves for a AR$6 corkage fee.

Also recommended:

Bamboo (☎ 497-8555; Junín 81; smoothies AR$6; ☺ 7am-8pm Mon-Sat) Cheery in apple green, this place does tasty breakfasts, sandwiches, iced fruit smoothies and salads to eat in or takeout – there's a little patio space, too.

Los Hornos (☎ 422-6066; San Juan 526; mains AR$13-26; ☺ lunch & dinner) Round the corner from the main eating drag, this does family-friendly *minutas* (quick meals), as well as tasty empanadas and *parrilla* choices at a good price.

Drinking & Entertainment

From Thursday to Saturday nights, most of the action is in the Abasto region, on Calle Lillo. Follow San Lorenzo west from the town center, and you'll hit the middle of the zone three blocks west of our map. There are dozens of bars and nightclubs to choose from – take your pick. Other popular *boliches* can be found in Yerba Buena, 6km west of the town center.

Künstner (☎ 497-5597; Crisóstomo Álvarez 456; ☺ lunch & 8pm-late) A blessed relief it is to step off this noisy, fume-filled street and into the gentle aromas of malt and hops. Four tasty beers are brewed in this convivial spot, which also serves fine cheap food such as *milanesas*, pasta and pizza.

Harris (cnr Laprida & Mendoza; ☺ 8am-late) On a busy corner, this is a popular hangout for smartly-dressed *tucumanos*. The interior is padded seats and elegant dark wood; outside, the tables and chairs are at the very top of the Coca-Cola range. Excellent mixed drinks and good coffee; the food is also more than passable.

Filipo (☎ 421-9687; Mendoza 501; licuados AR$8; ☺ 7am-1am) Glasses gleaming on the gantry, outdoor tables and bow-tied waiters make this a great cafe. The espresso is superlative, and the apple *licuados* (blended fruit drinks) deserve a prize.

Plaza de Almas (Maipú 791; mains AR$11-22; ☺ 8pm-late) This intimate and engaging multilevel place is popular with bohemian young *tucumanos* and is one of the best of Tucumán's many combination cafe-bar-restaurant-cultural centers. The short but interesting menu offers a range of kebabs and salads, among other choices.

Costumbres Argentinas (☎ 0381-15-643-9576; San Juan 666; ☺ 9:30pm-4am Wed-Sun) Though the address seems like a contradiction in terms, this unusual, popular and welcoming bar has an arty bohemian vibe and sometimes puts on live music. There's a big two-level beer garden out the back, which is the place to be on summer nights. Simple food is also available.

Centro Cultural Universidad Nacional de Tucumán (☎ 421-6024; 25 de Mayo 265) Art exhibitions, crafts for sale, a cafe, and regular theatrical and musical performances.

Cine Atlas (☎ 422-0825; Monteagudo 250) The last remaining central cinema.

Teatro Alberdi (☎ 422-9118; cnr Jujuy & Cristósomo Álvarez) The principal one of several Tucumán theaters.

Getting There & Away

AIR

Aerolíneas Argentinas (☎ 431-1030; 9 de Julio 110) has three to four daily flights to Buenos Aires' Aeroparque Jorge Newbery (AR$760). **LAN** (☎ 422-0606; Laprida 176) has two daily flights to Buenos Aires (AR$743), **Sol** (www.sol.com.ar) links Tucumán with Rosario, and **Aerosur** (☎ 453-9162; Rivadavia 137) flies three times weekly to Santa Cruz in Bolivia (AR$537).

BUS

Tucumán's **bus terminal** (Brígido Terán 350) is a major project with 60 platforms and plenty of shops and services. The bus **information booth** (☎ 430-6400) is outside, by the supermarket. A handy tourist office is opposite platform 12.

Sample destinations and fares:

Destination	Cost (AR$)	Duration (hr)
Bariloche	374	33
Buenos Aires	180	16
Cafayate	44	6½
Catamarca	32	4
Córdoba	106	7
Jujuy	62	5
La Quiaca	115	11
La Rioja	59	6
Mendoza	165	13
Posadas	200	18
Resistencia	138	12
Río Gallegos	499	40
Salta	55	4½
Salvador Mazza	110	10
San Juan	138	12
Santiago del Estero	23	2
Tafí del Valle	22	2½-3
Termas de Río Hondo	15	1

THE ANDEAN NORTHWEST

TRAIN

Argentina's trains aren't what they used to be, but Tucumán is still connected to Buenos Aires (via Santiago del Estero and Rosario) twice a week from the beautiful **Estación Mitre** (☎ 430-9220; www.ferrocentralsa.com.ar) in the northwest of town. Services frequently take hours longer than advertised, but it's an experience a little like stepping back in time and might appeal to those in no hurry or on a strict budget.

At time of research, trains were leaving Buenos Aires' Retiro station at 10.40am on Monday and Friday, arriving in Tucumán at around noon the next day. From Tucumán, trains left at 6pm on Wednesday (arriving at 7pm Thursday) and 8.50pm on Saturday, arriving at 10pm on Sunday.

The trip costs AR$45/70/130 in *turista* (2nd class)/1st class/Pullman (reclinable seats) or AR$400 for two in a sleeper.

Getting Around

Aeropuerto Benjamín Matienzo (TUC; ☎ 426-4906) is 8km east of downtown. It's tricky to get there by public transport; a *remise* costs around AR$22 from the town center.

For getting around the city, local buses (AR$1.50) clearly mark their major destinations on the front.

There are several car-rental places. A reliable choice is **Móvil Renta** (☎ 431-0550; www.movilrenta.com.ar; San Lorenzo 370).

AROUND TUCUMÁN

Until 1767 the ruins of **San José de Lules**, 20km south of Tucumán, was a Jesuit *reducción* (Indian settlement created by Spanish missionaries) among the region's Lule Indians. After the Jesuits' expulsion, the Dominicans assumed control of the complex, whose present ruins date from the 1880s and once served as a school. The small museum has replicas of colonial documents and a plethora of busts of various Argentine independence heroes. Buses to Lules, a pleasant site for an outing, depart from Tucumán's bus terminal.

The fertile, hilly area northwest of Tucumán is known as **Las Yungas**, and offers plenty of appealing day trips that get you out of the hot, busy city. The tourist offices offer good information on destinations, which include the reservoir of **El Cadillal** (Dique Celestino Gelsi) offering camping, swimming and windsurfing, or the **Parque Sierra de San Javier**, a university-operated reserve offering guided walks, including one to the small but pretty Río Noque waterfall. San Pedro (go to ticket booth No 69) runs regular buses from Tucumán's bus terminal to El Cadillal (AR$5.20, one hour), while San Javier (no ticket booth, leaves from platforms 57 to 58) runs to San Javier (where there are a few places to stay) and the reserve. Tucumán tour operators also run trips out here.

TAFÍ DEL VALLE

☎ 03867 / pop 3300 / elev 2100m

The lovely hilltown of Tafí is where the folk of Tucumán traditionally head to take refuge from the summer heat. The journey from the city is a spectacular one: about 100km northwest of Tucumán, the narrow gorge of the Río de los Sosas – with its dense, verdant subtropical forest on all sides – opens onto a misty valley beneath the snowy peaks of the Sierra del Aconquija. The precipitous mountain road is a spectacular trip; grab a window seat on the bus.

Tafí makes a fine spot to hang out for a few days, with crisp mountain air, many budget accommodations and a laid-back scene. There are also a couple of memorable historic ranches to stay at.

Orientation

Tafí's center is a triangle of three streets. Av Miguel Critto is the main street running east to west. If you turn left out of the bus terminal, you soon join it. Off it, Av Perón is the center of activity, and Belgrano climbs from Perón past the church. Most public services are near the unusual semicircular plaza.

Information

There's a *locutorio* at the bus terminal, one of several places offering phone calls and internet access.

Banco Tucumán (Av Miguel Critto) In the *municipalidad* building. Changes US dollars and has an ATM.

Tourist office (Av Miguel Critto; ☺ 8am-9pm) Tourist information at the junction of the pedestrian street.

Sights & Activities
CAPILLA LA BANDA

This 18th-century **Jesuit chapel** (☎ 421685; Av José Frías Silva; admission AR$2; ☺ 8am-6pm), acquired by the Frías Silva family of Tucumán on the Jesuits' expulsion and then expanded in the 1830s, was restored to its original configuration in the 1970s. Note the escape tunnel in the chapel. A small archaeological collection – consisting mostly of funerary urns, but also religious art of the Cuzco school, ecclesiastical vestments and period furniture that once belonged to the Frías Silvas – is on display in the **museum** next door.

The chapel is a short walk from downtown. Cross the river bridge and follow the road; you'll see it on your left after 750m.

HIKING

Several nearby peaks and destinations make hiking in the mountains around Tafí del Valle an attractive prospect; try 3000m **Cerro El Matadero**, a four- to five-hour climb; 3600m **Cerro Pabellón** (six hours); and 4500m **Cerro El Negrito**, reached from the statue of Cristo Redentor on RN 307 to Acheral. The trails are badly marked, and no trail maps are available; you can hire a guide for about AR$10 an hour. Ask for more information at the tourist office. An easier hike climbs **Cerro Pelado** for views over the town. The path starts on the left as soon as you've crossed the bridge. It takes about 1¼ hours to climb, and less to come down.

HORSEBACK-RIDING

Several people around town hire out horses (look for 'alquilo caballos' or 'cabalgatas') for rides in the valley. These start at about 10 pesos for half an hour. Readers have recommended the setup opposite the bus terminal, which also hires out quad bikes.

Tours

La Cumbre (☎ 421768; www.lacumbretafidelvalle.com; Perón 120) offers various two- to three-hour trips around the valley on 4WD tracks or taking in sights such as the menhir park near El Mollar and a traditional cheese factory (AR$70 to AR$90 per person). It also organizes more rigorous full-day trips and excursions to the Quilmes ruins.

Sleeping

There are many choices, including several budget places charging AR$30 per person for dorm rooms without bathroom. Prices rise about 25% in January, Easter and July when Tafí gets packed. Unheated rooms can get distinctly chilly at any time of year.

Hospedaje Celia (☎ 421170; Belgrano 443; r per person AR$28) Set back from the road 100m uphill

from the church, this place offers bright, white and comfortable enough rooms with private bathroom. There are minor inconveniences – no sockets in the rooms, for example – but the price is right.

Nomade Hostel (☎ 420179; www.nomadehostel.unlugar.com; Los Palenques s/n; dm/d AR$30/80; 🖳) Rustic, comfortable dorms with bathroom surround a courtyard with sierra views and artistic stone pillars and cartwheels. It's very friendly, breakfast is included and there's an HI discount. From the bus terminal, follow Critto past the tourist office and take the first left; the hostel's about 400m up this road.

Hostel la Cumbre (☎ 421768; www.lacumbretafidelvalle.com; Perón 120; dm/d without bathroom AR$40/80) The happy orange and ochre color of the courtyard and views from the roof terrace make this a good choice. The rooms are cramped but clean, and there's a decent kitchen and welcoming staff.

our pick **Estancia Los Cuartos** (☎ 0381-15-587-4230; www.estancialoscuartos.com; Critto s/n; s/d AR$125/189) Oozing character from every pore, this lovely spot with grazing llamas lies between the bus terminal and the town center. Two centuries old, it feels like a museum, with venerable books lining antique shelves, and authentic rooms redolent with the smell of aged wood and woolen blankets. There are rooms in a new annex that offer more comfortable beds but less history, although they remain true to the feel of the place. Traditional cheeses are also made here.

Hotel Tafí (☎ 421007; www.hoteltafiweb.com.ar; Belgrano 177; s/d AR$135/170; 🖳 🛜) Despair not when you see it from the street, for things improve once you get inside, with a ski-lodge feel and helpful staff. The medium-sized rooms have gleaming bathrooms, wood-tile floors, mountain views and tiny TVs. There's a pleasant rocky garden, and the huge fireplace makes the comfortable lounge area the place to be on a chilly night.

Hostería Lunahuana (☎ 421330; www.hosterialunahuana.com.ar; Av Miguel Critto 540; s/d AR$250/330; 🍽 🖳 🛜) This stylish and popular hotel has rooms decorated with flair – some have mezzanines accessed by spiral staircases. The whole place is decked out with interesting and tasteful decorations, and service is professional and friendly.

Las Tacanas (☎ 421821; www.estancialastacanas.com; Perón 372; s/d AR$280/310; 🖳 🛜) Impeccably preserved and decorated, this fabulous historic complex was once a Jesuit *estancia* and is a most memorable place to stay. The adobe buildings, more than three centuries old, house a variety of tasteful, rustic rooms with noble furniture and beamed ceilings. Though it's in the center of town, it feels like you're in a country retreat, and there's a warm welcome from the family that has owned it for generations.

Other options:

Camping Sauzales (☎ 421880; Los Palenques s/n; per tent & per car AR$10) Riverside campsite about 1km west of the plaza.

La Posada (☎ 421841; jjmiaposada@hotmail.com; Av Belgrano s/n; s/d AR$50/100) Small but comfy rooms opposite the church, some with balcony access. Good price, and warmly family run. Don't confuse with nearby Rosada.

Eating & Drinking

Bar El Paraíso (☎ 0381-15-587-5179; Perón 175; light meals AR$10-20; ☽ lunch & dinner) This cozy bar is where locals congregate to dine cheaply and watch football or martial arts films. There is a pleasant terrace overlooking the street.

Don Pepito (☎ 421764; Perón 193; mains AR$11-28; ☽ lunch & dinner) It looks touristy, the level of service varies, and it charges too much for extras, but the meat is truly excellent. Bypass the set *parrillada* (for one/two AR$23/45) and order off the menu. Kidneys, *bife de chorizo* or *chivito* (goat) are all fine choices and are served in generous portions. There's often live entertainment (AR$2 extra).

El Rancho de Félix (☎ 421022; cnr Belgrano & Juan de Perón; mains AR$15-25; ☽ lunch & dinner) This big, warm thatched barn of a place is incredibly popular for lunch. Regional specialties such as *locro* and *humitas* feature heavily on the menu, but *parrilla* and pasta are also on offer. It doesn't open evenings when things are quiet.

Kkechuwa (Perón s/n; ☽ 10am-midnight) Mediocre food options but a nice terrace where you can try the local artisanal beer range.

The bar-restaurant at the bus terminal is an unexpectedly smart place, and locals head down there to socialize even if they've no intention to travel.

Getting There & Away

Tafí's impressive **bus terminal** (☎ 421031; Av Miguel Critto) is 400m east of the town center. Empresa Aconquija has six to nine buses a day to Tucumán (AR$22, three hours). Buses head the other way to Santa María (AR$17,

two hours, four to six daily) and Cafayate (AR$24.50, four hours, three to four daily) via Amaicha del Valle and the Quilmes ruins turnoff.

The road from Tucumán is beautiful, and the road to Santa María, Quilmes and Cafayate is spectacular, crossing the 3050m pass known as Abra del Infiernillo (Little Hell Pass).

Getting Around

Hourly in summer (every three hours in winter), local Aconquija buses do most of the circuit around Cerro El Pelado, in the middle of the valley. One goes on the north side, another on the south side, so it's possible to make a circuit of the valley by walking the link between them.

AROUND TAFÍ DEL VALLE

There are several attractions in the valley around Tafí, including **Parque de los Menhires** (admission AR$5; ☽ 8am-6pm), a collection of more than 100 carved standing stones found in the surrounding area. They were produced by the Tafí culture some 2000 years ago, but they have been somehow stripped of dignity by being removed from their original locations. The site lies 12km south of Tafí, near the village of El Mollar.

Santa María

☎ 03838 / pop 10,800 / elev 1900m

This seductive little town lies on the route between Tafí del Valle and Cafayate, and is a handy base for exploring the ruins at Quilmes. It actually sits within Catamarca province and makes a fine stopover.

The plaza is the center of town, and lies nine blocks north of the bus terminal. A remarkably helpful **tourist office** (☎ 421083; ☽ 7am-11pm Mon-Fri, 8am-10pm Sat & Sun), with heroic opening hours, is located under the trees in the square itself. On one corner of the plaza, the recommended **Museo Arqueológico Eric Boman** (cnr Belgrano & Sarmiento; ☽ 9am-7:30pm Mon-Sat, 10am-1pm Sun) has a worthwhile collection of ceramics and gold and silver grave jewelry from this important archaeological zone. Ask to see the back room, where a whole lot more elaborately decorated funerary urns are stored. Next door is an **artesanía cooperative**, selling woven goods and other handicrafts at more-than-fair prices. On the edge of town, **Cabra Marca** (☽ 8am-5pm Mon-Sat) makes traditional goat's cheese, and is worth visiting for the free guided tour, which includes a chance to meet the horned beasts themselves.

There are many places to stay in town, including the welcoming **Residencial Pérez** (☎ 420257; hotelperez@hotmail.com; San Martín 94; s/d AR$50/80), with spotless rooms set around a viney courtyard behind a cafe near the plaza (no sign), and the somewhat surreal **Caasama** (☎ 421627; www.hotelcaasama.com.ar; cnr 9 de Julio & 25 de Agosto; s/d AR$135/160; ⚇ ⚇) by the bus terminal, which offers comfortable and very unusual accommodations in a colorful provincial government complex that includes a big pool, floodlit tennis court and pumping summertime *boliche*. You'll need to book ahead in summer months.

Eating options on the plaza include **El Colonial del Valle** (☎ 420897; cnr Esquiú & San Martín; meals AR$7-20; ⚇ lunch & dinner), a traditional and attractive *confitería* that serves good coffee and tamales, a set lunch for AR$13 and fuller meals in the upstairs dining room.

There are several buses daily to Tucumán (AR$32, five hours) via Tafí del Valle (AR$17, 1½ hours) and two daily to Cafayate (AR$13, two hours) via Quilmes. Three buses a week go to Belén (AR$20, five hours) via Hualfin. A *remise* from the terminal to the town center is AR$2.50.

Amaicha del Valle
☎ 03892 / pop 3214
On the main road between Tafí del Valle and Cafayate, this dusty settlement has a notable indigenous feel and, indeed, is famous for its **Pachamama** festival in February, which includes music, dancing and a llama sacrifice to bless the harvest. On the main road, the ornate and unusual **Museo de Pachamama** (☎ 421004; admission AR$10; ⚇ 8am-6pm) is a picturesque if locally controversial collection of indigenous art and artifacts in a sizable indoor-outdoor setting.

Amaicha is useful for getting to the ruins at Quilmes, and has several places to stay, including hostels and campgrounds. Buses between Tafí (AR$14, 1½ hours) and Cafayate (AR$14, 1½ to 2½ hours) stop here.

Quilmes
☎ 03892
Dating from about AD 1000, **Quilmes** (☎ 0381-15-443-6805; Argentines/foreigners AR$5/10; ⚇ 8am-7pm) was a complex indigenous urban settlement that occupied about 30 hectares and housed as many as 5000 people. The Quilmes locals sur-vived contact with the Inca, which occurred from about AD 1480 onward, but could not outlast the siege of the Spaniards, who in 1667 deported the last 2000 inhabitants to Buenos Aires.

Quilmes' thick walls underscore its defensive purpose, but clearly this was more than just a *pucará*. Dense construction sprawls both north and south from the central nucleus, where the outlines of buildings, in a variety of shapes, are obvious even to the casual observer. For revealing views of the extent of the ruins, climb the trails up either flank of the nucleus, which offer vistas of the valley once only glimpsed by the city's defenders. Be prepared for intense sun with no shade, and a large fly population keen on exploring your facial orifices.

In theory, there is a beautiful hotel and *confitería* at the site, as well as a museum. However, at the time of research, the government, local Diaguita community and concession holder were embroiled in a prolonged legal battle, so it was all closed. If it's open, friendly folk selling local ceramics will look after your bags and sell cold drinks.

GETTING THERE & AWAY
Buses from Cafayate to Santa María or Tafí del Valle will drop passengers at the junction, but from there you'll have to walk or hitchhike 5km to the ruins. Easier is to get off the bus at Amaicha del Valle, where jeeps will charge around AR$40 to the ruins, including waiting time. Often a few people are wanting to go, so you may end up paying less. *Remises* charge AR$40 for the half-hour journey from Santa María to Quilmes, more with waiting time. From Cafayate think AR$70.

SANTIAGO DEL ESTERO
☎ 0385 / pop 327,974 / elev 200m
Placid Santiago del Estero enjoys the distinction of the title 'Madre de Ciudades' (Mother of Cities) for this, founded in 1553, was the first Spanish urban settlement in what is now Argentina. Sadly, it boasts no architectural heritage from that period, but still makes a pleasant stopover.

Santiagueños (residents of Santiago del Estero) enjoy a nationwide reputation for valuing rest and relaxation over work. A popular Argentine joke claims that they are world hammer-throwing champions, for they prefer to be as far away from anything work related as possible. Nevertheless, there's plenty of bustle around the town center, particularly in the evenings when life orbits around the pretty plaza and its adjoining pedestrian streets.

Orientation & information

The town center is Plaza Libertad, from which Av Libertad, trending southwest to northeast, bisects the city. Street names change either side of Avs Libertad and Belgrano. The Río Dulce runs to the northeast of the town center. On the other side of the river, connected by bridges, is the twin town of La Banda.

Several downtown banks have ATMs, and internet places are widespread. There's free wi-fi in the plaza.

Municipal tourist office (☎ 422-9800; Plaza Libertad s/n; ✆ 8am-1pm & 5-9pm Mon-Fri, 9am-1pm & 5-9pm Sat) In a kiosk in the plaza itself.

Provincial tourist office (☎ 421-3253; www. turismosantiago.gov.ar; Av Libertad 417; ✆ 7am-2pm & 3-9pm Mon-Fri, 10am-1pm & 5-8pm Sat & Sun) On the plaza. Displays work by local artists.

Sights

The glitzy new development of **Complejo Cultural Santiago del Estero** is due to open on the plaza in late 2010 or early 2011. As well as performance spaces and a bridge linking it to the market, it will house three museums – the city historical museum, an art gallery and the **Museo de Ciencias Antropológicas y Naturales** (☎ 421-1380; Avellaneda 355; admission free; ✆ 8am-8pm Mon-Fri, 10am-7pm Sat). An excellent collection founded by two French archaeologist brothers, it is by far the most interesting thing to see in town. There's a stunning array of indigenous ceramics – mostly sizable, noble funerary urns used for secondary burial (the remains were put in the pot after decomposition) – as well as jewelry, flutes and a large case filled with ornate loom weights. There are also some impressive fossils of glyptodonts, an extinct family of creatures that somewhat resembled large armadillos.

Named for the city's founder and only 10 blocks from Plaza Libertad, the enormous eucalypt- and casuarina-filled **Parque Aguirre** has a small zoo, camping areas, a swimming pool and, on the far side, a new *costanera* (riverside road) along the erratic Río Dulce. It's a fine place for a wander, and has a few *confiterías* and bars that get lively on weekend evenings.

Tours

A competent and professional setup, **Sumaq** (☎ 421-3055; www.sumaqturismo.com.ar; Tucumán 39) is currently the only operator offering tours to the remote Parque Nacional Copo; it also offers good trips to other parts of northwestern Argentina. The office is in the same building as the Hotel Savoy – to get there, go through the restaurant and up a narrow spiral staircase.

Festivals & Events

Santiago's chaotic **Carnaval**, in February, resembles celebrations in the Quebrada de Humahuaca. During the entire last week of July, *santiagueños* celebrate the founding of the city. The centerpiece of this is the **Marcha de los Bombos**, a boisterous procession into the center of the city by some 2000 locals banging all manner of drums.

Sleeping

Campamento las Casuarinas (☎ 421-1390; Parque Aguirre; per person/tent/car AR$1/3/1) This municipal campground is normally a pleasant, shady and secure area, less than 1km from Plaza Libertad, but it can be oppressively crowded and deafeningly noisy on weekends.

Hotel Avenida (☎ 421-5887; avenidahotelsgo@yahoo .com.ar; Pedro León Gallo 405; s/d with bathroom AR$70/110, without bathroom AR$40/60; 🅿) You have to feel for these people: they set up a welcoming little hotel, beautifully decorated with indigenous art and right opposite the bus terminal. Then the city moved the bus terminal to the other side of town. Still, it's only a short walk to the town center.

Palace Hotel (☎ 421-2700; www.palacehotelsgo.com; Tucumán 19; s/d AR$135/200; 🅿 🛜) Just off the plaza on a pedestrian mall, this has slightly stuffy rooms with small bathrooms. If you don't mind street noise, ask for one at the front for a dose of natural light.

Hotel Savoy (☎ 421-1234; www.savoysantiago.com .ar, in Spanish; Tucumán 39; s/d AR$150/210; 🅿 🛜) With a sumptuous entrance and gorgeous spiral staircase, this place looks like a palace at first glance. Sadly, there are no four-poster beds or slaves fanning you with ostrich feathers, but the smallish rooms are comfortable, with decent showers, and the service is attentive. It's also excellently located.

Hotel Carlos V (☎ 424-0303; hotelcarlosv@arnet.com .ar; Independencia 110; s/d standard AR$250/340, d superior AR$450; 🅿 🖥 🛜 🅿) By far the most luxuri-

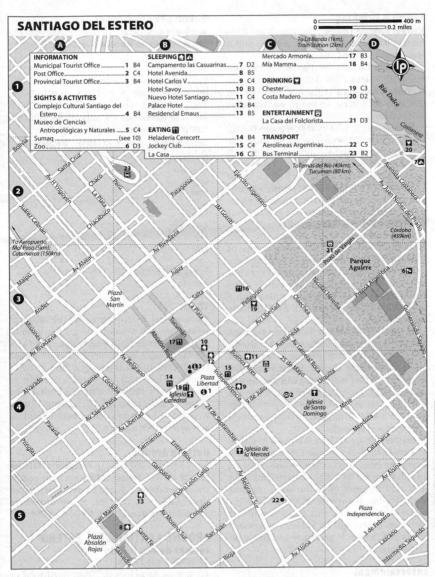

SANTIAGO DEL ESTERO

INFORMATION
Municipal Tourist Office **1** B4
Post Office **2** C4
Provincial Tourist Office................**3** B4

SIGHTS & ACTIVITIES
Complejo Cultural Santiago del
Estero **4** B4
Museo de Ciencias
Antropológicas y Naturales **5** C4
Sumaq ....(see 10)
Zoo **6** D3

SLEEPING
Campamento las Casuarinas **7** D2
Hotel Avenida.............................**8** B5
Hotel Carlos V.............................**9** C4
Hotel Savoy................................**10** B3
Nuevo Hotel Santiago..................**11** C4
Palace Hotel................................**12** B4
Residencial Emaus........................**13** B5

EATING
Heladería Cerecett.......................**14** B4
Jockey Club.................................**15** C4
La Casa.......................................**16** C3

Mercado Armonía.........................**17** B3
Mia Mamma.................................**18** B4

DRINKING
Chester.......................................**19** C3
Costa Madero.............................**20** D2

ENTERTAINMENT
La Casa del Folclorista..................**21** D3

TRANSPORT
Aerolíneas Argentinas...................**22** C5
Bus Terminal...............................**23** B2

ous option in town, this has a great central location and rooms with business-level facilities, large comfortable beds and carpet that could do with a color change. Some rooms have a balcony to really enjoy the city views. Superior rooms are larger and have a table and chairs. There's a gym and sauna as well as the indoor pool.

Also recommended:
Residencial Emaus (☎ 421-5893; Av Moreno Sur 675; s/d AR$55/90) Light and airy rooms with TV and benevolent management.
Nuevo Hotel Santiago (☎ 421-4949; nuevohotel santiago@arnet.com.ar; Buenos Aires 60; s/d AR$120/170; 🔁 🖳 📶) Smart impersonal place with good rooms, a block from the plaza.

THE ANDEAN NORTHWEST

Eating & Drinking

Mercado Armonía (Tucumán) Santiago's art deco market has food stalls, cheap eateries and a few *artesanía* shops upstairs.

Heladería Cerecett (Av Libertad 525; ice cream from AR$3; ☺ 11am-11pm) This *heladería* (ice-creamery) has some of the best ice cream in Santiago del Estero, served in no-nonsense surroundings.

Mía Mamma (☎ 429-9715; 24 de Septiembre 15; mains AR$15-34; ☺ lunch & dinner) Set back from the plaza, this is a discreet and reliable restaurant with well-dressed waiters who see to your every need. There's a fine salad bar with plenty of vegetables (AR$18, or AR$11 with a main) and a wide choice of food that includes enormous *parrilla* options as well as a tasty *arroz a la valenciana* (similar to paella).

Jockey Club (☎ 421-7518; Independencia 68; mains AR$18-34; ☺ lunch & dinner) Strangely empty of pint-sized horse riders, the staid atmosphere of the Jockey Club belongs to another era but belies the quality and welcome variety of its cuisine. Elaborate and tasty creations with a Spanish touch are accompanied by cordially formal service.

La Casa (☎ 421-0433; Av General Roca 475; mains AR$22-45; ☺ dinner daily, lunch Sat & Sun) This attractive conversion of stately house to restaurant also has streetside seating. It has many different interesting wines (you can also buy to takeout) and, as well as fairly-priced *parrilla* offerings, has more imaginative specials like pork on a bed of mustard mash, sundried tomatoes and spinach.

Chester (☎ 422-4972; cnr Pellegrini & Av General Roca; mains AR$15-36; ☺ noon-3:30pm & 7pm-1am) Everyone likes the booths, polished brass and dark wood of a British-style pub, but it doesn't transmit quite the same coziness when the bar is the size of a tractor warehouse. Nevertheless, this place is popular and offers decent-quality but very overpriced meals and drinks. It gets busy and lively on Friday nights.

Entertainment

La Casa del Folclorista (☎ 421-7518; Parque Aguirre, Pozo de Vargas; admission AR$10) To the east of town, this is a big barn of a *peña* that has live folk bands some evenings and cheap food. The music tends to kick off around 11pm.

Costa Madero (Costa del Río Dulce s/n; ☺ 8pm-late) A popular place for draft beer and snacks, with outdoor tables right by the river

Getting There & Away

Aerolíneas Argentinas (☎ 422-4335; 24 de Septiembre 547) flies daily to Buenos Aires (AR$689).

BUS

Santiago's shiny new **bus terminal** (☎ 422-7091; cnr Perú & Chacabuco) is six blocks northwest of Plaza Libertad. There's no convenient local bus into town, but it's only AR$4 in a taxi. Sample destinations and fares:

Destination	Cost (AR$)	Duration (hr)
Buenos Aires	157	13
Catamarca	35	4½
Córdoba	77	6
Jujuy	77	7
La Rioja	99	7
Mendoza	200	17
Resistencia	121	9
Rosario	109	10
Salta	68	6
San Juan	173	14
Termas de Río Hondo	8	1
Tucumán	23	2

TRAIN

Santiago del Estero (actually, the adjacent twin town of La Banda) is on the Buenos Aires–Tucumán train line, which runs twice weekly. Trains run from La Banda **station** (☎ 427-3918) to Tucumán (4½ hours) twice weekly. They also leave twice weekly to Buenos Aires' Retiro station (22 hours). The station is in the heart of La Banda; bus 17 does a circuit of Santiago's center before heading across the river to there.

Getting Around

Bus 15 (AR$1.25) goes to **Aeropuerto Mal Paso** (SDE; ☎ 434-3651; Av Madre de Ciudades), 6km northwest of downtown. A taxi from the city center costs AR$10. A taxi just about anywhere around town should cost AR$4 to AR$6.

AROUND SANTIAGO DEL ESTERO
Termas de Río Hondo
☎ 03858 / pop 27,838

Termas de Río Hondo, 70km northwest of its provincial capital Santiago del Estero, is famous for its thermal waters, and its nearly 200 hotels all have hot mineral baths. While it's very well known as a winter vacation destination for Argentines, it's of little interest unless you plan a spa treatment. The town has two unusual features: it has a triangular plaza (San Martín) as well as one of the country's few public monuments to Juan and Evita Perón. There are numerous shops selling tasty chocolates and *alfajores* (filled sandwich cookies).

The town has many banks, internet places and other tourist facilities. There's a **tourist office** (☎ 421571; www.lastermasderiohondo.com; Alberdi 245; ☒ 7am-9pm) on the main street.

There are numerous hotels and *hospedajes* strung out along the main street; most close from November to April, when those that remain open slash their prices. There's a huge quantity (if not variety) of restaurants.

The **bus terminal** (☎ 421513; Las Heras) is six blocks west of the plaza (where all buses also stop). Buses run regularly to Santiago del Estero (AR$8, one hour) and Tucumán (AR$15, one hour), as well as destinations further afield.

Parque Nacional Copo

Right in the northeast corner of Santiago del Estero province, on the edge of the Chaco, this 1150-sq-km national park was created in 2000. Like the Parque Nacional Chaco it is an important last redoubt of the quebracho colorado tree, of which there are some huge and noble examples in the park. Among the rich birdlife are several species of parrot, and unusual creatures include endangered tatú carretas (a large species of armadillo), ant-eaters and jaguars. When visiting the park, it's a sobering thought that this type of forest covered 80% of the province as recently as 1907. Less than a quarter remains.

Before entering the park, head first to the **ranger office** (☎ 03841-15-669206; drnoa@apn.gov.ar; San Francisco Solano s/n) in Pampa de los Guanacos (where there are simple accommodations). Daily buses run through here from Santiago del Estero and Resistencia. In the park itself, 24km west then north from Pampa, there's a simple camping area but no facilities. See p290 for tours to the park from Santiago del Estero.

CATAMARCA & LA RIOJA

Comparatively little visited by travelers, these provinces are great fun to explore, and are rich in scenery and tradition. Both were home to several important pre-Columbian cultures, mostly maize cultivators who developed unique pottery techniques and styles, and the region has many important archaeological sites.

The town of Catamarca has an immediacy and lively feel, while La Rioja's calm center and moving Tinkunaco celebration are also worth getting to know. Further towards the sierra, the remote poncho-making town of Belén feels miles from anywhere, while Chilecito has a fascinating mining heritage and is the base for several excellent excursions into the lofty mountains.

CATAMARCA

☎ 03833 / pop 171,923 / elev 530m

Vibrant Catamarca has a very different feel to other towns of this size in the region. The local authorities have been energetically promoting the province's natural products, and trade fairs showcasing wines, walnuts, olive oils and jams mean the city's hotels are often full.

San Fernando del Valle de Catamarca, to give the city its full name, has a lovely central plaza, and noble buildings dot the streets. To the west of town, the huge eucalypts of Parque Navarro scent the air and are backed by the spectacular sierra beyond.

Orientation

Nearly everything is in walking distance in the city center, an area 12 blocks square circumscribed by four wide avenues: Belgrano to the north, Alem to the east, Güemes to the south and Virgen del Valle to the west. The focus of downtown is the beautiful Plaza 25 de Mayo.

There are numerous internet and phone places around the central streets.

BBVA (Rivadavia 520) Cashes traveler's checks and has an ATM.

Municipal tourist office (☎ 437413; turismocatama rca@cedeconet.com.ar; Av República 446; ☒ 8am-9pm) Helpful place on the plaza. There's a desk in the bus terminal as well.

Provincial tourist office (☎ 437791; www.turismo catamarca.gov.ar; Av República 446; ☒ 7am-9pm Mon-Fri, 8:30am-9pm Sat-Sun) Near the plaza. Professional staff with excellent information on the whole province.

Sights

Dating from 1859, Catamarca's **Catedral Basílica de Nuestra Señora del Valle** (☒ 7am-9pm) shelters the Virgen del Valle, who is the patron of Catamarca and one of northern Argentina's most venerated images since the 17th century. The atmospheric cathedral also contains an elaborately carved altar to St Joseph, an ornate baroque pulpit and an exhibition of paintings of the Virgin. The cathedral overlooks Plaza 25 de Mayo, a truly beautiful square filled with robust jacaranda, araucaria, citrus and palm trees.

The fine **Museo Arqueológico Adán Quiroga** (☎ 437413; Sarmiento 450; admission AR$4; ☑ 7am-12:30pm & 3-8pm Mon-Fri, 9am-8pm Sat & Sun) is reason enough to come to Catamarca if you have an interest in Argentine indigenous culture. A superb collection of pre-Columbian ceramics from several different cultures and eras is on display. Some – in particular the black Aguada ceramics with their incised, stylized animal decoration – is of truly remarkable quality. A couple of dehydrated mummies found at 5000m are also present, as well as a spooky shrunken head from the Amazon, and trays used to snort lines of *rape* (finely ground tobacco). There's also a colonial and religious section.

Tours

Yokavil Turismo (☎ 430066; www.yokavilturismo.com .ar; Rivadavia 916) arranges tours to area attractions, including Gruta de la Virgen del Valle (AR$75), and trips to Belén, Londres and El Shincal ruins (AR$350). Kids go free. It's tucked away in an arcade.

Iskay Patatí (☎ 03833-15-531350; mharia23@hot mail.com) can hire you bikes or take you on guided bicycle tours to places such as the Gruta de Choya (p296).

Festivals & Events

The **Fiesta de Nuestra Señora del Valle** takes place for two weeks after Easter. In an impressive manifestation of popular religion and hordes of pilgrims come from the interior and from other Andean provinces to honor the Virgen del Valle. On her saint's day, December 8, she is similarly feted.

Sleeping
BUDGET

Autocamping Municipal (RP 4; per car/person AR$5/3; ☒) Four kilometers west of town, in the Sierra de Ambato foothills, this is a pleasant riverside spot. It's loud and crowded on weekends and holidays, and it has fierce mosquitoes. Take bus 101A (AR$1.75) from outside the Convento de San Francisco.

Residencial Avenida (☎ 422139; Av Güemes 754; s without bathroom AR$30, d with/without bathroom AR$58/45) With plenty of rooms arranged around a central courtyard, the Avenida, meters from the bus terminal, is a fine place to rest your legs and your pesos. Most of the rooms are excellent value, although some are a little rickety.

San Pedro Hostel (☎ 454708; www.hostelsanpedro .com.ar; Sarmiento 341; dm/d AR$30/100; ☐ 🛜 ☒) One of three hostels in town, this is a great spot, with a big back garden that includes a *parrilla* and a tiny pool. Dorms are OK (mattresses are foam) but the overall package and cheery vibe make this a real winner. It runs another hostel around the corner if it's full. Bikes available to rent for AR$10 per day.

Residencial Tucumán (☎ 422209; Tucumán 1040; s/d AR$70/100; ☒) This well-run, immaculately presented *residencial* has spotless rooms and is about a one-minute walk from the bus terminal. For this reason you might want to book ahead. Air-con costs a little more.

Sol Hotel (☎ 430803; solhotel@hotmail.com; Salta 1142; s/d AR$95/150; ☒ 🛜) Clean and welcoming, the Sol's bright, cheery rooms are an OK deal if you want to be near the bus terminal. Some are much better than others; ask to see a few.

Hotel Colonial (☎ 423502; Av República 802; s/d AR$120/160; ☒ 🛜) Cutely decorated in highland colonial style, with dimpled 'adobe' walls and cactus, this down-to-earth place represents value. The rooms are fairly ordinary, but there's space and everything works. Try to get one facing the rear for a bit more peace and quiet.

MIDRANGE & TOP END

Hotel Pucará (☎ 431569; www.hotelpucara.com.ar; Caseros 501; s/d AR$130/180; ☒ ☐) Style gurus need not apply. This peaceful hotel on the west side of town stands out for its gloriously kitschy faux-Chinese knickknacks and ruffled bedspreads. The china dog on the stairs appeals and appalls in equal measure, but the place is comfortable and well run.

Hotel Ancasti (☎ 435951; www.hotelancasti.com.ar; Sarmiento 520; s/d AR$204/258; ☒ ☐ 🛜) As ever, the handsome indigenous-art-inspired lobby of this upmarket central hotel is better than the rooms, which are comfortable but sparsely furnished, and showcase those toweling bedspreads normally seen in cheap *residenciales*. Cheerful service, mountain views, a gym and sauna, and excellent bathrooms go a long way to compensate.

Hotel Arenales (☎ 431329; www.hotel-arenales.com .ar; Sarmiento 542; s/d AR$220/265; ☒ ☐ 🛜 ☒) The straight-down-the-line Arenales is reliable rather than spectacular. The rooms could do

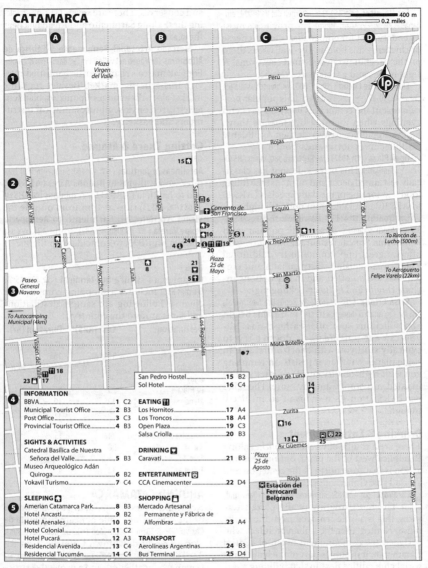

CATAMARCA

0 _____ 400 m
0 _____ 0.2 miles

INFORMATION	
BBVA	**1** C2
Municipal Tourist Office	**2** B3
Post Office	**3** C3
Provincial Tourist Office	**4** B3

SIGHTS & ACTIVITIES	
Catedral Basílica de Nuestra Señora del Valle	**5** B3
Museo Arqueológico Adán Quiroga	**6** B2
Yokavil Turismo	**7** C4

SLEEPING	
Amerian Catamarca Park	**8** B3
Hotel Ancasti	**9** B2
Hotel Arenales	**10** B2
Hotel Colonial	**11** C2
Hotel Pucará	**12** A3
Residencial Avenida	**13** C4
Residencial Tucumán	**14** C4

San Pedro Hostel	**15** B2
Sol Hotel	**16** C4

EATING	
Los Hornitos	**17** A4
Los Troncos	**18** A4
Open Plaza	**19** C3
Salsa Criolla	**20** B3

DRINKING	
Caravati	**21** B3

ENTERTAINMENT	
CCA Cinemacenter	**22** D4

SHOPPING	
Mercado Artesanal Permanente y Fábrica de Alfombras	**23** A4

TRANSPORT	
Aerolíneas Argentinas	**24** B3
Bus Terminal	**25** D4

THE ANDEAN NORTHWEST

with more color, and some of the windows have irritating fixed louvres, but the facilities and treatment of guests are good.

Amerian Catamarca Park (☎ 425444; www.amerian.com; República 347; d AR$509; ❄ ▯ ⊛ ▣) This upmarket hotel is well appointed and coolly modern. Grab a mountain-view room at the front of the building and you'll be content with your stay. Facilities include a gym, sauna and restaurant.

Eating

There's a row of eateries along the north side of the plaza. Cheap burger and *lomito* (steak sandwich) joints are along Güemes west of the bus terminal.

Los Hornitos (☎ 451937; Av Virgen del Valle 924; empanadas AR$2; ☽ 10am-10pm) The province's most legendary spot for empanadas – meat, cheese or chicken – this hole-in-the-wall cooks them on the street in two wood-fired clay ovens. A sight to see, and a Catamarca classic.

El Rincón de Lucho (☎ 457000; Av Puente Castillo 65; dishes AR$10-32; ☽ lunch & dinner) This popular *parrilla* east of the center gets lively on weekend evenings when there's a live *folklore* show. Follow República eastwards then Ave Puente Castillo curves northwards from it.

Open Plaza (☎ 404718; Av República 580; mains AR$10-32; ☽ 8am-late) This plaza-side spot has classically restrained decor and no-nonsense filling food. Go for one of the daily specials (AR$23 to AR$30), available from noon till night.

Los Troncos (☎ 434944; Mota Botello 37; dishes AR$10-36; ☽ lunch & dinner) Deservedly popular with locals, this typical restaurant and *parrillada* offers a great opportunity to try traditional Catamarcan cuisine. Tasty tamales and empanadas are on offer, and meaty options include *chivito* and *lechón* (suckling pig).

Salsa Criolla (☎ 433583; Av República 546; meals AR$45; ☽ lunch & dinner) On the plaza, this bright and solicitous spot offers a high-class all-you-can-eat *parrillada*. It doesn't try to cynically stuff you with chorizo first like in some places – rather, it insists on tempting you with high-quality cuts long after you've insisted you don't want any more. The salad bar (AR$20 on its own) isn't so inspired, though.

Drinking & Entertainment

There are a couple of weekend *boliches* along República west of the plaza, but the real pub action is in a zone north of the center on and around Ave Gobernador Galindez.

Caravati (☎ 426185; Sarmiento 683; ☽ 10am-midnight) The most inviting of the plaza's terraces, this is a little removed from the traffic noise. Named after the Italian architect who designed the cathedral and much of central Catamarca, it occupies part of the handsome social club edifice next to that building.

CCA Cinemacenter (☎ 423040; www.cinemacenter.com.ar; Av Güemes 850) Located in the bus terminal, this cinema screens the latest releases.

Shopping

Catamarca is enthusiastic in promoting its fine natural products; the region is well known for wines, olive oil, walnuts, and various jams and conserves. There are several shops stocking these along Sarmiento and Rivadavia near the plaza.

Mercado Artesanal Permanente y Fábrica de Alfombras (Av Virgen del Valle 945; ☽ 8am-1pm & 2-8pm) For Catamarca's characteristic hand-tied rugs, visit this artisans' market. Besides rugs, the market also sells a range of ponchos, blankets, jewelry, red onyx sculptures, musical instruments and basketry.

Getting There & Around

AIR

Aerolíneas Argentinas (☎ 424460; Sarmiento 589) has three weekly flights to Buenos Aires (AR$975) and to La Rioja (AR$211). A **minibus** (☎ 03833-15-685208; AR$23) runs at 1pm from outside the Hotel Arenales on Sarmiento to **Aeropuerto Felipe Varela** (☎ 430080, 435582), some 22km east of town on RP33, to coincide with flights.

BUS

Catamarca's spruce **bus terminal** (☎ 423415; Av Güemes 850) includes a shopping complex and cinema. Following are sample destinations and fares around the country:

Destination	Cost (AR$)	Duration (hr)
Belén	20	4½
Buenos Aires	175	16
Córdoba	73	5
Jujuy	96	10
La Rioja	25	2
Mendoza	125	10
Rosario	135	11
Salta	91	8
Salvador Mazza	142	15
San Juan	98	8
Santiago del Estero	35	4½
Tucumán	32	4

AROUND CATAMARCA

According to local legend, in 1619 the image of the Virgen del Valle appeared in **Gruta de Choya** (☽ 8:30am-7:30pm Mon-Fri, 8am-noon Sat & Sun), 7km north of downtown Catamarca on RP 32. The present image is a replica of that in Catamarca's cathedral, and a protective structure shelters the grotto itself. Empresa Cotca's bus 104 goes to the Gruta de Choya every 40 minutes (AR$1.75) from outside the San Francisco monastery.

Six kilometers west of town, not far from the campground, **Pueblo Perdido de la Quebrada** is the ruins of a 9th-century-AD settlement built by an indigenous group who had moved south from the puna, perhaps driven by extreme climatic conditions. There's not a great deal to see, however; only low foundation walls remain. Take bus 101A (AR$1.75) from outside the San Francisco monastery.

The Sierra de Famatina, the province's highest mountain range, is visible from the road to picturesque **Villa Las Pirquitas**, near the dam of the same name, 29km north of Catamarca via RN 75. The foothills en route shelter small villages with hospitable people and interesting vernacular architecture.

Free camping is possible at the basic river beach, where the shallows are too muddy for swimming. **Hostería Provincial Las Pirquitas** (☎ 03833-15-584944; s/d AR$30/50) is great value, with clean and comfortable rooms, and a bar with pool table and very cheap meals.

From Catamarca's bus terminal, Empresa Cotca's bus 201 leaves hourly for the village. You can catch it on Salta between Esquiú and Prado.

BELÉN
☎ 03835 / pop 11,003 / elev 1250m

Slow-paced little Belén feels like, and is, a long way from anywhere, and will appeal to travelers who like things small-scale and friendly. It's got an excellent place to stay and is one of the best places to buy woven goods, particularly ponchos, in Argentina. There are many *teleras* (textile workshops) dotted around town, turning out their wares made from llama, sheep and alpaca wool. The nearby ruins of El Shincal are another reason to visit.

Before the arrival of the Spaniards in the mid-16th century, the area around Belén was Diaguita territory, on the periphery of the Inca empire. After the Inca fell, it became the *encomienda* (colonial labor system) of Juan Ramírez de Velasco, founder of La Rioja, but its history is intricately intertwined with nearby Londres, a Spanish settlement that shifted several times because of floods and Diaguita resistance. More than a century passed before the priest José Bartolomé Olmos de Aguilera divided a land grant among veterans of the Diaguita wars, on the condition that they support evangelization in the area.

Orientation & Information
In the western highlands of Catamarca, Belén is 289km from the provincial capital and 180km southwest of Santa María.

There's a **tourist office** (☎ 461304; turismobelencat@gmail.com; ☼ 7am-1pm & 2-10pm Mon-Fri, 8am-10pm Sat, 9am-10pm Sun) by the bus terminal, and another at General Paz 180, which keeps similar hours.

Sights
The neoclassical brick **Iglesia Nuestra Señora de Belén** dates from 1907 and faces Plaza Olmos y Aguilera, which is well shaded by pines and colossal pepper trees. Up some stairs at the end of a little shopping arcade, the **Museo Cóndor Huasi** (cnr Lavalle & Rivadavia; admission AR$2; ☼ 9am-noon & 1-8pm Mon-Fri) has a well-presented archaeological collection, including some fine bronze axes, gold-leaf jewelry and an illustrated information panel (in Spanish) on hallucinogen use among the Diaguita people.

Festivals & Events
On December 20, the town officially celebrates its founding, **Día de la Fundación**, but festivities begin at least a week earlier with a dance at the foot of the Cerro de la Virgen, three blocks west of the plaza. A steep 1900m trail leads to a 15m statue of the Virgin, side by side with a 4.5m image of the Christ child.

Sleeping & Eating
Hotel Gómez (☎ 461250; Calchaquí 213; s/d AR$40/60) One of a handful of cheap hotels on the main road, this spot has a plant-filled patio and basic rooms with bathroom and TV. The welcome isn't exactly effusive, but that's life.

Hotel Belén (☎ 461501; www.belencat.com.ar; cnr Belgrano & Cubas; s/d AR$159/181; 🖭 🖳) It's hard to believe that this superstylish hotel exists in Belén (thank the enlightened Catamarca government of a few years back). The exposed rock bathrooms, with inlaid-tile mosaics on the floors and wall, and grotto-like, extremely comfortable rooms are unusual and a delight.

El Único (Roca 74; mains AR$12-34; ☼ lunch & dinner) A block and a bit west of the plaza, this is the best *parrilla* in town. It features an attractive *quincho* (thatch-roof hut), cheap *patero* wine and friendly service.

1900 (☎ 461100; Belgrano 391; mains AR$14-26; ☼ lunch & dinner) Beyond-the-call service is the key to this highly enjoyable restaurant a block down from the plaza. It's very popular, but it hates to turn people away, so a Tetris-like reshuffling of tables is a constant feature, bless 'em. Prices are more than fair, and there are a number of large platters designed to be shared. Well-mixed salads and juicy brochettes are highlights.

Shopping

There's a marquee off the plaza with a number of friendly *artesanía* stalls selling ponchos, camelid-wool clothing and foot-trodden local wine. For more upmarket woven goods, **Cuna del Poncho** (☎ 461091; Roca 144) has reasonable prices, accepts major credit cards and arranges shipping.

Getting There & Away

Belén's **bus terminal** (cnr Sarmiento & Rivadavia), one block south and one block west of the plaza, is sadly underused, and Catamarca (AR$20, four to five hours) is the only long-distance destination served daily at a reasonable hour (1pm). There's a night service to La Rioja (AR$30, five hours) and Córdoba (AR$83, 14 hours), as well as four buses a week to Santa María (AR$20, four hours) via Hualfin. For Salta and Tucumán, you can change at Catamarca or Santa María.

Hotel Belén has irregular minibus service to Catamarca.

AROUND BELÉN
Londres & El Shincal

Only 15km southwest of Belén, sleepy Londres (population 2134) is the province's oldest Spanish settlement. It dates from 1558, though it moved several times before returning here in 1612, and the inhabitants fled again during the Diaguita uprising of 1632. Its name (London) celebrated the marriage of the prince of Spain (and later King Philip II) to Mary Tudor, queen of England, in 1555. The **Festival Provincial de la Nuez** (Provincial Walnut Festival) takes place here the first fortnight of February.

Seven kilometers west of Londres, the Inca ruins of **El Shincal** (admission AR$5; ◷ 8am-sunset) are well worth visiting. Founded in 1470, the town occupied a commanding position in the foothills of the mountains, surveying the vast valley to the south. The setting is spectacular, with fantastic views and great atmosphere. The site was pretty thoroughly ruined when excavations began in 1991, but the *ushno* (ceremonial platform) and *kallanka* (possibly a barracks) have been restored, and you can climb two hillocks on either side of the central square. Aligned to the rising and setting sun, they probably served as both lookouts and altars. Entrance usually includes a tour by one of the welcoming family that lives here and looks after the site.

There are seven buses Monday to Saturday from Belén to Londres (AR$2), that continue to a spot a short walk from the ruins. There's a campground between Londres and the ruins, and a cabin complex. Londres also has a couple of basic *residenciales*.

Beyond Londres, you can head on south to Chilecito, 200km away in La Rioja province along RN 40, if you have transportation. The drive is a spectacular one, with the imposing Sierra Famatina to the west, and the road is excellent.

Hualfin

About 60km north of Belén via spectacular RN 40 is the grape-growing village of Hualfin. Surprisingly green and fertile in the midst of a barren landscape, it has an attractive pink chapel, dating from 1770, beneath a small promontory whose 142-step staircase leads to a mirador with panoramic views of cultivated fields and the distant desert. Next to the chapel is a small archaeological museum.

Two kilometers south, and a further 2km west, the **Termas de la Quebrada** is a small thermal bath complex; a little further south of the turnoff, amazing reddish rock formations stand proud above the usually dry river valley; the 'snowdrifts' visible on the mountains behind are actually cascades of fine white sand.

Hospedaje Alta Huasi (☎ 03835-15-696275; r per person AR$30), 1km along the Santa María road

---

WAY OUT WEST

If you like getting off the beaten track, you're sure to appreciate out-of-the-way **Antofagasta de la Sierra**, right up in the Andes in the far west of Catamarca province. This puna village sits at 3320m amid a spectacular landscape of guanacos, volcanoes, pumice fields, salt pans and lakes where flamingoes congregate. It's particularly worth visiting in early March for the livestock- and traditional culture–based **Fiesta de la Puna**. There's accommodation available, including the **Hostería de Antofagasta** (☎ 03835-471001; C Principal s/n; s/d AR$65/87). Buses run here from Catamarca at 6:15am Wednesday and Friday (AR$60, 12 hours), returning at noon on Monday and Friday.

from the church, offers simple accommodations. Around town, look for locally grown paprika sprinkled on creamy slices of goat's cheese.

Minibuses run twice daily from Belén to Hualfín (AR$7, 1½ hours) from Monday to Friday; Belén–Santa María buses (four a week) also stop here.

LA RIOJA

☎ 03822 / pop 143,684 / elev 500m

Encircled by the graceful peaks of the Sierra de Velasco, La Rioja is quite a sight on a sunny day. And there are plenty of sunny days: summer temperatures rise sky-high in this quiet, out-of-the-way provincial capital. Even if you're on a short highlights tour, you might consider stopping off here – it's halfway between Mendoza and Salta – to take a tour to the Talampaya and Ischigualasto national parks.

Juan Ramírez de Velasco founded Todos los Santos de la Nueva Rioja in 1591. The Diaguita tribe who lived here were converted and made peace with the conquerors (see boxed text, p301), paving the way for Spanish colonization of what Vásquez de Espinosa called 'a bit of Paradise.'

The city's appearance reflects the conflict and accommodation between colonizer and colonized: the architecture combines European designs with native techniques and local materials. Many early buildings were destroyed in the 1894 earthquake.

Orientation

At the base of the picturesque Sierra de Velasco, La Rioja is relatively small, with all points of interest and most hotels within easy walking distance of each other.

North–south streets change their names at San Nicolás de Bari, but east–west streets are continuous.

Information

BBVA (Av San Nicolás de Bari 476) Changes US dollars.
Mama Espuma (Av JD Perón 324; per load AR$15) Laundry.
Municipal Tourist Kiosk (Plaza 25 de Mayo; ☑ 8am-9:30pm) On the plaza itself.
Provincial tourist office (☎ 426345; www.larioja .gov.ar/turismo; Pelagio Luna 345; ☑ 8am-9:30pm) Helpful.
Telecentro (Av San Nicolás de Bari 502; per hr AR$2.50) On the plaza. Internet and telephones.

Sights
LANDMARK BUILDINGS

La Rioja is a major devotional center, so most landmarks are ecclesiastical. Built in 1623 by the Diaguita under the direction of Dominican friars, the picturesque **Convento de Santo Domingo** (cnr Pelagio Luna & Lamadrid; ☑ 9:30am-12:30pm & 6-8pm Mon-Fri) is Argentina's oldest monastery. The date appears in the carved algarrobo doorframe, also the work of Diaguita artists.

The curious neo-Gothic **Convento de San Francisco** (cnr 25 de Mayo & Bazán y Bustos; ☑ 7pm-9pm) houses the image of the Niño Alcalde, a Christ-child icon symbolically recognized as the city's mayor (see the boxed text, p301, for details).

The enormous and spectacular neo-Byzantine 1899 **catedral** (cnr Av San Nicolás de Bari & 25 de Mayo) contains the image of patron saint Nicolás de Bari, an object of devotion for both *riojanos* (people who live in La Rioja) and the inhabitants of neighboring provinces.

MUSEO FOLKLÓRICO

The hugely worthwhile **Museo Folklórico** (☎ 428500; Pelagio Luna 811; admission by donation; ☑ 9am-1pm & 4-8pm Tue-Fri, 9am-1pm Sat & Sun) is set in a wonderful early-17th-century adobe building, and has fine displays on various aspects of the region's culture. Themes include *chaya* (local La Rioja music) and the Tinkunaco festival, weaving (with bright traditional wallhangings colored with plant extracts) and winemaking. The *lagar* (stretched leather used for treading the grapes) is quite a sight, as is the room that deals with mythology, including a demanding series of rituals required to sell your soul to the devil hereabouts. The informative guided tour is excellent if your Spanish is up to it.

MUSEO INCA HUASI

A couple of blocks from the plaza, this curious **museum** (Alberdi 650; admission AR$2; ☑ 9am-1pm & 4-8pm, Sat 9am-1pm Tue-Fri), run by monks, has a notable collection of pre-Columbian ceramics from the region from a number of different cultures.

Activities & Tours

Several operators run excursions around the province, including visits to the Parque Nacional Talampaya, which invariably includes

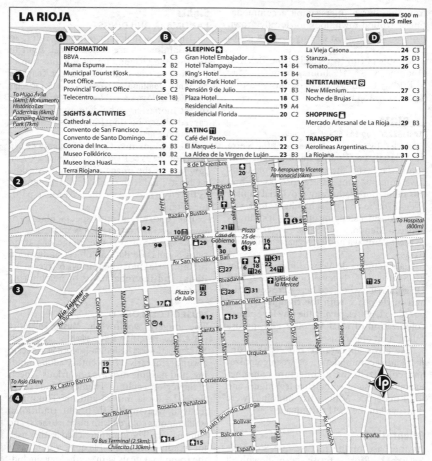

LA RIOJA

0 — 500 m
0 — 0.25 miles

INFORMATION
BBVA...**1** C3
Mama Espuma...........................**2** B2
Municipal Tourist Kiosk..........**3** C3
Post Office.................................**4** B3
Provincial Tourist Office.........**5** C2
Telecentro............................(see 18)

SIGHTS & ACTIVITIES
Cathedral...................................**6** C3
Convento de San Francisco....**7** C2
Convento de Santo Domingo..**8** C2
Corona del Inca........................**9** B3
Museo Folklórico....................**10** B2
Museo Inca Huasi....................**11** C2
Terra Riojana...........................**12** B3

SLEEPING
Gran Hotel Embajador...........**13** C3
Hotel Talampaya.....................**14** B4
King's Hotel.............................**15** B4
Naindo Park Hotel..................**16** C3
Pensión 9 de Julio..................**17** B3
Plaza Hotel..............................**18** C3
Residencial Anita....................**19** A4
Residencial Florida.................**20** C2

EATING
Café del Paseo.........................**21** C2
El Marqués...............................**22** C3
La Aldea de la Virgen de Luján...**23** B3

La Vieja Casona.......................**24** C3
Stanzza.....................................**25** D3
Tomato.....................................**26** C3

ENTERTAINMENT
New Milenium.........................**27** C3
Noche de Brujas......................**28** C3

SHOPPING
Mercado Artesanal de La Rioja...**29** B3

TRANSPORT
Aerolíneas Argentinas............**30** C3
La Riojana................................**31** C3

the nearby Parque Provincial Ischigualasto ('Valle de la Luna') in San Juan province. Rates vary according to numbers, but the 13-hour day trip to the two parks tends to cost around AR$180 to AR$210 per person. These companies also offer excursions to high, remote parts of the Andes in the west of the province (see boxed text, p305, for more information on these destinations).

A couple of operators:

Corona del Inca (☎ 422142; www.coronadelinca .ar; Pelagio Luna 914)

Terra Riojana (☎ 427-4160; www.terrariojana.com.ar; H Yrigoyen 240)

The La Rioja area has high drop-offs and thermals that make it a great zone for hang-gliding

and paragliding; world records for long flights have been set here. Get in touch with **Hugo Ávila** (☎ 451635, 03822-15-663296; www.vuelosaguilablanca .ar; Av Ramírez de Velasco, Km 7), who offers instruction and tandem flights.

Festivals & Events

La Chaya, the local variant of Carnaval, attracts people from throughout the country. Its name, derived from a Quechua word meaning 'to get someone wet,' should give you an idea of what to expect. A particular style of local music, *chaya*, is associated with the festival.

Taking place at noon December 31, the religious ritual of **El Tinkunaco** is one of Argentina's most interesting ceremonies (see the boxed text, opposite).

Sleeping

La Rioja's hotels often offer discounts if you pay cash and aren't afraid to bargain.

Residencial Anita (☎ 424836; Coronel Lagos 476; s/d AR$80/95; 🅿) Offering excellent value for two, the quiet and proper Anita is a few blocks away from the center in a residential district. Rooms are very clean, with spotless bathrooms, and the plant- and saint-filled patio and plump pet dog are bonuses. It's not the sort of place that will appreciate you rolling in pissed at 4am.

Pensión 9 de Julio (☎ 426955; cnr Copiapó & Dalmacio Vélez Sársfield; s/d AR$80/100; 🅿 🖳) Definitely a good deal, this place has clean and pleasant rooms in a central part of town. A shady, vine-covered patio overlooking the plaza of the same name is another bonus. The drawback is substantial traffic noise from exterior rooms.

Gran Hotel Embajador (☎ 438580; www.granhotel embajador.com.ar; San Martín 250; s/d AR$95/130; 🅿 🛜) This cheery place is very tidy; the rooms upstairs are larger and sunnier – a good thing if dark-red color schemes oppress you – and some have balconies. It offers plenty of value, and is popular as a result; reservations are advised.

Hotel Talampaya (☎ 422005; Av JD Perón 1290; s/d AR$140/250; 🅿 🖳 🛜 🅿) What was formerly the Hotel Turismo has been taken over by the nearby King's Hotel. The rooms are good at this price (especially the singles), and have excellent bathrooms and noisy balconies. There's also a good restaurant here.

King's Hotel (☎ 422122; Av Juan Facundo Quiroga 107; s/d AR$160/280; 🅿 🖳 🛜 🅿) Though the King's has a few gray hairs appearing, it still has atmosphere. The rooms have space and are comfortable enough, but the big pluses are the service, buffet breakfast and the pool, sundeck and gym.

Plaza Hotel (☎ 425215; www.plazahotel-larioja.com.ar; Av San Nicolás de Bari 502; s/d standard AR$228/261, s/d superior AR$320/341; 🅿 🖳 🛜 🅿) Right on the plaza, this hotel looks a great deal better from inside than out. Rooms overlooking the plaza are much nicer than those looking onto internal light wells. Superior rooms are also available; they have a newer feel and king-sized beds.

Naindo Park Hotel (☎ 470700; www.naindoparkho tel.com; Av San Nicolás de Bari 475; s/d AR$374/400; 🅿 🖳 🛜 🅿) Just off the plaza, and dominating it assertively, La Rioja's finest hotel has an excellent level of service and comfort and prices to match. The rooms are particularly spacious, and many have good views.

Also recommended:

Camping Alameda Park (☎ 03822-15-501977; Ruta 75, Km 9; campsites per person AR$10) Best and closest campground west of town; to get there, catch city bus 2 or 5 southbound on Perón.

Residencial Florida (☎ 03822-15-688170; 8 de Diciembre 524; s/d/tw without bathroom AR$30/50/60, s/d with bathroom AR$40/70) Dark but decent rooms with fan for a pittance.

Eating

Regional dishes to look for include *locro*, juicy empanadas, *chivito asado* (barbecued goat),

---

EL TINKUNACO – CONFLICT RESOLUTION IN THE 16TH CENTURY

The fascinating and moving Tinkunaco ceremony is a symbolic representation of the resolution of the clash of cultures that occurred at the founding of La Rioja. When Juan Ramírez de Velasco founded the city in 1591, he blithely ignored the fact that the land was owned and farmed by the Diaguita, who naturally took exception to their territory being carved up among Spanish settlers. They rebelled in 1593, and a bloody conflict was averted by the mediation of the friar Francisco Solano, later canonized for his efforts. The Diaguita trusted the cleric and listened to his message. They then agreed to down their arms on two conditions: that the Spanish *alcalde* (mayor) resign and that his replacement be the Christ child. The Spaniards agreed and peace was made. The new mayor became known as Niño Jesús Alcalde.

The Tinkunaco (the word means 'meeting' in Quechua) commemoration commenced not long after these historic events. Every year at noon on December 31, two processions – one representing the Spaniards, one the Diaguita – cross town and meet at the Casa de Gobierno. The 'Spaniards' are dressed as religious penitents and *alféreces* (lieutenants) with uniform and flag. The 'Diaguita,' or *aillis*, wear headbands with mirrors and ponchos. The processions meet, and solemnly all fall to their knees before the image of the Niño Jesús Alcalde, then embrace. It's a powerful moment with a deep message about cultural differences and compromises.

humitas, quesillo (a cheese specialty) and olives. Cheap local wines are a good bargain in restaurants.

Café del Paseo (☎ 422069; cnr Pelagio Luna & 25 de Mayo; light meals AR$7-22; ☺ breakfast, lunch & dinner) This is your spot on the corner of the plaza to observe La Rioja life. The cell-phone clique mingles with families and tables of older men chewing the fat over another slow-paced La Rioja day. It's a fine place to try Argentina's favorite mixed drink – Fernet Branca with cola.

El Marqués (Av San Nicolás de Bari 484; dishes AR$10-22; ☺ 8am-midnight Mon-Sat) No surprises are on the menu here at this simple but effective local eatery. Pasta, pizza, omelets and grilled meats are well prepared and fairly priced. The fruit *licuados* are delicious.

Tomato (☎ 424444; Rivadavia 569; dishes AR$15-25; ☺ lunch & dinner) Chunky *lomitos* and decent pizza and pasta with big flatscreen TVs and outdoor seating make this a popular choice near the plaza. There's good cheap Rioja wine on hand, too.

Stanzza (☎ 430809; Dorrego 1641; mains AR$15-34; ☺ lunch & dinner Tue-Sun) One of the best places to eat in town, this friendly neighborhood restaurant serves up imaginative seafood and Italian dishes in an intimate environment.

La Aldea de la Virgen de Luján (☎ 460305; Rivadavia 756; lunches AR$18-25; ☺ 7am-3pm & 7-11pm Mon-Sat, 10am-3pm Sun) Though serving good-value breakfasts and a fairly predictable range of dinner options, lunchtime is the place to be at this spot, when it offers a good range of regional specialties.

La Vieja Casona (☎ 425996; Rivadavia 457; mains AR$19-44) Cheerfully lit and decorated, this is a cracking place with a great range of regional specialties, creative house choices and a long menu of standard Argentine dishes – the *parrillada* here is of excellent standard. There's a fair selection of La Rioja wines, too, and wonderful smells wafting from the busy kitchen.

Entertainment

If you're up for a late night, there's a number of discos where you can show the locals your latest moves. Two of the most popular options are **New Milenium** (San Martín 82; ☺ Fri-Sat), opposite the Colegio Nacional, and packed and cheerful **Asia** (Av San Francisco; ☺ Fri-Sat). **Noche de Brujas** (San Martín 162) is a popular central bar-*boliche* with a Halloween theme.

Shopping

La Rioja has unique weavings that combine indigenous techniques and skill with Spanish designs and color combinations. The typical *mantas* (bedspreads) feature floral patterns over a solid background color. Spanish influence is also visible in silverwork, including tableware, ornaments, religious objects and horse gear.

Fittingly for a place named after Spain's most famous wine region, La Rioja wine has a national reputation.

La Rioja crafts are exhibited and sold at the excellent **Mercado Artesanal de La Rioja** (Pelagio Luna 792; ☺ 8am-noon & 4-8pm Tue-Fri, 9am-noon Sat & Sun), as are other popular artworks at prices lower than most souvenir shops.

Getting There & Away

AIR

Aerolíneas Argentinas (☎ 426307; Belgrano 63) flies three times weekly to and from Buenos Aires (AR$975), stopping in Catamarca (AR$211 from Catamarca to La Rioja) on the way out.

BUS

La Rioja's **bus terminal** (☎ 427991; Barrio Evita s/n) is an interesting building, picturesquely backed by the sierra. It's a long walk south from the center of town. Sample fares and destinations:

Destination	Cost (AR$)	Duration (hr)
Belén	37	5
Buenos Aires	173	22
Catamarca	25	2
Chilecito	22	3
Córdoba	54	6
Jujuy	121	11
Mendoza	100	8
Salta	117	10
San Juan	73	6
Santiago del Estero	99	7
Tucumán	59	6

For going to Chilecito, **La Riojana** (☎ 435279; Buenos Aires 154) minibuses run from its office in the center of town four times a day. The trip costs AR$30 and takes 2½ hours, a little quicker than the bus.

Getting Around

Aeropuerto Vicente Almonacid (☎ 427239) is 7km east of town on RP 5. An airport taxi costs around AR$25. A taxi from the bus terminal to the city center costs about AR$12.

AROUND LA RIOJA

According to legend, San Francisco Solano converted many Diaguita at the site of **Monumento Histórico Las Padercitas**, a Franciscan-built colonial adobe chapel now sheltered by a stone temple, 7km west of town on RN 75. On the second Sunday of August, pilgrims convene to pay homage to the saint. Buses 2 and 5 go to the site (AR$1.50)

Beyond Las Padercitas, RN 75 climbs and winds past attractive summer homes, bright-red sandstone cliffs, lush vegetation and dark-purple peaks whose cacti remind you that the area is semidesert.

CHILECITO

☎ 03825 / pop 29,453 / elev 1080m

With a gorgeous situation among low rocky hills and sizable snowcapped peaks, Chilecito, a stop on spectacular Ruta 40, is the province's second-largest settlement but still a small town. There are several interesting things to see, including the amazing abandoned cableway leading to a mine high in the sierra. With the intense heat, mining heritage and slopes around town dotted with cardón cactus, Chilecito can have a Wild West feel to it at times and is definitely the most appealing place to spend a few quiet days in this part of the country. It's also a useful base for worthwhile excursions into the sierra.

Founded as Villa Santa Rita in 1715 by Domingo de Castro y Bazán, who had been granted the land, it was little more than a hamlet until the mining took off in the late 19th century. It acquired the name Chilecito (Little Chile) because many from that country crossed the Andes to come and work the mines here.

Information

The plaza has three banks with ATMs.

Municipal tourist office (Pl Sarmiento s/n; ☯ 8am-9pm) In a kiosk on the plaza; helpful and friendly.

Provincial tourist office (☎ 422688; turismochil ecito@yahoo.com.ar; Castro y Bazán 52; ☯ 8am-9pm) Has enthusiastic staff and good material. There is also a small kiosk on Plaza Sarmiento.

Telecentro (Plaza Sarmiento; per hr AR$2) Phone cabins and internet access.

Sights

MUSEO DEL CABLECARRIL

The fascinating **Museo del Cablecarril** (suggested donation AR$5; ☯ 8:30am-12:30pm & 2:30-7:30pm) and cablecar station documents an extraordinary

engineering project that gave birth to the town of Chilecito at the beginning of the 20th century. To enable the mining of gold, silver and copper from the Sierra de Famatina, a German firm was contracted to construct a cablecar running from here, at the end of the railway line, to La Mejicana, at an altitude of 4603m, more than 3.5km above Chilecito and nearly 40km away. With nine stations, a tunnel and 262 towers, the project was completed in 1904. Men and supplies were carried to the mine, operated by a British firm, in four hours. WWI put an end to this Anglo-German cooperation and the line started to decay, although local miners continued using it until the 1930s.

The picturesque museum preserves photos, tools and documents from the cablecar and mine, as well as communications equipment, including an early cell phone. There's a detailed guided tour in Spanish, and you'll then be taken to the cablecar terminus itself – a rickety spiral staircase climbs to the platform, where ore carts now wait silently in line. It's worth going in the late afternoon, when the sun bathes the rusted metal and snowy sierras.

The museum is on the main road at the southern entrance to town, a block south of the bus terminal.

MUSEO MOLINO DE SAN FRANCISCO

Chilecito founder Don Domingo de Castro y Bazán owned this colonial flour mill, whose **Museo Molino de San Francisco** (J Ocampo 63; admission AR$3; ☯ 8am-12:30pm & 2:30-7:30pm) houses an eclectic assemblage of archaeological tools, antique arms, early colonial documents, minerals, traditional wood and leather crafts, banknotes, woodcuts, early cell telephones and paintings.

SAMAY HUASI

Joaquín V González, writer and founder of the prestigious La Plata university in Buenos Aires, used **Samay Huasi** (☎ 422629; samayhuasi@ arnet.com.ar; admission AR$5; ☯ 8am-6pm), a *finca* (ranch) 2km from Chilecito, as his country retreat. The verdant grounds counterpoint the rocky cactus hills around them. González' bedroom is preserved, as well as scrapbook material from his life. More interesting is a collection of paintings, mostly of the area; a canvas by González' friend Alberto Alice, *Claro de Luna,* stands out. Below is a somewhat depressing natural sciences, archaeology and mineralogy collection.

You can stay at the *finca*, which offers full-board accommodations for AR$70 per person. It needs to be booked in advance.

To get there, head out from town past the Chirau-Mita cactus garden and follow the main road as it bends around to the right. Keep going and you'll see the *finca* on your right.

LA RIOJANA WINERY

La Rioja is one of the best areas to taste the aromatic white torrontés, though it's far from the only wine the province has to offer. **La Riojana** (☎ 423150; www.lariojana.com.ar; La Plata 646; ☼ 8am-6pm Mon-Fri, 9am-1pm Sat) cooperative is the area's main wine producer, and a sizable concern. A good free tour (call or drop in to arrange a time; English is spoken) shows you through the bodega – think large cement fermentation tanks rather than rows of musty barrels – and culminates in a generous tasting.

CHIRAU-MITA

This impressive cactus garden and handsome museum was closed indefinitely at the time of research, but it's worth asking if it's opened again.

Sleeping

A new five-star hotel and casino, Hotel Famatina, unsurprisingly owned by the local governor, was rapidly being built at 19 de Febrero 351 at the time of research.

Hostel Paimán (☎ 429135; El Maestro 188; dm/s/d AR$35/50/80) With simple, comfortable rooms opening onto a quiet courtyard, and a welcoming owner, this is a friendly, relaxing place at a good price. There's a kitchen and laundry; prices include breakfast. You can also pitch a tent for AR$20.

Hotel Ruta 40 (☎ 422804; Libertad 68; s/d with bathroom AR$50/90, without bathroom AR$35/60; ✿) An excellent deal a couple of blocks from the plaza, this comfortable spot offers a variety of rooms with comfortable beds and clean spacious bathrooms. Look at a few – some look over a vine-covered patio to the hills beyond.

Hostal Mary Pérez (☎ 423156; hostal_mp@hotmail .com; Florencio Dávila 280; s/d AR$100/120) A neat little *residencial* in the northeast of town that is more like a family-run hotel. The place is spotless – you may get high on the smell of cleaning products – and rooms come with TV and phone.

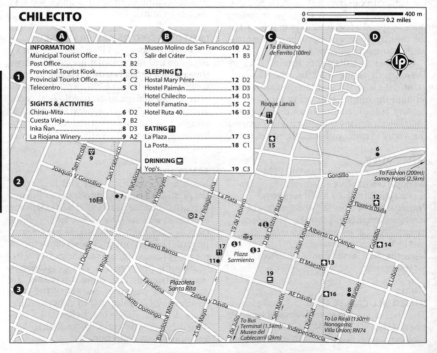

CHILECITO

0 ———— 400 m
0 ———— 0.2 miles

INFORMATION	
Municipal Tourist Office	1 C3
Post Office	2 B2
Provincial Tourist Kiosk	3 C3
Provincial Tourist Office	4 C2
Telecentro	5 C3

SIGHTS & ACTIVITIES	
Chirau-Mita	6 D2
Cuesta Vieja	7 B2
Inka Ñan	8 D3
La Riojana Winery	9 A2

Museo Molino de San Francisco	10 A2
Salir del Cráter	11 B3

SLEEPING	
Hostal Mary Pérez	12 D2
Hostel Paimán	13 D3
Hotel Chilecito	14 D3
Hotel Famatina	15 C2
Hotel Ruta 40	16 D3

EATING	
La Plaza	17 C3
La Posta	18 C1

DRINKING	
Yop's	19 C3

To El Rancho de Ferrito (100m)

Roque Lanús

To Fashion (200m); Samay Huasi (2.5km)

To Bus Terminal (1.5km); Museo del Cablecarril (2km)

To La Rioja (130m); Nonogasta; Villa Union; RN74

TRIPS AROUND CHILECITO

The western portion of La Rioja province is fascinating, with plenty of intriguing destinations in the sierras, and Chilecito is a launch pad for a range of excellent excursions. Parque Nacional Talampaya (below) is one appealing trip, which also takes in the Ischigualasto provincial park (p373) and crosses the picturesque Miranda pass. Northbound jaunts up RN 40 take in the ruins of El Shincal (p298) or the remote hot springs at Fiambalá, while for some serious 4WD mountain action, head up to the abandoned mine at La Mejicana (4603m), an ascent that takes in some amazing scenery and broad palette of colors, including a striking yellow river. Deeper into the sierras by the Chilean border is sizable Laguna Brava, a flamingo-filled lake surrounded by awesomely bleak and beautiful Andean scenery. Higher still, at 5600m, is the sapphire-blue crater lake of Corona del Inca, only accessible in summer.

Operators in town such as **Salir del Cráter** (☎ 423854; www.salirdelcrater.com.ar; 25 de Mayo 87), **Inka Ñan** (☎ 423641; www.inkanan.com.ar; Martínez 49) and **Cuesta Vieja** (☎ 424874; www.cuestavieja .com; Joaquín V González 467) run these trips, which cost around AR$150 to AR$250 per person depending on numbers. There's usually a minimum of two people, but it's always worth asking. Tailored multiday trips are available, too.

Hotel Chilecito (☎ 422201; hotel_acachilecito@hot mail.com; T Gordillo 101; s/d AR$117/156; ❄ ▢ ☏ ▣)
With a quiet location near where the town ends among rocky hills, this ACA establishment offers fine value for money. There's space to burn here, with a garden and cavernous recreation room (pool table). The rooms are light, bright and pleasant, with tiled floors and gleaming bathrooms. There's also a decent restaurant.

Eating & Drinking

La Plaza (☎ 422696; 25 de Mayo 58; mains AR$10-25; ❄ breakfast, lunch & dinner) Right on the plaza (as the name suggests), this warmly decorated restaurant specializes in tasty pizza and pasta. There are various set meals for AR$24 to AR$32, and all-you-can-eat pasta for AR$16.

El Rancho de Ferrito (☎ 422481; Av Pelagio Luna 647; mains AR$13-26; ❄ lunch & dinner) Seven blocks from the plaza, this inviting local restaurant is worth every step. You've seen the menu before – except for house specialties such as *cazuela de gallina* (chicken stew: yum), and local wines – but the quality, price and atmosphere make it truly excellent.

La Posta (☎ 425988; cnr 19 de Febrero & Roque Lanús; mains AR$22-59; ❄ lunch & dinner) Just the sort of place you wouldn't expect Chilecito to have, and here it is – an intimate, stylish restaurant warmly decorated and lined with shelves of deli products on sale. The dishes are innovative (stewed goat with torrontés, for example) and attractively presented. The taste doesn't quite live up to the service or decor, but it's pretty good, especially the empanadas cooked on the *parrilla*.

Yops (AE Dávila 70; ❄ 8am-2pm & 5pm-late Mon-Sat) Atmospheric and darkish, this bohemian spot is comfortably Chilecito's best cafe, serving fine coffee and decent mixed drinks. Watch the locals' epic chess battles.

Entertainment

If you're in Chilecito on a Saturday night, you'll want to check out castle-like **Fashion** (admission AR$10; ❄ 11pm-late Sat), the town's best *discoteca*. It's on the way to Samay Huasi about 1km out of town, and a lot of fun. Girls get in a little cheaper, and you may even win a motorbike or similar in the prize draw.

Getting There & Away

The new bus terminal is 1.5km south of the center, near the Museo del Cablecarril. There are regular services to La Rioja (AR$22, three hours), and beyond to Rosario, Buenos Aires and other cities. **La Riojana** (☎ 424710; Maestro 61) minibuses also do the La Rioja run for AR$8 more and in half an hour less. There are no buses north to Belén; to avoid the lengthy backtrack through La Rioja and Catamarca you could take a tour to Shinkal and stay in Belén.

PARQUE NACIONAL TALAMPAYA
☎ 03825 / elev 1300m

Though only a trickle of water winds through what, in the Quechua language, translates as the 'Dry River of the Trees,' the spectacular rock formations and canyons of this national park are evidence of the erosive action of far greater quantities of water. It's a dusty desert of scorching days, chilly nights, infrequent but torrential summer rains and gusty spring winds. The sandstone cliffs are amazing, as are the distant surrounding mountainscapes. Talampaya is adjacent to fossil-rich Parque Provincial Ischigualasto in San Juan province (p373) and it's easy to combine the two if you have transport.

Orientation & Information

Talampaya is 141km southwest of Chilecito via a combination of RN 40's scenic Cuesta de Miranda route, RP 18 and RP 26. Via RP 26, it is 58km south of Villa Unión and 58km north of Los Baldecitos, the turnoff to San Juan's Parque Provincial Ischigualasto.

The park's **visitor center** (☎ 470356; www.ta lampaya.gov.ar; ☽ 8am-6pm) is just off the RP 26; private vehicles are not allowed further into the park. Here you pay the AR$25 admission (AR$8 for Argentine citizens), and arrange guided visits to the park.

Sights & Activities

The focus of most visits is the spectacular **Cañón de Talampaya**, a usually dry watercourse bounded by sheer sandstone cliffs. Condors soar on the thermals, and guanacos, rheas and maras can be seen in the shade of the several varieties of algarrobo tree along the sandy canyon floor.

A series of enigmatic **petroglyphs** carved into oxidized sandstone slabs are the first stop on the standard 2½-hour visit (AR$65), followed by, in the canyon itself, such highlights as the **Chimenea del Eco**, whose impressive echo effect is a guaranteed hit, the **Catedral** formation and the clerical figure of **El Monje**.

Longer 4½-hour excursions (AR$95) also take in the more remote gorge of **Los Cajones**. Other trips to sites such as Ciudad Perdida and Los Chañares can be organized inside the park. The trips are in comfortable minibuses and there's little walking involved; nevertheless, take water and protection from the fierce sun.

Guided walks (AR$40 to AR$80) and trips on bicycles (AR$35 to AR$45) are also available; these can be more appealing if the heat's not too intense.

Sleeping & Eating

There are no accommodations in the park itself, but there's shadeless camping at the visitor center (AR$7 per person), which has decent toilets and showers. There's also a cafe here serving meals and cold drinks.

There are simple accommodations in Pagancillo, 29km north. A further 29km up the road, larger Villa Unión has several cabin and hotel options, some of them quite stylish.

Getting There & Away

Buses bound from La Rioja to Pagancillo and Villa Unión will leave you at the park entrance (AR$22, 3½ hours), from where it's only a 500m walk to the visitor center. The earliest bus leaves La Rioja at 7am, giving you plenty of time to make a day trip of it. There's a daily bus between Villa Unión, 58km up the road, and Chilecito (AR$22, three hours) over the spectacular Miranda pass. It leaves Villa Unión at 3pm; you can make it if you cadge a lift off someone in your tour group.

THE ANDEAN NORTHWEST

Córdoba & the Central Sierras

Argentina's second city is bursting with life. Home to not one but seven major universities, Córdoba has a young population that ensures an excellent nightlife and a healthy cultural scene. Art is one of the city's strong points, and the four major galleries here are truly world-class. The business center of the country's most populous province, Córdoba also boasts a fascinating history, owing its architectural and cultural heritage to the Jesuits, who set up shop here when they first arrived in Argentina.

Outside of the city, the rolling hill country of the Central Sierras is dotted with towns that could grab your attention for a day or a month. The region boasts five Jesuit missions that have been declared Unesco World Heritage sites, each of them located in quaint little satellite towns that are an easy day trip from the capital.

Adventure buffs won't be left twiddling their thumbs, either – the paragliding is excellent at La Cumbre and Merlo and there's fantastic trekking to be done in two national parks – the fossil-strewn Sierra de las Quijadas and the condor haven of Quebrada del Condorito.

Further to the southwest, the Valle de Conlara and Sierras Puntanas offer a real chance to get away from the crowds and into the heart of the countryside. Highlights include the caves and rock art at Inti Huasi, the palm-filled valley of Papagayos and the picturesque ex-mining village of Carolina. Public transportation in this part of the region is often rare and sometimes nonexistent, but the wealth of experiences that awaits far outweighs any inconvenience.

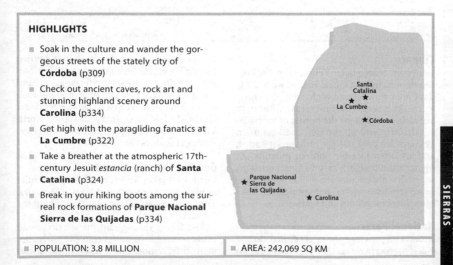

HIGHLIGHTS

- Soak in the culture and wander the gorgeous streets of the stately city of **Córdoba** (p309)

- Check out ancient caves, rock art and stunning highland scenery around **Carolina** (p334)

- Get high with the paragliding fanatics at **La Cumbre** (p322)

- Take a breather at the atmospheric 17th-century Jesuit *estancia* (ranch) of **Santa Catalina** (p324)

- Break in your hiking boots among the surreal rock formations of **Parque Nacional Sierra de las Quijadas** (p334)

Santa Catalina
★ ★
La Cumbre ★
★ Córdoba

Parque Nacional
★ Sierra de las Quijadas

★ Carolina

- POPULATION: 3.8 MILLION | - AREA: 242,069 SQ KM

Climate

Generally, November to February are the hottest months in the Central Sierras, when 29°C days are common and nights are pleasantly warm. This is also the rainy season, but days are sunny enough for the hordes of sunbathers that descend on the sierras all summer. Winters are cool but get little precipitation and are often nice for outdoor pursuits. At higher altitudes (such as in La Cumbre), light snowfall is not uncommon. Fall and spring get more rain than winter, but temperatures are often ideal for hiking and biking.

National Parks

In San Luis province, the rarely visited Parque Nacional Sierra de las Quijadas (p334) is an excellent alternative to the better-known Parque Provincial Ischigualasto (p373) in San Juan province: getting there is far easier, and you'll often have the desert canyons and rock formations all to yourself. Parque Nacional Quebrada del Condorito (p328) is well worth a day trip from Córdoba to see the impressive Andean condors the park protects.

Getting There & Around

Córdoba makes an excellent stop if you're heading south or southwest toward Mendoza. The city has bus connections throughout the country.

The towns throughout the sierras are all easily accessible by public transportation, but many tiny, remote towns and Jesuit *estancias* (ranches) can only be reached with your own wheels. The sierras' dense network of roads, many well paved but others only gravel, make them good candidates for bicycle touring; Argentine drivers here seem a bit less ruthless than elsewhere in the country. A mountain bike is still the best choice.

CÓRDOBA

☎ 0351 / pop 1.5 million / elev 400m

It's an old guidebook cliché, but Córdoba really *is* a fascinating mix of old and new. Where else will you find DJs spinning electro-tango in crowded student bars next to 17th-century Jesuit ruins?

In 2006 Córdoba was awarded the hefty title of Cultural Capital of the Americas, and it fits the city like a glove. Four excellent municipal galleries – dedicated to emerging, contemporary, classical and fine art respectively – are within easy walking distance of each other and the city center. The alternative film scene is alive and kicking. Young designers and artisans strut their stuff at a weekend crafts market that sprawls for blocks and is one of the best in the country. And if all this action is too much for you, quaint little mountain villages are a short bus ride away.

ORIENTATION

Córdoba is 715km northwest of Buenos Aires. Most colonial sites lie within a few blocks of Plaza San Martín, the city's urban nucleus. The commercial center is just northwest of the plaza, where the main pedestrian malls – 25 de Mayo and Rivera Indarte – intersect. Obispo Trejo, just west of the plaza, has the finest concentration of colonial buildings. Just south of downtown, Parque Sarmiento offers relief from the bustling, densely built downtown.

East–west streets change names at San Martín/Independencia and north–south streets change at Deán Funes/Rosario de Santa Fe.

INFORMATION
Internet Access
Cyber cafes are tucked into *locutorios* (telephone kiosks) throughout the center, and they're everywhere in Nueva Córdoba.

Stone (☎ 0351-15-547-6458; Av Marcelo T de Alvear 370; per hr AR$3; ☺ 10am-dawn) One of the grooviest cyber joints in town. Pizzas, drinks and empanadas, too.

Laundry
Trapitos (☎ 422-5877; Independencia 898; full service about AR$15)

Medical Services
Emergency hospital (☎ 421-0243; cnr Catamarca & Blvd Guzmán)

Money
Cambios (money-exchange offices) and ATMs are on Rivadavia north of the plaza; both are also at the main bus terminal and airport.

Cambio Barujel (cnr Rivadavia & 25 de Mayo) High commissions.

Maguitur (☎ 421-6200; 25 de Mayo 122) Charges 3% on traveler's checks.

Post
Main post office (Av General Paz 201)

Tourist Information
ACA (Automóvil Club Argentino; ☎ 421-4636; cnr Av General Paz & Humberto Primo) Argentina's auto club; good source for provincial road maps.

Casa Cabildo Tourist Information Office (☎ 428-5856; Independencia 30; ☺ 8am-8pm) Together provincial and municipal tourist boards maintain their main office in the historic Casa Cabildo.

Provincial tourist office airport (☎ 434-8390; Aeropuerto Pajas Blancas; ☺ 8am-8pm Mon-Fri); bus terminal (☎ 433-1980; ☺ 8am-9pm)

Travel Agencies
Asatej (☎ 422-9453; www.asatej.com; Av Vélez Sársfield 361, Patio Olmos, Local 319) On the 3rd floor of Patio Olmos shopping center. Nonprofit student travel agency with great staff. Open to all ages and nonstudents.

ESTANCIAS IN THE CENTRAL SIERRAS

From rustic little getaways to sprawling, atmospheric ranches, the Central Sierras offer a small but excellent selection of *estancias*.

Estancia El Viejo Piquete (p323) A cozy ranch house near La Cumbre with fabulous views over the Valle de Punilla.

Estancia La Estanzuela (p336) Wonderfully preserved, set on lush grounds.

Estancia Las Verbenas (p334) Set in a beautiful glade, it's a truly rustic experience.

La Ranchería de Santa Catalina (p324) Spend the night in the old slave quarters.

Puesto Viejo (p324) *Estancia* atmosphere at backpacker prices.

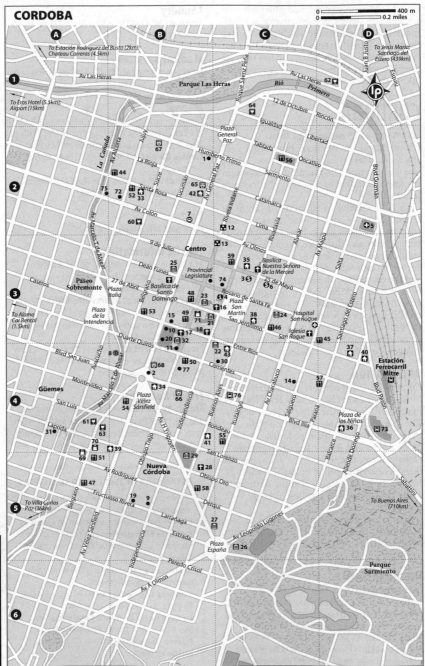

SIGHTS

There's plenty to see in Córdoba, so allow yourself at least a couple of days for wandering around. Most churches are open roughly from 9am to noon and from 5pm to 8pm. Museum opening hours change regularly depending on the season and the administration.

Centro

Downtown Córdoba is a treasure of colonial buildings and other historical monuments.

IGLESIA CATEDRAL

The construction of Córdoba's **cathedral** (cnr Independencia & 27 de Abril; guided visit AR$10; ☺ 9am-12:30pm & 4:30-7pm) began in 1577 and dragged on for more than two centuries under several architects, including Jesuits and Franciscans, and though it lacks any sense of architectural unity, it's a beautiful structure. Crowned by a Romanesque dome, it overlooks Plaza San Martín. The lavish interior was painted by renowned *cordobés* (Córdoban) painter Emilio Caraffa. Guided visits leave hourly between 9am and 5pm from Psje Santa Catalina 61, the entry on the north side of the cathedral.

MUSEO DE LA MEMORIA

A chilling testament to the excesses of Argentina's military dictatorship, this museum (San Jerónimo s/n; admission free; ☺ 9am-noon & 3-8pm Tue-Sun) occupies a space formerly used as a clandestine center for detention and torture. It was operated by the dreaded Department of Intelligence (D2), a special division created in Córdoba dedicated to the kidnap and torture of suspected political agitators and the 'reassignment' of their children to less politically suspect families.

The space itself is stark and unembellished, and the walls are covered with enlarged photographs of people who are still 'missing' after

30 years. There's not much joy here, but the museum stands as a vital reminder of an era that human-rights groups hope will never be forgotten.

MANZANA JESUÍTICA

Córdoba's beautiful Manzana Jesuítica (Jesuit Block), like that of Buenos Aires, is also known as the Manzana de las Luces (Block of Enlightenment), and was initially associated with the influential Jesuit order.

Designed by the Flemish Padre Philippe Lemaire, the **Iglesia de la Compañía de Jesús** (cnr Obispo Trejo & Caseros; admission free) dates from 1645 but was not completed until 1671, with the successful execution of Lemaire's plan for a cedar roof in the form of an inverted ship's hull. Lemaire, unsurprisingly, was once a boat builder. Inside, the church's baroque altarpiece is made from carved Paraguayan cedar from Misiones province. The **Capilla Doméstica** (Domestic Chapel; guided visits per person ARS6; 10am, 11am, 5pm & 6pm), completed in 1644, sits directly behind the church on Caseros. Its ornate ceiling was made with cowhide stretched over a skeleton of thick taguaro cane and painted with pigments composed partially of boiled bones. Guided visits leave from inside the Universidad Nacional de Córdoba.

In 1613 Fray Fernando de Trejo y Sanabria founded the Seminario Convictorio de San Javier, which, after being elevated to university status in 1622, became the **Universidad Nacional de Córdoba** (433-2075; Obispo Trejo 242; 9am-1pm & 4-8pm). The university is the country's oldest and contains, among other national treasures, part of the Jesuits' Grand Library and the **Museo Histórico de la Universidad Nacional de Córdoba** (433-2075; guided visits per person ARS10; 10am, 11am, 5pm & 6pm Tue-Sun). Guided visits are the only way to see the inside and are well worth taking. The guides let you wander through the Colegio and peek into the classrooms while students run around.

Next door, the **Colegio Nacional de Monserrat** (Obispo Trejo 294) dates from 1782, though the college itself was founded in 1687 and transferred after the Jesuit expulsion. Though the interior cloisters are original, the exterior was considerably modified in 1927 by restoring architect Jaime Roca, who gave the building its present baroque flare.

In 2000 Unesco declared the Manzana Jesuítica a World Heritage site, along with five Jesuit *estancias* throughout the province.

MUSEO HISTÓRICO PROVINCIAL MARQUÉS DE SOBREMONTE

It's worth dropping into this **museum** (433-1661/71; Rosario de Santa Fe 218; admission ARS3; 9am-2pm Mon-Sat), one of the most important historical museums in the country, if only to see the colonial house it occupies: an 18th-century home that once belonged to Rafael Núñez, the colonial governor of Córdoba and later viceroy of the Río de la Plata. It has 26 rooms, seven interior patios, meter-thick walls and an impressive wrought-iron balcony supported by carved wooden brackets.

CRIPTA JESUÍTICA

The Jesuits, at the beginning of the 18th century, built the **Cripta Jesuítica** (cnr Rivera Indarte & Av Colón; admission ARS3; 9am-3pm Mon-Fri). It was originally designed as a novitiate and later converted to a crypt and crematorium. Abandoned after the Jesuit expulsion, it was demolished and buried around 1829 when the city, while expanding Av Colón, knocked the roof into the subterranean naves and built over the entire structure. It remained all but forgotten until Telecom, while laying underground telephone cable in 1989, accidentally ran into it. The city, with a new outlook on such treasures, exquisitely restored the crypt and uses it regularly for musical and theatrical performances and art exhibits. Entrances lie on either side of Av Colón in the middle of the Rivera Indarte pedestrian mall.

MUSEO MUNICIPAL DE BELLAS ARTES DR GENARO PÉREZ

This **museum** (433-1512; Av General Paz 33; 10am-8pm Tue-Sun) is prized for its collection of paintings from the 19th and 20th centuries. Works, including those by Emilio Caraffa, Lucio Fontana, Lino Spilimbergo, Antonio Berni and Antonio Seguí, chronologically display the history of the *cordobés* school of painting, at the front of which stands Genaro Pérez himself. The museum is housed in Palacio Garzón, an unusual late-19th-century building named for its original owner; it also has outstanding changing contemporary art exhibits.

PLAZA SAN MARTÍN & AROUND

Córdoba's lovely and lively central plaza dates from 1577. Its western side is dominated by the white arcade of the restored **Cabildo** (colonial town-council building), completed in 1785 and containing three interior patios, as well as basement cells. All are open to the public as part of the **Museo de la Ciudad** (☎ 433-1543; Independencia 30; ☺ 9am-1pm & 3-7pm Tue-Sun), a block to the south.

Occupying nearly half a city block, the **Iglesia de Santa Teresa y Convento de Carmelitas Descalzas de San José** (cnr Caseros & Independencia; ☺ 6-8pm) was completed in 1628 and has functioned ever since as a closed-order convent for Carmelite nuns. Only the church itself is open to visitors. Once part of the convent, the **Museo de Arte Religioso Juan de Tejeda** (☎ 423-0175; Independencia 122; ☺ 9:30am-12:30pm Wed-Sat), next door, exhibits religious artifacts, as well as paintings by *cordobés* masters.

Nueva Córdoba & Güemes

Before the northwestern neighborhoods of Chateau Carreras and Cerro de las Rosas lured the city's elite to their peaceful hillsides, Nueva Córdoba was the neighborhood of the *cordobés* aristocracy. It's now popular with students, which explains the proliferation of brick high-rise apartment buildings. Still, a stroll past the stately old residences that line the wide Av H Yrigoyen reveals the area's aristocratic past.

Paseo del Buen Pastor (Av H Yrigoyen 325; ☺ 10am-8pm) is a cultural center/performance space, which was built in 1901 as a combined chapel/monastery/women's prison. In mid-2007 it was re-inaugurated to showcase work by Córdoba's young and emerging artists. There are a couple of hip cafe-bars in the central patio area where you can kick back with an Appletini or two. The attached chapel (which has been desanctified) hosts regular live-music performances – stop by for a program, or check Thursday's edition of the local newspaper *La Voz del Interior* for details.

While you're in the neighborhood, pop across the road to see the marvelous neo-Gothic **Parroquia Sagrado Corazón de Jesús de los Capuchinos** (cnr Buenos Aires & Obispo Oro), built between 1928 and 1934, whose glaring oddity is its missing steeple (omitted on purpose to symbolize human imperfection). Among the numerous sculptures that cover the church's facade are those of Atlases symbolically struggling to bare the spiritual weight of the religious figures above them (and sins and guilt of the rest of us).

Nueva Córdoba's landmark building, the **Palacio Ferreyra** (Av H Yrigoyen 551; ☺ 10am-8pm Tue-Sun) was built in 1914 and designed by Ernest Sanson in the Louis XVI style. The build-

ing itself is amazing, and has recently been converted into a fine-arts museum, featuring more than 400 works in 12 rooms spread over three floors. If you're into art or architecture, this place is a don't miss.

One of the city's best contemporary art museums is the neoclassical **Museo Provincial de Bellas Artes Emilio Caraffa** (☎ 433-3414; Av H Yrigoyen 651; ☺ 10am-8pm Tue-Fri, 10:30am-7pm Sat & Sun). It stands ostentatiously on the eastern side of Plaza España. Architect Juan Kronfuss designed the building as a museum and it was inaugurated in 1916. Exhibits change monthly. South of the museum the city unfolds into its largest open-space area, the **Parque Sarmiento**, designed by Charles Thays, the architect who designed Mendoza's Parque General San Martín.

Once a strictly working-class neighborhood, Güemes is now known for the eclectic **antique stores** and **artisan shops** that line the main drag of Belgrano, between Rodríguez and Laprida. Its weekend *feria artisanal* (p317), one of the country's best, teems with antique vendors, arts and crafts and a healthy dose of Córdoba's hippies. It's within the same block as the **Museo Iberoamericano de Artesanías** (☎ 433-4368; cnr Belgrano & Av Rodríguez; ☺ 10am-5pm Mon-Fri), which houses beautiful crafts from throughout South America. A good way back to the city center is along **La Cañada**, an acacia-lined stone canal with arched bridges.

COURSES

Córdoba is an excellent place to study Spanish; in many ways, being a student is what Córdoba is all about. Lessons cost about AR$60 per hour for one-on-one tuition or AR$600 to AR$800 per week in small classes.

Escuela Superior de Yoga (☎ 427-0712; Salguero 256) Offers yoga classes with monthly rates.

Facultad de Lenguas (☎ 433-1073/5, ext 30; Av Vélez Sársfield 187) Part of the Universidad Nacional de Córdoba.

SET Idiomas (☎ 421-1719; www.learningspanish.com .ar; Corrientes 21) Offers accommodation and afternoon activities at extra cost and discounts for extended study.

Tsunami Tango (☎ 15-313-8746; www.tsunamitango .blogspot.com; Laprida 453) Tango classes and *milongas* (tango halls) Tuesday to Saturday. The website lists times.

TOURS

City tours (in Spanish/English AR$30/50) Absorb Córdoba's rich history by taking one of the guided city tours that depart at 4:30pm Tuesday to Sunday from Casa Cabildo (p309). Reserve a day in advance if you want a tour in English.

Latitud Sur (☎ 425-6023; www.latitudsurtrek.com.ar; Fructuoso Rivera 70) Run by an enthusiastic young couple with boundless knowledge of both the sierras and the city, Latitud Sur offers mountain-bike, trekking, rock-climbing and horseback-riding tours throughout the Sierras de Córdoba, including day trips to Los Gigantes and Parque Nacional Quebrada del Condorito (p328). Prices range from AR$90 to AR$120, including transport, guide and lunch. Its city tours are outstanding, fun and only cost AR$25 per person.

FESTIVALS & EVENTS

During the first three weeks of April, the city puts on a large **crafts market** (locally called 'FICO') at the city fairgrounds, in the town's north near Chateau Carreras stadium. Bus 31 from Plaza San Martín goes there. Mid-September's **Feria del Libro** is a regional book fair.

SLEEPING

Hotels on and around Plaza San Martín make exploring the center a cinch, but you'll have to walk several blocks for dinner and nightlife. Hotels along La Cañada and in Nueva Córdoba, on the other hand, mean going out to dinner and hitting the bars is a simple matter of walking down the street.

Centro

Aldea Hostel (☎ 426-1312; www.aldeahostel.com; Santa Rosa 447; dm AR$32, d with/without bathroom AR$120/90; 🖳 🛜) It has plain but spacious rooms in a mildly inconvenient location. The patio, rooftop terrace and bar areas ooze atmosphere and the vibe is young and friendly.

Palenque Hostel (☎ 423-7588; www.palenquehostel .com.ar; Av General Paz 371; dm AR$35, d without bathroom AR$100; 🗷 🖳 🛜) By far the prettiest hostel in Córdoba, the Palenque occupies a classic old house and retains much of its original charm. Facilities are extensive, including laundry area, air-con and nightly cooking classes. Dorms are large, with plenty of room to move.

our pick **Hotel Garden** (☎ 421-4729; www.garden -hotel.com.ar; 25 de Mayo 35; s/d standard AR$80/110, deluxe AR$130/160; 🗷 🛜) About as central as it gets. Standard rooms are OK value, but the deluxe are several steps up in quality and a very good deal.

Hotel Quetzal (☎ 426-5117; www.hotelquetzal.com .ar; San Jerónimo 579; s/d AR$110/150; 🗷 🖳) Spacious, minimalistic, modern rooms are what's on offer here. Once the seemingly endless renovations are done, this should be a very tranquil option.

LOVE BY THE HOUR

Every city in Argentina has *hoteles por hora* (hourly rate hotels), where people take their secret lovers for a romp in the good old proverbial hay. They vary from cheap, nondescript *residenciales* (cheap hotels) to deluxe love pads with black lights, wall-to-wall mirrors, nonstop sex-TV, Jacuzzis and room-service menus featuring every imaginable sex toy under the sun. These deluxe versions are a part of under-the-table Argentine culture that possibly shouldn't be missed (provided you're traveling with a partner who's game, of course).

Córdoba boasts four deluxe *hoteles por hora* on the road to the airport, and if you haven't experienced one of these Argentine institutions, now's your chance. Although they're geared toward folks with cars, you can go in a taxi (trust us, we know). Here's a quick primer on how they work.

First, it's all about anonymity. As you drive into the hotel a big number flashes on a sign; that's your room number. Drive to the garage door with your number on it, pull in and close the garage door; if you're in a taxi, the driver will drop you in the garage and leave. Close the garage door and enter the room.

In five minutes the phone will ring, and the attendant will ask you if you'd like a complimentary beverage, which he or she then delivers through a tiny sliding door in the wall so no one sees anybody. When the attendant knocks on the door, you open it, take your drinks and pay for the room (AR$75 for two hours is the going rate). Ten minutes before your time is up, the attendant will courteously ring again to tell you it's time to get your gear back on.

Of the four hotels on the airport road, the best is **Eros Hotel** (Camino al aeropuerto, Km 5.5; AR$45 per hour). Rooms have Jacuzzis, bedside control panels, all the right TV channels and *all* the fun stuff. And it's impeccably clean.

A taxi costs about AR$20 each way from town. If you take one, call a *remise* (telephone taxi) from your hotel and have the driver pick you up later. They all know the drill – no pun intended.

Hotel Sussex (☎ 422-9070; www.hotelsussexcba .com.ar; San Jerónimo 125; s/d AR$200/250; 🅿 🛜 🏊) Another wonderful lobby (this one sporting vaulted ceilings, grand piano and fine art) leads on to more workaday rooms. At this price, you'd want to be getting plaza views.

Windsor Hotel (☎ 422-4012; www.windsortower.com; Buenos Aires 214; s/d from AR$412/473; 🅿 🛜 🏊) In a great downtown location, the Windsor is one of the few classic hotels in town with any real style. The lobby's all dark wood and brass, and the rooms have been tastefully renovated with modern fittings.

Nueva Córdoba & La Cañada

Le Grand Hostel (☎ 422-7115; www.legrandshostel.com; Buenos Aires 547; dm AR$39-50, d AR$110; 🅿 💻 🛜) The best-looking hostel in town would be a madhouse if it ever hit its 108-bed capacity, but until then it's an excellent option. Need a good night's sleep? Look elsewhere.

Hotel Viña de Italia (☎ 425-1678; www.hotelvina deitalia.com.ar; San Jerónimo 611; s/d AR$110/150; 🅿 💻) There's a bit of elegance left in this 150-room hotel, and the midsize rooms include TV, phone, air-con and heating. The rooms aren't nearly as graceful as the lobby, but they're still a good deal.

Hotel Viena (☎ 460-0909; www.hotelviena.com.ar; Laprida 235; s/d AR$170/200; 🅿 💻 🛜) This modern hotel in the heart of Nueva Córdoba offers bright, clean rooms and an excellent breakfast buffet. There are lots of nooks for sitting in the lobby area, and there's a restaurant on the premises. Good choice.

Hotel Heydi (☎ 422-2219; www.hotelheydi.com.ar; Blvd Illia 615; s/d AR$170/220; 🅿) This is the best of the bunch near the bus terminal: a modern, immaculate place with friendly, professional staff.

Amerian (☎ 420-7000; www.amerian.com; Blvd San Juan 165; r from AR$370; 🅿 💻 🛜 🏊) Straddling the border between the new town and the historic center, the Amerian is a big-business hotel with an excellent location and all the comforts. Sunset drinks at the bar by the rooftop pool are near obligatory.

EATING

Mercado Norte (cnr Rivadavia & Oncativo; ☯ Mon-Sat) Córdoba's indoor market has delicious and inexpensive food, such as pizza, empanadas and seafood. Browsing the clean stalls selling every imaginable cut of meat, including whole *chivitos* (goat) and pigs, is a must.

Bar San Carlos (Plazoleta San Roque, Salguero & San Jerónimo; set meals AR$12; ☯ lunch & dinner) Neighborhood *parrillas* (steak restaurants) are fast disappearing in Córdoba, but the San Carlos is one of the best, and still hanging in there. Get here reasonably early and beat the old guys out of a table on the small shady plaza.

Verde Siempre Verde (☎ 421-8820; 9 de Julio 36; mains from AR$15; ☯ lunch & dinner) Delicious vegetarian buffet that also serves set meals.

La Parrilla de Raul (Jujuy 278; mains AR$15-30; ☯ lunch & dinner) Of Córdoba's *parrillas,* this is probably one of the most famous. *Parrillada* (mixed grill) for two costs only AR$30, not including extras such as drinks or salad.

El Arrabal (☎ 460-2990; Belgrano 899; mains AR$18-30; ☯ lunch & dinner) One of the few old-style restaurants in Nueva Córdoba (OK, so it may be a reconstruction…), this place serves slightly pricey, imaginative regional and house specialties. It packs out for tango classes (AR$15) at 7pm nightly and the dinner tango show (AR$25) at 11pm Thursday to Saturday. Make a reservation.

El Ruedo (cnr Obispo Trejo & 27 de Abril; mains around AR$20; ☯ 8am-10pm) It doesn't stray too far from the steak, sandwich and pizza formula here, but the plaza-side spot under big shady trees is a winner, as are the *limonadas con soda* (lemon juice with soda water) on a hot day.

Qa'ra (Parana 206; mains from AR$20; ☯ lunch & dinner) Excellent Middle Eastern food provides a welcome dash of variety. The pretty courtyard is the place to be on a sunny day and the *picada* (sample plate) for two (AR$30) is a journey in deliciousness.

our pick Las Rías de Galicia (Montevideo 271; set lunch AR$20, mains AR$25-50; ☯ lunch & dinner) An upscale Spanish restaurant with the best value set lunch in town. Going à la carte gets you all sorts of goodies, including some excellent seafood selections.

Bursatil (San Jerónimo & Ituzaingó; mains AR$25-30; ☯ breakfast, lunch & dinner) Stylish, modern cafes are starting to pop up in the old part of town, and Bursatil is one of the finest. There's a cool modern interior, good coffee and a small, Asian-inspired menu.

Mega Doner (Ituzaingó 528; set meals AR$27-40; ☯ lunch & dinner) Conveniently located in Nueva Córdoba's bar district, this place specializes in real giro *doners*. Daily lunch specials are an excellent deal and there's outdoor seating.

La Nieta 'e La Pancha (☎ 468-1920; Belgrano 783; mains AR$30-35; ✷ dinner Tue-Fri, 4:30pm-1am Sat & Sun) Wonderful staff prepares and serves a changing menu of delectable regional specialties, creative pastas and house recipes. Be sure to save room for dessert. Check out the lovely upstairs terrace, which catches breezes and gives ample people-watching ops on the street below.

Alcorta (☎ 424-7452; Av Alcorta 330; mains AR$30-55; ✷ lunch & dinner) This upmarket *parrilla*, esteemed for its grilled meats (many say they're the best in town), also serves delicious pasta and fish. Try the *mollejitas al sauvignan blanc* (sweetbreads in a white wine sauce).

Sushi Club (Yrigoyen 419; mains AR$40; ✷ lunch & dinner) Sushi in Córdoba? Well, why not? The surroundings are hip, the prices reasonable and the wasabi hit is the real deal.

Looking to chow down with Córdoba's student crowd? Pull up a stool at any of the following, where the empanadas, beer and *locro* (spicy corn and meat stew) flow freely.

La Alameda (Obispo Trejo 170; empanadas AR$2.50, locro AR$12; ✷ lunch & dinner) Pull up a bench and wash down your homemade empanadas with some ice-cold beer. Then write some graffiti on the wall.

La Candela (Duarte Quiros 67; empanadas AR$2.50, locro AR$14; ✷ lunch & dinner) Rustic and wonderfully atmospheric, run by three cranky but adorable señoras.

La Vieja Esquina (cnr Belgrano & Caseros; empanadas AR$2.50, locro AR$17; ✷ lunch Mon-Sat) A cozy little lunch spot with stools and window seating. Order at the bar.

DRINKING

Córdoba's drink of choice is Fernet (a strong, medicinal-tasting herbed liquor from Italy), almost always mixed with Coke. If you don't mind a rough morning, start in on the stuff.

Nightlife in Córdoba basically divides itself into three areas – all the bright young things barhop in Nueva Córdoba – a walk along Rondeau between Avs H Yrigoyen and Chacabuco after midnight gives you a choice of dozens of bars, mostly playing laid-back electronic music.

North of the center, there's a string of live-music venues on Blvd Guzmán near the corner of Av General Paz.

Across the river on Av Las Heras between Roque Sáenz Peña and Juan B Justo (the area known locally as Abasto) are the discos and nightclubs. Go for a walk along here and you'll probably pick up free passes to some, if not all, of them.

Los Infernadas (Belgrano 631) A laid-back bar playing an eclectic range of music. Live music Thursday to Sundays and a big *patio cervecero* (beer garden) make this a standout.

But Mitre (www.butmitre.com; Av Marcelo T de Alvear 635) Extremely popular bar-cum–dance club on La Cañada. Check it out, especially on Thursday night.

Beep! (Sucre 171; admission incl drink AR$10; ✷ midnight-dawn Thu-Sat) The best gay club in the center is completely empty until 2am and completely slamming until sunup.

Ojo Bizarro (Igualdad 176; admission AR$8-13) In a semidodgy neighborhood, the Bizarro is one of the city's more bohemian hangouts. There's plenty of mood lighting, and a different DJ in each of the four rooms.

El Barranco (Av Las Heras 58; admission AR$6-12) In the busy Albasto scene, this live-music venue cum disco is a good place to start, if only for the fact that it gets a crowd before 1am. Fridays are Latin dance partiesl; on Saturdays there are live bands.

ENTERTAINMENT

La Voz del Interior, Córdoba's main newspaper, has a reasonably comprehensive entertainment section every Thursday with show times and the like.

On Friday nights, the city hosts the **Patio del Tango** (admission AR$10, with dance lessons AR$20) on the outdoor Patio Mayor of the historic Cabildo (weather permitting), kicking off with two-hour tango lessons. Times vary, so it's best to stop by the Casa Cabildo Tourist Information Office (see p309).

Cuarteto music (a Córdoba invention) is predictably big here and played live in many venues. Unfortunately, it's also the gangsta rap of Argentine folk music and tends to attract undesirable crowds. **La Sala del Rey** (Humberto Primero 439) is a respectable venue and the best place to catch a cuarteto show, on Sunday, when the hugely popular band La Barra often plays.

Centro Cultural Casona Municipal (☎ 428-5600; cnr Av General Paz & La Rioja; ✷ 8am-8pm Sun-Fri, 10am-10pm Sat) Shows contemporary and avante garde art, hosts concerts and offers month-long art and music courses.

Teatro del Libertador General San Martín (☎ 433-2319; Av Vélez Sársfield 365; admission AR$25-160; ✷ box office 9am-9pm) It's well worth going to a performance here, if only to see the opulence of the country's most historic theater. The theater was completed in 1891, and the floor was designed to be mechanically raised and leveled to the stage, so seats could be removed, allowing for grand parties for the aristocracy of the early 1900s.

Cineclub Municipal Hugo del Carril (☎ 433-2463; www.cineclubmunicipal.org.ar; Blvd San Juan 49; admission AR$6; ☻ box office 9am-late) For a great night (or day) at the movies, pop into this municipal film house, which screens everything from art flicks to Latin American award winners and local films. Stop by for a program. There's also live music and theatrical performances here.

SHOPPING

Antique stores line Calle Belgrano in barrio Güemes, where there is also a **feria artisanal** (artisans' market; cnr Rodriguez & Belgrano; ☻ 5-10pm Sat & Sun), one of the country's best. You'll find Argentine handicrafts at several stores downtown.

Paseo Colonial (Belgrano 795; ☻ 10am-9pm Mon-Sat, 5-10pm Sun) To find out what the city's hip young designers have been working on, slip into this little arcade, featuring a variety of small shops selling clothes, homewares and jewelry.

Talabartería Crespo (☎ 421-5447; Obispo Trejo 141; ☻ Mon-Sat) Leather goods made from *carpincho* (a large rodent that makes a beautifully spotted leather) are the specialty here. Sweaters, knives and *mate* (tealike beverages) paraphernalia grace the shelves as well.

GETTING THERE & AWAY
Air
Córdoba's international airport, **Ingeniero Ambrosio Taravella** (☎ 434-8390), charges a AR$116 departure tax on all international departures.

Aerolíneas Argentinas/Austral (☎ /fax 482-1025; Av Colón 520) has offices downtown and flies several times daily to Buenos Aires (from AR$400). **Lan** (☎ 452-3030; Av Alcorta 206) flies daily to Buenos Aires (AR$366) and Santiago, Chile (one-way AR$1600). **Sol** (☎ 0810-122-7765; www.sol.com.ar) flies to Rosario (AR$264), Tucumán (AR$254) and Mendoza (AR$250). **Andes Líneas Aéreas** (☎ 426-5809; www.andesonline.com; Colón 532) flies to Salta (AR$320) and Puerto Iguazú (AR$470). **Aero Chaco** (☎ 0810-345-2422;

www.aerochaco.net) flies to Resistencia (AR$341) and plans to add flights to El Calafate and Iguazú.

Bus
Córdoba's **bus terminal** (NETOC; ☎ 423-4199, 423-0532; Blvd Perón 300) is about a 15-minute walk from downtown. **Rede Ticket** (Obispo Trejo 327) sells tickets for all the major bus companies without charging commission. Its downtown location is handy for booking in advance.

Sierras del Córdoba, Sierras de Calamuchita and Transportes La Cumbre all serve Córdoba's mountain hinterlands, including Villa General Belgrano (AR$18, two hours) and Mina Clavero (AR$35, three hours). Their offices are on the top floor of the terminal. Other nearby destinations in the Sierras are easier and more quickly reached from the Mercado Sud minibus terminal (see p318).

There are several daily departures to the destinations listed following. Check the **bus terminal tourist office** (☎ 433-1980) for the best deals, cheapest fares and quality services.

Destination	Cost (AR$)	Duration (hr)
Bahía Blanca	160	12
Bariloche	254	22
Buenos Aires	160	10
Catamarca	73	5-6
Corrientes	175	12
Esquel	375	25
Formosa	166	12
Jujuy	176	12
La Rioja	73	7
Mendoza	100	10
Merlo	45	5½
Montevideo (Uruguay)	190	15
Neuquén	200	17
Paraná	67	6
Puerto Iguazú	296	22
Puerto Madryn	260	18-20
Resistencia	140	13
Río Gallegos	430	40
Rosario	71	6
Salta	182	12
San Juan	105	14
San Luis	65	6
San Martín de los Andes	292	21
Santiago del Estero	77	6
Tucumán	106	8

Several companies offer service to Chilean destinations, including Santiago (AR$180, 16 hours) and Valparaiso (AR$100, 16 hours), though most involve changing buses in Mendoza.

Minibus

Frequent minibuses leave from **Mercado Sud minibus terminal** (Blvd Illia, near Buenos Aires). Some of these go direct, while others stop at every little town along the way. It's worth asking, as this can shave an hour off your travel time.

In summer there may be direct buses to La Cumbrecita, but it will probably be quicker to go first to Villa General Belgrano.

Destination	Cost (AR$)	Duration (hr)
Alta Gracia	7	1
Capilla del Monte	23	3
Cosquín	13	1¼
Jesús María	9	1
La Falda	17	3
La Cumbre	20	3
Mina Clavero	35	3
Villa Carlos Paz	6	1
Villa General Belgrano	18	2

Train

Trains leave Córdoba's **Estación Ferrocarril Mitre** (☎ 426-3565; Blvd Perón s/n) for Rosario (AR$22/35/70 in *turista/primera*/Pullman class, eight hours) and Buenos Aires' Retiro station (AR$30/50/90/150 in *turista/primera*/Pullman/*camarote,* 15 hours) at 4:20pm and 8pm on Wednesday and Sunday. There is a dining car and bar on board. Tickets often sell out weeks in advance, especially in the *camarote* (two-person sleeping cabin), so book as soon as possible.

Trains to Cosquín (AR$6, two hours) leave from **Estación Rodríguez del Busto** (☎ 568-8979; Cardeñosa 3500) on the northwest outskirts of town at 10:50am daily. Buses A4 and A7 from the central plaza go to the station or it's an AR$18 taxi ride.

GETTING AROUND

The airport is 15km north of town via Av Monseñor Pablo Cabrera. Intercórdoba goes to/from the airport from the main bus station (AR$3). A taxi into town shouldn't cost you more than AR$25.

Buses require *cospeles* (tokens), available for AR$1.50 from nearly every kiosk in town.

Bike hire is available from **Córdoba Rent a Bike** (☎ 421-8012; cordobarentabike@gmail.com; San Martín 5), inside the lottery agency. Rates are AR$30/50 per half-/full day with an AR$400 deposit.

A car is very useful for visiting some of the nearby Jesuit *estancias* that cannot be reached

by bus. Depending on seasonal demand, economy cars cost around AR$200 with 200km. Try the following:

Alamo (☎ 499-8436; Sheraton Hotel, Duarte Quirós 1300)

Europcar (☎ 422-4867, 481-7683; Entre Ríos 70) Inside Hotel Dora.

THE CENTRAL SIERRAS

Nowhere near as visually spectacular as the nearby Andes, the Central Sierras more than make up for it by being way more hospitable. The area is dotted with little towns that are worth a quick visit or a longer stay, and is connected by an excellent road network with frequent bus services.

From the hippy-chic of paragliding capital La Cumbre to the over-the-top kitsch of Villa Carlos Paz, you'd have to be one jaded traveler not to find something to your liking here. Kicking back is easily done – the riverside village of Mina Clavero is a favorite, as are the ex-Jesuit centers of Alta Gracia and Jesús María. Things get decidedly Germanic down south, and the pedestrian-only La Cumbrecita is not to be missed for *spaetzle* (German egg noodles), bush walks and swimming holes.

VILLA CARLOS PAZ

☎ 03541 / pop 81,670 / elev 600m

Not everybody gets a chance to go to Vegas, but you might be able to satiate a little of your thirst for kitsch in this summer resort town 36km west of Córdoba. Villa Carlos Paz, set on the shores of so-called Lago San Roque (in reality a large reservoir), has architectural excesses including hotels shaped like pyramids and the Kremlin, and the town's pride and joy, a monstrous cuckoo clock (*reloj cu-cu* for the Spanish speakers out there). In summer, hordes of Argentines crowd Carlos Paz's lakeshores, pack its dance floors and whiz around in miniature trains on city tours. Foreigners generally find it less appealing.

A **telesilla** (chairlift; ☎ 422254; Sanchez & San Antonio; return ticket AR$20; ☯ 10am-6pm) takes you to the top of Cerro Carlos Paz for a bird's-eye view over town. There's a pricey cafe and a couple of short, well-signposted walking trails at the top.

The **tourist office** (☎ 436430; cnr San Martín & Yrigoyen; ☯ 7am-11pm summer, to 9pm rest of yr) distributes useful maps and guides to local services (which are plentiful).

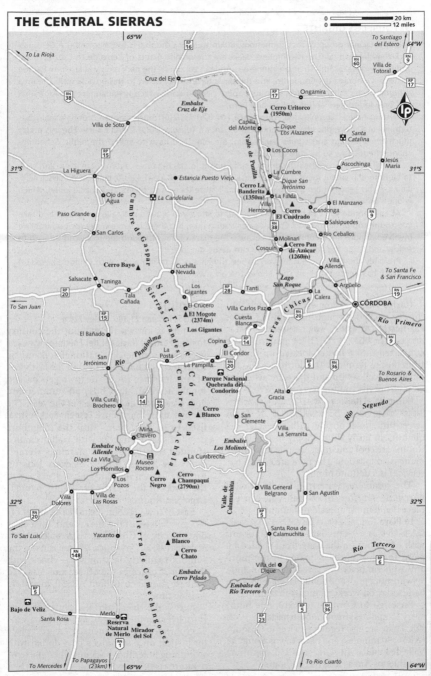

THE CENTRAL SIERRAS

DETOUR: LOS GIGANTES

This spectacular group of rock formations, 80km west of Córdoba, is fast becoming Argentina's rock-climbing capital. The two highest peaks are the granite giants of Cerro de La Cruz (2185m) and El Mogote (2374m). There are numerous Andean condors – the park is only 30km from Parque Nacional Quebrada del Condorito, and the birds have slowly taken to this area as well. The area is home to the tabaquillo tree, with its papery peeling bark, which is endangered in Argentina and only found here and in Bolivia and Peru.

Getting here is complicated. **Sarmiento** (☎ 0351-433-2161) buses leave Córdoba's main bus terminal at 8am Wednesday to Monday and 6am on Tuesday (AR$18, two hours). The bus pretty much turns around and comes back again, meaning you have to spend the night. Schedules change frequently, so be sure to check.

Get off at El Crucero (tell the driver you're going to Los Gigantes). From there it's a 3km walk to La Rotonda, where there is a super-basic **hospedaje** (☎ 03541-498370; camp site per person AR$6; dm AR$25, per person kitchen use AR$5) and a small store (beer, soft drinks and snacks only), which is open on weekends.

At La Rotonda you can hire guides (AR$40) to show you around the cave complexes and take you to the top of Cerro de La Cruz. It's not a long hike, but there is some tricky rock scrambling involved. Guides are recommended because the maze of trails through the rocks can be hard to follow and if the fog comes down, you can easily get lost.

Probably the best and easiest way to see the area is by taking a trip with Latitud Sur (p314) in Córdoba, whose excellent staff knows the area well.

Carlos Paz has some excellent hotels, but they're packed through the summer. **Carlos Paz Hostel** (☎ 436023; www.carlospazhostel.com.ar; Lugones 72; dm AR$40; 🛜 🖳) It's a modern house converted into a hostel, located up the hill from the bus terminal. The dorms are OK, the kitchen's well set up and there are awesome views from the rooftop terrace.

Nuevo Hotel Italiano (☎ 422202; www.nuevohotel italiano.com.ar; Uruguay 253; s/d AR$100/130; 🅿 🖳) A sweet little hotel oozing with character – a quantity in fairly short supply in this town. Rooms are cool and quiet, despite its central, main-road location. The pool area (with bar service) is a definite bonus.

The *costanera* (waterfront) is lined with *parrillas*, *tenedor libres* (all-you-can-eat places) and more upscale restaurants.

La Playa (Costanera s/n; mains AR$20-35; ⓧ breakfast, lunch & dinner) This laid-back restaurant, with tables out on the waterfront shaded by palm-thatch umbrellas, is one of the more atmospheric places to eat. Bonuses include a swimming pool and sandy lake beach. Live bands play on weekend nights in summer.

Buses go to Córdoba (AR$13, one hour, every 15 minutes) from the **bus terminal** (San Martín 400). There are also regular services to Cosquín (AR$6, 40 minutes) and other towns along the Valle de Punilla, Alta Gracia (AR$6, one hour) and Buenos Aires (AR$106, 11 hours).

COSQUÍN
☎ 03541 / pop 21,300 / elev 720m

Cosquín is known throughout the country for its **Festival Nacional del Folklore** (www.aqui cosquin.org), a nine-day national folk-music festival which has been held in the last week of January since 1961. The town gets packed for the festival, stays busy all summer and goes pleasantly dead the rest of the year. The slightly more hard-core **Cosquín Rock Festival** used to be held here, until the neighbors decided that teenagers with wallet chains, studded wristbands and piercings weren't really the tourist trade they were looking for. The festival relocated a few years ago to the banks of the nearby (and aptly named) Lago San Roque.

East of town, 1260m **Cerro Pan de Azúcar** offers good views of the sierras and, on a clear day, the city of Córdoba. An **aerosilla** (chairlift; return ticket AR$20; ⓧ 9am-1pm & 3-5pm) runs to the summit regularly in summer – check with the tourist office in the off season. A taxi to the base should cost about AR$50, including waiting time.

Across the river from the center of town (turn left after the bridge), Av Belgrano forms 4km of waterfront promenade – a great place for a stroll on a summer's day, dotted with swimming holes that pack out when the temperature rises.

The **municipal tourist office** (☎ 453701; www.cos quin.gov.ar; San Martín 560; ☒ 8am-9pm Mon-Fri, 9am-6pm Sat & Sun) has a good map of the town.

Sleeping & Eating

Residencial Ale (☎ 450232; Tucumán 809; s/d AR$45/70) A friendly, family-run budget option. Floors are wooden, beds old and there are no frills whatsoever.

Hospedaje Petit (☎ 451311; petithotel@infocosquin .com.ar; A Sabattini 739; s/d AR$80/100) Steepled roofs and lovely antique floor tiles in the lobby give way to some fairly ordinary, modern rooms in the interior. It's decent value, though – clean, spacious and central.

Hostería Siempreverde (☎ 450093; hosteriasiem preverde.com; Santa Fe 525; s/d AR$100/120) This lovely old house has good-sized, modern rooms out back. There's a big, shady garden and the breakfast/lounge area is comfortable and stylish.

San Martín, between the plaza and the stadium, is lined with cafes, restaurants and *parrillas*.

Confitería Munich (cnr San Martín & Sarmiento; sand wiches from AR$10; ☒ breakfast, lunch & dinner) An at mospheric plaza-side cafe-bar, the Munich is a great place to grab a table in the late afternoon and watch the world go by.

Mama Rosa (Perón & Catamarca; mains AR$25-35; ☒ lunch & dinner) The most frequently rec ommended *parrilla* looks like a barn from the outside, but the excellent service and warm atmosphere help lend it a touch of intimacy

Getting There & Away

There are many daily departures north to La Falda (AR$6, 45 minutes) and La Cumbre (AR$8, 1¼ hours); and south every 20 minutes to Villa Carlos Paz (AR$6, 40 minutes) and Córdoba (AR$10, 1¼ hours). There are a few departures daily for Buenos Aires (AR$107, 11 hours).

Trains depart for Córdoba's Estación Rodriguez del Busto (AR$6, 2½ hours) at 2pm daily.

LA FALDA

☎ 03548 / pop 16,300 / elev 934m

A woodsy resort town, La Falda is busier than its Central Sierra neighbors and not quite as interesting. It's worth a day or two, though, for walks in the hills and around the grounds of the defunct Hotel Eden.

La Falda's main **plaza** (cnr Sarmiento & Rivadavia) is a charming, tranquil affair, all the more so for being removed from the main drag. On weekends, and daily in summer, there's a **feria artisanal** (☒ daylight hr) here.

The **tourist office** (☎ 423007; www.lafalda.gov.ar; Av España 50; ☒ 8am-8:30pm) is very helpful and has excellent maps of the area.

Sights & Activities

A favorite **hiking** trail takes about two hours to the nearby summit of 1350m Cerro La Banderita. And since you're in town, take a guided tour of the once-extravagant, now-decaying **Hotel Eden** (admission by tour AR$20; ☒ 10am-noon & 2-4pm summer, 10am-noon & 2-4pm Fri-Sun winter), built in 1897, where the guest list included Albert Einstein, the duke of Savoy and several Argentine presidents. Inside the hotel is the **Miniature Train Museum**, a strangely captivat ing museum devoted to, you guessed it, very small trains. From the hotel, follow signs to **El Chorito**, a lookout with spectacular views out over the Sierras Chicas.

When the weather heats up, locals and tourists alike head for **7 Cascadas** (admission AR$5; ☒ daylight hr), which has three pools and a va riety of swimming holes under waterfalls that were created when the local dam was built. It's a 3km walk or AR$12 taxi ride from town.

Sleeping & Eating

Hostería Marina (☎ 422640; Güemes 144; r per person AR$40; ☒) The rooms are on the small side, but this is an excellent budget deal – clean and quiet, with a decent-sized swimming pool in the front yard.

Residencial Old Garden (☎ 422842; Capital Federal 28; s/d AR$120/150; ☒) Definitely one of the better accommodation deals in the country, this is a beautiful old house, lovingly maintained by the live-in owners. The whole place is charm ing, right down to the fuzzy dogs running around the large gardens.

our pick **La Bordolesa** (cnr Sarmiento & Saavedra; mains from AR$20; ☒ lunch & dinner) A laid-back, modern *parrilla* with two grills going – one inside and one out. If the weather's good, grab a table on the lawn and a platter of *picadas* (finger food: AR$25 for two) – it's a fine way to while away a few hours.

Meat dodgers will be very relieved at the sight of **Pachamama** (Av Eden 127; ☒ 9am-3pm), a vegetarian restaurant and health-food store on the main street.

Getting There & Away

The bus terminal sits on RN 38, just north of Av Eden. There are regular buses and minibuses south to Cosquín (AR$6, 45 minutes), Villa Carlos Paz (AR$9, 1¼ hours) and Córdoba (AR$17, two hours), and north to La Cumbre (AR$4.50, 30 minutes) and Capilla del Monte (AR$6, one hour). There are regular long-distance runs to Buenos Aires (from AR$110, 12 hours) and other destinations.

LA CUMBRE

☎ 03548 / pop 9800 / elev 1141m

A favorite getaway for Córdoba dwellers and foreigners alike, La Cumbre packs a lot of character into a small space. It's an agreeable little town due to its wide streets and mild mountain climate, and there are plenty of adventures to be had in the surrounding hills. The town gained worldwide fame when it hosted the 1994 World Paragliding Cup, and enthusiasts of the sport have made La Cumbre their home, giving the town an international feel. The launch site, 380m above the Río Pinto, provides a spectacular introduction to the sport and there are plenty of experienced instructors around, offering both classes and tandem flights.

Information

Banco de la Provincia de Córdoba (cnr López y Planes & 25 de Mayo) Has an ATM.
Tourist office (☎ 452966; www.lacumbre.gov.ar; Av Caraffa 300; ⏰ 8am-9pm Apr-Jun & Aug-Nov, to midnight Dec-Mar & Jul) Across from the bus terminal in the old train station. Friendly staff will supply a handy map of the town and surroundings.

Sights & Activities

Head to the south side of town to the road known as **Camino de los Artesanos**, where more than two dozen homes sell homemade goodies, from jams and chutneys to wool, leather and silver crafts. Most homes open from 11am to sunset.

There are excellent views from the **Cristo Redentor**, a 7m statue of Christ on a 300m hilltop east of town; from the Plaza 25 de Mayo, cross the river and walk east on Córdoba toward the mountains – the trail begins after a quick jut to the left after crossing Cabrera.

PARAGLIDING & SKY DIVING

Flying from the launch at Cuchi Corral (and hanging out by the Río Pinto afterward) is truly a memorable experience. The launch site (La Rampa) is about 10km west of town via a signed dirt road off the highway. Both Pablo Jaraba (El Turco) at **Taller de las Nubes** (☎ 03548-15-570951; www.cuchicorral.com) and **Fechu** (☎ 03548-15-574568) offer tandem flights and lessons. Everyone charges about the same. Tandem flights cost AR$250 for a half-hour; full courses cost AR$3000.

At the **Aeroclub La Cumbre** (☎ 452544; Camino a los Troncos s/n) you can arrange everything from tandem flights to ultralights. Ask for Andy Hediger (former paragliding world champion) or Hernán Pitocco (number four in the world in paragliding acrobatics). You can also test your nerves parachuting with **Nicolás López** (☎ 452544; www.redbullaerobatix.com, in Spanish).

HORSEBACK RIDING, TREKKING & MOUNTAIN BIKING

La Chacra (☎ 451703; Pje Beiró s/n) and Estancia El Viejo Piquete (opposite) offer horseback excursions lasting from a few hours to multiple days. Prices run about AR$90 for a half-day excursion and AR$450 for two days, including a full *asado* (barbeque) in the mountains.

Hacer Cumbre (☎ 452907; www.hacercumbre.com; Caraffa 270) rents good-quality mountain bikes (AR$60 per day) and offers guided rides in the breathtaking countryside around Cerro Ongamina, which you can combine with trekking, horseback riding and 4WD offroading. Day trips, including transfers and food, start at AR$500 for two people and become significantly cheaper if you get a group together.

Sleeping

The proprietors of the following places can arrange any activities available in La Cumbre.

Camping El Cristo (☎ 451893; Monseñor P Cabrera s/n; camp sites AR$10) Below the Cristo Redentor east of town, La Cumbre's exceptional campgrounds are only a short tramp from the center.

our pick **Hostel La Cumbre** (☎ 451368; www.hostel lacumbre.com; San Martín 186; dm AR$40, d with/without bathroom AR$130/120;) A couple of blocks behind the bus terminal, this converted English mansion is one of the most impressive hostels in the Sierras. Views from the front balcony are superb.

Hostería Plaza (☎ 451252; www.hosteriaplaza.com .ar; Cuesta 538; s/d AR$100/120;) A friendly, family-run hotel on a quiet street overlooking the plaza. Rooms are spacious, if not quite palatial, and the whole place is decked out with homey decorations. The small pool in the front yard can serve for a quick dip.

Estancia El Viejo Piquete (☎ 03548-15-635948; elviejopiquete@yahoo.com.ar; via Calle Mons Pablo Cabrera; d with full board AR$360) For a relaxing stay in a divine location about 2.5km north of town, treat yourself to a night or two at this remote three-room *estancia* with fabulous views over the Valle de Punilla. Horseback riding, hiking and other excursions are offered for guests and nonguests alike.

Eating & Drinking

Casa Caraffa (cnr Caraffa & Rivadavia; mains AR$20-30; ☯ lunch & dinner) An excellent main-street restaurant serving up delicious homemade pastas and a divine *bife de chorizo* (sirloin steak) with Roquefort sauce (AR$25).

Kasbah (Alberdi & Sarmiento; mains from AR$30; ☯ lunch & dinner) You may not be expecting a good Thai curry way out here, but this cute little triangular restaurant comes up with the goods. Also on offer is a range of Chinese and Indian dishes.

El Pungo (☎ 451378; www.elpungopub.com.ar; Camino de los Artesanos s/n; cover from AR$15; ☯ noon-late Sat & Sun) This somewhat legendary watering hole attracts musicians from all over the country (Argentine folk musicians Charly Garcia and Fito Paez have played here).

Getting There & Away

Buses depart regularly from La Cumbre's convenient **bus terminal** (General Paz, near Caraffa), heading northward to Capilla del Monte (AR$4, 30 minutes) or south to La Falda (AR$4.50, 30 minutes), Cosquín (AR$6, 1¼ hours), Villa Carlos Paz (AR$10, 1½ hours) and Córdoba (AR$20, 2½ hours). Minibuses (which take about half an hour less) are the fastest way to Córdoba. There is also direct service to Buenos Aires (AR$115, 12½ hours).

AROUND LA CUMBRE
Capilla del Monte

This attractive town (elevation 979m), 18km north of La Cumbre on the RN 38, not only attracts paragliders and outdoor enthusiasts to its surrounding countryside, but reputedly

---

CLOSE ENCOUNTERS

It's not just the freaks and hippies. Even normal-looking people in Capilla del Monte have stories about strange lights appearing in formation in the night skies over nearby Cerro Uritorco. The stories go way back, too. In 1935 Manuel Reina reported seeing a strange being dressed in a tight-fitting suit while he was out walking on a country road. In 1986 Gabriel and Esperanza Gómez saw a spaceship so big that its lights illuminated the surrounding countryside. The next day a burn mark measuring 122m by 64m was found at the point where it reportedly landed.

A couple of years later, 300 people witnessed another ship, which left a burn mark 42m in diameter. And in 1991, another burn mark was found. This one measured 12m in diameter, with a temperature of 340°C. Geologists were called in and they claimed that nearby rocks had recently been heated to a temperature of 3000°C.

Why all this activity around Capilla del Monte? This is where it gets really weird. One theory is that *Ovnis* (UFOs) visit the area because Cerro Uritorco is where the knight Parsifal brought the Holy Grail and the Templar Cross at the end of the 12th century. He did this to lay them beside the Cane of Order, which had been made 8000 years before by Lord Voltán of the Comechingones, the indigenous tribe that inhabited this region.

Another theory offers that they are drawn here because underneath Uritorco lies Erks, a subterranean city which, according to 'hermetic scientists' is where the future regeneration of the human species will take place. Inside you'll find the Esfera Temple and the three mirrors used to exchange data with other galaxies, and where you can see the details of the life of every human being.

The official explanation? Good ol' meteorological phenomena, caused by supercharged ion particles in the atmosphere, mixed in with a healthy touch of mass hysteria.

Whatever you believe, one thing's for sure – all this hype isn't hurting little Capilla del Monte's tourist industry one bit. Recently, the only people climbing Uritorco were goatherds and a few interested townsfolk. These days, numbers can approach 1000 per day, all hoping to catch a glimpse of the mysterious lights.

receives frequent visits from *Ovnis* (UFOs) as well, most frequently to the nearby 1950m **Cerro Uritorco** (admission AR$20), the highest peak in the Sierras Chicas. The 5km hike to the top affords spectacular views. Catch a taxi or walk the 3km to the base of the mountain. You must start the climb before midday, and begin your descent by 3pm.

Capilla del Monte itself has plenty of restaurants and lodging – the **tourist office** (☎ 03548-481903; www.capilladelmonte.gov.ar; cnr Av Pueyrredón & Buenos Aires) in the old train station has mounds of information. All that UFO activity has attracted its fair share of esoteric practitioners offering alternative treatments, massage and yoga retreats alongside Zen and Tantric temples. For more info on UFOs in the area, drop in to the **Centro de Informes Ovni** (☎ 482485; www.ciouritorco.org; ☼ 10am-4pm).

There is frequent bus service south to Córdoba (AR$30, three hours), stopping at all towns on the RN 38, and long-distance service to Buenos Aires.

Estancia Puesto Viejo

Billing itself as the only youth hostel set on an *estancia* in Argentina, this working **ranch** (☎ 03548-423809, 03548-15-566504; www.estanciapuestoviejo.com; dm/d AR$45/170) gives you the chance to live the gaucho dream without paying the deluxe prices that usually accompany it. All the farm-life activities are here – herding cattle, horseback riding etc, or you can just kick back and enjoy the scenery. Also on offer are 4WD tours to the little-visited Jesuit mission at La Candelaria, gold mine tours and trekking on Cerro Colorado. Simple, hearty meals (AR$55 per day) are available and you can use the kitchen.

Access is a little tricky – from La Cumbre you have to take a taxi (one way AR$120, 24km), but call first to see if the owners are in town and can give you a ride.

JESÚS MARÍA

☎ 03525 / pop 28,300

Sleepy little Jesús María earns its place on the map by being home to one of the most atmospheric Jesuit *estancias* in the region – the Unesco-listed **Museo Jesuítico Nacional de Jesús María** (☎ 420126; admission AR$10; ☼ 8am-7pm Tue-Fri, 10am-noon & 3-7pm Sat & Sun). The church and convent were built in 1618 and are set on superbly landscaped grounds. The Jesuits, after losing their operating capital to pirates off the Brazilian coast, sold wine they made here to support their university in colonial Córdoba. The museum has good archaeological pieces from indigenous groups throughout Argentina, informative maps of the missionary trajectory and well-restored (though dubiously authentic) rooms.

Jesús María is also home to the annual **Fiesta Nacional de Doma y Folklore** (www.festivaljesusmaria .com), a 10-day celebration of gaucho horsemanship and customs beginning the first weekend of January. The festival draws crowds from all over the country, and accusations of animal cruelty from animal-rights groups, who argue that whipping horses and making them perform acrobatics in front of noisy crowds under bright lights is tantamount to torture. Or to gaucho culture.

Most people do Jesús María as a day trip from Córdoba. Frequent minibuses (AR$9, one hour) leave Córdoba's Mercado Sud terminal and bus terminal (see p317) daily.

ESTANCIA SANTA CATALINA

☎ 03525

One of the most beautiful of the Sierra's Unesco World Heritage sites, the Jesuit *estancia* of **Santa Catalina** (☎ 421600; www.santacatalina .info; admission AR$5-15; ☼ 10am-1pm & 2-6pm Tue-Fri, closed Jan, Feb, Jul & Semana Santa), some 20km northwest of Jesús María, is a quiet, tiny place, where the village store occupies part of the *estancia*, and old-timers sit on the benches outside and watch the occasional gaucho ride past on a horse. Much of the *estancia* is off-limits to visitors, but guided **tours** (each site AR$5) are available, taking in the chapel, cloisters and novitiate, where unmarried slave girls were housed.

The grounds themselves, while a fraction of their former selves, are lovely and well maintained and you can easily while away an hour or two wandering around. Outside the *estancia*, around the back, is the original reservoir built by the Jesuits, now slowly being overtaken by tall-stemmed lilies.

Santa Catalina is the only Unesco World Heritage *estancia* still under private ownership. Part of the family owns and operates **La Ranchería de Santa Catalina** (☎ 424467, 03525-15-538957; r per person without bathroom AR$120), a lovely inn, restaurant (meals around AR$30) and crafts store in the *ranchería*. It has only two rooms, which occupy the former slave quarters and, while small, are carefully decorated and retain their original stone walls. Three more rooms with bathrooms are being constructed, using traditional techniques. The place is run by a friendly couple who are more than willing to fill you in on the illustrious story of the *estancia,* from Jesuit times to the present.

A taxi out here from Jesús María costs about AR$75.

ALTA GRACIA

☎ 03547 / pop 42,900 / elev 550m

Set around a 17th-century Jesuit reservoir, Alta Gracia is a tranquil little mountain town of winding streets and shady parks. The star attraction here is the 17th-century Jesuit *estancia,* whose exquisite church, nighttime lighting, and lovely location between a tiny reservoir and the central plaza make it one of the most impressive of Córdoba province's Unesco World Heritage sites. Revolutionary Che Guevara spent his adolescence in Alta Gracia and his former home is now a museum. Most visitors find a day enough and head back to Córdoba for the night.

The **tourist office** (☎ 428128; www.altagracia.gov.ar; Reloj Público, cnr Av del Tajamar & Calle del Molino; ◷ 7am-10:30pm summer, to 7pm winter) occupies an office in the clock tower.

Sights & Activities

THE JESUIT ESTANCIA

From 1643 to 1762, Jesuit fathers built the **Iglesia Parroquial Nuestra Señora de la Merced** (west side of Plaza Manuel Solares; admission free), the *estancia's* most impressive building. Directly south of the church, the colonial Jesuit workshops of **El Obraje** (1643) are now a public school. Beside the church is the **Museo Histórico Nacional del Virrey Liniers** (☎ 421303; www.museoliniers.org.ar; admission AR$10, Wed free; ◷ 9am-1pm & 3-7pm Tue-Fri, 9:30am-12:30pm & 3:30-6:30pm Sat, Sun & holidays), named after former resident Virrey Liniers, one of the last officials to occupy the post of Viceroy of the River Plate. If you want to know every last historical detail, guided tours in English (AR$30 per person; held at 10am, 11:30am, 3:30pm and 5pm) are available

---

THE LEGEND OF CHE GUEVARA

One of Cuba's greatest revolutionary heroes, in some ways even eclipsing Fidel Castro himself, was an Argentine. Ernesto Guevara, known by the common Argentine interjection 'che,' was born in Rosario in 1928 and spent his first years in Buenos Aires. In 1932, after Guevara's doctor recommended a drier climate for his severe asthma, Guevara's parents moved to the mountain resort of Alta Gracia, where the young Guevara would spend his adolescence.

He later studied medicine in the capital and, in 1952, spent six months riding a motorcycle around South America, a journey that would steer Guevara's sights beyond middle-class Argentina to the plight of South America's poor. The journal he kept during his trip, now known as *The Motorcycle Diaries,* hit bookstore shelves around the world and inspired the movie of the same name, staring Mexico's Gael García Bernal.

After his journey, Guevara traveled to Central America and fatefully landed in Mexico, where he met Fidel Castro and other exiles. Together the small group would sail to Cuba on a rickety old yacht and begin the revolution that overthrew Cuban dictator Fulgencio Batista in 1959. Unable to resign himself to the bureaucratic task of building Cuban socialism, Guevara tried, unsuccessfully, to spread revolution in the Congo, Argentina and finally Bolivia, where he was killed in 1967.

Today Che is known less for his eloquent writings and speeches than for his striking black-and-white portrait as the beret-wearing rebel – an image gracing everything from T-shirts to CD covers – taken by photojournalist Alberto Korda in 1960. Although these commercialized versions of Che are hardly a poke at the belly of global capitalism, they have managed to irritate some: Korda sued Smirnoff in 2000 for using his famous photograph to sell vodka, and a 1998 Taco Bell ad, in which a talking, beret-wearing Chihuahua barks 'Viva Gorditas' to a cheering crowd, sparked furor in Miami's Cuban-American community.

In 1997, on the 30th anniversary of Che's death, the Argentine government issued a postage stamp honoring Che's Argentine roots. You can take a look as the stamps, as well as other government-sponsored tributes from around the world, by visiting Alta Gracia's modest but lovely Museo Casa de Ernesto Che Guevara (see p326), inaugurated June 14, 2001, on what would have been Che's 73rd birthday.

and recommended – call to reserve one day in advance. If you just have a passing interest, each room has an information sheet in English, which gives you a fair idea of what's going on.

Directly north of the museum, across Av Belgrano, the **Tajamar** (1659) is one of the city's several 17th-century dams, which together made up the complex system of field irrigation created by the Jesuits.

MUSEO CASA DE ERNESTO CHE GUEVARA

In the 1930s, the family of youthful Ernesto Guevara moved here because a doctor recommended the dry climate for his asthma (see the boxed text, p325). Though Che lived in several houses – including the house in Rosario (p183) where he was born – the family's primary residence was Villa Beatriz, which was recently purchased by the city and restored as this **museum** (☎ 428579; Avellaneda 501; admission AR$5, Tue free; ⏲ 2-7pm Mon, 9am-7pm Tue-Sun). Its cozy interior is now adorned with a photographic display of Che's life, and a couple of huge photos commemorating a recent visit from Fidel Castro and Hugo Chávez. If you think you've been on the road for a while, check out the map detailing Che's travels through Latin America – whatever you think of the man's politics, you have to admit he was well traveled. A small selection of Che paraphernalia (including cigars, of course) is on sale.

ADVENTURE ACTIVITIES

Rent a Bike (☎ 494194; www.altagraciarentabike.com.ar) does pretty much what its name suggests, for AR$50 per day. Alta Gracia is a good place for bike riding – not much traffic and the two main sights are just far enough apart for it to be a pain to have to walk it.

If all Alta Gracia's history makes you feel like throwing yourself out of a plane, contact recommended local outfit **Paracenter** (☎ 03525-15-5413816; www.paracenter.com.ar), which offers tandem skydives for AR$500.

Sleeping & Eating

A number of hip cafe-bar-restaurants with sidewalk seating are scattered along Av Belgrano in the three blocks downhill from the Jesuit museum.

Alta Gracia Hostel (☎ 428810; www.altagraciahostel. com.ar; Paraguay 218; dm AR$35) Five short blocks downhill from the Jesuit museum, Alta Gracia's hostel offers a fair deal. Dorms are

roomy enough and the kitchen should meet your needs. One bizarre inconvenience: you can't check in until noon.

Hostal Hispania (☎ 426555; Av Vélez Sársfield 57; s/d AR$90/170; ✄ ✄) Located in a handsome late-19th-century wooden building, this place boasts spacious rooms that open onto a covered porch (complete with chaise longues) overlooking the large garden. The attached Spanish restaurant is worth a look in, too.

Sol de Polen (☎ 427332; www.hectorcelano.com.ar; Avellaneda 529; mains AR$10-15; ⏲ lunch & dinner) A few short steps from the Che museum, this Cuban-themed restaurant serves up a couple of Cuban dishes alongside all the Argentine standards. Friday nights there's live music and if you really like the place, it rents out basic double rooms at the back for AR$90.

our pick Morena (cnr Sarmiento & Funes; mains AR$25-40; ⏲ lunch & dinner) Some of the best eats in town are on offer in the lovely dining salon of this upscale restaurant, a couple of blocks uphill from the reservoir.

Getting There & Away

Minibuses depart regularly for Córdoba (AR$7, one hour) from in front of the clock tower near the main plaza. The **bus terminal** (Tacuarí at Perón) near the river also has departures for Córdoba, as well as Villa Carlos Paz (AR$6, one hour) and Buenos Aires (AR$160, 13 hours). Buses to Villa General Belgrano stop every hour on RP 5, about 20 blocks along Av San Martín from the center.

VILLA GENERAL BELGRANO

☎ 03546 / pop 7400 / elev 820m

More a cultural oddity than a full-blown tourist attraction, Villa General Belgrano flaunts its origins as a settlement of unrepatriated survivors from the German battleship *Graf Spee*, which sank near Montevideo during WWII.

The annual **Oktoberfest** (elevated in 1972 to status of Fiesta Nacional de la Cerveza; National Beer Festival; see http://elsitiode lavilla.com/oktoberfest, in Spanish), held during the first two weeks of October, draws beer lovers from all over the world. In summer the village slowly fills with holidaymakers enjoying the tranquil streets and evergreen-dotted countryside. Unless you're really excited about microbrew beer, *torta selva negra* (black forest cake) and goulash, Villa General Belgrano makes a fine day trip from Córdoba or nearby La Cumbrecita. Despite its decidedly Germanic flavor, you'd be lucky to hear any of the modern-day inhabitants speaking the language of the old country.

For an overview of the town, make your way up the **tower** (admission AR$2; ⊗ 9am-8pm) attached to the tourist office.

The **tourist office** (☎ 461215; www.vgb.gov.ar; Plaza José Hernández; ⊗ 8am-8:30pm) is on the main strip.

Activities

To go horseback riding, look for Sr Martinez, who sets up behind the bus terminal in summer and charges around AR$25 an hour. Otherwise contact **Pituco Sanchez** (☎ 463142), who offers horseback riding year-round at similar prices. **Fiedrich** (Roca 224) rents mountain bikes for AR$8/30 per hour/day.

If you're up for a stroll, a lovely path runs between Corrientes and El Quebracho alongside the Arroyo La Toma, a creek one block downhill from the main street.

Sleeping & Eating

In the December-to-March high season, hotel prices rise and rooms book quickly. Unless you book weeks before Oktoberfest, plan on hitting the festival as a day trip from Córdoba. There are numerous restaurants along the main strip of Julio A Roca and San Martín.

Albergue El Rincón (☎ 461323; rincon@calamu chitanet.com.ar; camp sites AR$10, dm AR$30, r per person AR$36) This beautiful Dutch-owned hostel, surrounded by forest, has excellent, spacious dorm rooms, outdoor and indoor kitchens, a *parrilla* and its own biodynamic farm. Outstanding breakfasts cost AR$10, and lunch and dinner AR$30. It's a good 1km walk from behind the bus terminal to the entrance gate; follow the signs.

Residencial Giovanni Luigi (☎ 462017; Ojo de Agua 35; s/d AR$70/90) An excellent little family-run spot right in the center of town. Rooms could be bigger, but the price can't be beat.

Posada Aitué (☎ 461476; www.elsitiodelavilla.com/ aitue; Sársfield 75; s/d from AR$140/170; ⊠ 🖳 🖳) This is a lovely Alpine-style chalet a short walk from the center. Pay another AR$60 and you get a sitting room, kitchenette and hydromassage bath.

Nissen (Julio A Roca 36; mains AR$15-25; ⊗ breakfast, lunch & dinner) A cute little cafe with sunny outdoor seating. Set-meal specials (AR$25) are a good deal.

Blumen (Julio A Roca 373; mains around AR$40; ⊗ lunch & dinner) With one of the widest menus in town, Blumen serves up good, tasty, if slightly expensive, dishes. It's a great spot for a few drinks – the huge shady beer garden is all wooden tables and pagodas, with plenty of space in between and the microbrew beer flowing readily.

Getting There & Away

The **bus terminal** (Av Vélez Sársfield) is uphill from San Martín, the main thoroughfare. Buses leave every hour for Córdoba (AR$18, two hours), and daily for Buenos Aires (AR$150, 11 hours). **Pajaro Blanco** (☎ 461709) has daily departures for La Cumbrecita (AR$18, two hours).

LA CUMBRECITA

☎ 03546 / pop 320 / elev 1300m

The pace of life slows waaaay down in this alpine-styled village, nestled in the forest in the Valle de Calamuchita. The tranquility is largely thanks to the town's pedestrian-only policy. It's a great place to kick back for a few days and wander the forest trails leading to swimming holes, waterfalls and scenic lookouts.

Visitors must park their cars in the dirt parking lot (AR$6) before crossing the bridge over Río del Medio by foot.

The helpful **tourist office** (☎ 481088; www .lacumbrecita.gov.ar; ⊗ 8:30am-9pm summer, 10am-6pm winter) is on the left, just after you cross the bridge into town.

Sights & Activities

The best reason to visit La Cumbrecita is to hike. Short trails are well marked and the tourist office offers a crude but useful map of the area. A 25-minute stroll will take you to **La Cascada**, a waterfall tucked into the mountainside. **La Olla** is the closest swimming hole, surrounded by granite rocks (people jump where it's deep enough). **Cerro La Cumbrecita** (1400m) is the highest point in town, about a 20-minute walk from the bridge. Outside town, the highest mountain is the poetically named **Cerro Wank** (1715m); a hike to the top takes about 40 minutes.

For guided hikes further into the mountains, as well as horseback riding (AR$60 for three hours), trout fishing and mountain biking, contact **Viviendo Montañas** (☎ 481172; Las Truchas s/n), which has an office on the main road in town. The company can also take you trekking to the top of **Cerro Champaquí** (2790m), the highest peak in the sierras, for about AR$100 per person.

If the whole Disneyland feel of La Cumbrecita isn't enough for you, check out **Peñon del Aguila** (☎ 0351-15-552-5232; www.penon delaguila.com.ar; adult/child AR$20/10; ❧ 11am-7pm daily in summer, weekends only rest of yr), a theme park offering 'alpine adventures.' Rappelling, ziplining, a canopy boardwalk, nature trails and waterfalls are all in abundance, cheerfully guided by folks in Tirolese outfits. The whole show wraps up with a sunset song-and-dance spectacular paying homage to Gambrinus, the king of beer. We kid you not.

Sleeping & Eating

La Cumbrecita has more than 20 hotels and *cabañas* in the surrounding hills; the tourist office is a good resource. Make reservations in summer (January and February), during Easter and during Villa General Belgrano's Oktoberfest (see p326).

Hostel El Viaje (☎ 15-573-5085; www.elviajelacum brecita.com; Calle Principal s/n; dm/d without bathroom AR$45/110) The only hostel in town is a cute, simple place, with a couple of three-bed dorms and one private room.

Hospedaje Casa Rosita (☎ 481003; Calle Principal s/n; s/d without bathroom AR$120/160) A humble little *hospedaje* (family home) set in a charming house by the river at the entrance to the village. If you can, go for room 1, which has a bay window overlooking the river.

Hotel La Cumbrecita (☎ 481052; www.hotelcum brecita.com.ar; s/d AR$130/260; ❧ ❧ ❧) Built on the site of the first house in La Cumbrecita, this rambling hotel has some excellent views out over the valley. Rooms aren't huge, but most have fantastic balconies. The extensive grounds include a gym and tennis courts. Half pensión (breakfast and dinner) is available for AR$30.

Confitería Tante Liesbeth (☎ 481079; ❧ 4-7:30pm Thu-Sun summer, 4-7:30pm Sat & Sun winter) On the north side of town, on the way to Cerro Wank, this is the village's most traditional teahouse, set creekside among the trees. It's about a 10-minute walk from the entrance to town.

El Paseo (mains AR$25-40; ❧ lunch & dinner Thu-Sun) Out by the La Olla swimming hole, this place serves up a good *parrilla*, plus all the Germanic standards. It's great for afternoon beer.

Restaurante Bar Suizo (Calle Pública s/n; mains AR$15-35; ❧ breakfast, lunch & dinner) Pull up a wooden bench under the pine tree and try some of the excellent Swiss German options such as *spaetzle* with wild mushroom sauce (AR$20).

Getting There & Away

From Villa General Belgrano, **Transportes Pajaro Blanco** (☎ 461709; cnr San Martín & Sarsfield), across and just downhill from the bus terminal, has departures to La Cumbrecita (AR$18, two hours, at 7am, 10am, noon, 4pm and 6:50pm Monday through Friday, and 8am, 10am, noon, 4pm and 6:50pm Saturday and Sunday). In summer there may be occasional minibuses from Córdoba's Mercado Sud terminal (see p318).

PARQUE NACIONAL QUEBRADA DEL CONDORITO
elev 1900-2300m

This national park protects 370 sq km of stunning rocky grasslands across the Pampa de Achala in the Sierras Grandes. The area, particularly the *quebrada* (gorge) itself, is an important condor nesting site and flight training ground for fledgling condors. A 9km, two-to three-hour hike from the park entrance at **La Pampilla** leads to the Balcón Norte (North Balcony), a cliff top over the gorge where you can view the massive birds circling on the thermals rising up the gorge. You can visit easily as a day trip from Córdoba or on your way to Mina Clavero.

Any bus from Córdoba to Mina Clavero will drop you at La Pampilla (AR$18, 1½ hours), where a trailhead leads to the gorge. To return to Córdoba (or on to Mina Clavero), flag a bus from the turnoff. Latitud Sur (p314) offers recommended day tours to the park.

For more information on the park, contact **Intendencia del PN Quebrada del Condorito** (☎ 03541-433371; www.quebradacondorito.com.ar; Sabattini 33) in Villa Carlos Paz.

MINA CLAVERO
☎ 03544 / pop 7350 / elev 915m

Really jumping in summertime, Mina Clavero pretty much empties out for the rest of the year, leaving visitors to explore the limpid streams, rocky waterfalls, numerous swimming holes and idyllic mountain landscapes at their own pace.

Mina Clavero is 170km southwest of Córdoba via RN 20, the splendid Nuevo

Camino de las Altas Cumbres (Highway of the High Peaks). It sits at the confluence of Río de Los Sauces and Río Panaholma, in the Valle de Traslasierra.

The Río Mina Clavero splits the town in two – if you arrive at the bus terminal and are headed for Andamundos Hostel or La Casa de Pipa, take the pedestrian bridge across the river – from there it's only a couple of blocks to the former and a short taxi ride to the latter. Otherwise you have to go the long way around.

The **tourist office** (☎ 470171; www.minaclavero.gov.ar; Av San Martín 1464; ☼ 7am-midnight Dec-Mar, 9am-9pm Apr-Nov) has standard brochures and a useful map of town.

Sights & Activities

Mina Clavero's *balnearios* (swimming areas) get mobbed in the summer, but are often empty the rest of the year. The magnificent, boulder-strewn gorges of the Río Mina Clavero are easily explored. A lovely *costanera* has been constructed, running from the pedestrian bridge all the way to the **Nido de Aguila**, the best swimming hole around – this makes for a great afternoon stroll. From there head west along the Río de Los Sauces and you'll hit **Los Elefantes**, a *balneario* named for its elephant-like rock formations. A 3km walk south along the river will take you to the village of **Villa Cura Brochero**, where you'll find black pottery that is characteristic of this region.

Traslasierra Aventura (☎ 471516; www.traslasierra.com/traslasierraaventura; San Martín 1241) offers tours of the nearby Comechingones mountains, condor spotting and horseback riding.

Sleeping

Many accommodations close around the end of March, when the town almost rolls up the sidewalks.

Andamundos Hostel (☎ 470249; www.andamundoshostel.com.ar; San Martín 554; dm/d AR$35/80; ▯) A rustic little setup a couple of blocks from the center of town. The big yard backing on to the river is a bonus.

Hotel Palace (☎ 470390; www.comprasvirtual.com/hotelpalace; Mitre 847; s/d AR$100/130) The highlight of this 40-room French-owned hotel is the huge backyard that slopes to the riverside. Shade trees and lounge chairs make it tough to leave the grounds. Rooms are slightly worn, but the garden makes up for it.

our pick **La Casa de Pipa** (☎ 470480; www.lacasadepipa.com; Hernán Cortés at Colón; s/d AR$150/200; ☼ closed May & Jun; ✕ ▤) This is a beautiful *hostería* (lodging house) set on mildly sloping grounds. There's plenty of shady spots, a good pool, a couple of barbecues and a lovely sunny breakfast room with views out over the mountains. It's about five blocks uphill from San Martín.

Hotel Rossetti (☎ 470012; www.hotelrossettiyspa.com.ar; Mitre 1434; all-inclusive packages per person AR$250; ✕ ▯ ▢ ▤) A sparkling hotel-spa complex in a slightly unfortunate location on a busy thoroughfare. Summer prices include meals, drinks and spa treatments. Off-season, doubles go for AR$160 (room only) and individual spa treatments cost AR$30 each.

Eating

Most of Mina Clavero's restaurants are along San Martín.

Palenque (San Martín 1191; mains AR$15-30; ☼ lunch & dinner) Funky works of art on the walls and live music on the weekends make this a popular spot. It's a great place for drinks and the snacks and meals are a good deal, too.

Cuba Bar (San Martín 1270; mains AR$20-35; ☼ lunch & dinner) Out the back of the Galeria Mina Clavero, the Cuba is noteworthy for three things – a decent music selection, a pool table and a great deck overlooking the river.

Don Alonso (cnr San Martín & Recalde; mains AR$20-35; ☼ lunch & dinner) The most frequently recommended *parrilla* in town, the Don serves up tasty empanadas and good-value set meals in front of the plaza.

Rincón Suizo (Champaqui 1200; mains AR$25-35; ☼ lunch & dinner) This comfy teahouse on the river prides itself on its homemade ice creams, delicious Swiss food (including fondue, raclette and ratatouille) and *torta selva negra*.

Getting There & Away

The **bus terminal** (Mitre 1191) is across the Río Mina Clavero from the town center. There are several daily buses to Córdoba (AR$31, three hours), Villa Carlos Paz (AR$21, 2½ hours) and at least three a day to Merlo (AR$45, 2½ to three hours). Minibuses to Córdoba are faster (AR$30, 2½ hours). **TAC** (☎ 470420) has daily service to Buenos Aires (AR$130, 13 hours). For destinations in San Juan and Mendoza provinces, go to nearby Villa Dolores (AR$12, one hour).

NONO & MUSEO ROCSEN

Operated by Juan Santiago Bouchon, an anthropologist, curator and passionate collector who first came to Argentina in 1950 as cultural attaché to the French embassy, this eclectic **museum** (☎ 03544-498218; www.museorocsen.org; admission AR$8; ☯ 9am-sunset) reveals just how strange the world really is. It contains more than 11,000 pieces, including antique motorcycles, mounted butterflies, Esso gas pumps, human skulls, Buddha statues, film projectors, Catholic altars, 19th-century instruments of torture, a shrunken head and a 1200-year-old Peruvian mummy. It's truly a one-of-a-kind museum, and requires plenty of time to explore.

The museum is 5km outside the pastoral village of **Nono**, a one-time indigenous settlement 8km south of Mina Clavero. There are regular minibuses from Mina Clavero to Nono's main plaza, from where you'll have to take a taxi (about AR$15 one way) or walk to the museum. If you do take a taxi, arrange for the driver to come back for you. A taxi from Mina Clavero to Nono costs AR$20.

SAN LUIS & AROUND

The little-visited province of San Luis holds a surprising number of attractions, made all the better by the fact that you'll probably have them all to yourself.

The province is popularly known as La Puerta de Cuyo (the door to Cuyo), referring to the combined provinces of Mendoza, San Luis and San Juan (see also the boxed text, p339).

The regional superstar is without doubt the Parque Nacional Sierra de las Quijadas, but the mountain towns along the Valle de Conlara and Sierras Puntanas are well worth a visit if you're looking to get off the tourist trail.

MERLO

☎ 02656 / pop 14,400 / elev 890m

At the top of the Valle de Conlara (see p335), the mountain town of Merlo is a growing resort known for its gentle microclimate (the local tourist industry buzzword) in a relatively dry area. The town is located 200km northeast of San Luis, tucked into the northeast corner of San Luis province.

The **municipal tourist office** (☎ 476078; www .villademerlo.gov.ar; Coronel Mercau 605; ☯ 8am-8pm) has maps and information on hotels and campgrounds.

Sights & Activities

For a sweeping view of the town and valley, head up to the Mirador del Sol. Buses leave from the old bus terminal and cost AR$4.50 for the 40-minute ride. If you've got your walking shoes on (or better, have a private vehicle), you can continue on this road another 12km to the Mirador de los Condores, which is up on the mountain ridge, and gives views in both directions. There's a **confitería** (mains AR$12-25) up here and if the wind is right, you can watch the parasailing maniacs taking off from the nearby launchpad.

Two kilometers from the center, in Rincon del Este, on the road to the Miradors, the **Reserva Natural de Merlo** (admission free; ☯ daylight hr) is a lovely spot for creekside walks up to a couple of swimming holes. The obligatory ziplines have been installed here and you can go whizzing through the canopy overhead for AR$30. **El Rincon del Paraiso** (set meals AR$15-30; ☯ breakfast & lunch), about 400m from the park entrance, is a beautiful, shady restaurant in the middle of the park – a great place for lunch or a couple of drinks.

Volando Bajo (☎ 476248; Pringles 459) is the most established of the plethora of tour operators in town. It offers tours to the nearby archaeological/paleontological park at Bajo de Veliz (half-day AR$80), and a trip combining the nature reserve, and Miradors de Sol and de los Condores (half-day AR$60). Tandem parasailing flights cost around AR$200 and last 20 to 30 minutes, depending on wind conditions.

Sleeping

Merlo Hostel (☎ 476928; Av del Sol 1025; dm AR$45; ▯ ▨) A sweet little family home–turned-hostel. Dorms could be bigger, but there are good hangout areas, it's an excellent, central location and this is one of the few true budget options in town.

Hostería Cerro Azul (☎ 478648; www.hosteriacer roazul.com.ar; cnr Saturno & Jupiter; s/d AR$120/150; ▨) This bright new hotel just off the main drag offers big rooms with spacious bathrooms and tiny TVs. The lounge-dining area is gorgeous, with high cathedral ceilings.

Hotel Casa Blanca (☎ 475320; www.casablancamerlo .com.ar; Av del Sol 50; s/d from AR$220/250; ▨ ▯ ▨) Undergoing a complete overhaul at the time of writing, this large business-style hotel right in the center is set on two hectares of woodsy grounds. It should be the best in town when it reopens.

Eating & Drinking

Cirano (Av del Sol 280; mains AR$15-30; ☺ lunch & dinner) Ignore the flashing fairy lights – there are some good-value eats on offer here, and an excellent set lunch or dinner for AR$20.

Giorgio (Av del Sol 558; mains AR$25-40; ☺ lunch & dinner) Some excellent, creative mixes here, along with hearty standards such as wild mushroom risotto (AR$28) and *bife de chorizo* (AR$25). Leave room for the tiramisu.

La Cerveceria (Av del Sol 515; ☺ 2pm-late) If you're looking for a beer, this is your spot – there's eight different types of microbrew on offer, plus the national and imported standbys, sidewalk seating and snacks.

Getting There & Away

Long-distance buses leave from the **new bus terminal** (RN 1 at Calle de las Ovejas), about eight blocks south of the town center. Departures include the following:

Destination	Cost (AR$)	Duration (hr)
Buenos Aires	120	12
Córdoba	43	6
El Volcán	17	4
La Toma	13	3
Mendoza	77	8
Mina Clavero	45	3
San Luis	35	4
Villa Carlos Paz	39	5

Getting Around

Local buses leave from the **old bus terminal** (☎ 492858; cnr Pringles & Los Almendres) in the center of town. There are departures for the Mirador del Sol (AR$5, 40 minutes), Piedra Blanca (AR$2, 20 minutes), Bajo de Veliz (AR$7, one hour), Papagayos (AR$3.50, one hour) and the nearby artisan village of Cerro de Oro (AR$2, 30 minutes).

Merlo Rent a Car (☎ 473949; www.merlorentacar .com.ar; cnr Av del Sol & Pelligrini) is the local car-rental operator.

SAN LUIS

☎ 02652 / pop 212,400 / elev 700m

Even people from San Luis will tell you that the best the province has to offer lies outside of the capital. That said, it's not a bad little town – there are a few historic sights here and the central Plaza Pringles is one of the prettiest in the country. The town's main nightlife strip, Av Illia, with its concentration of bars, cafes and restaurants, makes for a fun night out.

Orientation

On the north bank of the Río Chorrillos, San Luis is 260km from Mendoza via RN 7 and 456km from Córdoba via RN 148.

The commercial center is along the parallel streets of San Martín and Rivadavia between Plaza Pringles in the north and Plaza Independencia in the south.

Information

Several banks, mostly around Plaza Pringles, have ATMs.

ACA (Automóvil Club Argentino; ☎ 423188; Av Illia 401) Auto club; good source for provincial road maps.

Ciber Max (cnr Pedrera & Caseros; per hr AR$3; ☺ 8am-5am) For that late-night email binge. There are countless other cybercafes downtown.

Las Quijadas Turismo (☎ 431683; San Martín 874) Tours to Parque Nacional Sierra de las Quijadas, La Angostura and Inti Huasi.

Post office (cnr Av Illia & San Martín)

Regional hospital (☎ 422627; Av República Oriental del Uruguay 150) On the eastward extension of Bolívar.

Tourist office (☎ 423957, 423479; www.turismo .sanluis.gov.ar; intersection of Junín, San Martín & Av Illia; ☺ 8am-8pm) The helpful staff can supply a good map of the town and its attractions.

Sights & Activities

The center of town is the beautiful tree-filled Plaza Pringles, anchored on its eastern side by San Luis' handsome 19th-century **cathedral** (Rivadavia). Provincial hardwoods such as algarrobo were used for the cathedral's windows and frames, and local white marble for its steps and columns.

On the north side of nearby Plaza Independencia is the provincial **Casa de Gobierno** (Government House). On the south side of the plaza, the **Iglesia de Santo Domingo** (cnr 25 de Mayo & San Martín) and its convent date from the 1930s, but reproduce the Moorish style of the 17th-century building they replaced. Take a peek at the striking *algarrobo* (carob tree) doors of the attached **Archivo Histórico Provincial** around the corner on San Martín.

Dominican friars at the **mercado artesanal** (cnr 25 de Mayo & Rivadavia; ☺ 8am-1pm Mon-Fri), next to Iglesia de Santo Domingo, sell gorgeous handmade wool rugs as well as ceramics, onyx crafts and weavings from elsewhere in the province.

Also stroll over to the lovely former **train station** (Avs Illia & Lafinur) for a look at its green corrugated-metal roofs and decorative ironwork dating from 1884.

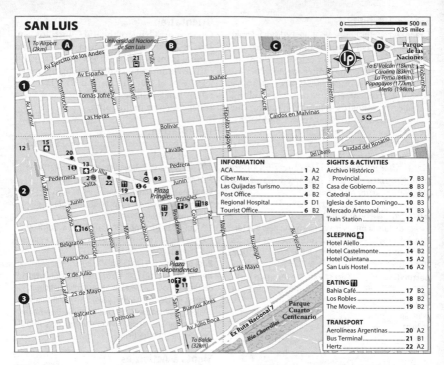

SAN LUIS

INFORMATION	
ACA	1 A2
Ciber Max	2 A2
Las Quijadas Turismo	3 B2
Post Office	4 B2
Regional Hospital	5 D1
Tourist Office	6 B2

SIGHTS & ACTIVITIES	
Archivo Histórico Provincial	7 B3
Casa de Gobierno	8 B3
Catedral	9 B2
Iglesia de Santo Domingo	10 B3
Mercado Artesanal	11 B3
Train Station	12 A2

SLEEPING	
Hotel Aiello	13 A2
Hotel Castelmonte	14 A2
Hotel Quintana	15 A2
San Luis Hostel	16 A2

EATING	
Bahia Café	17 B2
Los Robles	18 B2
The Movie	19 B2

TRANSPORT	
Aerolíneas Argentinas	20 A2
Bus Terminal	21 B1
Hertz	22 A2

Sleeping

San Luis' better hotels cater to a business crowd, filling up quickly on weekdays and offering discounts on weekends.

San Luis Hostel (☎ 424188; www.sanluishostel.com.ar; Falucho 646; dm/tw AR$35/100; 🖵 🐾) San Luis' best and most central hostel has it all, from pool table to DVD library, excellent kitchen and shady backyard with barbecue. The 16-person dorms (segregated for male and female) could be a bit more atmospheric, but apart from that it's pure gold.

our pick Hotel Castelmonte (☎ 424963; Chacabuco 769; s/d AR$80/110; 🐾 🛜) An excellent-value mid-range hotel. Its spacious rooms have wooden parquetry floors and firm new beds. While central, it's set back from the road, keeping things nice and quiet.

Hotel Aiello (☎ 425609; www.hotelaiello.com.ar; Av Illia 431; s/d AR$225/250; 🐾 🛜 🐾) With its low-slung hacienda vibe the Aiello has what so many of San Luis' hotels are lacking – character. It's all very comfortable here, with patios spread around and an excellent pool area featuring a kids' pool, a good-sized main pool and a shady grassy corner with deck chairs.

Hotel Quintana (☎ 438400; www.hotelquintana.com .ar; Av Illia 546; s/d AR$320/400; 🐾 🛜 🐾) The best setup hotel in town, the Quintana lays it all out for the business set with a serene lobby area leading on to restaurants, bars and a small pool area out back. Rooms are comfortable but nothing special.

Eating & Drinking

Traditional San Luis dishes include *empanadas de horno* (baked empanadas) and *cazuela de gallina* (chicken soup).

Bahia Café (cnr Pringles & Av San Martín; mains AR$15-25; 🕑 breakfast, lunch & dinner) For plaza-side cafe action and frenzied, middle-aged waiters, you can't go past the Bahia. At night they put tables out on the plaza in front, making it a great spot for drinks, snacks and people-watching.

The Movie (Av Illia 177; mains from AR$25; 🕑 11am-late) A vaguely cheesy 'theme restaurant' that actually turns out some pretty good food. Best thing – it's open very late for full meals and drinks.

Los Robles (Colón 684; mains AR$30-50; 🕑 lunch & dinner) One of the town's few upmarket *parril-*

las, this one has great atmosphere, attentive service and a menu that goes way beyond the usual offerings.

There are numerous laid-back bars along Av Illia. As is the deal all over the country, they start late and end late. Go for a stroll and see which one you like.

Getting There & Around
AIR
San Luis airport (☎ 422427/57) is 3km northwest of the center; taxis cost around AR$15.

Aerolíneas Argentinas (☎ 425671, 437981; Av Illia 472) flies daily to Buenos Aires (AR$463).

BUS & CAR
Unless it's suddenly moved to the old train station (corner of Avs Illia and Lafinur), San Luis' **bus terminal** (☎ 424021; España, btwn San Martín & Rivadavia) is about six blocks north of the main plaza. Provincial destinations, including Merlo (AR$18, four hours), El Volcán (AR$5, 30 minutes), Carolina (AR$12, two hours), Inti Huasi (AR$15, 2½ hours), La Toma (AR$8 1½ hours) and Balde (AR$4, 45 minutes), are served by local operators, whose ticket offices are in a separate building just in front of the main terminal complex.

There are long-distance departures daily to the destinations in the following table. For destinations such as Neuquén and Bariloche, you must head first to Mendoza or San Rafael.

Destination	Cost (AR$)	Duration (hr)
Buenos Aires	150	11
Córdoba	70	7
Mar del Plata	240	19
Mendoza	40	5
Paraná	120	13
Rosario	120	9
San Juan	45	5
San Rafael	50	5
Santa Fe	150	12

Hertz (☎ 15-549002; Av Illia 305) is the local car-rental agency.

AROUND SAN LUIS
Balde
☎ 02652
This small village, 35km west of San Luis, is remarkable only for its thermal baths. The municipal complex is a decidedly down-at-heel affair, while a new spa resort offers oodles of comfort in gorgeous surrounds.

Centro Termal Municipal (☎ 499319; Av Esteban Agüero s/n; 1hr baths per person AR$8, campsites AR$6, cabin for 2 people AR$75; ☉ baths 8am-6pm) is a budget-friendly alternative to Los Tamarindos up the road, offering small rooms with a bath and a bed to relax, rented by the hour. They're clean enough and decent value for a quick dip. Cabins (located across the road) are spacious for two, with kitchen facilities, but no thermal water piped in.

Los Tamarindos (☎ 15-664-6628; Av Esteban Agüero s/n; s/d AR$200/260, cabins s/d AR$230/300; ☉ baths 8am-6pm) is a wonderful thermal baths complex featuring a couple of public pools for day use – an outdoor one at 26°C (AR$15 per person) and a lovely, clean indoor one (AR$30 for both). The rooms here are standard, with small baths fed by hot spring water, but the cabins are a real treat – they're much more spacious and have a separate tub where you can get neck deep in the water. Hotel guests have access to the hot baths included in the price and there are a variety of spa treatments (mudpacks, massages etc) available. The whole complex is set on leafy grounds and is pure relaxation, especially midweek.

Regular buses run to and from San Luis' bus terminal to the bus terminal at Balde (AR$4, 45 minutes), which is a short walk to either of the complexes.

El Volcán
☎ 02652 / pop 1480
A small village nestled in the hills east of San Luis, El Volcán (there is no volcano here, by the way) is a laid-back summer getaway spot. The star attraction is the river that runs through the middle of town, where Balneario La Hoya, a series of natural rock pools, offers shady swimming spots and picnic areas.

El Volcán is close enough to San Luis to make it an easy day trip, but there are plenty of cabins for rent, especially during summer.

Hotel El Volcán (☎ 494044; Banda Norte s/n; s/d AR$180/200; ⊠ ☎) is the only real hotel in the village. It's a sprawling complex set on shady grounds that run down to the river. The hotel closes off-season – call ahead to make sure it's open. **El Mantial** (Balneario La Hoya; mains AR$15-22; ☉ breakfast, lunch & dinner) has decent food and great views out over the river. Portions are big and service is quick, if somewhat impersonal.

Regular buses run to and from San Luis' main bus terminal (AR$5, 30 minutes).

PARQUE NACIONAL SIERRA DE LAS QUIJADAS

Fans of the Road Runner cartoon will feel oddly at home among the red sandstone rock formations in this rarely visited **national park** (admission AR$25). The park comprises 1500 sq km of canyons and dry lake beds among the Sierra de las Quijadas, whose peaks reach 1200m at Cerro Portillo. Recent paleontological excavations by the Universidad Nacional de San Luis and New York's Museum of Natural History unearthed dinosaur tracks and fossils from the Lower Cretaceous, about 120 million years ago.

Despite the shortage of visitors here, access to the park is excellent: buses from San Luis to San Juan will drop visitors at the park entrance and ranger station (AR$20, 1½ hours) just beyond the village of Hualtarán, about 110km northwest of San Luis via RN 147 (San Juan is 210km to the northwest). At this point, a 6km dirt road leads west to a viewpoint overlooking the **Potrero de la Aguada**, a scenic depression beneath the peaks of the sierra that collects the runoff from much of the park and is a prime wildlife area. At the ranger station you can hire guides; two-hour, 3km treks to see the famous dinosaur footprints leave hourly between 9am and 4pm and cost AR$22 per person. Four-hour treks to a 150m-deep canyon in the park leave at 1:30pm and cost AR$35. A minimum group size of two people applies to both treks.

Other **hiking** possibilities in the park are excellent, but the complex canyons require a tremendous sense of direction or, preferably, the assistance of a local guide. Even experienced hikers should beware of summer rains and flash floods, which make the canyons extremely dangerous.

There's a shady **campground** (campsites free), near the overlook, and a small store with groceries and drinks, including very welcome ice-cold beer.

Buses from San Juan to San Luis pass every hour or so, but they don't always stop. It's sometimes possible to catch a lift from the park entrance to the overlook.

VALLE DE LAS SIERRAS PUNTANAS

From San Luis the RP 9 snakes its way northwards, following the course of the Río Grande. Along the way, small villages are slowly developing as tourist destinations while still retaining much of their original character. The picturesque mining town of Carolina and nearby Inti Huasi cave are highlights of the region, and the landscapes higher up in the valley, with their rolling meadows and stone fences, probably resemble the Scottish highlands more than anything you've seen in Argentina so far.

Estancia Las Verbenas

Set in a gorgeous glade in the Valle de Pancanta, this **estancia** (☎ 02652-430918; RP 9, Km 68; per person incl full board AR$108) does rustic to the hilt, with plenty of hearty food served up among animal-skin decoration and rough-hewn furniture. Rooms are basic but comfortable. Two-hour horseback-riding tours (AR$30 per person) to a nearby waterfall are bound to be a highlight of your stay here. The signposted entrance to the property is just after the bridge on the highway, from where it's another 4km to the farmhouse. If you're coming by bus, call and staff will pick you up from the highway.

Carolina

☎ 02651 / pop 230 / elev 1610m

Nestled between the banks of the Río Grande and the foothills of Cerro Tomalasta (2020m), Carolina is a photogenic little village of stone houses and dirt roads. Take away the power lines and you could be stepping back in time 100 years. The region boomed in 1785 when the Spanish moved in to exploit local gold mines that had first been used by the Inca. Nobody uses street addresses in Carolina – the town is small enough to navigate without them.

SIGHTS & ACTIVITIES

One of the quirkier museums in the country, **Museo de Poesia** (admission free; 10am-6pm Tue-Sat) honors San Luis' favorite son, poet Juan Cristofer Lafinur. The museum has a few artifacts from the poet's life, plus handwritten homages to the man by some of Argentina's leading poets.

Across the creek and up the hill from the poetry museum is a small **stone labyrinth**, set on the hilltop. It should provide you with an hour or so of entertainment (or, if your sense of direction is really bad, days of frustration).

Huellas Turismo (☎ 02652-490224; www.huellasturismo.com.ar) is the local tour operator – it can set you up with tours of the local gold mine

(AR$25, two hours), rock climbing and rappelling trips on Cerro Tomalasta, and tours of Inti Huasi, La Casa de la Piedra Pintada and La Angostura.

SLEEPING & EATING

Accommodation is improving in Carolina, but if you can't find a place, ask in the restaurants for a *casa de familia* (room in a private house with shared bathroom), which rents for around AR$25 per person.

Rincón del Oro Hostel (☎ 490212; Pringles s/n; dm AR$30) Set on a hilltop overlooking town, this great little hostel has a rustic, intimate feel despite its 57-bed capacity.

La Posta del Caminante (☎ 490223; www.lapostadelcaminante.com.ar; RP 9 s/n; s/d AR$150/180; ☒) Carolina's one hotel is set in a gorgeous stone building on the edge of town. A lovely seminatural rock swimming pool out the back completes the picture. The hotel is open mainly in summer, so if you're set on staying here, call ahead.

La Tomalasta (mains AR$15-20; ☒ breakfast, lunch & dinner) Good-value home-cooked meals. If it looks like it's closed, go around the back to the general store and ask them to open up.

GETTING THERE & AWAY

Regular buses run from Carolina to San Luis (AR$10, two hours), passing through El Volcán. Some continue on to Inti Huasi (AR$4, 30 minutes).

Around Carolina

INTI HUASI

This wide, shallow **cave** (admission free; ☒ daylight hr), whose name means 'house of the sun' in Quechua, makes an interesting stop, as much for the gorgeous surrounding countryside as the cave itself. Radiocarbon dating suggests that the cave was first inhabited by the Ayampitín some 8000 years ago. There are regular buses here from San Luis (AR$13, 2½ hours), passing through Carolina (AR$4, 30 minutes).

LA CASA DE LA PIEDRA PINTADA

Coming from Carolina, 3km before the Inti Huasi cave, a dirt track turns off to Paso de los Reyes. From the turnoff, it's an easy 5km signposted walk to **La Casa de la Piedra Pintada** (admission free), where more than 50 rock carvings are easily visible in the rock face. Follow the signs until you reach an open meadow at the base of Cerro Sololasta and you see the new cable-and-wood walkway up the cliff face that gives you access to the site. Once you're finished with the rock art, continue up the hill for spectacular views out over the Sierras Puntanas.

If you're unsure about getting here on your own, there's usually someone around at Inti Huasi who will guide you for a nominal fee.

LA ANGOSTURA

This site, 22km northeast of El Trapiche, holds one of the most extensive collections of indigenous rock art in the region. There's around 1000 examples here, painted and carved onto a shallow concave cliff face. Some are wonderfully preserved, while others fade with exposure to the weather. Keep an eye out for three mortar holes carved into the rock floor; they were most likely used to grind grain.

The site is tricky to access, even with a private vehicle. On the El Trapiche–Paso de los Reyes road, a signpost leads off to the right, through a closed (but not locked) gate. From there, it's 2.5km along a very bad dirt road to an abandoned stone farmhouse where the road ends.

The trail to the site is unmarked, but if you head uphill, veering right, you'll reach a stone bluff on the hilltop, giving excellent views over the valley. Descending on the right side of the bluff, you'll see the wire fence set up to protect the works of art.

Tour operators in Carolina (see opposite) and San Luis (see p331), including the San Luis Hostel (p332) come out here, but it's not a popular excursion – get a group together, or expect to pay top dollar.

VALLE DE CONLARA

Heading northeast to Merlo from San Luis, the landscape changes dramatically as the road climbs into the hills. Around La Toma the land is arid and desertlike, Papagayos has its own unique vistas, punctuated by palm trees, while Merlo (p330) is a lush mountain town.

La Toma

☎ 02655 / pop 6820

A dusty little town plonked down by the side of RP 20, La Toma owes its existence to the mineral riches in the surrounding hills. This is the only place in the world where green onyx is mined. The stone is soft and hard to work, so not much jewelry is made out of it, but several shops around town sell souvenirs made from green onyx and other local stones.

Tours of the local mines can be arranged at the **Cooperativa Telefónica office** (☎ 421400; Belgrano & Moreno; 2hr tours AR$25). Tours leave at 10am, Monday to Friday.

If you're interested in seeing the workshops (and the working conditions therein), drop in to **Onix Olimpia** (☎ 421732; H Yrigoyen & Av Centenario) and ask about a free tour. Workers will whip up a Holy Mary head right before your eyes, in about two minutes.

Hostería El Indio (☎ 421393; www.hosteriaelindio .com.ar; cnr Av San Martín & 7 de Mayo; s/d AR$66/88; ☒) is the best place to stay in town, featuring large, cool rooms with leopard-skin-print bedspreads.

Italia Hotel (Belgrano 644; mains AR$20-28; ☼ lunch & dinner) is the town's one true restaurant, serving up some reasonable set meals and tasty empanadas.

Estancia La Estanzuela

Set on a Jesuit mission dating from 1750, this gorgeous **estancia** (☎ 02656-420559; www.estanzuela .com.ar; per person with full board AR$220; ☒) has been left in near-original condition from the days when it was a working farm. Floors are wood or stone, walls are meter-thick adobe and many ceilings are constructed in the traditional gaucho style. The house is decorated like a museum, with antique furniture, paintings and family heirlooms galore. A small pond that the Jesuits built for irrigation serves for romantic rowboating outings and there is plenty of horseback riding and nature walking to be done. This is a very special – near-magical – place and the minimum three-night stay should not be hard to adhere to. Prices include meals, drinks and activities.

The property is located 2km off RP 1, between Villa del Carmen and Papagayos. The closest public transport is to Papagayos from Merlo (see below). Reservations are essential and must be made at least two days in advance. If you don't have your own transport, ask about getting picked up in Papagayos or San Luis.

Papagayos
☎ 02656 / pop 420

Possibly the last thing you're expecting to see in this part of the world is a valley full of palm trees, but that's exactly where this small town is situated. The town is located on the banks of the Arroyo Papagayos and has huge Caranday palms surrounding it, giving the area a certain notoriety for handicrafts made from their trunks and branches.

Small stores (mostly attached to workshops) selling these *artesanias en palma* are scattered around town. Rosa López (in front of plaza) has the best range. The tourist office can provide a map showing all the store locations, along with other local attractions.

The *arroyo* (creek) is a good place to cool off – its length is dotted with swimming holes. For a more formal swimming environment, the Balneario Municipal offers swimming pools, picnic and barbeque areas.

For horseback riding and trekking to local waterfalls and swimming spots out of town, ask at the tourist office or Hostería Los Leños.

The **Oficina de Turismo** (☎ 480093; www.papagayos .gov.ar; RP 1 s/n; ☼ 8am-8pm) is useful for contacting guides and arranging tours, and has decent maps of the town.

Hostería Los Leños (☎ 478289; www.hosterialoslen ios.com.ar; Av Comechingones 555; r AR$160; ☒) is the best-looking hotel in town, featuring fresh new rooms with spacious bathrooms and a good-sized swimming pool. Also on offer are excellent home-cooked meals (mains AR$20 to AR$30) and staff can set you up with a picnic lunch if you're off on a day trip.

From Papagayos' main plaza there are regular buses to Merlo (AR$3.50, one hour).

Mendoza & the Central Andes

This region, a long, narrow sliver of desert landscape jammed up against the eastern foothills of the Andes, gains its fame from all that is good about traveling in Argentina. To start with, this is where 70% of the country's wine is produced, and even if you have only a passing interest in the nectar of the gods, Mendoza is pretty much an obligatory stop on your itinerary. It's a lively, cosmopolitan city whose tasting rooms and wine stores are unrivaled in the country. In the surrounding area, hundreds of wineries offer tours – an educational (and occasionally intoxicating) way to spend an afternoon or a month.

If you can put your glass down for a minute, there's plenty more to keep you busy here. The nearby Andes are home to Aconcagua, the Americas' highest peak and a favorite for mountain climbers the world over. A couple of ski resorts give you the chance to drop into fresh powder with Argentina's jet set, or go off-piste on rugged Nordic or dogsledding expeditions. If none of that's ringing your bell, a slew of Mendoza-based operators offer rafting, mountain biking and paragliding, among other adventures.

To the north, San Juan province is often overlooked, but well worth a visit, as much for its small but important selection of wineries (producing some of the country's top syrah and whites) as for the Parque Provincial Ischigualasto, a near-surreal desert landscape whose cartoonlike eroded rock forms hold fossils dating from the first life forms to the Triassic era. Or make your way to Rodeo, one of the windiest places on earth, for some high-speed windsurfing action.

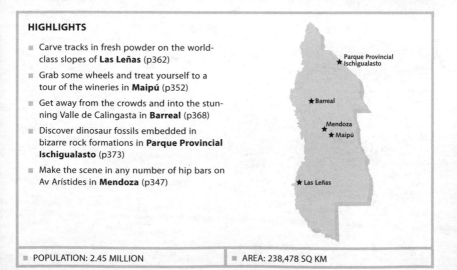

HIGHLIGHTS

- Carve tracks in fresh powder on the world-class slopes of **Las Leñas** (p362)
- Grab some wheels and treat yourself to a tour of the wineries in **Maipú** (p352)
- Get away from the crowds and into the stunning Valle de Calingasta in **Barreal** (p368)
- Discover dinosaur fossils embedded in bizarre rock formations in **Parque Provincial Ischigualasto** (p373)
- Make the scene in any number of hip bars on Av Arístides in **Mendoza** (p347)

★ Parque Provincial Ischigualasto

★ Barreal

Mendoza
★ ★ Maipú

★ Las Leñas

- POPULATION: 2.45 MILLION
- AREA: 238,478 SQ KM

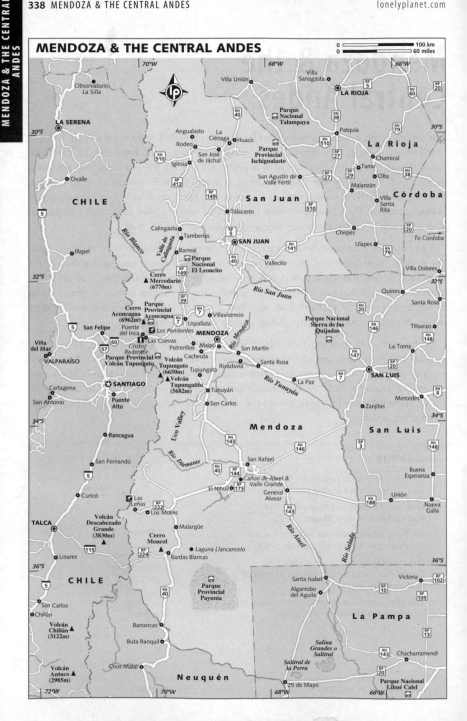

MENDOZA & THE CENTRAL ANDES

Climate

Mendoza and the Central Andes is definitely a year-round destination. The region gets little rain through most of the year. Summer (December to March) in Mendoza is hot and dry. This is climbing season for the region's highest peaks. Autumn is spectacular, thanks to the vivid colors of Mendoza's introduced trees and grapevines. Winter (June through to August) is ski season. Though the cities of Mendoza and San Juan never get snow, the highest passes to Chile close regularly during winter. Spring is lovely, with warm days and cool nights.

National & Provincial Parks

The region's most famous park is Parque Provincial Aconcagua (p356), home of 6962m Cerro Aconcagua, the highest peak outside the Himalayas. Nearby Parque Provincial Volcán Tupungato (p357) is another favorite climbing destination. For mind-blowing volcanic landscapes, visit the little-known Parque Provincial Payunia (p362) near Malargüe. In neighboring San Juan province Parque Provincial Ischigualasto (p373) is world famous for its dinosaur fossils as well as its spectacular desert rock formations. Also in San Juan, Parque Nacional El Leoncito (p371) occupies 76 sq km of dry Andean precordillera and is famous for its observatory and land sailing on the nearby flats of Pampa El Leoncito.

Getting There & Away

With flights to/from nearby Santiago (Chile), Mendoza has the region's only international airport. There are regular flights to Mendoza, San Juan and San Luis from Buenos Aires. During ski season there are usually flights to Malargüe, near Las Leñas ski resort. Bus transport is excellent throughout the province. If you're heading south to the Lake District, the fastest way can be to head to Neuquén city, but if you don't mind taking it slow, a seldom-explored section of RN 40 between Mendoza and Neuquén provinces can be a worthwhile detour.

MENDOZA

☎ 0261 / pop 929,000 / elev 703m

A bustling city of wide, leafy avenues, atmospheric plazas and cosmopolitan cafes, Mendoza is a trap. Even if you've (foolishly) only given it a day or two on your itinerary, you're bound to end up hanging around, captivated by the laid-back pace while surrounded by every possible comfort.

Ostensibly it's a desert town, though you wouldn't know unless you were told – *acequias* (irrigation ditches) that run beside every main road and glorious fountains that adorn every main plaza mean you'll never be far from the burble of running water.

Lively during the day, the city really comes into its own at night, when the bars, restaurants and cafes along Av Arístides fill up and overflow onto the sidewalks with all the bright young things, out to see and be seen.

All over the country (and in much of the world), the name Mendoza is synonymous with wine, and this is the place to base yourself if you're up for touring the vineyards, taking a few dozen bottles home or just looking for a good bottle to accompany the evening's pizza.

The city's wide range of tour operators also makes it a great place to organize rafting, skiing and other adventures in the nearby Andes.

Orientation

Mendoza is 1050km west of Buenos Aires via RN 7 and 340km northwest of Santiago (Chile) via the Los Libertadores border complex.

Strictly speaking, the provincial capital proper is a relatively small area with a population of only about 120,000, but the inclusion of the departments of Las Heras, Guaymallén and Godoy Cruz, along with nearby Maipú and Luján de Cuyo, swells the population of Gran Mendoza (Greater Mendoza) to nearly one million.

CUYO

The provinces of Mendoza, San Juan and, to some extent, neighboring San Luis (covered in the Córdoba & the Central Sierras chapter) are traditionally known as the Cuyo, a term which is derived from the indigenous Huarpe word *cuyum,* meaning 'sandy earth.' The Huarpes were the original practitioners of irrigated agriculture in the region, a legacy still highly visible throughout the region today. The term is one you'll encounter often, whether in the names of local bus companies, businesses and newspapers, or in everyday conversation.

MENDOZA

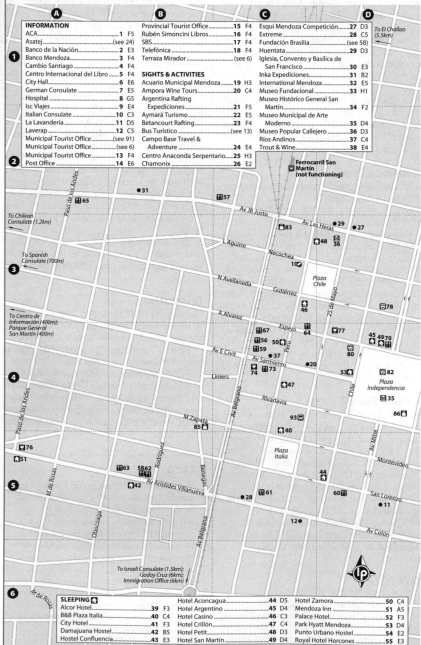

INFORMATION
ACA	1	F5
Asatej	(see 24)	
Banco de la Nación	2	E3
Banco Mendoza	3	F4
Cambio Santiago	4	F4
Centro Internacional del Libro	5	F4
City Hall	6	E6
German Consulate	7	E5
Hospital	8	G5
Isc Viajes	9	E4
Italian Consulate	10	C3
La Lavandería	11	D5
Laverap	12	C5
Municipal Tourist Office	(see 91)	
Municipal Tourist Office	(see 6)	
Municipal Tourist Office	13	F4
Post Office	14	E6
Provincial Tourist Office	15	F4
Rubén Simoncini Libros	16	F4
SBS	17	F4
Telefónica	18	F4
Terraza Mirador	(see 6)	

SIGHTS & ACTIVITIES
Acuario Municipal Mendoza	19	H3
Ampora Wine Tours	20	C4
Argentina Rafting Expediciones	21	F5
Aymará Turismo	22	E5
Betancourt Rafting	23	F4
Bus Turístico	(see 13)	
Campo Base Travel & Adventure	24	E4
Centro Anaconda Serpentario	25	H3
Chamonix	26	E2
Esquí Mendoza Competición	27	D3
Extreme	28	C5
Fundación Brasilia	(see 58)	
Huentata	29	D3
Iglesia, Convento y Basílica de San Francisco	30	E3
Inka Expediciones	31	B2
International Mendoza	32	E5
Museo Fundacional	33	H1
Museo Histórico General San Martín	34	F2
Museo Municipal de Arte Moderno	35	D4
Museo Popular Callejero	36	D3
Ríos Andinos	37	C4
Trout & Wine	38	E4

Ferrocarril San Martín (not functioning)

To El Challao (5.5km)

To Chilean Consulate (1.2km)

To Spanish Consulate (700m)

To Centro de Información (400m); Parque General San Martín (400m)

Plaza Chile

Plaza Independencia

Plaza Italia

To Israeli Consulate (1.5km); Godoy Cruz (6km); Immigration Office (6km)

SLEEPING
Alcor Hotel	39	F3
B&B Plaza Italia	40	C4
City Hotel	41	F3
Damajuana Hostel	42	B5
Hostel Confluencia	43	E3
Hotel Aconcagua	44	D5
Hotel Argentino	45	D4
Hotel Casino	46	C3
Hotel Crillón	47	C4
Hotel Petit	48	D3
Hotel San Martín	49	D4
Hotel Zamora	50	C4
Mendoza Inn	51	A5
Palace Hotel	52	F3
Park Hyatt Mendoza	53	D4
Punto Urbano Hostel	54	E2
Royal Hotel Horcones	55	E3

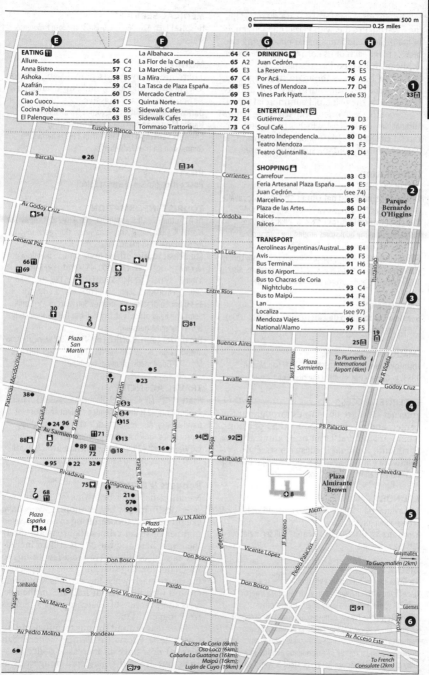

EATING
Allure	56	C4
Anna Bistro	57	C2
Ashoka	58	B5
Azafrán	59	C4
Casa 3	60	D5
Ciao Cuoco	61	C5
Cocina Poblana	62	B5
El Palenque	63	B5
La Albahaca	64	C4
La Flor de la Canela	65	A2
La Marchigiana	66	E3
La Mira	67	C4
La Tasca de Plaza España	68	E5
Mercado Central	69	E3
Quinta Norte	70	D4
Sidewalk Cafes	71	E4
Sidewalk Cafes	72	E4
Tommaso Trattoria	73	C4

DRINKING
Juan Cedrón	74	C4
La Reserva	75	E5
Por Acá	76	A5
Vines of Mendoza	77	D4
Vines Park Hyatt	(see 53)	

ENTERTAINMENT
Gutiérrez	78	D3
Soul Café	79	F6
Teatro Independencia	80	D4
Teatro Mendoza	81	F3
Teatro Quintanilla	82	D4

SHOPPING
Carrefour	83	C3
Feria Artesanal Plaza España	84	E5
Juan Cedrón	(see 74)	
Marcelino	85	B4
Plaza de las Artes	86	D4
Raíces	87	E4
Raíces	88	E4

TRANSPORT
Aerolíneas Argentinas/Austral	89	E4
Avis	90	F5
Bus Terminal	91	H6
Bus to Airport	92	G4
Bus to Chacras de Coria Nightclubs	93	C4
Bus to Maipú	94	F4
Lan	95	E5
Localiza	(see 97)	
Mendoza Viajes	96	E4
National/Alamo	97	F5

The city's five central plazas are arranged like the five-roll on a die, with Plaza Independencia in the middle and four smaller plazas lying two blocks from each of its corners. Be sure to see the beautifully tiled Plaza España.

Av San Martín is the main thoroughfare, crossing the city from north to south, and Av Las Heras is the principal commercial street.

A good place to orient yourself is the **Terraza Mirador** (free; ☺ 9am-1pm), which is the rooftop terrace at **City Hall** (9 de Julio 500), offering panoramic views of the city and the surrounding area.

Information

BOOKSTORES
Centro Internacional del Libro (☎ 420-1266; Lavalle 14) Small selection of classics and best-sellers in English.
Rubén Simoncini Libros (☎ 420-2988; San Juan 1108) One of many bookstores around the intersection of San Juan and Garibaldi; some English books in stock.
SBS (Gutiérrez 54) A large range of novels in English, Lonely Planet guidebooks, maps and wine-related literature. Also TOEFL resources and textbooks for Spanish students.

EMERGENCY
Servicio Coordinado de Emergencia (☎ 428-0000) Call for an ambulance.

IMMIGRATION
Immigration office (☎ 424-3512; Av San Martín 1859) In Godoy Cruz, south of the city center.

INTERNET ACCESS
Internet cafes are ubiquitous throughout the center, and all charge about AR$3 per hour. There are several large ones along the Av Sarmiento *peatonal* (pedestrian street).
Telefónica (cnr Avs Sarmiento & San Martín; per hr AR$3) Serves coffee and has phones, too.

LAUNDRY
La Lavandería (☎ 429-4782; San Lorenzo 352; full service about AR$15)
Laverap (☎ 423-9706; Av Colón 547; full service about AR$15)

MEDIA
La Guía This free monthly events magazine is a must-have if you plan on keeping up with Mendoza's hectic cultural scene. Pick up a copy at any tourist office.
Wine Republic (www.wine-republic.com) An excellent English-language magazine focusing on wine but also featuring good reviews of up-and-coming restaurants, Mendoza gossip and a couple of entertaining articles. Pick up a copy at Vines of Mendoza (p347) or Trout & Wine (p345).

MEDICAL SERVICES
Hospital (☎ 420-0600, 420-0063; cnr José F Moreno & Alem)

MONEY
There are many ATMs downtown. The following two banks are architectural landmarks; Banco Mendoza is massive.
Banco de la Nación (cnr Necochea & 9 de Julio)
Banco Mendoza (cnr Gutiérrez & San Martín)
Cambio Santiago (Av San Martín 1199) Charges 2% commission on traveler's checks.

POST
Post office (Av San Martín at Colón)

TOURIST INFORMATION
ACA (Automóvil Club Argentina; ☎ 420-2900; cnr Av San Martín & Amigorena) Argentina's auto club; good source for provincial road maps.
Municipal tourist offices (www.turismo.mendoza.gov .ar) bus terminal (☎ 431-5000, 431-3001; ☺ 7am-11pm); City Hall (☎ 449-5185; fax 449 5186; 9 de Julio 500; ☺ 8:30am-1:30pm Mon-Fri); Garibaldi (☎ 420-1333; Garibaldi sidewalk, near Av San Martín; ☺ 9am-9pm) The head office is at City Hall but the Garibaldi office is best for most questions.
Provincial tourist office (☎ 420-2800; www.turismo .mendoza.gov.ar; Av San Martín 1143; ☺ 8am-10pm Mon-Fri) Good maps, plenty of brochures.

TRAVEL AGENCIES
Asatej (☎ /fax 429-0029/30; mendoza@asatej.com.ar; Av Sarmiento 223) Recommended student and discount travel agency. Also representative of Argentina Rafting Expediciones, which is based in Potrerillos (p353).
Isc Viajes (☎ 425-9259; www.iscviajes.com; Av España 1016) Travel agent and Amex representative.

Dangers & Annoyances
Mendoza has long been one of Argentina's safer destinations, but economic woes have caught up here, too, resulting in an increased number of street crimes. Tourists are rarely the target here and the city is still an incredibly safe place, but there are a few things to watch out for. Bag snatching and pickpocketing (particularly when the victim is wandering around with their hands full) are on the rise, as is the practice of snatching MP3 players from joggers in the park.

The areas around the bus terminal and on Cerro de la Gloria (in Parque General San Martín) now have an increased police presence, but are still considered dangerous at night. Increased caution is recommended during the early afternoon, too, as police tend to take the siesta along with everybody else. There have been several reports of people picking locks on hostel lockers – if you have something really valuable, leave it at your hostel's reception or, better yet, in its safe.

Sights

MUSEO FUNDACIONAL & AROUND

Mendoza's **Museo Fundacional** (☎ 425-6927; cnr Alberdi & Videla Castillo, Ciudad Vieja; admission AR$10; ☼ 8am-8pm Mon-Sat, 3-10pm Sun) protects excavations of the colonial *cabildo* (town council), destroyed by an earthquake in 1861. At that time, the city's geographical focus shifted west and south to its present location. A series of small dioramas depicts Mendoza's history, working through all of human evolution as if the city of Mendoza were the climax (maybe it was).

Walk to the museum from downtown and you'll pass some bizarre sights near **Parque Bernardo O'Higgins**. First check out the **Acuario Municipal Mendoza** (Municipal Aquarium; ☎ 425-3824; cnr Ituzaingó & Buenos Aires; admission AR$7; ☼ 9am-9pm, to 10pm in summer). Nothing at this small underwater freak show seems to have changed since its inauguration in 1945 (except the algae levels on the glass). But it's hard not to gaze in awe at the motionless, tongueless albino frogs or the 'armored pig,' a very ugly fish from the Río Paraná. Skip the crocodile exhibit. Across the street, the **Centro Anaconda Serpentario** (☎ 425-1393; Ituzaingó 1420; adult/child under 12yr AR$7/4; ☼ 9:30am-1pm & 3:30-8pm) houses some 50 snakes (in small cages), including a giant yellow Burmese python.

OTHER MUSEUMS

Underground at the Plaza Independencia, the **Museo Municipal de Arte Moderno** (☎ 425-7279; Plaza Independencia; ☼ 9am-8pm Tue-Sat, 4-8pm Sun & Mon) is a relatively small but well-organized facility with modern and contemporary art exhibits. Free concerts and theatrical performances are usually held here on Sunday night at 8pm – stop by for the weekly program.

Museo Popular Callejero (Av Las Heras, btwn 25 de Mayo & Perú; ☼ 24hr) is an innovative sidewalk museum. It consists of a series of encased streetside dioramas with odd clay sculptures depicting changes in one of Mendoza's major avenues since its 1830 creation in a dry watercourse.

Museo Histórico General San Martín (☎ 425-7947; Remedios Escalada de San Martín 1843; admission AR$7; ☼ 9am-1pm & 4-8pm Mon-Fri) honors José de San Martín, the general who liberated Argentina from the Spanish and whose name graces parks, squares and streets everywhere in Argentina; the Libertador is especially dear to Mendoza, where he resided with his family and recruited and trained his army to cross into Chile. The museum is in a small arcade just off Av San Martín.

IGLESIA, CONVENTO Y BASÍLICA DE SAN FRANCISCO

Many *mendocinos* (people from Mendoza) consider the image at this **church** (Necochea 201; admission AR$5; ☼ 9am-1pm Mon-Sat) of the Virgin of Cuyo, patron of San Martín's Ejército de los Andes (Army of the Andes), miraculous because it survived Mendoza's devastating 1968 earthquake. In the Virgin's semicircular chamber, visitors leave tributes to her and to San Martín. A mausoleum within the building holds the remains of San Martín's daughter, son-in-law and granddaughter, which were repatriated from France in 1951.

PARQUE GENERAL SAN MARTÍN

Walking along the lakeshore and snoozing in the shade of the rose garden in this beautiful 420-hectare park is a great way to enjoy one of the city's highlights. Walk along Sarmiento/ Civit out to the park and admire some of Mendoza's finest houses on the way. Pick up a park map at the **Centro de Información** (☎ 420-5052, ext 22; cnr Avs Los Platanos & Libertador; ☼ 9am-5pm), just inside the impressive entry gates, shipped over from England and originally forged for the Turkish Sultan Hamid II. The park was designed by Carlos (Charles) Thays in 1897, who also designed Parque Sarmiento in Córdoba. Its famous **Cerro de la Gloria** has a monument to San Martín's Ejército de los Andes for its liberation of Argentina, Chile and Peru from the Spaniards. On clear days, views of the valley make the climb especially rewarding.

Activities

Once you've sucked down enough fine wine and tramped around the city a bit, get yourself into the Andes, Mendoza's other claim to fame, for some of the most spectacular mountain scenery you'll ever set eyes upon. Numerous agencies organize climbing and trekking expeditions, rafting trips, mule trips and cycling trips. For guides for Aconcagua, see p357.

Aymará Turismo (☎ 420-2064; www.aymaramendoza .com.ar; 9 de Julio 1023) Mule trips, trekking, rafting.

Betancourt Rafting (☎ 429-9665; www.betancourt .com.ar; Lavalle 35, Local 8) Rafting, mountain biking, paragliding.

Cabaña La Guatana (☎ 15-668-6801; www.criollos laguatana.com.ar; Maza 8001, Lulunta, Maipú) Horseback tours through the vineyards of Maipú.

Campo Base Travel & Adventure (☎ 425-5511; www.campobase.com.ar; Av Sarmiento 229) Offers all adventures imaginable from trekking to paragliding (AR$210) to more conventional day trips.

Oso Loco (☎ 630-0026; www.argentinaskitours.com; Darragueira 558, Chacras de Coria) Full-service ski tours and lessons in Spanish or English. Best quality ski-equipment rental in town. Also brokers a range of on-mountain accommodations, from budget to luxury. Summer activities include sandboarding in nearby Lavalle.

Ríos Andinos (☎ 429-5030; www.riosandinos.com.ar; Sarmiento 768) Based in Potrerillos, it specializes in rafting on Río Mendoza. Rafting trips cost AR$80 (35 minutes, Class I-II) to AR$230 (five hours, Class III-IV). Combined rafting and trekking AR$230 per day.

CLIMBING & MOUNTAINEERING

Mendoza is famous for Cerro Aconcagua, the highest mountain in the Americas, but the majestic peak is only the tip of the iceberg when it comes to climbing and mountaineering here. The nearby Cordón del Plata boasts several peaks topping out between 5000m and 6000m, and there are three important rock-climbing areas in the province: Los Arenales (near Tunuyán), El Salto (near Mendoza) and Chigüido (near Malargüe).

Pick up a copy of Maricio Fernandez' full-color route guide (Spanish only), *Escaladas en Mendoza*, at **Inka Expediciones** (☎ 425-0871; www.inka.com.ar; Av Juan B Justo 345, Mendoza). For up-to-date information, contact the **Asociación Argentina de Guiás de Montaña** (www.aagm.com.ar). See p357 for a list of the most experienced guides operating throughout the province.

For climbing and hiking equipment, both rental and purchase, visit **Chamonix** (☎ 425-7572; www.chamonix-outdoor.com.ar; Barcala 267).

SKIING & SNOWBOARDING

Los Penitentes (p355) has the best skiing near Mendoza, although further south, Las Leñas (p362) has arguably the best skiing in South America. For standard ski and snowboard equipment rental, try **Esquí Mendoza Competición** (☎ 429-7944; Av Las Heras 583), **Extreme** (☎ 429-0733; Av Colón 733) or any of the shops along Av Las Heras. All charge AR$40 to AR$60 per day for a skis-boots-poles package and about AR$70 per day for a snowboard with boots. Most rent gloves, jackets and tire chains, as well. If you're an intermediate or advanced skier, Oso Loco (see left) can set you up with much better equipment.

WHITE-WATER RAFTING

The major rivers are the Mendoza and the Diamante, near San Rafael. Most agencies mentioned earlier offer trips ranging from 35-minute runs (AR$90) or half-day descents (from AR$130) to overnight expeditions (from AR$500). Well-regarded **Argentina Rafting Expediciones** (☎ 429-6325; www.argentinaraft ing.com; Primitivo de la Reta 992, local 4) operates out of Potrerillos (p353) but you can book trips at its Mendoza office.

Courses

Fundación Brasilia (☎ 423-6917; www.fundacionbrasilia .com.ar; Av Arístides Villanueva 251) offers individual Spanish classes for AR$432/816 per 10/20 hours.

Tours

Huentata (☎ 425-7444; www.huentata.com.ar; Av Las Heras 699) is one of several conventional travel agencies that organize trips in and around town. Among the possibilities are half-day tours of the city (AR$45), and day tours of the Cañon del Atuel (AR$140), Villavicencio (AR$70) or the high cordillera around Potrerillos, Vallecito and Uspallata (AR$110).

Internacional Mendoza (☎ 423-2103; www.inter nacionalmendoza.com; San Martín 1020, Local 3) rents bikes for AR$40 for six hours, including a city map and MP3 player with audio bike tour of the city.

WINE TOURS

For the casual sipper, a self-guided tour of Maipú (see the boxed text, p352) or any of the bodega tours offered by various travel agencies around town will likely satisfy. Moving several rungs up the ladder, there are a couple of companies operating out of Mendoza offering deluxe wine tours. They're not cheap, but the benefits are obvious – small group sizes (usually no more than six people), a knowledgeable English-speaking guide (as well as the winery guides, whose English is sometimes rough and occasionally nonexistent) and access to some of the more exclusive (ie better quality) vineyards. Winemakers are much more likely to be getting the good stuff down off the top shelf for you on these tours, too. The two listed here also offer tours of the Valle de Uco (see p354), an important new wine-growing region 150km south of Mendoza that's near-impossible to explore by public transport and doesn't yet appear on any tour-agency itinerary.

Trout & Wine (☎ 425-5613; www.troutandwine.com; Espejo 266) organizes custom-designed full-day tours of Luján de Cuyo (AR$540), Maipú (AR$600) and the Uco valley (AR$640). Maximum group size of six, also offering private tours across the border to Chilean wineries. From November to March it runs fly-fishing tours in the Valle de Uco for AR$920, including all gear and a barbecue lunch out in the highlands accompanied by – you guessed it – some very fine wines.

Ampora Wine Tours (☎ 429-2931; www.mendozawinetours.com; Av Sarmiento 647) is a well-established operation that concentrates on midrange and top-end wines. It has tours leaving every day (sometimes two) to Luján de Cuyo and Maipú (AR$540) and the Uco valley (AR$600). Tours focus more on tasting than winemaking techniques.

Festivals & Events

Mendoza's biggest annual event, the **Fiesta Nacional de la Vendimia** (National Wine Harvest Festival), lasts about a week, from late February to early March. It features a parade on Av San Martín with floats from each department of the province, numerous concerts and folkloric events, and it all culminates in the coronation of the festival's queen in the Parque General San Martín amphitheater.

Sleeping

Note that hotel prices rise from January to March, most notably during the wine festival in early March. Some hostels in Mendoza will only rent you a bed if you buy one of their tours. None of these are listed below.

BUDGET

Punto Urbano Hostel (☎ 429-5281; www.puntourbanohostel.com; Av Godoy Cruz 332; dm/d AR$35/100;) Just north of the city center, this hostel maintains an air of intimacy despite its grand proportions. The dorms are regular, but the doubles are extremely good value – spacious, with wide-screen TVs and tastefully decorated bathrooms. The large backyard – good for smoking, drinking, barbecuing and generally hanging out – is an added bonus.

Mendoza Inn (☎ 438-0818; www.mendozahostel.com; Av Arístides Villanueva 470; dm/d from AR$43/120;) With a great location and friendly, bilingual staff, this is one of the city's better hostels. Common areas are spacious and the big shady backyard and pool are definite pluses.

Damajuana Hostel (☎ 425-5858; www.damajuanahostel.com.ar; Av Arístides Villanueva 282; dm/d from AR$50/150;) Another good-looking hostel on the Arístides strip, this one doesn't miss a beat with great common areas, an excellent pool/garden area and functional dorms and doubles. Staff are probably way cooler than you are, and not shy about letting you know it.

Hotel Zamora (☎ 425-7537; www.hotelzamora.netfirms.com; Perú 1156; s/d AR$80/100) With a lot more style than most in this price range, this sweet little family-run hotel offers comfortable rooms, a buffet breakfast and a charming courtyard with tinkling fountain and Spanish tilework.

Hostal Confluencia (☎ 429-0430; www.hostalconfluencia.com.ar; Av España 1512; s/d AR$80/100;) A hotel-hostel hybrid, the Confluencia has good rooms with private bathrooms as well as kitchen access, a spacious lounge and a good central location.

City Hotel (☎ 425-1343; http://cityhotelmendoza.tripod.com; General Paz 95; s/d AR$90/130) A family-run, back to basics budget hotel. There's a slight sag to the beds, but the bathrooms are spacious and recently renovated.

MIDRANGE

Hotel Casino (☎ 425-6666; Gutiérrez 668; s/d AR$100/120;) Facing on to Plaza Chile, the Hotel Casino offers some good, spacious rooms and some smallish, ordinary ones. They're all clean and comfortable, but have a look at a few before deciding.

Hotel Petit (☎ 423-2099; www.petit-hoteles.com.ar; Perú 1459; s/d AR$100/120;) An excellent, central location, friendly welcome and big buffet breakfast make up for the slightly cramped rooms at this clean but ageing hotel.

Alcor Hotel (☎ 438-1000; www.alcorhotel.com.ar; General Paz 86; s/d AR$130/150;) One block from busy Av Las Heras, this is a recently renovated hotel that has maintained a few of its original charms. Rooms are big, light and well proportioned, with some comfy touches. Discounts apply for stays longer than three days.

Royal Hotel Horcones (☎ 425-0045; www.hotelhor cones.com; Av Las Heras 145; s/d AR$130/165; ❄ 🖳 🛜) A good deal on very central, spacious rooms. The wallpaper could do with a change, but the parquetry floors and sunny patio area are winners.

Palace Hotel (☎ 423-4200; www.hotelpalace.com.ar; Av Las Heras 70; s/d AR$130/220; ❄) The fading '70s charm of this large hotel is compensated for by its great, central location and a few classy decorations left over from the good ol' days. Rooms are generously sized and those at the front boast views out over the busy avenue.

Hotel San Martín (☎ 438-0875; www.hsm-mza.com .ar; Espejo 435; s/d AR$190/230; ❄ 🖳 🛜 🐾) Fronting the plaza, this three-story brick hotel offers solid value. There's plenty of tasteful tile work and rooms are spacious and comfortable with modern bathrooms and big windows.

Hotel Crillón (☎ 429-8494; www.hcrillon.com.ar; Perú 1065; s/d AR$200/230; ❄ 🖳 🛜 🐾) This is a modern, unpretentious place with wood-floored rooms, firm beds, good bathrooms (complete with towel-warmers) and a great swimming pool across the street.

our pick **Hotel Argentino** (☎ 405-6300; www.argen tino-hotel.com; Espejo 455; s/d AR$240/270; ❄ 🖳 🛜 🐾) Right on the central plaza, this business-class hotel has some fine features, including large rooms and a decent-sized swimming pool. Pay extra for a balcony overlooking the plaza.

B&B Plaza Italia (☎ 423-4219; www.plazaitalia.net; Montevideo 685; r AR$320; ❄) This six-room B&B is hard to beat when it comes to friendliness and delicious breakfasts. The house is lovely, the owners (who speak English) are divine, and the living room is just right for reading. It's like being at home.

TOP END

Hotel Aconcagua (☎ 420-2083; www.hotelaconcagua .com; San Lorenzo 545; r from AR$308; ❄ 🖳 🛜 🐾) Four-star Hotel Aconcagua has it all, with manicurists and hairstylists on the premises, a sauna and pool and some multilingual staff. It's one of the biggest in town, built in 1978 for the football World Cup.

Park Hyatt Mendoza (☎ 441-1234; www.mendoza .park.hyatt.com; Chile 1124; r from AR$735; ste from AR$1675; ❄ 🖳 🛜 🐾) Facing Plaza Independencia, Mendoza's only five-star hotel is a real beauty,

and walk-in rates can be surprisingly affordable (from the splurge perspective), considering the quality and comfort of the ultrachic rooms.

Eating

Some of Mendoza's best restaurants, often with outdoor seating and lively young crowds, are along Av Arístides Villanueva, the western extension of Av Colón. West of Plaza Independencia, Av Sarmiento is lined with the city's most traditional, albeit touristy, *parrillas* (steak restaurants), while east of the plaza along the Sarmiento *peatonal*, you'll find numerous sidewalk cafes with outdoor seating. The Sarmiento cafes are required visiting for coffee. The renovated **Mercado Central** (cnr Av Las Heras & Patricias Mendocinas; ⏲ lunch & dinner) is a good hunting ground for cheap pizza, empanadas (small, stuffed pastries) and sandwiches.

Ashoka (Av Arístides Villanueva 275; mains AR$12-15; ⏲ lunch) A cute little hole-in-the-wall setup serving up a surprisingly wide range of vegetarian options. Order by the kilo, take-out or pull up a stool.

Quinta Norte (Av Mitre & Espejo; set meals AR$12-30; ⏲ lunch & dinner) Sidewalk dining right across from the plaza. The menu's not huge, but there are some good dishes and the AR$17 set lunches are some of the best in town. A great place to grab a coffee and recharge the batteries.

La Flor de la Canela (Av Juan B Justo 426; mains AR$17-20; ⏲ lunch & dinner) Need something spicy? Check out this authentic, bare-bones Peruvian eatery a few blocks from the center. What it lacks in atmosphere it makes up for in flavor.

Casa 3 (San Lorenzo 490; set meals AR$18; ⏲ lunch & dinner Mon-Sat) A hip little bar-restaurant that wouldn't look out of place in downtown Barcelona. There are sofas on the sidewalk, after-work happy hours and some good, inventive cooking.

Ciao Cuoco (Perú 747; mains AR$20-30; ⏲ lunch & dinner) The front courtyard of this charming little pasta restaurant is the place to be on a sunny day. Nighttime, enjoy the rustic decor inside. Also on offer is a good range of Italian-inspired dishes.

La Albahaca (Espejo 659; mains AR$22-35; ⏲ lunch & dinner) In a country where 'Italian' food is abundant but can often disappoint, this is the real deal. The fettuccine puttanesca (AR$26) is everything it should be.

Tommaso Trattoria (Av Sarmiento 762; mains AR$22-35; lunch & dinner) An excellent, trilingual (Italian, Spanish and English) menu featuring a good range of creative regional Italian dishes. The wine list is impressive and the tables out the front are the place to be on a balmy evening.

Cocina Poblana (Av Arístides Villanueva 217; dishes AR$25-30; lunch & dinner Mon-Sat) The very tasty, inexpensive Middle Eastern food (hummus, falafel, dolmas) here comes as a welcome break from all that steak. The shish kebab served with tabouleh salad is a definite winner.

El Palenque (Av Arístides Villanueva 287; mains AR$25-40; lunch & dinner Mon-Sat) Don't miss this superb, extremely popular restaurant styled after an old-time *pulpería* (tavern), where the house wine is served in traditional *pinguinos* (white ceramic penguin-shaped pitchers). The food and appetizers are outstanding, and the outside tables are always full and fun.

La Tasca de Plaza España (423-3466; Montevideo 117; mains AR$25-40; dinner) With excellent Mediterranean and Spanish tapas (mostly seafood), great wines, intimate atmosphere, good art and friendly service, La Tasca is one of Mendoza's best.

La Marchigiana (Patricias Mendocinas 1550; mains AR$25-40; lunch & dinner) Mendoza's most frequently recommended Italian restaurant. The decor may seem stark, but the service is warm and a few Argentine twists to the classic Italian menu keep things interesting.

La Mira (Av Belgrano 1191; mains AR$30-40; lunch & dinner) Delicious, innovative dishes in a relaxed and casual environment. Each dish comes as a full meal (some even with side orders of vegetables) and there's a small but respectable wine list.

our pick **Anna Bistro** (Av Juan B Justo 161; mains AR$30-50; lunch & dinner) One of Mendoza's best-looking restaurants, this one offers a wonderful garden area, cool music and some carefully prepared, creative dishes.

Allure (Av Belgrano 1169; mains AR$35-50; lunch & dinner) Excellent, freshly prepared dishes in modern, tranquil surrounds. The ambience is hyper-zen and the food doesn't quite live up to that level of creativity, but the smoked meats platter (AR$20) and mixed kebabs (AR$25) are mouth-wateringly good.

Azafrán (429-4200; Av Sarmiento 765; mains AR$50-70; lunch & dinner Mon-Sat) It's hard to figure what's the bigger draw here – the rustic-chic decor, the small but creative menu or the extensive wine list. Who cares? Enjoy them all.

Drinking

For a great night on the town, walk down Av Arístides Villanueva, where it's bar after bar; in summer, entire blocks fill with tables and people enjoying the night.

Por Acá (420-0346; Av Arístides Villanueva 557) Purple and yellow outside and polka-dotted upstairs, this bar-cum-lounge gets packed after 2am, and by the end of the night, dancing on the tables is not uncommon. Good retro dance music.

La Reserva (Rivadavia 34; admission free-AR$15) This small, nominally gay bar packs in a mixed crowd and has outrageous drag shows at midnight every night, with hard-core techno later.

WINE BARS

Wine is available pretty much everywhere in Mendoza (right down to gas stations), but there are a few places that specialize.

Vines of Mendoza (438-1031; www.vinesofmendoza.com; Espejo 567; 3-10pm) This friendly, central wine bar (where everybody, down to the security guards, seems to speak English) offers flights (tastings of five selected wines) and top-shelf private tastings. It also offers wine-appreciation classes which give you an idea of how to taste wine – a great idea before hitting the bodegas.

Juan Cedrón (Av Sarmiento 786) An intimate little combination wine bar/store. Occasional tastings and sidewalk tables.

Vines Park Hyatt (Chile 1124; 11am-midnight) In the superformal surrounds of Mendoza's best-looking hotel, this is a relaxed and intimate wine bar offering wine by the glass, cheese platters and tapas.

Entertainment

Check the tourist offices or museums for a copy of *La Guía*, a monthly publication with comprehensive entertainment listings. *Los Andes*, the daily rag, also has a good entertainment section.

DANCE CLUBS

Finding a dance floor generally means abandoning downtown for one of two areas: the northwest suburb of El Challao, or Chacras de Coria, along the RP 82 in the southern outskirts. The former is reached by bus 115 from Av Sarmiento. Chacras de Coria is reached from the stop on La Rioja between Catamarca and Garibaldi by taking bus 10, *interno* (internal route number) 19, or from the corner of 25 de Mayo and Rivadavia by taking bus 10, *interno* 15. In both cases simply asking the driver for *los boliches* (the nightclubs) is enough to find the right stop. The nightclubs in both El Challao and Chacras de Coria are all right next to each other, and you can walk along to take your pick from the ever-changing array. **Cariló** (Av Champagnat s/n, El Challao; admission AR$10-40; ☽ Wed-Sat) was the hot club at the time of research – with a bit of luck it may still be there by the time you arrive.

Something to watch for here: the Mendoza government has introduced a law that prohibits dance clubs from allowing patrons to enter after 2:30am, making timing a tricky balancing act – get there after the place starts to fill up (1am at the earliest), but before they stop letting people in.

Many visitors to Mendoza (and *mendocinos* for that matter) find the effort involved getting to these places far outweighs the fun they have while there, often opting for the smaller bars along Av Arístides Villanueva. One exception is **Gutiérrez** (Gutiérrez 435; admission AR$10-30), located right downtown. It's a big dance club, with various theme nights, including Tuesday's 'hostel night' and regular live music.

THEATER & LIVE MUSIC
Soul Café (☎ 425-7489; San Juan 456; admission AR$5-15) Grab a table and enjoy everything from live *rock en español* (Spanish-language rock) to jazz and theater. Shows start after 10pm.

The main theaters in town are **Teatro Quintanilla** (☎ 423-2310; Plaza Independencia), the nearby **Teatro Independencia** (☎ 438-0644; cnr Espejo & Chile) and **Teatro Mendoza** (☎ 429-7279; San Juan 1427).

GRABBING A BOTTLE: THE MENDOZA SHOPPING LIST

Time to put the beer down and see what all the fuss is about. That's right: wine. While nearly every restaurant in the country has some sort of wine list, choices often tend toward the lower end of the market and markups can be hefty. In all but the finest restaurants you can bring a bottle, pay a nominal corkage fee (between AR$5 and AR$10) and enjoy a sublime experience.

Something else worth considering is that, while it's illegal to post wine from Argentina, countries such as the USA and Canada have no restriction on how much you can bring home in your luggage, provided you pay duty. And duty can be as low as US$5 for 40 bottles for the US.

If you are planning on transporting wine, it's best to stop in at a specialty wine store (see opposite) where they can pack bottles to avoid breakage (remember that most airlines no longer allow bottles in hand luggage). If you're just looking for a bottle to have with dinner, supermarkets around town have an excellent selection in the less-than-AR$100 range. Listed below are some of our top picks. Don't worry about vintages – Mendoza's incredibly consistent weather means a good wine is a good wine, regardless of the year.

Reds
Sottano Malbec (AR$20) One of the bigger bargains on the market, with deep fruity flavors and a long, long finish.

La Celia Cabernet Franc (AR$40) From one of the oldest vineyards in the Vale de Uco, this one has heavy berry tones and a velvety texture.

Prodigo Malbec Reserva (AR$65) An intense floral nose and light touches of chocolate and vanilla.

Ruca Malen Kinien (AR$95) A delicious, complex wine combining hints of plum, berry and pepper. French oak ageing gives smoky, chocolatey tones.

Whites
Tempus Alba Tempranillo (AR$48) Mendoza's *other* signature grape shows off its delicate, cherry flavors and silky entrance.

Pulenta Estate La Flor Sauvignon Blanc (AR$30) A wonderful summer wine, with a delicate, intense balance of grapefruit and citrus.

Mil Piedras Sangiovese (AR$25) Hints of white chocolate and ripe fruits in this delicate, dry white.

Urban Uco Sauvignon Blanc (AR$20) Grassy and floral, with hints of citrus. Sweet apricot tones lead to a buttery, oaky finish.

Shopping
CRAFTS
Av Las Heras is lined with souvenir shops, leather shops, chocolate stores and all sorts of places to pick up cheap Argentine trinkets. Items made of *carpincho* (spotted tanned hide of the capybara, a large rodent) are uniquely Argentine and sold in many of the stores.

Plaza de las Artes (Plaza Independencia; ☾ 5-11pm Fri-Sun) Outdoor crafts market in the Plaza Independencia.

Feria Artesanal Plaza España (Plaza España; ☾ 5-10pm Fri-Sun) Crafts fair in Plaza España with mediocre-quality goods.

Raices (☎ 425-4118; Av España 1092) High-quality weavings, *mates* (tealike beverages), jewelry and more. There is another location nearby on Av Sarmiento 162.

WINE STORES
Unless you are looking for a very obscure top of the range bottle (or a sales assistant who knows what they're talking about), the best place to buy wine in town, in terms of price and variety, is the supermarket **Carrefour** (Avs Las Heras & Belgrano; ☾ 8am-10pm). The places listed below stock finer wines, have staff who speak at least a little English and can pack your bottles for shipping.

Juan Cedrón (Av Sarmiento 786) A small but well-chosen selection lines the walls. Doubles as a wine bar. Occasional tastings and sidewalk tables.

Marcelino (www.marcelinonline.com; cnr Benegas & M Zapata) An almost staggering array of mostly reds. They were one of the first to move into the potentially lucrative online sales arena.

Getting There & Away
AIR
Aerolíneas Argentinas/Austral (☎ 420-4185; Av Sarmiento 82) share offices; Aerolíneas flies several times daily to Buenos Aires (from AR$513). **Sol** (☎ 0810-444-4765; www.sol.com.ar) flies to Córdoba (AR$450) and Rosario (AR$392).

Lan (☎ 425-7900; Rivadavia 135) flies twice daily to Santiago, Chile (from AR$1300), the only international flights from Mendoza.

BUS
Mendoza is a major transport hub so you can travel to just about anywhere in the country. Mendoza's **bus terminal** (☎ 431-5000, 431-3001; cnr Avs R Videla & Acceso Este, Guaymallén) has domestic and international departures.

Domestic
Several companies send buses daily to Uspallata (AR$20, two hours) and Los Penitentes (AR$48, four hours), the latter for Aconcagua.

During the ski season several companies go directly to Las Leñas (about AR$80, seven hours); **Mendoza Viajes** (☎ 461-0210; Sarmiento 129) leaves from Av Sarmiento and 9 de Julio, rather than the terminal.

A number of companies offer a morning bus service to the Difunta Correa Shrine (p367; AR$25 return, departs 7:30am) in San Juan province; the journey is three hours each way and the bus waits three hours before returning. Buses to Maipú leave from the stop on La Rioja between Garibaldi and Catamarca.

There are daily departures from Mendoza's bus terminal to the destinations in the following table, and sometimes upwards of 10 to 20 per day to major cities. Prices reflect midseason fares.

Destination	Cost (AR$)	Duration (hr)
Bahía Blanca	210	16
Bariloche	240	20
Buenos Aires	200	13-17
Catamarca	140	10
Chos Malal	115	13
Córdoba	110	10
Jujuy	250	22
Maipú	1.50	45 mins
Malargüe	45	5
Mar del Plata	280	19
Neuquén	160	10-12
Resistencia	250	24
Río Gallegos	626	41
Rosario	190	12
Salta	270	18
San Juan	22	2½
San Luis	40	3½
San Rafael	22	3
Santa Fe	170-210	14
Tucumán	180	14
Zapala	135	16

International
Numerous companies cross the Andes every day via RN 7 (Paso de Los Libertadores) to Santiago, Chile (AR$85, seven hours), Viña del Mar (AR$85, seven hours) and Valparaíso (AR$85, eight hours). The pass sometimes closes due to bad winter weather; be prepared to wait (sometimes days) if weather gets extreme.

Several carriers have connections to Lima, Perú (AR$570, 60 to 70 hours), via Santiago, Chile, and there are at least two weekly departures to Montevideo, Uruguay (from AR$230, 25 hours), some with onward connections to Punta del Este and Brazil.

International buses depart from the main bus terminal. Companies are at the eastern end of the terminal.

Getting Around

TO/FROM THE AIRPORT

Plumerillo International Airport (☎ 448-2603) is 6km north of downtown on RN 40. Bus 68 ('Aeropuerto') from Calle Salta goes straight to the terminal.

BUS

Mendoza's **bus terminal** (☎ 431-5000, 431-3001; cnr Avs R Videla & Acceso Este, Guaymallén) is really just across the street from downtown. After arriving, walk under the Videla underpass and you'll be heading toward the center, about 15 minutes away. Otherwise, the 'Villa Nueva' trolley (actually a bus) connects the terminal with downtown.

Local buses cost AR$1.50 – more for longer distances – and require a magnetic Mendobus card, which can be bought at most kiosks in denominations of AR$2 and AR$5. Most *lineas* (bus lines) also have *internos* (internal route numbers) posted in the window; for example, *linea* 200 might post *interno* 204 or 206; watch for both numbers. *Internos* indicate more precisely where the bus will take you.

CAR

Rental-car agencies are at the airport and along Primitivo de la Reta.

Avis (☎ 447-0150; Primitivo de la Reta 914)

Localiza (☎ 429-6800; Primitivo de la Reta 936, Local 4)

National/Alamo (☎ 429-3111; Primitivo de la Reta 928)

AROUND MENDOZA

Sites in this section are Mendoza's closest major attractions, but you could easily visit Puente del Inca and Las Cuevas (near the Chilean border; see p357) in a day.

Wineries

Thanks to a complex and very old system of river-fed aqueducts, land that was once a desert now supports 70% of the country's wine production. Mendoza province is wine country, and many wineries near the capital offer tours and tasting. Countless tourist agencies offer day tours, hitting two or more wineries

in a precisely planned day, but it's also easy enough to visit on your own. Hiring a *remise* (taxi) is also feasible. Most winery tours and tastings are free, though some push hard for sales at the end, and you never taste the *good* stuff without paying. Malbec, of course, is the definitive Argentine wine.

With a full day it's easy to hop on buses and hit several of the area's most appealing wineries in the outskirts of neighboring Maipú, only 16km away. See the boxed text, p352, for a self-guided tour. For a look at what the cutting-edge wineries are doing, consider renting a car or going on a tour of the Valle de Uco – see p354. Another option is the area of Luján de Cuyo, 19km south of Mendoza, which also has many important wineries. Buses to Maipú leave from La Rioja, between Garibaldi and Catamarca in central Mendoza; buses to wineries in Luján de Cuyo leave from Mendoza's bus terminal.

Mendoza's tourist office on Garibaldi near Av San Martín provides a basic but helpful map of the area and its wineries. Also look for the useful three-map set *Wine Map: Wine and Tasting Tours* (Wine Map, 2004–05).

Bodega Escorihuela (☎ 0261-424-2744; www.escorihuela.com; cnr Belgrano & Pte Alvear, Godoy Cruz; ☒ tours 9:30am, 10:30am, 11:30am, 12:30pm, 2:30pm & 3:30pm), founded in 1884, is one of the country's oldest wineries. It has an art gallery, a restaurant and a famous barrel from Nancy, France, with an impressive sculpture of Dionysus. Take bus 'T' from Mendoza's Av Sarmiento at Av San Martín.

Luigi Bosca (☎ 0261-498-0437; www.luigibosca.com.ar; San Martín 2044, Luján de Cuyo; guided visits Mon-Sat by reservation only), which also produces Finca La Linda, is one of Mendoza's premier wineries. If you're into wine, don't miss it. Tours are available in Spanish and English. Take bus 380 (AR$2, one hour) from platform 53 in Mendoza's bus terminal.

The modern **Bodegas Chandon** (☎ 0261-490-9900; www.bodegaschandon.com.ar; RN 40, Km 29, Agrelo, Luján de Cuyo; guided visits Mon-Sat by reservation only) is popular with tour groups and known for its sparkling wines (champagne). Tours are available in Spanish and English. Take bus 380 (AR$2, one hour) from platform 53 in Mendoza's bus terminal.

Catena Zapata (☎ 0261-413-1100; www.catenawines.com; Calle Cobos 5519, Agrelo, Luján de Cuyo; visits/tours by appointment 10am-6pm Mon-Sat) is one of Argentina's most esteemed wineries. Tours are fairly mundane but are conducted in English, German or

GETTING THE JUICE ON MENDOZA WINE

Since the Jesuits first planted vines in northern Argentina more than 500 years ago, the wine industry here has been slowly developing and it wasn't so long ago that Argentine wine didn't even make a blip on the international radar.

The first major improvement came with the arrival of French, Italian and Spanish immigrants in the 19th century. True winemakers, these folks brought varieties from their home countries, replacing the Jesuit's *criollo* vines with 'noble' varieties such as merlot and cabernet sauvignon. The new grapes brought a minimal increase in quality, but even so, Argentine wine remained a very domestic product, often to be enjoyed with a big blast of soda to take the edge off.

Then, as if from nowhere, Argentine wines hit the world stage with a vengeance, and these days a Mendoza merlot has just as much (if not more) cachet than a comparably priced Chilean red.

There are a few reasons for this meteoric rise to fame: for one, the wine industry here is becoming more sophisticated. As domestic consumption drops (in favor of beer and, incredibly, soft drinks), more wineries are looking to export their product. At last count there were more than 300 wineries in the region exporting, a dramatic increase from the '60s, when only a handful did so.

Quality is another factor. Argentine wines are good and they just keep getting better. One of the keys to successful winemaking is controlled irrigation. A big rain before a harvest can spoil an entire crop, but winemakers in the desertlike Mendoza region don't have to worry about that. Nearly every drop of water is piped in – often using irrigation techniques developed by the Huarpe people – and comes as beautiful fresh snowmelt from the Andes.

Another advantage of the region is the variation in altitudes. Different grapes grow better at different heights, and the area around Mendoza has vineyards at between 900m and 1800m above sea level. Mendoza's flagship grape will probably always be malbec, but local winemakers are having good results with tempranilla, bonarda, syrah, chardonnay and sauvignon blanc.

Desert vineyards have another advantage – the huge difference between daytime and nighttime temperatures. Warm days encourage sugar production and help the grapes grow a nice thick skin. Cool nights ensure good acidity levels. Another bonus is low humidity levels, meaning bugs and fungus aren't a problem.

Overall quality is improving as techniques are refined. Back in the day, it was all about quantity, but now winemakers are looking to produce fewer grapes of higher quality. Better hygiene standards, the further replacement of old 'criollo' vines with 'noble' varieties such as malbec, cabernet sauvignon, merlot and syrah, and the practice of ageing wines in smaller oak barrels (with a lifespan of a few years) rather than large barrels (which would be used for up to 70 years) have all had positive effects.

And you can't talk about Argentine wines without talking price-to-quality ratio. The country's economic crash in 2001 was a boon for exporters as prices plummeted and Argentine wine all of a sudden became a highly competitive product. Land here is (relatively) cheap and labor so inexpensive that nearly every grape in the country is hand-picked, a claim that only the top-end wines in other countries can make.

For a list of recommended wines from the Mendoza region, see the boxed text, p348.

Spanish. Tasting – if you put down the cash – can be educational indeed. Get there by taxi (cheaper if you catch a bus to Luján de Cuyo and grab one from there).

Cacheuta
☎ 02624 / elev 1237m
About 40km southwest of Mendoza, in the department of Luján de Cuyo, Cacheuta is renowned for its medicinal thermal waters and agreeable microclimate.

Complejo Termal Cacheuta (☎ 429133; www.ter mascacheuta.com; RP 82, Km 41; admission Mon-Sat AR$20, Sun AR$25; 10am-6pm) This excellent, open-air thermal-baths complex is one of the best in the country, due to its variety of pools and dramatic setting on the side of a valley. Midweek is the best time to come as weekends get crowded with kids splashing around on the waterslide and in the wave pool and the air runs thick with the smoke from a thousand *parrillas*.

MAIPÚ: A GOURMET EXPERIENCE

The small town of Maipú, just out of Mendoza, is so packed with wineries, olive oil farms and other gourmet businesses that it's easy to hit five or six in a day. All offer tours and most finish proceedings with at least a small sampling of their produce.

Accordingly, a few companies in Maipú rent bikes and electric scooters, making a day tour of the area an excellent outing, and a lot more fun than the often rushed half-day wine tours on offer from Mendoza tour agencies.

To get to Maipú, catch the 173 bus from the bus stop on La Rioja in Mendoza and get off at the triangular roundabout. Bike-hire competition here is serious business (there have been fistfights in the street between operators) and the main companies are all within walking distance of each other. Go for a stroll and see who has the best wheels on the day. Among operators are **Coco Bikes** (☎ 0261-481-0862; Urquiza 1781; bikes/scooters per day AR$25/60), **Hugo Bikes** (☎ 0261-497-4067; Urquiza 2228; bikes per day AR$25) and **Bikes & Wines** (☎ 0261-410-6686; www.bikesandwines.com; cnr Urquiza & Montecaseros; bikes/scooters per day AR$25/50). All will supply you with a (basic) map of the area and some may offer to take you in a van to your furthest point, meaning you only have to ride the 12km back to base.

All of the following are open 10am to 5pm Monday to Friday and 10am to 1pm Saturday. Reservations are not necessary at any.

Carinae (☎ 0261-499-0470; www.carinaevinos.com; Aranda 2899; tours AR$15) is the furthest south you really want to go – it's a small, French-owned winery producing a lovely rosé and some good reds. Tour fees are deducted from any wine purchases you make.

Across the road is **LAUR** (☎ 0261-499-0740; www.laursa.com.ar; Aranda 2850; tours AR$5), a 100-year-old olive farm. The 15-minute tour tells you everything you need to know about olive oil production and is followed by a yummy tasting session.

Heading back to Urquiza, go past the big roundabout and venture north. The first winery you come to is **Di Tomasso** (☎ 0261-499-0673; Urquiza 8136; tours AR$15), a beautiful, historical vineyard dating back to the 1830s. The tour includes a quick pass through the original cellar section.

Heading north again, take a right on Moreno to get to **Viña del Cerno** (☎ 0261-481-1567; www.elcerno.com.ar; Moreno 631; tours AR$20), a small, old-fashioned winery supervised by its two winemaker owners. The underground cellar complex is atmospheric, but tastings can be a little rushed.

Back out on Urquiza, it's a little under 3km to Zanichelli, where you turn left and travel another 1km to get to **Almacen del Sur** (Zanichelli 709; set meals AR$35-120; ⏰ lunch). This working farm produces and exports gourmet deli goods that are grown and packed on the premises. Free tours of the production facilities are available. There's also an excellent restaurant here, serving delicious set lunches (the more expensive ones come accompanied by local wines) in a leafy garden setting.

Head back to Urquiza and continue north until you get to the big roundabout. Turn right and follow the signs to **Historia y Sabores** (Carril Gómez 3064). Seven families run this little chocolate- and liqueur-making operation. Tours are brief, but the lovely rustic surrounds and comfy bar (where you're invited to a free shot of liqueur) make it a worthwhile stop.

Along Urquiza, keep heading north until you get to where you got off the bus, take a right on Montecaseros and continue for 500m to reach **Bodega La Rural** (☎ 0261-497-2013; www.bodegalarural.com.ar; Montecaseros 2625; tours AR$10; ⏰ 9am-1pm & 2-5pm Mon-Fri). Winery tours here are fairly standard (and you probably have the idea by now) but the museum (admission free) is fascinating – there's a huge range of winemaking equipment from over the years on display, including a grape press made from an entire cowskin. Tours in Spanish leave on the hour. If you want one in English, call ahead, or you can simply walk around on your own.

There is lodging at the lovely **Hotel & Spa Cacheuta** (☎ 490152/3; www.termascacheuta.com; RP 82, Km 38; s/d with full board from AR$490/830; ⚊), where prices include a swimming pool, hot tubs, massage, in addition to optional recreation programs. Nonguests may use the baths for around AR$160 per person.

Campers can pitch a tent at **Camping Termas de Cacheuta** (☎ 482082; RN 7, Km 39; campsite per person AR$25).

Expreso Uspallata (☎ in Mendoza 0261-438-1092) runs daily buses to Cacheuta (AR$8, 1½ hours).

Potrerillos
☎ 02624 / elev 1351m

Set above the newly built Potrerillos reservoir in beautiful Andean precordillera, Potrerillos is one of Mendoza's white-water hot spots, usually visited during a day's rafting trip from the capital.

Located about 1km uphill from the ACA campground, **Argentina Rafting Expediciones** (☎ 482037; www.argentinarafting.com; Ruta Perilago s/n; day trips with transfer from Mendoza AR$280) offers rafting and kayaking on the Río Mendoza. Trips range from a 5km, one-hour Class II float to a 50km, five-hour Class III-IV descent over two days (from AR$500). Set up trips at the Mendoza **office** (☎ 0261-429-6325; Primitivo de la Reta 992, Local 4) or at the base here in Potrerillos.

El Puesto Hostel (☎ 02624-15-655-9937; www.el puestohostel.com.ar; Av Los Condores s/n; dm AR$40) This newish hostel has four- to six-bed dorms in a tranquil setting. Table tennis and darts are on hand to keep you entertained and hearty traditional meals are available (AR$25 to AR$40).

Camping del ACA (☎ 482013; RN 7, Km 50; campsites members/nonmembers AR$15/18, extra tent AR$8) offers shady sites near the reservoir just below the new town.

For delicious traditional cooking, don't miss friendly **El Futre** (☎ 482006; Ruta Perilago s/n; mains AR$15), at the same location as Argentina Rafting.

Villavicencio
☎ 0261 / elev 1800m

If you've ordered mineral water from any restaurant or cafe in Argentina, odds are you've ended up with a bottle of Villavicencio on your table. These springs are the source, and their spectacular mountain setting once hosted the prestigious thermal baths resort of the **Gran Hotel de Villavicencio** (admission free; ☉ 8am-8pm). Popular with the Argentine elite during the middle of the 20th century, the resort has been closed for more than a decade; promises have floated around for years that it would 'soon' reopen.

Panoramic views from the hair-raising winding turns leading to Villavicencio make the journey an attraction in itself. There is free camping alongside the attractive **Hostería**

Villavicencio (☎ 439-6487; meals AR$20-50), which has no accommodations but serves gourmet meals in charming surrounds.

There is no public transport to the valley. Nearly every tour operator in Mendoza offers half-day tours (AR$70) that take in the hotel grounds, the bottling plant and short walks in the surrounding countryside.

USPALLATA
☎ 02624 / pop 3550 / elev 1751m

A humble little crossroads town on the way to the Chilean border, Uspallata is an oasis of poplar trees set in a desolate desert valley. The polychrome mountains surrounding the town so resemble highland Central Asia that director Jean-Jacques Annaud used it as the location for the epic film *Seven Years in Tibet*.

The town first gained fame as a low-budget base for the nearby ski fields at Los Penitentes, but has recently been coming into its own with a few companies offering treks, horseback riding and fishing expeditions in the surrounding countryside.

There's a post office and a Banco de la Nación, which has an ATM. The tiny **tourist office** (☎ 420009; RN 7 s/n; ☉ 9am-8pm) is across from the YPF gas station. It has good information on local sights and activities and some very basic (but still useful) area maps.

Sights & Activities
A kilometer north of the highway junction in Uspallata, a signed lateral leads to ruins and a museum at the **Museo Las Bóvedas** (admission AR$3; ☉ 10am-7pm Tue-Sun), a smelting site since pre-Columbian times. An easy 8km walk north of town brings you to Cerro Tunduqueral, where you'll find sweeping views and Inca rock carvings.

Pizarro Expeditions (☎ 421-0003; www.pizarroexpedi ciones.com.ar) offers a range of outdoor activities, including horseback riding, mountain-bike tours, rock climbing, trekking and 4WD off-roading. Prices generally run at AR$90/160 for half-/full-day trips, depending on group size. It also rents mountain bikes for AR$10 per hour.

Fototravesías 4x4 (☎ 420185; www.fototravesias4x4 .com, in Spanish; day trips per person AR$50-100), near the main intersection, offers exciting 4WD tours in the surrounding mountains. The owner is a photographer and is especially amenable to ensuring travelers get good shots.

TOURING THE VALLE DE UCO

Seriously remote and woefully signposted, the Valle de Uco – home to some of Mendoza's top wineries – is best visited on a guided tour. If you've got the time and patience, though, you can easily rent a car in Mendoza to make the trip. Reservations are essential for touring any of the following 'must sees' in the region:

Pulenta Estate (☎ 0261-420-0800; www.pulentaestate.com; RP 86) A boutique winery started by the ex-owners of the Trapiche label. Tours of the beautiful modern facility focus on tasting, not production.

Andeluna Estate (☎ 02622-423226; RP 89, Km 11; ☽ tours 10:30am, 12:30pm & 3:30pm) Tastings of the wonderful wines produced here take place in a charming old-world style tasting room. There are also great mountain views from the patio.

La Azul (☎ 02622-423593; www.bodegalaazul.com.ar; RP 89 s/n) A small winery producing excellent malbecs. Tours are in Spanish only, but focus mainly on tasting – you're in and out in 20 minutes.

Salentein (☎ 02622-429000; www.bodegasalentein.com; RP 89 s/n) A state-of-the-art, Dutch-owned winery that's distinctive for its on-site contemporary-art gallery and its method of moving grapes and juice by hand and gravity, rather than by machine.

Francois Lurton (☎ 0261-441-1100; www.francoislurton.com; RP 94, Km 21) An ultramodern facility run by two French brothers from a famous winemaking family, producing one of the best Mendoza torrontés on the market. Excellent tours with impressive tasting areas and barrel room.

The valley is an easy day trip from Mendoza, but there are some wonderfully atmospheric places to stay out here, including **Tupungato Divino** (☎ 02622-448948; www.tupungatodivino.com.ar; cnr RP 89 & Calle los Europeos; s/d AR$495/570; ☒ ▯), **Posada Salentein** (☎ 02622-429000; www.bodegasalentein.com; RP 89 s/n; s/d with full board AR$1242/1383; ☒ ▯ ☎ ☒) and **Valle de Uco Lodge** (☎ 0261-429-6210; www.postalesdelplata.com/valledeuco.htm; Tabanera s/n, Tunuyán; r from AR$460; ☒ ▯ ☒).

If you're looking for a lunch stop, most of the above wineries offer gourmet meals. Otherwise, **Ilo** (cnr Cabral & Belgrano, Tupungato; mains AR$35-50; ☽ lunch & dinner) is generally considered the best in Tupungato – the good range of seafood dishes makes it a winemakers' favorite.

Sleeping & Eating

In the summer high season (when climbers from around the world descend on the area), reservations are wise.

Hostel Uspallata (☎ in Mendoza 0261-15-466-7240; www.hosteluspallata.com.ar; RN 7 s/n; dm/d AR$40/140) Friendly hostel 5km east of town with plain but comfortable rooms, a Ping-Pong table and a cafe. There's good hiking from the hostel. Ask the bus driver to drop you at the front before you hit Uspallata.

Hospedaje Mi Casa (☎ 420358; hospedajemicasa@hotmail.com; RN 7 s/n; s/d AR$60/90) A cute little *hospedaje* (family home) with very homey-feeling rooms and superfriendly owners. It's about 300m east of the junction, next to the post office.

Hotel Viena (☎ 420046; Av Las Heras 240; s/d AR$100/140) Making an extremely ordinary first impression, this little hotel actually has some of the cutest rooms in town. Lots of wooden furniture, big TVs and real floorboards await. Bathrooms are large and modern.

Hostería Los Cóndores (☎ 420002; www.loscondoreshotel.com.ar, in Spanish; Las Heras s/n; s/d AR$170/220;

☒ ☒) Close to the junction, this is the finest hotel in the center of town. There's plenty of space, modern furnishings, and a gut-busting breakfast buffet is included in the price.

Gran Hotel Uspallata (☎ 420006; www.granhoteluspallata.com.ar; RN 7, Km 1149; r from AR$260; ☒ ☒) Though it looks a bit shopworn since its Peronist glory days, this resort hotel, about 1km west of the junction, offers an interesting taste of old-school Argentine tourism and some serious attitude from the desk staff. The hallways are large, almost daunting, there's a bowling alley, and the rooms come complete with pink chenille bedspreads.

Café Tibet (cnr RN 7 & Las Heras; mains AR$12-25; ☽ breakfast, lunch & dinner) No visit to Uspallata would be complete without at least a coffee in this little oddity. The food is nothing spectacular, but the decor, comprising leftover props from the movie, is a must for fans of the surreal.

El Rancho (cnr RN7 & Cerro Chacay; mains AR$20-30; ☽ lunch & dinner) This is the coziest and most reliable *parrilla* in town, serving all the usual, plus a good roasted *chivo* (goat).

Getting There & Away

Expreso Uspallata (☎ 420045) runs several buses daily to and from Mendoza (AR$20, 2½ hours). Buses continue from Uspallata to Las Cuevas (AR$30, two hours), near the Chilean border, and stop en route at Los Penitentes, Puente del Inca and the turnoff to Laguna Los Horcones for Parque Provincial Aconcagua. They can be flagged from all of these locations on their return to Uspallata from Las Cuevas.

Andesmar has daily morning departures to Santiago (AR$70, six hours) and Valparaíso (AR$75, seven hours) in Chile.

All buses leave from the Expreso Uspallata office in the little strip mall near the junction.

LOS PENITENTES

☎ 02624

So named because the pinnacles resemble a line of monks, **Los Penitentes** (☎ 420229; www .penitentes.com) has both excellent scenery and snow cover (in winter). It's 165km west of Mendoza via RN 7, and offers downhill and cross-country skiing at an altitude of 2580m. Lifts (AR$75 to AR$155 per day) and accommodations are modern, and the vertical drop on some of its 21 runs is more than 700m. Services include a ski school (private lessons run around AR$130), equipment rentals (skis AR$75 per day, snowboards AR$95) and several restaurants and cafeterias. For transportation details, see above.

In high ski season (July and August) and during peak climbing season (December through to March), make reservations up to a month in advance for all of the following options.

Hostel Los Penitentes (☎ 0261-429-0707; www .penitentes.com.ar; dm AR$85) A cozy converted cabin, owned by Mendoza's HI Campo Base, it accommodates 38 people in extremely close quarters, and has a kitchen, wood-burning stove and three shared bathrooms. It's all good fun with the right crowd. Lunch and dinners are available for AR$20 to AR$30 each.

Hostería Los Penitentes (☎ in Mendoza 0261-438-0222; d with half-board AR$170) This modest *hostería* (lodging house) with plain, comfortable rooms has a restaurant and bar and offers full board with ski passes (AR$2300 per week with full board and unlimited skiing).

Refugio Aconcagua (☎ in Mendoza 0261-424-1565; www.refugioaconcagua.com.ar; r with half-board per person AR$170) There's nothing fancy about the rooms at this place, but they're an OK size and con-

sidering you're in the middle of the resort, with a private bathroom and two meals a day, they're a good deal. The restaurant here serves up big, hearty set meals (AR$25 to AR$40) and is open year-round.

Hotel & Hostería Ayelén (☎ in Mendoza 0261-427-1123; www.ayelen.net; s/d hostería AR$150/300, hotel AR$410/500) It's a four-star resort hotel with comfortable accommodations in the main hotel and cheaper rooms in the *hostería* alongside. The lobby and restaurant are great, but the wallpaper in the rooms could use a change.

PUENTE DEL INCA

☎ 0264 / elev 2720

One of Argentina's most striking natural wonders, this stone bridge over the Río de las Cuevas glows a dazzling orange from the sediment deposited by the warm sulfuric waters. The brick ruins of an old spa, built as part of a resort and later destroyed by flood, sit beneath the bridge, slowly yielding their form to the sulfuric buildup from the thermal water that trickles over, around and through it. Due to the unstable nature of the structure, the area has been closed off and you can't cross the bridge or enter the hot baths any more, but you can still get some fairly wild photos.

Puente del Inca enjoys a spectacular setting, and whether or not you climb, it's a good base for exploring the area. Trekkers and climbers can head north to the base of Aconcagua, south to the pinnacles of Los Penitentes, or even further south to 6650m Tupungato (p357).

About 1km before Puente del Inca (directly across from Los Puquios), the small **Cementerio Andinista** is a cemetery for climbers who died on Aconcagua.

In summer, free camping is possible at the nearby mini ski resort of **Los Puquios** (☎ 0261-429-5007; www.lospuquios.com.ar). There are two accommodations options at Puente del Inca.

Refugio La Vieja Estación (☎ 0261-452-1103; dm AR$40; meals AR$30) is a rustic hostel in Puente del Inca's old wooden train station, built in the late 1800s. It's popular with climbers during peak season but can be wonderfully quiet other times of the year. If you're up for some outdoor action, these are the guys to ask – they'll take you trekking for one to three days (AR$80 per day) in summer or point you in the direction of the best backcountry skiing in winter – a six-hour walk uphill for two hours of downhill, track-carving bliss.

Hostería Puente del Inca (☎ 420266; RN 7, Km 175; s/d AR$130/150) has comfortable rooms and a huge restaurant (with an overpowering smell of budget air-freshener) serving AR$30 set meals. It's the most comfortable in the area and fills up fast in climbing season.

For transportation details, see p355.

PARQUE PROVINCIAL ACONCAGUA

North of RN 7, nearly hugging the Chilean border, Parque Provincial Aconcagua protects 710 sq km of the wild high country surrounding the western hemisphere's highest summit, 6962m Cerro Aconcagua. Passing motorists (and those who can time their buses correctly) can stop to enjoy the view of the peak from **Laguna Los Horcones**, a 2km walk from the parking lot just north of the highway.

There's a ranger available at Laguna Los Horcones from 8am to 9pm weekdays, 8am to 8pm Saturday. There are also rangers at the junction to Plaza Francia, about 5km north of Los Horcones; at Plaza de Mulas on the main route to the peak; at Refugio Las Leñas, on the Polish Glacier Route up the Río de las Vacas to the east; and at Plaza Argentina, the last major camping area along the Polish Glacier Route.

Only highly experienced climbers should consider climbing Aconcagua without the relative safety of an organized tour.

Cerro Aconcagua

Often called the 'roof of the Americas,' the volcanic summit of Aconcagua covers a base of uplifted marine sediments. The origin of the name is unclear; one possibility is the Quechua term Ackon-Cahuac, meaning 'stone sentinel,' while another is the Mapuche phrase Acon-Hue, signifying 'that which comes from the other side.'

Italian-Swiss climber Mathias Zurbriggen made the first recorded ascent in 1897. Since then, the peak has become a favorite destination for climbers from around the world, even though it is technically less challenging than other nearby peaks. In 1985 the Club Andinista Mendoza's discovery of an Incan mummy at 5300m on the mountain's southwest face proved that the high peaks were a pre-Columbian funerary site.

Reaching the summit requires a commitment of at least 13 to 15 days, including acclimatization time; some climbers prefer the longer but more scenic, less crowded and more technical Polish Glacier Route.

Potential climbers should acquire RJ Secor's climbing guide Aconcagua (Seattle, The Mountaineers, 1999). The website www .aconcagua.com.ar and Mendoza government's website, www.aconcagua.mendoza.gov .ar, are also helpful.

Nonclimbers can trek to **base camps** and **refugios** beneath the permanent snow line. On the Northwest Route there is also the relatively luxurious **Hotel Refugio Plaza de Mulas** (☎ 02642-490442; www.refugioplazademulas.com.ar; dm/r per person AR$115/230, with full board AR$390/500; ♥ Nov-Mar), the highest hotel in the world.

PERMITS

From December to March permits are obligatory for both trekking and climbing in Parque Provincial Aconcagua; park rangers at Laguna Los Horcones will not permit visitors to proceed up the Quebrada de los Horcones without one. Fees vary according to the complex park-use seasons. Permits cost AR$170/300 for trekkers (three/seven days) and AR$1500 for climbers (20 days) during high season, from December 15 through to January 31; AR$150/220 for trekkers and AR$1000 for climbers during midseason, from December 1 to December 14 and February 1 through to February 20; and AR$150/220 (trekking) and AR$500 (climbing) in low season, from November 15 through to November 30 and February 21 through to March 15. Argentine nationals pay about 30% of overseas visitors' fees at all times. These fees climb (steeply) each year – check www.aconcagua.mendoza .gov.ar for the latest.

Organized tours rarely, if ever, include the park entrance fee. Fees must be paid in Argentine pesos or US dollars only, and you must bring your original passport with you when you pay the fee. The permit start-date takes effect when you enter the park.

All permits are available only in Mendoza at the provincial tourist office (p342).

ROUTES

There are three main routes up Cerro Aconcagua. The most popular one, approached by a 40km trail from Los Horcones, is the **Ruta Noroeste** (Northwest Route) from Plaza de Mulas, 4230m above sea level. The **Pared Sur** (South Face), approached from the base camp at Plaza Francia via a 36km trail from Los Horcones, is a demanding technical climb.

From Punta de Vacas, 15km southeast of Puente del Inca, the longer but more scenic **Ruta Glaciar de los Polacos** (Polish Glacier Route) first ascends the Río de las Vacas to the base camp at Plaza Argentina, a distance of 76km. Climbers on this route must carry ropes, screws and ice axes, in addition to the usual tent, warm sleeping bag and clothing, and plastic boots. This route is more expensive because it requires the use of mules for a longer period.

MULES

The cost of renting cargo mules, which can carry about 60kg each, has gone through the roof: the standard fee among outfitters is AR$520 for the first mule from Puente del Inca to Plaza de Mulas, though two mules cost only AR$800. A party of three should pay about AR$1100 to AR$1700 to get their gear to the Polish Glacier Route base camp and back.

For mules, contact Rudy Parra at Aconcagua Trek or Fernando Grajales, following. If you're going up on an organized tour, the mule situation is, of course, covered.

TOURS

Many of the adventure-travel agencies in and around Mendoza arrange excursions into the high mountains (see p343). It is also possible to arrange trips with some overseas-based operators.

The following are the area's most established and experienced operators.

Daniel Alessio Expediciones (www.alessio.com.ar) Located in Mendoza; contact online.

Fernando Grajales (www.grajales.net) Contact online.

Inka Expediciones (☎ 0261-425-0871; www.inka .com.ar; Juan B Justo 345, Mendoza) Fixed and tailor-made expeditions. Airport to airport costs AR$8500 to AR$11,000.

Rudy Parra's Aconcagua Trek (☎ /fax in Mendoza 0261-429-5007; www.rudyparra.com; Barcala 484) Contact Rudy by telephone. Rudy operates at nearby Los Puquios (p355) from December to March.

Several guides from the **Asociación Argentina de Guías de Montaña** (www.aagm.com.ar) lead two-week trips to Aconcagua, including **Pablo Reguera** (pabloreguera@hotmail.com) and **Mauricio Fernández** (info@summit-mza.com.ar).

All guides and organized trips are best set up online or by telephone *at least* a month in advance. Everything – guides, mules, hotels

etc – must be booked far in advance during peak climbing months.

Getting There & Away

The two park entrances – Punta de Vacas and Laguna Los Horcones – are directly off RN 7 and are well signed. The Los Horcones turnoff is only 4km past Puente del Inca. If you're part of an organized tour, transport will be provided. To get here by bus, take an early morning Expreso Uspallata bus (see p355) from Mendoza. Buses bound for Chile will stop at Puente del Inca, but often fill up with passengers going all the way through.

From Los Horcones, you can walk back along the RN 7 to Puente del Inca or time your buses and catch a Mendoza-bound bus back down.

LAS CUEVAS & CRISTO REDENTOR
☎ 02624 / elev 3200m

Pounded by chilly but exhilarating winds, the rugged high Andes make a fitting backdrop for Cristo Redentor, the famous monument erected after a territorial dispute between Argentina and Chile was settled in 1902. The view is a must-see either with a tour or by private car (a tunnel has replaced the hairpin road to the top as the border crossing into Chile), but the first autumn snowfall closes the route. You can hike the 8km up to El Cristo via trails if you don't have a car.

In the nearby settlement of Las Cuevas, 10km east of the Chilean border and 15km from Puente del Inca, **Arco de Las Cuevas** (☎ 420185; www.arcodelascuevas.com.ar; mains AR$30) has extremely basic bunks (AR$50) and only two bathrooms (which everyone in the restaurant uses as well). The restaurant, however, serves what one traveler called the 'best lentil soup ever.'

PARQUE PROVINCIAL VOLCÁN TUPUNGATO

Tupungato (6650m) is an impressive volcano, partly covered by snowfields and glaciers, and serious climbers consider the mountain a far more challenging, interesting and technical climb than Aconcagua. The main approach is from the town of **Tunuyán**, 82km south of Mendoza via RN 40, where the **tourist office** (☎ 02622-488097, 02622-422193; República de Siria & Alem) can provide info. Many of the outfitters who arrange Aconcagua treks can also deal with Tupungato (see left).

SAN RAFAEL

☎ 02627 / pop 116,280 / elev 690m

Arriving by bus at San Rafael's scruffy terminal, you're bound to be underwhelmed. Persevere, though – a few blocks away lies a busy, modern town whose streets are lined with majestic old sycamores and open irrigation channels. It's not exactly Mendoza, but it's getting there.

There is nothing to do in town (part of its allure) except wander its shady streets and plazas or while the day away in a cafe. There are, however, several esteemed wineries within biking distance that are well worth a visit. The city has also become a popular base for exploring (or driving through) the nearby Cañon del Atuel (p360) and for scenic rafting on the Río Atuel.

Orientation

San Rafael is located 230km southeast of the city of Mendoza via RN 40 and RN 143, and 189km northeast of Malargüe via RN 40. Most areas of interest in town are northwest of the Av H Yrigoyen and Av San Martín intersection.

Information

Banco de Galicia (Av H Yrigoyen 28) Several banks along Av H Yrigoyen have ATMs, including Banco de Galicia.
Cambio Santiago (Almafuerte 64) Charges 2.5% on traveler's checks.
Hospital Teodoro J Schestakow (☎ 424490; Emilio Civit 151)
Municipal tourist office (☎ 424217; www.sanrafael turismo.gov.ar; Av H Yrigoyen 745; 8am-8pm) Helpful staff and useful brochures and maps.
Post office (cnr San Lorenzo & Barcala)

Sights & Activities

San Rafael is flat (hence the proliferation of bike riders here), and when in Rome…get a bike. Several places around town rent out clunkers, but if you're looking for a smooth ride, try **Risco Viajes** (☎ 436439; Av H Yrigoyen 284; per day AR$80), who also offer standard local excursions to Valle Grande and nearby wineries, white-water rafting, mountain biking and other activities.

There are three wineries within walking or cycling distance of town offering free tours and tasting. Head west on RN 143, which has a welcome bike path along its side. The modern and highly regarded **Bianchi Champañera** (☎ 435600; www.vbianchi.com; cnr Ruta 143 & Valentín

Bianchi; 9am-noon & 2-5pm Mon-Fri) is the furthest west, but still only 6km away. Tours are friendly, offering visitors a glimpse into the making of sparkling wine (champagne), and English is spoken.

Only about 4km out, **Fincas Andinas** (Salafia; ☎ 430095; www.fincasandinas.com.ar; Av H Yrigoyen 5800; 9:30am-4pm Mon-Fri) makes excellent sparkling wine as well as malbec and cabernet. Guided visits take place every half an hour.

Halfway between Fincas Andinas and San Rafael, **Suter** (☎ 421076; www.sutersa.com.ar, in Spanish; Av H Yrigoyen 2850; short tours free; 9:30am-12:30pm & 1:30-5pm Mon-Fri) is a rather unromantic, modern affair, but a worthwhile stop for some discounted wine. For AR$150 you can set up a half-day tour, visiting the vineyards with an agronomist, tasting specialty wines and eating a big lunch in the vineyard.

If wineries and bikes aren't your thing, the nearby Cañon del Atuel (p360) is an easy, scenic day trip from San Rafael.

Sleeping

Hostel Tierrasoles (☎ 433449; www.tierrasoles.com.ar; Alsina 245; dm/d AR$40/110;) Simply the best-looking hostel in town has OK-sized dorms and a couple of good sitting areas. The inviting backyard (with barbecue for guest use) rounds out the picture.

Hotel Cerro Nevado (☎ 423993; www.cerroneva dohotel.com.ar; Av H Yrigoyen 376; s/d AR$65/130;) The best of the budget hotel picks, the Cerro Nevado offers good-sized rooms, dinky decorations and a super central location.

Hotel España (☎ 424055; www.hotelespanasrl.com.ar; Av San Martín 270; s/d from AR$85/110) It may not scream 'Spain,' but the mod 1960s-ish interior is definitely unique. Rooms in the 'colonial' sector open onto a delightful patio area, making them more attractive (and a better deal) than the spacious rooms in the pricier 'celeste' sector.

Hotel Jardín (☎ /fax 434621; www.hoteljardinhotel.com.ar; Av H Yrigoyen 283; s/d AR$115/140;) There is indeed a garden here – or better said, a courtyard – filled with baroque touches such as fountains and sculptures of nude Greek figures. Rooms face onto it and are big and comfortable, if slightly soulless.

our pick Hotel Regine (☎ 421470; www.hotelregine.com.ar; Independencia 623; s/d AR$200/250;) A bit of a walk from the center, but well worth it for the big stylish rooms. The palm-shaded pool/cafe/bar area is a real bonus.

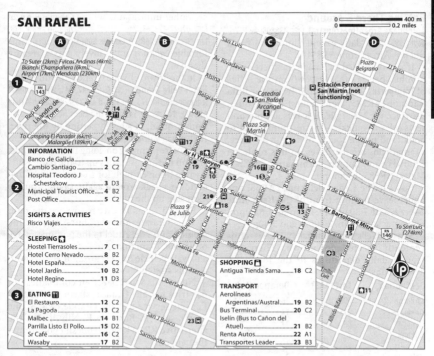

SAN RAFAEL

INFORMATION	
Banco de Galicia	1 C2
Cambio Santiago	2 C2
Hospital Teodoro J	
Schestakow	3 D3
Municipal Tourist Office	4 B2
Post Office	5 C2

SIGHTS & ACTIVITIES	
Risco Viajes	6 C2

SLEEPING	
Hostel Tierrasoles	7 C1
Hotel Cerro Nevado	8 B2
Hotel España	9 C2
Hotel Jardín	10 B2
Hotel Regine	11 D3

EATING	
El Restauro	12 C2
La Pagoda	13 C2
Malbec	14 B1
Parrilla Listo El Pollo	15 D2
Sr Café	16 C2
Wasaby	17 B2

SHOPPING	
Antigua Tienda Sama	18 C2

TRANSPORT	
Aerolíneas	
Argentinas/Austral	19 B2
Bus Terminal	20 C2
Iselín (Bus to Cañon del	
Atuel)	21 B2
Renta Autos	22 A1
Transportes Leader	23 B3

Camping El Parador (☎ 427983; Isla Río Diamante; campsites AR$23) Located about 6km south of downtown.

Eating & Drinking

Sr Café (Av San Martín 49; sandwiches AR$15, mains AR$20-28; ☼ breakfast, lunch & dinner) The most stylin' little cafe in the center, this is a good place for coffee and a sandwich anytime. Weekend nights, pull up an outside table and enjoy the live music.

La Pagoda (Av Bartolomé Mitre 188; tenedor libre AR$18; ☼ lunch & dinner) Anybody familiar with the all-you-can-eat scene in Argentina won't find too many surprises here, but the food (Argentine and Chinese) is fresh enough – get there early – and there's certainly plenty of it.

Wasaby (Av Moreno 31; mains AR$20-30; ☼ lunch & dinner) 'Asian food' quite often means medio-cre Chinese around these parts, but this little hole-in-the-wall turns out some surprisingly good dishes, and even a couple of Japanese-inspired options.

Malbec (cnr Av H Yrigoyen & Pueyrredón; mains AR$20-30; ☼ lunch & dinner) San Rafael's most frequently

recommended *parrilla* holds no surprises, but has a good range of pastas and salads and, yes, some big juicy steaks.

Parrilla Listo El Pollo (Av Bartolomé Mitre s/n; par-rilla AR$24; ☼ lunch & dinner) The roadside *par-rilla* is an Argentine classic and this one's a great example. Grab a sidewalk table (not that there's any choice) and knock elbows with taxi drivers while feasting on big cheap chunks of meat.

El Restauro (cnr Salas & Day; mains AR$25-40; ☼ din-ner) The snootiest restaurant around has some excellent dishes on offer using local ingre-dients and regional recipes. A fair wine list features local heavy hitters such as Suter and Bianchi.

Shopping

There are numerous crafts stores around town, all of which stock the usual souvenirs. For something a bit more authentic, pick up a pair of *bombachas* (commonly worn gaucho-influenced pants with button-cuff bottoms) for about AR$60 at friendly **Antigua Tienda Sama** (Godoy Cruz 123); they're subtle enough to wear anywhere.

Getting There & Around

Aerolíneas Argentinas/Austral (☎ 438808; Av H Yrigoyen 395) flies daily except Sunday to/from Buenos Aires (from AR$510).

If you're headed to Patagonia, there's one minibus per day that leaves from the office of **Transportes Leader** (☎ 421851; Perú 65) for Buta Ranquil (AR$85, eight hours) in Neuquén province via Malargüe. It leaves at 6pm and seats sell out quickly – it's recommended to book (and pay) a couple of days in advance. Tramat runs regular buses on this route on Thursday and Sunday, terminating in Chos Malal (AR$85, 10 hours).

Buses to the Cañon del Atuel (AR$8, one hour) leave from in front of the **Iselín office** (Suárez 255) at 7:30am, 12:40pm and 6:30pm, returning at 8:40am, 2:40pm and 7:40pm.

San Rafael's **bus terminal** (Suárez) is conveniently located downtown. There are regular daily departures to the following destinations.

Destination	Cost (AR$)	Duration (hr)
Bariloche	200	16
Buenos Aires	215	14
Córdoba	88	11
El Nihuil	7	1
Las Leñas	24	3
Malargüe	22	3
Mar del Plata	260	16
Mendoza	22	3
Neuquén	110	9
San Luis	50	4

Renta Autos (☎ 424623; www.rentadeautos.com.ar; Av H Yrigoyen 818) offers the best deals on car rentals in town.

CAÑON DEL ATUEL & VALLE GRANDE

South of San Rafael along the Río Atuel, RP 173 passes through a multicolored ravine that locals compare to Arizona's Grand Canyon, though much of the 67km **Cañon del Atuel** has been submerged by four hydroelectric dams. Nevertheless, there is white-water rafting on its lower reaches, and several operators at the tourist complex of **Valle Grande**, midway down the canyon, do short but scenic floats down the river, and other trips.

Sport Star (☎ 02627-15-581068; www.sportstar.com.ar; RP 173, Km 35) offers the widest range of activities, including trekking, horseback riding, kayaking, mountain-bike tours, canoes and rappelling.

There are numerous places to stay in Valle Grande itself. Some cater to large groups and are rather unpleasant, but the **Cabañas Río Azul** (☎ 02627-423663; www.complejorioazul.com.ar; RP 173, Km 33; campsites AR$20, cabañas from AR$180) has comfortable *cabañas* and a lovely grassy area by the river.

In the 'town' of Valle Grande, the three-star **Hotel Valle Grande** (☎ 02627-423541; www.hotelvallegrande.com; RP 173, Km 35; s/d AR$233/280, cabañas from AR$400; ⊠ ⊜ ⊛) offers the best accommodations around, in a lovely setting by the river. It also has a good restaurant.

If you're planning on going to Valle Grande, stay on the bus as it goes up to the dam, waits a while (long enough for a couple of photos) and turns back around again, saving you the 4km slog up the hill.

RP 173 turns to dirt road past the dam at Valle Grande, and continues through the scenic Cañon del Atuel to the podunk village of **El Nihuil**, 79km from San Rafael – you'll need a private vehicle or tour group if you want to see this stretch.

Numerous San Rafael tour companies run day trips to Valle Grande, starting at AR$90. For bus service to Valle Grande (AR$8, one hour), see left. Buses to El Nihuil take the alternative RP 144, which doesn't go through the canyon.

MALARGÜE

☎ 02627 / pop 24,300 / elev 1400m

Despite serving as a base for Las Leñas, one of Argentina's snazzier ski resorts, Malargüe is a mellow little town that even gets a little rough around the edges. For skiers it's a cheaper alternative to the luxury hotels on the mountain, and people staying here get a 50% discount on lift tickets (hotels provide vouchers) provided they rent their gear on the mountain. The dry precordillera that surrounds the town is geologically distinct from the Andes proper, and two fauna reserves, Payén and Laguna Llancancelo, are close by. Caving is possible at Caverna de Las Brujas and Pozo de las Animas. The nearby Parque Provincial Payunia (p362) is a 4500-sq-km reserve with the highest concentration of volcanic cones in the world.

Information

Banco de la Nación (cnr Av San Martín & Inalicán) One of several banks downtown with ATMs.

Post office (cnr Adolfo Puebla & Saturnino Torres)

Tourist office (☎ 471659; www.malargue.gov.ar; RN 40, Parque del Ayer; ⊗ 8am-11pm) Helpful tourist office with facilities at the northern end of town, on the highway.

Sights

Due to Malargüe's remote location, it's a great spot for stargazing, and the newly opened **Planetarium** (☎ 472116; Villegas & Aldeo; tours AR$10; ☺ 5-9pm) is an excellent, state-of-the-art complex featuring some freaky architecture and some reasonably entertaining audiovisual presentations.

Activities & Tours

Several companies offer excellent 4WD and horseback-riding excursions, and if you don't have a car, these are generally the best way to get into the surrounding mountains (see p362). Possible day trips include Caverna de Las Brujas (AR$100 per person, which includes AR$20 park entrance fee and obligatory guide), Los Molles (AR$70) and the marvelous Laguna Llancancelo (AR$80). One of the most exciting drives you might ever undertake is the 12-hour 4WD tour through Parque Provincial Payunia (AR$230); be sure your tour stops at all the sites – those that combine the visit with Laguna Llancancelo only visit half the sites in Payunia.

Amulén (☎ 02627-15-604130; Rodríguez 120) offers half-day horseback-riding or hiking trips to the spectacular **Volcán Malacara** (AR$100), which you should do your best to see. The company also offers a two-day trip through Parque Provincial Payunia complete with an *asado* (barbecue) under the stars.

Huarpes del Sol (☎ 02627-15-557878; www.huarpes delsol.com.ar; Av San Martín 85) has received excellent reports for its trips and the owner of **Karen Travel** (☎ /fax 470342; www.karentravel.com.ar; Av San Martín 54) speaks English – this company also gets rave reviews.

Sleeping

Malargüe has abundant, reasonably priced accommodations. Prices quoted here are for ski season (June 15 through to September 15) and drop by up to 40% the rest of the year. Get a discount voucher from your hotel if you plan to ski at Las Leñas. Singles are nonexistent during ski season, when you'll likely be charged for however many beds are in the room.

Camping Municipal Malargüe (☎ 470691; Alfonso Capdevila s/n; campsites AR$15) At the northern end of town, 300m west of Av San Martín, this is the closest place to camp.

Hostel Kathmandú (☎ 02627-15-414899; www.hos tel-kathmandu.com.ar; Torres 121; dm AR$35) Half a block from the plaza, this homey little hostel offers comforts such as hammocks, Ping-Pong table and an open fireplace.

Hostería La Posta (☎ 472079; Av San Martín 634; s/d AR$100/120) Budget hotels are very light on the ground in Malargüe, but this one is OK – the rooms are big and the family's friendly, though the mattresses sag somewhat.

Hotel Bambi (☎ 471237; Av San Martín 410; s/d AR$120/155) Friendly hotel with clean but faded rooms with basic bathrooms. It's the most comfortable place downtown.

Hotel de Turismo (☎ 471042; Av San Martín 224; s/d AR$120/160) The Turismo's a good standby – there are plenty of rooms (which are nothing special) so it rarely fills up. Downstairs, the restaurant-cafe lifts the tone with a few charming touches.

Hotel Pehuén (☎ 02627-15-587-7024; cnr Ruibal & A Puebla; s/d AR$150/180) Although the exterior is a lot better looking than the interior, the Pehuén still has some good-sized rooms (which vary – have a look at a few if you can) with fading carpet and floral bedspreads.

Hotel El Cisne (☎ 471350; cnr Civit & Villegas; s/d AR$180/200; ☒ ☍) A new, ultramodern hotel with a good central location. Rooms are big, with plenty of furnishings and attractive pine-lined ceilings.

Eating & Drinking

our pick **El Quincho de María** (Av San Martín 440; mains AR$15-35; ☺ lunch & dinner) The finest dining in the center is at this cozy little *parrilla* where everything from the gnocchi to the empanadas is handmade. Don't miss the mouth-watering shish kebabs for AR$30.

Don Gauderio (cnr Av San Martín & Torres; mains AR$16-30; ☺ breakfast, lunch & dinner) A hip little nouveau-rustic bar on the plaza. Meal-sized sandwiches are the standout here, but the pizzas and savory crepes deserve a mention, too.

La Posta (☎ 471306; Av General Roca 374; mains AR$20-30; ☺ lunch & dinner) A friendly neighborhood *parrilla*, La Posta comes up with the goods in the juicy steak, wine list and televised football department.

Getting There & Around

There are charter flights (AR$1950) to/from Buenos Aires in July and August only, from **Malargüe airport** (☎ 470098) at the southern end of town. They're usually sold as part of an accommodation package for Las Leñas, but if there's space, they can squeeze you in. Contact the **Las Leñas office** (☎ in Buenos Aires 011-4819-6000; www.laslenas.com; Cerrito 1186, 8th fl) for details.

From Malargüe's **bus terminal** (cnr Av General Roca & Aldao) there are several direct buses to Mendoza daily (AR$43, five hours), plus others requiring a change in San Rafael (AR$22, three hours). In summertime there's one departure daily for Los Molles (AR$12, one hour) and Las Leñas (AR$16, 1½ hours).

Transportes Leader (☎ 470519; cnr Avs San Martín & General Roca) has one minibus leaving for Buta Ranquil (AR$65, five hours) in Neuquén at 9pm Monday to Saturday. Seats sell out fast – it's recommended that you book (and pay) at least two days in advance. Tramat has the same route, leaving from the bus terminal on Thursdays and Sundays to Chos Malal (AR$65, six hours).

For winter transportation to Los Molles and Las Leñas ski resorts, contact any of the travel agencies listed, p361. They offer a roundtrip shuttle service, including ski rentals, from AR$60 to AR$90 per person.

AROUND MALARGÜE
☎ 02627

Geologically distinct from the Andean mountains to the west, the volcanically formed landscapes surrounding Malargüe are some of the most mind-altering in Argentina and have only recently begun to receive tourist attention. Visiting the following places is impossible without your own transportation, though Malargüe's excellent travel agencies can arrange excursions to all of them.

Just over 200km south of Malargüe on the RN 40, the spectacular **Parque Provincial Payunia** is a 4500-sq-km reserve with a higher concentration of volcanic cones (over 800 of them) than anywhere else in the world. The scenery is breathtaking and shouldn't be missed. The 12-hour 4WD tours or three-day horseback trips offered by most of the agencies in Malargüe (p361) are well worth taking.

Lying within its namesake fauna reserve about 60km southeast of Malargüe, **Laguna Llancancelo** is a high mountain lake visited by more than 100 species of birds, including flamingos.

Caverna de Las Brujas is a magical limestone cave on Cerro Moncol, 72km south of Malargüe and 8km north of Bardas Blancas

along RN 40. Its name means 'Cave of the Witches.' The cave complex stretches for 5km. Guided tours (admission and flashlights included in the price) take two to three hours. Tours depart with a minimum group size of two, although getting more people together will bring down the per-person cost. Check with tour operators in Malargüe for details.

Los Molles

Before Las Leñas took over as the prime ski resort in the area, Los Molles was the only place around where you could grab a poma (ski lift). These days it's a dusty windswept village that would be slowly sinking into obscurity if not for its reasonably priced accommodation alternatives for those wishing to be near, but not in, Las Leñas, and its favored status for rock climbers, hikers and other rugged outdoor types. The village straddles RP 222, 55km northwest of Malargüe. Karen Travel in Malargüe (p361) offers a range of activities in the dramatic countryside that surrounds the village.

Hostel Piriá (☎ 15-516757; dm AR$35) Across the bridge and up the valley from the highway, this little *refugio* offers reasonable dorms, a big common area, cheap meals and kitchen access. Also on-site, a 'mountain school' teaches rock climbing and ice climbing, depending on the season.

Hotel Los Molles (☎ 499712; www.losmolleshotel.com .ar; RP 222, Km 30; r per person AR$160) The most modern and best equipped of the hotels here, it features big rooms with balconies facing out over the valley. A decent restaurant serves good-value set meals (AR$30).

Buses heading between Malargüe (AR$12, one hour) and Las Leñas (AR$5, 30 minutes) pass through the village.

LAS LEÑAS
☎ 02627

Designed primarily to attract wealthy foreigners, **Las Leñas** (☎ 471100; www.laslenas.com; 🗓 mid-Jun–late-Sep) is Argentina's most self-consciously prestigious ski resort. Since its opening in 1983 it has attracted an international clientele who spend their days on the slopes and nights partying until the sun comes up. Because of the dry climate, Las Leñas has incredibly dry powder.

Its 33 runs cover 33 sq km; the area has a base altitude of 2200m, but slopes reach

3430m for a maximum drop of 1230m. Outside the ski season Las Leñas is also attempting to attract summer visitors who enjoy weeklong packages, offering activities such as mountain biking, horseback riding and hiking.

Las Leñas is 445km south of Mendoza and 70km from Malargüe, all via RN 40 and RP 222.

Lift Tickets & Rentals

Prices for lift tickets vary considerably throughout the ski season. Children's tickets are discounted about 30%. One-day tickets range from AR$137 in low season to AR$210 in high season (week passes are AR$734 to AR$1124). Also available are three-day, four-day, two-week and season passes. Anyone lodging in Malargüe receives a 50% discount on lift tickets provided they rent their ski gear on the mountain (make sure you get a voucher from your hotel).

Rental equipment is readily available and will set you back about AR$100 per day for skis and AR$70 per day for snowboards.

Sleeping & Eating

Las Leñas has a small village with four luxury hotels and a group of 'apart hotels,' all under the same management. They are generally booked as part of a weeklong package, which includes lodging, unlimited skiing and two meals per day. Despite the country's economic troubles, rates for foreigners staying in Las Leñas have changed little. All bookings are done either online at www.laslenas .com or centrally through **Ski Leñas** (in Buenos Aires 011-4819-6000/60; ventas@laslenas.com; Cerrito 1186, 8th fl).

Hotel Acuario (per person AR$3500-8000;) The most humble of the hotels here is still very comfortable, and, with 'only' 40 rooms, cozier than other options.

Hotel Escorpio (per person AR$3800-8250;) This 47-room hotel is nominally three stars, but still top-notch, with an excellent restaurant. Guests can use facilities at the Hotel Piscis.

Hotel Aries (s AR$5800-12,650, d AR$7250-15,800;) Aries is a four-star hotel with a sauna, gym facilities, a restaurant and luxuriously comfortable rooms.

Virgo Hotel & Spa (per person AR$6000-14,500;) The newest hotel in the village, this one goes all out, with a heated outdoor swimming pool, sushi bar, whirlpool bath and cinema.

Hotel Piscis (s AR$7330-17,000, d AR$9160-21,380;) The most extravagant of Las Leñas' lodgings is the five-star, 99-room Hotel Piscis. This prestigious hotel has wood-burning stoves, a gymnasium, sauna, an indoor swimming pool, the elegant Las Cuatro Estaciones restaurant, a bar, a casino and shops. Rates depend on time of the season, and are based on double occupancy.

Apart Hotel Gemenis (weekly per person AR$4200-6000) and **Apart Hotel Delphos** (weekly per person AR$4200-6000) offer similar packages without meals but do have well-equipped kitchenettes.

There are also small apartments with two to six beds and shared bathrooms, equipped for travelers to cook for themselves. Budget travelers can stay more economically at Los Molles, 20km down the road, or at Malargüe, 70km away.

Restaurants in the village run the comestible gamut, from cafes, sandwich shops and pizzerias to upscale hotel dining rooms. The finest restaurant of all is Las Cuatro Estaciones, in Hotel Piscis.

Getting There & Away

In July and August, there are charter flights (AR$1950) on Saturday from Buenos Aires to Malargüe, including transfers to and from Las Leñas. These are most commonly booked as part of an accommodation package with one of the Las Leñas hotels.

There is a bus service operating in season from Mendoza (AR$40, 6½ hours), San Rafael (AR$25, three hours) and Malargüe (AR$16, 1½ hours).

SOUTH ALONG THE RN 40

From Malargüe the RN 40 winds its way through rugged desert landscapes and into Neuquén province. Despite what many will tell you, there *is* public transport along this route. Tramat runs regular buses between Mendoza and Zapala twice a week and Transportes Leader runs minibuses between San Rafael and Buta Ranquil Monday to Saturday. See the Mendoza (p349), San Rafael (p360) and Malargüe (p361) sections for details. From Buta Ranquil there are connections to Neuquén and Chos Malal, but you may get stuck for the night. There's no real reason to be here, but there are a couple of cheap hotels, one nice accommodations option, and enough restaurants and cafes to keep you from starving.

MENDOZA & THE CENTRAL ANDES

SAN JUAN

☎ 0264 / pop 460,200 / elev 650m

Living in the shadow of a world-class destination like Mendoza can't be easy and, to its credit, San Juan doesn't even try to compete. Life in this provincial capital moves at its own pace, and the locals are both proud of and humble about their little town.

No slouch on the wine production front, San Juan's wineries are refreshingly low-key after the Mendoza bustle, and the province's other attractions are all within easy reach of the capital. Most come here en route to Parque Provincial Ischigualasto (p373).

In 1944 a massive earthquake destroyed the city center, and Juan Perón's subsequent relief efforts are what first made him a national figure. The city goes dead in summer, especially on Sunday, when all of San Juan heads to the nearby shores of Dique Ullum for relief from the sun.

Orientation

San Juan is 170km north of Mendoza via RN 40 and 1140km from Buenos Aires. Like most Argentine cities, San Juan's grid pattern makes orientation very easy; the addition of cardinal points – *norte* (north), *sur* (south), *este* (east) and *oeste* (west) – to street addresses helps even more. East–west Av San Martín and north–south Calle Mendoza divide the city into these quadrants. The functional center of town is south of Av San Martín, often referred to as Av Libertador.

Information

ACA (Automóvil Club Argentina; ☎ 422-3781; 9 de Julio 802) Argentina's auto club; good source for provincial road maps.

Banco de San Juan (cnr Rivadavia & Entre Ríos) Has an ATM.

Cambio Santiago (General Acha 52 Sur) Money exchange.

Cyber Neo (cnr Mitre & Entre Ríos; per hr AR$3) One of countless internet cafes in San Juan.

Hospital Rawson (☎ 422-2272; cnr General Paz & Estados Unidos)

Laverap (Rivadavia 498 Oeste; full laundry service about AR$13)

Post office (Av José Ignacio de la Roza 259 Este)

Provincial tourist office (☎ 422-2431, 421-0004; www.turismo.sanjuan.gov.ar, in Spanish; Sarmiento 24 Sur; ☻ 7am-8pm Mon-Fri, 9am-8pm Sat & Sun) Has a good map of the city and its surroundings plus useful information on the rest of the province, particularly Parque Provincial Ischigualasto.

Sights & Activities

If you need a little perspective on things, make your way up the **Lookout Tower** (cnr Mendoza & Rivadavia; admission AR$2; ☻ 9am-1pm & 5-9pm) for a sweeping view out over the town and surrounding countryside.

There's usually an open-air *milonga* (tango dance hall) in the Parque de Mayo on Friday, starting at 9pm – check with the tourist office if it's still going when you get here.

Museum hours change often, so check with the tourist office for updated information.

The **Casa Natal de Sarmiento** (☎ 422-4603; www.casanatalsarmiento.com.ar; Sarmiento 21 Sur; admission AR$5; ☻ 9am-7pm Tue-Fri, 9am-2pm Sat, 9am-9pm Sun) is named for Domingo Faustino Sarmiento, whose prolific writing as a politician, diplomat, educator and journalist made him a public figure both within and beyond Argentina. Sarmiento's *Recuerdos de Provincia* recounted his childhood in this house and his memories of his mother. The house is now a museum.

The most interesting specimen at the **Museo de Ciencias Naturales** (Museum of Natural Sciences; ☻ 9am-1pm) is the skeleton of the dinosaur Herrerasaurus from Ischigualasto, though

---

JUST A LOAD OF HOT AIR

While traveling through San Juan, especially in autumn and winter, you may become acquainted – through hearsay if not through experience – with one of the region's meteorological marvels: *el zonda*. Much like the Chinook of the Rockies or the foehn of the European Alps, the *zonda* is a dry, warm wind that can raise a cold day's temperature from freezing to nearly 20°C (68°F). The *zonda* originates with storms in the Pacific that blow eastward, hit the Andes, dump their moisture and come whipping down the eastern slopes, picking up heat as they go. The wind, which varies from mild to howling, can last several days; *sanjuaninos* (people from San Juan) can step outside and tell you when it will end – and that it will be cold when it does. It's a regular occurrence, giving the region – and the *sanjuaninos* – severe seasonal schizophrenia, especially during winter.

SAN JUAN

INFORMATION	
ACA	1 F3
Banco de San Juan	2 C2
Cambio Santiago	3 D2
Cyber Neo	4 C3
Hospital Rawson	5 F3
Laverap	6 B3
Post Office	7 D3
Provincial Tourist Office	8 C2

SIGHTS & ACTIVITIES	
Casa Natal de Sarmiento	9 C2
Lookout Tower	10 C2
Mario Agüero Turismo	11 D2
Museo de Ciencias Naturales	12 A1
Saitur Saul Saidel	13 D2

SLEEPING	
Albertina Hotel	14 D3
Hotel Alhambra	15 D2
Hotel Alkazar	16 D2
Hotel América	17 F4
Plaza Hotel	18 C3
San Juan Hostel	19 D3

EATING	
Baró	20 C2
Cereza Light	21 C2
de Sánchez	22 D2
Remolacha	23 C2
Soychú	24 C3

SHOPPING	
Mercado Artesanal Tradicional	25 A1

TRANSPORT	
Aerolíneas Argentinas/Austral	26 C2
Bus Terminal	27 F3
Classic	28 C2
Parque Auto Motor	29 B2

there are plenty of provincial minerals, fossils and other exhibits to mull over. The museum is next to the old train station on Av España at Maipú.

Museo de Vino Santiago Graffigna (☎ 421-4227; www.graffignawines.com; Colón 1342 Norte; ⏰ 9am-5:30pm Mon-Sat, 10am-4pm Sun) is a wine museum well worth a visit. It also has a wine bar where you can taste many of San Juan's best wines. Take bus 12A from in front of the tourist office on Sarmiento (AR$1.50, 15 minutes) and ask the driver to tell you when to get off.

Tour operators in San Juan provide lots of options for taking in the sights in and around town.

Mario Agüero Turismo (☎ 422-0840; General Acha 17 Norte) Offers organized tours including Parque Provincial Ischigualasto.

Saitur Saul Saidel (☎ 421-2222; www.saulsaidel.com; Av José Ignacio de la Roza 112 Este) Offers city tours and day trips to Ischigualasto (AR$250) and elsewhere.

Sleeping

San Juan Hostel (☎ 420-1835; www.sanjuanhostel.com; Av Córdoba 317 Este; dm AR$35, d with/without bathroom AR$95/70; ▢ 🛜) An excellent little hostel with a variety of rooms placed conveniently between the bus terminal and downtown. Good info on tours and local attractions, and a rooftop Jacuzzi rounds out the picture.

Plaza Hotel (☎ 422-5179; plazahotelsanjuan@hotmail.com; Sarmiento 344 Sur; s/d AR$90/120; 🛏) There's no plaza in sight, but the large, unrenovated rooms here represent fair value. Check out a few for better ventilation and light.

Hotel Alhambra (☎ 421-4780; www.alhambrahotel.com.ar; General Acha 180 Sur; s/d AR$100/140; 🛏 🛜) Cozy, carpeted rooms with splashes of dark wood paneling giving them a classy edge. Little touches such as leather chairs and gold ashtray stands in the hallways give it a kitschy appeal and the central location seals the deal.

Hotel América (☎ 421-4514; www.hotel-america.com.ar; 9 de Julio 1052 Este; s/d AR$110/130; 🛏 🛜) This is excellent value in a drab location. It conveniently offers excursions through an on-site tour operator and is a popular place with a good restaurant. Its swimming pool is located five blocks from the hotel.

Albertina Hotel (☎ /fax 421-4222; www.hotelalbertina.com; Mitre 31 Este; r AR$160; 🛏 ▢ 🛜) A slick, business-class hotel right on the plaza. Stay for more than two nights and you get free massages, gym access and yoga classes. The

tiny rooms are a bit of a letdown, but the bathrooms are big. Fair deal.

Hotel Alkazar (☎ 421-4965; www.alkazarhotel.com.ar; Laprida 82 Este; r from AR$230; 🛏 ▢ 🛜 🛒) San Juan's most upscale hotel teeters on corporate blandness, but pulls it off in the end, with big, stylishly decorated rooms. Services include a spa, sauna and on-site massage therapist.

Eating

Most restaurants are right downtown, and many of the city's hippest eateries are around the intersection of Rivadavia and Entre Ríos.

Cereza Light (cnr Mendoza & Laprida; juices AR$10; ⏰ breakfast, lunch & dinner) An otherwise unremarkable little cafe that deserves a mention for its excellent range of fruit and vegetable juices.

Baró (Rivadavia 55 Oeste; mains AR$18-24; ⏰ breakfast, lunch & dinner) This popular main-street cafe/restaurant has the best variety of pasta dishes in town and a relaxed atmosphere that make it a good stop for coffee or drinks at any time.

our pick Remolacha (cnr Av José Ignacio de la Roza & Sarmiento; mains AR$18-35; ⏰ lunch & dinner) One of the biggest *parrillas* in town, the dining room is extremely ordinary, but eating in the garden is a lush experience. Get a table by the picture windows looking into the kitchen and you'll be able to see your meal being hacked off the carcass before getting thrown on the flames. Excellent salads, too.

Soychú (Av José Ignacio de la Roza 223 Oeste; tenedor libre AR$20; ⏰ lunch & dinner Mon-Sat, lunch only Sun) Excellent vegetarian buffet attached to a health-food store selling all sorts of groceries and a range of teas. Arrive early for the best selection.

de Sánchez (Rivadavia 61 Oeste; mains AR$30-40; ⏰ lunch & dinner) San Juan's snootiest restaurant is actually pretty good. It has a creative menu with a smattering of seafood dishes, an adequate wine list (featuring all the San Juan heavy hitters) and a hushed, tranquil atmosphere.

Shopping

The **Mercado Artesanal Tradicional** (Traditional Artisans Market; Centro de Difusión Cultural Eva Perón) is an excellent local handicrafts market with an assortment of items for sale including ponchos and the brightly colored *mantas* (shawls) of Jáchal.

Getting There & Away

AIR

Aerolíneas Argentinas/Austral (☎ 421-4158; Av San Martín 215 Oeste) flies twice daily to Buenos Aires (AR$510) except Sunday (once only).

BUS

From San Juan's **bus terminal** (☎ 422-1604; Estados Unidos 492 Sur) there are international services to Santiago (AR$94, eight hours), Viña del Mar and Valparaíso, Chile, but they require a change of bus in Mendoza.

Except in summer, when there may be direct buses, service to Patagonian destinations south of Neuquén requires a change of bus in Mendoza, though through-tickets can be purchased in San Juan.

Various companies serve the following destinations daily.

Destination	Cost (AR$)	Duration (hr)
Barreal	36	4
Buenos Aires	210	14
Calingasta	33	3½
Catamarca	110	8
Córdoba	105	11
Huaco	30	3
Jujuy	220	20
La Rioja	80	7
Mendoza	22	3
Neuquén	185	15½
Pismanta	30	3
Rodeo	30	3½
Rosario	160	14
Salta	200	17
San Agustín de Valle Fértil	40	4½
San José de Jáchal	27	3
San Luis	40	5
Tucumán	150	13

Getting Around

Las Chacritas Airport (☎ 425-4133) is located 13km southeast of town on RN 20. A taxi or *remise* costs AR$30. For car rental, try **Classic** (☎ 422-4622; Av San Martín 163 Oeste) or **Parque Auto Motor** (☎ 422-6018; cnr Avs San Martín & España).

AROUND SAN JUAN

Dique Ullum

Only 18km west of San Juan, this 32-sq-km reservoir is a center for nautical sports: swimming, fishing, kayaking, waterskiing and windsurfing (though no rental equipment is available). *Balnearios* (beach clubs) line its shores, and hanging out for a day in the sun is part of being in San Juan. At night, many of the *balnearios* function as dance clubs. Bus 23 from Av Salta or bus 29 from the San Juan bus terminal via Av Córdoba both go hourly to the dam outlet.

Difunta Correa Shrine

At Vallecito, about 60km southeast of San Juan, the shrine of the Difunta Correa, a popular saint, is one of the most fascinating cultural phenomenons in all of Argentina, and visiting the shrine is a mandatory stop if you're in the area.

Empresa Vallecito goes daily from the bus terminal in San Juan to the shrine (AR$20 return, 1¼ hours each way) at 8:30am and 4pm Monday through to Saturday, and waits about an hour and 15 minutes before returning. On Sunday there are roundtrip buses at 8am, 10:30am, 11:45am, 3:30pm, 4:15pm and 7pm. Any other eastbound bus heading toward La Rioja or Córdoba will drop passengers at the entrance. There are also departures from Mendoza (see p349).

VALLE DE CALINGASTA

The Calingasta Valley is a vast smear of scenic butter cradled between the Andes and the rumpled, multicolored precordillera, and is one of the most beautiful regions in both San Juan and Mendoza provinces.

With the completion of two new reservoirs, the spectacular cliffside RP 12 is now closed. Most maps will show the old road, but drivers have to take RP 5 north to Talacasto, then the RP 149, which snakes around west and then south to Calingasta.

Calingasta

☎ 02648 / pop 8100 / elev 1430m

Calingasta is a small agricultural town shaded by álamos (poplars) on the shores of Río de los Patos. There's little to do, though a visit to the 17th-century adobe chapel **Capilla de Nuestra Señora del Carmen** makes a nice stop on the way to Barreal. Looming on the horizon 7km out of town is **Cerro El Calvario**, the site of an indigenous cemetery where several mummies have been found. One example can be seen in Calingasta's small **archaeological museum** (admission AR$4; ☒ 10am-1pm & 4-8pm Tue-Sat), just off the main plaza.

The folks at Calingasta's **tourist information office** (☎ 441066; www.calingastaturismo.gov.ar; RP 12), at the entrance to town from San Juan, are helpful for sights and lodging in the area.

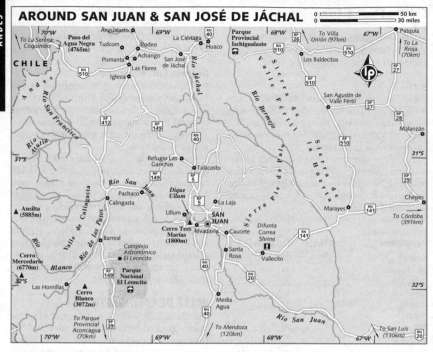

AROUND SAN JUAN & SAN JOSÉ DE JÁCHAL

If you wish to spend the night, lay your head at the modest **Hospedaje Nora** (☎ 421027; cnr Cantoni & Sarmiento; s/d AR$80/100), featuring simple but spacious rooms in a family house. Those in the building out the back are a better deal. There's a **municipal campground** (campsites AR$10) down by the river. The meals at **Doña Gorda** (Calle Principal; mains AR$15-30) will stave off your hunger – on offer are tasty empanadas and good-value set meals.

Two buses a day roll through town, heading for San Juan (AR$33, 3½ hours) and Barreal (AR$5, 30 minutes).

Barreal
☎ 02648 / pop 1900 / elev 1650m
Barreal's divine location makes it one of the most beautifully situated towns you'll likely ever come across. Sauces (weeping willows), álamos and eucalyptus trees drape lazily over the dirt roads that meander through town, and views of the Cordillera de Ansilta – a stretch of the Andes with seven majestic peaks ranging from 5130m to 5885m – are simply astonishing. Wandering along Barreal's back roads is an exercise in dreamy laziness.

Presidente Roca is the main drag through town, a continuation of RP 149 that leads from Calingasta to Barreal and on to Parque Nacional El Leoncito. Only a few streets have names; businesses listed without them simply require asking directions.

INFORMATION
Banco de la Nación (Presidente Roca s/n) Has an ATM.
IWS Comunicaciones (San Martín s/n; per hr AR$3) Internet access. Slow.
Tourist office (☎ 441066; turismo@calingasta.gov.ar; Presidente Roca s/n; ☼ 9am-1:30pm & 3-8pm) Located beside the main plaza; offers a list of excursion operators and accommodations.

SIGHTS & ACTIVITIES
Wander down to the **Río de los Patos** and take in the sweeping views of the valley and the **Cordillera de Ansilta**, whose highest peak, **Ansilta**, tops out at 5885m. To the south, **Aconcagua** and **Tupungato** are both visible, as is the peak of **Cerro Mercedario** (6770m).

At the south end of Presidente Roca is a sort of triangular roundabout. Follow the road east (away from the Andes) until it leads into the hills; you'll see a small shrine and you can **hike** into the foothills for more stunning views. Follow this road for 3km and you'll come to a mining site (the gate should be open). Enter and continue for 1km to reach a **petrified forest**.

White-water rafting is excellent – more for the scenery than for the rapids themselves – and most trips start 50km upriver at **Las Hornillas**. Contact **Condor Expediciones** (☎ 441144), the best-established rafting operator in town.

Las Hornillas (site of two *refugios* and a military outpost) also provides **climbing** access to the Cordón de la Rameda, which boasts five peaks over 6000m, including Cerro Mercedario. Climbing here is more technical than Aconcagua and many mountaineers prefer the area. Ramon Ossa, a Barreal native, is a highly recommended mountain guide and excursion operator who knows the cordillera intimately; contact him at **Cabañas Doña Pipa** (☎ 441004; www.fortunaviajes.com.ar). He can

---

RUTA DEL VINO DE SAN JUAN

San Juan's winery tourism industry isn't quite as developed as that of Mendoza, but in a lot of ways that's a good thing. There are no crowds for a start, and tours are occasionally conducted by the winemakers themselves. A few wineries have got together to promote the Ruta del Vino de San Juan (The San Juan Wine Route). The best way to do it, if you want to hit them all in one day, is by hire car. Starting from downtown San Juan, it's about a 40km return stopping at all the places listed here. It is feasible to do it by public transport and taxi, too. None of the wineries listed below require reservations.

The first stop on the route should be **Las Marianas** (☎ 0264-423-1191; www.bodegalasmarianas .com.ar; Calle Nuevo s/n; ⏱ 9am-1pm & 3:30-8pm). One of the prettiest wineries in the region, this one was built in 1922, abandoned in 1950 and reinstated in 1999. The main building is gorgeous, with thick adobe walls and a few examples of the original winemaking equipment lying around. The mountain views out over the vineyard are superb. If you're coming by bus, catch the 16 (AR$1.30, 40 minutes) near the corner of Santa Fe and Mendoza in San Juan. Get off at the corner of Calle Aberastain and Calle Nuevo, where you'll see a signpost to the winery (an 800m walk).

Making your way back to Calle Aberastain, turn right and follow the road south for 500m to **Viñas de Segisa** (☎ 0264-492-2000; www.saxsegisa.com.ar; Aberastain & Calle 15; ⏱ 10am-7pm Mon-Sat, 10am-2pm Sun). This stately old winery has more of a museum feel than others. The tour of the underground cellar complex is excellent and tastings are generous. This is one of the few wineries who actually admit to 'chipping' (adding oak chips to young wines to improve flavor).

If you're not up for a walk, now's the time to call a *remise* (taxi). If you are, make your way back north to Calle 14, turn right and continue for 5km until you hit RN 40. Turning left, after about 1km you'll come to **Fabril Alto Verde** (☎ 0264-421-2683; www.fabril-altoverde.com.ar; RN 40 btwn Calle 13 & 14; ⏱ 9am-1pm & 2:30-6:30pm Mon-Fri, 9am-1pm Sat), a big, state-of-the-art winery that sells 90% of its wine for export; tours here are in English or Spanish and come accompanied by a rather dreary promotional video. The award-winning organic brands Buenas Hondas and Touchstone are produced here.

Next, catch a 24 bus heading north on RN 40 up to Calle 11. Turning right down Calle 11 for 300m brings you to **Miguel Mas** (☎ 0264-422-5807; miguelmas@infovia.com.ar; Calle 11 s/n; ⏱ 9am-5pm Mon-Fri, 9am-1pm Sat). This small winery makes some of the country's only organic sparkling wine (champagne) and other wine. The whole process – apart from inserting the cork in bottles – is done by hand. Tours (in Spanish only) take you through every step of the process.

Making your way back out to RN 40, flag down a 24 bus, which will take you back to the bus terminal in San Juan.

If you've still got a thirst up when you get back to the bus terminal, consider hopping on bus 23 to check out one of South America's most curious wineries, **Cavas de Zonda** (☎ 0264-494-5144; www.cavasdezonda.com; Ruta 12 s/n, Zonda; ⏱ 9am-5pm Mon-Fri, 11am-5pm Sat & Sun), in a cave about 16km west of San Juan, via the RP 12, near the town of Zonda. This champagne-maker boasts having the only wine cellar in South America whose 'roof is a mountain' and, true or not, its temperatures are perfect for cellaring its excellent sparkling wines. And hey…it's a darn good marketing tool. Bus 23 leaves the San Juan bus terminal from platform 20 six times daily.

DIFUNTA CORREA

Legend has it that during the civil wars of the 1840s Deolinda Correa followed the movements of her sickly conscript husband's battalion on foot through the deserts of San Juan, carrying food, water and their baby son in her arms. When her meager supplies ran out, thirst, hunger and exhaustion killed her. But when passing muleteers found them, the infant was still nursing at the dead woman's breast. Commemorating this apparent miracle, her shrine at Vallecito is widely believed to be the site of her death.

Difunta literally means 'defunct,' and Correa is her surname. Technically she is not a saint but rather a 'soul,' a dead person who performs miracles and intercedes for people; the child's survival was the first of a series of miracles attributed to her. Since the 1940s her shrine, originally a simple hilltop cross, has grown into a small village with its own gas station, school, post office, police station and church. Devotees leave gifts at 17 chapels or exhibit rooms in exchange for supernatural favors. In addition, there are two hotels, several restaurants, a commercial gallery with souvenir shops, and offices for the nonprofit organization that administers the site.

Interestingly, truckers are especially devoted. From La Quiaca, on the Bolivian border, to Ushuaia in Tierra del Fuego, you will see roadside shrines with images of the Difunta Correa and the unmistakable bottles of water left to quench her thirst. At some sites there appear to be enough parts lying around to build a car from scratch!

Despite lack of government support and the Catholic Church's open antagonism, the shrine of Difunta Correa has grown as belief in her miraculous powers has become more widespread. People visit the shrine all year round, but at Easter, May 1 and Christmas, up to 200,000 pilgrims descend on Vallecito. Weekends are busier and more interesting than weekdays.

---

arrange trips to Cerro Mercedario and expeditions across the Andes in the footsteps of San Martín, including mules and equipment.

Explora Parques (☎ 0264-503-2008; www.territorio sandinos.com.ar; Mariano Moreno s/n) offers tours of El Leoncito national park, fishing trips and 4WD treks.

Barreal is best known for **carrovelismo** (land sailing), an exhilarating sport practiced on a small cart with a sail attached. Fanatics come from miles away to whizz around out on the gusty, cracked lake bed at Pampa El Leoncito, about 20km from town and adjacent to the national park. **Rogelio Toro** (☎ 0264-15-671-7196; dontoro.barreal@gmail.com) hires the necessary equipment and also gives classes.

For access to the *refugio* at Las Hornillas, climbing information, guide services and **mountain bike** rental, visit Maxi at **Cabañas Kummel** (☎ 441206; Presidente Roca s/n).

SLEEPING & EATING

Hostel Barreal (☎ 441144; Av San Martín s/n; 6-person cabaña AR$150) Has simple but delightful little *cabañas* with kitchens, leafy surrounds and plenty of shade trees.

Posada Don Lisandro (☎ 0264-15-505-9122; www .donlisandro.com.ar; Av San Martín s/n; s/d with shared bathroom AR$70/100) This new posada (inn) is actually a 100-year-old house. The original cane-and-mud ceilings remain, as do a few sticks of room furniture. There's a kitchen for guest use and lovely, shady grounds to lounge around in.

El Alemán (☎ 441193; d AR$180, 4-person cabaña AR$260; ☽ breakfast, lunch & dinner) Down by the river, with sweeping views of the Andes, this German/ Argentine-owned complex has some of the best-looking rooms in town. Cabins are more like small houses, spread out over the property and allowing for a sense of privacy. Rooms are cute and cozy. There's an excellent restaurant (mains AR$30 to AR$50) on the premises, serving hearty dishes and superb breakfasts made from the freshest ingredients.

Posada San Eduardo (☎ 441046; cnr San Martín & Los Enamorados; s AR$130-150, d AR$200-280) This handsome adobe inn offers refreshing rooms with whitewashed walls set around a beautiful shady courtyard. Rooms have a quiet elegance, with natural poplar bed frames and chairs. Pay a little extra and you get your very own fireplace.

Pizzería Clif (Presidente Roca s/n; mains AR$12-25; ☽ dinner) Won't be winning any decor design awards, but cooks up some decent pizzas and turns into a bar later on.

La Ramada (Presidente Roca s/n; mains AR$15-20; ☽ lunch & dinner) Offers a fairly standard range of meats and pastas and some delicious meat empanadas. Also a good selection of wines from the San Juan region.

GETTING THERE & AWAY

Barreal's right at the end of the line, but there are two departures per day for San Juan (AR$36, four hours), which pass through Calingasta (AR$5, 30 minutes).

Parque Nacional El Leoncito

The 76-sq-km Parque Nacional El Leoncito occupies a former *estancia* (ranch) 22km south of Barreal. The landscape is typical of the Andean precordillera, though it's drier than the valley north of Barreal. Lately, its primary attraction is the Pampa El Leoncito, where a dry lake bed makes for superb **land sailing**. The high, dry and wide-open valley rarely sees a cloud, also making for superb stargazing. Hence, the park is home to the **Complejo Astronómico El Leoncito** (www.casleo.gov.ar), which contains two important observatories: **Observatorio El Leoncito** (☎ 02648-441088; admission AR$7; ☺ guided visits 10am, 11am, 3pm, 4pm & 5pm) and **Observatorio Cesco** (☎ 02648-441087; admission AR$6; ☺ guided visits 10am, noon, 4pm & 6pm). Night visits must be reserved by contacting **Yafar Destinos** (☎ 0264-420-4052; Av Rioja 428 Sur) in San Juan.

Camping is not permitted, but in the northwest corner of the park, **Cascada El Rincon** is a lovely, small waterfall set in a shallow canyon. If you're looking for somewhere to picnic and splash around on a hot day, this is your spot.

There is no public transport to the park, and with 17km of entrance road added to the 22km to get here from Barreal, it's certainly too far to walk. If you don't have your own transportation, contact Ramon Ossa (p369) in Barreal, whose informative tours of the park have been heartily recommended.

SAN JOSÉ DE JÁCHAL

☎ 02647 / pop 21,000

Founded in 1751 and surrounded by vineyards and olive groves, Jáchal is a charming village with a mix of older adobes and contemporary brick houses. *Jachalleros* (the local residents) are renowned for their fidelity to indigenous and gaucho craft traditions; in fact, Jáchal's reputation as the Cuna de la Tradición (Cradle of Tradition) is celebrated during November's **Fiesta de la Tradición**. Except during festival season, finding these crafts is easier in San Juan.

Across from the main plaza the **Iglesia San José**, a national monument, houses the **Cristo Negro** (Black Christ), or Señor de la Agonía (Lord of Agony), a grisly leather image with articulated head and limbs, brought from Potosí in colonial times.

Jáchal's accommodation scene isn't what you'd call thriving, but the **Hotel San Martín** (☎ 420431; www.jachalhotelsanmartin.com; Echegaray 387; s/d AR$75/100, with shared bathroom AR$40/60; ☒ ☐), a few blocks from the plaza, does the job. It's not quite as contemporary as it looks from the outside, but rooms are big and comfortable and the bathrooms are modern.

La Taberna de Juan (San Martín s/n; mains AR$20-25; ☺ lunch & dinner) is a bright and cheery *parrilla* facing the plaza. Meat is the go here, but there's a range of pasta dishes and salads, too. Set lunches are particularly good value.

There are several daily buses to San Juan (AR$27, three hours) from Jáchal's **bus terminal** (cnr San Juan & Obispo Zapata).

AROUND SAN JOSÉ DE JÁCHAL

Rodeo

☎ 02647 / elev 2010m

Rodeo is a small, ramshackle town with picturesque adobe houses typical of the region, 42km west of San José de Jáchal. There are several *cabañas* and *hosterías* in town, and Pismanta is only about 20km away.

Rodeo has recently become famous – world famous – for **windsurfing**. The town is only 3km away from one of the best windsurfing sites on the planet: **Dique Cuesta del Viento**, a reservoir where, between mid-October and early May, wind speeds reach 120km/h nearly every afternoon, drawing surfers from around the globe. Even if you don't take to the wind, it's worth spending a day or two wandering around Rodeo and hanging out on the beach absorbing the spectacular views and watching the insanity of airborne windsurfers.

Inside the town hall, the **tourist office** (municipalidad_iglesia@yahoo.com.ar; ☺ 8am-8pm) provides a list of places to stay and information on local attractions.

On Playa Lamaral, on the shore of the reservoir, HI affiliate **Rancho Lamaral** (☎ 0264-15-660-1197; www.rancholamaral.com; dm/d AR$40/100) offers simple rooms in a refurbished adobe house, and offers windsurfing classes (one/three classes AR$100/270) and kitesurfing courses, and rents all equipment.

ourpick 50 Nudos (☎ 011-15-5759-0525; www.50nudos.com; Puque s/n; s/d AR$120/180) Follow the signs from the main street to these charming, rustic

---

DETOUR: HUACO

Continuing north from San José de Jáchal on RN 40, visitors pass through a beautiful landscape that is rich with folkloric traditions and rarely seen by foreigners. East of Jáchal, the RN 40 climbs the precipitous **Cuesta de Huaco**, with a view of Los Cauquenes dam, before arriving at **Huaco**, a sleepy village 36km from Jáchal whose 200-year-old Viejo Molino (Old Mill) justifies the trip. Some visitors get captivated by Huaco's eerie landscape and middle-of-nowhere atmosphere. If you're one of them, you can stay at **Hostería Huaco** (☎ 0264-421-9528; www.grupohuaco.com.ar; dm/r AR$35/120; ⛌ ⛩), a beautifully set up little hostel with great mountain views from the backyard pool.

One bus daily from Huaco heads to San Juan (AR$30, four hours), passing through Jáchal (AR$15, one hour) on the way.

Backtracking to RN 510 and heading westward, you pass through the town of Rodeo and into the department of Iglesia, home of the precordillera thermal baths of **Pismanta** (see below). RN 510 continues west to Chile via the lung-busting 4765m **Paso del Agua Negra** (open summer only). South of Pismanta, RP 436 returns to RN 40 and San Juan.

---

rooms. Optional are larger rooms with sitting area and breakfast served in your room.

La Surfera (Santo Domingo s/n; mains AR$15-30; ⛌ lunch & dinner) On the main street in the center of town, this laid-back restaurant/cafe/reggae bar is HQ for Rodeo's surprisingly large hippie community. Vegetarian meals are predictably good; meat dishes could be better.

From San Juan's bus terminal, there are several departures daily for Rodeo (AR$30, 5½ hours).

Pismanta
☎ 02647

Part of **Hotel Termas de Pismanta** (☎ 497091/02; www.pismantahotel.com.ar; s/d AR$150/270; ⛩) and recently refurbished, this thermal baths complex offers spacious if slightly run-down rooms. The baths are indoors, in small, clean, tiled cubicles. Temperatures range from 38°C to 45°C. Access to the baths is AR$10 for nonguests and there is a variety of spa treatments available.

If the complex is too pricey for a night, try **Hospedaje La Olla** (☎ 497003; r per person AR$30), a basic place with large rooms, low wooden ceilings and the odd animal skin thrown around for decoration. It's across the highway and up a side street from the thermal baths.

Iglesia SRL minibuses leave the San Juan bus terminal four times a week, and take RP 149 to Jáchal, stopping at Iglesia and Pismanta (AR$30, three hours).

SAN AGUSTÍN DE VALLE FÉRTIL
☎ 02646 / pop 6800

Reached via comically undulating highways that cut through the desert landscape, San Agustín de Valle Fértil makes an excellent base for trips to the nearby Parque Provincial Ischigualasto. It's a measure of just how dry the countryside is that this semiarid valley gets called 'fertile.'

Apart from visiting the park, there's not much to do around these parts, but the ponderous pace of life here, where people sit on the sidewalks on summer evenings greeting passersby, has mesmerized more than one visitor.

Orientation & Information

San Agustín lies among the Sierra Pampeanas, gentle sedimentary mountains cut by impressive canyons, 247km northeast of San Juan via RN 141 and RP 510, which continues to Ischigualasto and La Rioja. San Agustín is small enough that locals pay little attention to street names, so ask directions.

Cámara de Turismo (Mitre, btwn Entre Ríos & Mendoza) A private tourist office that has an office in the bus terminal.

Municipal tourist office (General Acha; ⛌ 7am-1pm & 5-10pm Mon-Fri, 8am-1pm Sat) Across from the plaza. Arranges car or mule excursions into the mountain canyons and backcountry. Also keeps an updated list of hotel prices.

Post office (cnr Laprida & Mendoza)

Turismo Vesa (☎ 420143; www.turismovesa.com; Mitre s/n) For tours to Parque Provincial Ischigualasto, Talampaya, El Chiflón and horseback riding.

Sleeping & Eating

Eco Hostel (☎ 420147; www.ecohostel.com.ar; Mendoza 42; dm/d AR$30/80; ⛩) With a great location half a block from the plaza and a tiny above-ground pool, this is one of the better hostels in town. Can arrange good-value tours to local sights, including Parque Provincial Ischigualasto.

Hostería & Cabañas Valle Fértil (☎ 420015; www.alkazarhotel.com.ar; Rivadavia s/n; s/d in hostería AR$170/200,

4-person cabaña AR$280) This place has the wraps on lodging in town, with a well-sited *hostería* above the reservoir and fully equipped *cabañas* nearby. The *hostería* also has a good restaurant (mains AR$20 to AR$35) serving food from 6am to 11pm. Both are reached from Rivadavia on the way to the river.

The *hostería* also owns the town's best campground, **Camping Valle Fértil** (Rivadavia s/n; sites AR$20). It's shaded by a monotone cover of eucalyptus trees, and gets very crowded during long weekends and holidays, but it's quiet enough off-season and midweek.

If the *hostería* is too much of a walk for you, there are good, simple restaurants along Rivadavia, leading west from the plaza. The plazaside **La Florencia** (cnr Mitre & Acha; mains AR$15-25; ☺ lunch & dinner) has a good range of *parrilla* offerings, including *chivito* (baby goat – order two hours in advance) and a delicious *lomo al roquefort* (beef with roquefort cheese sauce; AR$20).

Getting There & Away

From San Agustín's **bus terminal** (Mitre, btwn Entre Ríos & Mendoza) daily buses head to San Juan (AR$40, 4½ hours).

PARQUE PROVINCIAL ISCHIGUALASTO

Also known fittingly as **Valle de la Luna** (Valley of the Moon; www.ischigualasto.org; admission AR$40), this park takes its name from the Diaguita word for land without life. Visits here are a spectacular step – or drive, as the case may be – into a world of surreal rock formations, dinosaur remains and glowing red sunsets. The park is in some ways comparable to North American national parks such as Bryce Canyon or Zion, except that here, time and water have exposed a wealth of fossils (some 180 million years old, from the Triassic period).

The park's **museum** displays a variety of fossils, including the carnivorous dinosaur Herrerasaurus (not unlike Tyrannosaurus rex), the Eoraptor lunensis (the oldest-known predatory dinosaur) and good dioramas of the park's paleoenvironments.

The 630-sq-km park is a desert valley between two sedimentary mountain ranges, the Cerros Colorados in the east and Cerro Los Rastros in the west. Over millennia, at every meander in the canyon, the waters of the nearly dry Río Ischigualasto have carved distinctive shapes in the malleable red sandstone, monochrome clay and volcanic ash. Predictably,

some of these forms have acquired popular names, including **Cancha de Bochas** (The Ball Court), **El Submarino** (The Submarine) and **El Gusano** (The Worm) among others. The desert flora of algarrobo trees, shrubs and cacti complement the eerie landforms.

From the visitor center, isolated 1748m **Cerro Morado** is a three- to four-hour walk, gaining nearly 800m in elevation and yielding outstanding views of the surrounding area. Take plenty of drinking water and high-energy snacks.

Tours

All visitors to the park must go accompanied by a ranger. The most popular tours run for three hours and leave on the hour (more or less), with cars forming a convoy and stopping at noteworthy points along the way, where the ranger explains (in Spanish only) exactly what it is you're looking at.

If you have no private vehicle, an organized tour is the only feasible way to visit the park. These are easily organized in San Agustín (opposite). Otherwise ask the tourist office there about hiring a car and driver. Tour rates (not including entry fees) are about AR$220 per person from San Juan (through any travel agency in town), or about AR$80 per person from San Agustín. Tours from San Juan generally depart at 5am and return well after dark.

A variety of other tours (AR$20 per person) are available from the visitor center here. Options include spectacular full moon tours (2½ hours) in the five days around the full moon, treks to the summit of Cerro Morado (three to four hours) and a 12km circuit of the park on mountain bikes.

Sleeping & Eating

There is camping at the **visitor center** (campsite per person AR$5), which also has a *confitería* serving simple meals (breakfast and lunch) and cold drinks; dried fruits and bottled olives from the province are also available. There are toilets and showers, but because water must be trucked in, don't count on them. There's no shade.

Getting There & Away

Ischigualasto is about 80km north of San Agustín via RP 510 and a paved lateral to the northwest. Given its size and isolation, the only practical way to visit the park is by private vehicle or organized tour. Note that the park roads are unpaved and some can be impassable after rain, necessitating an abbreviated trip.

The Lake District

Home to some of the country's most spectacular scenery, the Lake District hosts thousands of visitors each year. People come to ski, fish, climb, trek and generally bask in the cool, fresh landscapes created by the huge forests, glacier-fed lakes and cute little alpine-style villages. Don't get the idea that the region is overrun, though – spaces are so wide here you'll only end up bumping shoulders with other travelers in the main population centers.

The city of Neuquén – the largest in the region – provides transportation links to all over the country. What it lacks in beauty it makes up for in surrounding attractions. Just out of town are some world-renowned paleontological sites and outstanding wineries. Way, way south is the resort town of Bariloche, with its picture-postcard location on the banks of the Lago Nahuel Huapi. This is ground zero for the outdoor adventure crew, both in summer and winter. Bariloche is the chief transportation hub for southern Patagonia and Chile, and a short ride from the laid-back hippie haven of El Bolsón.

Those looking to get off the track and away from the crowds won't find it hard to do here. Villa Traful and San Martín de los Andes, both lakeside villages nestled among pehuén (araucaria) forests fill up for a short time in summer and are blissfully quiet the rest of the year. To the north, the little-visited former provincial capital of Chos Malal makes an excellent base for exploring nearby volcanoes, lagoons and hot springs, as well as an important stopover for those traveling northwards on the RN 40 to Mendoza.

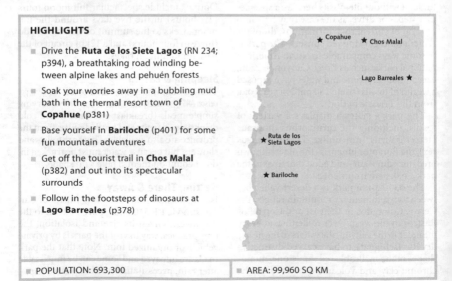

HIGHLIGHTS

- Drive the **Ruta de los Siete Lagos** (RN 234; p394), a breathtaking road winding between alpine lakes and pehuén forests
- Soak your worries away in a bubbling mud bath in the thermal resort town of **Copahue** (p381)
- Base yourself in **Bariloche** (p401) for some fun mountain adventures
- Get off the tourist trail in **Chos Malal** (p382) and out into its spectacular surrounds
- Follow in the footsteps of dinosaurs at **Lago Barreales** (p378)

★ Copahue   ★ Chos Malal

Lago Barreales ★

Ruta de los ★ Sieta Lagos

★ Bariloche

■ POPULATION: 693,300   ■ AREA: 99,960 SQ KM

THE LAKE DISTRICT

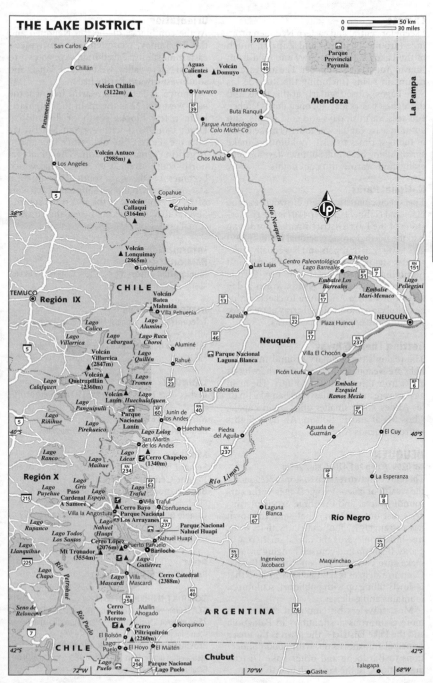

THE LAKE DISTRICT

Climate

Except for central and eastern Neuquén province (around Neuquén and Zapala), much of the Lake District is snowy and cold from June to August or September. The most scenic mountain roads (including the Ruta de los Siete Lagos) close regularly at this time, and the highest passes may not open until October. Fall sees warmish days and cold nights, and autumn leaves and fewer tourists make it one of the best times to visit. Wildflowers make spring hiking beautiful. Summer days are generally quite warm, with cool nights.

National Parks

The spectacular but often crowded Parque Nacional Nahuel Huapi (p410) is the cornerstone of the Lake District's parks. Bordering it to the north, Parque Nacional Lanín (p389) gets fewer trail trampers and has equally spectacular sights, including Volcán Lanín and humbling pehuén forests. The tiny Parque Nacional Arrayanes (p399) is worth a day trip from Villa la Angostura to check out its beautiful cinnamon-colored arrayán trees. See p78 for more on Argentina's parks.

Getting There & Away

The region's two primary ground transport hubs are Neuquén and Bariloche, where buses arrive from throughout the country. The main airports are in these cities, plus San Martín de los Andes, while smaller ones are in Zapala, Chos Malal and El Bolsón. All have flights to/from Buenos Aires.

NEUQUÉN

☎ 0299 / pop 261,420 / elev 265m

There are only two reasons to stop in Neuquén – the wealth of paleontological sites in the surrounding area, and the three excellent wineries just out of town. That said, the town has a strangely hypnotic effect, with its wide, tree-lined boulevards and liberal smattering of plazas. If you *do* find yourself hanging around, make sure you take a stroll through Parque Central, a strip of reclaimed railway land that is slowly filling up with public art, sculptures, fountains and galleries.

Most travelers hit Neuquén en route to more glamorous destinations in Patagonia and the Lake District – the town is the area's principal transport hub, with good connections to Bariloche and other Lake District destinations, to the far south and to Chile.

Orientation

At the confluence of the Río Neuquén and the Río Limay, Neuquén is the province's easternmost city. Paved highways go east to the Río Negro valley, west toward Zapala and southwest toward Bariloche.

Known as Félix San Martín in town, the east–west RN 22 is the main thoroughfare, lying a few blocks south of downtown. Don't confuse it with Av San Martín (ie sans the 'Félix'), the obligatory homage to Argentina's national icon. The principal north–south street is Av Argentina, which becomes Av Olascoaga south of the old train station. Street names change on each side of Av Argentina and the old train station. Several diagonal streets bisect the conventional grid.

Information

IMMIGRATION

Immigration office (☎ 442-2061; Santiago del Estero 466)

INTERNET ACCESS

Telecentro (Av Argentina at Ministro González; per hr AR$3; ☯ 24hr)
Telecentro del Comahue (Av Argentina 147; per hr AR$2)

LAUNDRY

Lavisec (Roca 137; wash & dry AR$15) Full service or DIY.

MEDICAL SERVICES

Regional hospital (☎ 443 1474; Buenos Aires 421)

MONEY

Several banks along Av Argentina, between Parque Central and Roca, have ATMs.
Banca Nazionale del Lavoro (cnr Av Argentina & Rivadavia)
Cambio Olano (cnr Juan B Justo & H Yrigoyen) Money exchange.
Cambio Pullman (Ministro Alcorta 144) Money exchange.

POST

Post office (Rivadavia & Santa Fe)

TOURIST INFORMATION

ACA (Automóvil Club Argentino; ☎ 442-2325; Diagonal 25 de Mayo at Rivadavia) Argentina's auto club; good source for provincial road maps.
Provincial tourist office (☎ 442-4089; www .neuquentur.gov.ar; Félix San Martín 182; ☯ 8am-10pm) Great maps and brochures.

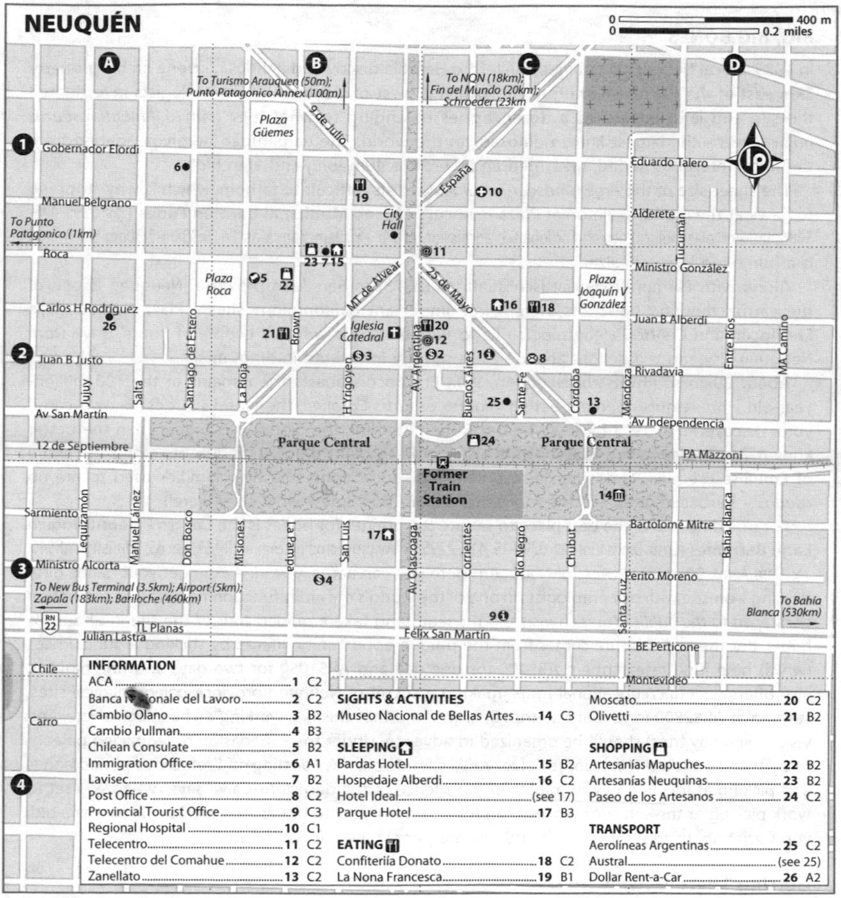
NEUQUÉN
0 400 m
0 0.2 miles
To Turismo Arauquen (50m); Punto Patagonico Annex (100m)
To NQN (18km); Fin del Mundo (20km); Schroeder (23km)
Plaza Güemes
9 de Julio
España
Gobernador Elordi
Eduardo Talero
Manuel Belgrano
To Punto Patagonico (1km)
City Hall
Alderete
Roca
Tucumán
Ministro González
Plaza Roca
MT de Alvear
25 de Mayo
Plaza Joaquín V González
Carlos H Rodríguez
Juan B Alberdi
Iglesia Catedral
Juan B Justo
Rivadavia
Jujuy
Salta
Santiago del Estero
La Rioja
Brown
H Yrigoyen
Av Argentina
Buenos Aires
Santa Fe
Córdoba
Mendoza
Entre Ríos
MA Camino
Av San Martín
Av Independencia
12 de Septiembre
Parque Central
Parque Central
PA Mazzoni
Former Train Station
Sarmiento
Bartolomé Mitre
Leguizamón
Manuel Láinez
Don Bosco
Misiones
La Pampa
San Luis
Av Olascoaga
Corrientes
Río Negro
Chubut
Bahía Blanca
Ministro Alcorta
Perito Moreno
To New Bus Terminal (3.5km); Airport (5km); Zapala (183km); Bariloche (460km)
Santa Cruz
To Bahía Blanca (530km)
RN 22
TL Planas
Julián Lastra
Félix San Martín
BE Perticone
Chile
Montevideo
Carro
INFORMATION
ACA 1 C2
Banca Nazionale del Lavoro 2 C2
Cambio Olano 3 B2
Cambio Pullman 4 B3
Chilean Consulate 5 B2
Immigration Office 6 A1
Lavisec 7 B2
Post Office 8 C2
Provincial Tourist Office 9 C3
Regional Hospital 10 C1
Telecentro 11 C2
Telecentro del Comahue 12 C2
Zanellato 13 C2
SIGHTS & ACTIVITIES
Museo Nacional de Bellas Artes 14 C3
SLEEPING
Bardas Hotel 15 B2
Hospedaje Alberdi 16 C2
Hotel Ideal (see 17)
Parque Hotel 17 B3
EATING
Confitería Donato 18 C2
La Nona Francesca 19 B1
Moscato 20 C2
Olivetti 21 B2
SHOPPING
Artesanías Mapuches 22 B2
Artesanías Neuquinas 23 B2
Paseo de los Artesanos 24 C2
TRANSPORT
Aerolíneas Argentinas 25 C2
Austral (see 25)
Dollar Rent-a-Car 26 A2

TRAVEL AGENCIES

Neuquén's dozens of travel agencies are almost all near downtown.

Turismo Arauquen (☎ 442-6476; www.arauquen.com; H Yrigoyen 720) Offers guided visits to paleontology sites of Lago Barreales, Plaza Huincul and Villa El Chocón for about AR$100 per person (minimum four), including the taxi fare; it's cheaper if you have your own vehicle.

Zanellato (☎ 443-0105; www.zanellatoviajes.com.ar; Av Independencia 366) Reliable for airline tickets and the like.

Sights

Just outside of town are three of the most important Patagonian wineries – **NQN** (☎ 489-7500; www.bodeganqn.com.ar; RP 7, Picada 15; ⏰ 9am-1pm & 2-4pm Mon-Fri, 10:30am-4:30pm Sat & Sun), **Fin del Mundo** (☎ 485-5004; www.bodegadelfindelmundo.com; RP 8, Km 9, San Patricio Del Chañar; ⏰ 10am-4pm Mon-Fri, 10am-5pm Sat) and **Schroeder** (☎ 508-6767; www.familiaschroeder.com; Calle 7 Nte, San Patricio del Chañar; admission AR$15; ⏰ 9am-5pm Mon-Fri, 10:30am-5:30pm Sat & Sun). Access to the vineyards is almost impossible without your own vehicle, but Turismo Arauquen can get you out there, often in combination with a paleontological tour.

Museo Nacional de Bellas Artes (☎ 443-6268; Bartolomé Mitre & Santa Cruz; ⏰ 10am-8pm Tue-Sat, 4-8pm Sun) showcases fine arts from the region and often features traveling exhibitions.

Sleeping

Neuquén's hotels mainly cater to the business set, and are fairly unexciting in all ranges and less than great value for budget travelers.

BIG, BIG BONES

In 1989 a local Neuquenian named Guillermo Heredia discovered a dinosaur bone on his property 7km east of the town of Plaza Huincul (which is west of Neuquén). Paleontologists investigated the site and later unearthed a dozen bones belonging to what they named *Argentinosaurus huinculensis* – the largest known dinosaur in the world. The gargantuan herbivore, dating from the mid-Cretaceous period, measured an incredible 40m long and 18m high.

The sheer size of the *Argentinosaurus huinculensis* is difficult to fathom, which is why stopping to gawk at the replica skeleton at Plaza Huincul's **Museo Municipal Carmen Funes** (☎ 0299-496-5486; museo@plazahuincul.gov.ar; Córdoba 55; admission AR$4; ✆ 9am-7pm Mon-Fri, 9:30am-7:30pm Sat & Sun) is a humbling lesson in size.

Along with Parque Provincial Ischigualasto (p373) in San Juan province, Neuquén is one of the earth's dinosaur hot spots. Here, three important paleontology sites – Plaza Huincul, Villa El Chocón and Centro Paleontológico Lago Barreales – lie within a couple of hours' drive from Neuquén city and will delight anyone even slightly interested in dinosaurs.

About 80km southwest of Neuquén, Villa El Chocón boasts the remains of the 100-million-year-old, 14m, eight-ton, meat-eating *Giganotosaurus Carolinii*, the world's largest known carnivore. Discovered in 1993 by fossil hunter Rubén Carolini, the dinosaur is bigger than the better known *Tyrannosaurus rex*. El Chocón is also home to giant dinosaur footprints along the shore of Embalse Ezequiel Ramos Mexía reservoir. (One local confessed how families used to fire up *asados* – barbecue grills – in the footprints before they knew what they were!)

For true dino freaks, the best place to satiate the hunger for bones is the **Centro Paleontológico Lago Barreales** (Costa Dinosaurio; ☎ 0299-15-418-2295; www.proyectodino.com.ar; RP 51, Km 65; admission AR$40; ✆ 9am-4pm), 90km northwest of Neuquén. Here you can actually work – as in get your hands dirty digging – on-site with paleontologists in one of the world's only fully functioning dinosaur excavation sites *open to the public*. You can visit the museum and take a guided tour of the site in about 1½ hours, but the real pleasure comes from the unique opportunity offered by sticking around. Prices (which help fund research) are AR$400 for one day and AR$1050 for two days and one night. It also offers scientific/educational tours, making a circuit of Neuquén province paleontoligical sites, starting at AR$2800 for a four-day trip. Bear in mind that this is a working archaeological site, and visits (even day trips) should be organized in advance. Under the supervision of renowned paleontologist and project director Jorge Calvo, you'll spend your days dusting off Cretaceous-period bones and picking at fossils, and your nights in the silence of the desert. As Calvo says, 'when you set to work picking at the soft rock, uncovering fossilized leaves and bones that are 90 million years old, you forget about the rest of the world – some people even forget to eat.'

Getting There & Away

From the bus terminal in Neuquén, **Cooperativa El Petroleo** (☎ 0299-446-2572) runs regular buses to Plaza Huincul (AR$20, 1¾ hours), and all buses between Neuquén and Zapala stop there. There are also regular buses to Villa El Chocón from Neuquén (AR$18, 1¼ hours). Centro Paleontológico Lago Barreales is a bit more difficult to reach; contact the site for driving directions or possible transportation options (there are no buses to the site), though tour companies from Neuquén (including Turismo Arauquen, see p377) come here. If you drive, take RP 51, not RN 7.

Punto Patagonico (☎ 447-9940; www.puntopatagonico.com; Roca 1694; dm/d AR$45/135; ☞) Neuquén's only hostel isn't a bad deal – it's well set up with comfy dorms. The only problem is the location, 17 blocks from downtown... once it gets its new, central **Annex** (Periodistas Neuquinas 94) up and running, it'll be a much better deal.

Hospedaje Alberdi (☎ 448-1943; JB Alberdi 176; s/d AR$80/140) A great location and its basic, comfortable rooms make this little hotel a good deal. Stay here and get 10% off your meal in the attached restaurant.

Parque Hotel (☎ 442-5806; Av Olascoaga 271; s/d AR$130/180) There are a few charming touches in the spacious, tile-floored rooms here. Some are showing their age, but most have views out over the busy street below.

Hotel Ideal (☎ 442-2431; www.interpatagonia.com/hotelideal; Av Olascoaga 243; s/d AR$150/200; ✄ ☞)

Not likely to win any design awards, but the medium-sized, unrenovated rooms here are clean and comfortable. Get one at the back for more peace.

Bardas Hotel (☎ 442-2403; www.bardashotel.com.ar; Roca 109; s/d AR$200/280; ❄ 📶) One of the smaller hotels in town is also one of the best looking. If it weren't in Neuquén you'd be tempted to call this a boutique hotel. Rooms are modern, but vary widely – generally those at the front are more spacious.

Eating & Drinking

The many *confiterías* (cafes) along Av Argentina are all pleasant spots for breakfast and morning coffee. There are numerous bars and *confiterías* in the area north of Parque Central and around the meeting of the diagonals.

Confitería Donato (cnr JB Alberdi & Santa Fe; snacks AR$12-20; 🕑 breakfast, lunch & dinner) Plenty of dark wood paneling and brass fittings give this place an old-time feel and the wraparound seats may have you lounging around for hours on end. The menu runs the usual *confitería* gamut, with plenty of sandwiches, cakes and coffee on offer. There is live music Friday to Sunday nights and the occasional tango show – drop in for the schedule.

Moscato (cnr JB Alberdi & Argentina; mains AR$20-30; 🕑 breakfast, lunch & dinner) The coolest cafe in town styles itself as a *café gourmet* – which is a stretch, but the set meals (AR$20) are a good deal and it's a good place for drinks at any time.

La Nona Francesa (☎ 430-0930; 9 de Julio 56; mains AR$39-50; 🕑 lunch & dinner) Some of Neuquén's finest dining can be found at this French-Italian trattoria – the pastas are all good, but the trout dishes are the standouts.

Olivetti (Brown 168; mains AR$40-60; 🕑 lunch & dinner) The fanciest restaurant in town has an impressive wine list and draws influences from French, Italian and Spanish cuisines. The set lunches (AR$42) are a worthy investment.

Shopping

Paseo de los Artesanos (Av Independencia, Parque Central; 🕑 10am-9pm Wed-Sun) Neuquén's largest selection of regional handicrafts is at this outlet, north of the old train station.

Artesanías Neuquinas (Brown 280) This provincially sponsored store offers a wide variety of high-quality Mapuche textiles and wood crafts.

Artesanías Mapuches (Roca 141) More quality local crafts.

Getting There & Away

AIR

Neuquén's **airport** (☎ 444-0525) is west of town on RN 22. **Aerolíneas Argentina/Austral** (☎ 442-2409/10/11; Santa Fe 52) flies to Buenos Aires (from AR$520) four times daily Monday to Friday and twice daily on weekends. **American Jet** (☎ 444-1085; www.americanjet.com.ar; Aeropuerto Presidente Perón) is the regional carrier, with flights to Chos Malal (AR$180) and Chapelco (AR$205) – the nearest airport to San Martín del los Andes and Junín de los Andes.

BUS

Neuquén is a major hub for domestic and international bus services. Accordingly, its newish **bus terminal** (☎ 445-2300; cnr Solalique y Ruta 22), about 3.5km west of Parque Central, is well decked out, with restaurants, gift stores and even a luggage carousel! To get downtown take either a Pehueche bus (AR$1.50; buy a ticket at local 41) or a taxi (AR$15).

Several carriers offer service to Chile: **Plaza** (☎ 446-5975) goes to Temuco (AR$120, 11 hours) via Zapala and Paso Pino Hachado. Andesmar goes daily to Osorno (AR$160, 11 hours).

Neuquén is a jumping-off point for deep-south, Patagonian destinations. Northern destinations such as Catamarca, San Juan, Tucumán, Salta and Jujuy require a bus change in Mendoza, though the entire ticket can be purchased in Neuquén.

The following table lists daily departures to nearly all long-distance destinations; provincial destinations are served numerous times daily.

Destination	Cost (AR$)	Duration (hr)
Aluminé	43	6
Bahía Blanca	77	7½
Buenos Aires	215	17
Chos Malal	64	6
Córdoba	230	16
El Bolsón	90	7
Esquel	117	10
Junín de los Andes	64	6
Mendoza	180	13
Puerto Madryn	114	11
Río Gallegos	430	29
Rosario	200	17
San Martín de los Andes	70	6
San Rafael	112	10
Viedma	80	8
Villa la Angostura	75	7
Zapala	35	3

Getting Around

Neuquén is a good province to explore by automobile, but drivers should be aware that RN 22, both east along the Río Negro valley and west toward Zapala, is a rough road with heavy truck traffic. On that note, try **Dollar Rent-a-Car** (☎ 442-0875; Carlos H Rodríguez 518), the only rental company downtown.

ZAPALA

☎ 02942 / pop 32,200 / elev 1200m

Taking its name as an adaptation of the Mapuche word *chapadla* (dead swamp), Zapala got off to a bad start, image-wise. Not much has changed. This is a humble little place where the locals amuse themselves with walks up and down the main street, punctuated by lengthy pauses on street corners.

The main excuse for rolling through town is to visit the nearby Parque Nacional Laguna Blanca (right), with its awesome array of birdlife, or to take advantage of the town's bus connections for the rarely visited northern reaches of the Lake District.

Zapala's **Centro Cultural** (San Martín & Chaneton; ☺ 5-10pm), in front of the plaza, hosts concerts and shows work by local artists and recently released Hollywood blockbusters.

Orientation & Information

Zapala's main drag is Av San Martín, which is an exit off the roundabout junction of RN 22 (which heads east to Neuquén and north to Las Lajas) and RN 40 (heading southwest to Junín de los Andes and north to Chos Malal).

Banco de la Provincia del Neuquén (San Martín & Etcheluz) Bank and ATM.

Laguna Blanca national park office (☎ 431982; lagunablanca@apn.gov.ar; Av Ejercito Argentino 217; ☺ 8am-3pm Mon-Fri) For information on Parque Nacional Laguna Blanca.

Tourist office (☎ 424296; RN 22, Km 1398; ☺ 7am-9pm) Located on the highway, 2km west of town center.

Festivals

Zapala's **Feria de la Tradición**, held in the second week in November, showcases regional culture, with plenty of folk music, gaucho horse skill demonstrations, handicraft exhibits and regional food on sale.

Sleeping & Eating

Zapala has very limited accommodations.

Hotel Pehuén (☎ 423135; Etcheluz & Elena de la Vega; s/d AR$85/150) Despite its (rather mysterious) two-star status, this is the best budget deal in town, conveniently near the bus terminal, with clean rooms, an attractive (classy, even) lobby and a good restaurant below.

Hotel Hue Melén (☎ 432109; www.hotelhuemelen .com; Almirante Brown 929; s/d AR$180/270; 🅿 🛜) You may be faintly surprised by the quiet stylishness of this hotel-casino complex. King-size beds, full bathtubs, contemporary art on the walls...it's wonderful what gambling money can buy you.

El Chancho Rengo (☎ 422795; Av San Martín & Etcheluz; sandwiches AR$12-20; ☺ breakfast, lunch & dinner) It's likely half the town saunters in here for an espresso each day. Outdoor tables and good coffee and sandwiches make it great for a light bite.

Mayrouba (Monti & Etcheluz; mains AR$20-40; ☺ breakfast, lunch & dinner) The best-looking restaurant in town also serves up some of the tastiest fare. There's shades of Middle Eastern influence on the menu and Patagonian faves such as smoked trout (AR$35). If you're up for a few drinks, it turns into a bar later on, with an impressive cocktail list.

Getting There & Away

The **bus terminal** (☎ 421370; Etcheluz & Uriburu) is about four blocks from Av San Martín. Buses for Mendoza (AR$165, 16 hours) and points along the RN40 leave on Monday, Friday and Sunday. During summer there are frequent departures for Copahue (AR$42, four hours). The destinations following have daily departures.

Destination	Cost (AR$)	Duration (hr)
Aluminé	33	3½
Buenos Aires	235	18
Chos Malal	37	3
Coviahue	35	3
Junín de los Andes	35	3
Laguna Blanca	15	½
Neuquén	35	3
San Martín de los Andes	38	3½
Temuco (Chile)	110	6
Villa Pehuenia	42	4½

PARQUE NACIONAL LAGUNA BLANCA

At 1275m above sea level and surrounded by striking volcanic deserts, Laguna Blanca is only 10m deep, an interior drainage lake that formed when lava flows dammed two small streams. Only 30km southwest of Zapala, the lake is too alkaline for fish but hosts many bird species, including coots, ducks, grebes, upland geese, gulls and even a few flamingos. The 112.5-sq-km park primarily protects the habitat of the black-necked swan, a permanent resident.

Starting 10km south of Zapala, paved and well-marked RP 46 leads through the park toward the town of Aluminé. If you're catching a bus, ask the driver to drop you off at the information center. For more bus details, see opposite. If you don't have your own transport, ask at the National Parks office in Zapala if you can get a ride out with the rangers in the morning. A taxi to the park should charge around AR$130, including two hours' waiting time.

There is a small improved campground with windbreaks, but bring all your own food. There's a visitor center (open in the morning) with information displays and maps of walking trails, but there's no place to eat.

COPAHUE
☎ 02948 / elev 2030m

This small thermal springs resort stands on the northeastern side of its namesake volcano among steaming, sulphurous pools, including a bubbling hot-mud pool, the popular **Laguna del Chancho** (8am-6pm; admission AR$10). The setting, in a natural amphitheater formed by the mountain range, is spectacular, but the town isn't much to look at.

Copahue has been gaining in popularity over the years, mainly with Argentine tourists, as the rapid growth in tourist infrastructure shows. Due to snow cover, the village is only open from the start of December to the end of April.

The village centers on the large, modern **Complejo Termal Copahue** (☎ 299-442-4140; www .termasdecopahue.com; Ortiz Velez; baths AR$20, spa treatments from AR$30), which offers a wide range of curative bathing programs.

Residencial Codihue (☎ 495151; codihue@futurtel .com.ar; Velez s/n; s/d ARS80/130) is the best budget option in town, with simple rooms just down the road from the thermal baths complex. Full board is available.

The best hotel in the village, **Hotel Termas** (☎ 495186; www.hoteltermascopahue.com.ar; Doucloux s/n; s/d from ARS210/300), features modern rooms, atmospheric common areas and an excellent restaurant serving traditional Argentine and regional foods.

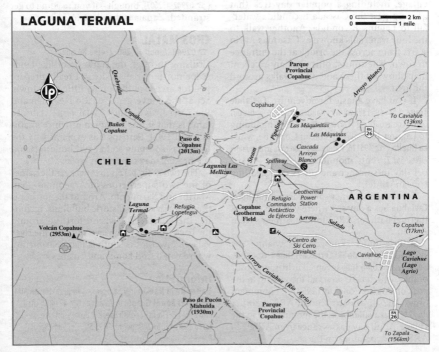

LAGUNA TERMAL

0 — 2 km
0 — 1 mile

Parrillada Nito (Zambo Jara s/n; mains AR$20-50; ☺ lunch & dinner) is the most frequently recommended *parrilla* (steak house) in town.

In summer, one bus daily runs to Neuquén (AR$73, seven hours) via Zapala (AR$42, four hours). There are no scheduled departures for the rest of the year.

CAVIAHUE

☎ 02948 / pop 580 / elev 1600m

On the western shore of Lago Caviahue, the ski village of Caviahue lies at the southeast foot of Volcán Copahue. A better-looking village than Copahue, this one is growing rapidly, too – construction noise fills the air during summer.

Information

Cyber Caviahue (Las Lengas s/n; per hr AR$4; ☺ 8am-1pm & 4-9pm) Internet access.

Oficina de Turismo (☎ 495036; www.caviahue-copahue.gov.ar; 8 de Abril s/n) In the municpalidad. Good maps and up-to-date info on local accommodations.

Activities

There are some good short walks from the village, including a popular day trek that goes up past the Cascada Escondida waterfall to Laguna Escondida. Another walk to the four waterfalls known as Cascadas Agrio starts from across the bridge at the entrance to town. The tourist office has an excellent map showing these and other walks around the area.

If you have a taste for adventure, **Caviahue Tours** (☎ 495138; www.caviahuetours.com; Av Bialous Centro Comercial local 11) organizes treks, including to Laguna Termal and Volcán Copahue, while **La Huella** (☎ 495116; viatursur@yahoo.com.ar; Bungalow Alpino Sur 2) rents mountain bikes for AR$50 per day in summer and offers dog-sledding trips in winter.

For those that fancy some pampering, **Hotel Caviahue** has a day spa where you can enjoy a thermal bath for AR$20 and treatments from AR$30.

A little under 2km west of Caviahue, the ski resort **Centro de Ski Cerro Caviahue** (☎ 495043; www.caviahue.com) has seven chairlifts, and four pomas, which take skiers all the way up to the peak of Volcán Copahue (2953m). Equipment hire (skis/snowboard around AR$70/80 per day) is also available on the mountain or in the village. Adult day passes range from AR$92 to AR$168, depending on the season.

Sleeping & Eating

Hebe's House (☎ 495238; www.hebeshouse.com.ar; Mapuche & Puesta del Sol; dm/d AR$80/150; ☺ Dec-Sep) With the only hostel for miles around, Hebe crams them in to cozy but cramped dorms. It's set in a cute alpine building and offers kitchen access, laundry facilities and plenty of tourist information. If you're coming in winter, book well ahead.

Hotel Caviahue (☎ 495044; hotelcaviahue@issn.gov.ar; 8 de Abril s/n; s/d AR$170/250) A rambling, older-style hotel set up the hill, with views out over the village, lake and mountains. It's the only hotel open in the village year-round. Rates drop around 30% off-season. Also on the premises is the only restaurant (mains AR$15 to AR$20) in town to stay open year-round.

Getting There & Away

One bus daily runs to Neuquén (AR$68, 6½ hours) via Zapala (AR$35, 3½ hours). If you're headed for Chos Malal, you can shave a couple of hours off your travel time by getting off in Las Lajas (AR$22, 2½ hours) and waiting for a bus there. Check your connection times with the bus company **Cono Sur** (☎ 02942-432607), though – if you're going to get stranded, Zapala is the place to do it.

CHOS MALAL

☎ 02948 / pop 12,200 / elev 862m

Cruising through the stark, desertlike landscape north of Zapala doesn't really prepare you for arrival at this pretty little oasis town. Set at the convergence of Río Neuquén and Río Curi Leuvú, Chos Malal's one claim to fame is that it was Neuquén province's capital until 1904. Perhaps this explains why the town has so many stately old buildings and the present-day capital has so few.

The two main plazas in town bear the names of the two superheroes of Argentina – San Martín and Sarmiento. Around the former is the majority of the historic buildings, including the Fuerte IV Division fort (go around the back for sweeping views out over the river valley). Five blocks south is Plaza Sarmiento, where you'll find banks and businesses.

Information

Banco de la Nación (cnr Sarmiento & Urquiza) Has an ATM.

Hospital Zonal Gregorio Avárez (☎ 421400; cnr Entre Ríos & Flores) English speaker usually on-site.

Laco (Sarmiento 280; per hr AR$3.50; ☺ 9am-8pm) Provides internet access.

LAGUNA TERMAL TREK

This day trip, which should be possible in around eight hours, is easy enough to do on your own, leaving from Copahue. Due to snow conditions, it's only possible from December to April unless you bring special equipment. If you'd like to take the side route to the peak of Volcán Copahue, it's recommended that you go with an experienced guide. Caviahue Tours (see opposite) is among the many tour operators offering guides on this route.

From the Hotel Valle del Volcán at the upper (southwest) edge of the village, cross the little footbridge and climb briefly past a lifesize statue of the Virgin. The well-worn foot track leads across a sparsely vegetated plain towards the exploded cone of Volcán Copahue, dipping down to lush, green lawns by the northern shore of the Lagunas Las Mellizas' western 'twin.' Follow a path along the lake's north side past black-sand beachlets and gushing springs on its opposite shore to reach the start of a steam pipeline, one to 1¼ hours from the village. The roaring of steam from the subterranean Copahue Geothermal Field entering the vapoducto and irregular explosive blasts of discharging steam can be heard along much of the trek. Cross the lake outlet – further downstream is a wide, easy ford – then cut up southwest over snowdrifts past a tarn to meet a 4WD track at the edge of a small waterlogged meadow. Turn right and follow this rough road up around left (or take a vague trail marked with white paint splashes to its right until you come back to the road on a rocky ridge below a wooden cross). The 4WD track continues westward up through a barren volcanic moonscape to end under a tiny glacier on the east flank of Volcán Copahue, 1¼ to 1½ hours from the pipeline.

Ascend southwest over bouldery ridges, crossing several small mineral-and-meltwater streams. To the northwest, in Chile, the ice-smothered Sierra Velluda and the near-perfect snowy cone of Volcán Antuco rise up majestically. From the third streamlet (with yellowy, sulphur-encrusted sides), cut along the slope below a hot spring then climb to the top of a prominent gray-pumice spur that lies on the international border. Ascend the spur until it becomes impossibly steep, then traverse up rightward over loose slopes into a gap to reach Laguna Termal, 1¼ to 1½ hours from the end of the 4WD track (3½ to 4¼ hours from Copahue).

Filling Volcán Copahue's eastern crater, this steaming hot lake feeds itself by melting the snout of a glacier that forms a massive rim of ice above its back wall. Sulphurous fumes often force trekkers to retreat from the lake, but these high slopes also grant a wonderful vista across the vast basin (where both villages are visible) between the horseshoe-shaped Lago Caviahue (Lago Agrio) and the elongated Lago Trolope to the northeast. From here, more experienced trekkers can continue up to the summit of Volcán Copahue.

To get back to Copahue, retrace your ascent route. If you have a decent map of the area, you can follow the Arroyo Caviahue (Río Agrio) and RN 26 back to town.

Warning

Particularly on windy days, acrid fumes rising from Laguna Termal can be overpowering due to sulphur dioxide gas (which attacks your airways). Approach the lake cautiously – don't even consider swimming in it. Less-experienced trekkers are advised to go with an organized tour (see opposite).

Tourist Information (☎ 421991; turnorte@neuquen.gov.ar; 25 de Mayo 89; ☻ 8am-8pm) Has good maps of the town and surrounds.

Activities

The only tour operator in town, **Tunduca** (☎ 422829; www.tunduca.com.ar; Jujuy 60) offers everything from fly-fishing, horse-back riding and rafting to day trips to the geysers and hot springs (p384) north of town and the rock carvings at Colo Michi-Co archaeological park (p384). It can also arrange five-day treks to the summit of Volcán Domuyo (4710m), the highest volcanic peak in Patagonia.

Sleeping & Eating

Most accommodations are located in between the two plazas.

Residencial Kallfü Küyen (☎ 421263; Jujuy 60; s/d AR$50/70) The best budget deal in town has clean, spacious rooms half a block from Plaza Sarmiento.

DETOUR: NORTH OF CHOS MALAL

Heading north from Chos Malal brings you to a couple of wonderful, rarely visited attractions. Public transportation is rare and often nonexistent, but if you have the time and patience, you'll be well rewarded.

Parque Archaeologico Colo Michi-Co

This small archaeological site features one of the most important collections of Pehuenche rock art in Patagonia. There are over 600 examples here, carved with symbolic figures and abstract designs. Getting to the site without a private vehicle is tricky. Buses leave Chos Malal at 8am Friday for the village of Varvarco (AR$30, three hours). From there, it's 9km south on the RP 39 to the Escuela Colo Michi-Co (buses will drop you off), where you'll see a signpost leading to the park, an 8km walk away. Bring everything – there's nothing out here.

If all that walking doesn't excite you, contact **Señora La Gallega** (☎ 02948-421329) in Varvarco – there aren't any *remises* (radio taxis) there, but the señora should be able to hook you up with a car and driver, charging around AR$5 per kilometer, plus waiting time. Hitchhiking is common practice in the area, but be prepared for long waits.

Aguas Calientes

These excellent, natural outdoor hot springs located at the foot of the Volcán Domuyo are spread over 20 sq km and feature three main sites. The main one at Villa Aguas Calientes is suitable for swimming; Las Olletas is a collection of bubbling mud pits and Los Tachos are geysers, spurting up to heights of 2m. The site is 40km north of Varvarco, where the last public transport terminates. If you don't have your own wheels, your best way of getting here is with Tunduca (p383) in Chos Malal. If you can get to Varvarco on your own, you can ask about hiring a driver with Señora La Gallega (see above).

Hostería Don Costa (☎ 421652; hostdoncosta@hotmail .com; s/d AR$100/120; ⊠ ▯ ☞) Attractive, modern rooms set well back from the road in case Chos Malal ever has a noisy night. Rooms are on the small side (like, door-bumping-bed small), but excellent value for the price. Get one upstairs for a balcony, sunlight and ventilation.

People in Chos Malal eat a lot of goat, and you may find yourself doing the same while you're there.

Bahia Café (Urquiza 305; breakfast AR$5, mains AR$18-30; ☯ breakfast, lunch & dinner) Just off Plaza Sarmiento, this cozy little cafe serves up the best coffee in town, along with hamburgers, sandwiches and pastas in a friendly, informal setting.

El Viejo Caicallén (General Paz 345; mains AR$20-35; ☯ lunch & dinner) The best *parrilla* in town is at this happy place, offering all sorts of meat dishes, pastas, salads and sandwiches, along with a couple of regional faves such as black butter trout (AR$35) and grilled goat (AR$30).

Getting There & Around

American Jet (☎ 299-444-1085; www.americanjet .ar) flies to and from Neuquén (AR$180) twice weekly.

Chos Malal is small enough to walk around, which is lucky – there's a serious taxi shortage. To get to the center of town from the bus terminal, walk two blocks down Neuquén and take a right on 25 de Mayo. Plaza Sarmiento is six blocks straight ahead.

Regular buses depart for Zapala (AR$37, three hours), Neuquén (AR$64, six hours) and Varvarco (AR$30, three hours). Three minibuses a day leave between 4:30pm and 5pm for Buta Ranquil (AR$18, two hours). Buses for Mendoza (AR$115, 13 hours) and points along the RN40 leave on Monday and Friday.

NORTH ALONG THE RN40

Following the RN40 north from Chos Malal gives you more wild desert scenery, tiny windswept towns and expansive, empty vistas. Despite what many will tell you, there *is* public transport along this route. Tramat runs regular buses between Zapala and Mendoza twice a week. Failing that, **Transportes Leader** (☎ in Buta Ranquil 02948-493268; cnr Malvinas & Jadull) runs minibuses between Buta Ranquil and San Rafael, Monday to Saturday. There's regular bus service from Neuquén and Chos Malal to

Buta Ranquil, where you may get stuck for the night. There's no real reason to be here, but there are a couple of cheap hotels, one nice one and enough restaurant-cafes to keep you from starving. See the Zapala (p380) and Chos Malal (opposite) sections for transportation details.

ALUMINÉ

☎ 02942 / pop 4300 / elev 400m

Time seems to have stopped for Aluminé, and although it's an important tourist destination, it is less visited than destinations to the south. The town itself has a very local flair, with the main plaza alive with families and children on weekends. Most of the buildings are whitewashed brick, faded with time, and the streets are nearly all dirt, all a relief from the chalet-lined streets of San Martín and Bariloche. Situated 103km north of Junín de los Andes via RP 23, it's a popular fly-fishing destination and offers access to the less-visited northern sector of Parque Nacional Lanín. The Río Aluminé also offers excellent white-water rafting and kayaking.

Information

Banco del Provincia del Neuquén (cnr Conrado Villegas & Torcuato Mordarelli) Bank and ATM.

Nex Sur (☎ 496027; Av RIM 26 848; per hr AR$4) Internet access; uphill from plaza.

Tourist office (☎ 496001; info@alumine.gov.ar; Christian Joubert, Plaza San Martín; ☺ 8am-8pm mid-Mar–Nov, 9am-9pm Dec–mid-Mar) For local info and maps, fishing permits, road conditions etc.

Sights & Activities

The nearby Mapuche communities of **Aigo** and **Salazar**, on the 26km rolling dirt road to **Lago Ruca Choroi** (in Parque Nacional Lanín), sell traditional weavings, araucaria pine nuts and, in summer, *comidas típicas* (traditional dishes). Salazar is an easy, signposted 12km walk or bike ride out of town – just follow the river. Aigo is another 14km along.

For rafting on the Río Aluminé (best in November), as well as kayaking, fly-fishing, trekking and rock climbing, contact **Aluminé Rafting** (☎ 496322; www.interpatagonia.com/alumineraft ing; Conrado Villegas 610).

Mali Viajes (☎ 496310), in front of the tourist office on the plaza, hires bikes for AR$12/50 per hour/day. During summer it offers scenic tours to Mapuche communities, circumnavigating Lago Ruca Choroi en route to Villa Pehuenia.

The tourist office keeps a list of available **fishing** guides and sells licenses (AR$75/250/350 per day/week/season).

Sleeping & Eating

If you're traveling in a group, the tourist office keeps a list of self-catering cabins – some just out of town – that offer good value for three or more people. High season coincides with the November-through-April fishing season.

Nid Car (☎ 496131; nidcaralumine@yahoo.com.ar; cnr Christian Joubert & Benigar; s/d AR$50/90) Very standard and slightly spacious rooms just uphill from the plaza. Cheapest in town and not a bad deal.

Hostería Aluminé (☎ 496174; www.hosterialumine .com.ar; C Joubert 336; s/d with bathroom AR$120/160, without bathroom AR$95/125; ☜) Probably a good-looking hotel once upon a time, the lobby and restaurant areas here are still impressive, but the rooms are functional and slightly drab. The attached restaurant (meals AR$18 to AR$30) serves good food, especially the mixed pasta dish with *salsa de piñon y hongos* (pine nut and mushroom sauce).

Hotel de la Aldea (☎ 496340; www.hoteldelaldea .com.ar; RP 23 & Crouzielles; s/d from AR$150/220; ☒) A sprawling brick wonderland out on the highway (a two-minute walk from the center of town), the Aldea is comfortable enough with modern, slightly cramped rooms. It's definitely worth paying the extra AR$40 for the river views.

Los Araucarias (cnr Candelaria & C Joubert; mains AR$22-35; ☺ lunch & dinner) This standard *parrilla* restaurant offers a down-home atmosphere and an impressive wine list.

Restaurante Sauco (Av RIM 26 & Candelaria; mains AR$20-30; ☺ dinner) It's a cozy little restaurant uphill from the plaza serving a range of trout dishes (the owner is a fly-fishing enthusiast), regional specialties, Patagonian oddballs, such as pickled rabbit, and your standard range of pasta, pizza, *parrilla* (mixed grill) and sandwiches.

Getting There & Away

Aluminé's **bus terminal** (☎ 496048) is just downhill from the plaza, an easy walk to any of the hotels listed here. Aluminé Viajes and Albus go daily to/from Neuquén (AR$43, six hours), Zapala (AR$33, three to 3½ hours), Villa Pehuenia (AR$20, one hour) and San Martín de los Andes (AR$45, 4½ hours).

VILLA PEHUENIA

☎ 02942 / pop 560 / elev 1200m

Villa Pehuenia is an idyllic little lakeside village on the shores of Lago Aluminé. There are several Mapuche communities nearby, including the community of Puel, located between Lago Aluminé and Lago Moquehue. The village lies at the heart of the Pehuen region, named of course after the pehuén (araucaria) trees that are so marvelously present. If you have a car, the Circuito Pehuenia is a great drive; it's a four- to six-hour loop from Villa Pehuenia past Lago Moquehue, Lago Ñorquinco, Lago Pulmarí and back around Lago Aluminé. Mali Viajes (p385) offers scenic back-road tours along this route in summer, starting from Aluminé.

The drive from Zapala on RP 13 via Primeros Pinos is spectacular with sweeping vistas across the high Pampa de Lonco Luan, where the tip of Volcán Lanín is visible off to the left and the double peaks of Volcán Llaima (3125m) in Chile.

Orientation & Information

Villa Pehuenia is 102km north of Junín de los Andes (via RP 23 and Aluminé) and 120km west of Zapala, via RP 13. Hosterías (lodging houses) and cabañas are spread around the Península de los Coihues, which dangles nearly 2km into Lago Aluminé. Most services such as supermarkets and restaurants are in and around the centro comercial (commercial center), which is just above the peninsula.

Banco de la Provincia del Neuquén (RP 13 s/n) Next to the police station; has an ATM.

Oficina de Turismo (☎ 498044; www.villapehuenia .gov.ar; RP 13 s/n) At the entrance to town, is extremely helpful and provides good maps of the region.

Sights & Activities

From the top of nearby **Volcán Batea Mahuida** (2010m) you can see eight volcanoes (from Lanín to the south to Copahue to the north) in both Argentina and Chile. Inside Batea Mahuida is a small crater lake. You drive nearly to the top (summer only) and then it's an easy two-hour walk to the summit. This is the location of the small Mapuche-operated **Batea Mahuida ski park** (☎ 02942-15-661527; www .cerrobateamahuida.com.ar; day pass AR$50-60), which is little more than a few snowy slopes with a T-bar and a poma. If you're a Nordic skier, you're in better luck – a circuit goes around the park, taking in awesome views of the volcano and lakes.

Brisas del Sur (☎ 02942-15-692737; www.brisas delsur.8m.com) gives boat tours of Lago Aluminé (AR$50, 1½ hours), leaving from the small peninsula in front of the Laguna El Manzano.

Los Pehuenes (☎ 498029; www.pehuenes.com.ar; Centro Comercial), the local adventure-tourism operator, offers rafting, trekking, horse-back riding and 4WD off-roading trips.

Sleeping & Eating

Many businesses in Villa Pehuenia close down off season. Those listed here are open year-round.

Hostería de las Cumbres (☎ 498097; r AR$170) Right down by the waterfront in the main part of town, this cozy little hostería has smallish rooms coming off way-narrow corridors. Lake views from the front rooms, however, make this one a winner.

Hostería la Balconada (☎ 02942-15-473843; www .hosterialabalconada.com.ar; r AR$395-425; 🔊) One of the finest, coziest accommodation options in town, this one sits out on a cliff on the peninsula. It's worth paying the extra AR$30 for the lake views.

Iñaki (☎ 498047; snacks from AR$12; 🕑 lunch & dinner) A cool little restaurant–tapas bar near the lakefront in the main part of town. Vegetarian food and good-value set meals are available. On a sunny day, the deck out front is the place to be.

Parrilla Los Troncos (☎ 498006; Centro Comercial; mains AR$20-35; 🕑 lunch & dinner) The most reliable parrilla in town cooks up some great burgers and excellent fries. Also parrilla, sandwiches and more. Staff can set you up with a packed lunch if you're off on an outing.

Between the centro comercial and the tourist office, the **Fabrica de Alfajores** (☎ 498090; RP 13 s/n; 🕑 9am-6pm daily in summer, weekends only rest of year) makes and sells delicious alfajores de piñon, (cookie-type sandwiches made with pine-nut flour) and serves up a mean cup of coffee or hot chocolate.

Getting There & Around

Exploring the area is tough without a car, though hitching is definitely feasible in summer. **Destinos Patagonicos** (☎ 498067; Centro Comercial) is the representative for Albus, the only bus company currently serving the village. There are daily buses to Zapala (AR$42, 4½ hours), Neuquén (AR$80, seven hours) and Aluminé (AR$20, one hour).

JUNÍN DE LOS ANDES

☎ 02972 / pop 12,000 / elev 800m

A much more humble affair than other Lake District towns, Junín's a favorite for fly fishers – the town deems itself the trout capital of Neuquén province and, to drive the point home, uses trout-shaped street signs. A couple of circuits leading out of town take in the scenic banks of the Lago Huechulafquen, where Mapuche settlements welcome visitors. Outside of peak season, these circuits are best done by private vehicle (or incredibly enthusiastic bike riders), but travel agents based here offer reasonably priced tours.

Orientation

Paved RN 234 (known as Blvd Juan Manuel de Rosas in town) is the main thoroughfare, leading south to San Martín de los Andes and 116km northeast to Zapala via RN 40. North of town, graveled RP 23 heads to the fishing resort of Aluminé, while several secondary roads branch westward to Parque Nacional Lanín.

The city center is between the highway and the river. Do not confuse Av San Martín, which runs on the west side of Plaza San Martín, with Félix San Martín, two blocks further west.

Information

ESSENTIALS

Banco de la Provincia de Neuquén (Av San Martín, btwn Coronel Suárez & General Lamadrid) Opposite the plaza.

Club Andino Junín de los Andes (Félix San Martín 358) Provides information on the Volcán Tromen climb as well as other excursions within the Lanín national park.

Park office (☎ 491160; Domingo Milanesio at Coronel Suárez; ☒ 9am-8:30pm Mon-Fri, 2:30-8:30pm Sat & Sun) Next to the tourist office. Has information on Parque Nacional Lanín.

Picurú Turismo (☎ 492829; www.picuruturismo.com.ar; Coronel Suárez 371) Recommended tour operator for trips into Parque Nacional Lanín and tours of Mapuche communities.

Tourist office (☎ 491160, 492575; www.junindel osandes.gov.ar; cnr Domingo Milanesio & Coronel Suárez; ☒ 8am-11pm Nov-Feb, 8am-9pm Mar-Oct) Enthusiastically helpful staff. Fishing permits and a list of licensed fishing guides available.

THE LAKE DISTRICT

JUNÍN DE LOS ANDES

0   200 m
0   0.1 miles

INFORMATION

Banco de la Provincia de Neuquén	1	B2
bits	2	C2
Ciclismo Maui	3	A1
Club Andino Junín de los Andes	4	B1
Laverap Pehuén	5	B2
Locutorio	6	C2
Park Office	7	C2
Picurú Turismo	8	B2
Post Office	9	C2
Tourist Office	(see 7)	

SIGHTS & ACTIVITIES

Museo Mapuche	10	C3

SLEEPING

Camping Laura Vacuña	11	D3
Hostería Chimehuín	12	D2
Residencial Marisa	13	A1
Rüpü Calel	14	C2
Tromen Hostel	15	A3

EATING

Offa	16	C2
Ruca Hueney	17	B2
Turi Centro	(see 7)	

TRANSPORT

Bus Terminal	18	A1

OTHER SERVICES

bits (Coronel Suárez 445 btwn Domingo Milanesio & Don Bosco; per hr AR$3) Internet access.

Ciclismo Maui (Felix San Martín 415) Rents mountain bikes for AR$10/50 per hour/day.

Laverap Pehuén (Ginés Ponte 340) Laundry services.

Locutorio (Domingo Milanesio 540) Phone service opposite the plaza.

Post office (cnr Coronel Suárez & Don Bosco)

Sights & Activities

Junín's surroundings are more appealing than the town itself, but the **Museo Mapuche** (cnr Ginés Ponte & Joaquín Nogueira; ☻ 10am-noon & 4-8pm Mon, Wed & Fri), which boasts Mapuche weavings and archaeological pieces, is well worth seeing.

About 3km west of town, near the end of Av Antártida Argentina, a wide dirt path called the **Vía Cristi** winds its way up the small Cerro de La Cruz (to get there, follow the cross) with impressive sculptures, bas-reliefs and mosaics vividly depicting the Conquest of the Desert, Mapuche legends, Christian themes and indigenous history.

The area around Junín is prime country for trout-fishing, and the Río Aluminé, north of Junín, is an especially choice area. Catch-and-release is obligatory. Fishing permits (AR$75/250/350 per day/week/season) are available through the tourist office.

Festivals & Events

In January the **Feria y Exposición Ganadera** displays the best of local cattle, horses, sheep, poultry and rabbits. There are also exhibitions of horsemanship, as well as local crafts exhibits, but this is the *estanciero's* (*estancia* owner's) show.

In July, the Mapuche celebrate their crafts skills in the **Semana de Artesanía Aborígen**.

The **National Trout Festival** takes place in November.

Sleeping

High season coincides with fishing season (November through April); during low season, prices are lower than those quoted here.

Camping Laura Vicuña (Ginés Ponte s/n; campsites per person AR$8, cabins AR$220) You won't find a much more sublime location for an urban campground: perched on an island in between two burbling creeks, with all the facilities, plus fully equipped cabins (three-night minimum).

Tromen Hostel (☎ 491498; tromen@fronteradigital .net.ar; Lonquimay 195; dm/d AR$30/80) A cozy little

hostel located upstairs in a family home. If the place ever fills up, it could get quite cramped, but it's a good deal nonetheless.

Residencial Marisa (☎ 491175; residencialmarisa@ jdeandes.com.ar; Rosas 360; s/d AR$75/110; ☞) The best little budget hotel in town offers spacious, clean rooms a couple of minutes' walk from the bus terminal.

Rüpú Calel (☎ 491569; Coronel Suárez 560; s/d AR$120/150) While they may look big and bare to some, the rooms here have a pleasing simplicity and are sparkling clean, as are the spacious bathrooms.

Hostería Chimehuín (☎ 491132; www.interpatagonia .com/hosteriachimehuin; cnr Coronel Suárez & 25 de Mayo; s/d AR$110/150) A beautiful spot a few minutes from the center of town. Book early and you'll have a good chance of snagging a room with a balcony overlooking the creek. Either way, rooms are big, warm and comfortable and the whole place has a tranquil air to it.

Eating

Junín has fairly mediocre restaurants, though local specialties such as trout, wild boar or venison may be available.

Turi Centro (Domingo Milanesio 590; mains AR$15-25; ☻ breakfast, lunch & dinner) You could hardly think of a less appealing name, but this bright, comfortable cafe by the tourist office is a good place for coffee and a sandwich.

Offa (Domingo Milanesio 520; mains AR$15-25; ☻ lunch & dinner) A cozy little pizza and burger bar, with a better atmosphere than most. There's a wide selection of pizzas on offer and a good music selection seals the deal.

Ruca Hueney (☎ 491113; cnr Colonel Suárez & D Milanesio; mains AR$20-35; ☻ lunch & dinner) Ruca Hueney, Junín's oldest restaurant, is reliable and has the most extensive menu in town. Portions are large; service is abrupt. There's a cheaper take-out counter next door in case you were thinking about a picnic at the park across the street.

Getting There & Away
AIR

Junín and San Martín de los Andes share Chapelco airport, which lies midway between the two towns (see p396). There are regularly scheduled flights to Buenos Aires and Neuquén. A *remise* (taxi) into town should run you about AR$30. Another option is walking the 1km out to the highway and flagging down a passing bus (AR$8, 25 minutes).

BUS

The **bus terminal** (☎ 492038; Olavarría & Félix San Martín) is three blocks from the main plaza. Ko-Ko has a service to Bariloche (AR$30, four to six hours) via both the paved Rinconada route (all year) and the dusty but far more scenic Siete Lagos alternative (summer only). El Petróleo goes three times a week to Aluminé (AR$32, three hours). To Mendoza you must change buses in Neuquén or Zapala. There are daily services to the following destinations:

Destination	Cost (AR$)	Duration (hr)
Bariloche	30	3
Buenos Aires	271	22
Neuquén	64	6
San Martín de los Andes	7	1
Zapala	35	3

PARQUE NACIONAL LANÍN

Dominating the view in all directions along the Chilean border, the snowcapped cone of 3776m Volcán Lanín is the centerpiece of this **national park** (www.parquenacionallanin.gov.ar; admission AR$30), which extends 150km from Parque Nacional Nahuel Huapi in the south to Lago Ñorquinco in the north.

Protecting 3790 sq km of native Patagonian forest, Parque Nacional Lanín is home to many of the same species that characterize more southerly Patagonian forests, such as the southern beeches – lenga, ñire and coihue. More botanically unique to the area, however, are the extensive stands of the broadleaf, deciduous southern beech, raulí, and the curious pehuén, or monkey puzzle tree (Araucaria araucana), a pine-like conifer whose nuts have long been a dietary staple for the Pehuenches and Mapuches. Note, though, that only indigenous people may gather piñones (pine nuts) from the pehuenes.

The towns of San Martín de los Andes, Junín de los Andes and Aluminé are the best bases for exploring Lanín, its glacial lakes and the backcountry.

Information

The Lanín national park office (p392) in San Martín produces brochures on camping, hiking and climbing in the park. Scattered throughout the park proper are several ranger stations, but they usually lack printed materials. The national park's website is full of useful information.

Lago Tromen

This northern approach to **Volcán Lanín**, which straddles the Argentine–Chilean border, is also the shortest and usually the earliest in the season to open for hikers and climbers. Before climbing Lanín, ask permission at the Lanín national park office in San Martín (p392) or, if necessary, of the *gendarmería* (border guards) in Junín. It's obligatory to show equipment, including plastic tools, crampons, ice axe and clothing – including sunglasses, sunblock, gloves, hats and padded jackets.

From the trailhead at the Argentine border station, it's five to seven hours to the **CAJA refugio** (capacity 14 people), at 2600m on the Camino de Mulas route; above that point, snow equipment is necessary. There's

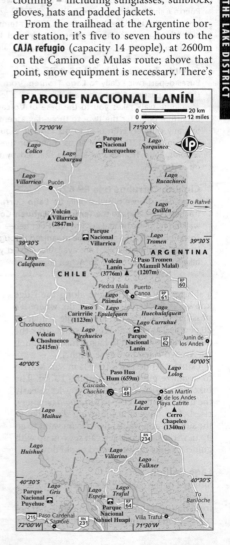

EXCURSIONS TO PARQUE NACIONAL LANÍN

In summer, buses leave the terminal in Junín several times a day for destinations within the national park, allowing you to hit the trails and camp in some beautiful areas. The buses run three 'circuits' and charge AR$15 for the return trip.

Lago Huechulafquen & Puerto Canoa (via RP 61)

From Puerto Canoa, on the north shore of the lake, there are three worthwhile hikes, including a 1½-hour roundtrip walk to the Cascada del Saltillo and a seven-hour roundtrip hike to **Cara Sur de Lanín** (south face of Volcán Lanín). For the latter, park rangers require you set out by 11am. Ranger stations are at both the entrance to Huechulafquen and at Puerto Canoa. From Puerto Canoa, the boat **Jose Julian** (☎ 02972-429264, 428029; www.catamaranjosejulian.com.ar) offers boat trips on the lake. Buses depart Junín's terminal twice in the morning (usually around 8am and 11am) and once in the afternoon (around 4pm). Be sure to catch the last bus back unless you plan to camp.

Circuito Tromen (via RN 23 & RP 60)

Buses depart twice daily to **Lago Tromen**, from where there is a 1½-hour roundtrip walk along the river, passing a fine araucaria forest and a lookout with fabulous views of the lake. Another 45-minute walk takes you to the base of **Volcán Lanín's Cara Norte** (north face). This is one departure point for the two- to three-day ascent of Lanín. Park rangers inspect equipment and test any climbers who plan to go without a guide. To hire a guide, contact the tourist office in Junín (p387). This is the access point for the CAJA *refugio* (shelter) and two military-owned *refugios*. Lago Tromen can also be reached by taking any bus that goes to Chile and getting off at Tromen.

Circuito Curruhué (via RP 62)

Buses depart once or twice daily for **Lago Curruhué** and **Lago Epulafquen**; near the latter is a trailhead that leads to the **Termas de Lahuen-Có** (☎ 424709; www.lahuenco.com), about one hour's walking from the head. Package tours out here – including transport, lunch and spa treatments – cost around AR$550 and can be organized through the center or through tour operators in town. Luxurious **rooms** (AR$925) are available, should you want to spend the night and you can also hike to the crater of Volcán Achen Niyeu.

a shorter but steeper route along the ridge known as the Espina del Pescado, where it's possible to stay at the **RIM refugio** (capacity 20 people), at 2450m. Trekkers can cross the Sierra Mamuil Malal to Lago Huechulafquen via Arroyo Rucu Leufu (see right).

Contact Andestrack (p393) in San Martín to organize guides for climbing Lanín. The hike usually takes two days: you leave early the first and stay at the RIM *refugio* (shelter), rise before dawn the following day, hike to the summit and walk down. If you want to go up in winter, Andestrack can set you up with guides to hike up and board or ski down.

Lago Quillén

Situated in the park's densest pehuén forests, this isolated lake is accessible by dirt road from Rahué, 17km south of Aluminé, and has many good **campsites**. Other nearby lakes include **Lago Rucachoroi**, directly west of Aluminé, and **Lago Ñorquinco** on the park's northern border. There are Mapuche reservations at Rucachoroi and Quillén.

Lago Huechulafquen

The park's largest lake is also one of its most central and accessible areas. Despite limited public transport, it can be reached from San Martín and – more easily – Junín de los Andes. RP 61 climbs from a junction just north of Junín, west to Huechulafquen and the smaller Lago Paimún, offering outstanding views of Volcán Lanín and access to trailheads of several excellent hikes.

From the ranger station at **Puerto Canoa**, a good trail climbs to a viewpoint on Lanín's shoulder, where it's possible to hike across to Paso Tromen or continue climbing to either of two *refugios*: the **RIM refugio** belongs to the army's Regimiento de Infantería de Montaña, while the **CAJA refugio** belongs to the Club Andino Junín de los Andes (p387). Both are fairly rustic but well kept and can be bases for attempts on the summit (for more detail, including information about permits, equipment and the *refugios*, see p389). The initial segment follows an abandoned road, but after about 40 minutes it becomes a pleasant woodsy trail along the **Arroyo Rucu Leufu**, an attractive mountain stream. Halfway to the *refugio* is an extensive **pehuén forest**, the southernmost in the park, which makes the walk worthwhile if you lack time for the entire route. The route to RIM's *refugio*, about 2450m above sea level, takes about seven hours one way, while the trail to CAJA's *refugio* takes a bit longer.

Another good backcountry hike circles **Lago Paimún**. This requires about two days from Puerto Canoa; you return to the north side of the lake by crossing a cable platform strung across the narrows between Huechulafquen and Paimún. A shorter alternative hike goes from the very attractive campground at **Piedra Mala** to **Cascada El Saltillo**, a nearby forest waterfall. If your car lacks 4WD, leave it at the logjam 'bridge' that crosses the creek and walk to Piedra Mala – the road, passable by any ordinary vehicle to this point, quickly worsens after a harsh winter. Horses are available for rent at Piedra Mala. Transportes Ko-Ko runs buses to Piedra Mala daily in summer from the San Martín bus terminal (p396).

Campsites are abundant along the highway; travelers camping in the free sites in the narrow area between the lakes and the highway must dig a latrine and remove their own trash. If you camp at the organized sites (which, though not luxurious, are maintained), you'll support Mapuche concessionaires who at least derive some income from lands that were theirs before the state usurped them a century ago. Good campsites include **Camping Raquithue** (per person AR$12) and **Bahía Cañicul** (AR$15).

Noncampers should treat themselves to a stay at **Hostería Refugio Pescador** (☎ in Puerto Canoa 02972-490210, in Junín de los Andes 02972-491132; www .patagon-fly-fishing.com; r per person incl full board AR$260) or the three-star **Hostería Paimún** (☎ 02972-491758; www.interpatagonia.com/hosteriapaimun; r per person incl full board AR$300); both cater to fishing parties.

Lago Lácar & Lago Lolog

From San Martín, at the east end of Lago Lácar, there is bus service on RP 48, which runs along the lake to the Chilean border at Paso Hua Hum. You can get off the bus anywhere along the lake or get off at Hua Hum and hike to Cascada Chachín; bus drivers know the stop. From the highway, it's 3km down a dirt road and then another 20 minutes' walk along a trail to the waterfall. It's a great spot for a picnic.

Fifteen kilometers north of San Martín de los Andes, Lago Lolog offers good fishing in a largely undeveloped area. You'll find pleasant, free camping at **Camping Puerto Arturo**. Transportes Ko-Ko runs four buses daily, in summer only, to Lago Lolog from San Martín (AR$5).

Getting There & Away

Although the park is close to San Martín and Junín, public transportation is not extensive; see p396 and opposite for details. With some patience, hitchhiking is feasible in high season. Buses over the Hua Hum and Tromen passes, from San Martín and Junín to Chile, will carry passengers to intermediate destinations but are often full.

SAN MARTÍN DE LOS ANDES

☎ 02972 / pop 28,000 / elev 645m

Like a mellower version of Bariloche, San Martín has two peak periods – winter for skiing at Cerro Chapelco and summer for trekking, climbing etc in nearby Parque Nacional Lanín. Brave souls also swim in the chilly waters of Lago Lácar on the western edge of town. Between these times, it's a quiet little town with a spectacular setting that retains much of the charm and architectural unity that once attracted people to Bariloche. A boat ride on the lake is pretty much a must if you're passing through, and if the snow's cleared (anytime from November onwards) and you're heading south, you should seriously think about leaving town via the scenically neck-straining Ruta de los Siete Lagos (RN 234), which runs south to Villa la Angostura, Lago Nahuel Huapi and Bariloche.

Orientation

Nestled in striking mountain scenery, San Martín de los Andes straddles the RN 234. Northbound RN 234 heads to Zapala via Junín de los Andes. Almost everything in

San Martín de los Andes is within walking distance of the *centro cívico* (civic center), and the shady lakefront park and pier are a delightful place to spend an afternoon. Av San Martín is the main commercial street, running northeast from the lakefront toward the highway.

Information

BOOKSTORES
Patalibro (☎ 421532; patalibro@yahoo.com.ar; Av San Martín 866) Good selection of books on Patagonia in Spanish; some Lonely Planet titles and novels in English. Carries the excellent *Sendas Y Bosques* park trail maps (AR$15).

INTERNET ACCESS
Athos (☎ 429855; Av San Martín 808; per hr AR$3) Internet access in kiosk, upstairs.

LAUNDRY
Laverap (☎ 428820; Capitán Drury 880; full service about AR$15)

MEDICAL SERVICES
Ramón Carrillo Hospital (☎ 427211; cnr Coronel Rohde & Av San Martín)

MONEY
Andina Internacional (☎ 427871; Capitán Drury 876) Money exchange, including traveler's checks.
Banco de la Nación (Av San Martín 687) Has an ATM.

POST
Post office (cnr Av Roca & Coronel Pérez)

TELEPHONE
Cooperativa Telefónica (Capitán Drury 761)

TOURIST INFORMATION
ACA (Automóvil Club Argentino; ☎ 429430; Av Koessler 2175) Good source for provincial road maps.
Lanín national park office (Intendencia del Parque Nacional Lanín; ☎ 427233; www.parquenacionallanin. gov.ar; Emilio Frey 749; ☽ 8am-2pm Mon-Fri) The office provides limited maps as well as brochures and information on road conditions on the Ruta de los Siete Lagos.
Nieves de Chapelco (☎ 427825; www.cerrochapelco. com; cnr M Moreno & Roca) Provides information and sells lift tickets for the Cerro Chapelco ski resort.
Tourist office (☎ 425500, 427347; www.smandes.gov .ar; cnr Av San Martín & M Rosas; ☽ 8am-9pm Apr-Nov, to 10pm Dec-Mar) Provides surprisingly candid information on hotels and restaurants, plus excellent brochures and maps.

TRAVEL AGENCIES
The agencies listed (below), as well as many others along Av San Martín, Belgrano and Elordi, offer standard services as well as excursions.

Sights

MUSEO PRIMEROS POBLADORES
Regional archaeological and ethnographic items such as arrowheads, spear points, pottery and musical instruments are the focus of this **museum** (M Rosas; admission AR$1; ☽ 2-7pm Mon-Fri), located two doors north of the tourist office, near Av Roca.

RUTA DE LOS SIETE LAGOS
From San Martín, RN 234 follows an eminently scenic but rough, narrow and dusty route past numerous alpine lakes to Villa la Angostura. It's known as the Ruta de los Siete Lagos (Seven Lakes Route) and its spectacular scenery has made the drive famous. Sections of the 110km route close every year due to heavy snowfalls – December to May is the best time to schedule this trip, but ask around for current conditions. Full-day tours from San Martín, Villa la Angostura and Bariloche regularly do this route, but there's also a scheduled bus service (p396) and, with a little forward planning, it's possible to drive/cycle it yourself (see p394).

Activities
Mountain biking is an excellent way to explore the surrounding area and a good way to travel the Ruta de los Siete Lagos. Rent bikes at **HG Rodados** (☎ 427345; Av San Martín 1061) for AR$30 to AR$55 per day.

The 2.5km steep, dusty hike to **Mirador Bandurrias** (admission AR$2) ends with awesome views of Lago Lácar; be sure to take a snack or lunch. Tough cyclists can reach the *mirador* (viewing point) in about an hour via dirt roads.

Walk, bike or hitch to **Playa Catrite**, 4km away down RN 234 (there's a bus three times daily in summer). This protected rocky beach has a laid-back restaurant with a nice deck

For rafting on the Río Meliquina, south of San Martín, or the Río Hua Hum to the west, contact **El Claro Turismo** (☎ 428876; www.elclarotur ismo.com.ar; Diaz 751) or **Lanín Turismo** (☎ 425808; www.laninturismo.com; Av San Martín 431). They both charge about AR$120 for the day trip, including transfers. The river is spectacular and suitable for kids.

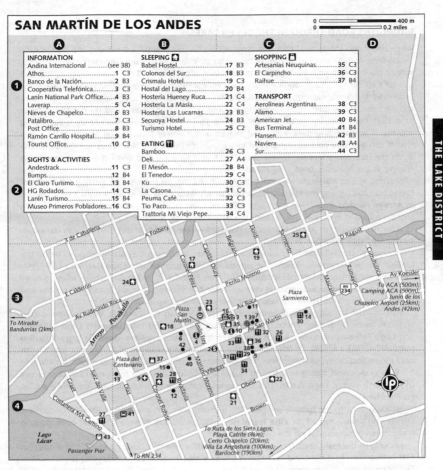

SAN MARTÍN DE LOS ANDES

INFORMATION
Andina Internacional ....(see 38)
Athos.......................................1 C3
Banco de la Nación.................2 B3
Cooperativa Telefónica...........3 C3
Lanín National Park Office......4 B3
Laverap..................................5 C4
Nieves de Chapelco.................6 B3
Patalibro................................7 C3
Post Office..............................8 B3
Ramón Carrillo Hospital.........9 B4
Tourist Office........................10 C3

SIGHTS & ACTIVITIES
Andestrack............................11 C3
Bumps...................................12 B4
El Claro Turismo....................13 B4
HG Rodados...........................14 B4
Lanín Turismo........................15 B4
Museo Primeros Pobladores...16 C3

SLEEPING
Babel Hostel...........................17 B3
Colonos del Sur......................18 B3
Crismalu Hotel.......................19 C3
Hostal del Lago......................20 B4
Hostería Hueney Ruca.............21 C4
Hostería La Masía...................22 C4
Hostería Las Lucarnas.............23 B3
Secuoya Hostel.......................24 B3
Turismo Hotel.........................25 C2

EATING
Bamboo..................................26 C3
Deli.......................................27 A4
El Mesón................................28 B4
El Tenedor..............................29 C4
Ku...30 C3
La Casona..............................31 C4
Peuma Café............................32 C3
Tío Paco.................................33 C3
Trattoria Mi Viejo Pepe..........34 C4

SHOPPING
Artesanías Neuquinas............35 C3
El Carpincho..........................36 C3
Raihue...................................37 B4

TRANSPORT
Aerolíneas Argentinas............38 C3
Alamo....................................39 C3
American Jet...........................40 B4
Bus Terminal..........................41 B4
Hansen..................................42 B3
Naviera..................................43 A4
Sur..44 C3

There are also excellent opportunities for trekking and climbing in Parque Nacional Lanín. **Andestrack** (☎ 420588; www.andestrack.com.ar; Roca 869) is a young, enthusiastic company that has been highly recommended for mountain biking, canoeing, snowshoeing and dog sledding in the park.

Fancy a day on the mountain? Easy. **Miramas** (☎ 411344; www.miramascanopy.com.ar) offers canopy tours, Nordic skiing and snowshoe expeditions from its base 30km out of San Martín. You can also stay out there, in basic but comfortable **dorms** (AR$50).

Skiing and snowboarding at nearby Cerro Chapelco attracts enthusiastic winter crowds (see p396). In San Martín, rental equipment is available at **Bumps** (☎ 428491; www.skienchapelco

.com.ar; Villegas 459) and many other places along San Martín. Ski gear rents for AR$60 to AR$90 per day and snowboards for AR$60 to AR$80. You can also rent equipment on the mountain.

Festivals & Events
San Martín celebrates its founding on February 4 with speeches, parades and other festivities; the **parade** itself is an entertainingly incongruous mix of military folks, firefighters, gauchos, polo players and foxhunters.

Sleeping
As a tourist center, San Martín is loaded with accommodations, but they're relatively costly in all categories, especially in summer high

RIDING THE ROAD THROUGH THE SEVEN LAKES

While there's no shortage of tour operators willing to take you on a quick day trip on the Ruta de los Siete Lagos from San Martín de los Andes to Villa la Angostura (see Map p411); the best way to do it is with your own wheels. It's a 110km trip, so it can be done in a day by car, but this isn't scenery to race through – there are a couple of lovely *hosterías* (lodging houses), some organized and 'bush' campgrounds along the way. If you've got the legs for it, a mountain-bike trip isn't out of the question. Depending on your pedal power, you could do the trip in three long days minimum, but factor in a lot more if you tend to get sidetracked by breathtaking scenery. If you're riding, take water and snacks, and if you're planning on camping, be aware that it can get very cold at night, even in summer. October and November are the best time to do the ride, for lack of traffic and dust. March and April are also good. If you're planning on staying at the *hosterías*, book well ahead.

Starting at San Martín de los Andes, head out of town on the RN 234, skirting the banks of Lago Lácar and passing the Mapuche town of **Curruhuinca**. After 20km you'll come to the lookout at **Arroyo Partido**. From here it's a 5km downhill coast to a bridge over the Río Hermoso. Two short climbs and 5km later, you'll reach the dark-blue **Lago Machónico**.

A further 5km brings you to a turnoff to the right, where it's 2km of dirt road to **Lago Hermoso**, surrounded by mixed ñire and radale forests and the southernmost strand of pehuén trees in the Parque Nacional Lanín. Colored deer are common in this area, as are hunters, so be on the lookout (for both) when walking in the woods. The charming **Refugio Lago Hermoso** (☎ 02944-15-569176; www.refugiolagohermoso.com; dm/r incl full board AR$225/450; ☺ Nov-Apr) is here, offering every comfort imaginable, including some very welcome hot showers, a good restaurant, canoes and horseback-riding trips. There are also organized and free campsites.

Entering the Parque Nacional Nahuel Huapi, it's 15km to the **Cascada Vullignanco**, a 20m waterfall made by the Río Filuco. Two kilometers on, the road runs between **Lago Villarino** and **Lago Falkner**, which has a wide sandy beach and free campsites. **Hostería Lago Villarino** (☎ 02972-427483; r AR$280; ☺ Nov-Mar), on the banks of Lago Falkner is a gorgeous place, with cozy rooms and cabins with fireplaces. Two kilometers further on is **Lago Escondido**, from where it's 8km of downhill zigzag to a turnoff to the left. Follow this side (dirt) road for 2km to get to the north end of **Lago Traful**. This is a popular camping and fishing spot, but there are no services here.

Heading back to the turnoff, say goodbye asphalt, hello dirt road. After 30km of undulating terrain, you'll see a turnoff for **Villa Traful** (see p397). It's 27km down a good dirt road, passing scenic bush campgrounds on the lakeshore.

Sticking to the main road, though, after 20km you'll come to a bridge and a disused *hostería*. Just before that, turn right and take the uphill road that ends at **Lago Espejo Chico** after 2km. The grassy banks of this emerald-green lake make it an excellent campground, but there are no facilities.

Continuing south, you'll catch glimpses of **Lago Espejo Grande** on the right through the trees. There are several lookouts along the road.

Five kilometers on, you'll see **Lago Correntoso**. There are cabins and *hosterías* here, but if you feel like pushing on, it's another 15km to a crossroads where you turn left, and 10km on asphalt to **Villa la Angostura** (p398).

season (January to March) and peak ski season (mid-July and August), when reservations are a must. Quality, however, is mostly high. In low season, prices can drop by 40%.

BUDGET

Camping ACA (☎ 427332; Av Koessler 2640; campsites per person with 2-person minimum AR$30) This is a spacious campground on the eastern outskirts

of town. However, you should try to avoid sites near the highway.

Playa Catrite (campsites per person AR$35) Good camping about 4km south of town.

Secuoya Hostel (☎ 424485; Rivadavia 411; dm AR$45, d without bathroom AR$110; ☐) Secuoya is a beautiful new hostel with plenty of space, free internet and an abundantly fitted-out kitchen. It's located in front of a park in a residential neighborhood, so there's plenty of tranquility on offer.

Babel Hostel (☎ 412120; www.babelhostel.com.ar; Roca 720; dm AR$50; 🖳 🛜) One of the more spacious hostels in town, with four-bed dorms, ample kitchen and lounge areas, and a huge backyard.

MIDRANGE & TOP END

Hostería Las Lucarnas (☎ 427085; Coronel Pérez 632; s/d AR$120/150) A sedate little *hostería* in the center of town. Wood-beamed ceilings and big bathrooms are definite bonuses; try for a spot upstairs.

Turismo Hotel (☎ 427592; www.interpatagonia.com/ hotelturismo; Mascardi 517; s/d AR$120/150; 🛜) A classic '70s ski lodge, right down to the stuffed deer's head and old-school pool table in the lobby. Rooms are comfortable enough, but best avoided if you have problems with glaring yellow paintjobs.

Hostal del Lago (☎ 427598; Coronel Rhode 854; s/d AR$140/160) This cute alpine house has been converted into a cozy hotel. There are only six rooms, and all are upstairs with sloping ceilings. There's plenty of space, a charming sitting area downstairs and super-friendly management.

Crismalu Hotel (☎ 427283; www.interpatagonia .com/crismalu; Rudecino Roca 975; s/d AR$150/180) This huge hotel hasn't been renovated since the '70s (or if it has, it was a very retro fitout), so green carpet and chunky room phones are the go. Get a room out front with a balcony overlooking the huge araucaria tree and you'll be happy.

Hostería Hueney Ruca (☎ 421499; www.hosteria hueneyruca.com.ar; cnr Obeid & Coronel Pérez; s/d AR$160/190) The big, terracotta-tiled rooms here look onto a cute, well-kept little backyard. Beds are big and firm and bathrooms spacious, with glass-walled shower stalls.

Colonos del Sur (☎ 427106; www.colonosdelsur.com.ar; Rivadavia 686; r AR$220) A big, modern hotel pleasingly constructed in the alpine style. Rooms are spacious and bright, with large modern bathrooms, firm beds and faux wooden floorboards.

Hostería La Masía (☎ 427688; www.hosterialama sia.com.ar; Obeid 811; s/d AR$250/300; 🛜) Taking the whole Edelweiss thing to the next level, La Masía offers plenty of dark-wood paneling, arched doorways and cast-iron light fittings. Rooms are big and comfortable and most have mountain views. Fireplaces warm the lobby,

and the owners are usually around to make sure everyone feels at home. Superb.

Eating & Drinking

Deli (☎ 428631; cnr Villegas & Costanera MA Camino; mains AR$15-35; ⏱ breakfast, lunch & dinner) Cheapest place on the lakeside with outdoor seating and reliable food. Good for afternoon beer and french fries. Very popular.

Tio Paco (☎ 427920; cnr Av San Martín & Capitán Drury; mains AR$20-40; ⏱ lunch & dinner) Great little bar-cafe with a full menu and a long list of mixed drinks, including coffee drinks (with booze), wine and cocktails. The menu's not all that exciting, but on a sunny day, the upstairs deck overlooking the main drag is the place to be.

Peuma Café (Av San Martín 853; mains AR$15-25; ⏱ lunch & dinner) If you're after that traditional ambience (and a televised soccer game), check out this local favorite – you can be sure that all the old guys in town will be there. The menu pushes all the right buttons, with steaks, pizzas and delicious raspberry waffles (AR$12).

El Tenedor (Villegas 760; set meal AR$22, all you can eat AR$45; ⏱ lunch & dinner) San Martín's *tenedor libre* (all-you-can-eat restaurant) holds its own, and throws venison and trout into the mix, along with good-value set meals.

Trattoria Mi Viejo Pepe (Villegas 725; mains AR$25-40; ⏱ lunch & dinner) For homemade pastas, this is the place to come. The huge range of sauces and styles is matched by a near-encyclopedic wine list.

La Casona (Villegas 744; mains AR$25-45; ⏱ lunch & dinner) The cozy atmosphere belies the wide menu, with some good twists on regional favorites. Try the boar stew in black-beer sauce (AR$37) or the lamb and wild mushroom risotto (AR$34).

Ku (San Martín 1053; mains AR$25-60; ⏱ lunch & dinner) The late-night favorite is this elegant restaurant, which serves up a good range of meats, homemade pastas and 'mountain food.'

Bamboo (cnr Belgrano & Villegas; mains AR$32-60; ⏱ lunch & dinner) One reader claims this up-market *parrilla* serves 'the best meat in all of Argentina.' We haven't tried all the meat in Argentina (yet), so you be the judge.

our pick El Mesón (Rivadavia 888; mains AR$35-40; ⏱ lunch & dinner) This cute little place has one of the most creative menus in town, with plenty of trout dishes, paella and a couple of vegetarian options.

Shopping

Many local shops sell regional products and handicrafts.

Artesanías Neuquinas (☎ 428396; M Rosas 790) Mapuche cooperative with high-quality weavings and wood crafts on offer.

El Carpincho (Capitán Drury 814) Specializes in gaucho regalia.

Raihue (☎ 423160; Av San Martín 436) Artisan knives, sweaters, leather, purses and ponchos.

Getting There & Away

AIR

Flights from **Chapelco airport** (☎ 428388; RN 234) to Buenos Aires cost about AR$680 with **Aerolíneas Argentinas** (☎ 427003/04; Capitán Drury 876). **American Jet** (☎ 411300; www.americanjet.com.ar; San Martín 555 local 2) flies to Neuquén (AR$205) daily except Monday and Thursday.

BOAT

Naviera (☎ 427380; naviera@smandes.com.ar) sails from the **passenger pier** (Muelle de Pasajeros; Costanera MA Camino) as far as Paso Hua Hum on the Chilean border, at 10am daily. A dock has been under construction for several years at Hua Hum – when it is completed, passengers will be able to disembark to cross the border there. For now, you have to get off at Chachin, about an hour's walk from Hua Hum. Departure times change annually; call the ferry company or check with the tourist office. The fare is AR$80/150 one way/return, plus AR$15 national park fee.

BUS

The **bus terminal** (☎ 427044; cnr Villegas & Juez del Valle) is a block south of the highway and 3½ blocks southwest of Plaza San Martín.

La Araucana goes to Villa Traful daily during summer (AR$25, 2½ hours). If you're heading to Villa La Angostura or Bariloche in summer, Transportes Ko-Ko regularly takes the scenic Ruta de los Siete Lagos (RN 234) instead of the longer but smoother Rinconada route (AR$23, 2½ hours).

To get to Aluminé you must first change buses in Zapala or Junín de los Andes (where there are three departures per week).

At 6am on Monday, Wednesday and Friday, Igi-Llaima takes RP 60 over Paso Tromen (also known as Mamuil Malal) to Temuco, Chile (AR$70, six hours), passing the majestic Volcán Lanín en route; sit on the left for views.

From San Martín there is direct service in summer via RN 231 over Paso Cardenal A Samoré (Puyehue) to Osorno and Puerto Montt in Chile.

There are frequent daily departures to the destinations listed following.

Destination	Cost (AR$)	Duration (hr)
Bariloche	37	4½
Buenos Aires	280	20-23
Junín de los Andes	7	1
Neuquén	65	6
Villa la Angostura	45	4
Zapala	38	3½

Getting Around

Chapelco airport (☎ 428388; RN 234) is midway between San Martín and Junín. **Al Sur** (☎ 422903) runs shuttles between San Martín and the airport; call for hotel pickup.

Transport options slim down during low season. In summer Transportes Airen goes twice daily to Puerto Canoa on Lago Huechulafquen (AR$17) and will stop at campgrounds en route. Albus goes to the beach at Playa Catrite on Lago Lácar (AR$5) several times daily, while Transportes Ko-Ko runs four buses daily to Lago Lolog (AR$5) in summer only.

San Martín has no lack of car-rental agencies.

Alamo (☎ 410811; Av San Martín 836, 2nd fl)
Hansen (☎ 427997; Av San Martín 532)
Sur (☎ 429028; Villegas 830)

CERRO CHAPELCO

Located 20km southeast of San Martín, **Cerro Chapelco** (☎ 02972-427845; www.cerrochapelco.com) is one of Argentina's principal winter-sports centers, with a mix of runs for beginners and experts, and a maximum elevation of 1920m. The **Fiesta Nacional del Montañés**, the annual ski festival, is held during the first half of August.

Lift-ticket prices vary, depending on when you go; full-day passes run from AR$95 to AR$185 for adults, AR$80 to AR$145 for children. The slopes are open from mid-June to early October. The low season is mid-June to early July and from August 28 to mid-October; high season is around the last two weeks of July.

The resort has a downtown information center (p392) that also sells lift tickets. Rental equipment is available on-site as well as in San Martín (p392).

THE MAPUCHE

The Lake District's most prevalent indigenous group, the Mapuche, originally came from Chilean territory. They resisted several attempts at subjugation by the Inca and fought against Spanish domination for nearly 300 years. Their move into Argentina began slowly. Chilean Mapuche were making frequent voyages across the Andes in search of trade as far back as the 17th century. Some chose to stay. In the 1880s the exodus became more pronounced as the Chilean government moved into Mapuche land, forcing them out.

Another theory for the widespread move is that for the Mapuche, the *puelmapu* (eastern land) holds a special meaning, as it is believed that all good things (such as the sun) come from the east.

Apart from trade, the Mapuche (whose name means 'people of the land' in Mapudungun, their language) have traditionally survived as small-scale farmers and hunter/collectors. There is no central government – each extended family has a *lonko* (chief), and in times of war families would unite to elect a *toqui* (axe-bearer) to lead them.

The role of *machi* (shaman) was and still is an important one in Mapuche society. It was usually filled by a woman, whose responsibilities included performing ceremonies for curing diseases, warding off evil, influencing weather, harvests, social interactions and dreamwork. The *machi* was also well schooled in the use of medicinal herbs, but as Mapuche access to land and general biodiversity in the region has decreased, this knowledge is being lost.

Estimates of how many Mapuche live in Argentina vary according to the source. The official census puts the number at around 300,000, while the Mapuche claim that the real figure is closer to 500,000.

Both in Chile and Argentina, the Mapuche live in humble circumstances in rural settings, or leave the land to find work in big cities. It is estimated that there are still 200,000 fluent Mapudungun speakers in Chile, where nominal efforts are made to revive the language in the education system. No such official program has been instituted in Argentina, and while exact numbers are not known, it is feared that the language here may soon become extinct.

Apart from loss of language, the greatest threat to Mapuche culture is the loss of land, a process that has been underway ever since their lands were 'redistributed' after the Conquest of the Desert and many Mapuche relocated to reserves – often the lowest-quality land, without any spiritual significance to them. As with many indigenous peoples, the Mapuche have a special spiritual relationship with the land, believing that certain rocks, mountains, lakes and so on have a particular spiritual meaning.

Despite a relatively well-organized land-rights campaign, the relocation continues today, as Mapuche lands are routinely re-assigned to large commercial interests in the oil, cattle and forestry industries. Defiant to the end, the Mapuche aren't looking like fading away any time soon. They see their cultural survival as intrinsically linked to economic independence, and Mapuche-owned and -operated businesses are scattered throughout the Lakes District.

Transportes Ko-Ko runs two buses each day (three in summer; AR$15 return) to the park from San Martín's bus terminal. Travel agencies in San Martín also offer packages with shuttle service, or shuttle service alone (AR$25); they pick you up at your hotel.

VILLA TRAFUL
☎ 02944 / pop 540 / elev 720m

This little village enjoys an almost achingly beautiful location surrounded by mountains on the southern banks of Lago Traful. The place really packs out in January, February and Easter, when booking accommodation three months in advance is advised. The rest of the year, you may just have it to yourself. Depending on what you're into, November, December, March and April are great times to be here.

Getting here is half the fun – Villa Traful is 80km north of Bariloche via unpaved RP 65. Continuing east of Traful along the Río Traful to RN 237, you roll through spectacular countryside with wild, towering rock formations very distinct from the areas to the south.

The **tourist office** (☎ 479099; www.villatraful.gov .ar; ☼ daily summer, Sat-Wed winter) is on the eastern side of the village.

THE LAKE DISTRICT

Banco de la Provincia de Neuquén in the middle of the village has an ATM that accepts Visa and MasterCard.

Sights & Activities

Guides can easily be hired through the tourist office for horseback riding and hiking in the surrounding mountains. Everything books quickly during fishing season (November to April) and in January and February.

Eco Traful (☎ 479139; www.ecotraful.blogspot.com) is a recommended agency that leads trips to Lagunas Las Mellizas (AR$120/160 per person walking/horseback) and Cerro Negro (AR$55 per person), and organizes boat rides and fishing trips.

CASCADAS DE ARROYO BLANCO & COA CÓ

These two waterfalls are a moderately easy, two-hour roundtrip walk from town that can be done without a guide. Walk uphill on the street running beside the *guardaparque* (park ranger) office and then follow the signs. From where the path forks at the open field it's 500m on the left to the 30m-high Coa Có. Return and take the other fork for 1km to the smaller Cascadas de los Arroyos Blancos. Far more spectacular than the actual waterfalls are the lookouts along the way, which give you a bird's-eye view of the forest, lake and mountains beyond.

LAGUNAS LAS MELLIZAS

Starting with a boat ride across the lake, this trek of moderate difficulty begins with a 2½-hour climb through cypress forests before reaching a lookout with views of the Lagunas Azul and Verde (Blue and Green Lagoons). If you've still got the legs for it, fording a stream gets you to an area with a variety of well-preserved Tehuelche rock paintings, dated at around 600 years old.

Eating & Sleeping

There are only a few places to stay unless you rent a *cabaña* (the tourist office has a complete listing).

Albergue & Camping Vulcanche (☎ 479028; www .vulcanche.com; campsites per person AR$15, dm AR$50, d without bathroom AR$130, cabañas AR$180) In a beautiful wooded area on the eastern edge of the village, this grassy campground and hostel has decent dorms, a good kitchen, and a huge living area overlooking the lake and mountains. The cabins, which come with kitchenette and bathroom, are a particularly good deal.

Hostería Villa Traful (☎ 479005; cabanastraful@ yahoo.com.ar; r per person AR$120) It's a pleasant little mom-and-pop-run operation on the western edge of town. Rooms are aging but comfortable, there's a good restaurant on the premises, and the owners organize boating and fishing trips.

our pick **Nancú Lahuén:** (mains AR$20-30; ☻ lunch & dinner) A cute little log cabin set up in the center of the village. Trout dishes are the specialty (try 'em with the almond sauce), but the menu stretches to *parrilla* and a good range of salads as well.

There are also a couple of restaurants tucked into the trees and a general store to buy groceries.

Getting There & Away

La Araucana has daily services to Villa la Angostura (AR$23, two hours) and summer services to San Martín de los Andes (AR$25, 2½ hours). There are services from Bariloche (AR$22, two hours) daily except Wednesday.

VILLA LA ANGOSTURA

☎ 02944 / pop 11,000 / elev 850m

An upmarket resort town on the northwestern shore of Lago Nahuel Huapi, Villa la Angostura provides accommodations and services for nearby Cerro Bayo, a small but popular winter-sports center.

It's worthwhile stopping by in summer, too, for lake cruises and walks in the small but incredibly diverse Parque Nacional Los Arrayanes (a small peninsula dangling some 12km into the lake), and because this is the southern starting point for the breathtaking trip along the Ruta de los Siete Lagos (Seven Lakes Route; see the boxed text, p394).

The village consists of two distinct areas: El Cruce, which is the commercial center along the highway, and La Villa, nestled against the lakeshore, 3km to the south. Though La Villa is more residential, it still has hotels, shops, services and, unlike El Cruce, lake access.

Orientation

Villa la Angostura is near the junction of RN 231 from Bariloche and RN 234 to San Martín de los Andes (100km). The junction gives the commercial strip of town the name of El Cruce (The Crossroads). Through town, RN 231 is known as Av Arrayanes and Av Siete Lagos. La Villa is a 3km walk toward the lake on Blvd Nahuel Huapi.

Information

Banco de la Provincia (Calle Las Frambuesas btwn Cerro Belvedere & Nahuel Huapi, El Cruce) Has an ATM.

HoraCero (☎ 495055; Av Arrayanes 45, El Cruce; internet per hr AR$4) Pizzeria with internet in back.

Park administration office (☎ 494152; Nahuel Huapi, La Villa)

Post office (Las Fucsias 40, lvl 3, El Cruce)

Tourist office (☎ 494124; www.villalaangostura.gov.ar; cnr Arrayanes & Av Siete Lagos, El Cruce; ⊗ 8:30am-9pm)

Sights & Activities

TREKKING, CYCLING & HORSEBACK RIDING

Several outfitters in town offer trekking, horseback riding and guided mountain-bike rides, and the tourist office provides information on each. Mountain biking is a great way to explore the surrounding area. **Cycling** (cnr Arrayanes & Las Mutisias) rents good quality bikes for AR$30/40 per half-/full day. For horseback riding (half-day to multiday trips), contact Tero Bogani at **Cabalgatas Correntoso** (☎ 02944-15-510559; www.cabalgatacorrentoso.com.ar; Cacique Antriao 1850), who brings the gaucho side of things to his trips. Prices start at AR$180 for a three-hour outing. For sailboat rides around the lake (which can be rippin' on a windy day), contact **Vela Aventura** (☎ 494834; www.vela-aventura .com.ar); a three-hour trip costs about AR$400 for up to four people.

La Angostura's **Museo Histórico Regional** (Nahuel Huapi & El Calafate; ⊗ 9:30am-5pm Tue-Sat, tours 11am, 1 & 3pm), on the road to La Villa, is worth popping into for a spot of Mapuche history, historical town photographs and old climbing relics.

PARQUE NACIONAL LOS ARRAYANES

This inconspicuous, often overlooked **park** (pedestrian/cyclist AR$20/30), encompassing the entire Quetrihué peninsula, protects remaining stands of the cinnamon-barked arrayán, a member of the myrtle family. In Mapudungun, language of the Mapuche, the peninsula's name means 'place of the arrayanes.'

The park headquarters is at the southern end of the peninsula, near the largest concentration of arrayanes, in an area known as **El Bosque**. It's a three-hour, 12km hike from La Villa to the tip of the peninsula, on an excellent **interpretive nature trail**; brochures are available in the tourist office at El Cruce. You can also hike out and get the ferry back from the point (p400), or vice versa. There are two small lakes along the trail. Regulations require hikers to enter the park before midday and leave it by 4pm in winter and around 6pm to 7pm in summer.

From the park's northern entrance at La Villa, a very steep 20-minute hike leads to two **panoramic overlooks** of Lago Nahuel Huapi.

CERRO BELVEDERE

A 4km **hiking trail** starts from Av Siete Lagos, northwest of the tourist office, and leads to an **overlook** with good views of Lago Correntoso, Nahuel Huapi and the surrounding mountains. It then continues another 3km to the 1992m summit. After visiting the overlook, retrace your steps to a nearby junction that leads to **Cascada Inayacal**, a 50m waterfall. If you're coming out here, get a map at the tourist office as the trails around here can be confusing.

CENTRO DE SKI CERRO BAYO

From June to September, lifts carry skiers from the 1050m base up to 1700m at this 'boutique' (read small but expensive) **winter resort** (☎ 494189; www.cerrobayoweb.com; full-day pass AR$94-165), 9km northeast of El Cruce via RP 66. All facilities, including rental equipment (AR$56 to AR$76), are available on-site.

Sleeping

Except for camping and Angostura's growing hostel scene, accommodations tend to be pricey; in summer, single rooms are almost impossible to find – expect to pay for two people.

Camping Cullumche (☎ 494160; moyano@uncu .edu.ar; Blvd Quetrihué s/n; campsites per person AR$20-25) Well signed from Blvd Nahuel Huapi, this secluded but large lakeside campground can get very busy in summer, but when it's quiet, it's lovely.

Italian Hostel (☎ 494376; www.italianhostel.com.ar; Los Marquis 215, El Cruce; dm AR$45; ⊛) With plenty of space and all the comforts you'd expect, this is the town's standout hostel. The kitchen is well equipped, you can use the *parrilla* and the lounge is comfy in a rustic kinda way. The only drawback – the 18-bed dorm.

Hostel La Angostura (☎ 494834; www.hostellaan gostura.com.ar; Barbagelata 157, El Cruce; dm/d AR$55/170; ⊛) Forget the short uphill slog to get here – it's worth it. Staying in this place feels like being out in the woods and there are great views from the balconies, a bar, ping-pong table, bike rental – the list goes on. Dorms are cramped but reasonable and have bathrooms.

Residencial Río Bonito (☎ 494110; riobonito@ciudad .com.ar; Topa Topa 260, El Cruce; s/d AR$120/150) Bright and cheery rooms in a converted family home a few blocks from the bus terminal. The big, comfortable dining/lounge area is a bonus, as are the friendly hosts.

Verena's Haus (☎ 494467; verenashaus@infovia .com.ar; Los Taiques 268, El Cruce; s/d AR$150/200; 🛜) With all the heart-shaped motifs and floral wallpaper, this one probably doesn't qualify as a hunting lodge, but it is a good deal for couples looking for a quiet, romantic spot. Rooms are big, spotless and packed with comfy features.

Hotel Angostura (☎ 494224; www.hotelangostura .com; Blvd Nahuel Huapi 1911, La Villa; s/d AR$210/250, bungalow AR$400-600; 🛜) Ignore the squishy rooms and the deer antler light fittings – this is an awesome location. It's perched up on a clifftop overlooking the bay and the national park; your biggest problem here is going to be neck crick from checking out the view – no matter which way you're walking.

Eating

There are several restaurants and *confiterías* in El Cruce along Los Arrayanes and its cross streets.

Gran Nevada (Av Arrayanes 106, El Cruce; mains AR$15-25; 🕐 lunch & dinner) With its big-screen TV (quite possibly showing a football game) and big, cheap set meals, this is a local favorite. Come hungry, leave happy.

Los Troncos (Av Arrayanes 67, El Cruce; mains AR$25-40; 🕐 breakfast, lunch & dinner) Specializing in 'mountain food,' this lovely little place serves up a range of tempting dishes, such as deer stew, trout with almond sauce and wild mushroom stew.

La Caballeriza (Av Arrayanes 44, El Cruce; mains AR$25-50; 🕐 lunch & dinner) The most upmarket *parrilla* in town has a good range of dishes, an intimate atmosphere and surprisingly reasonable prices.

La Encantada (☎ 495515; Cerro Belvedere 69, El Cruce; mains AR$30-50; 🕐 lunch & dinner) A cute little cottage offering all of your Patagonian and Argentine favorites. The food is carefully prepared and beautifully presented, and the atmosphere is warm and inviting. The *ojo de bife* (eye-fillet steak; AR$55) for two is a definite winner if you are a couple of carnivores.

La Buena Vida (Arrayanes 167; mains AR$35-50) A modern restaurant that is good for traditional dishes, along with some more exotic choices – try the Hungarian goulash, crepes, risotto or borscht.

Tinto Bistro (☎ 494924; Nahuel Huapi 34, El Cruce; mains AR$50-70; 🕐 lunch & dinner) Besides the fact that the food (regional cuisine prepared with European flair) is excellent, the owner, Martín Zorreguieta, is the brother of Máxima, princess of the Netherlands. Feast on that.

Getting There & Away

Villa la Angostura's **bus terminal** (cnr Av Siete Lagos & Av Arrayanes, El Cruce) is across the street from the tourist office in El Cruce. Some buses stop in El Cruce on runs between Bariloche and San Martín de los Andes.

For Chile, **Andesmar** (☎ 495217) goes over Paso Cardenal Samoré to Osorno (AR$80, 3½ hours).

There are numerous daily departures to Bariloche (AR$15, one hour) and two daily departures to Neuquén (AR$70, seven hours). Albus goes several times daily in summer to San Martín de los Andes (AR$45, four hours) by the scenic Ruta de los Siete Lagos. La Araucana has daily services to Villa Traful (AR$23, two hours).

Getting Around

La Villa and its surrounds are easily seen on foot, but if you're venturing further out, taxis are the best means of getting to the trailheads, although some are served by local buses. Both leave from the local bus terminal on Av Siete Lagos, just north of Av Arrayanes.

Transporte 15 de Mayo runs hourly buses from the terminal to La Villa (AR$1.30, 15 minutes), up Av Siete Lagos to Lago Correntoso (AR$1.30, 15 minutes), and south down Av Arrayanes to Puerto Manzano on Lago Nahuel Huapi (AR$1.30, 15 minutes). From July through September, and December through March, 15 de Mayo runs six or seven daily buses to the ski resort at Cerro Bayo (AR$10, one hour).

Two companies run daily ferries from the dock (next to Hotel Angostura in La Villa) to the tip of Quetrihué peninsula, Parque Nacional Los Arrayanes (one way AR$59 to AR$69, return AR$118 to AR$138, plus AR$20 national park entrance), meaning you can hike the peninsula and take the boat back (or vice versa). Purchase tickets at the dock before hiking out, to secure a space on the return. Check with the tourist office for ever-changing ferry times. The ride takes 45 minutes and you can put a bicycle on the boat.

BARILOCHE

☎ 02944 / pop 102,800 / elev 770m

Strung out along the shoreline of Lago Nahuel Huapi, in the middle of the national park of the same name, Bariloche (formally San Carlos de Bariloche) has one of the most gorgeous settings imaginable. This, combined with a wealth of summer and winter activities in the surrounding countryside, has helped it become, for better or worse, the Lake District's principal destination.

The soaring peaks of Cerros Catedral, López, Nireco and Shaihuenque (to name just a few) – all well over 2000m high – ring the town, giving picture-postcard views in nearly every direction.

These mountains aren't just for gazing, though – excellent snow coverage (sometimes exceeding 2m at the *end* of the season) makes this a winter wonderland, and a magnet for skiers and snowboarders from all over the world.

In summertime the nature buffs take over, hitting the hills to climb, hike trails, fish for trout and ride mountain bikes and horses.

There's so much fun to be had that this has become the destination for Argentine high school students' end of year celebrations. And if all this wasn't enough, Bariloche is also Argentina's chocolate capital and the only thing that approaches the amount of storefront window space dedicated to fresh chocolate is the infinite number of peculiar gnomes of all sizes and demeanors sold in nearly every shop downtown.

Officially founded in 1902, the city really began to attract visitors after the southern branch of the Ferrocarril Roca train line arrived in 1934 and architect Ezequiel Bustillo adapted Central European styles into a tasteful urban plan. Bariloche is now known for its alpine architecture, which is given a Patagonian twist through the use of local hardwoods and unique stone construction, as seen in the buildings of Bustillo's *centro cívico*.

The flip side of Bariloche's gain in popularity is uncontrolled growth: in the last two decades, the town has suffered as its quaint neighborhoods have given way to high-rise apartments and time-shares. The silver lining is that many accommodations have remained reasonably priced.

Orientation

Bariloche is 460km southwest of Neuquén via RN 237. Entering the town from the east, RN 237 becomes the Av 12 de Octubre (also called Costanera), continuing westward to the lakeside resort of Llao Llao. Southbound Calle Onelli becomes RN 258 to El Bolsón, on the border of Chubut province.

The principal commercial area is along Av Bartolomé Mitre. Do not confuse VA O'Connor (also known as Vicealmirante O'Connor or Eduardo O'Connor) with similarly named John O'Connor, which cross each other near the lakefront. Similarly, Perito Moreno and Ruiz Moreno intersect near Diagonal Capraro, at the east end of the downtown area.

Information

IMMIGRATION

Immigration office (☎ 423043; Libertad 191)

INTERNET ACCESS

El Refugio (Av Bartolomé Mitre 106, 1st fl; per hr AR$3) Upstairs; fast connection.

LAUNDRY

Laverap Quaglia (btwn Perito Moreno & Elflein; full service AR$12-16); Rolando (☎ 432628; btwn Av Bartolomé Mitre & Perito Moreno; full service AR$15)

MEDICAL SERVICES

Hospital (☎ 426100; Perito Moreno 601) *Long* waits, no charge.

Sanatorio San Carlos (☎ 429000/01/02, emergency 430000; Av Bustillo, Km 1; consultations AR$50) Excellent medical clinic.

MONEY

Banks with ATMs are ubiquitous in the downtown area.

Cambio Sudamérica (Av Bartolomé Mitre 63) Change foreign cash and traveler's checks here.

POST

Post office (Perito Moreno 175)

TOURIST INFORMATION

ACA (Automóvil Club Argentino; ☎ 423001; Av 12 de Octubre 785) Argentina's auto club; has provincial road maps.

Club Andino Bariloche (☎ 422266; www.activepatagonia.com.ar, www.clubandino.com.ar; 20 de Febrero 30; 9am-1pm & 4-8:30pm Dec-Mar, Mon-Fri only Apr-Nov) Best source of hiking information on Nahuel Huapi. Takes reservations and gives information on hikers' refuges in the park. For park details, see p410.

THE LAKE DISTRICT

BARILOCHE

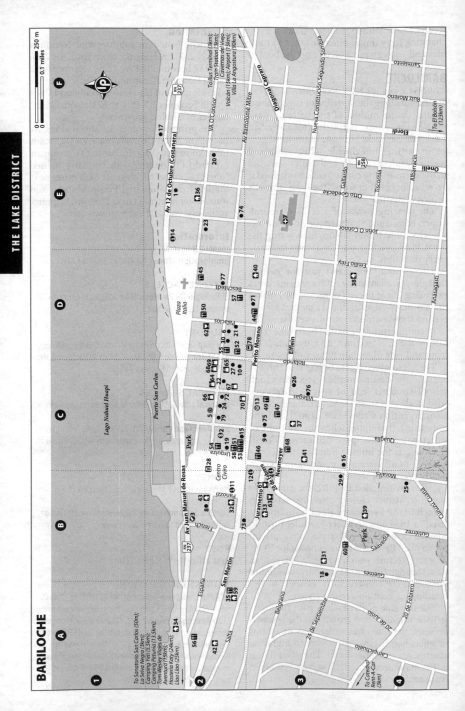

Municipal tourist office (☎ 429850; www.barilo chepatagonia.info; Centro Cívico; ⏱ 8am-9pm) It has many giveaways, including useful maps and the blatantly commercial but still useful *Guía Busch*, updated biannually and loaded with basic tourist information about Bariloche and the Lake District.

Nahuel Huapi national park office (Intendencia del Parque Nacional Nahuel Huapi; ☎ 423121; www .nahuelhuapi.gov.ar; San Martín 24; ⏱ 8am-4pm Mon-Fri, 9am-3pm Sat & Sun)

Provincial tourist office (☎ 423188/89; secturrn@ bariloche.com.ar; cnr Av 12 de Octubre & Emilio Frey) Has information on the province, including an excellent provincial map and useful brochures in English and Spanish.

TRAVEL AGENCIES
Hiver Turismo (☎ 423792; Av Bartolomé Mitre 387) One of numerous agencies along Av Bartolomé Mitre and immediate cross streets.

Sights
A stroll through Bariloche's **centro cívico**, with its beautiful log-and-stone buildings designed by architect Ezequiel Bustillo, is a must. Besides, posing for a photo with one of the barrel-toting Saint Bernards makes for a classic Argentine snapshot, and views over the lake are superb.

The buildings house the municipal tourist office and the **Museo de la Patagonia** (☎ 422309; Centro Cívico; admission by donation; ⏱ 10am-12:30pm & 2-5pm Tue-Fri, 10am-6pm Sat). The latter is filled with archaeological and ethnographic materials, life-like stuffed animals and enlightening historical evaluations on such topics as Mapuche resistance to the Conquest of the Desert.

Cavernas del Viejo Volcán (☎ 529909; Villegas 246, 1st fl, Bariloche; with/without transport AR$60/46; ⏱ tours 11:30am, 1:30pm & 3pm) is a cave complex, 15km east of Bariloche, which was inhabited for nearly 8000 years by the Mapuche and other tribes. Parts of the cave feature reasonably well-preserved rock-art specimens. A guided tour is compulsory, and takes you 130m into Cerro Leones then out onto the summit where there is a lookout with majestic views of the surrounding countryside. It is possible (but not a whole lot cheaper) to make your own way there on public transport. Either way, reservations are essential – contact the Bariloche office for more information.

Activities
Bariloche and the Nahuel Huapi region are one of Argentina's major outdoor recreation areas, and numerous operators offer a variety

of activities, particularly horseback riding, mountain biking and white-water rafting. The following have excellent reputations:

Overland Patagonia (☎ 456327; www.overlandpatagonia.com; Villegas 195) Numerous trips throughout Patagonia. Also ski transfers for AR$16 from any hotel in town.

Tom Wesley Viajes de Aventura (☎ /fax 435040; Av Bartolomé Mitre 385) Horseback riding, mountain biking; been long in the business. Also at Av Bustillo, Km 15.5.

MOUNTAINEERING & TREKKING

The national park office distributes a brochure with a simple map, adequate for initial planning, that rates hikes as easy, medium or difficult and suggests possible loops. Many of these hikes are detailed in Lonely Planet's *Trekking in the Patagonian Andes*.

Club Andino Bariloche (p401) provides loads of information (including on camping), and issues obligatory permits for trekking in Parque Nacional Nahuel Huapi. For AR$20, its *Mapa General de la Guía de Sendas y Picadas* is cartographically mediocre, but has good trail descriptions and is indispensable for planning. It sells three additional trekking maps, all of which include mountain-bike trails.

SKIING

Nahuel Huapi's ski resort, **Cerro Catedral** (☎ 409000; www.catedralaltapatagonia.com), was once South America's trendiest, and has been superseded only by Las Leñas (near Mendoza) and resorts in Chile. Las Leñas has far superior snow (dry powder), but it lacks Catedral's strong point: views. There's nothing like looking over the shimmering lakes of Nahuel Huapi from its snowy slopes.

Day passes run between AR$90 and AR$150, depending on the season. If you need lessons, stop into the ski schools at Cerro Catedral or Club Andino Bariloche (p401). Two-hour private lessons run at about AR$330. For rental equipment, try **Baruzzi Deportes** (☎ 424922; Urquiza 250) or **Martín Pescador** (☎ 422275; martinpescador@bariloche.com.ar; Rolando 257). Equipment is also available on-site. Sets of skis, boots and poles rent for between AR$54 and AR$70, and snowboarding gear between AR$75 and AR$98 per day, depending on the season.

MOUNTAIN BIKING

Bicycles are ideal for the Circuito Chico (though this 60km loop demands endurance; see p410) and other trips near Bariloche; most roads are paved and even the gravel roads are good. Mountain-bike rental, including gloves and helmet, costs AR$40 to AR$60 per day at a number of places. Try **Bikeway** (☎ 424202; www.bikeway.com.ar; VA O'Connor 867) or **Dirty Bikes** (☎ 425616; www.dirtybikes.com.ar; VA O'Connor 681). Guided tours with bilingual guides run at about AR$180 per day.

FISHING

Fly-fishing draws visitors from around the world to Argentina's accessible Andean-Patagonian parks, from Lago Puelo and Los Alerces in the south to Lanín in the north.

On larger lakes, such as Nahuel Huapi, trolling is the preferred method, while fly-fishing is the rule on most rivers. The season runs mid-November to mid-April. For more information, contact the **Asociación de Pesca y Caza Nahuel Huapi** (Hunting & Fishing Club; ☎ 421515; www.apcnh.com; cnr Costanera 12 de Octubre & Onelli). For rental equipment and guide hire, try Baruzzi Deportes or Martín Pescador (see left). Both offer guided fishing trips for about AR$1400 per day for one or two people (price is the same either way and includes all equipment, lunch, transport and guide). Fishing licenses (AR$75/250/350 per day/week/season) are required and available at these shops.

HORSEBACK RIDING

Most travel agencies along Av Bartolomé Mitre offer horseback-riding trips. For something special, contact the amiable Carol Jones at **Cabalgatas Carol Jones** (☎ 426508; www.caroljones.com.ar), who offers half-day horseback riding from her family *estancia* outside of town for AR$220 per person. The price includes transport to/from town and an excellent *asado* (barbecue grill) outside. She also offers multi-day pack trips by horse for AR$500 per person per day. Carol speaks English. All trips require a minimum of two people.

RAFTING & KAYAKING

Rafting and kayaking on the Río Limay and the Río Manso have become increasingly popular in recent years. The best time to be on the rivers is November through February, though you can raft October through Easter.

In business since 1991, **eXtremo Sur** (☎ 427301; www.extremosur.com; Morales 765) offers several trips on the Río Manso: the Manso Inferior (class II to III, AR$195 per person) is suitable for all ages; the Manso a la Frontera (class III to IV, AR$250 per person, ages 14 and up) is a fun and beautiful stretch of the river before the Chilean border. There's also a three-day Expedición Río Manso (class III to IV, AR$1350 to AR$1500), where you camp riverside at excellent facilities. For the last, *asados* and all food and drink are included in the price.

Aguas Blancas (☎ 432799; www.aguasblancas.com .ar; Morales 564) also has an excellent reputation and offers similar trips. It's located inside Albergue Patagonia Andina.

Pura Vida Patagonia (☎ 15-414053; www.puravida patagonia.com) offers kayaking trips on the Lago Nahuel Huapi, ranging from half-day stints to overnight camp-'n'-kayak trips, custom-designed to match your skill level.

PARAGLIDING

The mountains around Bariloche make for spectacular paragliding. If you wish to take to the sky, it will cost you around AR$260 for a 20-minute to half-hour tandem flight with, among others, **Luis Rosenkjer** (☎ 427588) or **Parapente Bariloche** (☎ 15-552403; Cerro Otto base).

Courses

La Montaña (☎ 524-212; www.lamontana.com; Elflein 251) is a recommended Spanish school.

Tours

Countless tourist agencies along and near Av Bartolomé Mitre, such as Catedral Turismo (see boxed text, p409), run minibus tours to the national park and as far south as El Bolsón. Prices range from AR$40 for a half-day trip along the Circuito Chico to AR$125 to San Martín de los Andes via the scenic Ruta de los Siete Lagos.

Overland Patagonia (opposite) offers a series of well-received camping tours; they range from the four-day Safari Siete Lagos (AR$900 food not included) to the 18-day Safari del Fin del Mundo (AR$6200 plus food), which goes all the way to Tierra del Fuego. Its local tours always offer a little more kick (such as hikes) than those offered by most agencies.

Adventure Center (☎ 428368; www.adventurecenter .com.ar; Perito Moreno 30) offers four-day trips down the fabled RN 40 as far as El Calafate for AR$500 per person. Trips run from the end of September to April. Prices include accommodation, but national park entries and food are separate.

Bariloche Moto Tours (☎ 462687; www.barilochemo totours.com) organizes custom-tailored motorbike tours to everywhere between southern Patagonia and northern Chile and beyond.

Espacio (☎ 431372; www.islavictoriayarrayanes.com; Av Bartolomé Mitre 139) offers cruises on Nahuel Huapi lake in its 40ft catamaran *Cau Cau* during summer. Reserve your place two days in advance.

Tren a Vapor (☎ 423858; www.trenhistoricoavapor .com.ar; ☻ Nov-Mar) runs full-day trips (a 40km circuit) in a five-wagon steam train built in 1912, stopping for photo ops at a bridge on the river Nirihau and Perito Moreno station, followed by two short guided walks to Laguna Los Juncos and Cerro Elefante. Buy tickets at the train station near the bus terminal. Fares are AR$90/135/220 for an adult in 2nd/1st/special class; AR$65/100/140 for a child.

Festivals & Events

For 10 days in August, Bariloche holds its **Fiesta Nacional de la Nieve** (National Snow Festival). In January and February the **Festival de Música de Verano** (Summer Music Festival) puts on several different events, including the **Festival de Música de Cámara** (Chamber Music Festival), the **Festival de Bronces** (Brass Festival) and the **Festival de Música Antigua** (Ancient Music Festival). On May 3 is the **Fiesta Nacional de la Rosa Mosqueta**, celebrating the fruit of the wild shrub used in many regional delicacies.

Sleeping

From camping and private houses to five-star hotels, Bariloche's abundant accommodations make it possible to find good value even in high season, when reservations are a good idea. Prices peak during ski season (July and August), drop slightly during high season (January and February) and are lowest the rest of the year. The following are high-season prices.

BUDGET

Bariloche has numerous excellent hostels; all those listed here arrange excursions in Nahuel Huapi and offer weekend *asados*.

La Selva Negra (☎ 441013; campingselvanegra@ speedy.com.ar; Av Bustillo, Km 2.9; campsites per person AR$33) Located 3km west of town on the road to Llao Llao, this is the nearest organized camping area. It has good facilities, and you can step outside your tent to pick apples in the fall.

our pick Hostel Patanuk (☎ 434991; www.patanuk
.com; Av JM Rosas 585; dm/d AR$40/120; ☞) Bariloche's
only lakefront hostel is a definite winner. Big
picture windows put you right in front of
the water and mountains. Hardwood floors,
a spacious kitchen and comfy lounge round
out the picture.

Hostel 1004 (☎ 432228; www.penthouse1004.com
.ar; San Martín 127, 10th fl, Bariloche Center bldg; dm AR$40,
d without bathroom AR$120; ☞) From the 10th floor,
this hostel has the most awesome views of any
of the hotels in town. Dorms are spacious,
with three or six beds and there's a giant living room, complete with sofas, fireplace and
big wooden tables. There's no sign; enter the
Bariloche Center, take the elevator to the 10th
floor and look for room 1004.

Hostel 41 Below (☎ 436-433; www.hostel41below
.com; Juramento 94; dm/d without bathroom AR$44/140;
🖳 ☞) Intimate, Kiwi-run hostel with clean
dorms, fine doubles (with good views) and
mellow vibe. The kitchen and common room
are excellent and it also offers great rooms
(AR$225/1350/4000 per day/week/month)
in a nearby apartment.

Hostel Pudu (☎ 429738; www.hostelpudu.com; Salta
459; dm/d AR$45/160; 🖳 ☞) Cool hostel run by a
young Argentine and an Irish couple. A bit
maze-like, but cozy and laid-back – with awesome views from every room. Great vibe, tiny
bar downstairs and small garden for *asados*.

Hospedaje Wikter (☎ 423248; www.hospedajewik
ter.com.ar; Güemes 566; s/d AR$60/80; ☞) Up the
hill away from the center, this friendly little
hospedaje offers spacious rooms in a bright,
modern building. Bathrooms are bigger than
most in this price range and some rooms have
good views.

Other campgrounds between Bariloche and
Llao Llao include **Camping Yeti** (☎ 442073; Av
Bustillo, Km 5.6; campsites AR$30) and **Camping Petunia**
(☎ 461969; Av Bustillo, Km 13.5; campsites AR$32).

MIDRANGE & TOP END
Hostería Katy (☎ 448023; www.gringospatagonia.com;
Av Bustillo, Km 24.3; s/d AR$125/250; 🖳 ☞) One of
the closest *hosterías* to the national park, this
one's set in a charming family home. It's a
family-run operation – the rooms are warm
and comfortable, with big bathrooms and
firm beds.

Hostería El Ciervo Rojo (☎ 435241; www.interpatago
nia.com/elciervorojo; Elflein 115; s/d AR$140/180; 🖳) Book
in advance if you'd like to shack up at this
pleasant, attractively restored *hostería*. Slate-

floored rooms with plenty of homey touches
and spacious bathrooms make it a popular
choice. Upstairs rooms are superior to those
downstairs. The lobby is excellent.

Hostería Ivalu (☎ 423237; Emilio Frey 535; s/d
AR$150/180) Up the hill overlooking town, this
friendly little *hostería* offers spacious, slightly
aging rooms, kept spotless by its friendly
owner.

Hostería La Paleta del Pintor (☎ 422220; 20 de
Febrero 630; s/d AR$150/180) Everything about this
place screams 'cute,' but the rooms are big
and airy, with small but spotless bathrooms
and big-screen TVs.

Hostería Adquintue (☎ 522229; www.interpat
agonia.com/adquintue; VA O'Connor 766; s/d AR$150/200)
Spacious, if slightly plain, rooms on the edge
of the busy downtown district. Good value
for the location.

Hotel 7 de Febrero (☎ 422244; www.hotel7defebrero
.com.ar; Perito Moreno 534; r from AR$250; ☞) Nothing
too exciting going on decor-wise, but the
rooms are big, the fittings new and overall
it's a good deal for the price. Pay another
AR$40 for a room out the back with stun-
ning lake views.

Hotel Carlos V (☎ 425474; www.carlosvpatagonia.com
.ar; Morales 420; s/d AR$216/285; 🖳 ☞) At first glance
a fairly standard business hotel, the Carlos V
has plenty of hidden charm. That, the central
location and the good-sized rooms make it
hard to beat.

Hotel Tirol (☎ 426152; www.hosteriatirol.com.ar;
Libertad 175; s/d AR$230/250; 🖳 ☞) Right in the
middle of town, this charming little lodge offers comfortable, spacious rooms. Those out
the back have spectacular views out over the
lake and to the mountain range beyond, as
does the bright sitting/breakfast area.

Hotel Panamericano (☎ /fax 425850; www.pana
mericanobariloche.com; San Martín 536; r from AR$600;
🖳 ☞ 🛉) Bariloche's biggest hotel (covering nearly three city blocks with over-street
bridges connecting the different sectors) pulls
out all the stops – a couple of restaurants, a casino, piano bar etc. Rooms are all you'd expect
for the price, with a couple of surprising flaws,
such as cracked tiles and fraying carpet.

Eating
Bariloche has some of Argentina's best food,
and it would take several wallet-breaking,
belt-bursting and intestinally challenging weeks to sample all of the worthwhile
restaurants. Regional specialties, including

cordero (lamb, cooked over an open flame), *jabalí* (wild boar), *ciervo* (venison) and *trucha* (trout), are especially worth trying.

BUDGET

Helados Jauja (Perito Moreno 14; ice cream AR$3-7) Ask anyone in town who serves the best ice cream in Bariloche and they'll reply with one word: 'Jauja.' Many say it's the best in the country.

Rock Chicken (San Martín 234; mains AR$15-25; 🕐 10am-late) Late night munchies? Midday junk-food cravings? The beef, burgers and fried chicken here won't be winning any culinary awards, but they get the job done.

Huang Ji Zhong (Rolando 268; mains AR$18-30; 🕐 lunch & dinner) There's exactly one Chinese restaurant in town, and it's not bad – all the usual suspects at decent prices.

La Esquina (Urquiza & Perito Moreno; mains AR$18-35; 🕐 breakfast, lunch & dinner) The most atmospheric *confitería* in town has good coffee, reasonably priced sandwiches and burgers, and some good regional specialties.

Corvina (VA O'Connor 511; mains AR$20-30; 🕐 lunch & dinner) The best vegetarian restaurant for miles around has a small but varied menu with a couple of Asian-inspired dishes. Has good-value set lunches (AR$28).

Los Tehuelches (Beschtedt 281; mains AR$20-30; 🕐 lunch & dinner) The best-value *parrilla* in town, this no-frills place attracts a lot more locals than tourists. The range of set meals is impressive and a *bife de chorizo* (sirloin) with salad for AR$25 is nothing to be sneered at in this town. The house red is not recommended, except for fans of the very rough hangover.

La Trattoria de la Famiglia Bianchi (☎ 421596; España 590; mains AR$20-50; 🕐 lunch & dinner) Finally, an Italian restaurant that offers something a little different. Excellent, creative pastas, a good range of meat dishes and some wonderful risottos, with ingredients such as seafood and wild mushrooms (AR$37).

MIDRANGE & TOP END

Map Room (Urquiza 248; mains AR$25-35; 🕐 11am-1am) A cozy little pub-restaurant with a good range of beers and some interesting menu items. The American breakfast (AR$28) is the real thing – a real belly-buster. Check out the 'after work' happy hours, when beers are half price.

Familia Weiss (Palacios 167; mains AR$25-45; 🕐 lunch & dinner) A popular family restaurant offering good-value regional specialties such as venison, trout and goulash. The picture menu's

handy for the Spanish-challenged, there's a good atmosphere and nightly live music.

La Marca (Urquiza 240; mains AR$25-55; 🕐 lunch & dinner) Upscale *parrilla* with reasonable (for Bariloche) prices. Choose from the impressive range of brochettes (shasliks) – beef, chicken, venison, lamb and salmon. On a sunny day, grab a garden table at the side.

our pick **Tarquino** (☎ 421601; 24 de Septiembre & Saavedra; mains AR$30-45; 🕐 lunch & dinner) Built entirely of Patagonian cypress, this esteemed restaurant resembles a hobbit house with its wood stairway, carved wooden doorway, fireplace and troll-like architecture. The small menu is almost entirely *parrillada* (including a delicious *cordero*, or grilled lamb), though a pasta and a trout dish grace the menu as well. One of Bariloche's best.

Días de Zapata (☎ 423128; Morales 362; mains AR$30-50; 🕐 lunch & dinner) A warm and inviting little Mexican restaurant. Dishes tend more toward the Tex Mex than you would think (the owners hail from Mexico City) but the flavors are good and the servings generous.

La Marmite (☎ 423685; Av Bartolomé Mitre 329; mains AR$30-50; 🕐 lunch & dinner) A trusty choice for Patagonian standards like trout and venison. Also the place to come for chocolate fondue (AR$70 for two), in case you haven't eaten enough of the stuff cold.

Cerros Nevados (Perito Moreno 338; all you can eat AR$35; 🕐 lunch & dinner) Every Argentine town has at least one gut-busting *tenedor libre*; Bariloche's lays it on thick, with plenty of *parrilla* items, pastas, salads and *fiambres* (cold meats).

El Boliche de Alberto (☎ 431433; Villegas 347; mains AR$35-50; 🕐 lunch & dinner) It's worth dining at this esteemed *parrilla* simply to see the astonished look on tourists' faces when a slab of beef the size of a football lands on the table; it's the AR$46 *bife de chorizo* (the AR$35 portion is plenty). If the place is full, check out the nearby sister restaurants at Elfein 49 and 158.

Drinking

For a rundown on cultural events, live music etc, pick up a copy of *La Puerta*, a free weekly events magazine available in cafes and bars around town.

Cruz Bar (cnr Juramento & 20 de Febrero) A laid-back little corner bar serving a good range of local microbrewery beers at excellent prices. The music's cool and the decor eclectic. Live DJs play on weekends.

Pilgrim (Palacios 167) This pub is a good place to knock back a few beers in a friendly atmosphere. Try the Cervezería Blest brews on tap.

South Bar (Juramento s/n) Mellow local pub where you can actually have a conversation while you drink your beer. Darts, too.

Shopping
CHOCOLATE
Bariloche is renowned for its chocolates, and dozens of stores downtown, from national chains to mom-and-pop shops, sell chocolates of every style imaginable. Quality of course varies, so don't get sick on the cheap stuff.

Mamuschka (☎ 423294; Av Bartolomé Mitre 298) Quite simply, the best chocolate in town. Don't skip it. Seriously.

Benroth (☎ 424491; Av Bartolomé Mitre 150) In our humble opinion, the best one after Mamuschka. Definitely try it.

La Mexicana (☎ 422505; Av Bartolomé Mitre 288) Bariloche's first chocolate store, started by the Ritter family in 1948, still produces delicious chocolates and fine *dulces* (jams). It's still owned by the same family, though the cocoa beans are no longer imported from Mexico, but from Ecuador and Brazil.

Abuela Goye (☎ 433861; Av Bartolomé Mitre 258) Another of Bariloche's long-time chocolate makers. Still small and still worth trying.

CLOTHING & CRAFTS
Arbol (☎ 423032; Av Bartolomé Mitre 263; ☉ Mon–Sat) For the latest in Patagonian fashion, drop by this Bariloche original, which produces beautifully designed fleeces, woolens, hats and jackets, as well as ceramics and decorative pieces. It has some beautiful clothing for women.

Huitral-Hue (☎ 426760; Villegas 250; ☉ Mon–Sat) Good selection of traditional ponchos, textiles and wool sweaters.

Paseo de los Artesanos (cnr Villegas & Perito Moreno) Local craftspeople display wares of wool, wood, leather, silver and other media here.

Getting There & Away
AIR
Aerolíneas Argentinas (☎ 422425; Av Bartolomé Mitre 185) has flights to Buenos Aires (AR$700) twice daily Monday through Wednesday and three times daily the rest of the week. In high season there are direct weekly flights to Córdoba and El Calafate and possibly Ushuaia.

LAN (☎ 431-077; www.lan.com; Av Bartolomé Mitre 500) flies to Chile and Buenos Aires, and **LADE**

(☎ 424-812; www.lade.com.ar; Villegas 480) covers southern destinations.

BOAT
It's possible to travel by boat and bus to Chile aboard the Cruce de Lagos tour. See the boxed text, opposite.

BUS
Bariloche's **bus terminal** (☎ 432860) and train station are east of town across the Río Ñireco on RN 237. Shop around for the best deals, since fares vary and there are frequent promotions. During high season, it's wise to buy tickets at least a day in advance. The bus terminal tourist office is helpful.

The principal route to Chile is over the Cardenal A Samoré (Puyehue) pass to Osorno (AR$80, five hours) and Puerto Montt (AR$80, six hours), which has onward connections to northern and southern Chilean destinations. Several companies make the run.

To San Martín de los Andes and Junín de los Andes, Albus, Transportes Ko-Ko and **Turismo Algarrobal** (☎ 427698) take the scenic (though often chokingly dusty) Ruta de los Siete Lagos (RN 234; see p392) during summer, and the longer, paved La Rinconada (RN 40) route during the rest of the year.

For northern destinations such as San Juan, La Rioja, Catamarca, Tucumán, Jujuy and Salta you'll probably have to go to Mendoza. Buses to northeastern destinations usually connect through Buenos Aires, though you could also head to Rosario where there are frequent services northeast.

The following services have at least three departures per day.

Destination	Cost (AR$)	Duration (hr)
Bahía Blanca	140	12–14
Buenos Aires	280	20–23
Córdoba	260	22
El Bolsón	25	2
Esquel	60	4½
Junín de los Andes	30	3
Mendoza	230	19
Neuquén	63	7
Puerto Madryn	175	14–18
Río Gallegos	320	28
Rosario	280	23–24
San Martín de los Andes	37	4
San Rafael	196	15
Trelew	220	13–19
Viedma	100	12
Villa la Angostura	14	1½

THE CRUCE DE LAGOS

One of Argentina's classic journeys is the Cruce de Lagos, a scenic 12-hour bus-and-boat trip over the Andes to Puerto Montt, Chile. Operated exclusively by **Catedral Turismo** (☎ 425444; www .cruceandino.com; Palacios 263; per person AR$880), the trip begins around 8am in Bariloche (departure times vary) with a shuttle from Catedral's office to Puerto Pañuelo near Hotel Llao Llao. The passenger ferry from Puerto Pañuelo leaves immediately after the shuttle arrives, so if you want to have tea at Llao Llao, get there ahead of time on your own (but make sure you bought your ticket in advance). Service is daily in the summer and weekdays the rest of the year. In winter (mid-April to September), the trip takes two days, and passengers are required to stay the night in Peulla, Chile, where the only hotel will cost you an additional AR$500. You may be able to stay at **Hotel Puerto Blest** (☎ 425443; r AR$320), which is a fair bit cheaper. Ask about this option at Catedral Turismo. If you just visit Puerto Blest (boats leave from Puerto Pañuelo) and are not overnighting as part of the two-day lake crossing, the hotel charges AR$220; essentially the price is higher for those who are taking the full lake crossing.

Bicycles are allowed on the boats, and sometimes on the buses (provided you dismantle them), so cyclists may end up having to ride the stretches between Bariloche and Pañuelo (25km), Puerto Blest and Puerto Alegre (15km), Puerto Frías and Peulla (27km), and Petrohué and Puerto Montt (76km); the tourist office may have info about alternative transport between Petrohué and Puerto Montt for cyclists hoping to avoid the ride.

In winter it's not possible to purchase segments of the trip (except between Puerto Pañuelo and Puerto Blest; AR$120). During summertime (from December to April), it's possible to buy just the boat sections (AR$725). Either way, if you're cycling, Catedral Turismo will cut your rate slightly since you won't be riding the buses. Though the trip rarely sells out, it's best to book it at least a day or two in advance.

TRAIN

The **Tren Patagonico** (www.trenpatagonico-sa.com.ar) leaves the **train station** (☎ 423172; 12 de Octubre 2400, downtown office at B Mitre 125 local 5), across the Río Ñireco next to the bus terminal. Departures for Viedma (16 hours) are 5pm Thursday and Sunday; fares range from AR$57 in *economica* to AR$229 in *cama* (1st-class sleeper). Departure times change frequently so it's best to check with the tourist office beforehand.

Getting Around

TO/FROM THE AIRPORT

Bariloche's **airport** (☎ 405016) is 15km east of town via RN 237 and RP 80. A *remise* costs about AR$50. Bus 72 (AR$2.50) leaves from the main bus stop on Perito Moreno (see following).

BUS

At the main local bus stop, on Perito Moreno between Rolando and Palacios, Codao del Sur and Ómnibus 3 de Mayo run hourly buses to Cerro Catedral for AR$1.50 one way. Codao uses Av de los Pioneros, while 3 de Mayo takes Av Bustillo. Some bus fares are cheaper when bought inside the **3 de Mayo ticket office** (☎ 425648; Perito Moreno 480), where you can also

pick up handy *horarios* (schedules) for all destinations.

From 6am to midnight, municipal bus 20 leaves the main bus stop every 20 minutes for the attractive lakeside settlements of Llao Llao and Puerto Pañuelo (AR$3, 40 minutes). Bus 10 goes to Colonia Suiza (AR$3, 50 minutes) 14 times daily. During summer three of these, at 8:05am, noon and 5:40pm, continue to Puerto Pañuelo, allowing you to do most of the Circuito Chico (p410) using public transport. Departure times from Puerto Pañuelo back to Bariloche via Colonia Suiza are 9:40am, 1:40pm and 6:40pm. You can also walk any section and flag down buses en route.

Ómnibus 3 de Mayo buses 50 and 51 go to Lago Gutiérrez (AR$6) every 30 minutes, while in summer the company's Línea Mascardi goes to Villa Mascardi/Los Rápidos (AR$3) three times daily. Ómnibus 3 de Mayo's Línea El Manso goes twice on Friday to Río Villegas and El Manso (AR$12), on the southwestern border of Parque Nacional Nahuel Huapi.

Buses 70, 71 and 83 stop at the main bus stop, connecting downtown with the bus terminal (AR$1.60).

CAR

Bariloche is loaded with the standard car-rental agencies and is one of the cheapest places to rent in the country. Prices vary greatly depending on season and demand, but usually come in around AR$200 per day with 200km.

Andes (☎ 431648; www.andesrentacar.com.ar; San Martín 162)

Budget (☎ 442482; www.budgetbariloche.com; B Mitre 717)

Catedral Rent-a-Car (☎ 441488; www.autoscatedral .com.ar; Pioneros 5645) Call for your car to be dropped off.

Hertz (☎ 423457; www.milletrentacar.com.ar; Quaglia 352)

HITCHHIKING

It's easy to hitch along Av Bustillo as far as Km 8, after which traffic thins out and catching a lift means waiting longer. In summer it's usually not to difficult to get around the Circuito Chico by thumb.

TAXI

A taxi from the bus terminal to the center of town costs around AR$12. Taxis within town generally don't go over the AR$6 mark.

PARQUE NACIONAL NAHUEL HUAPI

☎ 02944

One of Argentina's most-visited national parks, Nahuel Huapi occupies 7500 sq km in mountainous southwestern Neuquén and western Río Negro provinces. The park's centerpiece is Lago Nahuel Huapi, a glacial remnant over 100km long that covers more than 500 sq km. To the west, a ridge of high peaks separates Argentina from Chile; the tallest is 3554m Monte Tronador, an extinct volcano that still lives up to its name (meaning 'Thunderer') when blocks of ice tumble from its glaciers. During the summer months, wildflowers blanket the alpine meadows.

Nahuel Huapi was created to preserve local flora and fauna, including its Andean-Patagonian forests and rare animals. Tree species are much the same as those found in Parque Nacional Los Alerces (p465), while the important animal species include the huemul (Andean deer) and the miniature deer known as pudú. Most visitors are unlikely to see either of these, but several species of introduced deer are common, as are native birds.

Information

A good source of information about the park is the national park office in Bariloche (see p403).

For trekking maps and information about hiking in the region, see Lonely Planet's *Trekking in the Patagonian Andes*, by Carolyn McCarthy or, if you read Spanish, the locally published *Las Montañas de Bariloche*, by Toncek Arko and Raúl Izaguirre.

Circuito Chico

One of the area's most popular and scenic driving excursions, the Circuito Chico begins on Av Bustillo, on Bariloche's outskirts, and continues to the tranquil resort of **Llao Llao**, named for the 'Indian bread' fungus from the coihue tree. At **Cerro Campanario** (Av Bustillo, Km 18), the **Aerosilla Campanario** (☎ 427274) lifts passengers to a panoramic view of Lago Nahuel Huapi for AR$25.

Llao Llao's **Puerto Pañuelo** is the point of departure for the boat and bus excursion across the Andes to Chile, as well as to Parque Nacional Los Arrayanes on Península Quetrihué, though you can visit Los Arrayanes more easily and cheaply from Villa la Angostura (p398).

Even if you don't plan to spend a night in **Hotel Llao Llao** (☎ 448530; www.llaollao.com.ar; d from AR$1250, cabañas/studios AR$3300/3600; ▯ ▯ ▯ ▯ ▯), Argentina's most famous hotel, take a stroll around the grounds. From Llao Llao you can head across to **Colonia Suiza**, named for its early Swiss colonists. A modest *confitería* has excellent pastries, and there are several campgrounds.

The road passes the trailhead to 2076m **Cerro López**, a three-hour climb, before returning to Bariloche. At the top of Cerro López it's possible to spend the night at Club Andino Bariloche's **Refugio López** (www.cerrolopezbariloche .com.ar; dm about AR$40; ☉ mid-Dec–mid-Apr), where meals are also available.

Although travel agencies offer the Circuito Chico as a half-day tour (AR$47 through most agencies in Bariloche), it's easily done on public transportation or, if you're up for a 60km pedal, by bicycle (p404). Less enthusiastic cyclists can hop on a bus to Km 18.600 and rent a bike at **Bike Cordillera** (☎ 524828; www.cordillerabike .com). This way you'll bike much less, avoid busy Av Bustillo and take advantage of the loop's more scenic sections. Call ahead to reserve a bike.

Cerro Otto

Cerro Otto (1405m) is an 8km hike on a gravel road west from Bariloche. There's enough traffic that hitchhiking is feasible, and it's also

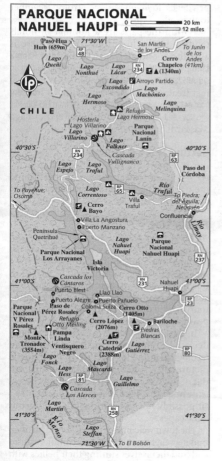

PARQUE NACIONAL NAHUEL HAUPI

a steep and tiring but rewarding bicycle route. The **Teleférico Cerro Otto** (☎ 441035; Av de Los Pioneros, Km 5) carries adult/child passengers to the summit for AR$55/25; a free bus leaves Bariloche from the corner of Av Bartolomé Mitre and Villegas or Perito Moreno and Independencia to the mountain base. Bring food and drink – prices at the summit *confitería* are nearly as painful as the walk up there.

Piedras Blancas (☎ 430417; www.piedrasblancasbariloche.com; Cerro Otto, Km 6) is the nearest ski area to Bariloche, and a popular area for summertime hiking.

There's a trail from Piedras Blancas to Club Andino's **Refugio Berghof** (☎ in Bariloche 422266; info@activepatagonia.com.ar; dm AR$40-50), at an elevation of 1240m; make reservations, since there

are only 20 beds. Meals are available here. The *refugio* also contains the **Museo de Montaña Otto Meiling** (guided visit AR$8), named for a pioneering climber.

Cerro Catedral

This 2388m peak (☎ 409000; www.catedralaltapatagonia.com), 20km southwest of Bariloche, is the area's most important snow-sports center, open from mid-June to mid-October. Several chairlifts and the **Aerosilla Cerro Bellavista** (AR$70) carry passengers up to 2000m, where there's a restaurant-*confitería* offering excellent panoramas.

There is a good mix of easy, intermediate and advanced skiing runs, with steep advanced runs at the top and some tree runs near the base. Lift lines can develop at this very popular resort, but the capacity is substantial enough that waits are not excessive.

The rates for lift passes vary from low to mid to high season, starting at AR$90 and going up to AR$150 per day for adults, AR$75 to AR$130 for children. One-week passes cost AR$430 to AR$750 for adults, and AR$380 to AR$650 for children. Basic rental equipment is cheap, but quality gear is more expensive. There are several on-site ski schools.

The **Aerosilla Lynch** (adult/child AR$45/30) also takes passengers up the mountain during summer, from 10am to 5pm daily except Monday. Several trekking trails begin near the top of the lift: one relatively easy four-hour walk goes to Club Andino's **Refugio Emilio Frey** (☎ in Bariloche 527966; info@activepatagonia.com.ar; dm AR$30-40), where 40 beds and simple meals (AR$25 to AR$35) are available, as are kitchen facilities (AR$10). This *refugio* itself is exposed, but there are sheltered tent sites in what is also Argentina's prime **rock-climbing** area. For more on rock climbing in the area, including guided trips and equipment hire, contact Club Andino in Bariloche (p401).

Hostería Knapp (☎ 460062; www.legendaryskihotel.com; r per person AR$280; ☞) is at the base of the lifts. Alternatively you can stay in Bariloche; public transport from there is excellent, consisting of hourly buses from downtown with Ómnibus 3 de Mayo (p409).

Monte Tronador & Pampa Linda

Traveling via Lago Mascardi, it's a full-day trip up a dusty, single-lane dirt road to Pampa Linda to visit the **Ventisquero Negro** (Black Glacier) and the base of Tronador (3554m).

The area around Tronador resembles, in some ways, California's Yosemite Valley – you have to set your sights above the hotels, *confiterías* and parking lots to focus on the dozens of waterfalls that plunge over the flanks of the extinct volcanoes.

From Pampa Linda – the starting point for several excellent hikes – hikers can approach the snow-line Club Andino **Refugio Otto Meiling** (☎ in Bariloche 422266; info@activepatagonia.com.ar; dm AR$30-40) on foot (about four to six hours' hiking time) and continue to Laguna Frías via the **Paso de las Nubes**; it's a five- to seven-hour walk to an elevation of 2000m. It's also possible to complete the trip in the opposite direction by taking Cerro Catedral's ferry from Puerto Pañuelo to Puerto Blest, and then hiking up the Río Frías to Paso de las Nubes before descending to Pampa Linda via the Río Alerce. The *refugio* itself prepares delicious meals (AR$15 to AR$42, kitchen use AR$15) and is well stocked with good wine and beer. You can hire a guide at the *refugio* to take you on a number of excursions, which range from a three-hour hike to a nearby glacier to the multiday ascent of Cumbre Argentina on Tronador.

Climbers intending to scale Tronador should anticipate a three- to four-day technical climb requiring experience on rock, snow and ice. Hostería Pampa Linda (right) arranges horseback riding in the area.

The road to Pampa Linda passes **Los Rápidos**, after which it becomes extremely narrow. Traffic is therefore allowed up to Pampa Linda until 2pm. At 4pm cars are allowed to leave Pampa Linda for the return trip. For AR$60 each way, Club Andino Bariloche (p401) has summer transport (end of November to April) to Pampa Linda at 8:30am daily, returning around 5pm. Buses depart from in front of Club Andino, and the 90km ride takes about 2½ hours. Park entry fees (AR$30) must be paid en route at the ranger station at Villa Mascardi (the bus stops so you can do this).

Sleeping

In addition to those campgrounds in the immediate Bariloche area, there are sites at Lago Gutiérrez, Lago Mascardi, Lago Guillelmo, Lago Los Moscos, Lago Roca and Pampa Linda. *Refugios* listed earlier charge AR$25 to AR$40 per night, about AR$10 for day use, and sometimes about AR$10 extra for kitchen

privileges. *Refugios* are open from December to the end of April.

Within the park are a number of hotels tending to the luxurious, though there is also the moderately priced **Hostería Pampa Linda** (☎ 490517; www.hosteriapampalinda.com.ar; s/d AR$280/390, incl half-pension AR$380/450). For a real treat, stay at the secluded **Hotel Tronador** (☎ 441062; www.hoteltronador.com; s/d from AR$400/460; ☾ Nov–mid-Apr), at the northwest end of Lago Mascardi on the Pampa Linda road.

Getting There & Around

For transport information from Bariloche, see p409. For road conditions in and around the national parks, call **Parque Nacional Estado de Rutas** (☎ 105) toll-free.

EL BOLSÓN

☎ 02944 / pop 27,000 / elev 300m

It's not hard to see why the hippies started flocking to El Bolsón back in the '70s. It's a mellow little village for most of the year, nestled in between two mountain ranges. When summer comes, it packs out with Argentine tourists who drop big wads of cash and disappear quietly to whence they came.

In the last 30-odd years El Bolsón has been declared both a non-nuclear zone and an 'ecological municipality' (are you getting the picture yet?). What's indisputable is that just out of town are some excellent, easily accessible hikes that take in some of the country's (if possibly not the world's) most gorgeous landscapes.

The town welcomes backpackers, who often find it a relief from Bariloche's commercialism and find themselves stuffing their bellies with natural and vegetarian foods and the excellent beer, sweets, jams and honey made from the local harvest.

Rows of poplars lend a Mediterranean appearance to the local *chacras* (farms), most of which are devoted to hops (El Bolsón produces nearly three-quarters of the country's hops) and fruits.

Motorists should note that El Bolsón is the northernmost spot to purchase gasoline at Patagonian discount prices.

Orientation

Near the southwestern border of Río Negro province, El Bolsón lies in a basin surrounded by high mountains, dominated by the longitudinal ridges of Cerro Piltriquitrón to the east

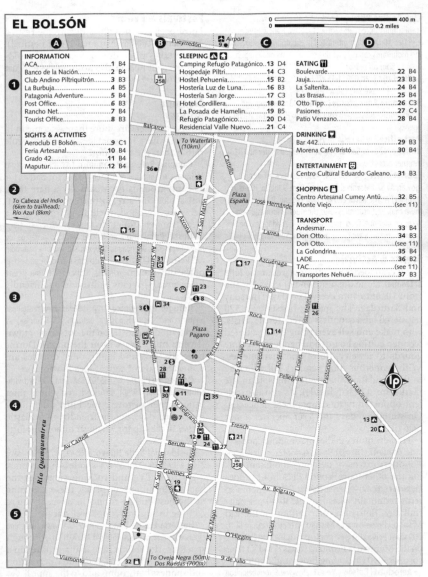

EL BOLSÓN

INFORMATION
ACA	1 B4
Banco de la Nación	2 B4
Club Andino Piltriquitrón	3 B3
La Burbuja	4 B5
Patagonia Adventure	5 B4
Post Office	6 B3
Rancho Net	7 B4
Tourist Office	8 B3

SIGHTS & ACTIVITIES
Aeroclub El Bolsón	9 C1
Feria Artesanal	10 B4
Grado 42	11 B4
Maputur	12 B4

SLEEPING
Camping Refugio Patagónico	13 D4
Hospedaje Piltri	14 C3
Hostel Pehuenia	15 B2
Hostería Luz de Luna	16 B3
Hostería San Jorge	17 C3
Hotel Cordillera	18 B2
La Posada de Hamelin	19 B5
Refugio Patagónico	20 D4
Residencial Valle Nuevo	21 C4

EATING
Boulevarde	22 B4
Jauja	23 B3
La Saltenita	24 B4
Las Brasas	25 B4
Otto Tipp	26 C3
Pasiones	27 C4
Patio Venzano	28 B4

DRINKING
Bar 442	29 B3
Morena Café/Bristó	30 B4

ENTERTAINMENT
Centro Cultural Eduardo Galeano	31 B3

SHOPPING
Centro Artesanal Cumey Antú	32 B5
Monte Viejo	(see 11)

TRANSPORT
Andesmar	33 B4
Don Otto	34 B3
Don Otto	(see 11)
La Golondrina	35 B4
LADE	36 B2
TAC	(see 11)
Transportes Nehuén	37 B3

and the Cordón Nevado along the Chilean border to the west. On the east bank of the Río Quemquemtreu, it is roughly midway between Bariloche and Esquel, each about 130km via RN 258 from Bolsón.

From the south, RN 258 enters town as Av Belgrano and becomes north–south Av San Martín through town. The principal landmark

is the ovoid Plaza Pagano. Most services are nearby.

Information

ACA (Automóvil Club Argentino; ☎ 492260; cnr Avs Belgrano & San Martín) Auto club; has provincial road maps.
Banco de la Nación (cnr Av San Martín & Pellegrini) Has an ATM.

Club Andino Piltriquitrón (☎ 492600; www
.capiltriquitron.com.ar; Sarmiento, btwn Roca & Feliciano;
⊙ Dec-Mar) Visitors interested in exploring the surrounding mountains can contact this office. Occasionally open
6pm to 8pm off season.

La Burbuja (☎ 02944-15-639241; Paso 425; wash & dry
AR$15; ⊙ Mon-Sat) Laundry service.

Patagonia Adventures (☎ 492513; www.patago
niaadventure.bolsonweb.com.ar; Pablo Hube 418) Travel
agency.

Post office (Av San Martín 2806)

Rancho Net (Av San Martín at Av Belgrano; per hr AR$3)
Internet access.

Tourist office (☎ 492604, 455336; www.elbolson
.gov.ar; Av San Martín & Roca; ⊙ 9am-9pm, to 10pm in
summer) At the north end of Plaza Pagano. It has a good
town map and brochures, plus thorough information on
accommodations, food, tours and services. Maps of the
surrounding area are crude but helpful. Superb staff.

Sights & Activities

Local craftspeople sell their wares at the **feria
artesanal**, along the south end of Plaza Pagano
from 10am to 4pm every Tuesday, Thursday
and Saturday. The market boasts over 320
registered (and countless unregistered) artists,
who make and sell everything from sculpted
wooden cutting boards and handcrafted *mate*
gourds to jewelry, flutes and marionettes.
With numerous food vendors (all adhering
to the regulation that everything sold in the
market must be handmade), it's also an excellent opportunity to sample local delicacies.
On sunny Sundays the *feria* operates about
half-tilt.

For adventures in the surrounding country-
side, **Grado 42** (☎ 493124; www.grado42.com; Av Belgrano
406) offers extensive trekking, mountain bik-
ing and other tours around El Bolsón, as does
Maputur (☎ 491440; Perito Moreno 2331), which also
rents mountain bikes for AR$30/40 per half-
/full day. Both also offer rafting on the Río
Manso. Trips on the Manso Inferior (class II to
III) cost AR$200 per person (including lunch);
on the Manso a la Frontera (class II to IV) trips
cost AR$290 (including lunch and dinner).

Aeroclub El Bolsón (☎ 491125; www.aeroclubelbolson
.8k.com; cnr San Martín & Puyrredon) offers aerial tours
of the area for AR$90 to AR$600 per per-
son on 10- to 110-minute scenic flights in a
Cessna 182. Clouds tend to form in the afternoon, so it's best to go in the morning for
stunning views of the national parks, lakes and
unexplored (and therefore unnamed) glaciers
of the region.

Festivals & Events

Local beer gets headlines during the **Festival
Nacional del Lúpulo** (National Hops Festival),
which takes place during four days in mid-
February. El Bolsón also hosts a weekend **jazz
festival** (www.elbolsonjazz.com.ar) in December.

Sleeping
BUDGET

Budget travelers are more than welcome in El
Bolsón, where reasonable prices are the rule
rather than the exception.

Camping Refugio Patagónico (☎ 15-635463; Islas
Malvinas s/n; campsites per person AR$20) Not bad as far
as campgrounds go – basically a bare field,
but a pleasant stream burbles alongside it.
Services are good, including *asados* and a
clean, modern toilet block.

Hostel Pehuenia (☎ 483010; www.hospedajepehue
nia.unlugar.com; Azcuénaga 140; dm/s/d without bathroom
AR$40/60/120; 🖵 🛜) The coziest and best setup
of the downtown hostels, this one has a great
living area, spacious bathrooms and friendly
hosts.

Refugio Patagónico (☎ 483628; www.refugiopat
agonico.com; Islas Malvinas s/n; dm/d AR$45/120; 🛜) A
sweet, modern hostel on the outskirts of town
(five minutes' walk from the plaza). Dorms
have six beds and bathrooms, doubles are
unheated (so not a great idea in winter).

Hospedaje Piltri (☎ 455305; Saavedra 2729; s/d without bathroom AR$70/90) Tucked away in a quiet
little corner of town, the Piltri's definitely
seen better days, but the friendly, enthusiastic
owner makes up for whatever minor comforts
may be lacking.

Residencial Valle Nuevo (☎ 492087; 25 de Mayo
2345; s/d AR$100/120) With spotless bathrooms,
big-screen TVs and rocking views out the
back onto mountain peaks, these are some
of the best budget rooms in town. If you're
coming in summer, book well ahead.

Hostería Luz de Luna (☎ 491908; www.luzdeluna
elbolson.com.ar; Dorrego 150; s/d AR$90/130) Although
spacious, the rooms here manage to retain a
pleasant, homelike feel. Individual decoration
and spotless bathrooms add to the appeal. Go
for one upstairs for better light and views.

our pick La Posada de Hamelin (☎ 492030; www
.posadadehamelin.com.ar; Granollers 2179; s/d AR$120/150)
A beautiful little rustic getaway. There are
only four rooms, but they're all gorgeous, with
exposed beams and rough hewn walls. The
sunny upstairs dining area is a great place to
munch on an empanada.

MIDRANGE & TOP END
Hostería San Jorge (☎ 491313; www.elbolson.com/san jorge; Perito Moreno & Azcuénaga; s/d AR$200/230) Big, spotless rooms, filling breakfasts and comfy inside and outside sitting areas make this a winner in this price range. English spoken.

Hotel Cordillera (☎/fax 492235; cordillerahotel@elbolson.com; Av San Martín 3210; s/d AR$220/300) Undergoing extensive renovations at the time of research, this will no doubt be El Bolsón's top hotel when it reopens. Get a room at the front for the views.

Eating
El Bolsón's restaurants lack Bariloche's variety, but food is consistently good value and often outstanding, thanks to fresh, local ingredients and careful preparation. *Trucha arco iris* (rainbow trout) is the local specialty.

The *feria artesanal* (opposite) is the best and most economical place to eat. Goodies here include fresh fruit, Belgian waffles with berries and cream, huge empanadas for AR$2, sandwiches, frittatas, *milanesa de soja* (soy patties), locally brewed beer and regional desserts.

La Salteñita (☎ 493749; Belgrano 515; empanadas AR$2-3; ☟ 10am-9pm) For spicy northern empanadas, try this cheap rotisserie.

Jauja (Av San Martín 2867; mains AR$20-50; ☟ breakfast, lunch & dinner) The most dependable *confitería* in town serves up all your faves with some El Bolsón touches (such as homemade bread and strawberry juice) thrown in. The daily specials are always worth checking out – the risotto with lamb and wild mushrooms is divine.

Otto Tipp (☎ 493700; cnr Roca & Islas Malvinas; mains AR$25-40; ☟ lunch & dinner in summer, dinner Wed-Sat rest of year) After a hard day of doing anything (or nothing for that matter) there are few better ways to unwind than by working your way through Mr Tipp's selection of microbrew beers. Guests are invited to a free sampling of the six varieties on arrival and there's a good selection of regional specialties on hand, such as smoked trout and Patagonian lamb cooked in black beer, should you happen to get peckish.

Patio Venzano (cnr Sarmiento & Pablo Hube; mains AR$25-40; ☟ lunch & dinner) On sunny days in the high season, you'll want to arrive a little early to guarantee yourself an outside table. No surprises on the menu (pasta, *parrilla*), but the atmosphere's a winner.

Boulevarde (cnr Av San Martín & Pablo Hube; pizzas AR$30; ☟ lunch & dinner) Excellent, thin-crust pizzas like you've probably been craving and a vaguely Irish-pub atmosphere. Around midnight the town's teen population rolls in and the party really starts.

Las Brasas (☎ 492923; cnr Av Sarmiento & Pablo Hube; mains AR$30-60; ☟ lunch & dinner) Probably the finest dining option in town. Las Brasas' signature dish is Patagonian lamb, but the place offers all your other *parrilla* favorites, plus a good variety of trout dishes.

Pasiones (cnr Belgrano & Beruti; mains AR$30-50; ☟ lunch & dinner) Specializing in excellent, homemade pastas, this sunny little spot has huge picture windows featuring some of the best views in town. Occasionally has live music.

Drinking & Entertainment
Morena Café/Bristó (☎ 455353; cnr Av San Martín & Pablo Hube) Friendly cafe-cum-bar that sometimes has live music.

Bar 442 (☎ 492313; Dorrego 442) This venue doubles as a disco on Friday nights and often has live music on Saturday nights.

Dos Ruedas (Av San Martín 2538) Laid-back pub with pool tables, sports on the big screen and a friendly atmosphere; south of the center.

Centro Cultural Eduardo Galeano (☎ 491503; cnr Dorrego & Onelli; admission varies) Small performance space featuring local (and sometimes international) theater, music and dance. Stop by for a program or ask around town.

Shopping
El Bolsón is a craft hunter's paradise. Besides the regular *feria artesanal* (opposite), there are several other outlets for local arts and crafts.

Centro Artesanal Cumey Antú (Av San Martín 2020) This outlet sells high-quality Mapuche clothing and weavings.

Monte Viejo (cnr Pablo Hube & Av San Martín) High-quality ceramics, wood crafts, silver, knives and Mapuche textiles.

Getting There & Away
AIR
LADE (☎ 492206; www.lade.com.ar; Sarmiento 3238) flies once a week to Bariloche (AR$76), Comodoro Rivadavia (AR$210) and Esquel (AR$76). All flights leave from El Bolsón's small **airport** (☎ 492066) at the north end of Av San Martín.

BUS
El Bolsón has no central bus terminal, but most companies are on or near Av San Martín.

Andesmar (☎ 492178; Av Belgrano & Perito Moreno) goes to Bariloche (AR$30, two hours) and Esquel (AR$35, two to three hours), and to points north of there, usually with a change in Neuquén (AR$96, eight hours).

TAC (☎ 493124; cnr Av Belgrano & Av San Martín) goes to Bariloche (AR$30, two hours) and Neuquén (AR$96, nine hours); the company sells tickets to Mendoza, Córdoba and other northern destinations, though you'll have to change buses in Neuquén.

Don Otto (☎ 493910; Av Belgrano 406) goes to Bariloche and Comodoro Rivadavia (AR$147, 11 hours), with connections in Esquel for Trelew and Puerto Madryn.

Transportes Nehuén (☎ 491831; cnr Sarmiento & Padre Feliciano) goes to El Maitén, Bariloche and Los Alerces.

Getting Around
BUS
Local bus service to nearby sights is extensive during the busy summer months, but sporadic in fall and winter, when you'll have to hire a taxi or take a tour. The tourist office provides up-to-date information. Local buses cost AR$1.50.

Transportes Nehuén (☎ 491831; cnr Sarmiento & Padre Feliciano) has summer bus services to many local destinations.

La Golondrina (☎ 492557; Pablo Hube & Perito Moreno) goes to Cascada Mallín Ahogado, leaving from the south end of Plaza Pagano; and to Lago Puelo, leaving from the corner of Av San Martín and Dorrego.

TAXI
Remises are a reasonable mode of transport to nearby trailheads and campgrounds. Companies include **Radio Taxi El Rusito** (☎ 491224), **Patagonia** (☎ 493907) and **Avenida** (☎ 493599); call for rides.

AROUND EL BOLSÓN
The outskirts of El Bolsón offer numerous ridges, waterfalls and forests for hikers to explore. With lots of time, and food and water, some of the following places can be reached by foot from town, though buses and *remises* to trailheads are reasonable. Mountain biking is an excellent way to get out on your own; for rentals try **Maputur** (see p414), in El Bolsón.

Cabeza del Indio
On a ridge-top 8km west of town, this metamorphic rock resembles a toothless hippie as much as it does a stereotypical profile of a 'noble savage,' from which the name 'Indian Head' was derived. The 7km trail up to the rock is reached by walking west on Azcuénaga from town. Part of it traverses a narrow ledge that offers the best views of the formation itself, but by climbing from an earlier junction you can obtain better views of the Río Azul and, in the distance to the south, Parque Nacional Lago Puelo.

Cascada Mallín Ahogado
This small waterfall, on the Arroyo del Medio, is 10km north of town, west of RN 258. Beyond the falls, a gravel road leads to Club Andino Piltriquitrón's **Refugio Perito Moreno** (☎ in El Bolsón 492600; per night with/without sheets AR$40/25), a great base for several outstanding hikes. The *refugio* has capacity for 80 people; meals are an additional AR$15.

From the *refugio*, it's 2½ hours to the 2206m summit of **Cerro Perito Moreno** (☎ 493912; lift pass AR$50, ski/snowboard rental AR$40/60). In winter there's skiing here at the Centro de Deportes Invernales Perito Moreno, where the base elevation is 1000m. The T-bar lifts reach 1450m and the installation of new chairlifts was well underway at the time of writing.

Downstream from the Cascada Mallín Ahogado, the Cascada Escondida waterfall is 8km from El Bolsón. There is a footpath beyond the bridge across the river at the west end of Av Pueyrredón.

Cerro Piltriquitrón
Dominating the landscape east of Bolsón, the 2260m summit of this granitic ridge yields panoramic views westward across the valley of the Río Azul to the Andean crest along the Chilean border. After driving or walking to the 1100m level (the 11km trip from El Bolsón costs about AR$45 by taxi), another hour's steep, dusty walk leads through the impressive **Bosque Tallado** (Sculpture Forest; admission AR$8) to the Club Andino's **Refugio Piltriquitrón** (☎ 492024; dm AR$25). Beds here are outstanding value, but bring your own sleeping bag. Moderately priced meals are available.

From the *refugio*, a steep footpath climbs along the rusted tow bar, then levels off and circles east around the peak before climbing precipitously up loose scree to the summit, marked by a brightly painted cement block. On a clear day the tiring two-hour climb (conspicuously marked by paint blazes) rewards the hiker with views south beyond Lago Puelo, northwest to Monte Tronador and, beyond the border, the snow-topped cone of Volcán Osorno in Chile. Water is abundant along most of the summit route, but hikers should carry a canteen and bring lunch to enjoy at the top.

Cerro Lindo

Southwest of El Bolsón a trail from Camping Río Azul (a small campground reached by a secondary road from El Bolsón) goes to **Refugio Cerro Lindo** (☎ 492763; dm AR$30; ☒ closed in winter), where you can get a decent bed; meals are extra. It's about four hours hike to the *refugio*, from which the trail continues to the 2150m summit.

El Hoyo

Just across the provincial border in Chubut, this town's microclimate makes it the local 'fresh fruit capital.' Nearby Lago Epuyén has good camping and hiking. La Golondrina in El Bolsón (opposite) has daily service to El Hoyo (AR$9, one hour).

Parque Nacional Lago Puelo

In Chubut province, 15km south of El Bolsón, this windy, azure lake is suitable for swimming, fishing, boating, hiking and camping. There are regular buses from El Bolsón in summer, but there's reduced service on Sunday and off-season, when you may have to hitchhike.

Peuma Hue (☎ 499372; www.peuma-hue.com.ar; s/d AR$100/120) is a lakeside resort complex nestled between two rivers with great views of the mighty Piltriquitrón mountain range. Rooms are heavy on the wood theme, but comfortable and spacious. Delicious meals are prepared with local organic ingredients where possible and the grounds are notable for the many species of native plants that the owners are seeking to help save from extinction. Book well ahead if you're coming in summer.

There are both free and fee campsites at the park entrance, including **Camping Lago Puelo** (☎ 499186; per person AR$15).

The Argentine navy maintains a trailer close to the dock, where the launch **Juana de Arco** (☎ 02944-15-633-838; juanadearcopaseos@elbolson.com) takes passengers across the lake to Argentina's Pacific Ocean outlet at the Chilean border (AR$90, three hours). For hardcore hikers heading to Chile, it's possible to continue by foot or horseback to the Chilean town of Puelo on the Seno de Reloncaví, with connections to Puerto Montt. This walk takes roughly three days. Contact the **Intendencia** (☎ 499432) in Lago Puelo for maps, trail conditions and recommended local guides.

For AR$60 the launches also take passengers to El Turbio, at the south end of the lake, where there's a campground.

EL MAITÉN

☎ 02945 / pop 4500

In open-range country on the upper reaches of the Río Chubut, about 70km southeast of El Bolsón, this small, dusty town is the end of the line for *La Trochita*, the old narrow-gauge steam train running between Esquel and El Maitén. It's also home to the workshops for La Trochita and a graveyard of antique steam locomotives and other railroad hardware – a train aficionado's dream.

Every February the **Fiesta Provincial del Trencito** commemorates the railroad that put El Maitén on the map and keeps it there; it now doubles as the **Fiesta Nacional del Tren a Vapor** (National Steam Train Festival). Drawing people from all over the province and the country, it features riding and horse-taming competitions, live music and superb produce and pastries, including homemade jams and jellies.

El Maitén has a helpful **tourist office** (☎ 495016; turismai@epuyem.net.ar).

Camping Municipal (☎ 495129; per person AR$16), directly on the river, gets crowded and noisy during the festival. **Hostería Refugio Andino** (☎ 495007; San Martín 1317; per person AR$40; ▣) is simple but clean and has an attached restaurant.

Getting There & Away

Transportes Jacobsen buses connect El Maitén with Esquel at 4pm Tuesday, Thursday and Saturday. There's a daily minibus service to and from El Bolsón with Grado 42 (see p414).

Train schedules change regularly for **La Trochita** (☎ 495190; www.latrochita.org.ar), so contact El Bolsón's tourist office (p413), Grado 42 in El Bolsón (p414), the train offices in either El Maitén or Esquel, or the tourist office in Esquel. At time of writing, full services between El Maitén and Esquel had been suspended indefinitely – check the website for the latest. Rest assured, though, you can still probably ride a section of the line on the three-hour **Paseos Turísticos** (AR$50), departing from Esquel on most days; see p460.

Patagonia

A star-riddled sky and snarled grasses dwarf the rider on the steppe as his horse closes the gap on the horizon. In South America's southern frontier, nature – long left to its own devices – grows wild, barren and beautiful. Spaces are large, as are the silences that fill them. For those who come here, an encounter with such emptiness can be as awesome as the sight of jagged peaks, pristine rivers and dusty backwater oases.

Though the paving of Ruta Nacional 40 (RN 40) is well underway – long stretches of the road are smooth enough for cycling, while others are uncomfortably rocky – the lonely highway, which has stirred affection in personalities as disparate as Butch Cassidy and Bruce Chatwin, still feels like a spellbinding road to nowhere. On the eastern seaboard, RN 3 shoots south, connecting oil boomtowns with the remains of ancient petrified forests, Welsh settlements and the spectacular Península Valdés. The map will tell you that Patagonia is a very large place, but motoring its distant horizons offers a whole other level of insight.

Then there is the other, trendy Patagonia: the tourist hubs studded with designer shops and reggae bars, where you will meet a dozen other travelers before one local. El Calafate and El Chaltén boast spectacular sights, but they remain a world apart from the mythical RN 40.

This chapter covers the region from its political start at the mouth of Río Negro, continuing through Chubut and Santa Cruz provinces south to the Strait of Magellan. Chile's Punta Arenas, Puerto Natales and Parque Nacional Torres del Paine are also included.

HIGHLIGHTS

- Gaze upon the blue-hued **Glaciar Perito Moreno** (p487) as icebergs crumble in thunderous booms
- Explore millennial forest in the eternal green of **Parque Nacional Los Alerces** (p465)
- Trek the toothy **Fitz Roy Range** (p478) near El Chaltén in the northern sector of Parque Nacional Los Glaciares
- See southern right whales up close in the waters of **Reserva Faunística Península Valdés** (p430)
- Ride the wide-open range and feast on fire-pit-roasted lamb at an **estancia** (p471)

★ Reserva Faunística Península Valdés

★ Parque Nacional Los Alerces

★ Estancias

★ Fitz Roy Range
★ Glaciar Perito Moreno

- POPULATION: 839,000
- AREA: 475,000 SQ KM

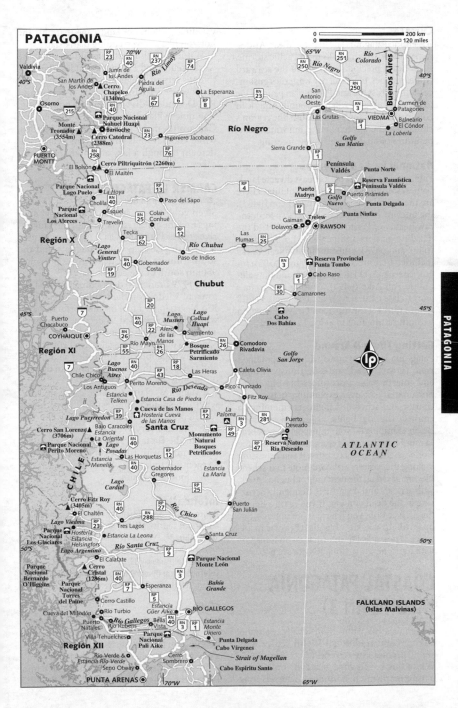

PATAGONIA

Climate

Argentine Patagonia sits in the Chilean Andes' rain shadow, which blocks most Pacific storms. After heavy precipitation falls on the seaward Andean slopes, powerful dry westerlies gust incessantly across the arid Patagonian plains. Due to oceanic influence where the South American continent tapers toward the south, the region's climate is generally temperate, but winter temperatures often drop well below freezing.

National Parks & Reserves

Patagonia's national parks boast diverse landscapes, solitude and incredible wildlife. There are the coastal treasures of Monte León (p453), the ancient forests of Los Alerces (p465), the raw beauty of Perito Moreno (p469), and the dazzling glaciers and peaks of Los Glaciares (p487 and p478). Outstanding Chilean parks included here are Torres del Paine (p505), remote Bernardo O'Higgins (p504) and the paleolithic Pali Aike (p499). Among Patagonia's world-class natural reserves, Península Valdés (p430) ranks at the top. Don't leave the region without setting foot in at least a couple.

Getting There & Around

Patagonia is synonymous with unmaintained *ripio* (gravel) roads, missing transport links and interminable uncomfortable bus rides. Fortunately, an ever-expanding network of charter and scheduled flights is emerging to connect the highlights, at least in summer. Before skimping on your transport budget, bear in mind that the region comprises a third of the world's eighth-largest country. If you're bussing it along the eastern seaboard, note that schedules are based on the demands of Buenos Aires, with arrivals and departures frequently occurring in the dead of night. If you're traveling in the high season, you'll have more options, but buses fill up quickly – buy tickets as far in advance as possible. For information on transport with tour operators along RN 40, see p462.

COASTAL PATAGONIA (ALONG RN 3)

Patagonia's cavorting right whales, penguin colonies and traditional Welsh settlements are all accessed by Argentina's coastal RN 3. While this paved road takes in some fascinating maritime history, it also travels long yawning stretches of landscape that blur the horizon like a never-ending blank slate.

Wildlife enthusiasts shouldn't miss the world-renowned Península Valdés, the continent's largest Magellanic penguin colonies at Reserva Provincial Punta Tombo and Río Deseado's diverse seabird population. The quiet villages of Puerto San Julián and Camarones make for quiet seaside retreats, while Gaiman tells the story of Welsh settlement through a lazy afternoon of tea and cakes.

CARMEN DE PATAGONES

☎ 02920 / pop 14,600

Steep cobblestone streets and colonial stylings breathe a little romance into this languid river town. Patagones, as it is known locally, is both the gateway into Patagonia and the southernmost city in Buenos Aires province, 950km south of the capital via RN 3.

In 1779 Francisco de Viedma founded the town of Viedma on the southern bank of the Río Negro, plus a fort on the northern bank, which later expanded to become Patagones. The region's first colonists hailed from the Spanish county of Maragatería in León (to this day, townspeople are still called *maragatos*) and fashioned their first dwellings in the side of the hills.

Patagones' claim to fame came in 1827, when its smaller and less-equipped forces repelled superior invaders during the war with Brazil. Every year, at the beginning of March, the **Fiesta del Siete de Marzo** celebrates this triumph with 10 days of *música folklórica* (Argentine folk music), parades and traditional food and crafts.

Information

Banco de la Nación (Paraguay 2) Has a 24-hour ATM.
Municipal tourist office (☎ 464819; www.patagones .gov.ar; Mitre 84; ⌚ 7am-7pm Mon-Fri, 10am-1pm & 6-9pm Sat & Sun Dec-Feb)
Post office (Paraguay 38)
Telefónica (cnr Olivera & Comodoro Rivadavia) *Locutorio* (private telephone office) and internet access.

Sights

Check out the eager tourist office for maps and brochures. Patagones has more historic buildings than most Patagonian towns and it's a pleasure to explore the town on foot.

Begin at **Plaza 7 de Marzo**; its original name, Plaza del Carmen, was changed after the 1827

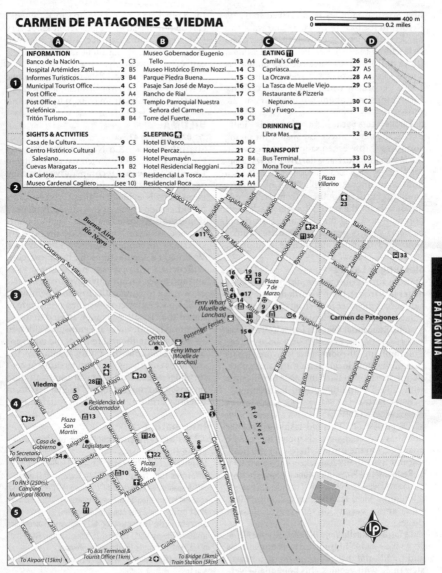

CARMEN DE PATAGONES & VIEDMA

0 — 400 m
0 — 0.2 miles

INFORMATION
Banco de la Nación................................**1** C3
Hospital Artémides Zatti......................**2** B5
Informes Turisticos...............................**3** B4
Municipal Tourist Office.......................**4** C3
Post Office...**5** A4
Post Office...**6** C3
Telefónica..**7** C3
Tritón Turismo.......................................**8** B4

SIGHTS & ACTIVITIES
Casa de la Cultura.................................**9** C3
Centro Histórico Cultural
  Salesiano...**10** B5
Cuevas Maragatas...............................**11** B2
La Carlota..**12** C3
Museo Cardenal Cagliero...........(see 10)

Museo Gobernador Eugenio
  Tello..**13** A4
Museo Histórico Emma Nozzi.........**14** C3
Parque Piedra Buena..........................**15** C3
Pasaje San José de Mayo...................**16** C3
Rancho de Rial.....................................**17** C3
Templo Parroquial Nuestra
  Señora del Carmen..........................**18** C3
Torre del Fuerte...................................**19** C3

SLEEPING
Hotel El Vasco......................................**20** B4
Hotel Percaz...**21** C2
Hotel Peumayén...................................**22** B4
Hotel Residencial Reggiani...............**23** D2
Residencial La Tosca...........................**24** A4
Residencial Roca..................................**25** A4

EATING
Camila's Café..**26** B4
Capriasca..**27** A5
La Orcava...**28** A4
La Tasca de Muelle Viejo....................**29** C3
Restaurante & Pizzeria
  Neptuno...**30** C2
Sal y Fuego...**31** B4

DRINKING
Libra Mas..**32** B4

TRANSPORT
Bus Terminal...**33** D3
Mona Tour...**34** A4

PATAGONIA

victory over the Brazilians. Salesians built the **Templo Parroquial Nuestra Señora del Carmen** in 1883. Its image of the Virgin, dating from 1780, is southern Argentina's oldest, and two of the original seven Brazilian flags captured in 1827 are on the altar. Just west of the church, **Torre del Fuerte** is the last vestige of the 1780 fort that once occupied the entire block.

Below the tower, twin cannons, once used to guard the Patagonian frontier, flank the 1960s **Pasaje San José de Mayo** staircase leading to the riverside. At the base of the steps, the **Rancho de Rial** (Mitre 94) is an 1820 adobe that belonged to the town's first elected mayor. Three blocks west, the **Cuevas Maragatas** (Maragatas Caves; Rivadavia s/n), excavated in the riverbank, sheltered the first Spanish families who arrived in 1779. Return to the base of the stairs and walk two blocks east, where the early-19th-century **Casa de la Cultura** (Mitre 27) was the site of a *tahona* (flour mill). Across the street, **La Carlota** (cnr Bynon & Mitre) is a former private residence (c 1800) decorated with typical 19th-century furnishings; ask about guided tours at the museum.

Parque Piedra Buena has a bust of Luis Piedra Buena, the naval officer responsible for saving countless shipwrecked sailors. A block west, the **Museo Histórico Emma Nozzi** (☎ 462729; admission AR$2; ☺ 10am-noon & 3-5pm Mon-Fri, 5-7pm Sat) houses an impressive collection of artifacts from Argentina's southern frontier, including details on the town's former black slave population. Along the river are recreational *balnearios* (river beaches), which are popular spots for swimming and picnics in summer.

Sleeping & Eating

Options for accommodations and dining are better in Viedma, but it's worth the short ferry ride across the river for a stroll on Carmen de Patagones' historic colonial waterfront.

Hotel Residencial Reggiani (☎ 461065; residencial reggiani@hotmail.com; Bynon 422; s/d/tr AR$80/140/180) This rambling 20-room home is favored for its friendliness and location on the main square. Rooms can be a bit dark and stale, but all come with cable TV and tidy private bathrooms.

Hotel Percaz (☎ 464104; www.hotelpercaz.com .ar, in Spanish; cnr Comodoro Rivadavia & Irigoyen; s/d/tr AR$108/153/189; ▣) This old-fashioned corner hotel has carpeted, no-frills rooms that can be cramped. On the upside, there's central heating and twice-daily housekeeping service.

Restaurante & Pizzeria Neptuno (Comodoro Rivadavia 310; mains AR$20-32; ☺ 8pm-late) This classic eatery, a longtime local favorite, serves up tortillas, pizza and a variety of well-prepared meat dishes.

La Tasca de Muelle Viejo (JJ Biedma 30; mains AR$26-32; ☺ dinner only) Whipping up tasty empanadas and traditional dishes like *puchero*, a hearty stew thick with veggies, this bohemian riverside cafe overflows with warm ambience.

Getting There & Around

Most travelers make bus, train and plane connections in Viedma. But many northbound buses also stop at Patagones' **bus terminal** (☎ 462666; cnr Barbieri & Méjico), with plenty of services to Bahía Blanca and Buenos Aires. Tickets

for Tren Patagónico (Viedma to Bariloche) can be purchased at the bus terminal. A very slow train operates once a week between Patagones and Bahía Blanca, though it gets cancelled periodically.

Two bridges connect Patagones with Viedma. A ferry crosses the river to Viedma (AR$1.50) every few minutes, from 6:30am to 10pm.

VIEDMA
☎ 02920 / pop 47,900

Sharing the lush Río Negro with sister city Carmen de Patagones, Viedma, the capital of Río Negro province, is comparatively bustling and prosperous. The difference between the two towns is evident in the ferry platforms on either side of the river – on the Patagones shore, the dilapidated staircase is made of brittle wood, while on Viedma's side, the platform and stairs are modern concrete. For travelers, Viedma is a less-picturesque but more convenient base with a greater number of services and amenities, an attractive riverfront, upscale cafes and a jogging path close to downtown.

In 1779 Francisco de Viedma put ashore to found the city after his men started dying of fever and lack of water at Península Valdés. In 1879 it became the residence of the governor of Patagonia and the political locus of the country's enormous southern territory. A century later, the radical Alfonsín administration proposed moving the federal capital here from Buenos Aires but was crushingly defeated.

Information

ATMs and internet cafes are in the center along Buenos Aires.

Hospital Artémides Zatti (☎ 422333; Rivadavia 351)

Informes Turisticos (☎ 427171; www.viedma.gov .ar, in Spanish; Av Francisco de Viedma 51) Offers local and regional information on the waterfront.

Post office (cnr 25 de Mayo & San Martín)

Secretaría de Turismo (☎ 422150; www.rionegrotur .com.ar; Caseros 1425) Located 15 blocks southwest of the plaza, with brochures for the entire province.

Tourist office (☎ 427171; bus terminal) Offers lodging and transportation details.

Tritón Turismo (☎ 431131; Ceferino Namuncurá 78) Changes traveler's checks, rents cars and runs tours.

Sights & Activities

Summer activities include kayaking on the Río Negro and weekend catamaran rides (AR$15). Ask individual launch operators at the pier about kayak rentals and river cruises.

The season for sport fishing on the Río Negro runs from November to early July, with rainbow trout (catch and release), silverside and carp. For information and licenses, consult Informes Turisticos, the **Direccion de Pesca de Río Negro** (☎ 420326), or fishing guides **Eduardo Urriza** (☎ 02920-15-626719) and **Constantino Mikitiuk** (☎ 426328).

In addition to exhibits on European settlement, the **Museo Gobernador Eugenio Tello** (☎ 425900; San Martín 263; admission free; �l 9am-4:30pm Mon-Fri, 4-6pm Sat) displays Tehuelche tools, artifacts, deformed skulls and skeletons.

The Salesian **Museo Cardenal Cagliero** (☎ 02920-15-308671; Rivadavia 34; admission free; �l 8am-1pm Mon-Fri) features incredible ceiling paintings and a neat fish-vertebrae cane (check out the cardinal's office). It is housed in the **Centro Histórico Cultural Salesiano**, the former Vicariato de la Patagonia, a massive 1890 brick structure on the corner of Colón.

Festivals & Events

In mid-January, the weeklong **Regata del Río Negro** (www.regatadelrionegro.com.ar) features the world's longest kayak race, a 500km paddle from Neuquén to Viedma.

Sleeping

Camping Municipal (☎ 02920-15-524786; RN 3 riverside at Río Negro; per person AR$6; �l Nov-Mar) This shady riverside campground, 10 blocks west of RN 3, offers drab gravel sites and hot showers. Arrive via taxi (AR$8) or take the Comarca bus from downtown.

Hotel El Vasco (☎ 430459; hotelelvasco@yahoo.com.ar; 25 de Mayo 174; s/d/tr AR$80/120/160; ☐) Since recently changing ownership, this centrally located hotel is comparatively bright and cheery. Rooms are small but spotless with hardwood floors and cable TV.

Residencial La Tosca (☎ 428508; residencialtosca@hotmail.com; Alsina 349; s/d/tr AR$95/130/175) La Tosca's dark lobby is decorated with strange statuary and the hotel seems to be growing shabbier as the years go by, but at least the rooms are clean with small TVs and private bathrooms.

Residencial Roca (☎ 431241; Roca 347; s/d/tr AR$103/160/225; ☒) This family-friendly hotel is a little off the beaten path, located several blocks away from Viedma's main attractions. The Roca isn't stylish but it's polished and hospitable, with spacious rooms and attentive desk service. Breakfast costs AR$10 extra.

Hotel Peumayén (☎ 425222/234; www.hotelpeumayen.com.ar; Buenos Aires 334; s/d/tr AR$120/150/210; ☐) This old business hotel is dated but well kept, with canary-yellow walls and carpeted rooms. Each floor has a small kitchen for *mate* (a tea-like beverage) breaks.

Eating & Drinking

Camila's Café (cnr Saavedra & Buenos Aires; snacks AR$10; �l breakfast, lunch & dinner; ☒) Its pleasant, homey atmosphere is best for breakfast, which branches out from *medialunas* (croissants) with fruit and egg plates.

La Ochava (☎ 426031; cnr Alsina & 25 de Mayo; sandwiches AR$20; �l breakfast, lunch & dinner) This cafe-pub is housed in an antique corner building with high ceilings and original woodwork. Try the *cerveza artesanal* (craft beer) and a steak, burger or sandwich while soaking up the old-fashioned atmosphere.

Capriasca (☎ 426754; Alvaro Barros 685; mains AR$28-35; �l lunch & dinner) Capriasca is a hit with local foodies thanks to its sophisticated menu based on staples like trout, beef and chicken, a good wine list, and a classy atmosphere with fine wood furniture and white linen tablecloths.

Sal y Fuego (☎ 431259; Av Villarino 55; mains AR$35-45) This hip riverfront hangout offers classic Argentine dishes with a few surprises, like chicken in sweet-and-sour plum sauce. In the afternoon, you can have coffee under the shade of a weeping willow at the adjoining Café del Sauce.

Libra Mas (☎ 427181; cnr Av Villarino & Saavedra; sandwiches AR$15; �l 9am-3am) Settle into a sleek white leather armchair at this modern restaurant and bar, perfect for sharing a *tabla* (cutting board with meat and cheeses) or fried calamari with drinks.

Getting There & Around

AIR

Aeropuerto Gobernador Castello (VDM; ☎ 422001) is 15km southwest of town on RP 51; a taxi to the center costs AR$8. **Aerolíneas Argentinas** (☎ 423033) flies twice a week to Buenos Aires (AR$600). **LADE** (☎ 424420) lands here on Mondays and Fridays en route to Comodoro Rivadavia (AR$260).

BOAT

From the pier at the foot of 25 de Mayo, a frequent ferry service (AR$1.50) connects Viedma and Carmen de Patagones from 6:30am until 10pm.

BUS

Viedma's **bus terminal** (☎ 426850) is 13 blocks southwest of the plaza, a 20-minute walk.

To Puerto Madryn, **Don Otto** (☎ 425952) and **El Cóndor** (☎ 423714) offer the best service. To Bariloche, **3 de Mayo** (☎ 425839) goes via RN 23, while **El Valle** (☎ 427501) takes longer via RN 22 and RP 6.

For Balneario El Cóndor (AR\$4, half-hour) and La Lobería (AR\$7, one hour), **Ceferino** (☎ 426691) leaves from Plaza Alsina six times daily in summer.

Destination	Cost (AR\$)	Duration (hr)
Bahía Blanca	35	3
Bariloche	110-150	14-15
Buenos Aires	160-250	13
Comodoro Rivadavia	142-160	10-13
Las Grutas	25	2½
Puerto Madryn	72-84	5-6
Trelew	75-85	8

TRAIN

Among the last of Argentina's great long-distance trains, **Tren Patagónico** (☎ 422130; www.trenpatagonico-sa.com.ar, in Spanish) offers service replete with dining and cinema cars. It crosses the plains to Bariloche (economy/1st class/Pullman/bed AR\$57/76/118/229, 17 hours) at 6pm on Fridays; children five to 12 years pay half price. Trains depart from the station on the southeast outskirts of town. Check the website for the current schedule, which changes often.

Tickets can also be purchased at **Mona Tour** (☎ 432492; www.monatour.com.ar; Laprida 145).

COASTAL RÍO NEGRO

La Ruta de los Acantilados occupies a beautiful stretch along Río Negro's 400km Atlantic coastline. Repeated wave action has worn the ancient cliff faces (three million to 13 million years old) to reveal a wealth of fossils. While the area teems with activity in the summer, it shuts down off-season.

Balneario El Cóndor, a resort 31km southeast of Viedma at the mouth of the Río Negro, has what's considered the largest parrot colony in the world, with 35,000 nests of burrowing parrots in its cliff faces. Don't miss the century-old lighthouse, Patagonia's oldest. Lodging options include **Hospedaje Río de los Sauces** (☎ 02920-497193; Calle 20 bis; d AR\$130) and the RV-friendly **Camping Ina Lauquen** (☎ 02920-497218; cnr Calle 87 & Costanera; per person AR\$8; 🖵), with grills, picnic tables, fast food and even internet.

There's a permanent southern sea-lion colony at **La Lobería** (Reserva Faunística de Punta Bermeja), 60km from Viedma, on the north coast of Golfo San Matías. The population peaks during spring, when males come ashore to fight other males and establish harems of up to 10 females. The females give birth from December onward. Visitors will find the observation balcony, directly above the mating beaches, safe and unobtrusive. Buses from Viedma pass within 3km of the colony.

At the northwest edge of Golfo San Matías, 179km west of Viedma along RN 3, the crowded resort of **Las Grutas** (The Grottos; www.balneariolasgrutas.com, in Spanish) owes its name to its eroded sea caves. Thanks to an exceptional tidal range, the beaches can expand for hundreds of meters or shrink to just a few. The **tourist office** (☎ 02934-497470; Galería Antares, Primera Bajada) has tide schedules. Buses leave hourly to San Antonio Oeste, 16km northeast, with more lodging.

Besides free meals for bus drivers, **Sierra Grande**, 125km south of Las Grutas, only has one thing going for it: gasoline at subsidized *precios patagónicos* (Patagonian prices). Almost everyone fills up their tank, grabs an uninspired snack and carries on.

PUERTO MADRYN

☎ 02965 / pop 57,791

This sheltered port facing Golfo Nuevo is the gateway to the wildlife sanctuary of Península Valdés. Fast growing with tourism and industry, it does retain a few small-town touches: the radio announces lost dogs and locals are welcoming and unhurried. Madryn holds its own as a modest beach destination, but from June to mid-December the visiting right whales take center stage. And from July to September the whales are so close they can be viewed without taking a tour – either from the coast 20km north of town or the 500m pier in town.

Founded by Welsh settlers in 1886, the town takes its name from Love Parry, Baron of Madryn. Statues along the *costanera* (seaside road) pay tribute to the Welsh: one to the role women have played, and the other, at the south end of town, to the Tehuelche, who helped the Welsh immigrants survive. Madryn's campus of the Universidad de la Patagonia is known for its marine biology department, and ecological centers promote conservation and education. The city is the second-largest fishing port in the country and home to Aluar, Argentina's first aluminum plant, built in 1974.

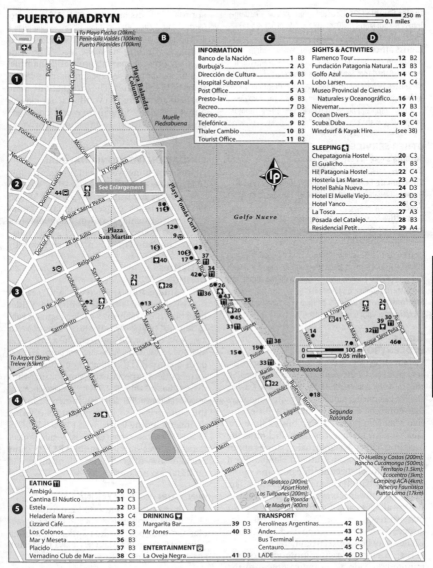

PUERTO MADRYN

INFORMATION		
Banco de la Nación	**1**	B3
Burbuja's	**2**	A3
Dirección de Cultura	**3**	B3
Hospital Subzonal	**4**	A1
Post Office	**5**	A3
Presto-lav	**6**	B3
Recreo	**7**	D3
Recreo	**8**	B2
Telefónica	**9**	B2
Thaler Cambio	**10**	B3
Tourist Office	**11**	B2

SIGHTS & ACTIVITIES		
Flamenco Tour	**12**	B2
Fundación Patagonia Natural	**13**	B3
Golfo Azul	**14**	C3
Lobo Larsen	**15**	C4
Museo Provincial de Ciencias		
Naturales y Oceanográfico	**16**	A1
Nievemar	**17**	B3
Ocean Divers	**18**	C4
Scuba Duba	**19**	C4
Windsurf & Kayak Hire	(see 38)	

SLEEPING		
Chepatagonia Hostel	**20**	C3
El Gualicho	**21**	B3
Hi! Patagonia Hostel	**22**	C4
Hostería Las Maras	**23**	A2
Hotel Bahía Nueva	**24**	D3
Hotel El Muelle Viejo	**25**	D3
Hotel Yanco	**26**	C3
La Tosca	**27**	A3
Posada del Catalejo	**28**	B3
Residencial Petit	**29**	A4

EATING		
Ambigú	**30**	D3
Cantina El Náutico	**31**	C3
Estela	**32**	D3
Heladería Mares	**33**	C4
Lizzard Café	**34**	B3
Los Colonos	**35**	C3
Mar y Meseta	**36**	B3
Placido	**37**	B3
Vernadino Club de Mar	**38**	C3

DRINKING		
Margarita Bar	**39**	D3
Mr Jones	**40**	B3

ENTERTAINMENT		
La Oveja Negra	**41**	D3

TRANSPORT		
Aerolineas Argentinas	**42**	B3
Andes	**43**	C3
Bus Terminal	**44**	A2
Centauro	**45**	C3
LADE	**46**	D3

PATAGONIA

Orientation

Puerto Madryn is just east of RN 3, 1371km south of Buenos Aires and about 65km north of Trelew. The action in town centers on the *costanera* and two main parallel avenues, Av Roca and 25 de Mayo. Bulevar Brown is the main drag alongside the beaches to the south.

Information

ESSENTIALS

Call centers and internet cafes abound in the center. Some travel agencies accept traveler's checks as payment for tours.

Banco de la Nación (9 de Julio 127) Has an ATM and changes traveler's checks.

Hospital Subzonal (☎ 451999; R Gómez 383)

Thaler Cambio (☎ 455858; Av Roca 497; ⊙ 9:30am-1pm & 6-8pm Mon-Fri, 10am-1pm & 7-9pm Sat & Sun) Poorer rates for traveler's checks.

Tourist office (☎ 453504, 456067; www.madryn .gov.ar/turismo, in Spanish; Av Roca 223; ⊙ 7am-10pm Mon-Fri, 8am-11pm Sat & Sun Dec-Feb, reduced hours off-season) Helpful and efficient staff, and there's usually an English or French speaker on duty. Check the *libro de reclamos* (complaint book) for traveler tips. There's another helpful desk at the bus terminal.

OTHER SERVICES
Burbuja's (☎ 472217; Gobernador Maíz 440; ⊙ closed Sun) Full- or self-service laundry.

Dirección de Cultura (Av Roca 444; showers AR$1.50) Showers available downstairs, beneath the Museo de Arte Moderno.

Post office (cnr Belgrano & Gobernador Maíz)

Presto-lav (☎ 451526; Blvd Brown 605) Laundry pickup and delivery available.

Recreo (cnr 28 de Julio & Av Roca) Stocks a good selection of regional books, maps and a few English-language novels and guidebooks. There is another branch on the corner of 25 de Mayo and Roque Sáenz Peña.

Telefónica (cnr Av Roca & 9 de Julio; ⊙ 8am-midnight) Big call center with internet access.

Sights
ECOCENTRO
Celebrating the area's marine treasures, **Ecocentro** (☎ 457470; www.ecocentro.org.ar; J Verne 3784; adult/child 12yr & under AR$32/20; ⊙ 9am-noon & 3-7pm Mon-Fri) is a masterpiece of interactive displays that combine artistic sensitivity with extensive scientific research. Exhibits explore the area's unique marine ecosystem, including the breeding habits of right whales, stories about dolphin sounds and southern elephant-seal harems, a touch-friendly tide pool and more. The building itself is equally impressive. The three-story tower acts as a library, with the top story – all glass and comfy couches – a great place to read, write or contemplate the fragile ocean community. Bring your binoculars: whales may be spotted from here.

It's an enjoyable 40-minute walk or 15-minute bike ride along the *costanera* to the Ecocentro. Shuttles run three times daily from the tourist office on Av Roca, or you can catch a Línea 2 bus to the last stop and walk 1km.

MUSEO PROVINCIAL DE CIENCIAS NATURALES Y OCEANOGRÁFICO
Feeling up strands of seaweed and ogling a preserved octopus are part of the hands-on approach of this **museum** (☎ 451139; cnr Domecq García & José Menéndez; admission AR$8; ⊙ 9am-noon & 3-7pm Mon-Fri, 3-7pm Sat & Sun) in the 1917 Chalet Pujol. A winding staircase leads into nine small rooms of marine and land mammal exhibits and preserved specimens, plus collections of Welsh wares. The explanations are in Spanish and geared to youth science classes, but it's visually informative and creatively presented. Twist up to the cupola for views of the port.

FUNDACIÓN PATAGONIA NATURAL
A well-run nongovernmental organization, **Fundación Patagonia Natural** (☎ 451920; www.pata goniatatural.org, in Spanish; Marcos A Zar 760; ⊙ 9am-4pm Mon-Fri) promotes conservation and monitors environmental issues in Patagonia. In a converted house, volunteers diligently nurse injured birds and marine mammals to health.

Activities
DIVING
With interesting shipwrecks and sea life nearby, Madryn and the Península Valdés have become Argentina's diving capitals. **Lobo Larsen** (☎ 470277, 02965-15-516314; www.lobolarsen .com; Av Roca 885, Local 2) and **Scuba Duba** (☎ 452699; www.scubaduba.com.ar, in Spanish; Blvd Brown 893) are both quality PADI-affiliated operators – the former offers a special excursion for first-time divers. **Golfo Azul** (☎ 471649; www.pinosub.com, in Spanish; H Yrigoyen 200) sells equipment. Most of the *balnearios* also have operators offering diving, including **Ocean Divers** (☎ 472569, 02965-15-660865; www.oceandivers.com.ar, in Spanish; Balneario Yoaquina). Dives start at around AR$150; some agencies also offer courses, night dives and multiday excursions.

WINDSURFING & KAYAKING
In high season, a hut next to Vernardino Club de Mar (p428) offers lessons and rents out regular and wide boards and kayaks by the hour. South of Muelle Piedrabuena, **Playa Tomás Curti** is a popular windsurfing spot.

BIKING & HIKING
Alpataco (☎ 451672; Av Roca 1848) rents good quality mountain bikes (AR$40 per day) and accessories. Several other outfitters along Av Roca advertise rentals and guided tours; inspect the gear before heading out on a long ride. Guide service **Huellas y Costas** (☎ 02965-15-637826; www.huellasycostas.com; Blvd Brown 1900) offers

coastal hiking, mountain biking, kayaking and camping adventures in small groups with bilingual guides.

Tours

Countless agencies sell tours to Península Valdés (p430), for AR$140 to AR$180 (not including the AR$45 park admission fee or whale watching, which ranges from AR$120 to AR$150). Most hotels and hostels also offer tours; it's always best to get recommendations from fellow travelers before choosing. Ask how large the bus was, if it came with an English-speaking guide, where they ate and what they saw where – different tour companies often visit different locations.

Those most interested in wildlife should bring binoculars and may find it more enjoyable to stay overnight in Puerto Pirámides (p430). Tours to Punta Tombo (p441) from Puerto Madryn cost about the same as those offered from Trelew (p437), but they require more driving time and thus less time with the penguins.

Recommended tour companies:

Flamenco Tour (☎ 455505; www.flamencotour.com; Av Roca 331) Offerings range from standard whale watching and snorkeling trips to stargazing 4WD journeys along the coast (telescopes and bilingual instruction included).

Nievemar (☎ 455544; www.nievemartours.com.ar; Av Roca 493) Amex representative. Excursions include whale watching and visits to sea-lion colonies and the petrified forest.

Sleeping

Book ahead, especially if you want a double room. If you are caught short, check with the tourist offices at the bus terminal or in town, where you'll find a comprehensive lodging list with prices that include nearby *estancias* (ranches) and rental apartments (double occupancy from AR$160 per day).

BUDGET

All hostels have kitchens and many offer pickup from the bus terminal, but most are a short, flat walk away.

Camping ACA (☎ 452952; Camino al Indio; s/d camp sites AR$25/30; ⏲ closed May-Aug) These 800 gravel camp sites are sheltered by trees to break the incessant wind. Although there are no cooking facilities, a limited selection of snacks (and sometimes prepared meals) is available. From downtown, city bus 2 goes within 500m of the campground; get off at the last stop (La Universidad).

Posada del Catalejo (☎ 475224; www.posadadelcatalejo.com.ar; Mitre 446; dm/d without bathroom AR$40/140, d with bathroom AR$170; ▣) Unlike many of Puerto Madryn's hostels, Posada del Catalejo is located in an old-fashioned building that makes the place feel more like a budget-friendly B&B. The small patio is a lovely place for coffee.

La Tosca (☎ 456133; www.latoscahostel.com; Sarmiento 437; dm AR$45, d AR$145-155; ▣) A cozy guesthouse where the owners greet you by name, La Tosca is the creation of a well-traveled couple. Although dorm beds are short, they sport good mattresses and convenient shelves. Perks include a grassy courtyard, bike rentals and an inviting common area.

Chepatagonia Hostel (☎ 455783; www.chepatagoniahostel.com.ar; Storni 16; dm/d AR$48/150; ▣) Just a stone's throw from the beach, this well-run hostel is owned by a friendly, youthful couple who book tours for guests and fire up the grill for barbecues twice a week. Adding to the appeal are free wi-fi, comfortable beds and the possibility of glimpsing a breaching whale from the hostel balcony.

our pick **Hi! Patagonia Hostel** (☎ 450155; www.hipatagonia.com, in Spanish; Av Roca 1040; dm/d AR$50/150; ▣) Reservations are essential at this cool and cozy suburban-style house featuring both private rooms and dorm beds with down comforters, a cocktail bar in the grassy courtyard, bike rental and twice-weekly barbecues. Friendly host Gaston creates a warm, social atmosphere and is more than happy to help travelers plan outdoor excursions.

El Gualicho (☎ 454163; www.elgualicho.com.ar, in Spanish; Marcos A Zar 480; dm/d AR$50/220; ▣) Boasting highly attentive staff and a sleek, contemporary lobby, this hostel draws the hip backpacker set. Dorms have wood-frame bunks and ample shared spaces, including an interior patio, a lively bar and comfy living and dining areas.

MIDRANGE & TOP END

Hostería Las Maras (☎ 453215; www.hosterialasmaras.com.ar; Marcos A Zar 64; s/d AR$150/220; ▣) Brick walls, exposed beams and wicker furniture create an intimate setting ideal for couples – in the lobby anyway. The guest rooms themselves aren't particularly cozy, just small, prim and serviceable. Superior rooms boast king-sized beds, flat-screen TVs and stylish design elements.

Residencial Petit (☎ 451460; hotelpetit@arnet.com
.ar; MT de Alvear 845; d AR$150) These immaculate
whitewashed motel rooms seem straight out
of Florida. The management is attentive and
rooms are furnished with desks and ceiling
fans. It's more than a 10-minute walk to the
costanera.

Hotel El Muelle Viejo (☎ 471284; www.muelleviejo
.com, in Spanish; H Yrigoyen 38; d/tr AR$160/190) A pleas-
ant couple keeps this older hotel shipshape,
with crisp linen curtains, plump beds and pale
wood furniture. The fluorescent lights lend
an institutional feel to the lobby; rooms have
bathtubs and cable TV.

Hotel Yanco (☎ 471581; hotelyanco@hotmail.com;
Av Roca 626; s/d/tr AR$158/190/260) This old-style
charmer has an ancient switchboard, an antique piano and accordion, and tidy rooms
that don't look all that much newer. The
rooms that face the *avenida* are noisy, while
whales have been spotted from those facing
the ocean.

La Posada de Madryn (☎ 453525; www.la-posada
.com.ar; Mathews 2951; s/d AR$250/280; 🖳) This mod-
ern inn amid rolling green lawns offers a quiet
alternative to lodging in town. Its tidy, light-
filled rooms with bright accents come with
cable TV; in the garden there's a pool and
parrilla (grill.)

Apart Hotel Los Tulipanes (☎ 471845; www.los-tu
lipanes.com.ar; Jones 150; d/tr AR$250/340; 🖳 🐾) Those
staying in town for more than a few days will
appreciate the spiffy kitchenettes and spacious
dimensions of these out-of-the-way (but close
to the beach) apartments. The pretty swimming pool doesn't hurt, either.

Hotel Bahía Nueva (☎ 450045/145; www
.bahianueva.com.ar; Av Roca 67; s/d AR$260/335; 🖳)
Stretching to resemble an English countryside retreat, the Bahía Nueva distinguishes
itself with a foyer library and flouncy touches.
Its 40 rooms are well groomed, but only a
few have ocean views. Highlights include
a bar with billiards and a TV (mostly to
view movies and documentaries), and tour
information.

Territorio (☎ 471496; Av Roca 33; www.australi
set.com.ar; d/tr AR$535/602, superior ste AR$945; 🖳)
Easily the region's most fashionable hotel,
Territorio is an ecofriendly boutique with 36
plush rooms and suites that all boast water
views. The Punta Cuevas location is a bit
of a trek from the center of Puerto Madryn,
but there's a cool cocktail bar and a contemporary spa.

Eating & Drinking
BUDGET & MIDRANGE

Heladería Mares (☎ 470705; Martin Fierro 85; ice cream
AR$10; 🕓 10am-midnight) Doing a brisk business
in creamy *helados* (ice creams), this excellent
beachfront parlor also offers delivery.

Lizzard Café (☎ 455306; cnr Av Roca & Av Gales;
snacks AR$10-25; 🕓 7am-2am) This popular cor-
ner cafe and eatery draws a young crowd in
the evenings for beer, pizza and sandwiches.
Hit your daily vegetable quota while you can
(fresh produce is often hard to come by in
Patagonia) with the salad heaped high with
egg, bell pepper, pineapple and olives.

Margarita Bar (☎ 475871; Roque Sáenz Peña; mains
AR$28-35; 🕓 11am-4am) With a trendy edge, this
low-lit brick haunt has a laundry list of cocktails,
a friendly bar staff and live music (such as jazz,
bossa nova or drumming) on Wednesdays.

Mr Jones (☎ 475368; 9 de Julio 116; mains AR$30-35;
🕓 dinner) With a wealth of yummy stouts and
reds, homemade pot pie and sausages, Mr Jones
will satiate your appetite for all things German.
The food is good and reasonably authentic.

Los Colonos (☎ 458486; cnr Av Roca & Storni; mains
AR$30-40; 🕓 lunch & dinner) Depending on your
perspective, the design of this corner restaurant – resembling an old wooden ship,
complete with a mini lighthouse near the entrance – is either corny or festive. We vote for
the latter, but maybe that's just because the
seafood is fresh and classically prepared.

our pick **Estela** (☎ 451573; Roque Sáenz Peña 27; mains
AR$30-42; 🕓 noon-2:30pm & 8pm-midnight Tue-Sun) The
sweet smell of garlic sautéeing in the kitchen
will stop you in your tracks if you're outside.
Billed as the town's best *parrilla* (steak restaurant), Estela also does pasta and fish in an
intimate, unpretentious setting often packed
with locals.

Vernardino Club de Mar (☎ 474289; www.vernardinoc
lubdemar.com.ar; Blvd Brown 860; mains AR$35-42; 🕓 breakfast,
lunch & dinner) With unbeatable beachfront atmosphere, Vernadino's white-linen tables are a hot
spot for drinks and wok dishes. Take a seat on
the patio in the early morning and you'll feel
like you're having breakfast on the sand.

Cantina El Náutico (☎ 471404; www.cantinaelnautico
.com.ar; cnr Av Roca & Lugones; lunch special AR$40) This
popular nook (see the photos of Argentine
celebs) offers old-fashioned ambience, from
the polished bar to the white linen. If you
share with a friend or two, the *paella de mar-
iscos* (rice and shellfish) is also practically
budget friendly.

TOP END

Mar y Meseta (☎ 458740; www.marymeseta.com.ar; Av Gales 32; mains AR$40-50; ☽ lunch & dinner) Colorful and cozy, this elegant seafood restaurant dishes up clever creations for a handful of tables. While the service is great, the food can be hit or miss: you can't go wrong, however, with the spaghetti in squid-ink sauce.

Plácido (☎ 455991; www.placido.com.ar; Av Roca 506; mains AR$42-55; ☽ lunch & dinner) This sleek new addition to Madryn's waterfront serves beautifully presented versions of traditional dishes such as shrimp in garlic and *cordero patagónico* (Patagonian lamb) in a minimalist setting. Try the shellfish sampler paired with a bottle of white from Bodega Fin del Mundo.

Ambigú (☎ 472451; www.ambiguresto.com.ar; cnr Av Roca & Roque Sáenz Peña; mains AR$45-52) With a focus on fresh ingredients and creative combinations, Ambigú masters a gamut of dishes, including seafood – try the *langostinos* (prawns) in sea salt – and pizza. The setting is an elegant renovation of a historic bank building, backlit by warm colors.

Entertainment

Bars and dance clubs come and go, so ask locals what's *de moda* (in) for the moment.

Rancho Cucamonga (cnr Blvd Brown & Jenkins) This up-all-night club has long been a hot spot for local partygoers. Twentysomethings fill the place to capacity in the wee hours of the morning when well-known DJs are spinning.

La Oveja Negra (H Yrigoyen 144) This intimate bar is decked in burlap and revolutionary paraphernalia – long live rock and folk – which keep the crowd bubbling at this fun bar.

Getting There & Away

Due to limited connections, it pays to book in advance, especially for travel to the Andes.

AIR

Though Puerto Madryn has its own modern airport, most commercial flights still arrive in Trelew (see p438), 65km south.

Aeropuerto El Tehuelche (PMY; ☎ 456774) is 5km west of town, at the junction with RN 3. From here, **LADE** (☎ 451256; Av Roca 119) puddle jumps to Esquel (AR$225), El Calafate (AR$474), Río Gallegos (AR$490) and Ushuaia (AR$616).

Newcomer **Andes** (☎ 452355; www.andesonline .com; Av Roca 624) has flights to Buenos Aires' Aeroparque (AR$558) several times a week.

Aerolíneas Argentinas (☎ 451998; Av Roca 427) flies only from nearby Trelew – but it does have a ticketing representative here.

BUS

Puerto Madryn's full-service **bus terminal** (☎ 451789; Doctor Avila, btwn Independencia & Necochea), behind the historic 1889 Estación del Ferrocarril Patagónico, has an ATM and a helpful tourist information desk. Bus timetables are clearly posted and large luggage lockers are available for rent.

Bus companies include **Andesmar/Central Argentino** (☎ 473764), **Don Otto** (☎ 451675), **28 de Julio** (☎ 472056), **Mar y Valle** (☎ 472056), **Que Bus** (☎ 455805), **Ruta Patagonia** (☎ 454572), **TAC** (☎ 474938) and **TUS** (☎ 451962).

The bus to Puerto Pirámides, operated by Mar y Valle (AR$16.50, 1½ hours), leaves at 9:45am and returns to Madryn at 6pm.

Some destinations served:

Destination	Cost (AR$)	Duration (hr)
Bariloche	145-190	14-15
Buenos Aires	240-290	18-20
Comodoro Rivadavia	60-88	6-8
Córdoba	180-240	18
Esquel	105-125	7-9
Mendoza	254-330	23-24
Neuquén	120-135	12
Río Gallegos	154-189	15-20
Trelew	10	1
Viedma	65-88	5-6

Getting Around

Renting a bicycle (see p426) is ideal for travel in and around town.

TO/FROM THE AIRPORT

Southbound 28 de Julio buses to Trelew, which run hourly Monday through Saturday between 6am and 10pm, will stop at Trelew's airport on request.

Radio taxis like **La Nueva Patagonia** (☎ 476000) take travelers to and from Madryn's airport for about AR$18, while **Eben-Ezer** (☎ 472474) runs a service (AR$35) to Trelew's airport.

CAR

A roundtrip to Península Valdés is a little over 300km. A group sharing expenses can make a car rental a relatively reasonable and more flexible alternative to taking a bus tour if you don't have to pay for extra kilometers – make sure that you understand the rental terms before handing over your credit card.

PATAGONIA

Rental rates vary, depending on the mileage allowance and age and condition of the vehicle. The family-owned **Centauro** (☎ 02965-15-340400; www.centaurorentacar.com.ar; Av Roca 733) gets high marks as an attentive and competitively priced rental agency. Basic vehicles run AR$268 per day, with insurance and 400km included.

Northbound motorists should note that the last gas station with cheap fuel is 139km north in Sierra Grande.

AROUND PUERTO MADRYN

Home to a permanent sea-lion colony and cormorant rookery, the **Reserva Faunística Punta Loma** (admission AR$25) is 17km southwest of Puerto Madryn via a good but winding gravel road. The overlook is about 15m from the animals, best seen during low tides. Many travel agencies organize two-hour tours (AR$80) according to the tide schedules; otherwise, check tide tables and hire a car or taxi, or make the trek via bicycle.

Twenty kilometers north of Puerto Madryn via RP 1 is **Playa Flecha** observatory, a recommended whale-watching spot.

RESERVA FAUNÍSTICA PENÍNSULA VALDÉS

Unesco World Heritage site Península Valdés is one of South America's finest wildlife reserves. More than 80,000 visitors per year visit this sanctuary, which has a total area of 3600 sq km and more than 400km of coastline. The wildlife viewing is truly exceptional: the peninsula is home to sea lions, elephant seals, guanacos, rheas, Magellanic penguins and numerous seabirds. But the biggest attraction is the endangered *ballena franca austral* (southern right whale). The warmer, more enclosed waters along the Golfo Nuevo, Golfo San José and the coastline near Caleta Valdés from Punta Norte to Punta Hércules are prime breeding zones for right whales between June and mid-December. For details on the region's ocean wildlife, see the boxed text (p434).

One doesn't expect lambs alongside penguins, but sheep *estancias* occupy most of the peninsula's interior, which includes one of the world's lowest continental depressions, the salt flats of Salina Grande and Salina Chica, 42m below sea level. At the turn of the 20th century, Puerto Pirámides, the peninsula's only village, was the shipping port for the salt extracted from Salina Grande.

About 17km north of Puerto Madryn, paved RP 2 branches off RN 3 across the Istmo Carlos Ameghino to the entrance of the **reserve** (admission AR$45; valid for 2 days). The **Centro de Interpretación** (☼ 8am-8pm), 22km beyond the entrance, focuses on natural history, displays a full right whale skeleton and has material on the peninsula's colonization, from the area's first Spanish settlement at Fuerte San José to later mineral exploration. Don't miss the stunning panoramic view from the observation tower.

If you are sleeping in Puerto Madryn but plan to visit the park on two consecutive days, ask a ranger to validate your pass before you exit the park so you can re-enter without charges.

Puerto Pirámides

☎ 02965 / pop humans 250, whales 400–600

Set amid sandy cliffs on a bright blue sea, this sleepy old salt port now bustles with tour buses and visitors clad in orange life jackets. Whales mean whopping and ever-growing tourism here, but at the end of the day the tour buses split and life in this two-street town regains its cherished snail's pace.

Av de las Ballenas is the main drag, which runs perpendicular to Primera (1era) Bajada, the first road to the beach, stuffed with tour outfitters. A small **tourist office** (☎ 495048; www .puertopiramides.gov.ar; 1era Bajada) helps with travelers' needs. Visitors can access the internet at **Telefónica** (Av de las Ballenas) and take out cash from the ATM at **Banco de Chubut** (Av de las Ballenas).

ACTIVITIES

While most visitors focus on whale watching, adventure options – including diving, snorkeling and mountain biking – continue to grow. Friendly **Patagonia Explorers** (☎ 02965-15-340619; www.patagoniaexplorers.com; Av de las Ballenas) offers guided hikes and short sea-kayaking trips (AR$190, two hours), as well as extended sea-kayaking expeditions lasting three, eight or 10 days – check the website or drop by its office for more information.

Area *estancias* offer **horseback riding**. But you don't have to stray far from town to find adventure: just join the local kids at the **sandboarding** hill at the end of the second road down to the beach.

Visitors can walk to the **sea-lion colony** less than 5km from town (though mostly uphill). It is a magnificent spot to catch the sunset,

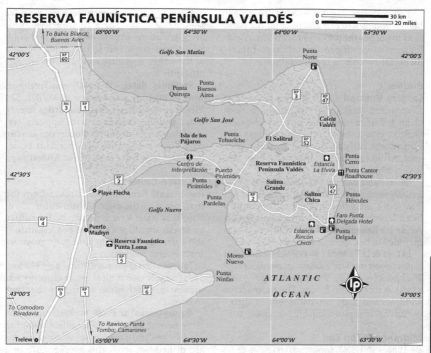

RESERVA FAUNÍSTICA PENÍNSULA VALDÉS

occasional whale sightings and views across the Golfo Nuevo toward Puerto Madryn. Be sure to time your visit with the tides (high tides finds all the sea lions swimming out to sea).

Whale Tours

This is the place to glimpse spy-hopping, breaching and tailing cetaceans on a **whale-watching excursion** (AR$120-180, under 12yr half price), arranged in Puerto Madryn or Puerto Pirámides. The standard trip lasts an hour and a half, but longer excursions are available, too.

When choosing a tour, ask other travelers about their experiences and check what kind of boat will be used: smaller, Zodiac-style inflatable rafts, seating around 20 people, offer more intimacy than the larger bulldozer variety. By law, outfitters are not allowed within 100m of whales without cutting the motor, nor allowed to pursue them.

Check your outfitter's policies. When the port is closed due to bad weather, tour bookings are usually honored the following day (although these days are more crowded). Outside of whale-watching season (June to

December), boat trips aren't worthwhile unless you adore sea lions and shorebirds.

The following is a partial list of reputable outfitters:

Bottazzi (☎ 495050; www.titobottazzi.com; 1era Bajada) If you can, arrange to explore the bay with Tito himself, an old sea dog with ample experience. Sunset cruises include a *picada* (shared appetizer plate) and glass of wine at Restingas afterwards. Also has an office in Puerto Madryn.

Hydrosport (☎ 495065; www.hydrosport.com.ar; 1era Bajada) In addition to whale watching, it runs dolphin-watching tours and has naturalists and submarine audio systems on board.

Whales Argentina (☎ 495015; www.whalesargentina .com.ar; 1era Bajada) Offers quality trips with a bilingual guide; also runs personalized excursions on a four-seater semi-rigid boat.

SLEEPING

If you're interested in watching wildlife, it's worth staying overnight instead of trying to see everything in a day-long sprint from Puerto Madryn. Campers gloat about hearing whales' eerie cries and huffing blow holes in the night – it can be an extraordinary experience.

You will have to get a voucher from your hotel if you plan to exit and re-enter the park, so as to not pay the park entry fee twice. Watch for signs advertising rooms, cabins and apartments for rent along the main drag.

Budget

Camping Municipal (☎ 495084; per person AR$6) Convenient, sheltered gravel camp sites with clean toilets, a store and hot pay showers (AR$2), down the road behind the gas station. Come early in summer to stake your spot. Avoid camping on the beach: high tide is very high.

Hostel Bahía Ballenas (☎ 02965-15-567104; www .bahiaballenas.com.ar; Av de las Ballenas s/n; dm AR$45; 🖳) You can't miss this bright but bare-bones brick hostel: the large 'Backpackers' sign on Av de las Ballenas will catch your eye. Rates include kitchen use and internet.

La Casa de la Tía Alicia (☎ 495046; http://lacasadela tiaalicia.blogspot.com; Av de las Ballenas s/n; per person AR$75) Backpackers praise the *buena onda* (good vibes) at this old tin house. The rooms have windows and share two bathrooms; a three-person cabin is also available for rent.

Midrange & Top End

De Luna (☎ 495083; www.deluna.com.ar; Av de las Ballenas s/n; d/cabin AR$200/350) Choose from spacious and inviting rooms in the main house, or a crunched but lovely guest cabin, perched above the house with excellent views.

Motel ACA (☎ 495004; www.motelacapiramides.com.ar; Av Roca s/n; s/d AR$240/295) The 16 noisy beachfront motel rooms have heating and cable TV. The attached restaurant, open to the public, serves fresh seafood and offers lovely views of the bay through huge glass windows.

our pick La Posta (☎ 495005; www.lapostapiramides .com.ar; 1era Bajada s/n; apartment for 4/5 people AR$260/300) These adorable cabin-style apartments, right in the middle of the action, fill up quickly in high season. It's easy to understand why when you see the cozy, clean interiors with exposed brick walls, simple wood furniture, cable TV and kitchenettes.

Del Nomade Hostería Ecologica (☎ 495044; www .ecohosteria.com.ar; Av de las Ballenas s/n; d AR$650; 🖳) This stylish ecofriendly lodge comprises eight rooms powered by solar energy and recycled water. Four rooms on the ground level offer private terraces; all come with heated floors, internet access, handmade soaps and other all-natural amenities.

Paradise (☎ 495030; www.hosteriaparadise.com.ar; 2da Bajada; d AR$830; 🖳) These 12 attractive, tiled, brick-walled rooms are expansive and cool. Some have views and Jacuzzi tubs. Outside of the whale-watching season, rates are significantly lower.

Restingas Hotel (☎ 495101; www.lasrestingas .com; 1era Bajada; d garden/oceanview AR$900/1175; 🖳) Mixed reviews beset this beachfront luxury hotel and spa. While service appears lax, watching whales from your bedroom is a big plus. Guests do praise the abundant buffet breakfast. Meals are available at AR$60.

EATING & DRINKING

Restaurants flank the beachfront, down the first street to the right as you enter town. Note that water here is desalinated: sensitive stomachs should stick to the bottled stuff. If self-catering, it's best to haul your groceries from Puerto Madryn.

Towanda (1era Bajada; mains AR$20-25; ⏱ 9am-6pm) This friendly cafe is ideal for an espresso and pressed sandwich while waiting for your tour to depart.

Quimey Quipan (☎ 458609; 1era Bajada; mains AR$20-35; ⏱ breakfast, lunch & dinner) Breakfast, towering sandwiches and no-frills set seafood menus are dished out from this average cafe to a steady stream of passersby.

La Estación (☎ 495047; Av de las Ballenas s/n; mains AR$25-38; ⏱ breakfast-late) This happy house is the spot to knock back drinks; there are also good pasta dishes and breakfast service.

El Refugio (☎ 495031; www.elrefugiopiramides.com .ar; Av de las Ballenas s/n; mains AR$30-45; ⏱ lunch & dinner) This small traditional eatery, filled with rustic wood tables, serves homemade local recipes and fresh fish. The owners also rent out simple apartments for two to five people; ask for prices and availability at reception.

GETTING THERE & AROUND

During summer, the Mar y Valle bus service travels from Puerto Madryn to Puerto Pirámides (AR$11, 1½ hours) at 9:30am and returns to Madryn at 6:30pm, with more limited services in the off-season. Bus tours from Puerto Madryn may allow passengers to get off at Puerto Pirámides.

Around Puerto Pirámides

If you're driving around the peninsula, take it easy. Roads are *ripio* and washboard, with sandy spots that grab the wheels. If you're in

---

THE LITTLE PRINCE

From an apartment in Manhattan in 1941, a French pilot and writer, in exile from the battlefields of Europe, scripted what would become one of the most-read children's fables, *The Little Prince*. Antoine St-Exupéry, then 40 years old, had spent the previous 20 years flying in the Sahara, the Pyrenees, Egypt and Patagonia – where he was director of Aeropostal Argentina from 1929 to 1931. Intertwined in the lines of *The Little Prince* and Asteroid B612 are images of Patagonia that stayed with him while flying over the barren landscape and braving the incessant winds.

It has become popular legend that the shape of Isla de los Pájaros, off the coast of Península Valdés, inspired the elephant-eating boa constrictor (or hat, as you may see it), while the perfectly conical volcanoes on the asteroid owe their shape to the volcanoes St-Exupéry flew over en route to Punta Arenas, Chile. The author's illustrations show the little prince on the peaks of mountains, unquestionably those in the Fitz Roy Range (one such peak now bears his name). And, possibly, meeting two young daughters of a French immigrant after an emergency landing in Concordia, near Buenos Aires, helped mold the character of the prince.

St-Exupéry never witnessed the influence his mythical royal character would enjoy. In 1944, just after the first publication of *The Little Prince*, he disappeared during a flight to join French forces-in-exile stationed in Algiers. His years in Patagonia also figure in two critically acclaimed novels, *Night Flight* and *Wind, Sand and Stars*, both worthwhile reads on long Patagonia trips.

---

a rental car, make sure you get all the details on the insurance policy. Hitchhiking here is nearly impossible and bike travel is long and unnervingly windy.

ISLA DE LOS PÁJAROS

In Golfo San José, 800m north of the isthmus, this bird sanctuary is off-limits to humans, but visible through a powerful telescope. It contains a replica of a chapel built at Fuerte San José. See the boxed text, above, to find out how this small island figures into Antoine de St-Exupéry's *The Little Prince*.

PUNTA DELGADA

In the peninsula's southeast corner, 76km southeast of Puerto Pirámides, sea lions and, in spring, a huge colony of elephant seals are visible from the cliffs. Enter the public dirt road right of the hotel for viewings.

The luxury **Faro Punta Delgada Hotel** (☎ 02965-458444, 02965-15-406304; www.puntadelgada.com; d incl half-/full board AR$1200/1550) occupies a lighthouse complex that once belonged to the Argentine postal service. Horseback riding, 4WD tours and other activities are available. Nonguests can dine at the upscale restaurant serving *estancia* fare (mains AR$35 to AR$75). Guided naturalist walks down to the beach leave frequently in high season.

With a prime location for wildlife watching, the refined **Estancia Rincón Chico** (☎ 02965-471733, 02965-15-688302; www.rinconchico.com.ar; d incl full board AR$2185; ⊗ Aug-Mar) hosts university marine

biologists, student researchers and tourists. Lodging is in a modern, corrugated-tin ranch house with eight well-appointed doubles and a *quincho* (thatched-roof building) for barbecues. In addition to guided excursions, there are paths for cycling and walking on your own.

PUNTA CANTOR & CALETA VALDÉS

In spring, elephant seals haul themselves onto the long gravel spit at this sheltered bay, 43km north of Punta Delgada. September has females giving birth to pups, while males fight it out defending their harem – making for dramatic sightings from the trails that wind down the hill. You may even see guanacos strolling along the beach.

Tour groups fill up the **Roadhouse** (☎ 02965-15-406183; www.laelvira.com.ar; meals AR$35), a decent self-service restaurant offering a salad bar, coffee, drinks and rest rooms. It is part of **Estancia La Elvira** (☎ 02965-15-669153; www.laelvira.com.ar; d AR$450), a comfortable lodging with a modern construction that lacks the romance of a seasoned guesthouse. Activities include horseback riding, agrotourism and nature strolls. A few kilometers north of the Roadhouse, there's a sizable colony of burrowing Magellanic penguins.

PUNTA NORTE

At the far end of the peninsula, Punta Norte boasts an enormous mixed colony of sea lions and elephant seals. Its distance means it is rarely visited by tour groups, and for that

PATAGONIA WILDLIFE

You don't have to be a whale groupie to be awed by the animals that gather along Southern Argentina's rugged coast. The chance to view up close a cast of wild characters – penguins, dolphins, killer whales, sea lions and elephant seals – makes these lonely Atlantic shores a must to visit.

Magellanic Penguin

What: Sphenicus magellanicus (in Spanish pingüino magellánico)
When: August to April; peak season December through February
Where: Península Valdés, Punta Tombo, Cabo Dos Bahías and Seno Otway (Chile)

Referred to locally as the jackass penguin for its characteristic braying sound, the Magellanic penguin has black to brown shading and two black-and-white bars going across the upper chest. It averages 45cm in height and weighs about 3.15kg. Winters are spent at sea, but males arrive on land in late August, followed by territorial fights in September as burrows and nests are prepared. In October females lay their eggs. Come mid-November, when eggs are hatched, males and females take turns caring for and feeding the chicks with regurgitated squid and small fish. In December it's a madhouse of hungry demanding chicks, adults coming in and out of the sea with food, and predatory birds trying to pick out the weaklings. In January chicks start to molt and take their first steps into the sea, and by February it's a traffic jam at the beach as chicks take to the water. By March juveniles start their migration north, followed in April by the adults.

Penguins are awkward on land, but in the water they are swift and graceful, reaching speeds of up to 8km/h. They are also naturally curious, though if approached too quickly they scamper into their burrows or toboggan back into the water. They will bite if you get too close. The least disruptive way to observe them is to sit near the burrows and wait for them to come to you.

Over a million pairs of these penguins exist, but their populations are threatened by human activity and oil spills.

Southern Right Whale

What: Eubalaena australis (in Spanish ballena franca austral)
When: June to mid-December; peak season September and October
Where: Golfo Nuevo and Golfo San José, Península Valdés

Averaging nearly 12m in length and weighing more than 27 tonnes, southern right whales enter the shallow waters of Península Valdés in the spring to breed and bear young. Females, which are larger than males, will copulate a year after giving birth. A female may pick out the best partner by fending off for hours the pack of males trailing her to see which one endures. For the past three decades, researchers have been able to track individual whales by noting the pattern of calluses, made white against the black skin by clusters of parasites found on the whale's body and head. Right whales don't have teeth, but trap krill and plankton with fringed plates (baleen) that hang from the upper jaw.

The slow-moving right whale was a favorite target of whalers because, unlike other species, it remained floating on the surface after being killed. After more than half a century of legal protection, South Atlantic right whale populations are now slowly recovering.

Killer Whale

What: Ornicus orca (in Spanish orca)
When: June to mid-December; peak season September and October
Where: Península Valdés

These large dolphins, with black with white underbellies, live in pods consisting of one male, a cluster of females and the young. Upon maturity, the young males leave the pod to create their own group. Males, which can reach more than 9m in length and weigh as much as 6000kg, live an average of 30 years, while females, substantially smaller at 7m and about 4000kg, live about 50 years, calving approximately every 10 years. The impressive dorsal fin can reach nearly 2m high.

Killer whales prey on fish, penguins, dolphins and seals, and will hunt in groups to prey upon larger whales. At Punta Norte on Península Valdés they hunt sea lions and elephant seals by almost beaching themselves and waiting for the waters to wash a few unfortunates their way. In the 1970s groups concerned with the livelihood of the sea lions requested the whales be shot, to either kill or scare them away, before they decimated the sea lion colonies. Fortunately, this reaction was short-lived and made clear the inevitability of the food chain.

Southern Sea Lion
What: *Otaria flavescens* (in Spanish *lobo marino*)
When: year-round
Where: widely distributed along Patagonia coasts
Aggressive southern sea lions feed largely on squid and the occasional penguin. No matter how tempting, don't approach them too closely for photo ops. The bull (male) has a thick neck and large head with longer hair around the neck, creating the appearance of a lion's mane. An adult male can weigh 300kg and measure 2m, while females weigh around 200kg. Bulls fight to control their harems and breed with up to 10 females per season. Females give birth once each season and are ready for mating again in less than a week. Unlike the elephant seal, pups nurse only from their mothers.

Southern Elephant Seal
What: *Mirounga leonina* (in Spanish *elefante marino*)
When: year-round; birthing and mating between September and November
Where: widely distributed along Patagonia coasts
Elephant seals take their common name from the male's enormous proboscis, which does indeed resemble an elephant's trunk. Bulls (males) reach nearly 7m in length and can weigh over 3500kg, but females are substantially smaller. They spend most of the year at sea, and have been observed diving to a depth of 1500m and staying submerged for over an hour in search of squid and other marine life. (The average dive depth and duration are 1000m and 23 minutes.)

Península Valdés has the only breeding colony of southern elephant seals on the South American continent. The bull comes ashore in late winter or early spring, breeding after the already pregnant females arrive and give birth. Dominant males known as 'beachmasters' control harems of up to 100 females, but must constantly fight off challenges from bachelor males. Females give birth to a pup once a year, each pregnancy lasting 11 months. For 19 days after the birth the female nurses the pup, during which time she will lose close to 40% of her body weight, while the pup's increases by 300%. Pups will sometimes nurse from other females. After the 19 days, the mother may breed again.

Commerson's Dolphin
What: *Cephalorhynchus commersonii* (in Spanish *tonina overa*)
When: year-round; breeding season November to February
Where: Puerto San Julián, Playa Unión and Puerto Deseado
Outgoing and acrobatic, the Commerson's dolphin is a favorite along shallow areas of coastal Patagonia. Adults are quite small, about 1.5m in length, and brilliantly patterned in black and white with a rounded dorsal fin. Young dolphins are gray, brown and black; the brown slowly disappears and the gray fades to striking white. In small groups, they play around the sides of boats, breaching frequently and sometimes riding the bow. Commerson's dolphins eat shrimp, squid and bottom-dwelling fish. In Argentina they are illegally captured to use as crab bait.

PATAGONIA

reason it offers visitors the treat of solitude. But the real thrill here is the orcas: from mid-February through mid-April these killer whales come to feast on the unsuspecting colonies of sea lions. The chances are you won't see a high-tide attack in all its gory glory, but watching their dorsal fins carving through the water is enough to raise some goosebumps.

There's a small but good museum focusing on marine mammals, with details on the Tehuelche and the area's sealing history.

TRELEW
☎ 02965 / pop 93,386

Though steeped in Welsh heritage, Trelew isn't a postcard city. In fact, this midsized hub, convenient to so many attractions, is poised to be touristy – but isn't. You might find that good or bad, but in its very uneventfulness Trelew does offer the traveler a welcome pause. After the obligatory visit to the city's top-notch dinosaur museum, you're free to frequent the ice-cream parlors, lounge on the verdant square and check out a few historic buildings. The region's commercial center, it is also a convenient base for visiting the Welsh villages of Gaiman and Dolavon. Founded in 1886 as a railway junction to unite the Río Chubut valley with the Golfo Nuevo, Trelew (tre-*ley*-ooh) owes its easily mispronounced name to the Welsh contraction of *tre* (town) and *lew* (after Lewis Jones, who promoted railway expansion). During the following 30 years, the railway reached Gaiman, the Welsh built their Salón San David (a replica of St David's Cathedral, Pembrokeshire), and Spanish and Italian immigrants settled in the area. In 1956 the federal government promoted Patagonian industrial development and Trelew's population skyrocketed.

Orientation
Trelew is 65km south of Puerto Madryn via RN 3. The center of town surrounds Plaza Independencia, with most services on Calles 25 de Mayo and San Martín, and along Av Fontana. East–west streets change names on either side of Av Fontana.

Information
ATMs and *locutorios* with internet are plentiful downtown and around the plaza.

ACA (Automóvil Club Argentino; ☎ 435197; cnr Av Fontana & San Martín) Argentina's auto club; good source for provincial road maps.

Marva Lavadero Sarmiento (Sarmiento 363) Self- and full-service laundry and dry cleaner.

Post office (cnr 25 de Mayo & Mitre)

Tourist office (☎ 426819; www.trelewpatagonia.gov .ar; Mitre 387; ☺ 8am-9pm) Helpful and well stocked, with some English-speaking staff.

Sights
The tourist office sometimes has an informative walking-tour brochure, in Spanish and English, describing most of the city's historic buildings.

MUSEO PALEONTOLÓGICO EGIDIO FERUGLIO
Showcasing the most important fossil finds in Patagonia, this natural-history **museum** (☎ 420012; www.mef.org.ar; Av Fontana 140; admission AR$23; ☺ 10am-6pm) offers outstanding life-sized dinosaur exhibits and more than 1700 fossil remains of plant and marine life. Nature sounds and a video accent the informative plaques, and tours are available in a number of languages. The collection includes local dinosaurs, such as the tehuelchesaurus, patagosaurus and titanosaurus. Museum researchers were part of an international team that discovered a new and unusual species called *Brachytrachelopan mesai*, a short-necked sauropod. Feruglio was an Italian paleontologist who came to Argentina in 1925 as a petroleum geologist for YPF.

Kids aged eight to 12 can check out the 'Explorers in Pyjamas' program, which invites kids to sleep over and explore the museum by flashlight. The museum also sponsors interesting group tours to **Geoparque Paleontológico Bryn Gwyn** (admission AR$8; ☺ 9am-4pm), in the badlands along the Río Chubut (25km from Trelew, or 8km south of Gaiman via RP 5). The three-hour guided visits are a walk through time, along a well-designed nature trail past a wealth of exposed fossils dating as far back as the Tertiary, some 40 million years ago.

OTHER MUSEUMS
Adjoined to the tourist office, the small visual-arts **Museo de Artes Visuales** (☎ 433774; Mitre 351; admission free; ☺ 8am-8pm Mon-Fri, 2-8pm Sat & Sun) features works on loan from the Museo Nacional de Bellas Artes in Buenos Aires, as well as polished relics from Welsh colonization.

In a former train station, the **Museo Regional Pueblo de Luis** (☎ 424062; cnr Av Fontana & Lewis Jones; admission AR$2; ☺ 8am-1pm & 3-8pm Mon-Fri) displays

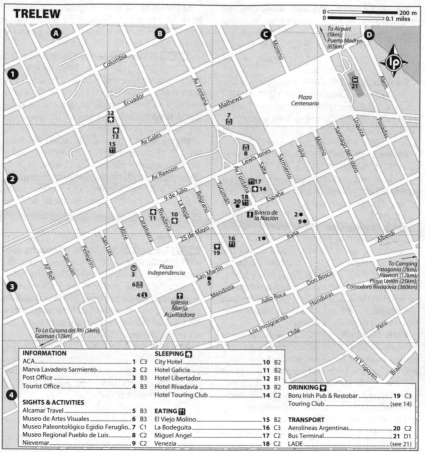

TRELEW

INFORMATION	
ACA	**1** C3
Marva Lavadero Sarmiento	**2** C2
Post Office	**3** B3
Tourist Office	**4** B3

SIGHTS & ACTIVITIES	
Alcamar Travel	**5** B3
Museo de Artes Visuales	**6** B3
Museo Paleontológico Egidio Feruglio	**7** C1
Museo Regional Pueblo de Luis	**8** C2
Nievemar	**9** C2

SLEEPING	
City Hotel	**10** B2
Hotel Galicia	**11** B2
Hotel Libertador	**12** B1
Hotel Rivadavia	**13** B2
Hotel Touring Club	**14** C2

EATING	
El Viejo Molino	**15** B2
La Bodeguita	**16** C3
Miguel Angel	**17** C2
Venezia	**18** C2

DRINKING	
Boru Irish Pub & Restobar	**19** C3
Touring Club	(see 14)

TRANSPORT	
Aerolíneas Argentinas	**20** C2
Bus Terminal	**21** D1
LADE	(see 21)

PATAGONIA

historical photographs, clothing and period furnishings of Welsh settlers.

Tours

Several travel agencies run excursions to Reserva Provincial Punta Tombo (around AR$150, plus AR$40 admission), some passing by Puerto Rawson on the way back to see *toninas overas* (Commerson's dolphins) when conditions are agreeable. The actual time at Punta Tombo is only about 1½ hours. Full-day trips to Península Valdés are also on offer, but going to Puerto Madryn first is a better bet: there are more options, prices are similar and there's less driving time.

Local agencies worth checking out include Amex representative **Nievemar** (☎ 434114; www

.nievemartours.com.ar, in Spanish; Italia 20), which accepts traveler's checks, and **Alcamar Travel** (☎ 421448; San Martín 146).

Festivals & Events

Gwyl y Glaniad On July 28 the landing of the first Welsh is celebrated by taking tea in one of the many chapels.
Eisteddfod de Chubut A Welsh literary and musical festival, held in late October. The tradition started in 1875.
Aniversario de la Ciudad October 20; commemorates the city's founding in 1886.

Sleeping

Trelew's accommodations are largely dated and geared toward the business traveler; in addition, spots fill up fast. Travelers can find more variety in nearby Puerto Madryn or Gaiman.

Camping Patagonia (☎ 02965-15-406907, 02965-15-350581; per person AR$8) Shady and spacious, this green campground has a small convenience store, electricity and hot showers, but limited public transport. It's 7km from town on RN 7, off the road to Rawson.

Hotel Rivadavia (☎ 434472; www.cpatagonia.com/rivadavia, in Spanish; Rivadavia 55; s/d/tr AR$105/130/145) Up on a hill, this small family-run hotel offers good value, though the rooms with gauzy curtains are somewhat faded. Breakfast (AR$13) is served in the TV-oriented lobby.

City Hotel (☎ 433951; hotelcitytrelew@speedy.com.ar; Rivadavia 254; s/d/tr AR$120/200/250; ⬛) There is not a speck of dust in this urban hotel, though it retains all the charm of a government institution. The 33 shuttered rooms are plain but comfortable and include TV. Parking is free.

Hotel Touring Club (☎ 433997/98; www.touringpatagonia.com.ar; Av Fontana 240; d AR$180; ⬛) Expectations are high when you climb the curved marble staircase of this historic hotel, but most of the grandeur is found in the lobby. Touring Club was once, supposedly, the fanciest hotel in Patagonia. Today, rooms are small but adequate, with a downside of lumpy mattresses and threadbare towels.

Hotel Libertador (☎ 420220; www.hotellibertadortw.com; Rivadavia 31; s/d AR$225/280; ⬛) Rooms in this business hotel are comfortable, with soft decor, firm beds and ample light, but no one ever updated the fire-engine red carpet! Tubs, phones and TVs come with all rooms. The buffet-style breakfast is complimentary but parking costs AR$12 extra.

Hotel Galicia (☎ 433802; www.hotelgalicia.com.ar, in Spanish; 9 de Julio 214; s/d/tr/q AR$342/457/495/570; ⬛) A marble staircase and gold trim bring a swanky touch to this popular hotel. The wood-paneled rooms have firm mattresses, carpet and cable TV. Staff are friendly and parking is included.

La Casona del Río (☎ 438343; www.lacasonadelrio.com.ar; Chacra 105; s/d AR$345/460; ⬛) Outside the city center on the bank of the Chubut River, this English-style B&B is a thoroughly charming refuge featuring a library, tennis court, gazebo and bikes available for rent. Guest rooms have antique wood furniture and cable TV.

Eating

Venezia (25 de Mayo 21; snacks AR$6; ⏲ 7:30am-10pm Mon-Sat, 9am-1pm & 4-8pm Sun) This bakery and ice-cream shop tempts passersby with a window view of mousses and chocolate creations to drool over.

La Bodeguita (☎ 437777; Belgrano 374; mains AR$25-38; ⏲ Tue-Sun) A popular stop for meats, pasta and seafood, this restaurant boasts attentive service and a family atmosphere.

our pick El Viejo Molino (☎ 428019; Av Gales 250; mains AR$28-35; ⏲ closed Mon) Iron lamps and brickwork restore the romance to this 1914 flour mill – a must if you're in town. On weekends it's packed, with the main attraction, the wood-fired *parrilla*, grilling steaks and even vegetables to perfection.

Miguel Angel (☎ 430403; Av Fontana 246; mains AR$32-38; ⏲ closed Mon) This chic eatery, outfitted with smooth tile and wood, departs from the everyday with savory dishes such as gnocchi and wild mushrooms, and popular sushi Wednesdays, but its staples are the homemade pasta and pizza.

Drinking

our pick Touring Club (☎ 433997/98; Av Fontana 240; snacks AR$12; ⏲ 6:30am-2am; ⬛) Old lore exudes from the pores of this historic *confitería*, from the Butch Cassidy 'Wanted' poster to the embossed tile ceiling and antique bar back. Even the tuxedoed waitstaff appear to be plucked from another era. It's too bad the sandwiches are only so-so, but it's worth stopping in for coffee or beers.

Boru Irish Pub & Restobar (☎ 0297-15-477-2416; Belgrano 341) This good-looking new pub, featuring a beautiful wood bar and a row of cozy red booths, serves up icy beer and plates piled high with french fries.

Getting There & Away

AIR

Trelew's **airport** (TRE; ☎ 428021) is 5km north of town off RN 3. Airport tax is AR$$18.

Aerolíneas Argentinas (☎ 420210; 25 de Mayo 33) flies direct daily to Buenos Aires (AR$857) and several times a week to Esquel (AR$425), Bariloche, Ushuaia (AR$1020) and El Calafate (AR$920).

LADE (☎ 435740), at the bus terminal, flies to Comodoro Rivadavia (AR$193) on Sundays.

BUS

Trelew's full-service **bus terminal** (☎ 420121) is six blocks northeast of downtown.

For Gaiman (AR$3.80), **28 de Julio** (☎ 432429) has 18 services a day between 7am and 11pm (reduced weekend services), with most continuing to Dolavon (AR$5, half-hour). Buses to Rawson (AR$3, 15 minutes) leave every 15 minutes.

PATAGONIA

Mar y Valle (☎ 432429) and 28 de Julio run hourly buses to Puerto Madryn (AR$10, one hour). Mar y Valle goes to Puerto Pirámides (AR$22, 2½ hours) daily at 8:15am, with additional service in summer. **El Ñandú** (☎ 427499) goes to Camarones (AR$20, three hours) at 8am on Monday, Wednesday and Friday.

Long-distance bus companies include **El Cóndor** (☎ 431675), **Que Bus** (☎ 422760), **Andesmar** (☎ 433535), **TAC** (☎ 431452), **TUS** (☎ 421343) and **Don Otto** (☎ 429496).

Of several departures daily for Buenos Aires, Don Otto has the most comfortable and most direct service. Only Don Otto goes to Mar del Plata, while TAC goes to La Plata. TAC and Andesmar service the most buses. For Comodoro Rivadavia there are a few daily departures with TAC, Don Otto or Andesmar, all of which also continue to Río Gallegos.

Destination	Cost (AR$)	Duration (hr)
Bahía Blanca	120-136	12
Bariloche	165-200	13-16
Buenos Aires	230-345	18-21
Caleta Olivia	72-85	6
Comodoro Rivadavia	62-82	5-6
Córdoba	170-225	19
Esquel	90-135	8-9
La Plata	192-223	19
Mar del Plata	197-240	17-21
Mendoza	210-305	24
Neuquén	115-162	10
Puerto Madryn	10	1
Río Gallegos	165-202	14-17
Viedma	79-95	8

Getting Around

From the airport, taxis charge AR$20 to downtown, AR$55 to Gaiman and AR$150 to Puerto Madryn. Car-rental agencies at the airport include **Hertz** (☎ 475247) and **Rent a Car Patagonia** (☎ 420898).

AROUND TRELEW

Rawson, 17km east of Trelew, is Chubut's provincial capital, but nearby **Playa Unión**, the region's principal playground, has the capital attraction: *toninas overas* (Commerson's dolphins; see p435). Playa Unión is a long stretch of white-sand beach with blocks of summer homes. Dolphin tours depart **Puerto Rawson** from April to December. For reservations, contact **Toninas Adventure** (☎ 498372; toninasadventure@msn.com).

Empresas Rawson and 28 de Julio buses depart from Trelew for Rawson (AR$2.50)

frequently from Monday to Friday and every 20 to 30 minutes on weekends. Get off at Rawson's plaza or bus terminal and hop on a green 'Bahía' bus, which heads to Puerto Rawson before turning around.

GAIMAN
☎ 02965 / pop 5753

Cream pie, dainty tea cakes, *torta negra* (a rich, dense fruit cake) and a hot pot of black tea – most visitors take an oral dose of culture when visiting this quintessential Welsh river-valley village. Today, about a third of the residents claim Welsh ancestry and teahouses persist in their afternoon tradition, even though their overselling sometimes rubs the charm thin.

Locals proudly recount the day in 1995 when the late Diana, Princess of Wales, visited Gaiman to take tea: naturally, competition was stiff between the rival teahouses. There's still a fair amount of grumbling about the fact that Diana's posse, due to security reasons, chose the large Ty Te Caerdydd over one of the more traditional establishments. The china and utensils used by the princess are still on display under a glass case at the teahouse, and though Lady Di is long gone, her afternoon visit to Gaiman is still a hot topic.

The town's name, meaning Stony Point or Arrow Point, originated from the Tehuelche who once wintered in this valley. After the Welsh constructed their first house in 1874, the two groups peacefully coexisted for a time. Later immigrant groups of criollos, Germans and Anglos joined the Welsh. Gaiman's homey digs provide great value for lodgers, but the town offers little in the way of diversion beyond quiet strolls past stone houses with rose gardens after a filling teahouse visit.

Orientation & Information

Gaiman is 17km west of Trelew via RN 25. The town's touristy center is little more than a criss-cross of streets snuggled between the barren hills and Río Chubut. Av Eugenio Tello is the main road, connecting the main town entrance to leafy Plaza Roca. Most of the teahouses and historic sites are within four blocks of the plaza. Across the river are fast-growing residential and industrial areas.

There's one ATM on the plaza at Banco del Chubut, but it does not always work, so bring cash. *Locutorios* and internet can be found along the main drag.

PATAGONIA

WELSH LEGACY

The Welsh opened the door to settling Patagonia in 1865, though the newfound freedom cost them dearly. Few had farmed before and the arid steppe showed no resemblance to their verdant homeland. After nearly starving, they survived with the help of the Tehuelche, and eventually occupied the entire lower Chubut valley, founding the towns and teahouses of Rawson, Trelew, Puerto Madryn and Gaiman.

Today about 20% of Chubut's inhabitants have Welsh blood, though it logically grows thinner with each generation – 'or pretty soon you're marrying your cousin,' jokes one descendant. What you wouldn't expect is that a recent revival of Welsh culture is dragging it back from the grave. According to Welsh historian Fernando Coronato, 'For the old principality of Wales, Patagonia meant its most daring venture.' This renewed bond means yearly British Council appointments of Welsh teachers and exchanges for Patagonian students. Curious Welsh tourists visit as if time-traveling in their own culture, thanks to Patagonia's longtime isolation.

Post office (cnr Evans & Yrigoyen) Just north of the river bridge.

Tourist office (Informes Turísticos; ☎ 491571; www .gaiman.gov.ar, in Spanish; Belgrano 574; ☼ 9am-8pm Mon-Sat, 11am-8pm Sun) Ask here for a map and guided tours of historic houses.

Sights

Gaiman is ideal for an informal walking tour, past homes with ivy trelliess and drooping, oversized roses. Architecturally distinctive churches and chapels dot the town. **Primera Casa** (cnr Av Eugenio Tello & Evans; admission AR$3) is the first house, built in 1874 by David Roberts. Dating from 1906, the **Colegio Camwy** (cnr MD Jones & Rivadavia) is considered the first secondary school in Patagonia.

The old train station houses the **Museo Histórico Regional Gales** (☎ 491007; cnr Sarmiento & 28 de Julio; admission AR$2; ☼ 3-6pm Tue-Sun), a fine small museum holding the belongings and photographs of town pioneers.

The **Museo Antropológico** (cnr Bouchard & Jones; admission AR$2) offers humble homage to the indigenous cultures and history. Ask the tourist office for access. Nearby is the 300m **Túnel del Ferrocarril**, a brick tunnel through which the first trains to Dolavon passed in 1914.

Don't miss **Parque El Desafío** (Av Brown 52; admission AR$10, children under 10yr free; ☼ 3-7pm Mon-Fri; 9am-7pm Sat & Sun), the perfect remedy to long-distance travel fatigue. Its octogenarian owner Joaquín Alonso, the 'Dali of Recycling,' spent 30,000 hours fashioning some 80,000 bottles, cans and soda containers into whimsical folk art. Though he created the park to entertain his grandchildren, adults can appreciate it just as well. Plaques (some translated into English) with folk sayings and quotes from

Seneca and Plato offer wit and reflection for all amid this symphony of junk. As one proclaims: *Si quieres vivir mejor, mezcla a tu sensatez unos gramos de locura* ('If you want to live better, mix up your sensibility with a few grams of craziness'). The park gained Guinness World Record status in 1998 as Earth's largest 'recycled' park. Visitors can't help but leave El Desafío (translated as 'the achievement') without a smile, a whimsical notion or whiff of inspiration, which is its own testament. It's at the western entrance to town.

Sleeping

Camping Bomberos Voluntarios (☎ 491117; cnr Av Yrigoyen & Moreno; per person AR$6, children under 12yr free) The volunteer firefighters put together this agreeable campground with hot-water showers and fire pits.

Dyffryn Gwyrdd (☎ 491777; Av Eugenio Tello 103; s/d/tr AR$100/120/140) This canary-yellow home creates an inviting atmosphere of bright and simple rooms with carpet, fans and throw pillows. The bathrooms are dated but spotless and there's a quiet bar and TV area.

our pick **Yr Hen Ffordd** (☎ 491394; www.yrhenffordd .com.ar; Jones 342; d AR$140) This charming B&B is run by a young couple who give you a set of keys to the front door so you can come and go as you please. Rooms are simple but cozy, with cable TV and private bathrooms with great showers. In the morning, work up an appetite for the divine homemade scones.

Hostería Gwesty Tywi (☎ 491292; www.hosteria -gwestytywi.com.ar; Chacra 202; s/d/tr/q AR$140/180/210/240; 🖳) Diego and Brenda run this wonderful Welsh B&B with large gardens and snug, frilly rooms. Breakfast includes a selection of jams, cold meats and bread. They are glad to help with travel planning and occasionally fire up the barbecue to the delight of guests.

Eating

Tarten afal, tarten gwstard, cacen ffrwythau, spwnj jam and *bara brith* and a bottomless pot of tea – hungry yet? Afternoon tea is taken as a sacrament in Gaiman – though busloads of tourists get dump-trucked in teahouses without warning. The best bet is to look for places without buses in front, or wait for their departure. Tea services usually run from 2pm to 7pm.

Breuddwyd (☎ 02965-15-697069; Yrigoyen 320; snacks/tea AR$10/40) A basic, more modern cafe whose best feature is the flower garden out back, brimming with blooms and a fountain. Ask about rooms for rent upstairs.

Gwalia Lan (☎ 02965-15-682352; cnr Av Eugenio Tello & Jones; mains AR$20-30; ☑ 8:30pm-midnight Tue-Sat, 12:30-3pm Sun) Considered Gaiman's best restaurant, it serves homemade pasta and well-seasoned meat dishes that are consistently good. Service is attentive.

El Ángel (☎ 491460; Rivadavia 241; mains AR$40-45) Combining sweet and savory in tasty concoctions, stylish Ángel is a favorite for romantic tête-à-têtes. Hours can be very sporadic so reserve ahead.

Ty Nain (☎ 491126; Yrigoyen 283; tea AR$45; ☑ closed May) It's been a decade since Ty Nain was written up in the *Washington Post* and *Los Angeles Times*, but the endorsements are still plastered on the front lawn. Inside an ivy-clad 1890 home, Ty Nain persists as one of the country's most traditional teahouses. The adjoining museum has some interesting Welsh artifacts.

Ty Cymraeg (☎ 491010; www.gaimantea.com; Matthews 74; tea AR$45) Teatime in this riverside house includes sumptuous pies and jams. The youngest member of the Welsh family that owns the place, an energetic twentysomething named Miguel, is happy to explain Welsh traditions from poetry competitions to the significance of carved wooden 'love spoons' – his knowledge adds significantly to the experience.

Plas y Coed (☎ 491133; www.plasycoed.com.ar; Jones 123; tea AR$50) Run by the original owner's great-granddaughter in a gorgeous brick mansion, Plas y Coed pleases the palette and senses, with friendly service, fresh cakes and serious crochet cozies for that steaming-hot pot. Rooms are also available for rent (doubles AR$180.)

Getting There & Away

During the week, 28 de Julio buses depart for Trelew (AR$3.80) frequently from Plaza Roca, from 7am to 11pm (fewer services on weekends). Most buses to Dolavon (AR$3.50) use the highway, but some take the much longer gravel 'valley' route. *Remise* (taxi) services are cheaper in Gaiman than in Trelew; the trip to Trelew costs around AR$110 for up to four passengers.

AROUND GAIMAN

To experience an authentic historic Welsh agricultural town, head to the distinctly nontouristy **Dolavon** (population 2500; www.dolavon.com.ar), 19km west of Gaiman via paved RN 25. Welsh for 'river meadow,' the town offers pastoral appeal, with wooden waterwheels lining the irrigation canal, framed by rows of swaying poplars. The historic center is full of brick buildings, including the 1880 **Molino Harinero** (☎ 02965-492290; romanogi@infovia.com.ar; Maipú 61; guided tour per person AR$10) with still-functioning flour mill machinery. It also has a cafe-restaurant, **La Molienda** (meals AR$35), serving handmade breads and pasta with local wines and cheeses. Call owner Romano Giallatini for opening hours.

RESERVA PROVINCIAL PUNTA TOMBO

Continental South America's largest penguin nesting ground, **Punta Tombo** (admission AR$40; ☑ dawn-dusk Aug-Apr) has a colony of more than half a million Magellanic penguins and attracts many other birds, most notably king and rock cormorants, giant petrels, kelp gulls, flightless steamer ducks and black oystercatchers.

Trelew-based travel agencies run day-long tours (around AR$150, not including entrance fee), but may cancel if bad weather makes the unpaved roads impassable. If possible, come in the early morning to beat the crowds. Most nesting areas in the 200-hectare reserve are fenced off: respect the limits and remember that penguins can inflict serious bites.

There's a bar and *confitería* on-site, but it's best to bring a picnic lunch.

Punta Tombo is 110km south of Trelew (180km south of Puerto Madryn) via well-maintained gravel RP 1 and a short southeast lateral. Motorists can proceed south to Camarones via scenic but desolate Cabo Raso.

CAMARONES

☎ 0297 / pop 1300

In the stiff competition for Patagonia's sleepiest coastal village, Camarones takes home the gold. Don't diss its languorous state: if you've ever needed to run away, this is one good option. Its empty beaches are conducive to strolling and the sociable townsfolk are masters of the art of shooting the breeze. It is also the closest hub to the lesser-known Cabo Dos Bahías nature reserve (right), where you can visit 25,000 penguin couples and their fuzzy chicks.

Spanish explorer Don Simón de Alcazaba y Sotomayor anchored here in 1545, proclaiming it part of his attempted Provincia de Nueva León. When the wool industry took off, Camarones became the area's main port for wool and sheepskins. The high quality of local wool didn't go unnoticed by justice of the peace Don Mario Tomás Perón, who operated the area's largest *estancia,* Porvenir, on which his son (and future president) Juanito would romp about. The town flourished as a port, but after Comodoro Rivadavia finished its massive port, Camarones was all but deserted.

The very helpful oceanfront **tourist office** (☎ 496-3040; Tomas Espora s/n) offers maps, good tips on scenic outings and lodging information. Contact **Jorge Kriegel** (☎ 496-3056) at Camping Municipal for fishing excursions and outings to see dolphins and nearby islands. Every February, Camarones hits its stride with the **Fiesta Nacional del Salmón,** a weekend of deep-sea fishing competitions featuring a free Sunday seafood lunch and the crowning of Miss Salmoncito.

In 2009, the paving of RN 1 meant the start of direct bus services from Comodoro Rivadavia. Tourism is increasing, at least to a moderate degree, so hurry to this coastal village now if you want to be able to say you knew Camarones way back when.

Sleeping & Eating

Camping Camarones (☎ 431500; San Martín; per person/vehicle AR$3/5) At the waterfront port, this peaceful campground offers shade to a few campers. Hot showers and electricity are other perks.

El Viejo Torino (☎ 496-3003; cnr Av Costanera & Brown; r per person AR$75) This attractive house down by the water is sometimes let out to long-term workers, but provides good-value rooms and meals on occasion.

Hotel Indalo Inn (☎ 496-3004; www.indaloinn.com .ar; cnr Sarmiento & Roca; d/cabin AR$270/370) Remodeled rooms are a bit of a squeeze, but feature good bedding and snug comforts. The showers are high pressure and breakfast includes *café con leche* (coffee with milk). The cabins run by the inn are more expensive but offer sea views.

Pick up groceries at **Mercado Mica** (cnr Roca & Sarmiento).

Getting There & Away

At a gas-station junction 180km south of Trelew, RP 30 splits off from RN 3 and heads 72km east to Camarones. For years, El Ñandú buses have departed for Trelew (AR$30, three hours) at 4pm on Monday, Wednesday and Friday, but services will likely be more frequent by the time you read this. For transport to Cabo Dos Bahías, chat with Don Roberto at Hotel Indalo Inn.

CABO DOS BAHÍAS

Thirty rough kilometers southeast of Camarones, the isolated **Cabo Dos Bahías** (admission AR$20; ☽ year-round) rookery attracts far fewer visitors than Punta Tombo, making it an excellent alternative. You'll be rewarded with orcas, a huge colony of nesting penguins in spring and summer, whales in winter and a large concentration of guanacos and rheas. Sea birds, sea lions, foxes and fur seals are year-round residents.

Inside the reserve, the friendly tourist complex **Caleta Sara** (☎ 0297-447-1118; campsites per person AR$20, dm AR$45; ☽ Sep-Feb) offers dorm beds with sheets and blankets in trailers, as well as camping. Cafeteria fare depends on the catch of the day. Car transfers can be arranged from the crossroads with RN 3 (AR$180) or Camarones (AR$100).

You can pitch a tent for free at Cabo Dos Bahías Club Náutico or on any of the beaches en route from Camarones.

COMODORO RIVADAVIA

☎ 0297 / pop 140,682

Surrounded by dry hills of drilling rigs, oil tanks and wind-energy farms, tourism in the dusty port of Comodoro (as it's commonly known) usually means little more than a bus transfer. What this modern, hardworking city does provide is a gateway to nearby attractions with decent services. It sits at the eastern end of the Corredor Bioceánico highway that leads to Coyhaique, Chile.

PATAGONIA

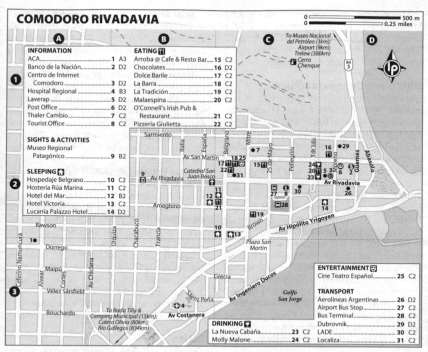

COMODORO RIVADAVIA

INFORMATION		
ACA	1	A3
Banco de la Nación	2	D2
Centro de Internet		
Comodoro	3	D2
Hospital Regional	4	B3
Laverap	5	D2
Post Office	6	D2
Thaler Cambio	7	C2
Tourist Office	8	C2

SIGHTS & ACTIVITIES		
Museo Regional		
Patagónico	9	B2

SLEEPING		
Hospedaje Belgrano	10	C2
Hostería Rúa Marina	11	C2
Hotel del Mar	12	B2
Hotel Victoria	13	C2
Lucania Palazzo Hotel	14	D2

EATING		
Arroba @ Cafe & Resto Bar	15	C2
Chocolates	16	D2
Dolce Barile	17	C2
La Barra	18	C2
La Tradición	19	C2
Malaespina	20	C2
O'Connell's Irish Pub &		
Restaurant	21	C2
Pizzeria Giulietta	22	C2

ENTERTAINMENT		
Cine Teatro Español	25	C2

TRANSPORT		
Aerolíneas Argentinas	26	D2
Airport Bus Stop	27	C2
Bus Terminal	28	C2
Dubrovnik	29	D2
LADE	30	C2
Localiza	31	C2

DRINKING		
La Nueva Cabaña	23	C2
Molly Malone	24	C2

Founded in 1901, Comodoro was once a transport hub linking ranches in nearby Sarmiento. In 1907 the town struck it rich when workers drilling for water struck oil instead. With the country's first major gusher, Comodoro became a state pet, gaining a large port, airport and paved roads. Today it is a powerhouse in the now-privatized oil industry. Although the recession hit hard in 2001, this boomtown rebounded with a flashy casino, elegant shops and hot rods on the streets.

Commerce centers on the principal streets Av San Martín and Av Rivadavia. Between Mitre and Belgrano Av, San Martín has upscale boutiques and shops unknown to most of Patagonia. A climb up 212m to the mirador atop **Cerro Chenque**, smack dab in the middle of the city, offers views to Golfo San Jorge.

Information

Locutorios abound around downtown.

ACA (Automóvil Club Argentino; ☎ 446-0876; cnr Dorrego & Alvear) Maps and road info.

Banco de la Nación (cnr Av San Martín & Güemes) Most of Comodoro's banks and ATMs, including this one, are along Av San Martín or Av Rivadavia.

Centro de Internet Comodoro (Rivadavia 245) Open till late.

Hospital Regional (☎ 444-2287; Av Hipólito Yrigoyen 950)

Laverap (Av Rivadavia 287) Centrally located laundry.

Post office (cnr Av San Martín & Moreno)

Thaler Cambio (Mitre 943) Changes traveler's checks.

Tourist office (☎ 447-4111; www.comodoro.gov .ar/turismo, in Spanish; Av Rivadavia 430; ✆ 8am-3pm Mon-Fri) Friendly, well stocked and well organized. A desk at the bus terminal is, at least in theory, open from 8am to 9pm.

Sights

MUSEO NACIONAL DEL PETRÓLEO

Intransigent petroleum fans should head to **Museo Nacional del Petróleo** (☎ 455-9558; admission AR$15; ✆ 9am-5pm Tue-Fri, 3-6pm Sat) for an insider look at the social and historical aspects of petroleum development. Don't expect balanced treatment of oil issues – the museum was built by the former state oil agency YPF (it is now managed by the Universidad Nacional de Patagonia). While its historical photos are interesting, the detailed models of tankers, refineries and the entire zone of exploitation are best left to the die hard. Guided tours are available.

The museum is in the suburb of General Mosconi, 3km north of downtown. Take a *remise* from downtown (AR$15) or bus 7 'Laprida' or 8 'Palazzo' (AR$1.80, 10 minutes); get off at La Anónima supermarket.

MUSEO REGIONAL PATAGÓNICO
Decaying natural-history specimens at this **museum** (☎ 477-7101; cnr Av Rivadavia & Chacabuco; admission free; ✆ 9am-6pm Mon-Fri, 11am-6pm Sat & Sun) nearly overshadow the small yet entertaining archaeological and historical items, including well-crafted pottery, spear points and materials on early South African Boer immigrants.

Tours

Several agencies arrange trips to Bosque Petrificado Sarmiento (p446) and Cueva de las Manos (p472).

Ruta 40 (☎ 446-5337; www.ruta-40.com) organizes well-informed and personalized 4WD trips on RN 40 and in other parts of Patagonia. It's run by Mónica Jung and Pedro Mangini, a dynamic duo who speak English, German and Italian.

The urban train tour **Circuito Ferroportuario** (admission free) takes visitors on a circuit from the tourist office to visit containers, warehouses, historical installations and workshops on the port.

Sleeping

Catering mainly to business travelers and long-term laborers, lodging here fits two categories: the ritzy and the run-down (and often full). Even the most basic double rooms are comparatively expensive here, so budget accordingly and keep your expectations low. Phone to reserve your spot well in advance if possible.

Camping Municipal (☎ 445-2918; Rada Tilly; www .radatilly.com.ar/turismo-camping.html, in Spanish; per person AR$5) At the windy beach resort of Rada Tilly, 15km south of Comodoro, this campground has sites with windbreaking shrubs. The wide beach is one of Patagonia's longest and there's a sea-lion colony near the south end below Punta del Marqués.

Hospedaje Belgrano (☎ 447-8439; Belgrano 546; s without bathroom AR$80, d with/without bathroom AR$180/100) This basic guesthouse may be the only budget option left in the city center: you can save some cash if you don't mind the stale smell of cigarettes in the hallways. Rooms are clean enough, but the space-saving shared bathrooms, with showerheads suspended over the toilets, leave something to be desired.

Hotel del Mar (☎ 447-2025; www.hotel-delmar.com .ar; Ameghino 750; s/d/tr without bathroom AR$90/160/195, with bathroom AR$150/210/270; 🖳) This simple but inviting small hotel offers bright rooms and a cozy lobby lined with faux-wood panels.

Hostería Rúa Marina (☎ 446-8777; Belgrano 738; s/d/tr/q AR$92/193/243/286) Wood-beamed ceilings and arched doorways add flair to this centrally located guesthouse – at least in the entryway. Once inside, the place feels more institutional, with small and often dark rooms. The best options have outside windows, like rooms 18, 19 and 20.

Hotel Victoria (☎ 446-0725; Belgrano 585; s/d/tr AR$210/245/275) If the aroma of baking pastries is any indication, the breakfast (AR$9) is worth the extra cost at Hotel Victoria, the friendliest on the block. Soothing, good-sized rooms have firm twin beds, desks and cable TV.

Lucania Palazzo Hotel (☎ 449-9300; www.lucania -palazzo.com, in Spanish; Moreno 676; s/d/ste AR$460/520/560; 🖳) Comodoro's answer to the Trump Towers, the sparkling Palazzo offers ocean views from every room and tasteful modern decor, although ventilation could be better.

Eating

Travelers will find a better selection of restaurants than hotels – the oil boom has bankrolled a taste for fine dining. You can find the free *Sabores del Sur* restaurant directory in some hotels.

Dolce Barile (cnr Belgrano & Av San Martín; snacks AR$3-10) This bright and contemporary corner cafe bustles with locals stopping in for a quick coffee and impeccably presented pastries.

Chocolates (Av San Martín 231; cones AR$8) Ice-cream junkies will appreciate this parlor's selection of velvety chocolate and rich *dulce de leche* flavors. If you're traveling with children, bring them here to ride the miniature carousel.

La Barra (☎ 446-6551; Av San Martín 686; mains AR$20-35) This modern cafe is a popular stop for an after-work *café con leche*. At mealtimes you'll find a good selection of salads, fancy burgers and meats, along with plenty of cocktails.

our pick Arroba @ Cafe & Resto Bar (cnr 25 de Mayo & Av San Martín; mains AR$25-35) This sleek resto-cafe has something for everyone: great coffee and pastries in the morning, salads and cheeseburgers for lunch, free wi-fi and smoothies in the afternoon, and a full bar – with sports on the flat-screen TVs – at night.

Malaespina (☎ 446-0667; 9 de Julio 859; mains AR$25-40; ☻ 10am-late Mon-Sat, 7pm-late Sun; ☐) A chic restaurant-bar catering to playful palates, Malaespina is lustrous and low lit with ample lounge space. A wide selection of gourmet salads and sandwiches fills the menu and a huge flat-screen TV shows *fútbol* (soccer) matches and music videos.

Pizzería Giulietta (☎ 446-1201; Belgrano 851; mains AR$30-35) The place for pizza, Giulietta also makes noteworthy spinach pasta and gnocchi, offered with your choice of several cream- or tomato-based sauces.

La Tradición (☎ 446-5800; Mitre 675; mains AR$32-48; ☎ closed Sun) This elegant *parrilla* grills excellent meats in a setting of white linens and oil paintings (literally, since their subjects are oil rigs!).

Drinking & Entertainment

Molly Malone (☎ 447-8333; cnr 9 de Julio & Av San Martín 292; mains AR$25-45) Run by the Golden Oldies rugby club, this funky little resto-pub is a pleasant stop for breakfast, set lunch or an evening Quilmes. The food's just average but the atmosphere is fun and inviting.

O'Connell's Irish Pub & Restaurant (☎ 444-2369; www.oconnells.com.ar; Belgrano 734; mains AR$28-35) This jovial pub serves up sandwiches, stews and hearty classics, such as chicken pot pie. During the nightly happy hour (7pm to 9pm) beer and cocktails are two for one.

La Nueva Cabaña (9 de Julio 821; ☻ 8pm-6am Tue-Thu, 10pm-6am Fri & Sat) This rustic pub and dance spot attracts a young crowd for *musica electronica*, rock, folk and pop.

Cine Teatro Español (☎ 447-7700; www.cinecr.com.ar, in Spanish; Av San Martín 668; admission AR$15) Stately, old-fashioned cinema offering a wide selection of Hollywood flicks.

Getting There & Away

The Corredor Bioceánico – RN 26, RP 20 and RP 55 – is a straight highway link to Coyhaique, Chile, and its Pacific port, Puerto Chacabuco. Developers are promoting this commercial transport route as an alternative to the Panama Canal, since the pass is open year-round and it is the continent's shortest distance between ports on both oceans. Paved RN 26, RP 20 and RN 40 lead to Esquel and Bariloche.

AIR

Aeropuerto General Mosconi (CRD; ☎ 454-8190) is 9km north of town.

Aerolíneas Argentinas (☎ 444-0050; Av Rivadavia 156) flies a couple of times daily to Buenos Aires (AR$398) and a couple of times a week to Neuquén (AR$1220).

Comodoro is the hub for **LADE** (☎ 447-0585; Av Rivadavia 360), which wings it at least once a week to Bariloche (AR$237), El Calafate (AR$248), Esquel (AR$178), Río Gallegos (AR$264), Trelew (AR$211), Ushuaia (AR$391), Viedma (AR$259) and Buenos Aires (AR$417) and points in between. Schedules and routes change as often as the winds.

BUS

The chaotic **bus terminal** (☎ 446-7305; Pellegrini 730) receives all buses plying RN 3. Stop at the helpful tourist desk for maps and travel assistance.

Most bus schedules are divided into northbound and southbound departures. **Andesmar** (☎ 446-8894) departs five times daily (between 1:15am and 3pm) for points north including Trelew, Rawson, Puerto Madryn and San Antonio Oeste, then heads inland toward Córdoba.

TAC (☎ 444-3376) follows the same route north through Patagonia but continues to Bahía Blanca, La Plata and Buenos Aires. **Etap** (☎ 447-4841) runs to Sarmiento four times daily, to Esquel and Río Mayo once daily, to Coyhaique on Wednesdays and Saturdays, and to Río Senguer four times weekly.

For Los Antiguos and connections to Chile Chico, via the town of Perito Moreno, **La Unión** (☎ 446-2822) has twice-daily services. **Marga** (☎ 447-0564) goes to Los Antiguos and to El Calafate in the evening. For other Chilean destinations, **Turibus** (☎ 446-0058) goes to Coyhaique on Wednesday and Saturday mornings.

Schedules are in constant flux; upon arrival at the bus station, ask at each bus line's desk for information on departure times.

Destination	Cost (AR$)	Duration (hr)
Bahía Blanca	160-225	15
Bariloche	118-160	14
Buenos Aires	282-430	24
Caleta Olivia	14-18	1
Esquel	60-75	8
El Calafate	110	8
Los Antiguos	65-80	6
Puerto Deseado	50	4-5
Puerto Madryn	59-88	6-8
Río Gallegos	118-147	9-11
Trelew	65-78	5-6
Viedma	125-180	10-13

Getting Around

Bus 8 'Directo Palazzo' (AR$1.80) goes directly to the airport from outside the downtown bus terminal.

Expreso Rada Tilly links Comodoro's bus terminal to the nearby beach resort (AR$3) every 20 minutes on weekdays and every 30 minutes on weekends.

Rental cars are available from **Avis** (☎ 454-9471; at airport) and **Localiza** (☎ 446-3526; Av Rivadavia 535). **Dubrovnik** (☎ 444-1844; www.rentacardubrovnik.com; Moreno 941) rents 4WD vehicles.

SARMIENTO

☎ 0297 / pop 10,000

Sarmiento is a sleepy, picturesque outpost of berry and cherry plantations, where half the roads are gravel and cars dodge the dogs napping in the middle of them. Once Tehuelche territory, Argentina's southernmost irrigated town has been an agricultural center since its founding in 1897. These days it is also an oil hub surrounded by derricks, a reality most farmers prefer to ignore. For the visitor, it is the gateway to the petrified forests, 30km southeast, and a tranquil spot for the road weary to rejuvenate. It sits between Lago Musters and Lago Colhué Huapi. As Comodoro's water source, Colhué Huapi has become a puddle of its former self and its compromised ecosystem is of serious concern to ecologists.

The eager **tourist office** (☎ 489-8220; turismo@coopsar.com.ar; cnr Infanteria 25 & Pietrobelli; ✆ 8am-7pm Mon-Fri, 11am-5pm Sat & Sun) is helpful and provides maps of town and region. Tourist agency **Santa Teresita** (☎ 489-3238; cnr Roca & Uruguay) makes excursions (AR$70) to see rock art at Alero de las Manos, 55km from Sarmiento. **Cabaña el Futuro** (☎ 489-3036) raises quarter horses and runs horseback-riding trips (AR$25 per hour) in summer.

Housed in the atmospheric old train station, the **Museo Regional Desiderio Torres** (20 de Junio 114; admission free; ✆ 10am-1pm & 5-8pm Mon-Sat, 10am-5pm Sun) offers interesting archaeological and paleontological displays, as well as indigenous artifacts with an emphasis on weaving. Just before the entrance to town on the way to the petrified forest, **Granja San José** (☎ 489-3733; tours AR$6) is a hydroponics farm selling exquisite jams.

Anglers can while away their time on **Lago Musters**, a 60m-deep, sandy-bottomed lake with good year-round fishing for trout, perch and silverside. Licenses are available at the tourist office.

Comfortable campsites can be found at **Camping Río Senguer** (☎ 489-8482; per tent/car/person AR$5/2/3), 1km from the center on RP 24. In town, find the mint-green facade of the well-scrubbed **Hotel Ismar** (☎ 489-3293; Patagonia 248; s/d/tr AR$80/120/140) for narrow motel rooms with linoleum floors.

Working cherry farm **Chacra Labrador** (☎ 489-3329, 0297-15-509-3537; www.hosterialabrador.com.ar; d AR$200) is a charming 1930s homestead offering bed and breakfast. Rooms are few but luxuriant, with big cozy beds, antique furniture, pots of tea and crackling fires. If you're driving, it's 10km west of Sarmiento (past the turnoff for town if you're coming from Comodoro), 1km before the Río Senguer bridge. Otherwise call for a pick up from town.

Sarmiento is 148km west of Comodoro along RN 26 and RP 20. Etap buses run daily to Comodoro Rivadavia (AR$15, two hours) at 8am, 1pm, 7pm and 10pm. Buses to Río Mayo (AR$26, 1½ hours) go at 9:30pm daily.

BOSQUE PETRIFICADO SARMIENTO

Fallen giants are scattered in a pale sandstone landscape at this **petrified forest** (admission AR$20; ✆ dawn-dusk), 30km southeast of Sarmiento. From the visitor center, a trail leads through ethereal grounds with the appearance of a lumberyard gone mad: 'wood' chips cover the ground and huge petrified logs, up to 100m in length and 1m wide, are strewn about. Unlike the petrified forest in Santa Cruz, these trunks were brought here by strong river currents from the mountainous regions about 65 million years ago. The most impressive area of the park has a handful of large trunks set against the red and orange striated bluffs. For travelers, this area is much more accessible than the Monumento Natural Bosques Petrificados (p450) further south.

Though tour buses do run between Sarmiento and the forest, readers report inconsistent service – it's much easier to come here with your own rental car, or ask at the tourist office in Sarmiento for *remise* rates for the 1½-hour roundtrip. Try to stay through sunset, when the striped bluffs of Cerro Abigarrado and the multihued hills turn brilliantly vivid.

CALETA OLIVIA

☎ 0297 / pop 37,000

Slightly seedy but nevertheless authentic, Caleta Olivia earns its living refining oil and processing fish. High winds plague the port, but are preferable to its sporadic dust storms. Located south of Comodoro on costal RN 3, Caleta Olivia is, however, a convenient place to change buses to more inspiring locales, such as the petrified forests, Puerto Deseado or Los Antiguos.

The port was built in 1901 as part of a plan to run the telegraph along the coast, and was named after the only woman on board that first ship to land here. Discovery of oil in 1944 turned the face of industry from wool and sheep to petroleum, as evidenced by the eerie 10m-high Monumento al Obrero Petrolero that lords over the downtown traffic circle.

Orientation

Entering town from the north, RN 3 becomes Av Jorge Newbery, then Av San Martín (the main thoroughfare), continuing after the traffic circle along southeast diagonal Av Eva Perón. The southwest diagonal Av Independencia, the center of teenage cruising, becomes RP 12. Most streets run diagonal to San Martín, except in the northeast quadrant. The port and pebbly beach are four blocks east of the traffic circle.

Information

Banks along San Martín have ATMs but don't change traveler's checks. *Locutorios* and internet cafes also line San Martín.

Post office (cnr 25 de Mayo & Yrigoyen)

Tourist office (☎ 485-0988; caletaolivia@santacruz .gov.ar; cnr San Martín & Güemes; ☽ 9am-6pm) Enthusiastic office near the monument, with maps of the town.

Sleeping & Eating

A housing shortage means oil workers are filling up the budget hotels and travelers may have a tough time finding a space. Rates are steep for what's on offer, and breakfast is usually extra. Av Independencia has lots of bars, cafes and ice-cream shops.

Camping Municipal (☎ 485-0988; Av Costanera s/n; per person/car AR$5/7) In an exposed gravel lot near the busy beach, the campground lacks privacy but has 24-hour security, hot showers and barbecue pits.

Posada Don David (☎ 485-7661; Yrigoyen 2385; d with/without bathroom AR$150/120) Fronted by a lively cafe filled with male drinkers, these basic rooms line a tight corridor. While the bathrooms need work, this posada (inn) is at least clean.

Quequén Aike (☎ 485-5503; Tierra del Fuego 865; d AR$180) Looking for a place to crash near the bus terminal? Try these tidy wood and brick cabins, located a stone's throw from the terminal's front door.

Hotel Capri (☎ 485-1132; Hernández 1145; s/d AR$180/220) For the better half of a century, the fun-loving owners have offered basic rooms (upstairs are best) off a central hallway.

Buonna Pizza (☎ 485-5550; Independencia 52; pizza AR$28) This family-friendly pizzeria provides an upbeat setting for pizza and empanadas, and it's less smoky than its nearby counterparts.

El Puerto (☎ 485-1313; Independencia 1060; mains AR$40-48) Crisp linens and elegant seafood platters are the order of the day. To get today's catch, ask waiters '¿Que es lo más fresco?'

Getting There & Away

The **bus terminal** (cnr Bequin & Tierra del Fuego) is 3km northwest of downtown (AR$8 by remise). The main north–south carriers leave for Comodoro Rivadavia (AR$20, one hour) hourly from 7am to 11pm, with fewer services on Sunday; and for Río Gallegos (AR$120, seven to 10 hours) four times daily between 8:30pm and 2am, passing Puerto San Julián (AR$75). **Sportsman** (☎ 485-1287) and **La Unión** (☎ 485-1134) serve Puerto Deseado (AR$50, three hours), Perito Moreno (AR$62, four hours) and Los Antiguos (AR$59, five hours) in the early morning and late afternoon. Check at the bus terminal for the latest time tables.

PUERTO DESEADO

☎ 0297 / pop 12,000

Some 125km southeast of the RN 3 junction, RN 281 weaves through valleys of rippling pink rock, past guanacos in tufted grassland, to end at the serene and attractive deep-sea-fishing town of Puerto Deseado. While the town is ripe for revitalization, it is also apparent that change takes a glacial pace here: witness the vintage trucks rusting on the streets like beached cetaceans. But the draw of the historic center, plus the submerged estuary of Ría Deseado (p450), brimming with seabirds and marine wildlife, make Puerto Deseado a worthy detour.

In 1520 the estuary provided shelter to Hernando de Magallanes after a crippling storm waylaid his fleet; he dubbed the area 'Río de los Trabajos' (River of Labors). In 1586 English privateer Cavendish explored the estuary and named it after his ship *Desire*, and this time the name stuck. The port attracted

PUERTO DESEADO

INFORMATION		
Banco de la Nación	1	C2
CIS Tour	2	C2
Dirección Municipal de Turismo	3	B2
Ecowash	4	D2
Hospital Distrital	5	C3
Post Office	6	C2

SIGHTS & ACTIVITIES		
Club Naútico	7	B3
Estación del Ferrocarril Patagónico	8	D2
Los Vikingos	9	B2
Museo Padre Beauvoir	10	C2
Museo Regional Mario Brozoski	11	C3
Sociedad Española	12	C2
Vagón Histórico	13	C2

SLEEPING		
Cabañas Las Nubes	14	B2
Hotel Isla Chaffers	15	C2
Hotel Los Acantilados	16	A2
Residencial Las Bandurrias	17	B2
Residencial Los Olmos	18	D2

EATING		
El Pingüino	19	D1
Maca	20	C2
Puerto Cristal	21	A2
Sushy Delicatessen	22	C2

DRINKING		
Quinto Elemento	23	C2

ENTERTAINMENT		
Jackaroe Boliche	24	C2

fleets from around the world for whaling and seal hunting, compelling the Spanish crown to send a squadron of colonists under the command of Antonio de Viedma. After a harsh winter, more than 30 of them died of scurvy. Those who survived moved inland to form the short-lived colony of Floridablanca. In 1834 Darwin surveyed the estuary, as did Perito Moreno in 1876.

Orientation

Puerto Deseado is two hours southeast of the RN 3 junction at Fitz Roy via dead-end RN 281. The center of activity is the axis formed by main streets San Martín and Almirante Brown.

Information

Banks, ATMs, *locutorios* and internet are all found along San Martín.

Banco de la Nación (San Martín & Almirante Brown)

CIS Tour (☎ 487-2864; San Martin 916) Handles local tours and flight reservations.

Dirección Municipal de Turismo (☎ 487-0220; www.puertodeseado.gov.ar, in Spanish; San Martín 1525; ☒ 10am-1pm & 5-8pm Mon-Fri) There's another English-speaking desk at the bus terminal, but its hours are limited.

Ecowash (☎ 487-0490; Piedra Buena 859; ☒ Mon-Sun) Full-service laundry.

Hospital Distrital (☎ 487-0200; España 991)

Post office (San Martín 1075)

Sights & Activities

A self-guided **walking tour** is a good start to catching the vibes of Deseado. Pick up a *Guía Historica* map (in Spanish) from either tourist office.

Puerto Deseado was once the coastal terminus for a cargo and passenger route that hauled wool and lead from Chilean mines from Pico Truncado and Las Heras, 280km northwest. Choo-choo fans can check out the imposing English-designed **Estación del Ferrocarril Patagónico** (admission by donation; ☒ 4-7pm Mon-Sat), off Av Oneto, built by Yugoslav stonecutters in 1908.

In the center of town, the restored 1898 **Vagón Histórico** (cnr San Martín & Almirante Brown) is famous as the car from which rebel leader Facón Grande prepared the 'Patagonia Rebellion.' In 1979 the car was almost sold for scrap, but disgruntled townspeople blocked the roads to stop the sale. A few blocks west is the attractive **Sociedad Española** (San Martín 1176), c 1915.

The **Museo Regional Mario Brozoski** (☎ 487-1358; cnr Colón & Belgrano; admission free; ☾ 10am-5pm Mon-Fri, 3-7pm Sat) displays relics of the English corvette *Swift*, sunk off the coast of Deseado in 1776. Divers continue to recover artifacts from this wreck, located in 1982. Named for a Salesian priest, **Museo Padre Beauvoir** (☎ 487-0147; 12 de Octubre 577; admission free; ☾ 10am-5pm Mon-Fri) shows an eclectic combination of native relics, stuffed birds and objects donated by pioneer families.

Paddling and windsurfing can be enjoyed in summer. On the waterfront, **Club Náutico** (☎ 0297-15-419-0468) rents boards and kayaks (summer only). Depending on current conditions, sport fishing can be an option; inquire at the pier.

Tours

Darwin Expediciones (☎ 0297-15-624-7554; www .darwin-expeditions.com; Av España 2601) Offers sea-kayaking trips, wildlife observation, and multiday nature and archaeology tours with knowledgeable guides. Its best seller is the tour of Reserva Natural Ría Deseado (AR$140). **Los Vikingos** (☎ 487-0020, 0297-15-624-5141/4283; www.losvikingos.com.ar; Estrada 1275) Offers excursions on land and sea. Tours, some led by marine biologists, include Reserva Natural Ría Deseado and Monumento Natural Bosques Petrificados.

Sleeping

Ask the tourist office about (relatively) nearby *estancias*.

Camping Cañadón Giménez (☎ 0297-15-673-6051; RN 281; per person/tent AR$4/15, cabins AR$100-125; ☾ year-round) Four kilometers northwest of town, but only 50m from the Ría Deseado, this campground is sheltered by forest and high rocky walls. Bare-bones cabins sleep four; the upgrade gets you heating and kitchen basics. Showers, hot water and simple provisions are available.

Residencial Las Bandurrias (☎ 487-0745; acantour@ speedy.com.ar; Estrada 1530; s/d AR$110/145) The cavernous dimensions give this tiled building a slightly institutional feel, but its plain rooms are kept impeccably clean.

Residencial Los Olmos (☎ 487-0077; Gregores 849; s/d/tr/q AR$120/160/210/240) A solid budget option kept shipshape by a vigilant matron, this brick house has 19 small rooms with TV, heat and private bathrooms.

Hotel Isla Chaffers (☎ 487-2246; cnr San Martín & Mariano Moreno; s/d/tr AR$150/190/230; ▣) This downtown hotel is pleasant and polished, if fraying

a bit around the edges. The ground-level cafe and bar, open to the public, is appealing for a hot chocolate when morning sunlight streams through the picture windows.

Hotel Los Acantilados (☎ 487-2167; cnr Pueyrredón & Av España; s/d standard AR$190/230, s/d superior AR$280/320; ▣) More inspiring from outside than in, these clifftop digs do boast an extensive lounge with fireplace: the perfect spot to chill out. Superior rooms and the dining room look out on the waterfront, while standard rooms are plain with dated bathrooms.

Cabañas Las Nubes (☎ 0297-15-403-2677; www.caba naslasnubes.com.ar; Ameghino 1351; d/q cabins AR$260/300) Currently the nicest lodgings in town, these deluxe two- and three-story wood and glass cabins bring you in reach of cloud nine. They sit on a hilltop, and some have ocean views and fully equipped kitchens.

Eating

Maca (☎ 487-2134; San Martín 1263; sandwiches AR$20; ☾ 1-3pm & 7:30-10pm Tue-Sun) This brick cafe serves cheesy pizza and sandwiches to fans of all ages. The ice cream comes highly recommended.

our pick Sushy Delicatessen (San Martín 1165; snacks AR$20; ☾ 9:30am-2pm & 4pm-2:30am Mon-Fri, closed Sat & Sun) This sophisticated wine bar and deli beckons weary travelers with bottles of good malbec and ample cheese plates. The decor is warm and stylish, with Patagonian vintages lining the walls and a few cozy nooks where you can read, write or plan the next leg of your trip.

El Pingüino (☎ 487-2105; Piedra Buena 958; mains AR$21-28; ☾ closed Sun) This local institution cooks up fresh fish and pasta in an animated setting kept in check by the gregarious owner. There's also a set menu and good wine list.

Puerto Cristal (☎ 487-0387; Av España 1698; mains AR$30-45; ☾ noon-3pm & 8pm-midnight, closed Wed lunch) Seafood looms large on the menu (fried calamari, paella and hearty soups) at this local classic. Ask for a table along the windows so you can fully appreciate the waterfront location.

Puerto Darwin (☎ 247554; www.darwin-expeditions .com; Av España 2581; mains AR$32-40; ☾ 9am-2am; ▣) Featuring sandwiches, *picadas* and fish dishes, this cool cafe run by Darwin Expediciones has an easygoing atmosphere and views of the port. It's a hike from downtown and street numbers aren't labeled: just keep walking along the water until you reach the other side of a fenced-in industrial area.

PATAGONIA

Drinking & Entertainment

Late-night drinking and dancing spots include the run-down pub **Quinto Elemento** (cnr Don Bosco & 12 de Octubre) and the swanky disco **Jackaroe Boliche** (Mariano Moreno 663), housed in an unfortunate building.

Getting There & Around

LADE (☎ 487-2674) flies to Comodoro Rivadavia on Wednesdays and Fridays (AR$260).

The **bus terminal** (Sargento Cabral 1302) is on the northeast side of town, nine long blocks and slightly uphill from San Martín and Av Oneto. Taxis to/from the center cost about AR$12.

There are five departures daily to Caleta Olivia (AR$50, three hours) around 4:15am, 6am, 1pm, 7pm and 7:30pm. All continue to Comodoro Rivadavia (AR$50, four hours). Sportman's evening bus to Comodoro Rivadavia is timed to link with Sportman connections to El Calafate. Leaving on the midday bus (which doesn't run Sunday) allows for the quickest connection to Perito Moreno and Los Antiguos. Travelers headed to San Julián must connect through Caleta Olivia. Schedules change frequently; inquire at the bus terminal about departures.

If you're thinking of getting off at godforsaken Fitz Roy (where locals claim the only thing to see is the wind!) to make progress toward Comodoro or Río Gallegos, think again: buses arrive at a demonic hour and the only place to crash is the campground behind Multirubro La Illusion.

Taxis (☎ 487-2288; 487-0645) aren't plentiful because the town isn't huge, but you may want to call for a ride from the bus station if it's cold or raining.

RESERVA NATURAL RÍA DESEADO

Flanked by sandy cliffs, these aquamarine waters create sculpted seascapes you won't forget. Moreover, it's considered one of South America's most important marine preserves. Ría Deseado is the unique result of a river abandoning its bed, allowing the Atlantic waters to invade 40km inland and create a perfect shelter for marine life. At the time of writing, the Isla de los Pingüinos archipelago was poised to become a national park, so expect more tourism in this naturally beautiful region as the new Parque Nacional Isla Pingüinos officially opens.

The marine life is abundant. Several islands and other sites provide nesting habitats for sea birds, including Magellanic penguins, petrels, oystercatchers, herons, terns and five species of cormorant. Isla Chaffers is the main spot for the penguins, while Banco Cormorán offers protection to rock cormorants and the striking gray cormorant. Isla de los Pingüinos has nesting rockhoppers and breeding elephant seals. Commerson's dolphins, sea lions, guanacos and ñandús (ostrichlike rheas) can also be seen while touring the estuary.

The best time to visit the reserve is from December to April. Darwin Expediciones (p449) runs circuits that take in viewing of Commerson's dolphins, Isla Chaffers, Banco Cormorán as well as a walk to a penguin colony (AR$140, 2½ hours). The main attraction of the all-day Isla de los Pinguinos excursion (AR$350) is the punked-out rockhopper penguins with spiky yellow and black head feathers, but the tour also includes wildlife watching, sailing and hiking. There's a four- to five-person minimum and tours leave depending on tides – usually early morning or midafternoon. Los Vikingos (p449) makes similar excursions with bilingual guides and organizes overland trips.

MONUMENTO NATURAL BOSQUES PETRIFICADOS

During Jurassic times, 150 million years ago, this area enjoyed a humid, temperate climate with flourishing forests, but intense volcanic activity buried them in ash. Erosion later exposed the mineralized *Proaraucaria* trees (ancestors of the modern *Araucaria*, unique to the southern hemisphere), up to 3m in diameter and 35m in length. Today, the 150-sq-km **Monumento Natural Bosques Petrificados** (Petrified Forests Natural Monument; admission free; ☯ 9am-9pm year-round) has a small visitor center, English-language brochure and short interpretive trail, leading from park headquarters to the largest concentration of petrified trees. Until its legal protection in 1954, the area was plundered for some of its finest specimens; please don't perpetuate this unsavory tradition.

The park is 157km southwest of Caleta Olivia, accessed from the good gravel RP 49, leading 50km west from a turnoff at Km 2074 on RN 3. There's no public transport directly to the park. Buses from Caleta Olivia will drop you at the junction, but you may wait several hours for a lift into the park. Los Vikingos (p449) runs tours from Puerto Deseado.

There's basic camping, as well as provisions, at **La Paloma**, 20km before the park headquarters. Camping in the park is strictly prohibited.

PUERTO SAN JULIÁN

☎ 02962 / pop 6143

The perfect desolate-yet-charismatic locale for an art film, this small town bakes in bright light and dust, in stark contrast to Bahía San Julián's startling blue. Considered the cradle of Patagonian history, the port of San Julián was first landed in 1520 by Magellan. His encounter with local Tehuelches provided the region's mythical moniker (see the boxed text, below). But he was not the last to make his mark – Viedma, Drake and Darwin all ventured onto this sandy spit. While its human history is proudly put forth, the landscape speaks of geologic revolutions, with its exposed, striated layers, rolling hills and golden cliffs.

Puerto San Julián's first non-native settlers came from the Falkland Islands (Islas Malvinas) with the late-19th-century wool boom. Scots followed with the San Julián Sheep Farming Company, which became the region's primary economic force for nearly a century. Recent growth has the city, 350km south of Caleta Olivia, developing like never before, with mining and seafood-processing industries. For travelers, the port is a relaxed and welcoming stop, as well as the place to see Commerson's dolphins.

Information

Banco Santa Cruz (cnr San Martín & Moreno) Has a Link ATM.

Dirección de Turismo (☎ 454396; www.sanjulian.gov.ar, in Spanish; Av San Martín 135; ⏰ 7am-9pm Mon-Fri, 5-9pm Sat & Sun) There's also a high-season kiosk at San Martín 500.

Post office (cnr San Martín & Belgrano)

Telefónica (cnr San Martín & Rivadavia) *Locutorio* with internet.

Sights & Activities

One small local adventure is to take a *remise* or your own poor abused rental car on the incredibly scenic 30km **Circuito Costero**, following Bahía San Julián on a dirt road. A series of golden bluffs divide beautiful beaches with drastic tides. The area includes a sea-lion colony and the penitent attraction of Monte Cristo (with its stations of the cross). If you are in your own vehicle, make sure it is equipped with a spare tire.

Relive Magellan's landing at **Museo Nao Victoria** (admission AR$12), a museum-cum-theme-park with life-sized figures cloaked in armor and shown celebrating Mass and battling mutiny. Reproductions of everyday items provide some interest. You can't miss it – it's at the port on a boat, a reproduction of the *Nao Victoria*.

The last census found 130,000 penguins inhabiting **Banco Cormorán**, which you can visit by boat. Two-hour excursions on Bahía San Julián (AR$110 per person) are run by a marine biologist-led team at **Expediciones Pinocho** (☎ 454600; cnr Mitre & 9 de Julio). The penguins stick around from September to April; when conditions permit, you'll be able to step off the boat and walk around an island where penguins swim, doze and guard their eggs. The tour also stops at **Banco Justicia**, to see the cormorant rookeries and other seabirds. From December to March there's a good chance you'll see the Commerson's dolphin (p435), known as the world's smallest dolphin.

PATAGONIA

BIG FEET, TALL TALES

Say 'Patagonia' and most think of fuzzy outdoor clothes, but the name that has come to symbolize the world's end still invites hot debate as to its origin.

One theory links the term 'Patagón' to a fictional monster in a best-selling 16th-century Spanish romance of the period, co-opted by Magellan's crew to describe the Tehuelche as they wintered in 1520 at Puerto San Julián. Crew member and Italian nobleman, Antonio Pigafetta, described one Tehuelche as 'so tall we reached only to his waist…He was dressed in the skins of animals skillfully sewn together…His feet were shod with the same kind of skins, which covered his feet in the manner of shoes…The captain-general [Magellan] called these people Patagoni.'

Another theory suggests that the name comes from the Spanish *pata*, meaning paw or foot. No evidence corroborates the claim that the Tehuelche boasted unusually big feet (it's possible that the skins they wore made their feet seem exceptionally large). But it's good fodder for the genre of travelers' tales, where first impressions loom larger than life.

Another option is **trekking** the coastline and checking out the abundant birdlife. If you have a friend (or make one), you can rent **tandem bicycles** (☎ 02962-15-532312; per hr AR$15) to explore the area. For more information on either activity, consult the tourist information kiosk.

Sleeping & Eating

Camping Municipal (☎ 452806; Magallanes 650; per person/car AR$3/5) On the waterfront at the north end of Vélez Sarsfield, this full-service campground has hot showers (AR$1.50), laundry and windbreaks.

Hostería Miramar (☎ 454626; hosteriamiramar@uvc .com.ar; San Martín 210; s/d AR$130/200; ⬚) Natural light fills this clean and cheerful waterfront hotel. Eleven rooms, including a family-sized apartment, have good-sized TVs, carpeted floors and somewhat dated mint-green decor.

Hotel Ocean (☎ 452350; San Martín 959; s/d/tr AR$140/180/200) This remodeled brick building has attractive, well-scrubbed rooms with firm beds and a backdrop of tropical tones. Friendly staff are happy to assist travelers – when you're tired and hungry and the bus has dropped you off in town around midnight (as it probably will), they'll help you find an open restaurant.

Hotel Bahía (☎ 453144; www.hotelbahiasanjulian .com.ar, in Spanish; San Martín 1075; s/d/tr AR$170/205/240; ⬚) This glass-front hotel feels decadent in a place like San Julián. Rooms are modern and beds firm, while TV and laundry service are perks. The cafe-bar is an appealing setting for breakfast or just coffee; it's also open to the public.

Costanera Hotel (☎ 452300; www.costanerahotel .com; 25 de Mayo 917; s/d/tr AR$185/220/255; ⬚) After major renovations, this waterfront mainstay feels new again. Double rooms are standard but tidy, and the restaurant is one of the better places to eat in town. The location across the street from the water doesn't hurt either.

La Rural (☎ 454066; Ameghino 811; mains AR$22-30) Service is friendly but the hearty food mediocre. Still, the whole town seems to congregate at this unpretentious spot. Fare ranges from meat and potatoes to grilled fish and pasta.

Restaurante Costanera Hotel (☎ 454192; 25 de Mayo 917; mains AR$32-38; ☾ lunch & dinner) On first glance, this spacious eatery looks like a sterile hotel restaurant. But at night, the place fills up with jovial locals and travelers sampling freshly caught fish and socializing over glasses of good red wine.

La Juliana (☎ 452074; Zeballos 1134; mains AR$40-50; ☾ dinner Tue-Sun) This renovated old home offers well-prepared versions of popular meals, but guests are mostly paying for the cool ambience.

Getting There & Away

BUS

Most RN 3 buses visit San Julián's **bus terminal** (☎ 452082; San Martín 1552) at insane hours. Before settling for a bus that will drop you off in the port at 4am, try **Don Otto** (☎ 452072), which delivers southbound travelers to San Julián at civilized evening hours. **Via Tac** (☎ 02966-15-638883) goes to Puerto Madryn (AR$132, 12 hours) via Trelew (AR$122). **Andesmar** (☎ 454403) goes to Comodoro Rivadavia (AR$65). **Taqsa** (☎ 454667) goes to Río Gallegos (AR$60), where travelers can make connections south. Taqsa also travels to Caleta Olivia (AR$55), Perito Moreno (AR$97) and Los Antiguos (AR$115).

There are slightly more expensive door-to-door service options, all operating Monday to Saturday in the early morning hours, for around AR$70. **Sur Servicio** (☎ 454044, in Comodoro Rivadavia 02962-454044; San Martín 1380) goes to Comodoro Rivadavia; **Gold Tour** (☎ 452265; San Martín 1075) goes to Río Gallegos; and **Cerro San Lorenzo** (☎ 452403; Berutti 970) serves Gobernador Gregores.

Bus schedules may change, so always confirm departures ahead of time.

ESTANCIA LA MARÍA

Some 150km northwest of Puerto San Julián on the Patagonia steppe, **Estancia La María** (www .arqueologialamaria.com.ar) is an important area of archaeological research, studied for clues of life in the Pleistocene epoch. It has 84 caves with excellently preserved rock paintings dating back 12,600 years. Three different cultures, predating the Tehuelche, created the *arte rupestre* (cave paintings), today seen as Patagonia's most important discovery of this kind. The only way to see these treasures is by guided tour (AR$130) with the *estancia* owners.

This is also a great opportunity for budget travelers to sample a night on an *estancia*. Contact the kind owners **Pepa and Fernando Behm** (☎ in San Julián 02962-452233, 02962-15-449827; Saavedra 1168; per tent incl hot shower AR$16, d with/without bathroom AR$98/60; ☾ Oct-May) for reservations and transport options. La María is accessed via RP 25 and RP 77.

PARQUE NACIONAL MONTE LEÓN

Inaugurated in 2004, this fine coastal national park protects over 600 sq km of striking headlands and archetypal Patagonian steppe, and 40km of dramatic coastline with bays, beaches and tidal flats. Once a hunting ground for nomads, and later frequented by the Tehuelche, this former *estancia* is home to abundant Magellanic penguins, sea lions, guanacos and pumas. Bring binoculars: the wildlife watching is prime.

Hiking along the coastline, with its unusual geographic features, is best when low tide exposes stretches of sandy and rocky beach. In October 2006 the park's signature landscape attraction, **La Olla** (a huge cavelike structure eroded by the ocean), collapsed from repeated tidal action. Accessible at low tide, **Isla Monte León** is a high offshore sea stack heavily mined for guano between 1933 and 1960. Now it has been recolonized by cormorants, Dominican gulls, skuas and other seabirds. Use caution and know the tide tables before setting out: the tidal range is great, exposed rocks are slippery and the water returns quickly.

Nature trails split off from the main road, leading to the coast. The **penguin trail** crosses the steppe, leading to an overlook of the rookery. It's forbidden to leave the trail, but seeing these 75,000 couples shouldn't be difficult. The roundtrip takes 1½ hours. Cars can reach the prominent cliff **Cabeza de León** (Lion's Head), where a 20-minute trail leads to the sea-lion colony.

There is free camping on the beach, with access to picnic tables, but visitors must bring their own water. The other option is the charming **Hostería Monte León** (☎ in Buenos Aires 011-4621-4784, in Ushuaia 02901-431851; www .monteleon-patagonia.com; s/d incl full board AR$800/1215; ☯ Nov-Apr), a refurbished century-old home that was the *casco* (ranch house) of an 1895 *estancia*, now run by the original owner's granddaughter. The four-bedroom house retains the spartan style of the Patagonian farmhouse, with iron-rod beds, basic tasteful furnishings and an open kitchen with iron wood stove. The *hostería* also offers all-day boat excursions and fly-fishing for steelhead.

The park entrance is 30km south of Comandante Luis Piedrabuena or 205km north of Río Gallegos, directly off RN 3. Watch for it carefully since signage is poor.

RÍO GALLEGOS

☎ 02966 / pop 79,114

Hardly a tourist destination, this coal-shipping, oil-refining and wool-raising hub is a busy port with a few merits worth mentioning. Since the reign of the Kirchners, the capital city of their home province has been spruced up and spit polished. Outside of town, visitors can find some of the continent's best fly-fishing, traditional *estancias* and amazingly low tides (retreating 14m). Traveler services are good here but most visitors quickly pass through en route to El Calafate, Puerto Natales or Ushuaia.

Gallegos' economy revolves around nearby oilfields, with coal deposits shipped to ocean-going vessels at Punta Loyola. Home to a large military base, the city played an active role during the Falklands War.

Information

ESSENTIALS

Banks on Av Roca have ATMs. Internet is widely available in cybercafes and restaurants.

ACA (Automóvil Club Argentino; ☎ 420477; Orkeke 10) Gas station, maps and traveler services.

Centro de Informes Turístico (☎ 422365; Av San Martín s/n; ☯ Oct-Apr) Useful info kiosk on median strip.

Hospital Regional (☎ 420289; José Ingenieros 98)

Immigration office (☎ 420205; Urquiza 144; ☯ 9am-3pm Mon-Fri)

Municipal tourist office (☎ 436920; www.riogalle gos.gov.ar; cnr Av Roca & Córdoba; ☯ 9am-3pm Mon-Fri) A desk at the bus terminal keeps longer hours.

Provincial tourist office (☎ 422702; www.santacruz .gov.ar, in Spanish; Av Roca 863; ☯ 9am-7pm Mon-Fri, 10am-1pm & 5-8pm Sat & Sun) Most helpful, with maps, bilingual staff and detailed info.

Thaler Cambio (Av San Martín 484; ☯ 10am-3pm Mon-Fri, 10am-1pm Sat) Changes traveler's checks.

OTHER SERVICES

Aike Lavar (☎ 420759; Corrientes 277) Serviced laundry.

Post office (Av Roca 893)

Telefónica (Av Roca 1328) One of several late-night *locutorios* on Av Roca with internet access.

Tur Aike (☎ 422436; turaiketurismo@ciudad.com.ar; Zapiola 63) Helpful for airline bookings.

Sights

The pretty **Plaza San Martín** offers quiet benches in the shade of poplars and purple-blossom jacarandas.

Satiate your appetite for dinosaur dioramas and modern art at **Museo Provincial Padre Jesús Molina** (☎ 423290; Av San Martín & Ramón y Cajal; admission

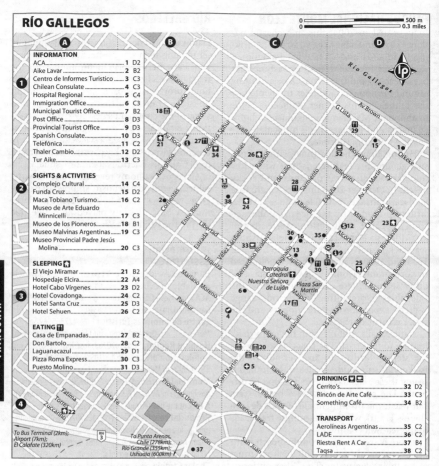

RÍO GALLEGOS

INFORMATION
ACA	1	D2
Aike Lavar	2	B2
Centro de Informes Turístico	3	C3
Chilean Consulate	4	C3
Hospital Regional	5	C4
Immigration Office	6	C3
Municipal Tourist Office	7	B2
Post Office	8	D3
Provincial Tourist Office	9	D3
Spanish Consulate	10	D3
Telefónica	11	D2
Thaler Cambio	12	D2
Tur Aike	13	C3

SIGHTS & ACTIVITIES
Complejo Cultural	14	C4
Funda Cruz	15	D2
Maca Tobiano Turismo	16	C2
Museo de Arte Eduardo Minnicelli	17	C3
Museo de los Pioneros	18	B1
Museo Malvinas Argentinas	19	C3
Museo Provincial Padre Jesús Molina	20	C3

SLEEPING
El Viejo Miramar	21	B2
Hospedaje Elcira	22	A4
Hotel Cabo Vírgenes	23	D2
Hotel Covadonga	24	C2
Hotel Santa Cruz	25	D3
Hotel Sehuen	26	C2

EATING
Casa de Empanadas	27	B2
Don Bartolo	28	C2
Laguanacazul	29	D1
Pizza Roma Express	30	C3
Puesto Molino	31	D3

DRINKING
Cerrito's	32	D2
Rincón de Arte Café	33	C3
Something Café	34	B2

TRANSPORT
Aerolíneas Argentinas	35	C2
LADE	36	C2
Riestra Rent A Car	37	B4
Taqsa	38	C2

free; ⓧ 9am-8pm Mon-Fri, 3-8pm Sat), offering exhibits on anthropology, paleontology, geology and fine arts. The Tehuelche ethnology exhibit includes fascinating photographs and local history.

With a mission to educate through art, **Museo de Arte Eduardo Minnicelli** (☎ 436323; Maipú 13; admission free; ⓧ 8:30am-7pm Tue-Fri, 2-6pm Sat & Sun) shows rotating exhibits from larger museums and paintings by Santa Cruz artists. It is also a good spot to get news on local cultural gatherings.

Perhaps a must-see for Brits, the **Museo Malvinas Argentinas** (☎ 420128; cnr Pasteur & San Martín; admission free; ⓧ 8am-noon Mon & Thu, 1-5:30pm Tue & Fri, closed Wed) gets inside the Argentine claim to the Islas Malvinas.

In a prefabricated 1890s metal-clad house shipped from England, the **Museo de los Pioneros** (☎ 437763; cnr Elcano & Alberdi; admission free; ⓧ 10am-8pm) has good displays on early immigrant life. **Funda Cruz** (G Lista 60) is another attractive, imported, prefabricated wooden house. Once a customs office, it now hosts cultural activities as well as a *salón de té* (teahouse).

Tours

The large penguin rookery at Cabo Vírgenes, 140km southeast of Río Gallegos, can be visited from October to March. Excursions can be booked through **Maca Tobiano Turismo** (☎ 422466; www.macatobiano.com; Av Roca 998); an eight-hour trip costs AR$145 (plus AR$10 park admission).

Sleeping

Since hotels cater mainly to business travelers, good-value budget accommodations are scarce.

Hospedaje Elcira (☎ 429856; Zucarino 431; dm AR$40, d with bathroom AR$120) This friendly hostel offers clean, homey dorms with kitchen access, and one double room. It's far from the center but just a 10-minute walk from the bus terminal.

Hotel Cabo Vírgenes (☎ 422134/41; hotelcabovirgenes@speedy.com.ar; Comodoro Rivadavia 252; s/d/tr AR$90/120/180) A good-value option just a few blocks from the river, this yellow house features tiled rooms off narrow hallways. With the exception of family rooms, most can be cramped, but all are quiet.

Hotel Covadonga (☎ 420190; hotelcovadongargl@hotmail.com; Av Roca 1244; d/tr/q with bathroom AR$120/150/180, d/tr without bathroom AR$85/120) Good value and grandmotherly, the tidy Covadonga has appealing large rooms with creaky floors, and a sunny living room with worn leather sofas. Rooms with private bathrooms are worth the upgrade. Cash discounts are offered.

El Viejo Miramar (☎ 430401; hotelviejomiramar@yahoo.com.ar; Av Roca 1630; d AR$150) Snug carpeted rooms and spotless bathrooms make this affable choice a good one. Its personable owner makes guests at ease. Rates include breakfast (but not a second cup of coffee).

Hotel Sehuen (☎ 425683; www.hotelsehuen.com, in Spanish; Rawson 160; s/d/tr/q AR$162/198/244/290) Boasting national-level service awards, modern Sehuen provides all-round good value. Bright and airy, the breakfast area has vaulted ceilings and the day's newspaper. Rooms are plain but well kept.

Hotel Santa Cruz (☎ 420601/2; http://usuarios.advance.com.ar/htlscruz; cnr Av Roca & Comodoro Rivadavia; s/d/tr AR$242/339/398; 🖥) Remodeling for a sleeker, suit-and-tie ambience, this downtown monolith is impeccably clean but currently a little short on charm (see the rubber shower curtains). There's a busy cafe downstairs.

Eating & Drinking

Pizza Roma Express (☎ 434400; Av San Martín 650; mains AR$15-25; ⏰ 11am-late) Cheap and casual, with service that's friendlier than you'll find elsewhere in town, this is where students and families dine on burgers, gnocchi and salads, and older gents share big bottles of cold Quilmes beer.

Puesto Molino (☎ 429836; Av Roca 854; pizza AR$28) This cozy local favorite, featuring an Italian-style pizza oven, is a solid choice for a set lunch or a lively dinner. Arrive early to get a table.

Don Bartolo (☎ 427297; Sarmiento 125; pizza AR$28; ⏰ lunch & dinner) Serious *parrilla* and stone-oven pizza with fresh toppings are the highlights here. Vegetarians will appreciate the create-your-own salad options.

Casa de Empanadas (☎ 444955; Sphur 78; dozen empanadas AR$30) Stock up for a long bus ride – or relax in your hotel room – with a box of piping hot empanadas from this tidy take-out joint. Don't miss the stromboli empanada and other creative options from the gourmet side of the menu.

Laguanacazul (☎ 444114; cnr G Lista & Sarmiento; mains AR$30-50; ⏰ closed Mon) Innovative and artsy, Laguanacazul dares to take Patagonian cuisine to new places, with stir-fried trout and pesto-encrusted lamb. The waterfront location is lovely and the interior quite stylish, but the service is chilly bordering on snobbish; it's not advisable to come in here wearing grubby backpacker clothes.

Rincón del Arte Café (☎ 420035; Bernardino Rivadavia 131; snacks AR$12; ⏰ 3-8pm Mon-Fri) Adjoining an excellent gallery, this ambient coffee shop gets the creative juices flowing. It features regular art talks and courses, and sells beautiful blown glass and jewelry.

Cerrito's (☎ 422501; cnr Moyano & Sarmiento; snacks AR$15; ⏰ 7am-9pm Mon-Fri) This pretty teahouse looks like a miniature castle a couple of blocks from the riverbank. Stop here for a civilized cup of Earl Grey and a pastry (or three.)

Something Café (☎ 431924; Sphur 40; tapas AR$30) This petite cafe and bar, comprising about 10 tables and a couple of bar stools, is a cozy spot for a hot chocolate or tapas and a glass of wine after a long day of travel.

Getting There & Away

AIR

Río Gallegos' **airport** (☎ 442340) is 7km northwest of town.

Aerolíneas Argentinas (☎ 422020/21; Av San Martín 545) flies daily to Buenos Aires (AR$820) and frequently to Ushuaia (AR$376). **LADE** (☎ 422316; Fagnano 53/57) flies several times a week to Río Grande (AR$114), El Calafate (AR$164), Comodoro Rivadavia (AR$264), Ushuaia (AR$227) and Buenos Aires (AR$447).

BUS

Río Gallegos' **bus terminal** (☎ 442159; cnr RN 3 & Av Eva Perón) is about 3km southwest of the center. Companies include **El Pingüino** (☎ 442169), **Líder** (☎ 442160), **Bus Sur** (☎ 442687), **Andesmar** (☎ 442195), **Sportman** (☎ 442595) and also **TAC** (☎ 442042). Companies going to Chile include **Ghisoni** (☎ 442687), **Pacheco** (☎ 442765) and **Tecni-Austral** (☎ 442427). **Taqsa** (☎ 423130; www.taqsa.com .ar, in Spanish; Estrada 71) beelines straight from the airport to Puerto Natales and El Calafate.

Destination	Cost (AR$)	Duration (hr)
Buenos Aires	380-530	36-40
Caleta Olivia	120	7-10
Comodoro Rivadavia	118-147	9-11
El Calafate	50-60	4-5
El Chaltén	72	9
Esquel	175	19
Los Antiguos	150-186	12-16
Puerto Madryn	154-189	15-20
Puerto Natales (Chile)	42	5-7
Puerto San Julián	50-60	4½
Punta Arenas (Chile)	60	5-6
Río Grande	105	7-8
Trelew	165-202	14-17
Ushuaia	150-175	12-14

Getting Around

It's easy to share metered taxis (AR$22) between downtown, the bus terminal and the airport. From Av Roca, buses marked 'B' or 'terminal' link the center and the bus terminal (AR$1.80).

Car rental is expensive due to the poor conditions of the roads to most places of interest. Despite exchange rates, rental deals are often better in Punta Arenas, Chile (see p498). For local rentals, try **Riestra Rent A Car** (☎ 421321; www.riestrarentacar.com; Av San Martín 1508).

ESTANCIAS AROUND RÍO GALLEGOS

Visiting a working *estancia* affords an intimate glimpse into the unique Patagonian lifestyle. These are not luxury hotels, but homes that have been converted into comfortable lodgings. Meals are often shared with the owners, and token participation in the daily working life is encouraged. For *estancias* in Santa Cruz province, contact the provincial tourist office in Río Gallegos (p453) or see www.estancias desantacruz.com.

Dedicated to anglers, **Estancia Güer Aike** (☎ in Río Gallegos 02966-423895, in Buenos Aires 011-4394-3486; truchaike@icqmail.com; 4 nights & 3 days regular/angler AR$1250/2600; ☼ Oct-Apr) has a lovely renovated lodge, Truchaike, enjoying 12km of private river frontage in a world-famous trout-fishing destination. It's at the junction of northbound RN 3 and westbound RP 5.

Estancia Monte Dinero (☎ 02966-428922; www .montedinero.com.ar; day trip AR$345, per person AR$495, incl full board AR$572; ☼ Oct-Apr), named for gold once found on the coast, is a comfortable, old-world lodging with intricate hand-painted doors, billiards and well-appointed rooms. Dudes see the typical *estancia* activities – dog demos, shearing etc – and can also take trips to nearby **Cabo Vírgenes**, where Magellanic penguins nest September through March. A museum at the *estancia* displays an intriguing assortment of goods salvaged from the wreckage of the ship that sunk soon after the family Greenshyls sailed here from Ireland in 1886. Travel agencies in Río Gallegos offer day trips to the *estancia* starting in mid-November, usually making a quick stop at the *estancia's casco*.

INLAND PATAGONIA (ALONG RN 40)

Save for the travel hubs of El Calafate and El Chaltén, rutted RN 40 is every bit a no-man's-land. It parallels the backbone of the Andes, where ñandús doodle through sagebrush, trucks kick up whirling dust and gas stations rise on the horizon like oases. It is the ultimate road trip.

The paving of RN 40 will clearly end the identity of a generation. At present, travel is long and hard but small hamlets along the way benefit. When the pavement settles, most motorists are likely to whiz from point A to point B, missing the quirky, unassuming settlements. For now, public transport stays limited to a few summer-only tourist shuttle services, and driving requires both preparation and patience.

RN 40 parallels the Andes from north of Bariloche to the border with Chile near Puerto Natales, then cuts east to the Atlantic Coast. Highlights include the Perito Moreno and Los Glaciares national parks, the rock art of Cueva de los Manos and remote *estancias*. This section picks up RN 40 in Esquel, from where it continues paved until south of Gobernador Costa, where it turns to gravel. From there on down, it's gravel most of the way, with slowly increasing numbers of paved sections, mainly near population centers.

ESQUEL

☎ 02945 / pop 36,000 / elev 570m

If you tire of the gnome-in-the-chocolate-shop ambience of Bariloche and other cutesy Lakes District destinations, regular old Esquel will feel like a breath of fresh air. Set in western Chubut's dramatic, hikeable foothills, Esquel mainly attracts visitors stopping over on their way to Parque Nacional Los Alerces and other Andean recreation areas. Most people zip through en route to Bariloche or Chile, but it's an easy-going and exceedingly friendly base camp for abundant adventure activities – the perfect place to chill for a few days after hard traveling on RN 40.

Founded at the turn of the 20th century, Esquel is the region's main livestock and commercial center. It's also the historic southern end of the line for *La Trochita*, the narrow-gauge steam train (see the boxed text, p461). The town takes its name from a term of the language of the Mapuche meaning either 'bog' or 'place of the thistles.'

Orientation

RN 259 zigzags through town to the junction with RN 40, which heads north to El Bolsón and south to Comodoro Rivadavia. South of town, RN 259 passes a junction for Parque Nacional Los Alerces en route to Trevelin.

Information

ACA (Automóvil Club Argentino; ☎ 452382; cnr 25 de Mayo & Av Ameghino) Inside YPF gas station; sells fishing licenses.
Banco de la Nación (cnr Av Alvear & General Roca) Has an ATM and changes traveler's checks.
Banco del Chubut (Av Alvear 1147) Has an ATM.
Biblioteca Publica (San Martín, btwn Mitre & Moreno; 🕒 8:30am-7:30pm) Free internet.
Cyber Club (Av Alvear 961; 🕒 10:30am-midnight Mon-Fri, noon-12:30am Sat, 4pm-midnight Sun) Internet access.
Hospital Regional (☎ 450009; 25 de Mayo 150)
Laverap (cnr General Roca & 9 de Julio; per load AR$12) Self- or full-service laundry.
Post office (cnr Avs Fontana & Alvear)
Tourist office (☎ 451927; www.esquel.gov.ar; cnr Av Alvear & Sarmiento; 🕒 7am-11pm) Well organized, helpful and multilingual, with an impressive variety of detailed maps and brochures.

Sights & Activities

Esquel's best attractions are of the outdoor variety, notably Parque Nacional Los Alerces and La Hoya. In town, there is **Museo de Culturas Originarias Patagónicas** (☎ 451929; Belgrano 330; admission by donation; 🕒 9am-noon Mon-Fri, also 3-5pm Tue, Thu & Sat), displaying a modest collection of Mapuche artifacts.

The Roca train station houses a free **train museum** (☎ 451403; www.latrochita.org.ar; cnr Roggero & Urquiza; 🕒 8am-2pm Mon-Sat). Even travelers arriving by bus or air should try to witness the arrival or departure of *La Trochita*, Argentina's famous narrow-gauge steam train. In summer, several tour agencies sell tickets for roundtrip rides on the antique train (see the boxed text, p461).

Esquel's nearby lakes and rivers offer excellent **fly-fishing**, with the season running from November to April. You can purchase a license at most gas stations, including the **YPF gas station** (cnr 25 de Mayo & Av Ameghino; 🕒 daylight hrs) that houses the ACA.

Full-day **white-water rafting** trips go to upper and lower sections of the glacial-fed Río Corcovado for float trips (class II) and serious white-water assaults (class IV). **Mountain biking** is a good way to get out of town and explore the surrounding hills and trails. For **skiing** information, see La Hoya (p461).

Tours

Numerous travel agencies, including **Limits Adventure** (☎ 455811; www.limitsadventure.com.ar; Av Alvear 1069), sell tickets for the Circuito Lacustre boat excursion in Parque Nacional Los Alerces (see p467); buying a ticket in Esquel assures a place on the often-crowded trip. Full-day excursions, including the lake cruise, cost AR$110 when sailing from Puerto Chucao or AR$140 from Puerto Limonao, including transfers to and from the park.

Excursions to El Bolsón/Lago Puelo and Corcovado/Carrenleufú (full day AR$85) are also offered. Half-day trips include La Hoya's winter-sports complex; the nearby Welsh settlement of Trevelin and the Futaleufú hydroelectric complex (AR$40); and the narrow-gauge railway excursion to Nahuel Pan.

For rafting and outdoor adventures, **Expediciones Patagonia Aventura** (EPA; ☎ 457015; www.epaexpediciones.com.ar, in Spanish; Av Fontana 482) offers myriad options on the Río Corcovado, 90km away. For class II and III rafting trips, choose either two hours on the river (with/without transport AR$150/100) or a full-day excursion that includes lunch (with/without

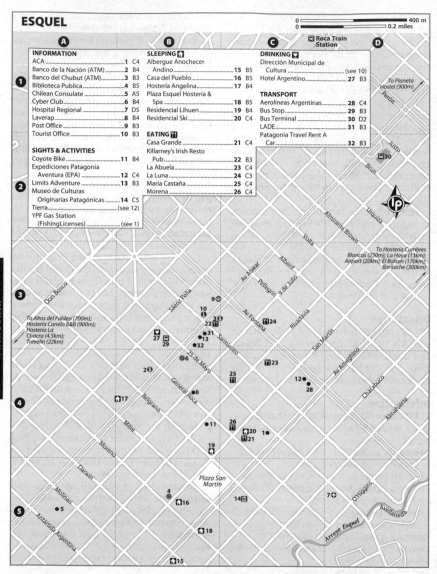

ESQUEL

INFORMATION	
ACA	1 C4
Banco de la Nación (ATM)	2 B4
Banco del Chubut (ATM)	3 B3
Biblioteca Publica	4 B5
Chilean Consulate	5 A5
Cyber Club	6 B4
Hospital Regional	7 D5
Laverap	8 B4
Post Office	9 B3
Tourist Office	10 B3

SIGHTS & ACTIVITIES	
Coyote Bike	11 B4
Expediciones Patagonia	
Aventura (EPA)	12 C4
Limits Adventure	13 B3
Museo de Culturas	
Originarias Patagónicas	14 C5
Tierra	(see 12)
YPF Gas Station	
(FishingLicenses)	(see 1)

SLEEPING	
Albergue Anochecer	
Andino	15 B5
Casa del Pueblo	16 B5
Hostería Angelina	17 B4
Plaza Esquel Hostería &	
Spa	18 B5
Residencial Lihuen	19 B4
Residencial Ski	20 C4

EATING	
Casa Grande	21 C4
Killarney's Irish Resto	
Pub	22 B3
La Abuela	23 C4
La Luna	24 C3
María Castaña	25 C4
Morena	26 C4

DRINKING	
Dirección Municipal de	
Cultura	(see 10)
Hotel Argentino	27 B3

TRANSPORT	
Aerolíneas Argentinas	28 C4
Bus Stop	29 B3
Bus Terminal	30 D2
LADE	31 B3
Patagonia Travel Rent A	
Car	32 B3

transport AR$185/140). Once you're there, you might want to take advantage of the peaceful surroundings: one interesting option is to stay at EPA's riverside hostel.

In summer EPA also offers canopy tours (full day AR$110 to AR$130, plus transfer AR$40), horseback riding and trekking at its mountain center, an attractive wooden

lodge (full pension AR$380) based in Parque Nacional Los Alerces. Guests have access to kayaks, and camping is also available here for AR$15 to AR$30 per person.

Ski rentals are available through several outfitters in town, including **Tierra** (☎ 454366; www.grupoepa.com, in Spanish; Av Fontana 482) for AR$40 to AR$90 per day, with performance skis at the high end. In summer, head to **Coyote Bike** (☎ 455505; Rivadavia 887) for mountain-bike rentals and trail details.

Festivals & Events
Semana de Esquel A weeklong February event that celebrates the city's 1906 founding.

Fiesta Nacional de Esquí (National Skiing Festival) Takes place in mid-September at La Hoya.

Sleeping
Thanks to the huge popularity of the nearby La Hoya ski area, there's no shortage of accommodation options in Esquel. The tourist office offers a long list of cabins and apartment-style hotels in all price ranges; while these mainly cater to families on ski vacations, they can be great alternatives for travelers seeking a temporary home base.

BUDGET
Casa del Pueblo (☎ 450581; www.esquelcasadelpueblo .com.ar, in Spanish; San Martín 661; dm/d/tr AR$45/100/130) Run with dedication and affection, this slightly sagging hostel offers cool shared spaces but would do well to dump the ashtrays. Connected with EPA tour agency, it has handy connections for active pursuits.

Albergue Anochecer Andino (☎ 450498; www .anochecerandino.com.ar, in Spanish; Av Ameghino 482; dm/d AR$45/140; 🖳) This friendly hostel features a handful of basic, clean rooms with shared bathrooms and a common area with a small DVD library. The owner, Federico, prepares dinners (AR$30) usually consisting of homemade pasta or pizza plus fresh bread and drinks.

Planeta Hostel (☎ 456846; www.planetahostel.com; Av Alvear 2833; dm/d AR$50/130; 🖳) The facilities at this small, brightly painted hostel are a cut above the usual: expect down comforters, a spotless and well-equipped communal kitchen and a flat-screen TV in the living area.

Residencial Lihuen (☎ 452589; www.lihuenpat agonia.com.ar; San Martín 820; s/d AR$110/130) These ample rooms are dated and mismatched but serviceable, with private bathrooms and cable TV. They're well located near the leafy Plaza San Martín.

Residencial Ski (☎ 451646; San Martín 961; s/d AR$110/140; 🖳) Clean and friendly Ski doesn't win any style points with its faux-wood paneling, but rooms include cable TV and parking is available.

MIDRANGE & TOP END
Hostería Angelina (☎ 452763; www.hosteriaangelina .com.ar; Av Alvear 758; s/d AR$160/200; 🖳) Hospitable and polished, with a courtyard fountain, Angelina follows international standards with professional service and a good breakfast buffet.

Hostería La Chacra (☎ 452802; www.lachacrapatago nia.com; RN 259, Km 5; d AR$200; 🖳 🐾) If you want a shot of local culture, nothing is better than this country lodging in a 1970s home with ample bright rooms, generous gringo breakfasts and thick down bedding. Get here via taxi or Trevelin bus – they pass hourly.

Altos del Faldeo (☎ 453108; www.altosdelfaldeo.com .ar, in Spanish; Amaya 45; d/tr/q apt AR$220/280/320, d/tr ste AR$200/300; 🖳) This guesthouse, consisting of several suites and apartments, delights travelers with details like Jacuzzis in each of the private bathrooms and top-notch service.

Hostería Canela B&B (☎ 453890; www.canelaesquel .com; cnr Los Notros & Los Radales, Villa Ayelén; d/tr AR$440/542, q apt AR$725; 🖳) This refined B&B, tucked away in a pine forest 2km outside the town center, is a hit with travelers who have a little extra to spend. Veronica and Jorge's lodge feels both cozy and elegant, with high wood-beamed ceilings and comfortable beds topped with pristine white linens.

Plaza Esquel Hostería & Spa (☎ 457002; www.pat agoniaandesgroup.com.ar; Av Ameghino 713; d/tr AR$300/350; 🖳) One of the newest hotels in Esquel, this attractive *hostería* in front of the plaza offers modern rooms with new fixtures.

Hostería Cumbres Blancas (☎ 455100; www .cumbresblancas.com.ar, in Spanish; Av Ameghino 1683; d AR$825; 🖳) While this inn is shiny and lavish, Cumbres Blancas does not surpass its packaged feel. Sportsmen and -women will enjoy having their own fly-casting pond and putting green for a few days. Rooms are decked out in crisp colors and fresh-feeling linens.

Eating
María Castaña (☎ 451752; cnr 25 de Mayo & Rivadavia; snacks AR$12; 🕙 9am-late) A favorite at this frilly cafe is waffles with *dulce de leche*; it's also good for breakfast, sandwiches and ice-cream sundaes. Grab an overstuffed chair in the back.

La Abuela (☎ 451704; Rivadavia 1109; mains AR$15; 🕙 lunch & dinner) Shoehorn yourself into this family nook decked out in lace tablecloths, and enjoy cheap gnocchi and home-cooked classics like *puchero* (vegetable and meat stew) with a carafe of passable house wine.

PATAGONIA

Morena (☎ 02945-15-693856; cnr San Martín & General Roca; mains AR$20-28; ☯ noon-midnight) Relaxed and warm, this brick yuppie watering hole is ideal for a glass of wine or cup of joe, plus decent sandwiches, pasta and pizza.

Killarney's Irish Resto Pub (☎ 457041; cnr Sarmiento & Av Alvear; mains AR$22-30; ☯ noon-late) Don't let the Irish-pub atmosphere fool you into thinking this is just a watering hole: Killarney's serves up good set lunches, too, and a range of hearty soups, salads and sandwiches with the Guinness.

La Luna (☎ 453800; Av Fontana 656; mains AR$22-30, pizza AR$35; ☯ noon-4pm & 7pm-1am) This homey rock'n'roll restaurant-bar offers tasty spinach pizza and heaped portions of steak and fries. The evening crowd spills out of wooden booths and brick nooks, drinking Patagonia's artisan beers.

our pick **Casa Grande** (☎ 02945-15-469712; General Roca 441; mains AR$30-38; ☯ lunch & dinner Wed-Mon) Dig into flavorful *jabalí* (wild boar), baked trout and lamb with roasted potatoes at this fine-dining spot, specializing in regional cuisine. The rambling house with burlwood chandeliers offers plenty of atmosphere.

Drinking & Entertainment

Dirección Municipal de Cultura (☎ 451929; Belgrano 330) Sponsors regular music, cinema, theater and dance.

Hotel Argentino (☎ 452237; 25 de Mayo 862; ☯ 4pm-5am) This lanky and lowbrow Wild West saloon is much better suited to drinking than sleeping, but by all means stop past: the owner is friendly, the 1916 construction is stuffed with relics and sculptures, and the place gets more than a little lively on weekends.

Getting There & Around

AIR

Esquel's **airport** (ESQ; ☎ 451676) is 20km east of town off RN 40. Taxis cost AR$35.

Aerolíneas Argentinas (☎ 453614; Av Fontana 406) flies to Bariloche (AR$1539) and Buenos Aires (AR$1256) several times a week.

LADE (☎ 452124; Av Alvear 1085) flies several times weekly to Bariloche (AR$132) and Comodoro Rivadavia (AR$178), and at least once a week to Puerto Madryn (AR$229) and El Calafate (AR$535).

BUS

Esquel's full-service **bus terminal** (☎ 451477/79; cnr Av Alvear & Brun) is close to the center.

Transportes Jacobsen (☎ 453528) goes to Futaleufú, Chile (AR$25, 1½ hours), at 8am and 6pm Monday and Friday. Buses go hourly to Trevelin (AR$3, 30 minutes), stopping near the corner of Av Alvear and 25 de Mayo on the way out of town. Buses to El Maitén (AR$22, two hours) leave at 1:30pm Tuesday, Thursday and Saturday, returning to Esquel at 4pm.

In summer, **Transportes Esquel** (☎ 453529) goes through Parque Nacional Los Alerces (AR$15, 1¼ hours) to Lago Futalaufquen at 8am and 4pm daily. The first bus goes all the way to Lago Puelo (AR$40, six hours), stopping in Lago Verde (AR$18) at 10:30am and Cholila at noon. If you plan on exploring the area by bus, purchase an open ticket, which allows passengers to make stops along the way between Esquel and Lago Puelo or vice-versa. Note that the service is reduced off-season.

There are daily departures to the following destinations:

Destination	Cost (AR$)	Duration (hr)
Bariloche	48-60	4¼
Buenos Aires	275-340	30
Comodoro Rivadavia	60-75	8-9
El Bolsón	30	2½
Neuquén	120	10
Puerto Madryn	105-125	7-9
Río Gallegos	175	19
Trelew	100	8-9

TRAIN

The narrow-gauge steam train *La Trochita* (also known by the Spanish diminutive *El Trencito*) departs from the diminutive **Roca train station** (☎ 451403; www.latrochita.org.ar; cnr Roggero & Urquiza; ☯ 8am-2pm Mon-Sat). There's a frequent tourist-oriented service to Nahuel Pan (see the boxed text, opposite). For the timeless *Old Patagonian Express* feeling, it's best to catch a bus to El Maitén for the less touristy excursion to Desvío Thomae, but this service is only available from time to time. Confirm schedules either online or via the tourist office.

CAR

Compact rental rates start around AR$100 a day, including 100km and insurance. Try **Patagonia Travel Rent A Car** (☎ 455811, 02945-15-692174; www.patagoniatravelrentacar.com, in Spanish; Av Alvear 1041), which has a good range of vehicles.

LA TROCHITA: THE OLD PATAGONIAN EXPRESS

Clearly an anachronism in the jet age, Ferrocarril Roca's **La Trochita** (☎ in Esquel 02945-451403; www.latrochita.org.ar), Argentina's famous narrow-gauge steam train, averages less than 30km/h on its meandering journey between Esquel and El Maitén – if it runs at top speed. Despite the precarious economics of its operations, the project has survived even the most concerted efforts to shut it down. In its current incarnation, subsidized by the city of Esquel and the governments of Río Negro and Chubut, *La Trochita* – which Paul Theroux facetiously called *The Old Patagonian Express* – provides both a tourist attraction and a service for local citizens.

Like many other state projects, completion of the line seemed an interminable process. In 1906 the federal government authorized the southern branch of the Roca line, between Puerto San Antonio on the Atlantic coast and Lago Nahuel Huapi. In 1922 Ferrocarriles del Estado began work on the narrow-gauge section; it didn't reach the halfway point of Ñorquinco until 1939. In 1941 the line made it to the workshops at El Maitén, and in 1945 it reached the end of the line at Esquel.

Since then, the line has suffered some of the oddest mishaps in railroad history. Three times within a decade, in the late 1950s and early 1960s, the train was derailed by high winds, and ice has caused other derailments. In 1979 a collision with a cow derailed the train at Km 243 south of El Maitén; the engine driver was the appropriately named Señor Bovino.

In full operation until 1993, *La Trochita*'s 402km route between Esquel and Ingeniero Jacobacci was probably the world's longest remaining steam-train line, with half a dozen stations and another nine *apeaderos* (whistle-stops). The Belgian Baldwin and German Henschel engines refilled their 4000L water tanks at strategically placed *parajes* (pumps) every 40km to 45km. Most of the passenger cars, heated by wood stoves, date from 1922, as do the freight cars.

During summer, the **Tren Turístico** (tickets AR$150; ☾ 10am Mon-Sat, additional 2pm departures Jan-Feb) travels from Roca station in Esquel to Nahuel Pan, the first station down the line, 20km east. At Nahuel Pan, the train stops for photo ops and a small artisan market – make sure you pick up a few piping hot *tortas fritas* pastries made by local women. The trip takes 45 minutes one way and space is tight: if you're squished between other tourists, escape to the cafe car for a hot chocolate.

AROUND ESQUEL

La Hoya

Only 13km north of Esquel, with a base elevation of 1350m, the winter-sports area of **La Hoya** (☎ 02945-453018; www.cerrolahoya.com, in Spanish; full-day lift pass AR$110) is a family-friendly favorite of Argentines and Chileans. The addition of new lifts has doubled the terrain and the powder skiing is some of Argentina's best.

The terrain consists of open bowls, with most trails located above the tree line, allowing for a longer season than most ski areas. While it's cheaper and less crowded than Bariloche, experienced skiers will find it smaller and comparatively tame. The season lasts from June until October, with the **Fiesta Nacional de Esquí** (Skiing Festival) held in the second week of September. Summer activity options include hiking, riding the chairlift and horseback riding.

Equipment can be rented on-site or at sport shops in Esquel, including Tierra (p458). Minibuses can take you to La Hoya from Esquel lodgings for around AR$25 per person; taxis may be a better deal for groups, though.

Cholila

Butch Cassidy, the Sundance Kid and Ethel Place tried settling down and making an honest living (see the boxed text, p464) near this quiet farming community outside the northeast entrance to Parque Nacional Los Alerces. Bruce Chatwin's travel classic *In Patagonia* recounts the tale. The bandits' partially restored homestead is just off RP 71 at Km 21, near the turnoff to the Casa de Piedra teahouse, 8km north of Cholila. Cholila's enthusiastic **Casa de Informes** (☎ 02945-498040/131; RP 71, at RP 15; ☾ summer only) has a helpful regional map and will gladly point you in the right direction.

Transportes Esquel buses from Esquel to El Bolsón pass close enough for a fleeting glimpse of the cabin on the west side of the highway, but visitors with their own vehicle or time to spare can stop for a look at the

SURVIVING RUTA NACIONAL 40

Patagonia's RN 40 is the quintessential road trip. No one gets anywhere fast here – the weather can be wily and the gravel loose. It can seem to go on forever. But it can also be magical when you've been rattling along for hours and the interminable flat line of steppe suddenly bursts open with views of glacial peaks and gem-colored lakes.

The road is half paved, and plans to finish the job are long overdue. When it is finished, the life that slow travel brought to the small roadside towns is bound to diminish. So, if you want to drive this dirt behemoth, now is the time to giddy up.

Conditions from December to March are generally fine, but heavy precipitation can render some parts inaccessible. Most of the mythic route's unpaved stretches are wide and compacted, although some of the paved sections already show serious wear. Just be thankful you didn't set out on a bike or motorcycle.

Be Prepared

Everyone should travel with necessary repair equipment. If renting a car, carry two full-sized *neumáticos* (spare tires) and make sure that the headlights work and that suspension, tires and brakes are in good shape. The gravel can puncture gas tanks, so be sure to have some extra fuel on hand, as well as oil and generous supplies of food and water. Gas is subsidized in Patagonia, so fill up the tank when you get the chance.

Dodging flying rocks can be difficult and many potential damages are not covered under the insurance policies offered by rental agencies. Those that aren't must be paid out of pocket. Be sure to check with the agency about coverage and deductibles.

Road Rules

The law requires that headlights be on during daylight hours. Respect speed limits: 65km/h to 80km/h is a safe maximum speed.

Sheep *always* have the right of way. While most will scurry out of the way, some are not so quick. Guanacos and ñandús are other potential hazards. Slow down, give them distance and watch out for unsigned *guardaganados* (cattle guards).

Driving Etiquette

Signal hello to oncoming drivers by flashing your headlights or raising an index finger with your hand on the steering wheel. An unwritten rule: stop to help anyone stranded on the side of the road. There's no 'roadside assistance' here and cell phones are useless in the mountains and along most west–east stretches. Along windy roads, toot your horn before barreling round blind curves.

When another car approaches, slow down and move to the side of the road to avoid stones flying out from under the wheels. For maximum security, consider adding a windshield screen for protection. Another recommendation is to cover headlights with transparent, industrial-strength tape to minimize the cracking should a stone hit.

overlapping log construction, typical of North America but unusual in this region. Without museum status, it remains locked, although the congenial caretaker, Daniel Sepulveda, is open to showing visitors around. Close any gates you open and ask permission from the caretaker before looking around or taking photographs.

Afterwards, you can follow the signs for 1km to the Calderón family's **Casa de Piedra** (☎ 02945-498056; RP 71, Km 20; ☺ Dec-Mar), a beautiful stone farmhouse offering tea, sweets and

preserves, as well as information. The hospitable Calderóns, of Spanish-Welsh-English-French-Basque-Mapuche descent, let double rooms for around AR$160 per person. Call ahead to let them know you are coming.

To drive back to Esquel, you can follow unpaved RP 71 north for 20km to the pavement at the first crossroads, and continue 116km on paved RN 40 to Esquel. On the way you will pass the **Museo Leleque** (☎ in Buenos Aires 011-4326-5156; www.benetton.com/patagonia; RN 40, Km 1440; ☺ 11am-5pm Thu-Tue Mar-Dec, to 7pm Jan & Feb,

Flash your headlights to signal a desire to pass. The car in front should slow down to let you by. If you're being overtaken, move over and slow down until the cloud of dust has settled. If you need to stop, don't slam on the brakes, which will send the car skidding along the road. Instead, slow down and use the gears to lower the speeds until you can safely park on the side of the road.

Letting Someone Else Deal with It

Several travel agencies coordinate two- to five-day minivan transport along RN 40 from El Calafate to Bariloche, via El Chaltén, Perito Moreno and Los Antiguos. Service follows fair weather, from mid-October/November to early April, depending on demand and road conditions. Pricier guided tours stretch the trip over four or five days, giving travelers the opportunity to get off the bus and explore the desolate landscape; if you're in a rush or have a limited budget, choose one of the latter options listed below for a quicker trip along the legendary highway.

Overland Patagonia (www.overlandpatagonia.com) offers trips down between El Calafate and Bariloche: AR$1680 for the five-day trip, including lodging.

Highly recommended outfitter **Las Loicas** (☎ 02963-490272; www.lasloicas.com; Lago Posadas) offers a five-day trip between El Chaltén and Perito Moreno that includes a bilingual guide, meals, four nights' accommodations, and visits to Cueva de las Manos and Parque Nacional Perito Moreno (AR$2100). The tours depart from both the northern and southern points just a few times each month; check the website for up-to-date schedules.

If you're really up for a road trip, contact **Ruta 40** (☎ 0297-446-5337; www.ruta-40.com; Comodoro Rivadavia). The small, multilingual outfitter takes travelers on eight-day journeys from Comodoro Rivadavia to Puerto Deseado and down RN 40, with stops at Cueva de las Manos and several lovely *estancias* before ending up in El Calafate. Consult for current rates and departure dates.

Quicker, more straightforward travel along RN 40 can be arranged through **Chaltén Travel** (☎ 011-4326-7282; www.chaltentravel.com; Sarmiento 559, piso 8, Buenos Aires), which runs northbound two-day shuttles, leaving at 8am from El Calafate, with accommodation in Perito Moreno. Southbound three-day shuttles leave Bariloche at 6:45am on odd-numbered days, with accommodations in Perito Moreno and El Chaltén. Buses stop in Los Antiguos as well. For the one-way trip, prices start at AR$450 per person (including accommodation). It's possible to hop on and off along the route, but space on the next shuttle is not reservable. Combinations to Puerto Madryn are also available for northbound travelers. Chaltén Travel has branches in **El Calafate** (☎ 02902-492212; Av Libertador 1174), **El Chaltén** (☎ 02962-493005; cnr Guemes & Lago del Desierto) and **Bariloche** (☎ 02944-423809).

The bus line **Taqsa** (☎ 0297-432675) now offers high-season service north and south between El Calafate and Bariloche, with stops in El Chaltén, Perito Moreno and Esquel. This new service isn't running smoothly just yet: Taqsa uses a full-size bus instead of a smaller shuttle, and, when we traveled, the journey from El Chaltén to Perito Moreno involved multiple breakdowns lasting several hours and a few chaotic bus changes. Theoretically, northbound buses will leave El Calafate on Monday and Thursday, stopping in El Chaltén at 11:25pm and arriving in Perito Moreno around 1:30pm the following day before ending up in Bariloche at 3am. See p478.

closed Wed), which has many Mapuche artifacts and narrates the history of the region from the perspective of the Benetton family.

TREVELIN

☎ 02945 / pop 6400 / elev 735m

Historic Trevelin (treh-*veh*-lehn), from the Welsh for town (*tre*) and mill (*velin*), is the only community in interior Chubut with a notable Welsh character. Easygoing and postcard pretty, this pastoral village makes a tranquil lodging alternative to the much busier Esquel (remember, everything is relative here), or an enjoyable day trip for tea. The surrounding countryside is ripe for exploration.

Orientation

Just 22km south of Esquel via paved RN 259, Trevelin's urban plan is unusual for an Argentine city: at the north end of town, eight streets radiate like the spokes of a wheel from Plaza Coronel Fontana. The principal thoroughfare, Av San Martín, is the southward extension of RN 259, which forks west 50km to the Chilean border and to Futaleufú, 12km beyond.

Information

Banco del Chubut (cnr Av San Martín & Brown) Just south of the plaza, with an ATM.

Gales al Sur (☎ 480427; www.galesalsur.com.ar; Patagonia 186) Esquel buses stop at this travel agency, which arranges tours.

Post office (Av San Martín) Just south of the plaza.

Telefónica (cnr Av San Martín & El Malacara) *Locutorio* next to Gales al Sur. Open late, with dial-up internet.

Tourist office (☎ 480120; www.trevelin.org, in Spanish; Plaza Fontana; ☺ 8am-9pm) Helpful, with a free town map, information on local hikes and English-speaking staff.

Sights & Activities

The **Museo Regional Molino Viejo** (☎ 02945-480189; cnr 25 de Mayo & Molino Viejo; admission AR$3; ☺ 11am-8:30pm Dec-Mar, to 6:30pm Apr-Nov) occupies the restored remains of a 1922 grain mill and is stuffed with interesting historic artifacts. Look for the antique bridal gown and the Welsh coffee cup designed for men who have mustaches. It's a couple of blocks east of the plaza, at the end of 25 de Mayo.

Horse lovers can pay their respects at **Tumba de Malacara** (☎ 480108; www.caballomalacara.com.ar; Malacara s/n; admission AR$10; ☺ 10am-8pm), the monument holding the remains of a brave horse whose swift retreat saved its owner's hide. As the story goes, town founder John Evans escaped with Malacara from murder-bent Araucanians, who were retaliating for an attack by the Argentine army during the Conquista del Desierto. It's two blocks northeast of Plaza Coronel Fontana. Here there's also the **Cartief Taid**, a museum replica of Evans' home.

Festivals & Events

An **artisan market** fills Plaza Coronel Fontana on Sundays in summer and on alternate Sundays the rest of the year. On March 19,

---

BUTCH & SUNDANCE'S PATAGONIAN REFUGE *Daniel Buck and Anne Meadows*

The only standing relics of Butch Cassidy and the Sundance Kid's South American adventure are the rough-hewn log ranch buildings by the Río Blanco in Chubut's Cholila Valley.

Butch and Sundance – and Sundance's chum, Ethel Place – arrived in the Cholila Valley in 1901, at a time when Argentina was attracting immigrants from all over the world and its government was eager to settle the sparsely populated southern territories. US newspapers rhapsodized about 'a land of wild apples and wild strawberries, of hill and dale, of beautiful scenery, of pastoral and mineral wealth.' Best of all, the land was free.

By all accounts, Butch and Sundance had every intention of giving up their delinquent ways and settling permanently in Cholila. They bought livestock, filed land petitions and built a ranch. In 1902 Butch wrote to a friend in Utah that 'the country is first class.' They had '300 cattle, 1500 sheep and 28 good saddle horses' and would soon be sending cattle over the Andes to a slaughterhouse in Chile.

Another hint of what their life was like comes from Primo Capraro, a Bariloche architect who spent a night with the trio in 1904 at their ranch. He later recalled: 'The house was simply furnished and exhibited a certain painstaking tidiness, a geometric arrangement of things, pictures with cane frames, wallpaper made of clippings from American magazines, and many beautiful weapons and lassos. The men were tall, slender, laconic and nervous, with intense gazes. The lady, who was reading, was well-dressed.'

Their neighbors, some of whose descendants still live in the valley, were from Chile, Wales, England, Ireland, Scotland and Texas. One of the Texans had even been a sheriff back home, but among expatriate settlers, amity was the rule. When the territorial governor came through on an inspection tour, Butch and Sundance hosted a party. The governor danced with Ethel while Sundance played guitar.

Their idyll was smashed in early 1905, when they were wrongly suspected of a bank robbery in Río Gallegos and forced to flee. A few months later, as a departing thumb-in-the-eye, they held up a bank in Villa Mercedes, near Mendoza. Ethel returned to the USA and vanished, while Butch and Sundance migrated to Chile and Bolivia. In November 1908, after a couple of years working in a mine camp, they robbed another mine's payroll and died in a shootout with a Bolivian military patrol.

the **Aniversario de Trevelin** celebrates the founding of the city. The biggest Welsh celebration of the year is the multilingual **Eisteddfod**, a festival that takes place at the end of October and sees bards competing in song and poetry. Other dates that bring out the Welsh flag include July 28, the date the first ship with 143 Welsh pilgrims docked in Patagonia in 1865. Every April 30, the community commemorates its decision to choose Argentine residency. November 25 marks the discovery of the valley, with a flurry of afternoon teas and an evening concert.

Sleeping

Circulo Policial (☎ 480947; Costanera Río Percy & Holdich; campsites per person AR$6; ☽ closed winter) These fine, grassy campsites offer some shade. From Av San Martín 600 block, walk two blocks west on Coronel Holdich and turn left down the gravel road. The Esquel bus goes beyond the plaza and stops at the intersection of Holdich and San Martín.

ourpick **Casaverde Hostal** (☎ 480091; www.casaverdehostel.com.ar; Los Alerces s/n; dm HI member/nonmember AR$40/50, d with bathroom AR$160, 6-person cabin AR$350; ▯) A convivial retreat perched above town, Casaverde is homey and helpful. Guests relax in the spacious rooms and sunny common areas, and wake up to breakfast (AR$12) with bottomless mugs of real coffee, homemade bread and jams. It's a 10-minute walk from the plaza, off Av Fontana.

Cabañas Oregon (☎ 480408; www.oregontrevelin.com.ar, in Spanish; cnr Av San Martín & JM Thomas; 4-person cabin AR$200) Scattered around an apple orchard on the south side of town, these appealing log cabins come with kitchen, TV and private bathroom.

Hostería Casa de Piedra (☎ 480357; www.casadepiedratrevelin.com, in Spanish; Brown 244; d/tr AR$250/290, 5-person apt AR$350, 6-person cabin AR$390) This stone lodge is a haven for anglers. A huge fireplace, tribal motifs and rustic touches create a warm ambience.

Cabañas Wilson (☎ 480803; www.wilsonpatagonia.com.ar; RP 259 at RP 71; 2-/6-person cabins AR$382/420) Savor the serenity surrounding these wood-and-brick cabins on the edge of town. The cabins include daily cleaning service, extra covers and a barbecue deck.

Eating

Just as visitors to Trelew flock to Gaiman, so visitors to Esquel head to Trevelin for Welsh

tea. Teahouses are typically open from 3pm to 8pm. Often the portions are big enough to share – ask first if it's OK.

Nain Maggie (☎ 480232; www.casadetenainmaggie.com; Perito Moreno 179; tea service AR$45; ☽ 10am-12:30pm & 3-8:30pm) Trevelin's oldest teahouse occupies a modern building but maintains high traditional standards. Along with a bottomless pot, there's outstanding cream pie, *torta negra* and scones hot from the oven.

La Mutisia (☎ 480165; Av San Martín 170; tea service AR$40) The only other teahouse where everything is reliably homemade.

Getting There & Away

The **bus terminal** (cnr Roca & RN 40), on a corner of the wheel, has buses to Comodoro Rivadavia (AR$53) at 11:30pm Sunday through Friday. **Gales del Sur** (☎ 480427; RN 259) has hourly buses to Esquel (AR$3, 30 minutes). Buses cross the border to Chile's Futaleufú (AR$22, one hour) on Mondays and Fridays at 8:30am and 6pm. Buses go to the village of Carrenleufú (AR$34, two hours), just before the border crossing to Palena in Chile, on Mondays, Wednesdays and Fridays at 10:30am.

PARQUE NACIONAL LOS ALERCES
☎ 02945

This collection of spry creeks, verdant mountains and mirror lakes resonates as unadulterated Andes. The real attraction, however, is the alerce tree *(Fitzroya cupressoides)*, one of the longest-living species on the planet, with specimens that have survived up to 4000 years. Lured by the acclaim of well-known parks to the north and south, most hikers miss this gem, which makes your visit here all the more enjoyable.

Resembling California's giant sequoia, the alerce flourishes in middle Patagonia's temperate forests, growing only about 1cm every 20 years. Individual specimens of this beautiful tree can reach over 4m in diameter and exceed 60m in height. Like the giant sequoia, it has suffered overexploitation because of its valuable timber. West of Esquel, this 2630-sq-km park protects some of the largest alerce forests that still remain.

Environment & Climate

Hugging the eastern slopes of the Andes, the peaks of Parque Nacional Los Alerces reach up to 2300m, bearing glaciers whose retreat formed the series of nearly pristine lakes and

PATAGONIA

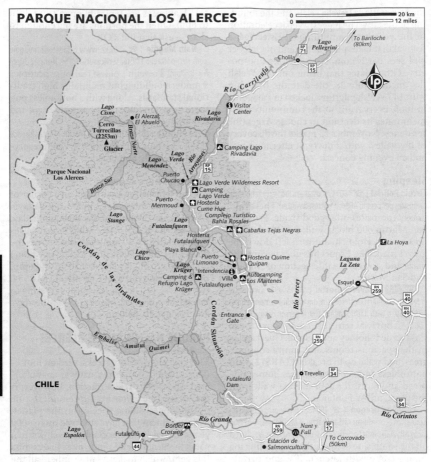

PARQUE NACIONAL LOS ALERCES

streams below. These lakes all drain southward via the huge hydroelectricity reservoir of Lago Amutui Quimei into the Río Futaleufú, which flows westward into Chile. The area offers beautiful vistas and excellent fishing.

Because the Andes are relatively low here, westerly storms deposit nearly 3m of rain annually. The park's eastern sector, though, is much drier. Winter temperatures average 2°C, but can be much colder. The summer average high reaches 24°C, but evenings are usually cool.

Plants & Animals

While its wild backcountry supports the seldom-seen huemul (Andean deer) and other wildlife, Los Alerces functions primarily as a trove of botanical riches. Besides the alerce, other important coniferous evergreens and deciduous broadleaf trees characterize the dense Valdivian forest, such as ñire, coihue and lenga. Most of the larger broadleaf tree species in the park belong to the genus *Nothofagus* (commonly known as southern beech), found only in the southern hemisphere. Hikers will find an almost impenetrable undergrowth of chusquea (a solid bamboo), coniferous cypress and the aromatic Chilean incense cedar. Another interesting species is the arrayán, whose foliage and peeling cinnamon-colored bark bear resemblance to the madrone (*Arbutus menziesii*) of the western US coastal states and British Columbia.

Information

During the high season (Christmas to Semana Santa) foreigners pay AR$30 admission. In Villa Futalaufquen you'll find the **Intendencia** (park office; ☎ 471015/20; ☼ 8am-9pm summer, 9am-4pm rest of year), where rangers have details about hiking, camping and guided excursions. Get your fishing permits here. The headquarters also house the **Museo y Centro del Interpretación**, a natural-history museum. The visitor center at the northern end of the park is only open December through February.

Activities

As well as sailing and hiking, travel agencies in Esquel offer fishing, canoeing, mountain-biking, snorkeling and horseback-riding tours.

SAILING

Traditionally, **Circuito Lacustre** is Los Alerces' most popular excursion and involves sailing from Puerto Limonao in the south of the lake system, up Lago Futalaufquen, then through the narrow channel of the Río Arrayanes to Lago Verde.

Low water levels now make it necessary to hike the short distance between Puerto Mermoud, at the north end of Lago Futalaufquen, and Puerto Chucao on Lago Menéndez. Launches from Puerto Chucao handle the second segment of the trip (1½ hours) to the northern nature trail **El Alerzal**, the most accessible stand of alerces. Another option (recommended) is to arrive to Puerto Chucao via a 1500m very scenic trail that crosses the bridge over Río Arrayanes.

The launch remains docked for over an hour at El Alerzal trailhead, sufficient for an unhurried hike around the loop trail that passes **Lago Cisne** and an attractive waterfall to end up at **El Abuelo** (Grandfather), a 57m-tall, 2600-year-old alerce.

From Puerto Limonao, the excursion costs AR$140; from Puerto Chucao it's AR$110. Departures are in the morning from Limonao and at midday from Chucao, returning to Chucao around 5pm and to Limonao at 7pm. In summer, purchase tickets in Esquel to ensure a seat.

HIKING

Because of fire-hazard, authorities allow camping only at authorized campsites. Even for short treks, it is compulsory to sign in at the one of the ranger stations before heading out.

Day hikes can be undertaken from several interpretive trails located near **Lago Futalaufquen**. There is also a 25km trail from **Puerto Limonao** along the south shore of Futalaufquen to **Refugio Lago Krüger** (p468), which can be done in a long day, or broken up by camping at **Playa Blanca**. Boat excursions from Puerto Limonao to Lago Krüger cost AR$110 per person.

For longer hikes, see Lonely Planet's *Trekking in the Patagonian Andes*.

Sleeping & Eating

En route to the park, watch for roadside signs advertising ideal picnic goods: homemade bread, delicious Chubut cheese, fresh fruit and Welsh sweets. In Villa Futalaufquen there are a couple of basic grocery stores and a summer-only restaurant, but it's best to bring your own provisions. The following accommodations are listed from north to south, not by price.

CAMPING

Los Alerces has several full-service, drive-in campgrounds, all of which have hot showers, grocery stores and restaurants on-site or nearby. Free (no services) and semi-organized campgrounds exist near most of these fee sites.

Camping Lago Rivadavia (☎ 454381; adult/child AR$15/8) These idyllic spots at Lago Rivadavia's south end are sheltered in the trees with picnic tables and a boat launch. There's an electricity hookup, too. It's 42km north of the Villa.

Camping Lago Verde (☎ 454421; campsites per person AR$20, 6-person cabin AR$1000) With deluxe remodeled cabins and full-service camping, this campground flanks the eastern shore of its namesake lake, 35km northwest of Villa Futalaufquen. Besides nearby Lago Verde Wilderness Resort, it's the only option on this tranquil lake.

Complejo Turístico Bahía Rosales (☎ 471044; campsites per person AR$20, 4-person refugio AR$180, 6-person cabin AR$400) This sprawling complex has flat campsites by the water, other lodging options and sporting facilities. At the north end of Lago Futalaufquen, it is 1.5km from the main road via a dirt path.

Autocamping Los Maitenes (☎ 471006; per person AR$18) On a slip of grass between the main road and the lake, these spots have lovely water views. Campsites include shade, electricity hookup and fire pits, 200m from the Intendencia.

PATAGONIA

Camping & Refugio Lago Krüger (☎ 02945-15-4424-7964; www.lagokrugger.com.ar; campsites per person AR$15, refugio incl full board per person AR$380) This relatively isolated lakefront *refugio* (rustic shelter) complex is accessible by the 25km trail that leaves from Hostería Futalaufquen (see p467), or by launch from Puerto Limonao.

CABAÑAS & HOSTERÍAS
With a group, cabañas can be an affordable option.

Lago Verde Wilderness Resort (☎ in Buenos Aires 011-4816-5348; www.hosteriaselaura.com; 2-/4-person cabins incl full board AR$1900/2300) Rustic yet ritzy, these raspy stone cabañas feature big cozy beds, panoramic forest views and earthy motifs. Anglers can rent motorized rafts to cast from the lake's every nook and cranny. A new gourmet restaurant and teahouse cater to travelers and guests. It's 35km north of the Villa.

Cabañas Tejas Negras (☎ 471012, 471046; tejas negras@infovia.com.ar; 4-/5-person cabins AR$500/700; ☺ year-round) With a lawn like a golf course and a handful of prim A-frames, Nilda and Hector have hosted guests for 40 years. Think retreat: there are no football matches on these greens where tranquility is savored.

Hostería Quime Quipan (☎ 471021; www.cpatagonia .com/quimequipan, in Spanish; d incl half-board AR$400-450 ☺ Nov-Apr) In a breathtaking setting, this old-fashioned guesthouse offers pleasant but dated rooms – splurge for those with lake views. Nonguests can dine at the cozy, sunlit restaurant (meals AR$45), an après-fishing pit stop.

Hostería Futalaufquen (☎ 02945-15-465941; www .brazosur.com.ar/hosteria.htm, in Spanish; d incl half-board AR$604-765, 4-/5-person apt AR$1236/1840) Exclusive and elegant, this country inn is on the quieter western shore of the lake, 4.5km north of the Villa at the end of the road. It offers nine well-appointed doubles and three log cabins (without kitchens). Activities – from kayaking to rappelling – abound; collapse by the fire afterwards with a plate of dessert. Reservations can be made at Sarmiento 635 in Esquel.

Getting There & Away
For information on getting to/from the park, see p460.

GOBERNADOR COSTA
☎ 02945 / pop 2000
When you find a town where a child snaps the tourist's picture (and not the reverse), you've discovered something of an anomaly.

This rusted little cattle town abuts the yawning stretch of RN 40 between Esquel and Río Mayo, at the intersection of RP 20 for Sarmiento and Comodoro Rivadavia. Some 20km west of town, RP 19 leads to **Lago General Vintter** and several smaller blue-ribbon lakes near the Chilean border; camping is possible along the shores.

Traveler services are few but reasonable. On the edge of fields, **Camping Municipal** (per person AR$6) has electricity and hot water. The motel-style **Mi Refugio** (☎ 491097; Av Roca s/n; s/d/tr/ q AR$60/85/105/130) has dark but clean rooms with central heating and TV. The downstairs grill is friendly and its food filling. If it's booked out, check **Residencial El Jair** (☎ 02945-15-680414; cnr San Martín & Sarmiento; per person AR$45), with basic rooms and special rates for families.

The **bus terminal** (Av Roca s/n) is next to Mi Refugio. Buses go to Esquel (AR$28), continuing to Bariloche, at 3:45am every day except for Saturday. For Comodoro Rivadavia (AR$65), buses leave at 11:30pm every day except Sunday. To reach Río Mayo, most buses skip this portion of bumpy (and boring) RN 40 by taking RP 20 south, paralleling Río Senguer to the Río Mayo cutoff.

RÍO MAYO
☎ 02903 / pop 3500 humans, 800,000 sheep
The national capital of sheep shearing is a surprisingly humdrum place, save for the petroleum workers and waylaid gauchos practicing their wolf-whistles on unsuspecting female *turistas*. This barren pit stop is 200km south of Gobernador Costa and 135km north of Perito Moreno.

The **Casa de Cultura** (☎ 420400; Ejército Argentino s/n; ☺ 9am-noon & 3-6pm) houses a tourist office, with information on local mountain-biking options. The town **website** (www.riomayo.gov.ar, in Spanish) has some useful information for visitors. **Banco del Chubut** (cnr Yrigoyen & Argentina) has an ATM.

January's **Festival Nacional de la Esquila** features merino wool–quality competitions and even guanaco shearing. But the main event is the long-anticipated crowning of the national sheep-shearing queen.

Camping Municipal (☎ 420400; Av E Argentino s/n; per vehicle AR$16) flanks the river. Run-down but respectable, the four-room **Aurora** (☎ 420193; Fontana 750; d without bathroom AR$75) is clean and cared for by a sweet-natured matron. It's around the corner from the YPF station.

The following lodgings both offer meals, otherwise the YPF is a good bet for a quick sandwich and coffee. Funky and rambling **El Viejo Kavadonga** (☎ 420020; San Martín 573; per person with/without bathroom AR$80/55) features rooms with good down covers but varying in quality. Its coveted feature is the orange vinyl bar. **Hotel Akatá** (☎ 420054; San Martín 640; per person AR$80; ☐) has internet but little else; its wood-panel rooms are dark and airless.

There are daily morning services from the **bus terminal** (☎ 420174; cnr Fontana & Irigoyen) to Comodoro Rivadavia, Sarmiento and Coyhaique (Chile). Schedules change regularly so check at the bus terminal. The only regularly scheduled services on the rugged stretch of RN 40 to Perito Moreno are summer-only backpacker shuttles (see p470).

PERITO MORENO
☎ 02963 / pop 3500

Those who confuse this dull agricultural village with the jaw-dropping national park of the same name or the glacier near El Calafate might wonder why the only tourist attraction is cruising the strip on Saturday night. Perito Moreno is a brief stopover en route to the more inviting Andean oasis of Los Antiguos. It also makes a good launching pad for visiting Cueva de las Manos and Parque Nacional Perito Moreno. The main drag, San Martín, leads north to RP 43 and south to RN 40; it's 128km south to Bajo Caracoles and 135km north to Río Mayo.

The town's glory came in 1898, when explorer Perito Moreno challenged Chile's border definition of *'divortum aquarum continental'* (which claimed the headwaters of Pacific-flowing rivers as Chilean territory) by rerouting the Río Fénix, which flows through town, to Atlantic-bound Río Deseado. The river and the area remained Argentine, and the town took his name.

Information
Avenida Kiosco y Anexo (Av San Martín 2147) At the time of writing, this was the only functional internet cafe in town. But repairs are supposedly underway at CTC (Perito Moreno 1062) and Ciber Café Loreto (Av Perón & Sarmiento).
Banco de la Nación (cnr San Martín & Perito Moreno)
Banco de Santa Cruz (cnr San Martín & Rivadavia) Has an ATM and changes traveler's checks.
Hospital Distrital (☎ 432040; Colón 1237)
Locutorio Call Center (Rivadavia 1057)

Post office (cnr JD Perón & Belgrano)
Tourist office (☎ 432732; peritomoreno@santacruzpatagonia.gob.ar; San Martín 1766; ☺ 7am-11:30pm Mon-Fri, 8am-3pm Sat & Sun) Helpful, with a surprising number of pamphlets and brochures. There is also a desk at the bus terminal.
Zoyen (☎ 432207; zoyenturismo@yahoo.com.ar; cnr San Martín & Saveedra) Good local travel agency with trips to Cueva de las Manos in high season.

Tours
The experienced **GuanaCondor Tours** (☎ 432117, 02963-15-452-6224; jarinauta@santacruz.com.ar; Perito Moreno 1087; ☺ 10am-noon & 4-8pm Mon-Wed & Sat, 5-8pm Sun) runs tours in summer to Cueva de las Manos (AR$150 per person), accessing the park via the former Estancia Los Toldos, with a challenging hike that adds considerably to the experience. Also ask about its trips to Monte Zeballos, a high mesa with excellent views, and the overnight trip to Paso Tehuelche.

Hugo Campañoli (☎ 432336) is a local guide who takes groups of three or more to Cueva de las Manos on day trips for AR$160 per person.

Also check out the shuttle services listed under Getting There & Away, p470.

Sleeping & Eating
Camping Municipal (Laguna de los Cisnes, off Mariano Moreno; campsites AR$30, plus AR$5 per person, 4-person cabañas per person AR$100) The cheapest option for backpackers is this campground with rustic cabins on the south side of town. It's shaded by breezy poplars and has hot showers.

Posada el Caminante (☎ 432204; Rivadavia 937; s/d/tr AR$120/160/200) The best bet in town, Señora Ethiel's inn fills up fast. This welcoming hostess has four spotless rooms with comfy beds, heating and private, modern bathrooms. An abundant breakfast (AR$10) is worthwhile, especially during fruit season.

Hotel Belgrano (☎ 432019; San Martín 1001; s/d AR$120/180) This big, boxy corner hotel has spacious concrete rooms with decent mattresses but not much ambience. Most folks shuffle in during the wee hours from Chaltén Travel shuttles. Breakfast is AR$10.

Hotel Americano (☎ 432074; San Martín 1327; s/d/tr AR$150/220/280) Cozy and family-run, Americano also has a decent restaurant. Rooms vary widely – some lack windows, others can be quite cozy – so ask to see a few before deciding. Breakfast is AR$12 extra.

PATAGONIA

ourpick **Salón Iturrioz** (cnr Rivadavia & San Martín; snacks AR$8) This charming brick corner cafe is the temporary home of antiques and photographs that will eventually be on display at the Museo Regional Cueva de las Manos (being built across the street.) Check out the artifacts, including a gorgeous old silver cash register, while waiting for your hot chocolate.

Restaurant Chee's 1 (☎ 432842; cnr 25 de Mayo & Laguna del Desierto; mains AR$25-35) This basic but cheerful corner joint doesn't offer a regular menu: it's just a few local ladies serving good daily specials like lasagna or steak alongside salads and bottles of inexpensive wine.

There are a couple of well-stocked *panaderías* (bakeries) and supermarkets along San Martín.

Getting There & Away
LADE (☎ 432055; San Martín 1065) flies to El Calafate, Río Gallegos, Río Grande and Ushuaia.

The bus terminal sits behind the YPF rotunda at the northern entrance to town. Taxis (AR$10) provide the only transport between here and the center, other than a flat 15-minute walk. Buses leave a few times daily for Los Antiguos (AR$25, 40 minutes), though departure times aren't reliable as they're usually scheduled to connect with incoming buses from RN 40, which are often delayed. In the afternoon, starting at 3:50pm, multiple buses also head for Comodoro Rivadavia (AR$75, five hours) via Caleta Olivia (AR$50, four hours). Buses to El Calafate (AR$180, 19 hours) via RN 3 go at 5:05pm, stopping at Caleta Olivia.

Several shuttle services also offering excursions serve travelers on RN 40. From November to April, **Chaltén Travel** (☎ /fax in El Calafate 2902-492-212/492-480; www.chaltentravel.com) goes north to Bariloche (11 hours), departing from Hotel Belgrano in Perito Moreno at 8pm on even-numbered days. Shuttles leave Hotel Belgrano at 8am to head south to El Chaltén (11 hours) on odd-numbered days. **Las Loicas** (☎ 02963-490272; www.lasloicas.com) leaves Perito Moreno a few days out of the month to take small groups on guided adventures down RN 40. The five-day tour includes all transfers, half-board accommodations and bilingual guides.

The bus company **Taqsa** (☎ 432675) now runs the entire stretch of RN 40 between El Calafate and Bariloche several times a week starting in the end of October, stopping at El Chaltén, Bajo Caracoles, Perito Moreno and Esquel

along the way. For more information on this service and all the other options listed here, see the boxed text, p463.

LOS ANTIGUOS
☎ 02963 / pop 2500
Situated on the windy shores of Lago Buenos Aires, the agricultural oasis of Los Antiguos is framed with rows of Lombardy poplars sheltering *chacras* (small independent farms) of cherries, strawberries, apples, apricots and peaches. Before the arrival of Europeans, ageing Tehuelche frequented this 'banana belt' – the town's name is a near-literal translation of the Tehuelche name *I-Keu-khon*, meaning 'Place of the Elders.' Travelers come to cross the border into Chile, but getting here via RN 40 can be an adventure in itself – and the stretch of road between Perito Moreno and Los Antiguos affords spectacular lake views.

Volcán Hudson's 1991 eruption covered the town in ash, but farms have bounced back. In summer **Lago Buenos Aires**, South America's second-biggest lake, is warm enough for a brisk swim. The stunning **Río Jeinemeni** is a favored spot for trout and salmon fishing.

Orientation
Los Antiguos occupies the delta formed by Río Los Antiguos and Río Jeinemeni, which constitutes the border with Chile. Most services are on or near east–west Av 11 de Julio, which heads west to the Chilean frontier at Chile Chico, the region's most convenient border crossing. Perito Moreno and RN 40 are 60km to the east.

Information
Banco de Santa Cruz (Av 11 de Julio 531) Has a 24-hour ATM.
Locutorio (Alameda 436) Also has internet.
Post office (Gregores 19)
Tourist information office (☎ 491261; www .losantiguos.gov.ar, in Spanish; Av 11 de Julio 446; ☼ 8am-8pm) Helpful, with a map of town and farms selling fresh produce.

Festivals & Events
The fun **Fiesta de la Cereza** (Cherry Festival), featuring rodeos and live music, celebrates its favorite crop during the second weekend of January. Artisan goods are sold and *peñas folkloricas* (Argentine folk music concerts) at private farms go on all night long – see the tourist information office for more information.

ESTANCIAS IN PATAGONIA

Most assume *estancias* are all about livestock, but these offbeat offerings prove otherwise.

A Wealth of Wildlife

- Meet the neighbors – that would be the penguins, seabirds and elephant seals – around Península Valdés' **Estancia Rincón Chico** (p433).
- Reel in the big one at the exclusive, world-renowned trout mecca **Estancia Güer Aike** (p456), near Río Gallegos.
- View the diverse fauna of Magellanic penguins, sea lions, guanacos and pumas at **Hostería Monte León** (p453).

Breathtaking Beauty

- Luxuriate among glaciers, lakes and the ragged Mt Fitz Roy in the exclusive **Hostería Estancia Helsingfors** (p490).
- Gallop the rugged splendor surrounding Parque Nacional Perito Moreno at the hospitable **Estancia Menelik** (p474).
- Hike narrow canyons and shout from the precipitous plateaus at **Estancia Telken** (p472).

Just Like Indiana Jones

- Travel back to the Pleistocene and explore 84 caves with prehistoric rock art at **Estancia La María** (p452), near Puerto San Julián.
- Trek to Unesco World Heritage site Cueva de las Manos from **Hostería Cueva de las Manos** (p472), via the serpentine red-rock canyon of Río de las Pinturas.

The Bargain Bin

- Grab your zzzs in a bunk bed and save some bucks: **Estancia Menelik** (p474), **La María** (p452) and **Estancia Casa de Piedra** (p473) all offer affordable *refugio* (rustic shelter) lodgings.

Sleeping & Eating

Camping Municipal (☎ 491265; RP 43; camping/cabins per person AR$5/45) Windbreaks help considerably at this lakeshore site 1.5km east of town. The windowless cabins have dorm-style accommodations, and hot showers are available in the evening.

Albergue Padilla (☎ 491140; San Martín 44; dm/d AR$40/100) Chaltén Travel shuttles deposit lodgers at this family-run institution after dark. The dorms share bathrooms (with plenty of hot water) and you'll have to shell out a few extra pesos for sheets and towels. The staff have RN 40 shuttle tickets and the latest details on Chilean border crossing and ferries.

Cabañas Rincon de los Poetas (☎ 491051; Patagonia Argentina 226; d/tr/q AR$120/140/150) These snug wooden cabins equipped with kitchenettes are nothing fancy, but they prove good value for couples and families. It's located two blocks from the center.

Hotel Los Antiguos Cerezos (☎ 491132; hotel_losantiguoscerezos@hotmail.com; Av 11 de Julio 850; s/d AR$120/150) Modern rooms all feature private bathroom and TV, and hearty meals satisfy a regular crowd of farmers, gauchos and businessmen.

Hostería Antigua Patagonia (☎ 491038; www .antiguapatagonia.com.ar, in Spanish; RP 43 Acceso Este; s/d AR$300/360, ste AR$390-440) This plush lakefront complex is decked out in rustic touches. Rooms feature four-poster beds and wooden trunks, though the snuggest spot is by the stone fireplace. It's 2km east of town.

our pick **Viva El Viento** (☎ 491109; www.vivaelviento .com; Av 11 de Julio 447; mains AR$25-35; 🕑 9am-9pm Oct-Apr) This stylish new cafe and restaurant – boasting fresh salads, strong coffee, free wi-fi and warm service by the Dutch owner and his Argentine girlfriend – is a traveler's oasis. The menu offers gourmet versions of classic dishes like milanesas, burgers, grilled salmon and steak.

Getting There & Around

The gradual paving of RN 40 and subsequent future services will keep transport options in flux, so get current information.

Various bus companies go to nearby Perito Moreno (AR$23, 40 minutes) several times daily, with multiple departures in the mid-afternoon. **Sportman** (☎ 491175; Senador Molina 690) has buses to Río Gallegos (AR$186, 16 hours) and Comodoro Rivadavia (AR$98, six hours) at 3:45pm daily; buses also go to El Calafate (AR$240) at 3:45pm Monday to Saturday. **La Unión** (☎ 491078; cnr Perito Moreno & Patagonia Argentina) buses head to Comodoro Rivadavia (AR$98) at 6am and 3pm Monday to Saturday and 4pm on Sunday; the company's minibuses also cross the border to Chile Chico (AR$10) on weekdays at noon.

From mid-November to March, **Chaltén Travel** (www.chaltentravel.com) goes to El Chaltén on even-numbered days at 9am, stopping first in Perito Moreno. See the boxed text, p463 for northbound schedules.

Ferry **El Pilchero** (☎ in Chile 56-67-411864) crosses Lago Buenos Aires daily from Chile Chico to Puerto Ibañez (CH$6000, vehicles CH$25,500 per meter, three to six hours), weather depending, on Monday at 8am, Thursday at 3:30pm, Friday at 5:30pm and Sunday at 2:30pm (this schedule is likely to change, so call ahead.) Alternatively, it's possible to continue overland around the lake's southern shore to Carretera Austral and Coyhaique.

Leiva Remise (☎ 491228) taxi service is useful when it's pouring rain and you need a ride to your hotel.

ESTANCIA TELKEN

A highlight of traveling along this stretch, **Estancia Telken** (☎ 02963-432079; telkenpatagonia@yahoo.com.ar; RN 40; campsites per person/tent AR$22, d with/without bathroom AR$380/305; ⌚ Oct-Apr) offers a welcoming repose in pretty countryside. This 1915 working sheep and horse ranch, 25km south of Perito Moreno, is run by the charming Coco and Petti Nauta. Coco's family is descended from Dutch settlers, while Petti hails from a New Zealand clan and spins many a yarn about ranch life. Delicious, abundant meals are served family style, and English and Dutch are spoken.

There are about 210 sq km of horseback riding and hiking possibilities, including a worthwhile meander along a creek bed up to the basalt plateau **Meseta de Lago Buenos Aires**. Ask Petti to take you to **Cueva de Piedra**, a small cave snuggled in a silent valley of guanacos, eagles and the occasional armadillo.

Controversial gold mining allowed by government concession has closed **Cañadon Arroyo del Feo** (a deep red-rock river canyon that narrows into steep ravines) to the public. This used to be an excellent opportunity to see well-preserved cave art that has been around for approximately 7000 years.

GuanaCondor Tours in Perito Moreno (p469) organizes trips here.

CUEVA DE LAS MANOS

The incredible rock art of **Cueva de las Manos** (Cave of the Hands; admission AR$50; ⌚ 9am-7pm) was proclaimed a Unesco World Heritage site in 1999. Dating from about 7370 BC, these polychrome rock paintings cover recesses in the near-vertical walls with imprints of human hands, drawings of guanacos and, from a later period, abstract designs. Of around 800 images, more than 90% are of left hands; one has six fingers.

The approach is via rough but scenic provincial roads off RN 40, abutting Río de las Pinturas. Drivers should have caution: guanacos are abundant, bounding across the steppe. There are two points of access: a more direct route via Bajo Caracoles, 46km away on the south side of the river; and another from Hostería Cueva de las Manos, on the north side, via a footbridge. Guides in Perito Moreno (p469) organize day trips, usually around AR$150 per person plus park entrance fee. The trip from Perito Moreno is about 3½ hours (one way) over rocky roads. Once you arrive at the caves, free guided walks are given every hour by knowledgeable staff. There's an information center and a basic *confitería* at the reception house near the southern entrance, but it's best to bring your own food.

On the doorstep of Argentina's best deposit of rock art, the budding **Hostería Cueva de las Manos** (☎ 02963-432730, in Buenos Aires 011-5237-4043; www.cuevadelasmanos.net; dm/d AR$106/400, cabin for 2/3/4/6 people AR$475/578/685/838; ⌚ Nov-Apr), formerly Estancia Los Toldos, is a short distance off RN 40, 52km south of Perito Moreno. Guests can stay in cabins, the *hostería* or a 20-person dormitory. Rooms are plain but well appointed, with hardwood details. Guests and tour groups can approach Cueva de los Manos via a scenic but challenging hiking trail (summer only) that starts from the *hostería*, descends the canyon and crosses Río de las Pinturas.

Rustic but welcoming **Estancia Casa de Piedra** (☎ 02963-432-199; off RN 40; campsites per person AR$30, dm AR$70; ☿ Dec-Mar), a basic ranch 76km south of Perito Moreno, has plain rooms and allows camping. It's a good spot for trekkers to hunker down: there are nearby volcanoes and you can take a beautiful day-long hike to the Cueva de las Manos via Cañon de las Pinturas. From the *estancia*, it's 12km to the canyon, then another 6km to the cave – estimate about 10 hours for the roundtrip trek. Hikers should get an early start and bring their own food; guides can be contracted here but the trail is clear enough to go without one.

BAJO CARACOLES

Blink and you'll miss this dusty gas stop. Little has changed since Bruce Chatwin described this hamlet as 'a crossroads of insignificant importance with roads leading all directions apparently to nowhere' in *In Patagonia* in 1975. If you're headed south, fill the tank, since it's the only reliable gas pump between Perito Moreno (128km north) and Tres Lagos (409km south). From here RP 39 heads west to Lago Posadas and the Paso Roballos to Chile.

Lodgers put on a brave face for **Hotel Bajo Caracoles** (☎ 02963-490100; d AR$150), a severely overpriced flophouse with old gas heating units that require a watchful eye. It also stocks basic provisions, serves decent coffee and has the only private telephone in town.

Heading south, RN 40 takes a turn for the worse: it's 100km to Las Horquetas, a blip on the radar screen where RN 40, RP 27 and RP 37 intersect. From here it's another 128km southeast via RP 27 to Gobernador Gregores.

PARQUE NACIONAL PERITO MORENO

Wild and windblown, Parque Nacional Perito Moreno is an adventurer's dream. Approaching from the steppe, the massive snowcapped peaks of the Sierra Colorada rise like sentinels. Guanacos graze the tufted grasses, condors circle above, and wind blurs the surfaces of aquamarine and cobalt lakes. If you come here, you will be among 1200 yearly visitors – that is, mostly alone. Solitude reigns and, save for services offered by local *estancias*, you are entirely on your own.

Honoring the park system's founder, this remote but increasingly popular park encompasses 1150 sq km, 310km southwest of the town of Perito Moreno. Don't confuse this gem with Parque Nacional Los Glaciares (home to the Perito Moreno Glacier) further south.

The sedimentary Sierra Colorada has a painter's palette of rusty hues. Beyond the park boundary, glacier-topped summits such as 3706m **Cerro San Lorenzo** (the highest peak in the area) tower over the landscape. The highest peak within the park is Cerro Mié (2254m).

Besides guanacos, the park is also home to pumas, foxes, wildcats, chinchillas and huemul (Andean deer). The abundant bird population includes condors, rheas, flamingos, black-necked swans, cauquén (upland geese) and caranchos (crested caracaras). Predecessors of the Tehuelche left evidence of their presence with rock paintings in caves at Lago Burmeister.

As precipitation increases toward the west, the Patagonian steppe grasslands along the park's eastern border become sub-Antarctic forests of southern beech, lenga and coihue. Because the base altitude exceeds 900m, weather can be severe. Summer is usually comfortable, but warm clothing and proper gear are imperative in any season. The water is pure but you must bring all food and supplies.

Information

Visitors must register at the park's information center on the eastern boundary; it's stocked with informative maps and brochures. Rangers offer a variety of guided hikes; they can also be contacted via the national parks office in Gobernador Gregores (p474), where it may be possible to arrange a ride.

Sights & Activities

Behind the information center, a one-hour interpretive trail leads to **Pinturas Rupestres**, a small number of cave paintings with interpretive signs in English. Consult park rangers for backpacking options and guided walks to the pictographs at **Casa de Piedra** on Lago Burmeister, and to **Playa de los Amonites** on Lago Belgrano, where there are fossils.

From Estancia La Oriental, it's a 2½-hour hike to the summit of 1434m **Cerro León**, from where there's a dazzling panorama.

Immediately east of the summit, the volcanic outcrop of **Cerro de los Cóndores** is a nesting site for the Andes' totem species. Pumas have also been spotted here and guanacos down below.

Sleeping & Eating

There are free campgrounds at the information center (barren and exposed; no fires allowed); at Lago Burmeister, 16km from the information center (more scenic and well sheltered among dense lenga forest; fires allowed); and at El Rincón, 15km away (no fires). None has showers, but there are pit toilets.

Estancia Menelik (☎ satellite phone 011-4152-5500, in Buenos Aires 011-4836-3502; www.cielospatagonicos.com; refugio per person AR$63, s/d/q AR$188/251/377; ☯ Oct-Mar) With a panorama of Parque Nacional Perito Moreno, this 1920 working ranch is a prime destination for horseback riding; highlights include overnight trips to the high camp of Veranada de Jones.

Getting There & Away

Public-transport options change often; check with tourist offices in Perito Moreno, Los Antiguos and El Calafate for updates. Las Loicas (see the boxed text, p463) can take travelers here from Perito Moreno. In summer hitchhiking is possible from the RN 40 junction, but the park is so large that getting to trailheads presents difficulties. From April to November the road becomes impassable at times. If you're driving, carry spare gas and tires.

GOBERNADOR GREGORES
☎ 02962 / pop 2521

Gobernador Gregores is a sleepy pit stop that beckons principally when your gas tank dips toward E. But as RN 40 is paved and re-routed here, its tourist services should expand in the coming years. For now, the hours of siesta remain holy.

Gregores is 60km east of RN 40 on RP 25. It's the nearest town to Parque Nacional Perito Moreno (still 200km west) and is an ideal spot to get supplies and arrange transportation. There's a **tourist office** (☎ 491192; San Martín 409; ☯ 8am-2pm Mon-Fri) and **national parks administration office** (☎ 491477; San Martín 882; ☯ 9am-4pm Mon-Fri).

Seventy kilometers west of town via RP 29, the waters of **Lago Cardiel** are well loved by anglers for blue-ribbon salmon and rainbow trout fishing. From the junction to the lake it's another 116km to **Tres Lagos**, where a jovial couple run a 24-hour YPF station, then another 123km west to El Chaltén.

Summer-only **Camping Nuestra Señora del Valle** (☎ 491398; cnr Roca & Chile; campsites AR$4) has showers, hot water and stone grills. Hot meals (*plato del día* AR$25) and firm beds are found at **Cañadón León** (☎ 491082; Roca 397; s/d/tr AR$110/135/170), with 11 tidy rooms that are ample and spotless. Reserve ahead if possible. Just outside town, the pleasing **Cabañas María Abril** (☎ 491016; Av Cañadon León 608; d without bathroom AR$100, d/tr/q AR$140/170/250) offers tranquility with a village of A-frames in the poplars.

Cerro San Lorenzo (cnr San Martín & Alberdi) buses leave for Puerto San Julián (AR$60, five hours) Monday to Saturday at 4pm or 6pm – ask at the office for exact departure times. **El Pulgarcito** (☎ 491474; San Martín 704) goes to Río Gallegos (AR$75, six hours) daily at 7am, while **El Pegaso** (☎ 491494; Pejkovic 520) goes to Río Gallegos (AR$78) at 4am Monday to Saturday.

EL CHALTÉN
☎ 02962 / pop 600

At the entrance to the northern sector of Parque Nacional Los Glaciares, the pretty village of El Chaltén serves the thousands of visitors who make summer pilgrimages to explore the range. It feels like a tourist town, at least in some ways – most buildings are cute, log cabin-like structures, and you'll see signs in English everywhere. But the packs of dogs roaming the streets are a reminder that this is a frontier town: it was slapped together in 1985 to beat Chile to the land claim. As Argentina's youngest town, it still has to sort out details such as roads and banks. Interestingly, for a place that still lacks some civic structure, environmental consciousness is a big priority – you'll see spiffy recycling bins all around town, a rare sight elsewhere in Argentina. Traveler services continue to evolve rapidly: the paving of RP 23 a few years ago has started making way for large-scale tourism.

El Chaltén is named for Cerro Fitz Roy's Tehuelche name, meaning 'peak of fire' or 'smoking mountain' – an apt description of the cloud-enshrouded summit. Perito Moreno and Carlos Moyano later named it after the *Beagle's* Captain FitzRoy, who navigated Darwin's expedition up the Río Santa Cruz in 1834, coming within 50km of the cordillera.

EL CHALTÉN

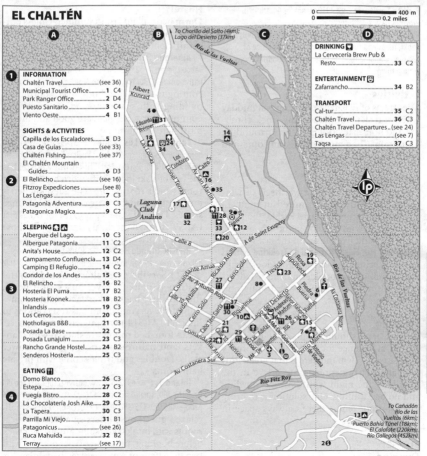

0 400 m
0 0.2 miles

To Chorillo del Salto (4km);
Lago del Desierto (37km)

To Cañadón
Río de las
Vueltas (6km);
Puerto Bahía Túnel (18km);
El Calafate (220km);
Río Gallegos (452km)

PATAGONIA

Capilla de los Escaladores, a simple chapel of Austrian design, memorializes the many climbers who have lost their lives to the precarious peaks since 1953.

Information

Technologically speaking, El Chaltén is a study in contrasts: there's no cell phone reception and an ATM that rarely works, but you're likely to pick up a good wi-fi signal in your hotel room and you won't have any problem finding a long-distance call center or gas station. Credit cards are almost useless, though some restaurants are starting to accept them, but traveler's checks, euros and US dollars are widely accepted. If you're coming from El Calafate, just take out the cash you'll need

there and skip the possible complications in El Chaltén. Surf www.elchalten.com for a good overview of the town.

Chaltén Travel (☎ 493092; cnr Av MM De Güemes & Lago del Desierto) Books airline tickets and offers weather-dependent internet service for AR$15 an hour.

Municipal tourist office (☎ 493270; comfomelchalten @yahoo.com.ar; Av MM De Güemes 174; ⏱ 8am-8pm) Friendly and extremely helpful, with lodging lists and good information on town and tours. English is spoken.

Park ranger office (☎ 493004/24; donations welcome; ⏱ 8am-7pm) Many daytime buses stop for a short bilingual orientation at this visitor center, just before the bridge over the Río Fitz Roy. Park rangers distribute a map and town directory and do a good job of explaining the park's ecological issues. Climbing documentaries are shown at 3pm daily – great for rainy days.

Puesto Sanitario (☎ 493033; AM De Agostini 70)
Provides basic health services.

Viento Oeste (☎ 493200; Av San Martín 898) Sells
books, maps and souvenirs and rents a wide range of
camping equipment, as do several other sundries shops
around town.

Activities

The streets of El Chaltén are empty at midday
when travelers are out hiking, rock climbing and horseback riding in the surrounding
mountains. For more details on tours and
excursions, see Activities, p478.

Festivals & Events

Every October 12, on the wet heels of winter and with the streets mired in mud, El
Chaltén celebrates **Fiesta del Pueblo**, the town
anniversary, with dancing in the school gym,
barbecues and live music. In the last week of
February the **Fiesta Nacional de Trekking** comes
to town, bringing a circus of outdoor freaks
for rock climbing, bouldering and woodcut-
ting competitions, as well as running and
mountain-bike races.

Sleeping

Reservations should be made at least one
month in advance for the January–February
high season – demand here is that great. Plus
it's particularly depressing to arrive in the
middle of the night with the wind howling
and no bed waiting. One solution is to bring
a bombproof tent – there's always space in
the campgrounds.

BUDGET

Camping

Campamento Confluencia (campsites free) A zero-
amenity campground across from the park
ranger office and visitor center.

Albergue del Lago (☎ 493010; Lago del Desierto 152;
campsites per person AR$20, dm AR$40) Partying seems
to be the priority of campers outside this hostel, which offers a shared kitchen and funky
showers.

Camping El Refugio (☎ 493221; Calle 3 s/n; campsites per person AR$20, dm AR$45) This private campground is attached to a basic hostel – hot
showers for campers are included in the fee.
Sites are exposed and there is some sparse
firewood (fires are OK).

El Relincho (☎ 493007; www.elrelinchopatagonia.com
.ar; Av San Martín 505; campsites per person AR$20) Another
private campground, similarly wind whipped.

Hostels

Dorm beds fill up fast in summer. Unless otherwise noted, thin walls, cramped dorms and
insufficient shared facilities are the norm.

Albergue Patagonia (☎ 493019; patagoniahostel@
yahoo.com.ar; Av San Martín 493; dm AR$50, d with/without
bathroom AR$230/140; ☉ Sep-May; ✗) This wel-
coming wooden farmhouse has a dormitory
building with spacious, modern dorms and
common areas. Services are good and the atmosphere is humming.

Condor de Los Andes (☎ 493101; www.con
dordelosandes.com; cnr Río de las Vueltas & Halvor Halvorsen;
dm/d AR$50/220; ☉ Oct-Apr) This homey hostel has
the feel of a ski lodge, with worn bunks, warm
rooms and a roaring fire. The guest kitchen is
immaculate and there are comfortable lounge
spaces. Dorm dwellers pay extra for breakfast
(AR$9), though the meal is included for those
staying in private rooms.

Rancho Grande Hostel (☎ 493092; www.ranchogran
dehostel.com; Av San Martín 724; dm/d/tr AR$60/140/160;
✗ ▣) Serving as Chaltén's Grand Central
Station (Chaltén Travel buses stop here),
this bustling backpacker factory has something for everyone, from bus reservations to
internet (AR$14 per hour) and cafe service.
Clean four-bed rooms are stacked with blankets, and bathrooms sport rows of shower
stalls. Doubles and triples come with private
bathrooms.

Inlandsis (☎ 493276; www.inlandsis.com.ar; Lago del
Desierto 480; small/large d AR$160/210, cabin for 2/3/4/6
people AR$300/325/350/400; ☉ Oct-Apr) This small,
relaxed guesthouse offers small, economical
rooms with bunk beds (some are airless, check
before booking) or larger, pricier doubles with
two twin beds or a queen-sized bed. Inlandsis
also has bilevel cabins with bathtubs, kitchens
and DVD players.

MIDRANGE

Posada La Base (☎ 493031; www.elchaltenpatagonia.com
.ar; Calle 10, No 16; d AR$160) These spacious, good-
value rooms all face outside and have kitchen
access. Large groups should book rooms 5 and
6, which share an inside kitchen with dining
area. The reception area has a popular video
loft with a multilingual collection.

our pick **Nothofagus B&B** (☎ 493087; www.not
hofagusbb.com.ar; cnr Hensen & Riquelme, s/d without bathroom AR$140/150, s/d/tr with bathroom AR$200/210/260;
☉ Sep-Apr; ✗) Attentive and adorable, this
chalet-style inn offers a great green retreat. It
is one of few Patagonian lodgings to separate

organic waste and replace towels only when asked. Wooden-beam rooms have carpet and some views, but most have bathrooms shared with one other room.

Hostería Koonek (☎ 493304; www.hosteriakoonek .com.ar; Lionel Terray 415; d/tr AR$230/270) Tidy and welcoming – and built next to a bluff popular with rock climbers – this guesthouse has eight rooms that accommodate up to four guests each. All come with private bathrooms that are tiny but clean.

TOP END

Anita's House (☎ 493288; www.anitashouse.com.ar; Av San Martín 249; cabin for 2/3/5 people AR$310/330/360; 💻) Ideal for families, these centrally located cabins are cozy and well equipped with kitchens, room service and cable TV.

Posada Lunajuim (☎ 493047; www.posadaluna juim.com.ar; Trevisán 45; s/d AR$350/410) Combining modern comfort with a touch of the off-beat, this artist-owned inn gets good reviews from guests. The halls are lined with the owner's monochrome sculptures and textured paintings, and a stone fireplace and library provide a rainy-day escape.

Senderos Hostería (☎ 493336; www.senderoshosteria .com.ar; Perito Moreno s/n; d/d AR$435/550; 🍷) This contemporary B&B offers wonderful amenities for trekkers with a little extra cash to spend on accommodations: a popular on-site wine bar and restaurant, rooms with great-looking wood furniture and impressive mountain views.

Hostería El Puma (☎ 493095; www.hosteriaelpuma .com.ar; Lionel Terray 212; s/d/tr AR$495/610/725) This luxury lodge with 12 comfortable rooms offers intimacy without pretension. The rock-climbing and summit photographs and maps lining the hall may inspire your next expedition, but lounging by the fireplace is the most savory way to end the day.

Los Cerros (☎ 493182; www.loscerrosdelchalten.com; Av San Martín s/n; s/d/tr AR$1058/1250/1632; 💬 Nov-Apr; 💻) This chic, top-end *hostería* perched on a hill has sweeping views of the valley. The style is tribal-modern with thick woven wall-hangings and natural fibers. The absence of TVs and phones in rooms is meant to bring you back to nature (but the gourmet meals and wine selections will surely zip you right back to civilization).

Eating & Drinking

Groceries, especially produce, are limited and expensive. Bring what you can from El Calafate.

Domo Blanco (☎ 493036; Av MM De Güemes s/n; ice-cream scoops AR$8; 💬 2pm-midnight) Homemade ice cream made with fruit harvested from a local *estancia* and calafate bushes in town.

La Chocolatería Josh Aike (☎ 493008; Lago del Desierto 105; snacks AR$8-18) This irresistible chocolate factory tells the story of local climbing legends on the walls. It makes for an intimate evening out, with options ranging from spirit-spiked hot cocoa to wine and fondue.

our pick **Fuegia Bistro** (☎ 493019; Av San Martín 342; mains AR$22-40; 💬 dinner Mon-Sat) Favored for its warm ambience and savory mains, this upscale eatery boasts good veggie options and a reasonable wine list. Try the homemade pasta with ricotta, spinach and fresh mushrooms, or trout with lemon.

Parrilla Mi Viejo (☎ 493123; Av San Martín 780; mains AR$22-40; 💬 lunch & dinner) If you're not in the mood for creative cuisine after a day in the mountains, head to this traditional steakhouse for grilled meat, french fries, salads, and a large selection of wine and dessert.

Estepa (☎ 493069; cnr Cerro Solo & Av Antonio Rojo; mains AR$25-45; 💬 noon-1am Tue-Sun) Local favorite Estepa cooks up consistent, flavorful dishes like lamb with calafate sauce, trout ravioli or spinach crepes.

Patagonicus (☎ 493025; Av MM De Güemes 57; pizza AR$28; 💬 closed Wed & May-Sep) The best pizza in town, with 20 kinds of pie, salads and wine served at sturdy wood tables surrounded by huge picture windows. Cakes and coffee are also worth trying.

La Tapera (☎ 493195; cnr Antonio Rojo & Riquelme; mains AR$30-42; 💬 lunch & dinner) As the name suggests, this new-on-the-scene eatery specializes in tapas. But wintry staples like pumpkin soup and grilled steak are also popular here; on cold days, you can sit so close to the open fireplace that you'll have to peel off a layer.

Terray (☎ 493095; www.hosteriaelpuma.com.ar; Lionel Terray 212; mains AR$32-48; 💬 7:30-10:30pm Oct-May) Named in tribute to the Chamonix guide who first climbed Fitz Roy, this high-end kitchen at Hostería El Puma cooks up hearty and original homemade meals like lima-bean risotto, chicken and grilled-fig salad, and lamb osso buco.

Ruca Mahuida (☎ 493018; Lionel Terray 55; mains AR$36-57; 💬 7-11pm) Some worry that this stone house with gourmet fare has lost its touch, but dishes like squash soufflé and salmon ravioli are a welcome departure from typical fare. The sheepskin benches, though, are pure Patagonia.

PATAGONIA

La Cervecería Brew Pub & Resto (☎ 493109; Av San Martín 320; snacks AR$18; ◷ lunch & dinner till late) That aprés-hike pint usually evolves into a night out in this humming pub with simpatico staff and a feisty female beer master. Savor a stein of unfiltered blond pilsner or turbid bock with pasta or *locro* (a spicy stew of maize, beans, beef, pork and sausage).

Entertainment

Zafarrancho, behind Rancho Grande Hostel (p476), is a bar-cafe that has internet and screens movies.

Getting There & Away

El Chaltén is 220km from El Calafate via newly paved roads. At the time of writing, a new bus terminal was about to open across from the tourist information office.

For El Calafate (AR$70, 3½ hours), **Chaltén Travel** (☎ 493005/92; cnr Av MM De Güemes & Lago del Desierto) has daily departures at 6:30am, 7am, 1pm and 6pm in summer from Rancho Grande Hostel. **Cal-tur** (☎ 493079; San Martín 520) and **Taqsa** (☎ 493068; Av Antonio Rojo 88) also make the trip, but neither company will take advance reservations. Service is less frequent off-season.

Las Lengas (☎ 493023/227; Antonio de Viedma 95) runs minivans at 5:30am to coastal destinations on RN 3, including Piedrabuena (AR$95, six hours), from where travelers can take transportation to Parque Nacional Monte León.

PARQUE NACIONAL LOS GLACIARES (NORTH)

Parque Nacional Los Glaciares is divided into geographically separate northern and southern sectors. El Chaltén (p474) is the gateway town for the northern part of the park; it's where you'll find all the operators for tours and activities mentioned in this section. El Calafate (p482) is the gateway town for the southern section of the park, which features the Perito Moreno Glacier.

In the northern part of the park, the **Fitz Roy Range**, with its rugged wilderness and shark-tooth summits, is the de-facto mountaineering mecca of Argentina. World-class climbers consider Cerro Torre and Cerro Fitz Roy epic ascents, notorious for brutal weather conditions. Occupying the northern half of Parque Nacional Los Glaciares, this area offers numerous well-marked trails for hiking and jaw-dropping scenery – that is, when the clouds clear.

Activities

HIKING

Before heading out on the trail, hikers should stop by the park ranger office for updated trail conditions. The most stable weather for hiking comes not in summer but in March and April, when there is less wind (and fewer people). During the winter months of June and July trails may be closed – check first with the park ranger office.

Experienced backpackers can register to hike in the remote areas, which require some route finding but reward by getting you off the central circuits and away from the crowds. A first-person ranger update is necessary for these hikes. For more information on hiking, read Lonely Planet's *Trekking in the Patagonian Andes*.

Laguna Torre

If you have good weather – ie little wind – and clear skies, make this hike (three hours one way) a priority, since the toothy Cerro Torre is the most difficult local peak to see on normal blustery days.

Hikers have the option of taking two different trails, which later merge. One starts at the northwestern edge of El Chaltén. From a signpost on Av San Martín, head west on Eduardo Brenner and right to find the signposted start of the track. The Laguna Torre track winds up westwards around large boulders on slopes covered with typical Patagonian dry-land plants, then leads southwest past a *mallín* (wet meadow) to a junction with a trail coming in from the left (see the following start) after 35 to 45 minutes.

If you start from the southern end of El Chaltén, follow Lago del Desierto west past the edge of town, then drop to the riverbed and continue past a tiny hydroelectric installation. At a signpost the route climbs away from the river and leads on through scattered lenga and ñire woodland (a small, deciduous southern beech species), with the odd wire fence to step over, before merging with a more prominent (signposted) path coming in from the right.

Continue up past a rounded bluff to the **Mirador Laguna Torre**, a crest giving you the first clear view up the valley to the extraordinary 3128m rock spire of Cerro Torre standing above a sprawling mass of intersecting glaciers. Look for the 'mushroom' of snow and ice that caps the peak. This precarious

formation is the final obstacle for hard-core climbers, who often spend weeks waiting for decent weather.

The trail dips down gently through beautiful stands of stout ancient lengas, before cutting across open scrubby river flats and old revegetated moraines to reach a signposted junction with the Sendero Madre e Hija, a shortcut route to Campamento Poincenot, 40 to 50 minutes on. Continuing up the valley, bear left at another signposted fork and climb over a forested embankment to cross a small alluvial plain, following the fast-flowing glacial waters of the Río Fitz Roy. You'll arrive at **Campamento De Agostini** (formerly Campamento Bridwell) after a further 30 to 40 minutes. This free campground (with pit toilet) gets busy; it

serves as a base camp for Cerro Torre climbers. The only other park-authorized place to camp in the vicinity is in a pleasant grove of riverside lengas below Cerro Solo.

Follow the trail along the lake's north side for about an hour to **Mirador Maestri** (no camping).

Laguna de los Tres

This hike to a high alpine tarn is a bit more strenuous (four hours one way). The trail starts from a yellow-roofed pack station, the former site of **Campamento Madsen**. After about an hour, there's a signed lateral to excellent free backcountry **campsites** at Laguna Capri. The main trail continues gently through windswept forests and past small lakes, meeting up with the trail from Lagunas Madre and Hija. Carrying on through wind-worn ñire forest and along boggy terrain leads to **Río Blanco** (three hours) and the woodsy, mice-plagued **Campamento Poincenot**, exclusively reserved for climbers. The trail splits before Río Blanco to head to Río Eléctrico (there is an alternative, parallel trail after Río Blanco but markings are sparse and it is not recommended). Stay left to reach a climbers' base camp. From here the trail zigzags steeply up the tarn to the eerily still, glacial **Laguna de los Tres** and an extraordinarily close view of 3405m Cerro Fitz Roy. Clouds even huddle in the rocky crevasses, whipping up with a change in wind. Be prepared for high, potentially hazardous winds and allow time for contemplation and recovery. Scurry down 200m to the left of the lookout for an exceptional view of the emerald-green **Laguna Sucia**.

Piedra del Fraile

At Campamento Poincenot, the trail swings west to Laguna de los Tres or northeast along Río Blanco to Valle Eléctrico and Piedra del Fraile (eight hours from El Chaltén; five hours from the Río Blanco turnoff). From the turnoff, the latter trail leads to **Glaciar Piedras Blancas** (four hours), the last part of which is a scramble over massive granite boulders to a turquoise lake with dozens of floating icebergs and constant avalanches on the glacier's face. The trail then passes through pastures and branches left up the valley along **Río Eléctrico**, enclosed by sheer cliffs, before reaching the private **Refugio Los Troncos** (campsites AR$35, refugio beds AR$70-150). Reservations are not possible since there are no phones – simply show up. The campground has a kiosk, restaurant and excellent services, and the owners can give information on recommended nearby trails.

Rather than backtrack to Río Blanco and the Laguna de los Tres trail, it's possible to head east, hopping over streams to RP 23, the route back to El Chaltén. You'll pass waterfall **Chorillo del Salto** on the way.

Buses to Lago del Desierto (right) drop hikers at the Río Eléctrico bridge (AR$50).

Loma del Pliegue Tumbado & Laguna Toro

Heading southwest from the park ranger office, this trail (four to five hours one way) skirts the eastern face of Loma del Pliegue Tumbado going toward Río Túnel, then cuts west and heads to Laguna Toro. It offers the best views of Cerros Torre and Fitz Roy. In fact, it's the only hike that allows views of both peaks at once. The hike is rather gentle, but be prepared for strong winds and carry extra water.

Lago del Desierto & Beyond

Some 37km north of El Chaltén is Lago del Desierto, near the Chilean border – a nice day-trip option when it's raining and there's no chance of catching a glimpse of the Fitz. A 500m trail leads to an overlook that often has fine views of the lake, surrounding mountains and glaciers.

Las Lengas (☎ 493023; Viedma 95) offers minibus service to Lago del Desierto, leaving El Chaltén at 8:30am and 3pm daily. The bus stops at Río Electrico (AR$50) and Los Huemules (AR$50) – so passengers can trek to Glaciar Huemul or do the boat trip (extra) – before continuing onto Lago del Desierto (AR$80). Ask about all-day trips that stay at the lake for six hours and return to El Chaltén in the evening. A *remise* charges around AR$180 roundtrip for three passengers, plus AR$10 per hour to wait. At the south end of the lake, travelers can dine in the inviting restaurant at **Hostería El Pilar** (☎ 493002; www.hosteriaelpilar.com.ar).

Patagonia Aventura (☎ 493110; www.patagonia-aventura.com.ar; per person AR$90) navigates Lago del Desierto. The alternative to the boat tour is a five-hour walking trek between the south end and the north end of the lake.

From the lake's north end, it's increasingly popular to walk or bicycle to the Chilean border post, with hundreds of travelers now using the crossing each year. It's particularly popular with cyclists traveling on to the Chilean frontier outpost Candelaria Mansilla via cargo boat from the southernmost outpost of Villa O'Higgins, in Chile's Aisén region. In Candelaria Mansilla a family offers meals, camping and basic farmhouse accommodations; bring Chilean pesos from El Calafate, if possible. If you leave El Chaltén first thing in the morning, it's possible to cross the Chilean border and reach Candelaria Mansilla in one long day.

A Chilean **excursion boat** (www.villaohiggins.com, in Spanish) offers a range of itineraries: travelers can do a roundtrip voyage from Candelaria Mansilla to see Glaciar O'Higgins (CH$50,000) on the Southern Ice Shelf, or opt for the longer trip to Villa O'Higgins (CH$60,000) via Puerto Bahamondez. From Puerto Bahamondez, bus service to Villa O'Higgins is CH$3000. The Villa O'Higgins **municipalidad** (☎ 56-7721-1849) may be able to help with further information and sleeping options. In El Chaltén, Albergue Patagonia (p476) and the tourist office can supply current details on this ever-evolving adventure option.

ICE CLIMBING & TREKKING

Several companies offer ice-climbing courses and ice treks, some including sleds pulled by Siberian huskies. **Fitzroy Expediciones** (☎ 493178; www.fitzroyexpediciones.com.ar; Av San Martín 56, El Chaltén) runs glacier-trekking excursions from AR$350 on the south face of Cerro Torre. The trek usually begins at 7am, starting with a 2½-hour walk along the Fitz Roy river valley and Lake Torre to Thorwood Camp, followed by three hours on the glacier and returning to the campground around 5pm. If you'd rather skip the walk from El Chaltén first thing in the morning, which can make for a very long day, camp out at Thorwood for the night before. The Fitzroy staff can help make arrangements; don't forget to bring extra food and water. Note that Fitzroy Expediciones does accept credit cards, unlike most businesses in town.

Another friendly and professional outfitter, **Casa de Guías** (☎ 493118; www.casadeguias.com.ar; Av San Martín 310, El Chaltén) has guides who are Argentine Association of Mountain Guides (AAGM) certified and speak English. They specialize in small groups and simple camps. Offerings include mountain traverses, mountain ascents for the very fit and rock-climbing classes.

Patagonia Aventura (☎ 493110; www.patagonia-aventura.com.ar, in Spanish; Av San Martín 56, El Chaltén) offers trekking (AR$350) and ice climbing ($400) on Glaciar Viedma. Trips include a six-hour hike with views of the glacier, a 2½-hour ice trek and all-day instruction in ice climbing. Ice trekkers get to trudge with their crampons through some truly awesome lunar landscapes of ice and learn the basics of safety on ice.

Multiday guided hikes over the Hielo Patagónico Continental (Continental Ice Field) offer a unique experience for those of us not versed in polar expeditions. Catering to serious trekkers, this route involves technical climbing, including use of crampons and some strenuous river crossings. Try **El Chaltén Mountain Guides** (☎ 493267; www.ecmg.com.ar; Rio de las Vueltas 218, El Chaltén); in addition to ice field traverse packages, starting at AR$2565, its

licensed guides run ice-climbing seminars (from AR$220) and ice-trekking day trips on Torre Glaciar (AR$300). Per-person rates decrease significantly if you're going with a friend or several; inquire at the office about pricing so before you book anything.

Certified guide **Paulo Gallego** (payosur@yahoo.com.ar) speaks English and French and commands fun treks for groups – or, in his own words, 'normal hikes' – that don't require complicated equipment or high fitness levels. His day rate (AR$460) is reasonable.

FLY-FISHING

The friendly guys at **Chaltén Fishing** (☎ 493185; www.chaltenfishing.com.ar, in Spanish; Av Antonio Rojo 88, El Chaltén) take anglers on half-day trips to Lago del Desierto or on full-day excursions that include a few hours at Laguna Larga. Equipment is provided; call for current rates and information on fishing licenses.

HORSEBACK RIDING

Horses can be used to trot round town and to carry equipment with a guide (prices negotiable), but are not allowed unguided on national-park trails. Outfitter **El Relincho** (☎ 493007; www.elrelinchopatagonia.com.ar; San Martín 545, El Chaltén) takes riders to the pretty valley of Río de las Vueltas (AR$160, three hours) and also offers more challenging rides up the Vizcacha hill followed by a barbecue on a traditional ranch (AR$320). Cabin-style accommodations are also available through the company (AR$370 for four people).

KAYAK & CANOE TRIPS

As El Chaltén grows, so do the aquatic offerings. **Fitzroy Expediciones** (☎ ☎ 493178; www.fitzroyexpediciones.com.ar; Av San Martín 56, El Chaltén) offers half-day guided kayaking trips on the Río de las Vueltas that stop for lunch at the company's attractive new 'adventure camp.' (Overnight stays are also available in the timber lodge and eight cabins, 17km north of town – ask at the office in El Chaltén for more information.) Travelers can also book two-day canoe and camping trips to Río La Leona.

LAKE CRUISES

Contact **Patagonia Aventura** (☎ 493110; www.patagonia-aventura.com.ar, in Spanish; Av San Martín 56, El Chaltén) about tourist launches from the Puerto Bahía Túnel on the north shore of Lago Viedma. The trip (per person AR$100, plus AR$50 transfer)

PATAGONIA

takes in impressive views of the 40m Glaciar Viedma, grinding from Cerro Fitz Roy. Boat trips leave at 3:30pm and last 2½ hours.

ROCK CLIMBING

Ice trekking may be the current novelty here, but even the most well-traveled rock climbers also delight in the dramatic terrain and exposed rock faces around the park. Outfitters around town rent equipment; try the friendly **Patagonia Mágica** (☎ 486261; www.patagoniamagica .com; Fonrouge s/n, El Chaltén), which runs one-day rock-climbing workshops for beginners on the natural rock-climbing walls near El Chaltén. Experienced climbers can go on expeditions on the Glaciar Laguna Torre with certified guides.

Sleeping

Free backcountry campgrounds are very basic, with one pit toilet. Bury human waste as far from water sources as possible. Some sites have dead wood with which to create windbreaks. Fires are prohibited. Water is pure as glacial melt; make sure all cleaning is done downstream from the campground and pack out all trash.

Getting There & Away

The national park is just outside El Chaltén, which is convenient if you're driving your own car; otherwise, most excursions offer transfers in and out of the park for around AR$40. For details of transportation to El Chaltén, see Getting There & Away, p478.

EL CALAFATE

☎ 02902 / pop 15,000

Named for the berry that, once eaten, guarantees your return to Patagonia, El Calafate hooks you with another irresistible attraction: Glaciar Perito Moreno, 80km away in Parque Nacional Los Glaciares. The glacier is a magnificent must-see, but its massive popularity has encouraged tumorous growth and rapid upscaling in the once-quaint El Calafate. At the same time, it's a fun place to be with a range of traveler services. The town's strategic location between El Chaltén and Torres del Paine (Chile) makes it an inevitable stop for those in transit.

Located 320km northwest of Río Gallegos, and 32km west of RP 11's junction with northbound RN 40, El Calafate flanks the southern shore of Lago Argentino. The main strip, Av del Libertador General San Martín (typically abbreviated to Av Libertador), is dotted with cutesy knotted-pine souvenir shops, chocolate shops, restaurants and tour offices. Beyond the main street, pretensions melt away quickly: muddy roads lead to ad-hoc developments and open pastures.

January and February are the most popular (and costly) months to visit, but as shoulder-season visits grow steadily, both availability and prices stay a challenge.

Information

INTERNET ACCESS

Cyberpoint (Av Libertador 1070; ☽ 24hr) Offers Skype on many computers.

LAUNDRY

Lava Andina (☎ 493980; Espora 88; per load AR$16)

MEDICAL SERVICES

Hospital Municipal Dr José Formenti (☎ 491001; Av Roca 1487)

MONEY

Withdraw your cash before the weekend rush – it isn't uncommon for ATMs to run out on Sundays.

Banco Santa Cruz (Av Libertador 1285) Changes traveler's checks and has an ATM.

Thaler Cambio (9 de Julio s/n; ☽ 10am-1pm Mon-Fri, 5:30-7:30pm Sat & Sun) Usurious rates for traveler's checks, but open weekends.

POST

Post office (Av Libertador 1133)

TELEPHONE

Cooperativa Telefónica (CTC; cnr Espora & Moyano) There's another branch on Av Libertador, near Perito Moreno.

TOURIST INFORMATION

ACA (Automóvil Club Argentino; ☎ 491004; cnr 1 de Mayo & Av Roca) Argentina's auto club; good source for provincial road maps.

Municipal tourist office (☎ 491090/466; www .elcalafate.gov.ar, in Spanish; cnr Rosales & Av Libertador; ☽ 8am-8pm) There's also a kiosk at the bus terminal; both have some English-speaking staff.

Parque Nacional Los Glaciares office (☎ 491005/755; www.parquesnacionales.gov.ar; Av Libertador 1302; ☽ 8am-7pm Mon-Fri, 10am-8pm Sat & Sun) Offers brochures and a decent map of Parque Nacional Los Glaciares. It's better to get info here than at the park.

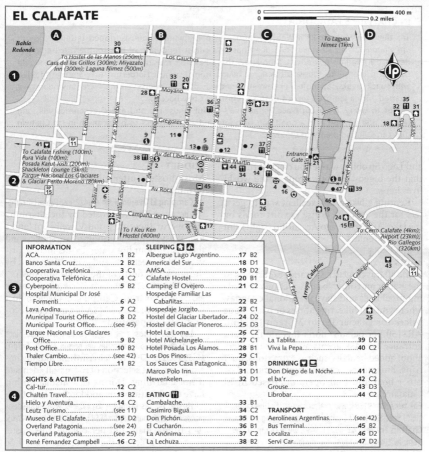

EL CALAFATE

0   400 m
0   0.2 miles

INFORMATION	
ACA	1 B2
Banco Santa Cruz	2 B2
Cooperativa Telefónica	3 C1
Cooperativa Telefónica	4 C2
Cyberpoint	5 B2
Hospital Municipal Dr José	
Formenti	6 A2
Lava Andina	7 C2
Municipal Tourist Office	8 D2
Municipal Tourist Office	(see 45)
Parque Nacional Los Glaciares	
Office	9 B2
Post Office	10 B2
Thaler Cambio	(see 42)
Tiempo Libre	11 B2

SIGHTS & ACTIVITIES	
Cal-tur	12 C2
Chaltén Travel	13 B2
Hielo y Aventura	14 C2
Leutz Turismo	(see 11)
Museo de El Calafate	15 D2
Overland Patagonia	(see 24)
Overland Patagonia	(see 25)
René Fernandez Campbell	16 C2

SLEEPING	
Albergue Lago Argentino	17 B2
America del Sur	18 D1
AMSA	19 D2
Calafate Hostel	20 B1
Camping El Ovejero	21 C2
Hospedaje Familiar Las	
Cabañitas	22 B2
Hospedaje Jorgito	23 C1
Hostel del Glaciar Libertador	24 D2
Hostel del Glaciar Pioneros	25 D3
Hotel La Loma	26 C2
Hotel Michelangelo	27 C2
Hotel Posada Los Álamos	28 B1
Los Dos Pinos	29 C1
Los Sauces Casa Patagonica	30 B1
Marco Polo Inn	31 D1
Newenkelen	32 D1

EATING	
Cambalache	33 B1
Casimiro Biguá	34 C2
Don Pichón	35 D1
El Cucharón	36 B2
La Anónima	37 C2
La Lechuza	38 B2

La Tablita	39 D2
Viva la Pepa	40 C2

DRINKING	
Don Diego de la Noche	41 A2
el ba'r	42 C2
Grouse	43 D3
Librobar	44 C2

TRANSPORT	
Aerolíneas Argentinas	(see 42)
Bus Terminal	45 B2
Localiza	46 D2
Servi Car	47 D2

TRAVEL AGENCIES

Most agents deal exclusively with nearby excursions and are unhelpful for other areas.
Tiempo Libre (☎ 491207; www.tiempolibreviajes.com.ar; 25 de Mayo 43) Books flights.

Sights & Activities

In shuffled disrepair, **Museo de El Calafate** (Av Libertador 575; admission by donation; ☉ 8am-7pm Mon-Fri, 10am-4pm Sat & Sun) displays arrowheads, stuffed penguins and early photographs. Don't miss the DVD on view, put on constant rotation at the museum, showcasing the greatest glacial ice ruptures at Perito Moreno in recent years.

Alongside the lakeshore, north of town, **Laguna Nimez** (admission AR\$2; ☉ 9am-9pm) is prime

avian habitat – and a great place to spot flamingos – but watching birds from El Calafate's shoreline on Lago Argentino can be just as good.

Hiking up **Cerro Calafate** (850m) is possible – follow Av Libertador east out of town to the second traffic circle and follow any of the direct roads towards the mountain, then work your way up. The route passes through marginal neighborhoods; while they are not considered dangerous, it is not exactly the ideal setting for hiking. To avoid them, ask a taxi to take you part way.

Anglers can take to the lakes with **Calafate Fishing** (☎ 496545; www.calafatefishing.com; Av Libertador 1826; ☉ 10am-7pm Mon-Sat), offering fun fly-fishing trips to Lago Roca (full day AR\$450)

IN CHATWIN'S PATAGONIA

'It's their Bible,' whispers a Welsh teahouse owner, spying a tourist-gripped tattered copy of *In Patagonia*. Over 30 years on, Bruce Chatwin's cubist rendering of this southern extreme has become a pilgrim's guide to it. Who knew that Chatwin's musings on errant wanderings would transform them into tourist attractions: hiking from Estancia Harberton to Viamonte (guided with snack breaks); taking tea in Gaiman (hundreds do it weekly); even the sacred mylodon cave (marred with a life-sized replica of this prehistoric Chewbacca).

Not to worry. It's a big place. Patagonia's willful landscape and exiled eccentrics will long remain, and anyone with a good pair of boots and a willingness to break them in (as Chatwin did) can still find plenty to discover.

---

and Lago Strobbel, where you can test rumors that the biggest rainbow trout in the world lives here.

Renting a **bike** is an excellent way to get a feel for the area and cruise the dirt roads by the lake. Albergue Lago Argentino (right) can advise on rentals.

Tours

Some 40 travel agencies arrange excursions to the glacier and other local attractions, including fossil beds and stays at regional **estancias**, where you can hike, ride horses or relax. Tour prices for Glaciar Perito Moreno (around AR$150 per person) don't include the park entrance fee. Ask agents and other travelers about added benefits, such as extra stops, boat trips, binoculars or multilingual guides. For other boat and tour operators based in El Calafate, see p488.

Cal-tur (☎ 491368; www.caltur.com.ar; Av Libertador 1080) Specializes in El Chaltén tours and lodging packages.

Chaltén Travel (☎ 492212/480; www.chaltentravel .com; Av Libertador 1174) Recommended tours to the glacier, stopping for wildlife viewing (binoculars provided); also specializes in RN 40 trips. Outsources some excursions to Always Glaciers (www.alwaysglaciers.com, in Spanish.)

Overland Patagonia (☎ 491243, 492243; www .glaciar.com) Operates out of both Hostel del Glaciar Libertador and Hostel del Glaciar Pioneros (see opposite); organizes recommended 'alternative' and full-moon trips to the glacier, plus guided hiking, camping and ice-trekking combos in El Chaltén.

Sleeping

In spite of abundant lodgings, there are always shortages here. Book ahead, even outside of high season. The core high season is January to February, although some places extend it from mid-October until April. Look for deep discounts in low season.

BUDGET

Most hostels offer pickup from the bus terminal.

Camping El Ovejero (☎ 493422; José Pantín 64; campsites per person AR$15-20) Hosted by the charming Humberto, these are woodsy, well-kept (and a little noisy) campsites. Showers are spotless and there is 24-hour hot water. Extras include private tables, electricity and grills. It's located by the creek just north of the bridge into town.

AMSA (☎ 492247; Olavarria 65; campsites per person AR$15) Not far from Camping El Ovejero, just south of the bridge, AMSA is a quiet and economical campground.

Los Dos Pinos (☎ 491271/632; www.losdospinos .com; 9 de Julio 358; campsites per person AR$20, dm/d/tr AR$50/200/250; 🖳) This labyrinthine lodging has a supermarket selection of rooms, all adequate if not charming. Dorms lack insulation but have clean bathrooms and kitchen facilities.

Hostel de las Manos (☎ 492996; www.hosteldelas manos.com.ar; Feruglio 59; dm AR$42, d with bathroom AR$205; 🖳) Immaculate and personable, this hostel alternative is across the footbridge from 9 de Julio. A wall of windows provides ample light. Dorms are small but doubles have white wood paneling, bright bedspreads and new fixtures.

Hospedaje Jorgito (☎ 491323; Moyano 943; dm/d/tr without bathroom AR$45/120/140) This home feels family oriented with vintage Barbies, doilies and synthetic flowers providing animated decoration. Rooms vary in size but are bright and well kept. Guests can use the large kitchen.

Albergue Lago Argentino (☎ 491423; www.losgla ciares.com/lagoargentino; Campaña del Desierto 1050; dm/d without bathroom AR$45/120, s/d with bathroom AR$140/180; 🖳) Run by well-traveled couple Javier and Veronica, this pink property offers clean but basic dorms. Its annex *albergue* is geared towards couples, with quiet garden rooms and breakfast in a plant-filled nook with antique wood stove.

Hostel del Glaciar Pioneros (☎ 491243; www.gla ciar.com; Los Pioneros 251; dm/d AR$46/170; 🖳) A 15-minute walk from town, this sociable hostel offers comfortable common areas and small dorms. From the outside, it looks like a green Victorian house, but step inside and you'll see that it's a huge backpacker complex.

Calafate Hostel (☎ 492450/2; www.calafatehostels .com; Moyano 1226; dm/s/d/tr/q AR$47/150/200/240/275; 🖳) Best suited to large groups, this mammoth log cabin ends up feeling blander than the competition. Double-bunk dorms are cozy, while the new annex features tidy brick doubles.

Hostel del Glaciar Libertador (☎ 491792; www .glaciar.com; Av Libertador 587; dm/d AR$53/274; ✂ 🖳) The best deals here are dorm bunks with thick covers. Behind a Victorian facade, modern facilities include a top-floor kitchen and a spacious common area with a plasma TV glued to sports channels.

Marco Polo Inn (☎ 493899; www.marcopoloinncala fate.com; Calle 405, No 82; dm/d/tr AR$55/200/220; 🖳) A relatively new addition with attentive service and spacious dorms featuring quilted bedspreads and wood-finished bunks. Doubles have bathrooms and extra amenities, such as hair dryers and TVs.

I Keu Ken Hostel (☎ 495175; www.patagoniaikeuken .com.ar; FM Pontoriero 171; dm/d AR$60/210; 🖳) These dorms are a bit pricier than others in town, and near the top of a steep hill – but travelers love the place anyway, thanks to the helpful owners, inviting common areas and first-rate barbecues.

America del Sur (☎ 493525; www.americahostel .com.ar; Puerto Deseado 151; dm/d AR$65/280; 🖳) This backpacker favorite boasts top-tier service and a stylish lodge setting with views. One thing you won't find here is solitude – it's bustling at every hour. All-you-can-eat barbecues are put on nightly (AR$35).

MIDRANGE
The tourist office has a complete list of *cabañas* and apartment hotels, which are the best deals for groups and families.

Hospedaje Familiar Las Cabañitas (☎ 491118; www.lascabanitascalafate.com; Valentín Feilberg 218; d/tr AR$170/220) Run by the endearing Giordano family, these storybook A-frames are somewhat dated but snug, with spiral staircases leading to loft beds. Sweet touches include English lavender and a sheltered dining patio brimming with plants.

Casa de los Grillos (☎ 491160; Las Bandurrias s/n; d with bathroom AR$230) A quiet B&B with fresh rooms, soft beds and attentive service. Guests can serve themselves coffee, tea and spring water in the dining nook. The backyard cabin offers shaggy bedspreads and all-new fixtures and appliances. A *quincho* (thatched-roof building) gives guests ample cooking and recreation space.

Hotel La Loma (☎ 491016; www.lalomahotel.com; Av Roca 849; s/d AR$160/190; 🐾) Colonial furnishings and a lovely rock garden enhance this rambling ranch-style retreat. While its exterior is nondescript, superior rooms are spacious and bright. Antiques fill the creaky hallways and the reception area boasts an open fire and plenty of books.

Newenkelen (☎ 493943; www.newenkelen.com.ar; Puerto Deseado 223; s/d/tr AR$208/262/300) Perched on a hill above town, this intimate option features a handful of immaculate brick rooms with tasteful bedding and mountain views.

TOP END
Luxury hotels are being added at a quick clip, though not all offer the same standard.

Posada Karut Josh (☎ 496444; www.posadakarut josh.com.ar; Calle 12, No 1882, Barrio Bahía Redonda; d/tr AR$260/310) This peaceful B&B has six light-filled rooms with bathrooms and large windows overlooking the mountains or the lake. An upscale continental breakfast is served in a dining room with a view.

our pick **Miyazato Inn** (☎ 491953; www.interpat agonia.com/miyazatoinn; Egidio Feruglio 150, Las Chacras; s/d AR$303/342; 🖳) This cozy B&B wins major points with travelers thanks to the friendly and personalized service of owners Jorge and Elizabeth. Resembling a simple Japanese inn and located a five-minute walk away from the center of town, Miyazato has five double rooms with private baths.

Hotel Michelangelo (☎ 491045; www.michelangelo hotel.com.ar; Moyano 1020; s/d AR$330/380; 🖳) Tour groups favor this Swiss chalet–style lodging in the center of town. Recently renovated, the place features a chic lobby and living area with stone fixtures and low lighting; the guest rooms are still somewhat dated with heavy drapes, floral bedspreads, high ceilings and full amenities.

Hotel Posada Los Álamos (☎ 491144; www.posada losalamos.com; Moyano 1355; s/d/ste AR$835/918/1345; 🖳) Calafate's original resort swims in luxury: plush rooms, overstuffed sofas, spectacular

PATAGONIA

gardens, tennis courts, putting greens and a spa. It's enough to make you almost forget about seeing that glacier.

Los Sauces Casa Patagónica (☎ 495854; www.casalossauces.com; Los Gauchos 1352/1370; d ARS950; 💻) With an award-winning restaurant, a full spa and spacious, immaculately manicured grounds where exotic birds roam and staff members zip by in golf carts, Los Sauces feels less like a hotel and more like a luxury compound. The interiors are gorgeous, with first-class beds, huge flat-screen TVs and stone bathrooms with jacuzzis.

Eating

Look for small shops selling fresh bread, fine cheeses, sweets and wine – there are several on the side streets that run perpendicular to Av Libertador – where you can fill up your picnic basket for the next day's excursion. Head to **La Anónima** (cnr Av Libertador & Perito Moreno) for cheap take-out and groceries.

Cambalache (☎ 492603; www.cambalacherestobar.com.ar; Moyano 1258; mains ARS20-30; 🕑 noon-midnight) This cheerful eatery, housed in a restored tin house, is a meeting place for young travelers who pile in for inexpensive wine and budget-friendly regional dishes like grilled steak and lamb stew.

La Lechuza (☎ 491610; www.lalechuzapizzas.com.ar; cnr Av Libertador & 1 de Mayo; pizza ARS25; 🕑 lunch & dinner Mon-Sat) A classic selection of empanadas, salads and pizza is served on round wooden plates – try the sheep cheese and olive pizza with a local microbrew. Watch for a new location on the eastern end of Av Libertador – and if the brownie with chocolate ganache and calafate ice cream is written on the dessert chalkboard, don't miss it.

Viva la Pepa (☎ 491880; Amado 833; mains ARS25-42; 🕑 10am-midnight Fri-Wed) Decked out in children's drawings, this cheerful cafe specializes in crepes but also offers great sandwiches with homemade bread (try the chicken with apple and blue cheese), fresh juice and gourds of *mate*.

La Tablita (☎ 491065; Coronel Rosales 24; mains ARS30-50; 🕑 lunch Thu-Tue, dinner daily) Steak and spit-roasted lamb are the stars at this satisfying *parrilla*, which is popular beyond measure. For average appetites a half-steak will do, rounded out with a good malbec, fresh salad or garlic fries.

our pick **El Cucharón** (☎ 495315; 9 de Julio 145; mains ARS35-40; 🕑 lunch & dinner) This sophisticated eatery, tucked away in a small space a few blocks off the main street, is a relatively undiscovered gem and an excellent place to try the regional classic *cazuela de cordero*. The trout with lemon sauce and grilled vegetables is delicious, too.

Pura Vida (☎ 493356; Av Libertador 1876; mains ARS35-52; 🕑 dinner Thu-Tue) Whole grains and abundant vegetarian dishes make this ambient eatery a traveler's treat. Try the gnocchi with saffron, rabbit with cream, or pumpkin stew served in an enormous gourd.

Casimiro Biguá (☎ 492590; www.casimirobigua.com; Av Libertador 963; mains ARS35-52; 🕑 11am-1am) With warm copper accents and a hustling staff, this chic eatery and *vinoteca* (wine bar) offers an impressive list of 180 Argentine wines. The chef creates wonderful homemade pasta, risotto, lamb stew, and grilled trout and steak. Two new locations have popped up nearby to accommodate the masses: a trattoria and a *parrilla*.

Don Pichón (☎ 492577; www.donpichon.com.ar; Puerto Deseado 242; mains ARS40-45; 🕑 lunch & dinner) For dinner with a view, it's hard to beat Don Pichón, perched high above the lake on the outskirts of town. The casual but classy lodge-style dining room features high wood-beamed ceilings and huge panes of glass revealing sweeping scenic views; the melt-in-your-mouth lamb is a huge hit with travelers. Call ahead to ask about complimentary shuttle pick-up.

Drinking

el ba'r (9 de Julio s/n; snacks ARS8-17; 🕑 breakfast & lunch) This trendy patio cafe is the hot spot for you and your sweater-clad puppy to order espresso, *submarinos* (hot milk with melted chocolate bar), green tea or sandwiches.

Grouse (☎ 491281; Av Libertador 351; drinks ARS12-25) This Celtic pub/karaoke hub aims to appeal to all whims. Look for live acts in summer, generous mixed drinks and cans of Guinness.

Librobar (☎ 491464; Av Libertador 1015; 🕑 Wed-Mon) Upstairs in the gnome village, this hip book-bar serves coffee, bottled beers and pricey cocktails. Peruse the oversized photography books on Patagonian wildlife or bring your laptop and take advantage of the free wi-fi.

Don Diego de la Noche (Av Libertador 1603; 🕑 until 5am) This perennial favorite serves dinner and features live music like tango, guitar and *folklórico* (Argentine folk music).

Getting There & Away

AIR

The modern **Aeropuerto El Calafate** (ECA; ☎ 491220/30) is 23km east of town off RP 11; the departure tax is US$38.

Aerolíneas Argentinas (☎ 492814/16; 9 de Julio 57) flies every day to Bariloche (AR$920), Ushuaia (AR$400), Trelew (AR$820), and Aeroparque and Ezeiza in Buenos Aires (AR$380 to AR$775).

LADE (☎ 491262; bus terminal) flies a few times a week to Río Gallegos (AR$147), Comodoro Rivadavia (AR$230), Ushuaia (AR$362), Buenos Aires (AR$429) and other smaller regional airports.

BUS

El Calafate's hilltop **bus terminal** (Av Roca s/n) is easily reached by a pedestrian staircase from the corner of Av Libertador and 9 de Julio. Book ahead in high season, as outbound seats can be in short supply.

For El Chaltén (AR$70, 3½ hours), several companies share passengers and leave daily at 7:30am, 8am and 6:30pm, stopping midway at Estancia La Leona for coffee and tasty pies.

For Puerto Natales (AR$65, five hours), **Cootra** (☎ 491444) departs at 8:30am daily, crossing the border at Cerro Castillo, where it may be possible to connect to Torres del Paine.

For Río Gallegos (AR$40 to AR$60, four hours), buses go daily at 3am, 4am, noon, 12:30pm and 2:30pm. **Freddy** (☎ 452671) and Interlagos offer connections to Bariloche and Ushuaia that require leaving in the middle of the night and a change of buses in Río Gallegos.

From mid-October to April, **Chaltén Travel** (☎ 492212/480; www.chaltentravel.com; Av Libertador 1174) goes to El Chaltén (AR$100 roundtrip, three hours) daily at 8am and 6:30pm. It also runs shuttles north along RN 40 to Perito Moreno and Los Antiguos (AR$220, 12 hours), departing on even-numbered days at 8am, to connect with onward service to Bariloche (AR$430, two days from El Calafate) the next morning. The same service also leaves from El Chaltén.

Getting Around

Airport shuttle **Ves Patagonia** (☎ 494355; www.vespatagonia.com.ar) offers door-to-door service (one way/roundtrip AR$24/40). There are several car-rental agencies at the airport.

Localiza (☎ 491398; www.localiza.com.ar; Av Libertador 687) and **Servi Car** (☎ 492541; www.servi4x4.com.ar; Av Libertador 695) offer car rentals from convenient downtown offices.

AROUND EL CALAFATE

From El Calafate, paved RN 40 cuts southeast across vast steppe for 95km, then jogs south at **El Cerrito** and turns to gravel. Staying on paved RP 5 means a slow-going, five-hour, 224km bore of a trip southeast to **Río Gallegos**. Halfway along RP 5, at Km 146, is the utilitarian **Hotel La Esperanza** (☎ 02902-499200; per person AR$75; ☺ year-round), a gas-station diner (daily special AR$30) with quick, friendly service. If you plan to stay, ask for a room in the newer cabin. From here, paved RP 7 connects back to RN 40 for the Chilean border crossing at Cerro Castillo–Cancha Carrera, Parque Nacional Torres del Paine and Puerto Natales.

PARQUE NACIONAL LOS GLACIARES (SOUTH)

Among Earth's most dynamic and accessible ice fields, **Glaciar Perito Moreno** is the stunning centerpiece of the southern sector of **Parque Nacional Los Glaciares** (admission AR$75). Locally referred to as **Glaciar Moreno**, it measures 30km long, 5km wide and 60m high, but what makes it exceptional in the world of ice is its constant advance – it creeps forward up to 2m per day, causing building-sized icebergs to calve from its face. In some ways, watching the glacier is a very sedentary park experience, but it manages to nonetheless be thrilling.

The glacier formed as a low gap in the Andes allowed moisture-laden Pacific storms to drop their loads east of the divide, where they accumulate as snow. Over millennia, under tremendous weight, this snow has recrystalized into ice and flowed slowly eastward. The 1600-sq-km trough of **Lago Argentino**, the country's largest single body of water, is unmistakable evidence that glaciers were once far more extensive than today.

While most of the world's glaciers are receding, Glaciar Moreno is considered 'stable.' Regardless, 17 times between 1917 and 2006, as the glacier has advanced, it has dammed the Brazo Rico (Rico Arm) of Lago Argentino, causing the water to rise. Several times, the melting ice below has been unable to support the weight of the water behind it and the dam

PATAGONIA

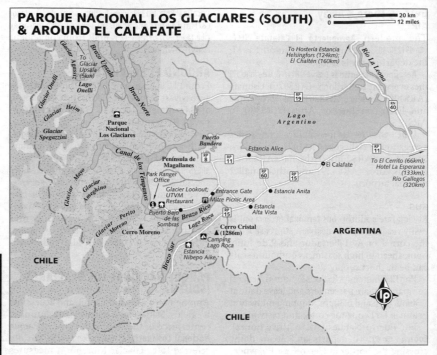

PARQUE NACIONAL LOS GLACIARES (SOUTH) & AROUND EL CALAFATE

has collapsed in an explosion of water and ice. To be present when this spectacular cataclysm occurs is unforgettable.

Visiting Glaciar Moreno is no less an auditory than a visual experience, as huge icebergs on the glacier's face calve and collapse into the **Canal de los Témpanos** (Iceberg Channel). This natural-born tourist attraction is ideally located at Península de Magallanes – close enough to guarantee great views, but far enough away to be safe. A series of recently improved catwalks and vantage points allow visitors to see, hear and photograph the glacier. Sun hits its face in the morning and the glacier's appearance changes as the day progresses and shadows shift.

A massive makeover is in the works at Glaciar Moreno. Plans are in the works for a new hotel located near the glacier lookout; a slick but chaotic new *confitería*, **Nativos** (☎ 499144), now serves cappuccino and sandwiches to sightseers. If you bring a picnic, remember that trash is difficult and costly to remove from the area – please pack yours out.

The main gateway town to the park's southern sector, El Calafate (p482), is 80km east of

the glacier by road. It's where you'll find all the operators for tours and activities mentioned in this section.

Activities
GLACIAR PERITO MORENO

Boat trips allow you to sense the magnitude of Glaciar Moreno, even though the boats keep a distance. **Hielo y Aventura** (☎ 02902-492094/205; www.hieloyaventura.com; Av Libertador 935, El Calafate) runs Safari Nautico (AR$45), a one-hour tour of Brazo Rico, Lago Argentino and the south side of Canal de los Témpanos. Catamarans crammed with up to 130 passengers leave hourly between 11:30am and 3:30pm from Puerto Bajo de las Sombras. Don't forget rain gear: it's often snowing around the glacier and you might get wet and cold quickly on the boat deck. Many travelers suggest getting on the last boat ride of the day and then viewing the glacier from the look-out platforms afterwards, when fewer visitors will crowd the catwalks.

Hielo y Aventura also offers minitrekking (AR$390, transfer AR$60) on the glacier, a five-hour trek for groups of up to 20, involving a quick boat ride from Puerto Bajo de las Sombras, a walk through lenga forests, a quick chat on glaciology and then a 1½-hour ice walk using crampons. For a more extensive trek, ask about the four-hour ice trek. Children under eight are not allowed; reserve ahead and bring your own food.

To see the glacier's main north face, **René Fernandez Campbell** (☎ 02902-491155; www.fernan dezcampbell.com; Av Libertador 867, El Calafate) operates 320-passenger boats (AR$50) from below the UTVM restaurant near the main lookout, hourly between 10:30am and 2:30pm.

Beyond a short walk that parallels the shoreline at the boat dock and climbs to the lookout area, there are no trails in this sector of the park accessible without boat transportation.

GLACIAR UPSALA & LAGO ONELLI

Glaciar Upsala – 595-sq-km huge, 60km long and some 4km wide in parts – can be admired for its monumental dimensions alongside the strange and graceful forms of the nearby icebergs. The downside is that it can only be enjoyed from the crowded deck of a massive catamaran: just you and nature and 300 of your closest friends. On an extension of the Brazo Norte (North Arm) of Lago Argentino, it's accessible by launch from Puerto Bandera, 45km west of Calafate by RP 11 and RP 8.

For the grand tour, **René Fernandez Campbell** (☎ 02902-492340; www.fernandezcampbell.com; Av Libertador 867, El Calafate) does an all-glacier tour (AR$295) from Punta Bandera, visiting Glaciar Upsala, Bahía Onelli and Glaciar Spegazzini. If icebergs are cooperating, boats may allow passengers to disembark at Bahía Onelli to walk 500m to iceberg-choked **Lago Onelli**, where the Onelli and Agassiz glaciers merge. Meals are expensive, but you can bring your own picnic.

LAGO ROCA

The serene south arm of Lago Argentino offers a great escape into lakeshore forests and mountains. Good hikes, pleasant camping and *estancia* accommodations occupy this most southerly section of the park, where most visitors rarely travel. No entrance fee is charged to access this section. Hikers can climb **Cerro Cristal**, a rugged but rewarding 3½-hour hike. It begins at the education camp at La Jerónima, just before the Camping Lago Roca entrance, 55km southwest of El Calafate along RP 15. On a clear day, you can see Glaciar Moreno and the Torres del Paine.

Horseback-riding trips with **Cabalgatas del Glaciar** (☎ 495447) offer glacier panoramas; they can also be booked through **Cal-tur** (☎ 02902-491368; Av Libertador 1080, El Calafate). **Leutz Turismo** (☎ 02902-492316; leutztur ismo@cotecal.com.ar; 25 de Mayo 43, El Calafate) takes visitors on day trips to Estancia Nibepo Aike (AR$155) from El Calafate. The morning or afternoon visits include tea, *mate* and fresh pastries, a sheep-shearing demonstration and an hour of horseback riding.

GLACIOLOGY 101

Ribbons of ice, stretched flat in sheets or sculpted by weather and fissured by pressure, glaciers have a raw magnificence that is mind-boggling to behold.

As snow falls on the accumulation area, it compacts to ice. The river of ice is slugged forward by gravity, which deforms its layers as it moves. When the glacier surges downhill, melted ice mixes with rock and soil on the bottom, grinding it into a lubricant that keeps pushing the glacier along. At the same time, debris from the crushed rock is forced to the sides of the glacier, creating features called moraines. Movement also causes cracks and deformities called crevasses.

The ablation area is where the glacier melts. When accumulation outpaces melting at the ablation area, the glacier advances; when there's more melting or evaporation, the glacier recedes. Since 1980, global warming has contributed greatly to widespread glacial retreat.

Another marvel of glaciers is their hue. What makes some blue? Wavelengths and air bubbles. The more compact the ice, the longer the path that light has to travel and the bluer the ice appears. Air bubbles in uncompacted areas absorb long wavelengths of white light so we see white. When glaciers calve into lakes, they dump a 'glacial flour' comprised of ground-up rock that gives the water a milky, grayish color. This same sediment remains unsettled in some lakes and diffracts the sun's light, creating a stunning palette of turquoise, pale mint and azure.

Sleeping & Eating

Camping Lago Roca (☎ 02902-499500; www.losglaciares
.com/campinglagoroca; per person AR$16, cabin dm for 2/4
AR$100/160) This full-service campground with
restaurant-bar, located a few kilometers past
the education camp, makes a good base to
explore the area. The clean concrete-walled
dorms provide a snug alternative to camping.
Hiking trails abound, and the center rents
fishing equipment and bikes and coordinates
horseback riding at the nearby *estancia*.

Estancia Nibepo Aike (☎ 02902-492797, in Buenos
Aires 011-5031-0755; www.nibepoaike.com.ar; RP 15, Km 60;
s/d incl full board AR$856/1332; ⊗ Oct-Apr) This work-
ing sheep and cattle ranch offers the usual
assortment of *estancia* highlights. In addition
to horseback riding, guests have the option to
explore the surroundings on two wheels from
the bicycle stash.

Hostería Estancia Helsingfors (☎ in Buenos Aires
011-4315-1222; www.helsingfors.com.ar; s/d AR$1446/2215;
⊗ Oct-Apr) The simply stunning location ogling
Cerro Fitz Roy from Lago Viedma makes for
lots of love-at-first-sight impressions. Intimate
and welcoming, this former Finnish pioneer
ranch is a highly regarded luxury destination,
though it cultivates a relaxed, unpretentious
ambience. Guests pass the time on scenic but
demanding mountain treks, rides and visits to
Glaciar Viedma. It's on Lago Viedma's southern shore, 170km from El Chaltén and 180km
from El Calafate.

Getting There & Away

Glaciar Perito Moreno is 80km west of El
Calafate via paved RP 11, passing through the
breathtaking scenery around Lago Argentino.
Bus tours (AR$110 roundtrip, AR$80 for
transport only) are frequent in summer – see
p484, or simply stroll down El Calafate's Av
Libertador. Buses leave El Calafate in the early
morning and afternoon, returning around
noon and 7pm.

CHILEAN PATAGONIA

Rugged seascapes rimmed with glacial peaks,
the stunning massifs of Torres del Paine and
howling steppe characterize the other side
of the Andes. If you have come this far, it
is well worth crossing the border. Chilean
Patagonia, a mountainous region sculpted
by westerly winds, consists of the isolated
Aisén and Magallanes regions, separated by

the southern continental ice field. This section covers Punta Arenas, Puerto Natales and
spectacular Parque Nacional Torres del Paine.
For in-depth coverage of Chile, pick up Lonely
Planet's *Chile & Easter Island*.

Most nationals of countries that have diplomatic relations with Chile don't need a visa
to enter the country. Upon entering, customs
officials will issue you a tourist card, valid
for 90 days and renewable for another 90;
authorities take it seriously, so guard it closely
to avoid the hassle of replacing it (in other
words, make sure that any small papers placed
in your passport stay there during your trip.)
If arriving by air, US citizens must pay a one-
time reciprocal entry fee of US$132, valid for
the life of the passport; Canadians pay US$132
and Australians US$61.

Temperature-sensitive travelers will quickly
notice a difference after leaving energy-rich
Argentina: in public areas and budget accommodations central heating is rare; warmer
clothing is the norm indoors.

Chile is slightly more expensive than
Argentina, and US cash is not as widely ac-
cepted. Prices here are given in Chilean pesos
(CH$).

PUNTA ARENAS

☎ 61 / pop 130,200

Today's Punta Arenas is a confluence of the
ruddy and the grand, witnessed in the elaborate wool-boom mansions, the thriving petro-
chemical industry and its port status. Visitors
will find it the most convenient base to travel
around the remote Magallanes region, with
good traveler services. In truth, the city's
increasing prosperity has sanded down and
polished off its former roughneck reputation.
Watch for more cruise-ship passengers and
trekkers to replace the explorers, sealers and
sailors of yesterday at the barstools – but save
a spot for the old guard.

Founded in 1848 as a penal settlement and
military garrison, Punta Arenas proved to be
conveniently situated for ships headed to Alta
California during the gold rush. The economy
foundered during its early years, taking off only
in the last quarter of the 19th century, after the
territorial governor authorized the purchase of
300 pure-bred sheep from the Falkland Islands
(Islas Malvinas). This successful experiment
encouraged the proliferation of sheep farming and, by the turn of the century, nearly two
million animals grazed the territory.

PUNTA ARENAS

0 — 400 m
0 — 0.2 miles

INFORMATION
British Consulate.....................................**1** C5
De Austro Internet..................................**2** C3
Hospital Regional...................................**3** B1
Information Kiosk.....................................**4** B4
Italian Consulate.....................................**5** A6
Lavasol...**6** C4
Netherlands Consulate............................**7** D3
Oficina de Turismo..................................**8** B4
Post Office...**9** C4
Spanish Consulate..................................**10** C4
Sur Cambios...**11** C4
Telefónica...**12** B4
World's End...**13** C4

SIGHTS & ACTIVITIES
Casa Braun-Menéndez.............................**14** C4
Cathedral...**15** B4
Cementerio Municipal.............................**16** D2
Club de la Unión..............................(see 14)
Fantastico Sur...**17** C4
Inhóspita Patagonia...............................**18** C4
Monument to Magellan.........................**19** C4
Museo Naval y Marítimo........................**20** C5
Museo Regional
  Braun-Menéndez..................................**21** C4
Museo Regional Salesiano......................**22** D2
Sociedad Menéndez Behety.............(see 23)
Turismo Aonikenk............................(see 50)
Turismo Comapa.....................................**23** C4
Turismo Pali Aike...................................**24** C5
Turismo Pehoé..**25** C4
Turismo Viento Sur................................**26** B4
Turismo Yamana.....................................**27** C5
Whale Sound...**28** C5

SLEEPING
Al Fin del Mundo....................................**29** C5
Amanecer Austral....................................**30** A5
El Conventillo...**31** C5
Hospedaje Independencia.......................**32** A5
Hostal Bustamante.................................**33** D4
Hostal Calafate......................................**34** C4
Hostal Carpa Manzano...........................**35** D2
Hostal de la Patagonia..........................**36** D4
Hostal Fitz Roy.......................................**37** C4
Hostal Terrasur......................................**38** D4
Hostel Keoken..**39** D2
Hotel Cabo de Hornos.............................**40** C4
Hotel Isla Rey Jorge...............................**41** B5
Hotel José Nogueira..........................(see 14)
Hotel Mercurio.......................................**42** B4
Hotel Plaza...**43** B4
Ilaia Hotel..**44** B3

EATING
Damiana Elena.......................................**45** D2
La Luna..**46** C5
La Marmita..**47** D3
Lomit's...**48** C4
O'Sole Mio...**49** C4
Pachamama..**50** C3
Sabores..**51** C3
Sotito's...**52** C5

DRINKING
El Madero...**53** C3
La Taberna.......................................(see 14)
Olijoe Pub..**54** C5

ENTERTAINMENT
Cine Estrella...**55** C3
Kamikaze...(see 53)

TRANSPORT
Adel Rent a Car/Localiza.........................**56** C4
Aerovías DAP..**57** C4
Budget..**58** C4
Bus Sur...**59** B4
Bus Transfer...**60** C4
Buses Fernández.....................................**61** B3
Buses Ghisoni...**62** C4
Buses Pacheco..**63** C4
Buses Pingüino..................................(see 61)
Central de Pasajeros...............................**64** C4
Hertz...**65** C4
LanChile..**66** C4
Lubag...**67** C4
Navimag...(see 23)
Queilen Bus.......................................(see 62)
Tecni-Austral.....................................(see 62)
Turibus...(see 61)
Turismo Comapa...............................(see 23)
Turismo Sandy Point..............................**68** C4

To Conaf (400m); Instituto de la Patagonia & Zona Franca (2.5km); Port (3km);
Transbordador Austral Broom (3km); Tres Puentes Ferry Terminal (3.5km);
Airport (15km);
Seno Otway
Pingüinera
(48km);
Puerto
Natales (247km)

PATAGONIA

Strait of Magellan
To Argentine Consulate (400m);
Puerto Hambre (53km); Fuerte Bulnes (60km)

Information

Travel agencies in the city center, along Roca and Lautaro Navarro, change cash and traveler's checks. All are open weekdays and Saturday, with a few open on Sunday morning. Banks with ATMs dot the city center.

ESSENTIALS

Conaf (☎ 223841; José Menéndez 1147) Has details on the nearby parks.

De Austro Internet (☎ 229297; Croacia 690, 1st fl; ☼ 9:30am-9pm) Internet access. Most cafes in town also have free wi-fi.

Hospital Regional (☎ 205000; cnr Arauco & Angamos)

Information kiosk (☎ 200610; www.puntaarenas.cl, in Spanish; Plaza Muñoz Gamero; ☼ 8am-7pm Mon-Sat, 9am-7pm Sun) South side of the plaza.

Oficina de Turismo (☎ 241330; www.sernatur.cl; Waldo Seguel 689; ☼ 8:15am-8pm Mon-Fri Dec-Feb, 8:15am-6pm Mon-Thu, 8:15am-5pm Fri rest of year) Has friendly, well- informed, multilingual staff, and lists of accommodations and transportation. Also has a list of recommended doctors.

Sur Cambios (☎ 225656; Lautaro Navarro 1001) Exchanges money.

OTHER SERVICES

Lavasol (☎ 243607; O'Higgins 969) Laundry service. Hostels do laundry for a bit less.

Post office (Bories 911)

Telefónica (Nogueira 1116)

World's End (☎ 213117; Plaza Muñoz Gamero 1011) Maps, photo books, souvenirs and Lonely Planet guides in English and Spanish.

Sights & Activities

PLAZA MUÑOZ GAMERO

In the heart of Punta Arenas, this central plaza is lined with magnificent conifers and surrounded by opulent mansions. Facing the plaza's north side is the Club de la Unión, which houses the former Palacio Sara Braun, now known as the **Casa Braun-Menéndez** (☎ 241489; admission CH$1000; ☼ 10:30am-1pm & 5-8:30pm Tue-Fri, 10:30am-1pm & 8-10pm Sat, 11am-2pm Sun). The nearby **monument** commemorating the 400th anniversary of Magellan's voyage was donated by wool baron José Menéndez in 1920. Just east is the former **Sociedad Menéndez Behety**, which now houses Turismo Comapa. The **cathedral** sits west.

RESERVA FORESTAL MAGALLANES

This **reserve** (admission free; ☼ daylight hrs), 8km from town, offers great hiking and mountain biking through dense lenga and coihue. A steady slog takes you to the top of Mt Fenton, where views are spectacular and winds impressively strong.

MUSEO REGIONAL BRAUN-MENÉNDEZ

This opulent **mansion** (☎ 244216; Magallanes 949; admission CH$1000, free Sun; ☼ 10:30am-5pm Mon-Sat, 10:30am-2pm Sun in summer, to 2pm daily in winter) testifies to the wealth and power of pioneer sheep farmers in the late 19th century. One of Mauricio Braun's sons donated the house to the state against other family members' wishes. The well-maintained interior is divided into two sections: one half is a regional historical museum (booklets with English descriptions are available); the other half displays the original exquisite French-nouveau family furnishings, from intricate wooden inlaid floors to Chinese vases.

The museum is most easily accessed from Magallanes. There's a cafe downstairs in what used to be the servants' quarters; it's a great place to have a pisco sour while soaking up the grandeur.

CEMENTERIO MUNICIPAL

Among South America's most fascinating cemeteries, **Cementerio Municipal** (main entrance at Av Bulnes 949; ☼ 7:30am-8pm) contains a mix of humble immigrant graves and flashy tombs under topiary cypresses. In death as in life, Punta Arenas' first families flaunted their wealth – wool baron José Menéndez' extravagant tomb is, according to Bruce Chatwin, a scale replica of Rome's Vittorio Emanuele monument. But the headstones also tell the stories of Anglo, German, Scandinavian and Yugoslav immigrants. There's also a monument to the Selk'nam (Ona) and a map posted inside the main entrance gate.

The cemetery is an easy 15-minute stroll northeast of the plaza, or you can catch any taxi *colectivo* (shared taxi with specific route) from in front of the Museo Regional Braun-Menéndez on Magallanes.

MUSEO NAVAL Y MARÍTIMO

Punta Arenas' naval and maritime **museum** (☎ 205479; Pedro Montt 981; adult/child CH$1800/1000; ☼ 9:30am-12:30pm & 3-6pm Tue-Sat) has varied exhibits on model ships, naval history, the unprecedented visit of 27 US warships to Punta Arenas in 1908, and a fine account of the Chilean mission that rescued British explorer Sir Ernest Shackleton's crew from Antarctica. The most imaginative display is a replica ship complete with bridge, maps, charts and radio room.

MUSEO REGIONAL SALESIANO
Especially influential in settling the region, the Salesian order collected outstanding ethnographic artifacts, but their **museum** (☎ 221001; Av Bulnes 336; admission CH$2000; ☼ 10am-12:30pm & 3-6pm Tue-Sun) touts their role as peacemakers between the Yaghan and Ona and settlers. The best materials are on indigenous groups and the mountaineer priest Alberto de Agostini.

INSTITUTO DE LA PATAGONIA
Pioneer days are made real again at the Patagonian Institute's **Museo del Recuerdo** (☎ 207056; www.umag.cl, in Spanish; Av Bulnes 01890; admission CH$1500; ☼ 8:30-11am & 2:30-6pm Mon-Fri), part of the Universidad de Magallanes. On display are a collection of antique farm and industrial machinery, a typical pioneer house and shearing shed, and a wooden-wheeled shepherds' trailer. The library has historical maps and a series of historical and scientific publications.

Tours
Worthwhile day trips include tours to the **Seno Otway pingüinera** (penguin colony; p499), 48km to the north. Tours (from CH$8000) leave at 4pm daily October through March, weather permitting.

Visits to the town's first settlements at **Fuerte Bulnes & Puerto Hambre** (admission CH$1000) leave at 10am. Both tours can be done in one day; by sharing a rental car and going at opposite times visitors can avoid the strings of tour groups. Most lodgings will help arrange tours – if they don't run their own operation.

Estancia Río Corey (www.estanciariocorey.com) offers day trips from Punta Arenas that consist of horseback riding and penguin observation along the Otway Sound.

Torres del Paine tours are abundant from Punta Arenas, but the distance makes for a very long day; it's best to head to Puerto Natales and organize transport from there.

If you have the time, a more atmospheric alternative to Seno Otway is the thriving Magellanic penguin colonies of **Monumento Natural Los Pingüinos** (p499) on Isla Magdalena. Five-hour tours on the *Barcaza Melinka* (adult/child CH$25,000) land for an hour at the island and depart the port on Tuesday,

Thursday and Saturday, December through February. Confirm times in advance. Book tickets through **Turismo Comapa** (☎ 200200; www .comapa.com; Magallanes 990) and bring a picnic.

Tours also go to destinations such as Parque Nacional Pali Aike.

Recommended agencies:

Fantastico Sur (☎ 710050; www.fantasticosur.com; Magallanes 960)

Inhóspita Patagonia (☎ 224510; Lautaro Navarro 1013) Offers trekking trips to Cabo Froward, the southernmost point on mainland South America.

Turismo Aonikenk (☎ 228332; www.aonikenk.com; Magallanes 619) English-, German- and French-speaking guides.

Turismo Pali Aike (☎ 223301; www.turismopaliaike .com; Lautaro Navarro 1129)

Turismo Pehoé (☎ 241373; www.pehoe.com; José Menéndez 918)

Turismo Viento Sur (☎ 226930; www.vientosur.com; Fagnano 565)

Turismo Yamana (☎ 221130; www.yamana.cl; Errázuriz 932) Kayaking trips on Magellan Strait.

Whale Sound (☎ 221076; www.whalesound.com; Lautaro Navarro 1163) Supports science with study-based sailing and kayak trips to the remote Coloane Marine Park.

Sleeping
Thanks to the cruise-ship traffic, there's an explosion of new hotels, B&Bs and hostels in Punta Arenas – too many to list, in fact. The following list is just a sample of the options in and around town. The rates at midrange and top-end establishments include breakfast but don't reflect the additional 18% IVA charge, which foreigners in Chile aren't required to pay if paying with US cash, traveler's checks or credit card. Off-season (mid-April to mid-October) rates can drop by up to 40%.

BUDGET
Hospedaje Independencia (☎ 227572; www.hostal independencia.es.tl; Av Independencia 374; campsites/dm CH$2000/5000) Shoestring travelers pack this cheaper-than-cheap lodging, run by a young couple. Rooms are good, the atmosphere is casual, and guests get kitchen use and reasonable bike rentals.

El Conventillo (☎ 242311; www.hostalelconventillo .com; Pasaje Korner 1034; dm CH$8500; 🖳) This cool brick hostel in the reviving waterfront district has remodeled carpeted dorms and clean row showers. Bright colors mask the fact that there is little interior light; rooms are windowless. Yogurt and cereal are part of a big breakfast.

Hostal Fitz Roy (☎ 240430; www.hostalfitzroy.com; Lautaro Navarro 850; dm/s/d/tr without bathroom CH$9000/14,000/22,000/27,000; 🖳) This country house in the city offers rambling, good-value rooms and an inviting, old-fashioned living room to pore over books or sea charts. Rooms have phones and TVs.

Hostel Keoken (☎ 244086; www.hostelkeoken.cl, in Spanish; Magallanes 209; s/d without bathroom CH$9000/23,800, with bathroom CH$15,000/24,900 🖳) Increasingly popular with backpackers, Hostel Keoken features comfortable beds topped with fluffy white down comforters and homemade pastries for breakfast. The center of town is a few minutes away on foot.

Amanecer Austral (www.amaneceraustral.cl; Boliviana 533; s/d CH$10,000/18,000, f ste CH$30,000; 🖳) Travelers praise the filling breakfast and silent but central location of this hostel-like guesthouse, where all rooms are private but most share bathrooms (the family suite has its own bathroom). Free car parking and laundry facilities add to the appeal.

Al Fin del Mundo (☎ 710185; www.alfindelmundo.cl; O'Higgins 1026; s/d/tr CH$16,700/28,000/36,500) On the 2nd and 3rd floors of a downtown building, these rooms are cheerful but due for recarpeting. All share bathrooms with hot showers and a large kitchen, as well as a living area with a large TV and DVD library.

Hostal Bustamante (☎ 222774; www.hostalbustamante.cl; Jorge Montt 847; s/d CH$25,000/30,000; 🖳) This quaint, slightly creaky wooden house boasts a sweeping staircase and a leafy breakfast room where tea and coffee are available to guests all day. Doubles are basic affairs with cable TV; each has a small private bathroom, many with gleaming new shower stalls that were recently added.

MIDRANGE

Hostal Calafate (☎ 241281; www.calafate.cl; Magallanes 922; s/d without bathroom CH$17,500/27,500, with bathroom CH$27,000/36,500; 🖳) This downtown hub bustles with traffic. Guests can choose from a selection of plain but good rooms that are not quite insulated from the street noise below. Perks include phones, TVs and central heating.

Hostal Terrasur (☎ 247114; www.hostalterrasur.cl; O'Higgins 723; s/d CH$24,000/30,000; 🖳) The slightly upscale Terrasur nurtures a secret-garden atmosphere, from its rooms with flowing curtains and flower patterns to the miniature green courtyard.

Hotel Mercurio (☎ 242300; www.chileaustral.com/mercurio; Fagnano 595; s/d/tr CH$26,000/35,000/50,000; 🖳) A well-kept and proper corner hotel with wide staircases and slightly dated stucco rooms. Staff are bilingual and very accommodating.

Hostal de la Patagonia (☎ 249970; www.ecotourpatagonia.com; O'Higgins 730; s/d CH$30,500/35,500) This unmistakable turquoise lodging offers a number of sunny rooms with light wood accents, and a decent buffet breakfast.

Hostal Carpa Manzano (☎ 710744; www.hotelcarpamanzano.com; Lautaro Navarro 336; s/d CH$35,500/43,100) These snappily colored rooms feature private bathroom, carpet and cable TV. A comfortable house, it's run more like a hotel, with uniformed staff and a certain formality.

Ilaia Hotel (☎ 223592; www.ilaia.cl; Ignacio Carrera Pinto 351; s/d CH$38,000/48,000) Ilaia is a hotel, yes, but it's also a high-concept retreat: yoga sessions and healthy breakfasts are on offer and the decor is ecochic (and TV-free.) The garden with fireplace – and a living area with picture windows facing the Strait of Magellan – are designed to promote quiet meditation.

Hotel Isla Rey Jorge (☎ 248220; www.hotelislareyjorge.com; 21 de Mayo 1243; s/d CH$43,100/53,300; 🖳) Elegant and relaxed, this 1918 house exudes character; we just wonder about the cannon on the lawn. Traditional British style fills 25 attractive rooms and a sun room for reading.

TOP END

Hotel Plaza (☎ 241300; www.hotelplaza.cl; Nogueira 1116; s/d CH$47,200/58,300; 🖳) This converted mansion boasts vaulted ceilings, plaza views and historical photos lining the hall. Inconsistent with such grandeur, the country decor is unfortunate. But service is genteel and the location unbeatable.

Hotel Cabo de Hornos (☎ 242134; www.hoteles-australis.com/cabo_hornos/html/ingles.asp; Plaza Muñoz Gamero 1039; s/d CH$83,700/99,000; ✕ 🖳) This smart business hotel begins with a cool interior of slate and sharp angles, but rooms are more relaxed, with bright color accents and top-notch views. The well-heeled bar just beckons you to have a whisky.

Hotel José Nogueira (☎ 711000; www.hotelnogueira.com; Bories 959; s/d CH$86,200/96,400; 🖳) This high-end hotel in the Sara Braun mansion lacks the original grandeur, but staff ghost sightings and the beautiful atrium dining room rescue some of the romance. Modern amenities combine with period furnishings in rooms.

Eating

The port's seasonal seafood is an exquisite treat: go for *centolla* (king crab) between July and November or *erizos* (sea urchins) between November and July. If heading to Torres del Paine, get groceries here beforehand.

Lomit's (☎ 243399; José Menéndez 722; mains CH$3000-4000; ☻ 10am-2:30am) Chile's answer to the side-car diner is this atmospheric cafe where cooks flip made-to-order burgers at a center-stage griddle.

Sabores (☎ 227369; Mejicana 702, 2nd fl; mains CH$3000-5000; ☻ 10:30am-midnight) Lacking pretension, this cozy second-story restaurant serves up hearty Chilean fare, grilled fish, pasta and seafood stews to a full house. Skip the house wine but don't miss the *machas a la parmesana* (razor clams baked in parmesan.)

La Luna (☎ 228555; www.laluna.cl; O'Higgins 1017; mains ARS4000-7000) This local favorite, known for fresh seafood dishes and a lively, colorful atmosphere, is becoming a little too touristy – but non-Spanish-speaking travelers will appreciate the multilingual staff when trying to decide between scallops stewed in garlicky sauce and *chupe de centolla* (crab casserole).

La Marmita (☎ 222056; Plaza Sampaio 678; mains CH$5000-8000; ☻ lunch & dinner Mon-Sat) Unbeatable for its ambience as well as its tasty fare, Marmita has fresh salads and hearty, home-cooked creations.

Sotito's (☎ 243565; O'Higgins 1138; mains CH$5000-10,000; ☻ lunch & dinner) This seafood institution is popular with moneyed locals and cruise-ship travelers in search of a classy king crab feast. The decor isn't inspiring but the cuisine won't disappoint.

our pick Damiana Elena (☎ 222818; Magallanes 341; mains CH$7000-9000; ☻ dinner Mon-Sat) This elegant restaurant is located in a romantic old house, off the beaten path in a residential neighborhood. The detour is worth it for the warm, sophisticated ambience and first-rate Chilean cuisine: highlights include the salmon ceviche and the grilled tilapia.

Also recommended:

O'Sole Mio (☎ 242026; O'Higgins 974) Casual eatery with a good selection of inexpensive pasta.

Pachamama (☎ 226171; Magallanes 619A) Bulk trail-mix munchies and organic products.

Drinking

La Taberna (☎ 241317; Sara Braun Mansion, Plaza Muñoz Gamero; ☻ 7pm-2am, to 3am weekends) This dark and elegant subterranean bar, with polished wood fixtures and cozy nooks reminiscent of an old-fashioned ship, is a classic old-boys' club. The rooms fill with cigar smoke later in the evening, but the opportunity to sip pisco sours in the classy Sara Braun Mansion shouldn't be missed.

Olijoe Pub (☎ 223728; Errázuriz 970; ☻ 6pm-2am) Leather booths and mosaic tabletops lend pretension, but this is your usual pub with good beer and bad service. Mix it up with the house special, Glaciar – a mix of pisco, *horchata* (cinnamon rice milk), milk and curaçao.

El Madero (Bories 655) A warm-up spot for clubbers, Madero gets packed with crowds sipping stiff drinks.

Entertainment

Kamikaze (☎ 248744; Bories 655; cover incl 1 free drink CH$3000) Tiki torches warm up this most southerly dance club and, if you're lucky, the occasional live rock band. Upstairs from El Madero.

Cine Estrella (Mejicana 777) Shows first-run movies.

Getting There & Away

The tourist offices distribute a useful brochure that details all forms of transport available.

AIR

Punta Arenas' airport (PUQ) is 21km north of town.

LanChile (☎ 241100, 600-526-2000; www.lan.com; Lautaro Navarro 999) flies several times daily to Santiago (CH$204,000) with a stop in Puerto Montt (CH$130,000), and on Saturday to the Falkland Islands (roundtrip CH$354,000). A new service goes direct to Ushuaia (CH$115,500) three times a week. For national flights, book ahead online for the best deals. **Aerolineas Argentina** (☎ 0810-222-86527; www.aerolineas.com.ar) offers flights to various cities in Argentina.

From November to March, **Aerovías DAP** (☎ 223340, airport 213776; www.dap.cl; O'Higgins 891) flies to Porvenir (CH$20,000) Monday through Saturday, and to Puerto Williams (CH$55,000) Wednesday through Saturday and Monday. Luggage is limited to 10kg per person. DAP also offers charter flights over Cape Horn (seven-passenger plane CH$1,825,000) and to other Patagonian destinations, including Ushuaia and El Calafate.

BOAT

The car ferry *Melinka*, operated by **Transbordador Austral Broom** (☎ 218100; www.tabsa.cl; Av Bulnes 05075), sails to Porvenir in Tierra

PATAGONIA

THE FALKLAND ISLANDS/ISLAS MALVINAS

☎ 500 / pop 3200 permanent nonmilitary, 600,000 sheep

The sheep boom in Tierra del Fuego and Patagonia owes its origins to a cluster of islands 500km to the east in the South Atlantic Ocean. Known as Las Islas Malvinas to the Argentines or the Falkland Islands to the British, they had been explored, but never fully captured the interest of either country until Europe's mid-19th-century wool boom. After the Falkland Islands Company (FIC) became the islands' largest landholder, the islands' population of stranded gauchos and mariners grew rapidly with the arrival of English and Scottish immigrants. In an unusual exchange, in 1853 the South American Missionary Society began transporting Yaghan Indians from Tierra del Fuego to Keppel Island to proselytize them.

Argentina has laid claim to the islands since 1833, but it wasn't until 1982 that Argentine President Leopoldo Galtieri, then drowning in economic chaos and allegations of corruption, decided that reclaiming the islands would unite his country behind him. However, British Prime Minister Margaret Thatcher (also suffering in the polls) didn't hesitate in striking back, thoroughly humiliating Argentina in what became known as the Falklands War. A severe blow to Argentina's nationalist pride, the ill-fated war succeeded in severing all diplomatic ties between the two nations.

On July 14, 1999, a joint statement issued by the British, Falkland Islands and Argentine governments promised closer cooperation on areas of economic mutual interest. In August 2001, British Prime Minister Tony Blair visited Argentina in an effort to further improve ties between the countries. Nevertheless, relations with Argentina remain cool, with most South American trade going via Chile.

Besides their status as an unusually polemical piece of property, what do the Falklands offer the intrepid traveler? Bays, inlets, estuaries and beaches create a tortuous, attractive coastline flanked by abundant wildlife. Striated and crested caracaras, cormorants, oystercatchers, snowy sheathbills and a plethora of penguins – Magellanic, rockhopper, macaroni, gentoo and king – share top billing with elephant seals, sea lions, fur seals, five dolphin species and killer whales.

Stanley (population 2000), the islands' capital on East Falkland, is an assemblage of brightly painted metal-clad houses and a good place to throw down a few pints and listen to island lore. 'Camp' – as the rest of the islands are known – hosts settlements that began as company towns (hamlets where coastal shipping could collect wool) and now provide rustic backcountry lodging and a chance to experience pristine nature and wildlife. Though there are 400km of roads, the islands have no street lights.

Planning

The best time to visit is from October to March, when migratory birds (including penguins) and marine mammals return to the beaches and headlands. The first cruise ships to South Georgia and Antarctica turn up in early November and the last ones depart around the end of March. It's worth visiting during the annual sports meetings, which feature horse racing, bull riding and sheepdog trials. The events take place in Stanley between Christmas and New Year, and on East and West Falkland at the end of the shearing season, usually in late February. Summer never gets truly hot (the maximum high is 24°C or 75°F), but high winds can bring a chill to the air. For more details, pick up Lonely Planet's *Antarctica* guide.

Information

Stanley's **Jetty Visitors Centre** (☎ 27019; jettycentre@horizon.co.fk), at the public jetty on Ross Rd, distributes excellent brochures describing activities in and around Stanley. The *Visitor Accommodation Guide* lists lodgings and camping areas around the Islands. Another helpful source of information is **Falkland Islands Tourism** (☎ 22215; www.visitorfalklands.com). In the UK, contact **Falkland House** (☎ 020-7222-2542; www.falklandislands.com; 14 Broadway, Westminster, London SW1H 0BH).

Visas & Documents

Visitors from Britain and Commonwealth countries, the EU, North America, Mercosur countries and Chile don't need visas. If coming from another country, check with the British consulate. All nationalities must carry a valid passport, an onward ticket and proof of sufficient funds (credit cards are fine) and pre-arranged accommodations. In practice, arrivals who don't have prebooked accommodations are held in the arrivals area while rooms are found.

Money

There's no ATM on the Falklands and only one bank in Stanley, so bring plenty of cash. Pounds sterling and US dollars in cash or traveler's checks are readily accepted, but the exchange rate for US currency is low. There's no need to change money to Falkland pounds (FK£), which are not accepted off the islands. In peak season, expect to spend US$150 to US$300 per day, not including airfare; less if camping or staying in self-catering cottages.

Getting There & Away

From South America, **LanChile** (www.lan.com) flies to Mt Pleasant International Airport (MPA; near Stanley) every Saturday from Santiago, Chile, via Puerto Montt, Punta Arenas and – one Saturday each month – Río Gallegos, Argentina. Roundtrip fares are CH$455,000 from Santiago and CH$354,000 from Punta Arenas with advance booking.

From **RAF Brize Norton** (www.raf.mod.uk/rafbrizenorton), in Oxfordshire, England, there are regular Royal Air Force flights to Mt Pleasant (18 hours, including a two-hour refueling stop on tiny Ascension Island in the South Atlantic). Roundtrip fares are UK£2222. Travelers continuing on to Chile can purchase one-way tickets for half the fare. Bookings from the UK can be made through the **Falkland Islands Government Office** (☎ 020-7222-2542; fax 020-7222-2375; travel@figo.u-net.com; Falkland House, 14 Broadway, Westminster, London SW1H 0BH). Payment can be by cash or by personal or bank check; credit cards are not accepted. On each flight only 28 seats are reserved for nonmilitary personnel.

Getting Around

From Stanley, **Figas** (☎ 27219; figas.fig@horizon.co.fk) serves outlying destinations in eight-seater aircraft. Travel within the Falklands costs around US$3 per minute.

Several Stanley operators run day trips to East Falkland settlements, including **Discovery Tours** (☎ 21027; www.discoveryfalklands.com) and **South Atlantic Marine Services** (☎ 21145; www .falklands-underwater.com).

Falkland Frontiers (☎ 51561; falklandfrontiers@horizon.co.fk) conducts fishing and wildlife tours. **Adventure Falklands** (☎ 21383; pwatts@horizon.co.fk) specializes in wildlife (featuring king, gentoo and Magellanic penguins) and historical tours.

Trekking and camping are feasible; however, there are no designated trails and getting lost is not unheard of. Always seek permission before entering private land.

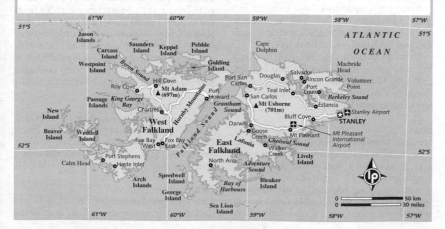

del Fuego (CH$4900, 2½ to four hours) from the Tres Puentes ferry terminal north of town; catch taxi *colectivos* in front of Museo Regional Braun-Menéndez. Boats usually depart in the early morning and return in the late afternoon; schedules and travel time depend on the mercurial weather. Make reservations to ferry your vehicle (CH$31,300) by calling the office.

A faster way to get to Tierra del Fuego is the Punta Delgada–Bahía Azul ('Cruce Primera Angostura') crossing, northeast of Punta Arenas. Broom ferries (CH$1600, 20 minutes) sail every 90 minutes between 8:30am and 11:45pm. Call ahead for vehicle reservations (CH$13,900).

Broom is also the agent for ferries from Tres Puentes to Puerto Williams (reclining seat/bunk CH$88,800/106,500 including meals, 38 hours), on Isla Navarino. Ferries sail three or four times per month on Wednesday only, returning Saturday, both at 7pm. Trust us, the extra cost of a bunk is worthwhile.

From September to May, **Cruceros Australis** (☎ in Santiago 02-442-3110; www.australis.com) runs breathtakingly scenic four- to seven-day luxury cruises aboard the 130-passenger MV *Mare Australis* and brand-new MV *Via Australis* from Punta Arenas through the Cordillera de Darwin, Parque Nacional Alberto de Agostini, the Beagle Channel and Puerto Williams to Ushuaia (Argentina), and back. Rates for four nights start from CH$979,000 per person (double occupancy) in low season (September–October and mid-March–April) and reach CH$2,025,000 for a high-season single. Most passengers only sail one leg. Departures from Ushuaia include a possibility of disembarking at Cape Horn. **Turismo Comapa** (☎ 200200; www.comapa.com; Magallanes 990) handles local bookings.

Navimag (☎ 200200; www.navimag.com; Magallanes 990), which runs ferries from Puerto Natales to Puerto Montt via the spectacular Chilean fjords, is also represented by Comapa. For fares and schedules, see p503.

BUS
A central terminal is perennially promised. In the meantime, buses depart from company offices, most within a block or two of Av Colón. Buy tickets at least a couple of hours (if not a day or two during summer) in advance. The **Central de Pasajeros** (☎ 245811; cnr Magallanes & Av Colón) is the closest thing to a central booking office.

For Ushuaia, Ghisoni continues direct, but travelers report Pacheco stops too long in Río Grande. In Río Grande, minivans (Lider or Transportes Montiel) go to Ushuaia throughout the day and may cost slightly less (depending on exchange rates) than a through ticket.

Companies and daily destinations include the following:

Bus Sur (☎ 614224; www.bus-sur.cl; José Menéndez 552) El Calafate, Puerto Natales, Río Gallegos, Río Turbio, Ushuaia and Puerto Montt.

Bus Transfer (☎ 229613; Pedro Montt 966) Puerto Natales and airport transfers.

Buses Fernández/Buses Pingüino (☎ 221429/812; www.busesfernandez.com; Armando Sanhueza 745) Puerto Natales, Torres del Paine and Río Gallegos.

Buses Ghisoni/Queilen Bus (☎ 223205; Lautaro Navarro 971) Río Gallegos, Río Grande, Ushuaia and Puerto Montt.

Buses Pacheco (☎ 242174; www.busespacheco.com; Av Colón 900) Puerto Natales, Puerto Montt, Río Gallegos, Río Grande and Ushuaia.

Tecni-Austral (☎ 222078; Lautaro Navarro 975) Río Grande.

Turibus (☎ 227990; www.busescruzdelsur.cl, in Spanish; Armando Sanhueza 745) Puerto Montt, Osorno and Chiloé.

Destination	Cost (CH$)	Duration (hr)
Puerto Montt	44,000	36
Puerto Natales	4500	3
Río Gallegos	7800	5-8
Río Grande	15,500	7
Ushuaia	26,000	10

Getting Around
TO/FROM THE AIRPORT
To get to Puerto Natales, there's no need to go into town since buses depart directly from the airport. **Turismo Sandy Point** (☎ 222241; Pedro Montt 840) runs door-to-door shuttle services (CH$3500) to/from town to coincide with flights. Buses Fernández does regular airport transfers (AR$3000), and Aerovías DAP also provides a shuttle service (CH$2000).

BUS & TAXI COLECTIVO
Taxi *colectivos,* with numbered routes, are only slightly more expensive than buses (about CH$700, or a bit more late at night and on Sundays), far more comfortable and much quicker.

CAR
Cars are a good option for exploring Torres del Paine, but renting one in Chile to cross the

border into Argentina can become prohibitively expensive due to international insurance requirements. If heading for El Calafate, it is best to rent your vehicle in Argentina. Purchasing a car to explore Patagonia has its drawbacks, as Chilean Patagonia has no through roads that link northern and southern Patagonia, so it is entirely dependent on the roads of Argentina or expensive ferry travel.

Punta Arenas has Chilean Patagonia's most economical rental rates, and locally owned agencies tend to provide better service. Recommended **Adel Rent a Car/Localiza** (☎ 235471/2, 09-882-7569; www.adel.cl; Pedro Montt 962) provides attentive service, competitive rates, airport pickup and good travel tips. Other choices include **Budget** (☎ 225983; O'Higgins 964), **Hertz** (☎ 248742; O'Higgins 987) and **Lubag** (☎ 710484; Magallanes 970).

AROUND PUNTA ARENAS
Penguin Colonies
There are two substantial Magellanic penguin colonies near Punta Arenas. Easier to reach is **Seno Otway** (Otway Sound), with about 6000 breeding pairs, about an hour northwest of the city. The larger (50,000 breeding pairs) and more interesting **Monumento Natural Los Pingüinos** is accessible only by boat to Isla Magdalena in the Strait of Magellan (see p493). Neither is as impressive as the larger penguin colonies in Argentina or the Falkland Islands. Tours to Seno Otway usually leave in the afternoon; however, visiting in the morning is best for photography because the birds are mostly backlit in the afternoon.

Since there is no scheduled public transport to either site, it's necessary to rent a car or join a tour. Admission to Seno Otway is CH$4500, while admission to Isla Magdalena is included in the tour price. Of the two options, the trip to Isla Magdalena is more often recommended. If driving independently, pay attention as you head north on Ruta 9 (RN 9) – it's easy to miss the small sign indicating the turn-off to the penguin colony.

Río Verde
☎ 61 / pop 300
About 50km north of Punta Arenas, a graveled lateral leads northwest toward Seno Skyring (Skyring Sound), passing this former sector of *estancias* before rejoining Ruta 9 at Villa Tehuelches at Km 100. Only visitors with a car

should consider this interesting detour to one of the region's best-maintained assemblages of Magellanic architecture.

Ranch life spills from the pores of **Estancia Río Verde** (☎ 311131/23; www.estanciarioverde.cl; Ruta Y50, Km 97), an interesting stop on the shores of Seno Skyring. English-speaking hosts Josefina and Sergio keep a relaxed atmosphere and manage to be gracious hosts while also running the ranch. A ride around the property affords a close look at operations on this sheep *estancia*, which also breeds fine Chilean horses. Sailing, fishing and sightseeing trips are also arranged. Passersby can stop for lunch (CH$15,000) and check out the small museum. It's 43km north of Punta Arenas via Ruta 9; follow gravel road Y50 to Km 97.

Río Rubens
Roughly midway between Villa Tehuelches and Puerto Natales on blustery, paved Ruta 9, Río Rubens is a fine trout-fishing area and, for travelers with their own transport, an ideal spot to break the 250km journey from Punta Arenas.

Hotel Río Rubens (☎ 09-640-1583; Ruta 9, Km 183; s/d CH$12,000/18,000, cabins CH$45,000) is a comfy, welcoming, old country-style inn that offers good rates but can be hard to contact. The restaurant serves outstanding meals, including lamb and seafood.

Parque Nacional Pali Aike
Rugged volcanic steppe pocked with craters, caves and twisted formations, Pali Aike, translated from the Tehuelche language, means 'devil's country.' This dry and desolate landscape is a 50-sq-km park along the Argentine border, west of the Monte Aymond border crossing to Río Gallegos. Lava rocks are red, yellow or green-gray, depending on their mineral content, while fauna includes abundant guanacos, ñandús, gray foxes, armadillos and bats. In the 1930s Junius Bird's excavations at 17m-deep **Cueva Pali Aike** (Pali Aike Cave) yielded the first Paleo-Indian artifacts associated with extinct New World fauna such as the milodón and the native horse *Onohippidium*.

The **park** (admission CH$2000) has several hiking trails, including a 1.7km path through the rugged lava beds of the **Escorial del Diablo** to the impressive **Crater Morada del Diablo**; wear sturdy shoes or your feet could be shredded. There are hundreds of craters, some as

PATAGONIA

high as a four-story building. There's also a 9km trail from Cueva Pali Aike to **Laguna Ana**, where there's another shorter trail to a site on the main road, 5km from the park entrance.

The *portería* (entrance gate) has a basic **refugio** (CH$6000) that holds four guests.

Parque Nacional Pali Aike is 200km northeast of Punta Arenas via Ch (rural road) 9, Ch 255 and a graveled secondary road from Cooperativa Villa O'Higgins, 11km north of Estancia Kimiri Aike. There's also an access road from the Chilean border post at Monte Aymond. There is no public transport, but Punta Arenas travel agencies (p493) offer full-day tours from CH$42,000.

PUERTO NATALES

☎ 61 / pop 15,800

On the windswept shores of Seno Última Esperanza (Last Hope Sound), this once-dreary fishing village now lives under assault by Gore-tex and Vibram soles, as it is the well-trodden hub of the continent's number-one national park, Torres del Paine. But Natales still manages to maintain backwater charm (especially in the shoulder seasons), even though the tourist industry is transforming its rusted tin shopfronts one by one into gleaming facades.

The town sits at the edge of a magnificent frontier of wilderness whose accessibility continually increases. The Navimag ferry through Chile's fjords ends and begins its trips here. Located 250km northwest of Punta Arenas via Ruta 9, Puerto Natales also offers frequent transport to El Calafate, Argentina.

Information
BOOKSTORES
World's End (☎ 414725; Blanco Encalada 226-A) Tip-of-the-world souvenirs, books and Torres trekking maps.

INTERNET RESOURCES
www.torresdelpaine.cl The best bilingual portal for the region.

LAUNDRY
Most hostels also offer laundry service.
Servilaundry (☎ 412869; Arturo Prat 337) Full-service laundry.

MEDICAL SERVICES
Hospital (☎ 411582; Pinto 537)

MONEY
Most banks in town have ATMs.
Gasic (Bulnes 692) Decent rates on cash and traveler's checks.

POST
Post office (Eberhard 429)

TELEPHONE & INTERNET ACCESS
Internet is widespread but slow throughout town.
Call Center Entel (Baquedano 270) Telephone office.

TOURIST INFORMATION
Conaf (☎ 411438; Baquedano 847) National parks service administrative office.
Municipal tourist office (☎ 614808; Bulnes 285; ☽ 8:30am-12:30pm & 2:30-6pm Tue-Sun) In the Museo Histórico, with attentive staff and region-wide lodgings listings.
Sernatur (☎ 412125; infonatales@sernatur.cl; Pedro Montt 19; ☽ 9am-7pm) Not as helpful as the municipal tourist office.

TRAVEL AGENCIES & TOURS
Most travel agencies ply similar services: park tours, maps and equipment rental. The following have some bilingual staff:
Antares Patagonia (☎ 414611; www.antarespatagonia.com; Barros Arana 111) Specializes in trekking in El Calafate, El Chaltén and Torres del Paine. Can facilitate climbing permits, science expeditions and made-to-order trips.
Baqueano Zamora (☎ 613530; Baquedano 534) Runs horseback-riding trips and owns the Posada Río Serrano in Torres del Paine.
Erratic Rock (☎ 410355; www.erraticrock.com; Baquedano 719) Offers good park information, talks and gear rentals. Guide service specializes in treks to Cabo Froward and Isla Navarino, as well as lesser-known destinations.
Fortaleza Expediciones (☎ 613395; www.fortalezapatagonia.cl; Tomás Rogers 235) Knowledgeable; rents camping gear.
Indomita Big Foot (☎ 414525; www.indomitapatagonia.com; Bories 206) Popular kayaking, trekking and mountaineering trips, plus ice- and rock-climbing seminars.
Knudsen Tour (☎ 414747; knudsentour@yahoo.com; Blanco Encalada 284) Well regarded, with trips to El Calafate, Torres del Paine and alternative routes along Seno Último Esperanza.
Path@gone (☎ 413291; Eberhard 595) Reserve *refugios*, campsites and transport to Torres del Paine.
Turismo 21 de Mayo (☎ 411978; www.turismo21demayo.cl, in Spanish; Eberhard 560) Organizes day-trip cruises and treks to the Balmaceda and Serrano glaciers.

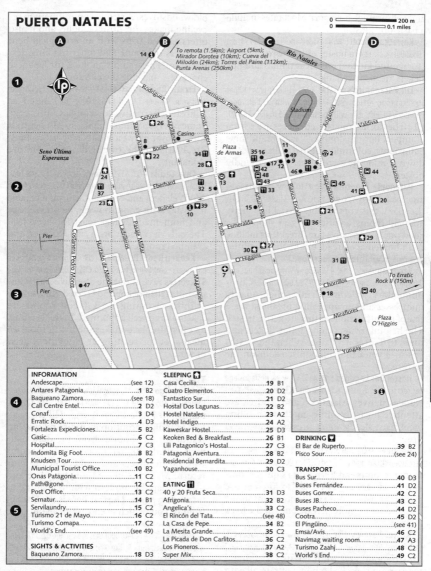

PUERTO NATALES

0   200 m
0   0.1 miles

PATAGONIA

INFORMATION	
Andescape	(see 12)
Antares Patagonia	1 B2
Baqueano Zamora	(see 18)
Call Centre Entel	2 D2
Conaf	3 D4
Erratic Rock	4 D3
Fortaleza Expediciones	5 B2
Gasic	6 C2
Hospital	7 C3
Indomita Big Foot	8 B2
Knudsen Tour	9 C2
Municipal Tourist Office	10 B2
Onas Patagonia	11 C2
Path@gone	12 C2
Post Office	13 C2
Sernatur	14 B1
Servilaundry	15 C2
Turismo 21 de Mayo	16 C2
Turismo Comapa	17 C2
World's End	(see 49)

SIGHTS & ACTIVITIES	
Baqueano Zamora	18 D3

SLEEPING	
Casa Cecilia	19 B1
Cuatro Elementos	20 D2
Fantastico Sur	21 D2
Hostal Dos Lagunas	22 B2
Hostel Natales	23 A2
Hotel Indigo	24 A2
Kaweskar Hostel	25 D3
Keoken Bed & Breakfast	26 B1
Lili Patagonico's Hostal	27 C3
Patagonia Aventura	28 B2
Residencial Bernardita	29 D2
Yaganhouse	30 C3

EATING	
40 y 20 Fruta Seca	31 D3
Afrigonia	32 B2
Angelica's	33 C2
El Rincón del Tata	(see 48)
La Casa de Pepe	34 B2
La Mesita Grande	35 B2
La Picada de Don Carlitos	36 C2
Los Pioneros	37 A2
Super Mix	38 C2

DRINKING	
El Bar de Ruperto	39 B2
Pisco Sour	(see 24)

TRANSPORT	
Bus Sur	40 D3
Buses Fernández	41 D2
Buses Gomez	42 C2
Buses JB	43 C2
Buses Pacheco	44 D2
Cootra	45 D2
El Pingüino	(see 41)
Emsa/Avis	46 C2
Navimag waiting room	47 A3
Turismo Zaahj	48 C2
World's End	49 C2

Turismo Comapa (☎ 414300; www.comapa.com; Eberhard 555; ⏰ 9am-1pm & 3-7pm Mon-Fri, 10am-2pm Sat) Navimag ferry and airline bookings.

Sleeping

For a small town, Puerto Natales brims with lodgings. Prices at nonbudget establishments don't reflect the additional 19% IVA (which foreigners don't have to pay if they use US dollars or credit cards). In the off-season, many places drop prices by as much as 40%. Reserve ahead if you are arriving on the ferry.

BUDGET

Many budget accommodations are in quirky family homes. Hostels often rent equipment and help arrange transport. Most rates include a basic breakfast.

Kaweskar Hostel (☎ 414553; Blanco Encalada 754; dm CH$3000) A bargain hostel with bare rooms, bag storage and kitchen use. Gear rentals and bus tickets are also available.

Lili Patagonico's Hostal (☎ 414063; www.lilipat agonicos.com; Arturo Prat 479; dm/d without bathroom CH$4500/10,000, d/tr with bathroom CH$16,000/24,000; 🖳) The dorms and shared spaces are a little cramped, but the doubles – with brand-new bathrooms, colorfully painted walls and cozy down comforters – are a steal at this friendly hostel.

Patagonia Aventura (☎ 411028; www.apatagonia .com; Tomás Rogers 179; dm/d CH$9000/21,000; 🖳) On the plaza, this comfortable hostel has small, ambient rooms, an attached gear shop and a good cafe with creative fare. Breakfasts include fresh homemade bread, but kitchen facilities are not available for guest use.

Yaganhouse (☎ 415553; www.yaganhouse.cl; O'Higgins 584; dm/d CH$10,000/$22,000; 🖳) Complimentary welcome drinks, high-quality mattresses and an appealing breakfast are a few of the attractions at this attractive hostel. The helpful owners can sell bus tickets and tours to Torres del Paine. When the weather's nice you can drink a pisco sour on the terrace.

Hostal Dos Lagunas (☎ 415733; www.hostadoslagu nas.com; cnr Barros Arana & Bories; dm/d CH$10,000/$25,000) Natales natives Alejandro and Andrea are attentive hosts, spoiling guests with filling breakfasts, steady water pressure and travel tips.

Residencial Bernardita (☎ 411162; www.residencial bernardita.cl; O'Higgins 765; s/d CH$12,000/20,000) Guests highly recommend Bernardita's quiet rooms and good service. There's also kitchen use and breakfast. Choose between rooms in the main house or more private ones in the back annex.

Hostel Natales (☎ 414731; www.hostelnatales.cl; Ladrilleros 209; dm/d/tr CH$15,400/44,000/64,000; 🖳) This tranquil green inn boasts tasteful and toasty rooms, decked out in neutrals, all with private bathroom. It doesn't have the energy of other hostels, but dorms are good value.

MIDRANGE
Cuatro Elementos (☎ 415751; www.4elementos.cl, in Spanish; Esmeralda 813; s/d/tr CH$25,000/30,000/42,000) Rooms are few and spare in this ecofriendly house crafted of recycled zinc, driftwood and

old woodstoves. A strong commitment to recycling makes this hostel unique, and it also offers guided trips with an ecological bent to Torres del Paine and other trekking destinations. There's no sign: look for Japanese characters marking the entrance.

Erratic Rock II (☎ 414317; www.erraticrock2.com; Benjamin Zamora 732; d CH$30,000; 🖳) Billed as a 'hostel alternative for couples,' this cozy home offers spacious doubles in soft neutrals with throw pillows and tidy new bathrooms. Breakfasts in the bright dining room are abundant.

Casa Cecilia (☎ 613560; www.casaceciliahostal.com; Tomás Rogers 60; d with/without bathroom CH$35,000/24,000; ✗) Well kept and central, Cecilia is a reliable mainstay with good showers, helpful service and homemade wheat toast for breakfast. The only drawbacks are a small kitchen and cramped rooms.

Keoken Bed & Breakfast (☎ 413670; www.keoken patagonia.com; Señoret 267; s/d CH$40,000/50,000; 🖳) Travelers rave about the attentive staff, simple but stylish decor and relaxed atmosphere at this welcoming B&B. Guest rooms are spacious and well appointed. In the evening, an open fireplace makes the living room an ideal spot for reading or enjoying a glass of wine.

TOP END
Hotel Indigo (☎ 413609; www.indigopatagonia.com; Ladrilleros 105; d/ste CH$132,000/147,000; ✗ 🖳) A pampered finale to your trip. Hikers head first to Indigo's rooftop Jacuzzis and spa, but restful spaces abound, from the dark hallways dotted with hammocks to plush rooms with down duvets and candles lit for your return. Materials like eucalyptus, slate and iron overlap the modern with the natural to interesting effect. The star here is the fjord in front of you, which even captures your gaze in the shower.

remota (☎ 414040, bookings in Santiago 02-387-1500; www.remota.cl; Ruta 9, Km 1.5; s/d 2 nights CH$750,600/1,047,000; 🖳 🖳) Unlike most hotels, the exclusive remota draws your awareness to what's outside: silence broadcasts the gusty winds, irregular window patterns imitate old stock fences and a crooked passageway pays tribute to *estancia* sheep corridors. Though rooms are cozy, you'll probably want to spend all your time at 'the beach' – a glass-walled barn room with lounge futons to gape at the wild surroundings.

Eating

La Picada de Don Carlitos (☎ 415496; Blanco Encalada 444; menú del día CH$3000; ☽ lunch & dinner) Hearty Chilean fare, like chicken and heaped mashed potatoes, is served at this down-home eatery bursting with locals at lunchtime. Try the fantastic *caldillo de congrio* (conger eel stew.)

Los Pioneros (☎ 410783; Pedro Montt 166; mains CH$3500-5000; ☽ lunch & dinner) This modest family-owned restaurant on the waterfront offers simple seafood dishes and lovely views of snow-capped mountains when the weather is clear. Try the grilled salmon or the *paila marina*, a flavorful seafood stew.

La Casa de Pepe (☎ 410950; www.lacasadepepe -chilespezialitaeten.de/index_e.htm; Tomás Rogers 131; mains CH$4500-6000; ☽ lunch & dinner) After a blustery day in Torres del Paine, pop by this homey German-style spot on the square for hearty *pastél de papas* (a baked potato and meat pie) or a huge roast beef sandwich.

El Rincón del Tata (☎ 614291; www.turismozaahj .co.cl/eltata.htm; Arturo Prat 236; mains CH$4500-7000; ☽ noon-late) This cozy bar-restaurant is a fine place to try calafate sours, the local specialty cocktail made with the berry of the same name. The menu offers a few unexpected dishes such as shawarma as well as appealing comfort food like pumpkin soup with chicken and carrots.

La Mesita Grande (Arturo Prat 196; pizza CH$5500; ☽ lunch & dinner) Happy diners share one long, worn table for outstanding thin-crust pizza, quality pasta and organic salads.

Afrigonia (☎ 412232; Eberhard 343; mains CH$5500-7000; ☽ lunch & dinner) If you're bored with local fare, try this romantic gem. Run by a Zambian/Chilean couple, its offerings include tasty mint lamb brochettes or chicken with creamy ginger sauce, spiced to your wishes.

Angelica's (☎ 410365; cnr Arturo Prat & Bulnes; mains CH$7000-8500) With an exposed kitchen, flickering candlelight and slick service, this central eatery clearly caters to tourists – but you probably won't care about that when the *corvino en papillote* (white fish marinated in white wine and baked in a foil packet) is melting in your mouth.

Looking to pick up your own groceries? Backpackers agree that Puerto Natales has better variety than either El Chaltén or El Calafate. Shoppers can hit **40 y 20 Fruta Seca** (☎ 210661; Baquedano 443) for dried fruits and nuts perfect for the trail. A couple of full-service supermarkets are also good places to stock up on snacks.

Drinking

El Bar de Ruperto (☎ 410863; cnr Bulnes & Magallanes; ▣) Ideal for a rainy day, this typical bar entertains you with foosball, chess and other board games. Guinness and other imports help you forget you're so far from home.

Pisco Sour (Ladrilleros 105, 2nd fl; ☽ 10am-11pm; ▣) For sunset cocktails, hit this stylish bar in the Hotel Indigo complex, with gaping views of the mountain-clad sound. Innovations on the bar's namesake drink shouldn't be missed: try the Nippon pisco sour (spiked with green tea).

Getting There & Away

AIR

Aerovías DAP (www.dap.cl) offers charter flights to El Calafate, Argentina, from the small airfield (PNT), a few kilometers north of town on the road to Torres del Paine. The closest LanChile office is in Punta Arenas (p495).

BOAT

For many travelers, a journey through Chile's spectacular fjords aboard Navimag's car and passenger ferry becomes a highlight of their trip. This four-day and three-night north-bound voyage has become so popular it should be booked well in advance.

You can also try your luck. To confirm when the ferry is due, contact Turismo Comapa (p501) a couple of days before your estimated arrival date. The *Magallanes* leaves Natales early on Friday and stops in Puerto Edén (or the advancing Glaciar Pía XI on southbound sailings) en route to Puerto Montt. It usually arrives in Natales in the morning of the same day and departs either later that day or on the following day, but schedules vary according to weather conditions and tides. Disembarking passengers must stay on board while cargo is transported; those embarking have to spend the night on board.

High season is November to March, mid-season is October and April and low season is May to September. Most folks end up in dorm-style, 22-bed berths, but often wish they had sprung for a private cabin. Fares vary according to view, cabin size and private or shared bathroom, and include all meals (including veggie options if requested while booking, but bring water, snacks and drinks anyway) and interpretive talks. Per-person fares range from CH$200,000 for a bunk berth in low season to CH$1,500,000 for a triple-A cabin in high season; students and seniors receive a 10% to 15% discount. Check online (www.navimag.com) for current schedules and rates.

BUS

Puerto Natales has no central bus terminal, though several companies stop at the junction of Valdivia and Baquedano. In high season book at least a day ahead, especially for early-morning departures. Services are greatly reduced in the off-season.

A new road has been opened to Torres del Paine and, although gravel, it is much more direct. Via Terra, which provides regular transportation service into and out of the park, uses the road, as do several tour operators. This alternative entrance goes alongside Lago del Toro to the Administración (park headquarters).

Buses leave for Torres del Paine two to three times daily at around 7am, 8am and 2:30pm. Many tour agencies will also offer seats on their minibuses for discounted prices if you don't want a guided tour but need a ride. If you are headed to Mountain Lodge Paine Grande in the off-season, take the morning bus (CH$9000) to meet the catamaran (one way CH$12,500, two hours). These schedules are in constant flux, so do double-check them before heading out.

Bus Sur goes to Río Gallegos, Argentina, on Tuesday and Thursday; El Pingüino goes at 11am Wednesday and Sunday. To El Calafate, Zaahj, Cootra and Bus Sur have the most services.

Companies and destinations include the following:

Bus Sur (☎ 614220; www.bus-sur.cl, in Spanish; Baquedano 668) Punta Arenas, Torres del Paine, Puerto Montt, El Calafate, Río Turbio and Ushuaia.

Buses Fernández/El Pingüino (☎ 411111; www .busesfernandez.com; cnr Esmeralda & Ramírez) Torres del Paine and Punta Arenas.

Buses Gomez (☎ 415700; www.busesgomez.com, in Spanish; Arturo Prat 234) Torres del Paine.

Buses JB (☎ 410242; busesjb@hotmail.com; Arturo Prat 258) Torres del Paine.

Buses Pacheco (☎ 414800; www.busespacheco.com; Ramírez 224) Punta Arenas, Río Grande and Ushuaia.

Cootra (☎ 412785; Baquedano 244) El Calafate daily at 7:30am.

Turismo Zaahj (☎ 412260/355; www.turismozaahj .co.cl, in Spanish; Arturo Prat 236/270) Torres del Paine and El Calafate.

Destination	Cost (CH$)	Duration (hr)
El Calafate	12,000	5
Punta Arenas	4500	2-3
Torres del Paine	9000	2
Ushuaia	30,000	12

Getting Around

Car rental is expensive and availability is limited; you'll get better rates in Punta Arenas or Argentina. Try **Emsa/Avis** (☎ 410775; Bulnes 632). **World's End** (☎ 414725; Blanco Encalada 226-A) rents bikes.

CUEVA DEL MILODÓN

Just 24km northwest of Puerto Natales, Hermann Eberhard discovered the remains of an enormous ground sloth in the 1890s. Nearly 4m tall, the herbivorous milodón survived on the succulent leaves of small trees and branches, but became extinct in the late Pleistocene. The 30m-high **cave** (admission CH$4000) pays homage to its former inhabitant with a life-size plastic replica of the animal. It's not exactly tasteful, but still worth a stop, whether to appreciate the grand setting and ruminate over its wild past or to take an easy walk up to a lookout point.

Camping (no fires) and picnicking are possible. Torres del Paine buses pass the entrance, which is 8km from the cave proper. There are infrequent tours from Puerto Natales; alternatively, you can hitchhike or share a taxi (CH$18,000). Outside of high season, bus services are infrequent.

PARQUE NACIONAL BERNARDO O'HIGGINS

Virtually inaccessible, O'Higgins remains the elusive and exclusive home of glaciers and waterfowl. The national park can only be entered by boat. Full-day boat excursions (CH$60,000 with lunch included) to the base of Glaciar Serrano are run by **Turismo 21 de Mayo** (☎ 061-411978; www.turismo21demayo.cl, in Spanish; Eberhard 560, Puerto Natales) and longer trips by **Path@gone** (☎ 061-413291; Eberhard 595, Puerto Natales).

You can access Torres del Paine via boat to Glaciar Serrano. Passengers transfer to a Zodiac (a rubber boat with a motor), stop for lunch at Estancia Balmaceda and continue up Río Serrano, arriving at the southern border of the park by 5pm. The same tour can be done leaving the park, but may require camping near Río Serrano to catch the Zodiac at 9am. The trip costs CH$85,000 with Turismo 21

de Mayo or **Onas Patagonia** (☎ 061-614303; www
.onaspatagonia.com; Blanco Encalada 211, Puerto Natales).
The trip includes the entrance fee to Parque
Nacional Bernardo O'Higgins, but not admission or further transportation within Torres
del Paine.

If you can't decide whether to ride, paddle
or climb in the national park, look to **Antares
Patagonia Adventure** (☎ 061-414611; www.antare
spatagonia.com; Barros Arana 111, Puerto Natales) – the
agency has teamed up with **Indomita Big Foot**
(☎ 061-414525; www.indomitapatagonia.com; Bories 206,
Puerto Natales) to offer new 'Multi-Activity Sport'
tours involving combinations of horseback
riding, kayaking, trekking and mountain biking. Rates start at CH$85,000 for the shortest
trip, a one-day kayak and horseback riding
excursion, all food and equipment included.

PARQUE NACIONAL TORRES DEL PAINE
☎ 61

Soaring almost vertically to nearly 3000m
above the Patagonian steppe, the Torres del
Paine (Towers of Paine) are spectacular granite pillars that dominate the landscape of what
may be South America's finest **national park**
(www.pntp.cl, in Spanish; high/low season in Chilean pesos
only CH$15,000/5000).

Before its creation in 1959, the park was
part of a large sheep *estancia,* and it's still
recovering from nearly a century of overexploitation of its pastures, forests and wildlife.
Part of Unesco's Biosphere Reserve system
since 1978, it shelters flocks of ostrich-like
rheas (known locally as ñandús), Andean
condors, flamingos and many other bird species. The park's conservation success is most
evident with the guanaco (*Lama guanicoe),*
which grazes the open steppe where its predator, the puma, cannot approach undetected.
After over a decade of effective protection
from poachers, the large and growing herds
of guanacos don't even flinch when humans
or vehicles approach.

For hikers and trekkers, this 1810-sq-km
park is an unequaled destination. Weather can
be wildly changeable. Some say you get four
seasons in a day here, and sudden rainstorms
and knock-down gusts are part of the hearty
initiation. Bring high-quality wet-weather
gear, a synthetic sleeping bag and, if you're
camping, a good tent.

Guided day trips from Puerto Natales
are possible, but permit only a bus-window

glimpse of what the park has to [c]
lovers should plan to spend any[...]
three to seven days to enjoy the[...]
other activities. Many travelers looking for
an overview of the park's highlights like to
enter the park with a guided tour and arrange
to be stay there instead of returning with the
group at the end of the day. Most tour operators are happy to help you arrange a plan like
this; just ask.

In 2005 a hiker burned down 10% of the
park using a portable stove in windy conditions. Sloppy camping has consequences. Be
conscientious and tread lightly – you are one
of more than 120,000 yearly guests.

Orientation & Information
Parque Nacional Torres del Paine is 112km
north of Puerto Natales via a decent but
sometimes bumpy gravel road. At Cerro
Castillo there is a seasonal border crossing
into Argentina at Cancha Carrera. From here
the road continues 40km north and west to
Portería Sarmiento, the main entrance where
fees are collected. It's another 37km to the
Administración and the **Conaf Centro de Visitantes**
(☺ 9am-8pm in summer), with good information
on park ecology and trail status. A new road
from Puerto Natales to the Administración
provides a shorter, more direct southern approach to the park.

The park is open year-round, subject to
your ability to get there. Transportation connections are less frequent in low season and
winter weather adds extra challenges to hiking. The shoulder seasons of November and
March are some of the best times for trekking.
In both months, the park is less crowded, with
typically windy conditions usually abating in
March. Internet resources include www.tor
resdelpaine.com and www.erraticrock.com,
with a good backpacker equipment list. **Erratic
Rock** (☎ 61-410355; www.erraticrock.com; Baquedano 719,
Puerto Natales) also holds an excellent information session every day at 3pm; go for solid
advice on everything from trail conditions
to camping. Travelers can also rent equipment onsite.

BOOKS & MAPS
The best trekking maps, by JLM and Luis
Bertea Rojas, are widely available in Puerto
Natales. For detailed trekking suggestions and
maps, consult Lonely Planet's *Trekking in the
Patagonian Andes.*

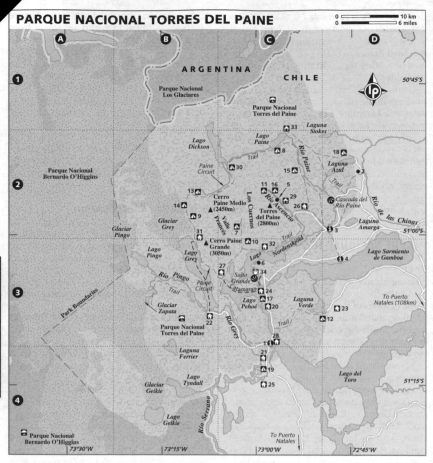

PARQUE NACIONAL TORRES DEL PAINE

Activities

HIKING

Torres del Paine's 2800m granite peaks inspire a mass pilgrimage of hikers from around the world. Most go for the circuit or the 'W' to soak in these classic panoramas, leaving other incredible routes deserted. Doing the Paine Circuit (the 'W' plus the backside of the peaks) requires seven to nine days, while the 'W' (named for the rough approximation to the letter that it traces out on the map) takes four to five. Add another day or two for transportation connections.

Most trekkers start either route from **Laguna Amarga** and head west. You can also hike from the Administración or take the catamaran from Pudeto to Lago Pehoé and start from

there; hiking roughly southwest to northeast along the 'W' presents more views of black sedimentary peaks known as Los Cuernos (2200m to 2600m). Trekking alone, especially on the backside of the circuit, is inadvisable and restricted by Conaf. Guided treks, which include all meals and accommodations at refugios or *hosterías,* are available through tour operators like **Antares Patagonia** (☎ 061-414611; www.antarespatagonia.com; Barros Arana 111, Puerto Natales) with prices starting around CH$925,000 for six days. Per person rates decrease significantly if you're traveling with three or more friends.

The 'W'

Most people trek the 'W' from right to left (east to west), starting at Laguna Amarga – accessible by a twice-daily 2½-hour bus ride from Puerto Natales. But hiking west to east – especially between Lago Pehoé and Valle Francés – provides superior views of Los Cuernos. To start the W from the west, catch the catamaran across Lago Pehoe, then head north along Lago Grey or Campamento Italiano, from which point excellent (and pack-free) day hikes are possible. The following segments are some of the W's most memorable.

Refugio Las Torres to Mirador Las Torres (Four hours one way) A moderate hike up Río Ascencio to a treeless tarn beneath the eastern face of the Torres del Paine proper. This is the closest view you will get of the towers. The last hour is a knee-popping scramble up boulders (covered with knee- and waist-high snow in winter). There are camping and *refugios* at Las Torres and Chileno, with basic camping at Campamento Torres. In summer stay at Campamento Torres and head up at sunrise to beat the crowds.

Refugio Las Torres to Los Cuernos (Seven hours one way) Hikers should keep to the lower trail as many get lost on the upper trail (unmarked on maps). There's camping and a *refugio*. Summer winds can be fierce.

Los Cuernos/Lago Pehoé to Valle Francés (Five hours one way) In clear weather, this hike is the most beautiful stretch between 3050m Cerro Paine Grande to the west and the lower but still spectacular Torres del Paine and Los Cuernos to the east, with glaciers hugging the trail. Camp at Italiano and at Británico, right in the heart of the valley.

Mountain Lodge Paine Grande to Refugio Lago Grey (Four hours one way from Lago Pehoé) This hike follows a relatively easy trail with a few challenging downhill scampers. The glacier lookout is another half-hour's hike away. There are camping and *refugios* at both ends.

Mountain Lodge Paine Grande to Administración (Five hours) Up and around the side of Lago Pehoé, then through extensive grassland along Río Grey. This is not technically part of the 'W,' but after completion of the hike you can cut out to the Administración from here and avoid backtracking to Laguna Amarga. Mountain Lodge Paine

Grande can radio in and make sure that you can catch a bus from the Administración back to Puerto Natales. You can also enter the 'W' this way to hike it east to west.

Paine Circuit
This loop takes in the 'W' (described earlier), plus the backside between Refugio Grey and Refugio Las Torres. The landscape is desolate yet beautiful. Paso John Garner (the most extreme part of the trek) sometimes offers knee-deep mud and snow. There's one basic *refugio* at Los Perros; the other option is rustic camping.

Many hikers start the Paine Circuit by entering the park (by bus) at Laguna Amarga, then hike for a few hours to Refugio & Camping Chileno. From this point, the circuit continues counter-clockwise, ending in Valle Frances and Los Cuernos. See the following for more details on hikes within the Paine Circuit.

Refugio Lago Grey to Campamento Paso (Four hours heading north, two hours going south) Hikers might want to go left to right (west to east), which means ascending the pass rather than slipping downhill.

Campamento Paso to Campamento Los Perros (Four hours) This route has plenty of mud and sometimes snow. Don't be confused by what appears to be a campsite right after crossing the pass; keep going until you see a shack.

Campamento Los Perros to Campamento Dickson (Around 4½ hours) A relatively easy but windy stretch.

Campamento Lago Dickson to Campamento Serón Six hours. As the trail wraps around Lago Paine, winds can get fierce and the trails vague; stay along the trail furthest away from the lake. It's possible to break the trek at Campamento Coiron, although it is currently recovering from the 2005 fire.

Campamento Serón to Laguna Amarga Four to five hours. You can end the trek with a chill-out night and a decent meal at Refugio Las Torres.

PATAGONIA

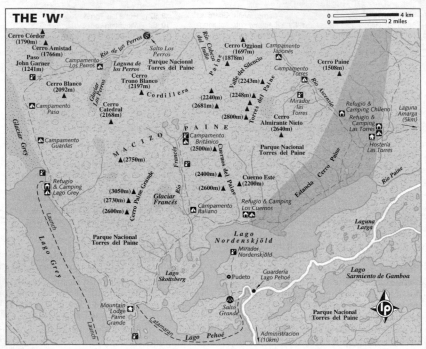

THE 'W'

Day Hikes

Walk from Guardería Lago Pehoé, on the main park highway, to **Salto Grande**, a powerful waterfall between Lago Nordenskjöld and Lago Pehoé. Another easy hour's walk leads to **Mirador Nordenskjöld**, an overlook with superb views of the lake and mountains. For a more challenging day hike, try the four-hour trek leading to **Lago Paine**, the northern shore of which is accessible only from Laguna Azul, in the park's east. The route offers tranquility and gorgeous scenery.

KAYAKING

Paddle your way to pristine corners of the park on multiday trips with **Indomita Big Foot** (☎ 061-414525; www.indomitapatagonia.com; Bories 206, Puerto Natales). Few see the sights around Río Serrano, and these trips aren't budget travel but they're great way to get up close to glaciers.

HORSEBACK RIDING

The park is certainly a beautiful place to ride. Due to property divisions within the park, horses cannot cross between the western sec-

tions (Lagos Grey and Pehoé, Río Serrano) and the eastern part managed by Hostería Las Torres (Refugio Los Cuernos is the approximate cut-off). **Baqueano Zamora** (☎ 061-613530; www.baqueanozamora.com, in Spanish; Baquedano 534, Puerto Natales) runs excursions to Lagos Pingo, Paine and Azul, and Laguna Amarga (half-day CH$21,000).

ROCK CLIMBING

Rock climbers of all levels should contact Rustyn Mesdag at **Erratic Rock** (☎ 061-410355; www.erraticrock.com; Baquedano 719, Puerto Natales). Expert guides have experience in many of the park's newer climbing areas; qualified climbers can join them for customized multiday trips, while beginners can get instruction and go on easier day climbs.

Sleeping & Eating

Make reservations! Arriving without them, especially in high season, limits you to camping in the few free options. Quoted rates include the Chilean VAT tax, which travelers can avoid (and therefore save some cash) if they pay in US dollars and show their passport to prove their citizenship in a foreign country. Travel agencies offer reservations, but it's best to deal directly with the various management companies (see Refugios, below).

Some *refugios* may require photo ID (ie a passport) upon check-in. Photocopy your tourist card and passport for all lodgings in advance to expedite check-in. Staff can radio ahead to confirm your next reservation. Given the huge volume of trekkers, snags are inevitable, so practice your Zen composure.

CAMPING

Camping at the *refugios* costs CH$4000 per site. *Refugios* rent equipment – tent (CH$6000 per night), sleeping bag (CH$3500) and mat (CH$1500) – but potential shortages in high season make it prudent to pack your own gear. Small kiosks sell expensive pasta, soup packets and butane gas. Sites administered by Conaf are free and very basic. Many campers have reported wildlife (in rodent form) lurking around campsites, so don't leave food in packs or in tents – hang it from a tree instead.

In addition to the campgrounds affiliated with well-known *refugios* or operated by one of the large management companies (see opposite), the following campgrounds are scattered about the park. Campamentos Británico, Italiano and Torres are located on the 'W.'

Campamento Británico Very basic, with pit toilets.

Campamento Italiano Has basic cooking facilities and bathrooms.

Campamento Laguna Verde Caters to groups; lots of facilities.

Campamento Los Perros On the Paine Circuit.

Campamento Paso Sheltered by forest; offers good views.

Campamento Serón Near Laguna Azul.

Campamento Torres Has a cooking area sheltered from the wind and rain.

Camping Lago Pehoé On the lake, with a restaurant and equipment rental.

Camping Laguna Azul Has rowboats for rent.

Camping Río Serrano Seven kilometers from Administración in Sector Serrano.

Camping Serrano Affiliated with Hotel Cabañas del Paine (see p510).

REFUGIOS

Refugio rooms have four to eight bunk beds each, kitchen privileges (for lodgers and during specific hours only), hot showers and

meals. A bed costs CH$19,000 to CH$26,000, sleeping-bag rental CH$3500 and meals CH$5500 to CH$10,000. Should a *refugio* be overbooked, staff provide all necessary camping equipment. Most *refugios* close by the end of April. Mountain Lodge Paine Grande is the only one that stays open year-round, but it has very limited operations.

For bookings, **Vertice Patagonia** (☎ 061-412742; www.verticepatagonia.cl) looks after Lago Grey and Lago Dickson and owns Mountain Lodge Paine Grande. **Fantastico Sur** (☎ 061-710050; www.fantasticosur.com; Esmeralda 661; ☺ 9am-1pm & 3-6pm Mon-Fri) owns Las Torres, Chileno and Los Cuernos, as well as their associated campgrounds.

Most of the following *refugios* also offer camping facilities when all beds are booked:

Refugio & Camping Chileno Situated on the peaceful Río Ascencio.

Refugio & Camping Lago Dickson On the Paine Circuit.

Refugio & Camping Lago Grey Near Cerro Paine Grande.

Refugio & Camping Las Torres Busy travel hub with horse rentals.

Refugio & Camping Los Cuernos On the shore of Lake Nordenskjöld.

Refugio Lago Paine Located in the park's far north.

HOTELS & HOSTERÍAS

The following have high-season prices listed (and, as noted earlier, prices are less if you pay in US dollars and show your foreign passport.)

Posada Río Serrano (☎ in Puerto Natales 061-613531; www.posadaserrano.com; dm CH$21,000, d with/without bathroom CH$75,000/55,000) Restored but still rustic, this rambling 19th-century ranch house has 13 rooms, a restaurant, a bar and a cozy living room focused on a fireplace. It's a popular base camp for horseback riding (arranged through the same company, Baqueano Zamora, that owns the posada) and fishing trips to nearby lakes and rivers.

Mountain Lodge Paine Grande (☎ 412742; www.verticepatagonia.cl; campsites per person CH$4500, dm CH$24,900, incl full board CH$45,000; ▢) Sometimes referred to as Pehoé (its predecessor), this boxy hotel reveals a smart interior made to give sublime Los Cuernos views to all rooms. Between Lago Grey and Valle Francés, it is a perfect day hike from either. It can also be reached by boat across Lago Pehoé. The lodge is partially open year-round and is a godsend to cold, wet winter hikers. It also offers camping.

PATAGONIA

Hostería Tyndall (☎ 239401; www.hoteltyndall.cl; d CH$70,000-80,000) This smart wooden lodge on the Río Serrano offers rooms or fully equipped cabins, as well as excursions for guests.

Hostería Mirador del Payne (☎ 226930; www.miradordelpayne.com; booking address Fagnano 585, Punta Arenas; s/d/tr CH$95,200/116,620/126,140) On the Estancia El Lazo in the seldom-seen Laguna Verde sector, this comfortable inn is known for its serenity, proximity to spectacular viewpoints and top-rate service – but not for easy park access. Activities include bird-watching, horseback riding and sport fishing. Call to arrange a ride from the road junction.

Hostería Pehoé (☎ 244506, in Santiago 02-235-0252; www.pehoe.cl; d CH$107,000) On the far side of Lago Pehoé, toward explora, this *hostería* is linked to the mainland by a long footbridge. It enjoys five-star panoramas of Los Cuernos and Paine Grande, but unfortunately the rooms are a bit dated. The restaurant and bar are open to the public.

Hotel Cabañas del Paine (☎ 220174; www.cabanasdelpaine.cl; d CH$124,800-142,800) On the banks of the Río Serrano, these modern wood cabins have hardwood details and offer views of the Paine massif and river. Meals are available from CH$12,500.

Hostería Lago Grey (☎ 410172; www.lagogrey.cl; booking address Lautaro Navarro 1061, Punta Arenas; d CH$174,000) Although at the outlet of iceberg-dotted Lago Grey, the crowded rooms at this year-round retreat are cut off from the views by thick windbreaking trees. The cafe (open to the public), however, overlooks the grandeur. Zodiac boat tours are available on the lake, but not to the glacier.

Hotel Las Torres (☎ 617450; www.lastorres.com; booking address Magallanes 960, Punta Arenas; d CH$135,000) A luxurious choice just 7km west of Guardería Laguna Amarga. Wings are interconnected by spacious living rooms with grand fireplaces. One end of the hotel has an interesting and educational interpretive center about the park. The restaurant serves elaborate dishes of salmon, crab and steak; the spa has a sauna and Jacuzzi. The rate listed covers just the room, but many guests stay for four or seven nights on all-inclusive packages; log on to the website for current rates.

explora (☎ in Santiago 02-206-6060; www.explora.com; d per person 4 nights incl full board & transfers CH$1,345,000; 🖳 🕿) Strutting with style, Torres del Paine's most sophisticated (and expensive) digs sit perched above the Salto Chico waterfall at the outlet of Lago Pehoé. Rates include airport transfers, full gourmet meals and a wide variety of excursions led by young, affable, bilingual guides. Views of the entire Paine massif pour forth from every inch of the hotel. But is it worth shelling out? Before you decide, check out the spa with heated lap pool, sauna, massage rooms and open-air Jacuzzi.

Getting There & Away

For details of transportation to the park, see p504. Going to El Calafate from the park on the same day requires joining a tour or careful advance planning, since there is no direct service. Your best bet is to return to Puerto Natales.

Getting Around

Buses drop off and pick up passengers at Laguna Amarga, at the Hielos Patagónicos catamaran launch at Pudeto and at Administración.

The catamaran leaves Pudeto for Mountain Lodge Paine Grande (one way/round trip per person CH$11,000/18,000) at 9:30am, noon and 6pm December to mid-March, at noon and 6pm in late March and November, and at noon only in September, October and April. Another launch travels Lago Grey between Hostería Lago Grey and Refugio Lago Grey (roundtrip CH$70,000, 1½ to two hours) a couple of times daily; contact the *hostería* for the current schedule.

Tierra del Fuego

A storied past of shipwrecks, failed religious missions and indigenous extinction contributes to the powerful mystique of this end-of-the-earth location. Travelers flock here to glimpse the furthest reaches of the continent, and ah – what a view it is! The barren northern plains of Tierra del Fuego give way to peat bogs and moss-draped lenga forests that rise into ragged snowy mountains. At Ushuaia, the Andes meet the southern ocean in a sharp skid, making way for the city before reaching a sea of lapping currents.

While assuming a complex and sometimes conflicted identity, Tierra del Fuego still manages to remain beautiful, ancient and strange. The curved bandera tree, waving like a hankie, is a reminder that it's the toying weather that defines this place and most travelers' visits to it.

While it is isolated and hard to reach, Tierra del Fuego is by no means cut off from the mainland. Ports bustle with commerce, oil refineries chug and adventure seekers descend in droves to fly-fish, hike and start Antarctic cruises. Separated from the mainland by the Strait of Magellan, this archipelago shared with Chile is comprised of one large island, Isla Grande de Tierra del Fuego, and many smaller ones, most of them uninhabited. This chapter covers both the Argentine and Chilean sections of the territory, including Chile's Isla Navarino.

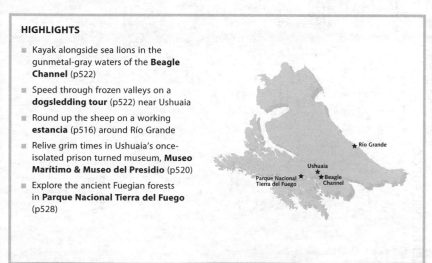

HIGHLIGHTS

- Kayak alongside sea lions in the gunmetal-gray waters of the **Beagle Channel** (p522)

- Speed through frozen valleys on a **dogsledding tour** (p522) near Ushuaia

- Round up the sheep on a working **estancia** (p516) around Río Grande

- Relive grim times in Ushuaia's once-isolated prison turned museum, **Museo Marítimo & Museo del Presidio** (p520)

- Explore the ancient Fuegian forests in **Parque Nacional Tierra del Fuego** (p528)

★ Río Grande

Ushuaia ★

Parque Nacional ★   ★ Beagle
Tierra del Fuego   Channel

TIERRA DEL FUEGO

- POPULATION: 106,000 (INCL CHILE) | - AREA: 47,992 SQ KM (ISLA GRANDE)

TIERRA DEL FUEGO

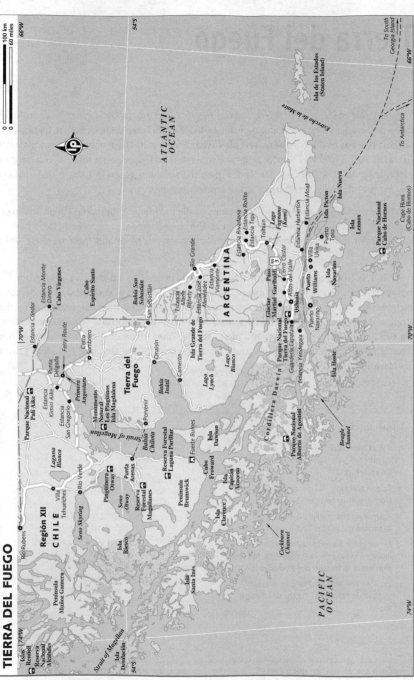

Climate

Unrelenting winds sweep the relatively arid northern plains of Isla Grande, while high rainfall supports dense deciduous and evergreen forests in the mountainous southern half. The maritime climate is surprisingly mild, even in winter, but its unpredictability makes foul-weather gear essential year-round. The Cordillera Darwin and Sierra de Beauvoir mountains, reaching up to 2500m in the west, intercept Antarctic storms, leaving the plains around Río Grande much drier than the storm-battered bogs characteristic of the archipelago's remote southern and western zones.

National Parks

Isla Grande is home to Parque Nacional Tierra del Fuego (p528), Argentina's first shoreline national park.

Getting There & Around

The most common overland route from Patagonia is via the ferry crossing at Punta Delgada (p495). Unlike the rest of Argentina, Tierra del Fuego has no designated provincial highways, but has secondary roads known as *rutas complementarias,* modified by a lowercase letter. References to such roads in this chapter are given as 'RC-a,' for example.

If renting a car in mainland Argentina, be aware that you must cross in and out of Chile a couple of times to reach Tierra del Fuego, and that this requires special documents and additional international insurance coverage. Most rental agencies can arrange this paperwork if given advance notice.

Visitors can fly into Río Grande or Ushuaia. Buses take the ferry from Chile's Punta Delgada; all pass through Río Grande before arriving in Ushuaia.

PORVENIR (CHILE)

☎ 61 / pop 5465

'Nothing happens in Porvenir,' proclaimed one Chilean, 'but that's exactly the point!' If you want a slice of home-baked Fuegian life, this is it. Most visitors come on a quick day trip from Punta Arenas that's often tainted by a touch of seasickness from the crossing. But spending a night in this rusted village of metal-clad Victorian houses affords you an opportunity to explore the nearby bays and countryside and absorb a little of the local life; bird-watchers will also enjoy the lively populations of cormorants, geese and seabirds.

Thanks to Porvenir's relative inaccessibility – during the low season, roads leading to the eastern mainland are often closed, and even the ferry crossing from Punta Arenas can be cancelled due to windy weather – the place seems to be lost in time.

Porvenir's heritage is rather peculiar. When gold was discovered in 1879, waves of immigrants arrived, many from Croatia, and most did not strike it rich. When sheep *estancias* (ranches) began to spring up, the immigrants found more reliable work. Chilotes (people from the Chilean island of Chiloé) appeared in droves for the fishing and *estancia* work, and the chance of a better life. Today's population is a unique combination of the two.

Information

Banco de Estado (cnr Philippi & Croacia) Has a 24-hour ATM.
Hospital (☎ 580034; Wood, btwn Señoret & Guerrero)
Post office (Philippi 176) Faces the plaza.
Telefónica (Philippi 277) Next to the bank.
Tourist office (☎ 580094/8; www.muniporvenir.com; Zavattaro 434; ⏰ 9am-5pm Mon-Fri, 11am-5pm Sat & Sun) Information is also available at the handicrafts shop on the *costanera* (seaside road) between Philippi and Schythe.

Sights

On the plaza, the intriguing **Museo de Tierra del Fuego** (☎ 581800; www.museoporvenir.cl; Zavattaro 402; admission CH$500; ⏰ 8am-5pm Mon-Thu, 8am-4pm Fri) has some unexpected materials on display, including Selk'nam skulls and mummies, musical instruments used by the mission Selk'nams on Isla Dawson and an exhibit on early Chilean cinematography.

Activities & Tours

Gold-panning, horseback-riding and 4WD tours can be arranged through the tourist office.
Cordillera Darwin Expediciones (☎ 580167, 09-888-6380; www.cordilleradarwin.com; Bahía Chilota s/n) organizes cool outings to view Peale's dolphins around Bahía Chilota in a traditional Chilote-style fishing boat (CH$15,000, including meals). Longer, well-recommended camping and horseback-riding trips include visits to Río Condor (three days/two nights CH$150,000), and an intense weeklong adventure that includes kayaking, *centolla-*(king crab) and fly-fishing, and riding to Glaciar Marinelli (groups of seven or more, November to May). Trips require a minimum number of participants. The office is in front of the ferry landing in a restaurant; ask for the tour guide Pechuga.

TIERRA DEL FUEGO

Sleeping & Eating

Residencial Colón (☎ 581157; Riobó 198; per person with shared bathroom CH$8000) Often filled with fisheries employees, this rickety pension offers the cheapest digs in town. Cheap meals can also be arranged.

Hotel Central (☎ 580077; Philippi 298; s/d CH$12,000/20,000) Facing Hotel Rosas, this unassuming option brims with matronly charm on the inside. Snug rooms have hardwood floors and good beds. There's a comfortable sitting area.

Hotel Rosas (☎ 580088; hotelrosas@chile.com; Philippi 296; s/d CH$14,000/20,000) Eleven clean and pleasant rooms offer heating and cable TV; some have wonderful views. Alberto, the owner, knows heaps about the region and arranges tours to Circuito del Loro, a historical mining site. The restaurant (*plato del día* CH$4000) gets crowded for meals, serving fresh seafood and more.

Hotel España (☎ 580160; www.hotelespana.cl; Croacia 698; s/d/tr CH$15,000/25,000/30,000) This rambling hotel has spacious, impeccably kept rooms with views of the bay. Rooms have Berber carpets, TV and central heating. There is a downstairs cafe and parking out the back.

El Chispa (☎ 580054; Señoret 202; plato del día CH$3500) In a century-old aquamarine firehouse, El Chispa packs with locals for salmon dinners, lamb and mashed potatoes, and other home-cooked fare. There are also several basic rooms (single/double CH$10,000/15,000) upstairs, often filled with workers. It's a couple of blocks uphill from the water.

Club Croata (☎ 580053; Señoret 542; mains CH$3500-6000; ☒ 11am-4pm & 7-10:30pm Tue-Sun) Formal to the verge of stuffy, this traditional restaurant nonetheless puts together good seafood meals at reasonable prices, in addition to Croat specialties such as pork chops with *chucrut* (sauerkraut). The polished pub section stays open until 3am.

Getting There & Away

Aerovías DAP (☎ 580089; www.dap.cl; Señoret near Gamero) flies to Punta Arenas (CH$20,000, 15 minutes) Monday to Saturday from November to March, with fewer flights in the low season. For the airport, 6km north of town, DAP runs a door-to-door shuttle (CH$1800) and taxis charge CH$3500.

Transbordador Austral Broom (☎ 580089; www.tabsa.cl) operates the car/passenger ferry *Melinka* to/from Punta Arenas (CH$4900/31,300 per person/vehicle, 2½ to four hours). It usually leaves at 9am but has some afternoon departures; check the current online schedule. The bus to the ferry terminal (CH$500), 5km away, departs from the waterfront kiosk an hour before the ferry's departure.

The gravel road east, along Bahía Inútil to the Argentine border at San Sebastián, is in good shape. From San Sebastián (where there's gas and a motel), northbound motorists should avoid the heavily traveled and rutted truck route directly north and instead take the route from Onaisín to the petroleum company town of Cerro Sombrero, en route to the crossing of the Strait of Magellan at Punta Delgada–Puerto Espora.

RÍO GRANDE

☎ 02964 / pop 68,776

A monster trout sculpture at the entrance to town announces that you have come to the de facto fly-fishing capital of Tierra del Fuego, with some of the world's best blue-ribbon angling for colossal sea-run trout. Exclusive fly-in lodges on nearby *estancias* lure guests, including Hollywood heavy hitters and former US presidents, with dreams of the big one. But if you didn't come with rod in hand, the longest that you will likely stay in windswept Río Grande is a few hours, before hopping on a bus to Ushuaia, 230km southwest.

As wool baron José Menéndez' sheep stations developed (see p516), Río Grande became a growing makeshift service town. In 1893 the Salesian order, under the guidance of Monseñor Fagnano, set up a mission in an unsuccessful attempt to shelter the Selk'nam from the growing infringement.

As a petroleum service center, the town has an industrial feel: even the public art looks like giant, grim tinker toys. Duty-free status, meant to foster local development, has brought in electronics manufacturing plants and wholesale appliance stores. During the Falklands War the military played an important role here; many local memorials pay tribute to fallen soldiers.

Information

Most visitor services are along Avs San Martín and Belgrano.

Banco de la Nación (cnr San Martín & 9 de Julio) Has an ATM; there are also several others nearby.

Don Pepe (cnr 9 de Julio & Rosales; ☒ 24hr) Supermarket with a burger grill, *locutorio* (telephone office) and internet access.

El Lavadero (Moreno 221) Laundry.

Farmacia Central (cnr San Martín & Piedrabuena; ☾ 24hr)

Instituto Fueguino de Turismo (Infuetur; ☎ 424326; www.tierradelfuego.org.ar; Espora 533; ☾ 9am-9pm) On the south side of the plaza.

Mariani Travel (☎ 426010; Rosales 281) Books flights and represents nearby *estancias*.

Municipal tourist kiosk (☎ 431324; rg-turismo@ netcombbs.com.ar; ☾ 9am-8pm) Helpful kiosk on the plaza, with maps, *estancia* brochures and fishing details.

Post office (Rivadavia, btwn Moyano & Alberdi)

Thaler Cambio (☎ 421154; Rosales 259) Changes traveler's checks.

Sights

In a restored *galpón* (sheepshearing shed), the **Museo de la Ciudad** (☎ 430414; Alberdi 555; admission free; ☾ 9am-5pm Mon-Fri, 3-7pm Sat) has impressive exhibits, from logging to military displays, postal communications to cartography, indigenous artifacts to yet another milodón (see p504 for a famous one), an extinct giant sloth.

Ten kilometers north of town on RN 3, the 1893 Misión Salesiano houses the **Museo Histórico y Natural Monseñor Fagnano** (☎ 421642; adult/child AR$2/1; ☾ 9-11:30am & 3-6pm Tue-Fri, 4-6pm Sat & Sun, 3-6pm Mon), an ethnographic museum with geological and natural-history exhibits. The mission's work to protect the Selk'nam dissolved with the indigenous group's eventual extinction. The mission then became an agrotechnical school, now considered the region's best. Visitors can buy fresh Salesian

---

GOLD DIGGER

In 1886 the villainous gold-seeker Julius Popper stumbled across the mouth of the Río Grande, home to Selk'nam (or Ona) people. After founding his own exploration company, Popper set up shop near the bay at San Sebastián and quite literally hit the goldmine when his team uncovered around 150 pounds of the precious metal. Popper's greed provoked a string of clashes between the foreign company and the indigenous community; naturally, Popper's team, armed with brand-new guns, won the battles, and the Chilean government had to step in. Julius Popper eventually died of poisoning in Buenos Aires, but not before he started a minting operation and had stamps created in his name in Tierra del Fuego.

---

cheeses and produce may be purchased in the tearoom. Horseback rides may be available, and students (female students were not admitted until 1997) conduct informal tours of the greenhouses and dairy farms. To get here, take *colectivo* (local bus) Línea B, which runs downtown every hour from San Martín.

Sleeping

Catering to suits and anglers, lodging tends to be overpriced, not to mention sparse. There are a number of cheap but unsavory lodgings; those worth recommending fill up fast. High-end places give discounts of 10% for cash payments.

Hostel Argentino (☎ 422546; www.hostelargentino .com; San Martín 64; dm AR$50; ☐) Locals and travelers kick back in this friendly hostel hosted by the effervescent Graciela. Guests get hot showers, a shared kitchen, breakfast and luggage storage. A new wing contains small, neat doubles with twin beds and fresh paint. Long-distance cyclists even have a spot to store their bikes inside.

Hotel Villa (☎ 424998; hotelvillarg@hotmail.com; San Martín 281; d/tr AR$240/280; ☐) Opposite Casino Status, this refurbished place has a popular restaurant, a dozen spacious and stylish rooms outfitted with down duvets, and breakfast with *medialunas* (croissants).

Posada de los Sauces (☎ 432895; www.posada delossauces.com.ar; Elcano 839; s/d/tr AR$250/325/390; ☐) Catering mostly to high-end anglers, this warm and professional hotel fosters a lodge atmosphere, with fresh scents and woodsy accents. Deluxe rooms have Jacuzzis. The upstairs bar-restaurant, decked out in dark wood and forest green, is just waiting for stogies and tall tales to fill the air.

Eating & Drinking

Epa!!! (☎ 425334; Rosales 445; mains AR$8-25) Deep leather booths and a curved bar mark this popular cafe-bar that sparks up when soccer is on the tube. The set lunch is well priced and there's a laundry list of cocktails to tempt the evening crowd.

our pick La Nueva Colonial (☎ 425353; cnr Lasserre & Belgrano; mains AR$18-30) Enough reason to delay your departure, chef Cesar's outstanding pasta dishes (we recommend the *sorrentinos* – large, round pastas – with pesto) are divine creations, served with fresh foccacia bread and a bottle of red. And if you don't like it, it's free (but a hard argument to make).

CONSULTING THE FUEGIAN TROUT ATLAS

You know a place takes fishing seriously when the tourism board posts a trout map online (www.tierradelfuego.org.ar/funcardio/trutamap.jpg). Hollywood stars, heads of state and former US presidents all flock to the desolate stretch of the island around Río Grande in search of the perfect day of angling. Usually they are in luck.

In 1933 pioneer John Goodall stocked the rivers around Río Grande with brown, rainbow and brook trout. Fish quickly populated the rivers and the sport-fishing industry took off. European brown trout ventured out to sea, returning to these rivers to spawn. Over the decades this back-and-forth migration has fostered one of the world's best sea-run trout-fishing areas, with some local specimens weighing in at 15kg. Rainbow trout from the western US are nearly as impressive, with individual fish reaching 9kg.

Fishing excursions are mostly organized through outside agents, many in the USA. 'Public' fishing rivers, on which trips can be organized, include the Fuego, Menéndez, Candelaria, Ewan and MacLennan. Many of the more elite angling trips are lodged in *estancias* (ranches), which snatch exclusive use of some of the best rivers.

There are two types of license. License 1 is valid for fishing throughout the province, except in the national park. Contact **Asociación Caza y Pesca** (☎ 02901-423168; cazapescaush@infovia.com .ar; Maipú 822) in Ushuaia, or **Club de Pesca John Goodall** (☎ 02964-424324; Ricardo Rojas 606) in Río Grande. License 2 is valid for fishing in the national park and in Patagonia areas. Contact the **National Parks office** (☎ 02901-421315; San Martín 1395) in Ushuaia and find more information on sport fishing in Argentina through the online portal **Pesca Argentina** (www.pescaargentina.com.ar, in Spanish). Other useful information:

Flies Rubber legs and woolly buggers.

License fees AR$75 per day or AR$350 per season, depending on where you fish.

Limit One fish per person per day, catch and release.

Methods Spinning and fly casting; no night fishing.

Season November 1 to April 15, with catch-and-release restrictions from April 1 to April 15.

El Rincón de Julio (☎ 02964-15-604261; Elcano 805; all you can eat AR$45) Dive into this ambient wood shack with seven tables for the best *parrilla* (steak restaurant) in town. It's in front of the YPF service station.

Karma Café Bar (cnr Lasserre & Belgrano; drinks AR$7) Ideal for a *café con leche* (coffee with milk) or glass of wine, this elegant nook has just a few tables. It's located next to La Nueva Colonial.

Getting There & Away

The **airport** (RGA; ☎ 420699) is off RN 3, a short taxi ride from town. **Aerolíneas Argentinas** (☎ 424467; San Martín 607) flies direct daily to Buenos Aires (AR$620). **LADE** (☎ 422968; Lasserre 445) flies a couple of times weekly to Río Gallegos (AR$174), El Calafate (AR$280) and Buenos Aires.

At the time of writing there was no central bus terminal, but plans for one were in the works. **Tecni-Austral** (☎ 432885, 430610; Moyano 516) goes to Ushuaia (AR$50, four hours, daily) from 6am to 8pm, with a stop in Tolhuin (AR$20, 1½ hours); to Río Gallegos (AR$95,

eight hours, daily); and to Punta Arenas (AR$90, eight hours) on Monday, Wednesday and Friday. **Buses Pacheco** (☎ 425611; 25 de Mayo 712) goes to Punta Arenas (AR$80, eight hours) several times a week.

A better option for Ushuaia (AR$60, four hours) and Tolhuin (AR$30, 1½ hours) is the door-to-door minivan service run by **Lider** (☎ 420003, 424-2000; Moreno 1056) and **Transportes Montiel** (☎ 427225; 25 de Mayo 712) several times daily. Call to reserve a seat; tickets must be paid for in person.

ESTANCIAS AROUND RÍO GRANDE

Much of Tierra del Fuego was once the sprawling backyard of wool baron José Menéndez. His first *estancia* – La Primera Argentina (1897), now known as **Estancia José Menéndez**, 20km southwest of Río Grande via RN 3 and RC-b – covered 1600 sq km, with over 140,000 head of sheep. His second and most-treasured venture was La Segunda Argentina, totaling 1500 sq km. Later renamed **Estancia María Behety** (☎ in Buenos Aires 011-4331-5061; www.maribety.com.ar, in Spanish) after his wife, it's still a working ranch,

17km west of Río Grande via RC-c. Besides boasting the world's largest shearing shed, it is considered a highly exclusive lodge, catering mainly to tour groups and elite anglers. Fishing lodge La Villa has six bedrooms and overlooks the Río Grande.

Several *estancias* in the area have opened to small-scale tourism, offering a unique chance to learn about the region's history and enjoy its magic. Reserve as far in advance as possible.

The sons of early settler Thomas Bridges (see p530) established **Estancia Viamonte** (☎ 02964-430861, 02964-15-616813; www.estanciaviamonte.com; per person with breakfast & dinner AR$550; ✷ Oct-Apr & by arrangement) in 1902 at the request of the Selk'nam, in part to protect the indigenous group. The Goodalls, descendents of the Bridges, now run it as a working ranch, with 22,000 head of sheep on 400 sq km. Guests stay in son Lucas' original dwelling, the Sea View, a comfortable English-style home within earshot of the crashing waves. Guided activity possibilities include horseback riding, hiking and fly-fishing the Río Ewan.

Croatian sheep ranch **Estancia Rivadavia** (☎ 02901-492186; www.estanciarivadavia.com; RC-h, Km 22; day tour/overnight package per person AR$420/875) has 100 sq km of valleys, lakes and mountains. Guests can participate in agrotourism as well as hikes to lakes and an adventure tour to the Río Claro. Notoriety found this remote spot

when Paraguayan general Lino Oviedo sought political refuge in Argentina during a 1999 stay. It's 100km from Río Grande; take RN 3 to RC-h (formerly Ruta 18) until Km 22.

Founded by Tierra del Fuego's first rural doctor, the Basque-Provençal-style **Estancia Tepi** (☎ 02964-427245, 02964-15-504-2020; www.estanciatepi.com.ar, in Spanish; RC-a, Km 5; day trip/B&B/full board per person AR$420/685/800; ✷ Dec-Mar) is a working, 100-sq-km ranch. Horseback riding is offered for all levels, with traditional Patagonian mounts heaped with sheepskins. The property also boasts thermal baths, treks and tours. It's 80km from Río Grande and 150km from Ushuaia.

The rustic and charismatic **Estancia Rolito** (☎ 02901-437351, 02901-432419; www.tierradelfuego.org.ar/rolito, in Spanish; RC-a, Km 14; r with half/full board per person AR$188/251) is very Argentine and very inviting. Guests rave about the horseback-riding trips and hikes through ñire and lenga forest. Day trips from Ushuaia (with Turismo de Campo) stop by for lunch or dinner and guided horseback riding. Rolito is 100km from Río Grande and 150km from Ushuaia.

TOLHUIN & LAGO FAGNANO
☎ 02901

Named for the Selk'nam word meaning 'like a heart,' Tolhuin (population 2000) is a lake town nestled in the center of Tierra del Fuego, 132km south of Río Grande and 104km northeast

---

FUEGIAN RITES OF PASSAGE

Part of traveling to Tierra del Fuego is searching for clues to its mystical, unknowable past. Souvenir shops sell a postcard of abstract intrigue: there's a naked man painted black. Fine horizontal white stripes cross his body from chest to foot. His face remains covered, hidden. So, what's this all about?

For people who lived exposed to the elements, dependent on their wits and courage, initiation ceremonies were a big deal. Those of the seafaring Yaghan (or Yámana) were surprisingly similar to those of the fierce northern neighbors they wanted little to do with, the nomadic hunters called Selk'nam (or Ona to the Yaghan). Both celebrated a male rite of passage that reenacted a great upheaval when the men stole the women's secrets to gain power over them. In the Kina, Yaghan men interpreted the spirits by painting their bodies with black carbon and striped or dotted patterns that used the region's white and red clays. The Selk'nam undertook their Hain ceremony similarly adorned, taking young men into huts where they were attacked by spirits. In related ceremonies men showed their strength to women by fighting the spirits in theatrical displays, each acting with the characteristics of a specific spirit. These manly displays did not always achieve their desired effect of subjugation: one account tells of spirits dispatched to menace female camps that instead evoked hilarity.

With European encroachment, these ceremonies became more abbreviated and much of their detailed significance was lost. When the last Hain was celebrated in the early 20th century in the presence of missionaries, it had already crossed over from ritual to theater.

of Ushuaia via smooth asphalt. This fast-growing frontier town of small plazas and sheltering evergreens fronts the eastern shore of Lago Fagnano, also known as Lago Kami. Most travelers tend to skip right over it, but if you are looking for a unique and tranquil spot, Tolhuin is well worth checking out.

Shared with Chile, the glacial-formed Lago Fagnano offers 117km of beach, with most of its shoreline remote and roadless. Plans to put a catamaran here are developing; look for this new cruising option, which might be combined with trekking on the far side of the lake. Otherwise, there is boating and fishing.

Tolhuin's nascent **tourist office** (☎ 492380, 492125; www.tierradelfuego.org.ar/tolhuin; Av de los Shelknam 80), behind the gas station, has information on local tours and rentals. Those coming from Ushuaia might get more complete information from Ushuaia's tourist office (p520). **Banco de Tierra del Fuego** (Menkiol s/n) has an ATM.

Sleeping & Eating

Camping Hain (☎ 02901-15-603606; Lago Fagnano; campsite per person AR$10, 8-person refugios AR$130) Located on Lago Fagnano, this excellent campground offers grassy sites sheltered with wooden windbreaks, a huge barbecue pit and a *fogon* (sheltered fire pit and kitchen area). There are bathrooms and showers with hot water.

La Posada de los Ramirez (☎ 02901-492137; Av de los Shelknam 411, Tolhuin; dm AR$50, 4-person cabin AR$180; 🖳) This welcoming family lodging sits in the center of town. The family's on-site restaurant (mains AR$35 to AR$40) serves pasta, local trout and meat dishes.

Hostería Kaikén (☎ 492372; www.hosteriakaiken .com.ar; Lago Fagnano, Km 2942; d AR$235-290, 2-person cabin AR$175; 🖳) This gorgeous lakeside inn is both refined and rustic, with beautiful colonial furniture, neutral tones and snug, down bedcovers. There's a stylish bar with panoramas of the lake and a dining room serving high-end cuisine.

Panadería La Unión (☎ 492202; www.panaderia launion.com.ar, in Spanish; Jeujepen 450, Tolhuin; snacks AR$3; 🕑 24hr) First-rate *facturas* (pastries) and second-rate Nescafé cappuccinos keep this roadside attraction hopping. You may or may not recognize the Argentine celebrities gracing the walls (hint: the men are ageing rock stars, the women surgically enhanced). Buses break here to pick up passengers and hot water for *mate* (a tealike beverage).

Getting There & Away

Throughout the day, buses and minivans passing along RN 3 (often full in high season) all stop at the Panadería La Union en route to Ushuaia or Río Grande (AR$30).

USHUAIA
☎ 02901 / pop 59,000

A busy port and adventure hub, Ushuaia is a sliver of steep streets and jumbled buildings set between the Beagle Channel and the snow-capped Martial Range. It's a location matched by few, and chest-beating Ushuaia takes full advantage of its end-of-the-world status as an increasing number of Antarctica-bound vessels call in to port. Its endless mercantile hustle knows no irony: the souvenir shop named for Jemmy Button (a native kidnapped for show in England), the ski center named for a destructive invasive species…you get the idea. That said, with a pint of the world's southernmost microbrew in hand, you can happily plot the dazzling outdoor options: hiking, sailing, skiing, kayaking and even scuba diving are just minutes from town.

Tierra del Fuego's comparatively high wages draw Argentines from all over to resettle here, and some locals lament the loss of the small-town culture that existed until recently. Meanwhile, expansion means a jumble of housing developments advancing in the few directions the mad geography allows.

History

In 1870 the British-based South American Missionary Society set its sights on the Yaghan (or Yámana), a nomadic tribe whose members faced brutal weather conditions almost entirely naked – they didn't have any permanent shelter to keep clothing dry, and believed that the natural oil of their skin was better protection than soaking wet animal fur. They were also a people whom Charles Darwin deemed 'the lowest form of humanity on earth.' (His statement, of course, carried less weight after the missionary Thomas Bridges learned the tribal language and proved its complexity in the first Yaghan-English dictionary, published in the late 19th century.) The mission made Ushuaia its first permanent Fuegian outpost, but the Yaghan, who had survived 6000 years without contact, were vulnerable to foreign-brought illnesses and faced increasing infringement by sealers, settlers and gold prospectors. Four Yámana were kidnapped by

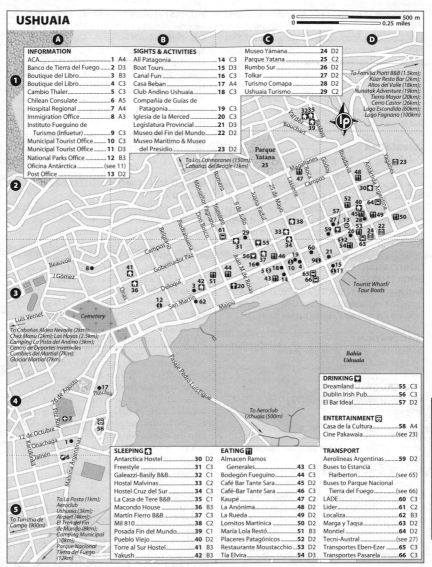

USHUAIA

0 — 500 m
0 — 0.25 miles

Parque
Yatana
25

To Los Cormoranes (150m);
Cabañas del Beagle (1km)

Beauvoir
J Gómez

Cemetery

To Cabañas Aldea Nevada (2km);
Chez Manu (2km); Las Hoyas (2.5km);
Camping La Pista del Andino (3km);
Centro de Deportes Invernales
Cumbres del Martial (7km);
Glaciar Martial (7km)

To La Posta (1km);
Aeroclub
Ushuaia (3km);
Airport (4km);
El Tren del Fin
del Mundo (8km);
Camping Municipal
(10km);
Parque Nacional
Tierra del Fuego
(12km)

To Turismo de
Campo (900m)

To Aeroclub
Ushuaia (500m)

Bahía
Ushuaia

Tourist Wharf/
Tour Boats

TIERRA DEL FUEGO

the naval captain Robert Fitz Roy – including a teenage boy who was later called 'Jemmy Button' – and shipped back to England to be educated and paraded around as examples of gentrified savages. One of the four natives died of disease immediately; after 15 months of public criticism, Fitz Roy agreed to return the Yámana to their homeland. The tribe died

out, and these days, the legacy of Ushuaia's original inhabitants has been reduced to shell mounds, Thomas Bridges' famous dictionary and the Jemmy Button souvenir shop. At the time of writing, one elderly Yámana woman was still alive on Isla Navarino; she's the last full-blooded Yaghan in existence and the only native speaker of the indigenous language.

Between 1884 and 1947 Argentina imitated Britain's example with Australia and made the city a penal colony, incarcerating many of its most notorious criminals and political prisoners here and on remote Isla de los Estados. In 1906 the military prison was moved to Ushuaia, and in 1911 it was combined with the Carcel de Reincidentes, which had incarcerated civilian recidivists since 1896. Since 1950 the town has been an important naval base.

Orientation

Paralleling the Beagle Channel, Maipú becomes Malvinas Argentinas west of the cemetery, then turns into RN 3, continuing 12km to Parque Nacional Tierra del Fuego. To the east, public access ends at Yaganes, which heads north to meet RN 3 going north toward Lago Fagnano. Most visitor services are on or near San Martín, a block from the waterfront.

Information

BOOKSTORES

Boutique del Libro (☎ 432117, 424750; 25 de Mayo 62) Comprehensive, multilingual selection of literature, guidebooks and pictorials; there's a branch at San Martín 1120.

IMMIGRATION

Immigration office (☎ 422334; Beauvoir 1536; ☽ 9am-noon Mon-Fri)

MEDICAL SERVICES

Hospital Regional (☎ 107, 423200; cnr Fitz Roy & 12 de Octubre)

MONEY

Several banks on Maipú and San Martín have ATMs.
Banco de Tierra del Fuego (San Martín 396) Best rates for traveler's checks.
Cambio Thaler (San Martín 778; ☽ 10am-1pm & 5-8pm Mon-Sat, 5-8pm Sun) Convenience equals slightly poorer exchange rates.

POST

Post office (cnr San Martín & Godoy)

TELEPHONE & INTERNET ACCESS

Internet access (around AR$4 per hour) is available at call centers along San Martín.

TOURIST INFORMATION

ACA (Automóvil Club Argentino; ☎ 421121; cnr Malvinas Argentinas & Onachaga) Argentina's auto club; good source for provincial road maps.

Instituto Fueguino de Turismo (Infuetur; ☎ 421423; www.tierradelfuego.org.ar; Maipú 505) On the ground floor of Hotel Albatros.
Municipal tourist office (☎ 432000, at airport 423970, outside of Tierra del Fuego 0800-333-1476; www.turismoushuaia.com, in Spanish; San Martín 674) Very helpful, with English- and French-speaking staff, a message board and multilingual brochures, as well as good lodging, activities and transport info. Also at the airport and pier.
National Parks office (Administración de Parques Nacionales; ☎ 421315; San Martín 1395; ☽ 9am-4pm Mon-Fri)

Sights

MUSEO MARÍTIMO & MUSEO DEL PRESIDIO

When convicts were moved from Isla de los Estados (Staten Island) to Ushuaia in 1906, they began building the national prison, which was finished in 1920. The spokelike halls of single cells were designed to house 380, but in the prison's most active period held up to 800. It closed as a jail in 1947 and now houses the **Museo Marítimo & Museo del Presidio** (☎ 437481; www.museomaritimo.com; cnr Yaganes & Gobernador Paz; adult/student AR$50/35; ☽ 10am-8pm). It's a fine port of call on a blustery day. Halls showing penal life are intriguing, but the informative plaques are only in Spanish. Two of the more illustrious inmates were author Ricardo Rojasand and Russian anarchist Simón Radowitzky.

Perhaps the most worthwhile part of the museum is the exhibit containing incredibly detailed scale models of famous ships, spanning 500 years and providing a unique glimpse into the region's history. In the courtyard are the remains of the world's narrowest-gauge freight train, which transported prisoners between town and work stations.

MUSEO YÁMANA

The small but carefully tended **Museo Yámana** (☎ 422874; Rivadavia 56; admission AR$18; ☽ 10am-8pm) offers an excellent overview of the Yámana (Yaghan) way of life. If you're interested in how the native people managed to survive the harsh weather conditions without clothing, why only the tribe's women knew how to swim, or how it's possible to keep a campfire going in a moving canoe, don't miss this museum. Expertly detailed dioramas (with details in English and Spanish) are based on accessible bays and inlets of the national park; coming here before hiking in the park will give you new bearings.

MUSEO DEL FIN DEL MUNDO

Built in 1903 for the territorial governor Manuel Fernández Valdés, this building was a branch of the Banco de la Nación up until 1979, when it was transformed into the **Museo del Fin del Mundo** (☎ 421863; www.tierradelfuego.org.ar/museo; cnr Maipú & Rivadavia; admission AR$20; ⏰ 9am-8pm). Exhibits on Fuegian natural history, stuffed birdlife, aboriginal life and the early penal colonies, and replicas of an early general store and bank, are of moderate interest.

PARQUE YATANA

Part art project, part urban refuge, **Parque Yatana** (Fundación Cultiva; ☎ 425212; cnr Magallanes & 25 de Mayo; admission AR$20; ⏰ 3-6pm Wed-Fri) is a city block of lenga forest preserved from the encroaching development by one determined family. After checking in, guests can walk the forest paths dotted with small benches.

HISTORIC BUILDINGS

The tourist office distributes a free city-tour map with information on many of the historic houses around town. The 1894 **Legislatura Provincial** (Provincial Legislature; Maipú 465) was the governor's official residence. The century-old **Iglesia de la Merced** (San Martín & Don Bosco) was built with convict labor. **Casa Beban** (cnr Maipú & Plúschow; admission free; ⏰ 10am-8pm Mon-Fri, 4-8pm Sat & Sun) was built in 1911 using parts ordered from Sweden, and sometimes hosts local art exhibits.

Activities

HIKING & CANOPY TOURS

Hiking possibilities should not be limited to Parque Nacional Tierra del Fuego; the entire mountain range behind Ushuaia, with its lakes and rivers, is a hiker's high. However, many trails are poorly marked or not marked at all, and some hikers who have easily scurried uphill have gotten lost trying to find the trail back down.

Club Andino Ushuaia (☎ 422335; www.clubandino ushuaia.com.ar, in Spanish; Juana Fadul 50; ⏰ 9am-1pm & 3-8pm Mon-Fri) sells a map and bilingual trekking, mountaineering and mountain-biking guidebook with rough maps and plenty of trail descriptions. The club occasionally organizes hikes and can recommend hiking guides. Unguided trekkers are strongly encouraged to register with the club or the tourist office before heading out – and check in after a safe return. In an emergency, contact the **Civil Guard** (☎ 103, 22108).

Compañía de Guías de Patagonia (☎ 437753; www .companiadeguias.com.ar; San Martín 654) organizes treks and is often recommended as a reliable information source. Tour companies (p524) also offer trekking tours.

Cerro Martial & Glaciar Martial

A hearty hike from the city center leads up to Glaciar Martial, with fantastic panoramas of Ushuaia and the Beagle Channel; in fact, the views are possibly more impressive than the actual glacier. Catch a taxi up the hill for under AR$25 or jump aboard one of the minivans that leave from the corner of Maipú and Juana Fadul every half-hour from 8:30am to 6:30pm (AR$20 roundtrip) to Cerro Martial. Or if you're up for an all-day hike, follow San Martín west and keep ascending as it zigzags. There are many hiker shortcuts, though you might not want to take your chances cutting through these neighborhoods where you're likely to encounter packs of wild dogs in the streets. When you arrive at the ski run 7km northwest of town, either take the **aerosilla** (AR$35; ⏰ 10am-4pm) chairlift or walk another two hours to make a full day of it. If you take the chairlift, when you get to the top you'll probably want to hike another hour uphill to get the best views.

The cozy **Refugio de Montaña** (snacks AR$7) here offers coffee, desserts and beer at the *aerosilla* base. The ski center there also rents equipment; inquire about snowshoes if there's fresh powder on the mountain. The weather is changeable so take warm, dry clothing and sturdy footwear.

Canopy tours (escuela@tierradelfuego.org.ar; Refugio de Montaña; AR$70-115; ⏰ 10am-5:15pm Oct-Jun) are run from the base of the *aerosilla* and offer an hour's worth of Tarzan time, zipping through the forest with 11 zip-line cables and two hanging bridges. The highest cable is 8m.

BOAT TRIPS

Navigating the Beagle Channel's gunmetal-gray waters, with glaciers and rocky isles in the distance, offers a fresh perspective and decent wildlife watching. On the wharf a string of operators hawk similar offerings: four-hour morning or afternoon excursions (AR$120 to AR$190) that visit the sea-lion colony at Isla de los Lobos and the extensive cormorant colonies at Isla de los Pájaros. An alternative tour takes hikers to the Parque Nacional Tierra del Fuego; they return via private transfer after hiking. Quality may vary: ask about the number of passengers, whether food is served and which sights are visited. A highlight is an island stop to hike and look at *conchales*, middens or shell mounds left by the native Yaghan. The tourist wharf is on Maipú between Lasserre and Roca; most outfitters offer two daily departures around 9:30am and 3pm.

Patagonia Adventure Explorer (☎ 02901-15-465842; www.patagoniaadvent.com.ar; tourist wharf) has comfortable boats with snacks and a short hike on Isla Bridges. For extra adventure, set sail in the 18ft sailboat. Full-day sail trips with wine and gourmet snacks or multiday trips are also available.

Resembling a bathtub toy, the sturdy but small vessel **Tres Marías Excursiones** (☎ 436416; www.tresmariasweb.com; tourist wharf) takes a maximum of eight passengers. It's the only outfitter with permission to land on Isla 'H' in the Isla Bridges natural reserve, which has shell mounds and a colony of rock cormorants.

Alternatively, try a more expensive catamaran trip or the historic 70-passenger **Barracuda** (☎ 437606), which chugs to the Faro Les Eclaireurs lighthouse and Isla de los Lobos and Isla de los Pájaros (AR$120, three hours).

From September through to May, **Cruceros Australis** (☎ in Santiago 02-442-3110; www.australis.com) runs luxurious four-day (starting from AR$3109/3925 per person in low/high season) and five-day sightseeing cruises to Punta Arenas and back, catering mostly to mature travelers. The Saturday departures from Ushuaia include the possibility of disembarking at Cape Horn. Low season is considered to be September to October and mid-March to April. The cruise visits many otherwise inaccessible glaciers, but time alone and hiking opportunities are limited; the focus is more on nature talks and group excursions. **Turismo Comapa** (☎ 430727; www.comapa.com; San Martín 245) handles local bookings for the cruises.

KAYAKING
Professional guide **Daniel Urriza** (☎ 433613, 02901-15-618777; danyurriza@hotmail.com; day trip per person AR$450) has plenty of experience; rounding Cape Horn in a kayak might be the most noteworthy. Excursions can be tailor-made, but generally you can expect to explore the channel, see penguins and sea lions, or head

to Lago Escondido. Kayaking is also a component of many tours to Parque Nacional Tierra del Fuego; see the Nunatak Adventure and Canal Fun listings (p524).

DOG SLEDDING
Wrap yourself in thermal layers and put Fido in the driver's seat. Outfitter **Nunatak Adventure** (☎ 430329; www.nunatakadventure.com; RN 3, Km 3018; guided ride AR$75) at Tierra Mayor takes dog sleds bumping across the valley floor on 2km and 6km rides. Your speed depends on the dogs (Siberian and Alaskan huskies) and conditions: heavy snow means a mild ride while gliding over packed snow feels a little like levitation.

Ski area **Altos del Valle** (☎ 422234; www.gatocuruchet.com.ar) teaches sledding and is the primary sponsor of popular annual dog-sled races at the end of August, where kids also compete. Owner Gato Curuchet was the first South American to participate in Alaska's Iditarod Trail Sled Dog Race.

SKIING
With the surrounding peaks loaded with powder, winter visitors should jump at the chance to explore the local ski resorts. Accessed from RN 3, resorts offer both downhill and cross-country options. The ski season runs from June to September, with July (during schools' winter vacation) the busiest month. Ushuaia's biggest ski event is the annual **Marcha Blanca**, a symbolic re-creation of San Martín's historic August 17, 1817 crossing of the Andes.

The largest resort is **Cerro Castor** (☎ 02901-15-605604/6; www.cerrocastor.com; full-day lift ticket adult/child AR$156/107), 26km from Ushuaia, with 15 runs spanning 400 hectares. Rentals are available for skis, boards, blades and cross-country skis. There's a good restaurant at the base and a summit lodge conducive to afternoon coffee breaks.

The closest ski area to Ushuaia, **Altos del Valle** (☎ 422234; www.gatocuruchet.com.ar) has good cross-country and snowshoeing areas, equipment rentals and full-moon trips. Extreme skiers can check out the snowcat skiing.

For a quick run near town, Club Andino Ushuaia (p521) runs cross-country and downhill slopes only 3km and 5km away. About 7km northwest of town, the family-oriented **Centro de Deportes Invernales Glaciar Martial** (☎ 421423, 423340) has downhill runs well suited for beginners; it also rents equipment.

ANTARCTICA: THE ICE

For many travelers, a journey to Antarctica represents a once-in-a-lifetime adventure. Despite its high price tag, it is much more than just a continent to tick off your list. You will witness both land and ice shelves piled with hundreds of meters of undulating, untouched snow. Glaciers drop from mountainsides and icebergs form sculptures as tall as buildings. The wildlife is thrilling: you will see thousands of curious penguins and an extraordinary variety of flying birds, seals and whales.

Tourism to the icy land of Antarctica is red hot and growing fast. In 2008 more than 38,000 tourists cruised the ice from Ushuaia – a stunning contrast to the continent's population of 5000 (summer) or 1200 (winter) scientists and staff. But travel here is not without its costs. On November 23, 2007, the hull of the MV *Explorer* was gashed by ice but evacuated successfully before sinking. The circumstances were highly unusual, although the incident will likely provoke further safety measures. We can only hope that careful management will ensure that this glorious continent remains unspoilt.

So long as you've got two or three weeks to spare, hopping on board a cruise ship is not out of the question. Some voyages take in the Falkland Islands and South Georgia (human population 10 to 20, estimated penguin population two to three million); some go just to the Antarctic Peninsula; others focus on retracing historic expeditions. A small but growing handful of visitors reach Antarctica aboard private vessels. All are sailboats (although obviously equipped with auxiliary engines).

The season runs from mid-October to mid-March, depending on ice conditions. It used to be that peak-season voyages sold out; now most trips do. When shopping around, ask how many days you will actually spend in Antarctica, as crossing the Southern Ocean takes up to two days each way. And how many landings will there be? The smaller the ship, the more landings there are per passenger (always depending on the weather, of course). Tour companies charge anywhere from US$7000 to US$70,000, although some ships allow walk-ons, which can cost as little as US$5000.

Due to Ushuaia's proximity to the Antarctic Peninsula, most cruises leave from here. Last-minute bookings can be made through **Ushuaia Turismo** (☎ 02901-436003; www.ushuaiaturismoevt .com.ar; ushuaiaturismo@speedy.com.ar; Gobernador Paz 865). Other travel agencies offering packages include **Rumbo Sur** (☎ 02901-422275; www.rumbosur.com.ar; San Martín 350), **All Patagonia** (☎ 02901-433622; www.allpatagonia.com; Juana Fadul 60) and **Canal Fun** (☎ 02901-437395; www.canalfun.com; 9 de Julio 118), though there are many more.

Check that your company is a member of **IAATO** (www.iaato.org), which mandates strict guidelines for responsible travel to Antarctica. The following are just a few companies that go to Antarctica.

Adventure Associates (www.adventureassociates.com) Australia's first tour company to Antarctica, with many ships and destinations.

Heritage Expeditions (www.heritage-expeditions.com) Award-winning New Zealand company that also goes to the Ross Sea/East Antarctica regions.

Peregrine Adventures (www.peregrineadventures.com) Offers unique trips that include visiting the Antarctic Circle, with kayaking and camping options.

Quark Expeditions (www.quarkexpeditions.com) Three kinds of ships, from an icebreaker to a 48-passenger small ship for close-knit groups.

WildWings Travel (www.wildwings.co.uk) UK-based company that focuses on bird-watching and wildlife in Antarctica.

For more information see Lonely Planet's *Antarctica* guidebook. Online, check out www.70south .com for up-to-date information and articles. In Ushuaia consult the very helpful **Oficina Antártica** (Antarctica tourist office; ☎ 02901-421423; infoantartida@tierradelfuego.org.ar) at the pier. And one last thing: bring more film and/or extra memory cards than you think you'll need. You'll thank us later.

Transportes Pasarela and Buses Alvarez run hourly shuttles (AR$30) from the corner of Juana Fadul and Maipú to the ski centers along RN 3, from 9am to 2pm daily. Each resort also provides its own transportation from downtown Ushuaia.

Tours

Many travel agencies sell tours around the region. You can go horseback riding, hiking, canoeing, visit Lagos Escondido and Fagnano, stay at an *estancia*, spy on birds and beavers, and even get pulled by huskies on a dog sled (winter only).

All Patagonia (☎ 433622; www.allpatagonia.com; Juana Fadul 60) Amex rep offering more conventional and luxurious trips.

Canal Fun (☎ 437395; www.canalfun.com; 9 de Julio 118) Run by hip young guys, these popular all-day outings include hiking and kayaking in Parque Nacional Tierra del Fuego (AR$500), the famous off-roading adventure around Lago Fagnano (AR$390), and a multisport outing around Estancia Harberton that includes kayaking around Estancia Harberton and a visit to the penguin colony (AR$625).

Compañía de Guías de Patagonia (☎ 437753; www.companiadeguias.com.ar; San Martín 654) Organizes full-day treks with climbing and ice-hiking on Glaciar Vinciguerra (AR$365), and two-day high-mountain treks to Cerro Alvear with glacier camping (ask for rates).

Nunatak Adventure (☎ 430329; www.nunatakadventure.com) Offers competitively priced adventure tours and has its own mountain base. Many travelers have liked the off-roading day trip to Lago Fagnano with canoeing and a full barbecue (AR$300).

Piratour (☎ 424834; www.piratour.com.ar; tourist wharf) Runs 20-person tours to Isla Martillo for trekking around Magellanic and Papúa penguins.

Rumbo Sur (☎ 422275; www.rumbosur.com.ar; San Martín 350) Ushuaia's longest-running agency specializes in more conventional activities.

Tolkar (☎ 431408/12; www.tolkarturismo.com.ar; Roca 157) Another helpful, popular, all-round agency, affiliated with Tecni-Austral buses.

Turismo Comapa (☎ 430727; www.comapa.com; San Martín 245) Confirm Navimag and Cruceros Australis passages here.

Turismo de Campo (☎ 437351; www.turismodecampo.com, in Spanish; Fuegia Basket 414) Organizes light trekking, Beagle Channel sailing trips and visits to Estancia Rolito near Río Grande. Also sells a wide variety of nine- to 12-night Antarctica passages.

Ushuaia Turismo (☎ 436003; www.ushuaiaturismoevt.com.ar; Gobernador Paz 865) Offers last-minute Antarctica cruise bookings.

Sleeping

Lodging is scarce in the January and February high season and during early March's Fin del Mundo Marathon. During these periods, reserving ahead is essential. Most lodgings offer free transfers in; check when you reserve. In winter those places that stay open drop their rates a bit. Most hotels offer laundry service.

The municipal tourist office (p520) has lists of B&Bs and *cabañas* (cabins), and also posts a list of available lodgings outside after closing time.

BUDGET

Hostels abound, all with kitchens and most with internet access. Rates typically drop 25% in the low season (April to October).

Camping Municipal (RN 3) Ten kilometers west of town, en route to Parque Nacional Tierra del Fuego, this free campground boasts a lovely setting but minimal facilities.

Camping La Pista del Andino (☎ 435890; www.lapistadelandino.com.ar, in Spanish; Alem 2873; campsite per person AR$22) A steep, uphill, 3km trek leads to this pleasant campground offering grassy or forested sites with views. While it's short on showers and toilets, perks include decent cooking facilities, a bar-restaurant, good common areas and bikes for rent (AR$25). It's at Club Andino Ushuaia's ski area. Call for free pickup from the airport or town center.

Torre al Sur Hostel (☎ 430745; www.torrealsur.com.ar; Gobernador Paz 1437; dm HI member/nonmember AR$46/49; ☐) Perched on a hilltop, this tower with gingerbread trim is ideal for eating in (see the large kitchen with stainless-steel countertops). Don't expect privacy: the small, mazelike dorm rooms can be noisy.

Hostel Cruz del Sur (☎ 423110; www.xdelsur.com.ar; Deloquí 636; dm AR$60; ☐) Cramped but cozy, this popular hostel lines its walls with old postcards and primary hues. The six- to eight-bed dorms (with heaters, thin mattresses and bedding) can get loud, and when filled to capacity the bathrooms are taxed to the max. But the welcoming hosts do a fine job of rounding up groups to explore nearby areas.

Freestyle (☎ 432874; www.ushuaiafreestyle.com; Gobernador Paz 866/868; dm AR$60; ☐) This five-star hostel boasts immaculate dorms with cozy fleece blankets, a marble-countertop cooking area, and a sprawling, sunny living room with leatherette sofas and gaping panoramic views. If it's howling outside, cue up a game of billiards or lounge in a comfy beanbag chair.

Yakush (☎ 435807; www.hostelyakush.com.ar; Piedrabuena 118; dm/d AR$60/180) Exuding warmth and skillfully adorned with whimsical drawings, this colorful hostel is well-kept and exceedingly friendly. It's a prime choice: dorms have fresh sheets and good beds, and social spaces include an ample upstairs lounge with futons and slanted ceilings.

La Posta (☎ 444650; www.laposta-ush.com.ar; Perón Sur 864; dm/d AR$60/180; 🖳) This cozy hostel and guesthouse on the outskirts of town is hugely popular with young travelers thanks to warm service, homey decor, two spotless open kitchens and fresh *medialunas* with coffee for breakfast. Another upside is La Posta's lovely location, half-surrounded by snowcapped mountains – the downside is that the place is far from the town center, but public buses and taxis are plentiful.

Antarctica Hostel (☎ 435774; www.antarcticahostel.com; Antártida Argentina 270; dm/d/tr AR$60/200/270; 🖳) An open floor plan and beer on tap make this trendy backpacker hub conducive to making friends. Guests play cards in the common room and cook in a cool balcony kitchen. The cement rooms are the biggest drawback; though ample in size, some smell of insecticide.

Los Cormoranes (☎ 423459; www.loscormoranes.com; Kamshen 788; dm/d/tr AR$60/250/300; 🖳) Mellower than the competition, this friendly HI hostel is a 10-minute (uphill) walk north of the center. Good, warm, six-bed dorms face outdoor plank hallways – making that midnight bathroom dash bearable. Modern doubles have polished cement floors and bright down duvets – the best is Room 10, with bay views. The abundant breakfast includes toast, coffee, do-it-yourself eggs and freshly squeezed orange juice.

MIDRANGE

Pueblo Viejo (☎ 432098; www.puebloviejo.info; Deloquí 242; s/d/tr AR$150/200/220; 🖳) This snug and relaxed eight-room lodging is great value and comprises two renovated houses (1920 and 1926) joined by a passageway. Tasteful rooms have firm mattresses and central heating; all share bathrooms. Cars can also be rented here; guests get discount rates.

Galeazzi-Basily B&B (☎ 423213; www.avesdelsur.com.ar; Valdéz 323; d AR$200; 🖳) The best feature of this elegant wooded residence is its warm and hospitable family. Rooms are small but offer a personal touch; some share a bathroom. Since beds are twin-sized, couples may prefer one of the modern cabins out the back. It's a peaceful spot, and where else can you practice your English, French, Italian and Portuguese?

La Casa de Tere B&B (☎ 422312; www.lacasadetere.com.ar; Rivadavia 620; d with/without bathroom AR$210/180) Tere showers her guests with attention in this beautiful modern home with great views. Its three tidy rooms fill up fast. Guests can cook, and there's cable TV and a fireplace in the living room. It's a short but steep walk uphill from the center.

Familia Piatti B&B (☎ 437104; www.interpatagonia.com/familiapiatti, in Spanish; Bahía Paraíso 812, Bosque del Faldeo; s/d/tr AR$225/275/350; 🖳) If idling in the forest sounds good, head for this friendly B&B with warm down duvets and native lenga-wood furniture. Hiking trails nearby lead up into the mountains. The friendly owners are multilingual (English, Italian and Portuguese) and can arrange transport and guided excursions.

Hostal Malvinas (☎ 422626; www.hostalmalvinas.net; Deloquí 615; s/d/tr AR$280/320/360) Representing good value but with no 'wow' factor, Malvinas offers standard hotel amenities at OK prices and happens to be central. The staff is hospitable and rooms are well kept – some have excellent harbor views. Clunky gas heaters, worn carpets and dated decor are the shortcomings. But you can enjoy hot drinks and pastries, available all day in the breakfast nook.

Martín Fierro B&B (☎ 430525; www.martinfierrobyb.com.ar; 9 de Julio 175; d AR$280) Spending a night at this charming inn feels like staying at the cool mountain cabin of a worldly friend who makes strong coffee and has a great book collection. The owner, Javier, personally built the interiors with local wood and stone; these days he cultivates a friendly, laid-back atmosphere where travelers get into deep conversations at the breakfast table.

TOP END

Posada Fin del Mundo (☎ 437345; www.posadafindelmundo.com.ar; cnr Rivadavia & Valdéz; d/tr AR$340/460) A friendly and well-traveled couple welcome guests into this lovely home. The enchantment starts with a snug living room with expansive water views. Eight fresh, tiled rooms tend toward the small side but beds are long. A big breakfast includes eggs, oatmeal, fruit and yogurt. The Fin del Mundo is on a quiet street, a good four-block walk uphill out of town.

Macondo House (☎ 437576; www.macondohouse.com; Gobernador Paz 1410; d AR$350) This sleek red house offers up a soothing refuge with dazzling views of the bay. Paper lanterns, geometric furniture and abstract art create a minimalist feel. Rooms have vaulted ceilings, TV and king-sized beds with down duvets.

Cabañas Aldea Nevada (☎ 422851; www.aldeanevada.com.ar; Martial 1430; d AR$380, 3-night minimum; ▣) You expect the elves to arrive here any minute. This beautiful patch of lenga forest is discreetly dotted with 13 log cabins with outdoor grills and rough-hewn benches contemplatively placed by the ponds. Interiors are rustic but modern, with functional kitchens, wood stoves and hardwood details.

Mil 810 (☎ 437710; www.hotel1810.com; 25 de Mayo 245; d/tr AR$410/475; ▣) This sleek boutique hotel plays with nature and modern style. It's not subtle: guests are first welcomed by a retention wall of river stones and a rock face trickling with water. Its 38 rooms feature brocade walls, rich tones, luxuriant textures and touches of abstract art. Rooms have flat-screen TVs and safes, and halls are monitored.

Cabañas del Beagle (☎ 432785; www.cabanasdelbeagle.com; Las Aljabas 375; 2-person cabin AR$480; ▨) Couples in search of a romantic hideaway delight in these rustic chic cabins with heated stone floors, crackling fireplaces and full kitchens stocked daily with fresh bread, coffee and other treats. The personable owner, Alejandro, wins high praise for his attentive service.

ourpick Cumbres del Martial (☎ 424779; www.cumbresdelmartial.com.ar; Martial 3560; r/ste AR$730/1093; ▣) A getaway that you may never want to leave, this stylish place sits at the base of the Glaciar Martial. Standard rooms have a touch of the English cottage, while the two-story wooden cabins are simply stunners, with stone fireplaces, Jacuzzis and dazzling vaulted windows. Lush robes, optional massages (extra) and your country's newspaper delivered to your mailbox are some of the delicious details.

Las Hayas (☎ 430710/8; www.lashayashotel.com; Martial 1650; d AR$1200, ste AR$1562-2320; ▣ ☎) Serving the likes of Nelson Mandela and Mercosur presidents, Ushuaia's only five-star resort is dramatically perched 3km above town. Its elegant, traditional rooms have fine monochrome patterns, some canopy beds and great bay views.

Eating

La Anónima (cnr Gobernador Paz & Rivadavia) A grocery store with cheap take-out.

ourpick Almacen Ramos Generales (☎ 427317; www.ramosgeneralesushuaia.com; Maipú 749; snacks AR$9) The real draw of this rustic-chic general store and cafe is its baked goods: the French pastry chef bakes crusty baguettes, croissants and chocolate cakes shaped like Magellanic penguins. Knock off a few postcards while lingering over a gourmet hot chocolate infused with *dulce de leche* (milk caramel) liqueur.

Lomitos Martinica (San Martín 68; mains AR$12-25; ⊙ 11:30am-3pm & 8:30pm-midnight) Cheap and cheerful dining at its best, this *parrilla* with grillside seating serves enormous *milanesa* (breaded fish) sandwiches and offers an economical lunch special.

Café-Bar Tante Sara (☎ 433710; www.cafebartantesara.com.ar; cnr San Martín & Juana Fadul; mains AR$22-35) Serving up burgers, cocktails and a killer grilled-chicken caesar salad, this popular corner bistro offers classic atmosphere. Tante Sara is so well-liked that even the sister branch, a few blocks away near the intersection of San Martín and Rivadavia, is often packed with locals having coffee and pastries.

Restaurante Moustacchio (☎ 423308; www.moustacchio.com.ar; cnr San Martín & Godoy; mains AR$25-40; ⊙ lunch & dinner) This classic corner restaurant serves fresh seafood dishes, fondue for two, fabulous crab omelettes, steaks, and wine by the glass or half-glass. Old-fashioned service and reasonable prices add to the appeal.

Bodegón Fueguino (☎ 431972; www.tierradehumos.com/bodegon; San Martín 859; mains AR$30-45; ⊙ Tue-Sun) A great gathering spot for wine and appetizers, this century-old Fuegian home is cozied up with sheepskin-clad benches, cedar barrels and ferns. A *picada* (shared appetizer plate) for two includes eggplant, lamb brochettes, crab and bacon-wrapped plums.

María Lola Restó (☎ 421185; Deloquí 1048; mains AR$35-48; ⊙ noon-midnight Mon-Sat) 'Satisfying' defines the experience at this creative cafe-style restaurant overlooking the channel. Locals pack this silver house for homemade pasta with seafood or strip steak in rich mushroom sauce. Service is good and portions tend toward humongous: desserts can easily be split.

Chez Manu (☎ 432253; www.chezmanu.com; Martial 2135; mains AR$45-55) If you are headed to Glaciar Martial, don't miss this gem on the way. Chef Emmanuel puts a French touch on fresh local ingredients such as Fuegian lamb or mixed plates of cold *fruits de mer*. The three-course set lunch is the best deal. Views are a welcome bonus. It's 2km from town.

Placeres Patagónicos (☎ 433798; www.patagoni cosweb.com.ar; cnr Godoy & Deloquí; mains AR$25-45) This cozy and stylish cafe-deli serves up wooden cutting boards piled high with homemade bread and mouth-watering local specialties: smoked trout, wild boar and salmon, to name just some. Coffee arrives steaming hot in a bowl-sized mug.

Tía Elvira (☎ 424725; www.tiaelvira.com; Maipú 394; mains AR$38-65; ☺ closed Sun) This highly regarded traditional venue produces seafood favorites such as grilled trout or scallops in garlic sauce. Before eating, take a peek at the small museum lining the entrance hall.

La Rueda (☎ 436540; San Martín 193; buffet AR$55) This good *tenedor libre* (all-you-can-eat restaurant) offers a variety of salads alongside tasty steaks and seafood grilled over coals in the window. Ordering a drink is mandatory with the buffet, which includes dessert.

Kaupé (☎ 422704; www.kaupe.com.ar; Roca 470; mains AR$45-58) For an out-of-body seafood experience, head to this candlelit house overlooking the bay. Chef Ernesto Vivian employs the freshest of everything and service is nothing less than impeccable. Good options include scallop ceviche, black sea bass in blackened butter, and mero (Patagonian sea bass) sashimi drizzled with soy.

Drinking

Geographically competitive drinkers should note that the southernmost bar in the world is not here but on a Ukrainian research station in Antarctica.

Dreamland (☎ 421246; cnr 9 de Julio & Deloquí; drinks AR$15; ☺ 11am-late; ⌨) The bar du jour, this ambient house mixes it up with DJs, free tango nights and happy hours. During the day it's a quiet cafe with good-value lunch specials.

Dublin Irish Bar (☎ 430744; www.dublinushuaia.com; cnr 9 de Julio & Deloquí) Dublin doesn't feel so far away with the lively banter and free-flowing drinks at this dimly lit foreigners' favorite. Look for occasional live music and be sure to try at least one of its three local Beagle beers.

El Bar Ideal (☎ 437860; cnr San Martín & Roca) After a cold day of boating or hiking, warm up with a pint and some lamb stew at this cozy corner pub. If you sit in the corner, you'll have water views; wood tables and a central bar fill up after dark.

Küar Resto Bar (☎ 437396; www.kuar.com.ar; Av Perito Moreno 2232; ☺ 6pm-late) This chic new log-cabin-style bar welcomes the 'after-ski' crowd for fresh cocktails, local beer and tapas. The interior is stylish but the real highlight, especially at sunset, is the jaw-dropping views over the water. You'll have to catch a cab; Küar is a few kilometers outside of town by the water.

Entertainment

Cine Pakawaia (☎ 436500; cnr Yaganes & Gobernador Paz; tickets AR$12) First-run movies are shown at the Presidio's fully restored hangar-style theater.

Casa de la Cultura (☎ 422417; cnr Malvinas Argentinas & 12 de Octubre) Hidden behind a gym, this center hosts occasional live-music shows.

Getting There & Away
AIR

Aerolíneas Argentinas (☎ 421218; Roca 116) jets several times daily to Buenos Aires (AR$983, 3½ hours), sometimes stopping in El Calafate (AR$700, 70 minutes).

LADE (☎ 421123; San Martín 542) has flights to Buenos Aires (AR$503), Comodoro Rivadavia (AR$373), El Calafate (AR$362) and Río Gallegos (AR$210). The airport departure tax is AR$25.

Chilean airline **Aerovías DAP** (www.dap.cl) offers charter-only flights to destinations in Patagonia, as well as flights over Cape Horn and trips to Chile's Frei base in Antarctica.

Aeroclub Ushuaia (☎ 421717, 421892; www.aeroclu bushuaia.org.ar) offers scenic 'flightseeing' tours (AR$200 to AR$400 per person).

BOAT

Charter boats anchored in Ushuaia's harbor may take passengers to Puerto Williams (AR$377) the next time they are heading out to sea.

A number of private yachts charter trips to Cape Horn, Antarctica and, less often, South Georgia Island. These trips must be organized well in advance. The trip around Cape Horn is the most popular weeklong charter and costs upwards of AR$5400 per person. A recommended option is **Mago del Sur** (☎ 02901-15-5148-6463; www.magodelsur.com.ar; charter per person per day AR$750), captained by Alejandro Damilano, whose lifetime of sailing ensures skill and safety at the helm. Individuals can join scheduled trips to Las Islas Malvinas, Antarctica, Cape Horn, Puerto Natales and beyond.

Cruises (p522) can offer transportation.

TIERRA DEL FUEGO

BUS

Ushuaia has no bus terminal. Book outgoing bus tickets as much in advance as possible; many readers have complained about getting stuck here in high season. Depending on your luck, long waits at border crossings can be expected.

Tecni-Austral (☎ 431408/12; Roca 157) and **Marga y Taqsa** (☎ 435453; Godoy 41) run buses to Río Grande (AR$50, four hours) most days of the week at 5am or 5:30am, stopping in Tolhuin. On alternating weekdays, the two bus lines offer onward connecting service to Punta Arenas (AR$140, 11 hours), with service to Río Gallegos (AR$145, 12 hours) on weekdays. Service is less frequent in shoulder season.

Lider (☎ 436421; Gobernador Paz 921) and **Montiel** (☎ 421366; Deloquí 110) run door-to-door minivans to Tolhuin (AR$30, 2½ hours) and Río Grande (AR$60, four hours) six to eight times daily, with fewer departures on Sunday.

Transportes Pasarela (☎ 433712; cnr Maipú & 25 de Mayo) runs roundtrip shuttles to Lago Esmeralda (AR$40), Lago Escondido (AR$90) and Lago Fagnano (AR$100), leaving around 10am and returning at 2pm and 6:30pm. If you're planning to stay overnight, ask to pay just one way (more likely if there are many people traveling) and arrange for pickup. Transportes Eben-Ezer offers a similar service and leaves from nearby.

For transport to Parque Nacional Tierra del Fuego, see p530.

Getting Around

Taxis to/from the modern airport (USH), 4km southwest of downtown, cost AR$18. Taxis can be chartered for around AR$60 per hour. There's a local bus service along Maipú.

Rental rates for compact cars, including insurance, start at around AR$185 per day (for 200km; rates for unlimited mileage start around AR$255); try Pueblo Viejo (p525) or **Localiza** (☎ 430739; Sarmiento 81). Some agencies may not charge for dropoff in other parts of Argentine Tierra del Fuego.

PARQUE NACIONAL TIERRA DEL FUEGO

Banked against the channel, the hushed, fragrant southern forests of Tierra del Fuego are a stunning setting to explore. West of Ushuaia some 12km along RN 3, **Parque Nacional Tierra del Fuego** (admission AR$50) was Argentina's first coastal national park and extends 630 sq km from the Beagle Channel in the south to beyond Lago Fagnano in the north. However, only a couple of thousand hectares along the southern edge of the park are open to the public, with a minuscule system of short, easy trails that are designed more for day-tripping families than backpacking trekkers. The rest of the park is protected as a *reserva natural estricta* (strictly off-limits zone). Despite this, a few scenic hikes along the bays and rivers, or through dense native forests of evergreen coihue, canelo and deciduous lenga, are worthwhile. For truly spectacular color, come in autumn when hillsides of ñire burst out in red.

Birdlife is prolific, especially along the coastal zone. Keep an eye out for condors, albatross, cormorants, gulls, terns, oystercatchers, grebes, kelp geese and the comical, flightless, orange-billed steamer ducks. Common invasive species include the European rabbit and the North American beaver, both of which are wreaking ecological havoc in spite of their cuteness. Gray and red foxes, enjoying the abundance of rabbits, may also be seen.

Hiking

After running 3242km from Buenos Aires, RN 3 reaches its terminus at the shores of Bahía Lapataia. From here, trails **Mirador Lapataia** (500m), with excellent views, and **Senda Del Turbal** (400m) lead through winding lenga forest further into the bay. Other short walks include the self-guided nature trail **Senda Laguna Negra** (950m), through peat bogs, and the **Senda Castorera** (400m), showcasing massive beaver dams, now abandoned, on a few ponds.

SENDA HITO XXIV

From Camping Lago Roca, a flat 10km (four-hour) roundtrip trek leads around Lago Roca's forested northeast shore to Hito XXIV – that number is *veinticuatro* in Spanish – the boundary post that marks the Argentina-Chile frontier. It is illegal to cross the frontier, which is patrolled regularly.

From the same trailhead you can reach **Cerro Guanaco** (973m) via the steep and difficult 8km trail of the same name; it's a long uphill haul but the views are excellent.

SENDA COSTERA

This 8km (four-hour) trek leads west from Bahía Ensenada along the coastline. Keep an eye out for old *conchales* (archaeologically

important mounds of shells left by Yaghan inhabitants), now covered in grass. The trail meets RN 3 a short way east of the park administration (*guardería*) center at Lapataia. From here it is 1.2km further to Senda Hito XXIV.

It might be tempting to roll up the cuffs and go clamming, but be aware that occasional red tides (*marea roja*) contaminate mollusks (such as clams and mussels) along the shore of the Beagle Channel.

SENDA PALESTRA
This 4km (three-hour) roundtrip trek from Bahía Ensenada follows a path eastward past an old copper mine to the popular rock-climbing wall of Palestra, near a *refugio* (rustic shelter) that is no longer in use.

SENDA PAMPA ALTA
The low heights of Pampa Alta (around 315m) grant long views across the Beagle Channel to Isla Navarino and Isla Hoste. RN 3 meets the trailhead 1.5km west of the Río Pipo and Bahía Ensenada road turnoffs (3km from the entrance gate). The 5km roundtrip trail first climbs a hill, passing a beaver dam along the way. Enjoy the impressive views at the lookout. A quick 300m further leads to a trail paralleling the Río Pipo and some waterfalls.

ISLA EL SALMÓN & LAGUNA NEGRA
From the road 2km southwest of Lapataia, a trail leads north along the western side of Río Lapataia to a fishing spot opposite Isla El Salmón. Laguna Negra, a lovely lake in the forest, is easily accessible via a 1km circuit loop signposted 200m past the trail to Isla El Salmón.

Sleeping & Eating
Campgrounds are the only lodging in the park. Most are free, lack services and get crowded, which means sites can get unreasonably messy. Do your part to take your trash out of the park and follow a leave-no-trace ethic. Camping Ensenada is 16km from the park entrance and nearest the Costera trail; Camping Río Pipo is 6km from the entrance and easily accessed by either the road to Cañadon del Toro or the Pampa Alta trail. Camping Las Bandurrias, Camping Laguna Verde and Camping Los Cauquenes are on the islands in Río Lapataia.

TIERRA DEL FUEGO

The only fee-based campground is **Camping Lago Roca** (per person with shower AR$9), 9km from the park entrance. It's also the only one that has hot showers, a good *confitería* (cafe offering light meals) and a tiny (expensive) grocery store. However, there's plenty of room in the park to rough it at wild sites. Note that water at Lago Roca is not potable; boil it before using.

Getting There & Away

Buses leave from the corner of Maipú and Juana Fadul in Ushuaia several times daily from 9am to 6pm, returning approximately every hour between 8am and 8pm. Depending on your destination, a round-trip fare runs ARS$50 to AR$60, and you need not return the same day. Private tour buses cost AR$100 for a roundtrip. Taxi fares shared between groups can be the same price as bus tickets.

The most touristy and, beyond jogging, the slowest way to the park, **El Tren del Fin de Mundo** (☎ 02901-431600; www.trendelfindemundo.com.ar; AR$95, plus park entrance fee) originally carted prisoners to work camps. It departs (sans convicts) from the Estación del Fin de Mundo, 8km west of Ushuaia (taxis AR$30 one way), three or four times daily in summer and once or twice daily in winter. The one-hour, scenic narrow-gauge train ride comes with historical explanations in English and Spanish. Reserve in January and February, when cruise-ship tours take over. If you are not a train fanatic, take it one way and return via minibus.

Hitchhiking to the park is feasible, but many cars will already be full.

ESTANCIA HARBERTON

Historic **Estancia Harberton** (☎ tours through Aves del Sur 01901-423213; www.estanciaharberton.com; tour AR$30; 🕙 10am-7pm Oct 15-Apr 15) was founded in 1886 by missionary Thomas Bridges and his family. As Tierra del Fuego's first *estancia* it contains the island's oldest house – still in use. The location earned fame from a stirring memoir written by Bridges' son Lucas, titled *Uttermost Part of the Earth* (see the boxed text, below). The *estancia* is now owned and run by the Goodalls, direct descendants of the Bridges.

Harberton is a working station, although only a handful of sheep and 1000 cattle remain on 200 sq km. The location is splendid and the history alluring. A one-hour guided tour (at 11am, 1:30pm, 3pm and 5pm) takes in the family cemetery and a garden where foliage names are given in Yaghan, Selk'nam and Spanish. There's also an abundant farm-house tea service (AR$30), complete lunch (AR$95), optional excursions to the Reserva Yecapasela penguin colony and a replica of a Yaghan dwelling. It's also a popular destination for bird-watchers.

TALES FROM THE UTTERMOST PART OF THE EARTH

Imagine a childhood where your backyard is the Beagle Channel, your playmates are unclothed Yaghans and your initiation into adulthood includes hunting wild bulls, saving ships from being wrecked off the coast and surviving bandit raids. Welcome to the life of E Lucas Bridges, as fraught and daring as any adventure penned by Stevenson or Krakauer.

Bridges' classic memoir, *Uttermost Part of the Earth,* starts with his British father establishing an Anglican mission in untamed Ushuaia. Little house on the prairie it wasn't. Once they moved from Ushuaia to remote Harberton, the family lived in lean-tos until a house could be shipped in pieces from England (it now stands as the oldest structure in Tierra del Fuego). Bridges spent the late 1800s growing up among the now-extinct Selk'nam and Yaghan people. He learned their languages and was one of the few who recorded indigenous customs with respect and insight.

By the time Bridges' book was published in 1948, the native population of Tierra del Fuego had nosedived to fewer than 150. *Uttermost Part of the Earth* captures the last years of Tierra del Fuego's native peoples and the island's transformation from an untouched wilderness to a frontier molded by fortune-seekers, missionaries and sheep ranching. After years out of print, the book's recent re-release rescues Tierra del Fuego's powerful history and wild landscape from oblivion, reminding us of the riches that still remain.

Though he is buried in Chacarita Cemetery in Buenos Aires, traces of Lucas Bridges live on throughout the island, from his family *estancia* of Harberton to his own Estancia Viamonte (near Río Grande) and the jagged peaks backing Ushuaia that bear his name.

Worth the trip is the impressive **Museo Acatushún** (www.acatushun.com; admission AR$15; ☼ hours vary), created by Natalie Prosser Goodall, a North American biologist who married into the family. Emphasizing the region's marine mammals, the museum has inventoried thousands of mammal and bird specimens; among the rarest specimens is a Hector's beaked whale. Much of this vast collection was found at Bahía San Sebastián, north of Río Grande, where a difference of up to 11km between high and low tide leaves animals stranded. Confirm the museum's opening hours with the *estancia*.

Volunteers and interns, mostly advanced university students studying tourism or biology, are taken on to work as tour guides and research assistants for the museum. Volunteers stay one month and are provided with food, lodging and the occasional opportunity to work in the field. Competition is fierce and preference is given to Argentines.

Harberton has no phones on-site so make reservations well in advance. With advance permission, free primitive camping is allowed at Río Lasifashaj, Río Varela and Río Cambaceres. Lodging is offered in the 1950 **Shepherds' house** (per person AR$455) and remodeled 1901 **Cook house** (with shared bathroom per person AR$265-342); three-course lunches and dinners cost an extra AR$95 each.

Harberton is 85km east of Ushuaia via RN 3 and rough RC-j, a 1½- to two-hour drive one way. Shuttles leave from the base of 25 de Mayo at Av Maipú in Ushuaia at 9am, returning around 3pm (AR$130 roundtrip); alternatively, take a taxi (around AR$400 roundtrip). Day-long catamaran tours are organized by agencies in Ushuaia.

PUERTO WILLIAMS (CHILE)
☎ 61 / pop 2500

Forget Ushuaia: the end of the world starts where colts roam Main St and yachts rounding Cape Horn take refuge. Naval settlement Puerto Williams is the only town on Isla Navarino, the official port of entry for vessels en route to Cape Horn and Antarctica, and home to the last living Yaghan speaker.

The village centers on a freshly sodded green roundabout and a concrete-slab plaza called the Centro Comercial. But just outside Puerto Williams is some of the Southern Cone's most breathtaking scenery. With over 150km of trails, Isla Navarino is a rugged, backpackers' paradise, with slate-colored lakes, mossy lenga forests and the ragged spires of the Dientes de Navarino. Trails lead past beaver dams, bunkers and army trenches as they climb steeply up into the mountains and deeper into forests. Some 40,000 beavers introduced from Canada in the 1940s now plague the island; they're even on the menu, if you can find an open restaurant.

Mid-19th-century missionaries, followed by fortune-seekers during the 1890s gold rush, established a permanent European presence here. The remaining mixed-race descendants of the Yaghan (Yámana) people are established in a small seaside village called Villa Ukika.

Information
Near the main roundabout, the Centro Comercial contains the post office, internet access, Aerovías DAP's representative and a couple of call centers. Money exchange (US cash only, US$100 minimum) and Visa advances are possible at Banco de Chile, where there is also an ATM.

Turismo SIM (☎ 621150; www.simltd.com) has details about the many sailing, trekking and expedition possibilities south of the 54th parallel, including Cape Horn, the Cordillera Darwin, Isla Navarino, South Georgia Island and the Antarctic Peninsula. The **municipalidad** (☎ 621011; O'Higgins 165) runs a rarely staffed **tourist info kiosk** (☎ 621012) at the roundabout.

Sights & Activities
Near the entrance to the military quarters is the original bow of the **Yelcho**, which rescued Ernest Shackleton's Antarctic expedition from Elephant Island in 1916.

The free **Museo Martín Gusinde** (☎ 621043; cnr Araguay & Gusinde; donation requested; ☼ 9am-1pm & 2:30-7pm Mon-Fri), honoring the German priest and ethnographer who worked among the Yaghans from 1918 to 1923, focuses on ethnography and natural history.

A 15-minute walk east of town along the waterfront leads to the settlement of Villa Ukika. Its modest crafts shop, **Kipa-Akar** (House of Woman), sells language books, jewelry and whale-bone knives. Ask a villager for help if it's closed.

Latin America's southernmost ethnobotanical park, **Omora** (www.cabodehornos.org), has trails with plant names marked in Yaghan, Latin and Spanish. Take the road to the right of the Virgin altar, 4km (an hour's walk) toward

Puerto Navarino. Donations help advocate for the creation of a Cape Horn Biosphere Reserve.

Hiking to **Cerro Bandera** affords expansive views of the Beagle Channel. Start this four-hour roundtrip at the Navarino Circuit. The trail ascends steeply through lenga to blustery stone-littered hilltops. For guided treks, contact **Turismo Shila** (☎ 621745; Plaza de Ancla s/n). Self-supported backpackers can continue on for the whole four- to five-day **Dientes de Navarino** circuit, enjoying impossibly raw and wind-swept vistas under Navarino's toothy spires. For details on trekking possibilities, refer to Lonely Planet's *Trekking in the Patagonian Andes*.

Many local lodgings can arrange tours of the island. For yacht tours to Antarctica and around the Beagle Channel, as well as trek-king, climbing and horse-riding expeditions, contact Turismo SIM (see p531).

Sleeping

Refugio El Padrino (☎ 621136; Costanera 267; dm CH$10,000) This clean, self-service hostel is located right on the channel; the views are sublime at sunset.

Hostal Lajuwa (☎ 621267; Villa Ukika; dm CH$12,000) These clean dorm-style rooms in the Yaghan community are a bit isolated but make for an interesting cultural exchange.

Residencial Pusaki (☎ 621116; Piloto Pardo 242; s/d CH$10,500/21,000) This fun family lodging is well cared for. Guests get kitchen privileges but shouldn't give up the chance to try owner Pati's fantastic seafood creations, which are also available to nonguests (mains CH$4000 to CH$4500).

Hotel Lakutaia (☎ 621733; www.lakutaia.cl; d CH$125,000) Three kilometers east of town toward the airport, this modern full-service lodge will arrange transportation from Punta Arenas, and can organize day hikes to the Navarino Circuit and trips to Cape Horn. The library contains tons of interesting history and nature references. Its only disadvantage is its isolation; you might leave without getting much of a feel for the quirky town of Puerto Williams.

Eating

Dientes de Navarino (Plaza de Ancla; mains CH$3000-3500) This hole-in-the-wall dining hall may offer few options but they are well prepared. Seafood platters, *combinados* (pisco brandy and colas) and box wine please the hungry.

Restaurant Cabo de Hornos (☎ 621067; Maragano 146; mains CH$3500-6500) With views over the town, this is the place to try local wild game (bea-ver, crab, goose, guanaco and rabbit), plus organic salmon, lamb and more traditional Magellanic meats.

Of the few supermarkets, Simon & Simon is the best, with fresher vegetables, fast food and great pastries.

Drinking

Club de Yates Micalvi (beer CH$2500; ☺ open late Sep-May) As watering holes go, this may be like no other. A grounded German cargo boat, the *Micalvi* was declared a regional naval mu-seum in 1976 and found infinitely better use as a floating bar, frequented by navy men and yachties.

Getting There & Away

Puerto Williams can be reached by plane or by boat. **Aerovías DAP** (☎ 621051; www.dap.cl; Plaza de Ancla s/n) flies to Punta Arenas (CH$65,000, 1¼ hours) at 11:30am Monday through to Saturday from November to March, with fewer flights in winter. DAP flights to Antarctica may make a brief stopover here.

The **Transbordador Austral Broom** (www.tabsa.cl) ferry *Patagonia* sails from the Tres Puentes sector of Punta Arenas to Puerto Williams three or four times a month on Wednesdays, with departures from Puerto Williams back to Punta Arenas on Saturdays (reclining seat/bunk CH$88,000/105,000 including meals, 38 hours). Travelers rave about the trip: if the weather holds there are good views on deck and the possibility of spotting dolphins or whales. Booking a bunk is worth the extra dollars, since passenger berths are small and the reclining Pullman seats not as comfortable as one might wish on such a long trip.

Zodiac boats head to Ushuaia daily from September to March; you'll have to pay dearly for the 40-minute ride. **Ushuaia Boating** (☎ 02901-436193; www.ushuaiaboating.com.ar; Godoy 190, Ushuaia) shuttles travelers back and forth for around CH$104,000. Also check with **Akainij** (☎ 621173; www.turismoakainij.cl; Centro Comercial Sur 156) for transport and related excursions around Puerto Williams. Departures are usually in the morning, with transfer buses first tak-ing passengers on the 52km stretch to Puerto Navarino. Private yachts making the trip can sometimes be found at the Club de Yates Micalvi.

Uruguay

Squished like a tiny grape between Brazil's gargantuan thumb and Argentina's long fore-finger, South America's smallest Spanish-speaking country is easily overlooked but well worth discovering. Ignored by the Spanish for its lack of mineral wealth, batted about like a ping-pong ball at the whim of its more powerful neighbors and bypassed by modern-day travelers, Uruguay has always been an underdog. Yet it remains a delightfully low-key, hospitable place where visitors can melt into the background and experience the everyday life of a different culture – whether caught in a cow-and-gaucho traffic jam on a dirt road to nowhere or strolling with *mate*-toting locals along Montevideo's beachfront.

For its diminutive size, Uruguay is surprisingly diverse. Cosmopolitan Montevideo is ex-periencing a renaissance of youthful energy while maintaining many long-standing cultural traditions. The streets erupt in a frenzy of drumming every February during Carnaval, and the newly renovated Teatro Solís is among dozens of venues hosting dance, music and theater year-round at astonishingly affordable prices. Seventeenth-century Colonia seduces visitors with its cobblestoned charms, while trendy Punta del Este draws glitterati from around the globe to its sandy beaches, chichi restaurants and party-till-you-drop nightclubs.

Whatever you do, don't limit yourself to these three tourist hubs. Get out under the big sky of Uruguay's vast interior, where fields spread out like oceans dotted with little cow and eucalyptus islands. Ride horses to a river at sunset, stargaze at a 19th-century *estancia* (ranch), or watch the moon rise over the dunes at Cabo Polonio's seal colony.

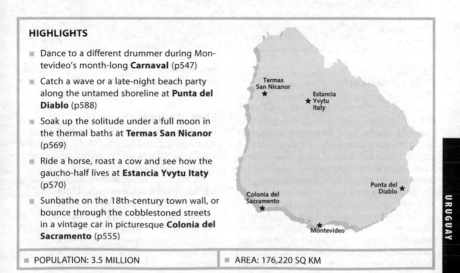

HIGHLIGHTS

- Dance to a different drummer during Mon-tevideo's month-long **Carnaval** (p547)
- Catch a wave or a late-night beach party along the untamed shoreline at **Punta del Diablo** (p588)
- Soak up the solitude under a full moon in the thermal baths at **Termas San Nicanor** (p569)
- Ride a horse, roast a cow and see how the gaucho-half lives at **Estancia Yvytu Itaty** (p570)
- Sunbathe on the 18th-century town wall, or bounce through the cobblestoned streets in a vintage car in picturesque **Colonia del Sacramento** (p555)

Termas San Nicanor ★

Estancia ★ Yvytu Itaty

Punta del Diablo ★

Colonia del Sacramento ★

★ Montevideo

- POPULATION: 3.5 MILLION
- AREA: 176,220 SQ KM

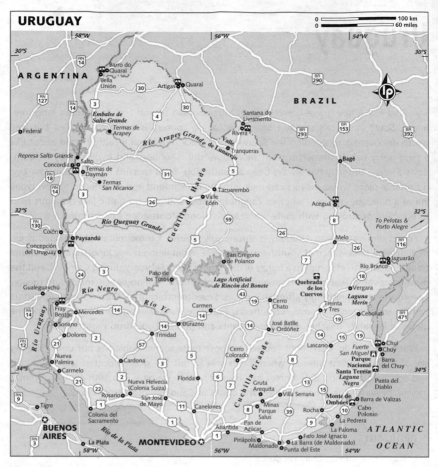

HISTORY
Early Settlement

Uruguay's aboriginal inhabitants were the Charrúa along the coast and the Guaraní north of the Río Negro. The hunting-and-gathering Charrúa discouraged European settlement for more than a century by killing Spanish explorer Juan de Solís and most of his party in 1516. In any event there was little to attract the Spanish, who valued these lowlands along the Río de la Plata only as an access route to gold and other quick riches further inland.

The first Europeans to settle on the Banda Oriental (Eastern Shore) were Jesuit missionaries near present-day Soriano, on the Río Uruguay. Next came the Portuguese, who established present-day Colonia in 1680 as a beachhead for smuggling goods into Buenos Aires. Spain responded by building its own citadel at Montevideo in 1726.

Birth of a Nation

For the next century the Portuguese and Spanish fought to get a foothold. Britain also joined the mix, briefly invading and occupying Montevideo in 1807.

Most of the Charrúa had fallen victim to introduced diseases and to the Europeans' relentless push for land. Then, on April 11, 1831, many of the remaining Charrúa accepted an invitation from a nephew of the Uruguayan president to a meeting at Salsipuedes. There, the Charrúa were surrounded, stripped of their arms and horses, and massacred.

As the 19th century dawned, anticolonial sentiments sparked the Uruguayan independence movement. José Gervasio Artigas, Uruguay's greatest national hero, allied with the United Provinces of the River Plate against Spain, but was unable to prevent Uruguay's takeover by Brazil. Exiled to Paraguay, Artigas inspired the famous '33 Orientales,' Uruguayan patriots under General Juan Lavalleja who, with Argentine support, crossed the Río Uruguay on April 19, 1825, and launched a campaign to liberate modern-day Uruguay from Brazilian control. In 1828, after three years' struggle, a British-mediated treaty established Uruguay as a small independent buffer between the emerging continental powers.

For most of the 19th century, Uruguay's independence was fragile. There was civil war between Uruguay's two nascent political parties, the Colorados and the Blancos (named, respectively, for the red and white bands they wore); Argentina besieged Montevideo from 1838 to 1851; and Brazil was an ever-present threat.

By the mid-19th century the economy was largely dependent on beef and wool production. The rise of the *latifundios* (large landholdings) and commercialization of livestock led to the gradual demise of the independent gaucho.

Prosperity then Decline

In the early 20th century, visionary president José Batlle y Ordóñez introduced such innovations as pensions, farm credits, unemployment compensation and the eight-hour work day. State intervention led to the nationalization of many industries, the creation of others and a new era of general prosperity. However, Batlle's reforms were largely financed through taxing the livestock sector, and when exports faltered mid-century, the welfare state crumbled.

By the 1960s economic stagnation and massive inflation were reaching crisis points, and social unrest was increasing, particularly in Montevideo, which had become accustomed to middle-class prosperity. In 1967 the country began sliding into dictatorship under President Jorge Pacheco, who outlawed leftist parties, closed newspapers and invoked state-of-siege measures in response to the 'Tupamaros' guerrilla movement – a clandestine socialist faction with roots in the urban middle class. At first the Tupamaros enjoyed public support, but this eroded quickly. After the movement executed suspected CIA agent Dan Mitrione and engineered a major prison escape, Pacheco put the military in charge of counterinsurgency. In 1971 Pacheco's chosen successor, Juan Bordaberry, handed control of the government to the army.

The military virtually eliminated free expression. Torture became routine, and more than 60,000 citizens were arbitrarily detained. The armed forces determined eligibility for public employment, subjected political offenses to military courts, censored libraries and even required prior approval for large family gatherings.

Attempts by the military to institutionalize their political role failed. Voters rejected a military-drawn constitution in 1980, and four years later elected Colorado candidate Julio María Sanguinetti as president under the existing constitution. Sanguinetti's election implied a return to democratic traditions, although he supported a controversial amnesty for military human-rights abuses, grudgingly ratified by voters in 1989.

Into the 21st Century

In March 2000, Uruguayans elected the outspoken Colorado Jorge Batlle Ibáñez, grandnephew of José Batlle y Ordóñez, as president. Ibañez immediately established himself as a maverick, dismissing the head of the army for suggesting that another coup might be in order, and promising to search for the remains of dissidents who disappeared under military rule. Decrying Uruguay's welfare state as cumbersome, he began implementing policies aimed at privatization and free trade. In response, the Frente Amplio (Broad Front) – a coalition of leftist parties – became a serious political contender, winning popularity for its antiprivatization, pro-welfare stance.

In July 2002, spillover from Argentina's economic crisis triggered a run on Uruguayan banks. Uruguayans watched in horror as their economy – previously one of the strongest in South America – crumbled and inflation (3.6% in 2001) rocketed to 40% by the end of 2002. The tourist industry (heavily reliant on prosperous Argentines) suffered. The peso plummeted in value, the economy minister resigned and the government declared a bank holiday to prevent further chaos.

PULP FRICTION: URUGUAY'S CELLULOSE WAR WITH ARGENTINA

Who could guess that a cellulose processing plant could provoke an international crisis? At the time of writing, Uruguayan-Argentine relations had reached a 50-year low, thanks to an ongoing dispute over Finnish paper company Botnia's pulp mill on the Río Uruguay north of Fray Bentos. Ever since plans for the mill were announced in 2005, Argentine environmental groups and government officials have been protesting that it will pollute the Argentine side of the river near Gualeguaychú. Uruguay's government, intent on safeguarding this major foreign investment, has steadfastly countered that the mill, governed by what it regards as strict international environmental standards, is perfectly safe.

On November 9, 2007, after multiple delays and inconclusive mediation efforts by King Juan Carlos of Spain, the pulp mill finally opened, only heightening tensions. As this book goes to press, the bridge between Fray Bentos and Gualeguaychú remains closed by Argentine protestors for the fifth straight summer (apart from a brief opening for a *fútbol* game between the two countries) and Argentina still has a case pending against Uruguay in the International Court of Justice, with a decision expected in mid 2010. Stay tuned!

What followed was a massive bailout – Ibañez' emergency measures (cutting public spending, increasing sales tax) were rewarded with a series of loans from the USA, the IMF and the World Bank totaling US$1.5 billion.

Recent Events

In March 2005 the leftist Frente Amplio swept to power under President Tabaré Vázquez, riding a wave of support from unions, youth and community groups. It was the first time in Uruguay's 175-year history that a third party had won the presidency. Things didn't start smoothly: Vázquez' early initiatives included seeking a free-trade deal with the USA (both surprising and alienating Uruguay's Mercosur trade partners), banning smoking in public (annoying pretty much everybody in this nicotine-crazed land) and granting leases to two foreign multinationals to build paper factories on the Río Uruguay (ruffling feathers with neighboring Argentina; see above).

On the home front, the Frente Amplio government has presided over numerous social changes, including the November 2007 legalization of abortion, the January 2008 sanctioning of civil unions between same-sex partners and an ambitious program called Plan Ceibal that has distributed internet-ready laptops to every student in the country.

Uruguayans gave the Frente Amplio a vote of confidence in November 2009, electing José Mujica as their new president. Despite his grandfatherly demeanor, Mujica was a controversial candidate, given his past as a Tupamaro guerrilla leader. As this book goes to press, Mujica is expected to continue much of Vázquez' left-leaning social agenda.

THE CULTURE
The National Psyche

The one thing that Uruguayans will tell you that they're *not* is anything like their *porteño* cousins across the water. In many ways they're right. Where Argentines can be brassy and sometimes arrogant, Uruguayans are more humble and relaxed. Where the former have always been a regional superpower, the latter have always lived in the shadow of one. Those jokes about Punta del Este being a suburb of Buenos Aires don't go down so well on this side of the border. There are plenty of similarities, though – the near-universal appreciation for the arts, the Italian influence and the gaucho heritage. Indeed, the rugged individualism and disdain that many Uruguayans hold for *el neoliberalismo* (neoliberalism) can be traced directly back to those romantic cowboy figures.

Lifestyle

Uruguayans like to take it easy and pride themselves on being the opposite of the hotheaded Latino type. Sunday's the day for family and friends, to throw half a cow on the *asado* (barbecue), sit back and sip some *mate* (a tealike beverage). The population is well educated, and there's strong public support for the arts. The gap between rich and poor is much less pronounced than in most other Latin American countries, although the economic crises of the early 21st century have put a strain on the middle class.

Population

With 3.5 million people, Uruguay is South America's smallest Spanish-speaking country. The population is predominately white (88%) with 8% mestizo (people with mixed Spanish and indigenous blood) and 4% black. Indigenous peoples are practically nonexistent. The average life expectancy (just over 76 years) is one of Latin America's highest. The literacy rate is also high, at 98%, while population growth is a slow 0.5%. Population density is 19.8 people per sq km.

Sports

Sexo, droga y Peñarol
Ni patria ni Dios... NACIONAL NA-
CIONAL
                 Montevideo graffiti

Uruguayans, like just about all Latin American, are crazy about soccer (*fútbol*). If you suddenly notice that all the streets are empty and the bars are full, you can bet there's a game on.

Uruguay has won the World Cup twice, including the first tournament, played in Montevideo in 1930. The most notable teams are Montevideo-based Nacional and Peñarol. If you go to a match between these two, sit on the sidelines, not behind the goal, unless you're up for some serious rowdiness.

The **Asociación Uruguayo de Fútbol** (☎ 02-400-7101; Guayabo 1531) in Montevideo can provide information on matches and venues.

Religion

Forty-seven percent of Uruguayans are Roman Catholic. About one-third are from other Christian denominations. There's a small Jewish minority, numbering around 18,000. Evangelical Protestantism has made some inroads and Sun Myung Moon's Unification Church owns the afternoon daily, *Últimas Noticias*.

Arts

Uruguay has an impressive literary and artistic tradition, and its small population produces a surprising number of talented artists and literary figures. Uruguay's most famous philosopher and essayist is probably José Enrique Rodó, whose 1900 essay *Ariel*, contrasting North American and Latin American civilizations, is a classic of the country's literature. Major contemporary writers include Juan Carlos Onetti, and poet, essayist and novelist Mario Benedetti. Onetti's novels *No Man's Land, The Shipyard, Body Snatcher* and *A Brief Life* are available in English translations, as is *The Tree of Red Stars*, Tessa Bridal's acclaimed novel set in Montevideo during the 1970s. Most young Uruguayans have a big soft spot for Eduardo Galeano, who has written many books and poems.

Probably the most famous Uruguay-related film is Costa-Gavras' engrossing *State of Siege* (1973), filmed in Allende's Chile, which deals with the Tupamaro guerrillas' kidnapping and execution of suspected American CIA officer Dan Mitrione. Among the best movies to come out of Uruguay recently are *Whisky* (2004), which won a couple of awards at Cannes, and *El Baño del Papa* (2007).

Theater is popular and playwrights such as Mauricio Rosencof are prominent. The most renowned painters are the late Juan Manuel Blanes and Joaquín Torres García. Sculptors include José Belloni, whose life-size bronzes can be seen in Montevideo's parks.

Tango is big in Montevideo – Uruguayans claim tango legend Carlos Gardel as a native son, and one of the best-known tangos, 'La Cumparsita,' was composed by Uruguayan Gerardo Matos Rodríguez. During Carnaval, Montevideo's streets reverberate to the energetic drumbeats of *candombe*, an African-derived rhythm brought to Uruguay by slaves from 1750 onwards. On the contemporary scene, several Uruguayan rock bands have won a following on both sides of the Río de la Plata, including Buitres, La Vela Puerca and No Te Va Gustar.

Access to the arts is relatively inexpensive. Museums are mostly free, and theater and music events often cost as little as UR$100. Even the very best seats for performances at Montevideo's elegant Teatro Solís rarely exceed UR$500.

FOOD & DRINK
Uruguayan Cuisine

Breakfast to a Uruguayan generally means *cafe con leche* (coffee with milk) and a *medialuna* (croissant) or two, followed by serious amounts of *mate*. Any later than, say, 10am huge slabs of beef are the norm, usually cooked over hot coals on a *parrilla* (grill or barbecue). The most popular cut is the *asado de tira* (ribs) but *pulpo* (fillet steak) is also good. Seafood is excellent on the coast.

DAY OF THE GNOCCHI

Most Uruguayan restaurants make a big deal out of serving gnocchi (or ñoquis as they're known locally) on the 29th of each month. In some places this is the only day you can get them.

The tradition dates back to tough economic times when everybody was paid at the end of the month. By the time the 29th rolled around, the only thing that people could afford to cook were these delicious potato dumplings. So, in their ever-practical way, Uruguayans turned a hardship into a tradition and the 29th has been the Day of the Gnocchi ever since. Bear this in mind next time you're paying US$25 a plate at your favorite Italian restaurant back home.

Uruguay's classic snack is a cholesterol bomb called the *chivito* (a steak sandwich with cheese, lettuce, tomato, bacon, ham, olives, pickles and more!). Vegetarians often have to content themselves with pizza and pasta, although there are a few veggie restaurants lurking about. Desserts are a dream (or nightmare, depending on your perspective) of meringue, *dulce de leche* (milk caramel), burnt sugar and custard. The same ingredients get recombined in endless configurations, with names such as *Principe Humberto* (Prince Humbert), *isla flotante* (floating island), *Massini* and *chajá*.

In major tourist destinations such as Punta del Este and Colonia, restaurants charge *cubiertos* (cover charges of UR$20 or more). Theoretically these pay for the basket of bread offered before your meal.

Drinks
ALCOHOLIC DRINKS
Local beers, including Pilsen, Patricia and Zillertal, are decent but nothing special. The 330mL bottles are rare outside tourist areas – generally *cerveza* (beer) means a 1L bottle and some glasses, which is a great way to meet your neighbors.

Tannat, a red wine produced primarily in Uruguay and southwestern France, is excellent and universally available.

Clericó is a mixture of white wine and fruit juice, while *medio y medio* (half and half) is a mixture of sparkling wine and white wine. A shot of *grappa con miel* (grappa with honey) is worth a try – you might just like it.

NONALCOHOLIC DRINKS
Tap water's OK to drink in most places, but bottled water is cheap if you have your doubts. Soft drinks are inexpensive: try the *pomelo* (grapefruit) flavor – it's very refreshing and not too sickly sweet. *Jugos* (juices) and *licuados* (juices mixed with milk or water) are available everywhere.

Coffee is generally good, coming mostly *de la máquina* (from the machine). Uruguayans consume even more *mate* than Argentines and Paraguayans. If you get the chance, try to acquire the taste – there's nothing like whiling away an afternoon passing the *mate* with a bunch of new-found friends.

ENVIRONMENT
The Land
Though one of South America's smallest countries, Uruguay not so small by European standards. Its area of 176,220 sq km is greater than England and Wales combined, or slightly bigger than the US state of Florida.

Uruguay's two main ranges of interior hills are the Cuchilla de Haedo, west of Tacuarembó, and the Cuchilla Grande, south of Melo; neither exceeds 500m in height. West of Montevideo the terrain is more level. The Río Negro flowing through the center of the country forms a natural dividing line between north and south. The Atlantic coast has impressive beaches, dunes, headlands and lagoons. Uruguay's grasslands and forests resemble those of Argentina's pampas or southern Brazil, and patches of palm savanna persist in the east, along the Brazilian border.

Wildlife
It seems fitting that Uruguay's name can be translated as 'river of the birds.' The country is rich in birdlife, especially in the coastal lagoons of Rocha department. Most large land animals have disappeared, but the occasional ñandú (rhea) still races across northwestern Uruguay's grasslands. Whales, fur seals and sea lions are common along the coast.

CLIMATE
Since Uruguay's major attraction is its beaches, most visitors come in summer. Along the coast, daytime temperatures average 28°C in January, and nighttime temperatures average 17°C. Along the Río Uruguay and in interior towns such as Tacuarembó, summer tempera-

tures can be smotheringly hot, with January highs commonly rising well above 30°C.

Annual rainfall, evenly distributed throughout the year, averages about 1m over the whole country. Between late April and November, strong winds sometimes combine with rain and cool temperatures (July's average temperature is a chilly 11°C).

NATIONAL PARKS

Uruguay's national parks are the military-administered Parque Nacional Santa Teresa (p589) and Parque Nacional San Miguel in Rocha department. Several other natural areas are nominally protected under the Sistema Nacional de Áreas Protegidas (SNAP; National System of Protected Areas) program – see the boxed text, p571.

GETTING THERE & AWAY

There are a few direct international flights to Montevideo (p553), but most airlines require a connection through Buenos Aires. Many visitors to Uruguay arrive by ferry from Buenos Aires, to either Colonia (p560) or Montevideo (p554).

MONTEVIDEO

☎ 02 / pop 1.3 million

Uruguay's capital and by far its largest city, Montevideo is a vibrant, eclectic place with a rich cultural life. Stretching nearly 20km from east to west, the city wears many faces, from its industrial port to the exclusive residential suburb of Carrasco near the airport. In the historic downtown business district, art deco and neoclassical buildings jostle for space alongside grimy, worn-out skyscrapers that appear airlifted from Havana or Ceauşescu's Romania, while to the southeast the shopping malls and modern high-rises of beach communities such as Punta Carretas and Pocitos bear more resemblance to Miami or Copacabana.

If you're coming from Colonia or Uruguay's northern beaches, Montevideo's polluted air and honking taxis may feel a bit jarring, but stick around. The capital's active and resurgent urban culture is a palpable force, and locals are justifiably proud to share it with you. In Ciudad Vieja, the heart of historic Montevideo, old buildings are being restored to make room for boldly painted cafes, hostels and galleries, while down by the port the municipal administration has spruced up the Mercado del

Puerto to accommodate a new city tourist office and Carnaval museum. Montevideo serves as administrative headquarters for Mercosur, South America's leading trading bloc, and the capital's many embassies and foreign cultural centers add to the international flavor. Meanwhile, the city's music, theater, art and club scenes continue to thrive, from elegant older theaters and cozy little tango bars to modern beachfront discos.

ORIENTATION

Montevideo lies almost directly across the Río de la Plata from Buenos Aires. For many visitors, the most intriguing area is the Ciudad Vieja, the formerly walled colonial grid straddling the western tip of a peninsula between the sheltered port and the wide-open river. Just east of the old town gate Puerta de la Ciudadela, the Centro (downtown) begins at Plaza Independencia, surrounded by historic public buildings of the republican era. Av 18 de Julio, a major thoroughfare and traditionally the capital's main commercial and entertainment zone, runs east from here through Plaza del Entrevero and Plaza Cagancha before reaching the Intendencia (town hall) at the Centro's eastern edge. Street numbering is easy to follow – each city block represents a range of 50 numbers. Note that some streets change their name on either side of Av 18 de Julio.

From Plaza del Entrevero, Av Libertador General Lavalleja leads diagonally northeast to the imposing Palacio Legislativo (Map p540), home of Uruguay's General Assembly. At the northeastern end of Av 18 de Julio are Montevideo's Tres Cruces bus terminal and Parque José Batlle y Ordóñez (both Map p540), home to the city's 75,000-seat soccer stadium. Running north–south from the bus terminal

---

TOP PLACES TO EXPERIENCE URUGUAY'S WIDE-OPEN SPACES

- Cabo Polonio (p586)
- Villa Serrana (p574)
- Valle del Lunarejo (p571)
- Quebrada de los Cuervos (p571)
- An *estancia* (p564)
- Laguna de Castillos (p586)
- Termas San Nicanor (p569)
- Sierra de las Ánimas (p573)

URUGUAY

MONTEVIDEO

to the beach and lighthouse at Punta Carretas is Bulevar Artigas, another major artery, while the nearby Av Italia becomes the Interbalnearia, the main highway east to Punta del Este and the rest of the Uruguayan Riviera.

Many points of interest lie beyond downtown. Westward across the harbor, 132m Cerro de Montevideo (Map p540) was a landmark for early navigators and still offers outstanding views of the city. Eastward, the Rambla, or waterfront road, leads past attractive Parque Rodó (Map p540) at the southern end of Bulevar Artigas, then snakes through a series of sprawling beach suburbs that are very popular with the capital's residents in summer and on weekends. These include Punta Carretas, Pocitos, Buceo (home of the yacht club) and Carrasco, an exclusive residential district near the airport.

INFORMATION
Bookstores
Availability of non-Spanish titles is limited.
Bookshop (☎ 401-1010; Rodó 1671) Montevideo's best selection of English-language novels and travel guidebooks; east of the Intendencia.

Librería Linardi y Risso (☎ 915-7129; Juan Carlos Gómez 1435) Good source for history, literature, out-of-print items and photo essays on Montevideo and Uruguay.

Librería Puro Verso Centro (☎ 901-6429; Av 18 de Julio 1199); Ciudad Vieja (☎ 915-2589; Peatonal Sarandí 675) Excellent Spanish-language bookstore-cafe with a small selection of novels in English.

Cultural Centers
Alianza Cultural Uruguay-Estados Unidos
(☎ 902-5160; www.alianza.edu.uy; Paraguay 1217) The USA-Uruguayan cultural center contains a bookstore, theater and library and sponsors special programs and lectures.

Alianza Francesa (☎ 400-0505; www.alliancefran caise.edu.uy, in Spanish; Bulevar Artigas 1229) About 2km east of Centro.

Centro Cultural de España (☎ 915-2250; www.cce .org.uy, in Spanish; Rincón 629) Spanish cultural center; it hosts art exhibits and other cultural events.

Complejo Multicultural Mundo Afro (☎ 916-8779; coordinacionoma@hotmail.com; Ciudadela 1229) Montevideo's Afro-Uruguayan community cultural center, upstairs in the Mercado Central just south of Plaza Independencia.

URUGUAY

Instituto Cultural Anglo-Uruguayo (☎ 902-3773; www.anglo.edu.uy; San José 1426) One of 47 branches around the country. Operates an English-language library and a theater.

Instituto de Cultura Uruguayo-Brasileño (☎ 901-1818; www.icub.edu.uy, in Spanish; Av 18 de Julio 994, 6th fl) Brazilian cultural center, with an excellent library.

Instituto Goethe (☎ 410-5813; www.goethe.de/mon tevideo, in Spanish & German; Canelones 1524) The German government's cultural center in Montevideo; east of Centro.

Instituto Italiano de Cultura (☎ 900-3354; www.iic montevideo.esteri.it, in Spanish & Italian; Paraguay 1177)

Emergencies
Ambulance (☎ 105)
Fire (☎ 104)
Police (☎ 109)
Tourist Police (☎ 0800-8226)

Immigration
Dirección Nacional de la Migración (☎ 916-0471; Misiones 1513; ☯ 9:15am-2:30pm Mon-Fri)

Internet Access
Most Montevideo accommodations have a guest computer in the lobby, free in-room wi-fi, or both.
Cyberia (☎ 908-8808; San José 933; per hr UR$15; ☯ noon-midnight Mon-Fri, 6pm-midnight Sat) Provides internet access, Skype and other digital services.

Laundry
Lavadero Mis Niños (☎ 903-0369; Andes 1333; wash & dry per load UR$90; ☯ 8am-8pm Mon-Fri, to 3pm Sat)

Media
Montevideo's leading dailies are *El País* (www .elpais.com.uy), *La República* (www.larepub lica.com.uy), *El Observador* (www.elobser vador.com.uy) and *Últimas Noticias* (www .ultimasnoticias.com.uy). The newsweekly *Búsqueda* (www.busqueda.com.uy) is also widely available at newsstands.

Medical Services
Hospital Británico (☎ 487-1020; Av Italia 2420) Highly recommended private hospital with English-speaking doctors; 2.5km east of downtown.
Hospital Maciel (☎ 915-3000; cnr 25 de Mayo & Maciel) The public hospital.

Money
Countless exchange houses line Av 18 de Julio, with rates posted. ATMs are everywhere, including at the bus terminal.

Banco Comercial (cnr Av 18 de Julio & Santiago de Chile) At eastern edge of downtown.
Banco de la Nación Argentina (Juan Carlos Gómez 1378) On Plaza Constitución.
Banco Santander (Av 18 de Julio 999) Opposite Plaza del Entrevero.
Cambio Gales (Av 18 de Julio 1046) Cashes traveler's checks.
Indumex (Tres Cruces bus terminal)

Post
Post office Centro (cnr Ejido & San José); Ciudad Vieja (Misiones 1328); Tres Cruces bus terminal (cnr Bulevar Artigas & Av Italia)

Telephone
Antel Telecentro Centro (cnr San José & Paraguay); Ciudad Vieja (Rincón 501); Tres Cruces bus terminal (cnr Bulevar Artigas & Av Italia)

Tourist Information
Municipal tourist office Centro (☎ 1950-3157, 1950-3171; cnr Av 18 de Julio & Ejido, 3rd fl; ☯ 10am-4pm Mon-Fri); Ciudad Vieja (☎ 916-8434; cnr Rambla 25 de Agosto & Maciel; ☯ 11am-5pm) City maps and general information about Montevideo.
National Tourism Ministry Carrasco airport (☎ 604-0386; ☯ 9am-8pm); Ciudad Vieja (☎ 188-5111; Rambla 25 de Agosto; ☯ 8am-6pm Mon-Fri); Tres Cruces bus terminal (☎ 409-7399; ☯ 8am-10pm Mon-Fri, 9am-10pm Sat & Sun) Provides information about Montevideo and destinations throughout Uruguay.

Travel Agencies
Turisport (www.turisport.com.uy) Centro (☎ 902-0829; San José 930); Pocitos (☎ 712-4797; Juan B Blanco 837) The local Amex representative.
Viajeros Sin Fronteras (☎ 916-5466; www.sinfronte ras.com.uy; Buenos Aires 618, Oficina 001) Student and youth travel specialist.

DANGERS & ANNOYANCES
While Montevideo is pretty sedate by Latin American standards, you should exercise caution as in any large city. Wallet- and purse-snatchings are not uncommon in Ciudad Vieja, and certain areas should be avoided at night, notably the Mercado del Puerto. You may also encounter some aggressive requests for cash along the pedestrian streets of Bacacay and Sarandí. Montevideo's *poli cia turística* (tourist police) patrol the streets throughout Ciudad Vieja and the Centro and should be able to help if you encounter any problems.

URUGUAY

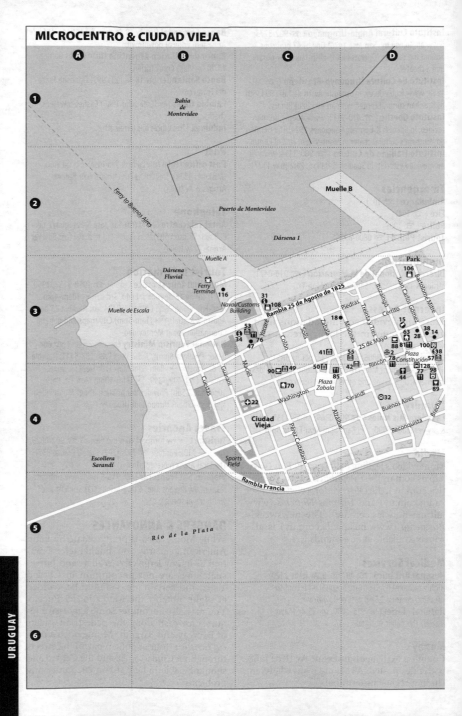

MICROCENTRO & CIUDAD VIEJA

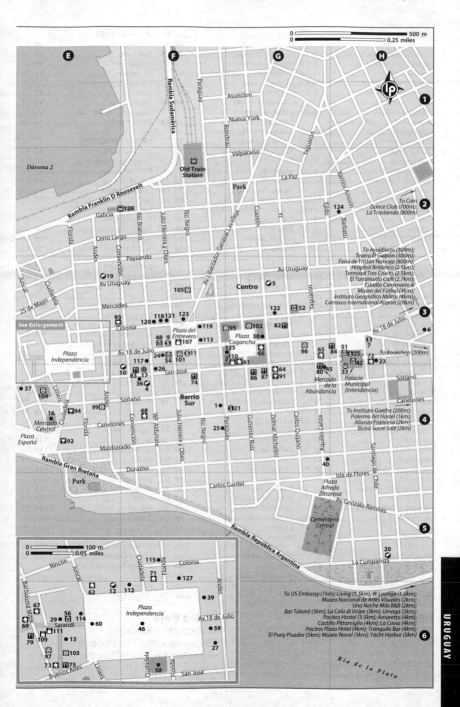

URUGUAY

SIGHTS

All sights below are listed from west to east.
Note that many Montevideo museums are
known by their acronyms. Admission is free
except where noted. Most museum exhibits
are in Spanish only.

Ciudad Vieja
MUSEO DEL CARNAVAL

This **museum** (☎ 916-5493; Rambla 25 de Agosto 218; admission URS\$50, free on Tue; ⏰ 11am-5pm Tue-Sun) houses
a wonderful collection of costumes, drums,
masks, recordings and photos documenting

the 100-plus-year history of Montevideo's Carnaval.

MERCADO DEL PUERTO

No visitor should miss Montevideo's old port market building, at the foot of Pérez Castellano, whose impressive wrought-iron superstructure shelters a gaggle of reasonably priced *parrillas* (steak restaurants; see p549). On Saturday afternoons in particular, it's a lively, colorful place where the city's artists, craftspeople and street musicians hang out.

MUSEO DE ARTE PRECOLOMBINO E INDÍGENA

This **museum** (MAPI; ☎ 916-9360; 25 de Mayo 279; ⏰ 1-6:30pm Mon-Fri, noon-5:30pm Sat) displays a permanent collection of artifacts and information about Uruguay's earliest inhabitants, along with rotating exhibits focused on native peoples of the Americas.

MUSEO DE ARTES DECORATIVAS

The Palacio Taranco, a wealthy merchant's residence dating from 1910, is now home to this **museum** (☎ 915-1101; 25 de Mayo 376; ⏰ 12:30-6pm Tue-Sat, 2-6pm Sun). The palatial building, designed by famous French architects Charles Girault and Jules Chifflot, is filled with ornate period furnishings, many brought over from Europe.

MUSEO HISTÓRICO NACIONAL

The National Historical Museum consists of three dispersed Ciudad Vieja houses. The centerpiece is 19th-century **Casa Rivera** (☎ 915-1051; Rincón 437; ⏰ 11am-5pm Mon-Fri, 10am-3pm Sat), the former home of Uruguay's first president and founder of the Colorado Party, Fructuoso Rivera. The collection of paintings, documents, furniture and artifacts traces Uruguayan history from indigenous roots through to independence.

The 18th-century **Museo Romántico** (☎ 915-5361; 25 de Mayo 428; ⏰ 11am-5pm Mon-Fri) is filled with paintings, porcelain, silver and antique furniture. **Casa Lavalleja** (☎ 915-1028; Zabala 1469), currently closed to the public, was the home of General Lavalleja from 1830 until his death in 1853.

PLAZA CONSTITUCIÓN

Also known as Plaza Matriz, this was the heart of colonial Montevideo. On its east side stands the **Cabildo** (finished in 1812), a neoclassical stone structure that contains the

Museo y Archivo Histórico Municipal (Municipal Archive & Historical Museum; ☎ 915-9685; Juan Carlos Gómez 1362; ⏰ 12:30-5:30pm Tue-Sun). Opposite the Cabildo is the **Iglesia Matriz**, Montevideo's oldest public building. It was begun in 1784 and completed in 1799.

MUSEO TORRES GARCÍA

This **museum** (☎ 916-2663; Sarandí 683; donation requested; ⏰ 9:30am-7:30pm Mon-Fri, 10am-6pm Sat) showcases the work of 20th-century Uruguayan painter Torres García, and has revolving exhibitions featuring other contemporary artists.

TEATRO SOLÍS

Just off Plaza Independencia, elegant **Teatro Solís** (☎ 1950 ext 3323; www.teatrosolis.org.uy, in Spanish; Buenos Aires 678) is Montevideo's premier performance space (see p552 and p553). First opened in 1856, and completely renovated during the past decade, it has superb acoustics. Regularly scheduled tours (Tuesday through Sunday) provide an opportunity to see the actual performance space without attending a show. Spanish-language tours are free on Wednesdays, UR$20 other days; English- and Portuguese-language tours cost UR$40.

Centro

PLAZA INDEPENDENCIA

In the middle of this downtown plaza is the **Mausoleo de Artigas**, whose above-ground portion is a 17m, 30-ton statue of the country's independence hero. Below street level, an honor guard keeps 24-hour vigil over Artigas' remains.

The 18th-century **Palacio Estévez**, on the south side of the plaza, was the Government House until 1985. On the east side of the plaza, the 26-story structure with the crazy beehive hairdo is **Palacio Salvo**, the continent's tallest building when it opened in 1927. At the west end of the plaza is the **Puerta de la Ciudadela**, a stone gateway that is one of the only remnants of the colonial citadel demolished in 1833.

MUSEO DEL GAUCHO Y DE LA MONEDA

Housed in the ornate Palacio Heber, the **Museo del Gaucho y de la Moneda** (☎ 900-8764; Av 18 de Julio 998; ⏰ 10am-5pm Mon-Fri) eloquently conveys the deep attachments and interdependent relationships between the gauchos, their animals and the land. The excellent collection features a range of artifacts from Uruguay's gaucho history, including horse gear, silver work, and *mates* and *bombillas* (metal straws with filters, used for drinking *mate*) in whimsical designs. Downstairs there is also a display of banknotes, coins, and exhibits about the volatile history of the Uruguayan economy.

MUSEO DE ARTE CONTEMPORÁNEO
Across from the gaucho museum, this tiny **museum** (MAC; ☎ 900-6662; Av 18 de Julio 965, 2nd fl; ☯ 2-8pm Tue-Sun, 2-6:30pm Mon) displays continually rotating exhibits of modern Uruguayan painting and sculpture.

MUSEO DE LA HISTORIA DEL ARTE
In the basement of Montevideo's Palacio Municipal (town hall, also known as Intendencia), the **Museo de la Historia del Arte** (MuHAr; ☎ 1950 ext 2191; Ejido 1326; ☯ noon-5:30pm Tue-Sun) features a wide-ranging collection of art – both originals and reproductions of famous pieces – from Egypt, Mesopotamia, Persia, Greece, Rome and numerous Native American cultures.

OTHER MUSEUMS
The Automóvil Club del Uruguay's **Museo del Automóvil** (☎ 902-4792; Colonia 1251, 6th fl; ☯ 2-7pm Tue-Sun) has a superb collection of vintage cars, including a mint 1910 Hupmobile.

Rotating contemporary photo exhibits can be seen at the **Centro Municipal de Fotografía** (CMDF; ☎ 1950 ext 1219; San José 1360; ☯ 10am-7pm Mon-Fri, 9:30am-2:30pm Sat). There are also two computers where visitors can browse the collection of 100,000 historic photos.

North of Centro
For great views out across the city, take the elevator to the top of the soaring, wedge-shaped **Torre Antel** (Map p540; ☎ 928-4417; Guatemala 1075; ☯ 3:30-5pm Mon, Wed & Fri, 10:30am-noon Tue & Thu), Montevideo's most dramatic modern skyscraper, northeast of the port. Free tours are available Tuesday and Thursday mornings, as well as Monday, Wednesday and Friday afternoons.

Dating from 1908, and still playing host to Uruguay's Asamblea General (legislative branch), the three-story neoclassical **Palacio Legislativo** (☎ 924-1783; www.parlamento.gub.uy; Av Libertador General Lavalleja) is one of Montevideo's most impressive landmarks. Guided tours (UR$60) are offered at 10:30am and 3pm every weekday.

Museo Blanes (Map p540; ☎ 336-2248; Av Millán 4015; ☯ 12:15-5:45pm Tue-Sun), housed in an old mansion in the suburb of Prado, shows the work of Uruguay's most famous painter, Juan Manuel Blanes, including many historical scenes of the Río de la Plata region.

East of Centro
A must-see for any soccer fan, the **Museo del Fútbol** (☎ 480-1259; Estadio Centenario, Av Ricaldoni s/n, Parque José Batlle y Ordóñez; admission UR$60; ☯ 10am-5pm Mon-Fri) displays memorabilia from Uruguay's 1930 and 1950 World Cup championships. The price of admission includes a tour of the stands, with good views of the playing field.

Uruguay's largest collection of paintings is housed in the **Museo Nacional de Artes Visuales** (MNAV; ☎ 711-6124; www.mnav.gub.uy; cnr Av Herrera y Reissig & T Giribaldi; ☯ 2-6pm Tue-Sun) in Parque Rodó. The large rooms are graced with works by Blanes, Cúneo, Figari and Torres García.

La Rambla & Eastern Beaches
La Rambla, Montevideo's multi-kilometer coastal promenade, is one of the city's defining elements, connecting downtown to the eastern beach communities of Punta Carretas, Pocitos, Buceo and Carrasco. This is Montevideo's social hub on Sunday afternoons, when the place is packed with locals cradling thermoses of *mate* and socializing with friends.

Castillo Pittamiglio (☎ 710-1089; Rambla Gandhi 633), on the Rambla between Punta Carretas and Pocitos, is the eccentric legacy of local alchemist and architect Humberto Pittamiglio. Its quirky facade alone is worth a look; Spanish-language tours of the interior (UR$50) are available at 4pm Tuesday and Thursday, and 5pm on Saturday.

Museo Naval (☎ 622-1084; cnr Rambla Costanera & LA de Herrera; ☯ 8am-noon & 2-6pm Fri-Wed), along the eastern waterfront in Buceo, traces the role of boats and ships in Uruguayan history, from the indigenous Charrúa's canoe culture to the dramatic sinking of the German *Graf Spee* offshore of Montevideo in 1939.

The **Yacht Harbor** in Buceo, just east of Pocitos beach, is a picturesque spot for a stroll and a popular Sunday afternoon hangout.

ACTIVITIES
Get yourself a **bike** at **Bicicletería Sur** (☎ 901-0792; Aquiles Lanza 1100; per hr/day UR$20/180; ☯ 9am-1pm & 3-7pm Mon-Sat) or one of the local hostels and

go cruising along the walking-jogging-cycling track that follows the riverfront Rambla. After about 2km you'll get to Playa Pocitos, which is best for **swimming** and where you should be able to jump in on a game of **beach volleyball**. A couple of bays further along at Puerto del Buceo you can get **windsurfing** lessons at the yacht club.

COURSES

The following Spanish and tango courses don't cater for the casual learner – you'd want to be staying at least a month to get your money's worth.

Academia Uruguay (☎ 915-2496; www.academia uruguay.com; Juan Carlos Gómez 1408; group/individual classes per hr UR$200/500) One-on-one and group Spanish classes. Also arranges homestays, private apartments and volunteer work.

Berlitz (☎ 901-5535; www.berlitz.com.uy; Plaza Independencia 1380) One-on-one Spanish classes.

Joventango (☎ 901-5561; www.joventango.org; Mercado de la Abundancia, Aquiles Lanza 1290) Tango classes for all levels, from beginner to expert.

TOURS

Most hostels and higher-end hotels can arrange city tours.

Starting at noon on Saturday, a photogenic (but stinky!) vintage bus makes half-hour circuits of the Ciudad Vieja (UR$25) from Plaza Constitución, with running commentary. Between 4pm and 8pm on Sunday, the same bus leaves regularly from Plaza del Entrevero.

FESTIVALS & EVENTS

Much livelier than its Buenos Aires counterpart, Montevideo's late-summer **Carnaval** is the cultural highlight of the year – see the boxed text, below.

At Parque Prado, north of downtown, Semana Criolla festivities during **Semana Santa** (Holy Week) include displays of gaucho skills, *asados* and other such events.

In the last weekend of September or first weekend of October, Montevideo's museums, churches, and historic homes all open their doors free to the public during the **Días del Patrimonio** (National Heritage Days).

CARNAVAL IN MONTEVIDEO

If you thought Brazil was South America's only Carnaval capital, think again! *Montevideanos* cut loose in a big way every February, with music and dance filling the air for a solid month.

Not to be missed is the early February **Desfile de las Llamadas**, an all-night parade of *comparsas* (neighborhood Carnaval societies) through the streets of Palermo and Barrio Sur districts just southeast of the Centro. *Comparsas* are made up of *negros* (persons of African descent) and *lubolos* (whites who paint their faces black for Carnaval, a long-standing Uruguayan tradition). Neighborhood rivalries play themselves out as wave after wave of dancers whirl to the electrifying rhythms of traditional Afro-Uruguayan *candombe* drumming, beaten out on drums of three different pitches: the *chico* (soprano), *repique* (contralto) and *piano* (tenor). The heart of the parade route is Isla de Flores, between Salto and Gaboto. Spectators can pay for a chair on the sidewalk (UR$40) or try to snag a spot on one of the balconies overlooking the street.

Another key element of Montevideo's Carnaval is the *murgas*, organized groups of 15 to 17 gaudily dressed performers, including three percussionists, who perform original pieces of musical theater, often satirical and based on political themes. (During the dictatorship in Uruguay, *murgas* were famous for their subversive commentary.) All *murgas* use the same three instruments: the *bombo* (bass drum), *redoblante* (snare drum) and *platillos* (cymbals). *Murgas* play all over the city, and also compete throughout February in Parque Rodó at the **Teatro de Verano** (Map p540; admission from UR$70). The competition has three rounds, with judges determining who advances and who gets eliminated.

The fascinating history of Montevideo's Carnaval is well documented in the city's **Museo del Carnaval** (p544). This is a great place to soak up some of the Carnaval feeling if you can't attend the real thing. On display are costumes, drums and photos, along with recorded music from Carnavals past.

Another great way to experience Carnaval out of season is by attending one of the informal *candombe* practice sessions that erupt in neighborhood streets throughout the year. A good place to find these is at the corner of Isla de Flores and Gaboto in Palermo. Drummers usually gather between 7pm and 7:30pm on Sunday nights. If you show up a little late, just follow your ears.

SLEEPING

Montevideo's burgeoning hosteling scene is a dream come true for budget travelers. The Centro is home to Montevideo's older, more established hotels. Beach communities such as Pocitos and Punta Carretas offer some appealing newer accommodations.

Ciudad Vieja

Posada al Sur (☎ 916-5287; www.posadaalsur. uy; Pérez Castellano 1424; dm UR$240-300, s UR$700-800, d UR$800-900; 🖳 🛜) A few blocks above Mercado del Puerto, this lovingly restored older building has one six-bed dorm and three private rooms. Discounts are available for friends traveling together or for extended stays. Proceeds help support the owners' ecotourism business.

Ciudad Vieja Hostel (☎ 915-6192; www.ciudadvie jahostel.com; Ituzaingó 1436; dm HI member/nonmember UR$290/330, r UR$840/990; 🖳 🛜) Only a few steps away from the old city's abundant nightlife, this hostel has friendly staff, a homey, hip atmosphere, and an appealing layout on two upper floors of an older Ciudad Vieja building. There are separate kitchens and lounging areas on each level, a DVD library, roof deck, bikes for rent, city tours and a helpful bulletin board of cultural events.

Spléndido Hotel (☎ 916-4900; www.splendidohotel .com.uy; Bartolomé Mitre 1314; s without breakfast & bathroom UR$360-600, d UR$560-1000, tr/q without bathroom from UR$700/880; 🖳 🛜) The faded but friendly Spléndido offers excellent value for budget travelers preferring privacy over a hostel-style party vibe. There's a remarkable variety of rooms, all with wi-fi. Pricier rooms have 5m-high ceilings and French doors opening to balconies, some overlooking Teatro Solís. Bars on the street below can get extremely noisy on weekends, and the Montevideo Philharmonic Orchestra rehearses next door some mornings (free concert anyone?).

Hotel Palacio (☎ 916-3612; www.hotelpalacio .uy; Bartolomé Mitre 1364; r UR$650, with balcony UR$750) This ancient hotel has sagging brass beds, antique furniture and a vintage elevator. Try for one of the two 6th-floor rooms; the views of the Ciudad Vieja from the large balconies are superb.

Plaza Fuerte Hotel (☎ 915-6651; www.plazafuerte .com; Bartolomé Mitre 1361; r UR$1600, ste UR$2400-2800; 🍴 🖳 🛜) Housed in a stately building dating to 1913, the Plaza Fuerte has red-carpeted marble stairs, decorative tile floors and dramatic views from its 5th-floor bar and terrace. All rooms have 5m-high ceilings; the suites (some split over two levels, some with Jacuzzis) are especially elegant.

Centro
BUDGET

Montevideo Hostel (☎ 908-1324; www.montevideo hostel.com.uy, in Spanish; Canelones 935; dm per person HI member/nonmember UR$280/320; 🖳 🛜) With musical instruments strewn everywhere, good internet facilities, a cellar bar, a nice fireplace and a spiral staircase connecting all three levels of the spacious central common area, this older hostel, managed by the same family for years, remains one of Montevideo's best budget options.

Che Lagarto Hostel (☎ 903-0175; www.chelagarto .com/hostels-in-uruguay.php; Plaza Independencia 713; dm UR$300, r with/without bathroom UR$1100/900; 🖳 🛜) Centrally located, in a cheerfully painted neoclassical building, Che Lagarto is part of a multihostel South American chain. The common areas and tiny kitchen are not as welcoming as at other area hostels, but front-room balconies have great views of Plaza Independencia. Book online for discounts of 20% to 40%.

Red Hostel (☎ 908-8514; www.redhostel.com; San José 1406; dm/s/d UR$320/700/1000; 🖳) The bright orange walls, roof deck, plants and natural light pouring in through stained-glass skylights make this Montevideo's cheeriest hostel, with an energetic, friendly young staff ready to answer any questions about local goings-on. Some of the internet computers are ready for retirement, and the TV room and kitchen could be a tad bigger, but it's highly recommended overall.

MIDRANGE & TOP END

Hotel Klee Internacional (☎ 902-0606; www.klee.com .uy; San José 1303; s/d/tr/ste UR$840/1160/1360/1600; 🍴) With solid three-star amenities and a great location directly across from the Mercado de la Abundancia, the Klee is a good midtown option.

Hotel Lancaster (☎ 902-1054; www.lancasterhotel .com.uy; Plaza Cagancha 1334; s/d/tr/ste UR$980/1200/ 1580/2640; 🍴 🛜) This centrally located three-star on Plaza Cagancha is good value. Despite the unpromising exterior and bland, functional lobby decor, the rooms are clean and comfortable, many with views of the square below.

Hotel Embajador (☎ 902-0012; www.hotelembajador .com; San José 1212; s/d from UR$1060/1380; ⊠ ▣ 🛜 🗟) The four-star Embajador offers comfortable accommodations without a monster price tag. There's wi-fi in all rooms, a rooftop pool and sauna, and plenty of other amenities.

Balmoral Plaza Hotel (☎ 902-2393; www.balmoral .com.uy; Plaza Cagancha 1126; s/d/tr from UR$1400/1600/1800; ⊠ ▣) All rooms have minibars, safes, big TVs and double-glazed, soundproof windows, and many have bird's-eye views of leafy Plaza Cagancha. You'll also find a garage, gym, sauna and business center.

Radisson Victoria Plaza (☎ 902-0111; www.radis son.com/montevideouy; Plaza Independencia 759; s/d/ste UR$4200/4600/5000; ⊠ ▣ 🛜 🗟) A true five-star hotel, with luxurious rooms, a 25m swimming pool, and remarkable city views from the 25th-floor restaurant. The central location on Plaza Independencia can't be beat.

East of Centro

Palermo Art Hostel (☎ 410-6519; www.palermoarthos tel.com; Gaboto 1010; dm UR$260-400, r UR$800; ▣ 🛜) Artsy, friendly Palermo compensates for its out-of-the-way location with welcoming touches such as colorfully painted rooms and pretty comforters. Wi-fi is available, and there's an attractive kitchen and a downstairs pub. It's also the perfect base for experiencing Montevideo's Sunday *candombe* drum sessions (see the boxed text, p547). HI members receive a 20% discount.

La Rambla & Eastern Beaches

Pocitos Hostel (☎ 711-8780; www.pocitos-hostel.com; Sarmiento 2641, Pocitos; dm UR$260-360, s/d UR$500/720; ▣) A few blocks from the Pocitos waterfront, this appealing new hostel squeezes several four- to six-bed dorms and a couple of doubles into a converted old home with fireplace, wood floors, high ceilings, guest kitchen, backyard barbecue and friendly staff.

Una Noche Más B&B (☎ 096-227406; www.unanoche mas.com.uy; Patria 712, Apt 2, Punta Carretas; s/d/tr UR$760/ 880/1200; ▣ 🛜) In beachside Punta Carretas, this is a great option for anyone seeking a 'homestay' experience in the big city. Friendly hosts Carla and Eduardo go out of their way to make guests feel welcome and also offer half and full board upon request. There's a two-night minimum stay.

Pocitos Plaza Hotel (☎ 712-3939; www.pocitospla zahotel.com.uy; Benito Blanco 640, Pocitos; s/d standard

UR$1780/1980, superior UR$2180/2500; ⊠ ▣ 🛜) This comfortable four-star is replete with services for the business traveler, although vacationers will also appreciate its sauna, sundeck and proximity to the beach. Superior rooms have sofas, whirlpool tubs and big closets.

Cala di Volpe (☎ 710-2000; www.hotelcaladivolpe .com.uy; cnr Rambla Gandhi & Parva Domus, Punta Carretas; s/d/ste from UR$2000/2200/3200; ⊠ ▣ 🛜 🗟) This classy newcomer across from the beach boasts one of Montevideo's most exclusive locations. Boutique features abound: comfy couches, writing desks, wi-fi, gleaming tile-and-marble bathrooms, and floor-to-ceiling picture windows with sweeping river views. There's a small rooftop pool and a nice restaurant.

EATING

Montevideo's restaurants are largely unpretentious and offer excellent value. Two of the most atmospheric places to eat are the converted market buildings. **Mercado del Puerto** (Pérez Castellano), on the Ciudad Vieja waterfront, is *the* classic place to eat in Montevideo. The densely packed *parrillas* here cater to every budget, competing like rutting elk to show off their obscenely large racks – of roasted meat and veggies, that is! Weekends are the best time to savor the market's vibrant, crowded energy, but lunching executives and tourists keep the place buzzing on weekdays, too. The more affordable and less touristy **Mercado de la Abundancia** (cnr San José & Aquiles Lanza), in the heart of downtown, features four low-key eateries surrounding an open space where locals come every Saturday night to tango, salsa and more.

Ciudad Vieja
BUDGET

Café Roldós (☎ 915-1520; Mercado del Puerto; sandwiches UR$40; ☯ 9am-5pm) This historic cafe in Mercado del Puerto is a perennial favorite. Since 1886 staff have been pouring their famous *medio y medio* (per bottle/glass UR$130/30), a refreshing concoction made from half wine, half sparkling wine. Throw in a few tasty sandwiches, and you've got a meal!

Rincón de Zabala (☎ 915-1617; Rincón 387; sandwiches UR$60-70, full meals incl dessert UR$135-155; ☯ 9am-5:30pm Mon-Fri; 🛜) This modern corner place serves up free wi-fi along with affordable breakfasts, sandwiches and cafeteria-style daily specials.

MIDRANGE & TOP END

Don Peperone (☎ 915-7493; Sarandí 650; dishes UR$130-250; ☽ 10am-late; ☏) This high-quality chain restaurant in Ciudad Vieja serves excellent, moderately priced food late into the night. Vegetarians will appreciate the unlimited salad bar for UR$205, including wine, coffee and dessert.

Cervecería Matriz (☎ 916-1582; Sarandí 582; dishes UR$130-290; ☽ 8am-1am Mon-Sat) Join the crowds enjoying beer and *chivitos* (goat) under the trees at this new eatery on Ciudad Vieja's most picturesque square. Brisk, friendly service and a good price–quality relationship add up to a fine experience.

Café Bacacay (☎ 916-6074; Bacacay 1306; dishes UR$170-360; ☽ 9am-late Mon-Sat) This chic little cafe across from Teatro Solís serves a variety of mouthwatering goodies: fish of the day with wasabi or *limoncello* (lemon liqueur) sauce, build-your-own salads with tasty ingredients such as grilled eggplant, spinach and smoked salmon, and a wide-ranging drinks menu. Desserts include chocolate cake, pear tart and lemon pie.

Delnorte (☎ 915-8267; Rincón 510; dishes UR$200-260; ☽ lunch Mon-Fri) The decor is minimalist, the soundtrack smooth and jazzy and the food superb at this Ciudad Vieja bistro. Everything, including the trademark fish cakes and steak pie, is prepared with loving care, and the house wines are excellent. Try the *ensalada con lomo* (a salad of spinach, escarole, sun-dried tomatoes, goat cheese and coriander-marinated sirloin with an Asian-inspired dressing).

La Silenciosa (☎ 915-9409; Ituzaingó 1426; dishes UR$250-390; ☽ lunch Mon-Sat, dinner Fri) With stone and brick walls, high ceilings and checkerboard marble floors, this restaurant has a fascinating history including stints as an 18th-century Jesuit seminary and as the tailor's shop where Carlos Gardel and other Uruguayan luminaries had their shirts made. The food is divine – from homemade pasta to scrumptious meat and fish dishes to desserts such as moist orange cake with green tea ice cream.

Centro
BUDGET

Pizza Subte (☎ 902-3050; Ejido 1327; pizzas UR$40-119; ☽ 10am-late Mon-Sat, 5pm-late Sun) Casually dressed families flock to this bright, boisterous 1950s-era pizzeria for reasonably priced pizzas, *milanesas* (breaded fish), *chivitos* and other Uruguayan standards.

Shawarma Ashot (☎ 900-7250; Zelmar Michelini 1295; dishes UR$60-100) This recently opened hole-in-the-wall, serving great falafel and other Middle Eastern treats, is a true labor of love for the owners, who work the counter here during the week, then on weekends return to work in their long-standing catering business.

La Vegetariana (☎ 902-3178; Yí 1369; per half-kg UR$100) Grab a plate and help yourself from the steam trays, salad bar and dessert table – it's not fine dining, but it's one of the few truly veggie options in this meat-crazed country.

Bar Hispano (☎ 908-0045; San José 1050; specials UR$125; ☽ 7am-1am) Old-school neighborhood *confiterías* (cafes offering light meals) like this are disappearing fast. The bow-tied, grouchy waiters can take pretty much any order you throw at them – a stiff drink to start the day, a full meal at 5pm or a chocolate binge in the early hours.

MIDRANGE & TOP END

El Rincón de los Poetas (☎ 901-5102; Mercado de la Abundancia; dishes UR$125-159; ☽ 11am-midnight Mon-Sat) Featuring the classic Uruguayan trinity of pasta, pizza and (of course) roast meat, this eatery with its red-and-white checked tablecloths epitomizes the Mercado de la Abundancia's cozy, relaxed ambience.

Ruffino Pizza y Pasta (☎ 908-3384; San José 1166; dishes UR$140-260; ☽ lunch & dinner Mon-Fri, dinner only Sat, lunch only Sun) Extremely popular for Sunday lunch, Ruffino's is a good midrange Italian option. Try the Caruso (mushroom and cream) sauce, a uniquely Uruguayan specialty named for Italian tenor Enrico Caruso, who visited Montevideo in 1915.

Los Leños Uruguayos (☎ 900-2285; San José 909; dishes UR$160-295; ☽ lunch & dinner) This tiny little restaurant is a favorite with the business set. It has a nice salad bar, and there's always a big rack of meat roasting on the fire up front. The lunchtime *menú ejecutivo* (UR$215) and *sugerencias del chef* (UR$195) are both great deals, including *cubierto*, main dish, dessert and coffee.

Club Brasilero (☎ 902-4344; Av 18 de Julio 994, 2nd fl; specials incl drink & dessert UR$180; ☽ 8am-10pm Mon-Sat) Inside the Brazilian cultural center, reasonably priced meals are served in an elegant 2nd-floor salon with high ceilings and stained glass. There's often live Brazilian music on Friday evenings.

East of Centro

Bistró Sucré Salé (☎ 402-7779; Blvd Artigas 1229, Parque Rodó; pastries from UR$40, sandwiches UR$50-85, dishes UR$225-315; 🕙 9am-7:30pm Mon-Fri, 10am-2pm Sat) Wonderful European influences abound at this little cafe behind the Alianza Francesa: French music, brioches, tarts, Illy espresso, Van Gogh posters, plus a courtyard with fountain, iron gazebo and climbing roses.

La Rambla & Eastern Beaches

Amaretto (☎ 711-9934; 21 de Setiembre 2998, Punta Carretas; salads/sandwiches UR$110/125; 🕙 8am-11pm) The obvious hook at this bakery-cafe is its tempting display of pastries, although the comfortable booth seating may entice you to linger over their reasonably priced soups, salads and sandwiches.

Tranquilo Bar (☎ 711-2127; 21 de Setiembre 3000, Pocitos; dishes UR$120-190; 🕙 10am-3am) This cozy corner bar, with its dark wood interior and outdoor terrace, makes an atmospheric spot for drinks and simple, affordable meals.

La Cavia (☎ 706-8253; 26 de Marzo 1000, Pocitos; dishes UR$135-245; 🕙 lunch & dinner) Since opening in late 2008, this *parrilla* has earned a devoted following for its classy but casual ambience, sidewalk seating and lunchtime *menú ejecutivo*, including main dish, salad, glass of wine, dessert and coffee, for UR$175.

Umaga (☎ 712-3141; cnr Luis de la Torre & Francisco Ros, Punta Carretas; dishes UR$250-370; 🕙 dinner Mon-Sat) Umaga offers a concise menu of beautifully presented gourmet dishes in a comfortable old Punta Carretas home done up in modern style. The innovative offerings range from grilled salmon with leeks and strawberries to desserts such as apple-cinnamon-clove roll flambed with grappa.

Bar Tabaré (☎ 712-3242; Zorrilla de San Martín 152, Punta Carretas; dishes UR$260-390; 🕙 8pm-late Mon-Sat) This tastefully remodeled traditional neighborhood bar, first opened in 1919, gets top marks for atmosphere and for its international array of salads, pasta, meat and fish. There's frequent live entertainment, featuring everything from tango to stand-up comedy.

DRINKING

Ciudad Vieja and Centro offer an intriguing mix of venerable old cafes and up-and-coming recent arrivals. Bars are concentrated along Bartolomé Mitre in Ciudad Vieja, and south of Plaza Independencia in the Centro.

Cafes

Café Irazú (☎ 915-7434; Juan Carlos Gomez 1315, Ciudad Vieja; 🕙 9am-9pm Mon-Fri, noon-7pm Sat) Take one sip and you'll understand why Irazú keeps winning awards for Uruguay's best coffee. There are also plenty of affordable light meal options, from sandwiches (UR$47 to UR$143) to mini-pizzas (UR$65 to UR$80) to *platos del día* (UR$135 to UR$150).

Oro del Rhin (☎ 902-2833; Convención 1403, Centro; 🕙 8:30am-8pm Mon-Sat) With over 75 years in business, you know they're doing something right! It's worth a visit just to ogle the gorgeous collection of cakes and pastries in the window.

Café Brasilero (☎ 915-8120; Ituzaingó 1447, Ciudad Vieja; 🕙 9am-8pm Mon-Wed, to 2am Thu & Fri) A delightfully old-fashioned 1877 cafe with little wooden tables and chairs, chandeliers, and historic photos and posters gracing the walls.

Diseño Café (☎ 916-0383; 25 de Mayo 263, Ciudad Vieja; 🕙 10am-7pm Mon-Sat) This stylish cafe in Ciudad Vieja has electric-purple walls, youthful energy and the artsy Imaginario Sur boutique next door.

Bars

Shannon Irish Pub (☎ 916-9585; www.theshannon.com.uy; Bartolomé Mitre 1318, Ciudad Vieja; 🕙 7pm-late) A perennial favorite, the Shannon pours a good pint and features live music every night, from rock to traditional Irish bands.

Fun Fun (☎ 915-8005; www.barfunfun.com; Ciudadela 1229, Mercado Central, Ciudad Vieja; 🕙 9pm-late Wed-Sat) Since 1895 this informal venue in the Mercado Central has been serving its famous *uvita* (a sweet wine drink) while hosting tango and other live music on a tiny stage. The front deck is very pleasant.

La Ronda (☎ 902-6962; Ciudadela 1182, Centro; 🕙 noon-late Mon-Sat, 7pm-late Sun) Ultracool Ronda is always animated and jam-packed. As a turntable spins hypnotic tunes, patrons straddle the windowsills between the dark interior plastered with vintage album covers and the sidewalk tables cooled by breezes off the Rambla.

Tras Bambalinas (☎ 903-2090; Ciudadela 1250, cnr Soriano; 🕙 9am-1am Mon, to 2am Tue-Thu, to 4am Fri & Sat) This newly opened pub sports a Carnaval theme: the decor features giant papier-mâché masks, costumes and photos from Carnavals past, and there's frequent live murga music (a choral-percussive style typical of Montevideo's Carnaval).

El Lobizón (☎ 901-1334; Zelmar Michelini 1264, Centro; ☺ 8pm-3am) Lobizón's cellar-bar atmosphere, free-flowing pitchers of sangría and *clericó*, and tasty snacks such as the famous *gramajo* (potatoes, ham and eggs) make it a very popular gathering place for young, artistic types.

ENTERTAINMENT

The useful weekly *Guía del Ocio* (UR$18; published Friday) lists Montevideo's cultural events, cinemas, theaters and restaurants. Websites with culture and entertainment listings include the following (all are in Spanish):

- www.aromperlanoche.com
- www.pimba.com.uy
- www.espectador.com
- www.cartelera.com.uy
- www.socioespectacular.com.uy

Nightclubs

W Lounge (☎ 712-2671; cnr Rambla Wilson & Sarmiento, Parque Rodó; ☺ midnight-7am Thu-Sat) With two dance floors accommodating 3000 people, this nightclub in Parque Rodó is *the* place to shake your thang to rock, *cumbia* and techno beats. A taxi from the center should cost about UR$80.

Kalú After Club (☎ 915-8916; Juan Carlos Gómez 1323, Ciudad Vieja; ☺ 3:30am onwards Sat & Sun) The party moves here after everything else closes in Ciudad Vieja; the last stragglers stumble out around noon.

La City (☎ 916-7782; Rincón 614, Ciudad Vieja; ☺ 10:30pm-7am Fri & Sat) People line up around the block to dance at this trendy club in the heart of Ciudad Vieja.

Cain Dance Club (☎ 099-600427; Cerro Largo 1833, Cordón; ☺ midnight-7am Sat & Sun) Montevideo's premier gay nightspot, Cain is a multilevel club with two dance floors playing everything from techno to Latin beats.

Living (☎ 402-3795; Paullier 1050, Parque Rodó; ☺ 9pm-late) An intimate venue for alternative sounds, Living often hosts lesser-known bands from Buenos Aires.

El Pony Pisador (☎ 915-7470; www.elponypisador .com.uy); Ciudad Vieja (Bartolomé Mitre 1324; ☺ 5pm-late Mon-Fri, 8pm-late Sat & Sun); Pocitos (José Iturriaga 3497; ☺ 8:30pm-late Thu-Sat) This thriving bar and disco has two locations in Montevideo featuring live music nightly; depending on the evening and the location, you may find yourself dancing to blues, Brazilian, flamenco, oldies, soul, Latin or rock covers in English and Spanish. The Pocitos branch occasionally also hosts stand-up comics.

La Bodeguita del Sur (☎ 901-1034; Soriano 840, Centro; ☺ 11pm-late Fri-Sun) For live salsa, hit this place on weekend nights.

Live Music & Dance

The legendary Carlos Gardel spent time in Montevideo, where the tango is no less popular than in Buenos Aires. Music and dance venues abound downtown.

Teatro Solís (☎ 1950 ext 3323; www.teatrosolis.org.uy, in Spanish; Buenos Aires 678, Ciudad Vieja; admission from UR$200) The city's top venue is home to the Montevideo Philharmonic Orchestra and hosts formal concerts of classical, jazz, tango and other music, plus music festivals, ballet and opera.

Sala Zitarrosa (☎ 901-7303; www.salazitarrosa.com .uy; Av 18 de Julio 1012, Centro) Montevideo's best informal auditorium venue for big-name music and dance performances, including zarzuela, tango, rock, flamenco and reggae.

Cine Teatro Plaza (☎ 901-5385; Plaza Cagancha 1129, Centro) It occasionally brings in big international acts such as Brazil's Milton Nascimento, France's Jean-Luc Ponty or American jazz virtuosos Mike Stern and the Yellowjackets.

El Tartamudo Café (☎ 480-4332; www.eltartamudo .com.uy; cnr 8 de Octubre & Presidente Berro, Tres Cruces; ☺ 9pm-late Tue-Sun) Performances at this place just east of Tres Cruces bus terminal run the gamut from rock to tango to *candombe* to jazz.

La Trastienda (☎ 402-6929; www.latrastienda.com .uy; Fernández Crespo 1763, Cordón; ☺ 9pm-late Wed-Sat) This popular club hosts an eclectic mix of international musicians, playing everything from rock to reggae, jazz to folk, tango to electronica.

Cinema

Cinemateca Uruguaya (☎ 900-9056; www.cinemateca .org.uy; Av 18 de Julio 1280; membership per month UR$180) For art-house flicks, this film club charges a modest membership allowing unlimited viewing at its five cinemas. It hosts the two-week Festival Cinematográfico Internacional del Uruguay in March or April, and smaller film festivals throughout the year.

The rest of Montevideo's cinema scene is concentrated in the shopping malls east of downtown.

Theater

Montevideo's active theater community spans many worlds: from classical to commercial to avant-garde.

Teatro El Galpón (☎ 408-3366; www.teatroelgalpon
.org.uy; Av 18 de Julio 1618, Centro; admission from UR$150)
Montevideo's most commercial theater al-
ways stages multiple shows concurrently; it's
northeast of the Intendencia.

Teatro Sobre Ruedas (☎ 900-8618; www.barro
negro.com; Bacacay 1318, Ciudad Vieja; admission UR$180)
Eighteen years old and going strong, this
company presents *Barro Negro*, an interactive
theater piece that literally takes place on a bus
whizzing through Montevideo's streets.

Teatro Victoria (☎ 901-9971; Rio Negro 1477, Centro;
admission from UR$120) This historic downtown
theater, north of Plaza del Entrevero, hosts
both theater and dance performances.

Teatro Solís (☎ 1950 ext 3323; www.teatrosolis.org
.uy, in Spanish; Buenos Aires 678, Ciudad Vieja; admission
from UR$100) Home to the Comedia Nacional,
Montevideo's municipal theater company.

Teatro Circular (☎ 901-5952; Rondeau 1388, Centro; admission from UR$120) Just north of Plaza Cagancha,
the venerable Circular has been open for over
50 years. It shows works by contemporary
playwrights from around the world.

Spectator Sports

Football, a Uruguayan passion, inspires large
and regular crowds. The main stadium, the
Estadio Centenario (Map p540; Av Ricaldoni, Parque José
Batlle y Ordóñez), opened in 1930 for the first
World Cup, in which Uruguay defeated
Argentina 4-2 in the title game.

SHOPPING

Central Montevideo's traditional downtown
shopping area is Av 18 de Julio. *Montevideanos*
also flock to three major shopping malls east
of downtown: Punta Carretas Shopping
(Map p540), Tres Cruces Shopping (above
the bus terminal; Map p540) and Montevideo
Shopping (Map p540) in Pocitos/Buceo.

Feria de Tristán Narvaja (Map p540; Tristán Narvaja,
Cordón) This colorful Sunday-morning outdoor
market is a decades-long tradition begun by
Italian immigrants. It sprawls from Av 18 de
Julio northwards along Calle Tristán Narvaja,
spilling over onto several side streets. You can
find used books, music, clothing, jewelry, live
animals, antiques and souvenirs in its many
makeshift stalls.

Saturday Flea Market (Plaza Constitución, Ciudad
Vieja) Every Saturday vendors take over Ciudad
Vieja's central square, selling antique door
knockers, saddles, household goods and just
about anything else you can imagine.

Manos del Uruguay Centro (☎ 900-4910; San José
1111); Ciudad Vieja (☎ 915-5345; Sarandí 668) This national cooperative is famous for its quality
goods, especially woolens.

Imaginario Sur (☎ 916-0383; 25 de Mayo 265, Ciudad
Vieja) This colorful, trendy shop features art,
fashion and design work by dozens of Uruguayan artists.

Hecho Acá (☎ 915-4341; cnr Rambla 25 de Agosto
& Yacaré, Ciudad Vieja) Woolen goods and other
handicrafts from around the country are
nicely displayed here.

Ayuídiscos (☎ 403-1526; 18 de Julio 1618, Centro)
This little store is an excellent source for
Uruguayan music of all kinds.

Corazón al Sur (☎ 901-1714; Plaza del Entrevero,
Centro) This kiosk downtown sells music CDs
by a wide variety of Uruguayan artists. It
sponsors live performances in the square
Friday through Sunday.

El Galeón (☎ 915-6139; Juan Carlos Gómez 1327, Ciudad
Vieja) With maps, engravings and rare books
piled everywhere, this place is fun to explore.

Casa Mario (☎ 916-2356; Piedras 641, Ciudad Vieja)
Specializing in Uruguayan leather since 1945,
Casa Mario is quite touristy but has a wide
selection.

Louvre (☎ 916-2686; Sarandí 652, Ciudad Vieja) The
Louvre has three floors packed with antiques,
including gaucho paraphernalia, paintings,
furniture and jewelry.

GETTING THERE & AWAY
Air

Montevideo's **Carrasco international airport**
(☎ 604-0272) is served by far fewer airlines than
Ezeiza in Buenos Aires.

Pluna, Sol and Aerolíneas Argentinas fly
frequently between Carrasco and Buenos
Aires' Aeroparque. Nonstop service from
Montevideo to other international destinations
is provided by Pluna (to Madrid and several
South American cities), American Airlines (to
Miami), Gol (to Porto Alegre, Brazil), Iberia
(to Madrid), LanChile (to Santiago), TACA
(to Lima) and TAM (to São Paulo).

Several airlines maintain offices in
Montevideo, but many do not have direct
flights to/from Uruguay.

Aerolíneas Argentinas (☎ 902-0828; Plaza Independencia 749 bis, Centro)

Air France/KLM (☎ 902-5013; Río Negro 1354, 1st fl,
Centro)

American Airlines (☎ 916-3929) Ciudad Vieja (Sarandí
699 bis); Pocitos (Benito Blanco 1261)

URUGUAY

Delta (☎ 900-7776; Colonia 981, 5th fl, Centro)

Gol (☎ 000-405-5127, 606-0901; Carrasco airport)

Iberia (☎ 908-1032; Colonia 975, Centro)

LanChile (☎ 902-3881; Colonia 993, 4th fl, Centro)

Pluna (☎ 902-1414; Colonia 1021, Centro)

Qantas/Alitalia (☎ 903-1760; Río Negro 1354, 4th fl, Centro)

Sol (☎ 000-405-210053; Carrasco airport)

TACA (☎ 900-2624; Plaza Independencia 831, Oficina 807, Centro)

TAM (Transportes Aéreos de Mercosur; ☎ 901-8451; Plaza Cagancha 1335, 8th fl, Centro)

United/Lufthansa (☎ 901-3370; Plaza Independencia 831, Oficina 409, Centro)

Boat

Buquebus (☎ 130; www.buquebus.com.uy; Centro cnr Colonia & Florida; Ciudad Vieja Terminal Puerto; Tres Cruces bus terminal cnr Bulevar Artigas & Av Italia) runs daily high-speed ferries direct from Montevideo to Buenos Aires (three hours). Turista class fares are UR$1765/1470 for adults/seniors and children aged 10 and under. There's a UR$720 surcharge for 1st-class travel.

Buquebus also offers less expensive bus-boat combinations to Buenos Aires via Colonia (slow boat UR$856/707 adult/seniors or child, 6¼ hours; fast boat UR$1117/877, 4¼ hours). Tickets can be purchased directly from Buquebus or at the **Ferryturismo office** (☎ 900-6617; Río Negro 1400) on Plaza del Entrevero.

Even more affordable are the bus-boat combinations offered by **Colonia Express** (www .coloniaexpress.com) Centro (☎ 901-9597; WF Aldunate 1341); Tres Cruces bus terminal (☎ 400-3939). Standard one-way fares for the 4¼-hour trip run UR$930 per person, but online advance bookings qualify for rates as low as UR$395.

Trans Uruguay (☎ 401-9350; www.transuruguay.com, in Spanish; Tres Cruces bus terminal, Boletería 32), with its partner Cacciola, runs a twice-daily scenic bus-launch service to Buenos Aires via the riverside town of Carmelo and the Argentine Delta suburb of Tigre. The eight-hour trip costs UR$629 one way.

Bus

Montevideo's modern **Tres Cruces bus terminal** (Map p540; ☎ 401-8998; cnr Bulevar Artigas & Av Italia) is about 3km east of downtown. It has tourist information, decent restaurants, clean toilets, a luggage check (UR$93 per 24 hours for up to three bags; first two hours free for passengers showing a ticket), public phones, ATMs and a shopping mall upstairs.

A taxi from the terminal to downtown costs UR$80 to UR$100. To save your pesos, take city bus CA1, which leaves Monday to Saturday from directly in front of the terminal (on the eastern side), traveling to Ciudad Vieja via Av Uruguay (UR$9, 15 minutes). On Sundays, head for the bus stop on the south side of the terminal and take bus 21, 64, 187 or 330, all of which go to Plaza Independencia via Av 18 de Julio (UR$16, 15 minutes).

For the beach neighborhoods of Punta Carretas and Pocitos, take city buses 174 and 183, respectively, from in front of the terminal (UR$16). A taxi to either neighborhood costs less than UR$100.

All destinations following are served daily (except as noted) and most several times a day. A small *tasa de embarque* (UR$5 to UR$15 surcharge) is added to the ticket prices. Travel times are approximate.

Destination	Cost (UR$)	Duration (hr)
International		
Asunción (Par)	2121	21
Buenos Aires (Arg)	760	10
Córdoba (Arg)	1493	15½
Curitiba (Bra)	2857	24
Florianópolis (Bra)	2347	18
Mendoza (Arg)	2010	24
Paraná (Arg)	1037	10
Pelotas (Bra)	1098	8
Porto Alegre (Bra)	1541	12
Santa Fe (Arg)	1085	12
Santiago de Chile	2747	28
São Paulo (Bra)	3303	28
Domestic		
Barra de Valizas	294	4½
Carmelo	235	3¼
Chuy	333	5½
Colonia	176	2¾
Fray Bentos	303	4½
La Paloma	235	3½
La Pedrera	245	4
Maldonado	137	2
Mercedes	274	4
Minas	117	2
Nueva Helvecia	127	2
Pan de Azúcar	98	1½
Paysandú	372	4½
Piriápolis	98	1½
Punta del Diablo	294	5
Punta del Este	142	2¼
Rocha	206	3
Salto	490	6½
Tacuarembó	382	4½
Treinta y Tres	284	4½
Villa Serrana	137	2½

EGA (☎ 402-5164) provides the widest range of service to neighboring countries, running buses once weekly to Santiago, Chile (Monday) and São Paulo, Brazil (Sunday), twice weekly to Asunción, Paraguay (Wednesday and Saturday), and daily except Saturday to Porto Alegre, Brazil. Service to Argentina is more frequent, with several companies competing and everyone offering daily service to Buenos Aires. Among other Argentine destinations, Córdoba has at least four departures a week, Rosario at least three, and Paraná, Santa Fe and Mendoza at least one.

GETTING AROUND
To/From the Airport
From **Terminal Suburbana** (☎ 1975; cnr Río Branco & Galicia), five blocks north of Plaza del Entrevero, Copsa buses 700, 701, 704, 710 and 711 run to Carrasco airport (UR$25, 45 minutes). Coming from the airport, look for the covered Copsa bus stop on a little island in front of the arrivals hall.

A taxi to the airport from downtown Montevideo costs about UR$400.

Bus
Montevideo's city buses go almost everywhere for UR$16 per ride. The *Guía de Montevideo Eureka* (UR$150), available at bookstores or kiosks, lists routes and schedules, as do the yellow pages of the Montevideo phone book. For additional information, contact **Cutcsa** (☎ 204-0000; www.cutcsa.com.uy).

Car
Avis, Hertz, Europcar and other international companies have counters at Carrasco airport. In downtown Montevideo, the following Uruguayan companies with nationwide branches offer good deals.
Multicar (☎ 902-2555; www.redmulticar.com; Colonia 1227, Centro)
Punta Car (☎ 900-2772; www.puntacar.com; Cerro Largo 1383, Centro)

Taxi
Montevideo's black-and-yellow taxis are all metered, and relatively cheap by world standards. It costs UR$22 to drop the flag (UR$26 at night and on Sunday) and just over UR$1 per unit thereafter. All cabbies carry two official price tables, one effective on weekdays, the other (20% higher) used at night (between 10pm and 6am), Sundays and holidays. Even

for a long ride, you'll rarely pay more than UR$150, unless you're headed to Carrasco airport (about UR$400 from downtown).

WESTERN URUGUAY

From Colonia's tree-shaded cobblestone streets to the hot springs of Salto, the slow-paced river towns of western Uruguay have a universally relaxing appeal, with just enough urban attractions to keep things interesting. Here, the border with Argentina is defined by the Río de la Plata and the Río Uruguay, and the region is commonly referred to as *el litoral* (the shore).

Further inland you'll find the heart of what some consider the 'real' Uruguay – the gaucho country around Tacuarembó, with *estancias* sprinkled throughout the rural landscape and some beautiful, rarely visited nature preserves.

COLONIA DEL SACRAMENTO
☎ 052 / pop 22,000
Colonia is an irresistibly picturesque town whose colonial-era Barrio Histórico is a Unesco World Heritage site. Pretty rows of sycamores offer protection from the summer heat, and the Río de la Plata provides a venue for spectacular sunsets. Colonia's charm and its proximity to Buenos Aires draw thousands of Argentine visitors; on weekends, especially in summer, prices rise and it can be difficult to find a room.

Colonia was founded in 1680 by Manuel Lobo, the Portuguese governor of Rio de Janeiro, and occupied a strategic position almost exactly opposite Buenos Aires across the Río de la Plata. The town grew in importance as a source of smuggled trade items, undercutting Spain's jealously defended mercantile monopoly and provoking repeated sieges and battles between Spain and Portugal.

Although the two powers agreed over the cession of Colonia to Spain around 1750, it wasn't until 1777 that Spain took final control of the city. From this time, the city's commercial importance declined as foreign goods proceeded directly to Buenos Aires.

Orientation
Colonia sits on the east bank of the Río de la Plata, 180km west of Montevideo, but only 50km from Buenos Aires by ferry. Its Barrio Histórico, an irregular colonial nucleus of

URUGUAY

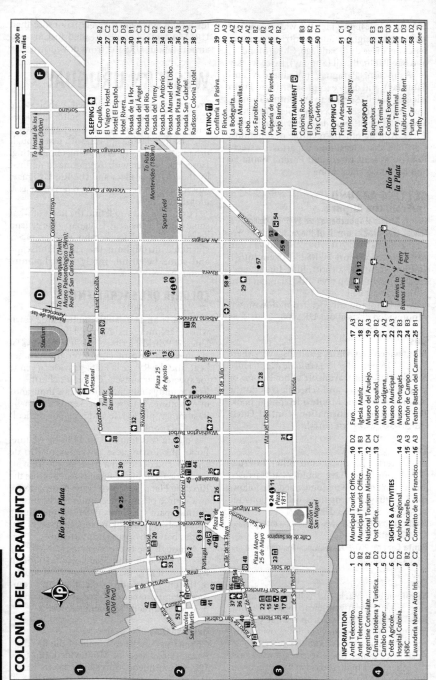

COLONIA DEL SACRAMENTO

SLEEPING 🏠	
El Capullo	26 B2
El Viajero Hostel	27 C2
Hostel El Español	28 C3
Hotel Rivera	29 D3
Posada de la Flor	30 B1
Posada del Ángel	31 C3
Posada del Río	32 C2
Posada del Virrey	33 B2
Posada Don Antonio	34 B2
Posada Manuel de Lobo	35 A3
Posada Plaza Mayor	36 A3
Posada San Gabriel	37 A3
Radisson Colonia Hotel	38 C1

EATING 🍴	
Confitería La Pasiva	39 D2
El Rincón	40 A3
La Bodeguita	41 A2
Lentas Maravillas	42 A2
Lobo	43 A2
Los Farolitos	44 B2
Mercosur	45 B2
Pulpería de los Faroles	46 A3
Viejo Barrio	47 B2

ENTERTAINMENT 🎭	
Colonia Rock	48 B3
El Drugstore	49 B2
Tr3s Cu4rto	50 D1

SHOPPING 🛍	
Feria Artesanal	51 C1
Manos del Uruguay	52 A2

TRANSPORT	
Buquebus	53 E3
Bus Terminal	54 E3
Colonia Express	55 D3
Ferry Terminal	56 D4
Multicar/Moto Rent	57 D3
Punta Car	58 D2
Thrifty	(see 2)

INFORMATION	
Antel Telecentro	1 C2
Antel Telecentro	2 B2
Argentine Consulate	3 B2
Cámara Hotelera y Turística	4 D2
Cambio Dromer	5 C2
Crédit Agricole	6 C2
Hospital Colonia	7 D2
HSBC	8 B2
Lavandería Nueva Arco Iris	9 C2
Municipal Tourist Office	10 D2
Municipal Tourist Office	11 B3
National Tourism Ministry	12 D4
Post Office	13 C2

SIGHTS & ACTIVITIES	
Archivo Regional	14 A3
Casa Nacarello	15 A3
Convento de San Francisco	16 A3
Faro	17 A3
Iglesia Matriz	18 B2
Museo del Azulejo	19 A3
Museo Español	20 B2
Museo Indígena	21 A2
Museo Municipal	22 B3
Museo Portugués	23 B3
Portón de Campo	24 B3
Teatro Bastión del Carmen	25 B1

narrow cobbled streets, occupies a small peninsula jutting into the river. The town's commercial center, around Plaza 25 de Agosto,
and the river port are a few blocks east, while
the Rambla Costanera (named Rambla de las
Américas at the edge of town) leads north along
the river to Real de San Carlos, another area of
interest. The diagonal Av Roosevelt becomes
Ruta 1, the main highway to Montevideo.

Information
ESSENTIALS

Cámara Hotelera y Turística (☎ 27302; cnr Av General Flores & Rivera; ☷ 11am-7pm, to 8pm in summer)
Adjacent to the main municipal tourist office; helps with
hotel bookings.

Cambio Dromer (cnr Av General Flores & Intendente
Suárez; ☷ 9am-7pm Mon-Fri, 9am-6pm Sat, 10am-1pm
Sun) Cashes traveler's checks.

Crédit Agricole (Av General Flores 299) One of several
ATMs along General Flores.

Hospital Colonia (☎ 22994; 18 de Julio 462)

HSBC (Portugal 183) Most convenient ATM in the
historical center.

Municipal tourist office (☷ 9am-7pm, to 8pm in
summer) Barrio Histórico (☎ 28506; Manuel Lobo 224);
Centro (☎ 26141; cnr Av General Flores & Rivera)

National Tourism Ministry (☎ 24897) Scheduled to
reopen inside the new ferry terminal.

OTHER SERVICES

Antel Telecentro Barrio Histórico (Av General Flores 172);
Centro (cnr Lavalleja & Rivadavia)

Lavandería Nueva Arco Iris (Intendente Suárez 196;
wash & dry per basket UR$100; ☷ 8am-noon & 2-6pm
Mon-Fri, 8am-noon Sat)

Post office (Lavalleja 226)

Sights & Activities
BARRIO HISTÓRICO

Colonia's Barrio Histórico is filled with visual
delights. It's fun to just wander the streets and
the waterfront. The most dramatic way to
enter is via the reconstructed 1745 city gate,
the **Portón de Campo** (Manuel Lobo). From here, a
thick fortified wall runs south along the Paseo
de San Miguel to the river, its grassy slopes
popular with sunbathers. Other famous streets
include the narrow, roughly cobbled **Calle de
los Suspiros** (Street of Sighs), lined with tile-
and-stucco colonial houses, and the **Paseo de
San Gabriel**, on the western riverfront.

Historic Colonia's two main squares are the
vast **Plaza Mayor 25 de Mayo** and the shady **Plaza
de Armas**, also known as Plaza Manuel Lobo.

The latter plaza is the home of Colonia's **Iglesia
Matriz**. The church, begun in 1680, is Uruguay's
oldest, though it has been completely rebuilt
twice. The plaza also holds the foundations of
a house dating from Portuguese times.

Off the southwest corner of Plaza Mayor
25 de Mayo are the ruins of the 17th-century
Convento de San Francisco, within which stands
the 19th-century **faro** (lighthouse; admission UR$15;
☷ 1pm-sunset Mon-Fri, 11am-sunset Sat & Sun). The
lighthouse provides an excellent view of the
old town.

The **Puerto Viejo** (Old Port) is now Colonia's
yacht harbor and makes for a very pleasant
stroll. The nearby **Teatro Bastión del Carmen**
(Rivadavia 223; admission free; ☷ 10:30am-10pm Tue-Sun)
is a theater and gallery complex incorporating
part of the city's ancient fortifications. It hosts
rotating art exhibits and periodic concerts.

Museums

A single UR$50 ticket covers admission to
Colonia's eight **historical museums** (☎ 25609;
museoscolonia@gmail.com; ☷ 11:15am-4:45pm). All
keep the same hours, but closing day varies
by museum as noted following.

The **Museo Portugués** (Plaza Mayor 25 de Mayo 180;
☷ closed Wed), in a beautiful old house, holds
Portuguese relics including porcelain, furniture, maps, Manuel Lobo's family tree and
the old stone shield that once adorned the
Portón de Campo.

The **Museo Municipal** (Plaza Mayor 25 de Mayo 77;
☷ closed Tue) houses an eclectic collection of
treasures including a whale skeleton, an enormous rudder from a shipwreck, historical time-
lines and a scale model of Colonia c 1762.

On the northwest edge of the plaza, the
Archivo Regional (Misiones de los Tapes 115; ☷ closed
Sat & Sun) contains historical documents along
with pottery and glass excavated from the
18th-century Casa de los Gobernadores on
nearby Plaza de Armas.

The **Casa Nacarello** (Plaza Mayor 25 de Mayo 67;
☷ closed Tue) is one of the prettiest colonial
homes in town, with period furniture, thick
whitewashed walls, wavy glass and original
lintels (duck if you're tall!).

The **Museo Indígena** (Comercio s/n; ☷ closed Thu)
houses Roberto Banchero's personal collection of Charrúa stone tools, exhibits on
indigenous history, and an amusing map upstairs showing how many European countries
could fit inside Uruguay's borders (it's at
least six!).

The dinky **Museo del Azulejo** (cnr Misiones de los Tapes & Paseo de San Gabriel; ☯ closed Thu) is a 17th-century stone house with a sampling of French, Catalan and Neapolitan tilework.

The **Museo Español** (San José 164; ☯ closed Thu), under renovation at the time of writing, has colonial pottery, clothing and maps.

The two-room **Museo Paleontológico** (Real de San Carlos; ☯ closed Mon-Wed) displays glyptodon shells, bones and other locally excavated finds from the private collection of self-taught palaeontologist Armando Calcaterra.

REAL DE SAN CARLOS

At the turn of the 20th century, Argentine entrepreneur Nicolás Mihanovich spent US$1.5 million building an immense tourist complex 5km north of Colonia at Real de San Carlos. The complex included a 10,000-seat bullring (alas Uruguay outlawed bullfights in 1912), a 3000-seat *frontón* (court) for the Basque sport of jai alai, a hotel-casino and a racecourse.

Only the racecourse functions today, but the ruins of the remaining buildings make an interesting excursion, and the adjacent beach is popular with locals on Sundays.

Tours

The tourist office outside the old town gate organizes good **walking tours** led by local guides. Spanish-language tours (UR$100 per person) leave at 11am and 3pm daily, with additional sunset tours on Friday and Saturday. For tours in other languages (UR$150 per person), contact the tourist office or Colonia's **Asociación de Guías Profesionales** (☎ 22309; asociacionguiascolonia@gmail.com).

Gabriel Gaidano (☎ 099-806106; 1929vintage@gmail.com; per 15min/hr UR$200/600) offers spins around town for up to four people in his 1929 Model A convertible. Look for him on Plaza de Armas.

Sleeping

Some hotels charge higher rates Friday through Sunday. Summer weekends are best avoided or booked well in advance.

BUDGET

Hostel El Español (☎ 30759; www.hostelelespaniol.com; Manuel Lobo 377; dm/d without bathroom UR$200/450, with bathroom UR$230/550; 🖵 🛜) Popular with young Latin Americans, this hostel's dark rooms are redeemed by the bright, spacious dining/internet area. HI members get 10% off. Breakfast costs UR$60 extra.

El Viajero Hostel (☎ 22683; www.elviajerocolonia.com; Washington Barbot 164; dm HI member UR$285-310, nonmember UR$320-360, tw HI member/nonmember UR$650/760, d HI member/nonmember UR$1100/1260; 🗷 🖵 🛜) With bike and scooter rental, horseback excursions, a bar for guests and air-con in all rooms, Colonia's newest hostel is brighter, fancier and somewhat cozier than the competition, but you may want to compare for yourself before plunking down the extra pesos.

Hostal de los Poetas (☎ 31643; www.guiacolonia.com.uy/hostaldelospoetas; Mangarelli 677; s/d/tr UR$400/640/880) This simple family-run place is a bargain, if you're willing to hoof it 1km out of town. The breakfast area, fireplace room and garden are charming.

MIDRANGE

Hotel Rivera (☎ 20807; riverahotel@adinet.com.uy; Rivera 131; s/d/tr/q UR$850/1200/1600/1900; 🗷 🛜) A stone's throw from the ferry and bus terminals, with clean rooms, cable TV and wi-fi, the Rivera is one of Colonia's least expensive midrange options.

Posada de la Flor (☎ 30794; www.posada-delaflor.com; Ituzaingó 268; r UR$1200-1600; 🗷) Serenely situated on a sycamore-lined street that ends at a small beach, the Flor's biggest draw is its upstairs terrace with lounge chairs overlooking the river.

Posada del Río (☎ 23002; www.hotelesencolonia.com; Washington Barbot 258; s/d/tr UR$850/1300/1700; 🗷) This peaceful place on a dead-end street is somewhat faded but still good value. The tiny upstairs breakfast room has partial river views.

Posada San Gabriel (☎ 23283; www.posadasangabriel.com.uy; Comercio 127; r downstairs/upstairs UR$1400/1500; 🗷 🖵 🛜) This sweet posada (inn) with stone walls, brass beds and wi-fi is surprisingly affordable given its prime location. Two upstairs rooms have river views.

Posada Don Antonio (☎ 25344; www.posadadonantonio.com; Ituzaingó 232; s/d/tr/ste UR$1200/1500/2000/3100; 🗷 🖵 🛜 🛁) Flip through the guest book at this spiffy new hotel and you'll find raves in multiple languages about the comfort of the beds, the friendliness of the staff and the generally welcoming atmosphere. The interior courtyard, complete with pool, makes a peaceful oasis only half a block from Colonia's main street.

Posada del Ángel (☎ 24602; www.posadadelangel.net; Washington Barbot 59; r standard/superior UR$1400/1900; 🗷 🖵 🛁) Cheerfully painted in yellow and periwinkle blue, this little hotel has amenities such as down comforters for rainy days and a swimming pool for the summer heat. Standard rooms are dark; it's worth splurging on one with a view.

TOP END

El Capullo (☎ 30135; www.elcapullo.com; 18 de Julio 219; s/d/tr UR$1200/1600/2200, cabaña UR$1800; ☒ ☜ ☒) Friendly English-speaking owners, a prime Barrio Histórico location, a grassy yard and a swimming pool are among the attractions at this newly remodeled colonial posada. Ask about their lovely cabaña, an entirely self-contained unit just 10 minutes outside of town.

Posada Manuel de Lobo (☎ 22463; www.posada manueldelobo.com; Ituzaingó 160; d/tr/ste UR$1600/1800/2200; ☒ ☜) The historical charms of this 150-year-old house include heavy wooden furniture, antique tilework, beamed ceilings, brick walls, fountains and twin patios out back. All rooms have wi-fi, and suites have Jacuzzis.

Posada del Virrey (☎ 22223; www.posadadel virrey.com; España 217; s/d from UR$1600/1900, ste s/d UR$3100/3400; ☒ ☜) The marble floors, stone walls, high ceilings and antique furniture in spacious rooms at this 1850 residence make you feel like a 'modern-day king,' as their motto says. There's wi-fi throughout, plus Jacuzzis, river views and (what else?) king-size beds in the upstairs suites.

Posada Plaza Mayor (☎ 23193; www.posadapla zamayor.com; Comercio 111; r from UR$2000, ste UR$3600; ☒ ☐ ☜) Near the river in the heart of historic Colonia, the Playa Mayor comprises two colonial houses. The stone-walled, high-ceilinged 19th-century Spanish rooms surround a beautiful courtyard with a fountain; the adjoining 18th-century Portuguese structure houses several lovely common areas.

Radisson Colonia Hotel (☎ 30460; www.radisson colonia.com; Washington Barbot 283; s/d weekends from UR$3480/4360, midweek UR$2300/2600; ☒ ☐ ☜ ☒) If you value chain-hotel comforts over colonial charm, the Radisson has what you're looking for. This all-in-one facility features two pools and a spacious deck overlooking the river, plus sauna, gym, solarium, children's play area and garage.

Eating

BUDGET

Los Farolitos (Av General Flores 268; chivitos from UR$75; ☒ noon-late) Specializing in *chivitos*, this no-nonsense hole-in-the-wall runs a booming business with locals.

Mercosur (☎ 24200; Av General Flores 252; mains from UR$99; ☒ 9am-1am) For low-priced fast food near the historic center, try this convenient corner eatery.

Confitería La Pasiva (☎ 28225; Av General Flores 444; dishes from UR$100; ☒ 8am-midnight) This bright, bustling chain *confitería* is great for breakfast, pizza or sandwiches any time of day.

MIDRANGE & TOP END

La Bodeguita (☎ 25329; Comercio 167; mini pizzas UR$75, dishes UR$150-320; ☒ dinner daily, lunch Sat & Sun) Nab a table out back on the sunny two-level deck and soak up the sweeping river views while drinking sangría or munching on La Bodeguita's trademark pizza.

Lentas Maravillas (☎ 20636; Santa Rita 61; sandwiches from UR$100, meals UR$260; ☒ 1-8:30pm Mon-Fri, noon-9pm Sat & Sun) Cozy as a friend's home, this is a dreamy spot to kick back with tea and cookies or a glass of wine and a sandwich between meals. Flip through an art book from owner Maggie Molnar's personal library and enjoy the incomparable river views, either from the upstairs fireplace room or the chairs on the grassy lawn below. Nightly dinner options vary according to the chef's whim.

Puerto Tranquilo (☎ 23475; Rambla de las Américas s/n; dishes UR$120-350; ☒ 10am-late Dec-Apr, 10am-sunset Fri-Sun May-Nov) Serving sandwiches, salads and freshly caught fish of the day, this 'resto-bar' 1km north of town makes a great getaway from historic Colonia's touristy madness. Survey the waterfront from the dining room or outdoor deck, or better yet, ask the waiter to bring your order down to the beach, where you can watch the sunset, beer in hand and music drifting down from the restaurant, while squishing sand between your toes.

El Rincón (☎ 099-675202; Misiones de los Tapes 41; dishes UR$170-280; ☒ lunch Thu-Tue) *Parrillada* (barbecue) is king at El Rincón. It's best enjoyed on a sunny weekend afternoon, lounging out back under a big tree between stone and red-stucco walls, listening to Brazilian music or tango, and watching the riverfront scene as the outdoor grill exudes intoxicating smoky smells.

Viejo Barrio (☎ 25399; Vasconcellos 169; dishes UR$180-270; ☒ lunch & dinner Thu-Mon, lunch Tue) Whether you're amused or annoyed by the eccentric waiter and his funny hats, Viejo Barrio remains a perennial old-town favorite thanks to its excellent homemade pasta and picturesque setting on historic Plaza de Armas.

Pulpería de los Faroles (☎ 30271; Misiones de los Tapes 101; dishes UR$180-290; ☷ noon-midnight) Specializing in seafood and pasta, this reader-recommended eatery has a rainbow of colorful tablecloths in the artsy interior dining room, plus a sea of informal outdoor seating on Plaza Mayor 25 de Mayo.

Lobo (☎ 29245; cnr Comercio & Calle de la Playa; dishes UR$200-370; ☷ noon-4pm daily, plus 8pm-late Fri & Sat) Lobo earns its reputation as one of Colonia's best restaurants with tasty creations such as *cordero marinado en vino tinto y miel con puré de hongos* (lamb marinated in red wine and honey with mushroom purée).

Entertainment

El Drugstore (☎ 25241; Portugal 174; ☷ noon-midnight) This corner place on Plaza de Armas, with frequent live music, is Colonia's most enjoyable, funkiest nightspot. It has vividly colored, eclectically decorated walls, an open kitchen, fridges painted with clouds and elephants, and a vintage car on the cobblestones doubling as a romantic dining nook. Half of the 24-page menu is devoted to drinks; the other half to tapas (from UR$115) and full meals (dishes UR$175 to UR$460), including a few vegetarian offerings.

Colonia Rock (☎ 28189; Misiones de los Tapes 157; ☷ 11:30am-1am) Always buzzing, this is Colonia's attempt at a Hard Rock Café. The restaurant-bar occupies a colonial building, with indoor and outdoor courtyard seating. There's live music here on Friday and Saturday nights.

Tr3s Cu4rto (☎ 29664; Alberto Méndez 295) Colonia's disco for the young and restless.

Shopping

Polished agate, ornate *mate* gourds and Portuguese-style ceramics are popular items.

Feria Artesanal (cnr Intendente Suárez & Daniel Fosalba; ☷ 10am-7pm or 8pm) This handicrafts market, open daily, is on the northern waterfront.

Manos del Uruguay (☎ 21793; Av General Flores 89; ☷ 11am-7pm) Colonia's branch of the national handicrafts store is in the Barrio Histórico.

Getting There & Away

BOAT

From the brand-new ferry terminal at the foot of Rivera, **Buquebus** (☎ 22975; www.buquebus.com.uy; cnr Manuel Lobo & Av FD Roosevelt) runs multiple daily ferries to Buenos Aires. There are two

slower boats daily (UR$735, three hours), plus three or more fast boats (UR$1010, one hour). Children and seniors get discounts of 15% to 25%. The 1st-class surcharge is UR$330 to UR$350.

Colonia Express (☎ 29677; www.coloniaexpress.com) runs less frequent but more affordable high-speed ferry service, with three departures Monday through Friday, two on Sunday and one on Saturday. Crossings take 1¼ hours. Day-of-departure fare is UR$620.

Both companies offer substantial advance-purchase discounts online.

Immigration for both countries is handled at the port before boarding.

BUS

Colonia's modern **bus terminal** (cnr Manuel Lobo & Av Roosevelt), with money-changing and internet facilities, is conveniently located near the port, within easy walking distance of the Barrio Histórico. The following destinations are served at least twice daily.

Destination	Cost (UR$)	Duration (hr)
Carmelo	78	1¼
Mercedes	176	3½
Montevideo	176	2¾
Nueva Helvecia	69	1
Paysandú	323	6
Salto	441	8

Getting Around

Walking is enjoyable in compact Colonia, but motor scooters, bicycles as well as gas-powered buggies are popular alternatives. Local buses go to the beaches and bullring at Real de San Carlos (UR$13) from along Av General Flores.

Colonia also makes a convenient starting point for touring western Uruguay by car – rates around UR$900 are available, and it's easy to get out of town. **Thrifty** (☎ 22939; Av General Flores 172; bicycle/scooter/golf cart per hr UR$60/140/240, per day UR$300/600/1000) rents everything from beater bikes to cars. Several other agencies rent cars and motorbikes near the bus and ferry terminals, including **Multicar/Moto Rent** (☎ 24893; Manuel Lobo 505) and **Punta Car** (☎ 22353; 18 de Julio 496).

NUEVA HELVECIA

☎ 055 / pop 10,000

Nueva Helvecia (also known as Colonia Suiza) is a quiet, pleasant destination with a demonstrably European ambience – where else in Uruguay would you find street names such as Guillermo (William) Tell and Frau Vögel? Lying 120km west of Montevideo, it was settled in 1862 by Swiss immigrants attracted by the temperate climate, good land, freedom of worship and opportunity to gain Uruguayan citizenship without renouncing their own. The country's first interior agricultural colony, Nueva Helvecia provided wheat for Montevideo's mills and today produces more than half of Uruguay's cheese.

Orientation

The center of town is Plaza de los Fundadores, with a clock made of flowers and a grandiose sculpture commemorating the original Swiss pioneers. Nueva Helvecia's hotel zone is a few kilometers southeast of the plaza.

Information

Antel (Dreyer 1127)
Banco de la República Oriental (Treinta y Tres 1210) Diagonally across from the central plaza.
Cyber Pez (☎ 47630; Treinta y Tres 1246; internet per hr UR$15; ☑ 9am-noon & 4-10pm Mon-Sat)
Hospital (☎ 44057; cnr 18 de Julio & C Cunier)
Post office (F Gilomen 1257)
Tourist information (Plaza de los Fundadores; ☑ 3-7pm Mon, Wed, Thu & Fri, 10am-2pm Sat & Sun) In the Movimiento Nuevas Generaciones building on the main square.

Festivals & Events

The best time to visit Nueva Helvecia is during one of its festivals. On August 1 the **Fiesta Suiza** attracts visitors from around the country for Swiss dances and artisan exhibits. Every October Uruguay's bovine bounty is on full display at **Expoláctea**, an agricultural festival featuring live music, cooking demos, wine- and cheese-tasting, kids' events and a giant fondue dinner. December's **Bierfest** celebrates the town's Alpine traditions, with music and dance performances, and of course enormous steins of beer.

Sleeping & Eating

Hotels are concentrated on the southeastern outskirts of town, making access difficult for those without a vehicle. Conveniently, most have their own restaurants.

Hotel del Prado (☎ 44169; www.hoteldelprado .info; Erwin Hodel s/n; dm with HI card UR$220, s/d/tr UR$450/750/1000; ☒) Dating from 1896, this 80-room hotel is a grand if declining build-

ing with balconies, a pool and some hostel rooms (HI card required for hostel rates). Its illustrious history is chronicled in old photos lining the walls.

Hostel Estancia El Galope (☎ 099-105985; www .elgalope.com.uy; Cno Concordia; r per person with/without HI card UR$600/700) At this new hostel a few kilometers southeast of Nueva Helvecia, experienced world travelers Mónica and Miguel offer guests a chance to settle into the relaxing rhythms of *estancia* life. Optional activities include horseback riding and cycling (free bikes provided). Pickup from the bus stop in nearby Colonia Valdense is available upon request.

Granja Hotel Suizo (☎ 44002; www.hotelsuizonueva helvecia.com, in Spanish; Av Federico Fischer 355; s/d from UR$1300/1700; ☒ ☒) Nueva Helvecia's oldest tourist hotel has ample grounds, a pool, a sauna and a renowned restaurant. All rooms have balconies, TV and heating.

Hotel Nirvana Resort & Spa (☎ 44081, in Montevideo 02-902-4124; www.hotelnirvana.com; Av Batlle y Ordóñez s/n; s/d from UR$2840/3380, half/full board supplement per person UR$420/840; ☒ ☒ ☜ ☒) Truly a world apart, ritzy Nirvana has two swimming pools, tennis courts, horseback riding, 25 hectares of beautifully landscaped grounds and a restaurant serving everything from *rösti* (Swiss potato pancakes) to chocolate fondue.

Don Juan (☎ 45099; cnr Treinta y Tres & 18 de Julio; dishes UR$130-250; ☑ lunch & dinner Tue-Sun) Start with homemade bread and butter, move on to Kasler (smoked pork) with sauerkraut and finish with Black Forest cake at this popular eatery opposite Nueva Helvecia's main square.

Getting There & Away

Some bus schedules refer to the town as Colonia Suiza. COT, Turil and Colonia offer frequent bus service to Montevideo (UR$127, two hours) and Colonia del Sacramento (UR$69, one hour). All three companies have offices near the plaza.

CARMELO

☎ 0542 / pop 17,000
Carmelo, dating from 1816, is a laid-back town of cobblestone streets and low old houses, a center for yachting, fishing and exploring the Paraná Delta. It lies opposite the delta just below the Río Uruguay's confluence with the Río de la Plata, 75km northwest of Colonia del Sacramento. Launches connect Carmelo to the Buenos Aires suburb of Tigre.

URUGUAY

Orientation

Carmelo straddles the Arroyo de las Vacas, a stream that widens into a sheltered harbor on the Río de la Plata. North of the *arroyo*, shady Plaza Independencia is now the commercial center. Most of the town's businesses are along 19 de Abril, which leads to the bridge over the *arroyo*, across which lies a large park with open space, camping, swimming and a huge casino.

Information

Antel (Barrios 329)
Banco Comercial (Uruguay 403) On Plaza Independencia.
Hospital (☎ 2107; cnr Uruguay & Artigas)
Municipal tourist office (☎ 2001; Casa de Cultura, 19 de Abril 246; ☯ 9am-6:30pm) Four blocks north of the bridge over the *arroyo*.
New Generation Cyber Games (Uruguay 373; internet per hr UR$20; ☯ 8am-3am)
Post office (Uruguay 360)

Sights & Activities

The *arroyo*, with large, rusty boats moored along it, makes for a great ramble, as does the 30-minute stroll out to the beaches across the bridge.

Just outside of town, **Bodega Irurtia** (☎ 2010; www.irurtia.com.uy; Av Paraguay, Km2.3) offers weekend tours (UR$240 to UR$400) of its chardonnay and pinot noir vineyards, plus tastings of its other award-winning varietals.

Festivals & Events

Local wines have an excellent reputation, and in early February the town hosts the **Fiesta Nacional de la Uva** (National Grape Festival).

Sleeping & Eating

Camping Náutico Carmelo (☎ 2058; Arroyo de las Vacas s/n; per tent UR$190; ☯ Dec-Mar) South of the *arroyo*, this seasonal campground with hot showers caters to yachties but accepts walk-ins too.

Hotel Rambla (☎ 2390; www.ciudadcarmelo.com/ramblahotel; Uruguay 55; s/d/tr from UR$560/740/960; ☒) The blocky Rambla won't win any design awards, but it's conveniently close to the launch docks. The upstairs doubles with balconies facing the *arroyo* are cheerier than the interior rooms.

Hotel Casino Carmelo (☎ 2314; www.hotelcasinocarmelo.com; Av Rodó s/n; s/d/ste UR$960/1360/1920; ☒ ☐ ☒) This hotel and casino across the *arroyo* is getting a bit worn around the edges, but the views toward the river are good. It has two pools, plus a small animal park with peacocks, flamingos and rheas.

Piccolino (☎ 4850; cnr 19 de Abril & Roosevelt; dishes UR$70-150; ☯ 9am-midnight) This corner place has decent *chivitos* and nice views of the square.

Fay Fay (☎ 4827; 18 de Julio 358; dishes UR$70-180; ☯ lunch & dinner Tue-Sun) Directly across from the square, this little family-run restaurant specializes in Uruguayan standards and homemade desserts.

Getting There & Away

Cacciola (☎ 7551; www.cacciolaviajes.com; Wilson Ferreira 263; ☯ 8am-7:30pm) runs twice-daily launches to the Buenos Aires suburb of Tigre. The one-way 2½-hour trip costs UR$429/391 for persons aged 10 and over/three to nine.

All the bus companies are on or near Plaza Independencia. **Chadre** (☎ 2987) has the most services, with seven daily departures to Montevideo (UR$235, 3½ hours), plus two to Colonia (UR$78, 1½ hours), Mercedes (UR$98, two hours), Fray Bentos (UR$137, 2¾ hours), Paysandú (UR$235, five hours) and Salto (UR$352, seven hours). For Colonia, **Berrutti** (☎ 2504; Uruguay 337) is a better bet, running buses almost hourly between 6am and 7pm.

FRAY BENTOS

☎ 056 / pop 24,000

Capital of Río Negro department, Fray Bentos is (or was!) the southernmost overland crossing over the Río Uruguay from Argentina.

This former company town, with its pretty riverfront promenade, was once dominated by an enormous English-owned meat-processing plant, now preserved as a museum. The big news here in recent years has been the construction of the controversial Botnia pulp mill northeast of town and the regular blockades of the bridge connecting Fray Bentos to Gualeguaychú, Argentina (see the boxed text, p536).

Information

Antel (Zorrilla 1127)
Credit Uruguay (cnr Treinta y Tres & 18 de Julio) One of several banks near central Plaza Constitución.
Hospital Salúd Pública (☎ 23511; cnr Oribe & Echeverría)
LA Cyber (18 de Julio 1106; internet per hr UR$20; ☯ 9am-10:30pm Mon-Sat, 4-10:30pm Sun) Just west of Plaza Constitución.
Municipal tourist office (☎ 22233; www.rionegro.gub.uy; 25 de Mayo 3400; ☯ 9am-6pm Mon-Fri, 9am-3pm Sat) North of Plaza Constitución.
Post office (Treinta y Tres 3271)

THE LITTLE BEEF CUBE THAT CIRCLED THE GLOBE

In 1865 the Liebig Extract of Meat Company located its pioneer South American plant southwest of downtown Fray Bentos. It soon became Uruguay's most important industrial complex. British-run El Anglo took over operations in the 1920s and by WWII the factory employed 4000 people, slaughtering cattle at the astronomical rate of 2000 a day.

Looking at the abandoned factory today, you'd never guess that its signature product, the Oxo beef cube, once touched millions of lives on every continent. On the factory's ground floor, the **Museo de la Revolución Industrial** brings this history to life with colorful displays painting a fascinating portrait of the company's scale and international influence. Oxo cubes sustained WWI soldiers in the trenches, Jules Verne sang their praises in his book *Around the Moon,* Stanley brought them on his search for Livingstone, Scott and Hillary took them to Antarctica and Everest. More than 25,000 people from over 60 countries worked here, and at its peak the factory was exporting nearly 150 different products, using every part of the cow except its moo.

Museum displays range from the humorous to the poignant: a giant cattle scale where school groups are invited to weigh themselves; or the old company office upstairs, left exactly as it was when the factory closed in 1979, with grooves rubbed into the floor by the foot of an accountant who sat at the same desk for decades.

Sights & Activities

Fray Bentos' star attraction, on the waterfront 2km west of town, is the **Museo de la Revolución Industrial** (☎ 23690; Barrio Histórico del Anglo; admission UR$20; ☉ 8am-5:30pm Tue-Fri, 10am-5:30pm Sat & Sun Mar–mid-Dec, to 7:30pm mid-Dec–Feb) – see the boxed text, above, for details. Guided tours (10am Monday to Saturday, plus variable scheduled afternoon tours) grant access to the intricate maze of passageways, corrals and abandoned slaughterhouses behind the museum.

The municipal **Museo Solari** (☎ 26748; Treinta y Tres s/n; admission free; ☉ 9am-7pm Mon-Fri, 1-7pm Sat & Sun) is on the west side of Plaza Constitución and features the satirical works of painter and engraver Luis Solari, many of which contain fanciful human figures with the heads of animals.

One block off the square, the 400-seat **Teatro Young** (cnr 25 de Mayo & Zorrilla) dates from the early 1900s and hosts cultural events throughout the year. Visits can be arranged at the theater itself or at the tourist office.

Sleeping & Eating

Balneario Las Cañas (☎ 24970; www.rionegro.gub.uy; tent site for 2/4/6 people UR$175/210/240, d/tr/q bungalows from UR$800/900/1000) This sprawling municipal facility on the riverfront 8km south of town offers a wide range of reasonably priced accommodations.

Nuevo Hotel Colonial (☎ 22260; 25 de Mayo 3293; s/d/tr/q with fan & without bathroom UR$350/400/530/600, with bathroom UR$400/500/590/640, s/d with air-con & bathroom UR$500/700; ✖ ☎) Long popular with budget

travelers, the Colonial is basic but well run, with wi-fi and high-ceilinged (if sometimes windowless) rooms surrounding a sunny interior patio.

La Posada del Frayle Bentos (☎ 28541; www.posadadelfraylebentos.com.uy; 25 de Mayo 3434; s/d/tr/q UR$770/1190/1640/2090; ✖ ☎ ☎) This lovely posada occupies a restored colonial building with patios, fountain, pool and bouganvilleas. Rooms are filled with modern amenities.

Wolves (☎ 23604; Barrio Anglo; dishes UR$65-130; ☉ lunch Tue-Sun) On the waterfront adjacent to Museo de la Revolución Industrial, Wolves serves pasta, *chivitos* and *milanesas* and makes a pleasant follow-up to a museum visit.

Pizzería 33 (☎ 28617; Treinta y Tres 3188; pizzas from UR$75; ☉ lunch & dinner) This popular place just off the main square has a bilingual menu and specializes in pizza, pasta and sandwiches.

Entertainment

Teatro Municipal de Verano (Parque Roosevelt, 18 de Julio) On the banks of the river, this open-air venue seats 4000 and has excellent acoustics. It hosts a diverse range of musical concerts.

Getting There & Around

Buses depart from the **bus terminal** (18 de Julio, btwn Varela & Blanes), 10 blocks east of central Plaza Constitución.

Several buses a day go to Mercedes (UR$29, 45 minutes) and Montevideo (UR$303, 4½ hours). Buses Chadre has two *línea litoral* (river route) buses daily in each direction: northbound, destinations include Salto (UR$215, four hours) and Paysandú (UR$98, two hours); southbound, they stop in Mercedes, Carmelo (UR$137, three hours) and Colonia (UR$215, four hours). ETA also has a midnight departure Monday and Thursday for Tacuarembó (UR$421, six hours).

At the time of research, all bus services to Gualeguaychú were still suspended due to the bridge closure between Uruguay and Argentina. With any luck, by the time you read this, ETA will be providing service again on this 1¼-hour route.

MERCEDES
☎ 053 / pop 44,000

Only 30km east of Fray Bentos, Mercedes is a livestock center and capital of the department of Soriano. There are cobblestoned streets and a small pedestrian zone around central Plaza Independencia, but the town's most appealing feature is its leafy waterfront along the south bank of the Río Negro.

Information
Antel (Roosevelt 681) Provides card-based internet service.
Banco Comercial (Giménez 719) ATM on Plaza Independencia.

Hospital Mercedes (☎ 22177; cnr Sánchez & Rincón)
Municipal tourist office (☎ 22733; turismosori ano@adinet.com.uy; Detomasi 415; ⏰ 12:30-6:30pm Mon-Fri Apr–mid-Dec, 8am-8pm daily mid-Dec–Mar) In a crumbling white building near the bridge to the campground.
Post office (cnr Rodó & 18 de Julio)

Sights & Activities
The waterfront area is Mercedes' biggest attraction. Principal activities are boating, fishing and swimming along the sandy beaches, or simply strolling along the Rambla (especially popular on Sunday afternoons).

On Plaza Independencia, the imposing **Catedral de Nuestra Señora de las Mercedes** dates from 1788. About 6km west of town is the **Museo Paleontológico Alejandro Berro** (☎ 23290; Zona Mauá; admission free; ⏰ 11am-5pm), displaying a substantial fossil collection in an old, white, castlelike building.

Sleeping
Camping del Hum (☎ 22733; Isla del Puerto; camping per person UR$20, plus per tent UR$40; ⏰ mid-Nov–Easter) Mercedes' spacious campground, one of the region's best, occupies half the Isla del Puerto

---

ESTANCIA TOURISM IN URUGUAY

Estancias, the giant farms of Uruguay's interior, are a national cultural icon and now a big contender for the tourist dollar. The Uruguayan Ministry of Tourism has designated 'Estancia Turística' as a distinct lodging category, and in recent years, dozens of such places have opened their doors, from traditional working farms to opportunistic wannabes. Typically, *estancias* organize daily activities with a heavy emphasis on horseback riding; many provide overnight accommodations as well. Most are difficult to reach without a vehicle, although they'll often pick guests up with advance notice.

The granddaddy of Uruguayan tourist *estancias* is **San Pedro de Timote** (☎ 031-08086; www .sanpedrodetimote.com.uy, in Spanish; r per person UR$2480; 🏊). Its remarkable setting, 14km up a dirt road from the town of Cerro Colorado, amid endless rolling cattle country, is greatly enhanced by the complex of historic structures, some dating back to the mid-1800s: a gracious white chapel, a courtyard with soaring palm trees, a library with gorgeous tilework, and a circular stone corral. Common areas feature parquet wood floors, big fireplaces and comfy leather armchairs. Two pools and a sauna add to the luxurious feel. Accommodation prices include three meals, afternoon tea and two daily horseback-riding excursions (plus night rides during the full moon). With 253 hectares of grounds, the possibilities are virtually limitless. Non-overnight guests can pay UR$1100 for lunch, afternoon tea and a horseback ride. Cerro Colorado is 160km northeast of Montevideo on Ruta 7.

Other tourist *estancias* covered in this book are listed under the city or town closest to them – our favorites include La Sirena, near Mercedes (see opposite), Guardia del Monte (p587) and Yvytu Itaty, near Tacuarembó (p570).

In Montevideo, **Lares** (☎ 02-901-9120; www.lares.com.uy; WF Aldunate 1320, Local 15) and **Cecilia Regules Viajes** (☎ 02-916-3011; www.ceciliaregulesviajes.com; Bacacay 1334, Local C) are travel agencies specializing in *estancia* tourism.

in the Río Negro. Connected to the mainland by a bridge, it offers excellent swimming, fishing and sanitary facilities.

Aparthotel La Armonia (☎ 25946; www.aparthotelarmonia.com; Haedo 222; s/d/tr without breakfast UR$380/750/880, 4-person apt UR$1100; ☒ ☜) With microwaves, coffee-makers, cable TV and wi-fi, the rooms and apartments at this family-run place are comfortable, although some suffer from cigarette smoke and street noise.

our pick **Estancia La Sirena** (☎ 02271, 099-102130; www.lasirena.com.uy, in Spanish; Ruta 14, Km 4.5; s with breakfast/half board/full board UR$1800/2000/2700, d with breakfast/half board/full board UR$1800/3200/4400) Surrounded by rolling open country 15km upriver from Mercedes, this *estancia* is one of Uruguay's oldest and most beautiful. The spacious 1830 ranch house, with its cozy parlor and fireplaces, makes a perfect base for relaxation and excursions to the nearby river on foot or horseback. The isolated setting is perfect for stargazing, and the homemade food, often cooked on a giant outdoor grill, is delicious. Hosts Rodney and Lucía Bruce speak English, French and Spanish.

Eating

Parador Rambla (☎ 20877; Rambla Costanera s/n; dishes UR$105-250; ☽ lunch & dinner Tue-Sun) This riverfront restaurant at the foot of Colón serves delicious Spanish specialties such as garlic prawns, *patatas bravas* (fried potatoes with a spicy sauce) and paella. The fabulous European-influenced desserts include chocolate crepes, tiramisu and orange flan.

Oveja Negra (☎ 22649; Lavalleja 178; dishes UR$180-250; ☽ dinner Mon-Sat, lunch Sun) One of Mercedes' best *parrillas*, Oveja Negra also merits a visit for its fine homemade pasta and extensive wine list.

Casa Bordó (☎ 29817; Paysandú 654; fixed-price meals UR$310-410; ☽ dinner Tue-Sat, lunch Sun) For a splurge, head for this plum-colored, French-themed restaurant above the main square. The prix-fixe menus include appetizer, dessert and main dishes such as vegetarian crepes or pork brochettes in rosemary-honey sauce with grilled vegetables.

Shopping

our pick **Lanas de Soriano** (☎ 22158; Colón 60; ☽ 9am-noon Mon-Sat, 3-7pm Mon-Fri) A rainbow of beautiful handmade woolens is available in this shop, hidden away in a residential neighborhood near the waterfront.

Getting There & Away

Mercedes' modern **bus terminal** (Don Bosco) is about 10 blocks from Plaza Independencia. It has a shopping center, a supermarket, an ATM, luggage storage and even an emergency medical clinic. A local bus (UR$8) leaves regularly from just in front of the terminal, making a circuit around the downtown area, including a stop in central Plaza Independencia.

All destinations following are served at least once daily.

Destination	Cost (UR$)	Duration (hr)
Buenos Aires (Arg)	561	7
Carmelo	101	2
Colonia	182	3
Fray Bentos	29	¾
Montevideo	274	3½-4½
Paysandú	123	2
Salto	273	4
Tacuarembó	392	6½

PAYSANDÚ

☎ 072 / pop 77,000

For most travelers, Uruguay's third-largest city is just a stopover en route to or from Argentina. Founded as a mid-18th-century outpost of cattle herders from the Jesuit mission at Yapeyú (in present-day Argentina), Paysandú gradually rose to prominence as a meat-processing center. Repeated sieges of the city during the turbulent 1800s (the last in 1864–65) earned it the local nickname 'the American Troy.'

Despite its turbulent history and its ongoing status as a major industrial center, modern-day Paysandú is easygoing and surprisingly sedate. To see the city's wilder side, visit during Carnaval or the annual week-long **beer festival** (held during Semana Santa).

Orientation

On the east bank of the Río Uruguay, Paysandú is 390km from Montevideo via Ruta 3 and 120km north of Fray Bentos via Ruta 24. The Puente Internacional General Artigas, 15km north of town, connects it with Colón in Argentina.

The center of activity is Plaza Constitución, six blocks north of the bus terminal. From here, 18 de Julio, the main commercial street, runs 2.5km west to the port. Except for a small developed area directly west of downtown, the entire riverfront remains open parkland due to regular flooding.

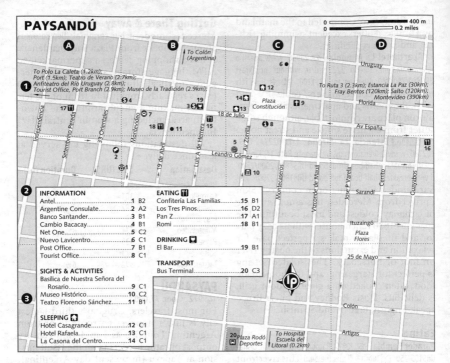

PAYSANDÚ

INFORMATION			EATING 🍴		
Antel	1	B2	Confitería Las Familias	15	B1
Argentine Consulate	2	A2	Los Tres Pinos	16	D2
Banco Santander	3	B1	Pan Z	17	A1
Cambio Bacacay	4	B1	Romi	18	B1
Net One	5	C2			
Nuevo Lavicentro	6	C1	DRINKING 🍷		
Post Office	7	B1	El Bar	19	B1
Tourist Office	8	C1			
			TRANSPORT		
SIGHTS & ACTIVITIES			Bus Terminal	20	C3
Basílica de Nuestra Señora del					
Rosario	9	C1			
Museo Histórico	10	C2			
Teatro Florencio Sánchez	11	B1			
SLEEPING 🛏					
Hotel Casagrande	12	C1			
Hotel Rafaela	13	C1			
La Casona del Centro	14	C1			

Information

Antel (Montevideo 875)

Banco Santander (18 de Julio 1137) One of several ATMs along Paysandú's main street.

Cambio Bacacay (18 de Julio 1039) Changes traveler's checks.

Hospital Escuela del Litoral (☎ 24836; Montecaseros 520) South of the bus terminal.

Net One (Leandro Gómez 1193; internet per hr UR$12; 🕐 24hr) Noisy with adolescent gamers, but open all night.

Nuevo Lavicentro (☎ 22826; Montecaseros 1043; per kilo UR$50; 🕐 8:15am-noon & 3:15-6:30pm Mon-Fri, 8:15am-noon Sat) Same-day laundry service.

Post office (cnr 18 de Julio & Montevideo)

Tourist office Centro (☎ 26220 ext 184; turismo@ paysandu.gub.uy; 18 de Julio 1226; 🕐 8am-7pm Mon-Fri, 9am-7pm Sat & Sun); Port (☎ 29235; plandelacosta@ paysandu.gub.uy; Av de Los Iracundos; 🕐 noon-6pm Mon-Fri, 2-7pm Sat & Sun) First office is on Plaza Constitución; latter is next to Museo de la Tradición.

Sights & Activities

Dating from 1860, chunky **Basílica de Nuestra Señora del Rosario** (Plaza Constitución) has one of the more ornately decorated interiors in Uruguay.

The 1876 **Teatro Florencio Sánchez** (☎ 26220 ext 170; 19 de Abril 926), Uruguay's oldest theater outside of Montevideo, has many original features (including the curtain) and hosts occasional music and dance events.

The **Museo Histórico** (☎ 26220 ext 247; Av Zorrilla 874; admission free; 🕐 8am-4:45pm Mon-Fri, 9am-1:45pm Sat) displays evocative images from the multiple 19th-century sieges of Paysandú. It includes images of women exiled to an island offshore watching the city's bombardment, the bullet-riddled shell of the cathedral and more.

In parkland near the riverfront, the **Museo de la Tradición** (☎ 23125; Av de Los Iracundos 5; admission free; 🕐 9am-5:45pm) features a small but well-displayed selection of anthropological artifacts and gaucho gear.

Sleeping

Hotel Rafaela (☎ 24216; 18 de Julio 1181; s/d/tr/q with fan & without bathroom UR$340/480/610/710, with air-con & bathroom UR$550/720/850/980; ❄) The Rafaela is decent value close to the main square; its rooms are dark but large, and some have their own small patios.

La Casona del Centro (☎ 22998; Av Zorrilla 975; s/d/tr/q UR$500/900/1200/1600; 🅿) Right on Plaza Constitución, La Casona offers clean, safe accommodations with a family vibe – the owners initially converted their grown kids' former bedrooms into guest space, and they've been expanding ever since.

Hotel Casagrande (☎ 24994; www.hotelcasagrande .com.uy; Florida 1221; s/tw/d UR$1100/1600/1775; 🅿 🖳 🛜) The extremely homey and conveniently located Casagrande is Paysandú's nicest downtown hotel. Comfy armchairs, marble tabletops and big brass beds are among the boutique hotel amenities justifying the higher price tag.

Estancia La Paz (☎ 02272; www.estancialapaz .uy; Ruta 24, Km 86.5; d with breakfast UR$1760, d with horseback riding, use of spa & half/full board UR$3600/4400; 🅿 🖳 🛜 🚗) The tennis courts, swimming pool and muzak-filled common areas feel incongruous among the historic buildings and pristine natural setting at this tourist *estancia* 30km south of Paysandú. Serious equestrians will appreciate the horseback-riding excursions, lasting from one day to a full week. Access is via a long dirt road: turn off at Km 86.5 on Ruta 24 or Km 336 on Ruta 3.

Eating & Drinking

Confitería Las Familias (☎ 22181; 18 de Julio 1152; chajá UR$40; 🕑 9am-8pm) If you've got a sweet tooth – and we mean a *really* sweet tooth – pull up a stool at this ancient bakery and sample one of Uruguay's classic desserts: *chajá* – a dentist-friendly concoction of sugary meringue, fruit and cream invented here in 1927.

Los Tres Pinos (☎ 41211; Av España 1474; dishes UR$70-270; 🕑 lunch & dinner Mon-Sat, lunch only Sun) The *parrilla* here is excellent; carnivores will appreciate specialties such as *chuletas de cerdo con puré de manzana* (pork chops with apple sauce) and *pollo patrón* (chicken stuffed with ham, pineapple and cherries).

Romi (☎ 42244; 19 de Abril 917; dishes UR$80-230; 🕑 lunch & dinner) This lively pizzeria-*parrilla*, directly across from Paysandú's historic theater, serves a full range of Uruguayan standards, from pasta to *milanesas*, pizza to grilled meat.

Pan Z (☎ 29551; cnr 18 de Julio & Setembrino Pereda; dishes UR$90-300; 🕑 lunch & dinner) Popular 'Panceta' serves pizza, *chivitos* stacked high with every ingredient imaginable, and tasty desserts such as strawberry cake and tiramisu.

El Bar (☎ 37809; Luis A de Herrera 955; 🕑 6:30am-late) This corner bar-cafe has a wide-ranging drinks menu and brings in occasional live music on weekends.

Entertainment

Polo la Caleta (☎ 30954; Av Brasil 259; 🕑 midnight-7am Fri & Sat) With five bars and two dance floors, this is the most popular of several late-night venues down by the port.

Further north along the waterfront, Paysandú's intimate, tree-encircled Teatro de Verano is just across the street from the larger Anfiteatro del Río Uruguay, which seats up to 20,000 people and hosts major concerts during Paysandú's annual beer festival. Check with the tourist office for details of upcoming events.

Getting There & Away

Paysandú's **bus terminal** (☎ 23225; cnr Artigas & Av Zorrilla) is directly south of Plaza Constitución. The following Uruguayan destinations are served at least once daily. International departures are less frequent, as detailed after the table.

Destination	Cost (UR$)	Duration (hr)
Asunción (Par)	2121	15
Buenos Aires	498	5½
Carmelo	237	5
Colón (Arg)	62	¾
Colonia	325	6
Concepción del Uruguay (Arg)	84	1½
Córdoba (Arg)	1049	10
Fray Bentos	100	2
Mercedes	120	2
Montevideo	372	4½
Paraná (Arg)	520	4½
Rosario (Arg)	648	6
Salto	117	2
Santa Fe (Arg)	560	5½
Tacuarembó	235	3½

Flecha Bus serves Buenos Aires, running comfy *coche-cama* (sleeper class) buses on Tuesdays and Saturdays, and *semi-cama* (semi-sleeper) services on other days.

EGA has services to Córdoba on Tuesday, Thursday and Sunday evenings via Rosario and Friday evenings via Paraná and Santa Fe. EGA also offers service to Asunción, Paraguay on Wednesday and Saturday afternoons. Empresa Paccot runs daily to Colón and Concepción del Uruguay.

URUGUAY

Getting Around

Bus 104, marked 'Zona Industrial,' runs every half-hour between downtown and the waterfront.

SALTO

☎ 073 / pop 105,000

Built near the falls where the Río Uruguay makes its 'big jump' (Salto Grande), Salto is Uruguay's second-largest city and the most northerly crossing point to Argentina. It's a relaxed place, surrounded by citrus orchards, with some 19th-century architecture and a pretty riverfront. People come here for the nearby hot springs, and the recreation area above the enormous Salto Grande hydroelectric dam.

Information

Antel (Grito de Asencio 33)

Banco Comercial (cnr Uruguay & Lavalleja) One of several banks at this intersection.

Cyberm@ni@ (☎ 23685; Uruguay 1082; per hr UR$18; ☽ 9am-midnight Mon-Sat) Air-conditioned internet access.

Hospital Regional Salto (☎ 32155; cnr 18 de Julio & Varela)

Lavadero Magnolias (Agraciada 786; per load UR$90) Same-day laundry service.

Post office (cnr Artigas & Treinta y Tres)

Tourist office (turismo@salto.gub.uy) bus terminal (☎ 40843; ☽ 6am-midnight); Centro (☎ 34096; Uruguay 1052; ☽ 8am-5:45pm Mon-Fri, 8am-12:45pm Sat)

Sights & Activities

There is free admission to each of Salto's museums.

The **Museo de Bellas Artes y Artes Decorativas** (☎ 29898; Uruguay 1067; ☽ 3-8pm Tue-Sat, 5-8pm Sun) displays a nice collection of Uruguayan painting and sculpture in a historic two-story mansion with a grand staircase, stained glass and back garden.

Housed in a historic market building, the **Museo del Hombre y la Tecnología** (☎ 29898; cnr Av Brasil & Zorrilla; ☽ 2-7pm Tue-Sun) features excellent displays on local cultural development and history upstairs, and a small archaeological section downstairs.

The **Teatro Larrañaga** (☎ 29898 ext 149; Joaquín Suárez 39; ☽ noon-6pm Mon-Sat), a red velvet-and chandelier-bedecked theater dating to 1882, is open for visits and hosts occasional dance and theater performances (UR$50 to UR$300).

Sleeping

Salto's downtown accommodation options are generally a bit faded; spiffier alternatives are at the many nearby hot springs (see opposite) and the five-star lakeside Hotel Horacio Quiroga.

Salto Hostel (☎ 37157; www.saltohostel.com; Uruguay 941; dm/d without bathroom UR$290/770; ☐ �;) In Salto's historic center, this comfortable new hostel features spacious common areas, convenient computer facilities and helpful staff. Front dorms have tall windows overlooking the busy main street – great for light and air circulation, but it can get noisy at night. The front desk sells discounted bus tickets to Montevideo, and HI members get 15% off room rates.

Gran Hotel Concordia (☎ 32735; www.granhotelconcordia.com.uy; Uruguay 749; r per person UR$600) This 1860s relic is a national historical monument and indisputably Salto's most atmospheric downtown hotel. A life-size wooden cutout of Carlos Gardel, who once stayed in room 32, greets you at the end of a marble corridor opening into a leafy courtyard filled with murals, sculptures and cats. Front rooms with tall French-shuttered windows overlook the courtyard. Back rooms flank a wrought-iron terrace shaded by climbing vines.

Hotel Horacio Quiroga (☎ 34411; www.hotelhoracioquiroga.com; Parque del Lago, Salto Grande; s/d/tr/q from UR$1820/2460/3080/3540, full board from UR$2620/4060/5480/6740; ☒ ☐ ☲) On the lake above the dam, the luxurious Quiroga has its own thermal baths and spa facilities. Lakeview rooms are especially nice, with balconies overlooking the swimming pools and flowery grounds planted with trees from around the world. Van transfers from town can be provided with advance notice.

Eating

La Trattoria (☎ 36660; Uruguay 754; dishes UR$65-190; ☽ lunch & dinner) Locals flock to this high-ceilinged downtown eatery for fish, meat and pasta. Sit in the wood-paneled dining room or people-watch from a sidewalk table on busy Calle Uruguay.

La Caldera (☎ 24648; Uruguay 221; dishes UR$80-190; ☽ lunch & dinner Tue-Sun) With fresh breezes blowing in off the river and sunny outdoor seating, this *parrilla* makes a great lunch stop; at dinnertime, the cozy interior dining room with its view of the blazing fire is equally atmospheric.

Casa de Lamas (☎ 29376; Chiazzaro 20; dishes UR$130-290; ☽ lunch & dinner Thu-Mon, dinner only Wed) Also near the waterfront, this swank eatery is housed in a 19th-century building painted an eye-catching shade of purplish-pink, with pretty vaulted brickwork in the dining room. It has several vegetarian offerings, and a *menú de la casa* (set menu) for UR$230.

Getting There & Away
BOAT
Transporte Fluvial San Cristóbal (☎ 32461; cnr Av Brasil & Costanera Norte) runs launches across the river to Concordia (UR$75/85 weekdays/Saturday, 15 minutes) four times daily except Sunday between 9:45am and 7:30pm.

BUS
Salto's **bus terminal** (☎ 36200; Salto Shopping Center, cnr Ruta 3 & Av Batlle), east of downtown, has ATMs, internet facilities and a supermarket. Flecha Bus runs one overnight bus daily to Buenos Aires (UR$559, 6½ hours) plus two daily buses to Concordia (UR$73, one hour), where you can connect to many other Argentine destinations. Chadre, Núñez and El Norteño offer services to Montevideo (UR$490, 6½ hours) and Paysandú (UR$117, two hours). Chadre also has twice-daily services to Colonia (UR$441, eight hours). On Mondays and Fridays direct buses run to Tacuarembó (UR$285, four hours).

AROUND SALTO
Represa Salto Grande
This massive **hydroelectric project** (☎ 26131; ☽ 7am-4:30pm) at Salto Grande, 14km north of town, provides 65% of Uruguay's electricity and is a symbol of national pride. Free hour-long guided tours of the dam visit both the Uruguayan and Argentine sides (no minimum group size, maximum wait 20 minutes). There's no public transport; a taxi from Salto costs about UR$700 roundtrip. En route, check out the stands selling freshly squeezed orange juice for UR$15 a liter!

Termas de Daymán
☎ 073
Eight kilometers south of Salto, Termas de Daymán is a Disneyland of thermal baths, the most developed of several such complexes in northwestern Uruguay. Surrounded by motels and restaurants, it's popular with Uruguayan and Argentine tourists, who roam the town's block-long main street in bathrobes.

The **Complejo Médico Hidrotermal Daymán** (☎ 69090; admission UR$150; ☽ 10am-7pm Mon-Fri, to 8pm Sat & Sun) provides body wraps, facials, massages, mud and chocolate treatments and physical therapy. A basic package including 30-minute massage costs UR$570. At the end of the hotel row are the **municipal baths** (☎ 69711; admission UR$70; ☽ 8am-11pm), a vast complex of pools interspersed with grassy picnic areas. **Acuamanía** (☎ 69222; www.acuamania.com, in Spanish; admission UR$150; ☽ 10:30am-6:30pm) is a water park with gargantuan slides.

The former monastery **La Posta del Daymán** (☎ 69801; www.lapostadeldayman.com; campsite per person UR$100, hostel/hotel r per person with breakfast UR$500/650, half board UR$730/880, full board UR$920/1070; ☏ ⌨) has everything – a campground, hostel, spacious hotel rooms, Jacuzzi, sauna, thermal swimming pool and good-value attached restaurant.

Hostal Canela (☎ 69121; www.hostalcanela.com.uy; Ruta 3, Km479; r per person HI member/nonmember UR$360/400; ☏ ⌨) is a family-run HI hostel with swimming pool on a quiet residential street 1km north of the springs.

Between 6:30am and 10:30pm Cottur operates hourly buses (UR$13.50) from Salto's port to the baths, returning hourly from 7am to 11pm. Stops in Salto are along Av Brasil outbound and Av 19 de Abril inbound.

Termas San Nicanor
Surrounded by a landscape of cows, fields and water reminiscent of a Flemish painting, **Termas San Nicanor** (☎ 0730-2209; www.sannicanor.com.uy, in Spanish; Ruta 3, Km 475; campsite per person UR$200, dm/r without bathroom per person UR$400/600, r with bathroom UR$1600, cabaña with kitchenette for 2/3/4 people UR$1800/2400/3000; ☏ ⌨) offers more tranquility than neighboring Daymán. Prized by New Agers, it has a gigantic outdoor thermal pool, plus camping, hostel and cabin accommodations, and a recently converted *estancia* house with gorgeous high-ceilinged rooms, large fireplaces and peacocks strolling the grounds. The 14km unpaved access road is just south of Termas del Daymán. **Santa Lucia Bus** (☎ 099-732368) runs four daily buses from Salto's **Terminal Rural** (☎ 32909; cnr Larrañaga & Latorre) to Termas San Nicanor (UR$50), via Termas de Daymán.

Termas de Arapey
In the middle of nowhere, 90km northeast of Salto, Termas de Arapey is another popular hot springs resort. Its multiple pools are surrounded by gardens, fountains and paths

leading down to the Río Arapey Grande. Despite the electric lighting and dizzying profusion of lodging options, the natural setting remains supremely serene.

Rooms at **Hotel Municipal** (☎ 0768-2441, in Salto 073-34096; www.hoteltermasdelarapey.com, in Spanish; s/d/tr UR$960/1320/1560, with half board UR$1210/1820/2310; ☒) have phone, satellite TV, and hot and cold thermal water. There are also cheaper motel and bungalow accommodations, plus camp-sites (UR$200 for up to two people, UR$80 each additional person).

Argentur runs one daily bus (two on Monday, Wednesday and Friday) from Salto to Arapey (UR$100, 1½ hours).

TACUAREMBÓ
☎ 063 / pop 54,000

This is gaucho country. Not your 'we pose for pesos' types, but your real-deal 'we tuck our baggy pants into our boots and slap on a beret just to go to the local store' crew. It's also the alleged birthplace of tango legend Carlos Gardel. Capital of its department, Tacuarembó has sycamore-lined streets and attractive plazas that make it one of Uruguay's most agreeable interior towns.

Orientation
In the rolling hill country along the Cuchilla de Haedo, Tacuarembó is 390km north of Montevideo. The town center is Plaza 19 de Abril, but the streets 25 de Mayo and 18 de Julio both lead south past the almost equally important Plazas Colón and Rivera.

Information
Antel (Sarandí 242)
Banco Santander (18 de Julio 258) One of several banks with ATMs near central Plaza Colón.
Departmental tourist office (☎ 27144; www .imtacuarembo.com/turismo; ☒ 7:30am-7pm Mon-Fri, 8am-noon Sat) Just outside the bus terminal.
Hospital Regional (☎ 22955; cnr Treinta y Tres & Catalogne)
Post office (Ituzaingó 262)

Sights & Activities
Tacuarembó's **Museo del Gaucho y del Indio** (cnr Flores & Artigas; admission free; ☒ 12:30-6:30pm Tue, Wed & Fri, 8:30am-6:30pm Thu, 1-5pm Sat & Sun) pays romantic tribute to Uruguay's gauchos and indigenous peoples. The collection includes stools made from leather and cow bones, elegantly worked silver spurs and other accessories of rural life.

Festivals & Events
In the first week of March, the colorful five-day **Fiesta de la Patria Gaucha** attracts visitors from around the country to exhibitions of traditional gaucho skills, music and other activities. It takes place in Parque 25 de Agosto, north of town.

Sleeping & Eating
Hotel Plaza (☎ /fax 27988; 25 de Agosto 247; s/d/tr/q UR$515/840/1150/1450; ☒ ⊛) Painted a bright and cheery yellow, with fish on the shower curtains and wireless internet in the rooms, the centrally located Plaza is the most welcoming place in town.

our pick **Yvytu Itaty** (☎ 08421, 099-837555; www .vivtiurismorural.com, yvytuitaty@hotmail.com; r per person incl full board, farm activities & horseback riding UR$1300) For a firsthand look at real gaucho life, this working *estancia* 50km southwest of Tacuarembó is warmly recommended. Since 2006, hosts Pedro and Nahir Clariget have been receiving overnight guests in their unpretentious ranch-style home and inviting them to participate in daily *estancia* routines. Pedro and his friendly cattle dogs delight in escorting guests around their 636-hectare domain on horseback, pausing en route to point out armadillos, ñandú nests and other local attractions. Back at the ranch, Nahir's tasty home cooking includes savory meat stews and traditional desserts such as *arroz con leche*. As you sip *mate* on the patio at sunset, don't be surprised to hear news of your visit broadcast on the local radio station – visitors in these parts are a big deal! Call in advance for driving directions or to arrange pickup at Tacuarembó's bus station (UR$1000 roundtrip).

La Rueda (☎ 22453; W Beltrán 251; dishes UR$65-190; ☒ lunch & dinner Mon-Sat, lunch Sun) With its thatched roof and walls covered with gaucho paraphernalia and animal skins, La Rueda is a friendly neighborhood *parrilla*.

Getting There & Around
The **bus terminal** (cnr Ruta 5 & Av Victorino Pereira) is 1km northeast of the center. A taxi into town costs about UR$50. Turil, Chadre and Nuñez offer direct service to Montevideo (UR$382, 4½ hours). Chadre and Toriani have direct but infrequent service to Salto (UR$284, four hours); an alternative is to take one of the twice-daily buses to Paysandú (UR$235, 3½ hours) and change for Salto there.

URUGUAY'S OFF-THE-BEATEN-TRACK NATURE PRESERVES

Uruguay's interior, with its vast open spaces, is a naturalist's dream. The Uruguayan government has designated several locations around the country as especially worthy of protection under its Sistema Nacional de Áreas Protegidas (SNAP) program. Alas, funding to actually preserve these areas is still sadly lacking, and tourist infrastructure remains rudimentary, but intrepid travelers will be richly rewarded for seeking out these little-visited spots. Here are two preserves that best capture the spirit of Uruguay's wild gaucho country.

Valle del Lunarejo

This gorgeous valley, 95km north of Tacuarembó, is a place of marvelous peace and isolation, with birds and rushing water providing the only soundtrack.

Enchanting **Posada Lunarejo** (☎ 099-826348; www.posadalunarejo.com, in Spanish; Ruta 30, Km 238; r with breakfast per person UR$540, other meals UR$200 each) occupies a lovingly restored 1880 building 2km off the main road, 3km from the river and a few steps from a garza (crane) colony. Further up the road, local guide Mario Padern's company **Balcones de Lunarejo** (☎ 0650-6353, 099-450653; Ruta 30, Km 230; tour with lunch UR$350/520 walking/horseback) leads hiking and horseback-riding tours from the canyon's edge down to a series of natural pools near the river's headwaters.

Valle del Lunarejo is served by Turil's twice-daily Montevideo-Tacuarembó-Artigas bus (from Montevideo UR$419, six hours; from Tacuarembó UR$92, 1½ hours). Ask to get off at the relevant kilometer marker. Posada Lunarejo can meet your bus if you call ahead.

Quebrada de los Cuervos

This hidden little canyon cuts through the rolling hill country 40km northwest of Treinta y Tres (325km northeast of Montevideo), providing an unexpectedly moist and cool habitat for a variety of plants and birds. There's a nature trail looping through the park (two hours roundtrip), plus a shady hilltop **campground** (per person UR$100) at park headquarters.

A perfect base for exploring this region is **Cañada del Brujo** (☎ 099-297448; www.pleka.com/delbrujo; dm UR$300, meals UR$130-190), an ultrarustic hostel in an old schoolhouse 12km from the park. Hostel owner Pablo Rado can take you hiking or horseback riding to nearby waterfalls and introduce you to the simple joys of gaucho life: living by candlelight, drinking *mate*, sleeping under a wool poncho, eating simple meals cooked on the wood stove and watching spectacular sunsets under the big sky. With advance notice, he'll meet you in Treinta y Tres and drive you to the hostel in his old VW bug (UR$250 per person).

Buses travel to Treinta y Tres from Montevideo, Chuy (p590), Minas (p574) and Maldonado (p576).

VALLE EDÉN

☎ 063

Valle Edén, a lush valley 24km southwest of Tacuarembó, is home to the **Museo Carlos Gardel** (☎ 23520 ext 30; admission UR$20; ☉ 9:30am-6pm). Reached via a drive-through creek spanned by a wooden suspension footbridge, and housed in a former *pulpería* (the general store/bar that used to operate on many *estancias*), the museum documents Tacuarembó's claim as birthplace of the revered tango singer – a claim vigorously contested by Argentina and France!

Accommodations in Valle Edén are available at **Camping El Mago** (☎ 27144; campsite per tent UR$30, per person UR$15). You can eat at the lovely historic mud-and-stone **Posada Valle Edén** (☎ 02345, 099-810567; www.posadavalleeden.com.uy; dishes UR$150-200) or stay in one of their modern *cabañas* (UR$1200) across the street.

Empresa Calebus runs infrequent buses from Tacuarembó to Valle Edén (UR$29, 20 minutes).

EASTERN URUGUAY

The gorgeous 340km sweep of beaches, dunes, forests and lagoons stretching northeast from Montevideo to the Brazilian border is one of Uruguay's national treasures. Still largely unknown except to Uruguayans and their immediate neighbors, this part of Uruguay lies nearly dormant for 10 months of each

URUGUAY

year, then explodes with summer activity from Christmas to Carnaval, when it seems like every bus out of Montevideo is headed somewhere up the coast. For sheer fun-in-the-sun energy, there's nothing like the peak season, but if you can make it here slightly off-season, you'll experience all the same beauty for literally half the price.

Near the Brazilian border, amid the wide-open landscapes and untrammeled beaches of Rocha department, abandoned hilltop fortresses and shipwrecks offer mute testimony to the time when Spain and Portugal struggled for control of the new continent. Where lookouts once scanned the wide horizon for invading forces, a new wave of invaders has taken hold, from binocular-wielding whale-watchers in Cabo Polonio to camera-toting celebrity-watchers in Punta del Este. This part of Uruguay has something for everyone: surfers flock to Punta del Diablo and La Paloma, ornithologists go cuckoo over the endless string of coastal lagoons, families with kids frolic in the waves at La Pedrera or Piriápolis, and party animals find their nirvana in the all-night club scene at Punta del Este.

PIRIÁPOLIS
☎ 043 / pop 8400
With its elegant old hotel and beach-front promenade backed by small mountains, Piriápolis is vaguely reminiscent of a Mediterranean beach town and is arguably Uruguay's most picturesque coastal resort. Less pretentious and more affordable than Punta del Este, it was developed for tourism in the 1930s by Argentine entrepreneur Francisco Piria, who built the imposing landmark Argentino Hotel and an eccentric hillside residence known as Castillo de Piria (Piria's Castle; opposite).

The surrounding countryside holds many interesting features, including two of Uruguay's highest summits.

Orientation
Piriápolis is very compact. Almost all the action happens near the beachfront, in the 10-block stretch between Av Artigas (the access road from Ruta 9) and Av Piria, where the coastline makes a broad curve southwards. Streets back from the beach quickly become residential. The Argentino Hotel is the town's most prominent landmark.

Information
Antel (cnr Dr Héctor Barrios & Buenos Aires; internet per hr UR$19; ☺ 9am-6pm)
Asociación de Promoción Turística (☎ 25055; www.turismopiriapolis.com; Paseo de la Pasiva; ☺ 9am-midnight Dec-Feb, 10am-6pm Mar-Nov) Brand-new office with helpful staff and public toilets, on the waterfront near Argentino Hotel.
Banco de la República (Rambla de los Argentinos, btwn Sierra & Sanabria) Convenient ATM.
Centro de Hoteles y Restaurantes de Piriápolis (☎ 22218; chyrp@adinet.com.uy; Rambla de los Argentinos; ☺ 9am-midnight Dec-Feb, 10am-6pm Mar-Nov) Adjacent to tourist office; provides local hotel info and booking assistance.
Lave-Lis (cnr Piria & Reconquista; wash & dry per load UR$85; ☺ 9am-9pm)
Post office (Av Piria s/n)

Sights & Activities
Swimming and **sunbathing** are the most popular activities, and there's good **fishing** off the rocks at the end of the beach, where Rambla de los Argentinos becomes Rambla de los Ingleses.

For a great view of Piriápolis, take the **chairlift** (adult/child UR$80/60; ☺ 9am-9pm) to the summit of **Cerro San Antonio** at the east end of town.

Sleeping
Prices below are for high season. Low-season rates are up to 50% less.

Hostel Piriápolis (☎ 20394; www.hostelpiriapolis.com; Simón del Pino 1106-36; dm/d/tr/q HI member UR$280/600/720/880, nonmember surcharge per person UR$100; 🖳 ☎) This 236-bed hostel, one of South America's largest, has several four-bed dorms, dozens of doubles and a guest kitchen. It's desolate as an airplane hangar when empty, but full of life (and often booked solid) in January and February.

Bungalows Margariteñas (☎ 22245; www.margaritenias.com; cnr Zufriategui & Piedras; d/tr/q UR$1250/1400/1600; 🖳) Near the bus terminal, this place has beautifully equipped, individually decorated bungalows that sleep two to four. Affable owner Corina speaks English and meets guests at the bus station upon request.

Hotel Colón (☎ 22508; www.hotelcolonpiriapolis.com; Rambla 950; r with/without waterfront view UR$1900/1760; 🖳) Built in 1910 by Francisco Piria, this faux-Tudor mansion by the waterfront boasts fine views, gorgeous art nouveau details and an old-fashioned sitting room with fireplace.

Hotel Rex (☎ 22543; Manuel Freire 968; www.hotelrex.com.uy; s/d UR$1060/1960; 🖳 🖳 ☎ 🖳) The Rex, with its colorful decor, immaculate housekeeping, brand-new swimming pool and location half a block from the beach, makes for a very comfortable stay.

Argentino Hotel (☎ 22791; www.argentinohotel .com.uy; Rambla de los Argentinos s/n; s/d with breakfast from UR$2160/3120, half board UR$2520/3840, full board UR$2800/4400; ❄ 🖳 🖳) Even if you don't stay here, you should visit this elegant 350-room European-style spa with two heated riverwater pools, a casino, ice-skating rink and other luxuries.

Eating

Most of Piriápolis' restaurants are within a block of the Rambla.

ourpick **Café Picasso** (☎ 22597; cnr Rojas & Caseros; dishes UR$100-220) Hidden down a residential backstreet several blocks from the beach, chef-owner Carlos has converted his carport into an informal restaurant with open-air grill. Locals chat astride plastic chairs and listen to tango recordings while Carlos cooks up some of the best fish anywhere on Uruguay's Atlantic coast. All mains come with mashed potatoes, mashed pumpkin, French fries or salad.

Restaurante Yoyo (☎ 22948; cnr Sanabria & Tucumán; dishes UR$120-295; ❄ lunch & dinner) Yoyo specializes in pizza and seafood and has live music in summer.

Terra Nova (☎ 27879; cnr Rambla de los Argentinos & Sanabria; dishes UR$130-410; ❄ 9am-midnight, to 3am in summer) Smack in the center of the waterfront promenade, this trendy *parrilla* with turquoise brick walls framing a blazing fire buzzes with activity year-round.

Getting There & Away

The **bus terminal** (cnr Misiones & Niza) is a few blocks back from the beach. COT and COPSA run frequent buses to Montevideo (UR$98, 1½ hours), Maldonado (UR$49, 40 minutes) and Punta del Este (UR$59, 50 minutes). COOM runs multiple buses daily to Minas (UR$69, 1¼ hours) and Pan de Azúcar, where there are connections to Rocha and other points northeast.

AROUND PIRIÁPOLIS
Castillo de Piria & Pan de Azúcar

North of town, visitors can tour **Castillo de Piria** (☎ 043-23268; Ruta 37, Km 4; admission free; ❄ 10am-5pm Tue-Sun), Francisco Piria's outlandishly opulent residence. One kilometer further up Ruta 37, the **Reserva de Fauna Autóctona** (Ruta 37, Km 5; admission free; ❄ sunrise-sunset) showcases native species

such as the capybara, gray fox and ñandú. From here, hikers can climb Uruguay's fourth-highest 'peak,' **Cerro Pan de Azúcar** (389m). The trail (three hours roundtrip) starts as a gradual dirt road, then narrows to a steep path marked with red arrows. Ask for directions at Parador Drago, in the reserve's parking lot.

Sierra de las Ánimas

Increasingly popular with Uruguayan hikers, the privately operated nature preserve **Sierra de las Ánimas** (☎ 094-419891; www.sierradelasanimas .com; Ruta 9, Km 86; ❄ weekends only) is just off the Interbalnearia, 25km toward Montevideo from Piriápolis. Activities include climbing to the 501m summit (Uruguay's second-highest), swimming in the **Espejo del Guardián** (a natural pool below a waterfall), mountain biking and camping. Coming from Montevideo by bus, get off at Parador Los Cardos restaurant and cross the highway.

SOS Rescate de Fauna Marina

Ten kilometers south of Piriápolis is Uruguay's premier marine-animal rescue and rehabilitation center, **SOS Rescate de Fauna Marina** (☎ 094-330795; sosfaunamarina@gmail.com; admission UR$50; ❄ by appointment). Run entirely by volunteers, its emphasis is on educating schoolchildren, who can assist with daily feedings and observe penguins, sea lions, turtles and other rescued wildlife. Visitors willing to support the center's mission with the requested UR$50 donation (or more) are welcome with advance notice.

MINAS
☎ 044 / pop 39,000

If Uruguay has been making you feel starved for hills, Minas will come as a welcome surprise. Surrounded by the lovely undulating landscape of the Cuchilla Grande in Lavalleja department, 60km north of Piriápolis, Minas is named for nearby granite quarries.

Information

Antel (Treinta y Tres 765; ❄ 8am-8pm) Opposite the bus terminal.
Cyber Arroba (☎ 32122; Treinta y Tres 591; internet per hr UR$15; ❄ 9am-2am Mon-Sat, 2:30pm-midnight Sun) Just off Plaza Libertad.
Municipal tourist office (www.lavalleja.gub.uy; ❄ 8am-7pm) bus terminal (☎ 29796; Treinta y Tres s/n); Plaza Libertad (☎ 20037; Roosevelt 625)
Post office (W Beltrán 612) At corner with 25 de Mayo.

Sights & Activities

Among the eucalyptus groves 10km west of town, **Parque Salus** (☎ 31652; Ruta 8, Km 109; admission free; ☼ 9am-5pm) is the source of Uruguay's best-known mineral water and site of the Patricia brewery. Buses for the complex (which includes an upmarket hotel, reasonable restaurant and small botanical garden) leave regularly from Minas' bus terminal (UR$19).

Gruta Arequita (☎ 02731; www.complejoarequita.com; tours UR$60; ☼ tours 11am & 4pm Mon-Fri, 11:30am, 3pm & 5pm Sat, Sun & holidays, or by arrangement) is a privately operated cave 10km north of town in beautiful Parque Arequita; there are accommodations here. Public buses (UR$25, 30 minutes) run to/from Minas at least once daily except Sunday (more in summer).

Festivals & Events

Every April 19, up to 70,000 pilgrims visit the **Cerro y Virgen del Verdún**, 6km west of town. The festival, dating back to the early 20th century, draws in pilgrims from all over Uruguay, who pack the mountains above Minas for a series of masses and other religious rituals.

Sleeping & Eating

Parque Arequita (☎ 02503; camping per person UR$64, 2-/3-/4-/6-bed cabañas without bathroom UR$250/345/440/700; ☒) This municipal-run park 11km north of town has grassy campsites and cabins set amid trees, hills and rocky outcroppings. Llamas and ñandús roam about, there's a cold-water swimming pool, and you can rent horses or hike to nearby Gruta Arequita.

Posada Verdún (☎ 24563; posadaverdun@hotmail .com; W Beltrán 715; s/d/tr/q UR$430/750/1100/1450, breakfast per person UR$80; ☒ ☎) Convenient for the bus terminal, this welcoming family-run posada has been in business for over 25 years. Simple, clean rooms come with cable TV, and there's a flowery patio. Recent additions include aircon, wi-fi and an on-site restaurant.

Confitería Irisarri (☎ 22639; Treinta y Tres 618; sandwiches UR$55-90; ☼ 9am-9pm) Family-run since 1898, this cafe on Plaza Libertad is famous for its *alfajores* (cookie sandwiches) and *serranitos* (sweets made from vanilla-flavored caramel, fruit pulp, chocolate and peanuts).

Kijoia (☎ 25884; Domingo Pérez 483; dishes UR$95-300; ☼ 11:30am-midnight) All you need is a whiff of the delightful smoky smell coming from this *parrilla* on Plaza Libertad to understand why it's so popular.

Getting There & Away

The **bus terminal** (Treinta y Tres) is between Sarandí and Williman. CUT and Minuano provide frequent services to Montevideo (UR$117, two hours). Minuano also runs twice daily to Treinta y Tres (UR$176, 2½ hours). COOM has several daily departures to Piriápolis (UR$69, 1¼ hours). Emtur goes to Maldonado (UR$78, 1½ hours) and Punta del Este (UR$88, 1¾ hours). Nuñez runs once daily to Chuy (UR$215, four hours).

VILLA SERRANA
☎ 0440

Those seeking an off-the-beaten-track retreat will love the serenity of this little village nestled in hills above a small lake, 25km northeast of Minas. Nearby attractions include **Salto del Penitente**, a 60m waterfall.

Picturesquely perched above the valley, **La Calaguala** (☎ 2955, 099-387519; www.lacalaguala.com, in Spanish; Ruta 8, Km 145; campsite UR$150, r per person with breakfast/half board/full board UR$530/730/1000, r superior per person extra UR$150) is a friendly family-run posada with attached restaurant; horseback-riding and hiking excursions can be arranged (use of the posada's two horses is free for guests). The slightly more expensive room with whirlpool tub and fireplace is extremely cozy on chilly nights.

The simple **ourpick Albergue Villa Serrana** (☎ 099-226911, 099-624098, in Montevideo 02-9005749; www.villaserranahostel.com; Camino Molle s/n; dm HI member/nonmember UR$170/210) has an intimate fairy-tale quality, with a thatched roof, fireplace and ladders climbing to sleeping decks under the eaves. There's a tiny guest kitchen (bring food). Advance notice is essential – in summer it's often fully booked; in the off-season you may be the only visitor and will need to fetch the key down the street.

COSU (☎ 044-22256) runs direct buses from Minas to Villa Serrana (UR$40, 30 minutes) at 9am and 5:30pm Tuesdays and Thursdays, returning at 9:45am and 6:15pm. On other days, any northbound bus from Minas that travels along Ruta 8 can drop you at Km 145, from where it's a stiff 4km uphill walk into town.

MALDONADO
☎ 042 / pop 62,000

Capital of its namesake department, Maldonado nowadays feels like Punta del Este's poor cousin. Dating from 1755, it has retained

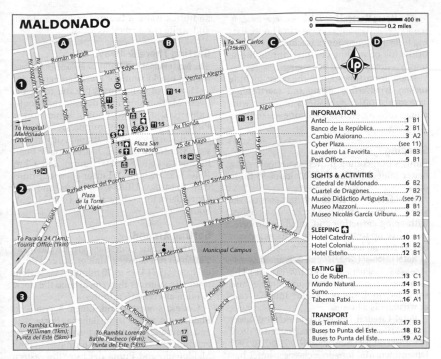

MALDONADO

INFORMATION	
Antel	1 B1
Banco de la República	2 B1
Cambio Maiorano	3 A2
Cyber Plaza	(see 11)
Lavadero La Favorita	4 B3
Post Office	5 B1

SIGHTS & ACTIVITIES	
Catedral de Maldonado	6 B2
Cuartel de Dragones	7 B2
Museo Didáctico Artiguista	(see 7)
Museo Mazzoni	8 B1
Museo Nicolás García Uriburu	9 B2

SLEEPING	
Hotel Catedral	10 B1
Hotel Colonial	11 B2
Hotel Esteño	12 B1

EATING	
Lo de Ruben	13 C1
Mundo Natural	14 B1
Sumo	15 B1
Taberna Patxi	16 A1

TRANSPORT	
Bus Terminal	17 B3
Buses to Punta del Este	18 B2
Buses to Punta del Este	19 A2

a few shreds of colonial atmosphere, but it's unlikely to keep you engaged for more than an afternoon.

Once considered an economical alternative to Punta, Maldonado's prices are no longer so attractive. However, there are a couple of nice museums and excellent restaurants that merit a visit.

Orientation

Maldonado is 30km east of Piriápolis. Other than the beaches south of the center, most points of interest are within a few blocks of its central Plaza San Fernando.

Information

Antel (Av Florida 786; ⏰ 9am-7pm)

Banco de la República (Av Florida 774) ATM on the main square.

Cambio Maiorano (Av Florida 860; ⏰ 9am-7:30pm Mon-Sat) One of many exchange houses found along Av Florida.

Cyber Plaza (☎ 223346; 18 de Julio 841; internet per hr UR$30; ⏰ 8am-2am)

Hospital Maldonado (☎ 225889; Ventura Alegre) West of the center.

Lavadero La Favorita (☎ 223763; Juan A Ledesma s/n) Laundry service just west of Sarandí.

Post office (18 de Julio 965)

Tourist office (☎ 230050; www.maldonado.gub.uy; Parada 24; ⏰ 8am-6pm Mar-Dec, 8am-midnight Jan & Feb) On beachside Rambla Claudio Williman.

Sights & Activities

The **Catedral de Maldonado** (Plaza San Fernando) was completed in 1895 after nearly a century of construction. On Rafael Pérez del Puerto, the **Plaza de la Torre del Vigía** features a colonial watchtower built with peepholes for viewing the approach of hostile forces.

Another colonial relic, the **Cuartel de Dragones** is a block of military fortifications with stone walls and iron gates, built between 1771 and 1797. Inside, the **Museo Didáctico Artiguista** (☎ 225378; admission free; ⏰ 10am-6pm) displays colorful maps tracing the peripatetic military campaigns of Uruguay's independence hero. Next door is the fine-arts **Museo Nicolás García Uriburu** (☎ 225378; cnr 25 de Mayo & 18 de Julio; admission free; ⏰ 10:15am-5:45pm Tue-Sun), an impressive collection of sculpture nicely displayed in two small wings.

URUGUAY

The **Museo Mazzoni** (☎ 221107; Ituzaingó 789; admission free; ☒ 10:15am-5:45pm Tue-Sun), in a house dating from 1782, provides a fascinating glimpse of the life of wealthy colonials through one family's furniture and belongings.

Popular pastimes along the coast include **surfing**, **windsurfing**, **diving** and **sportfishing**. The tourist office publishes a brochure with a map recommending sites for each of these activities.

Sleeping

Punta's burgeoning hostel scene makes it a better budget choice than Maldonado these days.

Hotel Esteño (☎ 225222; hotelesteno@hotmail.com; Sarandí 881; s/d UR$700/1300) The Esteño's rooms, with aging carpeting and small bathrooms, don't live up to the promise of its entryway, but its central location is convenient.

Hotel Colonial (☎ 223346; www.elhotelcolonial.com; 18 de Julio 841; s/d/tr/q UR$700/1400/1700/1900; ☐) The Colonial's rooms are clean and simple, and some overlook the plaza. The internet cafe downstairs is a bonus.

Hotel Catedral (☎ 242513; hotelcatedral@adinet .com.uy; Av Florida 830; s/d/tr/q without breakfast UR$1600/ 1900/2260/2780, with breakfast UR$1760/2200/2780/3360) Downtown Maldonado's classiest hotel has Japanese-pattern bedspreads, clean bathrooms and art posters in the hallways. Front rooms overlook the cathedral.

Eating

Mundo Natural (☎ 251697; Román Guerra 918; savory/sweet tartas (pies) UR$60/65; ☒ 10am-7pm Mon-Fri, 10am-2pm Sat) This cheerful hole-in-the-wall has been serving little vegetarian treats since 1992.

Sumo (☎ 223959; cnr Sarandí & Av Florida; dishes UR$78-290; ☒ 8am-1am) Perfectly situated for people-watching, this corner restaurant on Maldonado's main pedestrian thoroughfare is popular with local youth.

Lo de Ruben (☎ 223059; Santa Teresa 846; dishes UR$140-420; ☒ lunch & dinner) From humble origins selling sausages off a cart with his father over 20 years ago, Ruben has built one of the area's most wildly popular *parrillas* – a true local institution.

Taberna Patxi (☎ 238393; José Dodera 944; dishes UR$230-560; ☒ dinner Wed, lunch & dinner Thu-Sat, lunch Sun) Taberna Patxi serves fine Basque food with an emphasis on fish and shellfish. The delightfully rustic dining room features stone-and-brick walls, a beamed ceiling, and red-and-white checked tablecloths.

Getting There & Away

The **bus terminal** (☎ 225701; cnr Av Roosevelt & Sarandí) is eight blocks south of Plaza San Fernando.

Dozens of daily buses ply the route between Maldonado/Punta del Este and Montevideo (UR$137, two hours); some stop in Piriápolis (UR$59, 50 minutes), and most stop at Carrasco International Airport outside Montevideo. COT has two daily buses to Rocha (UR$88, 1½ hours) and Chuy (UR$215, 3½ hours). Emtur goes four times daily to Minas (UR$84, 1½ hours) and three times daily to Treinta y Tres (UR$215, 3½ hours).

Getting Around

Local buses (blue Codesa and green Maldonado Turismo) run between Maldonado and Punta del Este (UR$14, 15 to 30 minutes) via various routes. In summer they run around the clock, as often as every 15 minutes.

Codesa's westbound Línea 8 connects Maldonado with Punta Ballena, Portezuelo and Punta del Este's airport, while eastbound Línea 14 hits the bus terminals in both Maldonado and Punta del Este, the eastern beaches, La Barra and Faro José Ignacio. The fare on both lines is UR$28.

PUNTA DEL ESTE
☎ 042 / pop 7000

OK, here's the plan: tan it, wax it, buff it at the gym, then plonk it on the beach at 'Punta.' Once you're done there, go out and shake it at one of the town's famous clubs.

Punta del Este – with its many beaches, elegant seaside homes, yacht harbor, high-rise apartment buildings, pricey hotels and glitzy restaurants – is one of South America's most glamorous resorts and easily the most expensive place in Uruguay. Extremely popular with Argentines and Brazilians, Punta suffered a period of decline during the Uruguayan and Argentine recessions, but has come back with a vengeance.

Celebrity-watchers have a full-time job here. Punta is teeming with big names, and local gossipmongers keep regular tabs on who's been sighted where. Surrounding towns caught up in the whole Punta mystique include the famed club zone of La Barra to the east and Punta Ballena to the west.

PUNTA DEL ESTE

0 .... 400 m
0 .... 0.2 miles

INFORMATION
Antel..............................1 C3
Argentine Consulate.........2 C3
Banco de la República Oriental.3 C3
Cambio Gales....................4 D2
Centro de Hoteles y
  Restaurantes................(see 8)
HSBC..............................5 C2
Librería El Virrey...............6 D2
Municipal Tourist Office........7 D2
Municipal Tourist Office........8 C3
Municipal Tourist Office......(see 42)
National Tourism Ministry......9 D2
Post Office......................10 D2
Ultrarap 24.....................11 C3

SIGHTS & ACTIVITIES
Calypso Charters &
  Excursiones..................12 B3
Golden Bikes...................13 D2
La Mano en la Arena...........14 D2
Novo Turismo..................(see 42)

SLEEPING
1949 Hostel.....................15 C2
Bonne Étoile....................16 C3
El Viajero Brava Beach Hostel..17 D1
Hotel Galicia...................18 B4
Hotel Marbella.................19 D2
Hotel Tanger...................20 D2
Palace Hotel...................21 B4

Río de la Plata

Yacht
Harbor

EATING
Chivitería Marcos..............22 B3
El Milagro......................23 B4
El Pobre Marino................24 B4
Il Baretto......................25 B4
Kitty's Resto...................26 B3
La Fonda del Pesca............27 D2
La Nueva Avenida.............28 D1
Les Delices....................29 C2
Lo de Charlie..................30 B4
Lo de Tere.....................31 C3
Los Caracoles..................32 C2
Supermercado Disco..........33 B4
Virazón........................34 C2

To western beaches; Conrad Resort & Casino (300m);
Pluna (1km); Maldonado (5km); Caspueblo (15km);
Las Cumbres (15km); Medio y Medio (15km);
Punta Ballena (15km); Airport (20km)

To eastern beaches; Hotel Bravamar (300m);
El Diablito (500m); Sunvalleysurf (500m); Caix (800m);
Ocean Club (1km); La Lomita del Chingolo (1.5km);
Museo Ralli (2km); Camping San Rafael (8km);
Crobar (9km); La Barra (9km);
La Posta del Cangrejo (9km); Baby Gouda Deli Café (9km);
Museo del Mar (10km); Manantiales Hostel (11km)

ATLANTIC
OCEAN

DRINKING
C Bistro & Bar..................35 C2
Moby Dick......................36 B3

ENTERTAINMENT
Cine Libertador................37 C3
Mambo Club....................38 B3
Soho............................39 B3

SHOPPING
Feria Artesanal...............(see 8)
Manos del Uruguay............40 D2

TRANSPORT
Aerolíneas Argentinas.........41 D2
Bus Terminal...................42 D1
Dollar.........................43 D2
Multicar.......................44 C2
Punta Car......................45 D2
TAM...........................46 D2

Orientation

Punta itself is relatively small, confined to a narrow peninsula that officially divides the Río de la Plata from the Atlantic Ocean. The town has two separate grids: north of a constricted isthmus just east of the yacht harbor is the high-rise hotel zone; the southern area is largely residential. Street signs bear both names and numbers, though locals refer to most streets only by their number. An exception is Av Juan Gorlero (Calle 22), the main commercial street, universally referred to as just 'Gorlero' (not to be confused with Calle 19, *Comodoro* Gorlero).

Both Rambla Claudio Williman and Rambla Lorenzo Batlle Pacheco are coastal

URUGUAY

thoroughfares that converge at the top of the isthmus from northwest and northeast, respectively. Locations along the Ramblas are usually identified by numbered *paradas* (bus stops).

Information

BOOKSTORES

Librería El Virrey (☎ 448908; Calle 30, btwn Gorlero & Calle 20; ☺ 9am-2:30am Dec-Mar, 10am-9pm Thu-Tue Apr-Nov) Friendly staff and a small selection of English-language bestsellers.

INTERNET ACCESS

Internet places pop up like mushrooms each summer, but most close in the off-season. Wi-fi is available year-round at most hotels and many restaurants.

Antel (cnr Calles 25 & 24; per hr UR$19) The most dependable spot for internet access in low season.

LAUNDRY

Ultrarap 24 (☎ 445595; Calle 24, btwn Calles 19 & 21; wash & dry per basket UR$220 Dec-Mar, UR$160 Apr-Nov; ☺ 8:30am-midnight Dec-Mar, 9:30am-7pm Mon-Sat Apr-Nov)

MONEY

Punta's many banks and exchange offices are concentrated along Gorlero.

Banco de la República Oriental (cnr Gorlero & Calle 25) One of two ATMs on this corner.

Cambio Gales (cnr Gorlero & Calle 29) Changes traveler's checks.

HSBC (cnr Gorlero & Calle 28)

POST

Post office (Gorlero 1035)

TELEPHONE

Antel (cnr Calles 25 & 24)

TOURIST INFORMATION

Centro de Hoteles y Restaurantes (☎ 440512; www.puntadelestehoteles.com; Plaza Artigas; ☺ 8am-midnight Dec-Mar, 10am-6pm Mon-Sat Apr-Nov) Helps with hotel bookings.

Municipal tourist office (☎ 446510; www.maldonado.gub.uy; Plaza Artigas; ☺ 8am-midnight Dec 15-Mar 1, 8am-6pm rest of year) Maintains additional branches at bus station and at corner of Calle 31 and the Rambla.

National Tourism Ministry (☎ 441218; puntadeleste@mintur.gub.uy; Gorlero 942; ☺ 10am-10pm Dec-Mar, 10am-5pm Mon-Sat, noon-4pm Sun Apr-Nov)

Sights

BEACHES & ISLANDS

Beaches are the big daytime draw in sunny Punta, and there are plenty to choose from. On the west side of town, Rambla Artigas snakes along the calm **Playa Mansa** on the Río de la Plata, then passes the busy **yacht harbor**, overflowing with boats, restaurants, nightclubs and beautiful people, before circling around the peninsula to the open Atlantic Ocean.

On the eastern side of the peninsula the water is rougher, as reflected in the name **Playa Brava** (Fierce Beach); the waves and currents here have claimed several lives. Also on the Atlantic side, you'll find surfer-friendly beaches such as **Playa de los Ingleses** and **Playa El Emir**.

From Playa Mansa, heading west along Rambla Williman, the main beach areas are La Pastora, Marconi, Cantegril, Las Delicias, Pinares, La Gruta at Punta Ballena, and Portezuelo. Eastward, along Rambla Lorenzo Batlle Pacheco, the prime beaches are La Chiverta, San Rafael, La Draga and Punta de la Barra. In summer, all have *paradores* (small restaurants) with beach service.

Punta's most famous landmark is **La Mano en la Arena**, a giant sculpted hand protruding from the sand on Playa Brava (see opposite).

Boats leave every half-hour or so (daily in season, weekends in off-season) from Punta del Este's yacht harbor for the 15-minute trip to **Isla Gorriti**, which has excellent sandy beaches, a couple of restaurants and the ruins of **Baterías de Santa Ana**, an 18th-century fortification.

About 10km offshore, **Isla de Lobos** is home to the world's second-largest southern sealion colony (200,000 at last count), as well as South America's tallest lighthouse. The island is protected and can only be visited on an organized tour (see opposite).

OTHER SIGHTS

Casapueblo (☎ 042-578041; admission UR$120; ☺ 10am-sunset), at Punta Ballena, a jutting headland 15km west of Punta del Este, is Uruguayan artist Carlos Páez Vilaró's exuberantly whimsical **villa and art gallery**. Gleaming white in the sun and cascading nine stories down a cliffside, it's one of Uruguay's most unique attractions. Visitors can tour five rooms, view a film on the artist's life and travels, and eat up the spectacular views at the upstairs cafeteriabar. There's a hotel (p580) and restaurant, too. It's a 2km walk from the junction where Codesa's Línea 8 bus drops you.

THE HAND IN THE SAND

Punta del Este's most famous landmark is the monster-sized hand emerging from the sands of Playa Brava. *La Mano en la Arena* (Hand in the Sand), sculpted in iron and cement by Chilean artist Mario Irarrazabal in 1982, won first prize in a monumental art contest that year and has been a Punta fixture ever since. The hand exerts a magnetic attraction over visitors to Punta, who climb and jump off its digits and pose for thousands of photos with it every year.

Up close, the hand is starting to show its age. There's graffiti scrawled all over it, and its ungraceful cement base often gets exposed by shifting sands. But watch out – the hand's still likely to reach out and grab you!

Museo Ralli (☎ 483476; www.rallimuseums.org; cnr Curupay & Los Arrayanes; admission free; ☼ 5-9pm Tue-Sun Jan & Feb, 2-6pm Sat & Sun Oct-Dec, Mar & Apr), in the suburb called Beverly Hills, displays a wide-ranging collection of works by contemporary Latin American artists.

Museo del Mar (☎ 042-771817; Calle de los Corsarios, La Barra; adult/child UR$100/50; ☼ 10am-8:30pm Dec-Mar, 11am-5pm Apr-Nov) is 1km inland from the ocean at La Barra. Its diverse collection includes seashells, whale skeletons, kooky-looking fish, a pirate room for kids, and quotes about the sea from famous personages such as Da Vinci and Beaudelaire.

Activities

In summer, **parasailing** (UR$1250 per 12 minutes), **waterskiing** (UR$1000 per 15 minutes) and **jet skiing** (UR$1000 per 15 minutes) are possible on Playa Mansa. Operators set up on the beach along Rambla Claudio Williman between Paradas 2 and 20.

Sunvalleysurf (☎ 481388; www.sunvalleysurf.com; Parada 3, Playa Brava) rents wetsuits, surfboards, bodyboards and just about anything else you could want. It also offers surf and bodyboard lessons.

Golden Bikes (Calle 24, btwn Calles 28 & 29) rents bikes for UR$50/200 per hour/day.

Tours

Calypso Charters & Excursiones (☎ 446152, 094-443600; www.calypso.com.uy; cnr Rambla Artigas & Calle 21; tours adult/child UR$1200/600) One of several companies offering two-hour tours to Isla de Lobos.

Novo Turismo (☎ 493154; www.novoturismo.com, in Spanish; bus terminal) Runs city tours of Punta del Este and arranges excursions to surrounding attractions such as Casapueblo, Faro José Ignacio and Cabo Polonio.

Sleeping

In summer Punta is jammed with people, and prices are astronomical. In winter it's a ghost town, and places that stay open lower their prices considerably. Prices listed below are for high season. Because Punta is so much more expensive than other Uruguayan summer resorts, you'll find that hotels marked midrange actually charge top-end rates in summer. Off-season visitors will find prices more in keeping with the ranges defined at p591.

BUDGET

Camping San Rafael (☎ 486715; www.campingsan rafael.com.uy; sites per person UR$140-240, per vehicle UR$30; ☼ Nov-Apr) This campground, near the bridge to La Barra, has well-kept facilities on woodsy grounds, complete with store, restaurant, laundry, 24-hour hot water and other amenities.

El Viajero Brava Beach Hostel (☎ 480331; www.elvi ajerobravabeach.com; cnr Charrúa & Av Francia; dm HI member UR$280-420, nonmember UR$340-500, d HI member UR$1020-1700, nonmember UR$1200-2000; ✂ ▯ ⓢ) Punta's newest hostel bears all the trademarks of the popular El Viajero chain – colorful decor, a lively 24-hour bar, music-filled common areas and plenty of traveler perks, including laundry facilities, bike rentals and surfing lessons. The noisy, trafficky street corner location is rather dreary, but it's conveniently close to the bus station as well as the waves and nightlife of Playa Brava.

Manantiales Hostel (☎ 774427; www.manantiales hostel.com; Ruta 10, Km 164; dm HI member UR$280-440, non-member UR$320-520, d HI member UR$840-1760, nonmember UR$1000-2200; ☼ Nov–mid-Apr; ▯ ⓢ ⓡ) If you're here to surf or just chill out, this hostel 12km east of Punta, with its swimming pool and backstreet location 15 minutes on foot from Bikini Beach, is a great bet. It's a 400m walk to the main road, plus five/20 minutes by bus to La Barra/Punta. There's a good kitchen and surfboards can be hired for UR$400 per day.

1949 Hostel (☎ 440719; www.1949hostel.com; Calles 30 & 18; dm from UR$340; ▯ ⓢ) This ultracool hostel is a magnet for international youth, with hammocks out front, river views, surfboard rentals, breakfast till noon and a corner bar. Light sleepers who don't plan to party till dawn, beware: it can get pretty rowdy here – but the homey atmosphere and friendly staff still make this one of Uruguay's very best hostels.

La Lomita del Chingolo (☎ 099-758897; www .lalomitadelchingolo.com; Las Acacias btwn Los Eucaliptus & Le Mans; dm UR$420-580, d UR$1400-1920; ☐ ☎) With one six-person dorm and five private rooms, this relaxed place is in a residential neighborhood north of the center. Hospitable owners Rodrigo and Alejandra welcome guests with internet and kitchen facilities, tasty breakfasts, impromptu backyard barbecues and plenty of information about the local area.

MIDRANGE
Hotel Galicia (☎ 444992; www.hotelgalicia.com.uy; Plaza El Faro; s/d/tr UR$1300/1800/2200) This small two-star sits in a quiet residential district south of the port. Three of the cheerfully painted rooms face the plaza and have fine views of Punta's lighthouse.

Hotel Marbella (☎ 441814; www.hotelmarbella.tk; Calle 31, No 615; s/d/tr/q UR$1300/1800/2400/3000; ☒ ☎) Near the bus station, with cable TV and frigobar, this is depressingly about as affordable as downtown hotels get in Punta. Off-season prices halve, making it a better deal.

Hotel Bravamar (☎ 480559; www.hotelbravamar.com .uy, in Spanish; Parada 2, Playa Brava; s/d/tr UR$1400/1800/2400; ☒ ☎) One of the best deals on Playa Brava, the Bravamar has two rooms overlooking the beach…sort of. Unfortunately, the little red Astroturf terraces and intervening highway don't do much to enhance the view!

Palace Hotel (☎ 441919; palacepunta@hotmail.com; cnr Gorlero & Calle 11; s/d/tr/q UR$1800/1800/2600/3200, ste UR$3200; ☒ ☒) Just one block up from the yacht harbor, the Palace has a palm-shaded central courtyard and a pretty shared veranda overlooking Calle 11. Rooms are a bit dowdy, but it's hard to argue with the location.

Bonne Étoile (☎ 440301; www.hotelbonneetoile.com; Calle 20, btwn Calles 23 & 25; s/d/tr UR$2100/2300/2700; ☒ ☎) In a 1940s beach house adjoining a more modern six-story tower, Bonne Étoile has clean, spacious rooms, some with river views. The location between Gorlero and the port is hard to beat.

Hotel Tanger (☎ 441333; www.hoteltanger.com; Calle 31, btwn Calles 18 & 20; d/tr/q UR$2400/3800/4400; ☒ ☐ ☎ ☒) This recommended family-run hotel has ample, comfortable rooms with minibars, safes and wi-fi. The rooftop sundeck and swimming pool have good beach views.

TOP END
our pick Casapueblo (☎ 578611; www.clubhotel.com.ar; Punta Ballena; d/q apt without breakfast from UR$3000/6000, r with breakfast from UR$3700, d/q ste from UR$5400/10,900; ☒ ☐ ☎ ☒) Artist Carlos Páez Vilaró's whimsical, splurge-worthy architectural masterpiece is like a Mediterranean fantasyland. Rooms cascade down nine levels – numbered zero to negative nine – to a brilliant turquoise, mosaic-floored pool surrounded by a vast sun terrace.

La Posta del Cangrejo (☎ 770021; www.laposta delcangrejo.com; La Barra; r from UR$3600, ste UR$9200; ☒ ☐ ☎ ☒) This beachside hotel in the heart of La Barra has whitewashed adobe walls, an award-winning French restaurant and a poolside terrace within earshot of the ocean. The upstairs suites are especially alluring, with fireplaces, Jacuzzis, 29in TVs and nice sound systems.

Las Cumbres (☎ 578689; www.cumbres.com.uy; Ruta 12, Km 3.9, Laguna del Sauce; r UR$3800-5700, ste UR$7800-11,900; ☒ ☐ ☎ ☒) Near Punta Ballena, this understatedly luxurious hilltop paradise is eclectically decorated with treasures from the owners' world travels. Rooms abound with special features such as writing desks, fireplaces and outdoor whirlpool tubs. Hourlong spa treatments start from UR$960, and the tearoom terrace (open to the public) has magnificent sunset views.

Conrad Resort & Casino (☎ 491111; www.con radhotels.com; Parada 4, Playa Mansa; d from UR$10,000; ☒ ☐ ☎ ☒) If you're looking for five-star amenities in downtown Punta, the high-rise, ultramodern Conrad is the obvious choice. Better rooms have terraces with sea views, the pool and spa complex is fabulous, and the casino offers entertainment extravaganzas.

Eating
BUDGET & MIDRANGE
Supermercado Disco (☎ 445130; Calle 17, btwn Gorlero & Calle 24; ☺ 8am-10pm) For shelter from Punta's high prices, shop for groceries or grab a snack from the *rotisería* (delicatessen) here.

El Milagro (☎ 443866; Calle 17, btwn Gorlero & Calle 24; dishes UR$70-140; ☺ lunch & dinner) This humble *chivitería* and pizzeria is about as affordable as things get in Punta. There's a *menu del día* (daily fixed-meal special) for UR$70 and (gasp!) no cover charge.

La Fonda del Pesca (☎ 449165; Calle 29, btwn Gorlero & Calle 24; dishes UR$120-300; ☺ noon-11pm) A vividly painted hole-in-the-wall specializing in fish,

La Fonda also serves up plenty of local color. Owner-chef Pesca makes personal appearances at diners' tables to make sure they're enjoying themselves.

La Nueva Avenida (☎ 493229; cnr Joaquin Lenzina & Francia; dishes UR$130-310; ❤ closed Jun) Ask locals where to find an honest meal without breaking the bank, and they'll point you to this unpretentious eatery northeast of the bus station. The *milanesa Avenida* (breaded veal cutlet with fried egg, French fries and salad) for UR$195 is enough food for two!

Chivitería Marcos (☎ 449932; Rambla Artigas, btwn Calles 12 & 14; chivitos UR$160; ❤ 11am-4am Dec-Mar, 11am-4pm & 8pm-late Apr-Nov) Montevideo-based Marcos earned its fame building mega-sandwiches to order. Just tell the *chivito*-sculptor behind the counter which of the 12 toppings and nine sauces you want, then try to balance the thing back to your table.

Baby Gouda Deli Café (☎ 771874; Ruta 10, Km 161, La Barra; dishes from UR$160; ❤ noon-1am) An ultracool deli with an inviting outdoor deck, on the main drag in La Barra, a couple of blocks up from the beach.

El Pobre Marino (☎ 443306; cnr Calles 11 & 12; dishes from UR$175; ❤ lunch & dinner, closed Mon dinner & Tue May-Oct) Decked out with nets and glass floats, this is one of the few affordable sit-down places near the port – with a strong emphasis on seafood.

Les Delices (☎ 443640; cnr Calles 20 & 29; cakes from UR$185; ❤ 7:30am-8:30pm, closed May) Great juices, pastries, cakes and salads explain the success of this award-winning corner *confitería*.

TOP END

Kitty's Resto (☎ 446197; Marina 3-4; dishes UR$250-420; ❤ 10am-5pm Fri-Wed Apr-Nov, 8am-1am Dec-Mar) So close to the water, you might as well be dining on a yacht. Seafood is the specialty, but homesick travelers may also appreciate the full American breakfasts for UR$250.

Los Caracoles (☎ 440912; cnr Calles 20 & 28; dishes UR$250-460; ❤ lunch & dinner) Waiters in white jackets and bow ties set the classy tone at this popular corner *parrilla*.

Virazón (☎ 443924; cnr Rambla Artigas & Calle 28; dishes UR$265-595; ❤ 9am-late) Virazón serves great seafood. Grab a spot on the beachside deck, and have fun watching the waiters try to look dignified as they cross the street with loaded trays.

Lo de Charlie (☎ 444183; Calle 12, No 819; dishes UR$320-635; ❤ lunch & dinner Dec-Mar, dinner Wed-Mon,

lunch Fri-Sun Apr-Nov) Owned by a fishing buddy of local artist Carlos Páez Vilaró and decorated with some of his work, this is one of Punta's premier restaurants. The endless culinary delights include gazpacho, risotto, homemade pasta, fish and shellfish.

Lo de Tere (☎ 440492; Rambla Artigas, btwn Calles 19 & 21; dishes UR$340-890; ❤ lunch & dinner) Even with early-bird discounts of 20% to 40%, Tere's can put a hurtin' on your wallet (their wine list routinely lists vintages costing hundreds of US dollars!), but the food is truly world-class.

Il Baretto (☎ 447243; cnr Calles 9 & 10; dishes UR$395-630; ❤ lunch & dinner daily Dec-Mar, Thu-Sun Apr-Nov) Il Baretto's menu features some of the best pasta in Punta and desserts to die for. The lunchtime special (UR$395, including cover charge, main dish and either dessert or appetizer) counts as a good deal by Punta's extravagant standards.

Drinking & Entertainment

Bear in mind that it's social suicide to turn up at a nightclub before 2am here. A good place to meet up with other travelers beforehand is the bar of the 1949 Hostel (p579). In general, Punta's bars stay open as long as there's a crowd and sometimes have live music on weekends.

The most fashionable clubs are clustered in Punta's port area and along the beach road to La Barra. Ironically, considering Punta's reputation for nightlife, many clubs only stay open for the midsummer super-peak period. Also, clubs commonly change names or disappear altogether from year to year.

Moby Dick (☎ 441240; Calle 13, btwn Calles 10 & 12) A local fixture, this classic bar near the yacht harbor is where Punta's dynamic social scene kicks off every evening.

C Bistro & Bar (☎ 440130; Calle 29, btwn Calles 18 & 20) In downtown Punta, this place is open all year for drinks and live music (weekends only in low season).

Soho (☎ 447315; Calle 13, btwn Calles 10 & 12) Next door to Moby Dick, Soho is a dependable year-round dance spot pumping out techno beats (weekends only in low season).

Mambo Club (☎ 448956; cnr Calle 13 & Calle 10) Yet another nightspot down by the port, featuring Latin grooves. As the sign says, there's a party every summer night at the Mambo!

Crobar (☎ 099-121591; Camino Urquiza, La Barra; ❤ Dec 26-Jan 31) A dance place mixing DJs and live music, inland from La Barra on the road to San Carlos.

Medio y Medio (☎ 578791; Camino Lussich s/n, Punta Ballena) This jazz club and restaurant near the beach in Punta Ballena brings in performers from Uruguay, Argentina and Brazil.

Cine Libertador (☎ 444437; Gorlero 796) Open year-round with movies on two screens.

Also recommended are the following clubs along Playa Brava; all open nightly in peak season and weekends throughout the year.

Caix (☎ 098-637090; www.caixpunta.com; Parada 8, Playa Brava)

El Diablito (Parada 3, Playa Brava)

Ocean Club (☎ 484869; Parada 12, Playa Brava)

Shopping

Manos del Uruguay (☎ 441953; Gorlero, btwn Calles 30 & 31) This is the local branch of Uruguay's national cooperative, selling fine woolens.

Feria Artesanal (Plaza Artigas) A well-established artisan's fair on Punta's central square.

Getting There & Away

AIR

The **Aeropuerto Internacional de Punta del Este** (☎ 559777) is at Laguna del Sauce, 20km west of Punta del Este.

Pluna (☎ 492050; cnr Av Roosevelt & Parada 9; ☼ 9am-5pm Mon-Sat) offers the most frequent service from Punta to Buenos Aires' Aeroparque.

Aerolíneas Argentinas (☎ 444343; Edificio Santos Dumont, Gorlero, btwn Calles 30 & 31; ☼ 9am-11pm daily Dec-Mar, 10am-12:30pm & 2:30-6pm Mon-Fri, 10am-2pm Sat Apr-Nov) flies to Aeroparque several times daily in season, and once a day on Friday and Sunday off-season.

TAM (☎ 442920; Calle 29, btwn Gorlero & Calle 24; ☼ late Dec–mid-Feb) offers twice-weekly, summer-only flights from Punta to Asunción, Paraguay, with a stopover in Buenos Aires' Ezeiza airport.

BUS

Most services to Punta's **bus terminal** (☎ 494042; cnr Calle 32 & Bulevar Artigas) are an extension of those to Maldonado; see p576.

Getting Around

TO/FROM THE AIRPORT

COT runs direct minivans from the bus station to the airport (UR$90, 30 minutes), leaving 1½ hours before each flight. Alternatively, any Montevideo-bound bus will drop you at the airport entrance on the main highway (UR$45, 30 minutes), a 10-minute walk from the terminal.

BUS

See p576 for details of the frequent transport between Maldonado and Punta. *Micros* (minibuses) leave every 15 minutes in summer from Bay 1 at Punta's bus terminal and serve the eastern beaches and nightspots on Rambla Batlle Pacheco on their way to La Barra (UR$25, 20 minutes); others run to points west, including Punta Ballena and Piriápolis.

CAR

Car-rental outlets are ubiquitous near the bus terminal and along Gorlero. Some of the better deals include **Punta Car** (☎ 482112; cnr Bulevar Artigas & Pedro Risso), **Multicar** (☎ 443143; Gorlero 860) and **Dollar** (☎ 443444; Gorlero 961).

AROUND PUNTA DEL ESTE
Faro José Ignacio

The rich and famous flock to this increasingly fashionable little beachside town with a pretty lighthouse 30km east of Punta. There's limited tourist infrastructure, but if your goal is to luxuriate by the sea, it's hard to find a nicer place than **La Posada del Faro** (☎ 0486-2110; www.posadadelfaro.com; cnr de la Bahía & Timonel; r UR$5400-10,400; ☒ ▢ ▣). The pricier rooms have fireplaces and private ocean-view terraces. For fine beachside dining, **Parador La Huella** (☎ 0486-2279; Playa Brava; ☼ lunch & dinner Dec-Mar, lunch Fri-Sun, dinner Fri & Sat May-Nov) specializes in sushi, grilled fish and clay-oven-fired pizza. Two buses daily make the 45-minute trip from Punta (UR$49), stopping in the main square near the **tourist office** (☎ 0486-2409, 094-527300; www.ligadejoseignacio.org; ☼ 9am-2pm Fri-Mon).

ROCHA
☎ 047 / pop 27,000

Rocha is capital of its namesake department and a transport hub for visitors to nearby La Paloma.

There's a helpful departmental **tourist office** (☎ 23100; www.turismorocha.gub.uy; ☼ 10am-6pm Apr-Nov, 10am-8pm Dec-Mar) on Ruta 9, 2km from the center. All other services are concentrated near central Plaza Independencia, including **Antel** (cnr General Artigas & Rodó), the **post office** (18 de Julio 2085) and **Banco Comercial** (cnr General Artigas & 25 de Mayo).

Rocha's hotels can be handy if things get booked up in La Paloma. **Hotel Trocadero** (☎ 22267; 25 de Agosto 114; s/d/tr UR$765/1415/1825; ☒ ▢) has spacious rooms with parquet floors, cable TV, writing desks and 1950s-vintage bathrooms.

For a bite between buses, there are some decent restaurants surrounding the main square. **El Pato** (☎ 25636; cnr 25 de Mayo & Julian Graña; dishes UR$100-185; ☽ lunch & dinner) keeps the fires blazing day and night, cooking pizzas, grilled meat and fish.

All buses stop on Plaza Independencia. **Cynsa** (cnr Ramírez & 25 de Mayo) has frequent services to La Paloma (UR$36, 30 minutes). Both **Rutas del Sol** and **COT** (cnr Ramírez & 25 de Agosto) each run several buses daily to Montevideo (UR$206, three hours) and Chuy (UR$137, two hours). Rutas del Sol also serves Punta del Diablo (UR$98, 1½ hours); COT has three daily buses to Maldonado (UR$88, 1¼ hours) and Punta del Este (UR$98, 1½ hours), and also goes to Barra de Valizas (UR$88, 1½ hours), stopping en route at La Paloma, La Pedrera (UR$49, 45 minutes) and the Cabo Polonio turnoff (UR$88, 1¼ hours).

LA PALOMA
☎ 0479 / pop 3400

Placid La Paloma, 28km south of Rocha, is less developed, less expensive and much less crowded than Punta del Este. It has attractive sandy beaches, great surfing and almost every important amenity except for Punta's hyperactive nightlife. On summer weekends the town often hosts free concerts down on the beach, making accommodations bookings essential.

Orientation
La Paloma occupies a small peninsula at the south end of Ruta 15. Its center, flanking Av Nicolás Solari, is small and compact. Streets radiating diagonally from the town center are named after classical deities, making for funny-sounding intersections such as Eros and Adonis.

Information
Antel (Av Nicolás Solari)
Banco de la República (cnr Av Nicolás Solari & Titania) Has an ATM.
Cyber del Navío (Av del Navío; internet per hr UR$15; ☽ 12:30pm-late Mon & Tue, 10am-late Wed-Sun)
Lavadero La Esquina (☎ 8176; cnr Antares & Aries; wash & dry per basket UR$80; ☽ 10:30am-7pm Mon-Sat)
Liga de Fomento y Turismo (☎ 6088; Av Nicolás Solari; ☽ 10am-10pm daily mid-Dec–Easter, 10am-4pm Tue-Sun rest of year) On the traffic circle.
Post office (Av Nicolás Solari)

Sights & Activities
The 1874 completion of **El Faro del Cabo Santa María** (admission UR$15; ☽ 8am-sunset), the local lighthouse, marked La Paloma's genesis as a summer beach resort. The unfinished first attempt collapsed in a violent storm, killing 17 French and Italian workers who are buried nearby. Outside is a solar clock using shadows cast by the lighthouse.

The best surfing beaches are Los Botes, Solari and Anaconda southwest of town, and La Aguada and La Pedrera to the north. Ruben at the very friendly **Peteco Surf Shop** (☎ 099-626726; petecosurf@adinet.com.uy; Av Nicolás Solari, btwn Av El Sirio & Av del Navío) rents boards for UR$250 a day, offers surfing classes for UR$500 (including equipment) and even has a couple of beachfront houses to rent (see p584). His staff speaks English.

The **Organización para la Conservación de Cetáceos** (OCC; ☎ 099-124144; info@ballenasenuruguay .com) sponsors scientific research and educational initiatives aimed at conserving the southern right whale. It offers all-day whale-watching tours (UR$700 per person, 10-person minimum, best viewing in September).

Laguna de Rocha, an ecological reserve protected under Uruguay's SNAP program (see the boxed text, p571), is a vast wetland 10km west of La Paloma with populations of black-necked swans, storks, spoonbills and other waterfowl. Local guide **Cecilia Olivet** (☎ 098-745708; colivet9@adinet.com.uy) offers tours in Spanish.

Sleeping
Complejo Turístico La Aguada (☎ 6239; www.com plejolaaguada.com; Ruta 15, Km 2.5; campsite for 2/3/4/5 people UR$260/340/420/460, 2-/4-/6-/8-bed cabañas UR$840/1100/1600/2000) This complex of campsites and cabins just outside town offers excellent access to Playa La Aguada. Buses from Rocha and *micros* from town will stop in front.

La Paloma Hostel (☎ 6396; www.lapalomahostel .com; Parque Andresito; HI member/nonmember UR$290/390; ☽ closed variably in winter) Just north of town, this thatched-roofed hostel in shady Parque Andresito has large dorms with sleeping lofts, an indoor-outdoor kitchen and a lounge area with fireplace.

La Balconada Hostel (☎ 94-198686; www.labalco nadahostel.com; Centauro s/n; dm from UR$400; ☜) La Paloma's newest hostel has an enviable location a stone's throw from La Balconada beach. Take a taxi from the bus station and the hostel will pick up the tab. Long-term guests get extra perks such as free use of bikes and disco passes.

Hotel La Tuna (☎ 6083; hotellatuna@gmail.com; cnr Neptuno & Juno; s/d/tr URS$1000/1300/1800, 4-person apt URS$2200; 🛜) The building is an eyesore, and some rooms are oppressively dark, but you can't get much closer to the water without a boat. Four rooms face the ocean, as does the 3rd-floor dining room.

Hotel Casino Cabo Santa María (☎ 6004; www .cabosantamaria.com; Av Nicolás Solari; s URS$1020-1260, d URS$1200-1400; 🖳 🛜) This rambling hotel attached to La Paloma's casino offers a variety of accommodations; all rooms come with wi-fi, plus free use of beach towels, chairs and umbrellas. More expensive rooms include air-con or ocean views.

Hotel Bahía (☎ 6029; www.elbahia.com.uy; cnr Av del Navío & Av del Sol; s URS$1300-1500, d URS$1400-1600, tr URS$1700-2000; 🛜) For central location and overall comfort, Bahía is hard to beat. Rooms are clean and bright, with firm mattresses, bedside reading lights and wi-fi. Superior rooms cost URS$200 extra, with balconies and updated bathrooms.

De Cara al Sol (☎ 099-626726; petecosurf@adinet .com.uy; Playa La Aguada; house for 5/6 people URS$3000/3800; 🖳) Large families and vanloads of surfers will appreciate these fully equipped beach houses with kitchen, washing machine and cable TV, directly across from Playa La Aguada, rented out by Ruben at Peteco Surf Shop.

Eating

Except as noted, the places below are open year-round. Many additional eateries open in summer.

Pizzeria Dacarlis (☎ 7873; Av Nicolás Solari s/n; pizzas URS$58-210, dishes URS$120-310; 🕚 noon-late) For wood-fired pizza, try this popular eatery on La Paloma's main street.

Rotisería Chivitería 7 Candelas (☎ 8253; Av Delfín s/n; dishes URS$120-230; 🕚 8:30am-3am Dec-Mar, 10am-3:30pm & 7-11pm Thu-Sun Apr-Nov) This unpretentious local hangout serves *chivitos*, chicken and *milanesas*. Eat in the cheerfully decorated interior room or on the tree-shaded front patio.

Bahía Restaurante (☎ 6029; cnr Av del Navío & Av del Sol; dishes URS$185-355; 🕚 lunch & dinner) Repeatedly recommended by locals as La Paloma's best restaurant, the Bahía specializes in seafood.

Punto Sur (☎ 9462; Centauro s/n; dishes URS$190-320; 🕚 noon-3am Christmas-Easter) For seafood with an ocean view, this summer-only place on Playa La Balconada is the obvious choice, featuring tapas, paella, grilled fish and homemade pasta.

Entertainment

In summer, take a midnight stroll out toward Playa La Aguada and follow your ears to La Paloma's three lively dance clubs: Hippie, Arachanes and Pogo, lined up in a row like the thatched-roofed houses of the Three Little Pigs. Other entertainment options include:

Perla Negra (Av del Puerto) This in-town restaurant and pub also has occasional live music.

Cine La Paloma (Av Nicolás Solari) Has twin screens showing movies throughout the summer.

Centro Cultural La Paloma (Parque Andresito) Shows movies at 7pm every Friday in off-season, and hosts other cultural events.

Getting There & Around

All buses use the new bus terminal near Aries and La Paloma. At least seven daily buses serve Montevideo (URS$235, four hours). Other destinations include La Pedrera (URS$29, 15 minutes), the Cabo Polonio turnoff (URS$59, 45 minutes), Barra de Valizas (URS$59, one hour), Punta del Diablo (UR$117, two hours) and Chuy (UR$157, three hours). The most frequently served destination is Rocha (URS$32, 30 minutes), from where better connections are available.

LA PEDRERA
☎ 0479 / pop 1000

Beautifully sited La Pedrera is popular with artists, surfers and families. The main street entering from Ruta 10 dead-ends atop a bluff with magnificent long views north toward Cabo Polonio and south toward La Paloma. Tourist services are limited.

Sleeping & Eating

Rates drop dramatically in the off-season.

La Casa de la Luna (☎ 094-602271; www.lacasadela luna.com.uy; Ruta 10, Km 230; campsite per person URS$200-240, dm URS$300-560, d URS$500-600; 🖳) To reach this hostel north of town, get off any Cabo Polonio–bound bus at Km 230, then walk toward the coast, bearing left as you go. There's a guest laundry and a comfy common area with internet, DVD player and fireplace, plus three upstairs doubles with distant ocean views. Bikes and surfing classes are available.

LA PALOMA

INFORMATION
Antel	1 B3
Banco de la República	2 B4
Cyber del Navío	3 B3
Lavadero La Esquina	4 A2
Liga de Fomento y Turismo	5 B2
Post Office	6 B3

SIGHTS & ACTIVITIES
El Faro del Cabo Santa María	7 B4
Peteco Surf Shop	8 B3

SLEEPING
Hotel Bahía	9 B3
Hotel Casino Cabo Santa María	10 B3
Hotel La Tuna	11 C3
La Balconada Hostel	12 A3
La Paloma Hostel	13 B1

EATING
Bahía Restaurante	(see 9)
Pizzeria Dacarlis	14 B3
Punto Sur	15 A3
Rotisería Chivitería 7 Candelas	16 A2

ENTERTAINMENT
Centro Cultural La Paloma	17 B2
Cine La Paloma	18 B3
Perla Negra	19 B2

TRANSPORT
Bus Terminal	20 A2

El Viajero La Pedrera Hostel (☎ 2252; www.elvia jerolapedrera.com; cnr Calles 3 & 11; dm per person without bathroom UR$300-460, d with bathroom UR$1000-1600; ⏰ Nov-Mar; 🖥 ☎) This friendly, newly opened hostel sits in the town center, only 500m from La Pedrera's beach. The sundeck, hammocks, and outdoor barbecue all invite mingling with other travelers.

Posada del Barco (☎ 2028; posadadelbarco@adinet.com .uy; Playa del Barco; s/d/tr/q UR$1480/1900/2520/3140; ✖ ☎) This classy and comfortable place has sweeping views of La Pedrera's southern beach. Its annual Easter Week jazz festival attracts performers from Argentina, Brazil and Cuba.

El Club (Calle Principal; dishes UR$125-195; ⏰ 11am-late Dec-Mar) This restaurant-cafe exudes vibrant, youthful energy, with trendy music and decor,

an outdoor deck and a working antique foosball table. El Club doubles as La Pedrera's cultural and social center, hosting live music, art exhibitions, yoga and dance classes, children's events and an annual short-film festival in January.

Costa Brava (☎ 2051; dishes UR$150-350; ⏰ lunch & dinner daily Dec-Mar, dinner Fri & Sat, lunch Sat & Sun Apr-Nov) Perched atop the bluffs overlooking the Atlantic, Costa Brava is all about seafood accompanied by an unbeatable view.

Getting There & Away

Regular buses to La Pedrera leave from Rocha and La Paloma. Some stop only at the town entrance on Ruta 10, from where it's a 15-minute walk. Others continue down La Pedrera's main street to the beachfront.

CABO POLONIO

☎ 0470 / pop 500

Northeast of La Paloma at Km 264.5 on Ruta 10 lies the turnoff to Cabo Polonio, one of Uruguay's wildest areas and home to its second-biggest sea-lion colony, near a tiny fishing village nestled in sand dunes. In September 2009 the region was placed under the protective jurisdiction of Uruguay's SNAP program (see boxed text, p571).

Sights & Activities

Cabo Polonio's striking lighthouse, **Faro Cabo Polonio** (admission UR$15; ☉ 8:30am-sunset), provides a fabulous perspective on the point itself, the sea-lion colony, and the surrounding dunes and islands.

Wildlife viewing is excellent year-round. Below the lighthouse, southern sea lions (*Otaria flavescens*) and South American fur seals (*Arctocephalus australis*) frolic on the rocks every month except February. You can also spot southern right whales just offshore from late August to early October, penguins on the beach in July, and the occasional southern elephant seal (*Mirounga leonina*) between January and March on nearby Isla de la Raza.

Surfing classes (UR$350 per hour) are available in high season. Inquire at the shop with the crazy surfing penguin logo, in the square where trucks from Ruta 10 drop you off.

Local accommodations can arrange **horseback rides** (UR$150 to UR$250 per hour) along the beach and into the surrounding dunes.

Sleeping & Eating

Places listed here are open year-round. Many locals also rent **houses** (winter from UR$500, summer from UR$1000). The hardest time to find accommodation is during the first two weeks of January. Off-season, prices drop dramatically.

Cabo Polonio Hostel (☎ 099-000305; www.cabopoloniohostel.com; dm UR$500 mid-Dec–Feb, dm/d UR$320/880 Mar–mid-Dec) Lit by candlelight and limited solar power, this sweet little hostel is a total delight, with friendly hosts, hammocks overlooking the beach and a wood stove inside for cooking and staying cozy on stormy nights. Highly recommended for anyone wanting to appreciate Cabo's rustic simplicity.

Posada y Parador La Cañada (☎ 099-550595, 099-972410; posadalacaniada@gmail.com; dm with/without bathroom UR$750/600) Near the far end of Cabo Polonio's southern beach, this inviting posada mixes dorms and private rooms in a two-story house with spacious decks overlooking the dunes and ocean. Amenities include fishing gear, surfboards, a kids' play area and meals made with fresh seafood and organic produce from the owners' garden.

Posada Mariemar (☎ 5164, 099-875260; posadamariemar@hotmail.com; r downstairs/upstairs UR$1900/2000) In business for nearly half a century, Posada Mariemar is right on the beach, and all rooms have ocean views. The restaurant serves tasty fish and homemade *buñuelos de algas* (seaweed fritters). It's a few hundred meters north of the lighthouse; just look for the beautiful angel mural out front.

Getting There & Away

Buses between La Paloma and Barra de Valizas stop at the access road to Cabo Polonio, where waiting 4WD trucks offer rides across the dunes into town (UR$60, 30 minutes). Alternatively, you can walk from the bus stop to Cabo Polonio, a strenuous 7km hike taking about two hours (bring water). Other ways to reach Cabo Polonio include the pretty 12km beach walk from Barra de Valizas (see the boxed text, opposite) or organized tours originating in neighboring towns.

LAGUNA DE CASTILLOS

Northwest of Cabo Polonio is the Laguna de Castillos, a vast coastal lagoon that shelters Uruguay's largest concentration of ombúes, graceful treelike plants whose anarchic growth pattern results in some rather fantastic shapes. In other parts of Uruguay the ombú is a solitary plant, but specimens here – some of them centuries old – grow in clusters, insulated by the lagoon from the bovine trampling that has spelled their doom elsewhere.

At **Monte de Ombúes** (☎ 099-295177), on the lagoon's western shore (near Km 267 on Ruta 10), brothers Marcos and Juan Carlos Oliveros, whose family received this land from the Portuguese crown in 1793, lead 2½- to three-hour excursions (UR$250 per person, five-person minimum). Tours begin with a 20-minute boat ride through a wetland teeming with cormorants, ibis, cranes and black swans, followed by a hike through the ombú forest. Departures are frequent in summer (pretty well anytime five people show up); other times of year, phone ahead for reservations.

URUGUAY

ourpick Guardia del Monte (☎ 0475-9064; www
.guardiadelmonte.com; Ruta 9, Km 261.5, Laguna de Castillos;
r per person incl 4 meals and excursions UR$2000), over-
looking the lagoon's northern shore, is at
the end of a 10km dead-end road. This now-
tranquil hideaway was established in the 18th
century as a Spanish guard post to protect
the Camino Real and the coastal frontier
from pirates and Portuguese marauders.
The lovely *estancia* house still oozes history, from the parlor displaying some 18th-
century maps and bird drawings to the kitch-
en's Danish woodstove salvaged from an 1884
shipwreck. Guests can explore the lakeshore
and the surrounding ombú forest on foot
or on horseback. Tasty meals are served on
the ancient brick patio or in the cozy dining
room, where a roaring fire beckons on chilly
nights. Access to Guardia del Monte is from
Ruta 9, a few kilometers south of the town
of Castillos.

BARRA DE VALIZAS

This tiny beach town 4km off Ruta 10 has
largely escaped the development creeping
eastward from Punta del Este. Slow-paced
Valizas has friendly dogs and inquisitive
horses wandering the streets, and dunes
stretching toward Cabo Polonio.

The Valizas-Polonio area is rich in history.
This notoriously treacherous stretch of coastline caused numerous shipwrecks over the
centuries. South toward Cabo Polonio, the
tallest point on the horizon is 58m-high **Cerro
Buena Vista**, a rocky outcropping draped in
sand that once formed the border between
Spanish and Portuguese America, as agreed
in the Madrid Treaty of 1750. The base of the
stone that marked the border is still embedded here; the carved part bearing the names
of Spain and Portugal is displayed at Fortaleza
de Santa Teresa (p589), 35km north.

Businesses listed here are on Valiza's main
dirt street, which runs perpendicular to the
waterfront. The town's bus stop is on a parallel
street one block south.

The very basic **Valizas Hostel** (☎ 0475-4045;
hostelvalizas@hotmail.com; dm UR$280; ☺ Nov-Mar) has
multibed dorms, kitchen facilities and hot
showers.

Nearby are Supermercado El Puente (a
year-round grocery store) and **Restaurante
Hipocampo** (☎ 0475-4053, 099-828601; dishes UR$100-
190), open daily in summer and cooking meals
upon request in the off-season – just knock!

Rutas del Sol operates at least three buses
daily to/from Montevideo (UR$294, 4½
hours).

MAKING TRACKS ON URUGUAY'S NORTHERN BEACHES

With so many kilometers of uninterrupted white sand, Uruguay's northern department of Rocha
is a great place for beach walks.

Barra de Valizas to Cabo Polonio

This adventurous approach to Cabo Polonio allows you to fully appreciate the town's isolation
and the dramatic visual impact of its lighthouse. From Barra de Valizas, follow the beach south
to the river (about 20 minutes). Locals will ferry you across for about UR$50 – knock on doors if
necessary. From here it's a stunningly wild and beautiful 12km walk along the ocean. The beach
is more or less flat, but sand dunes rise steeply just inland. Depending on the season you may
see sea lions or whales offshore, or cows grazing on the dune grasses. Near the halfway mark,
you'll round a point and get your first view of Cabo Polonio's lighthouse, at the far end of a
seemingly endless beach. Follow the light into town.

Punta del Diablo to Parque Nacional Santa Teresa

From the Punta del Diablo bus stop, stroll down to the waterfront and turn north. Within half
an hour you'll cross over a point and descend to Playa Grande, a long sandy beach at the
southernmost edge of Parque Nacional Santa Teresa. Just beyond a wooden observation platform on the left, look for a campground and a road coming down to meet the beach. You can
continue exploring north along the beach (the road goes on for several kilometers), or follow
the road 45 minutes inland through a hilly eucalyptus forest to the Capatacía (park headquarters), where any Rutas del Sol or Cynsa bus will whisk you back to Punta del Diablo (UR$25,
15 minutes).

PUNTA DEL DIABLO
☎ 0477 / pop 1000

Once a sleepy fishing village, Punta del Diablo has long since become a prime summer getaway for Uruguayans and Argentines, and has increasingly established itself as the epicenter of Uruguay's backpacker beach scene. Waves of seemingly uncontrolled development have pushed further inland and along the coast in recent years, but the stunning shoreline remains largely intact, and the influx of outsiders has added an infectious dose of youthful energy. To escape the crowds, come outside the Christmas to February peak season.

Information & Orientation

Buses arrive in the town's traditional center, a sandy 'plaza' just inland from the ocean. From here, small dirt roads fan out in all directions. To get to the marina and the hostels listed following, head along the main street downhill 200m to the waterfront and continue northeast along the shoreline.

Note that at the time of research there were still no ATMs in Punta del Diablo. This was scheduled to change in early 2010, but it's still best to bring cash with you, as few businesses accept credit cards and the nearest big town is Chuy on the Brazilian border.

Sights & Activities

A big part of Punta del Diablo's appeal is simply taking life as it comes. During the day you can rent surfboards or horses along the town's main beach, or take the hour-long trek north to Parque Nacional Santa Teresa (see the boxed text, p587). In the evening there are sunsets to watch, spontaneous bonfires and drum sessions to drop in on…you get the idea.

On the shores of Laguna Negra, 10km northwest of town, the **Estación Biológica Potrerillo de Santa Teresa** harbors a rich variety of bird and plant life and several 3000-year-old indigenous burial mounds. Three-hour tours can be arranged by calling ☎ 0470-6028.

Sleeping

Cabañas are the accommodations of choice in Punta del Diablo. Note that this term applies to just about anything: from rustic-to-a-fault shacks to custom-built designer condos with all modern conveniences. Most *cabañas* have kitchens and require you to bring your own bedding. A couple of nice ones are listed here, but available offerings literally change month

to month. If you need help finding something, ask at the pharmacy, supermarket or newsstand in town, or check online at www .portaldel diablo.com.uy.

The town's hostel scene has also taken off dramatically in recent years, and there are several offerings beyond those listed below.

Please note that all prices listed here are for the period between Christmas and February, when rates skyrocket. Low-season rates may be as much as 75% cheaper.

La Casa de las Boyas (☎ 2074; www.lacasadelasboyas .com; Playa del Rivero; dm URS$400-660, apt URS$2400-2800; 🖳 🛜 🖳) Ten minutes' walk north of the bus stop, this hostel perched just above the beach offers a guest kitchen, a pool, dorms of varying sizes and two brand-new apartments equipped with kitchens.

El Diablo Tranquilo (☎ 2647; www.eldiablotranquilo .com; dm URS$440-560, d URS$1280-2320; 🖳 🛜) Setting the new standard for budget accommodations in Punta del Diablo, this exceptionally well-designed hostel is the brainchild of expat American Brian Meissner. Follow the devilish red glow through the entryway, past the animated crowd on the circular fireside couch, and you'll find a mix of dorms and cushy doubles, with many perks. Along with wi-fi, high-speed computers, hammocks, a guest kitchen and laundry service, there are Paypal cash advances, bike and surfboard rentals, yoga and language classes and horseback excursions. The hostel's bar-restaurant offers reasonably priced meals, with beach service, and the newest rooms above the restaurant have fireplaces, direct ocean views and great sound systems. Unsurprisingly, the average guest stay is nearly a week, and things can book up even in winter.

Del Norte Vengo y En El Sur Me Quedo (☎ 099-878357; jasypo2876@yahoo.com; d/q URS$1800/2000) Two blocks north of the bus stop, these colorful two-level *cabañas* have upstairs decks, ocean views, and satiny curtains and bedspreads. The young owners have lived in the US and speak good English.

Aieta & Yoquese (☎ 099-274604; www.portaldeldia blo.com.uy; cabañas URS$2400) These two beachfront *cabañas* sleep seven people each.

Eating

In high season, simply stroll the beachfront and you'll have your pick of seafood eateries and snack shacks by the dozen. Most restaurants, however, close down completely in winter. A dependable year-round choice is the lively bar-restaurant at El Diablo Tranquilo. Another off-season option is **Il Tano** (☎ 2690; Calle 9 btwn Calles 12 & 14), a restaurant in the Paseo del Rivero shopping area that brings in a rotating cast of local chefs Thursday through Sunday.

Getting There & Away

Rutas del Sol and Cynsa each run at least two daily buses from Punta del Diablo's bus stop to Montevideo (UR$294, five hours), Rocha (UR$98, 1½ hours) and Chuy (UR$49, one hour). For Parque Nacional Santa Teresa (UR$29, 15 minutes), take any Chuy-bound bus, and get off at either the Capatacía (park headquarters) or Fortaleza de Santa Teresa, near the park's northwestern corner.

If coming from Montevideo, make sure to take one of the buses that come directly into Punta del Diablo (at the time of research, these included Rutas del Sol buses leaving Montevideo at 7am and 2:30pm, and Cynsa buses leaving Montevideo at 8:40am and 4:15pm). Many other buses only stop at the town entrance on Ruta 9, which leaves you with a 4km walk into Punta del Diablo.

PARQUE NACIONAL SANTA TERESA

This **national park** (☎ 0477-2101; www.ejercito.mil .uy/cal/sepae/sta_teresa.htm), 35km south of Chuy, is administered by the army and attracts many Uruguayan and Brazilian visitors to its relatively uncrowded beaches. It offers 1200 dispersed campsites in eucalyptus and pine groves, a very small zoo and a plant conservatory. Bare-bones campsites cost UR$50/30 per person in summer/winter; developed sites with water and electricity cost UR$80/50. There are also various grades of *cabañas* for rent; in January, prices range from UR$1100 for a basic A-frame to UR$3220 for a fancier oceanfront unit; between March and November these rates get slashed in half.

Many buses between Chuy and Rocha stop at the Capatacía (park headquarters), where there's a phone, post office, market, bakery and **restaurant** (dishes UR$90-250; 10am-9pm).

The park's star attraction, 4km further north on Ruta 9, is the impressive hilltop **Fortaleza de Santa Teresa** (admission UR$15; 10am-7pm daily Dec-Mar, 10am-6pm Thu-Sun Apr-Nov), begun by the Portuguese in 1762 and finished by the Spaniards after its capture in 1793. At the park's northeastern corner is **Cerro Verde**, a coastal bluff protected under Uruguay's SNAP program (see the boxed text, p571).

CHUY

☎ 0474 / pop 11,000

Warning: if you're not on your way to or from Brazil, you're seriously lost, buddy. Turn around and go back. But while you're here you may as well check out the pirated CDs, contraband cigarettes and duty-free shops lining both sides of Chuy's main street.

Orientation

Av Artigas is the main drag into town from Ruta 9. Crossing north into Brazil, it becomes Av Argentina (for a full list of name changes, see the maps posted throughout town). Chuy's main square is one block south of the border. Running east–west along the border itself is the town's four-lane commercial thoroughfare, called Av Brasil on the Uruguayan side, Av Uruguaí on the Brazilian side.

Information

If proceeding into Brazil, complete Uruguayan emigration formalities at the **customs post** (Ruta 9), 1km south of town, where you'll also find the **National Tourism Ministry** (☎ 4599).

Uruguayan pesos are worthless any distance into Brazil. There are several exchange houses along the border and on Av Artigas. **Banco de la República Oriental** (cnr Av Artigas & Ventura) has an ATM across from the main square. The **post office** (Av Artigas 322) is a few blocks further south.

Sleeping & Eating

If you've got a long layover between buses, Chuy has several affordable hotels and eateries, plus a fancy tourist *estancia* west of town.

Hotel Vitoria (☎ 2280; Numancia 143; r per person UR$380) Simple, clean and family-run, it's far enough east of the hubbub to offer a decent night's sleep.

Fortín de San Miguel (☎ 6607; www.elfortin .com, in Spanish; Ruta 10, Km 10; s/d UR$1100/1600;) You'll think you've died and gone to – well, someplace much nicer than Chuy – when you see the palatial rooms and pool at this colonial-style *estancia* in verdant countryside across from Fuerte San Miguel. The attached restaurant is reasonably priced.

Panadería Gianinn (☎ 4390; cnr Av Artigas & Guaiba; snacks from UR$15; 7:30am-9pm) Just follow your nose to this aromatic bakery, which also sells sandwiches, yogurt and juice.

Miravos (☎ 4180; Av Brasil 507; dishes UR$120-340) Miravos serves a varied menu, with comfortable indoor booths and sunny sidewalk seating.

Getting There & Away

Bus companies **COT** (Olivera 111), **Cotec/Rutas del Sol** (Olivera 121) and **Cynsa/Núñez** (Olivera 125) operate out of adjoining offices half a block south of the border, just off the northwest corner of Chuy's central plaza. Several daily buses go to Montevideo (UR$333, 5½ hours), stopping at intermediate points along the coast. **Tureste** (Mauro Silva 109) serves Treinta y Tres (UR$157, three hours) twice daily from its office two blocks west of the plaza.

The Brazilian *rodoviária* (bus terminal) is at the corner of Venezuela and Chile, two blocks north of the border. Destinations include Rio Grande (R$34, four hours), Pelotas (R$37, four hours), Porto Alegre (R$74/87 regular/semidirect, seven hours) and São Paulo (R$225, 26 hours).

FUERTE SAN MIGUEL

This pink-granite **fortress** (Ruta 19, Km 9; admission UR$15; ◷ 10am-7pm daily Dec-Mar, 10am-6pm Thu-Sun Apr-Nov), 9km west of Chuy, was built in 1734 during hostilities between Spain and Portugal. Today it forms the centerpiece of Parque Nacional San Miguel. Its entrance, guarded by a moat, overlooks the border from a high, isolated point. When it's closed you can still glimpse the interior and visit the nearby **Museo Criollo/Museo Indígena**, with indoor and outdoor displays on gaucho, indigenous and pioneer life, and an impressive array of carts and machinery. When open, you can tour the fort's various rooms, reconstructed with period furnishings, and take in the views from the ramparts.

Cotec runs a few daily buses from Chuy to the fortress (UR$29, 10 minutes), or you can pay UR$100 for a taxi.

URUGUAY DIRECTORY

ACCOMMODATIONS

Uruguay has an excellent network of hostels and campgrounds, especially along the coast. Some offer discounts to ISIC or HI cardholders. General hostel information is available in Montevideo from **HI Uruguay** (☎ 02-900-5749; www.hihostels.com; Paraguay 1212). Other low-end options include *hospedajes* (family homes) and *residenciales* (budget hotels).

Posadas (inns) are available in all price ranges and tend to be homier than hotels. Hotels are ranked from one to five stars, according to amenities.

> **PRACTICALITIES**
>
> ■ Uruguay runs on 220V, 50Hz. The most common plug uses two round pins with no earthing/grounding pin.
>
> ■ Toilets are of the sit-down variety – dispose of used toilet paper in the wastepaper basket provided.
>
> ■ Newspapers are listed at p541.

Country *estancias turísticas* (marked with blue National Tourism Ministry signs) provide lodging on farms (see the boxed text, p564).

ACTIVITIES

Uruguay's Atlantic coast is a paradise for surfers and wildlife watchers. Punta del Diablo, La Paloma and Punta del Este all get excellent waves, while Cabo Polonio and the coastal lagoons of Rocha department are great for whale- and bird-watching, respectively.

Punta del Este is the place to head for the upmarket beach scene, bars and snazzier beach activities such as parasailing, windsurfing and jet skiing.

Horseback riding is very popular in the interior and can be arranged on most tourist *estancias* (see the boxed text, p564).

BOOKS

Compared with neighboring countries, surprisingly little material is available on Uruguay in English. William Henry Hudson's novel *The Purple Land* (1916) is a classic portrait of 19th-century Uruguayan life. A good starting point for looking at the politics of modern Uruguay is Martin Weinstein's *Uruguay, Democracy at the Crossroads*. For an account of Uruguay's Dirty War, see Lawrence Weschler's *A Miracle, A Universe: Settling Accounts with Torturers*. For a sympathetic explanation of the rise of the 1960s guerrilla movements, see María Esther Gilio's *The Tupamaro Guerrillas*.

For Uruguayan literature, see p537.

BUSINESS HOURS

Most shops open weekdays and Saturday from 8:30am to 1pm, then close until mid-afternoon and reopen until 7pm or 8pm. Banks are generally open weekday afternoons only.

If serving breakfast, restaurants open around 8am. Lunch is generally between noon and 3pm, and dinner is generally not eaten until after 9pm or even as late as midnight in urban areas. Bars may open as early as 6pm, but often remain empty until at least 1am, when everybody finally gets around to going out.

COSTS
Throughout this chapter, accommodations are generally categorized by price: budget (up to UR$750 per double), midrange (UR$750 to UR$1500 per double) and top end (over UR$1500 per double). Unless otherwise mentioned, prices include tax and are high-season rates. Please note that summertime prices in glitzy Punta del Este will often be at least double what you'd pay elsewhere in Uruguay.

For eating reviews, listings are categorized by the average price of a main course: budget (up to UR$125), midrange (UR$125 to UR$250) and top end (over UR$250).

Travelers' costs are somewhat higher than in Argentina.

COURSES
Cafes in tourist areas often have noticeboards advertising private Spanish lessons. Formal language classes and tango lessons are also available in Montevideo (see p547).

DANGERS & ANNOYANCES
Uruguay is still one of the safest countries in South America, but petty street crime in Montevideo has risen in recent years. Visitors to the capital should take precautions as in any large city (see p541).

EMBASSIES & CONSULATES
Unless otherwise specified, the following addresses and phone numbers are in Montevideo (area code ☎ 02); many are east and south of downtown.
Argentina Consulate (Map pp542-3; ☎ 902-8623; WF Aldunate 1281); Embassy (Map pp542-3; ☎ 902-8166; Cuareim 1470); Colonia (Map p556; ☎ 052-22093; Av General Flores 209); Fray Bentos (☎ 056-23225; Treinta y Tres 3237); Paysandú (Map p566; ☎ 072-22253; Leandro Gómez 1034); Punta del Este (Map p577; ☎ 446162; cnr Gorlero & Calle 19; ☒ mid-Dec–mid-Mar); Salto (☎ 073-32931; Artigas 1162)
Bolivia (☎ 708-3573; Prudencio de Pena 2469)
Brazil (Map pp542-3; ☎ 901-2024; Convención 1343, 6th fl); Chuy (☎ 0474-2049; Fernández 147)
Canada (Map pp542-3; ☎ 902-2030; Plaza Independencia 749, Oficina 102)

Chile (Map pp542-3; ☎ 916-2346; 25 de Mayo 575)
France (Map pp542-3; ☎ 1705-0000; Av Uruguay 853)
Germany (Map pp542-3; ☎ 902-5222; La Cumparsita 1435)
Israel (☎ 400-4164; Bulevar Artigas 1585)
Italy (☎ 480-7080; Jorge Canning 2535)
Japan (☎ 418-7645; Bulevar Artigas 953)
Netherlands (☎ 711-2956; Leyenda Patria 2880, 2nd fl)
Paraguay (☎ 707-2138; Bulevar Artigas 1256)
Peru (☎ 707-1420; Obligado 1384)
Spain (☎ 708-0048; Libertad 2738)
Switzerland (☎ 711-5545; Federico Abadie 2936, 11th fl)
UK (☎ 622-3630; Marco Bruto 1073)
USA (☎ 418-7777; Lauro Muller 1776)

FESTIVALS & EVENTS
Uruguay's Carnaval (see p547) lasts for over a month and is livelier than Argentina's. Semana Santa (Holy Week) has become known as Semana Turismo – many Uruguayans travel out of town, and finding accommodations is tricky during this time. Other noteworthy events include the beer festival in Paysandú (p565) and Tacuarembó's Fiesta de la Patria Gaucha (p570).

GAY & LESBIAN TRAVELERS
Uruguay has gotten more GLBT-friendly in recent years. In January 2008 it became the first Latin American country to recognize same-sex civil unions nationwide (in 2002 Buenos Aires had been the first Latin American city to recognize same-sex unions).

An excellent English-language web resource is **Out in Uruguay** (www.outinuruguay.com).

HOLIDAYS
Año Nuevo (New Year's Day) January 1
Epifanía (Epiphany) January 6
Viernes Santo/Pascua (Good Friday/Easter) March/April (dates vary)
Desembarco de los 33 (Return of the 33 Exiles) April 19; honors the exiles who returned to Uruguay in 1825 to liberate the country from Argentine support
Día del Trabajador (Labor Day) May 1
Batalla de Las Piedras (Battle of Las Piedras) May 18; commemorates a major battle of the fight for independence
Natalicio de Artigas (Artigas' Birthday) June 19
Jura de la Constitución (Constitution Day) July 18
Día de la Independencia (Independence Day) August 25
Día de la Raza (Columbus Day) October 12
Día de los Muertos (All Souls' Day) November 2
Navidad (Christmas Day) December 25

URUGUAY

INTERNET ACCESS

Internet cafes are commonplace in cities and larger towns; access costs UR$15 to UR$20 an hour. Many Antel (state telephone company) offices also provide internet for UR$19 an hour.

INTERNET RESOURCES

Mercopress News Agency (www.mercopress.com) Montevideo-based internet news agency.

National Tourism Ministry (www.turismo.gub.uy) Government tourist information.

Olas y Vientos (www.olasyvientos.com.uy, in Spanish) Everything you need to know about Uruguay's surf scene.

Uruguayan Embassy in Washington, DC (www .uruwashi.org) Historical, cultural and economic information on Uruguay.

LANGUAGE

Spanish is the official language and is universally understood. Uruguayans fluctuate between use of the *voseo* and *tuteo* in everyday speech (see the boxed text, p630), and both are readily understood. Along the Brazilian border, many people speak both Spanish and Portuguese, or speak *portuñol*, an unusual hybrid of the two. One common influence from Brazilian Portuguese is the Uruguayan usage of '*ta*,' short for '*está bien*' ('OK'), often in question form. See the Language chapter (p629) for more on Latin American Spanish.

LEGAL MATTERS

Illegal drugs are freely available in Uruguay, but getting caught with them is about as much fun as anywhere else in the world, and Uruguayan police and officials are not as bribe-hungry as many of their South American counterparts.

MAPS

ITMB (http://shop.itmb.ca) publishes a useful map depicting Montevideo on one side and Uruguay on the other. In Uruguay, Ancap service stations sell good road maps. Two other good sources in Montevideo are the **Automóvil Club del Uruguay** (☎ 02-1707; Yí 1422) and **Instituto Geográfico Militar** (☎ 02-481-6868; cnr 8 de Octubre & Abreu), east of the center.

MONEY

The unit of currency is the *peso uruguayo* (UR$). Banknote values are 20, 50, 100, 200, 500 and 1000. There are coins of 50 centavos, and one, two, five and 10 pesos.

US dollars are commonly accepted in major tourist hubs, where top-end hotels and even some budget accommodations quote US$ prices. However, beware of poor exchange rates at hotel desks. In many cases, you'll still come out ahead paying in pesos. Away from the touristed areas, dollars are of limited use.

Most upmarket hotels, restaurants and shops accept credit cards.

ATMs

In all but the smallest interior towns, getting cash with your ATM card is easy. Machines marked with the green Banred or blue Redbrou logo serve all major international banking networks, including Cirrus, Visa, MasterCard and Maestro.

ATMs dispense bills in multiples of 100 pesos. It's advisable to request smaller bills (ie take out UR$900 rather than UR$1000, UR$1900 rather than UR$2000 etc) to avoid getting stuck with large bills. The UR$1000 notes, in particular, can be difficult to change even in big cities.

Many ATMs dispense US dollars, designated as U$S, but only in multiples of US$100.

Exchange Rates

Exchange rates at press time included the following:

Country	Unit	UR$
Argentina	AR$1	4.94
Australia	A$1	17.35
Brazil	R$1	10.34
Canada	C$1	18.70
Euro zone	€1	25.75
Japan	¥100	20.75
UK	UK£1	28.60
USA	US$1	19.20

Exchanging Money

There are *casas de cambio* in Montevideo, Colonia, the Atlantic beach resorts and border towns such as Chuy. They keep longer hours than banks but often offer lower rates.

Traveler's Checks

Traveler's checks can still be cashed at some banks and *casas de cambio*, but you'll get better rates and avoid commissions by simply withdrawing cash on your ATM card.

POST

Postal rates are reasonable, though service can be slow. If something is truly important, send it by registered mail or private courier.

SHOPPING

Bargains include leather clothing and accessories, woolen clothing and fabrics, agates and gems, ceramics, woodcrafts and decorated *mate* gourds.

Bargaining isn't part of Uruguayan culture, and serious red-in-the-face, veins-out-on-forehead haggling is completely out of sync with the whole Uruguayan psyche. Chances are you're paying what the locals are.

TELEPHONE

Uruguay's country code is ☎ 598. Antel is the state telephone company, with offices in every town. There are also private *locutorios* (telephone offices) everywhere.

Public phones require prepaid cards, sold in values of 25, 50, 100 and 200 pesos, available at Antel offices or newspaper kiosks.

Many internet cafes have headphone-microphone setups and Skype installed on their computers.

Cell (Mobile) Phones

Rather than use expensive roaming plans, many travelers bring an unlocked cell phone (or buy a cheap one here) and simply insert a local SIM card. These are readily available at most kiosks, as are prepaid cards to recharge your credit.

Note that it's best to unlock your phone in your home country, since reliable providers of this service are hard to find in Uruguay. Also, Uruguayan SIM card rates are relatively steep (around UR$7 per minute, even for local calls). Long-term visitors can save money with a local roaming plan; for example, both Movistar and Ancel offer iPhone plans charging UR$2 to UR$4 per minute for international calls.

TOURIST INFORMATION

The **National Tourism Ministry** (www.turismo.gub .uy) operates 13 offices around the country. They distribute excellent free maps for each of Uruguay's 19 departments, along with specialized brochures on *estancia* tourism, Carnaval and other subjects of interest to travelers. Most towns also have a muncipal tourist office on the plaza or at the bus terminal.

TOURS

Tour operators in Montevideo can arrange *estancia*-based tours with an emphasis on horseback riding, birding and other outdoor activities. See the boxed text, p564 for more.

TRAVELERS WITH DISABILITIES

Uruguay is slowly beginning to plan for travelers with special needs. In Montevideo you'll find newly constructed ramps and dedicated bathrooms in high-profile destinations such as Plaza Independencia and Teatro Solis, and disabled access on the new CA1 bus line. However, there's still a long way to go. Many budget hotels have at least one set of stairs and no elevator. On the bright side, taxis are cheap and locals are glad to help however they can.

VISAS

Nationals of Western Europe, Australia, the USA, Canada and New Zealand automatically receive a 90-day tourist card, renewable for another 90 days. Other nationals may require visas. For extensions, visit the **Dirección Nacional de la Migración** (Map pp542-3; ☎ 02-916-0471; Misiones 1513; ☿ 9:15am-2:30pm Mon-Fri) in Montevideo, or local offices in border towns.

VOLUNTEERING

All Uruguayan organizations accepting volunteers require a minimum commitment of one month, and many require at least basic Spanish proficiency. Following are some Montevideo-based groups:

Academia Uruguay (☎ 02-915-2496; www.academia uruguay.com; Juan Carlos Gómez 1408) Language school offering volunteer opportunities in Montevideo.

Karumbé (☎ 098-614201; www.karumbe.org) Sea turtle conservation.

WOMEN TRAVELERS

Uruguayans are no slouches when it comes to *machismo*, but women are generally treated with respect, and traveling alone is safer here than in many other Latin American countries.

TRANSPORTATION IN URUGUAY

GETTING THERE & AWAY
Entering the Country

Uruguay requires passports of all foreigners, except those from neighboring countries (who need only national identification cards).

Passports are necessary for many everyday transactions, such as checking into hotels and cashing traveler's checks.

Air

International passengers leaving from Montevideo's Carrasco airport pay a departure tax of US$31. For addresses and telephone numbers of airline offices, see p553.

EUROPE

Both Iberia and the Uruguayan carrier Pluna have direct flights between Montevideo and Madrid. One-stop service is available from London to Montevideo on Iberia (via Madrid) and TAM (via São Paulo). Air France, KLM and Lufthansa connect Montevideo to other European destinations via Buenos Aires or São Paulo.

SOUTH AMERICA

There are frequent flights between Carrasco and Buenos Aires' Aeroparque, as well as between Aeroparque and Punta del Este. Pluna and Aerolíneas Argentinas offer the most flights.

Other South American countries served by direct flights from Montevideo include Brazil, Chile, Paraguay and Peru. See p553 for more details.

USA

American Airlines has direct flights between Montevideo and Miami. LanChile has flights from Los Angeles, Miami and New York with a change of planes in Santiago. Other airlines connect through Buenos Aires' Ezeiza airport or São Paulo, Brazil.

Land & Sea

Uruguay shares borders with the Argentine province of Entre Ríos and the southern Brazilian state of Rio Grande do Sul. Major highways and bus services are generally good.

ARGENTINA

The most common way of traveling between Uruguay and Argentina is by launch or ferry (the latter sometimes involving bus connections through Colonia). The three routes are: Montevideo to Buenos Aires (p554); Colonia to Buenos Aires (p560); and Carmelo to Tigre (p562).

By land, three bridges cross the Río Uruguay between Uruguay and Argentina: from Fray Bentos to Gualeguaychú (closed indefinitely at time of writing); from Paysandú to Colón; and from Salto to Concordia. Direct buses from Montevideo to Buenos Aires (traveling via Paysandú-Colón until the Fray Bentos-

Gualeguaychú bridge reopens) are slower and less convenient than the land/river combinations across the Río de la Plata.

BRAZIL

There are five land crossings between Uruguay and Brazil. The most popular one connects Chuy, Uruguay, to Chuí, Brazil (see p589). The remaining crossings, from east to west, are: Río Branco to Jaguarão; Aceguá to Bagé; Rivera to Santana do Livramento; Artigas to Quaraí; and Bella Unión to Barra do Quaraí. It's possible to use the latter crossing as a route to Iguazú Falls, but the trip through Brazil is slow and difficult.

GETTING AROUND

Bus

Buses are comfortable, fares are reasonable and distances are short. Most companies distribute free timetables. In the few cities that lack terminals, all companies are within easy walking distance of each other, usually around the main plaza.

Buses leave frequently for destinations all around the country, so reservations are unnecessary except during holiday periods. Be aware that on peak-travel dates a single company may run multiple departures at the same hour, in which case they'll mark a bus number on your ticket; check with the driver to make sure you're boarding the right bus, or you may find yourself in the 'right' seat on the wrong bus!

Most towns with central bus terminals have a fee-based left-luggage facility. Where there's no terminal you can usually leave your bags with the company you're ticketed to leave with later in the day.

Car & Motorcycle

Visitors to Uruguay who are staying less than 90 days need only bring a valid driver's license from their home country. Uruguayan drivers are extremely considerate, and even bustling Montevideo is quite sedate compared with Buenos Aires.

Uruguay imports all its oil. Unleaded gasoline cost UR$29.60 a liter at the time of research.

AUTOMOBILE ASSOCIATIONS

The **Automóvil Club del Uruguay** (☎ 02-902-4792; Av Libertador General Lavalleja 1532, Montevideo) has good maps and information.

HIRE

Economy cars rent for around UR$900 a day in the low season, with tax and insurance included. If you shop around, multiweek rentals can work out even less (as low as UR$700 per day), sometimes with discounts for cash payment. Online bookings are another potential money-saver. Note that most credit-card companies' automatic LDW (loss-damage-waiver) insurance covers rentals in Uruguay.

ROAD RULES & HAZARDS

Drivers are expected to use headlights in daytime on all highways. People will flash their lights to remind you. In most towns, alternating one-way streets are the rule, with an arrow marking the allowed direction of travel. Outside of Montevideo, most intersections have neither a stop sign nor a traffic light; right of way is determined by who reaches the corner first. This can be nerve-wracking for the uninitiated! Arbitrary police stops and searches are rare.

Outside the capital and coastal tourist areas, traffic is minimal and poses few problems. Roads are generally in good shape, but some interior roads can be rough. Keep an eye out for livestock and wildlife. Even in Montevideo's busy downtown, horse-drawn carts still operate, hauling trash or freight.

Hitchhiking

It's common to see locals hitchhiking in rural areas, as gas is expensive and relatively few people own cars. Safety is not as serious a concern as in most other countries, although foreigners looking to hitch a ride may encounter some raised eyebrows. See p620 for the risks of hitching.

Local Transportation

Taxis, *remises* (radio-dispatched taxis) and local buses are similar to those in Argentina. Taxis are metered, and drivers calculate fares using meter readings and a photocopied chart. Between 10pm and 6am, and on weekends and holidays, fares are 20% higher. There's a small additional charge for luggage, and passengers generally tip the driver by rounding fares up to the next multiple of five or ten pesos. City bus service is excellent in Montevideo and urban hubs such as Maldonado–Punta del Este, while *micros* (minibuses) form the backbone of the local transit network in smaller coastal towns such as La Paloma.

DIRECTORY

Directory

CONTENTS

ACCOMMODATIONS

Accommodations in Argentina range from campgrounds to five-star luxury hotels, with excellent options in all categories. At the more tourist-oriented hotels, staff members usually speak a smattering of English, though at more provincial accommodations you'll need to learn the Spanish basics.

All but the cheapest hotels have private bathrooms, and most hotels include breakfast – usually *medialunas* (croissants) and weak coffee or tea – in the price. Generally, assume both are included as you flip through listings in this book. Many hotels provide temporary luggage storage for travelers who have late-afternoon or evening flights or bus trips.

Some hotels, particularly pricier hotels in tourist hot spots such as Patagonia, operate on a two-tier price system (see the boxed text, below), charging foreigners more than nationals.

For apartment rentals in the capital, see p109. For information on relocating to Argentina, see p607. Also note that many hotels offer discounted rates for extended stays, usually a week or more. Make sure to negotiate this *before* you begin your stay.

Prices

Throughout this book, accommodations are generally categorized by price: budget (up to AR$180 per double), midrange (from AR$180 to AR$250 per double) and top end (over AR$250 per double). Prices in Argentina have increased steadily over the last several years (many places charge twice what they did in 2003), and they may continue to do so. To avoid getting price shock, it's helpful to supplement your book research with a good

---

TWO-TIER PRICING

With the devaluation of the peso in 2002, Argentina became a highly affordable destination practically overnight. With the subsequent upswing in tourism, however, the annoying two-tier pricing system emerged: businesses in certain areas (mostly in Buenos Aires, but also in Patagonia and parts of the Lake District) charge Argentines one price and foreigners a higher price, regardless of whether they're banking euros, pounds or dollars. While you won't find this everywhere, you will encounter it at some *estancias*, national parks, the national airline (Aerolíneas Argentinas) and upmarket hotels throughout the country.

Many accommodations quote prices in US dollars rather than pesos. This doesn't necessarily mean you're getting charged more than Argentines; the peso is just so unstable that places prefer to use a currency that isn't always fluctuating.

PRACTICALITIES

- Argentina uses the metric system for weights and measures.

- Electrical current is 220 volts, 50 cycles, and there are two types of electric plugs: either with two rounded prongs or with three angled flat prongs. Adapters from one to the other are available.

- Buenos Aires' two leading daily newspapers, available throughout Argentina, are *Clarín* (www .clarin.com, in Spanish) and *La Nación* (www.lanacion.com.ar, in Spanish). English-language dailies include the *Buenos Aires Herald* (www.buenosairesherald.com; available at newsstands in most large cities) and the *Argentimes* (www.theargentimes.com; look for it at various tourist destinations). Also see Media, p93.

- In Buenos Aires, tune into FM 92.7 for 24-hour tango or FM 98.3 for Argentine rock.

- In Argentine addresses, the word *local* refers to a suite or office. If an address has 's/n' – short for *sin numero* (without number) – the address has no street number.

---

dose of internet research. For information on the rising cost of travel in Argentina, see the boxed text (p19).

That said, in Buenos Aires you can land excellent accommodations for under AR$200, and throughout the country AR$130 will buy you a comfortable double room. Hostels in Buenos Aires charge AR$25 to AR$35 per bed and from around AR$90 for a private double. Rates are lower outside the capital: figure on about AR$22 for a dorm bed and AR$60 for a private double.

Accommodations prices in this book, to the best of our knowledge, all include tax and are general high-season rates (although not peak seasons like Christmas or Easter). Budget and midrange hotels almost always include taxes when quoting their prices. If you're inquiring on your own into a top-end hotel, however, be sure to ask: pricier hotels often quote fares before tax – a whopping 21%! High season is generally July and August (except in Patagonia), Semana Santa (Easter week) and January and February (when Argentines take their summer breaks). Outside these times, prices can drop anywhere from 20% to 40% from the rates quoted in this book.

Camping & Refugios

Camping can be one of the most splendid ways to experience Argentina, particularly the Lake District and Patagonia, where there are many good campgrounds. Nearly every Argentine city or town has fairly central municipal campgrounds, where you can pitch a tent for around AR$20 per night. These are hit-and-miss – sometimes delightfully

woodsy, sometimes crowded and ugly. Free campgrounds are often excellent, especially in the Lake District, although they lack facilities.

Private campgrounds usually have good facilities: hot showers, toilets, laundry, a barbecue for grilling, a restaurant or *confitería* (cafe), a small grocery store and sometimes even a swimming pool. Personal possessions are generally secure, since attendants keep a watchful eye on the grounds, but don't leave anything lying around unnecessarily.

For comfort, invest in a good tent before coming to South America, where camping equipment is costlier and often inferior, even in Argentina. A three-season sleeping bag should be adequate for almost any weather. A good petrol- or kerosene-burning stove is also a good idea, since white gas (called *bencina* in Spanish) is expensive and available only at chemical-supply shops, hardware stores and some camping stores in larger cities. Bring mosquito repellent, since many campgrounds are near rivers or lakes; the stuff is essential if you're camping in hotter places in north-central and northeast Argentina.

Backpacking and backcountry camping opportunities abound in and around the national parks, especially those in the Lakes District and the south. Some parks have *refugios* (basic shelters for hikers in the high country), which have some sort of cooking facilities and are filled with saggy but welcome bunks. Many *refugios* are free, but some do charge. They tend to fill up quickly in high season, so do your local research and arrive early to score a bed if necessary.

DIRECTORY

Estancias

Few experiences feel more typically Argentine than staying at an *estancia* (a traditional ranch, often called *fincas* in the northwest). *Estancias* are a wonderful way to spend time in remote areas of the country – and wine, horses and *asados* (traditional barbecues) are almost always involved. *Estancias* are especially common in the area around Buenos Aires, near Esteros del Iberá and throughout the Lake District and Patagonia. In the latter, they're often geared toward anglers. Costs rarely dip below AR$250 per day, but the rates generally include room, board and some activities. To easily locate many of the *estancias* covered in this book, see the boxed texts, p152, p309 and p471; in Uruguay, see p564). *Estancias* are also listed in Sleeping sections. If you're investigating *estancias* from within Argentina, the provincial tourist offices (p609) in Buenos Aires are an excellent resource. Helpful websites listing *estancias* around Argentina include www.estanciastravel.com and www.estanciasargentinas.com.

Those lacking the time, money or inclination to spend the night on an *estancia* can still experience one by partaking in a *día de campo* (day in the country). Offered by many of the *estancias* that offer accommodations, the *día de campo* usually consists of a giant *asado,* horseback riding and other traditional activities associated with *estancias*.

Hospedajes, Pensiones & Residenciales

Aside from hostels, these are Argentina's cheapest accommodations, and the differences among them are sometimes ambiguous – to the point that they're often simply called hotels. However, if you're flipping through a tourist office's list of accommodations, they won't fall into the 'hotel' category.

A *hospedaje* is usually a large family home with a few extra bedrooms (and, generally, a shared bathroom). Similarly, a *pensión* offers short-term accommodations in a family home, but may also have permanent lodgers. Meals may be available. *Residenciales* figure more commonly in tourist-office lists. In general, they occupy buildings designed for short-stay accommodations, although some (known euphemistically as *albergues transitorios*) cater to clientele who intend only *very* short stays – of two hours maximum. Prostitutes occasionally use them, but they're mostly used by young Argentine couples with no other indoor alternative or by someone who cannot, for whatever reason, get busy at home.

Rooms and furnishings at these accommodations are modest, often basic and usually clean, and rooms with shared bathrooms are the cheapest. *Hospedajes* and *residenciales* are usually as good as or better than one-star hotels.

Hostels

Hostels have sprouted up throughout Argentina like grass on the pampas, and nearly every town with tourist appeal has at least one. Most are excellent places to stay, where you can meet and hang out with fellow travelers, get travel advice and enjoy one of the fun *asados* that are practically de rigueur. Like hostels throughout much of the world, those in Argentina usually have common kitchens and living spaces, shared bathrooms and (more often than not) at least one private double. What's more, most hostels are run by enthusiastic, conscientious people who have a finger on the pulse of Argentine travel, meaning few establishments in all of Argentina are as helpful in finding out the best places to visit. But remember that Argentines are night owls and hostelers tend to follow suit, so earplugs can be handy indeed.

Many hostels offer private doubles that, if not for their predominantly dorm-room style accommodations, would fall into our midrange sections. Those who crave the camaraderie of a hostel but actually wish to sleep (and have their own bathroom) should consider these options. They can offer the best of both worlds: the community of a hostel and the privacy of a hotel.

Card-carrying **Hostelling International** (HI; www.hihostels.com) members can save from 10% to 20% at HI facilities. Other hostel networks include **minihostels** (www.minihostels.com) and **HoLa** (www.holahostels.com).

Hotels

Argentine hotels vary from depressing, utilitarian one-star places to luxurious five-star hotels. Oddly enough, many one- and two-star hotels can prove better value than three- and four-star lodgings. In general, hotels provide a room with private bathroom, often a telephone and usually a TV with cable. Sometimes they have a *confitería* or restaurant and almost always include breakfast in the price. In the top categories you will have room and laundry service, a swimming pool, a bar, shopping galleries and perhaps a gym (which, in the three- to four-star range, amounts to little more than a pile of dumbbells and a squeaky exercise bike).

Rentals & Homestays

House and apartment rentals can save you money if you're staying in one place for an extended period. In resort locations, such as towns along the Atlantic coast (Mar del Plata, Pinamar etc) or Bariloche, you can lodge several people for the price of one by seeking an apartment and cooking your own meals. Tourist offices and newspapers are good sources for listings. For rental resources in Buenos Aires, see p109.

During the tourist season, mostly in the interior, families rent rooms to visitors. Often these are excellent bargains, permitting access to cooking and laundry facilities and hot showers, as well as encouraging contact with Argentines. Generally, we do not cover homestays in this book, since they change regularly. Tourist offices in most smaller towns (but even in cities as large as Salta and Mendoza) maintain lists of such accommodations.

ACTIVITIES

Argentina has a cornucopia of outdoor activities, offering trekking in the Lake District and Patagonia, mountaineering in Mendoza and San Juan, plus snow sports, cycling and fishing. For more information, see p53.

BUSINESS HOURS

Traditionally, business hours in Argentina start at 8am and break at midday *siesta* (rest) for three or even four hours, during which people return home for lunch and a brief nap. After siesta, shops reopen until 8pm or 9pm. This schedule is still common in the provinces, but government offices and many businesses in Buenos Aires have adopted a more conventional 8am to 5pm schedule in the interests of 'greater efficiency.'

Throughout this book, we list opening hours for businesses only when they deviate from the standard business hours listed inside the front cover.

CHILDREN

Argentina is extremely child-friendly in terms of travel safety (except when it comes to car safety seats), health, people's attitudes and family-oriented activities. This is also a country where people frequently touch each other, so don't be surprised when your child is patted on the head or caressed on the cheek.

When it comes to public transport, Argentines are usually very helpful. It's common for someone sitting to give up a seat for a parent and child, and occasionally an older person may offer to put the child on his or her lap.

Most nonflashy restaurants provide a wide selection of food suitable for children (vegetables, pasta, meat, chicken, fish, French fries etc), but adult portions are normally so large that small children rarely need a separate order. Waiters are accustomed to providing extra plates and cutlery for children, though some places may add a small additional charge.

FUN FOR THE KIDS

Art museums? Boring. Churches (yawn). Bus rides – ouch. But worry not. There are plenty of ways to keep your kiddos' spirits high in Argentina. The following make great bargaining chips to keep the kids in check.

- Dinosaur exhibits – including multistory-tall skeletons and massive footprints – in Neuquén (see the boxed text, p378).
- Shopping for zany, unique and affordable kids clothes in Palermo Viejo, Buenos Aires (p131).
- Horseback rides during a stay on an *estancia* (opposite).
- Glaciar Perito Moreno and icebergs in Parque Nacional Los Glaciares (p478).
- Tandem paragliding flight in La Cumbre, Córdoba (p322).
- Two words: ice cream. It's outstanding in Argentina.

For what to do with kids in Buenos Aires, see p106.

DIRECTORY

Whatever you do, don't forget to take the kids out for ice cream – it's a real Argentine treat!

Breast-feeding in public is not uncommon, though most women are discreet and cover themselves. Poorly maintained public bathrooms may be a concern for some parents. Always carry toilet paper and baby wipes. While a woman may take a young boy into the ladies' room, it is socially taboo for a man to take a girl of any age into the men's room.

On buses, small children can share a seat with their parents to save money; on sleeper buses (see p618), this rarely proves uncomfortable.

CLIMATE CHARTS

From the scorching subtropical summers of Chaco and Formosa provinces, to the freezing, gale-force winter winds of Tierra del Fuego, Argentina has wildly varied climates. For information on the best time to visit the country, see p18.

COURSES

Since the devaluation of the peso, Argentina has become a hot destination in which to learn Spanish. Most opportunities for Spanish-language instruction are based in Buenos Aires (see p106), though larger cities such as Mendoza (p344) and Córdoba (p313) are also excellent places to kick-start or hone your Spanish. Córdoba is a city of students, meaning you will feel right at home going to school, and you will also find plenty of opportunities to set up learning exchanges with local students.

Small-group instruction or individual tutoring offer the best options for improving language skills, and are affordable options. Rates average about AR$60 to AR$75 per hour (one-on-one) or AR$600 to AR$800 per week.

Tango classes are hugely popular in Buenos Aires, where group lessons cost anywhere from AR$15 to AR$40. For more information see the boxed text, p125.

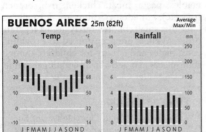

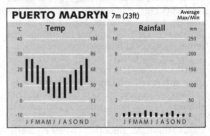

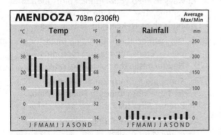

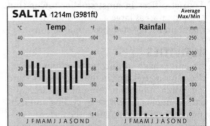

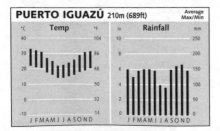

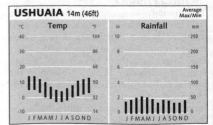

Cooking classes, both for Argentine and international cuisine, are available in Buenos Aires (see p106).

CUSTOMS REGULATIONS

Argentine officials are generally courteous and reasonable toward tourists. Electronic items, including laptops, cameras and cell (mobile) phones, can be brought into the country duty free, provided they are not intended for resale. If you're over 18 you may also bring in up to 2L of alcohol, 400 cigarettes and 50 cigars. If you're entering with expensive computer, photographic and/or other electronic equipment, you should play it safe and declare it. Folks rarely have problems entering with the usual electronic items.

If you're entering Argentina from a neighboring country, officials focus on different things. Travelers southbound from the central Andean countries may be searched for drugs, while those from bordering countries will have fruits and vegetables confiscated. Carrying illegal drugs will pretty much get you into trouble no matter which country you're coming from.

DANGERS & ANNOYANCES

For tourists, Argentina is one of the safest countries in Latin America. This isn't to say you should skip down the street drunk with your money belt strapped to your head, but with a little common sense you can visit Argentina's big cities as safely as you could London, Paris or New York. That said, crime has been on the rise.

Petty Crime

The economic crisis of 1999–2001 plunged a lot of people into poverty, and street crime (pickpocketing, bag-snatching and armed robbery) has subsequently risen, especially in Buenos Aires (see p94) and, more recently, Mendoza (see p342). Still, most people feel perfectly safe in the big cities. In the small towns of the provinces you'd have to *search* for a crook to rob you.

Bus terminals are the most common places tourists become separated from their possessions. For the most part bus terminals are safe, as they're usually full of families traveling and saying goodbyes, but they're also prime grounds for bag-snatchers. Always keep an eagle eye on your goods. This is especially true in Buenos Aires' Retiro station.

Other places to be wary are tourist destinations and sidewalk cafe or restaurant tables.

Pickets & Protests

Street protests have become part of daily life in Argentina, especially in Buenos Aires' Plaza de Mayo area, so it's wise to be aware of current political events. Generally these have little effect on tourists other than blocking traffic or making it impossible to see Buenos Aires' Plaza de Mayo and the Casa Rosada (where protests occur almost weekly). The country has many *gremios* or *sindicatos* (trade unions), and it seems that one of them is always on strike. Transportation unions sometimes go on strike, which can affect travelers directly by delaying domestic flights and bus services. It's always a good idea to keep your eye on the news before traveling.

Drivers

Being a pedestrian in Argentina is perhaps one of the country's more difficult ventures. Many Argentine drivers jump the gun when the traffic signal is about to change to green, drive extremely fast and change lanes unpredictably. Even though pedestrians at corners and crosswalks have legal right of way (ha!), very few drivers respect this and will hardly slow down when you are crossing. Be especially careful of buses, which can be reckless and, because of their large size, particularly painful.

Police & Military

The police and military have a reputation for being corrupt or irresponsible, but both are generally helpful and courteous to tourists. If you feel you're being patted down for a bribe (most often if you're driving), you can respond by tactfully paying up (see p604) or asking the officer to accompany you to the police station to take care of it. The latter will likely lead the officer to drop it – though it could lead you in to the labyrinthine bureaucracy of the Argentine police system. Pretending you don't understand Spanish may also frustrate a potential bribe.

Smoking

Many Argentines are heavy smokers, and you can't help but be exposed to it on the street. The good news for nonsmokers is that Argentina passed a smoking ban for restaurants, cafes, internet cafes, bars and other public places in 2006. Regulations and enforcement differ throughout the country. Smoking is prohibited on buses and all domestic flights.

DISCOUNT CARDS

The International Student Identity Card (ISIC) is available for AR$43 through the student and discount travel agency **Asatej** (Map pp84-5; ☎ 011-4114-7500; www.asatej.net; Florida 835, Room 320, 3rd fl, Buenos Aires). It can help travelers obtain discounts on public transportation and admissions to museums. Any official-looking university identification may be an acceptable substitute. An HI card, available for AR$60 at any HI hostel or the **HI office** (Map pp84-5; ☎ 011-4511-8723; www.hostels.org.ar; Florida 835, Room 319, 3rd fl, Buenos Aires), will get you discounts on your stay at any HI facility (see p598). The **minihostel** (www.minihostels.com) and **HoLa** (www.holahostels.com) cards work in a similar way for a different network of hostels.

Travelers over the age of 60 can sometimes obtain senior-citizen discounts on museum admissions and the like. Usually a passport with date of birth is sufficient evidence of age.

EMBASSIES & CONSULATES
Argentine Embassies & Consulates

Argentina has diplomatic representation throughout the world. A quick internet search will turn up the *embajada Argentina* (Argentine embassy) in your home country with nearest consulates to you.

Embassies & Consulates in Argentina

Following is a list of embassies and consulates, most of which are in Buenos Aires. Some countries have both an embassy and a consulate here, but only the most central location is listed.

Australia Buenos Aires (Map pp88-9; ☎ 011-4779-3500; Villanueva 1400, Palermo)

Bolivia Buenos Aires (Map pp84-5; ☎ 011-4394-1463; Corrientes 545, 2nd fl, Microcentro); Jujuy (Map p248; (☎ 0388-424-0501; Independencia 1098); La Quiaca (☎ 0388-422283; cnr Árabe Siria & 9 de Julio); Salta (Map p262; ☎ 0387-421-1040; Mariano Boedo 34)

Brazil Buenos Aires (Map pp84-5; ☎ 011-4515-6500; Carlos Pellegrini 1363, 5th fl, Retiro); Paso de los Libres (☎ 03772-425444; Calle Bartolomé Mitre 894 at Sarmiento); Puerto Iguazú (Map p227; ☎ 03757-421348; Córdoba 264)

Canada Buenos Aires (Map pp88-9; ☎ 011-4808-1000; Tagle 2828, Recoleta)

Chile Buenos Aires (Map pp84-5; ☎ 011-4331-6228; Diagonal Roque Sáenz Peña 547, 2nd fl, Microcentro); Bariloche (Map p402; ☎ 02944-423050; Av Juan Manuel de Rosas 180); Esquel (Map p458; ☎ 02945-451189; Molinari 754); Mendoza (off Map pp340-1; ☎ 0261-425-4844; Paso de los Andes 1147); Neuquén (Map p377; ☎ 0299-442-2727; La Rioja 241); Río Gallegos (Map p454; ☎ 02966-422364; Mariano Moreno 148); Salta (Map p262; ☎ 0387-431-1857; Santiago del Estero 965); Ushuaia (Map p519; ☎ 02901-430909; Jainén 50)

France Buenos Aires (Map pp84-5; ☎ 011-4315-4290; Santa Fe 846, 4th fl, Retiro); Mendoza (off Map pp340-1; ☎ 0261-423-1542; Av Houssay 790); Salta (Map p262; ☎ 0387-423-5797; Tucumán 380); Tucumán (Map p281; ☎ 0381-421-8202; Crisóstomo Álvarez 471)

Germany Buenos Aires (Map pp88-9; ☎ 011-4778-2500; Villanueva 1055, Belgrano); Mendoza (Map pp340-1; ☎ 0261-429-6539; Montevideo 127, 2nd fl, No 6); Posadas (Map p215; ☎ 0387-422-9088; Caeros 1874); Tucumán (off Map p281; ☎ 0381-425-5528; Remedios de Escalada 680, Yerba Buena)

Israel Buenos Aires (Map pp84-5; ☎ 011-4338-2500; Av de Mayo 701, 10th fl, Microcentro); Mendoza (off Map pp340-1; ☎ 0261-428-2140; Lamadrid 738)

Italy Buenos Aires (Map pp88-9; ☎ 011-4114-4800; Calle Billinghurst 2577, No 1425); Mendoza (Map pp340-1; ☎ 0261-520-1400; Necochea 712); Salta (Map p262; ☎ 0387-432-1532; Santiago del Estero 497); Tucumán (Map p281; ☎ 0381-422-3830; San Martín 623, 5th fl)

Japan Buenos Aires (Map pp84-5; ☎ 011-4318-8200; Bouchard 547, 17th fl, Microcentro)

Netherlands Buenos Aires (Map pp84-5; ☎ 011-4338-0050; Olga Cossettini 831, 3rd fl, Edificio Porteño II, Puerto Madero)

Paraguay Buenos Aires (Map pp84-5; ☎ 011-4814-4803; Viamonte 1851, Balvanera); Corrientes (☎ 03783-426576; Córdoba 969); Posadas (Map p215; ☎ 03752-423858; San Lorenzo 179); Puerto Iguazú (Map p227; ☎ 03757-424230; Córdoba 370)

Peru Buenos Aires (Map pp84-5; ☎ 011-4382-3916; Av Rivadavia 1501, Congreso)

Spain Buenos Aires (Map pp84-5; ☎ 011-4814-9100; Guido 1770, Recoleta); Mendoza (off Map pp340-1; ☎ 0261-425-3947; Agustín Alvarez 455); Río Gallegos (Map p454; ☎ 02966-422131; Av Roca 866); Rosario (Map p180; ☎ 0341-447-0100; Santa Fe 768)

UK Buenos Aires (Map pp84-5; ☎ 011-4808-2200; Dr Luis Agote 2412, Recoleta)

Uruguay Buenos Aires (Map pp84-5; ☎ 011-4807-3040; Av Las Heras 1915, Recoleta); Colón (☎ 03447-421999; San Martín 417); Concordia (Map p210; ☎ 0345-421-0380; Asunción 131); Gualeguaychú (Map p204; ☎ 03446-422466; Rivadavia 510)

USA Buenos Aires (Map pp88-9; ☎ 011-5777-4533; Colombia 4300, Palermo)

FOOD

For a mouthwatering idea of all the food you can eat while traveling in Argentina, see p61. Compared with Europe and North America, restaurant prices in much of Argentina are quite affordable. However, in places such as Buenos Aires and especially Patagonia, good-value meals are harder to come by.

Eating sections throughout this book are arranged by budget, with the most economical options listed first. Restaurants that charge up to AR$20 for a main course (what we abbreviate as 'mains' in listings) fall into the budget category. Budget restaurants are usually modest, often family oriented and, more often than not, serve Argentine standbys like pastas, *milanesas* (breaded fried veal or chicken) and sandwiches. Ordering house wine by the glass or *jarra* (carafe) keeps the price down. If you're pinching pesos, you can almost always find budget restaurants and keep your eating costs low (but remember there are a lot of Argentines trying to do the same).

Our midrange category includes restaurants that charge AR$20 to AR$40 for main courses. You can eat very well at midrange eateries and usually get out the door having spent under AR$60 for a complete meal, often including dessert and wine. Top-end restaurants charge over AR$40 for a main course. These are plentiful in Buenos Aires (thanks to all the money in the city and the higher cost of living) and in Patagonia (thanks to tourism and the region's isolation).

For the standard opening hours of restaurants, see the inside front cover.

GAY & LESBIAN TRAVELERS

Since the end of military rule, and with the declining influence of the Catholic church, Argentina has become increasingly gay-friendly. Buenos Aires is one of the world's top gay destinations – with dedicated hotels and B&Bs; bars, nightclubs and restaurants; and even gay cruises calling at the port. The capital is home to South America's largest annual gay pride parade and has numerous gay and lesbian organizations and clubs. In 2002 Buenos Aires became the first city in Latin America to legalize civil unions between same-sex couples, granting some civil-union rights similar to those held by heterosexual couples. And in Ushuaia on December 28, 2009, two Argentine men became the first same-sex couple to legally marry in Latin America.

Although Buenos Aires (and, to a lesser extent, Argentina's other large cities) is becoming increasingly tolerant, most of the rest of Argentina still feels uncomfortable with homosexuality. Homophobia rarely takes the form of physical violence, however; instead it manifests through inappropriate jokes and chatty disapproval any time the subject comes up. That said, gay people regularly travel throughout the country to return home with nothing but praise.

When it comes to public affection, Argentine men are more physically demonstrative than their North American and European counterparts. Behaviors such as kissing on the cheek in greeting or a vigorous embrace are innocuous even to those who express unease with homosexuality. Lesbians walking hand in hand should attract little attention, since heterosexual Argentine women frequently do so, but this would be very conspicuous behavior for men. When in doubt, it's best to be discreet.

For much more on what's gay in Buenos Aires, see the boxed text, p128.

Also check out the following websites:

Gayscape (www.gayscape.com) Handful of useful links on the Argentina page.

Global Gayz.com (www.globalgayz.com) Has a South America section full of news, tips and links about gay travel in the region, with a small section on Argentina.

International Lesbian and Gay Association (ILGA; www.ilga.org) Click 'Countries' and find the Argentina page for news and information. Also links to international lesbian, gay and transgender organizations.

Mundo Gay (www.mundogay.com) Noteworthy online publication out of Buenos Aires; club listings, chat, blog and more. Mostly for men, and all in Spanish.

HOLIDAYS

Government offices and businesses are closed on Argentina's numerous public holidays. If the holiday falls on a midweek day or weekend day, it's often bumped to the nearest Monday. Public transport options are also more limited and fill up fast. The following list does not include provincial holidays, which may vary considerably. For Argentina's best festivals and events, see p22.

January 1 New Year's Day

March 24 Día de la Memoria; anniversary of the day that started the 1976 dictatorship and subsequent Dirty War.

March/April Semana Santa (Easter week) – dates vary; most businesses close on 'Good Thursday' and Good Friday; major travel week.

April 2 Día de las Malvinas; honors the fallen Argentine soldiers from the Islas Malvinas (Falkland Islands) war in 1982.

May 1 Labor Day.

May 25 Revolución de Mayo; commemorates the 1810 revolution against Spain.

June 20 Día de la Bandera (Flag Day); anniversary of death of Manuel Belgrano, creator of Argentina's flag and military leader.

July 9 Independence Day

August 17 Día del Libertador San Martín; marks the anniversary of José de San Martín's death (1778–1850).

October 12 Día de la Raza (Columbus Day)

December 8 Día de la Concepción Inmaculada; religious holiday that celebrates the immaculate conception of the Virgin Mary.

December 25 Christmas Day

INSURANCE

In addition to health insurance (p622) and car insurance (p620), it's wise to purchase travel insurance that protects baggage, valuables and canceled flights. Keep in mind that some insurance policies do not cover certain 'high risk' activities, usually of the extreme sport type, which can be anything from rock climbing to paragliding. Be sure to read the fine print and choose a policy that best suits your needs.

Keep your insurance records separate from other possessions in case you have to make a claim (a good trick is to email them to yourself and keep them accessible in your Inbox). Worldwide travel insurance is available at www.lonelyplanet.com/travel_services. You can buy, extend and claim online anytime – even if you're already on the road.

INTERNET ACCESS

For Sleeping listings throughout this book, we've included a 🖳 symbol for those accommodations that provide internet access for their guests. If a hotel offers wireless service, our symbol is 🛜. For a list of recommended internet resources, see p21.

Rarely is an Argentine town – no matter how small – without an internet cafe. In cities, internet cafes seem to occupy every other building, with even the smallest *locutorios* (telephone centers) having a few computers. Internet cafes charge AR$4 to AR$6 per hour in most cities. To find the @ *(arroba)* symbol, try holding down the Alt key and typing 64. Or ask the attendant '¿*Cómo se hace la arroba?*' ('How do you make the @ sign?').

Open, free wireless networks (such as wi-fi) are commonplace at cafes and hotels throughout Argentina, even in small towns. Traveling with a laptop can be convenient, but unless you know what you're doing, it's fraught with potential problems. Remember, the power supply in Argentina (220 volts) may differ from that at home, so if your laptop doesn't have an internal voltage converter (many do), you'll have to purchase one. If you do buy a converter, be sure you buy one that's rated for the electronic devices you're using – the standard power converters sold at most luggage and travel stores are meant only for hairdryers, battery chargers and the like.

For more information on traveling with laptops and other electronics check out Steve Kropla's excellent website at www.kropla.com.

LEGAL MATTERS

Argentina presently enjoys civilian government, but the police and military both have a reputation for corruption and abuse of power. However, as a tourist it is very unlikely you will ever experience this if you obey the law. Police, however, can demand identification at any moment and for whatever reason. Always carry your documents and always be courteous and cooperative.

The legal drinking age is 18. Though it's not uncommon to see folks drinking beer on the street or in plazas, it's technically illegal to do so. Small-scale use of marijuana has recently been decriminalized, but it's always a good idea to be discreet. Cocaine and other substances that are illegal in the USA and most European countries are also illegal here. Though constitutionally a person is innocent until proven guilty, people can be held for years without a trial. If arrested, you have the constitutional right to a lawyer, a telephone call and to remain silent.

No Argentine in their right mind would directly offer a *coima* (bribe) to a police officer. However, things are often taken care of on the spot by asking '¿*Como podemos arreglar esto mas rápido?*' ('What can we do to expedite this situation?') or '¿*Puedo pagar la multa ahora*' ('Can I pay the ticket now?').

MAPS

Tourist offices throughout the country provide free city maps that are good enough for tooling around town. **International Travel Maps** (www.itmb.com) publishes fairly useful Buenos Aires and Argentina maps.

With offices in nearly every Argentine city, the Automóvil Club Argentino (ACA; p619) publishes excellent maps of provinces and cities that are particularly good for driving and trip planning. Card-carrying members of foreign automobile clubs can get discounts. Not as good but still handy are the red *Argenguide* maps, available at most YPF (gas or petrol) stations.

Geography nerds will adore the topographic maps available from the **Instituto Geográfico Militar** (Map pp88-9; ☎ 011-4576-5576; www.igm.gob.ar; Cabildo 381, Palermo, Buenos Aires; ☑ 7am-2pm Mon-Fri). These maps are difficult to obtain outside the capital.

MONEY

The Argentine unit of currency is the peso (AR$). Prices in this book are quoted in Argentine pesos unless otherwise noted. See the inside front cover for exchange rates. Also see p18 for information on costs.

Carrying cash and an ATM card is the way to go in Argentina.

ATMs

Cajeros automáticos (ATMs) are found in nearly every city and town in Argentina and can also be used for cash advances on major credit cards. They're the best way to get money, and nearly all have instructions in English. Almost all ATMs use Cirrus, Plus or Link systems. There may be limits per withdrawal (anywhere from AR$300 to AR$1000), but you can withdraw several times per day, up to perhaps AR$3000.

When getting cash out, consider withdrawing an odd number like 290 pesos, instead of 300. This will guarantee you some small bills; just *try* breaking a 100 peso note for a 10 peso sale – you'll get groans for sure.

Also, a fee of AR$11.46 may be charged on ATM transactions by the *local* bank (not including charges by your home bank, which are extra). Note that this is a *per transaction* fee, so consider taking out your maximum allowed limit – if you feel safe doing so.

Cash

Paper money comes in denominations of two, five, 10, 20, 50 and 100 pesos. One peso equals 100 *centavos*; coins come in denominations of one (rare), five, 10, 25 and 50 *centavos*, and one peso. At present, US dollars are accepted by many tourist-oriented businesses, but you should always carry some pesos.

Counterfeiting, of both local and US bills, has become a problem in recent years, and merchants are very careful when accepting large denominations. You should be too; look for a clear watermark or running thread on the largest bills. This is especially important in nightclubs or taxis (where you should avoid using large bills in the first place; see p136).

Changing large denomination bills is a huge problem throughout the country (and a major gripe for Argentines and tourists alike). Whenever you can, change your AR$100 and AR$50 bills at the bank to avoid problems. Large supermarkets and restaurants are good places to get rid of AR$100 bills. Taxi drivers, kiosks and small stores rarely change them, and you could easily find yourself without a means of paying.

Credit Cards

The most widely accepted credit cards are Visa and MasterCard, though American Express

---

SPARE SOME CHANGE...PRETTY PLEASE?

You will very quickly notice that change in small bills – but especially coins – is very hard to come by in Argentina, and especially Buenos Aires. Some vendors won't sell a small item if it involves giving up precious *monedas*. Theories abound as to why this problem exists, but the situation is certainly exacerbated by bus companies. Buses take only coins, which are never deposited at banks. Instead, they're sold on the black market for a 5% to 10% markup. In BA a magnetic card system is theoretically in the works to ease this ridiculous situation.

In the meantime, break large bills when making big transactions, like at restaurants. Save up a stash of small bills and coins for small purchases, and never give up coins unless you're begged to – and you will be. Some people line up in special queues at Retiro and Constitución train stations, where you can get up to AR$20 in coins without a 'fee.' (Surprisingly, banks only give out a few pesos' worth.) There's one silver lining – you won't be weighed down with too much change.

and a few others are also valid in many establishments. Before you leave home, warn your credit-card company that you'll be using it abroad or it may put a hold on the card thinking it was lost.

Some businesses add a *recargo* (surcharge) of 5% to 10% toward credit-card purchases. Also, the actual amount you'll eventually pay depends upon the exchange rate not at the time of sale, but when the purchase is posted to an overseas account, sometimes weeks later.

If you use a credit card to pay for restaurant bills, be aware that tips can't usually be added to the bill. Many lower-end hotels and private tour companies will not accept credit cards. Holders of MasterCard and Visa can get cash advances at Argentine banks and most ATMs.

Moneychangers

US dollars are by far the preferred foreign currency, although Chilean and Uruguayan pesos can be readily exchanged at the borders. Cash dollars and euros can be changed at banks and *cambios* (exchange houses) in most larger cities, but other currencies can be difficult to change outside Buenos Aires.

Taxes & Refunds

Under limited circumstances, foreign visitors may obtain refunds of the *impuesto al valor agregado* (IVA; value-added tax) on purchases of Argentine products upon their departure from the country. A 'Tax Free' (in English) window decal identifies merchants participating in this program. Hang on to your invoice and you can obtain refunds in Buenos Aires at Ezeiza, Aeroparque Jorge Newbery and the Buquebus terminal at Darsena Norte. For more information see the boxed text, p131.

Tipping & Bargaining

In restaurants it's customary to tip about 10% of the bill, but in times of economic distress (ie these days), many Argentines overlook the custom. In general, waiters are poorly paid, so if you can afford to eat out, you can afford to tip. Even a small *propina* (tip) will be appreciated, but note that restaurant tips can't be added to a credit card bill. Taxi drivers don't expect tips, but it's customary to round up to the nearest peso. Unlike many other South American countries, bargaining is generally not the norm in Argentina.

Traveler's Checks

Very high commissions are levied on traveler's checks, which are difficult to cash anywhere and specifically *not* recommended for travel in Argentina. Stores will *not* accept traveler's checks, and outside Buenos Aires it's even harder to change them.

PHOTOGRAPHY

For tips on how to photograph people, cities, landscapes and more, pick up a copy of Lonely Planet's easy-to-carry *Travel Photography* book by Richard I'Anson. Avoid taking photos of military or police, as you may have your camera confiscated.

Digital

If you're shooting digital and plan to be taking a lot of photos, invest in a portable hard drive. It's the best way to back up your files. If you don't plan to travel with a portable hard drive, you can easily back up your photos to CD, DVD or flash drive at an internet cafe (see p604). Nearly all internet cafes have at least one machine with usable USB ports and a CD burner.

Film

Film in Argentina is comparable to that in North America and Europe, both in quality and price. But it's generally cheaper to develop film here than it is in Europe or the USA. Developing quality is generally high, so do it before you leave for home and save yourself a bundle. For slide developing, you'll have fewer choices except in Buenos Aires.

POST

Correo Argentino (www.correoargentino.com.ar), the privatized postal service, has become more reliable over the years, but mail still regularly gets waylaid and occasionally gets lost. International letters and postcards under 20g cost AR$6; a letter from 20g to 150g costs AR$18. Certified *(certificado)* international letters under 20g cost AR$17; from 20g to 150g it's AR$29.

Domestic couriers, such as **Andreani** (www .andreani.com.ar) and **OCA** (www.oca.com.ar), and international couriers like DHL and FedEx are far more dependable than the post office. But they're also far more expensive. The last two have offices only in the largest cities, while the first two usually serve as their connections to the interior of the country.

If a package is being sent to you, expect to wait a long time for it to turn up within the system (or to receive notice of its arrival). Nearly all parcels sent to Buenos Aires go to the international Retiro office, near the Buquebus terminal. To collect the package you'll have to wait (sometimes hours) first to get it and then to have it checked by customs. There's also a small processing fee. Don't expect any valuables to make it through.

You can send packages under 2kg from any post office, but anything heavier needs to go through *aduana* (a customs office). In Buenos Aires, this office is near Retiro bus terminal and is called Correo Internacional (see p94).

RELOCATING TO ARGENTINA

After the devaluation of the peso in 2002, foreigners began moving to Argentina – where the cost of living for those earning dollars, euros or pounds was low – in huge numbers. Although prices for just about everything (including food, apartments and transportation) have been on the rise, Argentina is still a very popular destination for expats on the make. Levels of relocation vary: countless folks simply rent an apartment in Buenos Aires for a year or two and leave the country every three months to renew their visa. Others go the full route, purchasing property and jumping through the hoops of legal residency. Whatever you decide to do, don't expect to find work in Argentina, unless you're going to be employed by a foreign company (for more on work, see p612) or become an entrepreneur.

Opening a bank account in Argentina is a bit of a hassle. You can't just walk in with AR$1000 and open one. Requirements vary by bank, but generally you need the minimum equivalent of US$500, plus a passport and/or picture ID, proof of domicile (ie an electricity bill), plus – and here's the kicker – a CDI (a national ID card number) and/or CUIL/CUIT (employment and tax ID numbers). Obtaining these requires proof of residency and/or legal employment. Basically, if you just want to open an account to avoid withdrawal fees from your home-country bank, it may not be worth the trouble.

For those considering long-term relocation, including buying property, there are some excellent resources out there:

Argentina Residency & Citizenship Advisors (ARCA; www.argentinaresidency.com) Helps foreigners obtain legal residency and citizenship.

BABlackJumpers (http://groups.yahoo.com/group/BABlackJumpers/) Sometimes zany newsgroup for expats in Argentina.

BANewcomers (http://groups.yahoo.com/group/BANewcomers/) Yahoo newsgroup; good place to throw out questions to expats in Argentina.

Buenos Aires Expatriates Group (www.baexpats.org) Popular expat website.

Expatargentina (www.expatargentina.wordpress.com) One expat's eclectic musings on living in BA.

Just Landed (www.justlanded.com/english/Argentina) More info for expats.

Transitions Abroad (www.transitionsabroad.com) Excellent, longtime resource for folks living, working and studying abroad.

For a list of apartment rental services in Buenos Aires, see p109. For internet resources specific to Buenos Aires, see p93.

SHOPPING

Argentina is a great place to shop, especially for anyone traveling on strong foreign currencies. When it comes to fashion, Buenos Aires is one of the world's best cities to shop, with everything from boutique and independent designers, who sell their wares at street fairs, to big-name brands in BA's slickest shopping centers. The city's Palermo Viejo neighborhood is arguably the city's best area to shop.

Argentina is also famous for its leather, and downtown Buenos Aires is home to countless leather shops (p132) that cater to the tourist trade, selling leather jackets, handbags and shoes. Quality and prices can vary greatly, so shop around before buying.

Found everywhere, *mate* paraphernalia makes great souvenirs. Gourds and *bombillas* (metal straws with filters for drinking *mate*) range from inexpensive aluminum to elaborate and expensive gold and silver. Another great buy of the traditional sort is the gaucho (or criollo) knife. These usually have intricately woven leather or bone handles, and the blades vary widely. They're sold throughout the country, but the pampas town of Tandil (p150) is particularly famous for its cutlery.

In artisans *ferias* (fairs), found throughout Argentina, the variety of handicrafts is extensive and interesting. The best *ferias* are likely those in Córdoba (p317) and El Bolsón (p414). The Lake District town of Bariloche (p401) is best known for its local chocolate. In the province of Salta, the distinctive *ponchos de Güemes* make for memorable purchases.

DIRECTORY

Argentines are well read and interested in both national and world literature, and Buenos Aires has a good selection of general- and special-interest bookstores. Since the end of the military dictatorship, the capital has reestablished itself as a publishing center; April's Feria del Libro (book fair; p108) is South America's largest, with over 600 exhibitors drawing over a million visitors. Foreign-language books tend to be very expensive, however.

Wine, of course, is another fabulous buy, but bringing it home is no longer as easy as it once was, primarily because most international airlines now prohibit passengers from carrying bottles aboard. You can pack a few bottles into your checked luggage, but you'd better be sure they're well padded. **Anuva Wines** (www.anuvawines.com) will ship to many US states for a nominal fee.

For refunds on tax-free items, see Taxes & Refunds (p606).

SOLO TRAVELERS

Traveling alone can be one of the most rewarding experiences in life. You're far more likely to meet locals and fellow travelers – which is really what travel's all about – without the shell of companionship. Mind you, it can get lonely at times, and it's certainly nice to have a mate to watch your bags for you (or your back when you're snapping photos), but these benefits are often outweighed by the joy of meeting locals. Argentines are quick to invite solo travelers to an *asado* or elsewhere, and even quicker to strike up conversation. What's more, with Argentina's abundance of new hostels, you can easily hook up with other travelers when you're feeling lonely.

Traveling alone as a woman, unfortunately, inherently entails more risk than traveling solo as a man. But countless women safely travel solo in Argentina every day; it's one of the safest countries in South America to do so. For more information for women travelers, see p612.

TELEPHONE & FAX

Two companies, Telecom and Telefónica, split the country's telephone services. For emergencies dial ☎ 107, for police ☎ 101 (or ☎ 911 in some larger cities) and for fire ☎ 100. Directory assistance is ☎ 110.

The easiest way to make a local phone call is to find a *locutorio*, which has private cabins where you make your calls, and then pay all at once at the register. *Locutorios* can be found on practically every other block. They cost about the same as street phones, are much quieter and you won't run out of coins. Most *locutorios* are supplied with phone books.

To use street phones, you'll pay with regular coins or *tarjetas telefónicas* (magnetic phone cards available at many kiosks). You'll only be able to speak for a limited time before you get cut off, so carry enough credit.

The cheapest way to make an international call is to use a phone card (see opposite). International calls can also be made at *locutorios*.

Faxes are inexpensive, widely used in Argentina and available at most *locutorios*.

CALLING ONLINE

Services like **Skype** (www.skype.com) and **Google Voice** (www.google.com/voice) make calling home cheap. It's easily done at many internet cafes in Argentina.

CELL (MOBILE) PHONES

Argentina operates on the GSM 850/1900 network, so, if you have a triband GSM cell phone (sometimes called a 'world phone' in the USA), you should be able to use it in Argentina. If you plan to use your own provider, you probably have to contact the company to have your phone unlocked for international use. Unless you have a plan tailored specifically toward international use, your rates on calls made and accepted in Argentina will likely be high.

The best option with an unlocked triband GSM phone, however, is to purchase a SIM chip/card (about AR$15) and insert it into your phone; you'll get a local phone number this way. Then you pay to add credits as you need them. Both SIM chips and credits can be bought at many kiosks or *locutorios*; look for the *'recarga facil'* signs. Many Argentines use this system with their cell phones. Phone unlocking services are available; ask around.

If you plan to travel with an iphone or other G3 smart phone, prepare yourself – you may need to purchase an international plan to avoid being hit by a huge bill for roaming costs. Do an internet search for 'iphone international use' for current tips.

Another option is purchasing a new cell phone in Argentina. You can pick one up for as little as AR$150, usually with some minutes already on the phone – but most companies require you to sign a contract. Cell-phone rentals are also available in Buenos Aires.

Finally, you can rent or purchase an international phone or a prepaid international SIM card from one of numerous companies that likely operate in your home country.

This is a fast-changing field so check the current situation before you travel; take a look at www.kropla.com or do an internet search on GSM cell phones for the myriad of products on the market.

PHONE CODES

When dialing abroad from Argentina, you must first dial '00,' followed by the country code (see the boxed text, below). The *característica* (area code) for Buenos Aires is ☎ 011, and all telephone numbers in the Greater Buenos Aires area have eight digits. Area codes vary wildly throughout the provinces; those of larger cities have four digits (always beginning with a zero), followed by a seven-digit telephone number. Smaller towns have six-digit telephone numbers and five-digit area codes (again, always beginning with a zero). Basically, when calling from outside an area code, you're always going to dial 11 numbers.

Cellular phone numbers in Argentina are always preceded by '15.' After that simple fact, it gets confusing. Usually you just dial the regional code corresponding to the person's location, regardless of where the phone was purchased. Other times, the regional code you must dial depends on where the person bought the cellular phone. So you may have to try more than once to get through. Your best bet is starting with the regional code where the person is located, followed by '15,' then the number. If you're calling a cell phone from within the same regional code, you don't have to dial the regional code. We've listed regional

---

<table>
<tr><td>**CALLING ARGENTINA FROM ABROAD**</td></tr>
</table>

To call a number in Argentina from another country, dial your international access code, then the country code for Argentina (☎ 54), then the area code (without the zero) and number.

When dialing an Argentine cell phone from outside Argentina, dial your country's international access code, then ☎ 54, then ☎ 9, then the area code without the 0, then the number – leaving out the ☎ 15.

---

codes with cell numbers throughout this book, so always try that option first when calling from another region. For information on calling an Argentine cell phone from outside that country, see the boxed text, left.

Toll-free numbers begin with ☎ 0800.

PHONECARDS

Telephone calling cards are sold at nearly all kiosks and make domestic and international calls far cheaper. However, they must be used from a fixed line such as a home or hotel telephone (provided you can dial outside the hotel). They cannot be used at most pay phones. Some *locutorios* allow you to use them, and although they levy a surcharge, the call is still far cheaper than dialing direct. When purchasing one, tell the clerk the country you will call so they give you the right card.

TIME

Argentina is three hours behind GMT and generally does not observe daylight saving time (though this situation can easily change). When it's noon in Argentina, it's 10am in New York, 7am in San Francisco, 3pm in London and 1pm the next day in Sydney (add one hour to these times during daylight saving). Argentina tells time by the 24-hour clock.

TOILETS

Public toilets in Argentina are better than in most of South America, but there are certainly exceptions. For the truly squeamish, the better restaurants and cafes are good alternatives. Large shopping malls often have public bathrooms, as do international fast-food chains. Always carry your own toilet paper, since it often runs out in public restrooms, and don't expect luxuries such as soap, hot water and paper towels either. In smaller towns, some public toilets charge a small fee for entry.

TOURIST INFORMATION

Argentina's national tourist board is the Secretaría de Turismo de la Nación; its main office is in Buenos Aires (p94). Almost every city or town has a tourist office, usually on or near the main plaza or at the bus terminal. Each Argentine province also has its own representation in Buenos Aires. Most (though not all) of these are well organized, often offering a computerized database of tourist information, and are well worth a visit before heading for the provinces.

Another excellent source of information and a generally indispensable resource is **South American Explorers** (Map pp84-5; ☎ 5275-0137; www.saexplorers.org; Roque Saénz Peña 1142, 7A), which maintains a clubhouse in central Buenos Aires.

The offices listed here are all provincial tourist offices located in Buenos Aires (area code ☎ 011).

Buenos Aires (Map pp84-5; ☎ 011-4373-2508; www.bue.gov.ar; Av Callao 237)

Catamarca (Map pp84-5; ☎ 011-4374-6891; www.catamarca.gov.ar; Córdoba 2080)

Chaco (Map pp84-5; ☎ 011-4372-5209; www.chaco.gov.ar; Av Callao 322)

Chubut (Map pp84-5; ☎ 011-4382-2009; www.chubut.gov.ar; Sarmiento 1172)

Córdoba (Map pp84-5; ☎ 011-4371-1688; www.cba.gov.ar; 4373-4277; Av Callao 332)

Corrientes (Map pp84-5; ☎ 011-4394-7418; www.corrientes.gov.ar; San Martín 333, 4th fl)

Entre Ríos (Map pp84-5; ☎ 011-4328-2284; www.entrerios.gov.ar; Suipacha 844)

Formosa (Map pp84-5; ☎ 011-4381-7048; www.casadeformosa.gov.ar; Hipólito Yrigoyen 1429)

Jujuy (Map pp84-5; ☎ 011-4393-6096; www.casadejujuy.gov.ar; Av Santa Fe 967)

La Pampa (Map pp84-5; ☎ 011-4326-0511; www.lapampa.gov.ar; Suipacha 346)

La Rioja (Map pp84-5; ☎ 011-4815-1929; www.larioja.gov.ar; Av Callao 745)

Mendoza (Map pp84-5; ☎ 011-4371-7301, 4371-0835; www.mendoza.gov.ar; Av Callao 445)

Misiones (Map pp84-5; ☎ 011-4322-0686; www.misiones.gov.ar; Av Santa Fe 989)

Neuquén (Map pp84-5; ☎ 011-4343-2324; www.neuquen.gov.ar; Maipú 48)

Río Negro (Map pp84-5; ☎ 011-4371-7273; www.rionegro.gov.ar; Tucumán 1916)

Salta (Map pp84-5; ☎ 011-4326-1314; www.turismosalta.gov.ar; Roque Saénz Peña 933)

San Juan (Map pp84-5; ☎ 011-4382-9241; www.sanjuan.gov.ar; Sarmiento 1251)

San Luis (Map pp84-5; ☎ 011-5778-1621; www.sanluis.gov.ar; Azcuénaga 1087)

Santa Cruz (Map pp84-5; ☎ 011-4343-8478; www.casadesantacruz.gov.ar; 25 de Mayo 279)

Santa Fe (Map pp84-5; ☎ 011-4342-0408; www.santafe.gov.ar; 25 de Mayo 178)

Santiago del Estero (Map pp84-5; ☎ 011-4326-3733; www.sde.gov.ar; Florida 274)

Tierra del Fuego (Map pp84-5; ☎ 011-4328-7040; www.tierradelfuego.org.ar; Esmeralda 783)

Tucumán (Map pp84-5; ☎ 011-4322-0010; www.tucumanturismo.gov.ar; Suipacha 140)

With offices throughout the country, the Automóvil Club Argentino (ACA) is a useful source of good, up-to-date maps of provinces and cities that are useful for driving and trip planning. For more information, see p619.

TRAVELERS WITH DISABILITIES

Travelers with disabilities will find things somewhat difficult in Argentina. Those in wheelchairs in particular will quickly realize that many cities' narrow, busy and uneven sidewalks are difficult to negotiate. Crossing streets is also a problem, since not every corner has ramps and Argentine drivers don't have much patience for slower pedestrians, disabled or not. Nevertheless, Argentines with disabilities do get around, and in Buenos Aires there exist a few buses described as *piso bajo*, which lower to provide wheelchair lifts. Wheelchair curb ramps exist at many corners in Buenos Aires, but they're often broken beyond use.

Except at four- and five-star properties, hotels usually do not have wheelchair-accessible rooms (at least as they're known in other parts of the world), meaning doors are narrow and there is little space to move around inside the room. Bathrooms at midrange and budget hotels are notoriously small, making it difficult for anyone (disabled or not) to get around in. For truly accessible rooms, you'll have better luck in pricier hotels. Call ahead and ask specific questions – even if a hotel defines a room as wheelchair-accessible, it may not be up to standards to which you're accustomed.

Other than the use of Braille on ATMs, little effort has been dedicated to bettering accessibility for the blind. Stoplights are rarely equipped with sound alerts. The **Biblioteca Argentina Para Ciegos** (Argentine Library for the Blind; BAC; Map pp82-3; ☎ 011-4981-0137; www.bac.org.ar; Lezica 3909, Buenos Aires) maintains a Braille collection of over 3000 books, as well as other resources.

In Buenos Aires, **QRV Transportes Especiales** (☎ 011-4306-6635, 011-15-6863-9555; www.qrvtransportes.com.ar) offers private transport and city tours in vans fully equipped for wheelchair users. **BA Cultural Concierge** (www.baculturalconcierge.com) offers service for low-mobility travelers by helping with errands.

Also check out the following international organizations online, all of which offer links to other resources:

Access-able Travel Source www.access-able.com
Mobility International www.miusa.org

National Information Communication Awareness Network www.nican.com.au
Society for Accessible Travel & Hospitality www.sath.org

VISAS

Nationals of the USA, Canada, most Western European countries, Australia and New Zealand do not need visas to visit Argentina. In theory, upon arrival all non-visa visitors must obtain a free tourist card, good for 90 days and renewable for 90 more. In practice, immigration officials issue these only at major border crossings, such as airports and on the ferries and hydrofoils between Buenos Aires and Uruguay. Although you should not toss your card away, losing it is no major catastrophe; at most exit points, immigration officials will provide immediate replacement for free.

However, for information on Argentina's new entry fee, which particularly affects Americans, Canadians and Australians, see p614.

Dependent children traveling without *both* parents theoretically need a notarized document certifying that both parents agree to the child's travel. Parents may also wish to bring a copy of the custody form; however, there's a good chance they won't be asked for either document.

Very short visits to neighboring countries usually do not require visas. Despite what a travel agency might say, you probably don't need a Brazilian visa to cross from the Argentine town of Puerto Iguazú to Foz do Iguaçu and/or Ciudad del Este, Paraguay, as long as you return the same day. You should bring your passport, however, and double- check this information – ideally with someone who has done it recently. For more information on entering Brazil, see the boxed text (p225).

The same is true at the Bolivian border town of Villazón, near La Quiaca (see the boxed text, p259). Officials at the Paraguayan crossing at Encarnación, near Posadas (see the boxed text, p218), can charge a fine from crossers who don't have a Paraguayan visa (Australian, New Zealand, Canadian and US nationals need them).

Visa Extensions

For a 90-day extension on your tourist visa, visit the **Dirección Nacional de Migraciones** (immigration office; Map pp84-5; ☎ 011-4317-0200; Antártida Argentina 1355; ☑ 7:30am-1:30pm Mon-Fri) in Buenos Aires. You must do so during the week that your tourist visa is scheduled to expire. The fee is AR$300.

Another option if you're staying more than three months is to cross into Colonia or Montevideo (both in Uruguay) or into Chile for a day or two before your visa expires, then return with a new 90-day visa. However, this only works if you don't need a visa to enter the other country.

VOLUNTEERING

There are many opportunities for volunteering in Argentina, from food banks to *villas miserias* to organic farms to working with monkeys. Most Argentine NGOs provide volunteer opportunities for travelers, sometimes in the form of internships that can go toward tertiary degree credits.

Argentine organizations:

Conservación Patagonica (www.patagonialandtrust.org/volunteer.htm) Help to create a national park.
Eco Yoga Park One-of-a-kind; see the boxed text (p104).
Fundación Banco de Alimentos (www.bancodealimentos.org.ar) Short-term, simple work at a food bank.
Parque Nacional Los Glaciares (☎ 02962-430004) Summer work with park rangers in El Chaltén. Spanish language skills preferred.
Refugio del Caraya (www.volunteer-with-howler-monkeys.org)

Referral services:

Anda Responsible Travel (www.andatravel.com.ar)
Buenos Aires Volunteer (www.bavolunteer.org.ar)
Foundation for Sustainable Development (www.fsdinternational.org)
Fundación Fos (www.fundacionfos.org.ar) Volunteer in Córdoba.
La Montaña (www.lamontana.com/volunteer-work) Volunteer in Bariloche.
Organic Volunteers (www.organicvolunteers.org) Organic farming in Argentina.
Patagonia Volunteer (www.patagoniavolunteer.org) Opportunities in Patagonia.
South American Explorers (www.saexplorers.org/clubhouses/buenosaires)
Volunteer South America (www.volunteersouthamerica.net) List of NGOs.
WWOOF Argentina (www.wwoofargentina.com) Organic farming in Argentina.
Voluntario Global (www.voluntarioglobal.org.ar) Community volunteering.

DIRECTORY

WOMEN TRAVELERS

Being a woman traveling in Argentina is a challenge, especially if you are young, going it alone and/or maintaining an inflexibly liberal attitude. In some ways Argentina is a safer place for a woman than Europe, the USA and most other Latin American countries, but dealing with its machismo culture can be a real pain in the ass.

Some males brimming with testosterone feel the need to comment on a woman's attractiveness. This often happens when the woman is alone and walking by on the street; it occasionally happens to two or more women walking together, but never to a heterosexual couple. Verbal comments include crude language, hisses, whistles and *piropos* (flirtatious comments), which many Argentine males consider an art of complimenting a woman. *Piropos* are often vulgar, although some can be creative and even eloquent. Much as you may want to give them a kick where it counts, the best thing to do is completely ignore the comments. After all, many *porteñas* (women from Buenos Aires) do enjoy getting these 'compliments' and most men don't necessarily mean to be insulting; they're just doing what males in their culture are brought up to do.

Images of attractive woman are very often used for advertising – even for the most non-sexual product (like health care). This can get old quick, but those who make a conscious effort to not let it bother them are least affected.

On the plus side of machismo, expect men to hold a door open for you and always let you enter first, including getting on buses; this gives you a better chance at grabbing an empty seat, so get in there quick.

WORK

Argentina is short on jobs – many locals are unemployed or underemployed – and unskilled foreign travelers shouldn't expect to find much work other than teaching English (or perhaps working at an expat bar). Working out of an institute, native English speakers (certified or not) can earn about AR$20 to AR$30 per hour. When planning, you should take into account slow periods such as January and February, when many locals leave town on vacation. Most teachers work 'illegally,' heading over to Uruguay every three months for a new visa.

For job postings, check out www.craigslist.com and the classifieds in the English-language newspapers *Buenos Aires Herald* (www.buenosairesherald.com) or the *Argentimes* (www.theargentimes.com). You could also try posting on expat website forums such as www.baexpats.org.

Transportation

CONTENTS

GETTING THERE & AWAY

ENTERING THE COUNTRY

Entering Argentina is straightforward; immigration officials at airports are generally quick to the point and waste few words, while those at border crossings may take a little more time scrutinizing your passport before stamping it. Anyone entering the country is required to have a valid passport. Once you're in the country, police can still demand identification at any moment. It's a good idea to carry at least a photocopy of your passport around town at all times. For information on visa requirements, see p611.

When entering by air, you officially must have a return ticket, though this is rarely asked for once you're in Argentina. However, it is commonly asked for by the airline in the country of origin. Most airlines prohibit the boarding of any passengers without proof of onward travel, regardless of whether the person was sold a one-way ticket or not. They do this because the airline is responsible for flying you back home should you be denied entrance (which is highly unlikely) once you're in Argentina. For those planning to travel indefinitely, the only way out of this predicament is to buy a cheap, *fully refundable* onward flight (say, Mendoza to Santiago, Chile) and either use it or get the refund once you're in Argentina. The refund, however, can take months to process.

AIR

Argentina has direct flights between countries including North America, the UK, Europe, Australia, New Zealand, Japan, Italy, Spain and South Africa, and from all South American countries except the Guianas. Alternatively, you can fly to a neighboring country, such as Chile or Brazil, and continue overland to Argentina.

Airports & Airlines

Aerolíneas Argentinas, the national carrier, enjoys a good reputation for its international flights (although its domestic flights are prone to delay; see p616). Except for flights from Santiago, Chile to Mendoza or Córdoba, nearly all international flights arrive at Buenos Aires' **Aeropuerto Internacional Ministro Pistarini** (Ezeiza; ☎ 011-5480-6111, tourist information 011-4480-0224), which is about a 40-minute bus or taxi ride out of town. For information on how to get into town from Ezeiza, see p134.

Airports in several provincial capitals and tourist destinations are earmarked as 'international': this usually means they receive flights from neighboring countries. Basic information on most Argentine airports can be found online at **Aeropuertos Argentina 2000** (www.aa2000.com.ar).

THINGS CHANGE...

The information in this chapter is particularly vulnerable to change. Check directly with the airline or a travel agent to make sure you understand how a fare (and ticket you may buy) works and be aware of the security requirements for international travel. Shop carefully. The details given in this chapter should be regarded as pointers and are not a substitute for your own careful, up-to-date research.

Airports in Argentina include (but are not limited to) the following:
Bariloche (airport code BRC; ☎ 02944-405016)
Córdoba (COR; ☎ 0351-475-0871)
El Calafate (ECA; ☎ 02902-491-220)
Jujuy (JUJ; ☎ 0388-491-1103)
Mendoza (MDZ; ☎ 0261-520-6000)
Puerto Iguazú (IGR; ☎ 03757-421996)
Río Gallegos (RGL; ☎ 02966-442340)
Rosario (ROS; ☎ 0341-451-2997)
Salta (SLA; ☎ 0387-424-3115)
San Juan (UAQ; ☎ 0264-425-4133)
Tucumán (TUC; ☎ 0381-426-5072)
Ushuaia (USH; ☎ 0291-431232)

AIRLINES FLYING TO & FROM ARGENTINA
The following airlines fly to and from Argentina and are listed here with their telephone numbers in Argentina; all numbers that aren't toll-free are Buenos Aires numbers.
Aerolíneas Argentinas (airline code ARG; ☎ 0810-222-86527; www.aerolineas.com)
AeroSur (ASU; ☎ 011-4516-0999; www.aerosur.com)
Air Canada (ACA; ☎ 011-4327-3640; www.aircanada.ca)
Air France (AFR; ☎ 011-4317-4700; www.airfrance.com)
Alitalia (AZA; ☎ 0810-777-2548; www.alitalia.com)
American Airlines (AAL; ☎ 011-4318-1111; www.aa.com)
Avianca (AVA; ☎ 011-4322-2731; www.avianca.com)
British Airways (BA; ☎ 011-4320-6600; www.britishairways.com)
Continental (COA; ☎ 0800-333-0425; www.continental.com)
Copa (CMP; ☎ 0810-222-2672; www.copaair.com)
Delta (DAL; ☎ 0800-666-0133; www.delta.com)
Gol (GLO; ☎ 0810-266-3232; www.voegol.com.br)
KLM (KLM; ☎ 011-4317-4711; www.klm.com)
LAN (LAN; ☎ 0800-999-9526; www.lan.com)
Líneas Aéreas del Estado (LADE) (LDE; ☎ 0810-810-5233; www.lade.com.ar)
Lufthansa (DLH; ☎ 011-4319-0600; www.lufthansa.com)
Pluna (PUA; ☎ 011-4120-0530; www.pluna.com.uy)
Qantas Airways (QFA; ☎ 011-4114-5800; www.qantas.com)
TACA (TAI; ☎ 0810-333-8222; www.taca.com)
Transportes Aéreos de Mercosur (TAM; ☎ 0810-333-3333; www.tam.com.py)
United Airlines (UAL; ☎ 0810-777-8648; www.united.com.ar)

Tickets
From almost everywhere, South America is a relatively costly destination, but discount fares can reduce the bite considerably. Contacting a travel agency that specializes in Latin American destinations often turns up the best deals.

INTERCONTINENTAL (RTW) TICKETS
Some of the best deals for travelers visiting many countries on different continents are Round-the-World (RTW) tickets. Itineraries from the USA, Europe or Australia usually include five or six stopovers (including Buenos Aires). Similar 'Circle Pacific' fares allow excursions between Australasia and South America. These types of tickets are certain to have restrictions, so check the fine print carefully. For an idea of the varying fares and itinerary policies for both types of tickets, check out the following websites:
Air Brokers International (www.airbrokers.com) US based.
Airtreks (www.airtreks.com) US based.
Round the World Flights (www.roundtheworldflights.com) UK based.

Australia & New Zealand
Qantas flies from Auckland to Buenos Aires via Sydney. Aerolíneas Argentinas has direct flights to Buenos Aires from both Sydney and Auckland. Nondirect flights go via the USA or Santiago, Chile.

RECIPROCITY FEE & DEPARTURE TAXES

As of January 2010, citizens from some countries have to pay a 'reciprocity fee' *(tasa de reciprocidad)* when they land in Ezeiza. This is equal to what Argentines are charged for visas to visit those countries. These fees are US$131 for Americans, US$70 for Canadians and US$100 for Australians. The fee is payable in cash, credit card or traveler's check and is usually good for 10 years (per entry for Canadians, though – sucks, eh?). It's currently charged at Ezeiza only, but in the future will be collected at all immigration checkpoints.

When leaving Ezeiza on an international flight, passengers have to pay a departure tax. Tickets bought after March 2009, however, should have this tax included in the ticket price.

The main domestic airports that charge a departure tax are Trelew (AR$18), El Calafate (AR$38) and Ushuaia (AR$25).

CLIMATE CHANGE & TRAVEL

Climate change is a serious threat to the ecosystems that humans rely upon, and air travel is the fastest-growing contributor to the problem. Lonely Planet regards travel, overall, as a global benefit, but believes we all have a responsibility to limit our personal impact on global warming.

Flying & Climate Change

Pretty much every form of motor travel generates carbon dioxide (the main cause of human-induced climate change) but planes are far and away the worst offenders, not just because of the sheer distances they allow us to travel, but because they release greenhouse gases high into the atmosphere. The statistics are frightening: two people taking a return flight between Europe and the US will contribute as much to climate change as an average household's gas and electricity consumption over a whole year.

Carbon Offset Schemes

Climatecare.org and other websites use 'carbon calculators' that allow jetsetters to offset the greenhouse gases they are responsible for with contributions to energy-saving projects and other climate-friendly initiatives in the developing world – including projects in India, Honduras, Kazakhstan and Uganda.

Lonely Planet, together with Rough Guides and other concerned partners in the travel industry, supports the carbon offset scheme run by climatecare.org. Lonely Planet offsets all of its staff and author travel.

For more information check out our website: lonelyplanet.com.

Canada

Air Canada flies direct from Toronto to Buenos Aires. Booking flights with connections through a US carrier (such as American Airlines and Continental via Dallas, Houston, Los Angeles, Miami or New York) may offer more flexibility.

Europe

Direct services from London (and other cities) to Buenos Aires are available with Aerolíneas Argentinas and several other airlines. **Journey Latin America** (☎ 020-8747 3108; www.journeylatinamerica.co.uk) specializes in travel to Latin America and is a good place to start your inquiries.

Direct flights from Europe to Buenos Aires include Paris (with Air France), Madrid (Iberia and Aerolíneas Argentinas), Rome (Aerolíneas Argentinas) and Frankfurt (Lufthansa). Nondirect flights go via Sao Paolo, Brazil, or Santiago, Chile.

USA

The principal gateways are Atlanta, Chicago, Dallas, Houston, Los Angeles, Miami and New York. Aerolíneas Argentinas, American Airlines, Continental, Delta and United fly to Buenos Aires. Latin American travel specialist **eXito Travel** (☎ in US 800-655-4053; www.exitotravel.com)

offers some of the cheapest fares around, as well as personal service from an impressively well-informed staff.

LAND
Border Crossings

There are numerous border crossings from neighboring Chile, Bolivia, Paraguay, Brazil and Uruguay; the following lists are only the principal crossings. Generally, border formalities are straightforward as long as all your documents are in order. For info on necessary visas and documents, see p611.

BOLIVIA

La Quiaca to Villazón Many buses go from Jujuy and Salta to La Quiaca, where you must walk or take a taxi across the Bolivian border.

Aguas Blancas to Bermejo From Orán, reached by bus from Salta or Jujuy, take a bus to Aguas Blancas and then Bermejo, where you can catch a bus to Tarija.

Pocitos to Yacuiba Buses from Jujuy or Salta go to Tartagal and then on to the Bolivian border at Pocitos/Yacuiba, where there are buses to Santa Cruz.

BRAZIL

The most common crossing is from Puerto Iguazú (p226) to Foz do Iguaçu (p230). Check both cities for more information on the peculiarities of this border crossing, especially if you're crossing the border into Brazil only to see the other side of Iguazú Falls. For specifics, see the boxed text on p225. There are also border crossings from Paso de los Libres (Argentina; p212) to Uruguaiana (Brazil) to São Borja (Brazil).

CHILE

There are numerous crossings between Argentina and Chile. Except in far southern Patagonia, every land crossing involves crossing the Andes. Due to weather, some high-altitude passes close in winter; even the busy Mendoza–Santiago route over RN 7 can close for several days (sometimes longer) during a severe storm. Always check road conditions, especially if you have a flight scheduled on the other side of the mountains. The following are the most commonly used crossings:

Bariloche to Puerto Montt The famous, scenic 12-hour bus-boat combination runs over the Andes to Chile. It takes two days in winter. See the boxed text, p409.

El Calafate to Puerto Natales and Parque Nacional Torres del Paine Probably the most beaten route down here, heading from the Glaciar Perito Moreno (near El Calafate) to Parque Nacional Torres del Paine (near Puerto Natales). Several buses per day in summer; one to two daily in the off-season.

Los Antiguos to Chile Chico Those entering from Chile can access the rugged RN 40 from here and head down to El Chaltén and El Calafate. Best in summer, when there's actually public transport available.

Mendoza to Santiago The most popular crossing between the two countries, passing 6962m Aconcagua en route.

Salta to San Pedro de Atacama (via Purmamarca) Twelve-hour bus ride through the altiplano with stunningly beautiful scenery.

Ushuaia to Punta Arenas Daily buses in summer, fewer in winter, on this 12- to 18-hour trip (depending on weather conditions), which includes a ferry crossing at either Porvenir or Punta Delgada/Primera Angostura.

URUGUAY & PARAGUAY

There are two direct border crossings between Argentina and Paraguay: Clorinda (p240) to Asunción, and Posadas (p214) to Encarnación. From Puerto Iguazú, Argentina, you can also cross through Brazil into Ciudad del Este, Paraguay.

Border crossings from Argentine cities to Uruguayan cities include Gualeguaychú (p203) to Fray Bentos; Colón (p207) to Paysandú; and Concordia (p210) to Salto. All

involve crossing bridges. Buses from Buenos Aires to Montevideo and other waterfront cities, however, are slower and less convenient than the ferries (or ferry–bus combinations) across the Río de la Plata (see below). The crossing at Gualeguaychú is still closed due to conflict surrounding the construction of the Botnia pulp mill on the Uruguayan side of the river. For more information, see the boxed text, p536.

Bus

Travelers can bus to Argentina from most bordering countries. Buses are usually comfortable, modern and fairly clean. Crossing over does not involve too many hassles; just make sure that you have any proper visas (p611) beforehand.

RIVER

There are several river crossings between Uruguay and Buenos Aires that involve ferry or hydrofoil, and often require combinations with buses.

Buenos Aires to Colonia Daily ferries (one to three hours) head to Colonia, with bus connections to Montevideo (additional three hours). See p560.

Buenos Aires to Montevideo High-speed ferries carry passengers from downtown Buenos Aires to the Uruguayan capital in only 2¾ hours. See p554.

Tigre to Carmelo Regular passenger launches speed from the Buenos Aires suburb of Tigre to Carmelo in 2½ hours (services also go to Montevideo from Tigre). See p562.

SEA

Arriving in Argentina by sea is uncommon indeed, although Chilean company **Navimag** (www.navimag.com) operates the famous ferry from Puerto Montt, Chile (near Bariloche), down the length of Chilean Patagonia to Puerto Natales, Chile, near Parque Nacional Torres del Paine (due west of Río Gallegos).

GETTING AROUND

AIR
Airlines in Argentina

The national carrier, **Aerolíneas Argentinas/ Austral** (☎ 0810-222-86527; www.aerolineas.com), offers the most domestic flights, but it's not necessarily better than its competitors. In fact, the airline had a very bad reputation for delays in the past (though most recently it's improved).

Other airlines with domestic flights include **LAN** (LAN; ☎ 0800-999-9526; www.lan.com) and **Líneas Aéreas del Estado** (LADE; ☎ 0810-810-5233; www .lade.com.ar), the air force's passenger service. The latter has some of the least expensive air tickets (probably because its offices still have the same decor it did in 1974) and specializes in Patagonia; the airline has very few flights, however.

Most domestic airlines operate on a two-tier system, where foreigners pay more than locals for the same ticket. One way to avoid the higher fee Aerolíneas Argentinas charges foreigners is by taking advantage of the discounted airfares the airline offers to those who fly to Argentina with Aerolíneas. However, you must purchase these tickets from outside Argentina, usually at the time of purchasing your international flight. The promotion is most convenient for travelers who can set their schedule prior to visiting the country.

Nearly all domestic flights (except for LADE's hops around Patagonia) have connections only through **Aeroparque Jorge Newbery** (☎ 011-5480-6111; www.aa2000.com.ar), a short distance north of downtown Buenos Aires. Flying with certain airlines on certain flights can be financially comparable or even cheaper than covering the same distance by bus, but demand is heavy and flights, especially to Patagonian destinations during summer, are often booked out well in advance.

BICYCLE

If you dig cycling your way around a country, Argentina has some good potential. It will also save you some money: partnered with camping, cycling can cut the costs of your trip significantly. And of course you'll see the landscape in greater detail, you'll have far more freedom than you would if beholden to public transportation, and you'll likely meet more locals.

Road bikes are suitable for many paved roads, but byways are often narrow and surfaces can be rough. A *todo terreno* (mountain bike) is often safer and more convenient, allowing you to use the unpaved shoulder and the very extensive network of gravel roads throughout the country. Argentine bicycles are improving in quality, but are still far from equal to their counterparts in Europe or the USA.

There are two major drawbacks to long-distance bicycling in Argentina. One is the wind, which in Patagonia can slow your progress to a crawl. The other is Argentine motorists: on many of the country's straight, narrow, two-lane highways, they can be a serious hazard to cyclists. Make yourself as visible as possible, and wear a helmet.

Bring an adequate repair kit and extra parts (and the know-how to use them) and stock up on good maps (see p604), which is usually easier to do once you're in Argentina (there are plenty of places to get good maps in Buenos Aires). Even if you have 10 maps for a region, always confirm directions and inquire about conditions locally; maps can be unreliable and conditions change regularly. In Patagonia, a windbreaker and warm clothing are essential. Don't expect much traffic on some back roads.

For ideas on where you might want to ride, see p58.

Rental

Reasonable bicycle rentals (mostly mountain bikes) are available in many popular tourist destinations, such as along the Atlantic Coast, Mendoza, Bariloche and other towns throughout the Lake District and Córdoba's Central Sierras. Prices are by the hour or day, and are affordable.

Purchase

Many towns have bike shops, but high-quality bikes are expensive, and repair parts can be hard to come by. If you do decide to buy while you're here, you're best off doing so in Buenos Aires. Selection in other major cities – even Córdoba and Mendoza – is pretty slim, and prices for an imported bike (which you'll want if you're doing serious cycling) are much higher than in their country of origin. If you're staying for a while and you just need a bike for tooling around the city, you'll find Argentine bikes are good value. You can pick up a beach cruiser for under AR$600, and a multispeed townie for around AR$800.

BOAT

Opportunities for boat or river travel in and around Argentina are limited, though there are regular international services to/from Uruguay (see opposite) and to/from Chile via the Lake District (see p408). The classic sea

TRANSPORTATION

route south along the Patagonian Andes is the Navimag boat trip (see p616); although the journey is in Chile, many people combine the trip with a visit to Argentina. Further south, from Ushuaia, operators offer boat trips on the Beagle Channel in Tierra del Fuego; see p521.

Otherwise, if you must be on the water, head to the Buenos Aires suburb of Tigre (p137), where there are numerous boat excursions around the delta of the Río de la Plata.

BUS

If you're doing any serious traveling around Argentina, you'll become very familiar with the country's excellent bus network, which reaches almost everywhere. Buses are fast, surprisingly comfortable and can be a rather luxurious experience. It's the way most Argentines get around. Larger luggage is stowed in the hold below, security is generally good (especially on the 1st-class buses) and attendants tag your bags (and should be tipped). If you have a long way to go – say, Buenos Aires to Mendoza – overnight buses are the way to go, saving you a night's accommodations and the daylight hours for fun.

Hundreds of bus companies serve different regions but a few bigger lines (listed here) really dominate the long-haul business:

Andesmar (☎ 0261-429-5095, 011-6385-3031; www .andesmar.com) Serves the entire country.

Chevallier (☎ 011-4000-5255; www.nuevachevallier .com) Serves the entire country.

El Rápido International (☎ 0261-405-4344; www .elrapidoint.com.ar) Buenos Aires, Mendoza, Córdoba and Rosario. International service to Santiago and Viña del Mar (Chile) and Lima (Peru).

Via Bariloche (☎ 0800-333-7575; www.viabariloche .com.ar) Serves most destinations in La Pampa province, the Lake District and Patagonia.

Most cities and towns have a central bus terminal where each company has its own ticket window. Some companies post schedules prominently, and the ticket price and departure time is always on the ticket you buy. Expect (Argentine) restrooms, left luggage, fast-food stalls, kiosks and newspaper vendors inside or near almost every terminal. In larger destination cities they'll often have a tourist information office. There are generally few hotel touts or other traveler-hassling types at terminals; El Calafate is one notable exception.

A nearly comprehensive search engine for bus schedules and prices country-wide is www.plataforma10.com.

Classes

This is where it gets fun. Better bus lines such as Chevallier and Andesmar (not to mention dozens of others) have modern coaches with spacious, cushy seats, large windows, air-conditioning, TVs, toilets (though don't expect luxury here – and bring toilet paper) and sometimes an attendant serving coffee and snacks.

On overnight trips it's well worth the extra pesos to go *coche cama* (sleeper class), though the cheaper *coche semi-cama* (semisleeper) is definitely manageable. In *coche cama*, seats are wider, recline almost flat and are far more comfortable. If you want to lay totally flat, you can go *ejecutivo* (executive) or *coche super cama* (super sleeper), which is available on a few popular runs such as Buenos Aires–Córdoba and Buenos Aires–Rosario. If pinching pesos, *común* (common) is the cheapest class. For trips under about five hours, there's usually no choice and buses are *común* or beat-up *semi-cama*, which are both usually just fine.

Costs

Bus fares vary widely depending on season, class and company. Prices given in the Getting There & Away sections throughout this book are approximate and are mid- to high-season fares, generally in *semi-cama*. Patagonia runs tend to be the most expensive. Many companies accept credit cards. Following are sample fares from Buenos Aires:

Destination	Cost (AR$)
Bariloche	245
Comodoro Rivadavia	308
Córdoba	150
Mar del Plata	90
Mendoza	250
Puerto Iguazú	280
Puerto Madryn	270
Rosario	50

Reservations

Often you don't need to buy bus tickets ahead of time unless you're traveling on a Friday between major cities, when overnight *coche cama* services sell out fast. During holiday stretches, such as late December, January, July and August, tickets sell quickly, so you're best off buying yours ahead of time. As soon as you arrive somewhere, especially if it's a town with limited services, find out which companies go to your next destination and when, and plan your trip out around that.

When the bus terminal is on the outskirts of a big town or city, there are often downtown agencies selling tickets without commission. Some of these agencies are listed in this book – if not, ask at your hotel or the tourist office.

Seasonal Services

In the Lake District and northern Patagonia, bus services are outstanding during summer (November through March), when there are many microbus routes to campgrounds, along lake circuits, to trail heads and to other destinations popular with tourists. Outside summer, however, these services stop, and getting around becomes much more difficult.

In Patagonia the famed stretch of RN 40, or Ruta Nacional Cuarenta (Route 40), south of Gobernador Costa, is infrequently traveled, rough and has with zero public transport – well, almost. Recently, some businesses have sprung up offering seasonal service (really they're microbus tours) along the route. For more details, see the boxed text, p462.

CAR & MOTORCYCLE

Because Argentina is so large, many parts are accessible only by private vehicle, despite the country's extensive public transport system. This is especially true in Patagonia, where distances are great and buses can be infrequent. Besides, with your own wheels you can stop for photo ops or bathroom breaks at the side of the road whenever you want.

If you want to rent a motorcycle in Buenos Aires, check out **Motocare** (p136).

Automobile Associations

Whenever driving in Argentina, it's worth being a member (in fact, you may *already* be something of a member) of the **Automóvil Club Argentino** (ACA; Map pp88-9; ☎ 011-4802-6061; www.aca .org.ar, in Spanish; Av del Libertador 1850, Palermo, Buenos Aires), which has offices, gas stations and garages throughout the country, offering **road service** (☎ 0800-888-84253) and towing in and around major destinations. ACA recognizes members of most overseas auto clubs and grants them privileges including road service and discounts on maps and accommodations. Bring your card.

Bring Your Own Vehicle

Chile is probably the best country on the continent for shipping a vehicle from overseas, though Argentina is feasible. Getting the vehicle out of customs typically involves routine but time-consuming paperwork.

Driver's License & Documents

Technically you're supposed to have an International Driving Permit to supplement your national or state driver's license. If you are stopped, police will also inspect your automobile registration and insurance and tax documents, all of which must be up to date. Except in Buenos Aires, security problems are unusual.

Drivers of Argentine vehicles must carry their title document (*tarjeta verde* or 'green card'); if it's a rental, make sure it's in the glove box. For foreign vehicles, customs permission is the acceptable substitute. Liability insurance is obligatory, and police often ask to see proof of insurance at checkpoints.

Fuel

Nafta (gas) costs roughly AR$3.15 to AR$3.60 per liter. Avoid *normal* or *común* (regular) as it's usually low quality and hard to find. Super and *premium* (often called Fangio) are better choices. In Patagonia (where much of Argentina's oil fields are) gas prices are nearly half what they are elsewhere. *Estaciones de servicio* (gas stations) are fairly common (especially YPFs), but outside the cities keep an eye on your gas gauge. In Patagonia it's a good idea to carry extra fuel.

Rental

Renting a car in Argentina is a good option because it allows you the freedom to go and stop wherever you please, and to visit those backcountry places that buses don't. To rent a car, you must be at least 21 years of age and have a valid driver's license and a credit card. To drive you must have an International Driving Permit, but renters rarely ask for this.

The cheapest and smallest vehicles cost about AR$190 per day with 150km to 200km included. Unlimited-kilometer deals do exist but might be more expensive, depending on the destination. A 4WD vehicle is significantly more expensive. One of the cheapest places to rent a car is Bariloche; if you're heading down to Patagonia or plan to drive for a while, this is a good place to rent. Reserving a car with one of the major international agencies in your home country sometimes gets you lower rates.

Insurance

Liability insurance is obligatory in Argentina, and police ask to see proof of insurance at checkpoints. Fortunately, coverage is reasonably priced. If you plan on taking the car to neighboring countries, make sure it will remain covered (you'll have to pay extra). Among reputable insurers in Argentina are **Mapfre** (☎ 0800-999-7424; www.mapfre.com.ar) and **ACA** (☎ 011-4802-6061; www.aca.org.ar).

Purchase

If you are spending several months in Argentina, purchasing a car is an alternative worth exploring. If you resell the car at the end of your stay, it may turn out even more economical. On the other hand, any used car can be a risk, especially on Patagonia's rugged back roads, and the process of purchasing a car can be a real headache.

If you buy a car, you must deal with the exasperating Argentine bureaucracy. You must have the title (tarjeta verde), and license tax payments must be up to date. As a foreigner, you may find it useful to carry a notarized document authorizing your use of the car, since the bureaucracy moves too slowly to change the title easily. Argentines themselves rarely change the title over because of the expense involved.

As a foreigner without a DNI (national document) you may own a vehicle in Argentina; however, you theoretically cannot take it out of the country without a notarized authorization, which can be difficult to obtain.

Road Rules & Hazards

Anyone considering driving in Argentina should know that Argentine drivers are aggressive and commonly ignore speed limits, road signs and even traffic signals. That said, once you're out of the city, driving can be much more pleasant.

Most Argentine highways have a speed limit of 80km/h, and some have been raised to 100km/h or more, but hardly anybody pays attention to these – or any other regulations. During the pampas harvest season, pay particular attention to slow-moving farm machinery: it's not a hazard in its own right, but brings out the worst in impatient Argentine motorists. Night driving is not recommended; in many regions animals hang out on the road for warmth, and plowing into an Argentine cow is not fun.

Have on hand some emergency reflectors (balizas) and a 1kg fire extinguisher. Headrests are required for the driver and passengers, and seatbelts are now obligatory (though few wear them). Motorcycle helmets are also obligatory, although this law is rarely enforced.

You won't often see police patrolling the highways, but you will meet them at major intersections and roadside checkpoints where they conduct meticulous document and equipment checks. Equipment violations can carry heavy fines, but such checks are more commonly pretexts for graft. For instance, if the police ask to check your turn signals (which almost no Argentine bothers to use), brake lights or hand brake, it may well be a warning of corruption in progress. The police may claim that you must pay the fine at a local bank, which may not be open until the following day or (if it's on a weekend) until Monday. If you are uncertain about your rights, state in a very matter-of-fact manner your intention to contact your embassy or consulate, or feign such complete ignorance of Spanish that you're more trouble than the police think it's worth. It may be possible to pay the fine on the spot (wink, wink). Ask, '¿Puedo pagar la multa ahora?' ('Can I pay the fine now?').

HITCHHIKING

Hitchhiking (hacer dedo) is never entirely safe in any country in the world. Travelers who decide to hitch should understand that they are taking a small but potentially serious risk. People who do choose to hitch will be safer if they travel in pairs and let someone know where they are planning to go.

Along with Chile, Argentina is probably the best country for hitching in all of South America. The major drawback is that Argentine vehicles are often stuffed full with families and children, but truckers will frequently pick up backpackers. At the estaciones de servicio (gas stations) at the outskirts of large Argentine cities, where truckers gas up their vehicles, it's often easy to solicit a ride.

Women can and do hitchhike alone, but should exercise caution and especially avoid getting into a car with more than one man. In Patagonia, where distances are great and vehicles few, hitchers should expect long waits and carry warm, windproof clothing.

Having a sign will improve your chances for a pickup, especially if it says something like *visitando Argentina de Canada* (visiting Argentina from Canada), rather than just a destination. Argentines are fascinated by foreigners.

There are a few routes along which hitching is undesirable. RN 40, from El Calafate to Perito Moreno and Río Mayo, is one. Up north, the scenic route from Tucumán to Cafayate is difficult past Tafí del Valle. Throughout the Lake District, hitching is common, especially out in the country where locals regularly get around by thumbing it.

For good information (in Spanish) see www.autostopargentina.com.ar.

LOCAL TRANSPORTATION
Bus
Local Argentine buses, called *colectivos,* are notorious for charging down the street, gobbling up coins and spewing clouds of black smoke while traveling at breakneck speeds. Riding on one is a good way to see the cities and get around, providing you can sort out the often complex bus systems. Buses are clearly numbered and usually carry a placard indicating their final destination. Many identically numbered buses serve slightly different routes (especially in big cities), so pay attention to the placards. To ask 'Does this bus go (to the town center)?' say '¿*Va este colectivo (al centro)?*'

Most city buses operate on coins; you pay as you board. In some cities, such as Mendoza, you must buy prepaid bus cards or – in the case of Córdoba – *cospeles* (tokens). In both cases, they can be bought at any kiosk.

Subway
Buenos Aires is the only Argentine city with a subway system (known as the Subte), and it's the quickest way of getting around the city center. For details, see p136.

Taxi & Remise
The people of Buenos Aires (BA) make frequent use of taxis, which are digitally metered and cheap by US and European standards. Outside the capital, meters are common but not universal, and it may be necessary to agree upon a fare in advance. Drivers are generally polite and honest, but there are exceptions: be sure the meter is set at zero and be sure it's on. It is customary to round up the fare as a tip. In Buenos Aires, do not pay with large bills;

these can be deftly and quickly switched for a fake, or you may get fake bills in change. For more on taking taxis in BA, see p136.

Where public transportation is scarce, it's possible to hire a taxi with a driver for the day. If you bargain, this can actually be cheaper than a rental car, but always negotiate the fee in advance.

Remises are radio taxis without meters that generally offer fixed fares within a given zone. They are usually cheaper than taxis. They don't cruise the city in search of fares, as taxis do, but hotels and restaurants will phone them for you if you ask.

TRAIN
For many years there were major reductions in long-distance train service in Argentina, but recent years have seen some rail lines being progressively reopened. A good source for information is http://www.seat61.com /SouthAmerica.htm.

Long-distance trains have sleepers. Trains continue serve most of Buenos Aires and some surrounding provinces. Major lines further afield from BA currently in service:

Buenos Aires–Bariloche Via Bahía Blanca, Carmen de Patagones/Viedma. Note that the weekly Bahía Blanca–Carmen de Patagones leg is slow and periodically is cancelled.

Buenos Aires–Córdoba Via San Isidro, Tigre and Rosario.

Buenos Aires–Mar del Plata

Buenos Aires–Pinamar/Tandil

Buenos Aires–Posadas Via Concordia and Paso de los Libres.

Buenos Aires–Tucumán Via San Isidro, Rosario and Córdoba.

During the holiday periods, such as Christmas or national holidays, buy tickets in advance. Train fares tend to be lower than comparable bus fares, but trains are slower and there are fewer departure times and destinations. For details on which station each service departs from in Bunos Aires, see p134.

Train buffs will want to take the narrow-gauge *La Trochita* (see the boxed text, p461), which runs between Esquel and El Maitén. Another legendary ride is Salta's spectacular *Tren a las Nubes* (Train to the Clouds; p270); the service is more regular these days compared to a few years ago. A scenic stretch of track (and luxurious service aboard the *Tren Patagónico*) also connects the Lake District hub of Bariloche (p409) to Viedma (p424), on the Atlantic coast of Patagonia.

TRANSPORTATION

Health Dr David Goldberg

Medically speaking, there are two South Americas. Tropical South America covers most of the continent, and includes northern Argentina. Temperate South America takes in southern Argentina, Chile, Uruguay and the Falkland Islands (Islas Malvinas). The diseases found in tropical South America are comparable to those found in tropical areas in Africa and Asia. Particularly important are mosquito-borne infections, including malaria, yellow fever and dengue fever. These are generally not a significant concern in temperate South America, but in 2009 a dengue fever outbreak reached Buenos Aires (see p624).

Prevention is the key to staying healthy in Argentina. Travelers who receive the recommended vaccines and follow common-sense precautions usually come away with nothing more than a little diarrhea.

BEFORE YOU GO

Bring medication in its original, clearly labeled container. A signed, dated letter from your physician describing your medical conditions and medications, including generic names, is also a good idea. If carrying syringes or needles, be sure to have a physician's letter documenting their medical necessity.

INSURANCE

If your health insurance doesn't cover you for medical expenses abroad, consider getting extra insurance. Find out in advance if your insurance plan will make payments directly to providers or reimburse you later for overseas health expenditures. (In Argentina, doctors expect payment in cash.)

MEDICAL CHECKLIST

- acetaminophen (Tylenol) or aspirin
- adhesive or paper tape
- antibacterial ointment (eg Bactroban; for cuts and abrasions)
- antibiotics
- antidiarrheal drugs (eg loperamide)
- antihistamines (for hay fever and allergic reactions)
- anti-inflammatory drugs (eg ibuprofen)
- bandages, gauze, gauze rolls
- DEET-containing insect repellent for the skin
- iodine tablets (for water purification)
- oral rehydration salts
- permethrin-containing insect spray for clothing, tents and bed nets
- pocket knife
- scissors, safety pins, tweezers
- steroid cream or cortisone (for poison ivy and other allergic rashes)
- sunblock
- syringes and sterile needles
- thermometer

INTERNET RESOURCES

There is a wealth of travel health advice on the internet. For further info, the **Lonely Planet website** (www.lonelyplanet.com) is a good place to start. The **World Health Organization** (www.who.int/ith) publishes a superb book called *International Travel and Health*, which is revised annually and is available online at no cost. Another website of general interest is **MD Travel Health** (www.mdtravelhealth.com), which provides complete travel-health recommendations for every country and is updated daily.

RECOMMENDED VACCINATIONS

Since most vaccines don't produce immunity until at least two weeks after they're given, visit a physician four to eight weeks before departure. No vaccines are required for Argentina, but a number are recommended.

Vaccine	Recommended for	Dosage	Side effects
chickenpox	travelers who've never had chickenpox	2 doses 1 month apart	fever; mild case of chickenpox
hepatitis A	all travelers	1 dose before trip; booster 6-12 months later	soreness at injection site; headaches; body aches
hepatitis B	long-term travelers in close contact with the local population	3 doses over 6-month period	soreness at injection site; low-grade fever
measles	travelers who have never had measles or completed a vaccination course	1 dose	fever; rash; joint pains; allergic reactions
rabies	travelers who may have contact with animals and may not have access to medical care	3 doses over 3-4 week period	soreness at injection site; headaches; body aches
tetanus	all travelers who haven't had booster within 10 years	1 dose lasts 10 years	soreness at injection site
typhoid	all travelers	4 capsules by mouth, 1 taken every other day	abdominal pain; nausea; rash
yellow fever	travelers to the northeastern forest areas	1 dose lasts 10 years	headaches; body aches; severe reactions are rare

It's usually a good idea to consult your government's travel health website before departure, if one is available:

Australia (www.smartraveller.gov.au)
Canada (www.hc-sc.gc.ca/english/index.html)
UK (www.nhs.uk/livewell) Click on Travel Health in the drop-down menu.
USA (www.cdc.gov/travel)

FURTHER READING

For further information, see Lonely Planet's *Healthy Travel Central & South America.* If you're traveling with children, Lonely Planet's *Travel with Children* may be useful. The *ABC of Healthy Travel,* by E Walker et al, is another valuable resource.

IN TRANSIT

DEEP VEIN THROMBOSIS (DVT)

Blood clots may form in the legs (deep vein thrombosis or DVT) during plane flights, chiefly because of prolonged immobility. The longer the flight, the greater the risk. Though most blood clots are reabsorbed uneventfully, some may break off and travel through the blood vessels to the lungs, where they could cause life-threatening complications.

The chief symptom of DVT is swelling or pain of the foot, ankle or calf, usually – but not always – on just one side. When a blood clot travels to the lungs, it may cause chest pain and difficulty breathing. Travelers with any of these symptoms should immediately seek medical attention.

To prevent the development of DVT on long flights, you should walk about the cabin, perform isometric contractions of the leg muscles (ie flex the leg muscles while sitting), drink plenty of fluids and avoid alcohol and tobacco.

JET LAG & MOTION SICKNESS

Jet lag is common when crossing more than five time zones, resulting in insomnia, fatigue, malaise or nausea. To avoid jet lag try drinking plenty of (nonalcoholic) fluids and eating light meals. Upon arrival, get exposure to natural sunlight and readjust your schedule (for meals, sleep etc) as soon as possible.

Antihistamines such as dimenhydrinate (Dramamine) and meclizine (Antivert, Bonine) are usually the first choice for treating motion sickness. Their main side effect is drowsiness. An herbal alternative is ginger, which works like a charm for some people.

HEALTH

IN ARGENTINA

AVAILABILITY & COST OF HEALTH CARE

Good medical care is available in Buenos Aires (see p93), but may be variable elsewhere, especially in rural areas. Most doctors and hospitals expect payment in cash, regardless of whether you have travel health insurance.

If you develop a life-threatening medical problem, you'll probably want to be evacuated to a country with state-of-the-art medical care. (For an ambulance, call ☏ 107.) Since this may cost thousands of dollars, be sure you have insurance to cover this before you depart.

You can also try contacting your embassy for recommended medical services. Most pharmacies in Argentina are well supplied. Many medications that require a prescription in the USA and Canada are available over the counter, though they may be relatively expensive. If you're taking any medication on a regular basis, be sure you know its generic (scientific) name, since many pharmaceuticals go under different names in Argentina.

INFECTIOUS DISEASES

Dengue Fever

Dengue fever is a viral infection found throughout South America. It is transmitted by Aedes mosquitoes, which prefer to bite during the daytime and are usually found close to human habitations (often indoors). They breed primarily in artificial water containers, such as jars, barrels, cans, cisterns, metal drums, plastic containers and discarded tires. As a result, dengue is especially common in densely populated, urban environments.

In 2009, several thousand cases of dengue were reported in the northern provinces of Argentina, with Chaco and Catamarca being hit the worst. There were even a few dozen cases in Buenos Aires. Fortunately, relatively few deaths resulted. Dengue usually causes flulike symptoms, including fever, muscle aches, joint pains, headaches, nausea and vomiting, often followed by a rash. The body aches may be quite uncomfortable, but most cases resolve uneventfully in a few days. Severe cases usually occur in children under the age of 15 who are experiencing their second dengue infection.

There is no treatment for dengue fever except to take analgesics such as acetaminophen/paracetamol (Tylenol) and drink plenty of fluids. Severe cases may require hospitalization for intravenous fluids and supportive care. There is no vaccine. The cornerstone of prevention is insect protection measures (see p628).

Hepatitis A

Hepatitis A is the second-most-common travel-related infection (after traveler's diarrhea). It's a viral infection of the liver that is usually acquired by ingestion of contaminated water, food or ice, though it may also be acquired by direct contact with infected persons. The illness occurs throughout the world, but the incidence is higher in developing nations. Symptoms may include fever, malaise, jaundice, nausea, vomiting and abdominal pain. Most cases resolve without complications, though hepatitis A occasionally causes severe liver damage. There is no treatment.

The vaccine for hepatitis A is extremely safe and highly effective. If you get a booster six to 12 months later, it lasts for at least 10 years. You really should get it before you go to Argentina. The safety of the hepatitis A vaccine has not been established for pregnant women or children under two years; instead, they should be given a gammaglobulin injection.

Hepatitis B

Like hepatitis A, hepatitis B is a liver infection that occurs worldwide but is more common in developing nations. Unlike hepatitis A, the disease is usually acquired by sexual contact or by exposure to infected blood, generally through blood transfusions or contaminated needles. The vaccine is recommended only for long-term travelers (on the road more than six months) who expect to live in rural areas or have close physical contact with the local population. Additionally, the vaccine is recommended for anyone who anticipates sexual contact with the local inhabitants or a possible need for medical, dental or other treatments while abroad, especially if a need for transfusions or injections is expected.

The hepatitis B vaccine is safe and highly effective. However, a total of three injections are necessary to establish full immunity. Several countries added the hepatitis B vaccine to the list of routine childhood immunizations in the 1980s, so many young adults are already protected.

A SWINE OF A FLU

The H1N1 virus (commonly referred to as 'Swine Flu') was given a 'Phase 6' rating by the World Health Organization in June 2009. A 'Phase 6' alert means the virus is considered a global pandemic. Like most countries, Argentina was affected. From June to August 2009 (the country's winter) the virus was a serious issue, but the number of cases fell dramatically after the flu season was over.

At the time of research, airport staff in some countries were screening arriving passengers for symptoms of the H1N1 flu. Check with the embassy of the country you're visiting to see if they have imposed any travel restrictions. It's best not to travel if you have flu-like symptoms of any sort.

For the latest information, check with the World Health Organization (www.who.int).

Malaria

Malaria occurs in Argentina, but not the Falkland Islands (Islas Malvinas). It's transmitted by mosquito bites, usually between dusk and dawn. The main symptom is high spiking fevers, which may be accompanied by chills, sweats, headache, body aches, weakness, vomiting or diarrhea. Severe cases may involve the central nervous system and lead to seizures, confusion, coma and death.

For Argentina, taking malaria pills is strongly recommended for travel to rural areas along the borders with Bolivia (lowlands of Salta and Jujuy provinces) and Paraguay (lowlands of Misiones and Corrientes provinces). There is a choice of three malaria pills, all of which work about equally well. Mefloquine (Lariam) is taken once weekly in a dosage of 250mg, starting one to two weeks before arrival and continuing through the trip and for four weeks after return. The problem is that a certain percentage of people (the number is controversial) develop neuropsychiatric side effects, which may range from mild to severe. Atovaquone/proguanil (Malarone) is a newly approved combination pill taken once daily with food starting two days before arrival and continuing through the trip and for seven days after departure. Side effects are typically mild. Doxycycline is a third alternative, but may cause an exaggerated sunburn reaction.

In general, Malarone seems to cause fewer side effects than mefloquine and is becoming more popular. The chief disadvantage is that it has to be taken daily. For longer trips, it's probably worth trying mefloquine; for shorter trips, Malarone will be the drug of choice for most people.

Protecting yourself against mosquito bites is just as important as taking malaria pills (for recommendations, see p628), since none of the pills are 100% effective.

If you do not have access to medical care while traveling, you should bring along additional pills for emergency self-treatment, which you should take if you can't reach a doctor quickly and you develop symptoms that suggest malaria, such as high spiking fevers. One option is to take four tablets of Malarone once daily for three days. However, Malarone should not be used for treatment if you're already taking it for prevention. An alternative is to take 650mg of quinine three times daily and 100mg doxycycline twice daily for one week. If you start self-medication, see a doctor at the earliest possible opportunity.

If you develop a fever after returning home, see a physician, as malaria symptoms may not occur for months.

Rabies

Rabies is a viral infection of the brain and spinal cord that is almost always fatal. The rabies virus is carried in the saliva of infected animals and is typically transmitted through an animal bite, though contamination of any break in the skin with infected saliva may result in rabies. Rabies occurs in all South American countries.

The rabies vaccine is safe, but a full series requires three injections and is quite expensive. Those at high risk for rabies, such as animal handlers and spelunkers (cave explorers), should certainly get the vaccine. In addition, those at lower risk for animal bites should consider asking for the vaccine if they might be traveling to remote areas and might not have access to appropriate medical care if needed. The treatment for a possibly rabid bite consists of the rabies vaccine with rabies immune globulin. It's effective, but must be given promptly. Most travelers don't need rabies vaccine.

HEALTH

All animal bites and scratches must be promptly and thoroughly cleansed with large amounts of soap and water, and local health authorities contacted to determine whether or not further treatment is necessary. Also see Animal Bites, opposite.

Typhoid Fever

Typhoid fever is caused by ingestion of food or water contaminated by a species of salmonella known as *Salmonella typhi*. Fever occurs in virtually all cases. Other symptoms may include headache, malaise, muscle aches, dizziness, loss of appetite, nausea and abdominal pain. Either diarrhea or constipation may occur. Possible complications include intestinal perforation, intestinal bleeding, confusion, delirium or (rarely) coma.

Unless you expect to take all your meals in major hotels and restaurants, a typhoid vaccine is a good idea. It's usually given orally, but is also available as an injection. Neither vaccine is approved for use in children under two years.

The drug of choice for typhoid fever is usually a quinolone antibiotic such as ciprofloxacin (Cipro) or levofloxacin (Levaquin), which many travelers carry for treatment of traveler's diarrhea. However, if you self-treat for typhoid fever, you may also need to self-treat for malaria, since the symptoms of the two diseases may be indistinguishable.

Yellow Fever

Yellow fever is a life-threatening viral infection transmitted by mosquitoes in forested areas. The illness begins with flu-like symptoms, which may include fever, chills, headache, muscle aches, backache, loss of appetite, nausea and vomiting. These symptoms usually subside in a few days, but one person in six enters a second, toxic phase characterized by recurrent fever, vomiting, listlessness, jaundice, kidney failure and hemorrhage, leading to death in up to half of the cases. There is no treatment except for supportive care.

The yellow fever vaccine is strongly recommended for all travelers greater than nine months of age who visit the northeastern forest areas near the border with Brazil and Paraguay. For an up-to-date map showing the distribution of yellow fever in Argentina, go to the Centers for Disease Control (CDC) website at www.cdc.gov/travel/diseases /maps /yellowfever_map2.htm.

TRADITIONAL MEDICINE

Some common traditional remedies:

problem	treatment
altitude sickness	gingko
jet lag	melatonin
mosquito-bite prevention	eucalyptus oil; soybean oil
motion sickness	ginger

The yellow fever vaccine is given only in approved yellow fever vaccination centers, which provide validated International Certificates of Vaccination (yellow booklets). The vaccine should be given at least 10 days before any potential exposure to yellow fever and remains effective for approximately 10 years. Reactions to the vaccine are generally mild and may include headaches, muscle aches, low-grade fevers or discomfort at the injection site. Severe, life-threatening reactions have been described but are extremely rare. In general, the risk of becoming ill from the vaccine is far less than the risk of becoming ill from yellow fever, and you're strongly encouraged to get the vaccine.

Taking measures to protect yourself from mosquito bites (p628) is an essential part of preventing yellow fever.

Other Infections

Argentine hemorrhagic fever occurs in the pampas, chiefly from March through October. The disease is acquired by inhalation of dust contaminated with rodent excreta or by direct rodent contact.

Brucellosis is an infection of domestic and wild animals that may be transmitted to humans through direct animal contact or by consumption of unpasteurized dairy products from infected animals. Symptoms may include fever, malaise, depression, loss of appetite, headache, muscle aches and back pain. Complications may include arthritis, hepatitis, meningitis and endocarditis (heart-valve infection).

Chagas' disease is a parasitic infection that is transmitted by triatomine insects (reduviid bugs, which look like long-legged beetles), which inhabit crevices in the walls and roofs of substandard housing in South and Central America. In Argentina, Chagas' disease occurs north of latitude 44° 45'. Transmission is greatest during late spring (November and December). The triatomine insect lays its feces on human skin as it bites, usually at night. A person becomes infected when he or she unknowingly rubs the feces into the bite wound or any other open sore. Chagas' disease is extremely rare in travelers. However, if you sleep in a poorly constructed house, especially one made of mud, adobe or thatch, you should be sure to protect yourself with a bed net and a good insecticide.

Cholera is extremely rare in Argentina. A cholera vaccine is not recommended.

Hantavirus pulmonary syndrome is a rapidly progressive, life-threatening infection acquired through exposure to the excretions of wild rodents. Most cases occur in those who live in rodent-infested dwellings in rural areas. In Argentina, hantavirus infections are reported from the north-central and southwestern parts of the country.

HIV/AIDS has been reported from all South American countries. Be sure to use condoms for all sexual encounters.

Leishmaniasis occurs in the mountains and jungles of most South American countries. The infection is transmitted by sandflies, which are about one-third the size of mosquitoes. In Argentina, most cases occur in the northeastern part of the country and are limited to the skin, causing slowly growing ulcers over exposed parts of the body. A more severe type of Leishmaniasis disseminates to the bone marrow, liver and spleen. The disease may be particularly severe in those with HIV. There is no vaccine. To protect yourself from sandflies, follow the same precautions as for mosquitoes (see p628), except that netting must be finer mesh (at least 18 holes per 2.54cm or to the linear inch).

Louse-borne typhus occurs in mountain areas, and **murine typhus**, which is transmitted by rat fleas, occurs in warmer rural and jungle areas in the north.

Tick-borne relapsing fever, which may be transmitted by either ticks or lice, is caused by bacteria that are closely related to those which cause Lyme disease and syphilis. In Argentina, tick-borne relapsing fever occurs in the northern part of the country. The illness is characterized by periods of fever, chills, headaches, body aches, muscle aches and cough, alternating with periods when the fever subsides and the person feels relatively well. To minimize the risk of relapsing fever, follow tick precautions (see p628) and practice good personal hygiene at all times.

TRAVELER'S DIARRHEA

Tap water in Argentine cities and towns is generally safe to drink, but ask a local to be sure. If you have doubts, avoiding tap water unless it has been boiled, filtered or chemically disinfected (with iodine) will help to prevent diarrhea.

Only eat fresh fruits or vegetables if they're cooked or peeled. Also be wary of dairy products that might contain unpasteurized milk, and be highly selective when eating food from street vendors.

If you develop diarrhea, be sure to drink plenty of fluids, preferably an oral rehydration solution containing lots of salt and sugar. A few loose stools don't require treatment, but if you start having more than four or five stools a day, you should start taking an antibiotic (usually a quinolone drug) and an antidiarrheal agent (such as loperamide).

If diarrhea is bloody, persists for more than 72 hours or is accompanied by fever, shaking chills or severe abdominal pain, you should seek medical attention.

ENVIRONMENTAL HAZARDS
Animal Bites

Do not attempt to pet, handle or feed any animal, with the exception of domestic animals known to be free of any infectious disease. Most animal injuries are directly related to a person's attempt to touch or feed the animal.

Any bite or scratch by a mammal, including bats, should be promptly and thoroughly cleansed with large amounts of soap and water, followed by application of an antiseptic such as iodine or alcohol. The local health authorities should be contacted immediately for possible post-exposure rabies treatment, whether or not you've been immunized against rabies. It may also be advisable to start an antibiotic, since wounds caused by animal bites and scratches frequently become infected. One of the newer quinolones, such as levofloxacin (Levaquin), which many travelers carry in case of diarrhea, would be an appropriate choice.

Snakes and leeches are a hazard in some areas of South America. In the event of a bite from a venomous snake, place the victim at rest, keep the bitten area immobilized and move the victim immediately to the nearest medical facility. Avoid tourniquets, which are no longer recommended.

HEALTH

HEALTH

Mosquito Bites

To prevent mosquito bites, wear long sleeves, long pants, hats and shoes (rather than sandals). Bring along a good insect repellent, preferably one containing DEET, which should be applied to exposed skin and clothing, but not to eyes, mouth, cuts, wounds or irritated skin. Products containing lower concentrations of DEET are as effective, but for shorter periods of time. In general, adults and children over 12 years should use preparations containing 25% to 35% DEET, which usually lasts about six hours. Children between two and 12 years should use preparations containing no more than 10% DEET, applied sparingly, which will usually last about three hours. Neurologic toxicity has been reported from DEET, especially in children, but appears to be extremely uncommon and generally related to overuse. DEET-containing compounds should not be used on children under the age of two.

Insect repellents containing certain botanical products, including oil of eucalyptus and soybean oil, are effective but last only 1½ to two hours. DEET-containing repellents are preferable for areas where there is a high risk of malaria or yellow fever. Products based on citronella are not effective.

For additional protection, you can apply permethrin to clothing, shoes, tents and bed nets. Permethrin treatments are safe and remain effective for at least two weeks, even when items are laundered. Permethrin should not be applied directly to skin.

Don't sleep with the window open unless there is a screen. If sleeping outdoors or in accommodations that allow entry of mosquitoes, use a bed net, preferably treated with permethrin, with edges tucked in under the mattress. The mesh size should be less than 1.5mm. If the sleeping area is not otherwise protected, use a mosquito coil, which will fill the room with insecticide through the night. Repellent-impregnated wristbands are not effective.

Tick Bites

To protect yourself from tick bites, follow the same precautions as for mosquitoes, except that boots are preferable to shoes, with pants tucked in. Be sure to perform a thorough tick check at the end of each day. You'll generally need the assistance of a friend or mirror for a full examination. Ticks should be removed with tweezers, grasping them firmly by the head. Insect repellents based on botanical products, described earlier, have not been adequately studied for insects other than mosquitoes and cannot be recommended to prevent tick bites.

Water

Tap water is generally safe to drink in Argentine cities and towns. If you wish to purify water, vigorous boiling for one minute is the most effective means. At altitudes greater than 2000m, boil for three minutes.

Another option is to disinfect water with iodine. Add 2% tincture of iodine to 1L of water (five drops to clear water, 10 drops to cloudy water) and let stand for 30 minutes. If the water is cold, longer times may be required. Or buy iodine pills such as Globaline and Potable-Aqua, which are available at most pharmacies. Instructions should be carefully followed. The taste of iodinated water may be improved by adding vitamin C (ascorbic acid). Iodinated water should not be consumed for more than a few weeks. Pregnant women, those with a history of thyroid disease and those allergic to iodine should not drink iodinated water.

Of water filters, those with smaller pores (reverse osmosis filters) provide the broadest protection, but they are relatively large and are readily plugged by debris. Those with somewhat larger pores (microstrainer filters) are ineffective against viruses, although they remove other organisms. Manufacturers' instructions must be carefully followed.

TRAVELING WITH CHILDREN

When traveling with young children, be particularly careful about what you allow them to eat and drink, because diarrhea can be especially dangerous for them and because the vaccines for hepatitis A and typhoid fever are not approved for use in children under two years.

In general, children under nine months should not be brought to northeastern forest areas near the border with Brazil and Paraguay, where yellow fever occurs, since the vaccine is not safe in this age group.

Chloroquine, which is the main drug used to prevent malaria, may be given to children, but insect repellents must be applied in lower concentrations.

WOMEN'S HEALTH

You can find an English-speaking obstetrician in Argentina by asking at your embassy. However, medical facilities will probably not be comparable to those in your home country.

Language

CONTENTS

Spanish (known as *castellano* in Argentina and the rest of South America) is the official language and it is spoken throughout the country.

A number of immigrant communities have retained their languages as a badge of identity. In central Patagonia, for instance, there are pockets of Welsh speakers, but despite having undergone a bit of a revival in Argentina, the language is in danger of disappearing. Welsh cultural traditions remain strong in these regions, however, even reaching into the tourist industry.

English is studied, spoken and understood by many Argentines (especially in the capital). Italian is the language of the largest immigrant group and also understood by some, as is French. German speakers are numerous enough to support a weekly *porteño* newspaper, *Argentinisches Tageblatt*.

Argentina has over a dozen indigenous tongues, though some are spoken by very few individuals. In the Andean northwest, Quechua speakers are numerous, and most of these are also Spanish speakers. In the southern Andes, there are at least 40,000 Mapuche speakers. In northeastern Argentina, there are about 15,000 speakers of both Guaraní and Toba.

ARGENTINE SPANISH

In addition to their flamboyance, an Argentine's Italian-accented Spanish pronunciation and other language quirks readily identify them throughout Latin America and abroad. The most prominent peculiarity is the usage of the pronoun *vos* in place of *tú* for the informal 'you,' (see the boxed text, p630). Note that in Latin American Spanish, the plural of *tú* or *vos* is *ustedes*, not *vosotros* as in Spain. See also the next page for notes on the pronunciation of the letters *ll* and *y* in Argentine Spanish.

There are many vocabulary differences between European and Latin American Spanish, and among Spanish-speaking countries in the Americas. The speech of Buenos Aires, in particular, abounds with phrases from the colorful slang known as *lunfardo*. Although you shouldn't use *lunfardo* words unless you are confident that you know their every implication (especially in formal situations), you should be aware of some of the more common everyday usages (see the boxed text, p632).

Every visitor should make an effort to at least try to speak some Spanish; the basic elements are easily acquired. If possible, take a brief course before departure. Even if you can't speak very well, Argentines are gracious folk and will encourage your use of Spanish, so there is no need to feel self-conscious about vocabulary or pronunciation. There are many words similar to English, so if you're stuck, try Hispanicizing an English word – it's unlikely you'll make a truly embarrassing error. Do not, however, admit to being *embarazada* unless you are in fact pregnant. See the boxed text, p634, for other usages to avoid.

PHRASEBOOKS & DICTIONARIES

Lonely Planet's *Latin American Spanish* phrasebook is not only amusing but can also get you by in many situations. Another useful language resource is the *University of Chicago Spanish–English, English–Spanish Dictionary*. For a food and drink glossary, see p68.

LANGUAGE

EL VOSEO

Spanish in the Río de la Plata region differs from that of Spain and the rest of the Americas, most notably in the informal form of the word 'you.' Instead of *tuteo* (the use of *tú*), Argentines commonly speak with *voseo* (the use of *vos*), a relic from 16th-century Spanish requiring slightly different grammar. All verbs change in spelling, stress and pronunciation. Examples of verbs ending in *-ar*, *-er* and *-ir* are given below – the pronoun *tú* is included to illustrate the contrast. Imperative forms (commands) also differ, but negative imperatives are identical in both *tuteo* and *voseo*.

The Spanish phrases included in this book use the *vos* form. An Argentine inviting a foreigner to address him or her informally will say *Me podés tutear* (literally 'You can address me with *tú*'), even though they'll use the *vos* forms in subsequent conversation.

Verb	Tuteo	Voseo
hablar (speak): **You speak./Speak!**	*Tú hablas./¡Habla!*	*Vos hablás./¡Hablá!*
soñar (dream): **You dream./Dream!**	*Tú sueñas./¡Sueña!*	*Vos soñás./¡Soñá!*
comer (eat): **You eat./Eat!**	*Tú comes./¡Come!*	*Vos comés./¡Comé!*
poner (put): **You put./Put!**	*Tú pones./¡Pon!*	*Vos ponés./¡Poné!*
admitir (admit): **You admit./Admit!**	*Tú admites./¡Admite!*	*Vos admitís./¡Admití!*
venir (come): **You come./Come!**	*Tú vienes./¡Ven!*	*Vos venís./¡Vení!*

PRONUNCIATION

Latin American Spanish is easy, as most of the sounds are also found in English. If you follow our pronunciation guides (included alongside the Spanish phrases), you'll have no problems being understood.

Vowels

There are four sounds (**ai, ay, ow, oy**) that roughly correspond to diphthongs (vowel sound combinations) in English.

a	as the 'a' in 'father'
ai	as in 'aisle'
ay	as in 'say'
e	as the 'e' in 'met'
ee	as the 'ee' in 'meet'
o	as the 'o' in 'more'
oo	as the 'oo' in 'zoo'
ow	as in 'how'
oy	as in 'boy'

Consonants

Pronunciation of Spanish consonants is similar to their English counterparts. The exceptions are given in the following list.

kh	as the throaty 'ch' in the Scottish *loch*
ny	as the 'ny' in 'canyon'
r	as in 'run' but stronger and rolled, especially at the beginning of a word and in all words with *rr*
s	not lisped

The letter 'h' is always silent (ie never pronounced) in Spanish.

Note also that the Spanish **b** and **v** sounds are very similar – they are both pronounced as a very soft 'v' in English (somewhere between 'b' and 'v').

There are some variations in spoken Spanish across Latin America, the most notable being the pronunciation of the letter *ll*. In much of Latin America it is pronounced as 'y' (eg as in 'yes'), while in some parts of the continent it sounds like the 'lli' in 'million.' In Argentina and Uruguay, however, the letters *ll* and *y* are both pronounced as 'zh' (like the 's' in 'measure'), and in and around Buenos Aires as the 'sh' in 'shut.' We've used the former in our pronunciation guides as it's more widespread.

Word Stress

In general, Spanish words ending in vowels or the consonants *-n* or *-s* are stressed on the second-last syllable, while those with other endings have stress on the last syllable. Written accents denote stress, and override the rules above, eg *sótano* (basement), *América, porción* (portion).

In our pronunciation guides the stressed syllable is indicated with italics, so you needn't worry about these rules.

GENDER & PLURALS

In Spanish, nouns are either masculine or feminine, and there are rules to help determine gender. Feminine nouns generally end with -*a*, -*ad*, -*z* or -*ión*. Other endings, particularly -*o*, typically signify a masculine noun. Endings for adjectives change to agree with the gender of the noun they modify (masculine/feminine -*o*/-*a*). Where both masculine and feminine forms are included in this chapter, they are separated by a slash, with the masculine form given first, eg *perdido/a*.

If a noun or adjective ends in a vowel, the plural is formed by adding -*s*. If it ends in a consonant, the plural is formed by adding -*es* to the end of the word.

ACCOMMODATIONS

I'm looking	Estoy	e·stoy
for a ...	buscando ...	boos·kan·do ...
Where's a ...?	¿Dónde hay ...?	don·de ai ...
boarding house	una residencial	oo·na re·si·den·syal
hotel	un hotel	oon o·tel
youth hostel	un albergue	oon al·ber·ge
	de juventud	de khoo·ven·tood
I'd like a ...	Quisiera una	kee·sye·ra oo·na
room.	habitación ...	a·bee·ta·syon ...
double	doble	do·ble
single	individual	een·dee·vee·dwal
twin	con dos camas	kon dos ka·mas
How much is it	¿Cuánto cuesta	kwan·to kwes·ta
per ...?	por ...?	por ...
night	noche	no·che
person	persona	per·so·na
week	semana	se·ma·na

Does it include breakfast?
¿Incluye el desayuno?   een·kloo·zhe el de·sa·zhoo·no
Can I see the room?
¿Puedo ver la   pwe·do ver la
habitación?   a·bee·ta·syon
I don't like it.
No me gusta.   no me goos·ta
It's fine. I'll take it.
Está bien. La alquilo.   es·ta byen la al·kee·lo
I'm leaving now.
Me voy ahora.   me voy a·o·ra

cheaper	más económico	mas e·ko·no·mee·ko
discount	descuento	des·kwen·to
full board	pensión completa	pen·syon kom·ple·ta
private/shared	baño privado/	ba·nyo pree·va·do/
bathroom	compartido	kom·par·tee·do
too expensive	demasiado caro	de·ma·sya·do ka·ro

MAKING A RESERVATION
(for phone or written requests)

From ...	De ...
To ...	A ...
Date	Fecha
I'd like to book ...	Quisiera reservar ...
in the name of ...	en nombre de ...
for the nights of ...	para las noches del ...
credit card	tarjeta de crédito
expiry date	fecha de vencimiento
number	número
Please confirm ...	¿Puede confirmar ...?
availability	la disponibilidad
price	el precio

CONVERSATION & ESSENTIALS

Hello. (inf)	Hola.	o·la
Good morning.	Buenos días.	bwe·nos dee·as
Good afternoon.	Buenas tardes.	bwe·nas tar·des
Good evening/ night.	Buenas noches.	bwe·nas no·ches
Bye. (inf)	Chau.	chow
Goodbye.	Adiós.	a·dyos
See you later.	Hasta luego.	as·ta lwe·go
Yes./No.	Sí./No.	see/no
Please.	Por favor.	por fa·vor
Thank you.	Gracias.	gra·syas
Many thanks.	Muchas gracias.	moo·chas gra·syas
You're welcome.	De nada.	de na·da
Pardon.	Perdón.	per·don
Excuse me. (asking permission)	Permiso.	per·mee·so
Forgive me. (apologizing)	Disculpe.	dees·kool·pe

How are you?
¿Cómo está/estás?   co·mo es·ta/es·tas (pol/inf)
What's your name?
¿Cómo se llama?   ko·mo se zha·ma (pol)
¿Cómo te llamás?   ko·mo te zha·mas (inf)
My name is ...
Me llamo ...   me zha·mo ...
It's a pleasure to meet you.
Mucho gusto.   moo·cho goos·to
The pleasure is mine.
El gusto es mío.   el goos·to es mee·o
Where are you from?
¿De dónde es/sos?   de don·de es/sos (pol/inf)
I'm from ...
Soy de ...   soy de ...
Can I take a photo?
¿Puedo tomar una foto? pwe·do to·mar oo·na fo·to

LUNFARDO

Below are are some of the spicier *lunfardo* (slang) terms you may hear on your travels in Argentina.

boliche – disco or nightclub
boludo – jerk, asshole, idiot; often used in a friendly fashion, but a deep insult to a stranger
bondi – bus
buena onda – good vibes
carajo – asshole, prick; bloody hell
chabón/chabona – kid, guy/girl (term of endearment)
che – hey
diez puntos – OK, cool, fine (literally '10 points')
fiaca – laziness
guita – money
macanudo – great, fabulous
mango – one peso
masa – a great, cool thing
mina – woman
morfar – eat
pendejo – idiot
piba/pibe – cool young guy/girl
piola – cool, clever
pucho – cigarette
re – very, as in *re interestante* (very interesting)

¡Ponete las pilas! – Get on with it! (literally 'Put in the batteries!')
Me mataste. – I don't know; I have no idea. (literally 'You've killed me')
Le faltan un par de jugadores. – He's not playing with a full deck. (literally 'He's a couple of players short (of a team)')
che boludo – The most *porteño* phrase on earth. Ask a friendly local youth to explain.

DIRECTIONS

How do I get to ...?
  ¿Cómo puedo llegar a ...? ko·mo *pwe*·do zhe·*gar* a ...
Is it far?
  ¿Está lejos? es·ta le·khos
What's the address?
  ¿Cuál es la dirección? kwal es la dee·rek·*syon*
Can you show me (on the map)?
  ¿Me lo podría indicar me lo po·*dree*·a een·dee·*kar*
  (en el mapa)? (en el *ma*·pa)
Go straight ahead.
  Siga derecho. see·ga de·*re*·cho
Turn left/right.
  Volteé a la izquierda/ vol·*te*·e a la ees·*kyer*·da/
  derecha. de·*re*·cha

north	*norte*	*nor*·te
south	*sur*	soor
east	*este*	*es*·te
west	*oeste*	o·*es*·te
avenue	*avenida*	a·ve·*nee*·da
block	*cuadra*	*kwa*·dra
here	*aquí*	a·*kee*
there	*allí*	a·*zhee*
street	*calle*	*ka*·zhe

EATING OUT

I'd like to make a reservation.
  Quisiera hacer kee·*sye*·ra a·*ser*
  una reserva. oo·na re·*ser*·va
Do you accept credit cards?
  ¿Aceptan tarjetas a·*sep*·tan tar·*khe*·tas
  de crédito? de *kre*·dee·to
When do you serve meals?
  ¿A qué hora sirven a ke *o*·ra *seer*·ven
  comidas? ko·*mee*·das
A table for ..., please.
  Una mesa para ..., oo·na *me*·sa *pa*·ra ...
  por favor. por fa·*vor*
Can I see the menu, please?
  ¿Puedo ver el menú, *pwe*·do ver el me·*noo*
  por favor? por fa·*vor*
What do you recommend?
  ¿Qué me aconseja? ke me a·kon·*se*·kha
What's today's special?
  ¿Cuál es el plato del día? kwal es el *pla*·to del *dee*·a
What's the soup of the day?
  ¿Cuál es la sopa del día? kwal es la *so*·pa del *dee*·a
I'll try what he/she is having.
  Probaré lo que él/ella pro·ba·*re* lo ke el/e·zha
  está comiendo. es·*ta* ko·*myen*·do
I'm a vegetarian.
  Soy vegetariano/a. soy ve·khe·ta·*rya*·no/a
We'd like to share (the salad).
  Quisiéramos compartir kee·*sye*·ra·mos kom·par·*teer*
  (la ensalada). (la en·sa·*la*·da)
What's in this dish?
  ¿Qué ingredientes tiene ke een·gre·*dyen*·tes *tye*·ne
  este plato? *es*·te *pla*·to
Can I have a (beer), please?
  Una (cerveza), por favor. oo·na (ser·*ve*·sa) por fa·*vor*
Is service/cover charge included in the bill?
  ¿El precio en el menú el *pre*·syo en el me·*noo*
  incluye el servicio een·*kloo*·zhe el ser·*vee*·syo
  de cubierto? de koo·*byer*·to
That was delicious.
  Estaba buenísimo. es·*ta*·ba bwe·*nee*·see·mo
The bill, please.
  La cuenta, por favor. la *kwen*·ta por fa·*vor*

EMERGENCIES

Help!	¡Ayuda!	a·zhoo·da
Go away!	¡Déjeme!	de·khe·me

Call ...!	¡Llame a ...!	zha·me a ...
an	una	oo·na
ambulance	ambulancia	am·boo·lan·sya
a doctor	un médico	oon me·dee·ko
the police	la policía	la po·lee·see·a

It's an emergency.
Es una emergencia.   es oo·na e·mer·khen·sya
Can you help me, please?
¿Me puede ayudar,   me pwe·de a·zhoo·dar
por favor?   por fa·vor
I'm lost.
Estoy perdido/a.   es·toy per·dee·do/a
Where are the toilets?
¿Dónde están los baños?   don·de es·tan los ba·nyos

I'd like a ...	Quiero ...	kye·ro ...
knife	un cuchillo	oon koo·chee·zho
fork	un tenedor	oon te·ne·dor
spoon	una cuchara	oo·na koo·cha·ra

HEALTH

I'm sick.
Estoy enfermo/a.   es·toy en·fer·mo/a
I need a doctor.
Necesito un médico.   ne·se·see·to oon me·dee·ko
Where's the hospital?
¿Dónde está el hospital?   don·de es·ta el os·pee·tal
I'm pregnant.
Estoy embarazada.   es·toy em·ba·ra·sa·da
I've been vaccinated.
Estoy vacunado/a.   es·toy va·koo·na·do/a

I'm allergic to ...	Soy alérgico/a a ...	soy a·ler·khee·ko/a a ...
antibiotics	los antibióticos	los an·tee·byo·tee·kos
nuts	las nueces	las nwe·ses
penicillin	la penicilina	la pe·nee·see·lee·na

I'm ...	Soy ...	soy ...
asthmatic	asmático/a	as·ma·tee·ko/a
diabetic	diabético/a	dya·be·tee·ko/a
epileptic	epiléptico/a	e·pee·lep·tee·ko/a

I have (a) ...	Tengo ...	ten·go ...
cough	tos	tos
diarrhea	diarrea	dya·re·a
headache	dolor de cabeza	do·lor de ka·be·sa
nausea	náusea	now·se·a

LANGUAGE DIFFICULTIES

Do you speak English?
¿Habla/Hablas inglés?   a·bla/a·blas een·gles (pol/inf)
Does anyone here speak English?
¿Hay alguien que hable   ai al·gyen ke a·ble
inglés?   een·gles
I (don't) understand.
(No) Entiendo.   (no) en·tyen·do
How do you say ...?
¿Cómo se dice ...?   ko·mo se dee·se ...
What does ... mean?
¿Qué quiere decir ...?   ke kye·re de·seer ...

Could you please ...?	¿Puede ..., por favor?	pwe·de ... por fa·vor
repeat that	repetirlo	re·pe·teer·lo
speak more slowly	hablar más despacio	a·blar mas des·pa·syo
write it down	escribirlo	es·kree·beer·lo

NUMBERS

1	uno	oo·no
2	dos	dos
3	tres	tres
4	cuatro	kwa·tro
5	cinco	seen·ko
6	seis	seys
7	siete	sye·te
8	ocho	o·cho
9	nueve	nwe·ve
10	diez	dyes
11	once	on·se
12	doce	do·se
13	trece	tre·se
14	catorce	ka·tor·se
15	quince	keen·se
16	dieciséis	dye·see·seys
17	diecisiete	dye·see·sye·te
18	dieciocho	dye·see·o·cho
19	diecinueve	dye·see·nwe·ve
20	veinte	vayn·te
21	veintiuno	vayn·tee·oo·no
30	treinta	trayn·ta
31	treinta y uno	trayn·ta ee oo·no
40	cuarenta	kwa·ren·ta
50	cincuenta	seen·kwen·ta
60	sesenta	se·sen·ta
70	setenta	se·ten·ta
80	ochenta	o·chen·ta
90	noventa	no·ven·ta
100	cien	syen
101	ciento uno	syen·to oo·no
200	doscientos	do·syen·tos
1000	mil	meel
10,000	diez mil	dyes meel

FALSE FRIENDS

'False friends' are words that appear to be very similar but have different meanings in different languages. In some cases, these differences can lead to serious misunderstandings. The following is a list of some of these words in English with their Spanish cousins and their meaning in Spanish. Note that this list deals primarily with the Río de la Plata region, and usage may differ elsewhere in South America. Also, be careful with some words from Spain, like *coger,* which in Mexico and South America doesn't mean 'to get or catch' but it's a slang (and rude) term for 'to have sex.'

English	Spanish	Meaning in Spanish
actual	*actual*	current (at present)
carpet	*carpeta*	loose-leaf notebook
embarrassed	*embarazada*	pregnant
fabric	*fábrica*	factory
to introduce	*introducir*	to introduce (eg an innovation)
notorious	*notorio*	well known, evident
to present	*presentar*	to introduce (a person)
precise	*preciso*	necessary
preservative	*preservativo*	condom
sensible	*sensible*	sensitive
violation	*violación*	rape

SHOPPING & SERVICES

I'd like to buy ...
   Quisiera comprar ...   kee·*sye*·ra kom·*prar* ...
I'm just looking.
   Sólo estoy mirando.   so·lo es·*toy* mee·*ran*·do
May I look at it?
   ¿Puedo mirarlo?   *pwe*·do mee·*rar*·lo
How much is it?
   ¿Cuánto cuesta?   *kwan*·to *kwes*·ta
That's too expensive for me.
   Es demasiado caro   es de·ma·*sya*·do *ka*·ro
   para mí.   *pa*·ra mee
Could you lower the price?
   ¿Podría bajar un poco   po·*dree*·a ba·*khar* oon *po*·ko
   el precio?   el *pre*·syo
I don't like it.
   No me gusta.   no me *goos*·ta
I'll take it.
   Lo llevo.   lo *zhe*·vo

big/small	*grande/pequeño*	*gran*·de/pe·*ke*·nyo
more/less	*más/menos*	mas/*me*·nos

Do you accept ...?	*¿Aceptan ...?*	a·*sep*·tan ...
American dollars	*dólares americanos*	*do*·la·res a·me·ree·*ka*·nos
credit cards	*tarjetas de crédito*	tar·*khe*·tas de *kre*·dee·to
traveler's checks	*cheques de viajero*	*che*·kes de vya·*khe*·ro

I'm looking for (the) ...	*Estoy buscando ...*	es·*toy* boos·*kan*·do ...
ATM	*el cajero automático*	el ka·*khe*·ro ow·to·*ma*·tee·ko
bank	*el banco*	el *ban*·ko
bookstore	*la librería*	la lee·bre·*ree*·a
chemist	*la farmacia*	la far·*ma*·sya
embassy	*la embajada*	la em·ba·*kha*·da
exchange office	*la casa de cambio*	la *ka*·sa de *kam*·byo
general store	*la tienda*	la *tyen*·da
laundry	*la lavandería*	la la·van·de·*ree*·a
post office	*los correos*	los ko·*re*·os
(super)market	*el (super-) mercado*	el (*soo*·per·) mer·*ka*·do
tourist office	*la oficina de turismo*	la o·fee·*see*·na de too·*rees*·mo

What time does it open/close?
   ¿A qué hora abre/cierra?   a ke o·ra *a*·bre/*sye*·ra
I want to change some money/traveler's checks.
   Quiero cambiar dinero/   *kye*·ro kam·*byar* dee·*ne*·ro/
   cheques de viajero.   *che*·kes de vya·*khe*·ro
What is the exchange rate?
   ¿Cuál es el tipo de   kwal es el *tee*·po de
   cambio?   *kam*·byo
I want to call ...
   Quiero llamar a ...   *kye*·ro zha·*mar* a ...
Where's the local internet cafe?
   ¿Dónde hay un cibercafé   don·de ai oon sai·ber·ka·*fe*
   por acá?   por a·*ka*
I'd like to get internet access.
   Quisiera usar internet.   kee·*sye*·ra oo·*sar* een·ter·net

airmail	*correo aéreo*	ko·*re*·o a·*e*·re·o
black market	*mercado negro*	mer·*ka*·do *ne*·gro
letter	*carta*	*kar*·ta
registered mail	*certificado*	ser·tee·fee·*ka*·do
stamps	*estampillas*	es·tam·*pee*·zhas

TIME & DATES

What time is it?	*¿Qué hora es?*	ke o·ra es
It's one o'clock.	*Es la una.*	es la *oo*·na
It's (six) o'clock.	*Son las (seis).*	son las (seys)
half past (two)	*(dos) y media*	(dos) ee *me*·dya

SIGNS

Abierto	Open
Cerrado	Closed
Comisaría	Police Station
Entrada	Entrance
Información	Information
Prohibido	Prohibited
Salida	Exit
Baños	Toilets
Hombres/Caballeros	Men
Mujeres/Damas	Women

yesterday	*ayer*	a·*zher*
today	*hoy*	oy
now	*ahora*	a·o·ra
noon	*mediodía*	me·dyo·*dee*·a
tonight	*esta noche*	es·ta *no*·che
midnight	*medianoche*	me·dya·*no*·che
tomorrow	*mañana*	ma·*nya*·na
Monday	*lunes*	*loo*·nes
Tuesday	*martes*	*mar*·tes
Wednesday	*miércoles*	*myer*·ko·les
Thursday	*jueves*	*khwe*·ves
Friday	*viernes*	*vyer*·nes
Saturday	*sábado*	*sa*·ba·do
Sunday	*domingo*	do·*meen*·go
January	*enero*	e·*ne*·ro
February	*febrero*	fe·*bre*·ro
March	*marzo*	*mar*·so
April	*abril*	a·*breel*
May	*mayo*	*ma*·zho
June	*junio*	*khoo*·nyo
July	*julio*	*khoo*·lyo
August	*agosto*	a·*gos*·to
September	*septiembre*	sep·*tyem*·bre
October	*octubre*	ok·*too*·bre
November	*noviembre*	no·*vyem*·bre
December	*diciembre*	dee·*syem*·bre

TRANSPORTATION
Public Transportation

At what time	*¿A qué hora*	a ke *o*·ra
does the ...	*sale/llega*	*sa*·le/*zhe*·ga
leave/arrive?	*el ...?*	el ...
bus	*autobus*	ow·to·*boos*
plane	*avión*	a·*vyon*
ship	*barco*	*bar*·ko
train	*tren*	tren

I'd like a ticket to ...
  Quisiera un boleto a ...   kee·*sye*·ra oon bo·*le*·to a ...

What's the fare to ...?
  ¿Cuánto cuesta hasta ...?   *kwan*·to *kwes*·ta a·sta ...

1st class	*primera clase*	pree·*me*·ra *kla*·se
2nd class	*segunda clase*	se·*goon*·da *kla*·se
one-way	*ida*	*ee*·da
round-trip	*ida y vuelta*	*ee*·da ee *vwel*·ta
student's (fare)	*de estudiante*	de es·*too*·dyan·te
taxi	*taxi*	*tak*·see
airport	*el aeropuerto*	el a·e·ro·*pwer*·to
bus station	*la estación de*	la es·ta·*syon* de
	autobuses	ow·to·*boo*·ses
bus stop	*la parada de*	la pa·*ra*·da de
	autobuses	ow·to·*boo*·ses
luggage check	*guardería de*	gwar·de·*ree*·a de
room	*equipaje*	e·kee·*pa*·khe
ticket office	*la boletería*	la bo·le·te·*ree*·a
train station	*la estación de*	la es·ta·*syon* de
	ferrocarril	fe·ro·ka·*reel*

Private Transportation

I'd like to	*Quisiera*	kee·*sye*·ra
hire a ...	*alquilar ...*	al·kee·*lar* ...
4WD	*un todo terreno*	oon *to*·do te·*re*·no
bicycle	*una bicicleta*	*oo*·na
		bee·see·*kle*·ta
car	*un auto*	oon *ow*·to
motorbike	*una moto*	*oo*·na *mo*·to
hitchhike	*hacer dedo*	a·ser *de*·do
pickup (truck)	*camioneta*	ka·myo·*ne*·ta
truck	*camión*	ka·*myon*

Is this the road to ...?

¿Se va a ... por	se va a ... por
esta carretera?	es·ta ka·re·*te*·ra

Where's a gas/petrol station?

¿Dónde hay una	*don*·de ai *oo*·na
gasolinera?	ga·so·lee·*ne*·ra

Please fill it up.
  Lleno, por favor.   *zhe*·no por fa·*vor*

I'd like (20) liters.
  Quiero (veinte) litros.   *kye*·ro (*vayn*·te) *lee*·tros

diesel	*diesel*	*dee*·sel
gas/petrol	*gasolina*	ga·so·*lee*·na
leaded (regular)	*con plomo*	kon *plo*·mo
unleaded	*sin plomo*	seen *plo*·mo

(How long) Can I park here?

¿(Por cuánto tiempo)	(por *kwan*·to *tyem*·po)
Puedo estacionar aquí?	*pwe*·do es·ta·syo·*nar* a·*kee*

Where do I pay?
  ¿Dónde se paga?   *don*·de se *pa*·ga

ROAD SIGNS

Acceso	Entrance
Ceda el Paso	Give Way
Despacio	Slow
Dirección Única	One Way
Estacionamiento	Parking
Mantenga Su Derecha	Keep to the Right
No Adelantar	No Passing
Peaje	Toll
Peligro	Danger
Prohibido el Paso	No Entry
Prohibido Estacionar	No Parking
Salida de Autopista	Freeway Exit

I need a mechanic.

Necesito un mecánico.   ne·se·*see*·to oon me·*ka*·nee·ko

The car has broken down (in ...).

El carro se ha averiado   el *ka*·ro se a a·ve·*rya*·do
(en ...).   (en ...)

The motorbike won't start.

No arranca la moto.   no a·*ran*·ka la *mo*·to

I have a flat tyre.

Tengo un pinchazo.   *ten*·go oon peen·*cha*·so

I've run out of gas/petrol.

Me quedé sin gasolina.   me ke·*de* seen ga·so·*lee*·na

I've had an accident.

Tuve un accidente.   *too*·ve oon ak·see·*den*·te

TRAVEL WITH CHILDREN

Do you mind if I breast-feed here?

¿Le molesta que dé   le mo·*les*·ta ke de
de pecho aquí?   de *pe*·cho a·*kee*

Are children allowed?

¿Se admiten niños?   se ad·*mee*·ten *nee*·nyos

I need (a) ...	*Necesito ...*	ne·se·*see*·to ...
Do you have	*¿Hay ...?*	ai ...
(a) ...?		
babysitter	*una niñera*	*oo*·na nee·*nye*·ra
(who speaks	*(que habla*	(ke *a*·bla
English)	*inglés)*	een·*gles*)
car seat for	*un asiento*	oon a·*syen*·to
babies	*de seguridad*	de se·goo·ree·*dad*
	para bebés	*pa*·ra be·*bes*
child-minding	*un servicio*	oon ser·*vee*·syo
service	*de cuidado*	de kwee·*da*·do
	de niños	de *nee*·nyos
(disposable)	*pañales (de*	pa·*nya*·les (de
diapers/	*usar y tirar)*	oo·*sar* ee tee·*rar*)
nappies		
highchair	*una trona*	*oo*·na *tro*·na
milk formula	*leche en polvo*	*le*·che en *pol*·vo
potty	*una pelela*	*oo*·na pe·*le*·la
stroller	*un cochecito*	oon ko·che·*see*·to

Glossary

For an explanation of food-related terms, see p61; for some accommodation terms, p596, and for language in general, p629.

abuelos – grandparents

ACA – Automóvil Club Argentino, which provides maps, road service, insurance and other services, and operates hotels and campgrounds throughout the country

acequia – irrigation canal

aerosilla – chairlift

alcalde – mayor

alerce – large coniferous tree, resembling a California redwood, from which Argentina's Parque Nacional Los Alerces takes its name

apeadero – whistle-stop

arrayán – tree of the myrtle family, from which Argentina's Parque Nacional Los Arrayanes takes its name

arroyo – creek, stream

arte rupestre – cave paintings

asado – the famous Argentine barbecue

autopista – freeway or motorway

baliza – emergency reflector

balneario – any swimming or bathing area, including beach resorts, river beaches and swimming holes

balsa – ferry

bandoneón – an accordion-like instrument used in tango music

barra brava – fervent soccer fan; the Argentine equivalent of Britain's 'football hooligan'

bencina – white gas, used for camp stoves; also known as *nafta blanca*

bicho – any small creature, from insect to mammal; also used to refer to an ugly person

boleadoras – weighted, leather-covered balls attached to a length of thin rope, historically used as a hunting weapon by gauchos and some of Argentina's indigenous peoples; thrown at a guanaco or rhea's legs, they entangle the animal and bring it down

boliche – nightclub or disco

bombachas – a gaucho's baggy pants; can also mean women's underwear

bombilla – metal straw with filter for drinking *mate*

buena onda – good vibes

cabildo – colonial town council; also, the building that housed the council

cacerolazo – a form of street protest; it first occurred in December 2001 when people took to their balconies in Buenos Aires banging pots and pans *(cacerolas)* to show their discontent; the banging moved to the streets, then to cities throughout Argentina, and culminated in the resignation of President de la Rua

cajero automático – ATM

caldén – a tree characteristic of the dry pampas

camarote – 1st-class sleeper

cambio – money-exchange office; also *casa de cambio*

campo – the countryside; alternately, a field or paddock

característica – telephone area code

carnavalito – traditional folk dance

carpincho – capybara, a large (but cute) aquatic rodent that inhabits the Paraná and other subtropical rivers

carrovelismo – land sailing

cartelera – an office selling discount tickets

casa de cambio – money-exchange office, often shortened to *cambio*

casa de familia – family accommodations

casa de gobierno – literally 'government house,' a building now often converted to a museum, offices etc

castellano – the term used in much of South America for the Spanish language spoken throughout Latin America; literally refers to Castilian Spanish

catarata – waterfall

caudillo – in 19th-century Argentine politics, a provincial strongman whose power rested more on personal loyalty than political ideals or party affiliation

centro cívico – civic center

cerro – hill, mountain

certificado – certified mail

chacarera – traditional folk dance

chacra – small, independent farm

chamamé – folk music of Corrientes

chusquea – solid bamboo of the Valdivian rainforest in Patagonia

coche cama – sleeper class

coima – a bribe; one who solicits a bribe is a *coimero*

colectivo – local bus

combi – long-distance bus

comedor – basic cafeteria

común – common class

Conaf – Corporación Nacional Forestal, Chilean state agency in charge of forestry and conservation, including management of national parks like Torres del Paine

confitería – cafe serving light meals

conjunto – a musical band

Conquista del Desierto – Conquest of the Desert, a euphemism for General Julio Argentino Roca's late-19th-century war of extermination against the Mapuche of northern Patagonia

contrabajo – double bass

correo – post office

corriente – current

cospel – token used in public telephones

costanera – seaside, riverside or lakeside road or walkway

criollo – in colonial period, an American-born Spaniard, but now used for any Latin American of European descent; the term also describes the feral cattle and horses of the pampas

cruce – crossroads

cuatrerismo – cattle rustling

día de campo – 'day in the country,' spent at an *estancia;* typically includes an *asado,* horseback riding and use of the property's facilities

desaparecidos (los) – the disappeared; the victims (estimated at up to 30,000) of Argentina's *Guerra Sucia* who were never found

dique – a dam; the resultant reservoir is often used for recreational purposes; can also refer to a drydock

Dirty War – see *Guerra Sucia*

dorado – large river fish in the Paraná drainage, known among fishing enthusiasts as the 'Tiger of the Paraná' for its fighting spirit

duende – gnome

edificio – a building

ejecutivo – executive class

encomienda – colonial labor system, under which Indian communities were required to provide laborers for Spaniards *(encomenderos),* and the Spaniards were to provide religious and language instruction; in practice, the system benefited Spaniards far more than native peoples

epa – an exclamation meaning 'Hey! Wow! Look out!'

ERP – Ejército Revolucionario del Pueblo, a revolutionary leftist group in the sugar-growing areas of Tucumán province in the 1970s that modeled itself after the Cuban revolution; it was wiped out by the Argentine army during the *Guerra Sucia*

esquina – street corner

estación de servicio – gas station

estancia – extensive ranch for cattle or sheep, with an owner or manager *(estanciero)* and dependent resident labor force; many are now open to tourists for recreational activities such as riding, tennis and swimming, either for weekend escapes or extended stays

este – east

facón – a knife used by gauchos that is traditionally worn in the small of the back behind the belt

folklore – Argentine folk music; also known as folklórico

fútbol – soccer

gasolero – motor vehicle that uses diesel fuel, which is much cheaper than ordinary gasoline in Argentina

guardaganado – cattle guard (on a road or highway)

guardia – watchman

Guerra Sucia – the Dirty War of the 1970s, of the Argentine military against left-wing revolutionaries and anyone suspected of sympathizing with them; also referred to as the 'military period'

guitarrón – an oversized guitar used for playing bass lines

horario – schedule

ichu – bunch grass of the Andean altiplano

ida – one-way

ida y vuelta – roundtrip

iglesia – church

interno – internal bus-route number; also a telephone extension number

IVA – *impuesto al valor agregado;* value-added tax, often added to restaurant or hotel bills in Argentina

jejenes – annoying biting insects

jineteada – rodeo

libro de reclamos – complaint book

locutorio – private long-distance telephone office; usually offers fax and internet services as well

lunfardo – street slang

manta – a shawl or bedspread

manzana – literally, 'apple'; also used to define one square block of a city

maragatos – inhabitants of Carmen de Patagones

mate – tea made from *yerba mate* leaves; Argentina is the world's largest producer and consumer of *mate* and preparing and drinking the beverage is an important social ritual; the word also refers to the *mate* gourd the tea is prepared in

mazorca – political police of 19th-century Argentine dictator Juan Manuel de Rosas

mercado artesanal – handicraft market

meseta – interior steppe of eastern Patagonia

mestizo – a person of mixed Indian and Spanish descent

milonga – in tango, refers to a song, a dance or the dance salon itself

minutas – snacks or short orders

mirador – scenic viewpoint, usually on a hill but often in a building

monte – scrub forest; the term is often applied to any densely vegetated area

Montoneros – left-wing faction of the Peronist party that became an underground urban guerrilla movement in 1970s

municipalidad – city hall

nafta – gasoline or petrol

neumático – spare tire

norte – north

oeste – west

Ovnis – UFOs

parada – a bus stop
paraje – pump
parrilla – mixed grill or steak house; also *parrillada*
paseo – an outing, such as a walk in the park or downtown
pato – duck; also a gaucho sport where players on horseback wrestle for a ball encased in a leather harness with handles
peatonal – pedestrian mall, usually in the downtown area of major Argentine cities
pehuén – araucaria, or 'monkey puzzle' tree of southern Patagonia
peña – club that hosts informal folk-music gatherings
percha – perch, also means coathanger
picada – in rural areas, a trail, especially through dense woods or mountains; in the context of food, hors d'oeuvres or snacks
pingüinera – penguin colony
piqueteros – picketers
piropo – a flirtatious remark
piso – floor
porteño/a – inhabitant of Buenos Aires, a 'resident of the port'
precios patagónicos – Patagonian prices
precordillera – foothills of the Andes
primera – 1st class on a train
Proceso – short for El Proceso de Reorganización Nacional, the military's euphemism for its brutal attempt to remake Argentina's political and economic culture between 1976 and 1983
propina – a tip, for example, in a restaurant or cinema
pucará – in the Andean northwest, a pre-Columbian fortification, generally on high ground commanding an unobstructed view in several directions
pulpería – a country store or tavern
puna – Andean highlands, usually above 3000m
puntano – a native or resident of Argentina's San Luis province

quebracho – literally, 'ax-breaker'; tree common to the Chaco that's a natural source of tannin for the leather industry
quebrada – a canyon
quincho – thatch-roof hut, now often used to refer to a building at the back of a house used for parties

rambla – boardwalk
rancho – a rural house, generally of adobe, with a thatched roof
recargo – additional charge, usually 10%, that many Argentine businesses add to credit-card transactions
reducción – an Indian settlement created by Spanish missionaries during the colonial period; the most famous are the Jesuit missions in the triple-border area of Argentina, Paraguay and Brazil
refugio – a usually rustic shelter in a national park or remote area
remise – radio taxi without a meter that generally offers fixed fares within a given zone; also *remís*

riacho – stream
ripio – gravel
rotisería – take-out shop
rotonda – traffic circle, roundabout
RN – Ruta Nacional; a national highway
RP – Ruta Provincial; a provincial highway
ruta – highway

s/n -*sin número*, indicating a street address without a number
sábalo – popular river fish in the Paraná drainage
salar – salt lake or salt pan, usually in the high Andes or Argentine Patagonia
samba – traditional folk dance
semi-cama – semisleeper class
sendero – a trail in the woods
servicentro – gas station
siesta – lengthy afternoon break for lunch and, sometimes, a nap
Subte – the Buenos Aires subway system
sur – south
surubí – popular river fish frequently served in restaurants

tahona – flour mill
tapir – large hoofed mammal of subtropical forests in northern Argentina and Paraguay; a distant relative of the horse
tarjeta magnética – magnetic bus card
tarjeta telefónica – telephone card
tarjeta verde – 'green card'; title document for Argentine vehicles that drivers must carry
teleférico – gondola cable-car
telera – textile workshop
tenedor libre – all you can eat
todo terreno – mountain bike
tola – high-altitude shrubs in the altiplano of northwestern Argentina
torrontés – an Argentine white grape and wine
trapiche – sugar mill
turista – 2nd class on a train, usually not very comfortable

vicuña – wild relative of domestic llama and alpaca, found in Argentina's Andean northwest only at high altitudes
vino tinto – red wine
vinoteca – wine bar

yacaré – South American caiman, found in humid, subtropical areas
YPF – Yacimientos Fiscales Petrolíferos, Argentina's former national oil company
yungas – in northwestern Argentina, transitional subtropical lowland forest

zapateo – folkloric tap dance
zona franca – duty-free zone
zonda – a hot, dry wind descending from the Andes

The Authors

SANDRA BAO
**Coordinating Author,
Buenos Aires, The Pampas & the Atlantic Coast**

Born to Chinese parents and raised in Buenos Aires, Sandra reluctantly came to the US when she was nine. She arrived in Toledo, Ohio during winter (it had been summer in BA) – but the novelty of snow was fun. The travel bug bit her after college and she visited more than 50 countries – so getting a job with Lonely Planet was only natural. Sandra has returned to Argentina a dozen times since her childhood, seeing the country change a little or a lot each time, always learning something and always meeting great new people. She's the author of about 25 Lonely Planet guidebooks, including *Buenos Aires*.

GREGOR CLARK
Uruguay

Gregor's fascination with South America dates back to high school, when his Spanish teacher filled him with starry-eyed notions of hiking the Inca Trail. Since then he's traveled the continent from tip to tail, developing a special fondness for Uruguay while researching the past two editions of this book. Favorite memories this time around include riding the range near Tacuarembó, watching the full moon rise over San Nicanor hot springs and rediscovering Montevideo's vibrant urban culture. He has contributed to Lonely Planet's *Brazil* and *South America on a Shoestring* and written about Machu Picchu and Easter Island in *Middle of Nowhere*.

BRIDGET GLEESON
Patagonia, Tierra del Fuego

As a child, Bridget listened to her mother talk about hitchhiking across Bolivia and sailing to Colombia. But her own South American experience, as a Buenos Aires–based writer covering food, wine and luxury travel, has been somewhat more sedate: the last time she was in Patagonia writing a story, Bridget had a personal fly-fishing instructor and four-course meals prepared by a French chef. Needless to say, she jumped at the chance to seek adventure on this pilgrimage to Patagonia and Tierra del Fuego. Bridget is the author of Lonely Planet's *Buenos Aires Encounter*; she's also written for *Delta Sky*, *Continental* and AOL Travel.

LONELY PLANET AUTHORS

Why is our travel information the best in the world? It's simple: our authors are passionate, dedicated travelers. They don't take freebies in exchange for positive coverage so you can be sure the advice you're given is impartial. They travel widely to all the popular spots, and off the beaten track. They don't research using just the internet or phone. They discover new places not included in any other guidebook. They personally visit thousands of hotels, restaurants, palaces, trails, galleries, temples and more. They speak with dozens of locals every day to make sure you get the kind of insider knowledge only a local could tell you. They take pride in getting all the details right, and in telling it how it is. Think you can do it? Find out how at **lonelyplanet.com**.

ANDY SYMINGTON   Northeast Argentina, The Andean Northwest

Andy's relationship with Argentina is a story of four generations: his grandmother lived here in the 1920s, and her father had a *mate* plantation in Misiones. Andy first visited the country with his own father, the start of a long love affair with South America that has involved many trips all around the continent, a spell living and working in Buenos Aires, a deep-rooted respect for provincial Argentina that he renewed on this research trip, and a debatable addiction to barbecued intestines. Andy hails from Australia, lives in northern Spain, and has contributed to many Lonely Planet guidebooks.

LUCAS VIDGEN   Córdoba & the Central Sierras,
Mendoza & the Central Andes, The Lake District

Lucas started wandering away from his mother in shopping malls when he was five and has never really stopped. Since then he's lived, worked and traveled in more than 20 countries, many of which don't supply milk and crayons when you get lost. First captivated by Argentina's wide open spaces and cosmopolitan cities in 2001, he now jumps at any excuse to go back. Among other Lonely Planet titles, Lucas has contributed to *South America, Guatemala, Nicaragua* and *Central America*. He currently lives in Quetzaltenango, Guatemala where he publishes – and occasionally works on – the city's leading nightlife and culture magazine, *XelaWho*.

Behind the Scenes

THIS BOOK

The 7th edition of *Argentina* was researched and written by Sandra Bao (coordinating author), Gregor Clark, Bridget Gleeson, Andy Symington and Lucas Vidgen. Sandra, Gregor, Andy and Lucas also wrote the previous edition with assistance from Danny Palmerlee, Sarah Gilbert and Carolyn McCarthy. The Health chapter for this edition is based on text supplied by David Goldberg, MD. Also contributing to this edition were David Labi (*Going to a Fútbol Game* boxed text in the Buenos Aires chapter) and Daniel Buck and Anne Meadows (*Butch & Sundance's Patagonian Refuge* boxed text in the Patagonia chapter).

This guidebook was commissioned in Lonely Planet's Oakland office, and produced by the following:

Commissioning Editors Kathleen Munnelly, Emily Wolman
Coordinating Editor Evan Jones
Coordinating Cartographer Peter Shields
Coordinating Layout Designer Yvonne Bischofberger
Managing Editor Brigitte Ellemor
Managing Cartographers David Connolly, Hunor Csutoros, Alison Lyall
Managing Layout Designer Celia Wood
Assisting Editors Peter Cruttenden, Martine Power, Kristin Odijk, Anne Mulvaney, Angela Tinson, Jeanette Wall

Assisting Cartographers Joelene Kowalski, Anthony Phelan, Valeska Cañas, Andrew Smith
Assisting Layout Designers Frank Deim, Jacqui Saunders
Cover Research Naomi Parker, lonelyplanetimages.com
Internal Image Research Aude Vauconsant, lonely planetimages.com
Project Manager Rachel Imeson
Language Content Branislava Vladisavljevic, Annelies Mertens

Thanks to Juan Winata, John Taufa, Lisa Knights, Raphael Richards, Melanie Dankel

THANKS
SANDRA BAO

Many people deserve my gratitude. Graciela Guzmán, Sylvia Zapiola, Totty Pease, Alan Patrick, Jed Rothenburg and Madi Lang were among those who took on the tough job of helping me review restaurants in Buenos Aires. Sally Blake is an ace on the tango world, while Cintia Stella knows travel in Argentina like no one else. Thanks to Alejo Mendez Guerin for introducing me to the organic scene. *Gracias* also to Daniel Karlin, Gastón Cernadas, Steve Finder and Sammy Ward for entertaining me, plus answering my questionnaire. Judy Hutton and Katie Alley – I love how good you are. My coauthors helped me immensely, as

---

THE LONELY PLANET STORY

Fresh from an epic journey across Europe, Asia and Australia in 1972, Tony and Maureen Wheeler sat at their kitchen table stapling together notes. The first Lonely Planet guidebook, *Across Asia on the Cheap,* was born.

Travelers snapped up the guides. Inspired by their success, the Wheelers began publishing books to Southeast Asia, India and beyond. Demand was prodigious, and the Wheelers expanded the business rapidly to keep up. Over the years, Lonely Planet extended its coverage to every country and into the virtual world via lonelyplanet.com and the Thorn Tree message board.

As Lonely Planet became a globally loved brand, Tony and Maureen received several offers for the company. But it wasn't until 2007 that they found a partner whom they trusted to remain true to the company's principles of traveling widely, treading lightly and giving sustainably. In October of that year, BBC Worldwide acquired a 75% share in the company, pledging to uphold Lonely Planet's commitment to independent travel, trustworthy advice and editorial independence.

Today, Lonely Planet has offices in Melbourne, London and Oakland, with over 500 staff members and 300 authors. Tony and Maureen are still actively involved with Lonely Planet. They're traveling more often than ever, and they're devoting their spare time to charitable projects. And the company is still driven by the philosophy of *Across Asia on the Cheap*: 'All you've got to do is decide to go and the hardest part is over. So go!'

did 'World's Best Commissioning Editor' Kathleen Munnelly. Finally, love always to my godmother Elsa, husband Ben, parents David and Fung – and brother Daniel.

GREGOR CLARK

Thanks to the dozens of warm-hearted Uruguayans and resident expats who shared Uruguay's beauty with me, especially Lucia and Rodney Bruce, Pedro and Nahir Clariget, Dahianna and José Assanelli, Alicia Fernandez, Fernando Rocca, Alejandra Carrau Bergengruen, Danilo Ruglio and Luciana Mestre in Montevideo and Gloria in Colonia. Warm thanks also to my commissioning editor Kathleen Munnelly, coordinating author Sandra Bao and all the other great folks at Lonely Planet. Finally, big hugs to Gaen, Meigan and Chloe, whose love and companionship always make coming home the best part of the trip.

BRIDGET GLEESON

My research trip wouldn't have been half as fun without my delightful travel companion, Margaret Gleeson, who remained in high spirits during bus breakdowns on Ruta Nacional 40 and miniblizzards in Torres del Paine. Thank you to my friends and fellow journalists in Buenos Aires who offered invaluable travel advice, and to those I met on the road, particularly Miguel Clavero Owen and Izabela Ratajewska – and the kind stranger in Ushuaia who gave us a ride when we desperately needed one. A special thank you to Rodolfo Diaz for his constant support. Above all, I want to thank all of the Lonely Planet readers I met on the road: your sense of adventure has inspired me and renewed my passion for travel.

ANDY SYMINGTON

Many warm-hearted people made this trip a very pleasurable one, and some in particular went beyond the call of duty to provide information, advice and help. These include: Jorge Guasp, Héctor Morales, Sebastián Clerico, Gloria at El Palmar, the intelligent, helpful staff of numerous tourist information offices, and scores of taxi and *remise* (radio taxi) drivers generous with local information. Thanks too to Amy Chester and Pam Chen for helping taste all that Cafayate wine and to Magdalena Bidabehere, Laura Hoogen and Karin Idelson for great travel moments. Profuse thanks also to my family and, especially, Ruth Nieto Huerta, for their support, to Kathleen Munnelly and the Lonely Planet team, to Sandra Bao for coordinating the writing of the book, and to all my fellow authors.

LUCAS VIDGEN

Thanks first and foremost to Argentines in general for making a country that's such a joy to travel and work in. In particular, Charlie O'Malley in Mendoza was once again a great source of information and in Córdoba Ana Navarta provided some invaluable insights. I'd also like to thank Marcos Alvarez, Sergio Bianchi, Daniel Sierra, Crisitina Pereyra, Paula Moreno, Valeria Rubio and Dario Carri for tips and tricks along the way. And to all the readers who took the time to write in with updates from the road – we really do read all those emails, and they're always (mostly!) a great help. As always, thanks to América and Sofía, for being there, and particularly being there when I got back.

OUR READERS

Many thanks to the travelers who used the last edition and wrote to us with helpful hints, useful advice and interesting anecdotes:

A Katherine Adams, Xavier Alcober, Giuseppe Amato, Emanuela Appetiti **B** Victoria Barber, Lisa Barker, Rebecca Barnshaw, Rick Benito, Antony Benois, Antony Benois, Yvonne Bierings, Irene Billeter Sauter, Sian Bishop, Hanna Blander, Sven Boell, Jose Alberto Bogado, James Booth, Steve Brosnan, Rudy Buelens, Angela Burke **C** Sven C, Ray Calver, Christopher Carriero, Geoffrey Clifford, Miles Cohen, Nick Creagh-Osborne, Andrea Cross **D** Allan

BEHIND THE SCENES

Darwent, James Davey, Alexandra De Groote, Hector Del Olmo, Mark Draper, Meredith Dundas, Gerhard Ebner **E** Tim Edwards, Christine Ehrnsperger, Johan Elmström **F** Mick Falk, Francisco Ferrer, Stephan Formella, Jonathan Freeman, June Fujimoto, Alice and Chris Fuller **G** Peter Gernsheimer, Nili Grothe **H** Nicole Halbeisen, Daphne Hameeteman, Isabel and Andrew Heim Vadis, Michael Hentschke, Mirko Hohmann, Søren Holm, Esther Huijsmans, Esther Huijsmans, Gretchen Hurlbutt, Eric Hutchinson, Helene Hvid-Jensen **J** Eden Janzen, Johana Javrková, Susanna Jordan **K** Carolyn Kegeris, Bjarke Lindø Kristensen **L** Francois Laneuville, Cestmir Lang, Tim Laslavic, Gaetan Lauzon, Eva Lecat, Kar-Soon Lim, Don Lindsay, Jonathan Lischke **M** Christie Maccallum, Amanda Mallon, Monica Manjarin, Jack Martin, Fernando Martinez Latorre, Betsy Masi, Sandra Mathews, Margaret McAspurn, Elsa McCargar, Roberto McKenna, Mick Meegan, Michael Menz, Laura Merle, Nina Mobaek, Catherine Murphy **N** Carol Nanson, Bryce Newman, Rachel Newton, Kate Noble **O** Marla Olson **P** Andy Parkin, Rafel Pascual De La Cruz, Denisse Isabel Pastorino, Matt Pepe, Mercedes Perez, Peter Phillips, Neil Pike **R** Mohammad Husam Rezek, Lies Rijniers, Alejandro Rivera, Warren Rodwell, Patrick Roman, Sophia Rome, Jeff Rothman, Camiel Rouweler **S** Mathews Sandra, Debbie Schatz, Rainer Schlager, Christopher Schulz, Lisette Schulz, Selina Shah, Emma Shanley, Peter Shorett, Guillaume Sillon, Niels Smit, Dominik Spoden, Annette Suter, Helga Svendsen **T** Olivia Taylor, Nicola Thomson, Stephen Tonnison, Eliza Toornstra, Leon Tretjakewitsch, Kariina Tshursin, Denise Turcinov, Martina Und Thomas **V** Jorge Vallejos, Maximiliano Vallés, Alet Van'T Eind, Ine Van Der Stock, Marianne Van Der Walle, Stephanie Van Elven, Jan Willem Van Hofwegen, Tomarchio Vasta Gianluca, David Versteeg, Christy Visaggi **W** Tod Western, Robert Wilson, Ben Wintle **Z** Hardy Zantke, Oliver Zoellner

ACKNOWLEDGMENTS

Many thanks to the following for the use of their content:

Globe on title page ©Mountain High Maps 1993 Digital Wisdom, Inc.

Index

000 Map pages
000 Photograph pages

INDEX

INDEX

GreenDex

GOING GREEN

Sustainable travel is still a very new concept in Argentina, which doesn't stop plenty of travel entrepreneurs waving the eco flag. So how can you spot the difference between a genuinely sustainable option and an eco-con?

Our authors have highlighted choices that contribute to sustainable tourism in Argentina, whether it's by using alternative energy, supporting sustainable development in local and indigenous communities or helping to preserve Argentina's cultural and architectural heritage. Many of the options on this list are Argentine-owned and operated, and, in some way or other, most help travelers reach a deeper understanding of the cultural and natural environment they're in.

Green travel is becoming more important all the time, but it's not always easy for travelers, including us, to find sustainable options. You can help us improve this list by sending your feedback and recommendations to talk2us@lonelyplanet.com.au. To find out more about sustainable tourism at Lonely Planet, head to www.lonelyplanet.com/responsibletravel.

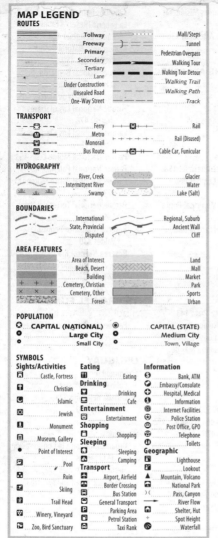

MAP LEGEND
ROUTES
- Tollway
- Freeway
- Primary
- Secondary
- Tertiary
- Lane
- Under Construction
- Unsealed Road
- One-Way Street
- Mall/Steps
- Tunnel
- Pedestrian Overpass
- Walking Tour
- Walking Tour Detour
- Walking Trail
- Walking Path
- Track

TRANSPORT
- Ferry
- Metro
- Monorail
- Bus Route
- Rail
- Rail (Disused)
- Cable Car, Funicular

HYDROGRAPHY
- River, Creek
- Intermittent River
- Swamp
- Glacier
- Water
- Lake (Salt)

BOUNDARIES
- International
- State, Provincial
- Disputed
- Regional, Suburb
- Ancient Wall
- Cliff

AREA FEATURES
- Area of Interest
- Beach, Desert
- Building
- Cemetery, Christian
- Cemetery, Other
- Forest
- Land
- Mall
- Market
- Park
- Sports
- Urban

POPULATION
- ○ **CAPITAL (NATIONAL)**
- ● **Large City**
- ● Small City
- ◎ **CAPITAL (STATE)**
- ● **Medium City**
- ● Town, Village

SYMBOLS
Sights/Activities
- Castle, Fortress
- Christian
- Islamic
- Jewish
- Monument
- Museum, Gallery
- Point of Interest
- Pool
- Ruin
- Skiing
- Trail Head
- Winery, Vineyard
- Zoo, Bird Sanctuary

Eating
- Eating

Drinking
- Drinking
- Cafe

Entertainment
- Entertainment

Shopping
- Shopping

Sleeping
- Sleeping
- Camping

Transport
- Airport, Airfield
- Border Crossing
- Bus Station
- General Transport
- Parking Area
- Petrol Station
- Taxi Rank

Information
- Bank, ATM
- Embassy/Consulate
- Hospital, Medical
- Information
- Internet Facilities
- Police Station
- Post Office, GPO
- Telephone
- Toilets

Geographic
- Lighthouse
- Lookout
- Mountain, Volcano
- National Park
- Pass, Canyon
- River Flow
- Shelter, Hut
- Spot Height
- Waterfall

LONELY PLANET OFFICES

Australia (Head Office)
Locked Bag 1, Footscray, Victoria 3011
☎ 03 8379 8000, fax 03 8379 8111
talk2us@lonelyplanet.com.au

USA
150 Linden St, Oakland, CA 94607
☎ 510 250 6400, toll free 800 275 8555
fax 510 893 8572
info@lonelyplanet.com

UK
2nd fl, 186 City Rd,
London EC1V 2NT
☎ 020 7106 2100, fax 020 7106 2101
go@lonelyplanet.co.uk

Published by Lonely Planet
ABN 36 005 607 983

© Lonely Planet 2010

© photographers as indicated 2010

Cover photograph: Cerro Torre in Parque Nacional Los Glaciares (North), Patagonia; Richard I'Anson/Lonely Planet Images. Many of the images in this guide are available for licensing from Lonely Planet Images: lonelyplanetimages.com.

Printed through Colorcraft Ltd, Hong Kong. Printed in China

Mixed Sources
Product group from well-managed forests and other controlled sources
www.fsc.org Cert no. SGS-COC-005002
© 1996 Forest Stewardship Council
FSC

R.C.L.

NOV. 2010

G

Although the authors and Lonely Planet have taken all reasonable care in preparing this book, we make no warranty about the accuracy or completeness of its content and, to the maximum extent permitted, disclaim all liability arising from its use.